CONTENTS

PREFACE

This second edition of *Undocumented DOS* is radically different from the first edition, which appeared three years ago. In addition to several new chapters on the interaction between DOS and Windows, on "other DOSs," and on disassembling DOS, other chapters have been completely overhauled, not only to accommodate MS-DOS 5.0, 6.0, and Microsoft's forthcoming "Chicago" operating system (DOS 7 and Windows 4), but also to reflect what we hope is a far more sophisticated understanding of DOS internals, and of the role of undocumented interfaces in the software industry.

DOS? In the 1990s?!

But what's the point of a new book on DOS? This is the 1990s, right? Windows programs are outselling DOS programs. Almost all new development of commercial products is targeting Windows rather than plain-vanilla DOS. Having produced the book *Undocumented Windows*, isn't a return to DOS, with its lame commands and boring user interface, a form of childish regression?

Not at all. First, all those nice-looking Windows applications are really just protected-mode DOS applications. Easily 99% of the world's Windows code runs on top of MS-DOS rather than on the NT operating system. For the forseeable future, Windows programmers will need a firm grasp of how DOS works, and of how Windows interacts with DOS.

Furthermore, plain-vanilla DOS is hardly dead. DOS is still the proper tool for many tasks, witness the large number of DOS programs such as Microsoft's own DBLSPACE.EXE that currently won't run under Windows. One well-known writer on Windows programming, who has publicly argued that "DOS Must Die!," nonetheless confesses to spending a major part of his working day at the C:\> prompt. One of the major computer magazines, whose editorial policy is that Windows is all-important, was until quite recently producing all this praise to Windows . . . using Xywrite, a positively ancient DOS word processor! MS-DOS may not win any awards, and DOS-based products may have a hard time attracting attention from the novelty-crazed trade press, but the fact is that DOS remains a suitable platform for many tasks.

And yet, while the journalist we just mentioned spends most of his time at the C:\> prompt, it's important to note that it's a C:\> prompt within a Windows DOS box. The Windows DOS box is a very different beast from DOS itself. One of the goals of this second edition of *Undocumented DOS* is to help software developers understand the huge changes that DOS has undergone in the last few years. Yes, DOS remains tremendously important, but in many ways it's a different DOS.

What's New?

The first edition of *Undocumented DOS* appeared in October 1990, just after the release of Windows 3.0 (July 1990), and a bit before the release of MS-DOS 5.0 (June 1991). We have thoroughly updated this new edition to cover MS-DOS 5, MS-DOS 6, and Windows 3.1.

The biggest change is the emphasis on the DOS/Windows connection. The book *Undocumented Windows* does not discuss this connection, because the connection is made at a low-level part of Windows, below the Windows kernel. A primary goal for this new *Undocumented DOS* is to introduce readers to DOSMGR, the Windows (Enhanced mode) interface to MS-DOS. This is a part of Windows that is really an extension to MS-DOS, providing the illusion to the rest of Windows that DOS is a pre-emptively multitasked operating system. With DOSMGR in place, MS-DOS does in fact become a pre-emptively-multitasked operating system.

DOSMGR is a Windows virtual device driver (VxD) that, as we'll see in Chapter 1, knows a lot about undocumented DOS functions and data structures. Even if you have no interest in Windows, DOSMGR is without a doubt the most important "user" of undocumented DOS. If nothing else, one can simply view Windows as a cool DOS program that makes a ton of undocumented DOS calls.

Windows Enhanced mode talks to MS-DOS using VxDs. One of the points we make in this book is that, in the 1990s, VxDs will play the same role for PC programmers that TSRs did in the 1980s. Think of VxDs as 32-bit protected-mode TSRs. Just as many programmers used TSRs to accomplish the otherwise impossible, soon VxDs will be how programmers "push the envelope." VxDs will become even more important in "Chicago," the next version of DOS/Windows.

So, here are some of the highlights of what is new in this second edition:

- The DOS/Windows connection, including DOSMGR (Chapter 1) and VxDs (Chapter 3).
- Calling undocumented DOS from protected-mode Windows programs (Chapter 3).
- The tight coupling of MS-DOS and Windows has caused Microsoft some problems with various U.S. government agencies, first the FTC, and now the Justice Department. DOS and Windows are sold separately, so Window's use of undocumented DOS calls may constitute what antitrust law calls a "tying arrangement." This will be solved in Chicago, but in the meantime, this subject is taken up in Chapter 1, and again in Chapter 4.
- This second edition emphasizes DOS internals more than the first edition did. Rather than presenting a random assortment of undocumented DOS calls, we try to show how DOS itself uses these calls internally to implement the documented functionality. Chapter 6 shows how to disassemble DOS, to see its implementation of the documented INT 21h calls.
- The file system chapter covers both DoubleSpace and Stacker (see Chapter 8).
- Of course, the chapter on memory, process, and devices now covers the memory management features introduced with DOS 5.0, including Upper Memory Blocks (see Chapter 7).
- Dave Maxey has rewritten his popular INTRSPY utility from scratch, incorporating many suggestions from users of the first version (see Chapter 5). For example, INTRSPY can now watch device-driver entry points and far function calls.
- Dave Maxey has also rewritten the Phantom network redirector from scratch, this time using C rather than Turbo Pascal. Phantom is now a full-blown XMS ram disk. We have also greatly expanded and rewritten our explanation of the network redirector (see Chapter 8).
- Jim Kyle has improved the DEVLOD utility, for loading device drivers from the command line (see Chapter 7).
- The TSR chapter discusses the "instance data" problem: how can TSRs loaded before Windows or another multitasker properly manage their state in multiple DOS boxes? (see Chapter 9)

- There's an all-new chapter on "other DOSs": DR DOS (now Novell DOS), the DOS box in OS/2, the DOS box in Windows NT, and even NetWare, whose NETX shell makes so many changes to the DOS INT 21h interface that it essentially qualifies as a different version of DOS (see Chapter 4).

- Ralf Brown has greatly expanded the appendix, not only to show the new undocumented functions in DOS 5 and DOS 6, but also to fill in many of the "unknown" fields of the first edition. We've also added cross-references to the complete Interrupt List on the accompanying disk, and to some of the figures and listings within the book itself.

- Microsoft has finally documented some previously-undocumented calls, and of course we make note of this. We also correct some errors in their new documentation for the old functions (see Chapter 1).

What Versions of DOS?

Of course, this edition covers MS-DOS 5.0 and 6.0. There's also a little on MS-DOS 6.2, and as much material as we could squeeze in on the forthcoming "Chicago" operating system (for example, Chapter 8 discusses long filenames).

As already noted, Chapter 4 discusses other versions of DOS, including DR DOS 5 and 6, Novell DOS 7, the DOS box in OS/2 2.x (which masquerades as DOS 20.x), and the DOS box in Windows NT.

One flaw in the book is that we don't say much about OEM versions of DOS, aside from a little bit on the most important OEM version, Compaq DOS. Fortunately, Geoff Chappell touches on OEM versions of MS-DOS in his book, *DOS Internals*. We do at least discuss Microsoft's OEM Adaptation Kit (OAK), which OEMs use to produce their own versions of DOS (see Chapter 6).

Is Any of This Useful?

I suppose the main question for a software developer contemplating a book on undocumented DOS functions and data structures is whether any of this is (as one U.S. news magazine would crassly put it) "news you can use." How is a book called *Undocumented DOS* going to help you in your job?

First, even if you never use a single undocumented DOS function or data structure in your programs, the real purpose of this book is not to incite you to use undocumented calls (in fact, we think you should try not to), but to help you understand how DOS works. A programmer who has a good mental image of what goes on during a file read or seek call, for example, and who understands how a file handle goes to the PSP, then the JFT, and on to the SFT (see Chapter 8), will be a better programmer.

Of course, there are those who say that knowing these implementation-dependent details makes you a *worse* programmer, because it contradicts the principle of "information hiding." However, it's interesting to note what Fred Brooks wrote about David Parnas's then-new notion of "information hiding" in his *The Mythical Man-Month: Essays on Software Engineering* (Addison-Wesley, 1975):

> D.L. Parnas of Carnegie-Mellon University has proposed a still more radical solution. His thesis is that the programmer is most effective is shielded from, rather than exposed to the details of construction of system parts other than his own. This presupposes that all interfaces are completely and precisely defined. While that is definitely sound design, dependence upon its perfect accomplishment is a recipe for disaster.

Exactly! "Information hiding" works only when all interfaces are completely and precisely defined. But this is almost impossible! In the absence of complete and precise interface definition, your best bet is to learn as much about the system as you possibly can.

Second, it is surprising (and unfortunate) how often DOS programmers actually do end up needing to use some undocumented feature. Four years ago, I got involved in the first edition of this book, not because I had any particular interest in undocumented interfaces, or any axe to grind against Microsoft's documentation department, but because in my job at Lotus I had run into a situation where undocumented DOS was the only solution to a problem, and the problem had to be solved because customers were demanding it.

Lotus has several excellent high-end CD-ROM products, including CD/Corporate, CD/Investment, CD/M&A (mergers and acquisitions), and so on. These products require the Microsoft CD-ROM extensions (MSCDEX). Our customers would load MSCDEX (which takes up a lot of memory) solely in order to run our products; as far as they were concerned, MSCDEX was part of our products. Unfortunately (but not surprisingly, given how it hooks into DOS), MSCDEX does not have a deinstall option. Customers really hated rebooting the machine to get rid of MSCDEX after running our products. They attempted to deinstall MSCDEX by using Kim Kokonnen's excellent MARK and RELEASE utilities, but this didn't work, because MSCDEX allocates drive letters, which MARK/RELEASE doesn't deallocate. Our customers wanted a NOMSCDEX utility. It turned out that the only way to write NOMSCDEX was to manipulate the DOS Current Directory Structure. As you can guess, this structure is undocumented, and so is the DOS function that lets you access it (see DRVSET.C in Chapter 8).

Given how MSCDEX patches into DOS, I'm not quite sure how NOMSCDEX, which merely undid MSCDEX's changes to the CDS, could have ever worked. In any case, it did work, and customers were happy with it. A more robust NOMSCDEX would have involved even more use of undocumented DOS.

Soon after, it became clear that our CD/Networker product (a CD-ROM network server) would need to use Microsoft's network redirector interface. Trying to get this from Microsoft proved impossible. At this point, David Maxey and I realized that, if Lotus couldn't get this information from Microsoft, probably no one else could either, and it would be useful to do an entire book on the subject of undocumented DOS. That the book turned out to be quite popular among PC programmers shows that, indeed, this material is useful. There are even a fair number of programmers at Microsoft who (frightening thought!) seem to rely on this book.

So, yes, this material is useful. One note of warning, however: *Before incorporating an undocumented DOS call into a commercial program, always double-check and triple-check that there isn't a documented way to achieve the same goal.* There often is. Even if the undocumented way seems more convenient (and it often will), it is better to use a documented function, since this makes your program more likely to work in future versions of DOS. Equally important, the less programs rely on undocumented DOS, the easier it is for Microsoft to produce future versions of DOS. Not incidentally, the same thing also makes it easier for companies other than Microsoft to produce DOS emulators. This topic is addressed in greater depth in Chapter 1. In any case, learning the undocumented way to accomplish some goal, and then figuring out a documented way, will also make you a better programmer.

What's With All the Legal Mumbo Jumbo?

The reader expecting a straightforward technical book may be wondering why Chapters 1 and 4 contain lengthy discussions of U.S. antitrust law, and why Chapter 6 has a whole section on the law surrounding reverse engineering. What the heck is this doing in a book for programmers?

For better or for worse, you can't view software so narrowly any more, if you ever could. In a book on undocumented programming interfaces, every now and then we have to stop staring at code and ask why a given interface isn't documented, and ask whether Microsoft might derive some larger benefit from this lack of documentation. We then have to ask the bigger question: is there anything "unfair" in this arrangement, given Microsoft's position both as the supplier of a "bottleneck" resource (the operating system), and as a key competitor with other applications and utilities that use that resource? These are not rhetorical questions; I sure wish I knew the answers to them.

These seemingly non-technical issues are particularly relevant, because an advance copy of some of the material in this book (early drafts of Chapters 1 and 4) were used by the U.S. Federal Trade Commission (FTC) during its three-year investigation into Microsoft. The FTC terminated its investigation, with the commissioners tied 2-2 over whether to issue an injunction against Microsoft. The U.S. Department of Justice (DOJ) has now taken up the Microsoft case.

At first, I viewed the FTC investigation with deep suspicion. The issue of undocumented interfaces seemed very narrow. While I felt Microsoft had failed to document interfaces that were vital to other software developers, this issue didn't seem to me particularly "FTC-able," as it were. Questions from an attorney at the FTC about what Microsoft might have "done" to Windows to make it incompatible with other versions of DOS, particularly Novell's DR DOS, struck me as ridiculous, for reasons I discuss in Chapter 1.

But after encountering the AARD code discussed in Chapter 1, and the Microsoft C compiler SetPSP warranty code discussed in Chapter 4, I had to change my mind about a lot of this. Still, I haven't made up my mind about these issues, as the reader will no doubt be able to tell from the somewhat confused and contradictory discussion in Chapter 1. While I still can't decide whether Microsoft is undermining the competitive process, or merely being super-competitive, the one thing I do know is that this is an important question for software developers, who each day become more dependent on Microsoft.

After Chapter 1 went to press, and after an article on this subject appeared in *Dr. Dobb's Journal*, I was able to meet with Brad Silverberg (Microsoft's vice president of system software) and Aaron Reynolds (a key developer of MS-DOS, Windows/386, and Windows Enhanced mode, and author of the AARD code discussed in Chapter 1). Microsoft's reply appears in the December 1993 issue of *Dr. Dobb's Journal*. Brad and Aaron did not persuade me that it's okay for Windows to be using DOS calls that Microsoft fails to document for other utilities vendors. Nor did they persuade me of the legitimacy of the AARD code's goal of warning users of non-Microsoft versions of DOS that running Windows on their system was "untested." While Brad and Aaron were no doubt thinking about how to reduce tech-support costs for Windows, the fact that the method they chose would unnecessarily damage Novell's reputation, with no real gain for Microsoft or its customers, seems not to have occurred to them.

I hope the reader (and the other authors) will indulge some of my attempts to take this discussion beyond the narrow confines of how to make undocumented DOS calls. The places in the book where an assembly-language disassembly listing appears directly adjacent a discussion of some antitrust case like *Siegel v. Chicken Delight* are my favorites. They also reflect my very mixed feelings about Microsoft's role in the software industry. Is Microsoft the software equivalent of Edison's Menlo Park "invention factory," or is it (as one prominent writer of programming books privately maintains) "The Dark Side of the Force"? Neither, or both.

How Do I Get In Touch with the Authors?

Returning to more immediately practical issues, many readers of this book will want to know how to contact the authors with questions, corrections, suggestions, and criticism. Many of the improvements in this second edition are the direct result of feedback from many readers of the first edition.

For any overall comments on the book, and on Chapters 1-4, 6, and 8, contact:

Andrew Schulman
CompuServe 76320,302
Internet 76320.302@compuserve.com

I edit a monthly "Undocumented Corner" in *Dr. Dobb's Journal,* and am always looking for new topics, and new writers. I am also starting a separate *UNDOC* newsletter. For details, see the READ.ME file on the accompanying disk. If you are interesting in learning more (such as the newsletter's price and frequency, which I have not yet decided upon), send your name and address, via normal mail (no email on this one, please), to:

Andrew Schulman
UNDOC
859 Massachusetts Avenue
Cambridge MA 02139

This is also the address to use if you want to contact the authors, but do not have email access. However, while I guarantee a response to email, I can't guarantee a response to "normal" (snail) mail.

For INTRSPY, Phantom, Chapter 5, or the network redirector section of Chapter 8, contact:

David Maxey
CompuServe 70401,3057
Internet 70401.3057@compuserve.com

Please note that the version of Phantom on the accompanying disk has two known bugs, which unfortunately we did not detect until the disk was already being produced: First, if DEVICE=HIMEM.SYS, Phantom requires DOS=HIGH; running Phantom under HIMEM without DOS=HIGH hangs the system. Second, Phantom allows only two directory levels; MD \DIR1\DIR2\DIR3 fails on a Phantom drive.

For DEVLOD, ENVEDT, Chapter 7, and Chapter 10, contact:

Jim Kyle
CompuServe 76703,762
Internet 76703.762@compuserve.com

For the TSR library and Chapter 9, contact:
Raymond J. Michels
CompuServe 72300,2414
Internet 72300.2414@compuserve.com

For the Interrupt List, contact:
Ralf Brown
Internet ralf@telerama.pgh.pa.us
CompuServe >INTERNET:ralf@telerama.pgh.pa.us

For updated versions of the Interrupt List, see the instructions in INTRLIST\INTER-RUP.1ST on the accompanying disk.

Did You Do This All By Yourselves?

Not exactly. The list of people who helped make this a better book is pretty long. The following people are not responsible for any of our errors or omissions (especially because we sometimes failed to implement their excellent suggestions!), but they are responsible for much of what is good in the second edition:

Bob Aitchison	Cartsen Bukhold Andersen	David Andrews
Paul Andrews	Dwayne Bailey	Steve Baker
Stewart Berman	Doug Boling	Paul Bonneau
John Brennan	Chuck Brewer	Peter Burch
Ron Burk	Barbara Cass	Frank Cavallito
David Chappell	Geoff Chappell	Peter Chew
Anton Chizhov	Norman D. Culver	E. Nicholas Cupery
John Desrosiers	drifkind	Ray Duncan
Grant Echols	Erick Engelke	Jon Erickson
John "Frotz" Fa'atuai	Klaus Fahnenstich	Tim Farley
Matthew Felton	Fran Finnegan	Klaus Flesch
Eric Fogelin	George Fulk	Isabele Gayraud
Gils Gayraud	Steve Gibson	Drew Gislason
David R. Glandorf	Barry Goldstein	John Hare
Rainer G. Haselier	Martin Heller	Robert Hummel
Tony Ingenoso	Ian Jack	Roger Jackson
Eduardo Jacob	Dave Jewell	Phil Jollans
Steven Jones	Mike Karas	Peter Kober
Kim Kokkonen	Dmitriy Kondratiev	Gene Landy
Jim Lerner	Bill Lewis	Charlie Little
Brian Livingston	Jay Lowe	Stephen Manes
David Markun	Mike Maurice	Phillipe Mercier
Ted Merecki	Graham Murray	Mike O'Connor
Walt Oney	Andrew Pargeter	Kirit Patel
Tim Paterson	Scott Pedigo	Jeff Peters
A. Padgett Peterson	Matt Pietrek	Mike Podanoffsky
Nathaniel Polish	Matthew Prete	Jeff Prosise
Dan Rangle	roedy	Art Rothstein
Wendy Goldman Rohm	Tim Rowe	Neil Rubenking
Gerald Sacks	Brett Salter	Murray Sargent

Hans Salvisberg	Arne Schäpers	Mitchell Schoenbrun
Peter Schultz	Larry Seltzer	Yishai Sered
Mike Shiels	Dan Silver	Barry Simon
Glen Slick	Richard Smith	Kyle Sparks
Mike Spilo	John Spinks	Glenn Stephens
Al Stevens	Andrew Tanenbaum	Stuart Taylor
Ray Valdés	Frank van Gilluwe	Terrence Vaughn
Robin Walker	Jerry Watkins	Martin Westermeier
Andy Wightman	Ben Williams	Bob Williamson
Dennis Williamson	Dan Winter	Clayton Wishoff
William T. Wonneberger	Dan B. Wright	Manfred Young
Richard Zigler	Kelly Zytaruk	

I am sure that I must have left someone's name off this list. If so, I am sorry. There are also several employees of Microsoft whose help we would like to acknowledge by name, but can't, because the company wants to make sure that you understand that Microsoft in no way endorses this book, or in any way helped with its contents. Thanks, guys!

While everyone I've just named has helped make this a better book, a few helped out to such an extent that they deserve special thanks:

Geoff Chappell	John "Frotz" Fa'atuai	Tim Farley
Gene Landy	Bill Lewis	David Markun
Larry Seltzer	John Spinks	

I hope to buy each of you several beers!

This book never would have happened without our literary agent, Claudette Moore, who is a genius for making things happen. Four years ago, when I was thinking about doing a book on undocumented interfaces in DOS, Windows, and OS/2, Claudette made the (only now obvious) point that I should start out with a book called *Undocumented DOS* and that separate books on other operating environments could be written at a later time. Thanks Claudette! Thanks too to John Paul Moore, for giving this project his blessing.

At Benchmark Productions, Andrew "Spike" Williams has orchestrated the transformation of this book from a motley collection of ASCII files into the attractive pages you see now. And he didn't punch me out once during this entire project. Spike was assisted by Jennifer Noble and, in the early stages, by Chris Williams. Chris arranged a special week-long undocumented retreat to the Clipper Ship Inn in Scituate, Massachusetts, where large chunks of Chapters 1 and 3 were written.

Our copy editor, Meredith Ruland, did a wonderful job transforming our technoid coredumps into reasonable English. She is responsible for any improvement in readability which will be found by you over what this was like in the first edition. (Clearly, she did not see that last sentence.)

A million thanks to Xavier Cazin for his work on the French edition, *Les coulisses du DOS*.

At Addison-Wesley, special thanks to Phil Sutherland, Claire Horne, Lisa Roth, and Doris Ruderman (Mrs.).

Thanks to my wife Amanda Claiborne, and my son, Matthew Jacob Schulman, for putting up with me the past few months.

Andrew Schulman
Cambridge MA

## CHAPTER 1

Undocumented DOS: The Madness Continues

by Andrew Schulman

Weighing in at less than 120K (a bit more if you include DBLSPACE.BIN from version 6.0), MS-DOS is one of the smallest operating systems still in use. Not coincidentally, it is also the world's most widely used operating system. Aficionados of more powerful systems might deride DOS's lack of features, but it is what DOS is *missing* that accounts in large part for its spectacular success. One estimate puts the number of commercial and internally-developed corporate applications for MS-DOS at more than 20,000. Estimates of the installed base of DOS systems range from 50 million to 100 million. Since some of these estimates appear in marketing literature, let's be conservative and call it 75 million. That's far more users than any other operating system. It is worth noting that (except for the few copies shipped on IBM machines) the Microsoft Corporation makes perhaps an average of $25 for each copy of this highly-leveraged small piece of code. In 1991 alone, Microsoft's revenues from MS-DOS (including retail sales of MS-DOS 5.0) were $617.5 million. What a sweet business!

On each of these 75 million or so machines, MS-DOS provides not only its familiar and contemptible user interface of the A> or C> prompt, but also a programmer's interface. Just as users make DOS requests by typing commands such as "DIR *.EXE" or "COPY *.* C:" (or, more likely these days, "WIN"), so programs make DOS requests—to open a disk file, to allocate memory, or even to terminate—by moving a function number into the Intel processor's AH register and issuing an INT 21h instruction. The MS-DOS programmer's interface consists of several software interrupts, the most important of which is INT 21h.

Just as MS-DOS itself is everywhere, technical documentation on how to program this ubiquitous piece of code turns up everywhere, too. Starting with the bible of DOS programming, Ray Duncan's superb *Advanced MS-DOS Programming*, information about DOS programming is readily available. In fact, it is almost *too* available. A medium-sized bookstore might carry half a dozen different books on how to make INT 21h calls. Are there really that many DOS programmers out there? Is there really that much to say about this little operating system?

Most DOS programming books, after a few chapters on input/output, disks and files, memory allocation, and perhaps error handling or compatibility/performance tradeoffs, contain a lengthy appendix listing the INT 21h calls. These lists start with INT 21h function 0 (Terminate Process), proceed to function 1 (Character Input With Echo), then to function 2 (Character Output), and then, not surprisingly, to functions 3, 4, 5, and so on.

Clearly, MS-DOS is a well-ordered world, where numerous books that are readily available carefully spell out all available functionality. MS-DOS is very small compared to many other computer operating systems, so it is possible to grasp DOS programming in its entirety. In contrast to the unfathomed depths of larger operating systems such as UNIX, MS-DOS is an apparently small, static world, in which everything there is to know already *is* known.

Well, not quite.

Open the Microsoft's official *MS-DOS Programmer's Reference* (either the DOS 5.0 version from 1991, or the DOS 6.0 version from 1993), and you will find many strange gaps in the INT 21h function numbers. For example, there are entries for function 51h (Get PSP Address) and function 54h (Get Verify State), with nothing at all said about numbers 52h and 53h in between. Other quasi-official references such as Duncan's *Advanced MS-DOS Programming* simply list the missing functions as "Reserved." So what are functions 52h and 53h? Two unused slots that Microsoft reserves for possible future use? Or perhaps some obsolete code that Microsoft no longer uses? Maybe something useful only to DOS itself?

Not exactly. If you turn to the appendix of this book, you will find the following entries:

```
INT 21h function 52h -- DOS 2+ -- Get SysVars (List of Lists)
INT 21h function 53h -- DOS 2+ -- Translate BIOS Parameter Block
```

(Actually, you will also find functions 50h and 51h because, until recently, these too were undocumented.)

One of these functions, INT 21h AH=52h, returns a pointer to the SysVars internal data structure in the DOS data segment. Practically every DOS utility in existence, whether written by Microsoft or by key third-party DOS vendors such as Central Point, Novell, Qualitas, Quarterdeck, Stac Electronics, and Symantec uses function 52h and SysVars (also known as the List of Lists). Yet the function really is undocumented. Microsoft uses it, all the major third-party utilities vendors use it, yet Microsoft has never acknowledged its existence. This is nuts! (Just plain nuts, or the monopolization of a vital resource? We'll try to answer this question in the course of this chapter.)

This is just one of many crucial holes in the programmer's interface to MS-DOS. There's a similar gap between functions 54h and 56h. This gap hides a crucial bit of functionality, function 55h (Create PSP). When DOS or Windows start a program, they use this function. Many third-party extensions to DOS, such as Phar Lap's 386|DOS-Extender, and NET.EXE in Microsoft's Windows for Workgroups (WfW; Microsoft removed NET.EXE from MS-DOS 6.0 at the last minute), use function 55h too.

Another hidden area of DOS is function 5Dh. The *MS-DOS Programmer's Reference* describes function 5D0Ah, which raises the inevitable question of whether there are other functions such as 5D00h, 5D01h, and so on. Not surprisingly, there are. In contrast to what the Microsoft official reference indicates, function 5Dh consists of 12 subfunctions that handle an assortment of tasks, including DOS calls over a network (Server Function Call) and support for DOS reentrancy (Get Swappable Data Area). In fact, the one 5Dh function that Microsoft does document has certain aspects that don't make much sense unless you know about the other ones.

Besides INT 21h, there are other DOS software interrupts, such as INT 2Fh, which contain entire undocumented subsystems. The most important of these is the Network Redirector (INT 2Fh function 11h), whose name is familiar even to many non-programmers who use DOS networking software; yet Microsoft has *never* documented this function's programming interface, despite years of repeated requests from developers.

These missing functions are merely the most apparent portion of undocumented DOS. The real core of undocumented DOS is its data structures: the DOS internal variable table (SysVars), the System File Table (SFT), the Current Directory Structure (CDS), and numerous other structures that this book describes in detail.

Although MS-DOS really is a small piece of code, it is nonetheless far from being a self-enclosed, static world. Like a tiny fractal equation whose graph is infinitely complex, this small piece of code called DOS contains many unexplained areas. Unexplained, at least, by Microsoft.

"Cruel Coding" and Tying Arrangements

As a concrete example of how undocumented DOS is used in the real world, consider Microsoft's tremendously-successful Windows operating environment, which runs on top of MS-DOS. Later in this chapter, we will see that Windows, especially in Enhanced mode, totally depends on in-depth knowledge of undocumented DOS functions and data structures, in particular INT 21h function 52h and SysVars. That Windows relies heavily on undocumented DOS is in itself an interesting avenue to explore in a book on undocumented DOS. But does this reliance have any wider implications?

The computer trade press has given a lot of attention to the question of whether Microsoft's position as an the leading supplier of PC operating systems has given its applications an "unfair advantage" over *applications* from other vendors. Much of the ruckus surrounding the book *Undocumented Windows* had to do with the fact that Microsoft applications were caught out using undocumented Windows functions. But the computer trade press may have been focused on the wrong issue. It is equally important to ask whether Microsoft's position as operating-systems supplier gives it an unfair advantage in bringing out *utilities* and *operating-system extensions* such as Windows and DoubleSpace.

The point will be made throughout this chapter that, even though they feel like "part of the operating system," and hence Microsoft's natural domain to do with as they see fit, in fact utilities and DOS extensions are some of the most fiercely competitive areas in the PC software marketplace. The existence of a large third-party aftermarket for these utilities and extensions shows that a large group of consumers considers them separate from the operating system. The question is, in competing for this market, whether Microsoft is abusing its monopoly position as nearly-sole supplier of the world's predominant operating system, and whether any advantage it derives from this position is an "unfair" one.

We can in part answer this question by looking at the relationship between Windows and MS-DOS. The DOS/Windows connection raises important issues for Microsoft. On the one hand, the company must avoid what is called a "tying arrangement," in which using one product (such as Windows) requires that you buy another product (such as MS-DOS) from the same company and prevents you in some way from buying a competitor's compatible product (such as Novell's DR DOS). Tying arrangements come under U.S. antitrust law, particularly section 3 of the Clayton Act, which explicitly prohibits as anti-competitive the lease or sale of a commodity "on the condition, agreement, or understanding that the lessee or purchaser thereof shall not use or deal in the goods . . . of a competitor or competitors of the lessor or seller, where the effect . . . may be to substantially lessen competition or tend to create a monopoly."

On the other hand, Microsoft very much wants to show that to properly run Windows, you need to upgrade to whatever is the latest release of MS-DOS. For example, the October 29, 1992 Microsoft "Reviewer's Guide" for DOS 6 states:

> *MS-DOS must be a superior platform for Windows*
> Windows has become a standard. More than half of all new PCs are shipped with Windows, and the number is growing. The Windows application market is approaching the size of the MS-DOS applications market. Given the widespread use of Windows, we plan to evolve MS-DOS over time to:
>
> - Provide the base technology that Windows needs to improve
> - Become more tightly integrated with Windows

Likewise, the README.WRI file included with Windows 3.1 states:

> *Running Windows with an Operating System Other Than MS-DOS*
> Microsoft Windows and MS-DOS work together as an integrated system. They were designed together and extensively tested together on a wide variety of computers and hardware configurations. Running Windows version 3.1 on an operating system other than MS-DOS could cause unexpected results or poor performance.

A key point here is that the pieces of this "integrated system" are currently sold separately (this will change in Microsoft's forthcoming "Chicago" operating system). Of course, there is nothing wrong in this. Cameras and film are sold separately, as are cars and tires, toasters and bread, and lamps and lightbulbs. But what if Kodak designed cameras that could only work properly with Kodak film, or that you could only have processed at Kodak processing centers? What if Kodak's camera division freely shared information with the company's film division, while withholding vital technical information from other, non-Kodak, film manufacturers and processors? The legality of this tie between Kodak cameras and Kodak film would then probably depend on whether this arrangement had a legitimate technical or business reason, or whether it existed for the sole purpose of excluding competition or potential competition. Answering such questions is no easy matter—a major reason why "vertical integration" antitrust cases typically take years and cost millions of dollars.

Has Microsoft created artificial ties between Windows and MS-DOS for the sole purpose of excluding competition? We will visit and revisit this question several times in the course of this chapter. But let's first establish what ties exist.

First, as noted earlier and as will be seen in more detail later, Windows makes extensive use of undocumented DOS functions and data structures, including INT 21h function 52h and SysVars.

Second, MS-DOS "knows about" Windows. As we will see later, there is a large and important undocumented INT 2Fh interface that MS-DOS 5.0 and 6.0 use to communicate with a key component of Windows known as DOSMGR. Because DOSMGR expects any DOS version 5.0 or higher to support this undocumented interface, which provides DOSMGR with information about DOS internals, all existing DOS workalikes to date, including DR DOS, pretend to be DOS 3.31. (As this book was going to press, we learned that Novell DOS 7.0 will return a DOS version number of 6.0 rather than 3.31. This means that Novell has implemented the undocumented DOSMGR interface.)

Third, Windows *patches* DOS. When Windows starts up, it overwrites some parts of DOS; when Windows exits, it (usually) backs these changes out. If you were to write a DOS 5.0 or 6.0 clone based entirely on the interface documented in the *Microsoft MS-DOS Programmer's Reference*, and if you failed to implement a lot of odd undocumented stuff, such as keeping certain internal values at specific memory locations, Windows wouldn't run on top of the clone.

Finally, pieces of MS-DOS sometimes patch Windows. For example, the WINA20.386 file that comes with DOS exists largely to replace some of the code found in the V86MMGR component of Windows 3.0. The VxD contained within Microsoft's EMM386.EXE also patches two routines in V86MMGR.

What all this means is that, while MS-DOS and Windows are sold as separate products, they are very tightly connected. Windows is not simply another third-party application that happens to run "on top of" DOS. Instead, it is a key *extension* of DOS and has intimate knowledge of undocumented DOS internals. MS-DOS knows when Windows is running and behaves differently when Windows is running that when your run-of-the-mill DOS-based word processor or spreadsheet is running.

It is good that Microsoft is making MS-DOS a better platform for Windows. If in the process this hurts non-Microsoft versions of DOS (such as Novell's DR DOS) or non-Microsoft competitors to Windows (such as Quarterdeck's Desqview), then so be it. There is a problem, however, if Microsoft has created *artificial* ties between Windows and MS-DOS. One obvious example would be putting code into Windows for the sole purpose of creating incompatibilities with DR DOS.

But another, less obvious, example would be failing to document functionality in DOS, which Microsoft itself uses in Windows. If Windows needs to use MS-DOS function 52h, for example, then failing to document DOS function 52h looks like an artificial tie—artificial because, if Windows has legitimate reasons for making the DOS call (which, we will see, it does), then Microsoft's persistent failure to document this DOS call can't be legitimate, at least as long as Windows and MS-DOS are separate products for which there is separate competition such as Quarterdeck's Desqview and Novell's DR DOS.

Windows and DR DOS

During the abortive three-year U.S. Federal Trade Commission (FTC) investigation into Microsoft (now taken up by the U.S. Justice Department), attorneys from the FTC were carefully looking at the relationship between MS-DOS and Windows. For example, *PC Week* (November 30, 1992), reporting on the FTC investigation, noted that:

> Another area of scrutiny is whether Microsoft modified Windows to prevent Novell's DR-DOS operating system from running with the graphical environment. DR DOS required updates to work with both Windows 3.0 and 3.1.

Certainly, there is a history of incompatibilities between Windows and DR DOS. But it is vital to filter out which of these incompatibilities are *not* Microsoft's fault. There is a vague, widespread notion that every incompatibility between Windows and DR DOS somehow reflects an attempt by Microsoft to clobber its competitors. The following letter to the editor of *PC Magazine* (September 15, 1992) is a good expression of this idea:

> In response to Microsoft's cruel coding, Windows 3.1 and DR DOS 6.0 are incompatible. A little message about the MS-DOS extender popped up whenever I typed "win" at the prompt in DR DOS. Luckily, update disks came from Digital Research and solved all my problems.

While it's unclear what "cruel coding" means exactly, the general idea is evidently that Microsoft introduces code into MS-DOS and/or Windows for the sole purpose of blocking its competitors, especially Novell. As we will see, this is not such a crazy idea. But it does not follow that every incompatibility between Windows and DR DOS therefore reflects back on Microsoft.

In this particular case, Microsoft is not at fault. The actual message that appears is "Standard Mode: Fault in MS-DOS Extender." This message comes from the Windows component DOSX.EXE, when you are trying to run Windows 3.1 in Standard mode on DR DOS 6.0; it does not occur in Windows 3.1 Enhanced mode. The term "Fault" here indicates a violation of one of the rules of protected mode; it usually indicates a bug in a program. Indeed, E-mail from one of the DR DOS developers reveals that, in fact, this one was DR DOS's problem:

> On the subject of Windows interaction with DOS, DR-DOS 6.0 did not function correctly with Windows 3.1; however, this was not related to any undocumented calls made by Windows. The problem was caused by an incompatibility in the EXEC handler (we caused the "NT" [nested task] flag to be set during the EXEC call as required by some old NEC processors; Windows DOS-X extender maintained the flags image when switching to protected mode and bang!).
>
> Windows 3.0 and 3.1 do make a number of undocumented calls to DOS if the version of DOS is 5.0 or higher. We are still [prior to Novell DOS 7.0] pretending to be version COMPAQ 3.31 so Windows does not use these calls. Under DOS 3.31 Windows is not as dirty as most networks, so it does not cause us any problems.

So much, at least in this case, for cruel coding! Yet the FTC's Bureau of Competition took the possibility of Microsoft "cruel coding" very seriously, for one of its attorneys asked us specifically about what Microsoft might have "put into" Windows to make it deliberately incompatible with DR DOS.

At first, this idea sounds completely ridiculous, and is reminiscent of the old, oft-repeated but never-proved drivel that MS-DOS 2.0 contained code to deliberately break Lotus 1-2-3. According to mythology, Microsoft's slogan was "DOS ain't done till Lotus don't run" (see, for example, Charles Ferguson and Charles Morris, *Computer Wars*, p. 66). No one has ever shown that DOS 2.0 in fact contained such code or even explained what it would look like. Perhaps:

```
if (exe_file == "123.EXE") then
    halt_and_catch_fire();
```

Microsoft's practice is, for better or for worse, usually exactly the opposite: to ensure that popular applications *run*, not break, under new releases of its operating systems, no matter what. The undocumented Windows GetAppCompatFlags() function (see *Undocumented Windows*, Chapter 5) is a perfect example of the insane lengths to which Microsoft goes to run popular applications, even from its competitors. Another good example is the ugly SETVER command in DOS 5, which compensates for the fact that many applications check for the DOS version in an incorrect manner. Finally, consider the fact that MS-DOS contains patches and workarounds for specific programs, including the Rational Systems DOS extender incorporated in Lotus 1-2-3.

In addition, while Windows and MS-DOS are tightly connected, the fact is that, in 386 Enhanced mode, they *need* to be. For example, while Windows can run multiple DOS boxes, there is only a single copy of DOS itself. While it is at first surprising to hear that DOS behaves differently when Windows Enhanced mode is running, it is important to realize that this DOS does this using documented function calls. When Windows starts up, it issues an INT 2Fh call with AX=1605h; when Windows exits, it issues an INT 2Fh with AX=1606h. MS-DOS 5.0 and 6.0 hook these calls to maintain (for Enhanced mode only) an IN_WINDOWS flag. But, as we'll see, while Microsoft does not document the way that MS-DOS 5.0 and 6.0 respond to these Windows calls, it does document the calls themselves, in its Windows Device Driver Kit (DDK). The Windows DDK is an admittedly obscure place to document information important to DOS programmers, but DOS programmers in the 1990s—even ones who resolutely "don't do Windows"—are going to have to get used to relying on the Windows DDK. Your DOS program may ignore Windows, but Windows will not ignore your program!

In short, it is hard to fault Microsoft for doing exactly what their advertising says they do, which is making MS-DOS into a better platform for Windows. A lot of the accusations against Microsoft sound like nothing more than scapegoating from the second-tier software companies such as Novell, Lotus, WordPerfect, and Borland, a lot of whose complaints about Microsoft resemble the way some Americans like to blame Japan for what are really our own domestic problems.

Now, it is true that, because of the undocumented interface shared by the Windows Enhanced mode DOSMGR VxD (inside WIN386.EXE) and MS-DOS 5.0 and 6.0, DOS emulators such as DR DOS—if they want to run Windows Enhanced mode—either must pretend to be an older version of DOS such as DOS 3.31, or they must reverse-engineer and implement this interface (as Novell DOS 7.0 has done). By failing to document this interface (which we will in part do for them later in this chapter!), Microsoft is allowing one of its products (MS-DOS) to essentially have "inside trading" with another one of its products (Windows). This is a major problem, but it has to do with undocumented interfaces, not "cruel coding." The fact remains that Windows did run on top of DR DOS 6.0, albeit a DR DOS 6.0 calling itself DOS 3.31. So what are all these accusations about Microsoft engineering Windows not to run on DR DOS? We'll see in a moment.

Systems Rivalry and Smoking Guns
No one would deny that Microsoft makes life difficult for its competitors (who of course are also often its customers; this gets into the separate "Chinese Wall" issue, which is discussed later in this chapter). But isn't that the nature of competition? A company should not be punished for so-called "predatory innovations," so long as these are really innovations and not attempts to inconvenience its rivals without "conveniencing" (so to speak) its customers.

How does one distinguish between the two? Surprisingly, there is some fascinating legal literature surrounding the issue of "deliberate incompatibilities." Many of the issues surrounding Microsoft's travails with the U.S. Federal Trade Commission have been dealt with before in cases involving companies such as Eastman Kodak and IBM. "Deliberate incompatibilities" form a fairly well-established part of antitrust law, going under monikers such as "tying arrangements," "non-price predation," and the (at first glance ridiculous-sounding) "predatory innovation."

While Microsoft wants to make MS-DOS a better platform for Windows, creating an *artificial* tie between Windows and MS-DOS for the sole purpose of hurting Novell would constitute predation.

The two crucial words here are "sole" and "artificial." Surely, Microsoft should be allowed to improve Windows, even in ways that might ultimately hurt DR DOS. This is a legitimate part of the competitive process, and whining about "predatory innovation" has rightly been rejected by the courts. For example, many manufacturers of so-called "plug compatibles" tried in the 1970s to have the courts characterize IBM's System/360 as "predatory innovation." The courts rejected these claims (along with, eventually, all of *U.S. v. IBM*, 1969-82), thereby "effectively requiring plaintiffs to prove that the defendant's design had no redeeming virtue for consumers" (Stephen F. Ross, *Principles of Antitrust Law*, 1993). (Techie's note: "consumers" is a synonym for "users.")

A fascinating article on this subject is "Predatory Systems Rivalry: A Reply" by James Ordover, Alan Sykes, and Robert Willig (*Columbia Law Review*, June 1983), who describe "systems rivalry" as follows:

> Suppose that company A manufactures a product system with two components, A1 and A2, each sold separately. Company A has monopoly power over A1, but company B competes in the market for the second component with its compatible offering, B2. Thus, consumers initially can use a product system comprised of either A1 and A2 or A1 and B2. Company A now introduces a new product system, A1' and A2', which serves roughly the same function for consumers as the old product system. Component B2, however, is incompatible with A1'. Furthermore, company A discontinues the sale of A1 or else reprices A1 substantially higher than before. As a consequence, consumers switch to the new product system and company B is driven from the market for component two.
>
> When, if ever, should the antitrust laws sanction company A for driving B out of the market?

There's a clear comparison here to Windows (A1), MS-DOS (A2), and DR DOS (B2). This scenario, which has nothing to do with operating-system software, underscores the fact that there's really little new in the questions surrounding Microsoft.

Normally, A driving B out of the market is what competition is all about. That's the goal of competition and should be protected. So how can you tell when this ceases to be honest competition and becomes predation? "Predatory Systems Rivalry" provides a good test:

> . . . the plaintiff must bear the burden of proof on this issue. To establish the illegitimacy of R&D expenses by a preponderance of the evidence, the plaintiff would most likely need a "smoking gun"—a document or oral admission that clearly reveals the innovator's culpable state of mind at the time of the R&D decision. Alternatively, the plaintiff could prevail if the innovation involves such trivial design changes that no reasonable man could believe that it had anything but an anticompetitive purpose.

This is what the question of the DOS/Windows connection boils down to: Has Microsoft done anything to Windows and/or MS-DOS for an anticompetitive purpose? Let's look at the closest thing we have to a "smoking gun."

The Windows AARD Detection Code

If you were one of the 15,000 Windows 3.1 beta testers, and if you happened to be using DR DOS rather than MS-DOS, you probably encountered the following, seemingly innocuous yet odd, error message generated by WIN.COM:

```
Non-Fatal error detected: error #2726
Please contact Windows 3.1 beta support
Press ENTER to exit or C to continue
```

As we'll see, this message is a visible manifestation of a piece of code in Windows whose implementation is technically slippery and evasive and which extensively uses undocumented DOS. Although it's difficult to gauge intent, this code doesn't appear to have a benign goal. Rather, its apparent purpose is to lay down arbitrary technical obstacles for "untested" DOS workalikes, DR DOS in particular.

The message first appeared with the release labeled "final beta release (build 61)" (dated December 20, 1991; the "Christmas beta"), and with "pre-release build 3.10.068" (January 21, 1992). Similar messages (with different error numbers) are produced in builds 61 and 68 by SETUP.EXE and by the versions of HIMEM.SYS, SMARTDRV.EXE, and MSD.EXE (Microsoft diagnostics) packaged with Windows. Although the error is non-fatal—that is, the program can continue running—WIN.COM's default behavior is to terminate the program, rather than continue.

The message itself first appeared in build 61, a late-stage beta, yet disappeared in the final retail release of Windows 3.1. However, the code that generates the message is present in the retail release, albeit in quiescent form, and executes every time you run Windows 3.1. In fact, we will see that one reason why Windows uses undocumented DOS function 52h is to implement the code that during the beta generated this error message on DR DOS.

It's significant that the message, which appeared when running on DR DOS (including a beta of an upcoming version, now named Novell DOS 7.0), did not appear when running on MS-DOS or PC-DOS. This raises the obvious question, what causes the error message?

There are many opponents of Microsoft who would jump to the immediate conclusion that this code *must* be the sign of a deliberate incompatibility inside Windows. Why else, they might say, would the message appear on DR DOS but not on MS-DOS? But until you know for sure exactly how the non-fatal error message is generated, it would be far more reasonable to assume that it's the manifestation of yet another bug in Novell's DR DOS. This wouldn't be the first time company N's bug had been misinterpreted as company M's "deliberate incompatibility."

Determining why the error message appears in DR DOS but not in MS-DOS requires examining the relevant code in WIN.COM that produces this message. However, this is easier said than none. Unlike a similar piece of code found in some versions of the Microsoft C compiler (see "Microsoft C Warranties and SetPSP(0)" in Chapter 4), the block of code in WIN.COM is XOR encrypted, self-modifying, and deliberately obfuscated, all in an apparent attempt to thwart disassembly.

The code also tries to defeat attempts to step through it in a debugger. For example, Figure 1-1 shows a code fragment in which WIN.COM points the INT 1 single-step interrupt at invalid code (the two bytes FFh FFh). WIN.COM does the same thing with INT 2 (nonmaskable interrupt) and INT 3 (debug breakpoint). This disassembly was produced by running Microsoft's DEBUG on the Windows 3.1 retail version of WIN.COM. As noted earlier, the same code is found in four other programs that ship with Windows.

Figure 1-1: The AARD Code in WIN.COM Attempts to Disable a Debugger

```
C:\DDJ\AARD>debug \win31\win.com
-u 3d0a
;;; Note that setting DS to 0; going to fiddle with intr vect table
7055:3D0A 33C0          XOR    AX,AX        ; AX = 0
7055:3D0C 8ED8          MOV    DS,AX        ; DS = 0
;;; ...
7055:3D12 A10400        MOV    AX,[0004]    ; get INT 1 offset
7055:3D15 2EA3D034      MOV    CS:[34D0],AX ; save away
7055:3D19 A10600        MOV    AX,[0006]    ; get INT 1 segment
7055:3D1C 2EA3D234      MOV    CS:[34D2],AX ; save away
7055:3D20 BBAC3F        MOV    BX,3FAC      ; set new INT handler ofs
7055:3D23 891E0400      MOV    [0004],BX
7055:3D27 8C0E0600      MOV    [0006],CS    ; set new INT handler seg

-u 3fac
6B30:3FAC FFFF          ??? DI              ; the new INT handler
6B30:3FAE CF            IRET                ;    is invalid code!
```

Yes, WIN.COM contains this code, which looks like something out of a teenage virus writer's nightmare. The code in Figure 1-1 would disable any attempt to set breakpoints in DEBUG. In Figure 1-1, we were still able to use DEBUG to examine this DEBUG-defeating code, because, rather than set breakpoints, we used the DEBUG unassembly command. Furthermore, WIN.COM's revectoring of INT 1-3 doesn't affect a modern debugger such as Nu-Mega's Soft-ICE, which runs the debugger and debuggee in separate address spaces. In any case, these attempts to throw pursuers off the track are in themselves quite revealing.

These attempts become far more effective later on, where the code is actually *encrypted*. WIN.COM passes the encrypted code through an XOR filter before execution. There is also a large amount of what we can only call "obfuscation". You can see this for yourself by using DEBUG to unassemble the Windows 3.1 retail version of WIN.COM or the SYSTEM\WIN.CNF file (dated March 10, 1992), which Windows 3.1 SETUP uses to build WIN.COM. Under DEBUG, the relevant code starts at offset 3CE2h and ends at 3FAEh:

```
C:\WIN31>type aard.scr
u 3ce2 3fae
q
C:\WIN31>debug win.com < aard.scr > aard.lst
```

Turning the resulting AARD.LST file into something reasonable will, we predict, cause you many hours of grief.

For some reason, while much of the code is XOR encrypted, it contains as plain-text a Microsoft copyright notice and the initials 'AARD' and 'RSAA', perhaps the programmer's signature. This has fueled speculation in the press (see, for example, Wendy Goldman Rohm, "Will the FTC Come to Its Senses About Microsoft's Mischief?," *Upside*, August 1993) that this code was written by none other than Aaron Reynolds, one of Micrsoft's most highly skilled and well-respected programmers and author of much of both MS-DOS and Windows Enhanced mode. Not surprisingly, this block of code has become known as "the AARD code."

A Gauntlet of Tests   Given the encryption and obfuscation, it would take far too long to present the actual AARD code. Figure 1-2 shows a pseudocode summary of the disassembled code. In essence, the AARD code (which, remember, is part of Windows, a product sold separately from MS-DOS) uses undocumented DOS functions and structures to check for genuine MS-DOS or PC-DOS.

Figure 1-2: Pseudocode of the AARD Code in WIN.COM

```
move (and fixup) code from 2D19h to 4E0h
call code at 4E0h
    call AARD code at 39B2h:
        -- see below
    IF (AX doesn't match 2000h)
        AND IF (control_byte is non-zero)     ;; added in retail
            THEN overwrite BYTE at 4E0h to a RET instruction
; ...
IF (byte at 4E0h is a RET instruction)
    THEN issue non-fatal error message

 call AARD code at 39B2h:
    point INT 1, 2, 3 and at invalid code to confuse debuggers
    call undocumented INT 21h AH=52h to get SysVars ("List of Lists")
    copy first 30h bytes of SysVars to stack
    copy first 4 bytes (DPB ptr) of copy of SysVars to stack
    IF DOS version >= 10.0 (i.e., OS/2)
        THEN don't set [bp+196h], so eventually OR AX, 2000h fails
    ELSE
        check fields in SysVars to ensure non-zero:
```

```
         SysVars[0] -- Disk Parameter Block (DPB)
         SysVars[4] -- System File Table (SFT)
         SysVars[8] -- Clock device
         SysVars[12h] -- Buffers header
         SysVars[16h] -- Current Directory Structure (CDS)
         SysVars[0Ch] -- CON device
         SysVars[22h] -- Device driver chain (NUL device next ptr)
IF no SysVars fields are zero (MS-DOS, or WIN.COM in DR DOS)
    THEN set [bp+196h] so that eventually OR AX, 2000h succeeds
ELSE some are zero (e.g., HIMEM.SYS in DR DOS)
    THEN don't set [bp+196h], so eventually OR AX, 2000h fails
copy code
jump to copied code
copy and XOR code
jump to copied and XORed code
;; the following crucial part was figured out by Geoff Chappell:
IF a redirector is running (INT 2Fh AX=1100h)
    AND IF default upper-case map (INT 21h AH=38h) in DOS
            data segment (undocumented INT 2Fh AX=1203h)
OR IF no redirector
    AND IF first System FCB header (SysVars[1Ah]) offset == 0
    THEN DOS is considered okay
ELSE (e.g., WIN.COM, SMARTDRV.EXE, etc. in DR DOS)
    THEN clear part of [bp+196h] so eventually OR AX, 2000h fails
restore previous INT 1, 2, 3
jump back to saved return address
```

As seen in Figure 1-2, the AARD code relies heavily on undocumented DOS functions and data structures. This code calls undocumented INT 21h function 52h to get a pointer to the DOS internal Sys-Vars structure, popularly known as the "List of Lists." SysVars contains pointers to other DOS internal data structures, such as the current directory structure (CDS) and system file table (SFT). The AARD code checks a number of these pointers in SysVars, ensuring that none are null.

Any moderately self-respecting DOS workalike must implement these internal DOS data structures in the same way that MS-DOS does and should pass unscathed through this initial set of tests. Indeed, if any of these initial tests *did* fail, Windows certainly would not run, given what we will see later is Windows's heavy reliance on these undocumented DOS data structures.

Interestingly, when this code is incorporated in a device driver such as HIMEM.SYS, it fails under DR DOS 5.0 and 6.0. These versions of DR DOS do not contain a genuine CDS and don't set up a simulated CDS until after device-driver initialization time. Thus, the Windows 3.1 beta HIMEM.SYS produces a non-fatal error message under DR DOS 5.0 and 6.0. Similarly, the AARD code fails under the Windows NT beta, where the DPB pointer in SysVars is null. Finally, the code fails in an OS/2 DOS box, where the DOS version number is 10.0 or greater (for example, OS/2 2.1 masquerades as DOS 20.10). The crucial and, appropriately, the most obfuscated test, however, appears at the end of the AARD test gauntlet, highlighted in Figure 1-3.

Figure 1-3: The Crucial AARD Test for DOS Legitimacy

```
IF a redirector is running (INT 2Fh AX=1100h)
    AND IF default upper-case map (INT 21h AH=38h) in DOS
            data segment (undocumented INT 2Fh AX=1203h)
OR IF no redirector
    AND IF first System FCB header (SysVars[1Ah]) offset == 0
THEN DOS is considered okay
```

This test, which was unraveled by Geoff Chappell (author of the book *DOS Internals*) first checks to see whether a network redirector (such as MSCDEX) is running. In this case, AARD checks that DOS's default upper case-map is located in the DOS data segment, which it locates by calling undocumented DOS INT 2Fh AX=1203h (see the appendix). If no redirector is running, AARD checks that the pointer to the first System File Control Block (FCB) is located on a paragraph boundary; that is, it has a 0 offset. AARD gets the pointer to the first System FCB from offset 1Ah in SysVars, which it retrieved earlier using undocumented DOS function 52h. All versions of MS-DOS pass this test; no version of DR DOS does.

To test whether this interpretation of the encrypted and heavily-obfuscated code is correct, Listing 1-1 shows MSDETECT.C. This program performs the same tests as the original AARD code, but without the obfuscations and with more informative "error" messages. MSDETECT succeeds under all versions of MS-DOS tested (Compaq DOS 3.31, MS-DOS 5.0, MS-DOS 6.0), and fails under all versions of DR DOS tested (DR DOS 5.0, DR DOS 6.0, beta Novell DOS 7.0). If it is running under DR DOS with a redirector, MSDETECT fails with the message "Default case map isn't in DOS data segment!" Otherwise it fails under DR DOS with the message "First System FCB not located on paragraph boundary!"

Listing 1-1: MSDETECT.C

```
/*
MSDETECT.C
Andrew Schulman, May 1993
From "Undocumented DOS", 2nd edition (Addison-Wesley, 1993)
See also Dr. Dobb's Journal, September 1993

A duplication of Microsoft's MS-DOS detection code from Windows 3.1
WIN.COM (WIN.CNF), SMARTDRV.EXE, HIMEM.SYS, SETUP.EXE, MSD.EXE

The original Microsoft code (with the initials 'AARD') is heavily XOR
encrypted and obfuscated. Here the encryptions and obfuscations have
been removed. The AARD code also attempts to disable debuggers by
pointing INT 1, 2, and 3 at invalid code (FFh FFh); this also has
been avoided here.

The original AARD code non-fatal error message has been replaced
with more informative messages about the exact "problem" (i.e.,
difference from MS-DOS).

Geoff Chappell deciphered the original code's tests (upper case map
segment, System FCB) in the case where the preliminary SysVars tests
fail. Some of this material is discussed in Geoff's forthcoming book,
"DOS Internals" (Addison-Wesley, 1993).

Optional command-line switches -DOREDIR and -NOREDIR have been added
to aid testing both crucial tests whether or not a redirector is
actually installed.

Build program with Microsoft C: cl msdetect.c
*/

#include <stdlib.h>
#include <stdio.h>
#include <string.h>
#include <dos.h>

typedef int BOOL;
typedef unsigned char BYTE;
typedef unsigned short WORD;
typedef unsigned long DWORD;
typedef void far *FP;

BYTE far *_dos_getsysvars(void);
FP _dos_getcasemap(void);
WORD _dos_getdataseg(void);
BOOL _dos_isredirector(void);

void fail(const char *s) { puts(s); exit(1); }

main(int argc, char *argv[])
{
    BYTE far *sysvars;
    int do_redir = -1;
```

```c
    // this is just to make testing easier
    // can fake presence or absence of a network redirector
    // to exercise both tests
    if (argc > 1 && argv[1][0] == '-')
    {
        char *s = strupr(&argv[1][1]);
        if (strcmp(s, "DOREDIR") == 0)
            do_redir = 1;
        else if (strcmp(s, "NOREDIR") == 0)
            do_redir = 0;
        else
            fail("usage: msdetect [-doredir] [-noredir]");
    }

    if ((sysvars = _dos_getsysvars()) == 0)
        fail("INT 21h AX=5200h returns 0!");

    if (_osmajor >= 0x0a)
        fail("DOS version >= 10; this is OS/2 (or early NT beta!)");

#define SYSVARS(ofs)           (*((FP far *) &sysvars[ofs]))
#define SYSVARS_TEST(ofs, msg)  if (! SYSVARS(ofs)) fail(msg)

    SYSVARS_TEST(0, "Disk Parameter Block (DPB) pointer is 0!");
    SYSVARS_TEST(4, "System File Table (SFT) pointer is 0!");
    SYSVARS_TEST(8, "CLOCK$ device pointer is 0!");
    SYSVARS_TEST(0x12, "BUFFERS header pointer is 0!");
    // next test fails in device-driver init (HIMEM.SYS) under DR DOS 6.0
    SYSVARS_TEST(0x16, "Current Directory Struct (CDS) ptr is 0!");
    SYSVARS_TEST(0x0C, "CON device pointer is 0!");
    SYSVARS_TEST(0x22, "Device chain ptr (from NUL) is 0!");

    if ((! _dos_isredirector()) && (do_redir == -1))
        do_redir = 0;

    // the following tests fail under DR DOS 5 and 6
    // (and under beta of Novell DOS 7)
    if (do_redir)
    {
        FP casemap;
        puts("Doing redirector test");
        casemap = _dos_getcasemap();
        if (FP_SEG(casemap) != _dos_getdataseg())
            fail("Default case map isn't in DOS data segment!");
        printf("case map @ %Fp\n", casemap);
    }
    else
    {
        puts("Doing no-redirector test");
        if (FP_OFF(SYSVARS(0x1A)) != 0)
            fail("First System FCB not located on paragraph boundary!");
        printf("System FCB ptr @ %Fp -> %Fp\n", sysvars+0x1a, SYSVARS(0x1A));
    }

    // if get here, everything checks out
    puts("All tests check out: must be MS-DOS");
    return 0;
}
// undocumented function
BYTE far *_dos_getsysvars(void)
{
    // could initialize ES:BX to 0:0 but the MS code doesn't do this
    _asm mov ax, 5200h
    _asm int 21h
    _asm mov dx, es
```

```
    _asm mov ax, bx
    // ES:BX retval moved into DX:AX
}
// formerly undocumented function
BOOL _dos_isredirector(void)
{
    BYTE retval;
    _asm mov ax, 1100h
    _asm int 2fh
    _asm mov retval, al
    return (retval == 0xFF);
}
// undocumented function
WORD _dos_getdataseg(void)
{
    _asm push ds
    _asm mov ax, 1203h
    _asm int 2fh
    _asm mov ax, ds
    _asm pop ds
    // retval in AX
}
// documented function: get far pointer to default case map
FP _dos_getcasemap(void)
{
    BYTE country_info[34];
    FP fp = (FP) country_info;
    _asm push ds
    _asm mov ax, 3800h
    _asm lds dx, dword ptr fp
    _asm int 21h
    _asm pop ds
    return *((FP far *) &country_info[18]);
}
```

A Gratuitous Gatekeeper   But what does "country information" like the DOS default upper case-map have to do with a network redirector? Good question! Why does a piece of Windows care whether this mapper is located in the DOS data segment? Good question! And why should it care whether the first System FCB is located on a paragraph boundary? What kind of "errors" are these, anyway?

In fact, the address of the default upper case-map has nothing to do with the network redirector, and no other part of Windows cares about what particular form is taken by DOS's default case-map or first System FCB pointers (System FCBs are discussed briefly in Chapter 8). Unlike the earlier part of the AARD test, which checks for internal DOS data structures on which Windows genuinely relies, this crucial part of the AARD code has no relation to the actual purpose of the five otherwise-unrelated programs into which it has been dropped. It is a wholly arbitrary test, with seemingly no purpose other than to smoke out non-Microsoft versions of DOS, tagging them with an appropriately vague "error" message.

Suitably, the section of the AARD code that performs this crucial test is the most heavily XOR encrypted and obfuscated. The test in Figure 1-3 is the crucial piece of information used by Windows to determine whether it is running on MS-DOS, or on a DOS "workalike."

This code checks some rather unimportant aspects of DOS. In fact, you can have an otherwise perfectly workable DOS, capable of running Windows, and yet not pass the above test for the specific location of the case map and System FCB. To check that the AARD code's test serves no technically useful purpose, you can use Microsoft's SYMDEB debugger to slightly alter ("denormalize") DOS's pointers to the default case-map and the System SFT. As you may recall, it's possible to change the outward form of a segment:offset pointer without necessarily changing what location it points to. Recall that, in real mode, a single memory location can be addressed by different pointers; there are many combinations of different segment and offset values that all resolve to the same physical address and are therefore equivalent. Not surprisingly, Windows is unaffected by this change to these pointers. As shown in Figure 1-4, the only software that noticed was MSDETECT and the AARD code in WIN.COM.

Figure 1-4: Making the AARD Code Fail

```
C:\UNDOC2\CHAP1>symdeb
Microsoft Symbolic Debug Utility
Windows Version 3.00
(C) Copyright Microsoft Corp 1984-1990
Processor is [80386]

;;; The first System FCB is stored in this configuration at 0116:0040,
;;; so "denormalize" the pointer at that location, changing it from
;;; 05E4:0000 to 05E0:0040. This points to the same exact location,
;;; but since the offset isn't zero the AARD test fails.

-dd 0116:0040 0040
0116:0040   05E4:0000
-ed 0116:0040 05E0:0040

;;; Now normalize the pointer for the default case map. I had to
;;; disassemble the code for INT 21h AH=38h to find where this is
;;; located. The pointer is stored here at 0116:12A8. Below, the
;;; pointer is changed from 0116:0CF5 to 01E5:0005. This points
;;; to the same exact location, but the segment isn't 0116 (DOS data
;;; segment) anymore, so the AARD test fails.

-dd 0116:12a8 12a8
0116:12A8   0116:0CF5
-ed 0116:12A8 01E5:0005
-q

C:\WINB61>win
Non-Fatal error detected: error #2726
Please contact Windows 3.1 beta support
Press ENTER to exit or C to continue

C:\UNDOC2\CHAP1>msdetect
Default case map isn't in DOS data segment!
```

These results are hardly surprising. Even a recent *Microsoft KnowledgeBase* article ("Replace Case Mapping Function with Proprietary Version," *Q49239*, April 29, 1993) reminds us that it is perfectly legitimate and documented for a DOS program to hook INT 21h AH=38h and replace the built-in case mapping function.

As has already been noted about half a dozen times, Windows relies heavily on undocumented DOS calls. This in itself is a problem, which we will take up later, but perhaps the AARD code is simply verifying that the underlying DOS in fact supports the undocumented DOS calls upon which Windows relies? Indeed, the early part of the AARD code does test for the presence of internal DOS data structures whose absence would certainly cause Windows to fail miserably. *If the AARD code stopped there, it would be very difficult to complain about this code.* However, DR DOS does not fail these tests in WIN.COM. DR DOS fails on the redirector/System FCB/case map test in Figure 1-3. And Windows does not rely on that behavior at all.

In other contexts (such as MSD's need to identify the operating system), it would be perfectly legitimate to walk internal DOS data structures to see that they were the same as would be expected under genuine MS-DOS. Or, if the AARD tested solely for those DOS internal data structures on which Windows actually relies, that too would be legitimate (though we still have to ask why Windows is relying on aspects of MS-DOS that Microsoft refuses to disclose to the rest of the software-development community). However, the fact that WIN.COM and other programs incorporating AARD code don't go on to make any use of the information gained in this way, other than to print the non-fatal error message, points to a deliberate incompatibility rather than a legitimate need to know some information about the underlying DOS.

The very non-fatality of the "error" further underlines the fact that it is not Windows's legitimate business to care whether it's running on genuine MS-DOS. If the program can continue running despite the detected "error," then how much of an error was it to begin with? Why should Windows possibly care where the default case map and first System FCB are located? It seems that the only "error" is that the user is running Windows on someone else's version of DOS.

Does Beta Code Really Matter?   The non-fatal error message appeared only in two widely-distributed beta builds of Windows. The retail version of Windows 3.1 does not produce it. So this is just dead history, right?

Not quite. Anyone with a copy of Windows 3.1 can hex dump WIN.COM or WIN.CNF and see the error message (including the mention of "beta support") and AARD and RSAA signatures. In other words, the crazy-looking AARD code paraphrased in Figure 1-2 executes every time you run Windows. The AARD code also remains in Windows SETUP and in the Windows version of SMARTDRV.EXE (it appears to have been removed from HIMEM and MSD).

It's perfectly natural for software to contain vestigial remnants of past implementations. For example, WIN.COM also refers to the short-lived MSDPMI utility from the Microsoft C 7.0 beta. But in the case of the AARD code, new instructions were *added* to the AARD portion of Windows 3.1 retail WIN.COM—instructions that weren't present in the beta.

In the retail version of WIN.COM, the AARD code contains additional instructions as well as a control byte. The control byte determines whether or not the error message appears; this byte is currently 0. As shown in Figure 1-5, when running the retail WIN.COM under DR DOS, you can easily use DR's version of DEBUG to turn on the control byte, and the message is issued just as under the beta versions. When running on DR DOS or an MS-DOS in which the FCB and/or case-map pointers have been suitably denormalized, changing the single byte at offset 16D4h in WIN.COM triggers the printing of the message.

Figure 1-5: Resurrecting the AARD Error Message in Windows 3.1 Retail

```
C:\DRDOS6>debug win.com
DEBUG v1.40      Program Debugger.
Copyright (c) 1985,1992 Digital Research Inc. All rights reserved

CPU type is [i486 in virtual 8086 mode]
-d 16d4 16d4
2271:16D0               00
-e 16d4 1
-g
Non-Fatal error detected: error #2726
Please contact Windows 3.1 beta support
Press ENTER to exit or C to continue
Program terminated.
```

Furthermore, don't dismiss this error message just because it only appeared in beta and not in the retail version. The sheer size of Microsoft's beta test programs makes them significant product releases in themselves. As noted earlier, there were 15,000 Windows 3.1 beta sites. Microsoft's beta tests are major industry events. Microsoft's beta releases go to their most important and influential customers, both large-volume purchasers and commercial and in-house software developers. Beta sites also include journalists at influential magazines such as *PC Week*, *InfoWorld* and *PC Magazine*. Many published evaluations are based on beta versions only. So it appears that Microsoft has used its extensive Windows beta program as a way to leverage MS-DOS against would-be competitors such as DR DOS.

So What?   A non-fatal error message in a beta version: that's it? If you have an axe to grind with Microsoft, you may have expected some more nakedly robber-baronesque behavior. If this is the worst that can be found, perhaps things aren't so bad after all. Note, however, that at least one other "smoking gun" has appeared: the amazing warranty-related error message in QuickC and Microsoft C 6.0, discussed in Chapter 4. While it's difficult to second-guess the precise goal of the encrypted and obfuscated AARD code, its results are clear enough. Windows beta sites that used DR DOS rather than MS-DOS would have been scared into not using DR DOS. ("Doctor, every time I do this I get a non-fatal warning." "Then stop doing it.")

Speculating further, a conceivable goal of the AARD code was to delay Novell's attempts to get out a version of DR DOS that is compatible with Windows 3.1. Recall that the AARD code was added to Windows toward the end of the beta test. The scenario runs as follows: Novell notices the message and panics that its customers will get weird errors whenever they run Windows 3.1. Its logical next step is to try to reverse-engineer WIN.COM in order to figure out why. However, the code has been deliberately written to obscure the precise test that is being conducted (and you thought those "Obfuscated C" contests served no practical purpose!).

The effect of the AARD code is to create a new and highly artificial test of DOS compatibility. The obfuscations and encryptions make it difficult for a competitor even to determine what is being tested. An indication that the AARD code's obfuscation was successful is the fact that a beta version of Novell's latest version of DR DOS fails the test, even though this version is otherwise far more compatible with MS-DOS than previous versions.

Still, it is hard to believe that Microsoft would exert such efforts to clobber something with as little market share (and as many problems) as DR DOS. DR DOS's brief place in the sun was due to the horrible MS-DOS 4.0 and PC-DOS 4.0 releases from IBM, and as soon as MS-DOS 5.0 came out any reason to use DR DOS pretty much evaporated, for retail customers, at least. But consider OEM purchasers, who must put a copy of DOS on every machine they sell. For every single non-IBM PC sold today, Microsoft extracts a tithe of something like $25. (Further, see Manes and Andrews, *Gates*, pp. 263–265, for a detailed discussion of Microsoft's per-machine rather than per-copy OEM pricing of MS-DOS.) Microsoft, not blind to Intel's experiences with AMD and Cyrix, fears any threat (no matter how lame) to this wonderful monopoly position.

Microsoft's Response   While Microsoft has provided no formal response to these accusations, Brad Silverberg, Microsoft's VP of Systems Software, was quoted in *Upside* (August 1993) as providing the following defense for the AARD error message: "Windows is designed for MS-DOS. If DR DOS is 100 percent compatible with MS-DOS as they claim, then it would never show up."

The implication is that if DR DOS gets an error message from Windows that MS-DOS doesn't get, then by definition it is Novell's fault and proof that DR DOS isn't 100% compatible (which it isn't, but that's another story: see Chapter 4). The problem with this argument is that, as seen in Figure 1-3, the AARD code's test for DOS compatibility is 100 percent artificial. By Microsoft's definition, only MS-DOS or something byte-for-byte identical with MS-DOS (and therefore in violation of copyright) is "100 percent DOS compatible."

As for why Microsoft disabled this code's output in the final shipping version of Windows 3.1, Silverberg told reporter Wendy Rohm "It wasn't worth the hassle." Rohm: "The hassle of?" Silverberg: "Of people like you asking me questions like this. [Laughs]" (*Upside*, August 1993).

Privately, a high-level manager at Microsoft has repeatedly told us that there can't be any malicious intent to the AARD code, because Microsoft is "agnostic" regarding DR DOS. This seems unlikely given the effort required to write this tricky code. Its presence in five otherwise unrelated programs also points to a fairly concerted effort, as it is unlikely that five so different programs are all maintained by the same person. In fact, the programs probably fall under the domain of several different product managers or divisions. Finally, this same Microsoft official has argued that the AARD code represented a legitimate effort by Microsoft to ensure compatibility and reduce technical-support costs for Windows. The AARD code, in other words, is really a form of quality control, to protect Windows' "goodwill." The argument goes something like this:

- Windows is not just any old DOS application but part of a "seamless" integarted system with MS-DOS. (This seems to be just another way of saying that Windows relies heavily on undocumented DOS internals.)
- Microsoft has no guarantee that other vendors' versions of DOS support all the DOS functionality that Windows requires.
- Microsoft is not obligated to test Windows on these others vendors' versions of DOS.
- Therefore, Microsoft needed a way for Windows to test for the presence of some other, i.e., untested, version of DOS and to warn the user of a *possible* problem, i.e., that the combination of Windows with this version of DOS was untested and was not guaranteed to work.
- The test had to be encrypted and obfuscated in some way, otherwise the other DOS vendor could easily circumvent the test by changing its DOS to conform to whatever the code was testing for, without doing anything else to make its DOS more compatible.

Note that this defense of the AARD code rests on Windows' use of undocumented DOS calls. According to the argument, the AARD is not deliberately incompatible. That is, it serves a legitimate purpose for consumers, because Windows depends so heavily on undocumented DOS calls and structures that Microsoft has no guarantee that Windows will work on anyone else's DOS. In other words, Windows rests on undocumented DOS calls, and the AARD code was an attempt to shore up this shaky foundation.

But in this case, why not test for the *specific* undocumented DOS functionality on which Windows relies? Why test for features that Windows doesn't care about? By constructing the totally contrived redirector/System FCB/case map test, Microsoft has constructed what looks very much like a deliberate incompatibility. The Windows beta produced a frightening-looking error message on DR DOS only because DR DOS failed to pass this contrived and well-hidden test. This does not look like a form of quality control or like mere protection of Windows' goodwill.

Documentation vs. Tying If Microsoft needs to exert quality control over how Windows runs on top of untested operating systems, surely there must be other, more reasonable, ways than by tying Windows to MS-DOS via warning messages and encrypted code. If Windows relies on some undocumented aspects of DOS, then Microsoft can *document* what it is that Windows requires of an underlying DOS. Instead of the AARD code, Microsoft could have issued a specification detailing the internal DOS calls and data structures that Windows requires. If DR DOS fails to meet these specifications, so be it. Or Microsoft could produce a TSR or other add-in to MS-DOS that provided a documented equivalent to the undocumented calls, similar to TOOLHELP.DLL in Windows. The alternative to Microsoft's tying of Windows and MS-DOS, in other words, is *documentation*.

Interestingly, when a company says that two of its products must be tied in some way, the courts have long held that the company can instead produce specifications of minimum quality standards. For example, in *Siegel v. Chicken Delight* (1971), where Chicken Delight required its franchisees to purchase all their supplies and mixes directly from Chicken Delight, a court held this tie to be unnecessary, as "effective quality control could be achieved by specification in the case of the cooking machinery and the dip and spice mixes." Similarly, Microsoft could document the "secret herbs and spices" (as it were) Windows expects of the underlying DOS. Without this, competition for DOS is not a "level playing field."

However, not everyone agrees that companies should be required to replace tying arrangements with documentation. For example, Robert Bork (a well-known judge whose views closely parallel those of the Chicago school of economics) in a section of his *The Antitrust Paradox* (1978) devoted to "Technological Interdependence or the 'Protection of Goodwill'" says that "the manufacturer is likely to understand the technical problems of his machines better than lessees" and that "the writing of specifications and the continual policing required to make sure they are complied with is also certain to be more expensive than supplying the related good oneself."

In other words, the "transaction costs" are too high for proper documentation and specifications, proper interfaces are too expensive, and the production of technically interdependent products is best handled within a firm ("supplying the related good oneself"), as an internal matter, rather than leaving it up to the market. So much for the "free market," which is apparently too inefficient! It follows from this, of course, that so-called "Chinese Walls" between the different divisions of such a firm are unnecessary. Likewise, it would follow that use of undocumented functions is a non-issue.

But there need to be "Chinese Walls," not only because Microsoft keeps claiming they exist, when they obviously don't (Microsoft uses its monopoly position as operating-systems supplier to leverage its competitive position as applications vendor), but also because this is *good engineering practice*. These nonexistent Chinese Walls are really nothing more than what software engineering calls "firewalls": narrow and well-documented interfaces. Despite the claims that tying arrangements are a nice, inexpensive alternative to proper documentation and public interfaces, engineering experience tells us otherwise.

Is it right for Microsoft to be able to use undocumented DOS calls in its Windows product? Is Microsoft obligated to either document all of these calls, or to erect a "Chinese Wall" (i.e., a well-defined, public interface!) between DOS and Windows? On the one hand, these are both pieces of *system* software; Windows is not (unless you consider it perhaps a Solitaire engine) an application. On the other hand, Windows competes (or did, before it won the GUI wars) with desktop shells from other companies. Microsoft can make its shell work better on top of DOS by both incorporating knowledge of DOS internals into Windows and by making DOS more Windows-compatible. No other company has that double luxury. Should Microsoft have this luxury or should it be required to spell out exactly how its products tie together?

Microsoft Windows Uses Undocumented DOS

Let's examine the DOS/Windows connection in greater detail. To properly cover this subject would require an entire, separate book (we know, because we wrote several hundred pages already and then put them aside for another book!), but certainly we can get some idea of what DOS and Windows have to say to each other. As everyone knows, Windows is itself a DOS program that you start by typing WIN at the DOS prompt or, just as likely, by putting WIN in your AUTOEXEC.BAT file. Actually, Windows is a whole collection of programs and drivers that WIN.COM kicks off.

Bootstrapping the protected mode, multitasking, graphical, windowed, dynamic linking, device-independent Windows operating environment on top of the feeble little single-tasking, real mode MS-DOS operating system is a tricky business that requires, not surprisingly, intimate knowledge of how MS-DOS works. This is knowledge that Microsoft uses to implement Windows but does not document for other vendors.

Let's look at exactly which undocumented DOS calls Windows makes. How do you find out what DOS functions, documented or undocumented, a program relies on? If you had access to the source code, you could just look at it. Chapter 6 discusses disassembly, but there is an easier way, if you're just interested in what DOS calls a program makes. The architecture of MS-DOS lets you hook into system interrupts, including INT 21h itself. Why not write a utility that hooks INT 21h and other DOS interrupts and that tells you whenever a program makes an undocumented DOS call?

David Maxey designed the program INTRSPY for this very purpose. It is an event-driven, script-driven DOS debugger that you can also use for many tasks that have nothing to do with undocumented DOS. Chapter 5 of this book describes a new, enhanced version of this program in detail. You can write an INTRSPY script that logs information to a file every time a program makes an undocumented DOS call. A very simple INTRSPY script that monitors some undocumented DOS calls, but that doesn't use many INTRSPY features, appears in Listing 1-2. This script includes only a few undocumented DOS calls. For example, the script does not intercept INT 2Ah critical-section functions because Windows generates so many of these functions that they would overflow the INTRSPY results buffer. Windows makes many other undocumented DOS calls besides those that UNDOC.SCR traps, but the few that UNDOC.SCR does trap are still quite a handful.

It is important to underline that what we're discussing here is undocumented DOS calls made by Windows. This is an entirely separate subject from that discussed in *Undocumented Windows*. That book covered the subject of undocumented calls in Windows itself; it also handled the controversial subject of which Microsoft applications use these calls. That book did not, however, go into how Windows itself boots on top of DOS, or what undocumented DOS functionality Windows relies upon.

Listing 1-2: INTRSPY Script UNDOC.SCR

```
;;
;; UNDOC.SCR
;;
intercept 21h
    function 52h on_exit output "2152: Get List of Lists: " ES ":" BX
    function 55h on_entry output "2155: Create PSP: " DX ", " SI
    function 53h on_exit output "2153: Translate BPB"
    function 5dh subfunction 06h
        on_exit output "215D06: Get DOSSWAP: " DS ":" SI
    function 60h
        on_entry output "2160: Canon File: " (DS:SI->byte,asciiz,64)
        on_exit sameline " ==> " (ES:DI->byte,asciiz,64)
;;
;; Use the next functions and ints 20h and 27h to show which
;; program made the undoc DOS call, and to show termination
;;
    function 4bh
        on_entry
            output "----------------------------"
            output (DS:DX->byte,asciiz,64)
    function 4ch on_entry output "----------------------------"
    function 31h on_entry output "--------- TSR -----------"
intercept 20h on_entry output "----------------------------"
intercept 27h on_entry output "--------- TSR -----------"
;;
;; Too many int 2Ah to show. Could use INTRSPY counters though.
;;
intercept 2fh
    function 13h
        on_entry output "2F13: Set Disk Handler " DS ":" DX
        on_exit sameline " (Prev: " DS ":" DX ")"
```

Figure 1-6 shows output from INTRSPY when starting Windows 3.1 Enhanced mode under MS-DOS 5.0.

Figure 1-6: Selected Windows 3.1 Enhanced Mode Undocumented DOS calls

```
C:\WIN31\WIN.COM
2152: Get List of Lists: 0116:0026
2152: Get List of Lists: 0116:0026
----------------------------
C:\WIN31\system\win386.exe
2F13: Set Disk Handler 338A:1AC5 (Prev: F000:9C13)
2F13: Set Disk Handler F000:9C13 (Prev: 338A:1AC5)
2F13: Set Disk Handler 338A:0AB8 (Prev: F000:9C13)
2F13: Set Disk Handler F000:9C13 (Prev: 338A:0AB8)
```

```
2152: Get List of Lists: 0116:0026
2152: Get List of Lists: 0116:0026
2F13: Set Disk Handler 338A:00B7 (Prev: F000:9C13)
2F13: Set Disk Handler F000:9C13 (Prev: 338A:00B7)
... tons of 2F/13 calls ...
2152: Get List of Lists: 0116:0026
215D06: Get DOSSWAP: 0116:0320
------------------------
 C:\WIN31\system\KRNL386.EXE
2152: Get List of Lists: 0116:0026
2155: Create PSP: 5576, 0100
```

In Figure 1-6, we see that when starting Windows in Enhanced mode, WIN.COM runs WIN386.EXE. WIN386.EXE is a collection of Windows virtual device drivers (VxDs). A few key VxDs are the Virtual Machine Manager (VMM), the MS-DOS Manager (DOSMGR), the MS-DOS Network Manager (DOSNET), the Virtual-8086 Mode Memory Manager (V86MMGR), the Virtual Programmable Interrupt Controller Device (VPICD), and the Virtual Block Device (BlockDev).

For the purposes of seeing the interaction between DOS and Windows, the key VxD is, as you might guess from its name, DOSMGR. When trying to understand why Windows calls the functions shown in Figure 1-6, DOSMGR is where we will spend most of our time. It isn't enough to say that Windows makes this or that undocumented DOS call because there really isn't any such single entity as Windows. Instead, Windows is a collection of many separate programs, libraries, drivers, and initialization files; it is important to pin the undocumented DOS calls made by Windows down to specific modules.

Another VxD, SHELL, launches KRNL386.EXE, which is a Windows DLL containing the kernel portion of the Windows application programming interface (API). For example, KRNL386 contains the Windows dynamic-linking code that knows how to load Windows executables, Windows device drivers (which are not the same as VxDs), and DLLs. KRNL386 launches other DLLs like USER and GDI. If the INTRSPY script also trapped calls to the DOS file open function (INT 21h AH=3Dh), the resulting log would show many files being accessed, including Windows EXE, DLL, DRV, and INI files. Eventually, whatever program is named in the SYSTEM.INI shell= setting comes up. By default, shell=progman.exe (Program Manager), but just as COMMAND.COM isn't the only possible shell for MS-DOS, PROGMAN.EXE isn't the only possible interface for the Windows desktop.

In Figure 1-6, it is clear that Windows (or, rather, various parts of Windows) calls INT 21h AH=52h (Get SysVars), INT 21h AH=55h (Create PSP), INT 21h AX=5D06h (Get SDA), and INT 2Fh AH=13h (Set Disk Handler). As noted earlier, Windows makes many additional undocumented DOS calls, but the few shown here are enough.

Let's briefly try to see why Windows is making these calls. INTRSPY only shows *what*. To see *why*, you need either to disassemble pieces of Windows with a product such as Windows Source from V Communications or to run Windows under a debugger such as Soft-ICE from Nu-Mega.

WIN.COM Walks the SFT

Why does WIN.COM call the undocumented Get SysVars function (INT 21h AH=52h)? This function returns a pointer in ES:BX to the internal SysVars structure within the DOS data segment. This structure in turn contains pointers to many other key internal DOS data structures, such as the Memory Control Block (MCB) chain, the System File Table (SFT) chain, the Current Directory Structure (CDS) table, and so on. For this reason, this structure is sometimes called the List of Lists.

WIN.COM actually contains four different calls to INT 21h AH=52h. Some of these are only invoked under certain circumstances, such as when you run Windows in Standard mode; others (including the call to INT 21h AH=52h we saw earlier in the AARD code) occur every time someone types "WIN". As one example, the disassembly of WIN.COM shows that WIN.COM uses the SysVars table to find the first SFT. WIN.COM then walks the SFT chain, counting the number of available files, to ensure that you have at least FILES=30 on your system. Figure 1-7 shows disassembly of this code. If this code looks strange, you may want to read Chapter 2 and then come back here.

Figure 1-7: WIN.COM Walks the SFT Chain

```
4C40:1828        mov ah,52h
4C40:182A        int 21h                      ; get sysvars into ES:BX
4C40:182C        xor ax,ax                    ; init number of files = 0
4C40:182E        les bx,dword ptr es:[bx+4]   ; sysvars[4]=ptr to first SFT
4C40:1832    DO_NEXT_SFT:
4C40:1832        add ax,es:[bx+4]             ; SFT[4] is number of files
4C40:1836        cmp word ptr es:[bx],0FFFFh  ; SFT[0]=ptr to next; at end?
4C40:183A        je short DONE                ; if so, done
4C40:183C        les bx,dword ptr es:[bx]     ; if not, walk linked list
4C40:183F        jmp short DO_NEXT_SFT
4C40:1841    DONE:                            ; done walking list of SFTs
4C40:1841        sub ax,1Eh                   ; 1Eh = 30
4C40:1844        jnc short loc_ret_0110       ; Complain if not FILES=30+
```

This code is very similar to the SFTWALK.C example in Chapter 8. In one sense, this use of undocumented DOS is no big deal; it almost seems trivial. You might ask, is this what all this "undocumented" fuss is about? The answer is yes. Many of the ways Microsoft uses undocumented DOS seem trivial in the same way.

But think for a moment about how you would get the FILES= value in a *documented* way. The obvious solution is to open the CONFIG.SYS file and read out the value. But that method is totally unreliable! A user could have booted the system with a low FILES= number, then changed CONFIG.SYS, thought about rebooting, but instead decided to run Windows. Many uses of the undocumented DOS and Windows functions are like this; they cover little petty things that can in fact make a big difference to the stability of a program. (Note: This is not to imply that Windows is in fact stable.)

BlockDev and INT 2Fh Function 13h

Back in Figure 1-6, the first set of calls from WIN386 is to INT 2Fh AH=13h, which, as noted in the appendix, is the DOS Set Disk Interrupt Handler function. The BlockDev VxD within WIN386 is making this call. BlockDev is new to Windows 3.1, replacing the Windows 3.0 virtual hard disk device. The FastDisk support in 3.1, which provides 32-bit disk access, relies on BlockDev. BlockDev needs to hook the BIOS disk interrupt, INT 13h, but in such a way that the procedure doesn't cut disk caches and the like that have already hooked INT 13h out of the action. BlockDev's INT 13h hook must be *retroactive*. Via INT 2Fh AH=13h, IO.SYS provides a way to retroactively hook INT 13h. Using this function, BlockDev can get its hooks in *below* any existing INT 13h handlers.

For a more complete discussion of BlockDev, FastDisk, and INT 2Fh function 13h, see Chapter 1 of Geoff Chappell's book *DOS Internals*.

DOSMGR: Windows' Connection to Undocumented DOS

The other WIN386 undocumented DOS calls in Figure 1-6 are coming from the DOSMGR VxD. This is where we get to the heart of Windows' connection to undocumented DOS. Just a few function calls appear in Figure 1-6, but since these functions return pointers to structures in the DOS data segment, the functions open up a vast amount of DOS internals to Windows.

In the disassembly in Figure 1-8, you can see that DOSMGR stores the return value from INT 21h AH=52h in several different ways. After calling INT 21h AH=52h (DOSMGR makes this call via an Exec_Int function provided by VMM; see Chapter 3), the ES register provides a handy way to get the value of DOS's data segment. DOSMGR stores this value in a variable we have called DOS_DS; DOSMGR also shifts the value left by four to form a 32-bit linear address, DOS_DS_LIN. To this, it adds BX to form a 32-bit linear address to the SysVars table, SYSVARS_LIN.

This is 32-bit code, by the way, so it might take some getting used to if you've spent too many years looking at 16-bit code. The key thing to remember is that a 32-bit register like EAX can address up to 4 gigabytes, so a single register can manipulate pointers to any location on the machine. DOS programmers need to become familiar with VxD code because, more and more, this is what DOS systems-level programming is going to look like. Chapter 3 includes a detailed examination of VxDs, including an explanation of Exec_Int, [ebp.Client_XXX], and other slightly odd-looking features of this code.

Figure 1-8: DOSMGR Saves Away SysVars

```
05A9E   mov [ebp.Client_AX],5200h    ; calling INT 21h AH=52h
05AA4   mov eax,21h                  ; (Get SysVars Table Address)
05AA9   VMMCall Exec_Int             ; via VMM Exec_Int function
05AAF   movzx eax, [ebp.Client_ES]
05AB3   mov DOS_DS,eax               ; save ES from 21/52, ignoring BX
05AB8   shl eax,4                    ; ES <<= 4
05ABB   movzx ebx,[ebp.Client_BX]    ; mov with zero-extend
05ABF   mov DOS_DS_LIN,eax           ; 32-bit linear address of DOS DS
05AC4   add eax,ebx                  ; now add in BX from 21/52
05AC6   mov SYSVARS_LIN,eax          ; 32-bit linear address of SysVars
```

Since SysVars is the gateway to most of the interesting DOS internal data structures, DOSMGR can do pretty much whatever it wants with DOS once DOSMGR has SYSVARS_LIN. Using SYSVARS_LIN, DOSMGR also sets up pointers to the DOS CDS table, the DOS device chain, the SFT chain, the MCB chain, and so on. But why would DOSMGR want to do that?

Windows Enhanced mode can run multiple preemptively multitasked DOS boxes. Each DOS box is actually a Virtual Machine (VM). All Windows programs run in a single VM, known as the System VM. Each VM has its own private address space, so that (for example) 1234:5678 in a DOS box usually has no relation to 1234:5678 in a Windows program, or to 1234:5678 in another DOS box.

Likewise, as shown in Figure 1-9, each VM can have its own DOS state, such as its own current drive and directory. In Figure 1-9, there are clearly multiple CDSes, because each DOS box is parked at a different current drive and directory.

Figure 1-9: Windows Enhanced Mode—Multiple CDS in Action

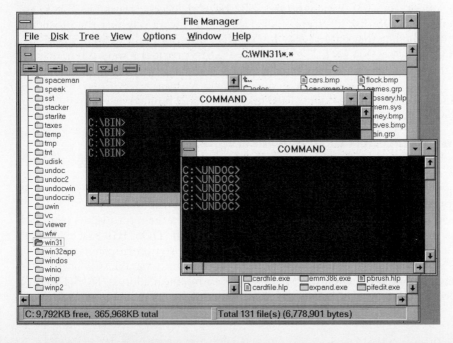

But there is only one copy of DOS! How does Windows Enhanced mode manage this? DOSMGR is the component of Windows responsible for maintaining the fiction that DOS is a multitasking operating system. Among its other responsibilities (which include being the DOS extender for Windows Enhanced mode), DOSMGR serves as a virtual DOS device, managing contention from multiple VMs for a single copy of DOS. Each DOS box thinks it has its own copy of DOS, and DOS thinks it is running some simple-minded application that happens to like to switch drives and directories a lot.

One of the mechanisms Windows uses to perform this feat is called "instance data." Normally, memory allocated before Windows loads is global—that is, it is mapped rather than copied into each VM. Thus, global memory is not private; all VMs share a single copy. Good examples of this memory include TSRs, device drivers, and all the data structures in DOS itself. In other words, the CDS would normally be global, shared by all VMs. To produce the desired effect shown in Figure 1-9, Windows Enhanced mode must "instance" the CDS. Instance data is the mechanism that lets Windows know which pieces of global memory should be private to each VM, while still located at the same address in each VM.

To instance the CDS, DOSMGR passes the address and size of the CDS to the VMM _AddInstanceItem function. But how does DOSMGR know where the heck in memory the CDS is located? By using undocumented DOS, naturally! In Figure 1-8, DOSMGR called INT 21h function 52h to get a pointer to SysVars; in Figure 1-10, DOSMGR uses SysVars to retrieve pointers to the DOS device chain, the CDS, and the DOS LASTDRIVE value, all of which are kept in SysVars (see Chapter 2).

At the start of Figure 1-10, DOSMGR calls the VMM Get_Cur_VM_Handle function, which returns, in the EBX register, the handle of the current virtual machine (VM), that is, a handle to the currently-running DOS box or to the System VM (which, again, is where all Windows applications run). This VM handle is the 32-bit linear address of a VM Control Block (VM_CB), a structure which contains, at offset 4, the 32-bit base address of the DOS box's or System VM's memory. Adding this base address onto a standard 20-bit (seg << 4 + ofs) address yields a unique 32-bit linear address that is valid across all VMs. For example, the code in Figure 1-10 figures out the linear address of the CDS within a given VM using the following calculation: vm_base + (FP_SEG(cds) << 4) + FP_OFF(cds). Chapter 3 discusses this somewhat complicated but important topic in more detail.

Figure 1-10: DOSMGR Saves Away Values from SysVars

```
; inside initialization code
05CBF    VMMCall Get_Cur_VM_Handle        ; get current VM handle into EBX
05CC5    mov ebx,dword ptr [ebx+4]        ; VM[4]=VM's base addr in memory
05CC8    add ebx,dword ptr SYSVARS_LIN    ; make a flat 32-bit linear addr
05CCE    mov eax,dword ptr [ebx+16h]      ; sysvars[16h] is CDS ptr
05CD1    movzx ecx,ax                     ; ecx = zero-extend (word) CDS ofs
05CD4    shr eax,10h                      ; eax = segment; discard offset
05CD7    shl eax,4                        ; linear addr of CDS segment
05CDA    add eax,ecx                      ; add in CDS offset
05CDC    mov CDS_LIN,eax                  ; 32-bit linear addr of CDS
05CE1    movzx eax,byte ptr [ebx+21h]     ; sysvars[21h]=LASTDRIVE
05CE5    mov LASTDRIVE,eax
05CEA    mov eax,dword ptr [ebx+22h]      ; sysvars[22h]=NUL dev (not ptr)
05CED    mov NEXT_DRIVER,eax              ; device_drv[0]=seg of next drvr
; ....
```

As an interesting side note, it is worth pointing out that DOSMGR sets up these variables once and doesn't check SysVars again. The code in Figure 1-10 is from the DOSMGR initialization; it is discarded once Windows is up and running. DOSMGR continues to use variables like CDS_LIN, LASTDRIVE, and NEXT_DRIVER throughout the entire Windows session.

However, utilities such as the QEMM programs FILES.COM and LASTDRIV.COM, resize and move DOS internal structures like the SFT and CDS. (The whole point is to run FILES or LASTDRIV with LOADHI.) Chapter 2 presents XLASTDRV, a clone of Quarterdeck's LASTDRIV. These programs work by updating the pointers in SysVars. But since DOSMGR only checks SysVars once, DOSMGR isn't set up for the SFT or CDS pointers to change, and it isn't prepared for the value of LASTDRIVE within SysVars to change either. So, while you can run FILES or LASTDRIV before Windows loads, running them from within an Enhanced mode DOS box is a recipe for disaster. (One of this book's technical reviewers writes, "Only an idiot would expect that to work!") These pointers in SysVars *can't* change once Enhanced mode is running, which means that all VMs have identical copies of these SysVars pointers. We'll take advantage of this fact in Chapter 3, in a Windows program, ENUMDRV.C, that displays the CDS in every VM (see Listing 3-27).

DOSMGR is completely dependent on the information it gets from SysVars, using pointers to the CDS, SFT, device chain, and so on, in so many places that it's difficult to summarize. The use of undocumented DOS in DOSMGR is far from trivial. The single call that DOSMGR makes to INT 21h AH=52h exposes a huge amount of DOS internals to DOSMGR, making it possible for DOSMGR to keep multiple DOS boxes relatively happy on top of a single copy of DOS.

CON CON CON CON CON

However, not everything DOSMGR needs to manipulate DOS internals is available in SysVars. For example, while SysVars contains a pointer to the SFT chain, and DOSMGR can determine the number of SFT entries by walking the SFT chain just as WIN.COM did back in Figure 1-7, SysVars does not provide the size of an SFT entry. DOSMGR needs to know the size of an SFT entry. Unfortunately, this size changes from one DOS version to the next (see Chapter 8 and the Appendix). Rather than using a lookup table to give the size of an SFT entry for each supported DOS version (an SFT entry is 3Bh bytes in DOS 4.0, 5.0, and 6.0, 35h bytes in 3.1-3.3, and 38h bytes in 3.0), DOSMGR figures out the size empirically. It opens CON five times, searches the first 512K of memory for the string CON, and then measures the span to the next occurrence of CON, and the next, and so on. DOSMGR then uses this span from one CON to the next as the size of an SFT entry.

KRNL386 and KRNL286 use this same loony technique too, as part of *growing* the SFT to get more file handles. The technique is loony because it is so easy for something to go wrong. Geoff Chappell reports having blown away a hard disk by creating a device driver with the string "CON CON CON CON CON" in it. DOSMGR and KRNL386 found the string, and thereafter assumed that SFT entries were four bytes wide!

Memory managers such as QEMM and 386Max contain utilities to move the SFT entries to upper memory, freeing up space in conventional memory. Because DOSMGR won't find the string of CONs in the first 512K of memory, these utilities can keep Windows from loading. If before starting Windows you run a utility that moves the SFT, Windows 3.1 can fail with the message "Unsupported DOS version," as though you had some DOS clone that internally didn't use SFTs.

To work around the problem of memory managers relocating the SFT tables to upper memory, *PC Magazine* ("Simulating SFT Entries," January 12, 1993) published a batch file that creates a string of CONs, 3Bh bytes apart, in conventional memory. You might wonder why DOSMGR doesn't end up manipulating these simulated SFT entries instead of the genuine ones. Fortunately, DOSMGR uses the five CONs just to get the size of an SFT entry; it then uses function 52h to find the entries themselves.

The Undocumented DOSMGR Callout API

As a more important example of how DOSMGR must sometimes supplement its use of undocumented DOS structures, let's return to the CDS table. To use the table, DOSMGR must know the size of an individual CDS entry for a single drive. Recall that, to instance the CDS, DOSMGR must pass CDS_LIN to _AddInstanceItem, together with the size in bytes of the CDS. From LAST-DRIVE, it knows the number of CDS entries, but it doesn't know how many bytes each entry is.

In most utilities that manipulate undocumented DOS, that information would be hard-wired. For example, the XLASTDRV program in Chapter 2 uses the DOS version number to determine whether a CDS entry is 51h bytes or 58h bytes. Feeling perhaps that this hard-wiring is too inflexible and that it leaves Windows *too* reliant on intimate knowledge of DOS internals, DOSMGR uses another mechanism to find the size of a CDS entry: to supplement its use of undocumented DOS, DOSMGR has a private interface to DOS 5.0 and higher.

As each VxD loads, it can issue a VxD initialization broadcast (INT 2Fh AX=1607h) with its VxD ID number in BX. VxDs that have broadcasts or that provide services to other programs have device ID numbers assigned by Microsoft. VMM, for example, has VxD ID 1, and DOSMGR has VxD number 15h. While Microsoft's Windows Device Driver Kit (DDK) *Virtual Device Adaptation Guide* (VDAG) clearly documents the INT 2Fh AX=1607h VxD initialization broadcast, Microsoft says absolutely nothing about the actual broadcasts or API functions supported by any of the VxDs built into Windows. In other words, Microsoft documents only the generic INT 2Fh mechanism; if you want to find out what notifications or APIs a piece of Windows such as DOSMGR provides, the DDK is silent.

Microsoft uses the DOSMGR VxD callout (INT 2Fh AX=1607h BX=15h) as a private interface between MS-DOS and Microsoft Windows. A Microsoft internal document, "API to Identify MS-DOS Instance Data" (undated), describes this interface, but it is not documented outside the company (apparently it was briefly available in beta versions of the QuickHelp files for the Windows 3.1 DDK). Actually, it's an API not only for getting instance data from DOS, but also for patching DOS. Even without Microsoft's internal document, several programmers have disassembled DOSMGR and MS-DOS to see what they have to say to each other.

This DOSMGR VxD callout (INT 2Fh AX=1607h BX=15h) provides several subfunctions, specified in the CX register; Table 1-1 lists these subfunctions. For further details, see the appendix entry for INT 2Fh AX=1607h as well as Geoff Chappell's book *DOS Internals*.

Table 1-1: DOSMGR VxD Callout Subfunctions

0	Query instance processing; get patch table
1	Set patches in DOS
2	Remove patches in DOS
3	Get size of DOS internal data structures
4	Query instanced data structures
5	Get device driver size

DOSMGR issues these calls (see for example the code in Figures 1-11 and 1-12), and MSDOS.SYS hooks INT 2Fh and responds to these calls. (Yes, MS-DOS 5.0 and 6.0 really do know about Windows!) For some of the functions, DOS is expected to pass back in DX:AX a sanity-check "signature" of A2AB:B97C, the significance of which eludes us. DOS 5.0 and 6.0 only implement subfunctions 0, 3, and 4. The implementation of subfunction 4 in DOS 5.0 and 6.0 is trivial; it indicates that *no* DOS data was instanced via this interface. On the other hand, should a future version of MS-DOS make heavier use of this interface and indicate that it has taken care of instancing DOS internal data structures itself, DOSMGR is ready for it, as shown in Figure 1-11:

Figure 1-11: DOSMGR Determines If MS-DOS Does Instancing

```
05B3C      mov [ebp.Client_AX],1607h  ; VxD callout
05B42      mov [ebp.Client_BX],15h    ; 15h = DOSMGR
05B48      mov [ebp.Client_CX],4      ; subfunc 4 = query inst data struct
05B4E      mov eax,2Fh
05B53      VMMCall Exec_Int           ; do INT 2Fh
```

```
05B59       cmp [ebp.Client_AX],0B97Ch ; make sure got funny signature
05B5F       jne short QUERY_PATCH_DOS
05B61       cmp [ebp.Client_DX],0A2ABh ; make sure got funny signature
05B67       jne short QUERY_PATCH_DOS
05B69       movzx eax,[ebp.Client_BX] ; bit mask of instanced items
05B6D       mov DOS_STRUCTS_INST,eax
        QUERY_PATCH_DOS:              ; now try subfunc 1
```

Table 1-1 shows that the DOSMGR callout API includes a subfunction to get the size of internal DOS data structures; as seen in the code fragment from DOSMGR in Figure 1-12, this subfunction is currently used only to get the size of a CDS entry.

Figure 1-12: DOSMGR Determines the Size of a CDS Entry

```
0618B       mov [ebp.Client_AX],1607h ; VxD callout
06191       mov [ebp.Client_BX],15h   ; 15h = DOSMGR
06197       mov [ebp.Client_CX],3 ; subfunc 3=get size of DOS data struct
0619D       mov [ebp.Client_DX],1     ; 1 = get CDS size
061A3       mov eax,2Fh
061A8       VMMCall Exec_Int
061AE       cmp [ebp.Client_AX],0B97Ch ; got weird signature?
061B4       jne short NO_CALLOUT   ;  if not, figure out CDS by hand
061B6       cmp [ebp.Client_DX],0A2ABh ; got weird signature?
061BC       jne short NO_CALLOUT   ;  if not, figure out CDS by hand
061BE       movzx eax,[ebp.Client_CX] ; call supported -- get CDS size
061C2       jmp short GOT_CDS_SIZE  ; if here, callout supported
061C4    NO_CALLOUT:               ; I'll do it myself without any help
061C4       mov eax,51h            ; CDS size = 51h bytes
061C9       cmp byte ptr DOS_MAJ,4
061D0       jb  short GOT_CDS_SIZE ; if DOS 3 skip next
061D2       add eax,7              ; add 7 bytes to CDS size for DOS 4+
061D5    GOT_CDS_SIZE:
061D5       mov CDS_ENTRY_SIZE,eax
061DA       mul dword ptr LASTDRIVE
061E0       mov CDS_SIZE,eax  ; CDS_SIZE=LASTDRIVE*CDS_ENTRY_SIZE
```

Only a small portion of the DOSMGR callout instance API is up and running; mostly it is used for patching (see Figure 1-13). For the most part, DOSMGR has to figure out how to instance DOS itself. It does so using undocumented DOS calls and knowledge of DOS internal data structures. For example, with the DOSMGR callout API MS-DOS could instance the CDS itself, but DOS 5.0 and 6.0 do not use this function, so DOSMGR has to do the work itself, as shown in Figure 1-13 (which is a continuation of Figure 1-12).

Figure 1-13: DOSMGR Instances the CDS

```
061D5    GOT_CDS_SIZE:
061D5       mov CDS_ENTRY_SIZE,eax                ; size of a CDS entry
061DA       mul dword ptr LASTDRIVE               ; number of entries
061E0       mov CDS_SIZE,eax                      ; size of entire CDS table
061E5       mov edx,dword ptr CDS_LIN             ; 0-base linear addr of CDS
; DOS_STRUCTS_INST set in figure 1-11
061EB       test    byte ptr DOS_STRUCTS_INST,1 ; does MS-DOS do the work?
061F2       jnz short MSDOS_DOES_INST            ;   jump if so
; ESI holds a pointer to an InstDataStruc
061F4       mov dword ptr [esi+8],edx             ; CDS_LIN
061F7       mov dword ptr [esi+0Ch],eax           ; CDS_SIZE
061FA       mov dword ptr [esi+10h],200h          ; inst type=ALWAYS_Field
06201       push    0
06203       push    esi                           ; push InstDataStruc
06204       VMMCall _AddInstanceItem              ; call VMM function
0620A       add esp,8                             ;   (cdecl call)
0620D       or  eax,eax                           ; did function succeed?
0620F       jz  short FAILURE
```

```
06211   MSDOS_DOES_INST:
; use tables from DOSMGR 2F/1607/15 callout
; .....
0628C   FAILURE:
0628C        VMMCall Fatal_Memory_Error              ; Windows can't run!
```

This code is interesting, not only as an illustration of the little information-sharing dance that DOS and Windows perform, but also as an illustration of what DOS systems programming will increasingly look like in years to come.

But there is something puzzling about the DOSMGR callout API. For example, since MS-DOS uses the API to pass DOSMGR the size of a CDS entry, why not also pass in the size of other DOS internal data structures, especially the SFT? We already saw the ridiculous "CON CON CON CON CON" effort that DOSMGR makes to find the size of an SFT entry. Given that the DOSMGR callout API exists, why doesn't DOSMGR make more use of it?

Perhaps the DOSMGR callout API was an *ad hoc* solution to problems of running Windows on OEM versions of MS-DOS. (One tech reviewer speculated, for example, that the Query CDS Size functionality was needed for HP and NEC versions of DOS.) But when we examine the DOSMGR interface it also seems if as someone had the excellent idea of creating an interface to decouple Windows (or at least DOSMGR) thoroughly from any knowledge of DOS internals and then thought better of it!

There have been persistent, unproven rumors that engineers at Microsoft have at various times created "portable" versions of Windows which were then scuttled by upper management. For example, Microsoft had a version of the Windows kernel that was "DPMI pure" and thus could run unaltered on OS/2. Currently, the Windows kernel is not a true DOS Protected Mode Interface (DPMI) client; as Matt Pietrek notes in his *Windows Internals* (p. 90), the kernel bypasses DPMI. This means that IBM must hack Windows to create a slightly-different WIN-OS/2 (see Chapter 4). However, Pietrek points out that the DPMI-pure version of the Windows kernel performed badly, and that this is the reason Microsoft bypassed DPMI. So, even if Microsoft upper management did conceivably have ulterior motives for making Windows non-portable, there were also sound engineering reasons.

In any case, you have to wonder whether the current half-way status of the DOSMGR interface isn't an example of Windows deliberate non-portability. On the one hand, a DOS 5.0 or higher workalike must implement the DOSMGR interface in order to run Windows Enhanced mode. On the other hand, once the DOSMGR interface is implemented, the DOS workalike must still be structured in such a way that it matches Windows' precise expectations of DOS internals. Far from decoupling Windows from DOS internals, the DOSMGR callout API in its current state serves only to bind Windows and MS-DOS more tightly together.

The program in Listing 1-3, NODOSMGR.C, helps illustrates this point. NODOSMGR hooks INT 2Fh and then spawns Windows. Inside its INT 2Fh handler, NODOSMGR uses the _chain_intr() function to pass through all calls, except DOSMGR callout API calls (AX=1607h BX=15h), which it ignores. By preventing MS-DOS from seeing Windows' calls to INT 2Fh AX=1607h BX=15h, NODOSMGR simulates the effect of running Windows on a version of DOS 5.0 or higher which fails to implement the undocumented DOSMGR interface.

Listing 1-3: NODOSMGR.C

```c
/*
NODOSMGR.C -- Simulate DOS 5+ without DOSMGR callout API
From "Undocumented DOS", 2nd edition (Addison-Wesley, 1993)
Andrew Schulman, June 1993
bcc -P- -2 nodosmgr.c
*/

#include <stdlib.h>
#include <stdio.h>
#include <process.h>
#include <dos.h>
```

```c
#pragma pack(1)

typedef struct {
#ifdef __TURBOC__
    unsigned short bp,di,si,ds,es,dx,cx,bx,ax;
#else
    unsigned short es,ds,di,si,bp,sp,bx,dx,cx,ax;       /* same as PUSHA */
#endif
    unsigned short ip,cs,flags;
    } REG_PARAMS;

volatile unsigned dosmgr_calls = 0;
int pass_through[10] = { 0 };   /* list of DOSMGR calls ok to pass to DOS */

#define DOSMGR_MAGIC_DX    0xA2AB
#define DOSMGR_MAGIC_AX    0xB97C

void interrupt far int2f(REG_PARAMS r);
void (interrupt far *old)(void);

void fail(char *s) { puts(s); exit(1); }

main(int argc, char *argv[])
{
    int i, func;

    if (argc < 2) fail("usage: nodosmgr [win] <func list to pass through>");

    for (i=2; i<argc; i++)
        if ((func = atoi(argv[i])) < 10)
        {
            pass_through[func]++;
            argv[i] = (void *) 0;
        }

    old = (void (interrupt far *)(void)) _dos_getvect(0x2F); // hook 2F
    _dos_setvect(0x2F, int2f);
    spawnvp(P_WAIT, argv[1], &argv[1]);       // run command (e.g., Windows)
    _dos_setvect(0x2F, old);                  // unhook 2F

    printf("%u calls to DOSMGR 2F/1607/15 interface\n", dosmgr_calls);
    return 0;
}

void interrupt far int2f(REG_PARAMS r)
{
    if ((r.ax == 0x1607) && (r.bx == 0x15))
    {
        dosmgr_calls++;
        if (pass_through[r.cx])
        {
            if (r.cx == 1)
            {
                r.bx = r.dx;                  // do just what DOS does
                r.dx = DOSMGR_MAGIC_DX;       // but don't pass down to DOS
                r.ax = DOSMGR_MAGIC_AX;
            }
            else
                _chain_intr(old);
        }
        // otherwise, don't pass down to DOS
    }
    else
        _chain_intr(old);
}
```

When NODOSMGR WIN is run on MS-DOS 6.0, Windows starts to come up, but then Windows aborts with the message "ERROR: Unsupported MS-DOS version." This is precisely the message that DOS 5.0 or higher workalikes get if they fail to implement the DOSMGR interface.

NODOSMGR has an option to pass through a specified DOSMGR subfunction. For example, running NODOSMGR WIN 0 blocks all subfunctions except CX=0 (Query instance processing; see Table 1-1), which is passed down to DOS. Passing through subfunctions 0, 2, 3, 4, or 5 still results in an "ERROR: Unsupported MS-DOS version" failure from Windows DOSMGR.

However, running NODOSMGR WIN 1 has an interesting effect: Windows runs! In other words, at least when running on genuine MS-DOS 5.0 or 6.0, only DOSMGR callout subfunction 1 (Set patches in DOS; see Table 1-1) seems to be absolutely necessary. And MS-DOS's implementation of this function is trivial, so trivial in fact that NODOSMGR doesn't even bother passing this function down to DOS. As you can see in Listing 1-3, NODOSMGR.C merely sets BX to DX and puts the NODOSMGR magic signature in DX:AX. This is all MS-DOS does in its handler for INT 2Fh AX=1607h BX=15h CX=1:

```
                        loc_4678:
FDC8:4678   8BDA            MOV BX,DX
FDC8:467A   EB0F            JMP loc_468B
; ...
                        loc_468B:
FDC8:468B   B87CB9          MOV AX,B97C
FDC8:468E   BAABA2          MOV DX,A2AB
```

So, simply by passing back a few magic numbers, we can eliminate the "ERROR: Unsupported MS-DOS version" message and allow Windows to run. At least empirically, the resulting Windows/DOS configuration seems stable (we're using it now to write this chapter, and have a few DOS boxes open along with Clock and Solitaire).

Of course, this is on top of a copy of genuine MS-DOS. In fact, subfunction 1 is *not* sufficient. If subfunction 0 is not passed down to MS-DOS, DOSMGR falls back on its own methods for patching DOS (see Chappell, *DOS Internals*, Chapter 2). The result is that (this will make more sense later) the DOS USER_ID field, rather than holding a virtual machine ID > 1 (see INT 2Fh AX=1683h), will instead be 0. This may have serious implications for file handling (see "Patching DOS"). Thus, both subfunctions 0 and 1 need to be passed down to DOS, by running NODOSMGR WIN 0 1.

These results raise the question of what purpose the DOSMGR callout API actually serves, and whether perhaps the actual "functionality" of DOSMGR resides almost entirely in these magic numbers. This in turn raises the possibility that the real purpose of the DOSMGR callout API is to tie Windows and MS-DOS 5.0 or higher in an artificial way, and that the rest of the interface is window dressing, as it were. This is purely a possibility, but one that is worth exploring.

This possibility is underlined by the fact that some pieces of the interface are not implemented by MS-DOS, and that some implementations are trivial. The current implementation of the interface in MS-DOS 6.0 looks like this (compare Table 1-1):

```
func 0: ret cx=1, es:bx -> DOS_DS:1022 (DOS var patch table)
func 1: ret bx=dx, dx:ax=magic
func 2: not handled
func 3: if (dx & 1) return cx=58h (CDS entry size), dx:ax=magic
func 4: ret dx = 0 (trivial)
func 5: get device driver size from MCB; ret dx:ax=magic
```

The real question is why DOSMGR requires that an underlying DOS 5.0 or higher implement this interface, when DOSMGR also contains tons of hard-coded assumptions about DOS internals. While it is highly unlikely that this interface was designed for the sole purpose of making Windows inhospitable to other DOSes, the result is certainly that the interface constitutes yet another obstacle to Windows portability, while providing very little benefit in return.

At the same time, there is also a positive lesson to be drawn from the DOSMGR callout API. The point has been made several times in this chapter that it is *good* for Microsoft to make DOS into a better platform for Windows. The impression was perhaps created that this requires intimate knowledge of Windows by MS-DOS, and of MS-DOS by Windows. Certainly that is the impression Microsoft wants to create. But the existence of the DOSMGR callout API (though not its current half-hearted implementation) shows that it would be possible to create a nice, clean, open interface between DOS and Windows. Were the DOSMGR callout API taken to its logical conclusion, Windows would no longer require intimate knowledge of DOS internals. All it would require would be an underlying DOS that handled the DOSMGR callout APIs.

Such an interface would not only be good engineering practice (remember modularity?), but it would also allow competition along this interface. Other DOSes could run Windows, and other multitasking environments could run on DOS. Even Microsoft would benefit from such a "Chinese Wall" in code ("Chinese Wall" is just another name for modularity), because it would allow Windows and DOS to be changed without affecting each other. On the other hand, this problem disappears in Chicago, where Windows 4 will not be sold separately from the underlying operating system.

Implementing DOSMGR Functions

The variable named CDS_SIZE in Figure 1-13 is used throughout DOSMGR. For example, DOSMGR uses it to implement a documented function, shown in Figure 1-14, that copies the CDS from one VM (specified in ESI) to another (specified in EBX). The SHELL VxD calls this DOSMGR function to initialize new VMs with the CDS of the System VM.

Figure 1-14: Implementation of DOSMGR_Copy_VM_Drive_State

```
        DOSMGR_Copy_VM_Drive_State  proc      near
01E13       pushad
01E14       mov esi,dword ptr [esi+4]    ; ESI=source VM; VM_CB[4]=base addr
01E17       add esi,dword ptr CDS_LIN    ; linear address of source VM CDS
01E1D       mov edi,dword ptr BUFFER     ; allocated with _HeapAllocate
01E23       mov ecx,dword ptr CDS_SIZE   ; number of bytes in CDS
01E29       cld
01E2A       rep movsb                    ; copy from source CDS to buffer
01E2C       mov esi,dword ptr BUFFER
01E32       mov edi,dword ptr [ebx+4]    ; EBX=target VM; VM_CB[4]=base addr
01E35       add edi,dword ptr CDS_LIN    ; linear address of target VM CDS
01E3B       mov ecx,dword ptr CDS_SIZE
01E41       cld
01E42       rep movsb                    ; copy from buffer to target CDS
01E44       popad
01E45       retn
        DOSMGR_Copy_VM_Drive_State  endp
```

Several other documented DOSMGR functions rely on undocumented DOS. For example, DOSMGR_Add_Device adds a DOS device driver onto the device chain for a VM. The function goes to offset 22h in SysVars; offset 22h is the header for the NUL device and the root of the device chain. The function then walks the device chain until it reaches the end of the list and links in the new device driver. This procedure works much like the DEVLOD program in Chapter 7, although DOSMGR_Add_Device only works with character device drivers. The Windows V86MMGR VxD uses DOSMGR_Add_Device to add its emulated EMM driver onto the DOS device chain, unless SYSTEM.INI includes the line NoEMMDriver=ON.

Figure 1-15 shows the complete code for DOSMGR_Add_Device. Most of the code here involves getting SysVars, getting the root of the device chain, finding the end of the device chain, and so on. The actual work of adding in the driver takes only a few lines (see the label ADD_DRIVER).

Figure 1-15: Implementation of DOSMGR_Add_Device

```
        DOSMGR_Add_Device    proc      near
00B1A       pushad
00B1B       mov esi,eax                  ; EAX = addr of device header
```

```
00B1D        shr  esi,4
00B20        shl  esi,10h
00B23        mov  si,ax
00B26        and  si,0Fh                  ; ESI = seg:ofs ptr to new dev
00B2A        or   ebx,ebx                 ; EBX = VM handle
00B2C        jnz  short GOT_VM
00B2E        VMMCall Get_Sys_VM_Handle    ; if VM=0, use System VM (global)
00B34    GOT_VM:
00B34        add  eax,dword ptr [ebx+4]   ; VM_CB[4] is addr of VM memory
00B37        mov  edi,eax                 ; EDI = linear addr of dev
00B39        test byte ptr [edi+5],80h    ; dev[5] is attrib
00B3D        jz   short ERROR             ; only character devices supported
00B3F        mov  edx,dword ptr LAST_DRV_LIN
00B45        or   edx,edx                 ; already have LAST_DRV_LIN var?
00B47        jnz  short NEXT_DRIVER       ; if so, walk to end of chain
00B49        mov  eax,SYSVARS_LIN
00B4E        or   eax,eax                 ; already have SYSVARS_LIN var?
00B50        jnz  short FIND_CHAIN_ROOT   ; if so, use NUL to find dev chain
00B52        mov  eax,reference_data      ; if not, another way to get sysvars?
00B57        shr  eax,10h
00B5A        mov  SYSVARS_LIN,eax
00B5F    FIND_CHAIN_ROOT:
00B5F        add  eax,dword ptr [ebx+4]   ; VM_CB[4]
00B62        mov  eax,dword ptr [eax+22h] ; in 3.1+, sysvars[22h] is NUL dev
00B65    NEXT_DRIVER:
00B65        movzx ecx,ax                 ; CX = offset of next driver
00B68        shr  eax,10h                 ; AX = segment of next driver
00B6B        shl  eax,4
00B6E        add  eax,ecx                 ; EAX = lin addr of next driver
00B70        mov  edx,eax                 ; EDX = 0-based lin addr
00B72        add  eax,dword ptr [ebx+4]   ; EAX = flat lin addr of next drv
00B75        mov  eax,[eax]               ; get far ptr to next drv
00B77        cmp  ax,0FFFFh               ; if segment=-1, at end of chain
00B7B        jne  NEXT_DRIVER             ;   otherwise, keep going
00B7D        mov  dword ptr LAST_DRV_LIN,edx  ; 0-based lin addr of last drv
00B83        mov  LAST_DRV_LIN_VM,eax     ; flat lin addr of last drv
00B88    END_OF_DEV_CHAIN:
00B88        add  edx,dword ptr [ebx+4]   ; EDX=flat lin addr of next drv too
00B8B        mov  eax,[edx]               ; get far ptr to next drv
00B8D        cmp  ax,0FFFFh               ; if segment=-1, at end of chain
00B91        je   short ADD_DRIVER        ; if so, can add in driver
00B93        movzx ecx,ax                 ; still not at end of dev chain!
00B96        shr  eax,10h                 ;   try same stuff again...
00B99        shl  eax,4
00B9C        add  eax,ecx
00B9E        mov  edx,eax
00BA0        jmp  short END_OF_DEV_CHAIN
00BA2    ADD_DRIVER:
; EDI holds the linear address of the new driver header
; EDX holds the linear address of the last driver header on the chain
; dword ptr [driver header + 0] is a real mode ptr to the next driver
00BA2        mov  dword ptr [edi],0FFFFFFFFh ;make new drv's next=-1 (end)
00BA8        mov  [edx],esi               ; link new drv into chain!
00BAA        clc                          ; carry clear = success
00BAB    DONE:
00BAB        popad
00BAC        retn
00BAD    ERROR:
00BAD        stc                          ; carry set = failure
00BAE        jmp  short DONE
    DOSMGR_Add_Device    endp
```

Unlike DEVLOD, this function does not call the device's initialization function. This behavior is documented in the DDK VDAG manual. Also unlike DEVLOD, this function adds a device to the end rather than to the front of the device list. As the DDK points out, this means that the service won't help replace an existing device.

The variables used in Figure 1-15 could have been set in a number of different ways elsewhere in DOSMGR. Given DOSMGR's reliance on the shifting sands of undocumented DOS, it is good that DOSMGR contains so much redundancy.

Again, the question is whether it is right for one Microsoft product (Windows) to rely so much on undocumented aspects of another Microsoft product (DOS). It is truly a good thing that Microsoft is bringing DOS and Windows closer together and integrating them so tightly, but you also have to remember that Microsoft still sells them separately. If Microsoft uses undocumented DOS calls in its own separate products such as Windows, shouldn't it document these calls? After all, the calls have proven to be useful. Doesn't its failure to document these calls or to provide new, clean, documented interfaces with equivalent functionality (like TOOLHELP.DLL in Windows) give Microsoft a gross advantage in bringing out products such as Windows? Is this advantage unfair? Remember, utilities may seem like part of the operating system, but they are one of the most active parts of the PC software market.

Think of Microsoft as a non-regulated company that owns 90% of the highways, and that is also a major producer of cars. Now imagine that Microsoft's cars use hidden features of its highways. This is not to suggest that Microsoft's cars are better than the competition's! The competition can use these hidden features too, but first they have to somehow find out about them. Many of these hidden features are well known and constitute a kind of folklore. But hiding them raises others' cost of using them, and there is always the danger that Microsoft will at some future date remove or change them.

Patching DOS   Rather than instancing, the private DOSMGR callout API mostly involves patching DOS. We really do mean patching here, not hooking an interrupt (though DOSMGR and other pieces of Windows do plenty of that too). The API writes over bits of DOS with REP MOVSB instructions.

In MS-DOS 5.0 and higher, MSDOS.SYS responds to an INT 2Fh AX=1607h BX=15h CX=0 call from DOSMGR by passing back in ES:BX a table with pointers to six DOS internal variables: SAVEDS, SAVEBX, INDOS, USER_ID, CRITPATCH, and UMB_HEAD. These names come from the Microsoft internal document on the DOSMGR API; presumably these names correspond to the actual variable names in the DOS source code (one of our tech reviewers writes, "they do!"). The patch locations are all in the same segment as the patch table itself, so only offsets are provided. Figure 1-16 shows a hex dump of the patch table in MS-DOS 5.0 and 6.0.

Figure 1-16: DOSMGR Patch Table in MS-DOS 5.0 and 6.0

```
-dw 0116:1022 102f
0116:1022   0005 05EC 05EA 0321 033E 0315 008C

Patch table at 0116:1022
DOS version 5.00
SAVEDS:     05ECh
SAVEBX:     05EAh
INDOS:      0321h
USER_ID:    033Eh
CRITPATCH:  0315h
UMB_HEAD:   008Ch
```

What does DOSMGR do with these pointers? Here again we see the half-hearted nature of the DOSMGR callout API. Basically, USER_ID and UMB_HEAD are the only variables of any great importance.

USER_ID is where DOS keeps the machine ID. As shown in Figure 1-17, DOSMGR's handler for the VM_Critical_Init message, which VMM sends out whenever a new virtual machine is starting up, smacks the new VM's ID number into this location in DOS. DOS in turn uses USER_ID to stamp the SFT entries for open files with the VM ID (see FILES.C in Chapter 8). We'll explain the cryptic variable names in a moment.

Figure 1-17: DOSMGR Patches the VM ID into DOS's USER_ID

```
; EBX contains the VM handle, a pointer to the VM control block (VM_CB)
mov eax, dword ptr [ebx+CB_VMID]          ; get VM ID # from VM CB
mov edx, dword ptr LIN_PATCH_USER_ID      ; linear addr of USER_ID
add edx, dword ptr [ebx+CB_High_Linear]   ; base address for VM's memory
mov [edx], ax                             ; smack in the VM ID #
```

In Figure 1-17, DOSMGR is patching the VM ID for the new VM right into DOS's data segment. As we will see later, DOS normally sets the machine ID to 0, but when DOS knows that Windows Enhanced mode is running, it skips this instruction. DOSMGR gets the address of USER_ID in the DOS data segment using the VxD callout patch table from Figure 1-16. Whenever a program opens a file, DOS places the program's PSP and the value of USER_ID into the file's SFT entry. Under Windows Enhanced mode, this means that each SFT entry carries not only the owner's PSP but also its VM ID. Thus, instead of identifying files with the combination of file handle and PSP, DOS under Windows Enhanced mode uses the combination of file handle, PSP, and VM ID. DOS needs to do this so that identical PSPs in different DOS boxes do not mistakenly appear as the same file owner. SYSTEM.INI settings such as UniqueDOSPSP= and PSPIncrement= also address this problem. The whole point behind this procedure is to keep distinct multiple DOS boxes running on top of a single copy of DOS.

The code fragment just shown from DOSMGR uses a variable labeled LIN_PATCH_USER_ID, which is the 32-bit linear address of the USER_ID patch location. VxDs are 32-bit programs, so they can reach anywhere in the machine, forming addresses of up to four gigabytes with a simple offset such as MOV [EDX], AX. Showing the code that DOSMGR uses to creates the LIN_PATCH_USER_ID pointer would require several pages, but in essence it goes through the steps shown in Figure 1-18. The pseudocode in Figure 1-18 may also help clarify some of the code shown in earlier figures.

Figure 1-18: DOSMGR Forms a Linear Address to DOS's USER_ID Variable

- Use the VMM function Exec_Int to generate an INT 21h AH=52h, which returns a pointer to the DOS SysVars table in ES:BX. Exec_Int makes these available in the Client_ES and Client_BX fields in a "client register structure" accessed off the EBP register (see Figure 1-8).
- Use the returned Client_ES and, ignoring Client_BX, create a DOS_DS variable.
- Shift DOS_DS left by 4 to form a DOS_DS_LIN variable (32-bit linear address of the DOS data segment).
- Use Exec_Int to generate an INT 2Fh AX=1607h BX=15h CX=0 (the DOSMGR VxD callout). DOS returns a pointer to the patch table in ES:BX.
- Shift Client_ES left by 4 and add in Client_BX, to get the 32-bit linear address of the patch table.
- Call VMM function Get_Cur_VM_Handle to get the VM handle, which is a 32-bit linear pointer to the VM control block (VM_CB). Offset 4 in the VM_CB is CB_High_Linear, which is the 32-bit base address of the VM's memory in the Windows linear address space.
- Add the VM CB_High_Linear onto the 32-bit address of the patch table, to get the true linear address of the patch table within the entire Windows address space. Call this LIN_PATCH_TAB.
- The remaining steps are easier to show as code:

```
mov esi, LIN_PATCH_TAB
mov ax, WORD PTR [esi+8]              ; 4th word is USER_ID
mov PATCH_USER_ID, ax
movzx eax, word ptr PATCH_USER_ID    ; zero-extend into EAX
add eax, dword ptr DOS_DS_LIN        ; add in linear addr of DOS DS
mov LIN_PATCH_USER_ID, eax
```

On its side of the conversation, MSDOS.SYS simply has an INT 2Fh handler that looks out for AX=1607h calls. NODOSMGR.C in Listing 1-3 puts its INT 2Fh handler ahead of this one in MSDOS.SYS. If DOS sees an INT 2Fh AX=1607h call with BX=15h, it checks the subfunctions in CX. For subfunction 0, it puts the address of a hardwired table (the one shown in Figure 1-16) into ES:BX.

Returning to the patch table itself, the next item is called CRITPATCH. To turn on critical sections in DOS prior to DOS 5.0, one had to patch a number of different locations in the DOS code. The patcher looked for the byte C3h (a RET opcode) and changed it to a 50h (the PUSH AX opcode). Starting with DOS 5.0, there is one central variable that all the DOS critical-section code checks. This variable is in the DOS data segment, which is crucial for DOS in ROM because you can't patch code in read-only memory. DOSMGR of course patches this location to turn on critical sections. (See the CRITSECT.C program in Chapter 9, and the appendix entry for INT 2Ah function 80h.) By the way, Windows is a good citizen and backs out all these patches when it exits ("well, usually," writes one of our tech reviewers).

Finally, UMB_HEAD, which Windows 3.0 does not use, is the address of a word where DOS records the paragraph address of the last arena header in conventional memory, that is, the base of the upper memory block (UMB) chain. This location is also instanced for each VM.

DOS Knows About Windows

As noted earlier, when Windows starts up, it issues an INT 2Fh call with AX=1605h; when Windows exits, it issues an INT 2Fh with AX=1606h. MS-DOS 5.0 and 6.0 hook these calls to maintain (for Enhanced mode only) an IN_WINDOWS flag. While Microsoft documents the 1605h and 1606h functions in the DDK *Device Driver Adaptation Guide*, the documentation states that this is to notify device drivers and TSRs that Windows is running. The documentation says nothing about the important fact that version 5.0 and 6.0 of MS-DOS itself respond to these Windows calls.

MS-DOS uses the INT 2Fh AX=1605h Windows initialization broadcast for a number of purposes. For example, if Windows 3.0 Enhanced mode is starting up, DOS 5.0 and 6.0 tell Windows to load the WINA20.386 file, which patches parts of the Windows V86MMGR. MS-DOS also uses the interface to inform Windows of certain instance data (Windows sure provides a lot of different ways to specify instance data!). Again, Microsoft documents this interface in the DDK, merely failing to note that MS-DOS itself uses the interface.

But DOS hooks the Windows broadcast, not only to tell Windows about instance data and VxDs, but also to maintain an internal flag that indicates whether Windows Enhanced mode is currently running. DOS doesn't care one way or the other about Standard mode. But when Windows Enhanced mode is running, MS-DOS wants to behave as if a network were running. If you think about it, multiple DOS boxes in Enhanced mode are very much like multiple machines on a network. As noted earlier, DOS has a machine ID number. The main INT 21h dispatch loop normally sets this ID to 0, indicating the current system (see Chapter 6). However, if DOS sets the IN_WIN3E flag, it doesn't set the machine ID number to 0. Instead, it uses the current DOS box's Virtual Machine ID number (see INT 2Fh AX=1683h). As we saw earlier, DOSMGR patches this VM ID number right into DOS, which then copies it into every SFT entry.

IO.SYS also tests the IN_WIN3E flag, and if Windows Enhanced mode is running, IO.SYS will, under certain circumstances, make a call into DOSMGR. In addition to the INT 2Fh AX=1607h initialization callout that VxDs can make, VxDs can also provide APIs. These APIs are available even to software that, like IO.SYS and (in DOS 6.0) DBLSPACE.BIN, was loaded before Windows. Basically,

VxD APIs provide a way for non-VxD code, even normal 16-bit DOS code, to have 32-bit protected mode VMM and VxD code executed on their behalf (see "Go Anywhere and Do Anything with 32-bit Virtual Device Drivers for Windows," *Microsoft Systems Journal*, October 1992). Calling INT 2Fh AX=1684h with the VxD ID (such as 15h for DOSMGR) in BX retrieves a VxD API entry point. The DDK documents this INT 2Fh mechanism. What Microsoft does not document are the actual INT 2Fh AX=1684h APIs provided by DOSMGR and other VxDs built into Windows. As with INT 2Fh AX=1605h and AX=1607h, the DDK documents only the general mechanism, not the way that Windows and DOS actually use the mechanism.

The undocumented DOSMGR API has six subfunctions. IO.SYS and DBLSPACE.BIN call subfunction 1; this subfunction uses the VMM Call_When_Not_Critical function to install a callback function that updates the timer (using Adjust_Execution_Time) after someone has held onto a critical section.

DOS also uses the broadcasts to set an internal flag to indicate whether to generate INT 2Ah AX=8001h and AX=8101h critical-section calls. Usually, DOS skips these calls, as there is no need to mark uninterruptible regions of code in a single-tasking operating system. The InDos flag is usually adequate (see Chapter 9). However, Enhanced mode effectively turns DOS into a genuine preemptively multitasked operating system.

Again, while it is at first surprising to hear that DOS behaves differently when Windows Enhanced mode is running, it is important to realize that DOS makes this change using documented function calls. The Microsoft DDK documentation should just state clearly that MS-DOS itself hooks this call.

DOSMGR and the SDA

Back in INTRSPY output in Figure 1-6, we saw that DOSMGR not only calls INT 21h AH=52h, but also calls INT 21h AX=5D06h. As noted in the appendix, this undocumented function returns a pointer to the DOS Swappable Data Area (SDA). The SDA is another internal data structure in the DOS data segment; it contains the current DOS state, including the current Program Segment Prefix (PSP), the current Disk Transfer Area (DTA), the InDOS flag, the current drive, the three DOS stacks, and so on.

DOSMGR calls INT 21h AX=5D06h because it needs to mark the SDA as instance data. Whereas DOSMGR has to go through various contortions to figure out the size of other DOS internal structures that must be instanced, it is easy to find out the size of the SDA. As noted in the appendix, INT 21h AX=5D06h, besides returning a pointer to the SDA, also returns the number of bytes that a program must always swap, and the number that a program need only swap when the InDOS flag is enabled.

DOSMGR passes these numbers directly to the VMM _AddInstanceItem function which, interestingly, accepts instance types of INDOS_Field and ALWAYS_Field. Given that the SDA itself is undocumented and that until recently the InDOS flag was as well, it is somewhat strange that the DDK documents these flags, especially because VMM appears to ignore them. But this is typical of the gross inconsistencies between the documentation for DOS and Windows. The Windows documentation frequently relies on a piece of DOS knowledge that is essential but undocumented.

DOSMGR and the InDOS Flag

As a good example, consider the DOSMGR_Get_IndosPtr function, documented in the Windows DDK. According to the DDK VDAG, this function "returns the linear address of the MS-DOS InDOS and ErrorMode flags." Inspection of the code in DOSMGR (see Figure 1-19) confirms that this is indeed exactly what the function does.

Figure 1-19: Implementation of DOSMGR_Get_IndosPtr

```
      DOSMGR_Get_IndosPtr proc    near
017D7   mov eax,INDOS_PTR
017DC   retn
```

```
      DOSMGR_Get_IndosPtr endp
; ...
; in initialization:
05A7A    mov [ebp.Client_AX],3400h ; set up client reg struct for call
05A80    mov eax,21h              ; call INT 21h AH=34h via Exec_Int
05A85    VMMCall Exec_Int         ;   (Get InDOS Flag Address)
05A8B    movzx eax, [ebp.Client_ES]
05A8F    shl eax,4               ; ES <<= 4
05A92    movzx ebx, [ebp.Client_BX] ; mov with zero-extend
05A96    dec ebx                 ; back up one to get ptr to CritErr
05A97    add eax,ebx             ; create 32-bit linear address
05A99    mov INDOS_PTR,eax        ; actually, both InDos and CritErr!
```

DOSMGR backs up the pointer returned from INT 21h AH=34h to get both the InDOS and CritErr flags into one convenient word-sized chunk, which can be used to test both InDos and CritErr in a single operation.

What's so undocumented about that? INT 21h AH=34h and the InDOS flag are documented (finally!) in the *MS-DOS Programmer's Reference* that Microsoft issued at the time it released DOS 5.0.

Not only was the code shown in Listing 3-15 written long before that but, more important, Microsoft's MS-DOS documentation is still missing a crucial detail. It fails to note that, in DOS 3.0 and higher, the byte before the InDos flag is the critical-error flag. Microsoft probably doesn't document this because, in some versions of DOS, the critical-error flag is located elsewhere (see the appendix). Yet Figure 1-19 shows that the documented DOSMGR_Get_IndosPtr function relies on this still-undocumented aspect of DOS. (Actually, as this book was going to press, we found that Microsoft's DOS programmer's reference *does* refer in one obscure place to the fact that the critical-error flag precedes the InDOS flag. In the words of Emily Latella, "Never mind!")

SYSTEM.INI Settings and Undocumented DOS

Not only does Microsoft have programmer's documentation for Windows that relies on things that are still undocumented in MS-DOS, but it also has *end-user* documentation for Windows that relies on things that are part of undocumented DOS.

That Windows relates in some way to DOS internals is clear even from a non-programmer's or end-user's perspective, because the Windows SYSTEM.INI configuration file can contain settings which relate to DOS functions and structures that are, or until recently were, undocumented. The SYSINI.WRI file that comes with Windows describes these settings, as does the *Windows Resource Kit* and *Windows for Workgroups Resource Kit* that Microsoft publishes:

```
[standard]
Int28Filter=10

[386Enh]
InDOSPolling=No
Int28Critical=True
PSPIncrement=2
ReflectDosInt2A=False
UniqueDOSPSP=True
```

For example, the SYSINI.WRI file (which, remember, is aimed at end-users, not programmers, and which comes with the retail version of Windows) contains the following description of ReflectDosInt2A:

> ReflectDosInt2A=<Boolean>
> Default: False
> Purpose: Indicates whether Windows should consume or reflect DOS INT 2A signals. The default means Windows will consume these signals and therefore run more efficiently. Enable this setting if you are running memory-resident software that relies on detecting INT2A messages.

Microsoft's programmer's documentation, even the latest programmer's reference for DOS 6.0, has no mention of INT 2Ah beyond the single tag "networks/critical sections." While apparently believing that DOS programmers don't need to know about INT 2Ah, Microsoft feels the need to say something about it to Windows end users.

In Windows Enhanced mode, DOSMGR and other VxDs check these SYSTEM.INI settings. The ReflectDOSInt2A= setting, along with an undocumented Modify DOSInt2A= setting, is also checked by DOSMGR, which contains an INT 2Ah handler. This handler, which the Windows Hook_V86_Int_Chain function installs, maps the INT 2Ah calls to appropriate functions provided by the Windows VMM. For example, the DOSMGR INT 2Ah handler calls Begin_Critical_Section to implement INT 2Ah AH=80h, End_Critical_Section to implement INT 2Ah AH=81h and AH=82h, and Release_Time_Slice to implement INT 2Ah AH=84h. If ReflectDOSInt2A= is set, then DOSMGR also passes down ("reflects") INT 2Ah calls to any INT 2Ah handlers that were installed before Windows.

KRNL386 Grows the SFT

Well, that's enough for DOSMGR. Popping back up to the INTRSPY results in Figure 1-6, we see that KRNL386.EXE, the Windows kernel, is finally running, and it too calls our old friend, INT 21h function 52h to get a pointer to SysVars.

KRNL386 uses SysVars to get a pointer to the System File Table chain. Windows makes such heavy use of files that it would be handy to keep a lot of them open at once, so KRNL386 tries to increase the number of SFT entries by using the same undocumented DOS hacks that utilities like Quarterdeck's FILES.COM and Jeff Prosise's UMBFILES use. (Actually, DOSMGR too can grow the SFT, depending on the value of the PerVMFiles= setting in SYSTEM.INI and on whether SHARE is loaded.)

KRNL386 increases the number of SFT entries during its initialization routine, BootStrap(). BootStrap(), an internal KRNL386 function, calls another internal function, GrowSFTToMax(), to do the dirty work. Chapter 1 of Matt Pietrek's book, *Windows Internals: Implementation of the Windows Operating Environment*, discusses BootStrap() and GrowSFTToMax(). Briefly, after calling INT 21h AH=52h, GrowSFTToMax() uses the DOS Protected Mode Interface (DPMI) to get a protected mode selector to SysVars and to the SFTs. After determining how many extra file entries it will create, GrowSFTToMax() multiplies this number by FileEntrySize and calls the Windows GlobalDosAlloc() function to allocate the new SFT block in conventional memory. This function then links the new SFT block onto the end of the existing SFT chain. Voilà! More SFT entries.

Where does FileEntrySize, the size of an SFT entry, come from? The appendix notes that an SFT entry is 38h bytes in DOS 3.0, 35h bytes in DOS 3.1–3.3, and 3Bh bytes in DOS 4.0 and higher. But DOSMGR does not rely on such hardwired knowledge. KRNL386's internal InitDosVarP() function calls yet another internal function, GetFileSize(). You'll never guess how KRNL386 figures out the size of an SFT entry. It opens up CON five times and searches the first 512k bytes of memory for the string "CON", just as we saw DOSMGR doing earlier. Pietrek's *Windows Internals*, which supplies pseudo-code for InitDosVarP(), explains GetFileSize() with the comment "Brrrr!!!!!" 'Nuff said.

KRNL386 and the PSP

Finally, KRNL386 calls undocumented INT 21h AH=55h, the Create PSP function.

As explained in Chapter 7, every process in DOS has a PSP; the DOS EXEC function (INT 21h AH=4Bh) automatically calls INT 21h AH=55h to create a PSP. The PSP contains process information, the most important of which is a pointer to the PSP's file table. All open files in DOS are associated with a particular PSP. The PSP's paragraph address also acts as an identifier for the process. For example, DOS Memory Control Blocks are generally owned by some PSP. When the process exits, any MCBs marked with the block's PSP are freed—unless, of course, the process exits via the DOS terminate-and-stay (TSR) function.

But that's DOS. Why is the Windows kernel creating PSPs? Because Windows isn't actually all that different from DOS. Windows is a protected mode DOS extender. Every process in Windows *also* has a PSP. When a process in Windows opens a file, its file handles are associated with, you guessed it, the PSP. When a Windows program allocates memory via GlobalAlloc(), the block of memory is (except for GMEM_SHARE allocations) associated with the PSP.

Now, PSPs do not contain enough information to hold the state of a Windows process, because Windows does a lot more than plain-vanilla DOS. For example, every running Windows program has its own current drive and directory; for dynamic linking, the program needs a link to its module; and Windows programs generally have message queues. There isn't room for any of this in the PSP, so Windows has another data structure, the Task Database (TDB). For symmetry, Windows calls the PSP a Process Database (PDB). (Actually, one of our tech reviewers writes that "PSPs are called PDBs in the DOS source code, too.") As both *Undocumented Windows* and *Windows Internals* explain, the TDB and PSP (PDB) are linked together. You can think of the TDB as an extended PSP.

Every time KRNL386 starts a new task, it creates a number of data structures for the task, including a PSP. This is a genuine DOS PSP, allocated in conventional memory, where DOS can get at it. Thus, every Windows program requires some low DOS memory (an insufficient amount of low memory can keep a Windows program from running, even if there is otherwise plenty of memory). After all, if the Windows program opens any files, DOS will need to get at a PSP to store the file handles, and PSPs must be located in low memory in order for DOS to find them. (An important side point is that any files opened by DLLs are actually associated with whatever task was running when the file was opened; DLLs aren't tasks and don't have PSPs.)

So, every time you run Solitaire, WinWord, Excel, Ami Pro, or any other Windows program, the kernel calls INT 21h function 55h. As explained in *Windows Internals*, this call involves the internal kernel functions, CreateTask() and BuildPDB(). Why then didn't we see a whole mess of INT 21h AH=55h calls back in Figure 1-6? Because only the first one gets passed down to real mode DOS; once Windows is up and running, KRNL386 handles these calls itself. You can still see the protected mode INT 21h AH=55h calls within Windows, however, if you run a Windows interrupt-trapping program, such as WISPY (I Spy for Windows) from *Undocumented Windows*.

There are many other aspects to Windows and the PSP that we unfortunately don't have room to get into here. For example, as noted in the appendix entry for the PSP (see INT 21h function 26h), Windows uses two unused fields in the PSP for its own purposes: The word at offset 42h forms a PDB chain, and offset 48h indicates whether a program running under Windows is an "old" DOS program or a (presumably new) Windows program. Chapter 3 discusses the Windows PSP in more detail.

Undocumented DOS and the Utilities Wars

Let us spread out from Windows to look at other systems software for the PC. How much do disk compression and disk repair programs, caches, memory managers, DOS extenders, networks, and so on rely on undocumented DOS calls?

DOS itself, and DOS utilities such as SUBST, JOIN, SHARE, PRINT, MEM, and the like, all use undocumented DOS calls. You can check this out for yourself by running any of these programs under INTRSPY (using UNDOC.SCR from Listing 1-2); these programs all call INT 21h function 52h and access SysVars. This is hardly surprising. After all, it was for DOS's own internal use that function 52h was created in the first place.

There's absolutely nothing wrong with this. Every operating system must, by its very nature, have undocumented aspects. One of the key purposes of an operating system is to shield users and programmers from complexity; and the operating system could hardly do that if its vendor documented every last detail of the system and every single function. But in the PC marketplace, utilities are almost like applications. Some of the fiercest competition and some of the largest sales come from utilities. It is not clear why they are so incredibly popular with consumers, but the fact is that inexpensive utilities take a surprisingly important place in lists of top-selling PC software. In a randomly selected issue of *PC Magazine* (March 16, 1993), the top five retail software packages included two utilities, QEMM-386 6.0 (Quarterdeck) and Stacker 3.0 (Stac Electronics).

The interesting thing is that all of these top-selling PC utilities rely on undocumented DOS functions and data structures. Many of the programs that make up QEMM, including BUFF-ERS.COM, FCBS.COM, FILES.COM, LASTDRIV.COM, LOADHI.COM, and MFT.EXE, call INT 21h function 52h. In Stacker, the programs FINDVOL.COM, CHECK.EXE, STACKER.COM, SWAPMAP.COM, and SCREATE.EXE call this most popular of undocumented DOS functions in order, for example, to find the DOS Disk Parameter Block (DPB) chain. Writing a competitive DOS utility without knowledge of undocumented DOS functions and data structures is impossible.

If utilities are a hot area of competition in the PC marketplace and yet if competing in this market depends on having information about DOS that Microsoft refuses to document, then Microsoft's refusal indicates a major problem. As new releases of MS-DOS incorporate functionality, such as memory management and disk compression, that once required separate products from other vendors but which probably belong in the operating system anyway, third-party utilities such as QEMM and Stacker must increasingly compete with DOS itself. Microsoft has a very large head start in producing software for this market, and its control over the operating-system documentation makes the playing field even more uneven.

On the other hand, lack of documentation hasn't yet kept anyone out of this market. It is, as we've noted, quite competitive. While Microsoft doesn't document everything about DOS that it should, programmers can pick up this information through reverse engineering or through sources such as this book. For all we know, this is how many programmers at Microsoft itself find out about DOS internals.

The way that utilities use undocumented DOS, as well as the way Windows uses it, is an important question. Is it right for Microsoft not to document functions that are *essential* for competing in the PC utilities market? While the ultimate answer to this question is far from clear, the raw facts are. As we did with Windows, we can poke around in the different utilities that come with DOS and see what use they make of functions that Microsoft doesn't document. To find examples of the key connection between undocumented DOS and PC utilities, we'll first look at SmartDrive, DoubleSpace, and EMM386; then we'll examine some of the formerly third-party utilities that have been incorporated into MS-DOS 5.0 and 6.0: MIRROR, DEFRAG, and Microsoft Anti-Virus.

Undocumented SmartDrive

Long referred to as DumbDrive because of its poor performance, Microsoft's SmartDrive disk cache has seen many improvements, to the point where it is now a viable alternative to commercial products such as PC-Kwik Cache. In DOS 6.0, you can load SMARTDRV.EXE at any time from the DOS command line, in contrast to the older SMARTDRV.SYS which you could only load as a device driver from CONFIG.SYS. On the other hand, the DOS 6.0 version of SMARTDRV.EXE also has an overly aggressive write-behind cache which can lead to data loss in the hands of inexperienced users.

SmartDrive calls INT 21h function 52h, but it seems like every program we look at uses this function, so this is no longer very interesting. What is more significant is the fact that SmartDrive itself has an undocumented API. For years, Windows programmers knew that Windows was able to grab memory back from SmartDrive temporarily. But how it did this, and how non-Microsoft programs could perform the same trick as Windows, was shrouded in mystery and confusion. Microsoft never documented this interface. but, after reverse engineering SmartDrive, Geoff Chappell revealed all in a January 1992 *Dr. Dobb's Journal* article, "Untangling SmartDrive." Chappell's article showed that programs could manipulate the SmartDrive cache using an IOCTL write (INT 21h AX=4403h) and could query SmartDrive using IOCTL read (INT 21h AX=4402h).

SmartDrive 4.0 and higher no longer use the IOCTL interface described by Chappell. SmartDrive now uses INT 2Fh AX=4A10h instead; this interface, sometimes referred to as the BABE interface based on the 0BABEh signature it uses, is also supported by PC-Cache 8.0 (see the Appendix). DOS 6.0 comes with a SMARTMON utility that uses this interface to measure various aspects of SmartDrive's performance. Jeff Prosise's MS-DOS Q&A column in *Microsoft Systems Journal* (September 1992) mentions this interface briefly, but Microsoft has not officially documented it; in any case *MSJ* showed only how to detect the presence of SmartDrive 4.0, not how to shrink its cache temporarily. (It appears that, to shrink the SmartDrive 4 cache, a program must pretend to be Windows by issuing the INT 2Fh AX=1605h and AX=1606h initialization and termination calls.)

Undocumented DoubleSpace

DoubleSpace, the disk compression utility provided by Microsoft in MS-DOS 6.0, is based on Vertisoft Systems' DoubleDisk. Its direct incorporation into DOS makes DoubleSpace formidable competition to add-in products such as the original disk compression utility, Stac Electronics' Stacker. It is widely rumored that Microsoft paid Vertisoft no money for DoubleDisk, offering instead the mere opportunity to market add-in products to MS-DOS 6.0. If true, this rumor sheds an interesting light on Microsoft's "deal, or be squashed" role as purchaser of technology from smaller software vendors.

DoubleSpace is truly integrated into MS-DOS. In MS-DOS 6.0, a new system file, DBLSPACE.BIN, joins IO.SYS and MSDOS.SYS. IO.SYS loads DBLSPACE.BIN before processing CONFIG.SYS, so DoubleSpace is transparent in a way that even the excellent Stacker product couldn't be (until DOS 6.0, where Stacker pretends to be DBLSPACE.BIN, thus sharing in same preload benefits as DoubleSpace; in essence, DOS 6.0 has created a new "preload" API). That DoubleSpace really is part of the DOS kernel, which is otherwise largely unchanged from DOS 5.0 to 6.0., is also shown by the fact that the SYS and FORMAT /S commands now copy DBLSPACE.BIN along with IO.SYS and MSDOS.SYS. DBLSPACE.BIN has two components, a disk space manager and a compress/decompress "engine" (see Chapter 8).

Amusingly, while Microsoft makes DoubleSpace's incorporation into the DOS kernel its major claim for MS-DOS 6.0 over the Stacker add-in, Microsoft tells its DOS licencees such as IBM that DoubleSpace is *not* part of MS-DOS! In this clumsy arrangement, the retail DOS 6.0 with DoubleSpace is called the "ValuePack," and so IBM does not get DoubleSpace. So much for Microsoft's claim that DoubleSpace, unlike Stacker, is "integrated" into MS-DOS! When it suits Microsoft's purposes, it regards DoubleSpace as wholly separate from MS-DOS.

Microsoft has perhaps learned some important lessons, because it is making available proper programmer's documentation for DoubleSpace. The "DoubleSpace System API Specification" documents the INT 2Fh AX=4A11h interface provided by DoubleSpace. Early versions of this specification described functions 3 and 4 merely as "This API is reserved for SmartDrive." However, after complaints from developers, Microsoft decided in the final version of the specification to document these calls, which SmartDrive uses to get and set device-driver entry points within DoubleSpace. These functions are useful for non-Microsoft disk caches.

Microsoft's "DoubleSpace Compressed Volume File Overview" describes the actual disk format of CVFs (see Chapter 8). The "Microsoft Real-time Compression Interface (MRCI) Specification" documents a new interface, MRCI (pronounced *merci*), which uses INT 2Fh AX=4A12. The MRCI specification also documents INT 1Ah AX=B001h for compression hardware.

The three DoubleSpace/MRCI documents are readily available on CompuServe, on the Microsoft Developer Network (MSDN) CD-ROM, and in the MS-DOS 6.0 version of the *MS-DOS Programmer's Reference*. It's worth contrasting the abundance of information Microsoft provides for DoubleSpace with the difficulty of finding programmer's documentation for Stacker.

The MRCI documentation is particularly interesting because, far from destroying a market, MRCI might create some interesting new possibilities for third-party disk compression vendors. MRCI defines an interface between compression clients and compression servers. For example, DoubleSpace's disk-space manager is a client, and its compress/decompress engine is a server. With the MRCI specification, third-party vendors can create new MRCI clients, such as disk defraggers, disk caches, backup programs, and network transports that know about DoubleSpace. These vendors could also create new MRCI hosts, such as disk-compression hardware similar to Stac Electronics' business before Stacker).

Still, not quite everything about DoubleSpace is documented, and the few remaining undocumented aspects of DoubleSpace appear to be at the center of Microsoft's legal battles with Stac Electronics. Stac originally sued Microsoft for patent infringement (Stac holds three disk-compression patents). Stac may have picked the wrong legal opponent, for Microsoft has turned around and charged Stac with trade-secrets violations and asked for an injunction to block shipments of Stacker 3.1 (*InfoWorld*, August 16, 1993). Such an injunction could, of course, put Stac out of business.

In MS-DOS 6.0, DBLSPACE.SYS /MOVE uses INT 2Fh AX=4A11h BX=FFFEh and BX=FFFFh to tell DBLSPACE.BIN to move itself. As noted earlier, INT 2Fh AX=4A11h is used by the documented DoubleSpace API. However, subfunctions FFFEh and FFFFh are not documented. Because of its tiny size (339 bytes), it is trivial to disassemble DBLSPACE.SYS, even with Microsoft's DEBUG. Some trade secret! DBLSPACE.SYS calls undocumented DoubleSpace function FFFFh to get DBLSPACE.BIN's relocation size and function FFFEh to tell DBLSPACE.BIN to move its to its final position in memory (see the Interrupt List on disk).

In MS-DOS 6.0, IO.SYS's "preloading" of DBLSPACE.BIN, before any drivers in CONFIG.SYS, involves another undocumented interface. Microsoft added hooks in IO.SYS to preload DBLSPACE.BIN (no other vendor can exercise this kind of control over MS-DOS). By naming itself DBLSPACE.BIN under MS-DOS 6.0, Stacker is able to get itself preloaded by IO.SYS. However, simply naming oneself DBLSPACE.BIN is not sufficient. Inspection of IO.SYS with Sourcer reveals that there is really a small "preload API." DBLSPACE.BIN contains a 2E2Ch signature at offset 12h, and a function pointer at offset 14h (there is also a documented MRCI information structure). After using INT 21h AX=4B03h (Load Overlay) to load DBLSPACE.BIN, IO.SYS checks the signature at offset 12h and calls the preload entry point at offset 14h. For example, subfunction BX=4 queries the preload-driver's size, which the preload program (such as DBLSPACE.BIN) must return in AX. IO.SYS calls subfunction 6 to tell the preload program to relocate itself to the top of memory:

```
mov   bx, 4              ; Query Size
call dword ptr cs:[PRELOAD_FUNC]
mov   bx, word ptr, cs:[MEMORY_END]
sub   bx, ax
cmp   bx, word ptr cs:[MEMORY_BASE]
jb    elsewhere
sub   word ptr cs:[MEMORY_END], ax
word es, word ptr cs:[MEMORY_END]
mov   bx, 6              ; Relocate
call dword ptr cs:[PRELOAD_FUNC]
mov   word ptr cs:[MEMORY_BASE], ax
```

IO.SYS appears to use preload subfunction 2 to tell DBLSPACE.BIN to mount drives. Of course, IO.SYS also uses the documented INT 2Fh AX=4A11h interface to communicate with DBLSPACE.BIN. Under MS-DOS 6.0, Stacker must implement the same APIs as DBLSPACE.BIN so that IO.SYS will preload Stacker as though it were DoubleSpace. Interestingly, Novell DOS 7 comes bundled with Stacker (which is widely held to be superior to DoubleSpace) and uses the same preload API to load a file called either STACKER.BIN or DBLSPACE.BIN.

In addition to implementing some important undocumented interfaces, DoubleSpace itself relies, not surprisingly, on undocumented DOS calls; given its competition with Stacker and SuperStor, this is important. Of course, as noted above, Stacker also uses undocumented DOS, and presumably SuperStor does too. And, as also noted, Stac's programmer's documentation for Stacker is nowhere as readily available as Microsoft's documentation for DoubleSpace. But isn't there a difference between a third-party vendor using undocumented DOS calls and Microsoft using them? And isn't there a difference between a third-party vendor failing to document its programming interfaces and Microsoft doing so? The courts have on occasion held that, even if a trade practice is legal in the hands of a small company, the same practice can be illegal in the hands of a monopolist.

Disassembly of DBLSPACE.BIN with Sourcer shows that DoubleSpace calls INT 21h function 52h, using offset 0 in SysVars to get a pointer to the DPB chain and offset 16h to get to the CDS table. DoubleSpace also makes a call to the undocumented DOSMGR VxD in Windows.

If DOS=HIGH, DBLSPACE.BIN tries to move parts of itself into the high memory area (HMA) at the beginning of extended memory. How does it do that? Programmers have frequently noted that there must be parts of the HMA that DOS doesn't use if, for example, the BUFFERS= setting is small. How does DBLSPACE.BIN get at these areas? It uses two undocumented calls, INT 2Fh AX=4A01h (Query Free HMA) and AX=4A02h (Allocate HMA Space; see the appendix). These functions were briefly noted, with a code sample, in *Microsoft Systems Journal* (March 1993), in Jeff Prosise's MS-DOS Q&A column. It is a depressing comment on the state of DOS that the ability to access an extra 6-7K (typically what is free in the HMA) is a useful feature, so this is another interface that Microsoft should formally document.

Undocumented EMM386.EXE

Compaq appears to have originally written Microsoft's memory manager, EMM386. EMM386 competes with third-party memory managers such as QEMM and 386Max.

EMM386 relies far more on knowledge of Intel 386 protected mode and virtual-8086 (V86) mode than on knowledge of undocumented DOS. This includes undocumented aspects of the Intel architecture, such as the 286 and 386 LOADALL instructions, which EMM386.EXE special-cases in its invalid opcode handler. For more on LOADALL, see the superb article by Robert Collins, "The LOADALL Instruction," which appeared in *TECH Specialist* (October 1991).

EMM386.EXE is actually a Windows virtual device driver (VxD). What we normally think of as the DOS utility, then, is just the real mode stub for an embedded VxD. The start of the file looks like a normal DOS executable. A Microsoft KnowledgeBase article, "Binding a TSR to a VxD" (Q74516), describes how to build this type of executable (SMARTDRV.EXE and INTERLNK.EXE use the same format).

The VxD portion of EMM386 is called LoadHi. Disassembly with Sourcer shows that, in addition to hooking the DOS Set Upper-Memory Link function (INT 21h AX=5803h) and hooking VxD functions such as _AddInstanceItem, _TestGlobalV86Mem, and DOSMGR_Instance_Device, the LoadHi VxD also *patches* routines in V86MMGR. This patching is evident when you do a strings dump of EMM386.EXE or another LoadHi device, such as 386MAX.VXD.

It's worth taking a closer look at LoadHi, since it is an example of how a DOS-provided utility such as EMM386 goes about patching Windows. According to the DDK, one of the functions VMM provides is Hook_Device_Service. This function allows any VxD to intercept any function that VMM or another VxD provides. This ability is typical of the far-reaching capabilities that VMM functions offer. Hook_Device_Service takes a function number (for example, Hook_Device_Service itself is function 010090h) and a pointer to the new intercepting function; Hook_Device_Service returns the *previous* handler for the function, a fact which DDK doesn't explain very well. The intercepting function typically uses the pointer to the previous handler to "chain." This is how LoadHi hooks the DOSMGR_Instance_Device_ call, for example. So far, so good.

Now, a VxD that wishes to *patch* VMM and VxD functions, rather than hook them, also uses Hook_Device_Service. The VxD passes in an invalid function pointer of -1, gets back the previous handler, then calls Hook_Device_Service a second time with the function pointer to the previous handler. Nothing has been changed, except the VxD now has the address of the code it wishes to patch. Generally the VxD compares some bytes at that address to see that the code matches what it expects; then it smacks in new code. The LoadHi portion of EMM386 uses this technique to patch the V86MMGR_Set_Mapping_Info and V86MMGR_Get_EMS_XMS_Limits functions. Under certain circumstances, the WINA20.386 VxD included with DOS uses the same Hook_Device_Service trick as EMM386 to patch the V86MMGR VxD in Windows 3.0.

That an MS-DOS utility patches Windows is the most extreme case one can imagine of the special relationship between these two products. But remember that 386Max and QEMM also include LoadHi, so here Microsoft shares information with at least some of its competitors. Novell's version of EMM386 in DR DOS also includes a LoadHi VxD, but Novell says that it never received the Windows 3.1 version of the LoadHi code or of the related Global Import Paging specification, and so they had to play DIY (do it yourself). Meanwhile, most other memory-management vendors had no problem getting these materials. The same thing seems to have happened with the XMS 3.0 specification. This is a good example of how the problem with Microsoft often isn't purely undocumented interfaces, but *discriminatory* documentation, which the company gives out to its customer-competitors on a case-by-case basis, as it sees fit.

This seems to be the case with EMM386. For example, EMM386 cooperates with V86MMGR, using an undocumented interface, sometimes called the "Windows/386 Paging Import" specification and sometimes called the "Global EMM Import" specification. While Microsoft has not documented this specification, it does appear to have shared this information with some other memory-management vendors. It's hard to imagine anyone else who would want this information anyway. (One tech reviewer writes, "Believe it or not, people want this information to help them take over from a memory manager." Sheesh!)

In addition, EMM386 provides a small API through INT 67h AX=FFA5h (see INTRLIST on the disk accompanying this book).

With all the unconventional things EMM386 does, remember that here Microsoft has at least some sort of sharing arrangement with the other memory-management vendors. (So perhaps it's a cartel problem rather than a monopoly problem!) Also, it is hard to see how any of EMM386's tricks give it a competitive advantage. EMM386 is, in fact, far more conservative than 386Max or QEMM, using fewer tricks, not more. EMM386's competitive advantage comes entirely from its being bundled free with the operating system, not from its use of undocumented secrets. Finally, is worth noting that the Microsoft Windows documentation contains a fairly clear statement of the advantages *and disadvantages* of EMM386 compared to other the third-party memory managers.

EMM386 is discussed in more detail in Geoff Chappell's *DOS Internals*.

Microsoft Anti-Virus

Starting with MS-DOS 5.0, Microsoft began incorporating formerly third-party utilities into the operating system. DOS 5.0 included the MIRROR, FORMAT, and UNDELETE utilities from Central Point Software, the makers of PC Tools, which competes with the Norton Utilities from Symantec. DOS 6.0 incorporates more utilities from Central Point, plus Symantec's DEFRAG, which is similar to SpeedDisk in the Norton Utilities. The Central Point utilities in DOS 6.0 include many Windows executables and DLLs. Apparently all Central Point received in exchange for licensing its tools to Microsoft was a license from Microsoft allowing Central Point to use the "look and feel" of the DOSSHELL (Newsbytes, June 12, 1991). Some deal!

We could spent days just looking at the different Central Point utilities included with MS-DOS 6.0. The inclusion in DOS of software that requires Windows is itself interesting; but let us focus on just one of these utilities, Microsoft Anti-Virus (MSAV). In a useful roundup of the utilities in MS-DOS 6.0, *PC Magazine* (April 13, 1993) noted that the inclusion of MSAV in DOS 6.0 is "a serious blow to the stand-alone antivirus software market." It is unclear how necessary all this antivirus software really is, given the extremely low incidence of verified virus sightings, but certainly this is a very active part of the PC software market.

MWAV.EXE, from Central Point's Anti-Virus for Windows, relies on many dynamic link libraries, including MWAVMGR.DLL (TSR manager), MWAVSCAN.DLL (virus scanning support), MWAVABSI.DLL (absolute disk I/O), MWAVDLG.DLL (dialogs), and so on. That DOS 6.0 now comes with Windows DLLs raises an intriguing question: Are these DLLs now part of MS-DOS? The names of the functions these DLLs export are plainly visible using utilities such as Microsoft's EXEHDR and Borland's TDUMP (locating functions in DLLs is discussed in agonizing detail in *Undocumented Windows*). For example, MWAVSCAN.DLL exports many named functions, including CPAV-_Scan_File_for_Viruses(), CPAV_Scan_Boot_for_Viruses(), CPAV_Kill_File_Virus(), and CPAV-_Kill_Boot_Virus(). Are these now part of DOS? Should they be documented? Who the heck knows?

It is good news, at any rate, that none of these Windows executables or DLLs seem to use undocumented Windows calls. Naturally, MWAVSCAN does lots of low-level stuff, making heavy use of DPMI, the formerly undocumented SetSelectorBase() and SetSelectorLimit() functions, and so on. On the other hand, MWAVMGR.DLL calls, or at least contains calls to, INT 2Fh AX=6282h and AX=6284h. As noted in INTRLIST, these functions are part of the PC Tools interface. Given the evident ties between Microsoft and Central Point, or at least the incorporation of so many former Central Point utilities into DOS 6.0, should this API now be considered part of MS-DOS?

One of the Windows anti-virus DLLs is MWAVABSI.DLL, a collection of functions for absolute disk I/O. This DLL exports about ninety named functions, including AIO_GetDDHeader(), AIO_GetFirstCluster(), AIO_GetNextCluster(), and AIO_PutNextCluster().

One function provided by MWAVABSI.DLL is AIO_GetListofLists(). Not surprisingly, this function calls INT 21h AH=52h (AIO_GetListofLists() uses the Windows DOS3Call() function to do the INT 21h). The presence of this function is further evidence, if any were needed, that Microsoft needs to document INT 21h AH=52h. But here, at least, there is no question of insider knowledge. Note that the function's name "ListofLists" comes from Ralf Brown's Interrupt List and general PC folklore, *not* from the MS-DOS source code, which labels this data structure SysInitVars.

Another unnamed export from MWAVABSI (ordinal 130) also calls INT 21h AH=52h and creates a protected mode pointer to the System File (SFT). Figure 1-20 shows the code. The code converts the real mode SFT segment to a protected mode selector, using DPMI function 0002h, which creates a permanent selector that no one can modify or free. While DPMI itself is hardly undocumented (the DPMI specification is readily available at no charge from Intel), Microsoft barely documents the presence of DPMI (version 0.9) within Windows. The Windows SDK contains a total of four pages on both the DOS extender and DPMI ("Windows Applications with MS-DOS Functions," *Programmer's Reference, Volume 1: Overview*, Chapter 20). This skimpy chapter, which also incorrectly claims that Windows supports version 1.0 of DPMI, lists a scant seven DPMI functions that Microsoft approves for use by Windows applications; function 0002h is not on the list. Microsoft's rendition of the golden rule would appear to be "Do as I say, not as I do."

Figure 1-20: MWAVABSI.DLL Creates a Protected-Mode Pointer to the SFT

```
7.087A    mov ah,52h                      ; most popular undoc function
7.087C    call far ptr DOS3CALL           ; call INT 21h
7.0881    mov ax, es:[bx+4]               ; sysvars[4]=SFT chain offset
7.0885    mov word ptr SFT_PTR, ax        ; save offset
7.0888    mov bx, es:[bx+6]               ; sysvars[6] -> SFT chain segment
7.088C    mov ax, 2                       ; DPMI Segment to Descriptor
7.088F    int 31h                         ;    input BX=real mode segment
7.0891    mov word ptr SFT_PTR+2, ax      ;    output AX=pmode selector
```

MWAVABSI.DLL makes extensive use of this protected-mode pointer to the SFT chain. For example, the exported AIO_UpdateSFTInfo( ) function of course uses SFT_PTR.

MWAVABSI.DLL raises yet again (though doesn't answer) the questions of whether it is right for MS-DOS to use undocumented functions in products that compete with third parties (recall *PC Magazine's* statement about the blow MSAV was going to deal to the anti-virus software market), and whether Microsoft needs to document the APIs exported from DLLs incorporated in MS-DOS 6.0. In any case MWAVABSI.DLL constitutes further proof that undocumented functions are useful and that it is crazy for Microsoft not to document INT 21h AH=52h. Crazy, or monopolistic?

Still, isn't it okay for Microsoft to use undocumented calls within the utilities that ship as part of MS-DOS? In the case of SHARE, PRINT, SUBST, and so on, the answer is obviously that it is okay. Every operating system *must* have undocumented internals! If every interface were documented, then the operating system wouldn't be doing its job of shielding developers from complexity.

But what about a utility bundled with the operating system, such as Microsoft Anti-Virus or DoubleSpace, that compete with already existing third-party products? Here the answer is less clear. *PC Magazine* (September 14, 1993) has complained that, "by adding these utilities, Microsoft has clouded the definition of exactly what an operating system should be." Many would disagree with this statement. What is separable from the operating system? The very existence of third-party products would seem to be the key test. Consumers have demonstrated a desire to purchase, in large numbers, utilities that compete with software that comes bundled free as part of MS-DOS. Even the Microsoft CD-ROM Extensions (MSCDEX) have competition, in a product from Corel Software. Where does the operating system stop and the third-party utilities aftermarket begin? At what point does Microsoft's use of an undocumented DOS call cease to be operating-system internals and turn into an advantage over competitors? At what point is the advantage unfair?

The answers seem to be clear when we get to products such as Windows, Windows for Workgroups, and other Microsoft products that are sold separately from MS-DOS. But even here there isn't a simple answer. If Microsoft bundles Windows with MS-DOS, as it will do with the forthcoming "Chicago" operating system, does the problem go away? Is bundling a good solution to the problem of tying? Perhaps. On the other hand, the continued existence of products such as Desqview testified to the desire that at least some consumers have to buy pieces of the operating system separately (somewhat like the aftermarket for automotive spare parts).

In the end, this much is clear: Today Windows and DOS are separate. Windows relies on INT 21h function 52h, SysVars, the CDS, the SFT, and other undocumented DOS calls and structures. Microsoft's failure to document these, or to provide documented equivalents, is monopolization, with no benefit to consumers and with harm to third-party developers.

No Problem?

The problems with undocumented DOS are that 1) some of these functions and data structures are absolutely crucial to DOS programming, 2) Microsoft uses these functions and data structures in its own software that competes with third-party utilities, and 3) programmers have repeatedly had to request that Microsoft document this material. While Microsoft did finally document a number of previously undocumented DOS functions when they released DOS 5.0, there are still many—INT 21h AH=52h in particular—for which Microsoft denies there is any problem.

Precisely *what* Microsoft denies has changed over time, though. On occasion, Microsoft representatives will deny even that undocumented DOS (or Windows, or OS/2, or...) calls even exist.

But usually what Microsoft denies is that Microsoft applications use or derive any advantage from these calls. For years, Microsoft has claimed that, between its operating systems and applications groups, there is "separation of church and state" or, using a term from the insider-trading scandals of the 1980s, a "Chinese Wall."

Stephen Manes and Paul Andrews discuss the Chinese Wall issue at length in their fine biography of Bill Gates (*Gates: How Microsoft's Mogul Reinvented an Industry—and Made Himself the Richest Man in America*, 1993). There have been other biographies of Gates and histories of Microsoft, but this is the first good one. This superb book is not a *People* magazine style report on Gates' life (who cares?), but rather an in-depth study on how Microsoft does business. On the question of the supposed Chinese Wall between Microsoft's two businesses, Manes and Andrews report:

> As far back as 1983, [Microsoft executive VP Steve] Ballmer had stated that "We have shown in the past that there is a very clean separation between our operating systems business and our applications software. It's like the separation of church and state. And if you don't play it straight, you can't expect to get the business." But except for Ballmer's favorite phrase, "get the business," it was hard to swallow. There had been no formal division between systems and apps until mid-1984.

Interestingly, all of the fears about Microsoft's applications conflicting with Microsoft's role as maintainer of the operating system were present at time of OS/2:

> But the ultimate worry about OS/2 was more insidious. *InfoWorld* columnist [now *PC Magazine* editor-in-chief] Michael Miller reported that "several developers I've talked to recently believe that Microsoft has an unfair advantage in developing applications that will run under OS/2. One has even whispered the ugly word 'antitrust.'". . .
> Microsoft's Adrian King insisted that "There are no undocumented interfaces in OS/2," then retreated to the position that "If there are any undocumented interfaces in OS/2, they are for operating system enhancement." Finally King admitted what was patently obvious: There were no official rules that truly separated the applications and systems sides of the company.

So here, too, Microsoft initially tried out the claim that there were no undocumented interfaces. In the case of OS/2 1.0, this claim was absurd. A good example is the DosPTrace() function, most of the command codes for which neither IBM nor Microsoft would document (see "Stalking GP Faults," *Dr. Dobb's Journal*, February 1990). As proof that undocumented functions never die, it is amusing to note that Microsoft hacked the code for DosPTrace() to create the important Windows WinDebug() function, which, naturally, Microsoft also fails to document (supposedly because the function is "going away," which doesn't in fact appear to be happening).

Returning to the supposed separation of Microsoft's applications from its operating systems and the "ugly word" antitrust, the *Gates* biography has a particularly revealing and balanced summary:

> In later years that claimed separation would be roundly derided and the "ugly word" [antitrust] increasingly spoken. "There is a kind of a wall but there is not a watertight wall, basically," a former Windows developer said. "It leaks when you get to Bill. . . . [And] when push comes to shove you're always going to be a little bit friendlier to the guy down in the next building than the guy off in Boston." If a Microsoft apps developer walked down the hall to a Windows developer and asked for a favor to make Excel run better, was that [violation of] antitrust?
> Besides, in the ego-dominated world of Microsoft, just asking for something didn't mean you'd get it. Windows developer Steve Wood . . . kept begging the languages group to give its C compiler some features he felt were desperately missing for Windows developers both in-house and out. The languages guys didn't care, and it was years before his wish list was implemented. (pp. 349–350).

To anyone who has ever dealt with both the Microsoft languages and operating systems groups, this last part rings especially true! There appears to be an intense rivalry, and something approaching intense dislike, between these two groups at Microsoft.

Unfortunately, though, the Chinese Wall didn't hold much water because, as was shown in *Undocumented Windows*, whatever separation did exist was completely informal and obviously not a matter of great importance to Microsoft. Willy nilly, somehow Microsoft applications such as Excel and Word for Windows ended up using undocumented Windows functions, even though Mike Maples, for example, had claimed (*InfoWorld*, December 30, 1992) that "the bigger issue would be, if we were using secrets or undocumented things, and we very consciously avoid that." It is important to stress that having its applications use undocumented functions was not a major or even a minor part of Microsoft's competitive strategy, but nonetheless the company's many claims to have some deliberate policy of *not* using these functions was shown to be totally bogus.

Having failed to deny convincingly that undocumented functions exist or that Microsoft uses them, Microsoft's third defense was that, sure, the functions exist and, sure, Microsoft applications use them, but the functions serve no useful purpose. Far from giving Microsoft an unfair advantage, so this argument goes, calling these functions actually puts it at a disadvantage. Oh yes, and war is peace. We have always been at war with Oceania.

This approach came out during the minor press furor created by *Undocumented Windows* (see for example, "Microsoft Rivals Boil Over Book About Windows," *Wall Street Journal*, September 1, 1992). Microsoft and its fanatically aggressive public relations firm Waggener-Edstrom issued several press releases on the topic ("Microsoft Statement on the Subject of Undocumented APIs," August 31, 1992; "Questions and Answers About Documented and Undocumented APIs," undated; and "Undocumented Functions," undated), which put forward this idea that calling undocumented functions puts Microsoft at a *disadvantage*.

Take, for example, the undocumented Windows function, GetTaskQueue(), which *Undocumented Windows* shows that Microsoft QuickC for Windows uses (yes, in the PC marketplace, compilers are applications). Microsoft's "Undocumented Functions" statement gave this function's status as "No equivalent, but useless." Elsewhere the Microsoft statement said that using GetTaskQueue() "is a major disadvantage," which is the same thing it says of every other undocumented function that Microsoft was caught calling.

While some of the undocumented functions that Microsoft applications call really *are* useless, representing obsolete code from older versions of Windows, this definitely was not the case with GetTaskQueue(). Disassembly of QCWIN.EXE shows that the program calls this undocumented function to determine if there is a message queue set up for the user's C program, running within the QCWIN integrated development environment. That is, QCWIN needs to determine whether the user's program has executed past the section of its startup code that calls InitApp() to establish a task queue. If an application doesn't yet have a task queue, sending it messages can cause bizarre behavior. QCWIN contains the following code:

```
if (GetTaskQueue(hTask) != 0)       // if there's a queue
    PostAppMessage(hTask, ...);     // send a message
DirectedYield(hTask);               // either way, do DirectedYield
```

Microsoft claims that the function SetMessageQueue() is a documented alternative to GetTaskQueue(), but whoever wrote that probably just looked up the word "queue" in an index. SetMessageQueue() simply sets the *size* of a message queue; it is no help with QCWIN's problem, which is to ensure that another task has a queue. Furthermore, one wonders, why if the documented function is such a good alternative to the undocumented one, QCWIN uses the undocumented one.

There are other examples besides GetTaskQueue(), but this is supposed to be a book about DOS, not Windows (though it's hard to keep them separate these days); so we'll move on. Microsoft's "we call these functions as a nice neighborly way of putting ourselves at a disadvantage and thereby leveling the playing field" argument basically isn't very effective.

We expect Microsoft's next defense to be that, sure, Microsoft uses these functions and, sure, they are useful, but that *everyone* uses them. In fact, one of Microsoft's statements on the undocumented Windows controversy notes that "MS-DOS has a number of undocumented APIs that are well-known, well-understood and used by ISVs" (independent software vendors). Well okay, but then why not document them?

DOS Documented

We'll address the subject of *why* Microsoft leaves crucial pieces of DOS functionality undocumented in a minute, but it's important to note first that the company has, to its credit, finally documented some of the most well-known and well-understood, previously undocumented functions.

In the summer of 1991, Microsoft Press issued the *Microsoft MS-DOS Programmer's Reference*, which includes the new INT 21h and INT 2Fh functions in MS-DOS 5.0. This book came out after the publication of the first edition of *Undocumented DOS*, and the Microsoft Press advertising headline for the programmer's reference was "DOS Documented." Microsoft released a nearly-identical version for MS-DOS 6.0 in the summer of 1993.

Indeed, the programmer's reference did document some previously undocumented calls. Most notably, Microsoft blessed the following previously-undocumented INT 21h functions:

- Function 1Fh (Get Default DPB)
- Function 32h (Get DPB)
- Function 34h (Get InDOS Flag Address)
- Function 4B01h (Load Program)
- Function 50h (Set PSP Address)
- Function 51h (Get PSP Address)
- Function 5D0Ah (Set Extended Error)

The new documentation for these old functions is, unfortunately, far from complete. One gets the sense that, to some extent, the point of this exercise for Microsoft was simply to claim that these functions are now documented. The new documentation for the previously undocumented INT 21h functions has the following problems:

- Functions 1Fh, 32h: The programmer's reference claims that these functions are only for DOS 5.0 and higher. In fact, these functions are present all the way back to DOS 2.0. This is an important piece of information, because a large number of DOS 3.x installations are still in use, and most PC disk utilities, which rely on function 32h, must be able to run on these machines. The DPB structure provided is only accurate for DOS 5.0 and higher. Basically, if you believe Microsoft's documentation, then disk utilities can only for written for DOS 5.0 and higher, which we know not to be the case.
- Function 34h: The documentation doesn't mention the critical-error flag located in the byte before the InDOS flag. As we saw earlier, the Windows DOSMGR relies on being able to decrement the return value from function 34h to get both the InDOS flag and critical-error flag into a single word.
- Function 4B01h: The documentation for the LOAD structure incorrectly reverses the order of the ldCIP and ldSSSP fields. Some errors are, of course, unavoidable, but the identical error had appeared earlier, in the book *Developing Applications Using DOS* by three IBMers, Ken Christopher, Barry Feigenbaum, and Shon Saliga (1990). Presumably Microsoft used this book as (uncredited) source material for the MS-DOS 5.0 programmer's reference. (The MS-DOS 6.0 programmer's reference does correct this error.) For a full explanation of function 4B01h, see Tim Paterson's "The MS-DOS Debugger Interface" in the first edition of *Undocumented DOS*.
- Function 5D0Ah: This function is documented only for DOS 4.0 and higher. In fact, it is present in 3.1 and higher. Furthermore, because the manual does not mention the other AH=5Dh

functions, the ERROR structure has a field that will, at best, baffle careful readers. According to the programmer's reference, errUID "identifies the computer, for errors that occur on remote computers." Huh, remote computers? Without documenting function 5D00h (Server Function Call) and its DOS parameter list structure (see the appendix), this statement makes little sense. The errUID field is actually the same as DOS's USER_ID field, discussed earlier in this chapter. Under Windows Enhanced mode, this field should thus contain the VM ID, which a DOS program can retrieve by calling INT 2Fh AX=1683h. If all this weren't enough to indicate that Microsoft's documentation for this function is a mess, the MS-DOS 5.0 programmer's reference also stated that the ERROR structure goes in DS:SI, when, in fact, it goes in DS:DX. This, at least, was fixed in the MS-DOS 6.0 programmer's reference.

Well, beggers can't be choosers, and it is good to have these functions finally brought into the official INT 21h fold.

In addition, Microsoft documented INT 28h (MS-DOS Idle Handler) and a number of INT 2Fh calls:

- Function 0106h (Get Printer Device; the first edition of *Undocumented DOS* incorrectly identified this call as "PRINT.COM: Check if Error on Output Device")
- Function 0600h (Get ASSIGN.COM Installed State)
- Function 1000h (Get SHARE.EXE Installed State)
- Function 1100h (Get Network Installed State)
- Function 1400h (Get NLSFUNC.EXE Installed State)
- Function 1A00h (Get ANSI.SYS Installed State)
- Function AD80h (Get KEYB.COM Version Number)
- Function AD81h (Set KEYB.COM Active Code Page)
- Function AD82h (Set KEYB.COM Country Flag)
- Function B000h (Get GRAFTABL.COM Installed State)
- Function B700h (Get APPEND.EXE Installed State)
- Function B702h (Get APPEND.EXE Version)
- Function B704h (Get APPEND.EXE Directory List Address)

Two interesting points emerge from the new Microsoft documentation. First, because INT 21h functions 34h, 4B01h, 50h, and 51h, according to the documentation, have existed as far back as DOS 2.0, it is clear, should there have been any doubt, that there really are such things as undocumented DOS calls, and useful ones at that.

Second, it is clear that using these undocumented functions was never unsafe. Rather than being changed or removed or blowing up on an end-user's machine, they were documented. Of course, we only have this 100% certainty of their safety in retrospect, but still, whenever previously undocumented functions become documented you have to wonder how solid the "don't use undocumented functions because they are unsafe" argument really is. We'll deal with this subject again shortly.

The *MS-DOS Programmer's Reference* left most of the useful undocumented DOS functions in their orphaned state. Of course, it doesn't document or even mention the core Get SysVars function, nor does it say anything about the CDS or SFT. The MCB structure is documented, under the name ARENA, but how one finds the root of the ARENA chain is never mentioned. Several important fields in the PSP are still undocumented. As noted earlier, only one INT 21h AH=5Dh function was documented. The network redirector is not mentioned, and the only redirector-related documented function was INT 2Fh AX=1100h. The entire INT 2Ah interface is absent beyond the single-line description, "Network/Critical Sections". All in all, aside from documenting some of the new functions in DOS 5.0, the programmer's reference didn't add very much to the store of DOS knowledge. (The DOS 6.0 version at least includes the DoubleSpace, CVF, and MRCI documentation in one handy place.) The book merely put Microsoft's grudging and belated approval on a small, already well-known, portion of it. As

Douglas Boling put it at the time, in the semi-independent *Microsoft Systems Journal* (January-February 1992): "We Knew That. Microsoft seems to have finally realized that a number of 'undocumented' functions were in fact documented everywhere but the MS-DOS technical reference."

Why Leave Functionality Undocumented?

Why didn't Microsoft do a better job with the DOS programmer's reference? Why, for example, given the functions's obvious importance in DOS programming, has it still not documented INT 21h function 52h and the List of Lists? Why are they still holding back on the network redirector specification? Why don't they document this INT 2Ah critical section stuff?

In one sense, Microsoft's reasons aren't really very different from the reasons other vendors' documentation doesn't always cover everything that a person would ever need to know. The difference is simply that Microsoft now plays such a central role in the software industry that, when Microsoft fails to document something important, this failure affects many more programmers much more deeply than if, say, Lotus failed to mention an @DATE function anomaly in 1-2-3.

One reason for insufficient documentation is simply a resource allocation problem. It is not easy finding qualified technical writers, and those who are qualified would probably rather write code. Any company that has had a difficult time finding good technical writers can sympathize with Microsoft's plight, and they can applaud Microsoft when it does find good people to write excellent documentation, such as that on the recent Microsoft Developer Network (MSDN) CD-ROM. (If you have the MSDN CD-ROM, check out in particular the excellent articles by David Long.)

Even if resource allocation problems were the sole reason for inadequate documentation, it puts the company's ever-outward expansion in a new light. Microsoft representatives have on several occasions clearly stated the company's desire to set all the key software standards. Microsoft wants to control every imaginable API, including areas such as telephony, copiers, fax, and television. There is, in itself, nothing wrong with this. However, if Microsoft wants to set every standard and control every API, it ought to make sure that it has the resources to maintain these standards and properly document these APIs.

In other words, one problem with Microsoft is simply that its eyes are bigger than its stomach. It seeks to control standards that it may not have adequate resources to document. The problem is, of course, not lack of money, but lack of personnel. Microsoft's policy of deliberately under-staffing projects to keep them "focused" is also at work here. Something has to "give," and documentation is a natural place to skimp. Especially when the existing documentation will satisfy, say, 85% of the users, it is difficult to make the huge effort necessary to supply what is needed by the remaining 15%. There are diminishing returns in documentation, just as there are in bug fixes.

Actually, this is not entirely a bad thing for the rest of the industry. If Microsoft's eyes are bigger than its stomach, and if Microsoft takes on projects for which it can do only an adequate job (one tech reviewer says "Microsoft has a talent for providing 85% solutions"), this situation opens up many niche opportunities for other companies. Microsoft's entry into the memory management market is a good example of this. At first, it was widely feared that the introduction of DOS 5.0 would shortly lead to bankruptcy filings from memory-management vendors such as Qualitas and Quarterdeck. Instead, even though memory management was included free of charge with DOS 5.0, the market for memory-management software expanded. Apparently utilities consumers know how to "look a gift horse in the mouth," as a Quarterdeck ad suggests. DOS 5.0 legitimized the idea of 386 memory managers, but did not itself provide more than an adequate memory manager. Companies such as Qualitas and Quarterdeck were able to exploit this contradiction. This book is itself a good example of how Microsoft's tendency to provide only partial solutions can create opportunities for others.

Another reason is that some of the things, like the network redirector, that Microsoft ought to bring out of the closet and document are more valuable to it in their undocumented "magic" state. Documentation is just documentation, but an important undocumented interface like the redirector is "technology." Microsoft has made the redirector source code available to selected vendors, apparently in exchange for things it wanted. It is hard to have such technology exchanges when the "technology" is nothing more than a chapter in a book.

There is a detectable pattern in the things that Microsoft doesn't document, as well as in the things it takes many years to document. The functions present in DOS 2.0 that they didn't document until DOS 5.0 are a prime example. Microsoft consistently underestimates the need that programmers have for low-level information about its operating systems. The unconscious Microsoft attitude seems to be that, if you aren't working at Microsoft, you shouldn't be messing around with SFT chains and CDS pointers in the first place ("What do they want to know that for?"). Of course, many people outside Redmond don't share this attitude, and eventually Microsoft has to break down and document at least some of the low-level interfaces that a lot of developers need. Microsoft may be showing some new openness in its Win32 SDK, which includes the source code for some key utilities, such as DLGEDIT, PVIEWER, SPY, and WALKER. Source code! What a concept!

Another reason Microsoft does not document some important functions is that, as one developer at Microsoft once put it, everyone at the company is "two releases ahead of reality." While third-party vendors need something that works on machines running DOS 5.0 today, developers at Microsoft are already thinking about, and preoccupied with, DOS 7.0 ("Oh, you can't use that, that's going away in DOS 7.0").

Microsoft, in other words, doesn't want to document things that it knows, or thinks, or hopes, or prays, will go away in some future version of the operating system. It is commendable that the company is so forward-looking, but this does little good to the third-party vendor whose programs have perhaps painted themselves into a corner and need to accomplish some low-level task *today*.

From Microsoft's perspective, documenting low-level functionality inhibits change, so it makes perfect sense to reserve entire areas of DOS and to tell developers that, if they somehow find out about these areas and use them, their programs might or might not work in future releases. Microsoft has a standard policy statement about programs that use undocumented DOS functions and data structures ("Regarding the Use of Undocumented MS-DOS Features," *Q34761*, September 5, 1988):

> Microsoft does not give out any information about undocumented system features. If calls, flags, or interrupts are undocumented, it is because they are not supported; we can give NO guarantee that they will exist in future releases of DOS. If you find out about these features (through articles or by chance) and begin using them in your programs, there is a real potential that your application will not work in future DOS versions. We strongly advise against using undocumented features for these reasons and will give out no information about their use.

Once a software developer documents some feature of a product, the developer is almost obligated to support that feature in future releases. Microsoft has enough problems maintaining features of MS-DOS that it has already documented. The persistence of such CP/M-compatible anachronisms as File Control Blocks (FCBs) and the structure of the DOS Program Segment Prefix (PSP) are good examples. The FCB is a good example of why operating-system internals should not be exposed to applications. Documenting features can make changing them difficult and can thus create anachronisms.

So far, Microsoft's reasons for failing to document key interfaces all look pretty mundane. None of it seems particularly vicious, conspiratorial, or even the product of much thought one way or the other.

But this passive-aggressive practice of neglecting to document certain well-known interfaces does have broader implications. The problem isn't "conspiracy," which seems to be the word that is invariably used to deride the notion that anything could possibly be rotten in Redmond. The idea of a conspiracy sounds ridiculous. But the problem isn't conspiracy, it's *monopoly*. Given Microsoft's 95% market share in PC operating systems, this sounds downright plausible. The problems with monopoly are well-known. Why should Microsoft be any different?

Documentation and Monopoly

What does Microsoft's position as monopoly supplier of DOS have to do with its failure to document key pieces of DOS? As noted earlier, the computer trade press may have wrongly focused on possible benefits that Microsoft applications derive from this arrangement and failed to note the benefits that DOS itself derives from undocumented interfaces.

To start, how has Microsoft managed to keep such a lucrative market as DOS almost entirely to itself? Simple economics would tell us that, given the relative simplicity of the DOS interface, and given the large amounts of money to be made by taking even a small piece of the DOS market away from Microsoft (see Chapter 4), Microsoft would have more competition for DOS. Why aren't there at least two or three other companies producing high-colume DOS workalikes, in the same way that many companies produce word processors? Why is the competition for DOS so lame?

One explanation is that the operating system might constitute a so-called "natural monopoly," that is, a market in which adding competitors drives prices up rather than down. Microsoft itself may believe that DOS is a natural monopoly. Manes and Andrews' biography quotes Bill Gates, at a Rosen Research Personal Computer Forum back in May 1981, discussing how volume and standards might lead to a natural monopoly:

> Why do we need standards? . . . It's only through volume that you can offer reasonable software at a low price. Standards increase the basic machine you can sell into. . . .
>
> I really shouldn't say this, but in some ways it leads, in an individual product category, to a natural monopoly: where somebody properly documents, properly trains, properly promotes a particular package and through momentum, user loyalty, reputation, sales force, and prices builds a very strong position within that product.

Gates probably understood this connection between volume and quality earlier than anyone else in the PC software industry (which industry, of course, he largely defined in the first place). Still, it is somewhat worrisome to hear Gates speaking of monopoly, even back in 1981. If the PC operating system is a natural monopoly, shouldn't it come under some form of government regulation, just like telephone service, the railroad, and electric utilities? The idea that Microsoft might consider the PC operating system a natural monopoly is particularly worrisome given the company's clear trend of putting more and more functionality into the operating system (particularly Windows) that was previously thought the province of applications (the Windows OLE 2.0 specification is a good example). Does this natural monopoly have any well-defined boundaries?

But it is difficult to see how there is any "natural" monopoly here. There are certainly many different ways to implement the documented DOS interface (we'll get to the undocumented parts of the interface in a moment). Surely the entrance of some strong competitors into this arena would drive prices down, not up. While developers would quite rightly not welcome the presence of multiple DOSs or multiple implementations of Windows (it would be a testing nightmare, at least at first), overall consumers would benefit by a highly competitive market for DOS. Just as competition from AMD and Cyrix (and now perhaps Motorola's PowerPC) has helped Intel speed up its product-development cycle, so too would competition for DOS make Microsoft more innovative.

DOS is relatively stagnant right now largely because of the lack of competition. And what little advance there has been since MS-DOS 4.0 has come *after* changes made in DR DOS (see Chapter 4). Of course, some of the relative stagnation in DOS is based on the need for backward compatibility. But if there were fierce competition for DOS, in the same way that there is for word processors and spreadsheets, Microsoft's "Chicago" would probably have been out by now. With little competition, Microsoft was able to dawdle over DOS and instead devote its efforts to exercises such as NT. The less competition it had for DOS, the more Microsoft was able to ignore DOS and simply milk it as a "cash cow."

The Microsoft near-monopoly on DOS provides little benefit to consumers, so it's not a natural monopoly. But then what explains the lack of competition in this lucrative market? The inconvenience to developers if there were more than one important DOS is one explanation. Microsoft's per-machine rather than per-copy OEM pricing of DOS is another. But an additional explanation, and one which will return us to the subject of undocumented interfaces, is the fear of incompatibility. A key to Microsoft's near-monopoly over DOS is the notion that the only possible DOS is MS-DOS. Because DOS itself is a rather small piece of code (which has been highly leveraged into an incredible business), and because implementing the documented portions of the DOS interface would be relatively simple (there are probably infinite ways to implement INT 21h AH=40h without infringing on Microsoft's copyright), Microsoft's DOS monopoly depends largely on this issue of "compatibility."

But compatible with what? It is relatively simple to be compatible with the documented DOS interface. Failure to do so is just a bug. So what does this "compatibility" mean?

In part, of course, compatibility is just marketing product-differentiation mumbo jumbo. Microsoft wants to promote the idea that MS-DOS is the only conceivable DOS. In this sense, "compatibility" is just another way of saying "anything else just isn't MS-DOS."

But an operating system must work as part of an integrated package together with other products. So there is something genuine to the issue of compatibility. It largely means compatibility with *undocumented* interfaces. After all, failing to be compatible with documented interfaces is just a bug. Microsoft can make a good argument that only MS-DOS implements all the undocumented DOS interfaces correctly, and that therefore only MS-DOS is "100% DOS compatible." This appears to be the core of Microsoft's defense of the AARD code in Windows, i.e., that if DR DOS were truly "100% DOS compatible," then it would pass the AARD test. As we saw earlier, the AARD test for 100% DOS compatibility depends entirely on undocumented interfaces. Producing a compatible DOS, then, is largely a matter of getting the undocumented interfaces right.

Because it is relatively easy for competitors to be compatible with a documented interface, companies try to create what Ray Valdés calls "artificial kingdoms" by selectively documenting only parts of their product interfaces. Consciously or not, Microsoft uses undocumented interfaces to shore up its dominance of the DOS market. Whenever an application follows the advice of this book and calls on undocumented DOS services and uses data structures internal to DOS, as many successful applications now do, it ties itself more closely to the MS-DOS binary, to that particular sequence of bytes, rather than to the DOS standard generally. Conversely, relying on undocumented calls and structures makes life more difficult for vendors of DOS workalikes.

But for Microsoft to derive any such benefit from undocumented interfaces, important applications have to use them. This would in turn mean that Microsoft would in some way actually have to encourage key vendors to use calls and structures that it doesn't document. Microsoft indeed does claim to help ISVs use undocumented calls when necessary. This has always raised the question of why Microsoft doesn't just document the calls. The possibility of using undocumented interfaces essentially as a form of product differentiation provides one answer to that question.

Indeed, many so-called "undocumented" interfaces are in truth "selectively documented" interfaces, in which Microsoft has selectively allowed some of its competitors and/or customers access to an interface, while denying similar access to other companies and to the rest of the developer community. There are numerous instances of this, including the network redirector, the Global EMM Import specification, and the LoadHi code for Windows 3.1.

Earlier, it was noted that "Chinese Walls" are really nothing more than what software-engineering texts sometimes call modularity or firewalls, that is, narrow, well-documented interfaces. But the software-engineering texts fail to mention that to properly document interfaces is also to throw them open to potential competition. Conversely, undocumented interfaces are a way of creating and reinforcing a *monopoly standard*.

Owning a crucial standard depends on publishing this standard and having others write to it. Otherwise the standard is worthless. But to publish a standard opens it up to potential competition from clones, workalikes, freeloaders, and so on. Is there any trick that would allow one to own a crucial standard, yet prevent or curtail or at least delay competition? MS-DOS shows that the answer is yes, and undocumented DOS interfaces, on which key applications rely, is part of how the trick works.

Fear of Undocumented DOS

We can see that MS-DOS includes a lot of undocumented functionality. Microsoft doesn't document these features because it wants the freedom to change or discard them in future versions of MS-DOS, and because, for the reasons just discussed, these features may be more useful to Microsoft in their undocumented form. Armed with *Undocumented DOS*, you now know all about these functions and data structures. It's interesting to know that MS-DOS returns the address of its internal variable table if you invoke INT 21h function 52h. But can you use this stuff in real programs?

Depending on who it is talking to, Microsoft generally says no, you can't. So do other programmers as well. After all, in many areas of computing, the use of reserved, undocumented, or unspecified features is a one-way ticket to unstable, nonportable software. Use of undocumented features is not generally part of any approved software-engineering curriculum. It is hard to believe that using undocumented features is often the only way to write stable and correct utilities for MS-DOS.

There is a certain mystique surrounding undocumented DOS, and some programmers have found it easiest to take the dogmatic view that programmers should never, ever use undocumented DOS functions in programs they plan to distribute to others. For example, the author of a well-written, well-organized, and enjoyable introduction to TSR programming (Thomas A. Wadlow, *Memory Resident Programming on the IBM PC*, 1987) writes:

> None of the programs in this book use the INDOS call, and for good reason. INDOS is "undocumented," a term that has two meanings. The first is, of course, that you cannot look it up in the DOS manual. The second is that Microsoft, the vendors of DOS, reserve the right to change or delete this function from subsequent versions of DOS. In fact, the INDOS call as shown here is useful only under DOS version 2.x (where x is any of the minor version numbers). In DOS version 3.x the call still exists, but has changed quite a bit from the older versions. In DOS 4.0, this function does something quite different; thus, calls to the INDOS function will fail miserably.
>
> For that reason, use of the INDOS function call or any undocumented DOS function is not recommended.

The DOS reference in the back of Wadlow's book has entire pages with only a note at the top such as:

```
AH = 034H (52)          Unsupported
INT 021H (33)           Universal function
```

The rest of the page is left blank!

A lot more than that can be said about INT 21h function 34h. If you have all the information about changes made from one DOS version to the next, then calls to the INDOS function will *not* "fail miserably." Ray Michels' TSRs from the first edition of *Undocumented DOS* used this then-undocumented function; and these programs work correctly in DOS 2.x, 3.x, 4.x, 5.x, and 6.x, in the DOS box of OS/2, and in Digital Research's DR DOS.

In fact, what happened with function 34h was that, far from failing miserably, Microsoft documented it. If the most useful undocumented calls are destined to become documented, then using such functions might do nothing more dangerous than give you a year or two jump on your more cautious competitors. Another good example of this is the Set/GetSelectorLimit/Base functions in Windows 3.0, which were so useful that Microsoft documented them in Windows 3.1. Was it a mistake to use them back when they were undocumented? In retrospect, clearly it wasn't. There is something of a

Heisenberg effect at work here. The reason that previously-undocumented functions become documented is that programmers start using them. Documentation is, to an extent, market-driven.

An informal poll seems to indicate that developers of commercial PC software—software that must maintain a high degree of reliability and compatibility, sometimes on millions of different machines—are in general less fearful of undocumented DOS than programmers whose work needs to run on only one or two machines. A curious paradox.

One explanation is simply that it is mostly mass-marketed shrink-wrapped utilities, rather than, say in-house databases or vertical market applications, that require undocumented DOS. Another explanation is that programmers who work for large commercial software houses can better afford the possible higher cost of working with undocumented DOS. Software that uses these functions perhaps requires more testing and more maintenance than that which uses "normal" DOS code.

In any event, attitudes toward undocumented DOS resemble current opinions about the "goto" construct in programming languages. Many professional programmers recognize that goto, possibly disguised as "longjmp," is sometimes necessary. Like goto, programmers should avoid undocumented DOS, but not when its use is unavoidable. Software construction involves tradeoffs and compromises, not fixed dogma. Software construction aspires to be engineering, not religion.

Even though use of undocumented API calls is particularly prevalent in widely distributed software packages for the PC, the idea persists that using these functions is somehow of use only to the home hobbyist, for fun. For example, *Peter Norton's Windows 3.0 Power Programming Techniques*, by Paul Yao and Peter Norton, says:

> It has been our experience that "undocumented goodies" are interesting to look at, but dangerous to include in software that is intended for general distribution.

While this is an excellent book, this particular statement is quite odd. Windows itself, as we've seen, relies heavily on undocumented DOS calls; and Windows was certainly intended for general distribution. More to the point, Peter Norton's own products, the Norton Utilities and the Norton Desktop for Windows, rely heavily on both undocumented DOS and Windows calls. Well, maybe Peter didn't read what Paul wrote.

Ain't Misbehavin'

As we've seen, a lot of systems software and utilities for the PC use undocumented DOS. With some exceptions like the Windows DOSMGR VxD, these programs tend to make just one or two undocumented DOS calls. This is somewhat like losing one's virginity, however: It takes only one undocumented DOS call to change the nature of a program.

Let's say that you start using one or two undocumented DOS calls in your program. What type of program do you have now? The chapter on "Compatibility and Portability" in Duncan's *Advanced MS-DOS Programming* categorizes MS-DOS applications by degrees of compatibility. Duncan unequivocally exiles programs that use undocumented DOS to the innermost circle of this DOS inferno:

> "Ill-behaved" applications are those that rely on undocumented MS-DOS function calls or data structures, interception of MS-DOS or ROM BIOS interrupts, or direct access to mass storage devices (bypassing the MS-DOS file system). These programs tend to be extremely sensitive to their environment and typically must be "adjusted" in order to work with each new MS-DOS version or PC model. Virtually all popular terminate-and-stay-resident (TSR) utilities, network programs, and disk repair/optimization packages are in this category.

The most important sentence here is the last one. If you write "ill-behaved" DOS applications, you are in good company. Indeed, the purpose of *Undocumented DOS* is to show how you too can write ill-behaved programs such as Microsoft Windows, the Norton Utilities, Stacker, and QEMM! All these programs do tend to be extremely sensitive to their environment. Some of them do have to be "adjusted" to work with each new MS-DOS version. Start using undocumented DOS, and that will be true of your software as well.

There problems already are a fact of life in the MS-DOS world. In fact, using undocumented DOS has many of the same benefits and liabilities as the standard practice of bypassing DOS and writing directly to the hardware. (Windows was supposed to eliminate that problem, but as *Undocumented Windows* showed, it traded that problem for another one: more undocumented interfaces.)

The need to use undocumented functions and data structures for many important tasks tells you much more about MS-DOS than it does about any sort of standard recommended engineering practice. Before we start knocking MS-DOS, though, let's not forget that, if for no other reason than that it has ridden on the coattails of the PC's wild success, DOS has succeeded in a way that no other, supposedly better, operating system can match. DOS, with all its warts, is an inescapable reality. Using undocumented DOS may not find a place in any software-engineering curriculum, but it is a good exercise in accommodating your principles to the real world.

Having said all this, let's see what we can salvage of good engineering practice as we make our descent into undocumented DOS. This book presents many techniques for using undocumented DOS in a relatively safe and reliable manner. Some of the techniques recommended in this book are:

- Rigorous checking of the MS-DOS version number (not so easy in DOS 5.0 and higher; see Chapter 2)
- Verifying the basic integrity of undocumented DOS internals by performing an undocumented DOS call and comparing its output with a known value
- Computing structure sizes dynamically as a double check for sizes computed from the DOS version number
- Never use an undocumented function or structure when there's a documented alternative! Devote some effort to looking for the documented alternative; don't just assume there isn't one.

Programs that use undocumented DOS are obligated to do a *better* job of DOS version checking, error checking, and basic sanity checking than many other programs that otherwise play by the book. (One of our tech reviewers writes, "This is the stupidest thing I've ever heard! All programs, whether they rely on undocumented features or not, have to do rigorous error checking!") Most of the programs in *Undocumented DOS* and its accompanying disk and work properly in MS-DOS versions 2.x, 3.x, 4.x, 5.0, and 6.0. Some of the programs have been ported to protected mode using DOS extenders. Many have been tested under different configurations, including Windows, SHARE, Desqview, QEMM, and 386Max, with various DOS components loaded into high memory.

Many of the programs in this book have also been tested under environments such as the DOS compatibility boxes found in OS/2 1.x and 2.0 and Novell's DR DOS (see Chapters 3 and 4). These environments may or may not matter to you, but it is important to gauge the quality of their support for undocumented DOS because any support they do provide *is completely intentional*. Unlike versions of MS-DOS itself, which may support one or another undocumented DOS feature simply out of inertia, these simulated DOS environments can only support an undocumented DOS function call or data structure if someone consciously puts it there.

So, there is a large collection of popular PC software that uses undocumented DOS. Are the vendors of all these programs going to get burned with the next version of DOS? It's instructive to read what Microsoft's one-time Chief Architect for System Software said about this issue (Gordon Letwin, *Inside OS/2*, 1988):

It may seem that if a popular application "pokes" the operating system and otherwise engages in unsavory practices that the authors or users of the application will suffer because a future release, such as OS/2, may not run the application correctly. To the contrary, the market dynamics state that the application has now set a standard, and it's the operating system developers who suffer because they must support that standard. Usually, that "standard" operating system interface is not even known; a great deal of experimentation is necessary to discover exactly which undocumented side effects, system internals, and timing relationships the application is dependent on.

In other words, when popular applications use undocumented DOS, ultimately it is Microsoft which suffers the inconvenience, not the application's developer. As noted earlier, Microsoft may also derive some benefit, in that the popular application has locked itself into MS-DOS. The real suffering may be done by vendors of would-be DOS workalikes. In any case, smaller developers, meanwhile, can ride the coattails of the larger developers. For better or for worse, if enough important applications use undocumented DOS, yesterday's undocumented hack becomes tomorrow's standard. The market has spoken. Amen.

## CHAPTER 2

Programming for Documented and Undocumented DOS: A Comparison

by Andrew Schulman

Let's pretend we work in the installation software group of a commercial software company. For some reason, we have been asked to produce a small utility that, when run from a DOS batch file, returns the number of logical drives on the system. This number corresponds to the LASTDRIVE statement in a user's CONFIG.SYS. Perhaps the company is installing software in a Novell NetWare 3.x environment, where LASTDRIVE determines the starting letter for network drives.

The utility is to be called LASTDRV.EXE, and the idea is that when the utility exits back to DOS, it should return a number corresponding to LASTDRIVE. For example, if LASTDRIVE=E, then LASTDRV.EXE should return the number five. This differs from other DOS utilities that return zero to indicate success and one (or more) to indicate an error. This number can be interrogated using the IF ERRORLEVEL facility in MS-DOS's demented batch language.

The LASTDRV utility should also display a string such as "LASTDRIVE=E", but in such a way that redirecting the program's output to the NUL bit bucket device will discard its output. For example, to make sure that there are at least six logical drives (that is, LASTDRIVE is F: or higher), someone in the batch files team of the installation software group (some large software companies work that way) would take our wonderful utility and incorporate it into the following batch file:

```
echo off
rem need6.bat
lastdrv > nul
if errorlevel 6 goto end
echo Requires at least six drives
:end
```

Now, how do we write LASTDRV.EXE? Trying to find the user's CONFIG.SYS file and then locate the LASTDRIVE statement is a very bad idea. Aside from the fact that LASTDRIVE didn't make its appearance until DOS 3.0 and that its use is optional because E: is the default LAST-DRIVE, we would have no guarantee that, once we locate a CONFIG.SYS file, it would be the one with which the system was booted. It also appears to be impossible to locate the boot drive reliably in MS-DOS prior to version 4.0 (in new versions of DOS, INT 21h function 3305h returns this value).

If we are writing in a high-level programming language like C or Pascal, it's unlikely that the compiler's subroutine library comes with a function that returns the number of drives. True, Microsoft C/C++ has the function _bios_equiplist(), and Borland C++ has the function biosequip(), both of which return the number of floppy drives. But what about fixed disks?

More important, we were asked to retrieve the number of DOS *logical* drives, so interrogating the PC's ROM BIOS does not meet the functional specification that management handed us for this brilliant utility. Logical drives also include RAM disks, network drives, CD-ROM drives, tape backup units, and the like. Logical, in other words, means both physical drives and *fictional* drives. As shown in Chapter 8 on the DOS file system, much of DOS's extensibility comes from the ability to have drive letters assigned to things that aren't really drives at all. In other words, a logical drive is an MS-DOS construct, having little to do with PC hardware or the ROM BIOS. How are we going to write the LASTDRV program?

Using the example of LASTDRIVE, this chapter looks at how to incorporate the information in the rest of the book into working code in C, 80x86 assembly language, Turbo Pascal, and BASIC. It also discusses the important issue of when *not* to use undocumented features, while showing that certain PC programming tasks absolutely require them.

In the course of this chapter, it will also become clear that exploiting undocumented features of MS-DOS usually requires only a few lines of code. On the other hand, programs that use undocumented DOS features must be more aware of the MS-DOS version number than code that uses only documented DOS. In particular, while undocumented MS-DOS *function calls* have remained remarkably stable from one version of DOS to another, the equally important DOS internal data structures vary wildly with each new release of the operating system. Programs that use undocumented DOS must somehow deal with this problem. In DOS 5.0 and higher, this issue is further complicated by the fact that the supposed DOS version number can be modified on a per-application basis. Gross!

This chapter assumes that you want to access undocumented DOS from a DOS program. While this assumption may at first sound obvious, more and more developers are writing for protected mode environments such as Microsoft Windows. Often these new programs must still talk to DOS, and sometimes they must even call undocumented DOS functions and access undocumented DOS data structures. The next chapter discusses this problem of accessing undocumented DOS from protected mode Windows.

Using Documented DOS Functions

Before examining how to use undocumented DOS in programs, let's review how to use documented DOS function calls. This detour into documented DOS—we might even say over-documented DOS because so much has been written about it—will pay off when we write programs using undocumented DOS. If you know all about calling DOS from your chosen programming language, skip to the section on "Using Undocumented DOS." Don't skip the entire chapter though, even if you read it all in the first edition. A lot has been added since then, including a program that modifies (not just examines) some DOS internal data structures, a peek at the disassembled source code for DOS, a discussion of hooking DOS, and a discussion of lots of new nastiness involving the DOS version number.

To learn how a program finds the value of LASTDRIVE, the first thing to do is browse through a reference book on the DOS programmer's interface, looking for an INT 21h function that returns the number of logical drives.

Flipping through Microsoft's official *MS-DOS Programmer's Reference*, we find that INT 21h function 0Eh, which selects the current disk drive in the system, also somewhat illogically (since the two have little to do with each other) returns the total number of drives:

```
Int 21H Function OEH
Select Disk
Selects the drive specified in DL (if valid) as the default drive.
Call with:
    AH = OEH
    DL = drive code (O=A, 1=B, etc.)
Returns:
    AL = number of logical drives in system
```

In single-drive IBM PCs with DOS 1.x and 2.x (present at more customer sites than you would like to think), DOS returns AL=2 because DOS supports two logical drives, A: and B:. These drives hang off the same single physical floppy drive. In DOS 3.x and higher, AL returns (a) the drive code corresponding to the LASTDRIVE entry in CONFIG.SYS (for example, six if LASTDRIVE=F:), (b) five, if there is no LASTDRIVE entry, or (c) the actual number of block devices on the system, if there are more than five.

This return value is what we want. Actually, it's *almost* what we want. In one important special case—DOS machines using Novell NetWare—the value Function 0Eh returns in AL is *not* equal to LASTDRIVE. Given the number of PC machines running Novell NetWare, this is an important exception to which we will return later in this chapter.

But how do we get the return value we want from this Select Disk function without also selecting a new current drive? The answer is obviously to specify the drive that is *already* current as the "new" one. Where do we find the current drive? Once again we flip through our DOS programmer's reference (DOS programming has a lot in common with using a mail-order or gardening catalog) until we stumble upon function 19h (Get Current Disk):

```
Int 21H Function 19H
Get Current Disk
Returns the drive code of the current, or default, disk drive.
Call with:
    AH = 19H
Returns:
    AL = drive code (0=A, 1=B, etc.)
```

It's simple to take all this information and turn it into a program. In the remainder of this section, we will produce versions of LASTDRV.EXE in assembly language, C, Turbo Pascal, and QuickBASIC. Throughout, we will call only thoroughly *documented* portions of the DOS programmer's interface, in preparation for our descent into the world of undocumented DOS.

DOS Calls from Assembly Language

The small assembly language program in Listing 2-1 shows how the reference material on DOS Functions 0Eh and 19h translates into a working version of LASTDRV.EXE. This code also uses DOS Function 09h to display output, which can be redirected to a file or to the NUL bit bucket. Finally, the program calls DOS Function 4Ch to exit to DOS, passing the numeric value of LASTDRIVE as the return code.

Listing 2-1: LASTDRV.ASM

```
; LASTDRV.ASM -- uses only documented DOS
; masm lastdrv;
; link lastdrv;

_STACK  segment para stack 'STACK'
_STACK  ends

_DATA   segment word public 'DATA'
msg     db      'LASTDRIVE='
dletter db      ?
        db      0dh, 0ah, '$'
_DATA   ends

_TEXT   segment word public 'CODE'
        assume cs:_TEXT, ds:_DATA, ss:_STACK

main    proc    near
        mov     ax, _DATA
        mov     ds, ax          ; set DS to data segment
        mov     ah, 19h         ; Get Current Disk function
        int     21h             ; call MS-DOS

        mov     dl, al          ; AL now holds current drive
        mov     ah, 0Eh         ; Select Disk function
        int     21h             ; call MS-DOS
        mov     bl, al          ; LASTDRIVE in AL; save in BL
```

```
        add     al, ('A' - 1)    ; convert to drive letter
        mov     dletter, al      ; insert into string

        mov     dx, offset msg   ; string in DS:DX
        mov     ah, 9            ; Display String function
        int     21h              ; call MS-DOS

        mov     ah, 4Ch          ; Return to DOS
        mov     al, bl           ; LASTDRIVE is exit code
        int     21h              ; call MS-DOS
main    endp
_TEXT   ends
        end main
```

You can assemble LASTDRV with any number of assemblers and then link it with any MS-DOS compatible linker, using the Microsoft Macro Assembler (MASM):

```
masm lastdrv.asm;
link lastdrv.obj;
```

Or, using Borland Turbo Assembler (TASM):

```
tasm lastdrv
tlink lastdrv
```

When run, the program produces the desired output; for example:

```
C:\UNDOC2\CHAP 2 > lastdrv
LASTDRIVE=M
```

DOS Calls from C

There is a problem making DOS calls using the C programming language. It's not that it is difficult to access MS-DOS services from C; the problem is there are too many different ways to do so. Not satisfied with one technique where a dozen techniques would do, C compiler manufacturers for the PC, such as Microsoft, Borland, Watcom, and MetaWare (one wonders how much longer the PC marketplace can support so many different good C compilers), offer a wide variety of techniques for calling MS-DOS and ROM BIOS services. Having so many different ways to perform the same operation is confusing.

The problem isn't really with the compilers, however. Ultimately, we have to ask why MS-DOS itself doesn't come with a set of standard include files, the way Windows does. The only thing approaching a standard programming interface for MS-DOS is the set of functions, such as _dos_setdrive(), _dos_allocmem(), and _dos_findfirst(), that appear in the Microsoft C/C++ DOS.H header file. Other C compiler vendors, such as Borland and Watcom, have adapted them as well.

On the other hand, this lack of standard programming facilities in MS-DOS has done nothing to stop MS-DOS's spectacular success; it may even have aided the success slightly because it gives programmers one more thing to muck around with. In any case, we need to discuss a few of the techniques that you can use to make MS-DOS calls from C, including the int86() and intdos() functions, inline assembly language, and register pseudo-variables.

int86()   For a long time, the most popular way of calling system services from C on the PC was to use the int86() functions, which invoke Intel 80x86 software interrupts. Compilers for the PC, such as Microsoft C/C++ and Borland C++, come with a DOS.H include file with prototypes for int86(), int86x(), intdos(), and so on. These functions work with two structures, union REGS and struct SREGS, which contain an *image* of the actual CPU registers. To see how functions such as int86x() are implemented, see the source code for your compiler's run-time library (for example, \BORLANDC\CRTL\CLIB\INT86.CAS).

Listing 2-2 shows LASTDRV.C, which uses int86(). This can be compiled with any Microsoft-compatible C compiler for the IBM PC, using either the full-screen or the command-line version of the compiler.

Listing 2-2: LASTDRV.C

```
/*
LASTDRV.C -- uses only documented DOS; illustrates int86()

Microsoft C/C++: cl lastdrv.c
Borland C++:     bcc lastdrv
*/

#include <stdio.h>
#include <dos.h>

main(void)
{
    union REGS r;
    unsigned lastdrv;
    r.h.ah = 0x19;              /* Get Current Disk */
    int86(0x21, &r, &r);       /* call MS-DOS */
    r.h.dl = r.h.al;           /* r.h.al now holds current drive */
    r.h.ah = 0x0E;             /* Select Disk */
    int86(0x21, &r, &r);       /* call MS-DOS */
    lastdrv = r.h.al;          /* r.h.al now holds number of drives */
    fputs("LASTDRIVE=", stdout); /* output string */
    putchar('A' - 1 + lastdrv); /* output drive letter */
    putchar('\n');             /* output newline */
    return lastdrv;            /* return drive number to MS-DOS */
}
```

The C source code in LASTDRV.C is almost half the length of the corresponding assembly language code in LASTDRV.ASM. On the other hand, the size of the executable grows from less than 600 bytes in assembly language to almost 5,000 bytes in C. Why does LASTDRV.C output the LASTDRIVE letter using putchar('A' - 1 + lastdrv) rather than putchar('A' + lastdrv)? Because, while functions 0Eh and 19h both deal with zero-based drive letters (0=A, 1=B, etc.), function 0Eh returns the number of drives, *not* the number of the last drive. Because DOS drive letters are zero-based, LASTDRV.C must subtract 1 from the number of drives to produce the number of the last drive, which can then be added to 'A' to produce the last drive letter (LASTDRIVE).

Inline Assembler   A better way to write PC system-level software in C is to use an inline assembler; that is, put Intel assembly language code directly in your C code. True, inline assembly code is inherently nonportable, but so are calls to int86(). You can't expect MS-DOS or ROM BIOS calls to work on non-Intel architectures anyway, so this is a perfect place to use inline assembly language.

Microsoft C/C++ and Borland C++ both include an inline assembler. There are a few differences between the Microsoft and Borland dialects. A key difference is that Borland does not allow labels in an _asm block. Both Borland and Microsoft put a scaled-down assembler right into their C compiler, but Borland can also (when compiling with the bcc -B switch) pass the inline assembler through to a separate assembler such as TASM or MASM, allowing you to include assembly language directives such as DB, assembly language macros, or 386 instructions directly in your C code. This task is far more difficult with Microsoft's inline assembler.

In LASTDRV2.C in Listing 2-3, note how the preprocessor directives ensure that the compiler can support an inline assembler. Most C compilers identify themselves with a preprocessor definition. Borland C++ provides both __BORLANDC__ and, for backward compatibility with the older Turbo C and Turbo C++ compilers, __TURBOC__. Microsoft C/C++ provides _MSC_VER, which contains the compiler version number, such as 700 (decimal) for 7.0.

Listing 2-3: LASTDRV2.C

```c
/* LASTDRV2.C -- uses only documented DOS; illustrates inline assembler */

#include <stdlib.h>
#include <stdio.h>

main()
{
    unsigned lastdrv;
#ifdef __TURBOC__
    asm mov ah, 19h         /* C-style comments only */
    asm int 21h
    asm mov dl, al
    asm mov ah, 0x0e        /* C-style hex */
    asm int 21h             /* assembly-style hex */
    asm xor ah, ah
    asm mov lastdrv, ax     /* refer to C variables */
#elif (defined(_MSC_VER) && (_MSC_VER >= 600)) || defined(_QC)
    _asm {
            mov ah, 19h         ; can include assembly-style comments
            int 21h             /* and C-style as well */
            mov dl, al          // and this style as well
            mov ah, 0x0E        ; can include C-style hex numbers
            int 21h             ; or assembly-style hex numbers
            xor ah, ah
            mov lastdrv, ax     ; can refer to C variables in _asm
            // Borland would not allow a goto/jmp label here!
            }
#else
#error Requires inline assembler
#endif

    fputs("LASTDRIVE=", stdout);
    putchar('A' - 1 + lastdrv);
    putchar('\n');
    return lastdrv;
}
```

The comments inside the _asm block show the odd mixtures of C and assembly language that you can produce. You do have to be careful when using inline assembly language. In particular, you must know your compiler's rules about preserving registers. For Microsoft and Borland, the rules are simple:

- You are free to change AX, BX, CX, DX, and ES.
- Inside a function, you can change BP.
- You must always put back any changes to the DI, SI, DS, SS, and SP registers, however.
- Because the compiler has no idea what you're doing with the registers, using the inline assembler turns off global optimizations. In this case, Microsoft C/C++ issues an "inline assembler precludes global optimizations" message.

Register Pseudo-Variables

Borland provides yet another way to write low-level code: register pseudo-variables. Not to be confused with C register variables, register pseudo-variables map onto the CPU registers but look like C variables. For example, assigning to _AX is the same as doing a MOV to the AX register. Listing 2-4 shows LASTDRV3.C, which uses register pseudo-variables to implement yet another LASTDRV utility.

Listing 2-4: LASTDRV3.C

```c
/* LASTDRV3.C -- uses only documented DOS;
illustrates register pseudo-variables */

#ifndef __TURBOC__
#error This program requires Borland C++ or Turbo C
```

```
#endif
#include <stdlib.h>
#include <stdio.h>
#include <dos.h>
main()
{
    unsigned lastdrv;
    _AH = 0x19;
    geninterrupt(0x21);
    _DL = _AL;
    _AH = 0x0E;
    geninterrupt(0x21);
    lastdrv = _AL;
    fputs("LASTDRIVE=", stdout);
    putchar('A' - 1 + lastdrv);
    putchar('\n');
    return lastdrv;
}
```

Note that geninterrupt(0x21) is *not* a function call but a compiler directive to emit an INT 21h directly into the compiled code. And, although the register pseudo-variables such as _AL are extremely handy, the code generated by the compiler of course uses the same CPU registers as your code, so you can't rely on values staying in the registers for very long.

DOS Library Functions

Actually, neither int86() nor _asm blocks are necessary here. As mentioned earlier, most C compilers for the PC provide a set of functions that map directly onto the most popular DOS functions. Microsoft C provides functions with names such as _dos_getdrive() and _dos_setdrive(), for instance; Borland C++ supports these as well as older Borland-specific functions such as getdisk() and set-disk(). The DOS lastdrive() function is thus (again with the important exception of Novell NetWare, which we discuss later) equivalent to setdisk(getdisk()):

```
printf("LASTDRIVE=%c\n", 'A' - 1 + setdisk(getdisk()));
```

If functions such as setdisk() and getdisk(), or _dos_setdrive() and _dos_getdrive(), didn't exist, it would be easy to create them. This is a major use for inline assembly language:

```
void _dos_setdrive(unsigned drive, unsigned *p_lastdrive)
{
    _asm mov ah, 0Eh
    _asm mov dl, byte ptr drive
    _asm int 21h
    _asm mov bx, p_lastdrive
    _asm xor ah, ah             /* Take 21/0E return value in AL, 0-extend */
    _asm mov word ptr [bx], ax  /* into AX, move into caller's pointer */
}
void _dos_getdrive(unsigned *p_currdriv)
{
    _asm mov ah, 19h
    _asm int 21h
    _asm mov bx, p_currdriv
    _asm xor ah, ah
    _asm mov word ptr [bx], ax  /* assuming near pointer! */
}
```

DOS Calls from Turbo Pascal

What about calling MS-DOS functions from other high-level languages? In some ways, it is much simpler to make these calls from other languages, such as Turbo Pascal, because you don't have to worry about which method to use. As noted earlier, having the wide variety of techniques available in C ultimately isn't so terrific, because programmers and writers end up spending too much time deciding which technique to use.

Calling DOS functions from Turbo Pascal requires the DOS unit, which includes the Registers variant record (similar to union REGS in C) and the MsDos() function. LASTDRV.PAS in Listing 2-5 shows this.

Listing 2-5: LASTDRV.PAS

```
{ LASTDRV.PAS -- uses only documented DOS }

program LastDrv;
uses Dos;
var
    r : Registers;
    lastdrive : Word;
begin
    with r do begin
        ah := $19;              { Get Current Disk }
        MsDos(r);
        dl := al;
        ah := $0E;              { Select Disk }
        MsDos(r);
        lastdrive := al;
    end;
    Writeln('LASTDRIVE=', Chr(Ord('A') - 1 + lastdrive));
    Halt(lastdrive);
end.
```

Note that Pascal's *with* construct allows us, for example, to refer to fields of the Registers record as *ah* rather than *r.ah*.

The command-line version of Turbo Pascal can turn LASTDRV.PAS can into LASTDRV.EXE:

```
tpc lastdrv.pas
```

True to Turbo Pascal's reputation for producing extremely tight code, the resulting Turbo Pascal executable file is only 2K. The smallest C version is about 4K.

There is a separate set of issues involved with making DOS calls from Turbo Pascal for Windows (TPW). For example, instead of using the DOS unit, you must use the WinDos unit. See Chapter 3 for an in-depth discussion of calling DOS from Windows programs. For TPW specifically, Neil Rubenking's excellent book, *PC Magazine Turbo Pascal for Windows Techniques and Utilities*, discusses this subject at length.

DOS Calls from BASIC

Finally, what about BASIC? LASTDRV.BAS, the version of LASTDRV in Listing 2-6, displays the LASTDRIVE letter and returns the numeric value of LASTDRIVE to the DOS ERRORLEVEL.

Listing 2-6: LASTDRV.BAS

```
REM LASTDRV.BAS -- uses only documented DOS
REM $INCLUDE: 'QB.BI'

SUB DOSEXIT(errorlevel)
    CLOSE
    DIM Regs AS RegType
    Regs.ax = &H4C00 + errorlevel    ' Terminate Process
    CALL INTERRUPT(&H21, Regs, Regs)
    PRINT "this is never executed"
END SUB

DIM Regs AS RegType
Regs.ax = &H1900                         ' Get Current Disk
```

```
CALL INTERRUPT(&H21, Regs, Regs)
Regs.dx = Regs.ax
Regs.ax = &H0E00                    ' Select Disk
CALL INTERRUPT(&H21, Regs, Regs)
lastdrv = Regs.ax AND &HFF
PRINT "LASTDRIVE="; CHR$(ASC("A") - 1 + lastdrv)
CALL DOSEXIT(lastdrv)
END
```

To turn this source code into an executable file, you can use either Microsoft QuickBASIC or the Microsoft BASIC 6.0 compiler. Using the BASIC 6.0 compiler, the command is:

```
bc /o lastdrv.bas;
link lastdrv,,,qb.lib;
```

If you are using Quick BASIC to produce a stand-alone executable file, the proper incantation is:

```
qb lastdrv.bas /L qb.qlb
```

Using the BC /O switch or producing a stand-alone executable file from within QuickBASIC is mandatory. Surprising as it seems, Microsoft BASIC has no provision for returning exit codes to DOS. In order to return the value of LASTDRV as the DOS ERRORLEVEL, LASTDRV.BAS uses the subroutine DOSEXIT(), which directly calls MS-DOS Function 4Ch (Terminate Process with Return Code) *and never returns*, thereby bypassing BASIC's normal exit routine. This does not work from an executable file that uses the BASIC run-time module (for example, BRUN60EP). Directly calling INT 21h function 4Ch from an executable that uses the BASIC run-time module can easily hang the machine.

There's another problem. Because the subroutine never returns after calling INT 21h function 4Ch, it does an end-run around BASIC's exit routine, and BASIC never gets to clean up after itself. The result is that the cursor is lost when you return to the DOS prompt. Thus, although this code shows how to make low-level system calls from Microsoft BASIC, it really isn't a useful piece of software. BASIC has many features going for it as a programming language, but returning exit levels to the operating system apparently is not one of them.

MS-DOS 5.0 and higher come with QBASIC. While an excellent addition to DOS in many ways, QBASIC unfortunately doesn't support the CALL INTERRUPT feature that LASTDRV.BAS uses. The CALL ABSOLUTE, POKE, and DEF SEG statements (see the MONEY.BAS sample program sometimes included with MS-DOS) could be used to implement LASTDRV, but this hardly seems worth the effort. And while having QBASIC included with DOS should have made it possible to do many fancy batch files in BASIC, unfortunately the QBASIC /RUN command causes too much screen flashing to be genuinely useful for creating batch-like utilities for DOS.

Using Undocumented DOS

Quarterdeck's expanded memory manager, QEMM, comes with a program called LASTDRIV.COM, one of whose uses is to report the value of LASTDRIVE. Interestingly enough, this program does not use documented function 0Eh. Instead, it uses undocumented Function 52h. We won't see why until later. For now, though, the point is simply that if Quarterdeck can do it, so can you.

What better place to start using undocumented DOS than with a program like LASTDRV whose operation we already know well? In the next section, we again show how to write the LASTDRV utility in assembly language, C, Turbo Pascal, and QuickBASIC, but this time using undocumented DOS. In particular, we highlight the larger role that the DOS version number plays when using undocumented DOS.

We just went through the process of using a standard DOS programmer's reference as if it were an office supply catalog or a handbook of mathematical functions, trying to find a tool that would help us write the LASTDRV utility. We never found a single function called Get Last Drive, but we did find two functions, Get Current Disk and Select Disk, that together achieve the same effect.

In other words, we saw lastdrive() is similar to setdisk(getdisk()). But there's something illogical in this. Why should DOS return the total number of drives when you set the current drive? MS-DOS presumably keeps the value of LASTDRIVE somewhere internally. Is there some way to find it?

Disassembling DOS

One thing we can do is disassemble the code for MS-DOS and see how it implements INT 21h function 0Eh, and especially how it produces the value that it returns in the AL register. Chapter 6 discusses DOS disassembly and DOS internals in greater detail, but it is worthwhile here to briefly look at what actually happens when we call INT 21h function 0Eh.

Chapter 6 shows how to locate this code in the first place, but for now you'll just have to take it on faith that the piece of code in Listing 2-7 below is the DOS handler for INT 21h function 0Eh. Microsoft's SYMDEB debugger, running under DOS 6.0 with DOS=HIGH, produced this disassembly. DEBUG, which comes with DOS itself, is harder to use and produces uglier results than SYMDEB.

Listing 2-7: SYMDEB Disassembly of INT 21h Function 0Eh in DOS 6.0

```
-u fdc9:4c68
FDC9:4C68 8AC2          MOV     AL,DL
FDC9:4C6A FEC0          INC     AL
FDC9:4C6C E8185E        CALL    AA87
FDC9:4C6F 7204          JB      4C75
FDC9:4C71 36A23603      MOV     SS:[0336],AL
FDC9:4C75 36A04700      MOV     AL,SS:[0047]
FDC9:4C79 C3            RET
```

This code is a little difficult to follow, so Listing 2-8 contains another version, suitably commented and decorated.

Listing 2-8: Commented Disassembly of INT 21h Function 0Eh

```
          select_disk_0E proc near
FDC9:4C68     MOV     AL,DL                      ; DL = zero-based drive code
FDC9:4C6A     INC     AL                         ; make one-based
FDC9:4C6C     CALL    i_select_disk              ; call internal function
FDC9:4C6F     JB      fail                       ; jump if carry
FDC9:4C71     MOV     DOS_DS:[CURRDRIVE],AL       ; 011E:0336
          fail:
FDC9:4C75     MOV     AL,DOS_DS:[LASTDRIVE]       ; 011E:0047
FDC9:4C79     RET
          select_disk_0E endp
```

The function labeled i_select_disk is not shown here, but, among other things, it calls the DOS internal set_drive function; this is the same piece of code that is invoked if you issue the undocumented INT 2Fh AX=1219h (Set Drive) call noted in the appendix. DOS can call this function directly, without needing an INT 2Fh. The set_drive function in turn calls two internal functions to manipulate the DOS internal Current Directory Structure (CDS): build_cds (INT 2Fh AX=121Fh) and set_drive_cds (INT 2Fh AX=1217h).

But notice that, even if i_select_disk sets the carry flag, indicating failure, select_disk_0E *still* returns the value of LASTDRIVE in AL. This means that we could pass any illegal drive number into INT 21h function 0Eh and still get back the value of LASTDRIVE. In Listings 2-1 through 2-6, the code that first called INT 21h function 19h to get the current drive wasn't strictly necessary, since all we care about is the LASTDRIVE return value. Of course, you don't want to pass in an arbitrary *valid*

drive number, because then DOS will do what you say and change to that drive. This would definitely not be a desirable side-effect for a LASTDRV utility! However, passing in an illegal drive number would work great.

This makes sense because, come to think of it, the Microsoft *MS-DOS Programmer's Reference*
didn't say anything about this function failing. There's nothing implementation-specific about always
returning the value of LASTDRIVE, even if the function fails. In retrospect, the DOS documentation was pretty clear that this is exactly what any implementation of INT 21h function 0Eh is supposed to do. It shouldn't have been necessary to look at the code to realize this. Nonetheless, seeing
the actual code does help make it clearer.

It should be possible, then, to pass some known invalid drive number in to the function and use
INT 21h function 0Eh purely as a Get Lastdrive function, rather than as a Select Disk function. Sure
enough, calling setdisk(0xFF) in Borland C++ works.

You can learn some other interesting facts about this DOS function from looking carefully at the code
in Listing 2-8, but these facts are dependent on the implementation. For example, the implementation in
Listing 2-8 keeps the carry flag set for failure and clear for success. But you cannot depend on this.

Note in Listing 2-8 that if function 0Eh succeeds, the function not only returns LASTDRIVE in
AL but also sets the value of an internal DOS variable we've called CURRDRIVE. The DOS Get
Current Disk function (INT 21h function 19h) that we called earlier to produce a value to pass to
INT 21h function 0Eh, does nothing more than return the value of this variable in AL:

```
-u fdc9:4c64
FDC9:4C64 A03603          MOV     AL,[0336]      ; DOS_DS:0336
FDC9:4C67 C3              RET
```

(If you are wondering about that INC AL in Listing 2-8, note that the i_select_disk function called
by select_disk_0E decrements AL, so the output produced by function 19h is a zero-based drive
number, just like the input expected by function 0Eh.)

To summarize, by disassembling DOS you can see more clearly how this DOS function works.
There are many other things we haven't looked at very closely that occur within i_select_disk. But it
any case we can see that select_disk_0E sets one internal DOS variable, CURRDRIVE and, no matter what, returns the value of another internal DOS variable, our old friend LASTDRIVE.

Let's look at these two variables for a moment. In this configuration, using DOS 6.0 with
DOS=HIGH, CURRDRIVE was located at 011E:0336. This location in memory is not arbitrary:
First, some Microsoft software accesses DOS data variables using hard-wired offsets into the DOS
data segment (as an example, see PSPTEST.C in Chapter 4). It will be very difficult for Microsoft to
move the location of these variables in future versions of DOS! Furthermore, CURRDRIVE is
located within an area of the DOS data segment that is sometimes treated as a data structure, the
Swappable Data Area (SDA). Undocumented DOS function INT 21h AX=5D06h returns a far
pointer to the SDA. In this configuration, the function returns 011E:0320, which means that
CURRDRIVE is located at SDA+16h. Sure enough, turning to the entry for INT 21h AX=5D06h
in the appendix reveals that DOS keeps the current drive value at offset 16h in the SDA. All is right
with the world.

What about LASTDRIVE? Listing 2-8 shows this byte at 011E:0047. Again, this is actually a
field in a larger internal structure in the DOS data segment, known as SysVars or the List of Lists.
INT 21h AH=52h returns a pointer to this structure; in this configuration, the function returns
011E:0026, which means that DOS keeps LASTDRIVE at SysVars+21h. If, for some reason, you want
to write a program that uses undocumented DOS to retrieve LASTDRIVE, this is just the information you're looking for.

Using the Interrupt List

So LASTDRIVE is just a byte stored at offset 21h by the address returned from INT 21h function 52h. We found this information by disassembling DOS. But there's another, easier, way to find out this kind of information: from Ralf Brown's Interrupt List! When you leaf through Ralf's appendix to this book you'll find DOS's internal location for LASTDRIVE in the middle of SysVars, or the List of Lists. However, it moved around a lot before DOS 4:

Table 2-1: Movement of LASTDRIVE Within SysVars

Offset	Size	Description	
10h	BYTE	number of logical drives in system	DOS 2.x
1Bh	BYTE	value of LASTDRIVE command in CONFIG.SYS (default 5)	DOS 3.0
21h	BYTE	value of LASTDRIVE command in CONFIG.SYS (default 5)	DOS 3.1-3.3
21h	BYTE	value of LASTDRIVE command in CONFIG.SYS (default 5)	DOS 4.x +

SysVars, or the DOS internal variable table, is probably the most important undocumented DOS data structure; and INT 21h function 52h, which returns in the ES:BX register pair a pointer to SysVars is, by far, the most important undocumented DOS function.

Note from Table 2-1 how the offset of the LASTDRIVE field within the DOS internal variable table changed from DOS 2.0 to DOS 3.0 to DOS 3.1. Disassembling just one version of DOS does not, of course, uncover this problem. This sort of undocumented DOS behavior is just what our programs have to deal with. What the offset will be in future versions is anyone's guess, and that, of course, is the whole problem with using undocumented DOS.

In future versions of DOS, the LASTDRIVE field might even disappear, breaking whatever programs depend upon its presence. The only comfort is that, should SysVars change radically, not only will our own programs start to fail but practically all important Microsoft software will break, too!

For example, the DOSMGR virtual device driver, crucial to the operation of Windows Enhanced mode, depends on finding LASTDRIVE at SysVars+21h (see Figure 1-10), which is one reason why Windows requires DOS 3.1 or higher and specifically does not run on DOS 3.0. The reliance of key pieces of Microsoft software, such as Windows 3.x, on the internal structure of DOS might make this internal structure unlikely to change. However, that perhaps is too much to hope for in a large company, where members of different groups may or may not talk with each other (see the discussion of Chinese Walls in Chapter 1).

In the midst of the changes to the position of LASTDRIVE within SysVars—and, if you look at the appendix entry for INT 21h Function 52h, massive changes throughout SysVars as a whole—one thing has remained constant: INT 21h function 52h itself.

```
INT 21 - DOS 2+ internal - GET SYSVARS
AH = 52h
Return:
    ES:BX -> DOS SysVars
```

From DOS 2.0 onward, this function has been as stable as any documented DOS function. Even simulated DOS environments, such as the DOS boxes in OS/2 2.0 and Windows NT, support it (see Chapter 4).

No Magic Numbers

Because the SysVars structure is so central to DOS programming, many books on the subject end up using INT 21h function 52h somewhere in their sample source code. However, because of their authors' possibly guilty feelings about using undocumented DOS in the first place, sometimes these books simply leave the code unexplained. For example, in the normally well-commented Turbo Pascal source code in an extremely useful book on LAN programming (Craig Chaiken's *Blueprint of a LAN*), the following code appears without any explanation:

```
regs.ah := $52;
intr($21, regs);
ofs := regs.bx + $22;
seg := regs.es;
while memw[seg:ofs] <> $ffff do
    ...
```

Here, the author is using INT 21h function 52h to get a pointer to SysVars and then using offset 22h in SysVars to get a pointer to the linked list of device drivers that DOS maintains. Obviously, the author needs to find some device in memory. What's so bad about that? Nothing, except the code appears out of nowhere, with no comment or explanation, like a small piece of magic. The code might as well have been commented "and then a miracle occurs," or even "you are not expected to understand this":

> *You are not expected to understand this* cav. [UNIX] The canonical comment describing something magic or too complicated to bother explaining properly. From an infamous comment in the context-switching code of the V6 UNIX kernel (Eric Raymond (ed.), *The New Hacker's Dictionary*, 1991).

To rely on INT 21h function 52h but not explain what it does seems far worse than using this undocumented call in the first place. As used above, 52h and 22h (and even FFFFh) appear to be random magic numbers. Let's see if we can't completely demystify INT 21h function 52h.

You can try out this function without even writing a program by using the DOS DEBUG utility. First assemble the DOS call and execute it:

```
C:\UNDOC2>debug
-a
775A:0100 mov ah, 52
775A:0102 int 21
775A:0104 nop
775A:0105
-g 104
AX=5200  BX=0026  CX=0000  DX=0000  SP=FFEE  BP=0000  SI=0000  DI=0000
DS=775A  ES=028E  SS=775A  CS=775A  IP=0104   NV UP EI PL NZ NA PO NC
775A:0104 90            NOP
```

The register dump shows that in this sample DEBUG session, ES:BX points to 028E:0026:

```
-d es:0026
028E:0020                   F0 75-8E 02 98 00 8E 02 A4 01      .u........
028E:0030  70 00 6E 01 70 00 00 02-00 00 49 0C 00 00 EE 0C   p.n.p.....I.....
028E:0040  00 00 6D 0A 00 00 03 05-12 00 F4 09 04 80 99 15   ..m.............
028E:0050  9F 15 4E 55 4C 20 20 20-20 20 00 90 43 17 8E 02   ..NUL     ..C...
028E:0060  47 17 8E 02 47 17 8E 02-43 17 8E 02 43 17 8E 02   G...G...C...C...
```

Aside from the NUL string at offset 0052, it is difficult to find our way around here. But if we hold the SysVars format (again, see INT 21h AH=52h in the Appendix) over the DEBUG dump, it all makes sense. Formatting the first four bytes, F0 75 8E 02, as a DWORD pointer, for example, comes out as 028E:75F0, a pointer to the first Disk Parameter Block (DPB):

Offset	Size	Description	
00h	DWORD	first Disk Parameter Block	028E:75F0
04h	DWORD	list of DOS file tables	028E:0098
08h	DWORD	pointer to CLOCK$ device driver	0070:01A4
0Ch	DWORD	pointer to CON device drive	0070:016E

Offset	Size	Description	
10h	WORD	max bytes/block	0200
12h	DWORD	first disk buffer	0C49:0000
16h	DWORD	Current Directory Structures	0CEE:0000
1Ah	DWORD	pointer to FCB table	0A6D:0000
1Eh	WORD	number of protected FCBs	0000
20h	BYTE	number of block devices	03
21h	BYTE	LASTDRIVE	05
22h	18 BYTEs	actual NUL device driver header	next dev: 09F4:0012
			attr: 8004h
			strat: 1599h
			intr: 159Fh
			name: 'NUL '
34h	BYTE	number of JOIN'ed drives	00

We can even see that the Turbo Pascal code quoted earlier was adding 22h to the value returned from Function 52h so that it could get a pointer to the NUL device, which is the head of DOS's device chain. This is one of the most popular uses of INT 21h function 52h, but clearly SysVars holds many other goodies. This is why it has also been called the DOS List of Lists.

Because the value of the LASTDRIVE field in SysVars is five, LASTDRIVE=E, which is the default value when CONFIG.SYS does not include a LASTDRIVE statement.

Having seen a little bit of what SysVars looks like, we can now retrace our steps in building the LASTDRV utility, this time using INT 21h Function 52h and the LASTDRIVE field within the DOS internal variable table. You may be thinking that this is a futile exercise because we already know how to get the value of LASTDRIVE using a completely safe and documented function that doesn't change with each new version of DOS. However, we will see later on that using the undocumented internal value of LASTDRIVE can actually be *more* reliable than using the documented function 0Eh return value, opening up some interesting possibilities. After all, Quarterdeck must have *some* reason for using Function 52h rather than function 0Eh.

Undocumented DOS Calls from Assembly Language

The small assembly language program in Listing 2-9 shows one how to translate the reference material on DOS Function 52h and SysVars into a working version of LASTDRV.EXE.

Listing 2-9: LASTDRV2.ASM

```
; LASTDRV2.ASM -- uses undocumented DOS
        assume cs:_TEXT, ds:_DATA, ss:_STACK
_STACK  segment para stack 'STACK'
_STACK  ends
_DATA   segment word public 'DATA'
msg     db      'LASTDRIVE='
dletter db      ?
        db      0dh, 0ah, '$'
_DATA   ends
_TEXT   segment word public 'CODE'
        public _lstdrv
_lstdrv proc    far
        push    si
        push    bx
        push    cx
        mov     si, 1Bh         ; assume DOS 3.0
```

```
        mov     ax, 3306h       ; Get (genuine) MS-DOS version
        xor     bx, bx          ; Don't know if func supported, so zero BX
        int     21h
        or      bx, bx          ; Is BX still zero, or did it get changed?
        jz      do_2130         ; Not supported, so call 21/30
        ; 21/3306 returns major=BL, minor=BH
        ; move into AX to make appear as if returned from 21/30
        mov     ax, bx
        jmp     short got_vers
do_2130:
        mov     ax, 3000h       ; Get MS-DOS version number
        int     21h             ; major=AL, minor=AH
got_vers:                       ; either did 21/3306 or 21/30
        cmp     al, 2
        jl      fail            ; Requires DOS 2+

        jne     dos3up          ; DOS 3+
        mov     si, 10h         ; DOS 2.x
        jmp     short get
dos3up: cmp     al, 3
        jne     ofs21
        and     ah, ah          ; DOS 3.0
        jz      get
ofs21:  mov     si, 21h         ; DOS 3.1+, DOS 4+

get:    mov     ah, 52h         ; Get SysVars
        xor     bx, bx          ; Zero out ES:BX so we can check
        mov     es, bx          ;    for NULL after INT 21h
        int     21h             ; list=ES:BX
        mov     cx, es
        or      cx, bx          ; Is ES:BX NULL?
        jz      fail            ; Function 52h not supported

        mov     al, byte ptr es:[bx+si]
        xor     ah, ah          ; return LASTDRIVE in AX
        jmp     short fini

fail:   xor     ax, ax          ; return 0 in AX
fini:   pop     cx
        pop     bx
        pop     si
        ret
_lstdrv endp

main    proc    near
        mov     ax, _DATA
        mov     ds, ax

        call    _lstdrv
        and     ax, ax          ; test for failure
        jz      done

        mov     bl, al          ; save LASTDRIVE in BL
        add     al, ('A' - 1)   ; convert LASTDRIVE to drive letter
        mov     dletter, al     ; insert into string

        mov     ah, 9           ; Display String
        mov     dx, offset msg
        int     21h
done:   mov     ah, 4Ch         ; Return to DOS
        mov     al, bl          ; exit code
        int     21h
main    endp
_TEXT   ends

        END     main
```

The main subroutine contains boring documented DOS code for displaying output and for exiting to DOS. All the really interesting code and all of the undocumented DOS is in the slightly convoluted _lstdrv subroutine, paraphrased in the following pseudocode:

```
offset := 1Bh;
ver := DosVersion();
if (ver.major < 2) return failure;
else if (ver.major == 2)                        offset := 10h;
else if (ver.major != 3 or ver.minor != 0) offset := 21h;
ListOfLists := GetListOfLists();
if (ListOfLists == NULL) return failure;
else                      return ListOfLists[offset];
```

The goal of the various DOS version number tests is to put the correct location of LASTDRIVE into the SI register, so that it can be added to the base address of SysVars that we get back from DOS undocumented Function 52h. The SI register is preloaded with the offset of LASTDRIVE for DOS 3.0, in a (somewhat foolish) attempt to reduce the large number of JMPs.

DOS Versionitis

Note how, in *all* DOS versions greater than 3.0, we store 21h into the offset. Usually when testing the DOS version number, it is useful to test for numbers *greater than or equal to* the highest known version (for example, version >= 6.0). Testing simply for equality (for example, version == 6.0) automatically shuts your application off from a future version such as DOS 7.0. For example, *PC Magazine* has published several utilities that check the DOS version with the JE instruction rather than with JB or JA. This guarantees that these utilities will have to be "revved" every time Microsoft comes out with a new version of DOS. Partially because many applications (even ones that use no undocumented calls at all) were too conservative with the DOS version number, Microsoft introduced the SETVER command.

By treating all DOS versions higher than 3.0 as one unit, obviously we are assuming that, for example, DOS 6.0 stores LASTDRIVE in the same place as DOS 3.3, which, in fact, it does. When dealing with undocumented DOS, you can either make this assumption or you can take the more conservative approach of halting the program under unknown versions of MS-DOS.

Sometimes—if only we knew when—the conservative approach is absolutely necessary. As an example, the first edition of this book contained code to access the DOS Swappable Data Area. The code used INT 21h AX=5D06h under DOS 3.x and INT 21h AX=5D0Bh under DOS 4.0 *and higher*. This code sounds fine, except that in DOS 5.0, Microsoft reverted to the DOS 3.0-style AX=5D06h call. This was the one part of *Undocumented DOS* that broke badly under DOS 5.0.

This "versionitis" is really the only problem with using undocumented DOS. If your application uses some of the less stable undocumented functions or data structures, perhaps you should use == rather than >= to test DOS version numbers. On the other hand, there are several double-checks your program could perform so that it is not simply left floundering in the shifting sands of DOS internals; you will see one such double-check later in this chapter.

When testing DOS version numbers, remember that DOS Function 30h counterintuitively returns the *major* version number in AL, the *low* portion of AX, and the minor version number is returned in AH, the *high* portion of AX. It is also important to remember that a version number such as 3.1 is actually 3.10. In the case of DOS 3.10, the minor version number in AH is neither 01h nor 10h, but 10 decimal (0Ah).

The most important point about the DOS version number, though, is that it might be *wrong*. The SETVER command allows the DOS version number returned from INT 21h function 30h to be set on an application-by-application basis. You can see which applications are being faked-out by typing SETVER at the DOS prompt. For example, in DOS 5.0 and 6.0 SETVER tells WINWORD.EXE and EXCEL.EXE—that is, the real mode DOS stubs of these Windows programs—that they are running under DOS 4.10. It's a sick world out there!

It is important to remember that SETVER changes nothing except the version number reported by INT 21h function 30h. SETVER doesn't change any other aspect of DOS behavior. WINWORD.EXE is still running under DOS 6.0, for example, but it *thinks* it's running under DOS 4.10. It is interesting to contrast this with another backwardly-compatible hack of Microsoft's, the undocumented GetAppCompatFlags() function in Windows. This function changes the actual behavior of Windows on a per-application basis (see *Undocumented Windows*, Chapter 5).

Because SETVER just changes the INT 21h function 30h version number, not the actual structure of DOS internals, programs that rely on undocumented DOS need to get the true DOS version number. Fortunately, DOS 5.0 and higher provides a documented way to do this. INT 21h function 3306h returns the true DOS version number in BX. (This function also reports on whether DOS is in ROM and whether DOS=HIGH.)

There is one complication here. INT 21h function 3306h is supported only in DOS 5.0 and higher. But you don't know whether you are actually running under DOS 5.0 or higher unless you call this function. One of the authors once wrote a piece of code in which he first called INT 21h AH=30h and then, if it reported the version number 5.0 or greater, he called INT 21h AX=3306h. This was incredibly stupid because the whole point is that INT 21h AH=30h may have been SETVERed to intentionally report some version number less than 5.0. But this means you must call INT 21h AX=3306h without knowing first whether the function is actually supported. And you can't rely on the carry flag being set if you call an unsupported INT 21h function.

As seen in Listings 2-9 (LASTDRV2.ASM) and 2-10 (LASTDRV4.C), the solution is to preload BX with zero before calling INT 21h AX=3306h. If the function isn't supported, BX will still be zero after issuing the INT 21h. If the function is supported, BX will be changed to the true DOS version number.

Who would have thought that something as simple as getting the DOS version number would be so complicated? But wait, it gets worse! The DOS box in OS/2 2.0 reports a DOS version number of 20.0; in OS/2 2.1, it's 20.10. Yet, as we see in Chapter 4, this environment generally behaves like DOS 5.0.

Finally, DR DOS 5.0 and 6.0 report the DOS version number as 3.31. Chapter 4 shows that there are undocumented DR DOS functions that return an actual DR DOS version code, rather than the simulated DOS version number.

The lesson here is that you should do whatever you can to minimize your dependence on specific versions of DOS because the DOS version number is a complete mess.

Accessing SysVars

At any rate, as you can see in the following chunk of code, once SI holds an offset appropriate to the version of DOS the program is running under, the rest is easy.

```
mov ah, 52h
int 21h
mov al, byte ptr es:[bx+si]
xor ah, ah
```

Actually, in LASTDRV2.ASM the code is slightly more complicated than this because we have taken the precaution of ensuring that undocumented INT 21h function 52h is really supported by checking that the pointer in ES:BX is not NULL. The ES:BX register pair is loaded with NULL prior to invoking INT 21h so that, in a really screwy simulated DOS environment that doesn't support this function, ES:BX will at least hold a reasonable value we can test for:

```
mov ah, 52h
xor bx, bx
mov es, bx
int 21h
mov cx, es
or cx, bx
jz fail
```

Note, however, that the code doesn't check whether INT 21h AH=52h set the carry flag (CF). Unless the documentation specifically says that a function sets or clears CF, the state of CF is undefined. The entry for INT 21h function 52h in the appendix to this book says nothing about CF. Thus, far from being an extra careful precaution, checking CF in fact would be a perfect example of relying on *undefined behavior*. Using undocumented DOS is completely different from relying on undefined behavior.

Although this version of LASTDRV looks completely different from the version that used only documented DOS calls, the result is similar. This version also displays and returns the value of LASTDRIVE. The difference is that now you're getting information straight from the horse's mouth by examining the DOS internal variable table.

Undocumented DOS Calls from C

This book has spent so much time on the LASTDRV utility and on various ways of performing DOS calls from C that you would think there would be nothing more to say. However, the following version, LASTDRV4.C (Listing 2-10), introduces a number of important topics, including the use of far pointers in C, the MK_FP() macro, testing the DOS version number, and using int86x() rather than int86().

Listing 2-10: LASTDRV4.C

```
/* LASTDRV4.C -- uses undocumented DOS */

#include <stdlib.h>
#include <stdio.h>
#include <dos.h>

#ifndef MK_FP
#define MK_FP(seg,ofs) \
    ((void far *)(((unsigned long)(seg) << 16) | (ofs)))
#endif

main()
{
    union REGS r;
    struct SREGS s;
    unsigned char far *sysvars;
    unsigned lastdrv_ofs;
    unsigned lastdrv;

    /* Try to get DOS version from 21/3306 call first, since
       this returns the true DOS version number. The 21/30 call
       used to set _osmajor, _osminor can be changed on a
       per-app basis with the DOS SETVER command. */
    r.x.ax = 0x3306;
    r.x.bx = 0;
    int86(0x21, &r, &r);
    /* See if 21/3306 actually supported. This is tricky because
       the behavior of unsupported calls is undefined. */
    if (r.x.bx != 0)  // BX has changed: func must be supported
    {
        _osmajor = r.h.bl;
        _osminor = r.h.bh;
        printf("21/3306 returns %u.%02u\n", _osmajor, _osminor);
    }

    /* Get offset for LASTDRIVE within SysVars */
    if (_osmajor < 2)                          return 0;
    else if (_osmajor == 2)                    lastdrv_ofs = 0x10;
    else if (_osmajor == 3 && _osminor == 0)   lastdrv_ofs = 0x1b;
    else                                       lastdrv_ofs = 0x21;

    /* Get DOS Lists of Lists */
    r.h.ah = 0x52;
    segread(&s);
```

```
    s.es = r.x.bx = 0;
    int86x(0x21, &r, &r, &s);
    /* make sure Function 52h is supported */
    if (! s.es && ! r.x.bx)
        return 0;
    sysvars = (unsigned char far *) MK_FP(s.es, r.x.bx);

    /* Get LASTDRIVE number */
    lastdrv = sysvars[lastdrv_ofs];

    /* OS/2 DOS compatibility box sets LASTDRIVE to FFh */
    if (lastdrv == 0xFF)
        return 0;

    /* Print LASTDRIVE letter */
    fputs("LASTDRIVE=", stdout);
    putchar('A' - 1 + lastdrv);
    putchar('\n');

    /* return LASTDRIVE number to DOS */
    return lastdrv;
}
```

If you contrast LASTDRV4.C with the earlier versions that used only documented DOS calls, you will notice a number of significant differences. Rather than call INT 21h function 30h to get the DOS version number, as the assembly language version did, LASTDRV4.C now uses the global variables _osmajor and _osminor, provided by most C compilers for the PC. In Microsoft C, Watcom C 386, and MetaWare High C 386, STDLIB.H declares these variables; in Borland C++, they are declared in DOS.H. It is important to remember that in DOS 3.3, for example, _osminor is 30 (decimal), not 3 and not 0x30. But note that even with _osmajor and _osminor, you must still call INT 21h function 3306h; if you're running under a version of DOS that supports this function, use its return value to possibly change _osmajor and _osminor.

Because DOS function 52h returns the address of SysVars in ES:BX, and because int86() doesn't handle segment registers such as ES, you need to use int86x() and struct SREGS. You don't need to pass any segment registers *into* Function 52h, so it seems as though it doesn't much matter what values struct SREGS holds before calling int86x(). Nonetheless, it is a good habit to call the segread() function to load the struct SREGS, as this example does, because if you ever try to move your code to a protected mode DOS extender, it will be crucial that you never load the segment registers with garbage values, even if these registers are seemingly not used.

Because SysVars is part of DOS and not located inside your program, it must be addressed with a four-byte (far) pointer. The C variable doslist is intended to hold this address and is declared as a *char far* *, rather than as a *char* *. This allows us to peek at and poke DOS's internal variable table, even from a C program that otherwise uses only two-byte (near) pointers.

After DOS Function 52h has returned the address of SysVars in ES:BX, int86x() returns it in s.es and r.x.bx. How do you move these into *char far *doslist*? LASTDRV4.C uses the macro MK_FP(), which, as its name implies, makes a far pointer from a segment and an offset. This handy macro is provided in the DOS.H include file with Borland C++ but, unfortunately, not with Microsoft C. LASTDRV4.C uses the C preprocessor to define a MK_FP() macro if one is not already present. While the definition of MK_FP() makes it appear as if it is performing a shift left (SHL), any good C compiler for the PC turns this code:

```
void far *fp = ((void far *)(((unsigned long)(seg) << 16) | (ofs)))
```

into this:

```
mov ax, _seg
mov dx, _ofs
mov word ptr _fp, dx
mov word ptr _fp+2, ax
```

You can examine your C compiler's output by compiling with the -Fa or -Fc switch in Microsoft C, for example, or the -S switch in Borland C++.

Rather than use the MK_FP() macro, in Microsoft C, you could also use the following construct:

```
FP_SEG(doslist) = s.es;
FP_OFF(doslist) = r.x.bx;
```

FP_SEG() and FP_OFF() are two other important macros for PC systems programming in C. Whereas MK_FP() constructs a far pointer from a segment and an offset, FP_SEG() and FP_OFF() perform the opposite operation. FP_SEG() extracts the segment of a far pointer, and FP_OFF() extracts the offset. Microsoft's versions of FP_SEG() and FP_OFF() are C lvalues and can therefore be assigned to.

This C version of LASTDRV also does a bit more work than the assembly language version. Before printing out the LASTDRIVE letter, LASTDRV4.C checks to see if LASTDRV is 0FFh. This is the value that the OS/2 1.10 DOS compatibility box (also known as the penalty box) uses for the LASTDRIVE field in its version of SysVars. A program running in this compatibility box thinks it is running under DOS 10.10, so you might think the program should simply fail if (_osmajor >= 10). However, the support for undocumented DOS has improved in each version of the DOS box, so there is no reason to cut yourself off unnecessarily from this simulated DOS environment. For instance, the DOS boxes in OS/2 2.0, which masquerade as DOS version 20.0, *do* provide proper support for LASTDRIVE and for most other fields in SysVars, as well. It is worth noting that, although the DOS version number is in the double digits, the OS/2 compatibility box closely resembles DOS 5.0 with SHARE.EXE loaded. (See Chapter 4 for details of DOS emulation in OS/2.)

What, No Structures?

To most C programmers, the big question in LASTDRV4.C is, "Where are the structures?!" You need only look at the entry for DOS Function 52h and SysVars in the appendix to see that all these offsets seem to cry out to be represented with a C structure. You might even ask why this book doesn't present an UNDOC.H include file!

The reason we do not have an UNDOC.H include file for you is that programs that use undocumented DOS functions should use only a few of them. An UNDOC.H file could be an invitation to overuse undocumented DOS calls. We don't want to promote undocumented DOS as yet another application programmer's interface (API), consisting of several hundred new functions and data structures.

There is an additional, more serious, problem with using data structures in undocumented DOS programming. This becomes clear as we discuss the next program, LASTDRV5.C (Listing 2-11), which uses a C structure to represent much of SysVars.

Listing 2-11: LASTDRV5.C

```
/* LASTDRV5.C */
#include <stdlib.h>
#include <stdio.h>
#include <dos.h>
#ifndef MK_FP
#define MK_FP(seg,ofs) \
    ((void far *)(((unsigned long)(seg) << 16) | (ofs)))
#endif
#pragma pack(1)
#define SYSVARS_DECR        12
typedef struct {
    unsigned shareretrycount, shareretrydelay;
    void far *currdiskbuff;
```

```
    void near *unreadcon;
    unsigned mcb;
    void far *dpb, far *filetable;
    void far *clock, far *con;
    union {
        struct {
            unsigned char numdrive;
            unsigned maxbytes;
            void far *first_diskbuff;
            unsigned char nul[18];
            } dos2;
        struct {
            unsigned char numblkdev;
            unsigned maxbytes;
            void far *first_diskbuff, far *currdir;
            unsigned char lastdrive;
            void far *stringarea;
            unsigned size_stringarea;
            void far *fcbtab;
            unsigned fcb_y;
            unsigned char nul[18];
            } dos30;
        struct {
            unsigned maxbytes;
            void far *diskbuff, far *currdir, far *fcb;
            unsigned numprotfcb;
            unsigned char numblkdev, lastdrive;
            unsigned char nul[18];
            unsigned numjoin;
            } dos31;    /* and higher */
        } vers;
    } SysVars;
main()
{
    union REGS r;
    struct SREGS s;
    SysVars far *sysvars;
    unsigned lastdrive;
    /* Try 21/3306 first */
    r.x.ax = 0x3306;
    r.x.bx = 0;
    int86(0x21, &r, &r);
    if (r.x.bx != 0)
    {
        _osmajor = r.h.bl;
        _osminor = r.h.bh;
    }

    /* No SysVars in DOS 1.x */
    if (_osmajor < 2) return 0;

    /* Get SysVars */
    r.h.ah = 0x52;
    segread(&s);
    s.es = r.x.bx = 0;
    intdosx(&r, &r, &s);
    if (! s.es && ! r.x.bx)
        return 0;
    sysvars = (SysVars far *) MK_FP(s.es, r.x.bx - SYSVARS_DECR);

    /* Get LASTDRIVE value, depending on DOS version */
    if (_osmajor == 3 && _osminor == 0)
        lastdrive = sysvars->vers.dos30.lastdrive;
    else if (_osmajor == 2)
        lastdrive = sysvars->vers.dos2.numdrive;
    else
```

```
        lastdrive = sysvars->vers.dos31.lastdrive;

    /* print LASTDRIVE letter, return LASTDRIVE number */
    printf("LASTDRIVE=%c\n", 'A' - 1 + lastdrive);
    return lastdrive;
}
```

From looking over struct SysVars, you should understand why this is sometimes called the List of Lists. Most of the fields are just pointers to other data structures, including the list of DOS Memory Control Blocks, the list of Drive Parameter Blocks, the DOS device chain, and the File Control Block table. Furthermore, in a complete SysVars structure, these other fields would each use, for example, FCB far * or DPB far *, rather than void far *.

The struct SysVars uses a C union to manage the differences between DOS versions. Unions help represent the changes that each version of DOS brought to SysVars. Each component of a C union is allocated storage starting at the beginning of the union, and the size of a union is the amount of storage necessary to represent its largest component. In other words, as in a variant record in Pascal, the components are overlaid. In the union vers within struct SysVars, the same block of memory can be viewed as a struct dos2, a struct dos30, or a struct dos31.

The line that reads #pragma pack(1) is essential. By default, C compilers for the PC align structures on word (two-byte) boundaries. For this C structure to correspond exactly with the layout of the DOS internal variable table, you need to pack the structure on byte boundaries. Otherwise, an unsigned char followed by an unsigned short would occupy four bytes, not three, and the structure would not reflect DOS's internal variable table.

Note that the program creates, not a struct SysVars, but a far *pointer* to a struct SysVars. The memory for the structure already exists inside DOS. Also, to get at some of the useful variables located just before the pointer returned from INT 21h function 52h, the program uses ES:BX-12 rather than ES:BX.

This example demonstrates a fundamental problem with using data structures when working with undocumented DOS: Structures are inflexible. The C compiler, seeing a reference such as doslist->vers. dos31.lastdrive, simply turns this reference into an offset into doslist. The *compiler* computes these offsets. The program itself does not compute the offsets while it is running, so the offsets don't change at run-time based on conditions such as different versions of an operating system.

You could use some of the simpler information-hiding features of C++ to create a ListOfLists structure that responded to the DOS version number. When working with undocumented DOS data structures, programmers often wish they weren't so unruly. One benefit of C++ is its ability to implement such wishful thinking by creating classes that manage and hide the complexity of underlying structures.

When using only one or two fields from an undocumented DOS data structure, however, and when placement of the fields within the structure differs from one DOS version to the next, it is best *not* to use data structures but to compute offsets instead. Structures may be self-documenting, but they are also static. Remember the convoluted expression in Listing 2-11 to extract the LASTDRIVE field from the appropriate component of the union vers in struct ListOfLists? Note how much simpler it is when you use offsets:

```
if (_osmajor == 3 && _osminor == 0) lastdrv_ofs = 0x1B;
else if (_osmajor == 2)             lastdrv_ofs = 0x10;
else                                lastdrv_ofs = 0x21;
lastdrv = doslist[lastdrv_ofs];
```

or:

```
lastdrv_ofs = (_osmajor == 3 && _osminor == 0) ? 0x1B :
              (_osmajor == 2) ?                   0x10 :
              /* otherwise */                     0x21 ;
lastdrv = doslist[lastdrv_ofs];
```

or the even more compact C expression, which also uses the C ?: ternary conditional operator, in the next version of this utility, LASTDRV6.C in Listing 2-12.

Listing 2-12: LASTDRV6.C

```
/* LASTDRV6.C */

#include <stdlib.h>
#include <stdio.h>
#include <dos.h>

#ifdef __TURBOC__
#define ASM asm
#elif defined(_MSC_VER) && (_MSC_VER >= 600)
#define ASM _asm
#else
#error Requires inline assembler
#endif

unsigned _dos_lastdrive(void)
{
    unsigned char far *sysvars;

    /* Try 21/3306 first */
    ASM mov ax, 3306h
    ASM xor bx, bx
    ASM int 21h
    ASM or bx, bx
    ASM jz osmajmin_ok
    ASM mov byte ptr _osmajor, bl
    ASM mov byte ptr _osminor, bh

osmajmin_ok:
    if (_osmajor < 2)
        return 0;

    ASM mov ah, 52h
    ASM int 21h
    ASM mov word ptr sysvars+2, es
    ASM mov word ptr sysvars, bx

    return sysvars[(_osmajor == 3 && _osminor == 0) ? 0x1B :
                   (_osmajor == 2) ?                    0x10 :
                   /* otherwise */                      0x21];
}

main()
{
    unsigned lastdrive = _dos_lastdrive();
    if (lastdrive == 0xFF)
        return 0;
    fputs("LASTDRIVE=", stdout);
    putchar('A' - 1 + lastdrive);
    putchar('\n');
    return lastdrive;
}
```

The other item of interest in LASTDRV6.C is the use of inline assembly within the function _dos_lastdrive(). The inline assembly language often seems like an invitation to produce extremely inline code—C programmers encountering inline assembly language for the first time seem to forget all about subroutines. Especially when working with the combination of undocumented DOS and inline assembler, you should remember to use subroutines. But also remember our earlier warning to preserve the DI, SI, DS, SS, and SP registers. The inline assembler in _dos_lastdrive() only changes AX, BX, and ES, so you're okay here. The name was chosen to conform to the Microsoft C naming convention (_dos_getdrive(), _dos_setdrive(), etc.).

Undocumented DOS Calls from Turbo Pascal

Turbo Pascal programs that make undocumented DOS calls are similar to those that make documented calls, except that, as with assembly language and C, such programs need to be especially aware of the version of MS-DOS under which they are running. The following program, LASTDRV2.PAS (Listing 2-13), uses the function DosVersion( ), added in Turbo Pascal 5.0.

Listing 2-13: LASTDRV2.PAS

```
{ LASTDRV2.PAS }

program LastDrv;
uses Dos;
var
    r : registers;
    lastdrv_ofs : Word;
    lastdrive : Word;
    vers : Word;
begin
    { determine offset of LASTDRIVE within SysVars }
    lastdrv_ofs := $21;
    vers := DosVersion;
    case Lo(vers) of
        0 : Halt(0); { DOS 1 }
        2 : lastdrv_ofs := $10;
        3 : if Hi(vers) = 0 then lastdrv_ofs := $1B;
    end;

    { Get pointer to SysVars }
    with r do begin
        ah := $52;
        es := 0; bx := 0;
        MsDos(r);
        if (es = 0) and (bx = 0) then
            Halt(0);
        lastdrive := Mem[es:bx+lastdrv_ofs];
    end;

    if lastdrive = $FF then
        Halt(0);

    { Print LASTDRIVE letter; return LASTDRIVE value }
    Writeln('LASTDRIVE=', Chr(Ord('A') - 1 + lastdrive));
    Halt(lastdrive);
end.
```

If you are working with a version of Turbo Pascal earlier than 5.0 and don't have the DosVersion( ) function, it is easy to write your own:

```
function DosVersion : Word;
var
    r : registers;
begin
    with r do begin
        ax := $3000;              {should call $3306 too!}
        MsDos(r);
        DosVersion := ax;
    end;
end;
```

Note that LASTDRV2.PAS uses the predefined Turbo Pascal array Mem[ ] to peek at SysVars. Mem[ ], MemW[ ], and MemL[ ] map onto the first megabyte of physical memory in the machine; you access them with a segment:offset index such as Mem[seg:ofs].

Rather than peek at a raw physical memory address with Mem[ ], you could use a data structure. Just as structures and unions can be used when making undocumented DOS calls from C, so variant records can be used from Turbo Pascal, as shown in LASTDRV3.PAS (Listing 2-14).

Listing 2-14: LASTDRV3.PAS

```pascal
{ LASTDRV3.PAS }
program LastDrv;
uses Dos;
type
    Dos20 = record
        numdrives : Byte;
        maxbytes : Word;
        first_diskbuff : Longint;
        nul : array [1..18] of Byte;
    end;
    Dos30 = record
        numblkdev : Byte;
        maxbytes : Word;
        first_diskbuff : Longint;
        currdir : Longint;
        lastdrive : Byte;
        stringarea : Longint;
        size_stringarea : Word;
        fcbtab : Longint;
        fcb_y : Word;
        nul : array [1..18] of Byte;
    end;
    Dos31 = record        { DOS 3.1 and higher }
        maxbytes : Word;
        diskbuff : Longint;
        currdir : Longint;
        fcb : Longint;
        numprotfcb : Word;
        numblkdev : Byte;
        lastdrive : Byte;
        nul : array [1..18] of Byte;
        numjoin : Word;
    end;
    ListOfLists = record
        shareretrycount : Word;
        shareretrydelay : Word;
        currdiskbuf : Longint;
        unreadcon : Word;
        mcb : Word;
        dpb : Longint;
        filetable : Longint;
        clock : Longint;
        con : Longint;
        case Word of
            20 : (dos20 : Dos20);
            30 : (dos30 : Dos30);
            31 : (dos31 : Dos31);
end;
var
    lastdrive : Word;
function GetLastDrive : Word;
var
    doslist : ^ListOfLists;
    r : registers;
    vers : Word;
```

```
begin
    { Get pointer to SysVars }
    with r do begin
        ah := $52;
        es := 0; bx := 0;
        MsDos(r);
        if (es = 0) and (bx = 0) then begin
            GetLastDrive := 0;
            Exit;
        end;
        doslist := Ptr(es, bx - 12);
    end;

    { LASTDRIVE offset depends on DOS version }
    GetLastDrive := doslist^.dos31.lastdrive;

    vers := DosVersion;
    case Lo(vers) of
        0 : GetLastDrive := 0; { DOS 1 }
        2 : GetLastDrive := doslist^.dos20.numdrives;
        3 : if Hi(vers) = 0 then
                GetLastDrive := doslist^.dos30.lastdrive;
    end;
end;
begin
    lastdrive := GetLastDrive;
    if lastdrive = 0 then
        Halt(0);
    Writeln('LASTDRIVE=', Chr(Ord('A') - 1 + lastdrive));
    Halt(lastdrive);
end.
```

LASTDRV3.PAS has nice self-documenting structures, but doesn't adjust itself to the DOS version number as well as LASTDRV2.PAS, which simply uses numeric offsets. This is the same tradeoff you face as when you are using the C programming language. One solution is to use the object-oriented features added to Turbo Pascal starting with version 5.5. Neil Rubenking's *PC Magazine Turbo Pascal 6.0 Techniques and Utilities* contains several in-depth discussions of using TP to create version-sensitive objects that map DOS internal data structures.

As noted earlier, making DOS calls is a little more complicated under Turbo Pascal for Windows. Naturally, making undocumented DOS calls can be a lot more complicated. The next chapter contains an in-depth discussion of making undocumented DOS calls and accessing DOS internal data structures from protected mode Windows programs; this focuses on C. For a discussion tailored to TPW, see the chapter on "Access to Real Mode" in Rubenking's *PC Magazine Turbo Pascal for Windows Techniques and Utilities*.

Undocumented DOS Calls from BASIC

The first BASIC version of the LASTDRV utility, which used only documented DOS calls, required a DOSEXIT() subroutine in order to return an exit code to MS-DOS. The second BASIC version of LASTDRV (Listing 2-15) uses the undocumented SysVars structure; this version requires a DOSVERSION() function so that it can determine the offset of LASTDRIVE within SysVars.

Listing 2-15: LASTDRV2.BAS

```
REM LASTDRV2.BAS
REM $INCLUDE: 'QB.BI'
DEF FNHI (x) = x \ &H100
DEF FNLO (x) = x AND &HFF

FUNCTION DOSVERSION
    DIM Regs AS RegType
    Regs.ax = &H3000                'should call &H3306 too!
```

```
        CALL INTERRUPT(&H21, Regs, Regs)
        DOSVERSION = Regs.ax
END FUNCTION

SUB DOSEXIT(errorlevel)
        CLOSE
        DIM Regs AS RegType
        Regs.ax = &H4C00 + errorlevel
        CALL INTERRUPT(&H21, Regs, Regs)
END SUB

REM based on DOS version number, find offset of LASTDRIVE
lastdrvofs = &H21
vers = DOSVERSION
IF FNLO(vers) << 3 THEN DOSEXIT(0)
IF (FNLO(vers) = 3) AND (FNHI(vers) = 0) THEN lastdrvofs = &H1B

REM get address of SysVars
DIM Regs AS RegTypeX
Regs.ax = &H5200
Regs.es = 0
Regs.bx = 0

REM to use current value of DS, set to -1
Regs.ds = -1
CALL INTERRUPTX(&H21, Regs, Regs)
IF (Regs.es = 0) AND (Regs.bx = 0) THEN DOSEXIT(0)

REM peek at LASTDRIVE field within SysVars
DEF SEG = Regs.es
lastdrv = PEEK(Regs.bx + lastdrvofs)
IF lastdrv = &HFF THEN DOSEXIT(0)

REM print LASTDRIVE letter, return LASTDRIVE number
PRINT "LASTDRIVE="; CHR$(ASC("A") - 1 + lastdrv)
CALL DOSEXIT(lastdrv)
END
```

Once INT 21h function 52h returns the address of SysVars in the ES:BX register pair, LASTDRV2.BAS uses DEF SEG and PEEK() to read the LASTDRIVE field. The earlier section on "DOS Calls from BASIC" includes instructions for compiling this code into a stand-alone executable. As noted there, the version of QBASIC included with MS-DOS unfortunately does not support CALL INTERRUPT.

When Not To Use Undocumented Features

The last few sections descended into the very depths of DOS simply to bring back a piece of information that was readily available all the while using DOS's well-documented function interface. This could be compared to an American who learns Japanese and then uses that newly acquired skill only to watch American movies dubbed into Japanese.

This provides us with a fine example of when *not* to use undocumented DOS. If there is a way to perform an operation using the documented DOS programmer's interface, use it. *Go out of your way* to use the documented interfaces. If there is a seemingly convenient way to accomplish some task using the undocumented calls described in this book, and a less convenient way involving only documented calls, use the documented calls. You'll see a good example of this in Chapter 7 where we discuss a brief temptation to use INT 29h.

The "Mount Everest" approach to programming—the desire to use a function simply because it is there—is fine when you are experimenting with a new operating system, but it has no place in commercial software. One of our worries in producing this book was that it might encourage the over-use of undocumented DOS. Please don't use undocumented DOS when documented DOS will do. Using undocumented calls and data structures ties your program to a particular implementation of the operating system, making it harder for the operating system to change, and making competition for DOS more difficult. The more programs depend on undocumented DOS, the more the whole industry will have to suffer under the backward-compatibility stranglehold of MS-DOS.

Having said all this, though, let's remember that lots of successful commercial software for the PC uses undocumented DOS features. Certain things can't be done using only the documented interfaces. This is somewhat analogous to the situation with direct hardware access. Clearly you should use direct hardware access only as a last resort, yet almost all successful PC software does some direct hardware access. A lot of DOS programming takes place in this area of "last resort."

Verifying Undocumented DOS

Actually, there is one good reason for using undocumented DOS even when there is equivalent documented functionality. It would be nice to have a way to perform a baseline validation of the usability of undocumented DOS in any given environment. Obviously, the best way to validate a value computed using undocumented DOS is to compare it to a known value with which it should be equivalent.

It seems we can't double-check the results of undocumented DOS against documented DOS because, if we could, we would be using documented DOS in the first place! To check that doslist->lastdrive really is equal to setdisk(getdisk()) or setdisk(0xFF), for example, seems pointless. But what if you were interested in some value other than LASTDRIVE from the SysVars? Then successfully comparing doslist->lastdrive against a known value might give your program enough confidence to proceed using undocumented DOS, whereas a mismatch would indicate that something was very wrong.

Therefore, you might want your programs to incorporate something similar to the following function, undos_dos_okay (Listing 2-16).

Listing 2-16: undoc_dos_okay()

```
BOOL undoc_dos_okay(void)
{
    unsigned char far *sysvars;
    unsigned lastdrv_doc;

    /* could do 21/3306, but if DOS version number from 21/30 doesn't
        accurately reflect genuine DOS version number, then test should
        fail, and undoc_dos_okay() should return FALSE */

    /* get offset for LASTDRIVE within DOS List of Lists */
    unsigned lastdrv_ofs = 0x21;
    if (_osmajor==2) lastdrv_ofs = 0x10;
    else if ((_osmajor==3) && (_osmajor==0)) lastdrv_ofs = 0x1b;

    /* Get DOS Lists of Lists */
    _asm mov ah, 52h
    _asm xor bx, bx
    _asm mov es, bx
    _asm int 21h
    _asm mov word ptr sysvars, bx
    _asm mov word ptr sysvars+2, es
    if (! sysvars) return FALSE;

    /* use documented DOS to verify results */
#ifdef __TURBOC__
    lastdrv_doc = setdisk(0xFF);    /* don't need getdisk() */
#else
    _dos_setdrive(0xFF, &lastdrv_doc);
#endif
    return (sysvars[lastdrv_ofs] == lastdrv_doc);
}
```

If undoc_dos_okay() returns TRUE in, say, DOS 8.0, it is no guarantee that all code that employs undocumented DOS will work. However, if undoc_dos_ okay() returns FALSE, there's a good chance that something is wrong with the underlying operating system, and that your code will have to work around this. For example, undoc_dos_okay() fails in the OS/2 1.10 DOS box, but succeeds in the vastly improved multiple DOS boxes of OS/2 2.0.

An interesting question is exactly what to test for. The test in Listing 2-16 is probably too liberal; a true undoc_dos_okay() would need to test for more than the value and location of LAST-DRIVE. But one can make a DOS test that is so stringent (and arbitrary) that only MS-DOS could hope to pass. A good example is the AARD code we examined in Chapter 1; this code is essentially Microsoft's version of undoc_dos_okay(). Another example is Microsoft's SetPSP(0) test, discussed in Chapter 4.

Making Modifications

We noted earlier that Quarterdeck's LASTDRIV.COM utility uses the undocumented rather than the documented technique for retrieving the value of LASTDRIVE. One reason for this seemingly outrageous flouting of the normal rules of good behavior is that LASTDRIV.COM can also be used to *change* the value of LASTDRIVE. This is a good example of something that requires undocumented DOS.

To change the value of LASTDRIVE is, of course, a simple matter. You've seen where this value is stored in DOS's data segment; changing the value would involve nothing more than writing rather than reading this memory location.

But to *usefully* change LASTDRIVE requires a little more work, dynamically adding or subtracting entries from DOS's internal drive table. For each logical drive, DOS maintains a Current Directory Structure. As explained in more detail in Chapter 8 (see the ENUMDRV.C sample program), the CDS marks the current working directory for each drive in the system. DOS allocates an array of these CDS structures; the pointer to this array is stored in SysVars, just like LASTDRIVE.

LASTDRIVE in fact is nothing more than the size of the CDS array. Quarterdeck's LASTDRIV.COM not only changes the value of LASTDRIVE but also relocates and resizes the CDS array. Indeed, the real purpose of LASTDRIV.COM is to re-allocate the CDS high in an upper memory block. The idea is that you put a small LASTDRIVE= value in CONFIG.SYS and later on LOADHI LASTDRIV.COM with a larger value. QEMM comes with similar utilities, such as FILES.COM and BUFFERS.COM, for relocating other DOS internal data structures reached from INT 21h function 52h.

How does all this work? One way to find out would be to disassemble QEMM's LASTDRIV, which is a tiny (2K) .COM file. Running it through Sourcer or another disassembler produces fairly understandable results, about 30 pages of assembly language code, much of which involves help and error messages. However, it isn't necessary to disassemble LASTDRIV. Running the program INTRSPY confirms that, hardly surprisingly, LASTDRV calls INT 21h function 52h. A few moments' thought about the problem of reallocating the CDS results in the pseudocode shown in Listing 2-17.

Listing 2-17: Pseudocode for Changing LASTDRIVE

```
get new_lastdrv from command line;
get sysvars from INT 21h AH=52h
set LASTDRV_OFS and CDS_PTR_OFS based on DOS version;
old_lastdrv = sysvars[LASTDRV_OFS];
old_cds = sysvars[CDS_PTR_OFS];
sizeof_cds_entry depends on DOS version;
new_cds = allocate(new_lastdrv * sizeof_cds_entry);  // LOADHI
disable interrupts;
memcpy(new_cds, old_cds, old_lastdrv * sizeof_cds_entry);
mark newly-formed CDS entries as invalid drives;
sysvars[LASTDRV_OFS] = new_lastdrv;
sysvars[CDS_PTR_OFS] = new_cds;          // do it!
enable interrupts;
```

```
// hope that no one has a dangling invalid pointer to old_cds!
// (in any case, can't free it because don't know how it was allocated)
```

Basically, reallocating the CDS is a matter of allocating a block of memory for the new CDS, copying the old CDS into it, and updating the CDS pointer and LASTDRIVE value in SysVars. It is easy to turn these steps into a working program. Listing 2-18 shows XLASTDRV.C, which for the most part just carries out the actions shown in the pseudocode.

Listing 2-18: XLASTDRV.C

```c
/*
XLASTDRV.C
Andrew Schulman, May 1993

bcc xlastdrv.c ..\chap3\iswin.c

Straightforward clone of QEMM LASTDRIV.COM utility, except:
-- Checks for presence of Windows Enh mode (DOSMGR hangs onto original
   CDS pointer from SysVars); refuses to run in DOS box
-- Checks for presence of Windows Std mode and task switcher (suggested
   by Ralf Brown). Otherwise, DOS box can be closed, thereby deallocating
   XLASTDRV's CDS!
-- Checks for presence of DesqView (suggested by Ralf Brown): the new
   CDS would be in remapped memory that isn't guaranteed to be around when
   a DOS call uses the CDS.
-- Uses sleazy hack to try to free up previously-created XLASTDRV CDSes
-- Uses "instant TSR" technique from Prosise UMBFILES
-- Provides -RESTORE command to put back original CDS pointer and LASTDRIVE
   from SysVars; uses sleazy hack entry to save these away.  This necessary
   for MSCDEX and other utilities and hold onto original SysVars pointers.
Ok, not such a straightforward clone after all!
*/

#include <stdlib.h>
#include <stdio.h>
#include <ctype.h>
#include <string.h>
#include <dos.h>
#ifdef __TURBOC__
#include <alloc.h>
#include <dir.h>
#else
#include <direct.h>
#endif

typedef unsigned char BYTE;
typedef unsigned short WORD;
typedef unsigned long DWORD;

#ifndef min
#define min(a,b)    (((a) < (b)) ? (a) : (b))
#endif

#ifndef MK_FP
#define MK_FP(seg,ofs) \
    ((void far *)(((DWORD)(seg) << 16) | (ofs)))
#endif

typedef struct {
    BYTE zero, far *orig_cds, orig_lastdrv, signature[];
    } SLEAZY_HACK;

#define GET_SLEAZY_HACK(cds, ld)    \
    ((SLEAZY_HACK far *) ((cds)+(((ld)-1)*sizeof_cds_entry)))
#define XLASTDRV_SIGN      "XLASTDRV sleazy hack"

// \undoc2\chap3\iswin.c
extern int is_win(int *pmaj, int *pmin, int *pmode);
```

```c
extern int detect_switcher(void);

void set_genuine_dos_vers(void);
BYTE far *get_sysvars(void);
void set_mcb_owner(WORD para, WORD owner);
void set_mcb_name(WORD para, char far *name);
int get_lastdrive_doc(void);
unsigned desqview(void);

void fail(char *s) { puts(s); exit(1); }

main(int argc, char *argv[])
{
    SLEAZY_HACK far *old_hack, far *new_hack;
    BYTE far *sysvars, far *old_cds, far *new_cds;
    unsigned int para;
    int lastdrv_ofs, cdsptr_ofs, new_lastdrv, old_lastdrv;
    int sizeof_cds_entry;
    int do_restore = 0;
    int dummy;

    if (argc < 2)
        fail("XLASTDRV [new value for lastdrv: A-Z] or -restore");

    if (is_win(&dummy, &dummy, &dummy))  // including Std mode (see Listing 3-29)
        fail("Sorry, XLASTDRV can't run under Windows");
    if (detect_switcher() != 0) // other than Std mode (see Listing 3-29)
        fail("Sorry, XLASTDRV can't run under a task switcher");
    if (desqview() != 0)
        fail("Sorry, XLASTDRV can't run under Desqview");

    // get new LASTDRV (or -RESTORE) from command line
    if (strcmp(strupr(argv[1]), "-RESTORE") == 0)
        do_restore = 1;
    else
        new_lastdrv = 1 + (toupper(argv[1][0]) - 'A');

    // possibly change _osmajor, _osminor; see if ok
    set_genuine_dos_vers();
    if ((_osmajor < 3) || (_osmajor >= 10))
        fail("Unsupported DOS version");

    // get offsets within SysVars
    if ((_osmajor == 3) && (_osminor == 0))
    {
        cdsptr_ofs = 0x17;
        lastdrv_ofs = 0x1b;
    }
    else
    {
        cdsptr_ofs = 0x16;
        lastdrv_ofs = 0x21;
    }

    // old_lastdrv = sysvars[lastdrv_ofs];
    if (! (sysvars = get_sysvars()))
        fail("Can't get SysVars");
    old_lastdrv = sysvars[lastdrv_ofs];

    // see if SysVars looks ok
    // get_lastdrive_doc() is wrong for Novell:  see Listing 2-19
    if (get_lastdrive_doc() != old_lastdrv)
        fail("Internal DOS data structures wrong?");
    if (old_lastdrv == 0xFF)
        fail("LASTDRIVE not supported");

    // old_cds = sysvars[cdsptr_ofs];
    old_cds = *((BYTE far * far *) &sysvars[cdsptr_ofs]);
```

```
// sizeof_cds_entry depends on DOS version;
if (_osmajor == 3)
    sizeof_cds_entry = 0x51;
else
    sizeof_cds_entry = 0x58;

if (do_restore)
{
    old_hack = GET_SLEAZY_HACK(old_cds, old_lastdrv);
    if (_fstrcmp(old_hack->signature, XLASTDRV_SIGN) != 0)
        fail("Can't restore original CDS!");
    _disable();
    _fmemcpy(old_hack->orig_cds, old_cds,
            min(old_lastdrv, old_hack->orig_lastdrv) * sizeof_cds_entry);
    *((BYTE far * far *) &sysvars[cdsptr_ofs]) = old_hack->orig_cds;
    sysvars[lastdrv_ofs] = old_hack->orig_lastdrv;
    _enable();
    printf("Restored CDS to %Fp (LASTDRIVE=%c)\n",
        old_hack->orig_cds,
        (old_hack->orig_lastdrv - 1) + 'A');
    goto free_old;
}

if (new_lastdrv != old_lastdrv)
    printf("Changing LASTDRIVE from %c to %c\n",
        (old_lastdrv - 1) + 'A',
        (new_lastdrv - 1) + 'A');

// temporarily bump up new_lasdtrv for signature entry
new_lastdrv++;

// new_cds = allocate(new_lastdrv * sizeof_cds_entry);
if (_dos_allocmem(1+((new_lastdrv * sizeof_cds_entry) >> 4),
    &para) != 0)
    fail("Insufficient memory");
new_cds = (BYTE far *) MK_FP(para, 0);

// This taken from Jeff Prosise, UMBFILES (PC MAG, 11/26/91)
// Instant TSR!  (MEM /D thinks XLASTDRV is TSR)
set_mcb_owner(para, para);
set_mcb_name(para, "XLASTDRV");

// mark newly-formed CDS entries as invalid drives;
_fmemset(new_cds, 0, new_lastdrv * sizeof_cds_entry);

printf("Moving CDS from %Fp to %Fp\n", old_cds, new_cds);

_disable();  // disable interrupts while moving CDS

// copy old CDS entries over to new CDS table
_fmemcpy(new_cds, old_cds,
    sizeof_cds_entry * min(new_lastdrv, old_lastdrv));

// put back actual new LASTDRIVE value requested by user
new_lastdrv--;

// use extra entry for signature, and to keep orig to restore
new_hack = GET_SLEAZY_HACK(new_cds, new_lastdrv);
old_hack = GET_SLEAZY_HACK(old_cds, old_lastdrv);
_fstrcpy(new_hack->signature, XLASTDRV_SIGN);
if (_fstrcmp(old_hack->signature, XLASTDRV_SIGN) == 0)
{
    // have done XLASTDRV before; copy orig values from old to new
    new_hack->orig_cds = old_hack->orig_cds;
    new_hack->orig_lastdrv = old_hack->orig_lastdrv;
}
else
{
    // this is first time we've run XLASTDRV
```

```
            new_hack->orig_cds = old_cds;
            new_hack->orig_lastdrv = old_lastdrv;
    }

    // plug new values into SysVars!
    *((BYTE far * far *) &sysvars[cdsptr_ofs]) = new_cds;
    sysvars[lastdrv_ofs] = new_lastdrv;

    _enable();    // new CDS in place; re-enable interrupts

    // hope that no one has a dangling invalid pointer to old_cds!
    // Windows does, MSCDEX does!
free_old:
    // if we allocated old one, we can free it
    if (_fstrcmp(old_hack->signature, XLASTDRV_SIGN) == 0)
    {
        if (_dos_freemem(FP_SEG(old_cds)) != 0)
            fail("Couldn't free up old CDS");
        else
            printf("Freed old XLASTDRV CDS at %Fp\n", old_cds);
    }

    return 0;
}
void set_genuine_dos_vers(void)
{
    union REGS r;
    r.x.ax = 0x3306;
    r.x.bx = 0;
    intdos(&r, &r);
    if (r.x.bx != 0)
    {
        _osmajor = r.h.bl;
        _osminor = r.h.bh;
    }
}
BYTE far *get_sysvars(void)
{
    union REGS r;
    struct SREGS s;
    r.h.ah = 0x52;
    segread(&s);
    s.es = r.x.bx = 0;
    intdosx(&r, &r, &s);
    return (BYTE far *) MK_FP(s.es, r.x.bx);
}
void set_mcb_owner(WORD para, WORD owner)
{
    *((WORD far *) MK_FP(para-1, 1)) = owner;
}
void set_mcb_name(WORD para, char far *name)
{
    _fmemcpy(MK_FP(para-1, 8), name, 8);
}
unsigned desqview(void)
{
    _asm mov ax, 2B01h
    _asm mov cx, 4445h    /* 'DE' */
    _asm mov dx, 5351h    /* 'SQ' */
    _asm int 21h
    _asm cmp al, 0FFh
    _asm je no_desq
    _asm mov ax, bx       /* BH=major, BL=minor */
    _asm jmp short done
```

```
no_desq:
    _asm xor ax, ax       /* return 0 */
done:;
    // return value in AX
}

int get_lastdrive_doc(void) // should adjust for Novell!
{
#ifdef __TURBOC__
    return setdisk(0xFF);
#else
    unsigned lastdrv_doc;
    _dos_setdrive(0xFF, &lastdrv_doc);
    return lastdrv_doc;
#endif
}
```

After XLASTDRV runs, DOS uses the new CDS it allocates, just as if it were DOS's own creation. Smacking the two new values into SysVars took care of this. However, if you run MEM /D or the UDMEM utility from Chapter 7, you will see that these utilities don't know that the CDS has moved. And it seems impossible to tell them it has! The QEMM LASTDRIV utility has the same problem. But aside from these problems, DOS accepts the new CDS as its own.

To reallocate the CDS high, just run LH XLASTDRV or LOADHIGH XLASTDRV. XLASTDRV can continue to allocate memory for the new CDS using the Microsoft and Borland _dos_allocmem() function, which calls INT 21h function 48h. If you run XLASTDRV under LOADHIGH, DOS attempts to allocate the memory from a UMB. While it would be easy enough to make XLASTDRV UMB-aware (see *PC Magazine*'s UMBFILES utility, for example), this step really isn't necessary. (For an explanation of how LOADHIGH works, see Chapter 7.)

What XLASTDRV *does* have to worry about is making sure that the memory for the new CDS stays around after the program exits. When XLASTDRV exits, DOS walks the Memory Control Block chain and frees up any blocks owned by XLASTDRV. It seems like overkill to make the program a TSR, so instead, after allocating a block of memory for the new CDS, XLASTDRV changes the block's owner so that DOS doesn't free the block when XLASTDRV exits. In essence, this procedure creates an "instant TSR." (See Chapter 7 for details of the MCB chain).

It is also nice to free up the old CDS. We can't free the original CDS owned by DOS, even though it's no longer in use, because we don't know how it was allocated. But we can free up any earlier CDSs that XLASTDRV itself created. To mark its own CDS allocations, XLASTDRV allocates an extra CDS entry and marks it with the signature "XLASTDRV sleazy hack." If XLASTDRV ever finds this signature in an old CDS, it knows it can delete the old CDS.

There is one serious problem with the otherwise clever technique of relocating internal DOS data structures to UMBs. Relocation depends on a completely voluntary convention, that the operating system, device drivers, and TSRs always go through SysVars. If a resident program gets a pointer to the CDS array from SysVars once during initialization and uses it thereafter without referring back to SysVars, the system fails spectacularly if XLASTDRV or any similar program comes along later and changes the CDS pointer in SysVars.

For example, the Microsoft CD-ROM Extensions (MSCDEX) save away a pointer to the CDS. If XLASTDRV changes the CDS location, MSCDEX can no longer find its CD-ROM drives. XLASTDRV provides a -RESTORE switch which puts the CDS back to its original location. Of course, any additional drives are lost, but at least MSCDEX works again.

Note in Listing 2-18 that XLASTDRV uses ISWIN.C from Chapter 3 (Listing 3-29) to see if Windows is running. Windows Enhanced mode does not follow this always-refer-to-SysVars convention at all. The DOSMGR VxD only checks SysVars once, during its initialization, and isn't prepared for the SFT or CDS pointers to change after this. As seen back in Listing 1-10, DOSMGR hangs on to these as linear addresses, and isn't prepared for LASTDRIVE to change. Thus, while running

FILES or LASTDRIV before Windows works fine, running either of them from within an Enhanced mode DOS box is a recipe for disaster. And because the code in DOSMGR that does call INT 21h AH=52h to check SysVars is discarded initialization code, there probably isn't even a way to indulge in that favorite activity, patching DOSMGR to do the right thing. These pointers in SysVars *can't* change once Enhanced mode is running. This means that all virtual machines have identical copies of these SysVars pointers. We'll actually take advantage of this fact in the next chapter, in a Windows program, ENUMDRV.C, that displays the CDS in every DOS box (see Listing 3-27).

This problem isn't just a Windows problem. In fact, the first edition of this book provided the "helpful" advice that programs, even TSRs, could check the List of Lists just once, during initialization, and thereafter hang onto and use pointers to the CDS, SFT, and so on. This advice is okay, assuming that these pointers don't change. But you've just seen how easy it is to write programs that make these pointers change! Hopefully no one else followed our advice in the first edition, but unfortunately Windows and MSCDEX have long followed the same logic.

XLASTDRV.C also checks for the presence of Windows Standard mode, for a task switcher such as the DOS shell, and for DesqView. Task switchers such as Standard mode and the DOS shell are not good places to run XLASTDRV, because the DOS box could be closed, thereby deallocating XLASTDRV's CDS! Under DesqView, XLASTDRV's new CDS would be in remapped memory that isn't guaranteed to be accessible when a DOS call actually uses the CDS. Basically, there are a lot of restrictions on moving DOS internal data structures.

An Important Special Case: Novell NetWare

There's an additional reason to use undocumented DOS for getting LASTDRIVE. In one situation, the documented method is actually less reliable than the undocumented method! On any of the many PCs that are Novell NetWare workstations, INT 21h function 0Eh doesn't return the value of LASTDRIVE; it returns the number 32, corresponding to the number of possible workstation drive mappings (drive letters A through Z, plus temporary drives with the silly names [, \,], ^, _, and '). Thus, under NetWare, the versions of LASTDRV that use undocumented DOS display correct values for LASTDRIVE, whereas the supposedly well-behaved version of LASTDRV that uses only documented DOS always prints out the following display:

```
C:\UNDOC2\CHAP2>lastdrv
LASTDRIVE='
```

Likewise, under NetWare our carefully written undoc_dos_okay() function returns FALSE. This happens not because undocumented DOS is broken but because documented function 0Eh is returning a strange value.

It is important to look into this situation. Novell is, by far, the largest supplier of PC local area network (LAN) software; its share of the PC LAN software market is probably twice that of its nearest competitor. Microsoft, king of the hill elsewhere in PC operating systems, has made few inroads into Novell's control over the PC networking market. If the version of LASTDRV that uses documented DOS doesn't work under Novell NetWare, it essentially doesn't work!

How does the NetWare shell running on a workstation change DOS so that INT 21h function 0Eh returns 32 instead of the value of LASTDRIVE? Easy. The shell hooks DOS and modifies the return value from Function 0Eh. You'll see exactly what "hooking DOS" means in a few moments. Chapter 4 also discusses the workings of the Novell workstation shell (NETX) in much more detail.

Novell's alteration to function 0Eh is unfortunate, but NetWare does provides an alternate function, INT 21h function DBh, which returns the correct value of LASTDRIVE. This is not part of undocumented DOS, so it does not appear in the appendix. However, INTRLIST on the accompanying disk describes this function. To be compatible with NetWare, we need to change our validity checking.

Instead of asserting that undocumented DOS is unusable simply because doslist->lastdrive != setdisk-(0xFF), the improved version of undoc_dos_okay() performs a slightly more complicated test, as shown in Listing 2-19.

Listing 2-19: OKAY.C

```
/*
OKAY.C -- basic test for validity of undocumented DOS
cl -DTESTING okay.c
*/

#include <stdlib.h>
#include <stdio.h>

#ifdef __TURBOC__
#include <dir.h>
#endif

typedef int BOOL;
#define FALSE    0
#define TRUE     (! FALSE)

BOOL netware(void);
unsigned lastdrv_netware(void);

BOOL undoc_dos_okay(void)
{
    unsigned char far *sysvars;
    unsigned lastdrv_doc;

    /* could do 21/3306, but if DOS version number from 21/30 doesn't
       accurately reflect genuine DOS version number, then test should
       fail, and undoc_dos_okay() should return FALSE */

    /* get offset for LASTDRIVE within DOS List of Lists */
    unsigned lastdrv_ofs = 0x21;
    if (_osmajor==2) lastdrv_ofs = 0x10;
    else if ((_osmajor==3) && (_osmajor==0)) lastdrv_ofs = 0x1b;

    /* Get DOS Lists of Lists */
    _asm mov ah, 52h
    _asm xor bx, bx
    _asm mov es, bx
    _asm int 21h
    _asm mov word ptr sysvars, bx
    _asm mov word ptr sysvars+2, es
    if (! sysvars) return FALSE;

    /* use documented DOS to verify results */
#ifdef __TURBOC__
    lastdrv_doc = setdisk(0xFF);
#else
    _dos_setdrive(0xFF, &lastdrv_doc);
#endif
    if (sysvars[lastdrv_ofs] == lastdrv_doc)
        return TRUE;
    else if (netware())
    {
        puts("Novell NetWare");
        if (lastdrv_doc != 32)
            puts("NetWare INT 21h 0Eh looks strange");
        return (sysvars[lastdrv_ofs] == lastdrv_netware());
    }

    return FALSE;
}

/*  Novell Return Shell Version function (INT 21h AH=EAh AL=01h)
    see INTRLIST on accompanying disk; also see Barry Nance,
    _Networking Programming in C_, pp. 117, 341-2. */
```

```
BOOL netware(void)
{
    char buf[40];
    char far *fp = buf;
    _asm push di
    _asm mov ax, OEA01h
    _asm mov bx, 0
    _asm les di, fp
    _asm int 21h
    _asm xor al, al
    _asm mov ax, bx
    /* if BX still 0, then NetWare not present; return in AX */
    _asm pop di
}
/*  Novell Get Number of Local Drives function (INT 21h AH=DBh).
    See INTRLIST on accompanying disk, or Charles Rose, _Programmer's
    Guide to NetWare_, p. 731. */
unsigned lastdrv_netware(void)
{
    _asm mov ah, 0DBh
    _asm int 21h
    /* AL now holds number of "local drives" (genuine LASTDRIVE) */
    _asm xor ah, ah
    /* unsigned returned in AX */
}

#ifdef TESTING
main()
{
    fputs("Undocumented DOS ", stdout);
    puts( undoc_dos_okay() ? "ok" : "not ok");
}
#endif
```

Function 0Eh isn't the only DOS function whose behavior Novell NetWare modifies. The NetWare shell inspects every INT 21h function request before DOS itself sees it. The shell decides whether to pass that function request along to DOS or to pass the request over the network to another machine, the server (which is not even a DOS machine). Finally, even if the shell decides to pass the INT 21h function request along to DOS, it gets to modify any registers before returning control to the application (such as LASTDRV) that called INT 21h in the first place. For further details on DOS differences under NetWare, see Chapter 4.

Hooking DOS: Application Wrappers

Seeing that NetWare changes DOS function 0Eh gives us an excuse to look into what it means for a program to "hook DOS." In order to hook DOS, all a program has to do is get the address of the current interrupt handler for INT 21h and then install its own handler for INT 21h. There's nothing difficult or undocumented about this capability. It's built right into DOS itself and is one of the key facilities that makes DOS extensible.

We can simulate NetWare's handling of function 0Eh and provide a realistic example of hooking DOS by using just a few lines of code. Generally programs that hook DOS, like Novell's workstation shells, are memory-resident. However, there is no reason such programs must be TSRs. As FUNC0E32 in Listing 2-20 shows, it is easier to build a program that instead acts as a shell or wrapper around another program (see Jim Kyle, "Application Wrappers," *PC Techniques*, June/July 1992). FUNC0E32 modifies Function 0Eh to return 32, just like NetWare, and then uses one of the C spawn() functions to run whatever program was specified on its command line. For example:

```
C:\UNDOC2\CHAP2>func0e32 lastdrv.exe
LASTDRIVE='
10 DOS calls
1 changed
```

Any version of LASTDRV that uses only documented DOS functions is fooled by FUNC0E32; but the versions that use undocumented DOS aren't. For example:

```
C:\UNDOC2\CHAP2>func0e32 lastdrv2.exe
LASTDRIVE=E
10 DOS calls
1 changed
```

FUNC0E32.C in Listing 2-20 consists of two functions. The function DOS() is our INT 21h handler. We want DOS() to get control each time anyone invokes INT 21h. DOS() changes the value that function 0Eh returns in AL to 32; the function also keeps count of how many INT 21h calls it has seen and how many it has changed. It is FUNC0E32 which produces the "10 DOS calls" and "1 changed" output above. In Listing 2-20, main() installs DOS() as the INT 21h handler, spawns the program named on the command line, and then restores the original INT 21h handler, which may be DOS itself but which, on most PCs, will be some other program that had earlier hooked DOS, such as NetWare.

Listing 2-20: FUNC0E32.C

```c
/* FUNC0E32.C -- take over INT 21h Function 0Eh; return 32 in AL */

#include <stdlib.h>
#include <stdio.h>
#include <process.h>
#include <dos.h>

#pragma pack(1)

typedef struct {
#ifdef __TURBOC__
    unsigned short bp,di,si,ds,es,dx,cx,bx,ax;
#else
    unsigned short es,ds,di,si,bp,sp,bx,dx,cx,ax;   /* same as PUSHA */
#endif
    unsigned short ip,cs,flags;
    } REG_PARAMS;
void _interrupt _far DOS(REG_PARAMS r);
void (_interrupt _far *old)(void);
unsigned long calls = 0;
unsigned long changed = 0;

void fail(char *s) { puts(s); exit(1); }

main(int argc, char *argv[])
{
    if (argc < 2)
        fail("usage: func0e32 [program name] <args...>");

    old = (void (interrupt far *)(void)) _dos_getvect(0x21);
    _dos_setvect(0x21, DOS);           /* hook INT 21h */
    if (spawnvp(P_WAIT, argv[1], &argv[1]) == -1) /* run command */
        puts("Can't run program!");
    _dos_setvect(0x21, old);           /* unhook INT 21h */

    printf("\n%lu DOS calls\n", calls);
    printf("%lu changed\n", changed);
    return 0;
}

void _interrupt _far DOS(REG_PARAMS r)
{
```

```
    _asm pusha
    calls++;
    if ((r.ax >> 8) == 0x0E)   /* if Function 0Eh... */
    {
        _asm popa
        (*old)();              /* first call old INT 21h handler */
        r.ax = 0x0E20;         /* then force #drives to 20h (32) */
        changed++;
    }
    else                       /* not for us */
    {
        _asm popa
        _chain_intr(old);      /* pass to old INT 21h handler */
    }
}
```

This code is important, not only to illustrate that it is perfectly legitimate (and completely documented!) for a company like Novell to change the return value from a DOS function, but also as an example of how to hook a DOS interrupt like INT 21h. Some undocumented DOS functions are not for you to call, but for you to *implement* so that DOS can call them (don't call us, we'll call you). Such functions are indicated in the appendix with the phrase "Called with" rather than "Call with." For example, the DOS network redirector, which, incidentally, Novell did not use until recently, is one such set of call-back functions. A network-redirector program takes over INT 2Fh and looks for calls to AH=11h, with subfunctions in AL.

Listing 2-20 shows you how to hook an interrupt with just a few lines of C code. The DOS.H header files provided by Microsoft, Borland, and other PC compiler vendors declares the functions _dos_setvect() and _dos_getvect(). The _interrupt keyword defines a C function as an interrupt handler. The compiler pushes an image of the CPU registers on a C interrupt handler's stack (see REG_PARAMS in Listing 2-20). Unfortunately, Borland orders the register image in a way that is inefficient on 286 and higher processors, whereas Microsoft puts the register image in PUSHA order. Either way, the interrupt handler can manipulate the registers using expressions such as r.ax = 0x0E20.

Of course, the new handler generally needs to call down to the previous handler. If the new handler needs to get control again after calling the previous handler, the new handler can simply call the old with an expression such as (*old)(). If the new handler doesn't need to regain control but instead wants to "chain" to the previous handler, it can call the function _chain_intr(), provided in both Microsoft C/C++ and, as a recent addition, in Borland C++. To see how _chain_intr() is implemented, check your compiler's run-time library source code (for example, \borlandc\ctrl\clib\chainint.asm).

FUNC0E32 is a rather specialized and contrived example of hooking DOS through an application wrapper. As another example of hooking DOS this way, consider the DOSVER program shown in Listing 2-21. This program takes over INT 21h function 30h and lets you muck with the DOS version number on an application-by-application basis. It is like the SETVER command, but less permanent in its effect.

Listing 2-21: DOSVER.C

```
/* DOSVER.C -- set different DOS version numbers */

#include <stdlib.h>
#include <stdio.h>
#include <process.h>
#include <dos.h>

#pragma pack(1)

void (interrupt far *old)();
unsigned dosver, old_bx, old_cx;

typedef struct {
```

```
#ifdef __TURBOC__
    unsigned short bp,di,si,ds,es,dx,cx,bx,ax;
#else
    unsigned short es,ds,di,si,bp,sp,bx,dx,cx,ax;    /* PUSHA order */
#endif
    unsigned short ip,cs,flags;
    } REG_PARAMS;
void interrupt far dos(REG_PARAMS r)
{
    if ((r.ax >> 8) == 0x30)
    {
        r.ax = dosver;
        r.bx = old_bx;
        r.cx = old_cx;
    }
    else
        _chain_intr(old);
}
void fail(char *s) { puts(s); exit(1); }
main(int argc, char *argv[])
{
    int new_major, new_minor;
    unsigned char old_major, old_minor;

    if (argc < 4)
        fail("usage: dosver <major> <minor> <command...>\n"
            "example: dosver 3 31 exe2bin devlod.exe devlod.com");
    if (! (new_major = atoi(argv[1])))
        fail("bad version number");
    if ((new_minor = atoi(argv[2])) < 10)      /* e.g. 3.1 to 3.10 */
        new_minor *= 10;
    dosver = (new_minor << 8) + new_major;

    _asm mov ax, 3000h
    _asm int 21h
    _asm mov old_major, al
    _asm mov old_minor, ah
    _asm mov old_cx, cx                     /* OEM, serial# */
    _asm mov old_bx, bx

    if ((new_major == old_major) && (new_minor == old_minor))
        fail("no change");

    printf("Changing DOS version from %u.%02u to %u.%02u\n",
        old_major, old_minor, new_major, new_minor);

    old = _dos_getvect(0x21);               /* save INT 21h */
    _dos_setvect(0x21, dos);                /* hook INT 21h */
    if (spawnvp(P_WAIT, argv[3], &argv[3]) == -1) /* run command */
        puts("Can't run program!");
    _dos_setvect(0x21, old);                /* unhook INT 21h */
    return 0;
}
```

In addition to its occasional usefulness with programs that are over-conservative in their response to the DOS version number, DOSVER and FUNC0E32 can also be lashed together to thoroughly mess up both INT 21h functions 30h and 0Eh and to see if the LASTDRV programs respond properly. For example, the following test, run under DOS 6.0, perversely sets the DOS version number to 3.31 and then makes function 0Eh return 32; but LASTDRV4 from Listing 2-10 recovers and gets the correct answer:

```
C:\UNDOC2\CHAP2>dosver 3 31 func0e32 lastdrv4
Changing DOS version from 6.00 to 3.31
```

```
21/30 returns 3.31
But 21/3306 returns 6.00
LASTDRIVE=M

45 DOS calls
0 changed
```

If you haven't written a C interrupt handler before, you may want to experiment with FUNC0E32.C or DOSVER.C, perhaps modifying them to count and display the number of different INT 21h calls. Try adding an additional INT 2Fh handler to count the number of INT 2Fh calls an application makes. This should take less than 100 lines of code, yet it would be a semi-useful scaled-down version of the INTRSPY program from Chapter 5.

On to Protected Mode

Frankly, it is a little difficult to take seriously all the little character-mode DOS programs we've developed in this chapter. In the 1990s, most new development on the PC is being done for Windows, or even for completely different non-DOS operating systems such as OS/2 and Windows NT. Little utilities that print LASTDRIVE=E almost seem like a joke. They have something of a hobbyist "look what I can do with my computer" feel to them.

But issues of MS-DOS systems programming and undocumented DOS really haven't gone away. Far from it. Windows applications running in protected mode often need to talk to DOS, TSRs, and device drivers. In Enhanced mode, developers often want some way for their Windows applications to get at something from a DOS box. OS/2 and NT emulate DOS, and it is important to know whether any of this undocumented DOS stuff works in these DOS emulations. Undocumented DOS hasn't gone away. As you'll see in the next two chapters, it's just become a lot more complicated.

## CHAPTER 3

Undocumented DOS Meets Windows

by Andrew Schulman

The previous chapter has shown how to call undocumented DOS functions and access undocumented DOS data structures from an assortment of programming languages. But in all cases the assumption was that the source for these calls and accesses was a real mode DOS program. Microsoft designed the MS-DOS operating system around the Intel 8088 microprocessor, and even on the hottest Pentium or 80486 processor with megabytes of memory, MS-DOS still runs in so-called real mode, limiting programs to a single megabyte of directly addressable memory. Yuk!

Fortunately, almost no hardware vendor makes 8088-based PCs anymore, and fewer and fewer developers write real mode DOS programs. The Windows application market is booming, and DOS-only development is relatively stagnant. More and more PC software is being delivered for Windows and other protected mode DOS extenders, rather than for plain vanilla DOS. In protected mode, programs can directly access multiple megabytes of memory on the 80286 and higher processors. The great innovation of Windows 3.x, and a major reason for its success, is that Windows programs run in protected mode.

But even with the move to Windows and protected mode, DOS definitely has not gone away. Windows' protected mode, multitasking, graphical, windowed, dynamic-linking, device-independent services sit atop DOS and are essentially extensions to DOS. While a Windows program runs in the protected mode of the 80286 and higher microprocessors and has transparent access to megabytes of extended memory, the program also maintains transparent access to DOS, even though DOS is still a real mode operating system. Windows programs can call DOS with a direct INT 21h or with the DOS3Call() function from the Windows API, or, more likely, by calling a compiler run-time library function, which in turn calls INT 21h.

When Windows 3.x runs a program, *DOS is still present*, ready for the program to call with a simple INT 21h. The job of a DOS extender such as Windows is to translate a protected mode program's INT 21h calls to something that real mode DOS can understand, and then to translate DOS's real mode replies back into something that the protected mode program can understand. (For a more complete discussion of DOS extenders and protected mode, see the second edition of *Extending DOS*, edited by Ray Duncan.)

Just as Windows programs use DOS to do file I/O, they can also use undocumented DOS to snoop around and modify the system. But while Windows programs have transparent access to the standard documented DOS functions for file I/O and the like, their access to undocumented DOS is generally *not* transparent. For example, whereas a protected mode Windows program can write to a file with an INT 21h AH=40h, without regard for the fact that the data to be written is probably located in extended memory, it is not so straightforward for a Windows program to call an undocumented function such as INT 21h AH=52h and then access a data structure such as the CDS. The

Standard and Enhanced mode DOS extenders built into Windows 3.0 and 3.1 do not support many undocumented DOS functions and data structures.

But in addition to being a DOS extender (that is, a provider of protected mode INT 21h services), Windows also provides an implementation of version 0.90 of the DOS Protected Mode Interface (DPMI). DPMI includes services for generating real mode interrupts from protected mode, mapping real mode memory into a protected mode program's address space, and so on. As this chapter details, a Windows program can use these services to access undocumented DOS because Windows programs are—whether or not they explicitly call DPMI—DPMI clients. Using DPMI, you can write the LASTDRV program from Chapter 2, for example, as a Windows program. Yet another version of LASTDRV!

Interestingly, rather than use DPMI, a Windows version of LASTDRV could instead use some until-recently undocumented Windows API functions to access the undocumented DOS data structures. Some of DPMI itself has a quasi-undocumented status within Windows. Windows itself uses a handful of undocumented DPMI functions. There are vast numbers of undocumented Windows API calls, though these are not addressed here since an entirely separate book, *Undocumented Windows*, deals with these calls. So there are plenty of undocumented aspects to Windows. What this chapter covers, however, is simply those aspects of Windows that in some way pertain to undocumented DOS.

Chapter 1 showed that Windows itself relies heavily on undocumented DOS and presented code fragments from the DOSMGR virtual device driver (VxD) that indicate how one would go about calling undocumented DOS from a VxD. This is important because VxDs are the future of DOS systems programming. While the present chapter focuses mostly on writing "normal" Windows applications that use undocumented DOS, it will also take an inside look at the code Windows Enhanced mode uses in its DOS extender and DPMI server. The end of the chapter will even present a sample VxD that provides transparent access to an undocumented DOS function that Windows does not otherwise support.

Several articles and books that have appeared since the release of Windows 3.0 have already discussed the use of DPMI to access undocumented DOS functions and data structures. However, Enhanced mode Windows introduces an additional wrinkle. In addition to providing protected mode, Enhanced mode provides a separate virtual machine for each DOS box and runs real mode programs in virtual 8086 mode, rather than in real mode. Each DOS box can have its own view of DOS, including separate instances or copies of DOS data structures such as the Current Directory Structure and Swappable Data Area.

For example, Figure 1-9 back in Chapter 1 showed two DOS boxes in Windows, one sitting at C:\BIN and one at C:\UNDOC; meanwhile, File Manager is sitting at C:\WIN31. In other words, Figure 1-9 shows multiple CDSs. One of the techniques this chapter presents is the enumeration of multiple VMs and instances of DOS data structures from a Windows program, or even from a DOS program running under Windows.

The general subject here is mixing real mode and protected mode. This sounds "impure," but until the millennium, when almost everything your program depends on will have already been ported to protected mode, in the real world today many programs depend on other components which haven't been, or can't be, ported to protected mode. For the forseeable future, the ability to get to real mode from protected mode should be a necessary and marketable skill. This is not especially unique to Windows, either: "mixing" in general is a necessary real-world engineering skill.

This chapter discusses many other topics, including: writing simple Windows programs without having to create windows or handle messages; using DPMI to write protected mode DOS programs; investigating the PSP and System File Tables under Windows; using INT 2Fh to call services provided by Windows VxDs; writing Windows VxDs; and examining how Windows implements its DOS extender and DPMI server.

Before we begin, a brief appeal to those DOS programmers who "don't do Windows": please don't skip this chapter! We will be dragging Windows down to the level of DOS systems programming here, so there's plenty even for the most die-hard fan of DOS and opponent of Windows. In this chapter, we will basically view Windows as little more than a protected mode version of DOS.

Calling Undocumented DOS from Windows

In Chapter 2, we built about 57 varieties of the LASTDRV utility, but each time we ended up with a real mode DOS program. The marketing department, responding to customer requests, now wants us to turn LASTDRV into a Windows program. This implies running in protected mode and somehow getting to the DOS internal data structure from protected mode. How do we proceed?

Windows and Printf()

The first problem is what to do with LASTDRIV's call to printf(). LASTDRV only needs to produce a single line of output, such as "LASTDRIVE=M". The amount of output is exactly the same as that for the classic "hello world" program, so writing the code shouldn't be too hard. However, all the standard books on Windows programming start by teaching you how to display "hello world" in Windows. The source code for this supposedly introductory program invariably takes about 80 lines of code and requires several other source files as well. Just displaying those eleven characters in Windows apparently requires calls to RegisterClass(), CreateWindow(), GetMessage(), BeginPaint(), TextOut(), and so on, as well as an understanding of the concepts behind each of these key Windows API functions. It seems that, by agreeing to marketing's request to port LASTDRV to Windows, we have bought into a big mess.

To survive as a PC programmer in the 1990s, you really do need to learn those Windows functions. However, that is a ridiculously difficult place to start. The biggest initial stumbling block for DOS programmers moving to Windows is the misconception that, to write a Windows program, even the simplest Windows program, you must first learn how to register window classes, create windows, handle messages, and so on.

Well, it just isn't necessary. Not only has Borland with its EasyWin library and Microsoft with QuickWin made it easy to port simple DOS programs to Windows, but even more important, there are Windows API functions which are high-level enough that you can use them to do an entirely self-contained, simple Windows application. Hello world? Despite what all the Windows programming books say, it's as simple as calling MessageBox()— well, that and using Windows' weird WinMain() entry point instead of the main() entry point that is used everywhere else in the world:

```
/* bcc -WS hello.c */
#include "windows.h"

#pragma argsused
int PASCAL WinMain(HANDLE hInstance, HANDLE hPrevInstance,
    LPSTR lpszCmdLine, int nCmdShow)
{
    MessageBox(0, "hello world", "My First Program", MB_OK);
    return 0;
}
```

That's it! Furthermore, the Windows MessageBox() function can produce an entire screen of output. Just put carriage returns in the string passed as the second parameter to MessageBox(). This makes it handy for tiny utilities like LASTDRV.

Alternatively, you can take advantage of Windows' multitasking and its interprocess messaging to use another program, such as Notepad, as your "display engine." For example, a Windows program can use the WM_SETTEXT message to blast text into some other window. This message can be sent to the other window with SendMessage(). For example, the following program launches Notepad and then sends the string "hello world" to Notepad's window. There's no intermediary text file.

```
/* bcc -WS hello2.c */
#include "windows.h"

#pragma argsused
int PASCAL WinMain(HANDLE hInstance, HANDLE hPrevInstance,
    LPSTR lpszCmdLine, int nCmdShow)
{
    if (WinExec("notepad.exe", SW_SHOWNORMAL) < 32)
        return FALSE;
    Yield();
    SendMessage(GetFocus(), WM_SETTEXT, O,
        (DWORD) (char far *) "hello world");
}
```

Using such primitive capabilities, it is easy to build Windows-specific versions of functions such as printf(). There is nothing magical about printf() or any other stdio function. As EasyWin and Quick Win show, it's possible to build stdio libraries on top of the Windows API. So why isn't there such a facility in Windows to begin with?

PRINTF.C and PRINTF.H in Listings 3-1 and 3-2 provide a rather hokey (one tech reviewer says the proper term is "gumby") but functional way to do simple Windows utilities like the ones we build in this chapter. A program that wants to use this facility should include "printf.h" and start off WinMain() by calling the open_display() function. The program can then freely call printf(). In PRINTF.C, printf() simply accumulates text until a call to show_display(). To build a program, just link it with PRINTF and compile for Windows. For example, in Borland C++ use bcc -W hello.c printf.c. Microsoft C/C++ users will also need a Windows .DEF file, unfortunately.

The show_display() function normally calls MessageBox(), but if there is more text than MessageBox() can handle, PRINTF.C uses WinExec() to fire up a copy of Notepad. PRINTF.C then sends the text to Notepad using the WM_SETTEXT message and the SendMessage() function mentioned earlier. The program does not create an intermediary file; it shoots the text directly in memory to Notepad. That one program can send text to another shows, incidentally, that Windows is genuinely message-based. Messages are a true form of interprocess communication, not just an elaborate way of describing a function call.

Listing 3-1: PRINTF.C

```
/*
PRINTF.C -- simple output for small Windows programs,
using MessageBox() or WinExec()/SendMessage().
From "Undocumented DOS", 2nd edition (Addison-Wesley, 1993)
*/

#include <stdlib.h>
#include <stdarg.h>
#include <string.h>
#include <windows.h>
#include <stdio.h>        // for vsprintf
#include "printf.h"

#define BUF_SIZE        2048

static char *str, *app;
static unsigned cap, len;
static int lines;

BOOL open_display(char *appname)
{
    app = appname;
    cap = 128;
```

```
    if (! (str = (char *) malloc(cap)))
        return FALSE;
    *str = lines = len = 0;
    return TRUE;
}
/* Maximum number of lines that MessageBox will hold */
static int max_lines(void)
{
    TEXTMETRIC tm;
    HWND hWnd = GetActiveWindow();
    HDC hDC = GetWindowDC(hWnd);
    if (hDC == NULL)
        return 0;
    GetTextMetrics(hDC, &tm);
    ReleaseDC(hWnd, hDC);
    return (GetSystemMetrics(SM_CYFULLSCREEN) /
        (tm.tmHeight + tm.tmExternalLeading)) - 5;
}

BOOL show_display(void)
{
    if (lines <= max_lines())
        MessageBox(NULL, str, app, MB_OK);
    else
        notepad(str);
    free(str);
    return TRUE;
}

static BOOL append(char *s2)
{
    char *s3;
    if (((len += strlen(s2)) < cap) && strcat(str, s2))
        return TRUE;
    cap = len + 128;
    if (! (s3 = (char *) malloc(cap)))
        return FALSE;
    strcpy(s3, str);
    strcat(s3, s2);
    free(str);
    str = s3;
    return TRUE;
}

int nlines(char *s2)
{
    int c, n = 0;
    while ((c = *s2++) != 0)
        if (c == '\n')
            n++;
    return n;
}

int printf(const char *fmt, ...)
{
    static char s2[BUF_SIZE];
    int len;
    va_list marker;
    va_start(marker, fmt);
    // Following uses vsprintf() rather than KERNEL wvsprintf()
    // because wvsprintf() requires that all %s parameters
    // be FAR; e.g., printf("%s\n", (char far *) "hi")
    len = vsprintf(s2, fmt, marker);
    lines += nlines(s2);
    va_end(marker);
    append(s2);
    return len;
```

```
}
BOOL notepad(char far *s)
{
    HWND notepad;
    HWND edit_ctrl;
    if (WinExec("notepad.exe", SW_SHOWNORMAL) < 32)
        return FALSE;
    notepad = FindWindow(NULL, "Notepad - (untitled)");
    edit_ctrl = GetFocus();
    SendMessage(notepad, WM_SETTEXT, 0, (DWORD) (char far *) app);
    SendMessage(edit_ctrl, WM_SETTEXT, 0, (DWORD) (char far *) s);
    return TRUE;
}

#ifdef TESTING
int PASCAL WinMain(HANDLE hInstance, HANDLE hPrevInstance,
    LPSTR lpszCmdLine, int nCmdShow)
{
    int i;
    open_display("GetSystemMetrics");
    for (i=0; i<37; i++)
    {
        printf("%d\t%d\r\n", i, GetSystemMetrics(i));
        Yield();
    }
    show_display();
}
#endif
```

Listing 3-2: PRINTF.H

```
/* PRINTF.H */

BOOL open_display(char *appname);
BOOL show_display(void);
#ifdef __cplusplus
extern "C"
#endif
int printf(const char *fmt, ...);
BOOL notepad(char far *s);
```

There are several alternatives to using this weird version of printf( ). As noted above, Borland C++ comes with an EasyWin library that provides C stdio functions for Windows. To use EasyWin, you just take a DOS program—one that has main( ) instead of WinMain( ) as its entry point—and compile for Windows—for example, bcc -W hello.c. To build a program with QuickWin in Microsoft C/C++, compile with the cl -Mq switch. In addition, the book *Undocumented Windows* comes with a more extensive stdio library for Windows, WINIO, which provides many features beyond those in EasyWin or QuickWin, including the ability to write event-driven programs while still using stdio functions.

Once we have some version of printf( ) for Windows, it is easy to move LASTDRV to Windows. For example, using PRINTF.C in Listing 3-1, we hacked one of the versions of LASTDRV.C from Chapter 2 so it started off with WinMain( ) instead of main( ). Otherwise, the program does the usual undocumented DOS stuff of calling INT 21h Function 52h and indexing into SysVars. We might as well add a few more lines of output. The result is a Windows version of LASTDRIV.C, shown in Listing 3-3. Since so many programs here use the get_sysvars( ) function, it has been moved into a separate file, SYSVARS.C, in Listing 3-3a.

Listing 3-3: LASTDRIV.C for Windows

```
/* LASTDRIV.C:  bcc -W lastdriv.c printf.c */

#include <stdlib.h>
#include <dos.h>
```

```
#include "windows.h"
#include "printf.h"   // see Listing 3-1, 3-2

void maybe_change_osmajmin(void)
{
    _asm mov ax, 3306h
    _asm xor bx, bx
    _asm int 21h
    _asm or bx, bx
    _asm jz osmajmin_ok
    _asm mov byte ptr _osmajor, bl
    _asm mov byte ptr _osminor, bh
osmajmin_ok:;
}

/* get_sysvars() */
#include "sysvars.c"

#ifdef __cplusplus
extern "C" int PASCAL WinMain(HANDLE hInstance, HANDLE hPrevInstance,
    LPSTR lpszCmdLine, int nCmdShow);
#endif

int PASCAL WinMain(HANDLE hInstance, HANDLE hPrevInstance,
    LPSTR lpszCmdLine, int nCmdShow)
{
    BYTE far *sysvars;
    BYTE lastdrive;
    open_display("LASTDRIVE");
    sysvars = get_sysvars();
    printf("SysVars @ %Fp\n", sysvars);
    maybe_change_osmajmin();
    printf("DOS %u.%02u\n", _osmajor, _osminor);
    lastdrive = sysvars[(_osmajor == 3 && _osminor == 0) ? 0x1B :
                        (_osmajor == 2) ?                  0x10 :
                        /* otherwise */                    0x21];
    printf("LASTDRIVE=%c\n", 'A' + lastdrive - 1);
    show_display();
    return 0;
}
```

Listing 3-3a: SYSVARS.C

```
/* SYSVARS.C */
BYTE far *get_sysvars(void)
{
    _asm xor bx, bx
    _asm mov es, bx
    _asm mov ah, 52h
    _asm int 21h
    _asm mov dx, es
    _asm mov ax, bx
    // return value in DX:AX
}
```

Compiling the program (for example, bcc -W lastdriv.c printf.c) results in a Windows executable, LASTDRIV.EXE. Given that the premise of this chapter is that Windows applications must do something special to access undocumented DOS, and given that we have done nothing special here, you would fully expect LASTDRIV to blow up or otherwise do something foolish when you run it under Windows.

Actually, though, LASTDRIV works fine. Figure 3-1 shows that LASTDRIV not only looks like a little Windows program, but the results look reasonable too. In this configuration, LASTDRIVE=M is the correct answer.

Figure 3-1: Running LASTDRIV Under Windows

LASTDRIVE

SysVars @ 1007:0026
DOS 6.00
LASTDRIVE=M

OK

The address for SysVars may look a little funny but hey, the program worked. So what's the problem?

It Doesn't Really Work!

That LASTDRIV got the correct answer was actually just dumb luck. Getting the value of LASTDRIVE out of SysVars just happens to be one of the very few undocumented things that work transparently in a protected mode Windows program. It is in one sense unfortunate that this was the first example we showed because it leads to the expectation that everything will "just work." In fact, this belief was the source of the truly foolish statement in the first edition of *Undocumented DOS* that "Programs written for Microsoft Windows 3.0 can make undocumented DOS calls without any special handling" (p. 70). Not! This statement was written after extensive testing with nothing more than, you guessed it, LASTDRIV.

That LASTDRIV works under Windows is misleading. To see why, let's try another, seemingly similar, program, CURRDRIV. Just as LASTDRIV uses INT 21h Function 52h and SysVars to get the value of LASTDRIVE, instead of calling documented Function 0Eh to get this value, CURRDRIV uses INT 21h Function 5D06h and the Swappable Data Area to get the current drive, rather than calling documented Function 19h. (As noted in Chapter 2, Function 19h in MS-DOS just returns the value of the SDA field.) Listing 3-4 shows CURRDRIV.C. Because we call get_sda() numerous times in this chapter, this function has been moved into a separate file, GETSDA.C (Listing 3-4a).

Listing 3-4: CURRDRIV.C for Windows (Fails!)

```
/* CURRDRIV.C:  bcc -W currdriv.c printf.c */

#include <stdlib.h>
#include <dos.h>
#include "windows.h"
#include "printf.h"

/* get_sda() */
#include "getsda.c"

BYTE get_doc_currdrive(void)
{
    _asm mov ah, 19h
    _asm int 21h
    _asm xor ah, ah
    // return value in AX
}

void do_currdrive(void)
{
    BYTE far *sda;
    BYTE currdrive;
    BYTE doc_currdrive;

    sda = get_sda();
```

```
    printf("SDA @ %Fp\n", sda);

    /* Following line gets wrong results! (Unless if UNDOSMGR.386,
       which supports 21/5D06 in protected mode, is installed.) */
    currdrive = sda[0x16];
    printf("CURRDRIVE=%c (from SDA)\n", 'A' + currdrive);

    doc_currdrive = get_doc_currdrive();
    if (currdrive != doc_currdrive)
        printf("Something wrong! CURRDRIVE=%c\n",
            'A' + doc_currdrive);
}

#ifdef __cplusplus
extern "C" int PASCAL WinMain(HANDLE hInstance, HANDLE hPrevInstance,
    LPSTR lpszCmdLine, int nCmdShow);
#endif

int PASCAL WinMain(HANDLE hInstance, HANDLE hPrevInstance,
    LPSTR lpszCmdLine, int nCmdShow)
{
    open_display("CURRDRIVE");
    do_currdrive();
    show_display();
    return 0;
}
```

Listing 3-4a: GETSDA.C

```
BYTE far *get_sda(void)
{
    _asm push ds
    _asm push si
    _asm mov ax, 5d06h
    _asm int 21h
    _asm jc error
    _asm mov dx, ds
    _asm mov ax, si
    _asm jmp short done
error:
    _asm xor ax, ax
    _asm xor dx, dx
done:
    _asm pop si
    _asm pop ds
    // return value in DX:AX
}
```

CURRDRIV.C really does seem just like LASTDRIV.C. Each program calls an undocumented function, and each program extracts a byte value from a DOS internal data structure whose address the function returns. While LASTDRIV worked, though, CURRDRIV produces totally wrong results, as Figure 3-2 shows.

Figure 3-2: CURRDRIV Messes Up

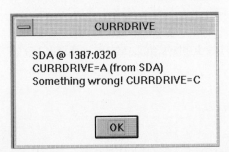

CURRDRIVE

SDA @ 1387:0320
CURRDRIVE=A (from SDA)
Something wrong! CURRDRIVE=C

OK

Not only are the results wrong (CURRDRIV showed drive A: as the current drive, whereas the documented Function 19h returned C:), but running multiple copies of CURRDRIV produces even stranger results. The address displayed for the SDA is different each time. For example, one run of the CURRDRIV showed an address of 1E97:0320 for the SDA, whereas Figure 3-2 shows an address of 1387:0320 for the SDA (the segment for which looks wrong anyhow). The SDA does *not* move around! Something is clearly wrong with the idea that Windows programs can just call any old undocumented DOS function and access any old internal DOS data structure.

At the end of this chapter (see Listing 3-31), we'll write a VxD that changes Windows in such a way CURRDRIV gets correct results. Without this VxD, however, CURRDRIV gets bogus results.

The Dreaded GP Fault

"But, I don't ever call INT 21h Function 5D06h. I've never used the SDA. The only undocumented DOS function I could see using is Function 52h, and the only structure I'm interested in is SysVars. LASTDRIV.C showed that those work." End of story, right?

No. Let's next try grabbing something other than LASTDRIVE out of SysVars. A good example is the pointer to the System File Table chain at offset 4 in SysVars. As Chapter 1 mentions, programs like WIN.COM that need to get the value of FILES= reliably usually do so by walking the SFT chain. SFTWALK.C in Listing 3-5 is a real mode DOS program that uses this technique.

Listing 3-5: SFTWALK.C for Real Mode DOS

```
/* SFTWALK.C -- count FILES= by walking SFTs */

#include <stdlib.h>
#include <stdio.h>
#include <dos.h>

typedef unsigned char BYTE;
typedef unsigned short WORD;

/* get_sysvars() -- see Listing 3-3a */
#include "sysvars.c"

typedef struct _sft {
    struct _sft far *next;
    WORD num;
    // other stuff not used here
    } SFT;

main()
{
    BYTE far *sysvars = get_sysvars();
    SFT far *sft = *((SFT far * far *) &sysvars[4]);
    int files = 0;
    while (FP_OFF(sft) != 0xFFFF)
    {
        files += sft->num;
        printf("SFT @ %Fp -- %u files\n", sft, sft->num);
        sft = sft->next;
    }
    printf("FILES=%d\n", files);
}
```

In addition to printing out the FILES= value, SFTWALK also displays the address and number of files, for each SFT in the chain. For example:

```
SFT @ 0116:00CC -- 5 files
SFT @ 05EB:0000 -- 40 files
FILES=45
```

This output was correct. In this configuration, CONFIG.SYS had FILES=45. However, before we've even turned this into a Windows program, just running the same real mode SFTWALK.EXE in a DOS box under Windows produced interesting results, claiming FILES=55 and showing an extra SFT with 10 entries:

```
SFT @ 0116:00CC -- 5 files
SFT @ 05EB:0000 -- 40 files
SFT @ 1295:0004 -- 10 files
FILES=55
```

We will explore this issue later. For now, the curious reader should check out the description of the Windows SYSTEM.INI PerVMFiles= setting in a reference such as the *Microsoft Windows for Workgroups Resource Kit.*

To start porting SFTWALK.C to Windows, let's for variety use Borland's EasyWin. This requires no change to the source code; merely recompile with bcc -W sftwalk.c. Or you can modify SFTWALK.C to use PRINTF.C from Listing 3-1; it makes no difference.

Either way, when the Windows version of SFTWALK runs, it doesn't work as the seemingly similar LASTDRIV did. Nor does it even produce incorrect results the way CURRDRIV did. Instead, SFT-WALK bombs, producing a general protection violation, or GP fault, as Figure 3-3 shows. In Windows 3.0, the message refers instead to an "Unexpected Application Error," the dreaded UAE.

Figure 3-3: Windows Version of SFTWALK GP Faults

```
        Application Error
SFTWALK caused a General Protection Fault in
module SFTWALK.EXE at 0001:01A4.
```

If SFTWALK is compiled with debugging symbols and run under a debugger such as Turbo Debugger or Soft-ICE/Windows (WINICE), the debugger catches the GP fault and highlights the offending code in SFTWALK.C:

```
files += sft->num;

les bx, [bp-8]
add cx, es:[bx+4]   ; GP fault occurs here!
```

The GP fault is just an interrupt (INT 0Dh) that the microprocessor sends to an application when it has violated one of the many "rules of the road" in protected mode. These rules are what make this processor mode protected in the first place. For example, segments in protected mode have specified sizes, and if a program reads or writes to an offset past that size, the processor decides that the program has violated protection and issues a GP fault.

One rule of protected mode is that you can't load any arbitrary number into a segment register. It must be a special number, called a *selector*, which corresponds to a processor data structure called a *descriptor*. Most randomly-generated numbers, if used as ssss:oooo pointers and dereferenced (that is, their ssss portion loaded into a segment register such as ES), will GP fault. In any given configuration, most numbers *don't* correspond to descriptors; the address space is sparse. This is largely where the protection comes from; its protection is only probabilistic. Randomly draw enough numbers from a hat, and one of them will happen to be a valid selector. In practice, though, this protection works pretty well. In contrast to the havoc it would wreak in real mode, the following insane program is 99-44/100% likely to be terminated with a GP fault in protected mode:

```
main()
{
    unsigned char far *fp;
    for (;;)
    {   // see Listing 2-10 for MK_FP()
        unsigned far *fp = MK_FP(rand(), rand());
```

```
        *fp = 666;
    }
}
```

The lesson is that protected mode pointers must correspond to descriptors. These descriptors are eight-byte structures, maintained generally by an operating system such as Windows and used by the chip itself whenever a new value is loaded into a segment register. A descriptor contains information about a segment, such as the specified size of the segment. The size actually, is stored as the *limit*, that is, as the size minus one, that is, as the last valid byte offset within the segment. Besides the segment's limit, a descriptor also contains a segment's attributes (code/data, read/write, and so forth), and its *base address*.

This notion of base address is crucial for this chapter. We will rely on it heavily to get to undocumented DOS data structures from protected mode. Recall that in real mode, address ssss:oooo corresponds to the memory location (ssss * 10h) + oooo, so that 1007:0000, for example, points to memory location 10070h. Protected mode introduces a small but crucial change. There are still ssss:oooo pointers, but the ssss part means something entirely different.

In essence, protected mode introduces an extra level of indirection in memory addressing. A selector value such as 1007h, for example, is an index into a descriptor table. This value is not in any way related to physical memory location 10070h. Actual memory addresses are instead found inside the descriptor, in its base-address field. If you actually wanted to get to a memory location such as 10070h, a protected mode pointer such as 1007:0000 would do you absolutely no good at all. Instead, you would need a selector whose descriptor had a *base address* of 10070h. The value of the selector itself would be irrelevant. Remember, the selector just represents an index into a descriptor table.

It is important to note that a base address is not necessarily a physical memory address, that is, a value that the processor can put on the bus. If paging is enabled on the 80386 or higher, it is instead a *linear address*. This corresponds to yet another set of tables, and yet another level of indirection. Page tables contain either an actual physical address or an indication that a page is not present; this is the basis for virtual memory (see "Exploring Demand-Paged Virtual Memory in Windows Enhanced Mode," *Microsoft Systems Journal*, December 1992).

Fortunately, 99% of this is transparent. Programs load values into segment registers, just like in real mode, and the processor takes care of reaching out to the correct part of memory. It is also fortunate, with all these extra tables and levels of indirection, that the processor contains several caches, which save it from having to consult these tables every time you read or write memory.

So where are we? Our three programs, LASTDRIV, CURRDRIV, and SFTWALK, all do more or less the same thing, yet we get three wildly different results. LASTDRIV works properly, SFTWALK GP faults, and CURRDRIV doesn't GP fault but instead produces bogus results. What can we conclude about the Windows DOS extender's support for undocumented DOS?

- LASTDRIV works, so the SysVars pointer must be valid. The program didn't GP fault, so SysVars must be a valid protected mode pointer. INT 21h AH=52h returned this pointer, so in Windows protected mode, this function must return a protected mode pointer to SysVars.
- CURRDRIV doesn't GP fault, so the SDA pointer must at least be legal. It's a legitimate protected mode pointer. But the results are bogus! Conclusion: it must actually point, not to the SDA, but to somewhere else. Thus, INT 21h AX=5D06h in Windows protected mode returns a protected mode pointer, but not to the SDA.
- SFTWALK GP faults because the SFT pointer is invalid in protected mode. That means it must have been a real mode pointer. But we got this pointer out of SysVars, to which INT 21h AH=52h returned a valid protected mode pointer. Conclusion: in Windows protected mode, INT 21h AH=52h returns a protected mode pointer to SysVars, but any pointers inside SysVars itself are still real mode, and will need to be translated.

The implications of the earlier discussion of descriptors and selectors for getting at undocumented DOS data structures from protected mode Windows should now be clear. To get at the SFT, for instance, you can't load the real mode address of the SFT into ES:BX and expect it to work. Instead, you must allocate a descriptor, put the real mode address of the SFT into the descriptor's base address field, and then use whatever selector corresponds to that descriptor as the ssss portion of your protected mode ssss:oooo pointer. We're getting a good bit ahead of ourselves here, but in the Windows API the function AllocSelector() allocates both a descriptor and a selector; the formerly undocumented function SetSelectorBase() sets the base address. We will be relying heavily on these functions in this chapter.

A DPMI Shell

To gain a better understanding of what is going on and what we can do about it, let's forget about Windows programs for a moment and look at DPMI programming. Using the DPMI services that Windows Enhanced mode provides, real mode DOS programs can switch into protected mode. While Windows Standard mode also provides DPMI, it is only accessible to Windows programs, not to programs running in the Standard mode DOS box. Memory managers such as 386MAX and, via an add-in, QEMM, also provide DPMI services.

Before we launch into using DPMI, it's worth noting an error in the Microsoft Windows SDK documentation. The very brief SDK discussion of DPMI ("Windows Applications with MS-DOS Functions," *Programmer's Reference, Volume 1: Overview*, Chapter 20) states that Windows 3.0 and later support DPMI 1.0. This is not true. Both Windows 3.0 and 3.1 support version 0.9 of the DPMI specification. Furthermore, not all DPMI functions are supported, especially in Standard mode. On the other hand, Enhanced mode does support a few DPMI 1.0 functions, via commonly-available VxDs. The SDK also claims that only seven DPMI functions are required for Windows applications. This certainly isn't true either. What a mess! Fortunately, the functions we'll need here are stable across all the different DPMI implementations.

We can use DPMI to take the DOS versions of LASTDRIV, CURRDRIV, and SFTWALK and execute them in protected mode. By running in protected mode but sticking to character mode DOS, we can separate the Windows-specific issues from the more general protected mode issues. Comparing the behavior of the protected mode DOS versions of these programs with the behavior of the Windows versions also yields some important insights about Windows.

A normal real mode DOS program can easily switch itself into protected mode using one DPMI call, INT 2Fh AX=1687h. Moving the DPMI-specific code into a separate "shell," which makes this call and then hands off control to the rest of the program, can make using DPMI even easier. In DPMISH.C (Listing 3-6), main() calls the function real_main(), then uses DPMI to switch into protected mode, and then calls pmode_main(). DPMISH expects an application such as LASTDRIV to supply real_main() and pmode_main(), and to #include DPMISH.H (see Listing 3-7). Besides DPMISH, the program also needs to link with CTRL_C, a tiny assembly language module which assists with Ctrl-C handling (see Listing 3-8).

Listing 3-6: DPMISH.C

```
/*
DPMISH.C
Shell to run a simple C program in protected mode under DPMI
Andrew Schulman, February 1993
from "Undocumented DOS", 2nd edition (Addison-Wesley, 1993)
(Changed version of DPMISHEL, from MSJ, Oct. 1992, Dec. 1992)

Does Ctrl-C handling: see CTRL_C.ASM
Must be compiled small model to use C run-time library
Calls real_main(), switches into protected mode, then calls pmode_main()

To build a DPMI app:
```

```
bcc -2 -DDPMI_APP foo.c dpmish.c ctrl_c.asm
*/

#include <stdlib.h>
#include <stdio.h>
#include <dos.h>
#include "dpmish.h"

void _dos_exit(int retval)
{
    _asm mov ah, 04ch
    _asm mov al, byte ptr retval
    _asm int 21h
}

// Call the DPMI Mode Detection function (INT 2Fh AX=1686h) to see
// if we are *already* running in protected mode under DPMI.
// See 3.1 DDK _Device Driver Adaptation Guide_, pp. 585-586
int dpmi_present(void)
{
    unsigned _ax;
    _asm mov ax, 1686h
    _asm int 2Fh
    _asm mov _ax, ax /* 2F/1686 ret 0 if DPMI is present */
    return (! _ax);  /* turn it around so 0 if *not* present */
}

// Call the DPMI function for Obtaining the Real to Protected Mode
// Switch Entry Point (INT 2Fh AX=1687h), to determine if DPMI is
// available and, if so, switch into protected mode by calling
// the Switch Entry Point. See DPMI 0.9 spec.
int dpmi_init(void)
{
    void (far *dpmi)();
    unsigned hostdata_seg, hostdata_para, dpmi_flags;
    _asm push si
    _asm push di
    _asm mov ax, 1687h              /* test for DPMI presence */
    _asm int 2Fh
    _asm and ax, ax
    _asm jz gotdpmi                 /* if (AX == 0) DPMI is present */
    _asm jmp nodpmi
gotdpmi:
    _asm mov dpmi_flags, bx
    _asm mov hostdata_para, si    /* paras for DPMI host private data */
    _asm mov word ptr dpmi, di
    _asm mov word ptr dpmi+2, es /* DPMI protected mode switch entry point */
    _asm pop di
    _asm pop si

    if (_dos_allocmem(hostdata_para, &hostdata_seg) != 0)
        fail("can't allocate memory");

    dpmi_flags &= ~1;   /* this is a 16-bit protected mode program */

    /* enter protected mode */
    _asm mov ax, hostdata_seg
    _asm mov es, ax
    _asm mov ax, dpmi_flags
    (*dpmi)();
    _asm jc nodpmi     /* carry set if error */
    /* in protected mode now:  segment registers changed! */
    return dpmi_present();   /* double check */
nodpmi:
    return 0;
}

void dpmi_setprotvect(int intno, void (interrupt far *func)(void))
```

```
{
    _asm mov ax, 0205h
    _asm mov bl, byte ptr intno
    _asm mov cx, cs       /* word ptr func+2 */
    _asm mov dx, word ptr func
    _asm int 31h
}
// INT 23h handler under DPMI can't do the usual DOS INT 23h stuff
// needs to be on page locked with 31/0600??
// problem:  compiler has hard-wired (real mode) _loadds!

#if 1
// pull in CTRL_C.ASM (Listing 3-8)
#ifdef __cplusplus
extern "C" void interrupt far ctrl_c(void);
#else
extern void interrupt far ctrl_c(void);
#endif
#else
int ctrl_c_hit = 0;

void interrupt far ctrl_c(void)
{
    ctrl_c_hit++;
}
#endif

main(int argc, char *argv[])
{
    int ret;
    // actually, if already in pmode, real_main() still runs
    // (this is for debugging under 286|DOS-Extender)
    if (real_main(argc, argv) != 0)
        return 1;
    flushall(); // flush all buffers before switch into protected mode
                // so I/O redirection works properly

    if (dpmi_present())
        printf("Already in protected mode\n");
    else if (dpmi_init())
        printf("Switched into protected mode via DPMI\n");
    else
        fail("This program requires DPMI");

    // now in protected mode: segment registers have changed

    dpmi_setprotvect(0x23, ctrl_c); // install Ctrl-C handler
    ret = pmode_main(argc, argv);   // call the application's pmode_main
    flushall();                     // flush all buffers before exiting
    _dos_exit(ret);                 // must exit via 21/4C!
}
```

Listing 3-7: DPMISH.H

```
/*
DPMISH.H -- see DPMISH.C
Andrew Schulman, February 1993
from "Undocumented DOS", 2nd edition (Addison-Wesley, 1993)
*/

#ifdef __BORLANDC__
#ifndef __SMALL__
#error DPMISH requires small model
#endif
#else /* Microsoft C */
#ifndef M_I86SM
#error DPMISH requires small model
```

```
#endif
#endif
#ifndef DPMI_APP
#define DPMI_APP
#endif

#ifdef __BORLANDC__
#define _dos_allocmem(x,y)  (allocmem(x,y) != -1)
#endif

void _dos_exit(int retval);
int dpmi_present(void);
int dpmi_init(void);

/* unfortunately, the app has to check Ctrl-C itself! */
extern int ctrl_c_hit;

/* these functions to be defined by app */
extern int real_main(int argc, char *argv[]);
extern int pmode_main(int argc, char *argv[]);
extern void fail(const char *s, ...);  // app's fail() must call _dos_exit()
```

Listing 3-8: CTRL_C.ASM

```
; CTRL_C.ASM -- for use with DPMISHEL

dosseg
.model small

public _ctrl_c_hit
public _ctrl_c

.data
_ctrl_c_hit dw  0

.code
_ctrl_c proc far
    inc _ctrl_c_hit    ; using app's DS
    iret
_ctrl_c endp
end
```

A program that uses this facility starts off in main() in DPMISH.C. As its first activity, main() calls the program's real_main() function. The program uses this function to perform any initialization that must occur in real mode. If real_main() returns zero, main() takes this as an indication that it is okay to switch into protected mode. Main() next calls dpmi_present() to see if the program is somehow *already* in protected mode. It uses INT 2Fh AX=1686h to perform this test. *In a Windows program, dpmi_present() would always return TRUE*—this is largely what distinguishes Windows programs from DOS programs running under Windows. Windows programs are automatically DPMI clients. We won't get into how a DOS program might somehow have started off in protected mode already, other than to note that Phar Lap Software's 286|DOS-Extender can help run these DPMISH programs under a Windows debugger such as CodeView or Turbo Debugger.

Assuming that real_main() says it's okay to switch to protected mode and that dpmi_present() doesn't say we're already in protected mode, DPMISH next calls dpmi_init(). This function uses INT 2Fh AX=1687h to get the DPMI Real to Protected Mode Switch Entry Point, and then calls this function, switching the program into protected mode. In DPMISH.C, this appears as (*dpmi)(). It is interesting to step over this line of code in WINICE (most other debuggers blow up when you step over this line). The (*dpmi)() call causes the program's segment registers to suddenly change out from under it. The tiny test program in Listing 3-9 (DPMITEST.C) shows this change. This program calls the same function, print_regs(), from both real_main() and pmode_main().

Listing 3-9: DPMITEST.C

```
/*
DPMITEST.C
bcc -DDPMI_APP -2 dpmitest.c dpmish.c ctrl_c.asm

Sample output:
CS=165Ch DS=17D5h
Switched into protected mode via DPMI
CS=0097h DS=008Fh
*/
#include <stdlib.h>
#include <stdio.h>
#include <dos.h>
#include "dpmish.h"

void print_regs(void)
{
    struct SREGS s;
    segread(&s);
    printf("CS=%04Xh DS=%04Xh\n", s.cs, s.ds);
}
void fail(const char *s, ...)           { puts(s); _dos_exit(1); }
int real_main(int argc, char *argv[])   { print_regs(); return 0; }
int pmode_main(int argc, char *argv[])  { print_regs(); return 0; }
```

Naturally, the new protected mode selectors that DPMI creates and loads into CS, DS, and SS on the program's behalf have base addresses that correspond to the program's initial real mode segment addresses. In the output from DPMITEST shown at the top of Listing 3-9, selector 0097h happened to have a base address of 165C0h, and selector 008Fh had a base address of 17D50h. You can verify this in WINICE or (getting ahead of ourselves again) with the DPMI Get Segment Base Address function (INT 31h AX=6). By the time DPMISH calls a program's pmode_main() function, the program is running in protected mode. The environment in which pmode_main() runs, then, is just like that of a Windows program, except that the program is in character mode and the familiar versions of functions such as printf() still work. This is why DPMISH is handy, even given the existence of libraries such as EasyWin, QuickWin, and WINIO, or the ease of cobbling together a Windows printf() from the MessageBox() function.

But the DPMISH program call C run-time library routines only if it is compiled in small model. Many of these library routines end up making INT 21h calls, thereby using Windows' protected mode DOS extender. DPMISH simply assumes that the presence of DPMI also means that protected mode INT 21h is present. This questionable assumption is discussed below; in practice it works. But why small model? Because, as you've just seen, the program that uses DPMISH is going to have its segment registers changed out from under it. The program cannot hang onto any far pointers after executing the (*dpmi)() call to switch into protected mode. The C run-time library undoubtedly does hang onto pointers for buffers and so on, so we use a small model to make sure these won't be far pointers with segments in them that will become invalid after the jump into hyperspace (oops, protected mode).

Trying Out Undocumented DOS from DPMISH Programs

We now take the Windows version of LASTDRIV and modify it to also run under DPMISH. We take the code that LASTDRIV executes inside of WinMain() or main() and move the code to a separate function, do_lastdrive(). The DPMI_APP version of LASTDRIV then calls do_lastdrive() from both real_main() and pmode_main(). Listing 3-10 shows this new version of LASTDRIV.

Listing 3-10: LASTDRIV for DPMI or Windows

```
/*
LASTDRIV.C
```

```
Windows:   bcc -W lastdriv.c printf.c
DPMI:      bcc -DDPMI_APP -2 lastdriv.c dpmish.c ctrl_c.asm
*/

#include <stdlib.h>
#include <dos.h>
#ifdef DPMI_APP
#include <stdio.h>
#include "dpmish.h"

typedef unsigned char BYTE;
#else
#include "windows.h"
#include "printf.h"
#endif

void maybe_change_osmajmin(void)
{
    _asm mov ax, 3306h
    _asm xor bx, bx
    _asm int 21h
    _asm or bx, bx
    _asm jz osmajmin_ok
    _asm mov byte ptr _osmajor, bl
    _asm mov byte ptr _osminor, bh
osmajmin_ok:;
}

/* get_sysvars() -- see Listing 3-3a */
#include "sysvars.c"
void do_lastdrive(void)
{
    BYTE far *sysvars;
    BYTE lastdrive;
    sysvars = get_sysvars();
    printf("SysVars @ %Fp\n", sysvars);
    maybe_change_osmajmin();
    printf("DOS %u.%02u\n", _osmajor, _osminor);
    lastdrive = sysvars[(_osmajor == 3 && _osminor == 0) ? 0x1B :
                        (_osmajor == 2) ?                  0x10 :
                        /* otherwise */                    0x21];
    printf("LASTDRIVE=%c\n", 'A' + lastdrive - 1);
}

#ifdef DPMI_APP
void fail(const char *s, ...) { puts(s); _dos_exit(1); }

int real_main(int argc, char *argv[])
{
    printf("In real mode:\n");
    do_lastdrive();
    printf("\n");
    return 0;
}

int pmode_main(int argc, char *argv[])
{
    printf("In protected mode:\n");
    do_lastdrive();
    return 0;
}
#else
// Windows program
#ifdef __cplusplus
extern "C" int PASCAL WinMain(HANDLE hInstance, HANDLE hPrevInstance,
    LPSTR lpszCmdLine, int nCmdShow);
#endif

int PASCAL WinMain(HANDLE hInstance, HANDLE hPrevInstance,
```

```
            LPSTR lpszCmdLine, int nCmdShow)
{
    open_display("LASTDRIVE");
    do_lastdrive();
    show_display();
    return 0;
}
#endif
```

The DPMI version of LASTDRIV works, just as the Windows version did. There seems to be some commonality between Windows programs and protected mode DOS programs. But while the DPMI version of LASTDRIV gets the same correct LASTDRIVE=M answer from pmode_main() as from real_main(), the address that INT 21h Function 52h returns for SysVars in protected mode is different. The program's output looks like this:

```
C:\UNDOC2\CHAP3>lastdriv
In real mode:
SysVars @ 0116:0026
DOS 6.00
LASTDRIVE=M

Switched into protected mode via DPMI
In protected mode:
SysVars @ 00AF:0026
DOS 6.00
LASTDRIVE=M
```

Note that SysVars was located at 0116:0026 in real mode but at 00AF:0026 in protected mode. Did SysVars move? No, of course not. Instead, this is just another confirmation of what you saw before: INT 21h Function 52h in Windows returns a protected mode pointer to SysVars. If a debugger such as WINICE is used to run LASTDRIV, you can see that 00AFh is, in fact, a protected mode selector with the base address 01160h. In other words, it addresses exactly the same memory as real mode pointer 0116:0026. Below, LDT is the WINICE command for inspecting selectors; LDT refers to the Local Descriptor Table:

```
:ldt 00af
00AF    Data16    Base=00001160    Lim=0000FFFF    DPL=3    P    RW
```

We can also use DPMISH to turn CURRDRIV into a protected mode DOS program. It's not worth showing the code here because it relates to the code in Listing 3-4 in the same way that Listing 3-10 relates to Listing 3-3. We just hack the code in WinMain() so that pmode_main() calls it.

This protected mode DOS version of LASTDRIV gets an incorrect answer, just like the Windows version did. Oddly enough, the same thing happens even if you run CURRDRIV under a different DPMI server, such as 386MAX 6.0. The important lesson here, and the reason for this long detour into DPMISH, is that protected mode DOS programs running under Windows behave just like character mode Windows programs. The environment for pmode_main() in a DPMISH program is a lot like WinMain(). A DPMISH program—or any other DOS program that switches itself into protected mode with INT 2Fh AX=1687h—is a lot like a character mode Windows program. Turning this around, the point is really that *Windows programs are nothing more than protected mode DOS programs*. Windows is just a protected mode extension to DOS. Still wondering why we're talking so much about Windows in a book on DOS?

The Windows DOS Extenders

Since MS-DOS is not a protected mode operating system, how can there even be such things as protected mode DOS programs? The illusion of a protected mode version of DOS must be *faked*.

This is the role of the DOS extender. In Windows Enhanced mode, the DOS extender is contained in the DOSMGR VxD, which we discussed at length in Chapter 1, and which makes such heavy use of undocumented DOS. The DPMI server in Enhanced mode—that is, the code that services functions such as INT 2Fh AX=1687h and the DPMI INT 31h API—is provided by the Virtual Machine Manager. VMM and DOSMGR are both part of WIN386.EXE (DOS386.EXE in Chicago). In Standard mode, DOSX.EXE contains both the DOS extender and the DPMI server.

The documentation for the DOS extenders in Windows is the scant four-page chapter on "Windows Applications with MS-DOS Functions" in the Windows 3.1 SDK *Programmer's Reference, Volume 1: Overview*. In addition to the largely inaccurate description of DPMI noted earlier, the documentation also provides a too-short list of DPMI functions available to Windows programs. This chapter then lists both "unsupported" and "partially supported" DOS functions. The section on partially supported functions contains some important notes about IOCTL calls (INT 21h AH=44h). There is no mention of any supported or unsupported ROM BIOS functions. No mention is made one way or the other of important DOS extensions such as MSCDEX. The documentation does make the important point that "if a software-interrupt function is completely register-based without any pointers, segment registers, or stack parameters, that function should work with Windows running in protected mode."

Besides this SDK documentation, there is an internal Microsoft document, "MS-DOS API Extensions for DPMI Hosts" (October 31, 1990), which devotes about thirty pages to this same subject. The brief chapter in the SDK appears to have been boiled down from this more extensive document. For example, the 1990 document discusses 32-bit DOS extenders. The DOS file read and write calls (INT 21h AH=3Fh and 40h) have the count register (ECX) extended to 32 bits, allowing 32-bit programs to perform DOS file I/O of more than 64K bytes at a time. The Enhanced mode DOS extender provides this 32-bit support (one of our tech reviewers tells us this 32-bit support is "totally bogus"). The document also discusses the Ctrl-Break (INT 23h) and critical error (INT 24h) handlers under Windows. Finally, there is a substantial discussion of ROM BIOS functionality, including low-level disk access (INT 13h) in protected mode. Microsoft should update this documentation for Windows 3.1 and make it available to all developers.

Given the paucity of documentation for the Windows DOS extenders, we're on our own trying to figure out what they support. How good is this fake protected mode DOS? One good test is of course what undocumented functionality this DOS supports. From LASTDRIV and CURRDRIV, we've gathered that Windows supports Function 52h in protected mode and does not support Function 5D06h. But how can we be sure? And what does "support" and "not support" mean here, anyway?

The small program in Listing 3-11, UNDOC.C, helps clarify this question. UNDOC can be built as a Windows program using EasyWin, Quick Win, or WINIO, or hacked slightly to use PRINTF.C from Listing 3-1. The program merely prints out the addresses of some important DOS internal data structures, as returned from various INT 21h functions or as found within SysVars.

Listing 3-11: UNDOC.C

```
/* UNDOC.C */
#include <stdlib.h>
#include <dos.h>
#include <stdio.h>

/* get_sysvars() -- see Listing 3-3a */
#include "sysvars.c"

void far *get_sft(void)
{
    unsigned char far * far *sysvars = get_sysvars();
    return *(sysvars+1);    // sysvars[4]
}

void far *get_dpb(void)
{
    unsigned char far * far *sysvars = get_sysvars();
    return *sysvars;        // sysvars[0]
}
```

```
void far *get_cds(void)
{
    unsigned char far *sysvars = (unsigned char far *) get_sysvars();
    return *((void far * far *) &sysvars[0x16]);
}
/* get_sda() -- see Listing 3-4a */
#include "getsda.c"
unsigned char far *get_indos(void)
{
    _asm mov ah, 34h
    _asm int 21h
    _asm mov dx, es
    _asm mov ax, bx
}
main()
{
    printf("SysVars @ %Fp\n", get_sysvars());        // supported!
    printf("CDS @ %Fp\n", get_cds());
    printf("SFT @ %Fp\n", get_sft());
    printf("DPB @ %Fp\n", get_dpb());
    printf("SDA @ %Fp\n", get_sda());                 // not!
    printf("InDOS @ %Fp\n", get_indos());             // now doc!
    if (get_indos() != (get_sda() + 1))
        printf("Something funny with SDA and InDOS!\n");
    return 0;
}
```

Figure 3-4 shows output from UNDOC. Because the InDOS flag is kept at offset 1 in the SDA, the address that get_sda() (INT 21h AX=5D06h) returns should be one less than the address get_indos() (INT 21h AH=34h) returns. DOS function 34h, which returns the address of the InDOS flag, was finally documented in DOS 5.0 (see Chapter 1), so it is reasonable to expect that the Windows DOS extenders would support this function. But UNDOC's output shows that the get_sda() and get_indos() return values are inconsistent. As we suspected, Windows doesn't support Function 5D06h.

Figure 3-4: UNDOC Under Windows

```
SysVars @ 1007:0026
CDS @ 06B2:0000
SFT @ 0116:00CC
DPB @ 0116:1368
SDA @ 1E67:0320
InDOS @ 1007:0321
Something funny with SDA and InDOS!
```

That UNDOC is able to successfully extract values from SysVars indicates that, as noted before, get_sysvars() (INT 21h AH=52h) must be returning a valid protected mode pointer. The pointers that UNDOC displays within SysVars, however, look like real mode pointers; the WINICE debugger confirmed, for example, that the CDS was at 06b2:0000. The level of support for Function 52h is, of necessity, somewhat uneven.

Notice, however, that, whatever the level of support Windows provides for the functions that UNDOC calls, the program does not GP fault. A GP fault occurs when you dereference an invalid pointer. UNDOC *displays* some pointers which are invalid in protected mode, but does not *dereference* them. There is a difference between printf("%Fp", fp) and *fp.

It is instructive to run UNDOC in Enhanced mode under the debug version of Windows. Recall from Chapter 1 that Windows Enhanced mode sits atop WIN386.EXE, which is a collection of VxDs. The Enhanced mode DOS extender is part of the DOSMGR VxD which, in turn, is contained in WIN386.EXE. The Windows Device Driver Kit contains a debug version of WIN386, which displays many more messages and which is slower than the retail version of WIN386. If you run UNDOC under the debug WIN386 and in turn run Windows under a low-level debugger such as WINICE or Microsoft's WDEB386, the DOSMGR DOS extender issues the following message:

```
WARNING: DOS INT 21 call AX=5D06 will not be translated.
         Use of this call is not supported from Prot
         mode applications.
```

DOSMGR also displays this message if you run a protected mode version of the CURRDRIV program.

Oddly enough, if you are a Borland C++ user even *compiling* UNDOC.C, or any other program for that matter, produces this same message! It turns out that Borland C++ assumes that all DPMI servers support INT 21h AX=5D06h in protected mode. It is not clear why Borland calls this function, but under Windows the function is returning the wrong value. Perhaps this is why Borland C++ occasionally blows up when it runs under Windows or another DPMI host. (A reviewer says "Actually, it is because Borland doesn't lock the pages for its interrupt handlers.")

Actually, Borland C++ is making a much bigger assumption than merely support for INT 21h AX=5D06h in protected mode. When running under DPMI, it assumes that all of INT 21h is supported in protected mode. But protected mode INT 21h is not part of the DPMI specification; it is provided by a DOS extender, which is something entirely different from a DPMI server. (As noted above, in Windows Enhanced mode the DPMI server is in VMM, and the DOS extender is in DOSMGR.) Running Borland C++ under the debug WIN386 also produces many occurrences of the message "Protected mode EMS calls not supported," so apparently BCC is making INT 67h calls in protected mode too (why?).

In practice, it is a fairly reasonable assumption that the presence of DPMI means that you also have protected mode INT 21h. As we saw, DPMISH also makes this assumption, which is why you can use the C run-time library's printf(), and other C run-time library() functions that depend on INT 21h, even after the program has switched into protected mode. For example, calling printf() in protected mode eventually calls the DOS Write File function (INT 21h AH=40h). The Windows DOS extender provides a protected mode version of this function. DPMISH and Borland C++ simply assume this will work. Borland C++ got burned on Function 5D06h, but for the most part this assumption is valid under Windows.

On the other hand, it is not a *necessary* assumption. As we will see in more detail shortly, DPMI provides services such as INT 31h AX=0300h (Simulate Real Mode Interrupt) to call down to real mode. Any program that uses DPMI, rather than assume there's reliable support for INT 21h in protected mode, can instead call INT 21h in real mode. For example, the first edition of *Undocumented DOS* (pp. 74-80) contained a DPMI sample program, LDDPMI, that was actually far more cautious than we've been here in DPMISH. Instead of using the C run-time library's printf(), and thereby relying on the barely documented DOS extender in Windows, LDDPMI.C included the functions pmode_putchar(), pmode_puts(), and pmode_printf(), which called down to real mode INT 21h using INT 31h AX=0300h.

Given the poverty of Microsoft's documentation for the Windows DOS extenders, it is probably a good idea to be conservative and make protected mode calls only to those INT 21h functions that Microsoft's documentation states are actually supported. This would mean that, even though our get_sysvars() function in Listing 3-3a seems to work, it would be safer not to trust this function. We will produce a different version of get_sysvars() later in this chapter (see Listing 3-18). Certainly, get_sda() *must* be changed (see Listing 3-27).

Inside the DOSMGR DOS Extender

But how can you find out exactly what function one of the Windows DOS extenders supports? We have danced around this issue enough; how can we actually see what the Windows DOS extender is doing? By looking at the code, of course. In Chapter 1, we examined the DOSMGR VxD to see which undocumented DOS functions it calls. You can also see which protected mode undocumented DOS calls it supports, and how. This will help clarify what is meant by "support" or "not support." For Standard mode, you would need to examine DOSX.EXE; here, we'll focus entirely on the Enhanced mode DOS extender in DOSMGR. As in Chapter 1, DOSMGR was disassembled using the author's Windows Source product from V Communications.

DOSMGR is a piece of 32-bit protected mode code running at Ring 0, which is the highest privilege level. Windows applications making INT 21h calls, on the other hand, are generally 16-bit and run at Ring 3, which is the lowest privilege level. These two types of code are worlds apart. How does DOSMGR arrange to have its protected mode INT 21h handler run whenever a Windows program opens a file, for example?

Among the many other things it does during the Sys_Critical_Init event, DOSMGR installs a protected mode INT 21h handler, using the VMM Set_PM_Int_Vector function. The address DOSMGR passes to Set_PM_Int_Vector is that of a callback, which programs that call INT 21h fom protected mode end up using to (unknowingly) call code in the VxD. As shown in Listing 3-12, the VMM Allocate_PM_Call_Back function creates this callback.

Listing 3-12: Installing the Enhanced Mode DOS Extender

```
06F5C        mov eax, 21h               ; INT 21h
06F71        mov esi, PM_INT21          ; address of DOS extender! (see Listing 3-13)
06F76        call    SetPMIntVect       ; PM = protected mode
; ...
     SetPMIntVect:
06F8B        mov edx,eax                ; reference data = 21h
06F8D        VMMCall Allocate_PM_Call_Back
06F93        mov ecx,eax                ; segment:offset of callback
06F95        xchg    eax,edx            ; EAX = interrupt number (21h)
06F96        movzx   edx,dx             ; EDX = handler offset
06F99        shr ecx,10h                ; CX = handler segment
06F9C        VMMCall Set_PM_Int_Vector
```

The protected mode INT 21h handler that DOSMGR installs in this way will be called any time a Windows program (or a DOS program running in protected mode, like one of our DPMISH creations) makes an INT 21h call. As shown in Listing 3-13, the code for this handler, PM_INT21, is very simple.

Listing 3-13: The Enhanced Mode DOS Extender

```
          PM_INT21:
00C48        VMMCall Simulate_Iret
00C4E        movzx eax, [ebp.Client_AH]       ; get INT 21h func #
00C52        cmp eax, 6Ch                     ; is it one we know?
00C55        ja short UNKNOWN_FUNC
00C57        movzx edx, byte ptr FUNC_TYPE[eax]   ; get func type
00C5E        mov edx, dword ptr XLAT_MACRO[edx*4]  ; get V86MMGR script
00C65        VxDCall V86MMGR_Xlat_API         ; run the script
00C6B     UNKNOWN_FUNC:
00C6B        mov edx, INT21_DEFAULT           ; default script
00C70        VxDCall V86MMGR_Xlat_API         ; run the script
```

In other words, the DOSMGR protected mode INT 21h handler looks to see if the function number specified in AH is valid. If it is, DOSMGR uses the AH function number as an index into the first of two tables. This first table groups the DOS functions into different categories, according to their input and output register usage (the function's "signature") and whether or not they need any special treatment.

For example, functions 39h (Create Directory), 3Ah (Delete Directory), and 3Dh (Open File) all take strings in DS:DX; they return values in AX, as well as the carry flag. DOSMGR handles protected mode calls to all three functions in the same way. It takes the string from DS:DX, copies it to a transfer buffer in conventional memory, switches to real mode (actually V86 mode), puts the real mode address of the transfer buffer into DS:DX, reissues the INT 21h call, and then jumps back to protected mode. Given that the many different INT 21h functions actually require only a handful of different treatments, it makes sense to classify them according to type. This is very similar to what one would do in Remote Procedure Call (RPC) over a network. In many ways, writing a DOS extender is similar to RPC programming.

DOSMGR then takes this INT 21h function type and uses it to index into a second table, which holds offsets to translation macros. The V86MMGR VxD (also part of WIN386.EXE) provides an API Translation service, documented in the Windows DDK, which helps build DOS extenders and other API translation ("xlat") layers. The V86MMGR service is actually a set of script macros defined in the DDK header file V86MMGR.INC, and the V86MMGR_Xlat_API function is a little interpreter that runs these script macros. (They sure do like p-code over at Microsoft.) V86MMGR also provides access to the transfer buffer (xlat buffer) in conventional memory. The SYSTEM.INI [386Enh] XlatBufferSize= setting, documented in the *Windows for Workgroups Resource Kit*, controls the size of this buffer; its default size is 8k bytes (4k in Windows 3.0).

DOSMGR uses V86MMGR XLAT API script macros to implement the DOS extender. The BIOSXLAT VxD also uses these macros, for example to support INT 13h disk calls in protected mode. As the simplest example, consider a function that requires no special handling, such as INT 21h AH=30h (Get Version). DOSMGR can just have this call passed down ("reflected") to DOS. DOSMGR does so using the following very simple V86MMGR macro:

```
Xlat_API_Exec_Int 21h
```

V86MMGR.INC defines Xlat_API_Exec-Int like so:

```
Xlat_Exec_Int EQU 000h
Xlat_API_Exec_Int MACRO Int_Number
    db Xlat_Exec_Int
    db Int_Number
    ENDM
```

Thus, the DOS extender's code for the default INT 21h handler is simply the two bytes 00h 21h, the address of which DOSMGR passes to V86MMGR_Xlat_API. These macros can make disassembly of DOSMGR a bit difficult; however, V Communications has an XLAT utility that translates these macros.

What does V86MMGR_Xlat_API do with these bytes? It uses the first one as an index into a table of handlers and then increments past the first byte, leaving the specific handler to deal with any remaining bytes. It then calls the handler, by "returning" to it:

```
      V86MMGR_Xlat_API      proc near
0015B  push    eax                    ; EDX = pointer to script
0015C  movzx   eax,byte ptr [edx]  ; get command code from first byte
0015F  inc edx                        ; move past it
00160  mov eax,dword ptr XLAT_FUNCTAB[eax*4]    ; find handler
00167  xchg    eax,[esp]              ; put its address on stack
0016A  retn                           ; "return" to it
      V86MMGR_Xlat_API      endp
```

Listing 3-14 shows V86MMGR's handler for Xlat_API_Exec_Int, which reflects protected mode software interrupts to V86 mode.

Listing 3-14: V86MMGR Code to Handle Xlat_API_Exec_Int

```
0016B  push    eax
0016C  movzx   eax,byte ptr [edx]  ; get byte #2 (INT num) from script
0016F  VMMcall Begin_Nest_V86_Exec ; set up for V86 mode
00175  VMMcall Exec_Int             ; interrupt number is in EAX
```

```
0017B    pop eax
0017C    VMMcall End_Nest_Exec
```

The functions Begin_Nest_V86_Exec, Exec_Int, and End_Nest_Exec are all described in the VMM section of Microsoft's DDK documentation. Begin_Nest_V86_Exec sets the current virtual machine to V86 mode, Exec_Int simulates a specified interrupt in the VM, and End_Nest_Exec returns everything to normal. We could, of course, now take apart VMM and see how *these* functions, too, are implemented but, while fascinating, this would take us rather far afield. However, we will look at VMM a little later to see how it implements some of the DPMI functions.

Note that Windows runs DOS not in real mode but in V86 mode. VMM or any Windows VxD may trap software interrupts, IN or OUT instructions, memory access, and so on from DOS. This means that many actions DOS takes will cause it to pop back into the Windows VMM.

The simplest-possible protected mode INT 21h call in Enhanced mode takes the route we've just described. DOSMGR gets the INT 21h call, figures out that it doesn't need to do anything special, and uses a script to tell V86MMGR to reflect the INT 21h call to V86 mode. V86MMGR figures out what DOSMGR is asking it to do and then asks VMM to switch to V86 mode, reissue the INT 21h, and switch back to protected mode.

Yes, all this happens every time a Windows program makes even the simplest INT 21h call. And we glossed over many details, such as how the PM callback actually makes the transition from 16-bit protected mode at Ring 3 into 32-bit protected mode at Ring 0. But you get the idea.

You might think that INT 21h calls don't happen very often in protected mode. However, the DDK debug version of WIN386.EXE includes a DOSMGR debug command ("Display DOS trace profile") to log the number of INT 21h calls. In just a few seconds, this command typically logs several *thousand* DOS calls. The most popular are INT 21h AH=2Ch (Get Time), AH=2Ah (Get Date), AH=4Fh (Find Next), and AH=50h (Set PSP). It's a wonder that Windows runs as fast as it does.

Windows does try to minimize this activity. For example, because every task in Windows has an associated PSP, you would think that the kernel would call INT 21h AH=50h (Set PSP) whenever it switched to a given task. In fact, as noted in *Undocumented Windows* (pp. 346-347), the kernel puts off making the Set PSP call until the task has made some other DOS call (which unfortunately happens pretty frequently). Given the confusion caused by having the genuine DOS current PSP out of sync with the Windows PSP, it is hard at first to see why the kernel does this—until you contemplate all the activity that occurs behind the scenes even for a simple INT 21h call such as Set PSP.

Actually, the Set PSP function is a good example of something that requires a little extra special handling from DOSMGR. INT 21h AH=50h expects a PSP address in BX. In protected mode, of course, it makes sense for this to be the protected mode selector to a PSP. DOSMGR reissues the INT 21h in V86 mode, but because DOS of course can't handle protected mode PSPs, it must first convert the PSP in BX to a real mode segment address, using the VMM _SelectorMapFlat function.

As another example of a function for which DOSMGR must provide special handling, consider INT 21h AH=25h (Set Interrupt Vector). When called in protected mode, this function naturally sets a protected mode interrupt vector. This means it *cannot be reflected* to DOS running in V86 mode. Instead, DOSMGR must handle the call itself by translating it into a call to the VMM Set_PM_Int_Vector function (this is the same function that DOSMGR used back in Listing 3-12 to install its own INT 21h protected mode callback). If you actually want to install a real mode interrupt handler from protected mode, you must call down to real mode by hand, for example by using the DPMI Simulate Real Mode Interrupt call, which we will describe later.

Likewise, INT 21h AH=48h (Allocate Memory Block) should, in protected mode, allocate extended memory and return protected mode selectors. It wouldn't make sense for a protected mode version of this function to allocate conventional memory and return a real mode paragraph address, so again DOSMGR can't call down to V86 mode. Instead, DOSMGR handles 21/48 by calling VMM functions such as _PageAllocate, _Allocate_LDT_Selector, and _SetDescriptor. If this handling of INT 21h calls in "VxD land" (without calling down to V86 mode) were taken to its logical conclusion Windows wouldn't need DOS at all. This is what Chicago provides, via VxDs such as VFAT.386.

How DOSMGR Handles Undocumented DOS Calls

So how does DOSMGR handle undocumented DOS functions? We already saw what it does with Set PSP calls, but this call was finally documented in DOS 5.0, so it's no longer a good example. Let's return to our old friend, Function 52h. As we all know by heart, this function takes no parameters and returns a far pointer to SysVars in ES:BX. We've seen that Windows somehow transparently makes this work in protected mode, since calling INT 21h AH=52h in protected mode gets back a valid protected mode pointer to SysVars. Well, it semi-transparently sort of works, since SysVars itself contains real mode pointers; but DOSMGR is doing the best that is humanly possible. DOSMGR can't very well modify SysVars to make it contain protected mode pointers, since this would immediately crash DOS.

How does DOSMGR give us the illusion of a protected mode DOS that even supports Function 52h? The DOSMGR script that handles Function 52h looks like this:

```
Xlat_API_Return_Ptr ES, BX
Xlat_API_Exec_Int 21h
```

DOSMGR also uses this same exact macro to handle the newly documented INT 21h AH=34h (Get InDOS Flag Address), which also takes no parameters and returns a far pointer in ES:BX. You can see how grouping the INT 21h functions into categories and using the V86MMGR XLAT API facility make it a bit easier to implement a DOS extender.

Xlat_API_Return_Ptr is explained in the DDK. Its job is to take a real mode pointer in the specified registers (here, ES:BX) and turn it into a protected mode pointer. The DDK notes that, although this macro is placed before the Xlat_API_Exec_Int macro in an XLAT script, V86MMGR actually creates the returned address after simulating the interrupt. Showing how V86MMGR implements Xlat_API_Return_Ptr would take us too far off the subject, even for this book, so we'll simply note that it first runs the next line of the script (here, Xlat_API_Exec_Int 21h), and then fiddles with the VM's client register structure (the Xlat_API_Return_Ptr macro turns ES and BX into Client_ES and Client_BX). For 16-bit software, the VMM Map_Lin_To_VM_Addr function, documented in the DDK, does the actual real- to protected-mode pointer conversion.

This last detail is important and is a good example of why it is sometimes helpful to know such low-level implementation details. The DDK documentation for Xlat_API_Return_Ptr says "For 16-bit protected mode apps, this macro creates an LDT selector if an appropriate selector does not already exist." What it doesn't discuss is how these selectors ever get freed. Once you know that Xlat_API_Return_Ptr is implemented using Map_Lin_To_VM_Addr, you can turn to the DDK documentation for that function and see that it says, plain as day, that "A virtual device must *never* free a selector that is returned by this service. For this reason, this service should be used sparingly."

This sounds bad, but it actually makes a lot of sense. In the case of providing a protected mode forgery of INT 21h AH=52h, how would DOSMGR know when we were done using SysVars and that the protected mode pointer to it, created with Xlat_API_Return_Ptr and thus with Map_Lin_To_VM_Addr, could be freed? There is no way to know, which is an inherent problem with transparency. But there remains a real danger that this service could consume selectors (of which only 8,192 are available) that would never be freed until the DOS box was thrown away, perhaps by a user who had started noticing weird behavior. Map_Lin_To_VM_Addr tries to avoid this danger by keeping a list of all selectors it has created; it tries to fulfill a request by returning some previously allocated selector, rather than allocating a new one.

DOSMGR uses the same Xlat_API_Return_Ptr macro to handle the recently documented INT 21h functions, 1Fh (Get Default DPB) and 32h (Get DPB), and also to handle functions 1Bh (Get Default Drive Data) and 1Ch (Get Drive Data). Because V86MMGR doesn't know the size of the returned data structures when calling Map_Lin_To_VM_Addr, V86MMGR always automatically gives the selector a limit of FFFFh (64K). Again, these selectors stick around until the VM is shut down.

All this sounds a lot like the DPMI Segment to Descriptor function (INT 31h AX=2), the documentation for which warns, "Descriptors created by this function can never be modified or freed. For this reason, the function should be used sparingly." The reason this sounds so familiar is that VMM implements the DPMI call using Map_Lin_To_VM_Addr. Unfortunately, the DPMI function provides a very easy way to turn real mode addresses into protected mode addresses, and so the function is abused and overused. Later in this chapter, when we need to convert real mode addresses to protected mode, we will use a better technique.

Where were we? Right, we were trying to see how DOSMGR handles undocumented Function 52h. The use of V86MMGR macros introduces a level of indirection. If we remove that level and show just the underlying VMM function calls, the protected mode implementation of this function would look like the code shown in Listing 3-15. Of course, this same code would also work for any other function, such as INT 21h AH=34h, that also needs an Xlat_API_Return_Ptr ES, BX and an Xlat_API_Exec_Int 21h. Similar code appears later in this chapter in the UNDOSMGR.ASM source code for a VxD that transparently supports INT 21h AX=5D06h in protected mode.

Listing 3-15: Direct Implementation for INT 21h Functions 34h and 52h

```
VMMcall  Simulate_Iret
VMMcall  Begin_Nest_V86_Exec
mov      eax, 21h
VMMcall  Exec_Int                 ; reflect INT 21h to V86 mode
VMMcall  Resume_Exec              ; do it now!
movzx    eax, [ebp.Client_ES]     ; get V86 ES inside nest
VMMcall  End_Nest_Exec
shl      eax, 4                   ; make linear address
mov      ecx, 0FFFFh              ; 64k segment
VMMcall  Map_Lin_To_VM_Addr       ; create permanent selector
mov      [ebp.Client_ES], cx      ; return selector to caller in DS
```

We knew already that somehow Function 52h did the right thing in protected mode; Listing 3-15 shows exactly how. We also know that Function 5D06h does the wrong thing, but we don't know why. Nor do we know what the DOSMGR code for INT 21h AX=5D06h looks like. DOSMGR uses a separate table to handle this function because there are many INT 21h AH=5Dh subfunctions (only one of which is documented). For example, the documented Set Extended Error function (AX=5D0Ah), which expects a 16h-byte buffer in DS:DX (not DS:SI, as claimed by the official, accept-no-substitutes *MS-DOS Programmer's Reference* for DOS 5), is handled this way:

```
Xlat_API_Fixed_Len DS, DX, 16h
Xlat_API_Exec_Int 21h
```

The Function 5Dh table also contains a handler for AX=5D06h (Get SDA). Here it is:

```
Xlat_API_Exec_Int 21h
```

That's it! Because this function is undocumented and, unlike Function 52h, rather obscure, DOSMGR does nothing at all other than reflect the INT 21h down to V86 mode. What this means is that, on returning from calling INT 21h AX=5D06h in protected mode, our segment registers will be *unchanged*. In other words, the function doesn't return random garbage; it returns the correct offset for the SDA, and the segment in DS will be whatever it was before the call. Borland C++ and CURRDRIV, which were calling this function in protected mode, were looking at some offset in their own data segments!

What have we learned here? First, there should be no mystery about how INT 21h is supported in protected mode. The DOS extender (in this case, DOSMGR) reissues INT 21h calls in V86 mode—many other DOS extenders switch into genuine real mode—and converts pointers between real mode and protected mode. Sometimes (for example, with file I/O or directory calls) this requires copying data to and from a conventional memory transfer buffer.

The whole point is to make the illusion of protected mode DOS as transparent as possible for the major DOS functions, even undocumented ones like Function 52h. But there are limits to transparency. The best example is how Windows supports Function 52h. Calling this function in protected mode does return a valid protected mode pointer to SysVars, but SysVars itself, of necessity, still contains real mode pointers. Even the protected mode support for some documented DOS functions such as IOCTL has similar limitations.

Another limitation of transparency is that the DOS extender has no idea exactly how a program that calls a DOS function is going to use the returned data. This is the problem with any of the DOS functions, documented or undocumented, which return pointers to data and which DOSMGR uses Xlat_API_Return_Ptr to implement. DOSMGR can't free the protected mode selector/descriptor for the returned pointer.

"Support" means the function tries to do the right thing in protected mode. If MS-DOS were a genuine protected mode operating system, how would function X behave? But it is not always clear what the right thing is. For example, it makes sense for Function 25h in protected mode to install a protected mode interrupt handler, but often even a protected mode program still wants to install a real mode handler. A larger problem is that the number of functions that might reasonably be considered part of the *de facto* DOS specification is nearly infinite. Many vendors besides Microsoft use INT 21h (see Novell NetWare in Chapter 4); there are a vast number of functions such as MSCDEX that employ INT 2Fh. There's no way that DOSMGR or any other DOS extender could possibly hope to support every one of these functions, that is, to make them work transparently in protected mode.

Do Your Own XLAT

But whether DOSMGR or any other DOS extender supports or doesn't support a particular DOS function in protected mode, or whether it supports or doesn't support a function in the way that would be convenient for your program, actually isn't a big deal. You can provide your own non-transparent support. Instead of calling the function in protected mode, your Windows program can switch back to V86 mode and call the function from there, just as DOSMGR would do if it supported the function in the first place. Likewise, you can translate pointers between protected mode and real mode, just as DOSMGR would do. And unlike DOSMGR, which can't free returned pointers, you can, because you know when you are done using them. In other words, whatever the DOS extender doesn't automatically take care of for you, you can take care of for yourself.

How? DOSMGR uses V86MMGR, which in turn uses services provided by VMM. The key VMM services API translation eventually ends up using are Begin_Nest_V86_Exec, Exec_Int, Map_Lin_To_VM_Addr, and so on (see Listing 3-15). You can access these functions too, because Windows provides a convenient layer, callable by normal applications, on top of these VMM functions. This application-callable layer is none other than DPMI. What DOSMGR does transparently, or would if it supported a given function, you can do by hand, using DPMI. In Enhanced mode, DPMI is a way to let normal Windows and protected mode DOS applications use some of the functionality of VMM. Of course, VMM is just one implementation of the DPMI specification, though it is the canonical implementation with which all the others are compatible.

DPMI does not satisfy every need. If DPMI does not supply the necessary functionality, you can also write a VxD, as we will do later in the UNDOSMGR.386 example at the end of this chapter.

DPMI Programming

Because DOS extenders can't support every conceivable DOS function in protected mode, protected mode programs need the ability to generate real mode software interrupts. This requires switching into real or V86 mode, reissuing the interrupt, and switching back into protected mode. DPMI provides functions for low-level mode switching (INT 31h AX=0305h and 0306h), but fortunately

DPMI also provides a higher-level function, Simulate Real Mode Interrupt (INT 31h AX=0300h), which takes care of the low-level mode switching for you. We use this function extensively in the remainder of this chapter.

For those occasions when you need to call a real mode function with a far pointer address, DPMI also provides two Call Real Mode Procedure functions (INT 31h AX=0301h and 0302h). All of these functions are documented in the DPMI specification (available free of charge from Intel), in Ray Duncan's *Extending DOS* and in Al Williams' *DOS and Windows Protected Mode*.

While very few people use Windows 3.0 any more, and even fewer use Windows 3.0 Standard mode, we probably ought to note that INT 31h functions 0300h, 0301h, and 0302h crashed Windows 3.0 Standard mode. According to a Microsoft article ("Three DOSEX Functions Not Reentrant in Std Mode," MSKB Q70891), this was fixed in the Windows 3.0a update.

INT 31h AX=0300h is slightly confusing because you use this software interrupt to generate (actually, simulate; you'll see what this means below) in real or V86 mode the software interrupt, such as INT 21h AH=52h or AX=5D06, that you are actually interested in. You use one software interrupt to simulate another.

But simulating real mode interrupts is just half the problem. It is important to note that using INT 31h AX=0300h to call INT 21h AX=52h or AX=5D06h in real or V86 mode *will yield real mode pointers*. The fact that you are calling the real mode software interrupt using DPMI does not change this. Thus, protected mode programs also require the ability to map these real mode pointers into the protected mode address space, that is, to convert real mode pointers to something valid in protected mode. When we're done, we'll have protected mode pointers to data structures in conventional memory. Sometimes, as with SysVars, these structures will in turn contain additional real mode pointers which also must be mapped before a protected-mode program can use them.

How are real mode pointers translated to protected mode? We saw earlier that, behind the scenes, DOSMGR uses Xlat_API_Return_Ptr, which in turn uses Map_Lin_To_VM_Addr to create permanent selectors. This corresponds exactly to the DPMI Segment to Descriptor function (INT 31h AX=2), which is indeed very convenient, but which Windows Enhanced mode implements using Map_Lin_To_VM_Addr, which in turn creates selectors that can never be modified or freed. We need a different technique so that we can free these things when we're done with them. Each descriptor is only eight bytes, so this doesn't sound like a big deal; but each VM only gets 8,192 descriptors (and therefore, selectors) because descriptor tables are limited to 64K. In Standard mode, for reasons we won't get into here, there are only 4,096 available descriptors. In short, explicitly freeing mapped real mode pointers when you're done with them is essential. Windows will *not* free these for you when your program terminates.

Actually, one solution is not to allocate new protected mode pointers in the first place. Windows preallocates several selectors to popular memory locations. These selectors are available for use by Windows programs and drivers. These predefined selectors, which have names such as __0000H, __0040H, and __B000H, are described in Chapter 5 of *Undocumented Windows*. Apparently as a "favor" to the Rational Systems DOS extender used by Lotus 1-2-3, Windows also supplies selector 40h, which is a "bimodal" selector (i.e., the selector * 10h equals its base address) to the BIOS data area at 400h. As Matt Pietrek shows in Chapter 1 of his *Windows Internals*, when the Windows kernel initializes, it creates these selectors using INT 31h AX=0002. Unfortunately, these predefined selectors only cover a portion of the real mode address space. Also, they are only available to Windows programs; protected mode DOS programs can't get at them.

But it is silly to worry too much about these predefined selectors because you can easily create your own protected mode selectors that map real mode addresses. This requires three DPMI functions: Allocate LDT Descriptors (INT 31h AX=0), Set Segment Base Address (INT 31h AX=7), and Set Segment Limit (INT 31h AX=8). As shown below, you allocate a descriptor/selector and then set its base to correspond to the real mode address. You should set the limit of the base to the size of the data structure you're interested in, rather than blindly make everything 64K, as DOSMGR has no choice but to do (it has no way of knowing which offsets your program will want to use). Setting a smaller limit, one that is exactly the size of the structure you're using, helps catch off-by-one errors and similar bugs. Rather than use DPMI, Windows programs can use three Windows API functions: AllocSelector(), SetSelectorBase(), and SetSelectorLimit(). The last two functions were at one point undocumented, so *Undocumented Windows* (Chapter 5) examines them in detail. Having created the protected mode selector, you can turn it into a usable far pointer with a macro such as MK_FP() (Borland C++ DOS.H) or MAKELP() (WINDOWS.H).

Remember that we want to be able to free one of these mapped protected mode selectors when we're done with it. INT 31h AX=1 (Free LDT Descriptor) provides this ability; the equivalent Windows API function is FreeSelector().

The LASTDRIV, CURRDRIV, and SFTWALK programs printed out various addresses returned from INT 21h Functions 52h and 5D06h. The pointers that our protected mode programs use, however, will of course be protected mode addresses, created using the DPMI or Windows API functions just mentioned. The ssss portion of these ssss:oooo far pointers is the selector whose base address we set to the real mode address we're interested in. (Got it?) The ssss value itself is more or less meaningless; it is just an index into a descriptor table. Printing out these protected mode addresses, then, will not be very useful. We'll need some way, given one of these protected mode addresses, to get back its base address, from which we can recreate the real mode address we actually want to display. This is provided by the DPMI Get Segment Base Address function (INT 31h AX=6), or by the once-undocumented Windows API function, GetSelectorBase(). Of course, only base addresses less than one megabyte (or 10FFEFh to be exact) have real mode equivalents.

Finally, a few undocumented DOS functions expect us to pass them buffers, which they will fill with information. For example, INT 21h AH=60h (Truename) works this way. To call the Truename function from protected mode, we must simulate the real mode interrupt. But that is not enough. The buffer address we pass to INT 21h AH=60h must be a *real mode* address. This in turn means that the address must be in conventional memory, below one megabyte; otherwise, how could DOS access it? Yet our program must manipulate the conventional memory buffer with a protected mode pointer.

As noted earlier, the V86MMGR already contains such a transfer buffer, which DOSMGR accesses all the time to implement all the documented file I/O and directory calls. We can allocate our own such "xlat buff," using the DPMI Allocate DOS Memory Block function (INT 31h AX=0100h). This function returns both the real mode segment (paragraph) address of a conventional memory block, as well as an equivalent protected mode selector. Programs read and write to the xlat buffer using the protected mode selector; they then pass the real mode paragraph address to DOS. INT 31h AX=0101h (Free DOS Memory Block) frees these buffers. The equivalent Windows API functions are GlobalDOSAlloc() and GlobalDOSFree().

So that's it. To access undocumented DOS from protected mode Windows, you need the following functions:

- Allocate LDT Descriptors (31/0000) or AllocSelector()
- Free LDT Descriptor (31/0001) or FreeSelector()
- Get Segment Base Address (31/0006) or GetSelectorBase()
- Set Segment Base Address (31/0007) or SetSelectorBase()
- Set Segment Limit (31/0008) or SetSelectorLimit()
- Allocate DOS Memory Block (31/0100) or GlobalDOSAlloc()
- Free DOS Memory Block (31/0101) or GlobalDOSFree()
- Simulate Real Mode Interrupt (31/0300) (no Windows API equivalent)

Now, these functions have been discussed in many other places. A number of good articles describe how to use DPMI to access real mode DOS from protected mode Windows, for those times when the Windows DOS extender doesn't do the work for you. It may seem that we could have just mentioned these eight functions at the beginning of this chapter and been done with it, without looking at how DOSMGR is implemented or how Windows programs are just protected mode DOS applications (DPMI clients), and without spending so much time looking at what happens when you *don't* use these DPMI functions. However, many times programmers use these DPMI functions in a cookbook fashion, without understanding what they actually do, or why you use one of them and not another. For example, we've often seen programmers try to use INT 31h AX=6 or GetSelectorBase() to call the DOS Truename function from protected mode and waste large amounts of time because it doesn't work. In the long run, it pays to understand what you are doing.

Hiding DPMI

Actually, though, having taken so long just to get to the point where most treatments of this subject usually start, we're now going to spend very little time looking at these eight DPMI functions. Instead, we're going to hide them beneath a higher-level, easier-to-use, interface.

For example, to map in a real mode address, you shouldn't have to worry about combining three different DPMI functions. We're going to implement a map_real() function and be done with it. This function just takes a real mode pointer and the number of bytes you will want to look at from protected mode; it returns an equivalent protected mode pointer. When you are done using the protected mode pointer, you can free it with free_mapped_real():

```
void far *prot_ptr = map_real(real_ptr, number_of_bytes);
// use prot_ptr
free_mapped_real(prot_ptr);
```

Let's continue to hide DPMI. Using one interrupt (INT 31h AX=0300h) to generate another (such as INT 21h AH=52h) is confusing. But calling a function to generate an interrupt isn't confusing at all. DOS programmers used to do this all the time with functions such as int86x() (see Chapter 2). We're going to implement a real_int86x() function that works just like int86x() but that generates a real mode software interrupt from protected mode. We can use this function together with map_real() to accomplish most of what we need. For example:

```
union REGS r;
struct SREGS s;
void far *real_sysvars;
void far *prot_sysvars;
memset(&s, 0, sizeof(s));
r.h.ah = 0x52;
real_int86x(0x21, &r, &r, &s);
real_sysvars = MK_FP(s.es, r.x.bx);
prot_sysvars = map_real(real_sysvars, number_of_bytes);
// access SysVars via prot_sysvars
free_mapped_real(prot_sysvars);
```

These functions, real_int86x() and map_real(), form the core of a library of routines, PROT.C and PROT.H (see Listings 3-16 and 3-17) for protected mode programming with Windows or any other DPMI server. In a Windows program, PROT.C uses Windows API functions such as AllocSelector() and SetSelectorBase(). In a DOS-based DPMI program, PROT.H maps these to PROT.C functions such as dpmi_alloc_selector() and dpmi_set_selector_base(), which provide C wrappers for the appropriate DPMI INT 31h calls.

Listing 3-16: PROT.C

```
/*
PROT.C
Routines for protected mode programming with Windows and DPMI
Andrew Schulman, February 1993
from "Undocumented DOS", 2nd edition (Addison-Wesley, 1993)
```

```c
(Changed version of PROTMODE, from MSJ, Oct. 1992, Dec. 1992)
Requires 286+ instruction set (e.g., bcc -2 or cl -G2)
*/

#include <stdlib.h>
#include <string.h>
#include <dos.h>
#ifndef DPMI_APP
#include "windows.h"
#endif
#include "prot.h"
/**********************************************************************/
static WORD mapped = 0;       // to ensure don't have selector leak

WORD get_mapped(void)   { return mapped; }
/**********************************************************************/
static DWORD base = 0;        // for data in other VMs

void set_base(DWORD b)  { base = b; }
DWORD get_base(void)    { return base; }
/**********************************************************************/
void far *map_linear(DWORD lin_addr, DWORD num_bytes)
{
    WORD sel;

    /* allocate a selector similar to our current DS
       (i.e., a data selector) */
    _asm mov sel, ds
    if ((sel = AllocSelector(sel)) == 0)
        return (void far *) 0;

    /* set the base and limit of the new selector; variable "base"
       allows access to data in other VMs */
    SetSelectorBase(sel, base + lin_addr);
    SetSelectorLimit(sel, num_bytes - 1);

    mapped++;

    /* turn into a far pointer */
    return MK_FP(sel, 0);
}

void free_mapped_linear(void far *fp)
{
    FreeSelector(FP_SEG(fp));
    mapped--;
}

void far *map_real(void far *fp, DWORD size)
{

    return map_linear(MK_LIN(fp), size);
}
/**********************************************************************/
/* Performs a real mode interrupt from protected mode */
BOOL dpmi_rmode_intr(WORD intno, WORD flags,
    WORD copywords, RMODE_CALL far *rmode_call)
{
    // ignore flags
    _asm    push di
    _asm    push bx
    _asm    push cx
    _asm    mov ax, 0300h        // simulate real mode interrupt
    _asm    mov bx, intno        // interrupt number, flags
    _asm    mov cx, copywords    // words to copy from pmode to rmode stack
    _asm    les di, rmode_call   // ES:DI = address of rmode call struct
```

```c
    _asm   int 31h             // call DPMI
    _asm   jc error
    _asm   mov ax, 1           // return TRUE
    _asm   jmp short done
error:
    _asm mov ax, 0             // return FALSE
done:
    _asm pop cx
    _asm pop bx
    _asm pop di
}
/********************************************************************/
int real_int86x(int intno, union REGS *inregs, union REGS *outregs,
    struct SREGS *sregs)
{
    RMODE_CALL r;
    memset(&r, 0, sizeof(r)); // initialize all fields to zero: important!
    r.edi = inregs->x.di;    r.esi = inregs->x.si;
    r.ebx = inregs->x.bx;    r.edx = inregs->x.dx;
    r.ecx = inregs->x.cx;    r.eax = inregs->x.ax;
    r.flags = inregs->x.cflag;
    r.es = sregs->es;         r.ds = sregs->ds;
    r.cs = sregs->cs;
    // NOTE: r.ss=r.sp=0 so that DPMI host provides real mode stack!
    if (! dpmi_rmode_intr(intno, 0, 0, &r))
    {
        outregs->x.cflag = 1;   // error: set carry flag!
        return 0;
    }
    sregs->es = r.es;         sregs->cs = r.cs;
    sregs->ss = r.ss;         sregs->ds = r.ds;
    outregs->x.ax = r.eax;  outregs->x.bx = r.ebx;
    outregs->x.cx = r.ecx;  outregs->x.dx = r.edx;
    outregs->x.si = r.esi;  outregs->x.di = r.edi;
    outregs->x.cflag = r.flags & 1; // carry flag
    return outregs->x.ax;
}
int real_int86(int intno, union REGS *inregs, union REGS *outregs)
{
    struct SREGS sregs;
    memset(&sregs, 0, sizeof(sregs));
    return real_int86x(intno, inregs, outregs, &sregs);
}

int real_intdos(union REGS *inregs, union REGS *outregs)
{
    return real_int86(0x21, inregs, outregs);
}

int real_intdosx(union REGS *inregs, union REGS *outregs,
    struct SREGS *sregs)
{
    return real_int86x(0x21, inregs, outregs, sregs);
}
/********************************************************************/
WORD lar(WORD wSeg) // load access rights
{
    _asm lar ax, wSeg
    _asm jnz error
    _asm shr ax, 8
    _asm jmp short done; // value in AX
error:
    return 0;               // can't be a valid AR
done:;
}
```

```
void far *lin_to_real(DWORD lin_addr)
{
    if (lin_addr > 0x10FFEFL)   /* allow HMA pointers up to FFFF:FFFF */
        return NULL;            /* not accessible in real mode */
    else
    {
        WORD seg, ofs;
        seg = (lin_addr > 0x100000L) ? 0xFFFF : (lin_addr >> 4);
        ofs = lin_addr - ((DWORD) seg << 4L);
        return MK_FP(seg, ofs);
    }
}

void far *get_real_addr(void far *fp)   /* prot to real */
{
    DWORD base;
    if (lar(FP_SEG(fp)) == 0)
        return NULL;     /* not a valid pointer */
    base = GetSelectorBase(FP_SEG(fp));
    return lin_to_real(base + FP_OFF(fp));
}
/*********************************************************************/
BOOL alloc_real_seg(DWORD bytes, WORD *ppara, WORD *psel)
{
    DWORD dw = GlobalDosAlloc(bytes);
    if (! dw) return 0;
    *ppara = HIWORD(dw);
    *psel = LOWORD(dw);
    return 1;
}

BOOL free_real_seg(WORD sel)
{
    return (GlobalDosFree(sel) == 0);
}
/*********************************************************************/
#ifdef DPMI_APP
WORD dpmi_alloc_selector(void)
{
    _asm xor ax, ax
    _asm mov cx, 1
    _asm int 31h
    _asm jc error
    _asm jmp short ok
error:
    return 0;
ok:;
    // return value in AX
}
WORD dpmi_free_selector(WORD sel)
{
    _asm mov ax, 1
    _asm mov bx, sel
    _asm int 31h
    _asm jc error
    _asm jmp short ok
error:
    return sel; // act like the Window function
ok:
    return 0;
}

WORD dpmi_set_selector_base(WORD sel, DWORD base)
{
    _asm mov ax, 7
```

```c
    _asm mov bx, sel
    _asm mov cx, word ptr base+2
    _asm mov dx, word ptr base
    _asm int 31h
    _asm jc error
    _asm jmp short ok
error:
    return sel;
ok:
    return 0;
}
WORD dpmi_set_selector_limit(WORD sel, DWORD limit)
{
    _asm mov ax, 8
    _asm mov bx, sel
    _asm mov cx, word ptr limit+2
    _asm mov dx, word ptr limit
    _asm int 31h
    _asm jc error
    _asm jmp short ok
error:
    return sel;
ok:
    return 0;
}
DWORD dpmi_get_selector_base(WORD sel)
{
    _asm mov ax, 6
    _asm mov bx, sel
    _asm int 31h
    _asm jc error
    // return CX:DX in DX:AX
    _asm mov ax, dx
    _asm mov dx, cx
    _asm jmp short done
error:
    return 0;    // problem: instinguishable from 1-byte segment!
done:;
}
/* C interface to LSL (Load Segment Limit) instruction */
#pragma warn -rvl
WORD lsl(WORD sel)
{
    if (! sel) return 0;    /* workaround 386 bug: Hummel, p.471 */
    _asm lsl ax, sel
}
DWORD dpmi_get_selector_limit(WORD sel)
{
    // no DPMI function; use LSL; should use 32-bit LSL though!
    return (DWORD) lsl(sel);
}
DWORD dpmi_dos_alloc(DWORD bytes)
{
    DWORD retval;
    WORD paras = (bytes >> 4) + 1;
    _asm mov ax, 0100h
    _asm mov bx, paras
    _asm int 31h
    _asm jc error
    _asm mov word ptr retval, ax
    _asm mov word ptr retval+2, dx
    return retval;
error:
```

```
    return OL;
}
WORD dpmi_dos_free(WORD sel)
{
    _asm mov ax, 0101h
    _asm mov dx, sel
    _asm int 31h
    _asm jc error
    return 0;
error:
    return sel;
}
#endif
```

Listing 3-17: PROT.H

```
/*
PROT.H -- see PROT.C
Andrew Schulman, February 1993
from "Undocumented DOS", 2nd edition (Addison-Wesley, 1993)
*/

#ifndef _PROT_H
#define _PROT_H

#ifdef DPMI_APP
typedef int BOOL;
typedef unsigned char BYTE;
typedef unsigned short WORD;
typedef unsigned long DWORD;
#define LOWORD(dw)      ((WORD)(dw))
#define HIWORD(dw)      ((WORD)((DWORD)(dw) >> 16))
#else
#include "windows.h"
#endif

void far *map_real(void far *fp, DWORD size);
void set_base(DWORD b);
DWORD get_base(void);
void far *map_linear(DWORD lin_addr, DWORD num_bytes);
void free_mapped_linear(void far *fp);
WORD get_mapped(void);
void far *get_real_addr(void far *fp);
BOOL alloc_real_seg(DWORD bytes, WORD *ppara, WORD *psel);
BOOL free_real_seg(WORD sel);

#define free_mapped_real(x)      free_mapped_linear(x)

#ifndef MK_FP
#define MK_FP(seg, ofs) \
    ((void far *) (((unsigned long) (seg) << 16) | (ofs)))
#endif

#define MK_LIN(fp) \
    (((DWORD) FP_SEG(fp) << 4) + FP_OFF(fp))

typedef struct {
    unsigned long edi, esi, ebp, reserved, ebx, edx, ecx, eax;
    unsigned flags, es, ds, fs, gs, ip, cs, sp, ss;
    } RMODE_CALL;

BOOL dpmi_rmode_intr(WORD intno, WORD flags,
    WORD copywords, RMODE_CALL far *rmode_call);

int real_int86x(int intno, union REGS *inregs, union REGS *outregs,
    struct SREGS *sregs);
int real_int86(int intno, union REGS *inregs, union REGS *outregs);
int real_intdos(union REGS *inregs, union REGS *outregs);
int real_intdosx(union REGS *inregs, union REGS *outregs,
```

```
          struct SREGS *sregs);
// to be defined by application;
// if DPMI_APP, app's fail() must call _dos_exit!
extern void fail(const char *s, ...);

#ifdef DPMI_APP
#define AllocSelector(x)        dpmi_alloc_selector()
#define FreeSelector(x)         dpmi_free_selector(x)
#define SetSelectorBase(x,y)    dpmi_set_selector_base((x), (y))
#define SetSelectorLimit(x,y)   dpmi_set_selector_limit((x), (y))
#define GetSelectorBase(x)      dpmi_get_selector_base(x)
#define GetSelectorLimit(x)     dpmi_get_selector_limit(x)
#define GlobalDosAlloc(x)       dpmi_dos_alloc(x)
#define GlobalDosFree(x)        dpmi_dos_free(x)

WORD dpmi_alloc_selector(void);
WORD dpmi_free_selector(WORD sel);
WORD dpmi_set_selector_base(WORD sel, DWORD base);
WORD dpmi_set_selector_limit(WORD sel, DWORD limit);
DWORD dpmi_get_selector_base(WORD sel);
DWORD dpmi_get_selector_limit(WORD sel);
DWORD dpmi_dos_alloc(DWORD bytes);
WORD dpmi_dos_free(WORD sel);
#endif
#endif
```

In addition to real_int86x(), there are the real_int86(), real_intdos(), and real_intdosx() functions. All of these functions in turn call dpmi_rmode_intr() and do little more than convert from the union REGS and struct SREGS structures (DOS.H; see Chapter 2) to a DPMI-specific RMODE_CALL structure. The dpmi_rmode_intr() function, also in PROT.C, provides a C wrapper for the DPMI Simulate Real Mode interrupt function (INT 31h AX=0300h). Of course, you can call dpmi_rmode_intr() directly if you prefer this to real_int86x().

About the only item worthy of note is that real_int86x() zeros out all fields in the DPMI RMODE_CALL structure and in particular forces the SS:SP fields in the structure to zero. This tells the DPMI host to provide a real mode stack, rather than expecting us to provide one. Note also that the segment-register fields in the structure should contain values that are meaningful in real mode. It is not useful for a protected mode program to initialize these fields with the values of the actual segment registers (from segread() for example), because these are protected mode values which real mode would interpret incorrectly.

The map_real() function is more interesting. As noted earlier, this function hides the work of three DPMI functions. Actually, map_linear() is the function that does all the work; map_real() consists of just a single call to map_linear(), using the MK_LIN() macro from PROT.H. Employing the familiar rule of real mode addressing (linear = (seg * 10h) + offset), MK_LIN() converts a segment:offset real mode address to a so-called *linear address*. A linear address is an index into the protected mode address space. If paging is enabled, as is usually the case in Windows Enhanced mode, then it is not necessarily a physical address. This is an important issue, but one that need not concern us right now.

The map_linear() function calls INT 31h AX=1 or AllocSelector() to allocate a new protected mode selector; the function also calls INT 31h AX=7 or SetSelectorBase() to set the new selector's base address to the linear address parameter. Optionally, map_linear() can add in a base value; we'll use this later (see Listing 3-23, for example) for accessing data in other virtual machines. By default, the base is zero, so map_linear() creates selectors that map data in the current VM. The function next calls INT 31h AX=8 or SetSelectorLimit() to set the new selector's limit to the size that was requested (actually, to one less than the size requested, since the limit is not the size of the segment but its last valid byte offset; a one-byte segment has a limit of zero, for example). Finally, the function uses the MK_FP() macro to turn this selector into a far pointer.

The resulting far pointer is just as usable in protected mode as regular far pointers are in real mode. For example, to access four bytes at linear address 12345h, in real mode you could just create a pointer with the value 1234:0005 or 1230:0045 or any number of other segment:offset combinations. To access this data in protected mode, you need to call map_linear(0x12345L, 4); this returns a segment:offset far pointer whose offset is zero and whose segment is some essentially meaningless number (an index into a descriptor table). But the segment's underlying base address will be 12345h. If you think about it, when we create far pointers all we really care about is getting to some memory location; we don't actually care what values the pointer's segment and offset have. If the pointer ends up letting us read or write to 12345h, it could be 0666:6660 for all we care. Think of map_real() as creating protected mode pseudonyms for real mode pointers.

The map_linear() function also increments a count of mapped selectors; free_mapped_linear() decrements this counter; you can query the counter with get_mapped(). AllocSelector() really does allocate a precious resource, one that is *not* automatically deallocated when you program exits. It is crucial that we free up every selector we allocate. By checking that get_mapped() returns zero just before your program terminates, you can ensure that you have been a good citizen.

Fixing SFTWALK

We can use the real_int86x() and map_real() routines to redo our earlier applications. It would be tedious (even for this book) to rewrite all three, so we'll just redo SFTWALK.C from Listing 3-5 and leave LASTDRIV.C and CURRDRIV.C as exercises for the reader. Listing 3-18 shows the new version of SFTWALK.C. This program can be linked with a library, DPMI_APP.LIB, containing the DPMISH, CTRL_C, and PROT modules shown earlier (Listings 3-6, 3-7, and 3-16). In addition to the DPMI_APP code, SFTWALK now also includes code for making a Windows version. The Windows version, to be discussed later, is built by linking with WIN_APP.LIB, which contains the PRINTF (Listing 3-1) and PROT modules. WIN_APP.LIB of course does *not* include the DPMISH module.

Listing 3-18: SFTWALK.C (Fixed for Protected Mode)

```
/*
SFTWALK.C -- Count FILES= by Walking SFTs
Version #2, uses real_int86x() and map_real() in PROT.C
Andrew Schulman, March 1993
From "Undocumented DOS", 2nd edition (Addison-Wesley, 1993)

DPMI program:
bcc -c -DDPMI_APP -2 dpmish.c prot.c ctrl_c.asm
tlib dpmi_app-+dpmish.obj-+ctrl_c.obj-+prot.obj
bcc -DDPMI_APP -2 sftwalk.c dpmi_app.lib

Windows program:
bcc -c -W -2 -DWINDOWS printf.c prot.c
tlib win_app-+printf.obj-+prot.obj
bcc -W -2 -DWINDOWS sftwalk.c win_app.lib
*/

#include <stdlib.h>
#include <string.h>
#include <dos.h>

#ifdef DPMI_APP
#define PROT_MODE
#include "dpmish.h"
#include "prot.h"
#endif

#ifdef WINDOWS
#define PROT_MODE
#include "windows.h"
#include "prot.h"
#include "printf.h"
```

```
#else
#include <stdio.h>
#endif

typedef unsigned char BYTE;
typedef unsigned short WORD;

// moved here (and changed) from SYSVARS.C
BYTE far *get_sysvars(void)
{
#ifdef PROT_MODE
    union REGS r;
    struct SREGS s;
    r.h.ah = 0x52;
    /* do not pass in garbage for seg regs, but don't use
       segread() either! Use memset to initialize to zero. */
    memset(&s, 0, sizeof(s));
    s.es = r.x.bx = 0;
    real_int86x(0x21, &r, &r, &s);
    return (BYTE far *) map_real(MK_FP(s.es, r.x.bx), 0xFFFF);
#else
    _asm xor bx, bx
    _asm mov es, bx
    _asm mov ah, 52h
    _asm int 21h
    _asm mov dx, es
    _asm mov ax, bx
    // return value in DX:AX
#endif
}

typedef struct _sft {
    struct _sft far *next;
    WORD num;
    // other stuff not used here
    } SFT;

int do_sftwalk(void)
{
    BYTE far *sysvars;
    SFT far *sft, far *next;
    WORD num_mapped;
    int files = 0;

    if (! (sysvars = get_sysvars()))
        return 0;
    sft = *((SFT far * far *) &sysvars[4]);
    next = sft;
#ifdef PROT_MODE
    sft = (SFT far *) map_real(sft, sizeof(SFT));
#endif
    while (FP_OFF(sft) != 0xFFFF)
    {
        files += sft->num;
#ifdef PROT_MODE
{
        // print out, using saved real mode address
        // (printing out the protected mode address isn't helpful)
        printf("SFT @ %Fp -- %u files\n", next, sft->num);
        next = sft->next;                  // save ptr to next
        free_mapped_real(sft);             // zap old one
        if (FP_OFF(next) == 0xFFFF)        // at end of list
            break;
        sft = (SFT far *) map_real(next, sizeof(SFT));  // map new one
}
#else
```

```
            printf("SFT @ %Fp -- %u files\n", sft, sft->num);
            sft = sft->next;
#endif
    }
    printf("FILES=%d\n", files);

#ifdef PROT_MODE
    free_mapped_real(sysvars);
    if ((num_mapped = get_mapped()) != 0)
        printf("Didn't free all selectors! %u remaining!\n", num_mapped);

    return num_mapped;
#else
    return 0;
#endif
}

#ifdef DPMI_APP
void fail(const char *s, ...) { puts(s); _dos_exit(1); }
real_main(int argc, char *argv[]) { return 0; }

pmode_main(int argc, char *argv[]) { return do_sftwalk(); }
#else
// Windows program
#ifdef __cplusplus
extern "C" int PASCAL WinMain(HANDLE hInstance, HANDLE hPrevInstance,
    LPSTR lpszCmdLine, int nCmdShow);
#endif

int PASCAL WinMain(HANDLE hInstance, HANDLE hPrevInstance,
    LPSTR lpszCmdLine, int nCmdShow)
{
    int retval;
    open_display("SFTWALK");
    retval = do_sftwalk();
    show_display();
    return retval;
}
#endif
```

Notice that SFTWALK not only calls map_real() for SysVars, but also calls the function for each SFT pointer. The root SFT pointer in SysVars is a real mode pointer, as is each next SFT pointer in the linked list. Whereas the real mode version of SFTWALK can follow the list with a simple sft = sft->next, the protected mode version has to go to considerably more trouble. Note that, while it would be nice to write sft = map_real(sft->next, sizeof(SFT)), this code would be incorrect because it would consume selectors. Remember, map_real() allocates a selector. We must stick in a call to free_mapped_real(). Before passing the SFT pointer to free_mapped_real(), however, we must first pull out the pointer to the next SFT. Walking real mode linked lists from protected mode is a little tricky. It is important enough to get this right that SFTWALK calls get_mapped() before exiting and will complain if there are any outstanding allocated selectors.

With these changes, SFTWALK now works in protected mode. It doesn't complain, so we are freeing all allocated selectors. And it produces the same output as the real mode version. Actually, that part is slightly tricky too. Printing out the SFT pointer that SFTWALK uses would not be helpful, because it is a protected mode value and gives us no indication of where the SFT actually is. In fact, displaying the protected mode SFT pointers usually displays the same address over and over because as soon as this program frees a selector, it allocates a new one. Usually the program ends up reusing the same selector. Therefore, SFTWALK prints out the real mode SFT pointer value *before* converting the pointer to protected mode with map_real(). Remember the point made earlier that there's nothing wrong with displaying real mode pointer values in protected mode; you just can't dereference them.

SFTWALK could instead have used the get_real_addr() function from PROT.C to retrieve the underlying real mode pointer from one of the protected mode pointers. However, the resulting real mode pointer is not necessarily in its most familiar form. Many real mode segment:offset combinations converge on the same linear address, so the real-to-linear function is not reversible. One linear address can yield many different segment:offset combinations, and the one that get_real_addr() generates may not be the same as the one that was fed into map_real(). They do have the same linear address, of course.

Inside the DPMI Server in VMM

The underlying DPMI or Windows functions used in real_int86x() and map_real() are sufficiently well hidden that we can now forget about them and proceed with writing DPMI or Windows programs that use undocumented DOS.

But since we are so dependent on these underlying DPMI functions, it pays to ask what in fact they actually do, and what part of Windows provides them. Who is hooking INT 31h in protected mode (and INT 2Fh in V86 mode), and what do they do when one of these DPMI functions gets called?

In Standard mode, the DPMI server is part of DOSX.EXE, along with the DOS Extender. DOSX is a fascinating program in its own right, a general-purpose DOS extender and DPMI server not really tied to Windows. But our focus here is on Enhanced mode, since that is what the vast majority of Windows users are running. The Enhanced mode DPMI server is part of VMM which, you may recall, is the Virtual Machine Manager upon which all VxDs (including DOSMGR) are ultimately based. VMM is the first 32-bit component in WIN386.EXE. An examination of VMM could be the subject of entire books (especially since, with Microsoft's forthcoming Chicago, this topic will grow in importance), but for now we'll look only at the DPMI server inside VMM. What really goes on when we make a DPMI call in Enhanced mode?

First, VMM hooks INT 2Fh in both V86 and protected mode. The INT 2Fh hook is used not only to handle DPMI calls such as Function 1686h (Get CPU Mode, used in dpmi_present() in Listing 3-6) and Function 1687h (Obtain Real-to-Protected Mode Switch Entry Point, used in dpmi_init() in Listing 3-6), but also to handle non-DPMI INT 2Fh calls. The calls constitute the only API that Windows provides to non-Windows applications. Microsoft documents most of these calls, but unfortunately in a very obscure location (Appendix C, "Windows Interrupt 2Fh Services and Notifications," in the Windows 3.1 DDK *Device Driver Adaptation Guide*).

A number of these functions are just thin layers on top of VMM. For example:

- INT 2Fh AX=1680h (Release Current VM-Time Slice; documented in the *MS-DOS Programmer's Reference* as the MS-DOS Idle Call) does little more than call the VMM Release_Time_Slice function.
- INT 2Fh AX=1681h (Begin Critical Section) calls VMM Begin_Critical_Section
- INT 2Fh AX=1682h (End Critical Section) calls VMM End_Critical_Section
- INT 2Fh AX=1683h (Get Current Virtual Machine ID) extracts the VM ID from the VM control block (CB) of the current VM. (For the VM CB, see VMWALK.H in Listing 3-24 later in this chapter.)
- INT 2Fh AX=1686h (Get CPU Mode) checks the VMSTAT_PM_EXEC bit in the current VM CB's status field.

VMM makes no distinction between the DPMI and non-DPMI INT 2Fh calls. From looking at the VMM code, DPMI appears to have started simply as a way for VMM to export some of its functionality to less privileged clients; only later did it become a separate specification shaped by vendors outside Microsoft.

We are more interested in the DPMI INT 31h functions. To install a protected mode INT 31h handler, VMM calls Allocate_PM_Call_Back and Set_PM_Int_Vector (the DDK documents all these VMM functions, as does Daniel Norton's book *Writing Windows Device Drivers*). The main INT 31h handler is just a few lines of code, using a jump table to get to handlers for the specific DPMI function groups (AH=0 for LDT management services, AH=1 for DOS memory management services, AH=2 for interrupt management services, AH=3 for translation services, and so on). These handlers in turn invoke other handlers for the specific DPMI functions (AX=0 for Allocate LDT Descriptor, AX=1 for Free LDT Descriptor, and so on).

For example, the DPMI Segment to Descriptor function (INT 31h AX=2) was described earlier as nothing more than a layer on top of the VMM Map_Lin_To_VM_Addr function. Here's what the VMM code for this function actually looks like:

```
        DPMI_0002:                        ; Segment to Descriptor
0A897       movzx eax, [ebp.Client_BX]    ; BX=real mode segment address
0A89B       shl eax,4                     ; EAX=linear address now
0A89E       mov ecx,0FFFFh                ; ECX=limit (make 64k)
0A8A3       VMMcall Map_Lin_to_VM_Addr
0A8A9       jc DPMI_ERROR
0A8AF       mov [ebp.Client_AX],cx        ; return selector to caller in AX
0A8B3       jmp DPMI_OK
```

Unfortunately, the DPMI function we're most interested in, Simulate Real Mode Interrupt (INT 31h AX=0300h), is sufficiently complicated that to show its implementation in full detail would require more space than we have here. We can summarize the function's operation, however, by noting that it makes the following sequence of VMM calls:

```
Push_Client_State
Begin_Nest_V86_Exec
Simulate_Int (or Exec_Int)
Resume_Exec
End_Nest_Exec
Pop_Client_State
```

This looks a lot like what Xlat_API_Exec does when DOSMGR asks it to reflect INT 21h to V86 mode (See Listing 3-15). In fact these functions are a lot alike. Remember, by using DPMI you are just doing by hand what DOSMGR or another DOS extender does, or would do, transparently. In essence, the DPMI Simulate Real Mode Interrupt function sets up the VM for V86 mode and tells VMM to simulate an interrupt. Simulate means that, rather than use an actual INT instruction, VMM gets the appropriate interrupt handler's address from the low-level interrupt vector table and shuffles the stack so that, when the VM runs in Resume_Exec, it returns to this address.

The three DPMI functions used to build map_linear() and map_real()—AllocSelector (INT 31h AX=0), SetSelectorBase (INT 31h AX=7), and SetSelectorLimit (INT 31h AX=8)—are easier to describe, though again it would be tedious to show the actual VMM code. The AllocSelector call is based on the VMM _Allocate_LDT_Selector function, documented in the DDK. This call also uses _BuildDescriptorDWORDs. The two SetSelectorX calls are built using _GetDescriptor and _SetDescriptor.

Interestingly, the equivalent Windows API functions are *not* implemented using the DPMI calls. Instead, these functions bang directly on the LDT. *Undocumented Windows* (Chapter 5) shows the code for these two functions. According to Matt Pietrek's *Windows Internals* (Chapter 2), the Windows kernel bypasses DPMI for performance reasons. A version of the Windows KERNEL that purely used DPMI was apparently built at one time, but Microsoft found it to be too slow (and, perhaps, too portable to other operating systems). Of course, the rest of us are still supposed to use DPMI instead of banging directly on descriptor tables.

In any case, the code *Undocumented Windows* shows for these functions is extremely simple. You could, if you cared to, implement your own SetSelectorX and GetSelectorX functions, without using Windows or DPMI, by directly manipulating the LDT. There is no reason to, but it shows that, here at least, there isn't any big mystery about what is happening behind the scenes.

Basically, then, the DPMI functions used to implement map_real() are just conveniences. The DPMI Simulate Real Mode Interrupt call, however, carries out a lot of semi-magical tasks that we probably could never carry out on our own.

Back to Windows Programming

Having used map_real() and real_int86x() in DPMI programs, we can now return to Windows programming and use these same two functions. In a Windows application, map_real() uses the Windows API functions rather than the DPMI INT 31h functions; real_int86x() continues to use the DPMI function, which has no Windows API equivalent. Windows applications can call DPMI functions because, as noted before, Windows applications are just DPMI clients. They are essentially the same as the DOS programs we built with DPMISH, except that someone (the Windows kernel) has already called INT 2Fh AX=1687h and switched into protected mode for them. And they have a fancier user interface, they use a different EXE file format, and under Enhanced mode all run together in a single virtual machine (called the System VM) rather than in separate DOS boxes ("and cost a lot more to develop," adds one tech reviewer).

Okay, so there are a lot of differences between Windows programs and protected mode DOS programs. But even so, you can profitably view Windows applications as nothing more than fancy-looking DPMI clients, and everything we learned about using DPMI in protected mode DOS programs applies to Windows applications. The real_int86x() and map_real() functions can help turn most undocumented DOS utilities into bona fide Windows applications.

Windows and the SFT

Back in Listing 3-18, SFTWALK was built as a DPMI program using DPMI_APP.LIB. WIN_APP.LIB can now help turn SFTWALK into a Windows program, one that doesn't GP fault and that correctly determines the DOS FILES= value, just as the real mode and DPMI versions did. Figure 3-5 shows the Windows version of SFTWALK.

Figure 3-5: SFTWALK as a Windows program

```
SFT @ 0116:00CC -- 5 files
SFT @ 05EB:0000 -- 40 files
SFT @ 23C6:0000 -- 82 files
FILES=127
```

This is certainly a nice contrast to the GP fault message in Figure 3-3, but note that this output is different from that produced by the DPMI_APP version or by the real mode version when run outside Windows under plain vanilla DOS. We get three different results from SFTWALK:

	MS-DOS	Windows DOS box	Windows application
SFT #1	0116:00CC (5)	0116:00CC (5)	0116:00CC (5)
SFT #2	05EB:0000 (40)	05EB:0000 (40)	05EB:0000 (40)
SFT #3	none	1295:0004 (10)	23C6:0000 (82)
FILES=	45	55	127

What has happened? The differences shown in the table depend not on the type of application, but rather on *where* the application is run. For DOS boxes (VMs other than the System VM), Windows Enhanced mode has a PerVMFiles= setting whose default is 10. DOSMGR adds an extra private SFT to each DOS box. Note that DOSMGR can do this only if the DOS SHARE utility is not loaded. SHARE must be able to enumerate all open files, and it wouldn't be able to if DOS boxes had their own private SFTs. In the System VM, the Windows kernel tries to add a much larger extra SFT to use as a file-handle cache. Chapter 1 discussed this topic in the sections "CON CON CON CON CON" (remember that craziness?) and "KRNL386 Grows the SFT." SFTWALK lets us see the results of Windows' manipulation of the SFT chain.

With each Windows VM adding its own private SFT, Windows must instance the "next" pointer at the end of the pre-Windows SFT chain. In the examples we've been looking at here, this pointer would be the DWORD at 05EB:0000. Unlike a DOS internal data structure such as the CDS, the entire SFT is *not* instanced; only this link from the global SFT to the private ones is (see "Instanced Data Management in Enhanced Mode Windows," MSKB Q90796, and "Limits on the Number of Open Files," MSKB Q81577). The SFT-link instancing code in DOSMGR looks like this:

```
06377    mov eax, SFT_PTR              ; end of pre-Windows SFT chain
0637C    mov dword ptr [esi+8],eax     ; esi is Inst struct
0637F    mov dword ptr [esi+0Ch],4     ; 4 bytes = SFT ptr link
06386    mov dword ptr [esi+10h],200h  ; instance flag = ALWAYS_Field
0638D    push   0
0638F    push   esi
06390    VMMCall _AddInstanceItem
```

It's not clear why Windows goes to such trouble over the SFT. Modifying SFTWALK to print out the actual file names in each SFT or porting the FILES program from Chapter 8 (Listing 8-19), shows that, no matter how many Windows applications you run at the same time, only a small portion of the enlarged SFT is in use. The SYSTEM.INI [boot] section has a CachedFileHandles= setting, which defaults to 12. Increasing this number appears to have no effect, at least in Windows 3.1. Generally the SFT contains the names of only the files used by the most recently opened large application. This cache is supposed to help with Windows' dynamic linking (see the FlushCachedFileHandle() description in Chapter 5 of *Undocumented Windows*).

Walking the Device Chain

In the same way that SFTWALK follows the linked list of SFTs from protected mode Windows, we can put together a Windows program that walks the DOS device chain. You can build DEV.C, shown in Listing 3-19, either for real mode DOS or protected mode Windows. When built for Windows, the program of course uses the real_int86x() and map_real() functions from PROT.C. However, to reduce the number of #ifdef WINDOWS preprocessor directives, DEV.C employs a number of macros, such as MAP() and FREE_MAP(), which call the appropriate functions under Windows but which do nothing under DOS. Figure 3-6 shows output from DEV.

Listing 3-19: DEV.C for Windows or DOS

```
/*
DEV.C -- display MS-DOS device chain -- for Windows
Andrew Schulman, March 1993

Real mode DOS:  bcc dev.c

Windows:
bcc -c -2 -DWINDOWS -W prot.c printf.c
tlib win_app-+prot.c-+printf.c
bcc -2 -DWINDOWS -W dev.c win_app.lib
*/

#include <stdlib.h>
#include <stdio.h>
#include <string.h>
#include <dos.h>
#ifdef WINDOWS
#include <windows.h>
#include "prot.h"
#include "printf.h"
```

```c
#endif

#ifdef WINDOWS
char *app = "Walk DOS Device Chain";
#define puts(s)          MessageBox(NULL, s, app, MB_OK)
#endif

// this fail() not suitable for a DPMI_APP (which would
// need to do a _dos_exit()
void fail(const char *s, ...) { puts(s); exit(1); }

#ifndef MK_FP
#define MK_FP(seg, ofs) \
    ((void far *) (((unsigned long) (seg) << 16) | (ofs)))
#endif

#ifdef WINDOWS
#define MAP(ptr, bytes)       map_real((ptr), (bytes))
#define FREE_MAP(ptr)         free_mapped_linear(ptr)
#define GET_REAL(ptr)         get_real_addr(ptr)
#define YIELD()               Yield()
#else
#define MAP(ptr, bytes)       (ptr)
#define FREE_MAP(ptr)         /**/
#define GET_REAL(ptr)         (ptr)
#define YIELD()               /**/
#endif

/* some device attribute bits */
#define CHAR_DEV    (1 << 15)
#define INT29       (1 << 4)
#define IS_CLOCK    (1 << 3)
#define IS_NUL      (1 << 2)

#pragma pack(1)

typedef struct DeviceDriver {
    struct DeviceDriver far *next;
    unsigned attr;
    unsigned strategy;
    unsigned intr;
    union {
        unsigned char name[8];
        unsigned char blk_cnt;
        } u;
    } DeviceDriver;

typedef struct {
    unsigned char misc[8];
    DeviceDriver far *clock;
    DeviceDriver far *con;
    unsigned char misc2[18];
    DeviceDriver nul;   /* not a pointer */
    // ...
    } ListOfLists;  // DOS 3.1+

ListOfLists far *get_doslist(void)
{
    union REGS r;
    struct SREGS s;
    memset(&r, 0, sizeof(r));
    memset(&s, 0, sizeof(s));
    r.x.ax = 0x5200;
#ifdef WINDOWS
    /* If Windows, call undocumented DOS INT 21h Function 52h via DPMI
       "Simulate Real Mode Interrupt" call (INT 31h AX=0300h), and return
       the resulting real mode pointer. */
    real_int86x(0x21, &r, &r, &s);
#else
    int86x(0x21, &r, &r, &s);
```

```
#endif
    return (ListOfLists far *) MK_FP(s.es, r.x.bx);
}

#ifdef WINDOWS
#ifdef __cplusplus
extern "C" int PASCAL WinMain(HANDLE hInstance, HANDLE hPrevInstance,
    LPSTR lpszCmdLine, int nCmdShow);
#endif

int PASCAL WinMain(HANDLE hInstance, HANDLE hPrevInstance,
    LPSTR lpszCmdLine, int nCmdShow)
#else
int main(int argc, char *argv[])
#endif
{
    ListOfLists far *doslist;
    DeviceDriver far *dd;
    DeviceDriver far *next;

#ifdef WINDOWS
    if (! (GetWinFlags() & WF_PMODE))
        fail("This program requires Windows Standard or Enhanced mode");

    // could also do protected mode DOS version with DPMI
#endif

    if (! (doslist = get_doslist()))
        fail("INT 21h Function 52h not supported");

#ifdef WINDOWS
    /* get protected mode pointer to DOS internal variable table */
    doslist = (ListOfLists far *) map_real(doslist, sizeof(ListOfLists));

    open_display(app);
#endif
#define PARANOID
#ifdef  PARANOID
    /* This block of code just double-checks that everything is ok */

    /* NUL is part of DOSLIST, not a pointer, so don't need to map */
    if (_fmemcmp(doslist->nul.u.name, "NUL     ", 8) != 0)
        fail("NUL name wrong");
    if (! (doslist->nul.attr & IS_NUL))
        fail("NUL attr wrong");

    /* CON is pointer, so need to map */
    dd = (DeviceDriver far *) MAP(doslist->con, sizeof(DeviceDriver));
    if (_fmemcmp(dd->u.name, "CON     ", 8) != 0)
        fail("CON name wrong");
    if (! (dd->attr & CHAR_DEV))
        fail("CON attr wrong");
    FREE_MAP(dd);

    /* CLOCK$ is also pointer, so need to map */
    dd = (DeviceDriver far *) MAP(doslist->clock, sizeof(DeviceDriver));
    if (_fmemcmp(dd->u.name, "CLOCK$  ", 8) != 0)
        fail("CLOCK$ name wrong");
    if (! (dd->attr & IS_CLOCK))
        fail("CLOCK$ attr wrong");
    FREE_MAP(dd);
#endif /*PARANOID*/

    /*
        Print out device chain:  thanks to the MAP, FREE_MAP, GET_REAL,
        and YIELD macros, this works in real mode DOS or in protected mode
        Windows. Old real mode only code looked like this:
            do {
```

```
                printf("%Fp\t", dd);
                if (dd->attr & CHAR_DEV)
                    printf("%.8Fs\n", dd->u.name);
                else
                    printf("Block dev: %u unit(s)\n", dd->u.blk_cnt);
                dd = dd->next;
            } while (FP_OFF(dd->next) != -1);
    */
    for (dd = &doslist->nul;;)
    {
        printf("%Fp    ", GET_REAL(dd)); /* print real mode addr */
        if (dd->attr & CHAR_DEV)
        {
#ifdef __BORLANDC__
            // Borland C++ printf can't handle non-terminated strings
            char buf[9];
            _fmemcpy(buf, dd->u.name, 8);
            buf[8] = '\0';
            printf("%s\r\n", buf);
#else
            printf("%.8Fs\r\n", dd->u.name);
#endif
        }
        else
            printf("Block dev: %u unit(s)\r\n", dd->u.blk_cnt);
        next = dd->next;             /* get next pointer */
        /* first time through, this will free selector to doslist */
        FREE_MAP(dd);                /* THEN free rmode seg */
        if (FP_OFF(next) == 0xFFFF) /* is there a next? */
            break;
        dd = (DeviceDriver far *) MAP(next, sizeof(DeviceDriver));
        YIELD();    /* no message loop in this program, so yield */
    }

#ifdef WINDOWS
{
    WORD mapped;
    if (mapped = get_mapped())
        printf("Error!: %u remaining mapped selectors!\r\n", mapped);
    show_display();
    return mapped;  /* 0 indicates success */
}
#else
    return 0;
#endif
}
```

Figure 3-6: DEV Under Windows

```
011A:0008    NUL
1A51:0002    Block dev: 1 unit(s)
1A52:0004    Block dev: 6 unit(s)
1A53:0006    Block dev: 3 unit(s)
CC2C:0000    DBLSSYS$
1328:0000    MSCD001
C8B4:0000    MS$MOUSE
02DD:0000    Block dev: 1 unit(s)
029B:0002    386MAX$$
029A:0000    EMMXXXX0
026E:0000    SETVERXX
0255:0000    Block dev: 6 unit(s)
0072:0003    CON
0073:0005    AUX
0074:0007    PRN
0075:0009    CLOCK$
```

```
0076:000B       Block dev: 3 unit(s)
0077:000B       COM1
0078:000D       LPT1
0079:000F       LPT2
007B:0008       LPT3
007C:000A       COM2
007D:000C       COM3
007E:000E       COM4
1B3E:0000       EMMXXXX0
```

An item worthy of note here is the second EMMXXXX0 (expanded memory) device at the very end of the list. As noted in Chapter 1 (see "Implementing DOSMGR Functions"), V86MMGR uses the DOSMGR_Add_Device function to add its emulated EMM driver onto the end of the DOS device chain.

Truename

So far, we've been calling undocumented DOS functions from Windows with real_int86x(), and mapping a returned real mode pointer with map_real(). This works fine for functions such as INT 21h AH=52h, but it isn't always the appropriate way to call an undocumented DOS function from protected mode.

For example, the undocumented DOS Truename function (INT 21h AH=60h) expects a pointer to an ASCIIZ path name in DS:SI; this function places the "canonical" fully-qualified version of the path name in a buffer pointed at by ES:DI. Windows does not support this function in protected mode, so you must use real_int86x() or some other derivative of INT 31h AX=0300h to make the INT 21h AH=60h call from real or V86 mode. But when setting up the registers for the real mode call, what values do you put in DS:SI and ES:DI? You obviously can't use protected mode pointers because the whole point of using DPMI Function 0300h is to generate a real or V86 mode interrupt. A protected mode pointer would be misinterpreted by DOS as a real mode pointer. Obviously, then, you must put real mode pointers in DS:SI and ES:DI. But where do you get these real mode pointers? A moment's consideration will reveal that our old standbys, map_real() and get_real_addr(), are not useful here.

Consider how a truename() function would work if there were a nice C interface to DOS:

```c
char *src = "c:\\this\\is\\some\\path";
char dest[128];
if (truename(src, dest))
    printf("Truename of %s is %s\n", src, dest);
```

In real mode DOS, the truename() function could be implemented more or less like this (see Chapter 8 for a better version):

```c
char far *truename(char far *src, char far *dest)
{
    _asm push ds
    _asm push di
    _asm push si
    _asm les di, dest
    _asm lds si, src
    _asm mov ah, 60h
    _asm int 21h
    _asm pop si
    _asm pop di
    _asm pop ds
    _asm jc error
    return d;
error:
    return (char far *) 0;
}
```

In protected mode, we want truename() to work the same way. Internally, the function will somehow have to turn the src and dest parameters into real mode pointers. How? In a protected mode program, src and dest will almost certainly be located in extended memory.

But there *isn't* any real mode equivalent to a protected mode pointer whose selector has a base address in extended memory. Thus, it seems there is no way for truename() to reliably convert its protected mode parameters to real mode for use by DOS. In fact, there isn't. What truename() must do is take the ASCIIZ string to which src points and *copy* it into an xlat buffer located in conventional memory. Truename() must pass the real mode address of this buffer to DOS. And it needs to create another buffer into which DOS can copy Function 60h's results. Before returning, truename() must again copy, this time from the conventional memory results buffer to the caller's dest pointer.

The real question, then, is how to allocate conventional memory from a protected mode program. There are numerous ways to do this. For example, you could use real_int86x() to call the DOS allocation function (INT 21h AH=48h). Calling INT 21h AH=48h in protected mode generally allocates extended memory, and certainly returns protected mode selectors; but calling the function from real or V86 mode with real_int86x() would of course yield the real mode paragraph address of a block of conventional memory. You could then use map_real() to get a protected mode selector to this conventional memory. You would manipulate the conventional memory block with the protected mode address and pass the original real mode paragraph address to DOS. The conventional memory block then acts as a transfer buffer.

Fortunately, there is an easier way to allocate conventional memory from protected mode. The DPMI Allocate DOS Memory Block function (INT 31h AX=0100h) allocates a conventional memory block and returns both the real mode paragraph address and protected mode selector pieces that you need to treat the block as a transfer buffer. DPMI also provides Free DOS Memory Block (INT 31h AX=0101h) and Resize DOS Memory Block (INT 31h AX=0102h) functions. The Windows API provides two similar functions, GlobalDOSAlloc() and GlobalDOSFree(). Of course, there's nothing magical about these functions. They don't do anything you couldn't do yourself. For example, Allocate DOS Memory Block is simply a nested V86 Exec_Int of INT 21h AH=48h.

PROT.C (Listing 3-16) provides an alloc_real_seg() function as a wrapper around either the DPMI or Windows DOS-allocation functions. It's easier to show how to use this function than to explain it. TRUENAME.C, in Listing 3-20, contains a protected mode truename() function and a small WinMain() testbed for trying it out. Simply run TRUENAME with a command line argument (yes, Windows programs can have command lines), and TRUENAME displays a message box with the results.

Listing 3-20: TRUENAME.C for Windows

```
/*
TRUENAME.C -- for Windows
Andrew Schulman, February 1993
bcc -W -DWINDOWS -2 truename.c win_app.lib
*/

#include <stdlib.h>
#include <stdio.h>
#include <string.h>
#include <ctype.h>
#include <dos.h>
#include "windows.h"
#include "printf.h"
#include "prot.h"
#define DEST_OFS    128
#define SRC_OFS     0
void fail(char *s) { MessageBox(NULL, s, "TRUENAME", MB_OK); exit(1); }

/* see real mode version in DISKSTUF.C (Listing 8-4) */
char far *truename(char far *src, char far *dest)
{
```

```
    RMODE_CALL r;
    char far *s2, far *fp;
    WORD para, sel;

    /* INT 21h AH=60h doesn't like trailing or leading blanks */
    while (isspace(*src)) src++;
    s2 = src;
    while (*s2) s2++;
    s2--;
    while (isspace(*s2)) *s2-- = '\0';

    /* Alloc 256 bytes conventional memory:  first 128 to transfer in src;
       second half to transfer back dest */
    if (! alloc_real_seg(256, &para, &sel))
        fail("Couldn't allocate conventional memory!");

    fp = (char far *) MK_FP(sel, SRC_OFS);
    _fstrcpy(fp, src);  /* use prot-mode sel addr in program */

    /* Generate real mode 21/60 */
    memset(&r, 0, sizeof(r));
    r.eax = 0x6000;
    r.ds = r.es = para;  /* pass real mode para addr to DOS */
    r.esi = SRC_OFS;
    r.edi = DEST_OFS;
    if (! dpmi_rmode_intr(0x21, 0, 0, &r))
        fail("DPMI real mode interrupt failed!");   //oops, should call free_real_seg

    if (r.flags & 1)    /* If carry set */
        _fstrcpy(dest, "<Invalid>");
    else
        _fstrcpy(dest, (char far *) MK_FP(sel, DEST_OFS));

    /* copied to caller's dest; don't need conventional-memory
       transfer buffer anymore */
    if (! free_real_seg(sel))
        fail("Couldn't free conventional memory!");

    return dest;
}
int PASCAL WinMain(HANDLE hInst, HANDLE hPrevInst,
    LPSTR lpszCmdLine, int nCmdShow)
{
    char buf[128], dest[128];

    if (! (GetWinFlags() & WF_PMODE))
        fail("This program requires Windows Enhanced or Standard mode");

    if (! lpszCmdLine && *lpszCmdLine)
        fail("syntax: truename <pathname>");
    sprintf(buf, "TRUENAME %Fs", lpszCmdLine);
    open_display(buf);
    printf("%Fs\n", truename(lpszCmdLine, dest));
    show_display();
    return 0;
}
```

For example, if you had run the DOS command SUBST F: C:\FOO before starting Windows, then running TRUENAME F:\BAR would produce the results, C:\FOO\BAR.

Note what the protected mode version of truename() does. After allocating 256 bytes with alloc_real_seg(), it copies the src string to the conventional memory buffer, using the buffer's protected mode address. Truename() then calls INT 21h AH=60h in real mode, passing in the buffer's real mode address. When Function 60h returns by way of the DPMI simulated real mode interrupt call), truename() copies DOS's reply to the caller's dest and frees up the transfer buffer. Truename() hides all this activity from its callers. It is almost as if DOSMGR implemented Function 60h in the first place.

Windows and the PSP

There's something annoying about porting programs such as TRUENAME to Windows. After you get all the simulated real mode interrupts and map-real calls and so on correct, you're left with something that isn't very different from what you could do much more easily under DOS. You're going through a lot of extra work just to produce the same old results.

When porting old DOS utilities to Windows, don't do such a blind port. You must consider how whatever you're looking at may change under Windows. A good example is the classic MEM utility, which walks and displays the DOS Memory Control Block chain. Chapter 7 presents an extensive example of such a utility, UDMEM. Naturally, we could take UDMEM and turn it into a Windows program, using map_real() to create temporary protected mode pointers to each MCB. But what would be the point of that? Windows memory management is quite different from that of plain vanilla DOS. A Windows version of UDMEM wouldn't reveal anything about Windows and wouldn't shed any new light on the MCB chain either.

One of the things that MEM utilities display are PSPs. If you do a blind port of UDMEM or a similar utility to Windows, you naturally still see PSPs for all the TSRs loaded before Windows, and you see ones for core Windows executables such as WIN.COM, WIN386.EXE, and KRNL386.EXE; but something is clearly missing. As noted earlier, every Windows task has an associated PSP. Well then, where are these PSPs? They must be in conventional memory because these must be genuine, *bona fide* PSPs. As we noted earlier, a Windows task's open files belong with its PSP, just as under real mode DOS. Yet a simple-minded Windows port of UDMEM won't find the PSPs for Windows programs. Why? Because, while the Windows kernel allocates these PSPs in conventional memory (otherwise, they wouldn't function as PSPs), it suballocates them out of one large conventional memory pool. Walking the MCB chain won't locate these Windows PSPs.

There is a separate chain of Windows PSPs associated with the Windows task database chain and linked through back pointers in an otherwise unused field at offset 42h in the PSP. The WinOldAp module, responsible for running ostensibly old DOS programs under Windows, employs another previously unused field at offset 48h to mark PSPs belonging to DOS boxes. Simply porting the DOS code for a MEM utility to Windows would miss these Windows-specific fields in the PSP.

Listing 3-21 shows a Windows PSP viewer, WINPSP.C. This program does what it can using the normal MCB chain, and then it uses the Windows ToolHelp library to walk the TDB chain. WINPSP.C extracts a protected mode PSP pointer from offset 60h in the TDB (see *Undocumented Windows*, Chapter 5). Finally, the program directly walks the Windows PSP chain, using the back pointers stored at offset 42h.

Listing 3-21: WINPSP.C Walks the Windows PSP Chain

```
/*
WINPSP.C
Andrew Schulman, April 1993
From "Undocumented DOS", 2nd edition (Addison-Wesley, 1993)

Uses EasyWin:
bcc -W -2 winpsp.c prot.c toolhelp.lib
*/

#include <stdlib.h>
#include <stdio.h>
#include <string.h>
#include <dos.h>
#include "windows.h"
#include "prot.h"
#include "toolhelp.h"
```

```
#ifdef __cplusplus
extern "C" BOOL FAR PASCAL IsWinOldApTask(HANDLE hTask);
#else
extern BOOL FAR PASCAL IsWinOldApTask(HANDLE hTask);
#endif

#define MAP(ptr, bytes)     map_real((ptr), (bytes))
#define FREE_MAP(ptr)       free_mapped_linear(ptr)
#define GET_REAL(ptr)       get_real_addr(ptr)

#pragma pack(1)

typedef struct {
    BYTE type;
    WORD owner;     /* PSP of the owner */
    WORD size;
    BYTE unused[3];
    BYTE name[8];   /* in DOS 4+ */
    } MCB;
WORD get_first_mcb(void)
{
    RMODE_CALL r;
    memset(&r, 0, sizeof(r));
    r.eax = 0x5200;
    if (dpmi_rmode_intr(0x21, 0, 0, &r))
    {
        // Extract seg of first MCB from SysVars. Note that this is
        // at sysvars[-2]. You can't call map_real() on sysvars, and
        // then back up 2! You must map in sysvars-2 to begin with.
        WORD far *tmp = (WORD far *) MAP(MK_FP(r.es, (WORD) r.ebx-2), 2);
        WORD first_mcb = *tmp;
        FREE_MAP(tmp);
        return first_mcb;
    }
    else
        return 0;
}

WORD count_open_files(BYTE far *jft, WORD num_files)
{
    WORD open_files = 0;
    BYTE far *fp;
    int i;
    // count number of open files in a Job File Table (JFT)
    for (i=0, fp=jft; i<num_files; i++, fp++)
        if (*fp != 0xFF)
            open_files++;
    return open_files;
}

void display_psp(WORD psp_seg, BYTE far *psp, MCB far *mcb)
{
    BYTE far *real_jft;
    BYTE far *prot_jft;
    WORD num_files;

    printf("%04X\t%04X", psp_seg, mcb->size);
    if (_osmajor >= 4)
    {
        char buf[9];
        _fmemcpy(buf, mcb->name, 8);
        buf[8] = '\0';
        if (*buf)
            printf("\t%-8s", buf);
    }
    real_jft = *((BYTE far * far *) &psp[0x34]);
    num_files = *((WORD far *) &psp[0x32]);
    prot_jft = (BYTE far *) MAP(real_jft, num_files);
```

```
    printf(" \t%Fp (%u files, %u open)\n",
        real_jft, num_files,                    /* print real mode addr */
        count_open_files(prot_jft, num_files)); /* use pmode addr */
    FREE_MAP(prot_jft);
}

void fail(char *s) { printf("%s\n", s); exit(1); }

main()
{
    TASKENTRY te;
    BYTE far *maybe_psp;
    MCB far *mcb;
    WORD mcb_seg;
    WORD mapped;
    BOOL ok;

    printf("-----------------------\nDOS apps:\n");

    // walk DOS MCB chain, looking for PSPs
    if (! (mcb_seg = get_first_mcb()))
        fail("Can't get MCB chain!");
    for (;;)
    {
        mcb = (MCB far *) MAP(MK_FP(mcb_seg, 0), sizeof(MCB));
        maybe_psp = (BYTE far *) MAP(MK_FP(mcb_seg + 1, 0), 512);
        if (*((WORD far *) maybe_psp) == 0x20CD) // look like a PSP?
        {
            if ((mcb_seg + 1) == mcb->owner)        // regular DOS app PSP
                display_psp(mcb_seg + 1, maybe_psp, mcb);
        }
        FREE_MAP(maybe_psp);
        if (mcb->type == 'Z')
            break;                              // end of list
        mcb_seg = mcb_seg + mcb->size + 1;      // walk list
        FREE_MAP(mcb);
    }

    FREE_MAP(mcb);                              // free last one
    mapped = get_mapped();
    if (mapped != 0)
        printf("ERROR! %u mapped selectors remaining!\n", mapped);

    printf("-----------------------\nWindows apps:\n");

    // now walk Windows task list, and extract PSPs
    te.dwSize = sizeof(te);
    ok = TaskFirst(&te);
    while (ok)
    {
        BYTE far *tdb = (BYTE far *) MK_FP(te.hTask, 0);
        WORD prot_psp = *((WORD far *) &tdb[0x60]);
        WORD real_psp = GetSelectorBase(prot_psp) >> 4;
        if (*((WORD far*)MK_FP(prot_psp,0))==0x20CD) // really a PSP?
        {
            BYTE far *psp = (BYTE far *) MK_FP(prot_psp, 0);
            BYTE far *real_jft = *((BYTE far * far *) &psp[0x34]);
            WORD num_files = *((WORD far *) &psp[0x32]);
            BYTE far *prot_jft = (BYTE far *) MAP(real_jft, num_files);

            // Windows-specific fields in PSP!
            WORD back_ptr = *((WORD far *) &psp[0x42]);
            WORD flags = *((WORD far *) &psp[0x48]);

            printf("%04X\t \t%-8s", real_psp, te.szModule);

            if (IsWinOldApTask(te.hTask) && (! (flags & 1)))
                fail("IsWinOldApTask flag weirdness!");
            putchar( (flags & 1) ? '*' : ' ' );    // IsWinOldApTask

            printf(" \t%Fp (%u files, %u open)\n",
```

```
            real_jft, num_files,    // print out real mode addr
            count_open_files(prot_jft,num_files)); // use pmode addr
        FREE_MAP(prot_jft);
    }
    ok = TaskNext(&te);
}
printf("------------------------\nFollow PSP backlinks:\n");
{
    WORD prot_psp, real_psp, next_psp;
    BYTE far *psp;

    prot_psp = GetCurrentPDB();
    while (prot_psp != 0)
    {
        real_psp = GetSelectorBase(prot_psp) >> 4;
        next_psp = *((WORD far *) MK_FP(prot_psp, 0x42));
        printf("%04X (%04X) -> %04X\n", prot_psp, real_psp, next_psp);
        prot_psp = next_psp;
    }
}

return 0;
}
```

Figure 3-7 shows sample WINPSP output. In addition to displaying the real mode paragraph address for each PSP and its name, WINPSP shows the size in paragraphs of the MCB based, non-Windows PSPs. Since Windows PSPs don't have MCBs, the size field is blank. Any number here would be meaningless anyway, since Windows programs can allocate gobs and gobs of extended memory. WINPSP also shows the address of the all-important Job File Table (JFT) associated with each PSP and displays the size of the JFT. Finally, WINPSP walks the JFT to determine the number of open files for each process.

Figure 3-7: Sample Output from WINPSP

```
DOS apps:

118D    0094    COMMAND     118D:0018 (20 files, 5 open)
1242    0102    DOSKEY      1242:0018 (20 files, 5 open)
1345    020D    WINICE      1345:0018 (20 files, 5 open)
155D    0055    win         155D:0018 (20 files, 5 open)
15BF    0341    win386      15BF:0018 (20 files, 5 open)
190D    85F3    KRNL386     27BA:0000 (32 files, 18 open)
------------------------
Windows apps:
257C            WINOLDAP*   257C:0018 (20 files, 5 open)
269C            DRWATSON    269C:0018 (20 files, 5 open)
4672            WINFILE     256A:0000 (30 files, 5 open)
2702            SH          2702:0018 (20 files, 5 open)
2734            WINPSP      2734:0018 (20 files, 5 open)
------------------------
Follow PSP backlinks:
11CF (2734) -> 1297
1297 (2702) -> 12F7
12F7 (269C) -> 1437
1437 (257C) -> 1817
1817 (4672) -> 00C7
00C7 (190D) -> 0000
```

WINPSP.C uses the Windows-specific flag word at offset 48h in the PSP to determine when it has a DOS box; it marks these with an asterisk. Windows itself uses this field in the useful undocumented IsWinOldApTask() function (see *Undocumented Windows*, Chapter 5). We use IsWinOldApTask(), as well as the ability to get at DOS boxes from Windows, in Listing 3-28 below. WINPSP displays all

DOS boxes with the name "WINOLDAP"; it would of course be more useful to display the name of whatever program is running in that DOS box, or at least the DOS box's window title.

Peeking at DOS Boxes from a Windows Program

Speaking of DOS boxes, it would be nice if Windows programs had an easier time getting at them. While it's a good thing that each virtual machine in Enhanced mode has its own address space—a pointer such as 1234:5678 in a DOS box has no relationship to 1234:5678 in another DOS box or in a Windows program—on the other hand, this makes it difficult for Windows programs to communicate with non-Windows programs. Such communication would be extremely useful, given that Enhanced mode provides preemptive multitasking for non-Windows programs. (Windows programs are only cooperatively multitasked.)

Fortunately, while each VM has its own segment:offset address space, all the VMs are connected at a lower level, in the linear address space. By mapping in linear addresses belonging to DOS boxes, a Windows program can peek or poke data in other VMs. Likewise, protected mode DOS applications can map in linear addresses to access data on the Windows side of the fence.

For example, we noted a second ago that it would be useful if WINPSP could give the name of the program currently running (or currently suspended) in each DOS box. To do this, WINPSP would need to get the *high linear* address for each DOS box (more on high linear addresses in a moment), add this address onto the linear address for different DOS internal data structures and then create usable protected mode pointers to these structures with the map_linear() function from PROT.C (Listing 3-16). Listing 3-22 presents pseudocode for these steps.

Listing 3-22: Pseudocode for Examining the Current PSP in Other VMs

```
sda = get_sda();
for each DOS box
    high_lin = somehow get DOS box's high linear address;  // see below

    // make linear address from SDA pointer
    sda_lin = MK_LIN(sda);

    // add together to get linear address of SDA in DOS box
    vm_sda_lin = high_lin + sda_lin;

    // make protected mode pointer to SDA in DOS box
    vm_sda = map_linear(vm_sda_lin, size of SDA);

    // extract current PSP from DOS box's SDA
    vm_curr_psp = vm_sda[0x10];
    free_mapped_linear(vm_sda);     // done with SDA

    // get linear address of current PSP in DOS box
    #define SEG_TO_LIN(x)    ((x) * 0x10)
    vm_curr_psp_lin = high_lin + SEG_TO_LIN(vm_curr_psp);

    // make protected mode pointer to current PSP in DOS box
    vm_psp = map_linear(vm_curr_psp_lin, size of PSP);

    // extract environment segment from DOS box's current PSP
    env_seg = vm_psp[0x2C];
    free_mapped_linear(vm_psp);     // done with PSP

    // make protected mode pointer to current environment in DOS box
    vm_env_lin = high_lin + SEG_TO_LIN(env_seg);
    vm_env = map_linear(vm_env_lin, 0xFFFF);

    do usual stuff to walk env to find program name (see Chapter 7);
    display program name;
    free_mapped_linear(vm_env);
```

Let's go over that again. From a program running in one VM (either a Windows program or a DOS program), we want to be able to get at data in other VMs. For example, a Windows program might want to access DOS internal data structures such as the SDA or SysVars or CDS in a DOS box. Because of the way that DOSMGR works, many of these structures *must* be at the same real mode segment:offset address in each VM. As Chapter 1 noted, DOSMGR assumes that even structures such as the CDS are not going to move. You can flatten this real mode segment:offset address into a linear address, using the familiar *linear = (segment * 10h) + offset* rule (MK_LIN; see Listing 3-17). To find the structure in a particular VM, you must add this linear address onto the VM's high linear address.

This high linear address is the offset of the VM's address space within the entire Enhanced mode address space. The key point is that this address is valid even when the VM is not running. For example, data located at linear address 12345h when a VM is running is always located at high_lin + 12345h when the VM is not running. The current VM's memory has a base address of 0. We've been using such linear addresses all along, but since we've always been examining data in our own VM, without even thinking about it, we were able to ignore the high_lin part. After all, if our program was running, then its VM was, by definition, the current VM.

So where do we get the all-important high linear address for each VM? Leaving aside for the moment how a program gets one of these addresses, note that debuggers such as WINICE display such addresses:

```
:vm
VM Handle    Status      High Addr    VM ID       Client Regs
805CF000     00004000    81800000     00000002    804B0F70
80481000     0000F062    81400000     00000001    80010D50
```

This shows two VMs. VM ID 1 is always the System VM, where all Windows applications run. Any other VM is a DOS box. We can see that the System VM's high linear address is the number 81400000h, and that there is one DOS box (VM ID 2), which has the high linear address 81800000h. In other words, in this example the DOS box's memory starts at 81800000h. A Windows program could peek and poke this memory by calling map_linear() on that address. You can now see why we needed a map_linear() function separate from map_real(). From these enormous numbers, you can also see that linear addresses are not necessarily physical addresses (this machine doesn't have two gigabytes of memory!).

Notice that WINICE displays a *VM handle*. VM handles are unique identifiers for each VM. But a VM handle is more than that. The number happens to be the linear address of the VM's *control block*. The VM control block is a large data structure, only a few fields of which are documented, containing all the fields that the WINICE VM command above happens to show, including the VM's high linear address. (Listing 3-24 below includes a VM_CB structure that shows this and other fields.) Given a VM handle then, one can get a high linear address. The following code fills in for the "somehow get DOS box's high linear address" line in Listing 2-22:

```
DWORD vm_handle = somehow_get_vm_handle();
VM_CB far *vm_cb = map_linear(vm_handle, sizeof(VM_CB));
DWORD high_lin = vm_cb->high_linear;
free_mapped_linear(vm_cb);
```

So now all we need is some way to get VM handles. This is the only difficult part. Fortunately, there is a way. VMM provides several functions, all documented in the DDK, that return VM handles, including Get_Cur_VM_Handle (get current VM), Get_Next_VM_Handle (follow the VM chain), and Get_Sys_VM_Handle (get System VM). Each of these functions returns a VM handle in the EBX register.

Great! Now if only there were some way we could call these functions from a Windows or DOS program. Unfortunately, VMM and VxD functions do not appear in the WINDOWS.H header file. They don't yet seem to be part of the normal Windows programming repertoire.

Fortunately, we can still call these or any other VMM or VxD functions from a normal Windows or DOS program. Recall that normal programs inadvertently call VMM and VxDs all the time. VxDs such as DOSMGR allocate callbacks and attach these to interrupts. Whenever a Windows program calls INT 21h, for example, it suddenly ends up running some 32-bit Ring 0 code in DOSMGR. Well, normal programs can *intentionally* call into VxDs too. Windows provides a documented Get Device Entry Point Address function (INT 2Fh AX=1684h) which, given the ID number of a VxD, returns a function pointer that the program can call to access services provided by the VxD.

This means that, for example, we could write a VxD to provide VM handle services to Windows and DOS programs. A program might call function 1 to get the current VM handle, function 2 to get the next VM, and function 3 to get the System VM handle. The VxD would of course implement these functions by calling the VMM services, thereby acting as a surrogate for the Windows or DOS program. Clearly, VxDs aren't just for devices.

We can do even better than this, though. Why write a VxD just to get at three functions? Next week or next month, we'll want to get at a different three functions. It is instead possible to implement a *generic VxD*, which lets Windows and DOS programs access *any* function in VMM or a VxD. Here, we use the generic VxD only to get at the three VMM handle functions provided by VMM. This barely shows off the capabilities of the generic VxD, which could be the subject of an entire book. For a taste of the other things the generic VxD can do, an explanation of how it works, and a look at its source code, see "Call VxD Functions and VMM Services Easily Using Our Generic VxD," *Microsoft Systems Journal*, February 1993.

So how do we fill in that somehow_get_vm_handle() pseudocode above? This is provided by VMWALK.C and VMWALK.H, shown in Listings 3-23 and 3-24. VMWALK provides a vmwalk() function, which takes a function pointer, walkfunc. Using the generic VxD, VMWALK uses Get_Sys_VM_Handle and Get_Next_VM_Handle to enumerate all VM handles. For each virtual machine, vmwalk() maps in the VM handle to form a VM_CB pointer, copies it, and calls the passed-in walkfunc. The walkfunc now has a VM handle and a copy of a VM_CB, including the high linear address, and can do what it wants.

Listing 3-23: VMWALK.C

```
/*
VMWALK.C -- Enumerates VM handles, using generic VxD
Andrew Schulman, February 1993
From "Undocumented DOS", 2nd edition (Addison-Wesley, 1993)
*/

#include <stdlib.h>
#include <string.h>
#include <dos.h>
#ifdef WINDOWS
#include "windows.h"
#endif
#include "prot.h"
#include "vxdcalls.h"
#include "vmwalk.h"

int vmwalk(WALKFUNC walkfunc)
{
    DWORD sys_vm = GetSysVMHandle();
    void far *vm_cb;
    VM_CB my_vm_cb;
    DWORD vm;
    int num_vm;
    for (vm=sys_vm, num_vm=0;; num_vm++)
    {
        set_vm(0);  // in case app fiddled with it
        vm_cb = map_linear(vm, sizeof(VM_CB));
        _fmemcpy(&my_vm_cb, vm_cb, sizeof(VM_CB));
        free_mapped_linear(vm_cb);
        if (! (*walkfunc)(vm, &my_vm_cb))
```

```
                  return num_vm;
            if ((vm = GetNextVMHandle(vm)) == sys_vm)
                break;  // circular list
        }
        return num_vm;
}
DWORD GetSysVMHandle(void)
{
    VxDParams p;
    p.CallNum = Get_Sys_VM_Handle;
    return (VxDCall(&p)) ? p.OutEBX : 0;
}
DWORD GetCurVMHandle(void)
{
    VxDParams p;
    p.CallNum = Get_Cur_VM_Handle;
    return (VxDCall(&p)) ? p.OutEBX : 0;
}
DWORD GetNextVMHandle(DWORD vm)
{
    VxDParams p;
    p.CallNum = Get_Next_VM_Handle;
    p.InEBX = vm;
    return (VxDCall(&p)) ? p.OutEBX : 0;
}
// The next functions do nothing but add vm_cb->CB_High_Linear
// onto a linear address, but they make it a lot easier to work with
// multiple VMs.
DWORD get_vm_base(DWORD vm)
{
    VM_CB far *vm_cb;
    DWORD base;
    if (vm == 0) return 0;  // stay in current VM
    vm_cb = (VM_CB far *) map_linear(vm, sizeof(VM_CB));
    base = vm_cb->CB_High_Linear;
    free_mapped_linear(vm_cb);
    return base;
}

void set_vm(DWORD vm)    // sets base address for map_linear
{
    set_base(get_vm_base(vm));
}

void far *map_real_vm(DWORD vm, void far *fp, WORD bytes)
{
    return map_linear(get_vm_base(vm) + MK_LIN(fp), bytes);
}

void far *map_linear_vm(DWORD vm, DWORD lin_addr, WORD bytes)
{
    return map_linear(get_vm_base(vm) + lin_addr, bytes);
}

#ifdef TESTING
#include <stdio.h>
BOOL walkfunc(DWORD vm, VM_CB far *vm_cb)
{
    printf("%08lX    VM #%lu  lin=%08lXh   crs=%08lXh\n",
        vm,
        vm_cb->CB_VMID,
        vm_cb->CB_High_Linear,
        vm_cb->CB_Client_Pointer);
    return 1;
}
```

```
void fail(const char *s, ...) { printf("%s\n", s); exit(1); }
#ifdef DPMI_APP
#pragma argsused
int real_main(int argc, char *argv[])    { return 0; }
#pragma argsused
int pmode_main(int argc, char *argv[])   { return vmwalk(walkfunc); }
#else
int main()                               { return vmwalk(walkfunc); }
#endif
#endif /*TESTING*/
```

Listing 3-24: VMWALK.H

```
/*
VMWALK.H -- See VMWALK.C
Andrew Schulman, February 1993
From "Undocumented DOS", 2nd edition (Addison-Wesley, 1993)
*/

// the first four fields are documented in DDK VMM.INC
typedef struct {
    DWORD CB_VM_Status;
    DWORD CB_High_Linear;
    DWORD CB_Client_Pointer;
    DWORD CB_VMID;
    BYTE other[0x100];   // e.g., vm->next at VM+68h
    } VM_CB;             // Virtual Machine Control Block

// Known VM_CB offsets in Windows 3.1:
// 00h   status
// 04h   high linear
// 08h   client pointer
// 0Ch   VM ID
// 14h   Get_Last_Updated_VM_Exec_Time return
// 18h   page tables
// 64h   Get_Cur_PM_App_CB return
// 68h   Get_Next_VM_Handle return
// BCh   instance data struct
// 10Ch  A20 wrap flag

// For more on the VM CB, see the two-part article by
// Kelly Zytaruk in Dr. Dobb's Journal, Dec. 1993 and Jan. 1994
#define NEXT_VM(vm_cb)  *((DWORD far*)(((BYTE far*)vm_cb)+0x68))

typedef BOOL (*WALKFUNC)(DWORD vm, VM_CB far *);
int vmwalk(WALKFUNC walkfunc);
extern BOOL walkfunc(DWORD vm, VM_CB far *vm_cb);    // app to provide

#ifndef DPMI_APP
// for Windows-based WVMWALK (without generic VxD; 3.1 Win apps only!)
typedef BOOL (*WWALKFUNC)(HWND hwnd, char *title, DWORD vm,
    VM_CB far *vm_cb);
int wvmwalk(WWALKFUNC walkfunc);
extern BOOL wwalkfunc(HWND hwnd, char *title, DWORD vm, VM_CB far *vm_cb);
#endif

DWORD GetSysVMHandle(void);
DWORD GetCurVMHandle(void);
DWORD GetNextVMHandle(DWORD vm);

void set_vm(DWORD vm);   // sets base address for map_linear
void far *map_real_vm(DWORD vm, void far *fp, WORD bytes);
void far *map_linear_vm(DWORD vm, DWORD lin_addr, WORD bytes);
```

Given a VM handle, the GetNextVMHandle() function returns the next VM in the chain; vmwalk() starts off its VM enumeration by calling GetSysVMHandle(). The VM list is circular, so when vmwalk() finds itself with the System VM handle again, it is finished.

But how do GetSysVMHandle() and GetNextVMHandle() work in the first place? These functions are wrappers around calls to VxDCall(). This function (we'll see the code for it in a moment) is the C interface to the generic VxD. It expects to be passed a VxDParams structure, which contains all the information the generic VxD needs to make a VMM or VxD call on an application's behalf.

For example, the DDK documents Get_Next_VM_Handle as taking a VM handle in the 32-bit EBX register and returning the next VM handle, also in the EBX register. The VxDParams structure contains an image of the 32-bit registers for both function input and output. It also contains a CallNum field, which holds the function's magic number. Get_Next_VM_Handle is defined in an include file as 0x01003BL. These function numbers include the VxD ID number; VMM is considered to be VxD 1.

Any program that wants to use the generic VxD must #include VXDCALLS.H, and link with VXDCALLS.C (see Listings 3-25 and 3-26). The generic VxD itself is the file VXD.386, which must be installed with a line such as device=c:\undoc2\chap3\vxd.386 in the [386Enh] section of SYSTEM.INI.

Listing 3-25: VXDCALLS.C

```
/*
VXDCALLS.C -- C interface to generic VxD (VXD.386)
Andrew Schulman, February 1993
From "Undocumented DOS", 2nd edition (Addison-Wesley, 1993)
Abbreviated from version in Microsoft Systems Journal, February 1993
*/

#ifndef DPMI_APP
#include "windows.h"
#endif

#include <dos.h>
#include "vxdcalls.h"

static void far *API = 0;
static BOOL API_is_V86 = 1;
static char *requires_msg = "This program requires VXD.386";

extern void fail(const char *s, ...);

/* Get entry point for the VxD API using Int 2Fh AX=1684h */
api_entry GetVxDAPI(WORD vxd_id)
{
    _asm push di
    _asm mov ax, 1684h
    _asm mov bx, vxd_id
    _asm xor di, di
    _asm mov es, di
    _asm int 2fh
    _asm mov ax, di
    _asm mov dx, es
    _asm pop di
    // returns in DX:AX
}

// This is only accurate with DPMI
BOOL IsProtMode(void)
{
    unsigned _ax;
    _asm mov ax, 1686h
    _asm int 2Fh
    _asm mov _ax, ax
    return (! _ax);
}

/* check if generic VxD installed */
BOOL GenericVxDInstalled(void)
{
```

```c
    return (GetVxDAPI(Generic_Dev_ID) != (api_entry) 0);
}
static void InitVxDAPI(void)
{
    if (! API)
    {
        if (! (API = GetVxDAPI(Generic_Dev_ID)))
            fail(requires_msg);
        API_is_V86 = (! IsProtMode());
    }
    else if (API_is_V86 && IsProtMode())
    {
        // API was last set in V86 mode, and we are now in protected mode
        API = GetVxDAPI(Generic_Dev_ID);     // get PM API
        API_is_V86 = 0;
    }
}
BOOL VxDCall(VxDParams far *fp)
{
    InitVxDAPI();

    _asm push es
    _asm les bx, dword ptr fp
    _asm mov ax, VXD_VxDCall
    _asm call dword ptr [API]
    _asm pop es
    _asm jc Error
    return TRUE;
Error:
    return FALSE;
}
BOOL VxDPushCall(VxDPushParams far *fp)
{
    InitVxDAPI();

    _asm push es
    _asm les bx, dword ptr fp
    _asm mov ax, VXD_VxDPushCall
    _asm call dword ptr [API]
    _asm pop es
    _asm jc Error
    return TRUE;
Error:
    return FALSE;
}
```

Listing 3-26: VXDCALLS.H

```c
/*
VXDCALLS.H -- See VXDCALLS.C
Andrew Schulman, February 1993
From "Undocumented DOS", 2nd edition (Addison-Wesley, 1993)
Abbreviated from version in Microsoft Systems Journal, February 1993
*/

#ifdef DPMI_APP
typedef int BOOL;
typedef unsigned short WORD;
typedef unsigned long DWORD;
#endif

#ifndef FALSE
#define FALSE    0
#define TRUE     (! FALSE)
#endif
```

```
/* Structure used with VxDCall */
typedef struct {
    DWORD CallNum;
    DWORD Reserved1;
    DWORD InEAX, InEBX, InECX, InEDX, InEBP, InESI, InEDI;
    DWORD Reserved2, Reserved3;
    DWORD OutEAX, OutEBX, OutECX, OutEDX, OutEBP, OutESI, OutEDI;
    WORD  OutFS, OutGS;
    DWORD OutEFLAGS;
    } VxDParams;

/* Structure used with VxDPushCall */
typedef struct {
    DWORD CallNum;
    DWORD NumP;
    DWORD P[10];
    DWORD OutEAX, OutEDX;
    } VxDPushParams;


#define CARRYFLAG           1
#define ZEROFLAG            (1 << 6)
#define OVERFLOWFLAG        (1 << 11)

/* VxD ID assigned by vxdid@microsoft.com */
#define Generic_Dev_ID      0x28c0
/* Functions supplied by VXD.386 */
#define VXD_Version         0
#define VXD_VxDCall         1
#define VXD_VxDPushCall     3
/*
W3MAP.H is a boring file generated from w3map -verbose:
#define Get_VMM_Version     0x010000L
#define Get_Cur_VM_Handle   0x010001L
#define Test_Cur_VM_Handle  0x010002L
#define Get_Sys_VM_Handle   0x010003L
#define Test_Sys_VM_Handle  0x010004L
....
#define Call_When_Idle      0x01003AL
#define Get_Next_VM_Handle  0x01003BL
#define Set_Global_Time_Out 0x01003CL
...
etc.
*/
#include "w3map.h"   /* available on disk */

/* function calls */
typedef void (far *api_entry)(void);

api_entry GetVxDAPI(WORD vxd_id);
BOOL GenericVxDInstalled(void);
BOOL VxDCall(VxDParams far *fp);
BOOL VxDPushCall(VxDPushParams far *fp);
```

VxDCall() does little more than take the VxDParams structure, passed in by a function such as GetNextVMHandle(), and pass the structure in ES:BX to the generic VxD entry point. VxDCall() calls InitVxDAPI() to initialize this entry point, if necessary, by calling GetVxDAPI(). GetVxDAPI() is just a wrapper around INT 2Fh AX=1684h. The generic VxD's ID is 28C0h; Microsoft assigns these VxD IDs.

With all the scaffolding in place, we are now ready to use the VMWALK facility to build a Windows program that examines data in DOS boxes. ENUMDRV.C, shown in Listing 3-27 (this is getting ridiculous!), is a Windows application that displays the Current Directory Structure (CDS) in all VMs. ENUMDRV calls vmwalk() to install a walkfunc, cleverly called walkfunc(), which, for each VM, gets a pointer to the CDS and prints out all the drives and the current directory on each drive.

ENUMDRV uses the CURRDRIVE field from the SDA to indicate the current drive in each VM. As we know, there is a documented DOS function that returns the current drive, but calling this function returns only the current drive for the caller, that is, for the current VM. It is possible to call DOS functions in other VMs, but it is considerably easier in this case to just grope the other VM's SDA. So it turns out that the foolishness back in Listing 3-4 about getting the CURRDRIVE value out of the SDA, rather than calling the documented DOS function (which then just gets the value out of the SDA) maybe wasn't such a dumb idea after all.

Listing 3-27: ENUMDRV.C Displays the CDS in All VMs

```
/*
ENUMDRV.C
Version of ENUMDRV for multiple VMs in Windows Enhanced mode
Andrew Schulman, April 1993
from "Undocumented DOS", 2nd edition (Addison-Wesley, 1993)

DPMI version:
bcc -2 -DDPMI_APP -c vxdcalls.c vmwalk.c iswin.c
tlib dpmi_app+vxdcalls.obj+vmwalk.obj+iswin.obj
bcc -2 -DDPMI_APP enumdrv.c dpmi_app.lib

Windows version (uses EasyWin):
bcc -2 -W -DWINDOWS enumdrv.c prot.c vxdcalls.c vmwalk.c

WVMWALK version (uses EasyWin; no generic VxD):
bcc -W -DWINDOWS -DUSE_WVMWALK -2 enumdrv.c wvmwalk.c prot.c
*/

#include <stdlib.h>
#include <stdio.h>
#include <string.h>
#include <dos.h>

#ifdef WINDOWS
#include "windows.h"
#else
#define DPMI_APP
#include "dpmish.h"
#endif

#include "prot.h"
#ifndef USE_WVMWALK
#include "vxdcalls.h"
#endif
#include "vmwalk.h"

#define NETWORK       (1 << 15)
#define PHYSICAL      (1 << 14)
#define JOIN          (1 << 13)
#define SUBST         (1 << 12)
#define REDIR_NOT_NET (1 << 7)   /* CDROM */

typedef unsigned char BYTE;
typedef unsigned short WORD;
typedef unsigned long DWORD;
typedef BYTE far *DPB;       // provide actual DPB struct if needed

#pragma pack(1)

typedef struct {
    BYTE current_path[67];  // current path (_MAX_PATH != 67)
    WORD flags;             // NETWORK, PHYSICAL, JOIN, SUBST
    DPB  far *dpb;          // pointer to Drive Parameter Block
    union {
        struct {
            WORD start_cluster; // root: 0000; never accessed: FFFFh
            DWORD unknown;
            } LOCAL;        // if (! (cds[drive].flags & NETWORK))
        struct {
```

```c
            DWORD redirifs_record_ptr;
            WORD parameter;
            } NET;          // if (cds[drive].flags & NETWORK)
        } u;
    WORD backslash_offset;  // offset in current_path of '\'
    // DOS4 fields for IFS
    // 7 extra bytes...
    } CDS;                  // Current Directory Structure
CDS far *currdir(unsigned drive);
void set_vm(DWORD vm);

#define ENHANCED_MODE   3

// see ISWIN.C
extern int is_win(int *pmaj, int *pmin, int *pmode);

void fail(const char *s, ...)
{
    puts(s);
#ifdef DPMI_APP
    _dos_exit(1);
#else
    exit(1);
#endif
}

static void far *sysvars_real = 0;
static void far *sda_real = 0;
static int currdir_size = 0;

#ifdef DPMI_APP
// going to do initialization from real mode (real_main())!
#define CALL_DOS(x,y,z)     int86x(0x21, x, y, z)
#else
#define CALL_DOS(x,y,z)     real_int86x(0x21, x, y, z)
#endif

void far *get_sysvars(void)
{
    union REGS r;
    struct SREGS s;
    memset(&r, 0, sizeof(r));
    memset(&s, 0, sizeof(s));
    r.h.ah = 0x52;
    CALL_DOS(&r, &r, &s);
    return MK_FP(s.es, r.x.bx);
}

void far *get_sda(void)
{
    union REGS r;
    struct SREGS s;
    memset(&r, 0, sizeof(r));
    memset(&s, 0, sizeof(s));
    r.x.ax = 0x5d06;
    CALL_DOS(&r, &r, &s);
    return (r.x.cflag) ? (void far *) 0 : MK_FP(s.ds, r.x.si);
}

void do_init(void)
{
#ifndef USE_WVMWALK
    if (! GenericVxDInstalled())
        fail("This program requires the generic VxD (VXD.386)\n"
            "Put device=vxd.386 in [386Enh] section of SYSTEM.INI");
#endif

    // assumes SysVars at same address in all VMs
    // but CDS not necessarily at same address!
```

```
    if (! (sysvars_real = get_sysvars()))
        fail("21/52 failed: can't get SysVars!\n");

    // assumes SDA at same address in all VMs
    if (! (sda_real = get_sda()))
        fail("21/5D06 failed: can't get SDA!\n");

    // problem!  Microsoft C QuickWin defines _osmajor, _osminor
    // with the Windows version, not the DOS version!!
    _asm mov ax, 3000h
    _asm int 21h
    _asm mov byte ptr _osmajor, al
    currdir_size = (_osmajor >= 4) ? 0x58 : 0x51;
}
#ifdef WINDOWS
int main(int argc, char *argv[])
{
    if (! (GetWinFlags() & WF_PMODE))
        fail("This program requires Windows 3.x Enhanced mode");

    do_init();
#ifdef USE_WVMWALK
    return wvmwalk(wwalkfunc);
#else
    return vmwalk(walkfunc);
#endif
}
#else
int real_main(int argc, char *argv[])
{
    int maj, min, mode;

    puts("ENUMDRV -- Enumerate CDS in all Windows VMs");
    puts("From \"Undocumented DOS\", 2nd edition (Addison-Wesley, 1993)\n");

    if ((! is_win(&maj, &min, &mode)) || (maj < 3) ||
        (mode != ENHANCED_MODE))
        fail("This program requires Windows 3.x Enhanced mode");

    do_init();  // call in real mode
    return 0;   // okay to switch into protected mode
}

int pmode_main(int argc, char *argv[])
{
    vmwalk(walkfunc);
    return 0;
}
#endif

#ifdef USE_WVMWALK
BOOL wwalkfunc(HWND hwnd, char *title, DWORD vm, VM_CB far *vm_cb)
#else
BOOL walkfunc(DWORD vm, VM_CB far *vm_cb)
#endif
{
    CDS far *cds, far *dir;
    BYTE far *sysvars;
    BYTE far *cds_real;
    BYTE far *sda;
    DWORD total, notmapped;
    int lastdrv, currdrv;
    int i;
    static DWORD sys_vm = 0;
    static DWORD cur_vm = 0;
#ifndef USE_WVMWALK
    if (! sys_vm) sys_vm = GetSysVMHandle();
    if (! cur_vm) cur_vm = GetCurVMHandle();
```

```
#endif
#define CDS_OFS        0x16
#define LASTDRV_OFS    0x21
    // Set the base address. Could also have used map_linear_vm
    // or map_real_vm. This one call to set_base will affect all
    // subsequent calls to map_linear.
    set_base(vm_cb->CB_High_Linear);
    sysvars = (BYTE far *) map_real(sysvars_real, LASTDRV_OFS+1);

    // Note: does _not_ assume that CDS at same address in all VMs!
    // But moving a CDS breaks in Windows anyway, because DOSMGR assumes
    // that CDS never moves after Windows initialization. *Sigh*
    cds_real = *((BYTE far * far *) &sysvars[CDS_OFS]);
    lastdrv = sysvars[LASTDRV_OFS];
    free_mapped_linear(sysvars);

    printf("\n%s (VM %lu) -- CDS at %08lX\n",
        (vm == sys_vm) ? "System VM" :
        (vm == cur_vm) ? "Current VM" :
        /* default */    "DOS Box",
        vm_cb->CB_VMID,
        vm_cb->CB_High_Linear + MK_LIN(cds_real));
#define CURRDRV_OFS    0x16
    // get current drive for this VM from SDA:0016
    // for System VM, will depend on current task
    // (each Windows app has its own current drive/directory)
    // already did set_base(vm_cb->CB_High_Linear);
    sda = (BYTE far *) map_real(sda_real, CURRDRV_OFS+1);
    currdrv = sda[CURRDRV_OFS];
    free_mapped_linear(sda);

    // map in cds_real for this VM, print out, free it
    cds = (CDS far *) map_real(cds_real, lastdrv * currdir_size);
    for (i=0; i<lastdrv; i++)
    {
        dir = (CDS far *) (((BYTE far *) cds) + (i * currdir_size));
        if (dir->flags)
        {
            // highlight current drive for this VM
            printf( (i == currdrv) ? "==> " : "    " );

            printf("%c\t%-50Fs", 'A' + i, dir->current_path);
            if (dir->flags & REDIR_NOT_NET) printf("REDIR_NOT_NET ");
            else if (dir->flags & NETWORK) printf("NETWORK ");
            if (dir->flags & JOIN) printf("JOIN ");
            if (dir->flags & SUBST) printf("SUBST");
            printf("\n");
        }
    }
    free_mapped_linear(cds);
    set_base(0);    // restore
    return TRUE;
}
```

Figure 3-8 shows output from ENUMDRV. By looking at all the VMs, this program provides a telling demonstration that Windows maintains multiple current drives and directories by instancing the CDS. The CDS is at the same segment:offset address in each VM (though ENUMDRV does not in fact depend on this). But observe that each one is different. It is worth contrasting this with, for example, the SFT, which is not instanced, aside from the link to the PerVMFiles= and GrowSFT segments, discussed earlier.

Figure 3-8: ENUMDRV Shows the CDS in Each Windows VM

```
System VM (VM 1) -- CDS at 81410DB0
    A    A:\
```

```
      B    B:\
==>   C    C:\SICE
      D    D:\
      E    E:\
      F    F:\
      G    G:\
Current VM (VM 2) -- CDS at 81810DB0
      A    A:\
      B    B:\
==>   C    C:\UNDOC2\CHAP3
      D    D:\
      E    E:\
      F    F:\
      G    G:\
```

If you look at ENUMDRV.C, you will notice that you can use it to build a DPMI_APP, a Windows application (using EasyWin or QuickWin), or a Windows application with something called WVMWALK. However, you cannot build this multiple-VM ENUMDRV as a real mode DOS program because, while a real mode program could easily call the generic VxD to enumerate VM handles, the program couldn't call map_linear() to access them.

What is WVMWALK? It turns out that a Windows application can bypass the generic VxD entirely and use an extremely slimy hack to enumerate VM handles. Remember, we're using the generic VxD here only to get a few VM handles. Everything else, such as turning the VM handle into a usable VM_CB structure and then using the high linear field, comes from using the map_linear() function provided by PROT.C.

The extremely slimy hack goes like this: It is possible to enumerate DOS boxes from a Windows program. WINPSP.C showed how to walk the Windows task list and determine if IsWinOldApTask. You can alternatively walk the window list using GetWindow(), find the task for each window using GetWindowTask(), and then call the undocumented IsWinOldApTask() function to see if you have a DOS box. Paul Bonneau of the *Windows/DOS Developer's Journal* (and now of Microsoft) found that, in Windows 3.1, offset 0FCh in a DOS box's data segment holds the DOS box's VM handle (see *Windows DOS Developers Journal*, December 1992). This makes it possible to write a VM_FROM_HWND() macro and use it as the basis for a Windows-based facility to enumerate VM handles.

The resulting code, WVMWALK.C, is shown in Listing 3-28. Of course, this code is utterly dependent on the VM handle staying at offset 0FCh, so it is unlikely to work in any version of Windows other than 3.1. You can link WVMWALK with ENUMDRV to form a Windows version of ENUMDRV that doesn't require the generic VxD (see the instructions at the top of Listing 3-27).

Listing 3-28: WVMWALK.C, a Slimy Hack to Enumerate VM Handles from Windows

```c
/*
WVMWALK.C -- Version of VMWALK for Windows 3.1
Andrew Schulman, April 1993
From "Undocumented DOS", 2nd edition (Addison-Wesley, 1993)
*/

#include <stdlib.h>
#include <string.h>
#include <dos.h>
#include "windows.h"
#include "prot.h"
#include "vmwalk.h"

// see W/DDJ, December 1992 (this is Paul Bonneau's doing!)
// see also MSJ, February 1993, p. 30
#define VM_FROM_HWND(hWndDosBox) \
    *((LPDWORD) MK_FP(GetWindowWord(hWndDosBox, GWW_HINSTANCE), 0x0FC))

// since undoc, missing from some import libs, so do run-time link
static BOOL (FAR PASCAL *IsWinOldApTask)(HANDLE hTask) = 0;
```

```
// from Undocumented Windows, p. 304
BOOL IsDosBox(HWND hWnd)
{
    if (! IsWinOldApTask) // one-time init
        if (! (IsWinOldApTask = (BOOL (FAR PASCAL *)(HANDLE))
            GetProcAddress(GetModuleHandle("KERNEL"),"ISWINOLDAPTASK")))
                fail("Can't find KERNEL.IsWinOldApTask");
    return (*IsWinOldApTask)(GetWindowTask(hWnd));
}

typedef BOOL (*WWALKFUNC)(HWND hwnd, char *title, DWORD vm, VM_CB far *vm_cb);

int wvmwalk(WWALKFUNC walkfunc)
{
    char buf[0x50];
    VM_CB dummy;
    HWND hwnd;
    int num_vm;

    if (((WORD) GetVersion()) != 0x0A03)
        return 0;          // only works in Windows 3.1
    if (! (GetWinFlags() & WF_ENHANCED))
        return 0;          // only works in Enhanced mode

    hwnd = GetActiveWindow();
    GetWindowText(hwnd, buf, 0x50);

    // Can't get handle for System VM, but that is VM the Windows
    // app is running in! So make a dummy VM_CB and pass that
    // (actually, COULD get System VM by walking VM next ptrs):
    memset(&dummy, 0, sizeof(dummy));
    dummy.CB_High_Linear = 0;      // current VM!
    dummy.CB_VMID = 1;             // System VM is always VM 1
    if (! (*walkfunc)(hwnd, buf, 0, &dummy))
        return 0;
    num_vm = 1;

    hwnd = GetWindow(hwnd, GW_HWNDFIRST);
    while (hwnd)
    {
        if (IsDosBox(hwnd) && GetWindowText(hwnd, buf, 0x50))
        {
            DWORD vm = VM_FROM_HWND(hwnd);
            VM_CB far *vm_cb = (VM_CB far *)
                map_linear(vm, sizeof(VM_CB));
            VM_CB my_vm_cb;
            _fmemcpy(&my_vm_cb, vm_cb, sizeof(VM_CB));
            free_mapped_linear(vm_cb);
            if (! (*walkfunc)(hwnd, buf, vm, &my_vm_cb))
                return num_vm;
            set_base(0);  // in case app changed base
        }

        hwnd = GetWindow(hwnd, GW_HWNDNEXT);
    }
    return num_vm;
}

#ifdef TESTING
#include <stdio.h>

BOOL wwalkfunc(HWND hwnd, char *title, DWORD vm, VM_CB far *vm_cb)
{
    printf("%04Xh\t%08lXh\t\"%s\"\n", hwnd, vm, title);
    printf("    VM #%lu    st=%08lXh    lin=%08lXh    crs=%08lXh\n\n",
        vm_cb->CB_VMID,
        vm_cb->CB_VM_Status,
        vm_cb->CB_High_Linear,
        vm_cb->CB_Client_Pointer);
```

```
      return 1;
}
main()
{
    return wvmwalk(wwalkfunc);
}
#endif
```

Aside from its extreme version dependence, there is a problem with WVMWALK: It does not get a handle for the System VM. However, this is not a major problem. This technique only works for Windows applications, and Windows applications run in the System VM. By definition, when a Windows application, such as a WVMWALK version of ENUMDRV, is running, the System VM *is* the current VM, so the program doesn't need the high linear address anyway. It can access its own CDS or whatever with a base of zero, just as we did all along when we innocently didn't know about VM handles, high linear base addresses, and other deviltry. WVMWALK concocts a dummy VM_CB for the System VM. Furthermore, by using the next pointer stored at offset 68h in each VM_CB to walk the VM linked list, it might be possible to locate the System VM, which is VM ID #1.

Actually, you could even use Bonneau's VM_FROM_HWND() technique in conjunction with the generic VxD. In Figure 3-8, it would be nice to have some more identification for each VM, such as its window title. Meanwhile, the WVMWALK version, since it starts with a window handle, is able to display window titles (see Figure 3-9). You could combine the two techniques to produce a single, more useful display. After all, most users don't think of VMs or even of DOS boxes; they think of the applications they are running.

Figure 3-9: WVMWALK Version of ENUMDRV

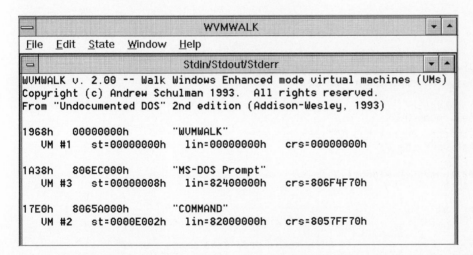

Note finally that ENUMDRV can also be built as a DPMI_APP. There is a twist here, however. We earlier built several utilities that required DPMI, and these could actually run not only in Windows but under any DPMI host, such as 386MAX 6.0 and higher. With ENUMDRV, though, we have a DOS program that, because of VMWALK and VXDCALLS, really does require Windows Enhanced mode. ENUMDRV uses the function is_win() to ensure it is running under Enhanced mode. Listing 3-29 shows ISWIN.C.

Listing 3-29: ISWIN.C: DOS Code to Check for Windows

```c
/*
ISWIN.C
Detecting Windows mode, version from DOS
Andrew Schulman, February 1993
bcc -DSTANDALONE iswin.c
*/

#include <stdlib.h>
#include <stdio.h>
#include <dos.h>

#define REAL_MODE            1
#define STANDARD_MODE        2
#define ENHANCED_MODE        3

#define SYSTEM_VM            1

int detect_switcher(void)
{
    int retval = 1;
    _asm push di
    _asm push es
    _asm xor bx, bx
    _asm mov di, bx
    _asm mov es, bx
    _asm mov ax, 4b02h
    _asm int 2fh
    _asm mov cx, es
    _asm or cx, di
    _asm je no_switcher
done:
    _asm pop es
    _asm pop di
    return retval;
no_switcher:
    retval = 0;
    goto done;
}
// a lot more complicated than you would have thought!
int is_win(int *pmaj, int *pmin, int *pmode)
{
    unsigned short retval;
    int maj=0, min=0, mode=0;

    /* make sure someone, anyone has INT 2Fh */
    if (_dos_getvect(0x2F) == 0)
        return 0;

    /* call 2F/160A to see if Windows 3.1+ */
    _asm mov ax, 160ah
    _asm int 2fh
    _asm mov retval, ax
    if (retval == 0)                    /* AX=0 if Windows running */
    {
        _asm mov mode, cx               /* CX=2 means Std; CX=3 means Enh */
        _asm mov byte ptr maj, bh       /* BX = major/minor (e.g., 030Ah) */
        _asm mov byte ptr min, bl
        *pmaj = maj;
        *pmin = min;
        *pmode = mode;
        return 1;
    }

    /* call 2F/1600 to see if Windows 3.0 Enhanced mode or Windows/386 */
    _asm mov ax, 1600h
    _asm int 2fh
    _asm mov byte ptr maj, al
```

```c
    _asm mov byte ptr min, ah
    if ((maj == 1) || (maj == 0xFF))       /* Windows/386 2.x is running */
    {
        *pmaj = 2;                 /* Windows/386 2.x */
        *pmin = 1;                 /* don't know; assume 2.1? */
        *pmode = ENHANCED_MODE; /* Windows/386 sort of like Enhanced */
        return 1;
    }
    else if (! ((maj==0) || (maj==0x80))) // AL=0 or 80h if no Windows
    {   /* must be Windows 3.0 Enhanced mode */
        *pmaj = maj;
        *pmin = min;
        *pmode = ENHANCED_MODE;
        return 1;
    }

    /* call 2F/4680 to see if Windows 3.0 Standard or Real mode; but,
       this could be a "3.0 derivative" such as DOSSHELL task switcher! */
    _asm mov ax, 4680h
    _asm int 2fh
    _asm mov retval, ax
    if (retval == 0)               /* AX=0 if 2F/4680 handled */
    {
        /* make sure it isn't DOSSHELL task switcher */
        if (detect_switcher())
            return 0;
        *pmaj = 3;
        *pmin = 0;

        /* either have Windows Standard mode or Real mode; to
           distinguish, have to do fake Windows broadcasts with
           2F/1605. Yuk! We'll avoid that here by assuming
           3.0 Standard mode. If you really want to distinguish
           3.0 Standard mode and Real mode, see _MSJ_, March 1991,
           p. 113; and MS KB articles Q75943 and Q75338 */
        *pmode = STANDARD_MODE;
        return 1;
    }

    /* still here -- must not be running Windows */
    return 0;
}

#ifdef STANDALONE
main()
{
    int maj, min, mode=0;
    if (! is_win(&maj, &min, &mode))
        printf("Windows is not running\n");
    else if (maj == 2)
        printf("Running Windows/386 2.x\n");
    else
        printf("Running Windows %u.%02u (or higher) %s mode\n",
            maj,
            min,
            (mode == REAL_MODE) ?     "Real" :
            (mode == STANDARD_MODE) ? "Standard" :
            (mode == ENHANCED_MODE) ? "Enhanced" :
            /* don't know */ "???");

    if (mode == ENHANCED_MODE)
    {
        unsigned short vm;
        /* call 2F/1683 to see if DOS app running in System VM; if so,
           this must be some hacked version of Windows like MSDPMI,
           or we must be running inside WINSTART.BAT */
        _asm mov ax, 1683h
        _asm int 2fh
```

```
      _asm mov vm, bx
      if (vm == SYSTEM_VM)
          printf("Running DOS app in System VM: "
                 "Must be WINSTART.BAT or hacked Windows!\n");
      else
          printf("VM #%u\n", vm);
    }
    /* could also call 2F/160C to check for Windows in ROM */
    return mode;    /* can be tested with ERRORLEVEL */
}
#endif
```

Something as seemingly simple as checking for Windows turns out to be so complicated that it requires 150 lines of code!

Undocumented DOS and DesqView

by Ralf Brown

With all this talk about Windows, what about other multitasking windowing environments for DOS, such as Quarterdeck's DESQview?

Although no special preparations are required to access undocumented DOS functions or data from a program running under the DESQview multitasker, task switching should be disabled when modifying DOS data structures through any method other than INT 21h calls.

DESQview serializes access to DOS via INT 21h, thus automatically avoiding problems with DOS data structure modifications. If a program directly modifies DOS internal data, however, a task switch could occur while the data is being modified. Ordinarily, one could just disable interrupts while making the modifications, but this will not work on 386 and higher processors. QEMM (used in DESQview/386) and other memory managers virtualize the interrupt flag, with the result that DESQview is able to task switch even while interrupts appear to be disabled. Therefore, task switching must be explicitly disabled by asserting a critical section using TopView API calls. While IBM's TopView has gone to the land of the cut-out bins (you can purchase TopView for $4.95 at a store called Weird Stuff in Sunnyvale, CA; a TopView SDK there costs $7.95), its API still lives on in DESQview, as well as in Sunny Hill Software's TaskView/OmniView.

Listing 3-30: DESQVIEW.C (Actually, More Like TopView)

```
static int TopView = 0 ;
void check_TopView(void)
{
    union REGS regs ;
    regs.x.ax = 0x1022 ;            /* get TopView version */
    regs.x.bx = 0 ;
    int86(0x15,&regs,&regs) ;
    TopView = regs.x.bx ;           /* nonzero if TopView or compatible */
}
void TopView_begincrit(void)
{
    union REGS regs ;
    if (TopView)
    {
        regs.x.ax = 0x101B ;            /* start critical section */
        int86(0x15,&regs,&regs) ;
    }
}
```

```
void TopView_endcrit(void)
{
    union REGS regs ;
    if (TopView)
    {
        regs.x.ax = 0x101C ;            /* end critical section */
        int86(0x15,&regs,&regs) ;
    }
}
```

These three functions are used in the following manner: call check_TopView() once near the beginning of the program to initialize the TopView variable. Then, each time a DOS data structure is to be modified, surround the code performing the modification by calls to TopView_begincrit() and TopView_endcrit(), which disable and enable task switching, respectively.

This chapter's discussion of Windows focused entirely on *peeking* at DOS internal data structures, so the question of critical sections never came up. However, Ralf's point about *modifying* structures in DESQview actually applies with equal force to Windows, at least when a DOS box's Background execution bit is set. Programs that modify DOS internal data should use the Begin Critical Section (INT 2Fh AX=1681h) and End Critical Section (INT 2Fh AX=1682h) calls, which the Windows DDK documents. On the other hand, a useful Microsoft KnowledgeBase article, "Using the Interrupt 2Fh Critical Section Services" (Q78151) notes that, despite their names, these functions "do not prevent a task switch from occurring" and "impact task switching only in a limited way." Sheesh! If you absolutely, positively must guarantee that a sequence of code will not be interrupted and switched away from, you need to put the code in a VxD.

A Brief Introduction to VxD Programming

Speaking of VxDs, we've seen so many VxD code fragments, both here and in Chapter 1, that we really need to look briefly at a complete, albeit small, VxD.

UNDOSMGR.ASM (Listing 3-31) is the 32-bit assembly-language source code for UNDOSMGR.386, a virtual device driver that provides *transparent* support in protected mode for a single undocumented DOS function, INT 21h AX=5D06h (Get SDA). Earlier in this chapter, we saw how a program running under Windows can use DPMI to call this function from protected mode. Because the program must explicitly use DPMI to access the function, this form of support is, of course, non-transparent.

However, if UNDOSMGR.386 is installed with a line such as device=c:\undoc2\chap3\-undosmgr.386 in the [386Enh] section of SYSTEM.INI, suddenly INT 21h AX=5D06h is supported in protected mode, and protected mode programs no longer need to access it via DPMI. They can just call the function as they would in real mode, and the UNDOSMGR VxD takes care of everything. With UNDOSMGR installed, a straight protected mode port of CURRDRIV.C (Listing 3-4) works properly, and Borland C++ no longer generates error messages from the debug version of DOSMGR.

Listing 3-31: UNDOSMGR.ASM

```
; UNDOCMGR.ASM
; Sample VxD that provides one undocumented DOS function (21/5D06)
;       in protected mode
; Andrew Schulman, April 1993
; From "Undocumented DOS", 2nd edition (Addison-Wesley, 1993)
.386p
INCLUDE VMM.INC
INCLUDE V86MMGR.INC
```

```
;**********************************************************************
;           V I R T U A L   D E V I C E   D E C L A R A T I O N
;**********************************************************************
Declare_Virtual_Device UNDOSMGR, 1, 0, \
    Control_Proc, \
    Undefined_Device_ID, \
    Undefined_Init_Order, , ,\

;**********************************************************************
;                 O N L Y   D A T A   S E G M E N T
;**********************************************************************
VxD_DATA_SEG

Prev_Int21Pmode     dd  0
Prev_Int21Pmode_Seg dw  0

VxD_DATA_ENDS

;**********************************************************************
;         M O V E A B L E   C O D E   S E G M E N T
;**********************************************************************
VxD_CODE_SEG

BeginProc   Int21Pmode
    mov     eax, [ebp.Client_EAX]
    cmp     ax, 5D06h
    je      short Do_GetSDA

Default:
    movzx   ecx, Prev_Int21Pmode_Seg     ;; *NOT* mov cx!!
    mov     edx, Prev_Int21Pmode
    VMMcall Simulate_Far_Jmp
    jmp     short Fini

Do_GetSDA:

IFDEF BYPASS_V86MMGR
    ; sample code to show how this looks with raw VMM calls
    VMMcall Simulate_Iret
    VMMcall Begin_Nest_V86_Exec
    mov     eax, 21h
    VMMcall Exec_Int               ; reflect INT 21h to V86 mode
    VMMcall Resume_Exec            ; do it now!
    movzx   eax, [ebp.Client_DS]   ; get V86 DS inside nest
    VMMcall End_Nest_Exec
    shl     eax, 4                 ; make linear address
    mov     ecx, 0FFFFh            ; 64k segment
    VMMcall Map_Lin_To_VM_Addr     ; create permanent selector
    mov     [ebp.Client_DS], cx    ; return selector to caller in DS
ELSE
    VMMcall Simulate_Iret
    mov     edx, OFFSET32 GetSDA_API
    VxDcall V86MMGR_Xlat_API
ENDIF

Fini:
    clc
    ret

GetSDA_API:
    Xlat_API_Return_Ptr DS, SI
    Xlat_API_Exec_Int 21h
EndProc     Int21Pmode

VxD_CODE_ENDS

;**********************************************************************
;             L O C K E D   C O D E   S E G M E N T
;**********************************************************************
VxD_LOCKED_CODE_SEG

BeginProc   Control_Proc
```

```
    Control_Dispatch Device_Init, Do_Device_Init
    clc
    ret
EndProc     Control_Proc

VxD_LOCKED_CODE_ENDS
;**********************************************************************
;              P M   I N I T   C O D E   S E G M E N T
;**********************************************************************
VxD_ICODE_SEG

BeginProc   Do_Device_Init
    ; get previous pmode INT 21h handler, so can chain
    mov     eax, 21h
    VMMcall Get_PM_Int_Vector
    mov     Prev_Int21Pmode, edx        ; offset
    mov     Prev_Int21Pmode_Seg, cx     ; segment

    ; turn Int21 handler into pmode callback
    xor     edx, edx
    mov     esi, OFFSET32 Int21Pmode
    VMMcall Allocate_PM_Call_Back
    jc      short Done
    ; segment:offset callback address in EAX

    ; install pmode Int21 handler
    mov     ecx, eax
    movzx   edx, ax
    shr     ecx, 10h
    mov     eax, 21h              ; eax = intno
    VMMcall Set_PM_Int_Vector
Done:
    ret
EndProc     Do_Device_Init

VxD_ICODE_ENDS
;**********************************************************************
;          R E A L   M O D E   I N I T I A L I Z A T I O N
;**********************************************************************
VXD_REAL_INIT_SEG

; just a stub real_init procedure
real_init proc near
    xor ax, ax
    xor bx, bx
    xor si, si
    xor edx, edx
    ret
real_init endp

VXD_REAL_INIT_ENDS
    END
```

VxDs are 32-bit Linear Executable (LE) files, which the standard Microsoft assembler and linker currently can't build. To turn UNDOSMGR.ASM into UNDOSMGR.386, you will need Microsoft's MASM5, LINK386, and ADDHDR utilities, and Microsoft's all-important VMM.INC header file, included with the Windows DDK and with the "VxD Lite" package available on the MSDN CD-ROM. MK_VXD is a handy batch file for making simple VxDs:

```
rem MK_VXD.BAT
set include=\ddk\include
masm5 -p -w2 %2 %1;
link386 %1,%1.386,,,%1.def
addhdr %1.386
```

For example, run MK_VXD UNDOSMGR or MK_VXD UNDOSMGR -DBYPASS_V86MMGR (see below for an explanation of BYPASS_V86MMGR). You will also need UNDOSMGR.DEF, provided on the accompanying disk.

How does UNDOSMGR work? The Declare_Virtual_Device statement near the top of UNDOSMGR.ASM establishes the function Control_Proc as UNDOSMGR's event handler. Control_Proc, further down in UNDOSMGR.ASM, is interested in only one event, Device_Init. Control_Proc establishes the Do_Device_Init function as the handler for the Device_Init event. Do_Device_Init patches UNDOSMGR into the protected mode INT 21h handler chain. It calls the VMM function Get_PM_Int_Vector to retrieve the previous handler's address and calls Set_PM_Int_Vector to install the UNDOSMGR handler. This handler, called Int21Pmode, is of course 32-bit Ring 0 code that is not normally callable from "normal" 16-bit programs running under Windows. UNDOSMGR passes the address of Int21Pmode to the VMM Allocate_PM_Call_Back function, which returns a protected mode "callback" that *is* callable from normal programs. By passing the address of this callback to Set_PM_Int_Vector, UNDOSMGR guarantees that, every time any program running under Windows issues an INT 21h in protected mode, the call will go to UNDOSMGR's Int21Pmode handler.

That's the end of UNDOSMGR's initialization. Now it lies dormant, its Int21Pmode handler waiting for protected mode INT 21h calls. Each time it is called, Int21Pmode checks to see if the function it handles (INT 21h AX=5D06h) has been called, by comparing [ebp.Client_EAX] with 5D06h. If the caller has requested some other INT 21h function, Int21Pmode chains to the previous INT 21h handler with a Simulate_Far_Jmp (this was taken from the DDK's VDMAD sample source code for chaining protected mode interrupts).

If the caller (such as CURRDRIV or Borland C++) actually did request an INT 21h AX=5D06h in protected mode, UNDOSMGR.ASM has two ways of handling the call. If assembled with BYPASS_V86MMGR, UNDOSMGR makes "raw" VMM calls, very similar to those we saw back in Listing 3-15, when we were discussing the implementation of DOSMGR. UNDOSMGR contains code that is nearly identical to that in DOSMGR and in fact is really just DOSMGR's evil baby brother. If assembled without the BYPASS_V86MMGR switch, UNDOSMGR uses the V86MMGR Xlat API, passing the address of a tiny GetSDA_API "script" to the V86MMGR_Xlat_API function. Either way, UNDOSMGR reflects the INT 21h down to V86 mode and then translates DS into a protected mode selector, using Xlat_API_Return_Ptr with V86MMGR, or Map_Lin_To_VM_Addr with direct VMM calls.

Timing DOS Calls

Clearly, VxDs provide a lot of power to extend the Windows DOS extender and provide other system services. VxD programming in many ways is to DOS systems programming in the 1990s what TSRs were to DOS programming in the 1980s. But notice that every single protected mode INT 21h call passes though UNDOSMGR's Int21Pmode function, even though UNDOSMGR is only interested in the AX=5D06h Get SDA call. What is the overhead for installing UNDOSMGR? What effect does it have on INT 21h calls other than AX=5D06h? We can measure the impact of UNDOSMGR, and the performance impact of the entire VMM/VxD mechanism, with a small DPMI program, DOSSPEED.C, which simply issues a large number of very simple INT 21h calls. DOSSPEED runs this DOS-call loop once in real (or V86) mode, then switches to protected mode and runs the loop again. It displays the number of seconds used to make the INT 21h calls. Listing 3-32 shows DOSSPEED.C.

Listing 3-32: DOSSPEED.C

```
/*
DOSSPEED.C -- time DOS operations
Andrew Schulman, May 1993
From "Undocumented DOS", 2nd edition (Addison-Wesley, 1993)
bcc -DDPMI_APP -2 dosspeed.c dpmi_app.lib
*/
```

```c
#include <stdlib.h>
#include <stdio.h>
#include <dos.h>
#include <time.h>
#include "dpmish.h"
void dosspeed(unsigned long iter)
{
    time_t t1, t2;
    unsigned long i;

    time(&t1);
    for (i=0; i<iter; i++)
    {
        _asm mov ah, 2Ah           /* get date */
        _asm int 21h
        _asm mov ah, 2Ch           /* get time */
        _asm int 21h
        _asm mov ah, 51h           /* get PSP */
        _asm int 21h
        _asm mov ax, 3000h         /* get version */
        _asm int 21h
    }
    time(&t2);
    printf("%lu calls in %lu seconds\n", iter * 4, t2 - t1);
}
void fail(const char *s, ...) { puts(s); _dos_exit(1); }
int real_main(int argc, char *argv[])
{
    printf("real mode: ");
    dosspeed((argc < 2) ? 10000 : atol(argv[1]));
    return 0;
}
int pmode_main(int argc, char *argv[])
{
    printf("prot mode: ");
    dosspeed((argc < 2) ? 10000 : atol(argv[1]));
    return 0;
}
```

On a standard 80386SX/20 laptop, DOSSPEED turned in the following times for 10,000 iterations of the four calls to INT 21h AH=2Ah, AH=2Ch, AH=30h, and AX=51h (recall from our earlier discussion that these four functions are typically called very frequently):

MS-DOS 5 (no memory manager)	5 seconds
MS-DOS 5 (386MAX or EMM386)	8 sec
MS-DOS 5 (Windows Enhanced mode DOS box)	13 sec
386MAX DPMI client	23 sec
Windows Enhanced mode DPMI client	26 sec
W Enh mode, with UNDOSMGR.386 installed	29 sec
Novell DOS 7 with KRNL386.SYS	20+ sec
Novell DOS 7, in DPMI	50+ sec

As with any hastily-concocted benchmark, one can conclude from these figures whatever one wants. However, it does seem clear, first that there is a small but noticeable overhead for installing VxDs that hook frequently used software interrupts and that, more importantly, there is a large and very noticeable overhead for running in V86 mode under Windows Enhanced mode, and an even larger and more noticeable overhead for making DOS calls from protected mode. As a fitting conclusion to this chapter on porting DOS programs to protected mode, perhaps DOSSPEED is trying to tell us that, as long as Windows has to call down to real-mode DOS, the best way to make a lot of DOS calls from protected mode is not to make them at all.

## CHAPTER 4

Other DOSs: From DR DOS and NetWare to MVDMs in OS/2 and Windows NT

For better or worse, the MS-DOS INT 21h programming interface has become a worldwide computing standard, in much the same way that programming languages such as C or C++ are standards. There is no committee to oversee the DOS standard—it is a proprietary standard controlled by Microsoft—but many other companies have reimplemented the DOS interface. DOS executables can now run on many operating systems besides MS-DOS, including UNIX, OS/2, and Microsoft's own Windows NT.

The same thing is starting to happen with Windows executables, which can now run under several UNIX environments, such as the Windows Application Binary Interface (WABI) from Sun Microsystems' SunSelect division (based on earlier work by Praxsys Technologies). In fact, Sun is promoting the idea of a "Public Windows Interface" (PWI) to put the Windows API into the public domain (*Dr. Dobb's Journal*, August 1993, p. 154). While Sun and its backers at Borland, IBM, Quarterdeck, Wordperfect, and other companies clearly have their own motives for this odd PWI idea, one could argue that DOS and Windows are now sufficiently generic, and sufficiently important, to deserve something like ANSI standards committees.

Even when DOS executables do run where nature intended them to run, under DOS, it isn't always Microsoft's MS-DOS. In addition to several smaller companies such as Datalight and General Software, which produce clones or work-alikes of DOS for the embedded systems market, there is Novell of Provo, Utah, makers of NetWare. In 1991, Novell purchased Digital Research Inc. (DRI), originator of the CP/M operating system from which MS-DOS itself was cloned, and makers of a competitor to MS-DOS called DR DOS. DR DOS has been renamed Novell DOS. Given the dominant position of Novell's NetWare in the network operating system market, Novell DOS may provide some much-needed competition to Microsoft's MS-DOS.

What does it mean to clone DOS? From other parts of this book, you know that you can't just haul out Microsoft's *MS-DOS Programmer's Reference*, implement each function, and proclaim yourself finished. This would result in a DOS under which almost no popular PC application would run! Looking just at the INT 21h calls, you would have to implement the ever-popular function 52h. And this would mean implementing at least some of the SysVars (List of Lists) structure. If you wanted to run any networking software, you would have to implement the DOS side of the network redirector interface (INT 2Fh AH=11h; see Chapter 8). And if you wanted to run Windows, and thereby run WinWord and Excel, you would have to do a Swappable Data Area and function 5D06h, plus loads of other stuff that should be implementation details, but which in fact are part of the *de facto* DOS specification.

In implementing a version of DOS, a company might have some good ideas about how to implement different data structures. Tough luck! You had better have an MS-DOS style Current Directory Structure for the drive/directory table, a System File Table for open files, Memory Control Blocks, and so on. At least you need copies of them, enough to keep different applications happy, and then some mechanism for transferring state from these dummy DOS structures to whatever internal structures your system actually uses.

Even worse, if you were creating a DOS workalike you would need to keep a number of supposedly internal variables at certain fixed locations in your DOS's data segment. For example, later in this chapter we'll see that some of Microsoft's C compilers depend on the presence of a flag at offset 4 in the DOS data segment and expect the current PSP to be stored in the same segment at either offset 2DEh or 330h (see listing 4-4).

All in all, the interface between DOS applications and DOS is very wide. The DOS specification, in fact, is really the applications themselves. Any self-respecting DOS workalike must, by definition, support whatever the popular PC applications do.

This problem of implementation details that turn into specification requirements is not unique to DOS. Anyone who has worked in the compatibility business, trying to get applications from one environment to run in some other environment, knows how you go about such emulation. You take the old applications that your new environment must run, and you try to run them. When the applications bomb or when something goes wrong, you make some change or addition to your operating system. The specification, in other words, is inferred from the applications. You see what the applications expect of their environment, and you provide it.

In his famous book of essays on software engineering, *The Mythical Man-Month*, Fred Brooks has a good discussion of compatibility with *de facto* standards:

> . . . an implementation can serve as a formal definition. When the first compatible computers were built, this was exactly the technique used. The new machine was to match an existing machine. The manual was vague on some points? 'Ask the machine!' A test program would be devised to determine the behavior, and the new machine would be built to match. . . .
>
> Using an implementation as a definition has some advantages. All questions can be settled unambiguously by experiment. Debate is never needed, so answers are quick. Answers are always as precise as one wants, and they are always correct, by definition. Opposed to these one has a formidable set of disadvantages. The implementation may over-prescribe even the externals. . . . In an unpoliced system all kinds of side effects may appear, and these may have been used by programmers. When we undertook to emulate the IBM 1401 on System/360, for example, it developed that there were 30 different "curios"—side effects of supposedly invalid operations—that had come into widespread use and had to be considered as part of the definition.
>
> . . . the *de facto* definition will often be found to be inelegant in these particulars precisely because they have never received any thought. This inelegance will often turn out to be slow or costly to duplicate in another implementation. For example, some machines leave trash in the multiplicand register after a multiplication. The precise nature of this trash turns out to be part of the *de facto* definition, yet duplicating it may preclude the use of a faster multiplication algorithm.

In this chapter we look at the work of several companies engaged in the game of DOS compatibility. These companies must figure out and then reproduce the different "curios" (one might even say "trash") of the *de facto* DOS definition. Novell DOS (formerly DR DOS) must of course be as close as possible to MS-DOS, while providing additional features at a lower cost. In this chapter, we see how close Novell DOS comes to this goal.

Novell NetWare is not a clone of DOS, but as we already saw briefly in Chapter 2, it hooks DOS and makes some important alterations to it, so discussing NetWare in more detail while we discuss

Novell DOS makes sense. In fact, we'll see that Novell NetWare makes so many changes to the INT 21h interface that, even though it seems to run "on top of" DOS, it effectively *replaces* DOS, and thereby fully qualifies as an "other DOS."

IBM OS/2 2.x and Windows NT most definitely do not hook or in any other way sit on top of DOS; they completely replace it. But market reality dictates that these environments run DOS programs out of the box. This ability is called *binary compatibility*, in contrast to the much simpler goal of source compatibility. In fact, users may for some time employ such environments primarily for the purpose of running old DOS or Windows software. This requires that the new operating system either emulate DOS or run a copy of genuine DOS within a virtual machine. Either way, an important question is whether DOS programs that access undocumented DOS data structures or call undocumented DOS functions will run in these environments. Undocumented DOS is an excellent test of DOS compatibility. Achieving compatibility with documented interfaces is fairly easy, so when you hear discussions of "DOS compatibility" or "Windows compatibility," it's really support for the undocumented interfaces that's being discussed.

An interesting point emerges from all this. It is often *in Microsoft's interest* for major applications (not necessarily or even primarily its own) to use undocumented DOS features, as this ties these applications to Microsoft's own versions of DOS (note especially that IBM's license to the DOS source code runs out in September 1993). After all, what is really the difference between Microsoft's DOS and anyone else's, except that Microsoft has guaranteed better support for the funky undocumented things that DOS applications do? For Microsoft, undocumented DOS is thus an interesting form of product differentiation.

From CP/M to DR DOS to Novell DOS

The funny thing is, MS-DOS itself started out as a clone of the CP/M operating system from DRI. The story has been told many times of how Tim Paterson (a coauthor, incidentally, of the first edition of this book), now at Microsoft but in 1980 an engineer at Seattle Computer Products, in two months wrote Quick and Dirty DOS (QDOS), how this became 86-DOS, to which Microsoft purchased non-exclusive rights, and how this became MS-DOS 1.0, for the then-new IBM PC. Stephen Manes and Paul Andrews' history of Microsoft, Gates, has all the details, even a photograph of the original Seattle Computer order form for Microsoft's purchase of 86-DOS sales rights. Price? $50,000.

Quick, dirty, and cheap. As Andrew Tanenbaum notes in his superb textbook on *Modern Operating Systems*, "If anyone had realized that within 10 years this tiny system that was picked up almost by accident was going to be controlling 50 million computers, considerably more thought might have gone into it."

Somewhat understandably, Digital Research was upset when it found that Microsoft's new operating system for the IBM PC was a clone of CP/M. Apparently Digital's Gary Kindall even considered suing IBM over the similarity of MS-DOS to CP/M. Microsoft would be similarly upset today if someone came out with a graphical environment that happened to provide the same API as Windows.

There is no question about MS-DOS's large-scale borrowing from CP/M. As Tim Paterson would write somewhat later in "An Inside Look at MS-DOS" (*Byte*, June 1983), "The primary design requirement of MS-DOS was CP/M-80 translation compatibility."

An early article by David Cortesti ("CP/M-86 vs. MSDOS: A Technical Comparison," *Dr. Dobb's Journal*, July 1982) compared MS-DOS with both CP/M-80 (for the Intel 8080) and CP/M-86 (for the 8086), showing not only where MS-DOS properly emulated CP/M functions, but also where there were differences. For example, function 9 outputs strings terminated with a '$' character in both systems, but CP/M expanded tabs and MS-DOS didn't. In any case, the '$' itself is a reminder of MS-DOS's CP/M roots. To this day, MS-DOS contains many holdovers from its early start as a CP/M clone. The PSP, for example, is nothing more than a CP/M base page.

However, even in the beginning there were crucial differences between the two systems. MS-DOS did not, as is widely claimed, mimic every last CP/M function call. For example, MS-DOS did not implement CP/M function 12 (0Ch) to get the system version number. Somewhat unaccountably, MS-DOS instead used (and still uses) function 0Ch to read the keyboard.

The crucial difference was in the file system. In an important departure from the CP/M file system, MS-DOS internally used a file allocation table (FAT), a scheme borrowed from Microsoft stand-alone BASIC. Paterson's original goal was to make the FAT memory resident at all times, eliminating the multiple disk reads that CP/M often made just to find where a file's data was located. As Ray Duncan noted at the time in his "16-Bit Software Toolbox" column (*Dr. Dobb's Journal*, November 1982), "although the systems appear very similar to the casual user, they use drastically different allocation schemes to manage disk files. This has surprisingly large effects on the speed of disk operations."

So MS-DOS began life as an enhanced clone of CP/M. Digital Research, makers of CP/M, went on to build many other operating systems, such as Concurrent CP/M, FlexOS, GEM, Concurrent DOS, Multiuser DOS, and finally DR DOS. DR DOS was intended as a complete replacement for MS-DOS. The cloners were now being cloned by the original clonees!

DR DOS also shows its CP/M roots. For one thing, the DR DOS disks and manuals carry copyright dates going back to 1976! Some of the code in DR DOS may even go back to the original CP/M code base. And while you won't see old CP/M terms such as PIP or CCP in the DR DOS manuals, and while the DR DOS debugger unfortunately is not called DDT, the DR DOS kernel is still called BDOS, just as in olden days.

For example, the HIDOS.SYS device driver has a /BDOS option to relocate the DR DOS kernel to the HMA or to a UMB. Interestingly, this option is more flexible than MS-DOS 5.0's DOS=HIGH command and appeared much earlier. While providing more features than Microsoft, sooner than Microsoft, DR DOS still clings a bit to its CP/M heritage, at least in its naming conventions.

None of this would matter very much, except for the fact that Novell acquired Digital Research (for $80 million) in July 1991. DR DOS, now renamed Novell DOS, may share in some of the success of Novell's NetWare. Netware dominates the network operating system market, far surpassing any of Microsoft's so far feeble attempts at providing network software. Novell's purchase of DR DOS is now widely regarded as a mistake, since DR DOS sales have dropped dramatically since the Novell purchase. However, this drop is likely due not to Novell's purchase of DR, but to Microsoft's release of MS-DOS 5.0. DR DOS had its brief moment in the sun in late 1990 and early 1991, when Digital had DR DOS 5 and all Microsoft had was the terrible MS-DOS version 4, engineered largely by IBM.

DR DOS is the only major competition for MS-DOS, which says a lot about Microsoft's role since the DR DOS share is quite small. DR claimed to have sold more than 1,500,000 copies of DR DOS 5.0 in 1991, admitting that this success was largely based on the clear inferiority of MS-DOS 4.0. Novell believes that DR DOS now holds 8-11% of the DOS market; *PC Magazine* (April 27, 1993) says the DR DOS share is 5%. In 1991, when Microsoft sold $617.5 million worth of MS-DOS, DRI's total revenues were $45.5 million. Assuming that DRI sold nothing but DOS, and assuming roughly equal prices for DR DOS and MS-DOS, this would give DR DOS about 7% of the DOS market. DR DOS's presence is stronger in Europe than in the United States, possibly in part because DR DOS comes out of Novell's European Development Centre in Hungerford, England.

DR DOS doesn't at first give the impression of being very important, and more than one reviewer of this book asked why we were bothering to talk about it in the first place. Angrily rejecting DR DOS's claims to MS-DOS compatibility, one reviewer (no, not a Microsoft employee) dismissed the idea of anyone "actually checking for the presence of this rather imperfect clone" and bluntly told us, "I see no reason why journalists should cooperate with DR's desire to have programmers share their development and marketing costs." This reflects a general feeling that DR DOS is Brand X and pretty much irrelevant. For example, in an article on operating system choices for the 1990s (*PC Magazine*, January 15, 1991), Charles Petzold placed DR DOS in the "Interesting-But-Does-It-Really-Matter Department."

But consider the economics of DOS. For example, in its 1991 fiscal year, which ended June 1991, Microsoft had total revenues of $1,843 million. Of this, Windows (though not Windows applications like Excel and Word!) brought in $260 million (14.1%). Meanwhile, MS-DOS (OEM plus retail sales; again, no applications) brought in more than twice that much, $617.5 million, which represents a whopping one-third of Microsoft's revenues.

Now notice that if a company takes only 5% of this business from Microsoft, it has made $30 million. One could run a 300-person company on sales like those. As noted earlier, in 1991 DRI had total revenues of $45.5 million. At the time, it had 290 employees.

With its reemergence as Novell DOS, this alternative to MS-DOS may become more important. This is not only because Novell DOS is a better name than DR DOS and because Novell DOS has stronger ties to NetWare, but also because Novell DOS is, as you will see, much more compatible with undocumented aspects of MS-DOS than were either DR DOS 5.0 or 6.0.

Why would anyone buy DR DOS rather than MS-DOS? Once reason is the price of DR DOS to computer manufacturers, who must bundle a copy of DOS with each machine. Microsoft makes between $10 and $25 for each OEM copy of MS-DOS; DR DOS's OEM price is lower (Manes and Andrews' *Gates* mentions a 1988 price of $6 for DR DOS). Thus a manufacturer might consider bundling DR DOS rather than MS DOS, for the same reason that they might consider using a 386 chip from AMD or Cyrix rather than from Intel.

On the other hand, it is a sign of Microsoft's hegemony that it is next to impossible to find any machines bundled with DR DOS rather than MS-DOS. Isn't it surprising that Microsoft has no competition in this tremendously lucrative market for the copies of DOS bundled on every single PC? This may in part be due to Microsoft's OEM pricing of MS-DOS on a per-machine rather than a per-copy basis. As Manes and Andrews note in their extensive discussion of MS-DOS OEM pricing, "per-machine deals made it virtually impossible to crack the DOS monopoly. If you were already paying a royalty to DOS on every machine you made, you weren't likely to offer a different operating system except as a high-priced option" (*Gates*, p. 263).

Another possible reason to buy DR DOS might be that DR DOS generally leads MS-DOS in features. The time line in Table 4-1 makes this clear:

Table 4-1: Novell and DRI vs. Microsoft: A Timeline

August 1990	DR DOS 5.0 (HIDOS=ON, etc.)
June 1991	MS-DOS 5.0 (DOS=HIGH, etc.)
July 1991	Novell purchase of Digital Research
September 1991	DR DOS 6.0 (data compression, etc.)
September 1991	NetWare Lite
October 1992	Windows for Workgroups 3.1
April 1993	MS-DOS 6.0 (DoubleSpace, etc.)
April 1993	Preannouncement of Novell DOS 7.0 and NetWare 4.0

DR DOS could load the DOS kernel into high memory almost a year before MS-DOS, and it came bundled with disk compression (SuperStor, from AddStor) well over a year before MS-DOS. Microsoft came out with Windows for Workgroups (WfW) some months after the newly merged Novell and DRI were bundling NetWare Lite with DR DOS—though both WfW and NetWare Lite lag far behind Artisoft's LANtastic in the peer-to-peer networking race. DR DOS appears to have been ROMable long before MS-DOS. And what is perhaps the most important "innovation" of MS-DOS 5.0—its retail availability to consumers, rather than only to OEMs for bundling with their machines—also comes from DR DOS. DR DOS 5.0 was the first retail DOS.

Basically, if you want to find out what features the next version of MS-DOS might support, you can look at the current version of DR DOS. However, it is not necessarily true that Microsoft simply copies ideas from DR DOS. For that to be true, there would need to be more of a time lag between each DR DOS release and the subsequent release of the MS-DOS version with similar features.

Microsoft has been accused of carefully orchestrating leaks about future versions of MS-DOS in an attempt to create what in the industry is called FUD (fear, uncertainty, and doubt) regarding DR DOS. For example, in October 1990, shortly after the release of DR DOS 5.0, and long before the eventual June 1991 release of MS-DOS 5.0, stories on feature enhancements in MS-DOS started to appear in *InfoWorld* and *PC Week*. Brad Silverberg, Vice President of Systems Software at Microsoft and General Manager of its Windows and MS-DOS Business Unit, wrote a forceful letter to *PC Week* (November 5, 1990), denying that Microsoft was engaged in FUD tactics ("to serve our customers better, we decided to be more forthcoming about version 5.0") and denying that Microsoft cops features from DR DOS: "The feature enhancements of MS-DOS version 5.0 were decided and development was begun long before we heard about DR DOS 5.0. There will be some similar features. With 50 million MS-DOS users, it shouldn't be surprising that DRI has heard some of the same requests from customers that we have."

Well, if you say so, Brad. But anyway, what is so bad about Microsoft's trying to match features provided earlier in DR DOS? We should feel thankful to DR DOS for whatever little competition it gives MS-DOS and for whatever pressure it puts on Microsoft to keep improving DOS. The improvements both companies are making to DOS are minor enough as it is. The present stagnation of DOS is a sorry example of what often happens under conditions of near-monopoly. But with its planned Chicago operating system (DOS 7.0, Windows 4.0), Microsoft will hopefully make some of the required major improvements to DOS and leapfrog way past Novell.

We were discussing why someone might buy DR DOS rather than MS-DOS. In making such a decision, it is important to remember that DR DOS is not MS-DOS. As we see in this chapter, DR DOS not only has features not found in MS-DOS but also has many compatibility differences, in both documented and undocumented areas of the DOS interface.

However, Novell DOS 7.0 is a major revamping of the operating system. Novell has reworked many of DR DOS's internals, and the new Novell DOS product is now much more compatible with MS-DOS. Coupled with the major redesign of NetWare 4.0, it will be interesting to see if Novell can use its clearly dominant NetWare to boost its DOS, perhaps by tightly integrating Novell DOS and NetWare.

The DR DOS Version Number

The first (and sometimes the only) question many programmers have about DR DOS is, when you are running under DR DOS, which *version* of DOS are you running under? This is an important enough point that the *DR DOS 6.0 Optimization and Configuration Tips* manual has a whole section on the DR DOS 6.0 version numbers. This user's manual notes that DR DOS "will appear to be COMPAQ DOS 3.31 to applications and drivers." What this means is that in DR DOS 5.0, 6.0, and Novell DOS 7.0, the DOS Get Version function (INT 21h AH=30h) returns the value 1F03h (3.31).

Since DR DOS is actually more capable than 3.31, this is an interesting case of masquerading downward, in much the same way that 386 machines usually pretend to be 8086s. There is a nice Irish term for such deliberate regression, "the poor mouth" (also the title of a hilarious book by Flann O'Brien), which means making a pretense of being poor or in bad circumstances to gain advantage for oneself from creditors or prospective creditors. We don't know about the creditors part, but given that DR DOS generally leads MS-DOS in features, it is surprising to learn that DR DOS puts on the poor mouth and goes out into the world not as DOS 5.0 or 6.0, but as DOS 3.31.

One reason of course is that so many DOS programs do version checking improperly that it doesn't pay to have a high version number. This is largely the reason for the otherwise idiotic SETVER command in MS-DOS. So many programs check simple-mindedly for DOS 3.0, for example, rather than for DOS 3.0 *and higher*, that they need to be fooled into thinking that DOS 5.0 is really DOS 3.0. (Incidentally, there isn't a DR DOS equivalent to SETVER.)

A major reason DR DOS sticks to the DOS 3.31 version number is that this makes it much easier to run Microsoft Windows. Other DOS clones, such as General Software's Embedded DOS and Datalight's ROM DOS, also stay at the 3.31 version number, largely to run Windows. As Chapter 1 discussed, the DOSMGR component of Windows Enhanced mode expects to be able to carry out a lot of back-door communications with any DOS that reports version 5.0 or higher. (As we were going to press, Novell announced that Novell 7 would report DOS version 6.0; Novell DOS 7 implements the DOSMGR interface.)

Given that all DR and Novell DOS versions report themselves as DOS 3.31, applications have a difficult time determining when they are running under DR DOS rather than MS-DOS. Of course, if DR DOS were close enough to MS-DOS, this wouldn't matter. However, there are enough differences that sometimes it matters a great deal.

For example, Stac Electronics' *Stacker 2.0 User's Guide* has a short appendix, "Programming with Stacker" (mostly as a teaser for the Stacker API, which must be licensed separately from Stacker), containing sample code to detect Stacker drives (see the ENUMDRV program in Chapter 8). This source code carries the following interesting comment:

```
; This function uses the removable media IOCTL call [21/4408] to
; detect Stacker drives. However, under DR DOS 5.0, the get
; logical device call (440EH) is used, since DR DOS does NOT
; pass these [4408h] calls through to the Stacker device driver.
```

If you examine the code itself, however, you can see that it checks simply for a DOS version of 3.31, thereby improperly lumping together everything, whether DR DOS or not, that reports this version number. Clearly, it would be better if there were a genuine DR DOS detection method.

As another example, DR DOS 5.0 users had problems running XtreeGold 2.0. According to the makers of Xtree, "Digital Research has not strictly followed all the published MS-DOS standards in some of their implementations" ("DR DOS 5.0 provokes compatibility quarrel," *PC User*, July 17, 1991). According to DRI, Xtree was getting the current directory, not from a documented MS-DOS function, but from the undocumented Current Directory Structure. As explained below, until Novell rewrote the DR DOS kernel, the CDS in DR DOS would always hold the *root* rather than the current directory. The solution was for XtreeGold to differentiate in its code between DR DOS and MS-DOS (or perhaps just to start using the documented Get Current Directory call).

Undocumented Novell DOS

So how can a DOS program determine that it is running under DR DOS and not MS-DOS or Compaq 3.31? In Chapter 1, we saw how Microsoft's AARD code in Windows differentiates between genuine MS-DOS and non-Microsoft DOS workalikes. Clearly, this is not a standard way of testing for an environment.

DR DOS has two environment variables, OS and VER, which are set to values such as OS=DRDOS and VER=6.0. But it would be foolish to rely on these, as any user can use SET VER= or SET OS= to remove or change these variables. Indeed, the VER command in DR DOS displays "DR DOS Release XXX", with XXX coming from the VER environment variable that any user can change. Relying on these variables is a bad idea.

Novell DOS has several undocumented extensions to INT 21h AH=43h and AH=44h. The AH=43h functions (some of which Novell does document) are used for elementary password security and for Undelete/DelWatch. Some of the AH=44h functions, INT 21h AX=4410 through AX=4418 are obsolete, as these are already running into the documented MS-DOS IOCTL codes, which currently go up to AX=4411h (Query IOCTL Device). However, these functions have equivalents in the range AX=4450h through AX=4458h, which Novell will continue to support. Table 4-2 shows the DR DOS extensions to INT 21h; see the appendix and INTRLIST on disk for further details.

Table 4-2: DR DOS INT 21h Functions

AX=4302h	Get Access Rights (documented in DR DOS 6.0+)
AX=4303h	Set Access Rights and Password (documented)
AX=4304h	Get Encrypted Password
AX=4305h	Set Extended File Attributes
AX=4306h	Get File Owner
AX=4307h	Set File Owner
AX=4380h	Undelete Pending Delete file (Novell DOS 7.0)
AX=4381h	Purge Pending Delete file (Novell DOS 7.0)
AX=4451h	Concurrent DOS Install Check
AX=4452h	Get DR DOS Version
AX=4454h	Set Global Password
AX=4456h	DR DOS History Buffer Control
AX=4457h	Get/Set Share/HiLoad Status
AX=4458h	Get Pointer to Internal Variable Table
AX=4E00h	(CX=88h) Find First Deleted File
AX=4F00h	(if 4Eh had CX=88h) Find Next Deleted File

The function we want here is INT 21h AX=4452h (Get DR DOS Version). It is probably not coincidental that 4452h is the ASCII code for the initials 'DR'. Under DR DOS and Novell DOS, this function returns a DR product code in AX (and, in Novell DOS 7.0, a release code in DX). Elsewhere, such as under MS-DOS, this function should return with the carry flag set and/or with the value in AX unchanged. The DRI multitasking products such as Concurrent DOS and Multiuser DOS use a similar function, INT 21h AX=4451h.

The existence of this DR DOS detection method has unfortunately been a closely guarded DRI secret. Arne Schäpers reports being told by DRI's then head of sales in Germany, "I just had a big OEM customer on the phone who asked me if there is any way to detect DR DOS. I had to tell him there is none because the two systems [MS-DOS 3.31 and DR-DOS 5.0] are absolutely the same."

Novell has recently relaxed this ridiculous policy of pretending that DR DOS is identical to MS-DOS, though it is still difficult to get a copy of the DR DOS *System and Programmer's Guide* (DR product #1182-2013-001), the very existence of which is sometimes even denied. (DR DOS programmer's documentation should by now be fairly readily available through Novell's developer relations group in Austin TX.) In any case, while documenting a few DR DOS specific functions such as AX=4302h and AX=4303h (see Table 4-2) and the TaskMAX INT 2Fh AH=27h interface, this manual doesn't provide the single piece of information that most developers want about DR DOS, which is how to detect that you're running under it.

The DRI product codes are not simple DOS version numbers. Instead, they indicate the code for the BDOS kernel. These numbers go all the way back to function 12 in CP/M-80. Table 4-3 shows the key version numbers.

Table 4-3: 1067h and All That: Novell/DR BDOS Product Codes

1063h	DR DOS 3.41
1065h	DR DOS 5.0
1067h	DR DOS 6.0
1070h	DR PalmDOS
1071h	DR DOS 6.0 March 1993 update for WfW
1072h	Novell DOS 7.0
1466h	DR Multiuser DOS 5.1
1467h	Concurrent DOS 5.1

As you can see, single-user (though possibly multitasking, such as Novell DOS 7.0) operating systems use version 10h, and multiuser systems use 14h. Function 4452h only works under the single-user systems such as DR DOS, and 4451h works only under the multiuser systems such as Concurrent DOS. DR PalmDOS is an OEM version of DR DOS for palmtop computers. Many of the DOS compatibility improvements found in Novell DOS 7.0 were in fact first introduced in Palm-DOS. The DOS compatible kernel is also present in the March 1993 "business update" of DR DOS, so programs that need the newer BDOS can check for 1070h or higher (that is, AH > 10h or (AH == 10h and AL >= 70h)).

All this can be wrapped up in a C-callable is_drdos() function, shown in listing 4-1 (IS_DRDOS.C). You can incorporate this code into other programs or (by compiling it with -DSTANDALONE) run it as a stand-alone test. You might contrast the straightforward nature of this code with the strangeness of MSDETECT.C in Chapter 1.

Listing 4-1: IS_DRDOS.C

```
/*
IS_DRDOS.C
Andrew Schulman, January 1993
With changes by John (Frotz) Fa'atuai of Novell, February 1993
From "Undocumented DOS", 2nd edition (Addison-Wesley, 1993)

To link with other programs:  bcc -c is_drdos.c
To make standalone test:      bcc -DSTANDALONE is_drdos.c
*/

#include <stdlib.h>
#include <stdio.h>
#include <dos.h>

typedef unsigned short WORD;

/* EDC = European Development Centre, Novell Digital Research
   Systems Group, Hungerford, England */
WORD EDC_product_codes(WORD api_function)
{
    _asm mov ax, api_function
    _asm stc                      /* set carry flag */
    _asm int 21h
    _asm jc no_drdos              /* carry set: function not supported */
    _asm cmp ax, api_function
    _asm je no_drdos              /* AX unchanged: function not supported */
have_drdos:
    _asm jmp short done           /* carry clear and AX changed */
no_drdos:
    _asm xor ax, ax               /* not supported, return AX=0 */
done:;
    /* return value in AX */
}
WORD is_drdos(void)
{
    WORD product_code;

    /* Try the single-user API call */
    if ((product_code = EDC_product_codes(0x4452)) != 0)
        return product_code;

    /* Try the multi-user API call */
    if ((product_code = EDC_product_codes(0x4451)) != 0)
        return product_code;

#if 1
    /* The following seems like a bad idea, because the documented
       calls already go up to AX=4411h (Query IOCTL Device)! */
#else
```

```
    /* Try an _old_and_obsolete_ single-user API call */
    if ((product_code = EDC_product_codes(0x4412)) != 0)
        return product_code;
#endif

    /* still here:  definitely no DR DOS! */
    return 0;
}
#ifdef STANDALONE
main()
{
    WORD EDC_product;

    if ((EDC_product = is_drdos()) == 0)
        printf("Single- or Multi-user DR DOS not running\n");
    else
    {
        switch (EDC_product)
        {
            case 0x1060: printf("DOS Plus"); break;
            case 0x1063: printf("DR DOS 3.41"); break;
            case 0x1064: printf("DR DOS 3.42"); break;
            case 0x1065: printf("DR DOS 5.0"); break;
            case 0x1067: printf("DR DOS 6.0"); break;
            case 0x1070: printf("DR DOS PalmDOS"); break;
            case 0x1071: printf("DR DOS 6.0 March 1993 update"); break;
            case 0x1072: printf("Novell DOS 7.0"); break;

            case 0x1432: printf("Concurrent PC-DOS 3.2"); break;
            case 0x1441: printf("Concurrent DOS 4.1"); break;
            case 0x1450: printf("Concurrent DOS/XM 5.0 or "
                                "Concurrent DOS/386 1.1"); break;
            case 0x1460: printf("Concurrent DOS/XM 6.0 or "
                                "Concurrent DOS/386 2.0"); break;
            case 0x1462: printf("Concurrent DOS/XM 6.2 or "
                                "Concurrent DOS/386 3.0"); break;
            case 0x1466: printf("DR Multiuser DOS 5.1"); break;
            case 0x1467: printf("Concurrent DOS 5.1"); break;
            default:     printf("Unknown DR DOS version"); break;
        }
        printf(" (BDOS %04Xh)\n", EDC_product);
        printf("Providing DOS interface %u.%02u\n", _osmajor, _osminor);
    }
    return (EDC_product);
}
#endif
```

IS_DRDOS has been tested under MS DOS 5.0 and 6.0, where it correctly outputs "Single- or Multi-user DR DOS not running," and under DR DOS 5.0, 6.0, Novell DOS 7.0, and under Concurrent DOS/386 2.01 (which one of the authors purchased at the Weird Stuff Warehouse in Sunnyvale CA, home of dead hardware and software, for $14.95).

Of course, many of the utilities that come with DR DOS and Novell DOS call function 4452h to ensure they are indeed running under DR DOS. For example, if you take COMMAND.COM or SHARE.EXE from DR DOS 6.0 and try to run them under MS-DOS 6.0, they will complain "Incorrect version of operating system." Unfortunately, this is not done consistently. For example, the MEM utility from DR DOS 6.0 runs under MS-DOS, and while it generally produces correct results, the /S (Show system structures) option fails to ensure that it is indeed running under DR DOS; running DR's MEM/S under MS-DOS hangs the system.

Watching DR DOS

Assuming one already knows about the undocumented DR DOS functions, how does one go about determining which DR DOS utilities use them? The INTRSPY utility, presented in Chapter 5, is perfect for this. The DRDOS.SCR script shown in listing 4-2 lets INTRSPY watch some selected DR DOS functions. In addition to the INT 21h extensions from Table 4-2, DRDOS.SCR also reports on INT 2Fh AX=12FFh, which the MEMMAX utility uses.

Listing 4-2: INTRSPY Script for Selected DR DOS Functions

```
; DRDOS.SCR
intercept 21h
    function 43h on_entry
        if (al > 1)
            output "21/43/" al
    function 44h on_entry
        if (al > 11h)
            output "21/44/" al
    function 4bh on_entry
        output (DS:DX->byte,asciiz,64)
intercept 2fh
    function 12h
        subfunction 0FFh on_entry
            output "2F/12FF/" bx "/" cx "/" dx
```

Figure 4-1 shows sample INTRSPY output, when running the simple MEM and MEMMAX utilities in DR DOS 6.0.

Figure 4-1: Undocumented DR DOS Calls from MEM and MAXMEM (DR DOS 6.0)

```
A:\MEM.EXE
21/44/52
21/44/52
21/44/58
2F/12FF/0006/0000/0000
21/44/58
2F/12FF/0006/0000/0000
21/44/58
21/44/58
21/44/57
21/44/56
21/44/56
21/44/57
21/44/56
21/44/56
A:\MEMMAX.EXE
2F/12FF/0006/0000/0000
2F/12FF/0006/0000/0000
2F/12FF/0006/0000/0000
21/44/57
21/44/56
21/44/56
```

To effectively use INTRSPY, however, you must already know what you are looking for. INTRSPY is good for telling us that MEM and MAXMEM call INT 21h AX=4452h, for example, but to write DRDOS.SCR we had to know already that DR DOS makes IOCTL calls with function numbers greater than 11h. How does one figure that out?

Disassembling DR DOS

Through disassembly of the DR DOS files, of course. The system files in DR DOS are called IBMBIO.COM and IBMDOS.COM. The command interpreter is, of course, COMMAND.COM.

Disassembly with a tool such as Sourcer shows, for example, that COMMAND.COM calls INT 21h AX=4452h, AX=4456h, AX=4457h, and AX=4458h. IBMDOS.COM provide these calls.

You can also disassemble the separate utilities shipped with DR DOS, such as MEM.EXE and MEMMAX.EXE. However, Novell compresses these programs with PKLITE, an executable-file compressor from PKWARE. To disassemble the files, you must first uncompress them with the PKLITE -x switch. PKLITE is readily available electronically, for example from the IBMSYS forum on CompuServe.

A good starting place is the MEMMAX utility, which in DR DOS enables, disables, and displays the status of upper, lower, and video memory. Even after expansion with PKLITE -x, MEMMAX.EXE is only 2K. Disassembly with Sourcer produces a small fifteen-page listing, in which it is easy to find the code that handles the MEMMAX switches, such as +U to open upper memory for HILOAD, -U to close it, +V to map memory into video memory space, -L to close the first 64K of memory (similar to LOADFIX in MS-DOS), and so on.

Using a MEMMAX.LST file, you can see, for example, how DR DOS enables and disables upper memory. Because DR DOS 5.0 and 6.0 do not implement the MS-DOS 5.0 AH=58h functions for upper memory control (Novell DOS 7.0 does), MEMMAX contains inline code to manipulate the MCB chain. It calls INT 21h AH=52h to get a far pointer to SysVars (of which DR DOS, as we will see, maintains a partial version), and uses SysVars[-2] to get a far pointer to the MCB chain.

Similar to INT 21h AX=5803h BX=1 in MS-DOS 5.0 and higher, MEMMAX enables upper memory by walking to the end of the MCB chain and replacing the last MCB's 'Z' flag with an 'M', thereby linking in the secondary upper memory MCB chain. To disable UMBs, it finds the last block below A000h and replaces the 'M' with a 'Z'. For sample code, see listing 4-3 later in this chapter. This listing also shows how one could do UMB links without the INT 21h AH=58h functions.

To implement its /V, +V, and -V video memory switches, MEMMAX does not use inline code. Instead it calls an undocumented function, INT 2Fh AX=12FFh BX=6 DX=0, with subfunction numbers in CX:

```
0       get status of video memory space (memmax /v)
1       map memory into video memory space (memmax +v)
2       unmap memory from video memory space (memmax -v)
```

These INT 2Fh AX=12FFh are handled inside HIDOS.SYS.

How Close Is DR DOS to MS-DOS?

DR DOS is quite close to MS-DOS. Most DOS programs, including low-level systems software such as Windows and network software such as (of course) NetWare, will run with DR DOS. The *DR DOS 6.0 Optimization and Configuration Tips* manual notes that DR DOS is generally compatible with applications that require 3.31 or higher and that follow the standard conventions for DOS programming. These standard conventions include "support for larger than 32 MB partitions using the COMPAQ Extended Interrupt 25 and 26 convention." However,

> Some applications have been designed to go beyond those conventions and actually attempt to directly manipulate DOS data structures or replace sections of the operating system code with their own. These applications depend on having intimate knowledge of each DOS version they detect and have been written to react differently for each of these versions. If an application uses this type of technique, the manufacturer will have to design the application to take the DR DOS 6.0 operating system into account as well.

But in most cases it is actually not the application's responsibility to conform to DR DOS, but DR DOS's responsibility to conform to the application because, as we noted earlier, that is how *de facto* standards work. It is DR DOS that must conform to the conventions of DOS programming, not the other way around. Hence, the new Novell DOS 7.0 kernel.

Indeed, with each release DR DOS has incorporated support for more and more of the *de facto* DOS programming standards. DR DOS started out as Concurrent DOS; DR stripped out the concurrent and multiuser parts and added in an MS-DOS compatibility layer. Additional MS-DOS compatibility was added with each release, as it seemed to be needed. One gets the feeling that DRI put off supporting one or another undocumented DOS internal data structure, such as the Current Directory Structure, for as long as it could. This produced some compatibility problems, such as those noted earlier with Xtree. In Novell DOS 7.0, however (or actually, any BDOS >= 1070h), there is finally a very close work-alike to MS-DOS 3.31. Note, however, that even these newer versions do not pass the highly-arbitrary test made by Microsoft Windows' AARD detection code, discussed in Chapter 1.

A technical support engineer at Novell reports that "many of our escalated technical support problems with developers are a result of differences that DR DOS 6.0 has with respect to the techniques used within *Undocumented DOS*." Presumably some of these problems are due to errors in the first edition of this book, but in some cases DR DOS 6.0 was simply not sufficiently compatible with undocumented but widely-used aspects of MS-DOS.

Clearly, life would be much easier for Novell and other builders of DOS work-alikes if DOS applications would restrict themselves to the documented DOS interface. Seen in this light, the widespread use of undocumented DOS is really to Microsoft's advantage! Novell would certainly prefer if applications avoided using undocumented DOS calls and data structures. But the same technical support engineer just quoted also reports that at Novell, "'word' internally is that NetWare Lite 1.x was developed almost exclusively from *Undocumented DOS*." This reflects a common situation. Many developers at major PC software houses suffer because of the widespread use of undocumented DOS calls (and suffer, frankly, because of the widespread use of this book!). Yet, at the same time, these companies use these calls themselves. They just wish everyone *else* would show some restraint! Of course, Microsoft sets the standard here, with its do-as-I-say-not-as-I-do attitude to undocumented calls.

SysVars, the Current Directory Structure, and the Redirector

We've already noted that Novell's own MEMMAX and HIDOS programs rely on the core INT 21h AH=52h undocumented function, so this function and at least some of its associated SysVars structure clearly must be present in DR DOS. Many of the programs from other parts of this book will run under DR DOS. Windows will run on top of DR DOS (though, as noted several times already, for this to happen DR DOS 5 and 6 must pretend to be DOS 3.31). Clearly, DR DOS is a close approximation to even the undocumented portions of MS-DOS.

However, under DR DOS 5.0 and 6.0, some of the internal data structures visible through undocumented DOS calls are *read only*. The structures exist to keep applications happy, but DR DOS does not actually use these structures. Applications that *modify* rather than merely query these structures may be in for a rude shock.

For example, the XLASTDRV utility from Chapter 2 modifies the CDS pointer and LASTDR-IVE fields in SysVars. XLASTDRV appears at first to run fine under DR DOS. Function 52h returns a pointer to SysVars, and SysVars contains what appears to be a valid CDS pointer and a LASTDR-IVE value; XLASTDRV successfully modifies both values. However, this has no useful effect on the system. If the value of LASTDRIVE in CONFIG.SYS was E, and if XLASTDRV changes the LASTDRIVE value in SysVars to F, the highest valid drive is *still* E. Quarterdeck's LASTDRIV.COM utility from QEMM likewise has no effect on the number of actual drives under DR DOS 5.0 and 6.0.

The problem is that DR DOS 5.0 and 6.0 keep their genuine current directory and drive information elsewhere, merely supplying enough of a CDS to satisfy programs that a CDS does indeed exist. DR DOS 5.0 and 6.0 internally store the current directory based on its first cluster, rather than on its ASCII name. DR DOS 6.0 rebuilds the fictitious CDS at appropriate times from DRI's genuine internal drive table, and likewise the internal table is sometimes updated from the CDS, but DRI believed that sufficiently few applications needed the full pathname that it could get away without updating this. The pathname field of the CDS always holds the drive's root (for example, C:\) rather than the actual current directory. The caused the problem with Xtree noted earlier. Likewise, the ENUMDRV program from Chapter 8 won't work under DR DOS 5.0 or 6.0.

You might think that DR DOS should not have to support something as sick as direct access to (and even modification of) the CDS, but in fact it *does* have to support this. So finally the new BDOS kernel found in PalmDOS, the DR DOS 6.0 March 1993 update, and Novell DOS 7.0 have a genuine CDS. Changing the CDS pointer and LASTDRIVE values in SysVars really does change the DOS drive table.

Whatever CDS support DR DOS 5.0 and 6.0 did provide was primarily for use by network redirectors which, as Chapter 8 explains, rely on the CDS. Even without a genuine CDS, DR DOS 5.0 and 6.0 were compatible with most commercial redirectors, though not with our Phantom redirector from Chapter 8. Perhaps most commercial redirectors do not use the CDS pathname field in quite the same way as our Phantom.

In PalmDOS and Novell DOS 7.0, the network compatibility is greatly improved. For example, WfW would not run on DR DOS 5.0 and 6.0 (apparently WfW relies on an obscure field in the SDA), but it does run on PalmDOS and Novell DOS 7.0.

The System File Tables and SHARE

Since version 5.0, DR DOS has used a System File Table structure that is nearly identical to that found in MS-DOS. The FILES program from Chapter 8 works fine under DR DOS. DR DOS even supports the same internal INT 2Fh AX=1216h function as MS-DOS to return the address of an individual SFT entry.

DR DOS provides SHARE.EXE, but its internal SHARE structures are radically different from those in MS-DOS. DR DOS doesn't use the SHARE hooks located in front of the first SFT (see SHARHOOK.C in Chapter 8), nor does it use the SHARE fields in the SFT (see the appendix). These differences are present even in Novell DOS 7.0. According to a developer at Novell, "We believe that there are enough problems with the design of the SHARE interface that we have continued to implement SHARE in a different way."

DR DOS does, of course, provide the INT 2Fh AX=1000h SHARE install check. DR DOS 5.0 and 6.0 (but not Novell DOS 7.0) have the ability to turn SHARE support off and on. However, this has no effect on the return value from INT 2Fh AX=1000h. As noted in Chapter 8, this function is now next to worthless as a genuine SHARE install check because Windows hooks INT 2Fh and reports that SHARE is installed, whether or not it is. To truly determine that SHARE is installed, you must use INT 21h AH=5Ch (Lock/Unlock File), as recommended in Microsoft's programmer's reference. Function 5Ch will set the carry flag and return with AX=1 (invalid function) if SHARE is not installed; this also works in DR DOS (see SHARHOOK.C in Chapter 8).

Memory Control Blocks

DR DOS 5.0 and higher use Memory Control Blocks just like those found in MS-DOS. In fact, the DR DOS MCBs even have an owner ID field with the program name, just as in MS-DOS 4.0 and above, even though DR DOS otherwise tries to behave like DOS 3.31. DR DOS also adds two MCB owner types: 0006h to indicate an XMS UMB, and 0007h to indicate an "excluded" UMB.

We saw earlier that, in the MEMMAX utility and elsewhere, DR DOS itself relies on its ability to access the MCB chain from offset -2 in SysVars. As also noted earlier, DR DOS 5.0 and 6.0 do not implement the MS-DOS 5.0 AH=58h functions for upper memory control, so MEMMAX contains inline code to manipulate the MCB chain. Arne Schäpers, author of a massive book from Germany on DOS programming; and a contributor to much of the DR DOS information in this chapter, has written two generic UMB link functions in Turbo Pascal that work both in MS-DOS 5.0 and higher and in DR DOS 5.0 and higher. These are shown in Listing 4-3.

Listing 4-3: Generic UMB Link Functions

```
{ from Arne Schapers, "DOS 5 fur Programmierer", pp. 684-688 }

{ Returns TRUE if UMBs are linked in, works for MS-DOS 5, MS-DOS 6.0,
DR-DOS 5.0, and DR-DOS 6.0 }
Function GetUMBLink: Boolean;
var Regs: Registers;
    MCB: MCBPtr; p: ^Word;
begin
  if TrueDosVersion = $3203 then { DR-DOS 5.0 }
  begin
    { GetDosDataArea calls INT 21h AH=52h }
    p := GetDosDataArea; Dec(LongInt(p),2);
    MCB := Ptr(p^,0);  { DOS Data Area, offset - 2 }
    while MCB^.Flag <> 'Z' do  { walk MCB chain }
      MCB := Ptr(Seg(MCB^)+1+MCB^.Size,0);
    GetUMBLink := Seg(MCB^)+MCB^.Size > $A000;
  end else
  begin
    Regs.AX := $5802;  { Function: "Get UMB Link State" }
    Intr($21,Regs);
    if Regs.Flags and FCarry <> 0 then GetUMBLink := False
      else GetUMBLink := (Regs.AL <> 0);  { TRUE if UMBs linked in }
  end;
end;

{ Tries to link UMBs in, works with MS- and DR-DOS 5.0/6.0 }
Procedure SetUMBLink(LinkState: Boolean);
var Regs: Registers;
    MCB: MCBPtr; p: ^Word;
    NextMCB: Word; Done: Boolean;
begin
  if DosVersion = $3203 then { DR-DOS 5.0 }
  begin
    p := GetDosDataArea; Dec(LongInt(p),2);
    MCB := Ptr(p^,0);  { DOS Data Area, offset - 2 }
    Done := False;
    { walk MCB chain to < $9FFF }
    while (MCB^.Flag <> 'Z') and not Done do
    begin
      NextMCB := Seg(MCB^)+1+MCB^.Size;
      if NextMCB >= $9FFF then Done := True
        else MCB := Ptr(NextMCB,0);
    end;
    if NextMCB < $9FFF then NextMCB := Seg(MCB^)+1+MCB^.Size;
    if (NextMCB = $9FFF) and  { MCB with ID of MEMMAX on $9FFF? }
      (MCBPtr(Ptr(NextMCB,0))^.OwnerPSP = $0007) then
    begin
      if LinkState then MCB^.Flag := 'M'
        else MCB^.Flag := 'Z';
    end
      else DosError := 1;  { "Function not supported" }
  end else
  begin        { MS-DOS }
    Regs.AX := $5803; { Function: "Set UMB Link" }
    Regs.BX := Ord(LinkState);
    Intr($21,Regs);
    if Regs.Flags and FCarry <> 0 then DosError := Regs.AX
      else DosError := 0;
  end;
end;
```

Only DR DOS 5.0 and 6.0 require these replacements, as Novell DOS 7.0 implements the DOS 5.0 INT 21h AX=5802h and AX=5803h functions.

TSRs and the Swappable Data Area

DR DOS implements all the formerly-undocumented functions commonly used by memory resident DOS programs. These functions include INT 21h AH=34h (Get InDOS flag), AH=50h (Set PSP), AH=51h (Get PSP), AX=5D0Ah (Set Extended Error Information), and INT 28h (Keyboard Idle). DOS TSRs run under DR DOS without incident.

DR DOS even implements undocumented DOS function INT 21h AX=5D06h, which returns a pointer to the Swappable Data Area. Some TSRs use this to swap the DOS state (see Chapter 9). While the fields in the SDA are not the same as in MS-DOS, most programs don't look at individual fields in the SDA. They just swap the entire structure, using the swap-InDOS and swap-always sizes returned from function 5D06h. This appears to work under all versions of DR DOS, though naturally the entire DOS state is not in fact kept in the SDA. But this is true in MS-DOS as well. Writing SDA-swapping TSRs is risky business.

Additional DR DOS and Novell DOS Functionality

Having looked at how DR DOS falls just slightly short of MS-DOS in implementing various undocumented DOS functions and structures, let's take a moment to look at what *additional* functionality DR DOS provides for programmers.

The most important extra DR DOS function is of course the DR DOS detection call (INT 21h AX=4452h) discussed above. While there are a number of other undocumented DR DOS functions, it seems unlikely that programmers would want to write DR DOS-specific software; the only thing that makes using undocumented DOS worthwhile is a large market. It is more likely that programmers would want to take advantage of some larger documented interfaces provided in DR DOS and Novell DOS, such as the DelWatch/Undelete APIs, which Novell documents in a specification on "File and Directory Salvage for DOS Media."

TaskMAX, the multitasking interface added in DR DOS 6.0, has a set of INT 2Fh AH=27h functions, documented in the *DR DOS 6.0 System and Programmer's Guide* (August 1991). INTRLIST on the accompanying disk also describes these calls. For example, INT 2Fh AX=2704h registers a new task manager; the ViewMAX GUI interface uses this call to replace the TaskMAX pop-up menu system.

In Novell DOS 7.0, KRNL386.SYS provides true preemptive multitasking capabilities. If KRNL386.SYS is loaded, Novell DOS 7.0 also provides DPMI services, supporting either the 0.90 or 1.0 version of the DPMI specification. All the DPMI_APP programs from Chapter 3 run under Novell DOS 7.0 if KRNL386.SYS is loaded with DPMI support enabled.

Novell DOS 7.0 also provides a new interface called the DOS Protected Mode Services (DPMS). A DPMS toolkit with full documentation is available from Novell; also see the Interrupt List on disk (INT 2Fh AX=43E0h).

The name DPMS sounds a lot like DPMI—and also like the common American acronym for premenstrual syndrome—but it has little to do with either. DPMS is a set of services that allow DOS TSRs and device drivers to move themselves into extended memory and run in protected mode. The idea behind DPMS is to make it very easy to port TSRs and device drivers to protected mode. For example, the DPMS toolkit comes with a sample protected mode VDISK.

DPMS is significant because Novell will be using it for its own utilities, not only in Novell DOS 7.0, but also in NetWare Lite. Novell plans to use DPMS for disk cache and compression software, CD-ROM extensions, resident workstation management utilities, workstation shells, redirectors, and requestors.

Protected Mode DOS

DPMS is just one part of a general move toward protected mode DOS. Of course, for years there have been DOS extenders such as Phar Lap's 286|DOS-Extender and 386|DOS-Extender. DOS extenders continue to grow in importance—witness the incorporation of Phar Lap's 386|DOS-Extender in most of Microsoft's new application software for DOS, including FoxPro, Microsoft C, Visual C++, and Microsoft FORTRAN.

However, DPMS illustrates a somewhat newer trend: moving pieces of the operating system itself into protected mode. In addition to Novell, whose DPMS is likely to play an important role in Novell DOS 7.0 and NetWare Lite, other companies are also working on moving TSRs and device drivers out of conventional memory and into protected mode.

In version 3 of its NetRoom memory management utility, Helix Software has introduced a "Cloaking API." Like DPMS, Cloaking is a method for moving TSRs and device drivers into protected mode. Helix has gone beyond this, providing cloaked versions of the system BIOS and video BIOS, both co-developed with Award Software. According to Helix, the cloaked BIOSs occupy only 8K of conventional memory instead of the normal 96K. The extra 88K becomes available as UMBs. The Cloaking API works as an extension to the EMS and XMS interfaces in real mode and uses INT 2Ch in protected mode.

Probably the most important effort to move pieces of DOS into protected mode is coming from Microsoft itself in Windows for Workgroups (WfW). While WfW may be relatively insignificant as networking software, it includes a number of virtual device drivers (see Chapters 1 and 3) that replace parts of MS-DOS. WfW 3.11 includes VSHARE.386, VREDIR.386, and VFAT.386, which contain 32-bit protected mode code for SHARE, the network redirector, and even the FAT file system. These VxDs are all also part of Microsoft's Chicago, which will provide an entire protected-mode operating system.

Novell NetWare

Novell's most significant product is not its DR DOS, of course, but its network operating system, NetWare, which holds about 70% of the PC network software market. With MS-NET, LAN Manager, and WfW, Microsoft has made three attempts to break into this market, but to date Microsoft's dominance in other PC systems software areas has not carried over to network operating systems. As networks increase in importance, so will the war between Microsoft and Novell.

How does NetWare relate to DOS? NetWare file servers are not DOS machines at all. They run the NetWare operating system, which has a proprietary file system and which, in NetWare 3.0 and higher, supports non-preemptive multitasking and a form of dynamic linking called NetWare Loadable Modules (NLMs).

On client workstations, however, the NetWare shell (NETX) runs atop DOS. When a DOS program tries to open a file, for example, NetWare detects whether the file is actually located on a file server rather than on the local hard disk. File access to NetWare drives is redirected to the NetWare file server. As we will see, NETX's radical changes to the INT 21h interface, where it effectively *replaces* large parts of DOS, justifies its inclusion in this chapter on "other DOSs".

As Chapter 8 discusses in detail, DOS provides an undocumented INT 2Fh interface for writing such software called, not surprisingly, the network redirector interface. However, NetWare did not start using the network redirector interface until version 4.0.

NETX and INT 21h

In NetWare 2.0 and 3.0, the workstation shell hooks INT 21h and looks for relevant calls. Novell sometimes calls this a "shell" or "front-end requester" because NETX hooks interrupts in front of DOS. If DOS can handle a request, NETX chains to the previous INT 21h handler; otherwise, NETX sends a NetWare request packet to the appropriate file server. The NetWare shell communicates with the file server using the "proprietary" (read: undocumented) NetWare Core Protocol (NCP). The shell sends NCP packets to the file server using Novell's low-level IPX protocol.

NetWare also hooks INT 17h (printing), INT 24h (critical error), and INT 2Fh. To keep track of tasks, it must also hook the old INT 20h and INT 27h termination and TSR routines.

To determine when a file-open call (INT 21h AH=3Dh or AH=6Ch) must be handled by a NetWare file server rather than locally by DOS, NETX consults the *drive mapping*. Any file-open requests involving drive C: might refer to the local hard disk, while a file-open request for F:\FOO.BAR might in fact refer to the file FOO.BAR on a volume such as FS1/SYS:PUBLIC on a file server. To maintain the workstation's drive mappings, NETX uses several tables: the Drive Flag Table, Drive Handle Table, and Drive Connection ID Table. Novell documents all these in the *NetWare System Interface Technical Overview* (Chapter 5: Connection and Workstation Environment Services; Chapter 7: Directory Services).

Each table has 32 entries that correspond to a workstation's 32 drives. These are drives A: through Z: plus six additional temporary drives with drive letters [, \,], ^, _, and ' (unfortunately, Drew Major and the other designers of NetWare had apparently not read Dr. Seuss's children's book *On Beyond Zebra*, which has precise information on the letters that come after Z). Whenever NETX's INT 21h handler intercepts a file or directory request, it can consult the Drive Flag Table to see if the specified or implied drive is local or remote. For remote drives, NETX can then use the Drive Connection ID table to find the file server to which the workstation drive is mapped. For local drives, NETX chains to the previous INT 21h handler.

When a DOS program opens a file on a NetWare server, it gets back a file handle. Just as in DOS without NetWare, this file handle is an index into the Job File Table (JFT) associated with the program's PSP. As discussed in Chapter 8, JFT entries are normally indices into the System File Table. Under NetWare, however, a file handle can be a negative number, starting with FEh and working backward, which represents a reverse index into the internal file handle table that NETX maintains. In this way, files opened on NetWare servers bypass the SFT. In recent versions of NetWare, the reverse file handles stop at the FILES= number specified in CONFIG.SYS. This means that the maximum number of open files under NetWare can be *reduced* by having a large value such as FILES=250 in CONFIG.SYS. (Like many of the other NETX modifications to standard DOS practice, this one goes away in the NetWare 4.0 DOS Requester, where Novell uses the DOS redirector, thereby doing away with the need for separate file handles.)

Transparency is of course the goal here. A DOS program should be able to access files on a NetWare server using exactly the same DOS calls it uses to access local files; it should not need to be aware of the difference.

On the other hand, some applications will need to be NetWare-aware. NetWare provides a large set of function extensions to INT 21h; this is another reason why NetWare hooks INT 21h. For example, INT 21h AX=EF00h is Get Drive Handle Table, AX=EF01h is Get Drive Flag Table, AX=EF02h is Get Drive Connection ID Table, and AX=EF04h is Get File Server Name Table.

Consider the ENUMDRV program in Chapter 8, which walks the DOS Current Directory Structure, displaying the current directory for each drive. Assuming that such a program is really useful in the first place (doubtful), when running under NetWare it would be important for ENUMDRV to look beyond the CDS. A NetWare-aware version of ENUMDRV could walk each of the NETX tables in the same that it now walks the CDS. It could also call INT 21h AX=E201h (Get Directory Path) to turn directory handles into readable directory pathnames. Actually, while

ENUMDRV could use NetWare API calls to inspect the NETX tables, it would be easier to determine the names of redirected network drives and printers with DOS function INT 21h AX=5F02h (Get Assign-List Entry; see NETDRV.C in Chapter 8). This works because NETX handles the INT 21h AH=5Fh call.

Programming NetWare with the extended INT 21h calls is an enormous subject. For more information, see Charles Rose's *Programmer's Guide to NetWare* or the "Novell's Extended DOS Services" chapter in Barry Nance's *Network Programming in C*. Ralph Davis' *NetWare Programmer's Guide* discusses the same subject, but using Novell's somewhat defective NetWare C Interface library, rather than with direct INT 21h calls.

NetWare 4.0 and the Network Redirector

NetWare 4.0 has a completely new architecture. As Novell notes, "technology outgrew the roughly eleven-year-old NETX shell." Apparently one reason Novell wanted to move to an INT 2Fh AH=11h redirector, and away from hooking INT 21h, is that it became tiresome to modify NETX every time a new version of DOS came out. NETX is very dependent on the DOS version, witness the many versions such as NET3, NET4, NET5, and so on; DOS 6.0 uses the SETVER command to tell NETX that it is supposedly running under DOS 5.0.

One of Novell's goals for NetWare 4.0 was to make the workstation client software more modular. Just as there are NLMs on the server side, NetWare 4.0 introduces Virtual Loadable Module (VLMs) on the client side. A VLM is something like a dynamic link library, an overlay that can be loaded and unloaded depending upon which functionality a user needs. (A VLM developer's kit is available from Novell developer services in Austin, Texas.)

NetWare 4.0 includes a NETX.VLM module, which provides backward compatibility with the old front-end requester. However, this is only loaded optionally, for applications that specifically require it. The required module is REDIR.VLM, which is a standard INT 2Fh DOS redirector.

Since this is a redirector, there isn't much more we need to say about it here. Chapter 8 discusses this DOS standard at length. Whereas a front-end requestor such as NETX effectively bypasses DOS and all the undocumented DOS structures such as the CDS and SFT, a redirector is fully part of DOS. Instead of hooking INT 21h ahead of DOS, a redirector is *called by* DOS. This means that all drives, whether local or remote, are maintained through the CDS; the SFT maintains all files, whether local or remote. Because a redirector doesn't bypass these DOS data structures, programs such as ENUMDRV wouldn't need to change at all for NetWare 4 though of course one might still want to know the NetWare name of the underlying file server and volume).

On the other hand, NetWare's new workstation client is not a 100% redirector. Yes, it implements the INT 2Fh redirector interface, but it still also hooks INT 21h, even if NETX.VLM isn't loaded. Novell must continue hooking INT 21h to support NetWare extensions such as the INT 21h AH=F2h interface (see below). Novell's engineers refer to an INT 21h hooker as a Shell and, of course, to one that implements the INT 2Fh interface as a Redirector. The new DOS client, which is both a Shell and a Redirector, is called the "Novell DOS Requestor."

You might wonder how a redirector version of NetWare can support the funny NetWare drives [through ' (27-32), since the DOS CDS uses LASTDRIVE=Z as the maximum drive letter. A Novell READVLM.TXT file notes somewhat coyly that "DR DOS could be enhanced to allow these drives to be treated as valid by providing a new option for the LASTDRIVE= parameter in CONFIG.SYS (for example: LASTDRIVE=32). Similarly, MS-DOS could also be enhanced if Microsoft decides to adopt any changes made to DR DOS." Of course, we could also enhance the XLASTDRV utility from Chapter 2 in this way.

On the other hand, perhaps the NetWare drives > Z: just aren't that important. Novell has all along intended these drives for internal use by programs that need to temporarily map a drive, and not generally for end-users. Novell has long warned developers that the temporary drive mappings might go away. In their place, Novell suggests using direct Universal Naming Convention (UNC; see Chapter 8) \\server\volume\path filespecs. For instance, rather than mapping drive "[:" to "FS1/SYS:MYDIR\" and then accessing your temporary files there, you instead can access them using the path "\\FS1\SYS\MYDIR". This functionality is available in NETX, though apparently with some problems in some DOS functions, notably Rename.

How NETX Changes INT 21h

We've seen that NetWare adds many functions to the INT 21h interface. Novell documents some of these, and others are undocumented but well known through disassembly or through inspection of the readily available source code to Novell's NetWare C Interface library. Because the NetWare extensions to INT 21h are such a large topic, we will instead look here at what changes NetWare makes to the standard INT 21h functions. The following discussion is based on information kindly provided by engineers at Novell, and on a disassembly of NETX.EXE using the techniques discussed in greater detail in Chapter 6.

Of course, all of the NETX's modifications to INT 21h should disappear in the NetWare 4 redirector (though, as we noted earlier, even this redirector will still have to hook INT 21h in order to support NetWare extensions to INT 21h such as the F2 interface). The interesting question, then, is what market penetration NetWare 4 will achieve, and how long it will take for the DOS-modifying NetWare versions 2 and 3 to disappear.

NETX.COM hooks INT 21h and puts its own code ahead of almost every single DOS function. In fact, it is easier to list the functions that NETX *doesn't* change than to enumerate all the ones it changes. The following are the only INT 21h functions that NETX does *not* special case: 0Dh, 18h, 1D-20h, 24h, 2Ah-30h, 32h, 34h, 35h, 37h, 38h, 49h, 51h-53h, 58h, 59h, 5Dh. NETX modifies all other DOS functions in some way. For example, NetWare intercepts all file I/O and directory calls, with those intended for NetWare file servers turned into NCP requests, as described above. This is why we are discussing NetWare, which runs on top of DOS, in a chapter on other DOSs. NETX replaces so much of DOS that, by running under the NetWare shell, you are effectively running under a different version of DOS. Incidentally, your programs can use INT 21h AX=EA01h to determine if they are running under the NetWare shell (see the netware_shell() function in PSPTEST.C in Listing 4-4 below).

The following is a list of some of the less immediately obvious changes that NETX makes to the DOS INT 21h interface.

- *Special Standard Handler for Redirection* (INT 21h functions 1, 2, 6, 7, 8, 9, 0Ah, 0Bh, 0Ch). For all the DOS character I/O calls, NETX needs to see if there has been redirection to or from a network file (for example, "FOO > G:\BAR.BAR", where FOO is a program that calls INT 21h AH=9 to display a string, and where G: represents a NetWare file server). If there is redirection to or from a network file, NETX temporarily substitutes a token that routes the I/O to a @!NETW!@ device that handles the redirection.

- *Select Disk* (INT 21h function 0Eh). This is the example we looked at in Chapter 2. Whereas plain-vanilla DOS returns the LASTDRIVE value in AL, NETX always returns 32, representing the size of the three NETX drive tables described above. The actual number of local drives is available under NetWare with INT 21h AH=DBh (see Listing 2-19 in Chapter 2). As a sample of the NetWare code, Figure 4-2 shows the NETX handler for INT 21h AH=0Eh.

Figure 4-2: NETX Handler for INT 21h AH=0Eh (Select Disk)

```
4491:1BD6    SELDISK_OE:
4491:1BD6        push es
4491:1BD7        cmp dl,20h        ; drive >= 32?
4491:1BDA        jae PASS_OE_TO_DOS ;   yes: chain to previous INT 21h
4491:1BDC        mov bl,dl         ;   no: put drive # into BX
```

```
4491:1BDE        xor bh,bh
4491:1BE0        test cs:DRV_FLAG_TAB[bx],83h    ; is it a NetWare drive?
4491:1BE6        jz PASS_OE_TO_DOS               ; no: chain
4491:1BE8        mov cs:CURR_DRV,dl              ; yes: set NETX curr drive
; ... some NetWare TASK stuff ...
4491:1C04    PASS_OE_TO_DOS:
4491:1C04        pop es
4491:1C05        pop bx
4491:1C06        pushf
4491:1C07        call cs:INT21    ; chain to previous INT 21h
4491:1C0C        mov al,20h       ; force 21/0E return LASTDRIVE=32 (20h)
4491:1C0E        iret
```

- *Delete File* (INT 21h function 13h). MS-DOS allows a read-only file to be deleted using the FCB delete call; NetWare does not allow this.

- *Set Interrupt Vector* (INT 21h function 25h). NETX substitutes its INT 24h Critical Error handler in place of COMMAND.COM's so that network errors are semi-intelligent. However, with the DOS Requester in NetWare 4.0, Novell no longer establishes its own INT 24h handler; instead, Novell provides an error-message string through the INT 2Fh AH=05h call that COMMAND.COM makes to expand a critical error message (see the appendix).

- *Parse Filename* (INT 21h function 29h). DOS will signal an error if an invalid drive number is specified. This invalid drive number may be an attempt by the user to reconnect to a network drive, so NETX intercepts the error return and, if it has no connections, attempts to build a connection and map the selected drive to the SYS:LOGIN directory.

- *EXEC* (INT 21h function 4Bh). To run programs located on the file server, and also to support the semi-obsolete "execute-only" attribute which NetWare can place on server files, NETX hooks EXEC and turns it into an NCP file-open call, with an "Open for EXEC" bit set. Because NETX hooks the EXEC call, it also calls the DOS Set Execution State function (INT 21h AX=4B05h), which among other things allows DOS to do SETVER checking. In his *DOS Internals* (Chapter 5), Geoff Chappell speculates that, since Novell uses the 21/4B05 call, and since no Microsoft software appears to, even when they should (for example, debuggers), it is possible Microsoft may have created this function specifically for Novell.

- *Set PSP* (INT 21h function 50h). NETX changes two unused values in the PSP, at offsets 003Eh and 003Fh. (You may recall from Chapter 1 that Windows also uses two unused locations in the PSP; fortunately, they are different locations from the ones NETX uses!) According to Tim Farley, author of a forthcoming book, *Undocumented NetWare* (Addison-Wesley, 1994), NETX uses the byte at 3Eh in the PSP as a flag. If set to 0CEh, NETX knows this PSP has already been initialized. If not already set to 0CEh, NETX changes the value to 0CEh and then initializes the byte at 3Fh to a Novell task ID. Since these are unused fields in the PSP, this is all fine and dandy, except that some programs call INT 21h AH=50h with a PSP of zero. Unfortunately, some versions of NETX do not check for this condition and consequently smack a CEh into 0000:003E and a Novell task number into 0000:003F, thereby wiping out the upper two bytes of the vector for INT 0Fh, which is the LPT1: hardware interrupt!

Microsoft C Warranties and SetPSP(0)

Who, you might ask, would do a Set PSP of zero? Why, Microsoft, of course! Some releases of Microsoft QuickC, Programmer's Workbench (PWB), and Microsoft C 6.0 Setup contain a DOS detection function that tests for the presence of "genuine" MS-DOS by calling INT 21h AH=50h to set the PSP to 0, then checking the current_psp field in the SDA (see Chapter 6) to see if it has become set to 0. Microsoft's code then does the same thing with a PSP of 0FFFFh (-1). Running these versions of the C compiler under NetWare thus trashes not only the INT 0Fh vector, but also some other location that depends on whether the A20 line is enabled. If A20 is off, FFFF:003E wraps around to 0000:002C, which holds the INT 0Bh vector; COM2 uses INT 0Bh. Imagine someone's surprise when, after compiling a program with QuickC under NetWare, their communications package fails! The DOS world, as a constant reminder of how "too many cooks spoil the soup," is full of interesting interactions like this. It almost makes you wish that Microsoft had even more of a monopoly!

We had heard rumors that QuickC performed such a test, but found it so difficult to believe we had to check it out for ourselves. Digging out a copy of version 2.51 of the Microsoft QuickC compiler with QuickAssembler, we found that the QuickC README.DOC file actually refers obliquely to this test, saying that the product "prints a warning message when a nonstandard version of DOS is detected. The /nologo option prevents this message from being printed." Indeed, QC.EXE (dated April 6, 1990) contains the following message, which sounds strangely reminiscent of some of the unfair trade practices explicitly banned by the Clayton antitrust act:

```
WARNING: This Microsoft product has been tested and certified for use
only with the MS-DOS and PC-DOS operating systems. Your use of this
product with another operating system may void valuable warranty
protection provided by Microsoft on this product.
```

Remember, this message is coming from a Microsoft C compiler, not from part of MS-DOS. It's no wonder that, shortly after bringing this warranty-related warning message to the attention of an attorney at the U.S. Federal Trade Commission (FTC), one of the authors started hearing rumors that the FTC's consumer-affairs bureau had suddenly become involved in the investigation of Microsoft, and that the Magnuson-Moss Warranty Act had entered the picture.

While it's a good thing that this message can be turned off, what about those calls to SetPSP(0) and SetPSP(-1)? Recall that, when this code was written, the Set PSP function wasn't even documented; yet Microsoft's C compilers compete with products from other vendors. Testing whether Set PSP modifies a certain fixed spot in the DOS data segment is just the sort of underhanded use of insider knowledge that Microsoft applications are not supposed to be taking advantage of—particularly when the sole purpose of this code is to make Microsoft C users think they shouldn't run versions of DOS other than Microsoft's. You could make a good case that it *is* dumb to bother with anything except genuine MS-DOS, but it is inappropriate, and possibly even restraint of trade, for Microsoft's C products to try to convince you of this point.

To see if QC.EXE really includes such code, we first ran it under the following INTRSPY script:

```
; psp0.scr
intercept 21h
    function 50h on_entry
        if ((bx == 0) || (bx == 0FFFFh))
            output "SET PSP " bx " from " CS ":" IP
```

Sure enough, INTRSPY produced the following output, indicating that the current PSP was being set to 0 and -1 (FFFFh):

```
SET PSP 0 from 9E33:016F
SET PSP FFFFh from 9E33:0177
```

Using the CS:IP addresses the INTRSPY script displays, we used WINICE to disassemble the code. Figure 4-3 shows the results.

Figure 4-3: Microsoft QuickC DOS Detection Code

```
:u &9e33:014e
; this is in the middle of some sort of "is dos okay?" function
9E33:0000014E    MOV     AH,52
9E33:00000150    INT     21              ; get DOS DS into ES; ignore BX
9E33:00000152    MOV     AX,ES:[0004]    ; DOS_DS[4] = SDA type
9E33:00000156    CMP     AX,0001
9E33:00000159    JA      018C            ; hmm, DOS_DS[4] > 1 is ok; DOS 2?
9E33:0000015B    SHL     AX,1
9E33:0000015D    MOV     SI,AX           ; AX is 0 or 2
9E33:0000015F    MOV     SI,[SI+0134]    ; QC knows CURR_PSP ofs in DOS_DS
9E33:00000163    MOV     AH,51           ;    [134h] = 02DE; [136h] = 0330h
9E33:00000165    INT     21
9E33:00000167    MOV     DX,BX           ; save current PSP in DX
9E33:00000169    XOR     BX,BX           ; BX = PSP = 0
9E33:0000016B    MOV     AH,50
9E33:0000016D    INT     21              ; SetPSP(0)
9E33:0000016F    CMP     ES:[SI],BX      ; see if DOS_DS[CURR_PSP] matches
9E33:00000172    JNZ     0183            ;    no: not MS-DOS
9E33:00000174    DEC     BX              ; BX = PSP = -1
9E33:00000175    INT     21              ; SetPSP(-1)
9E33:00000177    CMP     ES:[SI],BX      ; see if DOS_DS[CURR_PSP] matches
9E33:0000017A    JNZ     0183            ;    no: not MS-DOS
9E33:0000017C    MOV     BX,DX
9E33:0000017E    INT     21              ; restore PSP
9E33:00000180    JMP     018C
9E33:00000182    NOP
; not_msdos:
9E33:00000183    MOV     BX,DX           ; problem: no match
9E33:00000185    INT     21
9E33:00000187    XOR     AX,AX           ; return false = 0
9E33:00000189    JMP     018F
9E33:0000018B    NOP
; is_msdos:
9E33:0000018C    XOR     AX,AX           ; ok: match
9E33:0000018E    DEC     AX              ; return true = -1
; done:
9E33:0000018F    POP     ES
; ...
:dw &9e33:0134 0136
9E33:00000134    02DE    0330
```

This code definitely is taking advantage of inside knowledge, and is using a narrow definition of DOS compatibility. For example, QuickC wants to find the address of the current_psp field in the DOS data segment. While also undocumented, the common way to get this in third-party code would be to call INT 21h AX=5D06h to get a pointer to the Swappable Data Area and then look at offset 10h. Instead, the code calls INT 21h AH=52h to get the DOS data segment into ES (ignoring the SysVars offset in BX), then uses a little-known value at offset 4 in the DOS data segment to determine whether there is a DOS 3.0-style SDA or a DOS 4.0-style SDA. Based on this, the program uses hard-wired offsets for the current PSP in the DOS data segment (offset 02DEh in DOS 3.0, and offset 0330h in DOS 4.0 and higher).

Despite the supposed "separation of church and state" between applications programmers and operating systems programmers at Microsoft, the use of DOS_DS[4] reveals an intimate knowledge of the DOS code. Unlike many other features of undocumented

DOS which are open secrets, the SDA type indicator at DOS_DS[4] has not been publicized at all. To our knowledge, the only place this has been discussed in print has been in the writings of Geoff Chappell (see the discussion of "Direct Access to Kernel Data" in Chapter 13 of his *DOS Internals*). The code for SHARE and other DOS utilities relies on DOS_DS[4], but it is certainly odd to see it showing up in the code for QuickC, which is an application, and doubly odd to see it being put to such seemingly malicious use.

Listing 4-4 shows a short C program, PSPTEST.C, that duplicates the nasty QuickC code. Of course, PSPTEST first checks to see if NETX is running; if it is, PSPTEST asks the user if they really want to run the test, since SetPSP(0) under NETX may corrupt their system.

Listing 4-4: PSPTEST.C

```
/*
PSPTEST.C
Andrew Schulman, June 1993
From Undocumented DOS, 2nd edition (Addison-Wesley, 1993)
*/

#include <stdlib.h>
#include <stdio.h>
#include <ctype.h>
#include <conio.h>
#include <dos.h>
#ifndef MK_FP
#define MK_FP(seg, ofs) \
    ((void far *) (((unsigned long) (seg) << 16) | (ofs)))
#endif

typedef int BOOL;
typedef unsigned char BYTE;
typedef unsigned short WORD;

#pragma warn -rvl
WORD _dos_getpsp(void)
{
    _asm mov ah, 51h
    _asm int 21h
    _asm mov ax, bx
}

void _dos_setpsp(WORD psp)
{
    _asm mov bx, word ptr psp
    _asm mov ah, 50h
    _asm int 21h
}

#pragma warn -rvl
WORD _dos_getds(void)
{
    _asm mov ah, 52h
    _asm int 21h
    _asm mov ax, es
    // ignore SysVars offset in BX
}

// Novell Return Shell Version function (INT 21h AH=EAh AL=01h)
// see INTRLIST on accompanying disk; also see Barry Nance,
// _Networking Programming in C_, pp. 117, 341-2.
BOOL netware_shell(void)
{
    char buf[40];
    char far *fp = buf;
    _asm push di
    _asm mov ax, 0EA01h
    _asm mov bx, 0
```

```
    _asm les di, fp
    _asm int 21h
    _asm xor al, al
    _asm mov ax, bx
    // if BX still 0, then NetWare not present; return in AX
    _asm pop di
}
void fail(const char *s) { puts(s); exit(1); }
main()
{
    BYTE far *dos_ds;
    WORD far *curr_psp_ptr;
    WORD psp;

    dos_ds = (BYTE far *) MK_FP(_dos_getds(), 0);
    switch (dos_ds[4])
    {
        case 0:  curr_psp_ptr = (WORD far *) (dos_ds + 0x02DE); break;
        case 1:  curr_psp_ptr = (WORD far *) (dos_ds + 0x0330); break;
        default: puts("DOS_DS[4] > 1"); goto okay;
    }

    if (netware_shell())
    {
        puts("Under NETX, SetPSP(0) can corrupt your system.");
        fputs("Still want to continue? [Y/N] ", stdout);
        if (toupper(getch()) != 'Y') fail("\nbye");
        putchar('\n');
    }

    psp = _dos_getpsp();
    if (*curr_psp_ptr != psp)
        fail("Curr_PSP field wrong!");

    _dos_setpsp(0);
    if (*curr_psp_ptr != 0)
    {
        _dos_setpsp(psp);
        fail("SetPSP(0) test failed");
    }

    _dos_setpsp(-1);
    if (*curr_psp_ptr != -1)
    {
        _dos_setpsp(psp);
        fail("SetPSP(-1) test failed");
    }

    _dos_setpsp(psp);
    puts("SetPSP(0) and SetPSP(-1) tests succeeded");
okay:
    return 0;
}
```

It's worth noting that this program succeeds, not only under MS-DOS 3.0 and higher, but also under DR DOS 5.0 and higher. In other words, DR DOS keeps the current PSP at exactly the same location, DOS_DS[02DEh], as DOS 3.0 does. What a coincidence!

PSPTEST also succeeds under the old Concurrent DOS/386 2.01, which doesn't implement the DOS_DS[4] flag. QuickC also runs in this environment. If you examine the code, you will notice that any environment with DOS_DS[4] > 1 is okay; presumably this is because QuickC has to run on DOS 2.x, which didn't implement the DOS_DS[4] flag. In fact, it's unclear under what circumstances you would have a DOS clone in which (DOS_DS[4] == 0 but DOS_DS[2DEh] != CURR_PSP) or (DOS_DS[4] == 1 but DOS_DS[330h] != CURR_PSP).

In summary, the SetPSP(0) code seems to package up all the problems of undocumented DOS in a nutshell: we have NetWare hijacking unused fields in the PSP (or perhaps not: see below), NetWare failing to think through all the implications of hooking INT 21h, Microsoft applications accessing undocumented DOS kernel data, and Microsoft applications testing for the presence of non-Microsoft operating systems in what certainly looks like a classic tying arrangement (see Chapter 1).

What about that Novell task ID? According to an engineer at Novell, NetWare uses this ID to keep track of multiple programs running on a single workstation. Just to make things interesting, this field in the PSP was apparently reserved for Novell *by Microsoft*. Microsoft's source file for the PSP, PDB.H from the OEM Adaptation Kit [OAK; see Chapter 6] contains a "PDB_Novell_Used" field and the comment "Novell shell (redir) uses these." The task ID starts at 1 for the master copy of COMMAND.COM and increments for each task loaded that does DOS I/O. Some programs are never assigned a task ID by NETX.

- *TRUENAME* (INT 21h function 60h). NETX hooks the TRUENAME function, and uses it to return a UNC \\server\volume\path name. Thus, you can call TRUENAME to get the underlying server and volume name for a NetWare drive.

Again, all these NETX modifications to INT 21h basically present us with a different version of DOS. On the other hand, these modifications go away starting in NetWare 4.0.

Undocumented NetWare

NetWare has vast amounts of undocumented functionality, enough to fill an entire book. As noted earlier, Tim Farley's *Undocumented NetWare* is scheduled for publication in 1994. In the meantime, it is interesting to consider the following:

- *NetWare server file system.* The physical file system used on NetWare file servers is proprietary, which makes it difficult to write a product such as Norton Utilities or PC Tools for NetWare file servers. At least one vendor (OnTrack) has reverse-engineered the NetWare file system.
- There are many *undocumented NLM calls*, the names of which appear in the Watcom linker that Novell ships. Many of these undocumented calls have an FE_ prefix (FileEngine). These calls would be useful for writing alternate file systems or for utility vendors interested in continuous backup, server antivirus software, and the like.
- *NetWare Lite.* The API for NetWare Lite appears to be completely undocumented. The Interrupt List on the accompanying disk has a few NetWare Lite functions, such as INT 2Fh AX=B809h (an install check both for NetWare Lite and LANtastic), AX=D800h (CLIENT.EXE install check), and AX=D880h (SERVER.EXE install check). This may all change with Personal NetWare, which is basically the next release of NetWare Lite. The server component will be based on the same NCP protocol as NetWare, not on the special Lite protocol, which means it will work with the VLM-based common client for DOS being shipped with NetWare 4.0. Currently, you must practice polygamy, loading both NETX to be a NetWare client and CLIENT.EXE to be a Lite client. With the common client you will be able to use one TSR instead of two. Rumor has it that Novell DOS 7.0 will virtually incorporate Personal NetWare for DOS and that the peer-to-peer server will use DPMS.
- The *NetWare Core Protocol.* Novell considers NCP "proprietary." While NCP is immediately visible to anyone with a network sniffer such as General Software's The Snooper, or even

Novell's own LANanlyzer, Novell has never publicly documented the protocol. A partial discussion appears in *Novell's Guide to NetWare LAN Analysis* by Laura Chappell (Sybex/Novell Press, 1993). General Software's The Snooper comes with full C source code, including an NCP.C module. For more information on NCP, see Pawel Szczerbina's article, "Novell's 'Unclean Hands': The NetWare Core Protocol (NCP)," *Dr. Dobb's Journal*, November 1993.

■ *The F2 interface.* As noted earlier, NETX extends INT 21h to provide many NetWare-specific functions. While Novell documents many of the extensions, some, including INT 21h AH=F2h are not documented. This allows programs to issue raw NCPs to the file server. (F2 isn't required to issue raw NCPs; as the *Dr. Dobb's Journal* article cited above notes, you can directly use IPX.) A friend at Microsoft complains (talk about the pot calling the kettle black!), "This still hasn't really been documented, although they have released a few code fragments that quietly use the interface. This was in response to developers who were [expletive deleted] that they could not do something that some Novell utility could do." However, Novell does seem committed to supporting F2 and has provided attendees of its "BrainShare" developer's conference with information on the interface, though at the same time keeping NCP information (without which F2 is useless) under wraps. An engineer at Novell supplied the following information on the F2 interface:

```
RawNPRequest          ;242 (F2)
** undocumented **
Generic function used to send raw NCP requests. Documented in part
by the Erase Files function for purging files (INT 21h AX=F244h)
input:
    AL      NCP function request code
    DS:SI   Request List
    CX      Request Length (in bytes)
    ES:DI   Reply List
    DX      Reply Length (in bytes)
output:
    AL   Return code
```

Other undocumented INT 21h calls include AttachHandle (AH=B4h), an interface Novell provides to give DOS file access to NetWare files, including on Macintosh, OS/2, and UNIX; GetIData (AH=B5h), an interface provided for the VNETWARE.386 Windows VxD (with subfunctions in AL to get instance data, start and end virtual machines, and so on); and ReturnCommandComPointers (AH=BAh), used to edit the master environment "COMSPEC" and "PATH" parameters.

The function to edit the master environment is interesting, given the difficulty noted in Chapter 10 of finding the master environment. According to an engineer at Novell, they use code directly out of the Spontaneous Assembly library, as this code seems to work best. Novell changes the PATH when you log in, to include your search drives in the list. Obviously, to make this change, Novell must find the master environment. According to one user, this makes for some real nastiness if you try to LOGIN to Novell while shelled out of another program. So now Novell is providing an (undocumented) way to let other programs let NetWare find the master environment block for them.

OS/2 2.x: "A Better DOS Than DOS"?

When OS/2 1.0 first appeared in 1987-88, Microsoft and IBM, along with many PC software developers, thought OS/2 would replace MS-DOS and take over the desktop. OS/2 1.x had a real mode DOS compatibility box (commonly referred to as the DOS coffin, penalty box, or Chernobyl box), which ran some DOS software and on which much work was spent. But it is indicative that many at the time thought this would fade away as all DOS programs were flushed out of circulation and replaced by new OS/2 programs.

Soon reality set in. IBM almost overnight ceased to be the most important force in the software industry, Microsoft went back to doing Windows, and it became clear that OS/2 would take its place as one of several operating system solutions and would in no way replace DOS. In fact, things look downright bad for OS/2. However, OS/2 2.0, which comes from the Personal Software Products (PSP) division of IBM (likely to be spun off as a separate company), includes dramatic improvements to the DOS compatibility box, to the extent that IBM now claims that OS/2 provides "a better DOS than DOS."

In some ways, this claim is valid. OS/2 2.x provides multiple, preemptively multitasked DOS boxes, called Multiple Virtual DOS Machines (MVDMs), with more available memory than is generally available in real mode DOS, and with better protection than real mode DOS affords. The secret to this is that OS/2 2.x, like Windows Enhanced mode and Windows NT, runs DOS and DOS applications in the virtual 8086 (V86) mode of the 80386 and higher processors, rather than in real mode.

With V86 mode, all sorts of DOS magic is possible. The claim to be a better DOS than DOS is true then, but only in the sense that *any* V86 DOS emulation is better than DOS itself. But it is also important to remember (see the DOSSPEED program in Chapter 3) that V86 DOS emulation is, necessarily, *slower* than genuine DOS. (According to one tech reviewer, "IBM claims that DOS sessions actually enhance the performance of DOS programs"!) Fortunately, Intel's new Pentium processor has enhancements to V86 mode intended to improve performance by reducing the number of traps to the V86 monitor (see "Undocumented Pentium," below).

Undocumented Pentium

Intel's Pentium processor, commonly known as the 586 or P5, includes enhancements to virtual 8086 mode that will improve performance by reducing the number of times programs running in V86 mode trap to the protected mode V86 monitor. The VME bit in the new CR4 control register enables these enhancements, which include the new Virtual Interrupt Pending (VIP) and Virtual Interrupt Flag (VIF) bits in the Pentium EFLAGS register.

Unfortunately, Intel's *Pentium Processor User's Manual* provides no further information on these important-sounding enhancements to V86 mode. Appendix H (Advanced Features) says that such information is "considered Intel confidential and proprietary and have not been documented in this publication. This information is provided in the *Supplement to the Pentium Processor User's Manual* and is available with the appropriate non-disclosure agreements in place." According to Spencer Katt's occasionally-reliable "Rumor Central" column in *PC Week* (May 24, 1993), the length of the NDA is fifteen years!

Clearly, the VIF bit in EFLAGS is intended to eliminate the need for trapping into protected mode every time a program running in V86 mode executes a CLI or STI instruction. Having to maintain a virtual interrupt flag has been one of the most serious performance problems with V86 mode. According to the DPMI specification, "Since *cli* and *sti* are privileged instructions, they will cause a protection violation and the DPMI provider will simulate the instruction. Because of the overhead involved in processing the exception, *cli* and *sti* should be used as little as possible. In general, you should expect either of these instructions to require at least 300 clocks." 300 clocks! The new VIF bit in EFLAGS sounds like an excellent idea.

According to *Microprocessor Report* ("Intel Reveals Pentium Implementation Details," March 29, 1993), the infamous Appendix H "is supplied only to selected operating-systems vendors." Presumably, users of V86 mode, such as Microsoft, IBM, Novell, Qualitas, and Quarterdeck, will have no trouble getting their hands on the necessary documentation from Intel and incorporating these Pentium enhancements into their software. Then it will just be a question of when end-users actually get machines with Pentium processors!

There are many interesting and important aspects to MVDMs in OS/2 2.0. Here, however, we focus exclusively on how well OS/2 emulates MS-DOS, emphasizing, of course, its support for undocumented DOS functions and data structures. For more information on MVDM technology, see the chapter on compatibility in Harvey Deitel and Michael Kogan's *The Design of OS/2* (Addison-Wesley, 1992).

MVDMs and VDDs

OS/2 MVDMs sound at first a lot like DOS boxes in Windows Enhanced mode. In both environments, DOS programs make normal INT 21h calls and INT 2Fh calls, do INs and OUTs to ports, read and write memory locations, and do all the other messy stuff that DOS programs like to do. A virtual machine monitor catches these events and hands them off to virtual device drivers (VxDs in Windows, but abbreviated as VDDs in both OS/2 and Windows NT), which virtualize whatever device the DOS program thinks it's directly banging on.

These devices aren't necessarily pieces of hardware. For example, just as Windows has the V86MMGR VxD to emulate the XMS and EMS specifications (that's right, XMS calls in Windows aren't handled by HIMEM.SYS; V86MMGR emulates XMS), likewise, OS/2 2.x doesn't use HIMEM.SYS or an EMM driver. Instead, it has the VDDs VXMS.SYS and VEMM.SYS. In OS/2, VDPMI.SYS provides the DOS Protected Mode Interface; VDPX.SYS provides optional protected mode INT 21h services (similar to DOSMGR in Windows).

Of course, some VDDs in OS/2, like some VxDs in Windows, do virtualize actual devices. For example, there are VPIC.SYS (similar to VPICD in Windows), VTIMER.SYS (VTD in Windows), VMOUSE.SYS (VMD in Windows), VKBD.SYS (VKD in Windows), and so on. There are many similarities to Windows Enhanced mode, right down to the file format these virtual device drivers use. In Windows, VxDs use the undocumented Linear Executable (LE) file format. In OS/2, VDDs use the LX file format, which is a hacked version of LE. LX, at least, is partially documented (see EXE386.H on the OS/2 2.x SDK CD-ROM). VDDs in OS/2 2.x (like VxDs in Windows) run in Ring 0 kernel mode, unlike NT VDDs, which (we'll see later) run in Ring 3 user mode.

DOS application support in OS/2 is almost infinitely extensible through VDDs, in the same way that VxDs can provide any type of service to programs running under Windows. By hooking software interrupts, a VDD in OS/2 could provide new APIs to DOS programs. Just as VxDs in Windows can call services from VMM or other VxDs, OS/2 VDDs have at their disposal a set of Virtual Device Helper (VDH) functions. For example, VDDs can hook V86 interrupts with VDHInstallIntHook() and protected mode interrupts with VDHSetVPMIntVector(); a DOS program's I/O port access can be controlled with VDHInstallIOHook(). (The *OS/2 2.0 Virtual Device Driver Reference* (IBM publication #s10g-6310) documents these VDH functions, as does the VDD chapter of Steven J. Mastrianni's book *Writing OS/2 2.0 Device Drivers in C.*)

All this is very similar to VxD programming in Windows Enhanced mode. This is not surprising, since Microsoft wrote much of this code before the IBM-Microsoft divorce. When Microsoft trashes OS/2 in public, it is mostly deriding its own earlier work.

But there is one very crucial difference between OS/2 MVDMs and Windows Enhanced mode. We saw in Chapters 1 and 3 that Windows reflects many DOS calls down to MS-DOS in V86 mode. But in OS/2 *DOS isn't there at all*. This is a rather obvious point, but it bears repeating: OS/2 does not run on top of DOS. DOS is nowhere in sight. Any INT 21h calls that a DOS program makes under OS/2 must be handled by OS/2 itself. Windows (at least without VFAT.386) handles file

I/O calls by doing a little API translation and then calling down to DOS in V86 mode; but OS/2 must turn all DOS file I/O calls into calls to the OS/2 kernel. For example, INT 21h AH=3Dh calls must be handled by the OS/2 DosOpen() function; AH=3Fh must be handled by DosRead(), and so on.

But DOS programs running under OS/2 really do think they are running under a version of DOS. They can use all the documented INT 21h and INT 2Fh functions and many of the undocumented ones. They can even make an INT 21h AH=30h call and get back a DOS version number.

So What Version of DOS Is This DOS Emulation Pretending To Be?

In OS/2 2.0, INT 21h AH=30h returns 0014h (DOS 20.00); in OS/2 2.10, it returns 0A14h (DOS 20.10). This is in keeping with an OS/2 tradition: The DOS box in OS/2 1.x proclaimed itself to be DOS 10.x. The original thinking here was probably that there never *would* be a genuine DOS 10.x. But what with minor upgrades such as MS-DOS 6.0 being given major version number increases, and with genuine major upgrades such as MS-DOS 7.0 on the horizon, it seems possible that one day there will be a DOS 10.0. But 20.0, at least, does seem a bit inconceivable. Actually, one of our reviewers says, "As for possibility of genuine MS-DOS >= 10.0, look at SETVER: it can only handle up to version number 9.99. Thus, MS-DOS has no plans to ever reach DOS 10!"

The 20.x version number is useful for telling DOS applications they are in fact running under OS/2 2.x, but what MS-DOS version is OS/2 *emulating*? The return value from INT 21h AX=3306h (Get Actual MS-DOS Version) isn't much help here, as it returns the same value as INT 21h AH=30h; but the mere presence of function 3306h, which came about with DOS 5.0, tells us that OS/2 is generally acting like MS-DOS 5.0 or higher. Unfortunately, there is no call to get the simulated DOS version. An engineer at IBM reports that:

> The OS/2 1.0 DOS box was originally a copy of DOS 3.3 modified (mostly removing things). OS/2 2.0 was targeted to emulate DOS 5.0. We looked at the functional specification for DOS 4 and DOS 5.0 and listed work which needed to be done. Most items on the list were completed. The largest item not finished was the FC command. [FC is a simple file-compare utility; is this some kind of joke?] When we finished we noticed that there were little things such as new INT 21h IOCTL calls [INT 21h AX=4410h and AX=4411h] that weren't in the spec. The stated emulation in our publications is DOS 5.0 compatible.

Just like MS-DOS 5.0 and higher, the OS/2 2.x MVDM can produce fake DOS version numbers on a per-application basis; this is controlled by the DOS_VERSION setting. With DOS_VERSION, applications that are confused by the idea of DOS 20.0 can be told they are running under DOS 5.0, or whatever. DOS_VERSION is just like SETVER in MS-DOS, except that DOS_VERSION includes not only the executable name and major.minor version number, but also the number of times to fake the version number (255 means "always fake"). Apparently, early beta versions of MS-DOS 5.0 also had this same fake-count value. As with SETVER, changing the DOS_VERSION field does nothing to make OS/2 compatible with that version of DOS. It simply determines what value INT 21h AH=30h will return when called by the specified application.

DOS_VERSION is just one of many settings in the OS/2 MVDMs. For example, DOS_LASTDRIVE determines the number of available drives in a VDM. OS/2 does not use a Current Directory Structure, even in the DOS box; the OS/2 kernel handles all INT 21h file I/O and directory calls. Therefore, this setting has roughly the same purpose as LASTDRIVE= in a DOS CONFIG.SYS, but its effect on the system is different. Multiple VDMs can run simultaneously, each with a different DOS_LASTDRIVE.

DOS_FILES seems as though it would be similar to the FILES= statement in DOS CONFIG.SYS. As discussed in Chapter 8, in MS-DOS FILES= sets the size of the System File Table (SFT); a file handle in MS-DOS is an index into the program's Job File Table (JFT), which in turn holds indices into the SFT. But OS/2 MVDMs don't have SFTs. While a file handle is still an index into the

JFT, the JFT holds OS/2 file handles, not SFT indices. From a DOS program's perspective, the SFT under OS/2 is infinite (much greater than 255 entries). Thus, changing the SFT size is meaningless in an OS/2 VDM. What DOS_FILES does, then, is increase the size of the VDM's JFT, using the OS/2 DosSetMaxFH() function, which is similar to INT 21h AH=67h in DOS.

Another example is DPMI_DOS_API, which controls whether the DOS Protected Mode Interface provided in the MVDM should also provide DOS calls in protected mode. As we saw in Chapter 3, DPMI and protected mode INT 21h are separate services. WIN-OS/2 requires both DPMI and DPMI_DOS_API; so do applications such as Borland C++ that interpret the presence of DPMI to mean that protected mode INT 21h is automatically available.

There is nothing special about these settings; they are simply registered and queried by VDDs, using documented VDH functions (see "Registering OS/2 DOS Settings," below). For example, VDPX.SYS registers DPMI_DOS_API; VBIOS.SYS registers DOS_LASTDRIVE and DOS_FILES; and DOSKRNL registers DOS_VERSION. In a sense, these are just like SYSTEM.INI settings in Windows Enhanced mode, which any VxD is also free to establish.

Registering OS/2 DOS Settings

There is a VDD call VDHRegisterProperty (yes, it's documented in the OS/2 DDK), to set-up a DOS Setting. Any VDD, whether system supplied or user written, can register a property. One of the pieces of information you must supply is whether the property can be changed at any time or only before the VDM is created. DOS Settings can be viewed as similar to DOS CONFIG.SYS processing, except that in DOS, unlike with OS/2 MVDMs, none of the settings can normally be changed once the machine is up and running. (We've seen in other chapters, of course, how to modify LASTDRIVE= by changing Sys-Vars, or how to modify FILES= by adding new tables to the SFT chain.)

The following minimal VDD demonstrates a user-written DOS Setting. It doesn't do anything but add GEORGE_FULK to your notebook for DOS Settings. The two reserved fields are really case-sensitive help. Unfortunately, the current PMVDMP.DLL (which runs the notebook) ignores them. The reader will not be surprised to learn that this code was supplied by George Fulk, an engineer at IBM who contributed much of the information on OS/2 MVDMs in this section. John Hare, also of IBM, supplied additional information.

```
; GEO_FULK.ASM
.386P
;-----------------------------------------------
ASSUME   CS:CSEG, DS:FLAT, SS:FLAT, ES:FLAT
CSEG     SEGMENT  DWORD USE32 PUBLIC 'CODE'
Validate proc    near
         xor     eax,eax
         ret
Validate endp
CSEG     ENDS
;-----------------------------------------------
ASSUME   CS:CINIT_TEXT
DSEG     SEGMENT DWORD USE32 PUBLIC 'DATA'
PROPERTYNAME    db         "GEORGE_FULK",0
DSEG     ENDS
;-----------------------------------------------
EXTRN    VDHREGISTERPROPERTY: NEAR
CINIT_TEXT       SEGMENT DWORD USE32 PUBLIC 'CODE'
_VDDInit proc near
         push    ebp
         mov     ebp, esp
```

```
;------ register the DOS setting
        push    offset FLAT:PROPERTYNAME
        push    0         ;reserved
        push    0         ;reserved
        push    0         ;=boolean
        push    0         ;="other", non-system VDD
        push    1         ;=only change before VDM creation
        push    0         ;=default value, =off
        push    0         ;no range checking for boolean
        push    offset FLAT:Validate
        call    VDHREGISTERPROPERTY
        or      eax,eax                   ;if VDH called fails,
        jz      short InitDone            ; then fail the VDD init.
        dec     eax                       ;init!=0 means success
InitDone :                                ;init==0 means failure
        leave
        ret
_VDDInit endp
;-----------------------------------------
CINIT_TEXT   ENDS
        END     _VDDInit
```

Loading a Genuine DOS

As an alternative to using DOS emulation, OS/2 2.x can also load an actual copy of MS-DOS. The IBM *Installation Guide* has an appendix, "Running Specific DOS from Within OS/2 2.0," which describes what to do if you have software (such as DOS LAN Requester) that must run within an actual ("specific") copy of DOS 4.0 rather than with OS/2 DOS emulation. The procedure involves creating a DOS boot diskette, then creating a diskette image (.IMG file) with the OS/2 VMDISK utility, and then installing the OS/2 FSFILTER.SYS device, which allows the specific copy of DOS running in DOS box to access the OS/2 file system.

FSFILTER is just a DOS device driver that hooks INT 21h. How then does it communicate with the OS/2 kernel? Disassembly of FSFILTER reveals some calls to INT 66h, with AX=1 and SI pointing to strings such as VCOM, VDISK, and VLPT. However, this doesn't seem sufficient for a DOS device driver running at Ring 3 in V86 mode to communicate with OS2KRNL running at Ring 0 in protected mode. FSFILTER uses HLT instructions to communicate with OS2KRNL. We asked one of the IBM MVDM engineers how this works:

> HLT is our magic pill. The HLT instruction is a Ring 0 instruction; since V86 mode is Ring 3, a trap occurs. A part of OS2KRNL called EM86 (Emulation 8086) receives the fault and takes action. EM86 looks at the registers and the two bytes following the HLT and determines that this is a special request and not a real HLT instruction. The code uses a *SVC xxx* macro, where xxx is the ordinal number of the function to call in OS2KRNL; the dispatcher in MVDM (part of OS2KRNL) knows all the valid xxx calls.
>
> Many opcodes that 8086 provides are now Ring 0 only, and EM86 emulates the 8086 actions of these privileged instructions. If a special request HLT is found, MVDM (also part of OS2KRNL) is given the request for dispatching and action. There is a second magic pill EM86 uses, the ARPL instruction. VDD stubs use the ARPL; DOSKRNL and FSFILTER use HLT.

More similarities to Windows! Windows Enhanced mode uses ARPL, for the same reasons, in the Install_V86_Break_Point function. Later on we'll see that DOS device drivers running under Windows NT can use a very similar mechanism, invalid opcodes, for communicating with NT VDDs.

Even though OS/2 can use FSFILTER to run an actual DOS in V86 mode, emulating DOS is preferable. For one thing, running an actual copy of DOS makes it more difficult to control polling in the DOS kernel, which wastes cycles. In addition, FSFILTER must catch DOS calls at a lower level than the normal DOS emulation code.

OS/2 2.x and Undocumented DOS

IBM's OS/2 *Compatibility Information* booklet, while noting that many DOS and Windows programs run under OS/2 2.0, notes, however, that "some applications, usually because of their design or because they use undocumented interfaces, will not operate properly with OS/2 2.0."

As examples of DOS software that won't run in this "better DOS than DOS," IBM goes on to list "application programs that directly address the physical sectors of OS/2 managed non-removable DASD" (in other words, the Norton Utilities!), timing-sensitive DOS programs, VCPI clients (OS/2 *does* support the XMS, EMS, and DPMI specifications), DOS debuggers that set 386 hardware breakpoints on 386 (DR0-DR7 register access), and Windows programs that rely on VxDs; this includes any Win32s application, since OS/2 can't load W32S.386.

It's worth noting that more and more Windows applications require a VxD or Win32s. For example, Microsoft Visual C++ comes with three VxDs: CVW1.386, DOSXNT.386, and MMD.386. *PC Week* (April 26, 1993) had an extremely confused discussion of OS/2's inability to run VC++, indicating that VC++'s need for VxDs was somehow "inexplicable." Attorneys at the FTC appeared at one point to interpret this to mean that VC++ perhaps required the VxDs simply to keep VC++ from running under OS/2. There is no evidence for this at all. CVW1.386 is Nu-Mega's VxD for running the CodeView debugger on a single screen, and DOSXNT.386 is used by the Phar Lap DOS extender used by the VC++ command-line tools. If major Windows applications won't run under OS/2 because the applications require a VxD, then it seems to be IBM's responsibility either to write a VxD loader for WIN-OS/2 or to develop OS/2 VDD equivalents for the most important Windows VxDs.

OS/2 2.1 has improved support for DOS and Windows: You can launch DOS programs from WIN-OS/2, and Windows Enhanced mode is supported to the extent of running WINMEM32 applications. Still no VxDs, however. (Note, incidentally, that programs that require VxDs won't run under Windows NT either.)

On the question of timing-sensitive applications, one of the MVDM developers at IBM writes,

> All well-behaved DOS applications [one tech reviewer asks, "what is a well-behaved DOS application?"] should run in MVDM. The only exception is an application that requires hardware capabilities beyond our capacity. For instance, we virtualize everything, including I/O ports. As a result we can only handle 1000 interrupts/second. Some applications want a much higher rate. The Links golf game produces sound by driving 16000+ interrupts/sec. With virtualization we could never obtain that rate. One suggestion I've received is to add an option (i.e., DOS Setting) to give exclusive control of a piece of hardware to one session (i.e., sound I/O ports). No other session in the system could use those I/O ports, but we could increase the interrupt rate dramatically.

It is important to know what kind of low-level support DOS emulation provides. The whole reason for these elaborate virtualization schemes is that popular PC applications bypass approved methods, making low level calls instead of high level ones, accessing I/O ports and memory locations instead of making DOS calls, and so on. This is necessary in the DOS world. The performance boost from bypassing DOS is one reason why these programs became popular in the first place. However, it also puts a great burden on the developers of environments such as OS/2, Windows NT, and Windows Enhanced mode.

If all applications played by the rules, life would be easy for DOS emulations. You wouldn't need all this elaborate device virtualization in the first place. Operating systems such as OS/2 could trap INT 21h and that would be it; once inside the INT 21h handler, everything could be done in native 32-bit mode. Virtualization, while impressive (hooking an I/O port just like it was an interrupt: amazing!), can lead to lower performance.

Given that use of low-level code is a fact of life in DOS software, let's focus on what support OS/2 provides for undocumented DOS. The following useful telegraphic summary comes from an engineer at IBM:

We are supposed to support all documented INT 20h-2Fh calls, and most of the undocumented ones too. We are close, but not quite there. There are a couple of documented calls we don't have done yet. The undocumented ones are (as a wild guess) 50% there.

Network redirectors: not yet.

All internal data structures are the same as DOS 5.0, but some are read-only and others are just dummy placeholders. That doesn't mean that they are all used, just they have the same position and appearance. Many of the values are read-only.

CDS no, SFT no (except for the INT 2Fh AX=1216h call, which we fake). Of course, the OS/2 file system has a CDS, but we do not maintain one in the DOS box.

Can we run MSCDEX? Nope; MSCDEX is a redirector. Note however, that the VCDROM.SYS VDD for CD-ROMs does support the MSCDEX INT 2Fh calls.

TSRs work just fine. No known problems or restrictions.

Low-level DOS disk utilities should work on diskettes but not on the hard disk. No absolute disk writes [INT 26h] are permitted to the hard disk. Unless an application issues a call to lock a device, no multitasking operating-system can permit this.

Basically, then, OS/2 MVDMs provide a read-only List of Lists (SysVars) and SDA, but no CDS or SFT and no network redirector. Running some of the programs from other parts of this book under OS/2 2.0 confirms this point:

- OKAY (Chapter 2) works, so INT 21h AH=52h is supported, and SysVars has a valid LASTDRIVE value in the correct location.
- UDMEM (Chapter 7) works, so SysVars also contains a pointer to a valid MCB chain. Of course, this MCB chain represents only one megabyte of VDM memory, not the entire OS/2 address space.
- DEV (Chapter 7) works, so SysVars contains a valid NUL device header, pointing to a valid device header chain. This is only the DOS device driver chain for the VDM, including device headers added by VDHSetDosDevice (see below). OS/2 physical device drivers (PDDs) have a separate chain, which is not visible to DOS programs (see Art Rothstein, "Walking the OS/2 Device Chain," *Dr. Dobb's Journal*, August 1990); there is a separate VDD chain.
- FILES (Chapter 8) fails, confirming that the SFT is absent in the VDM. Note, however, that OS/2 itself does have SFT and Master File Table (MFT) structures, which are used by OS/2 applications (see Deitel and Kogan, *The Design of OS/2*, p. 236).
- ENUMDRV (Chapter 8) reports "can't get CDS." Again, OS/2 itself does have a CDS structure, which it maintains on a per-process basis in the Per-Task Data Area (PTDA; see Deital and Kogan, p. 236).
- PHANTOM (Chapter 8) fails, confirming that the network redirector interface isn't supported.
- TSRs (Chapter 9) work, including those that use the SDA.
- Other programs that work include TRUENAME (INT 21h AH=60h), ROOTS (PSP parent chain), INSTCMD (INT 2Fh AH=AEh installable commands), ENVEDT (master environment), and INTRSPY (intercepting interrupts).

How about DOS device drivers? OS/2 itself does not load DOS device drivers. If a DEVICE= statement appears in CONFIG.SYS for what is determined to be a DOS device driver, then the DEVICE= or DEVICEHIGH= is placed in the default DOS_DEVICE setting; these settings apply only to VDMs. Thus, MVDM would load a DOS device driver in each VDM. Only character DOS drivers are supported. For example, to load ANSI.SYS into a VDM you have a choice. Either place

DEVICE=C:\OS2\MDOS\ANSI.SYS in CONFIG.SYS so it will be loaded into all VDMs, or add C:\OS2\MDOS\ANSI.SYS to the DOS_DEVICE setting for the particular VDMs into which you want it loaded.

OS/2 provides a VDHSetDosDevice() function, which links a DOS device driver header into the chain of drivers to be passed to a DOS session on VDM creation. For example, the VXMS.SYS VDD uses this function to leave a fake XMSXXXX0 stub DOS driver in the VDM address space. This is similar to the DOSMGR_Add_Device function in Windows Enhanced mode, which we discussed in Chapter 1.

We asked one of the MVDM developers at IBM to summarize what DOS programmers can do to help their programs run in DOS emulation environments such as OS/2:

> In the two years I've worked in DOS Emulation I've seen an unbelievable number of bad programs. I've come up with a real quick, simple test of whether a DOS program is ill-behaved. On a DOS machine, run the program. Then load SHARE and try it again. You can't believe how many programs fail even on a genuine DOS machine with SHARE loaded. The single biggest offender is INT 21h AX=3D00h (open compatibility mode). Compatibility mode was the biggest mistake DOS 3.0 could have possibly made. If I had to give DOS programmers suggestions on programming, number one on my list would be never, never, never use 3D00h. Why? Compatibility mode changes meaning under different environments. A compatibility mode open on one LAN will not behave the same on a different LAN, or on no LAN.
>
> Other suggestions:
>
> Check return codes (i.e., the carry flag). You can't believe how many program never do this!
>
> Avoid using the volume-label bit mixed with other bits in the Find First/Next calls. DOS introduced some hasty bugs here.
>
> Don't expect dumb things to always work. For example, opening a file and, while it is open, trying to delete it; or opening a file with read/write access on a read-only media such as CD-ROM.

New OS/2 Services for Old DOS Programs

Now that we have some idea of the support OS/2 provides for the standard DOS interface, what sort of new functionality does OS/2 provide to DOS programs?

The OS/2 API is very extensive, but it is not directly available to DOS programs running under OS/2, just as Windows API calls aren't available to DOS programs running under Windows. However, OS/2 does define a number of extensions to INT 21h that make selected portions of the OS/2 API accessible to DOS programs running in a VDM. Using these INT 21h extensions, a DOS program running under OS/2 could access some of the otherwise-unavailable OS/2 kernel functionality described in IBM's *OS/2 2.0 Control Program Programming Guide*.

First, there is the set of functions OS/2 1.x added as part of the Family API (FAPI), mostly to support Extended Attributes (EAs):

```
INT 21h AX=5702h    DosQueryPathInfo() (1.1+) and DosQueryFileInfo() (1.2+)
INT 21h AX=5703h    DosSetPathInfo() (1.1+) and DosSetFileInfo() (1.2+)
INT 21h AX=6C01h    DosOpen2()
INT 21h AH=6Dh      DosMkDir2()
INT 21h AH=6Eh      DosEnumAttrib()
INT 21h AH=6Fh      DosQMaxEASize()
```

The INT 21h AX=5702h and AX=5703h Extended Attribute functions are the most important. These allow a DOS program to indirectly call the OS/2 DosSet/QueryPath/FileInfo functions, which are described in detail in IBM's documentation. Interestingly, IBM's DOS 4.0 also supported these INT 21h Extended Attribute calls. To use the INT 21h calls, see the Interrupt List on disk;

any additional information can be inferred from Chapter 5 on Extended Attributes in IBM's *Control Program Programming Guide*. (As a side note, it's worth pointing out that any programs that hook the normal MS-DOS INT 21h AH=57h Get/Set File Date and Time functions will need to explicitly ignore these OS/2 Extended Attribute functions.)

JOIN and SUBST are provided in DOS boxes under OS/2, but they are implemented quite differently from JOIN and SUBST in real mode DOS, where they muck around with DOS internals. Since JOIN and SUBST are built into the OS/2 file system as kernel services, the JOIN and SUBST commands for OS/2 DOS boxes need to call into the kernel, using INT 21h AH=61h:

```
; OS/2 INT 21h AH=61h JOIN/SUBST function
AH = 61h
AL = 0 (List), 1 (Add), 2 (Delete)
BX = drive number
CX = size of buffer
SI = 2 (JOIN), 3 (SUBST)
ES:DI -> buffer
BP = 'dg' magic signature
```

DOS programs running under OS/2 can access *named pipes*, using the normal DOS open, read, write, and close (INT 21h AH=3Dh-40h) calls on files such as \PIPE\PipeName or \\SERVER\PIPE\PipeName. For named-pipe support beyond the basics, there is a standard (though undocumented) LAN Manager local named pipes interface:

```
INT 21h AX=5F32h      DosQNmPipeInfo
INT 21h AX=5F33h      DosQNmPHandState
INT 21h AX=5F34h      DosSetNmPHandState
INT 21h AX=5F35h      DosPeekNmPipe
INT 21h AX=5F36h      DosTransactNmPipe
INT 21h AX=5F37h      DosCallNmPipe
INT 21h AX=5F38h      DosWaitNmPipe
INT 21h AX=5F39h      DosRawReadNmPipe
INT 21h AX=5F3Ah      DosRawWriteNmPipe
```

OS/2 2.0 itself uses these named pipe functions to implement DOS clipboard transfer and DOS dynamic data exchange (DDE). OS/2 2.1 instead uses the VWIN.SYS VDD, which improves performance. For more information on these functions, see Mike Shiels's article, "The Undocumented LAN Manager and Named Pipe APIs for DOS and Windows" (*Dr. Dobb's Journal*, April 1993).

OS/2 2.x makes major extensions to DOS using INT 21h AH=64h. The handler for INT 21h AH=64h first looks at the CX register. If CX=636Ch ('cl', a developer's initials), then it's an OS/2 function. If not, then the handler jumps to the code for DOS extended open (INT 21h AH=6Ch); this is a work-around for a bug in FAPI that issued INT 21h AH=64h rather than AH=6Ch for the DosOpen2() function.

If OS/2's INT 21h AH=64h handler finds the CX magic signature, it examines the BX register. If BX=0, then this is a special request (see below). Otherwise, BX is the DOSCALLS ordinal number of an OS/2 API DosXXX function to execute.

OS/2 API functions, like Windows API functions, are exported from dynamic link libraries (DLLs); each DLL export has an "ordinal number" (given in decimal). For example, the OS/2 Dos32StartSession() API function is DOSCALLS.37. DOSCALLS is the module name for the OS/2 kernel; many of these functions are in fact provided by OS2KRNL, rather than by DOSCALLS.DLL, but they still have DOSCALLS ordinal numbers. INT 21h AH=64h expects a DOSCALLS ordinal number in BX (0 is not a valid ordinal number, which is why this indicates a special request). However, not every OS/2 DOSCALLS function is callable from a DOS program via INT 21h AH=64h; this interface supports only a specific small set of OS/2 APIs:

```
INT 21h AH=64h BX=DOSCALLS ordinal (decimal) CX=636Ch
BX=37 (25h)      Dos32StartSession (see below)
```

```
BX=130 (82h)    Dos32GetCP
BX=167 (A7h)    Dos32QFSAttach
BX=191 (BFh)    Dos32EditName
BX=203 (CBh)    Dos32ForceDelete
BX=324 (144h)   Dos32CreateEventSem
BX=325 (145h)   Dos32OpenEventSem
BX=326 (146h)   Dos32CloseEventSem
BX=327 (147h)   Dos32ResetEventSem
BX=328 (148h)   Dos32PostEventSem
BX=329 (149h)   Dos32WaitEventSem
BX=330 (14Ah)   Dos32QueryEventSem
BX=331 (14Bh)   Dos32CreateMutexSem
BX=332 (14Ch)   Dos32OpenMutexSem
BX=333 (14Dh)   Dos32CloseMutexSem
BX=334 (14Eh)   Dos32RequestMutexSem
BX=335 (14Fh)   Dos32ReleaseMutexSem
BX=336 (150h)   Dos32QueryMutexSem (?)
BX=337 (151h)   Dos32CreateMuxWaitSem (?)
BX=338 (152h)   Dos32OpenMuxWaitSem
BX=339 (153h)   Dos32CloseMuxWaitSem
BX=340 (154h)   Dos32WaitMuxWaitSem
BX=341 (155h)   Dos32AddMuxWaitSem
BX=342 (156h)   Dos32DeleteMuxWaitSem (?)
BX=343 (157h)   Dos32QueryMuxWaitSem (?)
```

The most useful of these functions is DosStartSession( ), which a DOS program can use to start up other programs, including even OS/2 programs. The ability to launch OS/2 programs is not available with the DOS EXEC (INT 21h AH=4Bh) function, which will simply run the MZ portion of any file passed to it, so the following is quite useful:

```
DosStartSession
Entry:
    AH = 64h
    BX = 37 (25h)
    CX = 636Ch ('cl' signature)
    DS:SI = STARTDATA structure
Exit:
    AX = return code
```

The STARTDATA structure is the same one used by OS/2 programs that call DosStartSession( ) and includes the program name, title, command-line arguments, environment, session type (windowed, full screen, etc.), icon, initial (x, y) position and size, and so on. For the format of the STARTDATA structure, see Chapter 7 (Program Execution Control) of IBM's *OS/2 2.0 Control Program Programming Guide*.

In OS/2 2.1, LINK386 uses this INT 21h AH=64h DosStartSession call to implement a clever new undocumented switch, /RUNFROMVDM. Normally the OS/2 linker binds an OS/2 application with a DOS stub that just prints a "This program requires OS/2" error message and exits. /RUNFROMVDM links in a stub that issues this INT 21h AH=64h DosStartSession call. Windows badly needs something like this! (Microsoft C's WXSRVR.EXE and WX.EXE present one solution to this problem, but really this functionality needs to be built into Windows itself.)

Returning to the other INT 21h AH=64h functions, if CX=636Ch but BX=0 (not a valid DOSCALLS ordinal number), then the DX register indicates a special function. The Interrupt List on the accompanying disk describes these calls in more detail:

```
INT 21h AH=64h BX=0 CX=636Ch DX=subfunction
DX=0    Enable Automatic Title Bar Switch
DX=1    Set Session Title Bar
DX=2    Get Session Title Bar
DX=3    Get LASTDRIVE (used by WIN-OS/2)
DX=4    Get Size of PTDA JFT (used by WIN-OS/2)
```

```
DX=5     Get OS/2 SFT Second Flags Word (print spooling?)
DX=6     Unload DOSKRNL Symbols and Load Program  (debugging)
DX=7     Get WIN-OS/2 Call Gate Address
DX=8     Get Loading Message (used by NLS)
```

As a final example of functionality that OS/2 provides to DOS programs, the OS/2 2.x VIDEO_SWITCH_NOTIFICATION setting enables and disables the INT 2Fh AH=40h screen-switch API from OS/2 1.x. By default, OS/2 doesn't issue the INT 2Fh AH=40h calls (VIDEO_SWITCH_NOTIFICATION is off), because issuing them has some implications for Super VGA and XGA displays. Windows also supports these screen-switch functions, which are documented in the Windows DDK; see INTRLIST on disk for further details.

This completes our whirlwind tour of the additional interrupt-based APIs that OS/2 provides to DOS programs. Remember, however, that any VDD can provide this sort of functionality to DOS programs running in an OS/2 VDM, so really we've just looked at what happens to come built-in to OS/2. This is very similar to the situation with Windows Enhanced mode, where the additional functionality that VxDs can provide to DOS programs is potentially infinite, even if it is currently fairly limited. Someone just has to write a VxD in Windows or a VDD in OS/2 to make new APIs available. Of course, they also have to consider whether the benefits of the additional functionality are worth the additional overhead of the virtual device driver (remember DOSSPEED in Chapter 3?).

DOS Emulation Under Windows NT

Windows NT is Microsoft's latest attempt to build a "real man's" operating system, with genuine thread-based preemptive multitasking, demand-paged virtual memory, built-in networking, an improved file system, security, cross-CPU portability, and symmetric multiprocessing. Windows NT runs not only on Intel 80386 and higher processors but also on RISC processors such as the MIPS R4000. All these groovy features require at least eight (more realistically, 12 or 16) megabytes of memory.

For the foreseeable future, NT will be a niche product. According to *Barron's* (April 5, 1993), Rich Barth, a product manager for Windows NT at Microsoft "says flat-out that over the next two years, 80% of the people using PCs won't need the kind of computing power NT provides." Microsoft intends NT, not as a replacement for MS-DOS or Windows, but as a way to perhaps conquer new non-PC markets currently owned by companies such as IBM and Novell. Even Microsoft's executive VP, Steve Ballmer, "acknowledges that when NT is introduced it will at first be little more than a niche business" (*New York Times*, May 26, 1992). Mike Maples, another Microsoft executive VP, more recently reiterated the company's not-so-great expectations for NT by noting, "If you don't know why you need NT, then you don't need it" ("Microsoft Soft-Peddling Its Latest," *New York Times*, May 24, 1993). In the next few years, perhaps fewer than 20% of existing Windows 3.1 users will move over to Windows NT.

For programmers considering whether to "bet the farm" on NT, this point is really important! Microsoft has been absolutely explicit about how NT will play a relatively small role in the PC market-place for some time, how it will *not* replace Windows 3.1, and how it is intended especially for network server machines. Developers would do well to pay careful attention to what Microsoft is actually saying about NT and not simply pick up on the *amount* they're talking about it. Frankly, Windows NT could turn out to be another OS/2. Yawn.

It is important to distinguish NT from the Win32 API, Microsoft's intended successor to the 16-bit Windows API. Whatever happens with NT, Win32 seems like a clear winner. Win32 is not at all tied to NT. A subset runs today on Windows 3.1 Enhanced mode (Win32s), and a larger subset will run on Chicago (DOS 7.0 and Windows 4.0), scheduled for release in 1994. In contrast to the prodigious memory requirements of NT, Microsoft's slogan for Chicago is "runs great in four megabytes."

Generally, when developers say they are writing an NT application, they really mean they are writing a Win32 application.

Just as Win32 applications don't run only on NT, conversely NT does not only run Win32 applications. Think of NT as a motherboard, into which you can plug multiple daughterboards; in NT terminology, these are "subsystems." Win32 is just one NT subsystem; others are WOW (Win16 on Win32, responsible for running 16-bit Windows programs on NT), an OS/2 1.x subsystem, a POSIX subsystem, and of course an MS-DOS subsystem, called NTVDM.

As in OS/2 2.x, the term VDM means Virtual DOS Machine. Like OS/2 and Windows Enhanced mode, NT runs real mode DOS programs in virtual 8086 mode, at the chip's lowest privilege level, Ring 3. As you will see, there are a number of similarities between the NTVDM subsystem and the MVDM layer in OS/2 2.x. This is hardly surprising because, before Microsoft's divorce from IBM and its abandonment of OS/2, Microsoft worked on OS/2 MVDM. The NTVDM team at Microsoft is led by Matthew Felton, who, according to Helen Custer's *Inside Windows NT*, had previously worked on OS/2's DOS compatibility environment. Matt has been kind enough to provide much of the following material. Other material in this section comes from a talk by Sudeep Bharati on "Virtual Device Driver Support on Windows NT" at Microsoft's NT device driver developer's conference (October 1992). Yes, like OS/2 2.x and Windows Enhanced mode, NT also has virtual device drivers; as in OS/2, these are called VDDs rather than VxDs. However, unlike Windows VxDs and OS/2 VDDs, NT VDDs run in Ring 3 user-mode, rather than in Ring 0 kernel-mode. NT has separate kernel-mode device drivers that run in Ring 0.

The Client/Server Model

As with MVDM in OS/2, the goal of NTVDM is to run DOS applications without DOS. Old DOS programs continue to make DOS INT 21h calls, but these are somehow serviced using Win32 calls. In the remainder of this chapter, we try to make this "somehow" part a little more concrete.

As an example, consider a simple program written in C that uses standard C run-time library functions such as fopen(), fread(), fwrite(), and fclose(). If this program is built with a C compiler for DOS, the resulting executable contains DOS calls such as INT 21h AH=3Dh or AH=6Ch to open the file, AH=3Fh to read, AH=40h to write, and AH=3Fh to close. The program uses the DOS 'MZ' executable file format. With a 32-bit C compiler for NT, this program could be recompiled for Win32 without changing a single line of source code. The end result would be a Win32 'PE' (Portable Executable) file containing Win32 API calls. For example, instead of using INT 21h AH=3Dh or AH=6Ch to open files, the recompiled Win32 version would contain calls to the Win32 CreateFile() function (yes, in Win32 existing files are opened with CreateFile()). The ability to target multiple operating systems from a single piece of C source code is called *source compatibility*. It is not very difficult to achieve.

While extremely useful for programmers, source compatibility is not much help to end-users. To satisfy this larger and more important group of people, a new operating system must supply *binary compatibility* with executables for older popular operating systems. NT must be able to take old DOS executables containing INT 21h calls and use these INT 21h calls as some sort of a signal that the application wants to call CreateFile(), ReadFile(), WriteFile(), and so on. You could say that a call to INT 21h AH=3Dh turns into a call to CreateFile().

There is not merely some minor semantic difference between INT 21h AH=3Dh and CreateFile(). Not only is DOS really absent, but a DOS program running under NT may not even be running on an Intel 80x86 machine. NT supports DOS emulation on RISC machines too. Even on Intel machines, the hard disk may not have been formatted using the old DOS file allocation table (FAT) format. NT also supports OS/2's high performance file system (HPFS) and a new NT file system (NTFS). How can an old DOS program be made to work with all this new, non-DOS, non-FAT, possibly non-Intel, stuff?

Actually, this isn't all that different from something that already takes place today under DOS. The DOS network redirector allows DOS INT 21h file I/O and directory calls to be serviced using files and directories located on other machines. As explained in Chapter 8, these other machines are probably not even running DOS. All a DOS program knows is that it issues the right INT 21h AH=3Ch incantation to open a file and low and behold, it gets back a file handle. Most programs hardly care where the file handle came from. If the handle represents a file located on a NetWare file server, a MIPS R4000, a Sun SparcStation, or a Macintosh, that makes no difference.

This network redirection sounds the same as what must go on when you run a DOS application on a non-DOS operating system such as NT. And, except for the fact that the DOS client and the Win32 server may be located on a single machine, it *is* the same. NT is built around the client/server model. Rather than have the operating system provide APIs directly, all APIs are instead provided by subsystem servers, which are just more or less normal user-mode applications.

Supporting DOS INT 21h fits in nicely with the idea—which NT borrows from the Mach operating system—that APIs, and other facilities normally regarded as part of the operating system, can instead be provided by user-mode applications. In other words, NT services a DOS application's INT 21h calls in much the same way that it services a Win32 application's Win32 calls with a subsystem. For a clear explanation of the NT client/server architecture, see Helen Custer's book *Inside Windows NT*, particularly the chapter on protected subsystems. For client/server operating systems in general (and an in-depth study of Mach), see Andrew Tanenbaum's brilliant *Modern Operating Systems*.

NTVDM, NTIO, and NTDOS

To see in more detail how NT runs DOS applications without DOS, possibly without the FAT file system, and possibly without an Intel processor, let's look at what happens when a user starts a DOS program under NT.

Windows NT runs programs with the Win32 CreateProcess() API. When a user clicks on a program's icon in the NT Program Manager, CreateProcess() is called, even if the program is a DOS program or a 16-bit Windows application.

CreateProcess(), or perhaps one of the lower-level undocumented functions that it invokes (see "Undocumented NT," later in this chapter) inspects each .EXE file to see the type of program it has been asked to run. All .EXE files have two-byte signatures (magic) indicating their type. Win32 executables use Microsoft's Portable Executable file format and have a 'PE' signature. Both Win16 and OS/2 1.x executables use the New Executable file format and have 'NE' signatures; there is an additional target-operating-system flag in the executable header that distinguishes Windows and OS/2 1.x programs. Both the NE and PE formats are supersets of the old DOS executable format, which starts with an 'MZ' signature, the initials of Microsoft's Mark Zbikowski. Thus, if CreateProcess() is handed an executable with only an 'MZ' signature, CreateProcess() knows it is dealing with a DOS program. The same is true, of course, for .COM files, which have no header at all. An 'NE' header with Windows as the target is a Win16 executable.

CreateProcess() deals with both DOS and Win16 executables by looking up a command line in the NT registry. By default, this command line tells CreateProcess() to instead run a Win32 executable, NTVDM.EXE, and pass it the name of the original DOS or Win16 program in which the user is actually interested. In other words, clicking on the DOS program FOO.EXE results in the execution of the command "NTVDM FOO.EXE".

NTVDM.EXE is not a DOS program but a user-level Win32 application. It creates a VDM in which a DOS program or Win16 program can run in V86 mode. In this VDM, it loads and starts NTIO.SYS, a real mode DOS file, at address 0070:0000. NTIO.SYS loads another file, NTDOS.SYS, and then processes CONFIG.SYS. If CONFIG.SYS contains HIMEM.SYS and a DOS=HIGH statement, some of the code is moved to the portion of the VDM that lies just above one megabyte.

The names NTIO.SYS and NTDOS.SYS should sound familiar. These are hacked versions of IO.SYS and DOS.SYS, which form the core of MS-DOS 5.0 (see Chapter 6). While modified for NT, they are still real mode DOS programs; these files represent the 16-bit side of the NT DOS emulation layer. There is also a hacked copy of COMMAND.COM, which processes AUTOEXEC.BAT. The program that the user asked to run is loaded in this environment.

Magic Pills and Bops

How do the NT files NTIO.SYS and NTDOS.SYS differ from the DOS files IO.SYS and MSDOS.SYS? For one thing, Microsoft has removed all hard-wired assumptions about the FAT file system. As an example of the changes made to IO.SYS and MSDOS.SYS to create NTIO.SYS and NTDOS.SYS, consider the following code fragment from MSDOS.SYS in DOS 5.0:

```
mov ds, cs:DOS_DS
lds si, dword ptr ds:PTR_CURRCDS
test word ptr [si.CDS_ATTRIB], NET_REDIR    ; test [si+43h], 8000h
```

The equivalent code in NTDOS.SYS looks like this:

```
mov ds, cs:DOS_DS
lds si, dword ptr ds:PTR_CURRCDS
db 0C4h, 0C4h, 50h, 13h
```

On Intel processors, C4h C4h is an illegal instruction (it decodes as LES AX,SP). Executing this illegal code in V86 mode causes a trap into whatever protected mode software is acting as the V86 monitor. In NT, this monitor is NTVDM.EXE.

Remember HLT in OS/2 2.x, which one of the IBM engineers quoted earlier in this chapter described as OS/2's magic pill, or ARPL, which is used for the same purpose in Windows Enhanced mode? These weird instructions are used to make the transition from V86 mode to protected mode. This is necessary because we have 16-bit real mode code that we somehow want to service from 32-bit protected mode. Well, C4h C4h is the NTDOS magic pill.

C4h C4h is described in the file ISVBOP.H in the NT device driver kit (DDK). BOP stands for BIOS operation, which is Microsoft's somewhat poorly-chosen name for this mechanism that allows 16-bit real mode code, such as DOS device drivers, to call down to 32-bit protected mode code, such as NTVDM and NT VDDs.

ISVBOP.H defines three macros supporting third-party bops:

```
RegisterModule      db C4h, C4h, 58h, 0
UnRegisterModule    db C4h, C4h, 58h, 1
DispatchCall        db C4h, C4h, 58h, 2
```

Any DOS software running under NT can use these macros (which are documented in the NT DDK *Win32 User-mode Driver Reference* and the *Win32 User-mode Driver Design Guide*) to communicate with a 32-bit protected mode dynamic link library. In NT, VDDs are nothing more than DLLs and thus can call any Win32 API functions, such as CreateFile(), ReadFile(), and so on. RegisterModule() expects the ASCIIZ name of a DLL and of a Dispatch routine in the DLL. It returns a handle which the 16-bit DOS program can then pass to DispatchCall() to call into the 32-bit DLL. Clearly, this can help DOS programs indirectly call Win32 functions.

Looking back at the code fragment from NTDOS.SYS, you can see that it is using C4h C4h, but the code is not calling any of the three macros from ISVBOP. As noted earlier, ISVBOP supports third-party bops. Microsoft has its own bops that NTIO.SYS, NTDOS.SYS, and COMMAND.COM use:

```
BOP_DOS             C4h, C4h, 50h        Used in NTIO.SYS, NTDOS.SYS
BOP_WOW             C4h, C4h, 51h        Win16 on Win32
BOP_XMS             C4h, C4h, 52h
```

```
BOP_DPMI                C4h, C4h, 53h
BOP_CMD                 C4h, C4h, 54h        COMMAND.COM to CMD.EXE?
BOP_DEBUGGER            C4h, C4h, 56h
BOP_REDIR               C4h, C4h, 57h        Used to be 55h
BOP_3RDPARTY            C4h, C4h, 58h        See ISVBOP.H: RegisterModule, etc.
BOP_NOSUPPORT           C4h, C4h, 59h        Host warning dialog box
BOP_GRABTIMER           C4h, C4h, 5Bh        Check whether timer INTs required
BOP_KBD                 C4h, C4h, 5Ch        temporary?
BOP_VIDEO               C4h, C4h, 5Dh        temporary?
BOP_NOTIFICATION        C4h, C4h, 5Eh        16-bit to 32-bit notification
BOP_UNIMPINT            C4h, C4h, 5Fh
BOP_SWITCHTOREALMODE C4h, C4h, FDh
BOP_UNSIMULATE          C4h, C4h, FEh        End execution of code in a VDM
```

Using illegal instructions, Microsoft has thus defined its own little pcode-like bop instruction set. NTIO.SYS and NTDOS.SYS use these bops, especially BOP_DOS, essentially as SVC (supervisor) calls.

Bops Through History

Microsoft's use of illegal instructions to make the hyperspace jump from 16-bit real mode to 32-bit protected mode sounds like an *ad hoc* hack that someone came up with in five minutes. It's not. In fact, this bop technique of using an illegal instruction as a supervisor call dates back over twenty years to IBM's VM/360 operating system, where a nonexistent instruction, often referred to as DIAGNOSE, was used to force an exception within a virtual machine, so that the exception could be caught by the VM kernel and interpreted as a service request.

For more information on the history of this great hack, see the letters to the editor in *Windows/DOS Developer's Journal*, July 1993 (pp. 99-100). These letters were prompted by an excellent earlier article on NT VDDs (Paula Tomlinson, "Windows NT Virtual Device Drivers for Hardware-Dependent 16-Bit Applications," *Windows/DOS Developer's Journal*, May 1993), which included a short sidebar on bops ("The VDD Backdoor").

Where do these calls go? DOS software from third-party vendors uses bops to communicate with VDDs. For example, the NT DDK documentation (see the chapter on "Virtual Device Drivers for MS-DOS Applications That Use Special Hardware") shows how to use the RegisterModule and DispatchCall bops to call down to a VDD that supports something like a FAX board or a 3270 communications board.

But bops are really much more general purpose than that. Any DOS program could use bops to call down to a VDD "surrogate" that called Win32 APIs on the DOS program's behalf. If the bop is placed in a DOS device driver or TSR, then normal DOS programs that call the device driver or TSR will end up using the bop without even being aware of it—this transparency, of course, is the whole idea. Bops can thus be used as thunks or as the transport layer for a form of remote procedure call (RPC).

What is NTVDM.EXE?

Microsoft's own bop handlers are located in NTVDM.EXE which, when we last left it, had started a VDM and loaded NTIO.SYS and NTDOS.SYS. When these hacked versions of DOS 5.0 issue a bop (such as C4h C4h 50h 13h in the NTDOS.SYS code fragment above), it is handled in NTVDM.EXE.

NTVDM (like any PE executable) can be examined with a utility such as Microsoft's COFF.EXE (COFF stands for Common Object File Format, a UNIX standard upon which PE is based).

COFF.EXE can even be run under DOS, using Phar Lap Software's TNT, a 32-bit DOS extender that runs NT executables under MS-DOS. For example:

```
tnt \mstools\bin\coff -dump -exports -imports \nt\i386\ntvdm.exe
```

(Actually, as this book was going to press, Microsoft replaced COFF.EXE with LINK32.EXE.) Examination of NTVDM.EXE with COFF shows that NTVDM exports a number of functions for use by VDDs, such as VDDInstallIOHook(), VDDInstallMemoryHook(), and so on (the NT DDK documents these functions). NTVDM also imports functions from KERNEL32.DLL, USER32.DLL, and GDI32.DLL. These dynamic link libraries contain the functions documented in the Win32 SDK. Naturally (this is Microsoft systems software, after all), NTVDM.EXE also imports a number of undocumented functions from KERNEL32, such as ExitVDM, GetNextVDMCommand, RegisterConsoleVDM, and VDMConsoleOperation, and uses an NtVdmControl function from NTDLL.DLL. You will see later that NTDLL.DLL is home for the undocumented "native" NT API.

NTVDM.EXE contains a number of components:

DEM32 is the 32-bit side protected mode side of DOS emulation (DEM). When NTIO.SYS or NTDOS.SYS issue a bop, it comes to DEM32.

NTVDM also contains an *instruction execution unit* (IEU), which handles all the DOS program instructions, such as IN, OUT, and INT, that are illegal under DOS emulation. For example, INT 21h is an illegal instruction in Ring 3. "Illegal" simply means that this instruction will cause a trap into NTVDM, which will, in turn, use this trap as its opportunity to do DOS emulation.

On non-Intel machines, the IEU contains an entire 80x86 emulation, which supports everything up to 80286 protected mode and is built around the Insignia Solutions Inc.'s SoftPC-AT. There are different versions of NTVDM.EXE for different processors. For example, in addition to the Intel version (\I386\NTVDM.EXE), there is also one for the R4000 (\MIPS\NTVDM.EXE). However, the exact same NTIO.SYS and NTDOS.SYS files used on Intel machines are used on MIPS machines.

As noted earlier, NTVDM exports functions for use in VDDs. These are documented in the NT DDK *Win32 User-mode Driver Design Guide* (see the chapter, "Virtual Device Drivers for MS-DOS Applications That Use Special Hardware") and in the *Win32 User-mode Driver Reference*.

NTVDM not only exports functions for use by VDDs. It also contains all the VDDs for a standard PC, such as the keyboard, mouse, video, timer, interrupt controller (PIC), and so on. These VDDs allow a DOS application running under NT to think that it is banging on I/O ports, writing to memory locations, and doing all sorts of other bare-metal activities. Meanwhile, it may not even be executing on a PC or an Intel processor! The term "virtual" means just that. The VDD, using NTVDM functions such as VDDInstallIOHook() and VDDInstallMemoryHook(), *acts* like the known low-level interface to a piece of hardware. The actual hardware may or may not exist. To maintain the integrity of other applications, the DOS applications cannot be allowed to "party" (in Microsoft lingo) with the actual hardware, even if it does exist. An exception is a DOS application running full-screen in the foreground, which will be allowed to directly bonk video memory.

All this sounds a lot like OS/2 and Windows Enhanced mode. It is similar, except that those systems are limited, practically speaking, to Intel machines. (This is not much of a limitation, since the RISC machines that NT runs on currently have such a small market share as to be almost irrelevant.) In addition, NT VDDs are really just user-mode (Ring 3) Win32 DLLs, not privileged Ring 0 parts of the kernel like Windows VxDs and OS/2 VDDs. Because they are just user-mode Win32 DLLs, VDDs like NTVDM.EXE can call any Win32 API—another difference from Windows VxDs, which cannot make direct Windows API calls.

So how do all these pieces this fit together?

NTVDM.EXE creates a VDM, starts NTIO.SYS and NTDOS.SYS in the VDM, and starts the DOS application that the user wants to run. The DOS application makes INT 21h calls, which go to NTDOS.SYS, which bops down to NTVDM. NTVDM contains VDDs; additional VDDs can handle any non-standard interfaces that NTVDM doesn't support. NTVDM and VDDs are Win32 DLLs, so they can make Win32 API calls on the DOS program's behalf.

In particular, NTVDM calls functions in KERNEL32.DLL. KERNEL32 contains not only the 32-bit widened versions of Windows API functions from KRNL386.EXE, but also a set of new Win32 API functions intended to replace the DOS functions that Win16 applications use. KERNEL32.DLL contains functions such as CreateFile, ReadFile, WriteFile, CloseFile, CopyFile, MoveFile, CreateDirectory, SetCurrentDirectory, RemoveDirectory, DeviceIoControl (IOCTL), and so on. Note that these names aren't the actual names of the functions exported from KERNEL32.DLL. For example, CreateFile is actually CreateFileA() (ASCII file names) and CreateFileW() (W = wide = Unicode file names). NTVDM uses KERNEL32 to carry out a DOS program's file I/O and directory requests.

KERNEL32.DLL also contains a set of Console functions to support character mode Win32 programs (why doesn't Windows have something like Console?). NTVDM uses the KERNEL32 Console to carry out a DOS program's stdin, stdout, and stderr I/O.

Returning to the example of a DOS program that calls INT 21h AH=3Dh or AH=6Ch to open a file, we said that this must somehow be turned into a call to CreateFile(). The "somehow" part should now be a little clearer. The call goes to NTDOS, which bops down to NTVDM.EXE, which then calls CreateFile() on the DOS program's behalf.

But what happens after that? CreateFile() returns a four-byte file handle. This cannot be returned as is to the DOS program, which is expecting a two-byte number in AX. Instead, the four-byte Win32 file handle is stored in the NTDOS SFT, which Microsoft has modified from the DOS original. Just as under DOS, the SFT index is then stored in the DOS program's JFT associated with its PSP. The JFT index is then returned to the DOS program as the file handle. In other words:

```
MS-DOS:  file handle -> JFT -> SFT
NTDOS:   file handle -> JFT -> modified SFT -> Win32 file handle -> ?
```

The NTDOS file handle mechanism is similar to that used in the OS/2 2.x MVDM. In OS/2, the "?" part happens to reference the OS/2 JFT, SFT, and MFT; presumably something similar happens in NT. For now, the point is simply that NTDOS takes in DOS file I/O requests and returns the necessary information. Unless an application pokes around in undocumented DOS structures such as the SFT and CDS, it shouldn't care that NTDOS is bopping down to NTVDM, which in turn is calling CreateFile() in KERNEL32, and so on.

DOS 5.50

Of course, the sort of programs we're writing in other parts of this book *do* care about the structure of SFTs and other undocumented DOS structures. So we had better take a few minutes to see what support NTDOS provides for such ill-behaved DOS programs.

According to the NT DDK, "The application layer cannot tell that it is not running in a native MS-DOS environment." That is true of most DOS applications, but some will definitely fail in this emulated DOS environment. On the other hand, we saw that the 16-bit side of DOS emulation under NT is based on a hacked version of MS-DOS 5.0, so the emulation is quite close. Even many of the ill-behaved programs from this book run fine under NT. Remember also that this same DOS-based code runs on non-Intel machines and can access NTFS as well as the FAT file system.

But what version of DOS is this, anyway? OS/2 2.x MVDM advertises itself as DOS 20.0, so initially NTDOS returned 30.0 from the INT 21h AH=30h Get Version call. However, this caused many DOS programs that checked for DOS >= 10.0 to fail with error messages such as "This program can't run in an OS/2 DOS box." The same programs were happy to run when NTDOS returned a 5.x version number, so NTDOS now returns 5.0 from the INT 21h AH=30h. This at first sounds like a very bad move because it makes NTDOS difficult to distinguish from genuine MS-DOS 5.0. However, under NTDOS the function to get the genuine DOS version (INT 21h AX=3306h) returns 50 (32h) as a minor version. Thus, NTDOS is currently DOS 5.50. This minor version of 50 is hard-wired into the NTDOS version of COMMAND.COM.

What undocumented DOS functionality does this DOS 5.50 support? Microsoft has said that NTDOS will implement all popular undocumented DOS functions but will not support DOS programs that depend on internal "structures." This appears to be accurate.

INT 21h AH=52h is of course supported, as is some of the SysVars data structure. For example, SysVars[-2] points to the head of the MCB chain for the VDM. The UDMEM program from Chapter 7 works very nicely under NTDOS, as does the WINPSP program from Chapter 3. Of course, these programs see only the memory chain for the first megabyte of the VDM.

Just as NTDOS provides an MCB chain, there is also a DOS device chain, with the NUL device rooted at the proper location in SysVars. As a result, the DEV program from Chapter 7 also runs nicely under NTDOS, as does the WINDEV program from Chapter 3. According to Custer's *Inside Windows NT*, NT uses symbolic links to turn DOS block device names into NT device names.

In the INT 21h AH=3Dh example above, we noted that NTDOS modifies the SFT to store four-byte Win32 file handles. In other words, NTDOS has an SFT, but it is substantially different from the one in MS-DOS. In NTDOS, all file operations are really being carried out on the Win32 side of the DOS emulation layer. The DOS SFT structure only needs to contain the 16-bit DOS state. As a result, each SFT entry is a bit smaller in NTDOS (21h bytes instead of 3Bh bytes). NTDOS does maintain the SFT pointer in SysVars. Running SFTWALK (see listing 3-5) indicates that NT automatically sets FILES=255.

The CDS in NTDOS is substantially different from the CDS in MS-DOS. NTDOS ignores the LASTDRIVE value in SysVars (recall that in MS-DOS LASTDRIVE holds the number of entries in the CDS array). Instead, NTDOS maintains one CDS for each physical drive and one for all the remote drives, switching the single redirected CDS as needed. As a result, the OKAY program (Listing 2-19), which tests that the LASTDRIVE field in SysVars is the same as the LASTDRIVE return value from INT 21h AH=0Eh, reports "Undocumented DOS not ok." Similarly the ENUMDRV program from Chapter 8 usually fails with a "can't get CDS" message because the value of LASTDRIVE is too low.

Without a proper CDS and with a bogus value for LASTDRIVE, how do DOS network redirectors work? Certainly the Phantom program from Chapter 8 does not work under NT, though perhaps Phantom is more dependent on the CDS than most redirectors. NTDOS comes with a VDMREDIR.DLL, and also with an alternate 16-bit redirector.

How about TSRs? Here the story is a lot better. All the TSRs from Chapter 9 work under NTDOS, including those that rely on INT 21h AX=5D06h and the Swappable Data Area. The only difference from MS-DOS is NTDOS's slightly nonnutritive handling of TSR hotkeys. When a TSR terminates using INT 21h AH=31h or INT 27h, a message pops up regarding the Windows NT memory-resident program support. The message indicates that you can press the TSR's hotkey or press ^Z to get back a command prompt. You are supposed to be able to hotkey into your TSR from a DOS program, but this seems at first only to work on an occasional basis.

In fact, TSR hotkeys *do* work—but only from inside DOS applications. When you are sitting at a command prompt in NT, it may look like a DOS prompt, but it's not. You're running CMD.EXE, which is a Win32 Console program. A VDM remains attached to this Console window, but in a dormant fashion. When you run a DOS binary, the VDM wakes up and does its thing. TSR hot keys work only when a DOS application is actually running. CMD.EXE, which provides the C:\> prompt, is not a DOS program! If you want continuous access to a TSR, then you should not press ^Z to return to the C:\> prompt. Instead, get yourself a new Console window, leaving the current one dedicated for the TSR.

While CMD.EXE is a Win32 program, it can run not only Win32 programs and, as you've seen, DOS programs, but also Win16, character-mode OS/2 and POSIX programs. Having one command prompt for everything is a welcome departure from the lame DOS command prompt in Windows Enhanced mode, which is unable, without a lot of extra help, to run Windows programs. Microsoft calls CMD.EXE the Single Command Shell (SCS). At the same time, NT still needs the real mode COMMAND.COM to process DOS batch files and generally to hang around in case DOS programs need it. For example, the undocumented COMMAND.COM backdoor (INT 2Eh) is available under NTDOS. For example, the TEST2E program from Chapter 10 works very nicely.

Of course, undocumented DOS calls are just one example of bad behavior from DOS programs that an environment such as NTDOS has to try to support, without compromising the integrity of the whole system. Another good example is the popular category of disk maintenance programs such as the Norton Utilities and PC Tools. It's simply impossible for NTDOS to allow such programs to write to the hard disk. If you have a favorite DOS undelete or defrag utility, you'll have to boot genuine MS-DOS to run it.

NT currently won't even let a DOS program have direct *read* access to the hard disk. The rationale is that a DOS application would expect to find FAT disk structures, whereas in fact there might be on NTFS or HPFS. There may be a way in the future for NT to provide DOS programs with read access to hard disks, but write access is "out of the question," says one of the NTDOS developers.

In fact, there are pretty strict limitations on what even a native Win32 application can do to the hard disk. Programs such as the Norton Utilities or PC Tools could be ported to Win32, but the user would have to be logged in as administrator to open the hard disk. Direct disk access is initiated with a call to CreateFile(), using a file name such as \\.\C: for drive C:. Furthermore, to write to the hard disk, the application would need to lock it with DeviceIoControl() FSCTL_LOCK_VOLUME. This lock would succeed only if there were no other open handles on the drive. The paging swap file creates an open handle, so you could never write or repair the disk with the swap file. Bummer! Looks like even most die-hard NT fanatics will still need MS-DOS for a while, if only to repair the massive hard disks NT needs.

Additional NTDOS Functionality

Having seen that NTDOS does an excellent job of supporting existing DOS functions, including the undocumented ones, and only a so-so job of supporting DOS internal data structures, we need to work at new functionality for DOS programs. Do DOS programs derive any positive benefits from running under NT? Certainly, DOS programs are going to run slower under NT than under genuine MS-DOS. Do they get anything in return, or is NTDOS just a way to avoid having two machines on your desk or needing a DOS boot diskette?

We already mentioned CMD.EXE, the single command shell, and its ability to run all manner of applications. What we didn't mention, but what seems very important, is that CDM allows different types of programs to *interact*. CMD.EXE allows *pipes* between all the different types of programs it runs. For example, you can mix DOS and Win32 programs on a single command line. An interesting article in the *Windows/DOS Developer's Journal* (John Richardson, "Escape from POSIX," *W/DDJ*, April 1993) even shows how non-Win32 programs can use these anonymous pipes to request services of Win32 programs.

Of course, a Win16 application—which, as we've seen in Chapter 3, is really just a fancy form of protected mode DOS application and DPMI client—can interact with Win32 applications using the clipboard and dynamic data exchange. Unfortunately, NT does not allow any further mixing. For example, Win32 programs cannot directly use Win16 DLLs, and Win16 programs cannot directly call Win32 DLLs. The word "directly" is important here because numerous indirect methods, such as named shared memory and DDE, are available.

While the NT services to DOS programs look rather sparse, it's important to remember the third-party bops that Microsoft supports. Using the RegisterModule and DispatchCall bops mentioned earlier, real mode DOS code running under NT can call down to a VDD, which in turn can call any arbitrary Win32 API function on the DOS program's behalf. The NT DDK CD-ROM provides some good examples in the APPINTS, COM_VDD, DOSIOCTL, and VDMINTS sample programs.

On the other hand, if someone is prepared to modify their DOS program to use bops and is prepared to write a VDD to act as a Win32 surrogate for the DOS program, they should probably bite the bullet and port their program to Win32. The third-party bops are probably most useful in a limited number of cases where the DOS software simply cannot be ported to Win32, but where there is an opportunity to either modify a small portion of it or to supply a DOS device driver or TSR that bops down to a VDD.

Undocumented NT

The goal of this chapter has been to discuss "other DOSs," avoiding major discussions of any other aspect of NetWare, OS/2, or NT. But in the case of Windows NT, it's difficult to resist a small peek at the broader topic of undocumented NT functions. Not only because many readers (and Microsoft too) have asked us when *Undocumented NT* is coming out, but because the topic of undocumented NT helps clarify the nature of the NT operating system.

In connection with NT, Microsoft has produced massive amounts of programmer's documentation. This documentation states quite clearly that its subject is the Win32 API, that is, functions such as (to pick a few at random) CreateFileMapping(), MoveWindow(), and FloodFill(), exported from KERNEL32.DLL, USER32.DLL, GDI32.DLL, and other Win32 dynamic link libraries.

This is *not* the NT API! To repeat the point made earlier, Win32 and NT are not the same thing. Large subsets of the Win32 API run on platforms other than NT, for example, on Windows 3.1 Enhanced mode (Win32s) and Chicago. On NT, Win32 is really just one subsystem. And NT supports APIs other than Win32—the DOS emulation we looked at is a perfect example. Win32 is a bit privileged in that (as we saw) it is used to implement other subsystems. It is also a required part of the NT configuration, whereas all the other subsystems are optional and only kick in if you load an application that needs them. But in many ways, Win32 relates to NT in much the same way that DOS emulation does. It's a subsystem.

The beauty of NT, like Mach, is that many features traditionally associated with the operating system kernel, such as API provision, have been moved into more or less normal applications, which can be preempted, paged, located on other machines, and so on. It's not at all clear how many people really need this, but it's certainly cool.

So if Win32 and the other subsystems are all user-level code, where is the operating system kernel? It definitely isn't in KERNEL32.DLL, which really is, confusingly enough, not kernel-mode but user-mode code. We saw that the NTVDM subsystem is implemented in part using KERNEL32.DLL, but how is KERNEL32.DLL itself implemented? And what was that NTDLL.DLL file that NTVDM.EXE also used?

Much of the genuine "native" NT API is exported from NTDLL.DLL. For example, Helen Custer's excellent *Inside Windows NT* mentions many NT objects, such as Processes, Threads, Files, Events, and so on, and refers to the types of operations these objects provide, such as Create, Open, Close, Query, and Wait. But, understandably, the book doesn't discuss *where* to find these objects and operations.

If you examine NTDLL.DLL with a PE dump utility, you will see that NTDLL exports many of the NT functions whose existence one would infer from *Inside Windows NT*. For example, here's a small portion of the NTDLL export table:

```
61      62      0000b810      NtConnectPort
62      63      0000b820      NtContinue
63      64      0000b830      NtCreateDirectoryObject
64      65      0000b840      NtCreateEvent
65      66      0000b850      NtCreateEventPair
66      67      0000b860      NtCreateFile
67      68      0000b870      NtCreateKey
68      69      0000b880      NtCreateMailslotFile
69      70      0000b890      NtCreateMutant
70      71      0000b8a0      NtCreateNamedPipeFile
71      72      0000b8b0      NtCreatePagingFile
72      73      0000b8c0      NtCreatePort
73      74      0000b8d0      NtCreateProcess
74      75      0000b8e0      NtCreateProfile
75      76      0000b8f0      NtCreateSection
76      77      0000b900      NtCreateSemaphore
77      78      0000b910      NtCreateSymbolicLinkObject
78      79      0000b920      NtCreateThread
79      80      0000b930      NtCreateTimer
80      81      0000b940      NtCreateToken
81      82      0000cd40      NtCurrentTeb
82      83      0000b950      NtDelayExecution
83      84      0000b960      NtDeleteKey
84      85      0000b970      NtDeleteValueKey
85      86      0000b980      NtDeviceIoControlFile
86      87      0000b990      NtDisplayString
87      88      0000b9a0      NtDuplicateObject
88      89      0000b9b0      NtDuplicateToken
```

You won't find any of these functions in the Win32 SDK, or even in the NT DDK documentation (some are mentioned in passing in DDK\INC\NTDDK.H and NTSTATUS.H). They really are undocumented. On the other hand, most of these functions do have documented equivalents in the Win32 API, so it's not clear how important undocumented NT really is to most programmers. For example, in early beta versions of NT, Microsoft's PVIEW (Process View) utility relied heavily on functions in NTDLL.DLL, but by the March 1993 beta, much of the functionality upon which PVIEW relied had been incorporated into the Win32 API.

Still, even if every NTDLL.DLL function has equivalent functionality in Win32 (which is not the case), it is profitable to look at this file because it helps solidify much of the material Custer presents in her book.

So is NTDLL.DLL the genuine core of NT? Hardly. Looking back at the excerpt of the NTDLL export table, you may notice something odd. The third column shows the virtual address for each function; most of the functions are only 10h bytes apart! Microsoft sometimes likes to brag about its "tight code," but it's unlikely that it has implemented each NT function in only 16 bytes. Disassembly of almost any portion of NTDLL shows what is really going on. For example:

```
NtCreateProcess proc far
    mov eax, 1Ah
    lea edx, dword ptr [esp+4]
    int 2Eh
    retn 20h
NtCreateProcess endp

NtCreateProfile proc far
    mov eax, 1Bh
    lea edx, dword ptr [esp+4]
    int 2Eh
    retn 1Ch
NtCreateProfile endp

NtCreateSection proc far
    mov eax, 1Ch
    lea edx, dword ptr [esp+4]
```

```
        int 2Eh
        retn 1Ch
NtCreateSection endp
```

It goes on like this, for hundreds and hundreds of functions. Most of the functions in NTDLL.DLL are little more than wrappers around INT 2Eh calls, with function numbers in EAX.

Just as there needs to be a way for 16-bit real mode code running in a DOS application to make a SVC-like call down to the 32-bit protected mode subsystem code in NTVDM, there also needs to be a way for code running in user-level (Ring 3) 32-bit protected mode code to make a SVC-like call down to the NT kernel running at Ring 0. NTDLL uses INT 2Eh instructions to call down to the NT kernel. (Naturally, this protected mode INT 2Eh has nothing to do with the INT 2Eh call that real mode COMMAND.COM provides as its backdoor.)

When NTDLL issues an INT 2Eh, it is handled by NTOSKRNL.EXE, the NT operating system kernel, or by NTKRNLMP.EXE, the multiprocessor version of the NT kernel. These files too can be examined with COFF -DUMP or a similar utility. NTOSKRNL exports almost 600 functions, such as (to pick a bunch at random):

```
CcGetFileObjectFromBcb()
ExQueueWorkItem()               ; Ex = General executive routine
FsRtlRegisterUncProvider()      ; Fs = File system
IoAdapterObjectType()           ; Io = I/O subsystem
IoStartNextPacket()
KeWaitForMultipleObjects()      ; Ke = Kernel
MmMapIoSpace()                  ; Mm = Memory management
NtCreateFile()
NtVdmControl()
ObQueryNameString()             ; Ob = Object management
PsThreadType()                  ; Ps = Process structure
RtlGetHeapUserValue()           ; Rtl = Run-time library (user mode)
SeOpenObjectAuditAlarm()        ; Se = Security
ZwReadFile()                    ; Zw = Windows NT system service
```

This is what the NT API looks like. It is important to note that the NT DDK *Kernel-mode Driver Reference* and *Kernel-mode Driver Design Guide* do document some of these NTOSKRNL functions, and that some also are prototyped in DDK header files such as NTDDK.H.

NTOSKRNL imports functions from HAL.DLL, which contains the NT Hardware Abstraction Layer. HAL in turn imports functions from NTOSKRNL. Despite the picture painted in most architectural diagrams of Windows NT, HAL is far from being the only hardware dependent piece of NT; this is simply a goal.

NT internals is a major topic and (if NT goes anywhere) deserves its own book, so we will leave the reader dangling here and return to the topic of undocumented MS-DOS.

## CHAPTER 5

INTRSPY: A Program for Exploring DOS

by David Maxey

Several places in this book refer to the program INTRSPY. Chapter 1, for example, uses INTRSPY to find which DOS programs make undocumented DOS function calls. Chapter 8 uses INTRSPY to explore the workings of the MS-DOS network redirector. Chapter 10 refers to an INTRSPY script that helps us figure out how the INT 2Fh Function AEh (Installable Command) interface works.

In this chapter, we examine INTRSPY in detail. The program has evolved significantly from the version that accompanied the first edition of this book. In addition to intercepting interrupts, INTRSPY can now also snoop on device driver Strategy and Interrupt routines and on far-call entry points such as those used by XMS.

After explaining how INTRSPY differs from other debuggers, this chapter presents a quick sample session that should be sufficient to get you started using INTRSPY; the program itself is on the disks that accompany this book. After this guided tour, a more formal user's guide to the program is presented, followed by an examination of several sample scripts. The second half of the chapter looks at the current specification for INTRSPY, discusses some of the issues involved in its implementation, and finally discusses plans for its commercial future.

Why a Script-Driven, Event-Driven Debugger?

INTRSPY is an event-driven debugger. It takes over one or more interrupt vectors or far-call entry points and, when the interrupt is generated or the entry point is called, performs some action. This sets it apart from more conventional debuggers, such as DEBUG, CodeView, or Turbo Debugger, which are generally driven by a user's keystrokes.

Such a program is essential, not only for exploring undocumented DOS, but also for many other debugging tasks on the PC. For example, what do you do if a program exits unexpectedly because it can't find some configuration file, but the program's error messages don't tell you which file it couldn't find? Just intercept INT 21h and monitor the different functions involved with opening, creating, or finding files.

There are now several other DOS debuggers that intercept interrupts, allowing you to look into the DOS and/or BIOS activity on your PC. The excellent Soft-ICE and Soft-ICE/Windows debuggers from Nu-Mega have a BPINT command that allows a breakpoint to set on the occurrence of any interrupt; because it uses Virtual-8086 mode, Soft-ICE can also trap events such as port I/O (BPIO) and memory accesses (BPM). Another interrupt driven debugger is INTRCPT from Hackensack Software, makers of the INTERVUE interrupt list viewer on the disk accompanying this book. CodeProbe from General Software is a new DOS interrupt and event analyzer similar to the same company's network protocol analyzer, The Snooper. Finally, the venerable PCWATCH program by James H. Gilliam and Larry K. Raper, once distributed by

IBM as part of its Personally Developed Software series, is still available (contact Personally Developed Software, Wallingford CT).

What sets INTRSPY apart from other DOS monitoring programs is its use of a *scripting language* for intercepting interrupts. INTRSPY knows very little about any particular DOS or BIOS call. It doesn't know that INT 21h Function 3Dh is the Open File function; it doesn't know that this function takes the ASCIIZ path name of a file to open to in the DS:DX register pair, or that, if successful, the function returns a file handle in the AX register. Rather than hard-wire such protocol knowledge into the program, INTRSPY's scripting language lets the user provide such knowledge.

The benefit is that the program is open-ended. If you want to monitor some undocumented region of DOS that this book doesn't mention, you can. If you want to examine some little-known DOS subsystem, you just write a script. Furthermore, because the INTRSPY language includes support for strings and structures, you can produce meaningful output rather than raw register dumps.

INTRSPY is currently for real-mode DOS only. To watch interrupts occurring in protected mode under Windows, you can use the BPINT command in Soft-ICE/Windows or INTRSPY's baby brother for Windows, WISPY (Windows I Spy), in Chapter 4 of *Undocumented Windows*.

A Guided Tour

Let's first run through a quick session with INTRSPY. It makes sense to start with something that doesn't involve undocumented DOS, so we will pretend we are interested in tracking down which files a program opens. One could, of course, disassemble the program or run it under a debugger, but it makes more sense to treat the program as a "black box" and simply see which DOS file calls it makes. In other words, in this case one should study the program as a behavioral, rather than a Freudian, psychologist. INTRSPY is perfect for this sort of exploration.

For example, the following commands could be used to find out which files Microsoft C (MSC) 7.0 uses when compiling the tiny, industry-standard HELLO.C program:

```
intrspy
cmdspy compile fopen.scr
cl hello.c
cmdspy report
```

This code first loads INTRSPY, which is a memory resident program. It then uses CMDSPY to compile an INTRSPY script called FOPEN.SCR. As explained below, CMDSPY communicates with the resident INTRSPY program. Then the Microsoft CL program is run. Finally, the code produces a report (which we also could have sent to a file using DOS file redirection, as in CMDSPY REPORT > CL.LOG). As for the FOPEN.SCR script itself, Listing 5-1 shows a very simple version which traps only calls to INT 21h Function 3Dh (Open File).

Listing 5-1: FOPEN.SCR (simple version)

```
; FOPEN.SCR
intercept 21h
    function 3dh      ; Open File
        on_entry
            output "OPEN " (ds:dx->byte,asciiz,64)
        on_exit if (cflag == 1)
            sameline " [FAIL " ax "]"
```

This script instructs INTRSPY to intercept INT 21h and trap all calls to AH=3Dh (Function 3Dh, the DOS handle-based file open function). On entry to the call, INTRSPY should output the string "OPEN ", plus the ASCIIZ string pointed to by the DS:DX register pair; a maximum of 64 bytes will be stored. The pointer operator (->) indicates that DS:DX is to be used as a pointer to an area of memory that should be treated as bytes. Sixty-four bytes should be stored and formatted on output as an ASCIIZ string. On exit from INT 21h AH=3Dh, if the carry flag is set, the script tells INTRSPY it should output, on the same line, the string "FAIL" and the value of the AX register, enclosed in square brackets. Note in Figure 5-1 how the on_entry clause corresponds to the parameters expected by INT 21h Function 3Dh, and how the on_exit clause corresponds to its possible error return value.

Figure 5-1: The DOS Open Function and a Corresponding INTRSPY Script

```
INT 21h Function 3Dh                          intercept 21h function 3dh
Open File                                     on_entry output "OPEN  "
Call with:
    AH = 3Dh
    AL = access mode
    DS:DX -> seg:ofs of ASCIIZ pathname       (ds:dx->byte,asciiz,64)
Returns:                                      on_exit
    CARRY = clear if function successful
        AX = handle
    CARRY = set if function unsuccessful      if (cflag == 1)
        AX = error code                       sameline " [FAIL " ax "]"
```

The output from INTRSPY goes, not directly to your screen, but into a results buffer. The default buffer size is 8K. This can be overridden on the INTRSPY command line (for example, INTRSPY -r16000). After running CL HELLO.C, the command CMDSPY REPORT produced the results shown in Figure 5-2.

Figure 5-2: INTRSPY FOPEN Results for CL HELLO.C

```
OPEN    \msc700\bin\CL.EXE
OPEN    \msc700\bin\ms32krnl.dll
OPEN    CON
OPEN    CON
OPEN    C:\msc700\bin\CL.EXE
OPEN    C:\UNDOC2\CHAP5\C13216.EXE [FAIL 2]
OPEN    C:\msc700\bin\C13216.EXE
OPEN    C:\UNDOC2\CHAP5\015592sy [FAIL 2]
OPEN    C:\UNDOC2\CHAP5\015592sy
OPEN    C:\UNDOC2\CHAP5\015592gl [FAIL 2]
OPEN    C:\UNDOC2\CHAP5\015592gl
OPEN    C:\UNDOC2\CHAP5\015592ex [FAIL 2]
OPEN    C:\UNDOC2\CHAP5\015592ex
OPEN    C:\UNDOC2\CHAP5\015592in [FAIL 2]
OPEN    C:\UNDOC2\CHAP5\015592in
OPEN    C:\UNDOC2\CHAP5\015592st [FAIL 2]
OPEN    C:\UNDOC2\CHAP5\015592st
OPEN    C:\UNDOC2\CHAP5\hello.c
OPEN    C:\UNDOC2\CHAP5\stdio.h [FAIL 2]
OPEN    C:\msc700\include\stdio.h
OPEN    C:\UNDOC2\CHAP5\q23.exe [FAIL 2]
OPEN    C:\msc700\bin\q23.exe
OPEN    C:\msc700\bin\q23.exe
OPEN    015592gl
OPEN    015592ex
OPEN    015592in
OPEN    015592st
OPEN    hello.obj [FAIL 2]
OPEN    hello.obj
OPEN    015592sy
OPEN    C:\UNDOC2\CHAP5\015592lk [FAIL 2]
OPEN    C:\UNDOC2\CHAP5\015592lk
OPEN    C:\UNDOC2\CHAP5\link.exe [FAIL 2]
OPEN    C:\msc700\bin\link.exe
OPEN    C:\msc700\bin\link.exe
OPEN    C:\msc700\bin\link.exe
```

```
OPEN  C:\msc700\bin\link.exe
OPEN  C:\msc700\bin\link.exe
OPEN  015592lk
OPEN  hello.obj
OPEN  \msc700\lib\OLDNAMES.LIB
OPEN  \msc700\lib\SLIBCE.lib
OPEN  \msc700\lib\OLDNAMES.LIB
OPEN  C:hello.exe [FAIL 2]
OPEN  C:hello.exe
OPEN  C:\UNDOC2\CHAP5\CMDSPY.EXE
```

Whew! All that just to compile HELLO.C! MS32KRNL.DLL is a hacked Win32 portable executable (PE) file that MSC 7.0 uses. The temporary files with sy, ex, gs, ls, in, st, pr, and lk suffixes relate to different phrases of compiling: symbols, expressions, global optimization, local optimization, and so on.

If you still have Microsoft C 6.0, you might try the -qc option to do a quick compile. Instead of the barrage of file activity you get with a full optimizing compile, the INTRSPY results (as shown in Figure 5-3) are much shorter. No wonder the -qc switch is faster! Unfortunately, -qc doesn't have the same effect in MSC 7.0.

Figure 5-3: INTRSPY FOPEN Results for CL -QC HELLO.C

```
OPEN qcc.exe [FAIL 0002]
OPEN hello.obj
OPEN hello.c
OPEN c:/c600/include\stdio.h
OPEN 007281lk [FAIL 0002]
OPEN link.exe [FAIL 0002]
OPEN c:\c600\bin\link.exe
OPEN 007281lk
OPEN hello.obj
OPEN c:\c600\lib\SLIBCE.lib
OPEN C:hello.exe
OPEN C:hello.exe
OPEN C:\DOS\COMMAND.COM
```

What has been accomplished here? With a seven-line INTRSPY script, we have created a file-open logging utility which would otherwise have taken many more lines of code (and, more important, a good several hours of programmer's time) to write and debug in C, assembly language, or Pascal.

Still, this FOPEN.SCR file is only a minimal implementation of a file-logging utility. For example, simply by typing CL, you must be generating lots of file system activity as DOS first tries to find and then execute CL.EXE. Furthermore, the log doesn't show any files being created. Nor does it look for more exotic versions of the file-open function, such as INT 21h AH=0Fh (FCB Open) and AH=6Ch (Extended Open/Create).

All we need to do is to trap some additional functions, as shown in the beefed-up version of FOPEN.SCR in Listing 5-2. To show the DOS command lines with which programs are EXECed, FOPEN.SCR uses an INTRSPY STRUCTURE that represents the parameter block used by the DOS EXEC function. It also uses a STRUCTURE to represent the part of the DOS File Control Block that it's interested in.

Listing 5-2: FOPEN.SCR Watches File Open, Create, Find, and Exec

```
; FOPEN.SCR
structure param_blk fields
    env_seg (word,hex)
    args (dword,ptr)

structure fcb fields
    drive_num (byte,char)
    filename (byte,char,8)
    ext (byte,char,8)
```

```
; etc.
intercept 21h
    function 0Fh      ; Open File with FCB
        on_entry
            output "FCBOP " (ds:dx->fcb.filename) "." (ds:dx->fcb.ext)
        on_exit if (al == 0FFh)
            sameline " [FAIL]"
; ------------------------------------------
    function 3ch      ; Create File
        on_entry
            output "CREAT " (ds:dx->byte,asciiz,64)
        on_exit if (cflag == 1)
            sameline " [FAIL " (ax, dec) "]"
; ------------------------------------------
    function 3dh      ; Open File
        on_entry
            output "OPEN  " (ds:dx->byte,asciiz,64)
        on_exit if (cflag == 1)
            sameline " [FAIL " (ax, dec) "]"
; ------------------------------------------
    function 4bh      ; Execute Program
        subfunction 00h
            on_entry
                output "EXEC  "
                    (ds:dx->byte,asciiz,64)                    ; program
                    (es:bx->param_blk.args->byte,pascal,128) ; cmdline
            on_exit if (cflag == 1)
                sameline " [FAIL " (ax, dec) "]"
; ------------------------------------------
    function 4eh      ; Find First File
        on_entry
            output "FIND  " (ds:dx->byte,asciiz,64)
        on_exit if (cflag == 1)
            sameline " [FAIL " (ax, dec) "]"
; ------------------------------------------
    function 6Ch      ; Extended Open/Create
        on_entry
            output "XOPEN " (ds:si->byte,asciiz,64)
        on_exit if (cflag == 1)
            sameline " [FAIL " (ax, dec) "]"
```

The first INTRSPY STRUCTURE statement corresponds to the first two fields (the only ones that matter here) of the parameter block that INT 21h Function 4Bh Subfunction 00h expects from the ES:BX register pair. FOPEN.SCR outputs the DOS command line, or the first 64 bytes of it, with this expression:

```
(es:bx->param_blk.args->byte,pascal,64)
```

This indicates that the ES:BX pair points to an area of memory that should be treated as a param_blk structure, and that we are interested in the args field. FOPEN.SCR then uses another arrow (->) to indicate that args, which was defined as (dword, hex), points to a string. A Pascal designation, (which reflects how strings are stored in Pascal) is different from ASCIIZ, in that its first byte is a length count. This corresponds exactly with the command tail used by MS-DOS.

Now, of course, INTRSPY produces even more output (a small fragment of which is shown in Figure 5-4) describing the activity generated by the simple command CL HELLO.C.

Figure 5-4: Detailed INTRSPY FOPEN Results for CL HELLO.C

```
FIND   cl.??? [FAIL 18]
FIND   \bin\cl.??? [FAIL 18]
FIND   \dos\cl.??? [FAIL 18]
FIND   \borlandc\bin\cl.??? [FAIL 18]
```

```
FIND   \watcomc\bin\cl.??? [FAIL 18]
FIND   \msc700\bin\cl.???
OPEN   \msc700\bin\CL.EXE
EXEC   \msc700\bin\CL.EXE hello.c
OPEN   \msc700\bin\ms32krnl.dll
OPEN   CON
OPEN   CON
... lots of OPENs, as in Figure 5-2 ...
OPEN   C:\msc700\bin\q23.exe
OPEN   C:\msc700\bin\q23.exe
EXEC   C:\msc700\bin\q23.exe
OPEN   015592gl
OPEN   015592ex
... more OPENs, as in Figure 5-2 ...
OPEN   C:\msc700\bin\link.exe
OPEN   C:\msc700\bin\link.exe
EXEC   C:\msc700\bin\link.exe @@"015592lk"
OPEN   C:\msc700\bin\link.exe
OPEN   C:\msc700\bin\link.exe
... yet more OPENs, as in Figure 5-2 ...
OPEN   \msc700\lib\OLDNAMES.LIB
OPEN   C:hello.exe
FIND   cmdspy.???
CREAT  hello2.log
OPEN   C:\UNDOC2\CHAP5\CMDSPY.EXE
EXEC   C:\UNDOC2\CHAP5\CMDSPY.EXE report
```

The first thing Figure 5-4 shows is that, before the actual execution of CL.EXE itself, COM-MAND.COM must first find it. The series of failed calls to the DOS Find First function show COM-MAND.COM looking along the PATH in many subdirectories before it finally finds CL.EXE. If you were going to be using Microsoft C a lot, it would probably be a good idea to optimize your PATH by moving C:\MSC\BIN forward a little.

INTRSPY can be likened to a protocol analyzer for PC software interrupts, where INTRSPY itself only knows about raw interrupts, registers, and interrupts, and where the user's scripts impose the necessary higher level interpretation to understand what is actually going on.

Device Drivers

INTRSPY also provides a script-driven approach to watching block and character mode device driver calls, using the same INTERCEPT command used to hook interrupts:

```
INTERCEPT STRATEGY("devname")    ; Character mode device
INTERCEPT INTERRUPT("d:")        ; Block mode device
```

Block-mode device drivers support data transfers to and from devices a block at a time, usually for random access storage devices such as hard disks, and are identified by a drive letter. Character mode device drivers provide stream (character by character) access to devices such as communications channels. They are also used to provide interfaces to system facilities such as XMS that may need to get loaded early on during system initialization. DOS includes built-in block-mode device drivers for the floppy and hard disk drives, for example, while HIMEM.SYS implements a character-mode device driver for managing XMS extended memory. The names of these character-mode drivers are displayed by programs such as DEV from Chapter 7.

Listing 5-3 (DD.SCR) shows how you might record device driver calls to any device driver. Note that, while you can monitor calls to both the Strategy and Interrupt entry points to the device driver, generally it is only useful to monitor the Strategy routine. DOS does not exploit the separation in drivers between Strategy and Interrupt; as soon as DOS calls the Strategy routine, it calls the Interrupt routine. Unlike operating systems such as OS/2 and NT, DOS does not provide overlapped (asynchronous) I/O.

Listing 5-3: DD.SCR Watches Calls to Device Drivers

```
; DD.SCR -- watch any device driver named on command line
; CMDSPY COMPILE DD C:
; CMDSPY COMPILE DD EMMXXXX0
structure requ fields
    len (byte, hex)
    subunit (byte, hex)
    cmd (byte, hex)
    status (word, hex)
    ; other stuff depends on packet
intercept strategy("%1")
    on_entry
        if ((es:bx->requ.cmd) == 0) output "00 - init"
        if ((es:bx->requ.cmd) == 1) output "01 - media check"
        if ((es:bx->requ.cmd) == 2) output "02 - build bpb"
        if ((es:bx->requ.cmd) == 3) output "03 - ioctl input"
        if ((es:bx->requ.cmd) == 4) output "04 - input"
        if ((es:bx->requ.cmd) == 5) && (#5 == 0)     ; often a lot of these
             output "05 - nondestruc input"
        if ((es:bx->requ.cmd) == 5)
            incr #5
        if ((es:bx->requ.cmd) == 6) output "06 - input status"
        if ((es:bx->requ.cmd) == 7) output "07 - input flush"
        if ((es:bx->requ.cmd) == 8) output "08 - output"
        if ((es:bx->requ.cmd) == 9) output "09 - output w/verify"
        if ((es:bx->requ.cmd) == 0Ah) output "0A - output status"
        if ((es:bx->requ.cmd) == 0Bh) output "0B - output flush"
        if ((es:bx->requ.cmd) == 0Ch) output "0C - ioctl output"
        if ((es:bx->requ.cmd) == 0Dh) output "0D - device open"
        if ((es:bx->requ.cmd) == 0Eh) output "0E - device close"
        if ((es:bx->requ.cmd) == 0Fh) output "0F - removeable media"
        if ((es:bx->requ.cmd) == 10h) output "10 - output until busy"
        ; 11h and 12h are missing from DOS 5 Programmer's Reference
        if ((es:bx->requ.cmd) == 11h) output "11 - stop output"
        if ((es:bx->requ.cmd) == 12h) output "12 - restart output"
        if ((es:bx->requ.cmd) == 13h) output "13 - generic ioctl"
        if ((es:bx->requ.cmd) == 14h) output "14 - unused"
        if ((es:bx->requ.cmd) == 15h) output "15 - unused??"
        if ((es:bx->requ.cmd) == 16h) output "16 - unused"
        if ((es:bx->requ.cmd) == 17h) output "17 - get logical device"
        if ((es:bx->requ.cmd) == 18h) output "18 - set logical device"
        if ((es:bx->requ.cmd) == 19h) output "19 - ioctl query
        if ((es:bx->requ.cmd) > 19h) output (es:bx->requ.cmd) " - UNKNOWN"
        ; could also handle CD-ROM driver commands
; intercept interrupt("%1")
;   on_entry
;       output "Interrupt entry point polled"
run "%2 %3 %4 %5 %6 %7 %8 %9"
report
```

This script introduces some additional features of the INTRSPY language. The "%1" in the script operates in the same way it would in a batch file; it acts as a parameter, specified on the command line and substituted into the script when it is compiled. The RUN statement is equivalent to running a command from the DOS command line except that, in an INTRSPY script, RUN can help reduce the amount of background noise from programs you currently aren't interested in. CMDSPY runs the command as soon as it finishes compiling the script. Finally, the REPORT statement is similar to running CMDSPY REPORT.

To see what commands are sent to the A: block driver during a simple command such as VOL A:, you could issue the following at the DOS command prompt:

```
C:\UNDOC2\CHAP5>cmdspy compile dd a: "command /c vol a:" > tmp.tmp
```

This kitchen sink command compiles DD.SCR to watch drive A:, issues the internal command, VOL A: (hence the COMMAND /C), and redirects CMDSPY's output to TMP.TMP. The output would look something like that shown in Figure 5-5. The first line is output from the VOL command itself; the rest of the output comes from CMDSPY.

Figure 5-5: DD.SCR Output for VOL A:

```
 Volume in drive A has no label
(Handler for calls to 0070:06F5 was already stopped.)
File: DD.SCR
Line 12: intercept strategy("a:")
                  ***
Warning: Same block device driver supports multiple drives.
1214 bytes of code generated for 'a:' driver strategy script

Running program: C:\DOS\command.COM...
Run completed.

05 - nondestruc input
01 - media check
04 - input
04 - input
04 - input
04 - input
04 - input
04 - input
04 - input
04 - input
01 - media check
04 - input
13 - generic ioctl
01 - media check
04 - input
04 - input
04 - input
08 - output
08 - output

Counter #5  : 2
All other counters zero.
```

Another feature of INTRSPY that DD.SCR uses is a counter. There will often be so many calls to a driver with command 5 (nondestructive input) that the INTRSPY results buffer would immediately fill up with these if you displayed a line of output for each one. Therefore, DD.SCR only displays the first nondestructive input call and uses all the rest only to increment a counter (INCR #5 in Listing 5-3).

Sixteen counters are available, identified by #1 through #16. Each is a 32-bit value that may be incremented (INCR), decremented (DECR), or reset to zero (ZERO) within a script. They may also be compared in IF statements and used as elements in OUTPUT or SAMELINE statements. We picked #5 here simply because it matches the command number for nondestructive input. At the end of an INTRSPY report, CMDSPY displays any active counters. In Figure 5-5, we can see that there were only two such calls; in some cases, there will be thousands.

With many character-mode device drivers such as XMSXXXX0, you won't see much activity. As noted earlier, these are often coded as device drivers only to get them installed early for use by other device drivers. In the case of XMS, in fact, Microsoft has a non-device driver version of HIMEM.SYS called XMSMMGR.EXE; it is used for Windows 3.1 SETUP when the user doesn't have HIMEM.SYS or another XMS driver installed. But some of these drivers *do* deal with device driver packets, particularly generic IOCTL calls. For example, EMMXXXX0 and 386MAX$$ have generic IOCTL calls that are used by Windows. For these, on the other hand, it is probably easier to watch calls to INT 21h AH=44h rather than inspect the lower level device driver packets.

Watching XMS

While interrupts and device driver entry points account for much of the communications between software in the PC, it is by no means all. To use XMS, for example, a program makes an initial call to INT 2Fh AX=4310h, and the address returned in ES:BX is then used for all subsequent calls for XMS services. Simply intercepting INT 2Fh and watching for AX=4310h will not get you very far.

XMS calls can be intercepted in an INTRSPY script using another form of the INTERCEPT command. In this case, the interrupt number or device driver name is replaced by the special keyword XMS, as seen in the XMSWATCH script in Listing 5-4.

Listing 5-4: XMSWATCH.SCR

```
; XMS.SCR
structure move fields
    len (dword,hex)
    src (word,hex)
    src_ofs (dword,hex)
    dest (word,hex)
    dest_ofs (dword,hex)
intercept xms
    function 0 on_entry output "XMS 00 - get xms version number"
    function 1 on_entry output "XMS 01 - request HMA " dx
    function 2 on_entry output "XMS 02 - release HMA"
    function 3 on_entry output "XMS 03 - global enable A20"
    function 4 on_entry output "XMS 04 - global disable A20"
    function 5 on_entry output "XMS 05 - local enable A20"
    function 6 on_entry output "XMS 06 - local disable A20"
    function 7 on_entry incr #1 ;; Query A20 state - Too many of these!
    function 8 on_entry output "XMS 08 - query free extended memory"
               on_exit sameline " -> " ax
    function 9 on_entry output "XMS 09 - allocate extended memory " dx
    function 0Ah on_entry output "XMS 0A - free extended memory " dx
    function 0Bh on_entry output "XMS 0B - move extended memory "
               (ds:si->move.len)
               " from " (ds:si->move.src) "/" (ds:si->move.src_ofs)
               " to " (ds:si->move.dest) "/" (ds:si->move.dest_ofs)
    function 0Ch on_entry output "XMS 0C - lock extended memory " dx
    function 0Dh on_entry output "XMS 0D - unlock extended memory " dx
    function 0Eh on_entry output "XMS 0E - get handle info"
    function 0Fh on_entry
               output "XMS 0F - realloc extended memory " dx "," bx
    function 10h on_entry output "XMS 10 - request UMB " dx
    function 11h on_entry output "XMS 11 - release UMB " dx
    function 12h on_entry output "XMS 12 - realloc UMB"
include "prog"
```

To keep it trim, Listing 5-4 only includes the XMS version 2.0 specification calls. Without much more effort, you could include the additional version 3.0 calls.

The last line of XMSWATCH.SCR shows another INTRSPY feature: Common scripts may be included using the INCLUDE statement, just as you might use #include in C or {$i} in Turbo Pascal. The PROG.SCR file, shown in Listing 5-5, records the start of program execution. Later in the chapter, a more extensive version, EXEC.SCR, provides an INTRSPY machine monitor. In its PROG.SCR form, it is a very useful file that you will include in many of your scripts, since it indicates exactly what proportion of the material your primary script is recording actually relates to a particular program.

Listing 5-5: PROG.SCR

```
; PROG.SCR
intercept 21h function 4bh on_entry
    output "-----------------------------------------"
    output (ds:dx->byte,asciiz,64)
```

Using XMSWATCH while Windows is starting up, the XMSWATCH results show, for example, that Windows grabs all free extended memory. It calls XMS function 8 to query the size of the largest block of available extended memory, and then calls XMS function 9 to allocate that largest available block.

Rather than output a line for each call to XMS function 7 (Query A20 State), a counter is used. Programs such as Windows typically call this function thousands of times in a very brief period. Logging the occurrence of each of these would produce a very monotonous report.

In most uses of XMSWATCH, most of the report will be devoted to XMS function 0Bh (Move). In one run, for example, the report ran to over 1000 lines, some 950 of which were function 0Bh. This result is much as you might expect, that being the workhorse function of the XMS interface. XMSWATCH shows how many bytes were moved, with the source and destination output as xxxx/yyyyzzzz. If xxxx is zero, it represents a conventional memory address, yyyy:zzzz. Otherwise, xxxx is an extended memory handle, and yyyyzzzz is a 32-bit offset into the extended memory block (EMB).

Unfortunately, there is a gap in the XMS call trapping for a brief period during the Windows load process. Because Windows takes over responsibility for XMS, and because, as a result, it does some patching of entry points, INTRSPY must temporarily disengage itself while Windows makes the transition to 386 Enhanced mode.

The way that INTRSPY knows that Windows is starting is through the useful Int 2Fh function 16h API provided by Windows. Among other things, this interface provides hooks to allow TSRs to not only detect the starting and stopping of Windows, but to perform any necessary preparations and even tell Windows not to load, should that be necessary. The MULTI shell that will be presented in Chapter 9 uses this mechanism because of incompatibilities between MULTI and Windows.

Subfunction 05h is called by Windows startup code while it is still in real mode in both enhanced and standard mode. Subfunction 08h is called only in enhanced mode and informs TSRs that the Windows startup is complete. A symmetrical pair of calls, subfunctions 09h and 06h notify TSRs that enhanced mode is closing down and that Windows closedown is complete, respectively. INTRSPY disables the XMS hook during startup and closedown to allow the V86MMGR module of Enhanced mode Windows to install an ARPL instruction at the XMS entrypoint. This instruction will generate an exception, which Windows traps to receive control. INTRSPY then reinstalls its own patch, allowing it to intercept XMS calls before passing them on to Windows.

Dynamic Hooks

INTRSPY also provides a means for watching calls to any function location, not just XMS. In fact, XMS is simply a reserved entry point identifier or hook. You may specify your own hooks for other addresses that you wish to intercept. This feature is very powerful and allows the trapping of callbacks.

Using the INTRSPY HOOK facility, for example, a script can be written to watch the completion of NetBIOS requests. In NetBIOS, an application can communicate asynchronously over the network; that is, it can perform other processing while NetBIOS goes about the business of sending or receiving data. One way to accomplish this is by specifying a post routine as one of the parameter fields in the NetBIOS Control Block (NCB) that is passed to Interrupt 5Bh when requesting a NetBIOS network communications service. At the completion of whatever task has been requested, NetBIOS calls the post routine, notifying the application.

The most significant difference between previous INTERCEPT commands and the entry point identifier variation is that the address that is to be intercepted is supplied, not at compile time, but as a result of another event. This is achieved using a HOOK statement with the same identifier, as shown in Listing 5-6 (NETBIOS.SCR).

Listing 5-6: NETBIOS.SCR

```
; NETBIOS.SCR
structure ncb fields
    cmd                 (byte)
    rc                  (byte)
    loc_sessno          (byte)
    name_no             (byte)
    buffer              (dword,ptr)
    buflen              (word,dec)
    dest_name           (byte,char,16)
    srce_name           (byte,char,16)
    rto                 (byte, dec)
    sto                 (byte, dec)
    post_routine        (dword,ptr)
    adap_no             (byte)
    cmd_rc              (byte)
    reserved            (byte,hex,14)
intercept post_routine
    on_entry
        output ""
        output "-------------------------------------"
        output "Post routine triggered for NCB at " es ":" bx
            " - completed " (es:bx->ncb.cmd_rc)
intercept 5ch
    on_entry
        output ""
        output "===================================="
        output "NCB at " es ":" bx " submitted" (es:bx->ncb)
        if ((es:bx->ncb.cmd) > 127)
            output "Command is NOWAIT "
        if ((es:bx->ncb.cmd) > 127) && ((es:bx->ncb.post_routine) != 0)
            hook post_routine = (es:bx->ncb.post_routine)
            sameline "- Post routine used"
    on_exit
        output "On exit AL is " al
```

The first INTERCEPT statement refers to an identifier, post_routine. When the script is compiled, there is no address associated with post_routine, since the NCB, whose post routine we want to trap, has not yet been created. However, our second INTERCEPT statement is watching NetBIOS interrupts (INT 5Ch). When the application interrupts NetBIOS to submit the NCB for processing, the intercept can determine if a post routine has been specified, that is, if the POST field in the supplied NCB structure is non-NULL. If a post routine has been specified, the HOOK statement uses the address in the POST field as the address to be watched by the post_routine intercept.

INTRSPY's different treatment of intercepts of interrupts on the one hand and entry point identifiers on the other can be likened to the difference between static and dynamic linking. Static linking establishes the addresses for function calls between modules when a program is built. Dynamic linking only establishes those inter-module call addresses at run time. In the same way, INTRSPY links interrupt and device driver INTERCEPT statements to the appropriate addresses at compile time, but links an entry point identifier script to the appropriate address when the associated HOOK statement within another INTERCEPT is invoked.

In Listing 5-6, notice how an entire NCB structure resulted from the single statement ES:BX->NCB. When so asked, INTRSPY will take care of displaying every field in a structure, including the field's name. The resulting output can be seen in Figure 5-6, which shows output from NETBIOS.SCR for a single NetBIOS command. As can be seen from the NCB.CMD field, the command was A2h; this is a Send Broadcast Datagram (22h), with the no-wait bit (80h) set. The NCB was located at 0CDD:0DDA. The actual data to send was located at 0CDD:0048 (NCB.BUFFER); 18 (decimal) bytes were to be sent (NCB.BUFLEN). We could of course have displayed the contents of this buffer as well.

Figure 5-6: Output from NETBIOS.SCR for a NetBIOS Command

```
NCB at 0CDD:0DDA submitted
NCB.CMD                        : A2
NCB.RC                         : 00
NCB.LOC_SESSNO                 : 00
NCB.NAME_NO                    : 02
NCB.BUFFER                     : 0CDD:0048
NCB.BUFLEN                     : 18
NCB.DEST_NAME                  :
NCB.SRCE_NAME                  :
NCB.RTO                        : 0
NCB.STO                        : 0
NCB.POST_ROUTINE               : 0B6B:003B
NCB.ADAP_NO                    : 00
NCB.CMD_RC                     : 00
NCB.RESERVED                   : 00  00  00  00  00  00  00  00  00  00  00
  00  00  00
Command is NOWAIT - Post routine used
--------------------------------------
Post routine triggered for NCB at 0CDD:0DDA - completed 00
On exit AL is 00
```

Since the goal of this example is to illustrate the INTRSPY HOOK statement, the important thing in Figure 5-6 is at the end, where the post routine was called at some later point for the initial no-wait (asynchronous) send broadcast datagram command. As can you see, the completion code (NCB.CMD_RC) was zero, indicating success.

The above is a useful example of the HOOK function's use in watching callback functions, but there is a significant caveat associated with its use in at least the NetBIOS context. The problem, as always, manifests itself when running under Windows enhanced mode. Since an application running in a DOS window may not be in memory at the precise moment that its NetBIOS event completes, a virtual device driver (VNETBIOS.VXD) is installed to undertake, among other things, the virtual memory manipulation and task switching necessary to synchronize the VM and the callback. In order to do this, the INT 5Ch that the application issues to submit the NCB is intercepted by the VxD, and the post routine address is replaced with the protected mode address of a thunk that will be invoked before the post routine is called. Additionally, the buffer address is converted to the address of a protected mode holding buffer until the real-mode callback can be called.

The above should not matter, you might think, given that INTRSPY is running in the same DOS window and, to all intents and purposes, replaces the application temporarily. Using the ON_ENTRY clause should allow us to pick up any addresses before they are modified. Unfortunately not. Windows gets there first, using an ARPL instruction (V86 breakpoint) and passes control back to the VM's real mode interrupt handler chain. Thus, even in the ON_ENTRY clause we are too late. This all means that, in a DOS box, hooking a NetBIOS callback will not lead to the desired results and will in all likelihood crash the VM.

Note the similarity here to our earlier problems with XMS. For a program like INTRSPY, Windows enhanced mode is a tough application with which to be compatible!

INTRSPY User's Guide

INTRSPY is actually two programs, INTRSPY.EXE and CMDSPY.EXE, whose operating instructions follow.

Using INTRSPY.EXE
The following command is used to run INTRSPY.EXE:

```
INTRSPY [-rnnnn] [-?]
```

where -rnnnn specifies the amount of memory INTRSPY is to allocate for compiled script and result storage (default is 8K). For example, the following command runs INTRSPY with an allocation of 24,000 bytes of code and results space:

```
C:\UNDOC2\CHAP5>INTRSPY -r24000
```

Using CMDSPY.EXE
The following command is used to run CMDSPY.EXE:

```
CMDSPY   [COMPILE [d:][path]inptfile[.ext] [param-1 [param-2 .. ]]]
         [REPORT]
         [RESTART]
         [FLUSH]
         [STOP]
         [UNLOAD]
```

where:

- COMPILE compiles a script and instructs INTRSPY to begin monitoring interrupts and entry points, as well as storing results specified in inptfile.ext, which contains script source in the form defined below. Any currently active script is stopped, and the results area is flushed. If the extension is omitted, .SCR (script) is assumed. For example, the following DOS command line compiles the script TEST.SCR:

  ```
  C:\UNDOC2\CHAP5>CMDSPY COMPILE TEST
  ```

- REPORT instructs INTRSPY to return the results accumulated since the script was compiled or since the last time a CMDSPY FLUSH was issued (see below). CMDSPY formats the results in the results buffer, as specified in the current script, and writes them to STDOUT. The display can be redirected to a file. For example,

  ```
  C:\UNDOC2\CHAP5>CMDSPY REPORT > TEST.LOG
  ```

- STOP instructs INTRSPY to stop monitoring interrupts and entry points, but to preserve the results area.
- RESTART instructs INTRSPY to restart monitoring interrupts and entry points (after a STOP or REPORT command) on the basis of the currently compiled script.
- FLUSH instructs INTRSPY to clear the results area, but to leave the current script active.
- UNLOAD instructs the INTRSPY TSR to *attempt* to unload itself from memory. Any active script is stopped. There are circumstances under which INTRSPY cannot be unloaded.

Script Language
The script language allows nine main constructs:

- INCLUDE, which includes another input file.
- STRUCTURE, which defines a data structure.
- INTERCEPT, which specifies an interrupt number, device driver strategy, interrupt routine, or an entry point identifier to be used with a HOOK statement. It also specifies optional

function and subfunction numbers or ranges, together with the entry and exit processing to be done when the intercept is triggered.

- RUN, which allows a DOS program to be EXECed from within the script and a built-in debugger to be used within intercepts.
- GENERATE, which allows interrupts to be generated, usually to obtain an address to be associated with an entry point identifier.
- REPORT, FLUSH, STOP, and RESTART, all of which work exactly like their command line counterparts.

Syntax

A script file is an ASCII file. All white space is ignored, except within literal strings used for results output. Thus, indentation and multiple lines may be used for readability or lack thereof, as the user sees fit. Line endings are only used to delimit comments, which begin with a semicolon anywhere on a line. The placeholders %1 through %9 can appear anywhere in a script and are replaceable from the DOS command line. The following is thus a valid INTRSPY script:

```
; INTERCEPT.SCR
intercept %1
    function %2
        %3 %4 %5 %6 %7 %8 %9
```

This script could be used for one-shot queries that didn't deserve their own separate scripts. For example,

```
C:\>cmdspy compile intercept 21h 52h on_exit output es ":" bx
```

The simplest possible valid INTRSPY script is thus:

```
; SCRIPT.SCR
%1 %2 %3 %4 %5 %6 %7 %8 %9
```

This requires that the entire script be placed on the DOS command line:

```
C:\>cmdspy compile script intercept 21h function 52h on_exit output es ":" bx
```

INCLUDE Syntax

The following syntax is used for INCLUDE statements:

```
INCLUDE "[d:][path]inptfile[.ext] [param-1 [param-2...]]"
```

This syntax includes the specified file and substitutes param-1, param-2, anD so forth, in the source for the strings %1, %2 ... %N, respectively, where found. If the extension is omitted, .SCR is assumed. Some examples:

```
include "%1"          ; include script named on command line
include "foo"         ; include foo.scr
include "foo %1"      ; include foo.scr, passing arg from cmdline
include "foo bar"     ; include foo.scr, passing arg "bar"
```

STRUCTURE Syntax

Some example structures, such as param_blk and fcb in Listing 5-2 (FOPEN.SCR) and requ in Listing 5-3 (DD.SCR), were shown earlier.

To formally define STRUCTURE, first define a *field definition* as:

```
field-type [,field-disp-type [,field-dup]]
```

where:

- *field-type* can be BYTE, WORD, DWORD, or a previously defined structure name.

- *field-disp-type* can be HEX, BIN, DEC, OCT, PTR, CHAR, PASCAL (a string with the count as its first byte), ASCIIZ (a zero-terminated string), DUMP (a combination of HEX and ASCII), or STRUCT (if field-type was a structure name).
- *field-dup* is the number of elements if the field should be treated as an array, or the length of the field in, for example, a string. In the case of a field being defined within a structure definition, field-dup may be a numeric literal or one of the predefined constants. In the case of a definition within an output element (see INTERCEPT syntax), field-dup may also refer to a register (reg8, reg16, sreg). Then, STRUCTURE syntax looks like this:

```
STRUCTURE struct-name FIELDS
     field-name1 (field-definition)
     [field-name2 (field-definition)]
                .
                .
     [field-nameN (field-definition)]
```

Note that struct-name must be a unique structure identifier, and that field-name must be unique within struct-name. There are thirty significant characters for both struct-name and field-name—and indeed for any INTRSPY symbol. This number should be adequate for almost any application.

INTERCEPT Syntax

Many examples of INTERCEPT statements were presented in the first portion of this chapter, but let us now formally define INTERCEPT. To begin with, let us define an intercept-element as an interrupt number, a device driver strategy, interrupt routine, or an entry-point-identifier. For example:

```
INTERCEPT 21h               ; intercept an interrupt
INTERCEPT STRATEGY("foo")   ; intercept device driver Strategy routine
INTERCEPT INTERRUPT("foo")  ; intercept device driver Interrupt routine
INTERCEPT hook_proc         ; intercept entry-point-identifier (see below)
```

Then, define an *output element* as:

```
REGS or
reg_or_flag or
(reg_or_flag, field-disp-type) or
#counter or
(#counter, field-disp-type) or
"string literal" or
(segval+/-seg_adjust:ofsval[additional-offset]->memory-reference) or
predefined-constant or
(predefined-constant, field-disp-type)
```

where:

- *reg_or_flag* is the name of an 8- or 16-bit register or a flag.
- a *flag* is identified by xFLAG, where x may be one of the following: D (direction), I (interrupt), T (trap), S (sign), Z (zero), A (auxiliary), P (parity), or C (carry). For example, CFLAG or AFLAG.
- *#counter* is one of the built-in 32-bit count registers identified by #1 through #16.
- *segval* is any register, numeric constant, or built-in constant.
- *seg-adjust* is an optional numeric constant to be added to or subtracted from the segment value. For example, (es-1:0->mcb).
- *ofsval* is any register, numeric constant, or built-in constant.
- *[additional-offset]* is an optional numeric literal increment or decrement. For example, (es:bx[-12]->list_31).
- *memory-reference* is one of the following:

  □ BYTE/WORD/DWORD, field-disp-type, field-dup (both defined in STRUCTURE above).

- ☐ struct
- ☐ struct.field
- ☐ struct.dword-field->memory-reference, where dword-field means that the field to be used as a pointer must have been defined, as DWORD struct and field must be predefined.

- *predefined-constant* is one of those defined in the section "Predefined Constants", below.

Define an *action-statement* as one of the following:

- OUTPUT output-element [output-element [output- element ...]], which starts on a new line.
- SAMELINE output-element [output-element [output-element ...]], which attempts to append elements to an existing line of output.
- STREAM reg8-name, which outputs raw ASCII characters from the 8-bit register specified.
- DEBUG, which, if the intercept occurs during a RUN statement, enters a pop-up debugger.
- INCR #counter, which increments the specified 32-bit count register.
- DECR #counter, which decrements the specified 32-bit count register.
- ZERO #counter, which resets the specified 32-bit count register to zero.
- HOOK entry-point-identifier = hook-spec, where '=' may be replaced by the word 'TO', and hook-spec may be: reg:reg or (segval+/-seg-adjust:ofsval[additional-offset]->memory-reference), where memory reference may not include a field-disp-type or field-dup.

Define a *test-clause* as:

```
(operand operator operand)
```

where operand may be a:

```
reg_or_flag or
#counter or
(segval+/-seg-adjust:ofsval[additional-offset]->memory-reference) or
predefined-constant
```

where memory-reference is one of the following:

- BYTE/WORD/DWORD
- struct.field, where field must be defined as a non-dup BYTE/WORD/DWORD
- struct.dword-field->memory-reference, where dword-field means that the field to be used as a pointer must have been defined, as DWORD struct and field must be predefined.

and where operator may be == (equal), != (not equal), > (greater than), >= (greater than or equal to), < (less than), or <= (less than or equal to).

Next define an *if-clause* as follows:

```
IF test-clause [AND test-clause [OR test-clause [... ]]]
   [action-statements]
```

where && may be used interchangeably with AND, and || may be used interchangeably with OR.

Add the two keywords ON_ENTRY and ON_EXIT, to describe pre- and post-processing of an intercept.

Finally, the two additional keywords FUNCTION and SUBFUNCTION provide a shorthand and self-documenting form of IF (AH == nn) and IF (AL == nn). However, those tests would likely produce incorrect results at the post-processing stage, since AX may have been modified, so the FUNCTION and SUBFUNCTION keywords recall the values that AH and AL had on entry to the intercept:

```
FUNCTION ah-value
   SUBFUNCTION al-value
```

Then, INTERCEPT syntax looks like this:

```
INTERCEPT [intercept-element]
    [action-statements]
    [test-clauses]
    [FUNCTION fnctn-number [fnctn-number ...]
        [action-statements]
        [test-clauses]
        [SUBFUNCTION sfnctn-number [sfnctn-number... ]
            [action-statements]
            [test-clauses]
                [ON_ENTRY
                    [action-statements]
                    [test-clauses]]
                [ON_EXIT
                    [action-statements]
                    [test-clauses]]]
        [SUBFUNCTION sfnctn-number [sfnctn-number... ]
            .
            .
            .   ]
    [FUNCTION fnctn-number [fnctn-number ... ]
        .
        .
        .   ]
```

Although the ON_ENTRY and ON_EXIT keywords are shown within the scope of the SUB-FUNCTION level in the implied block hierarchy, they need not be; they could have been shown at a higher level, below INTERCEPT, with FUNCTION and SUBFUNCTION as lower levels in that hierarchy. For example:

```
INTERCEPT intercept-element
    ON_ENTRY
        FUNCTION fnctn-number
            ... etc. ...
```

GENERATE Syntax

The GENERATE construct allows an interrupt to be generated from within a script. This allows scripts to be self-contained (see LSTOFLST.SCR, Listing 5-8). Without it, some other program must be run to generate the wanted interrupt.

The GENERATE construct shares some of the INTERCEPT syntax. There is an ON_ENTRY section and/or an ON_EXIT. The difference is that in GENERATE one or the other section is required. The ON_ENTRY clause allows for the setting up of registers for the interrupt, and the ON_EXIT clause currently allows the use of only one statement, the HOOK command referred to in the INTERCEPT syntax.

The syntax of the ON_ENTRY clause, where hook-spec is as defined in the INTERCEPT section, is simple:

```
ON_ENTRY
    reg = value [, reg = value[, reg = value]]
```

The syntax of the ON_EXIT clause is

```
ON_EXIT
    HOOK entry point-identifier = hook-spec
    [HOOK entry point-identifier = hook-spec]
    ...
```

RUN Syntax

The RUN syntax looks like this:

```
RUN "[d:][path]program[.ext] [parm1 [parm2 ...]]"
```

If the extension is omitted, first an .EXE and then a .COM file is searched for, either in d:path if specified or on the DOS search PATH if both drive and path are omitted. Substitute param-1, param-2, and so forth, in the source for the strings %1, %2, ... %N, respectively, where found. For example,

```
RUN "cl hello.c"
RUN "%1 %2 %3 %4 %5 %6 %7 %8 %9"
```

If the second example were embedded in a script called TEST.SCR, the syntax from the DOS command line might look like this:

```
C:\UNDOC2\CHAP5>CMDSPY COMPILE TEST cl hello.c
```

Because DOS programs can be run normally from the DOS command line while an INTRSPY script is active, the RUN statement is necessary only when (a) you want to investigate a program without possible interference from COMMAND.COM; (b) you want an entirely self-contained script; or (c) you want to use the DEBUG statement.

REPORT, STOP and RESTART Syntax
REPORT, STOP, and RESTART take no parameters.

DEBUG Syntax
If its associated intercept occurs during a RUN statement, the DEBUG statement invokes a simple interactive debugger that allows access to some of CMDSPY's output capabilities from a command line. Debugger commands are as follows:

- R—Displays the registers as they were when the caller generated the interrupt but also reflects any modifications made using the M (Modify) command. It replicates the REGS output element type.
- D segval+/-seg-adjust:ofsval[additional-offset]->memory-reference—Displays an area of memory. The argument to the command is an output-element, but without the parentheses.
- M register-name = new-value—Modifies the contents of a register to be new-value, which may be any numeric literal.
- C—Cancels all register modifications and returns all register contents to their values at entry.
- X—Exits the debugger. If modifications have been made, X allows the modifications either to be canceled or allowed to remain in effect.
- The up- and down-arrow keys recall previous commands for editing. The command line is fully editable using the normal editing keys. <ESC> clears the command line, which is permanently in Insert mode.

An INTRSPY script that invokes the debugger might look like this:

```
; OPEN.SCR
intercept 21h
    function 3dh
        on_entry
            debug "INT 21h Function 3Dh - Open File"
    run "%1 %2 %3 %4 %5 %6 %7 %8 %9"
```

Note that the debugger is available only within a script that uses a RUN statement. As noted earlier, a RUN statement can contain either a string literal (for example, RUN "CL HELLO.C") or parameters replaceable from the DOS command line. In this example, you might then type the following at the DOS prompt:

```
C:\UNDOC2\CHAP5>cmdspy compile open cl hello.c
```

At the first call to INT 21h Function 3Dh, you would be in the debugger, as shown in Figure 5-7.

Figure 5-7: The INTRSPY Debugger

```
==========================================================================
==                         INTRSPY DEBUGGER                             ==
==========================================================================
 AX   BX   CX   DX   BP   SI   DI   DS   ES    SS:SP      CS:IP     FLAGS
3D00 371E 0000 0437 3094 33F0 0BE0 4173 4173 4173:308E  3C34:3BD9 odItsZaPc
>>d ds:bx->byte,asciiz,64
C:\MSC\BIN\c1.err
>>x
```

Note that at the debugger prompt (>>) you can type in expressions similar to those enclosed in INTRSPY scripts. As noted earlier, the DEBUG statement only invokes the debugger when located in a script with a RUN statement; without RUN, DEBUG is a NOP.

Predefined Constants

The following constants are provided within the script language and the debugger:

- OS_MAJOR and OS_MINOR—The major and minor DOS version number, obtained from INT 21h Function 30h (Get Version).
- LOL_SEG and LOL_OFS—The segment and offset portions of the DOS List of Lists (SysVars), obtained from INT 21h Function 52h (SysVars).
- SDA_SEG and SDA_OFS—The segment and offset portions of the address of the primary Swappable DOS Area, obtained from INT 21h Function 5D06h (Get Swappable DOS Area). This is useful in exploring the network redirector and for querying values such as the current PSP. For example,

```
intercept 21h
    function 50h
        on_entry
            if (bx != (sda_seg:sda_ofs[10h]->word))
                output "PSP changed to" bx
```

Error Messages

CMDSPY Compilation Messages   CMDSPY generates explicit script compiler error and warning messages and identifies where problems lie. The following shows sample CMDSPY output when an error is encountered:

```
File: BAD.SCR
Line 2:     field1      (word, ptr, 3)
                               ***
Error: PTR format can only be used with DWORD fields.
```

The first line shows that BAD.SCR was the file CMDSPY was compiling when it encountered the error. The next line shows that it was in line two of the file, and the asterisks show the token that was in error. The last line is the error message. The following shows one of the warning messages that do not stop compilation, but that draw attention to something that may be important and that may affect the results that you expect:

```
File: DD_INTR.SCR
Line 3: intercept interrupt("A:")
                            ***
Warning: Same block device driver supports multiple drives.
16 bytes of code generated for 'A:' driver interrupt script
```

In this example, the compiler has found that the same device driver handles not only A: but presumably B: and C:, as well. Thus the results that you obtain will relate not only to A:, but also to other drives. This condition is not an error, so compilation proceeds.

CMDSPY and INTRSPY In Operation   Both CMDSPY and INTRSPY respond to a -? or /? command line switch with a summary of their command line options. In addition, they generate various operational messages, many of which are purely informational, but some of which are errors. All err on the side of verbosity, so I will only deal with some of the more interesting messages here.

One message you encounter frequently if you are watching INT 21h and use STOP or UNLOAD to terminate the script is

```
Cannot disable current INTRSPY Int 21h handler.
It is handling the DOS Exec of CMDSPY.
Try again immediately and it will disable successfully!
```

When INTRSPY is watching INT 21h, all INT 21h calls, even those functions that are not the subject of the script, are intercepted. Those that need no processing for the script are simply passed on. However, the path for the return from DOS when it has completed a function is back through the INTRSPY INT 21h handler. Since CMDSPY itself is run by the DOS command interpreter issuing a function 4Bh (EXEC), the handler cannot be unloaded until that function has returned. The handler can be, and is, unplugged from INT 21h so that subsequent INT 21h calls do not pass through it. Thus, the second time the CMDSPY STOP or UNLOAD command is issued, the handler can be unloaded successfully.

The following message needs more in the way of intervention to overcome:

```
Cannot disable current INTRSPY script.
Remove any subsequently loaded TSRs and try again...
```

To generate this message, compile the 2F.SCR file included on the accompanying disk, as if to investigate the PHANTOM program presented in Chapter 8. Then load PHANTOM. Finally, attempt to stop the 2F script by typing CMDSPY STOP. The "Cannot disable..." message is generated because, before restoring the INT 2Fh vector that was in place before the 2F.SCR handler was installed, CMDSPY checks that the current vector for the interrupt still points at our handler. If it does not—as in this situation where PHANTOM, a redirector, has installed itself in the chain—to remove the 2F.SCR handler from memory would be disastrous. PHANTOM, in order to keep up its responsibility to prior INT 2Fh handlers, has stored the previous vector, an address in our resident code, and will pass INT 2Fh calls on to it. If our 2F.SCR handler were to unload, the contents of memory at the address that PHANTOM chains to would be indeterminate.

The appropriate action in this case, of course, is to type PHANTOM -U to unload it. At this point, our handler is restored to the head of the INT 2Fh handler chain and can safely unload in turn. Similar action would need to be taken to unload other TSRs that have installed after INTRSPY.

INTRSPY Utility Scripts

Let's now take a look at some mini-applications built using the INTRSPY language.

UNDOC

To begin, let us focus on how INTRSPY quickly shows which undocumented DOS calls a program makes. Some of this material was presented in Chapter 1, but then we were interested only in the final results, not in INTRSPY itself. Here, we focus on just two pieces of system software, the Microsoft CD-ROM Extensions (MSCDEX) and the NetWare shell (NET5). A step-by-step account is given in Figure 5-8. This figure shows some CMDSPY output, which we have until now been omitting as uninteresting.

Figure 5-8: INTRSPY UNDOC.SCR Watching MSCDEX and NET5

```
C:\BIN> intrspy                              (1)
8192 bytes allocated for code and results.
```

```
INTRSPY v2.00 loaded.

C:\BIN> cmdspy compile undoc                         (2)
715 bytes of code generated for Int 21h script
65425 bytes of code generated for Int 20h script
65425 bytes of code generated for Int 27h script
27 bytes of code generated for Int 2Eh script
UNDOC.SCR compiled successfully.
2928 bytes of space used for code and overhead.
5264 bytes of results space available.
Handler for Int 21h started.
Handler for Int 20h started.
Handler for Int 27h started.
Handler for Int 2Eh started.

C:\BIN>mscdex /d:xrw1001 /l:g                        (3)
MSCDEX Version 2.20
Copyright (C) Microsoft Corp. 1986, 1987, 1988, 1989, 1990. All rights reserved
    Drive G: = Driver XRW1001 unit 0

C:\BIN> cmdspy report                                (4)
Handler for Int 21h stopped.
Handler for Int 20h stopped.
Handler for Int 27h stopped.
Handler for Int 2Eh stopped.
UNDOC.SCR compiled successfully.

----------------------- Start of Report ----------------------

------------------------                             (5)

C:\BIN\MSCDEX.EXE
2152: Get List of Lists: 011C:0026
--------- TSR -----------                            (6)
C:\BIN\CMDSPY.EXE
2152: Get List of Lists: 011C:0026

----------------------- End of Report ----------------------

All counters zero.

148 bytes of results reported.

Intrspy returned successful status.

C:\BIN> cmdspy flush                                 (7)
INTRSPY Buffer flushed.

C:\BIN> net5                                         (8)

    .
    .

C:\BIN> cmdspy report                                (9)
Handler for Int 21h stopped.
Handler for Int 20h stopped.
Handler for Int 27h stopped.
Handler for Int 2Eh stopped.
UNDOC.SCR compiled successfully.
----------------------- Start of Report ----------------------

------------------------
C:\NOVELL\NET5.COM
2134: InDOS flag: 0116:0321
2134: InDOS flag: 0116:0321
2152: Get List of Lists: 0116:0026
2150: Set PSP: 0486
2150: Set PSP: 0B5B
--------- TSR -----------
2151: Get PSP: 0486
2152: Get List of Lists: 0116:0026
```

```
------------------------
C:\BIN\CMDSPY.EXE
2152: Get List of Lists: 0116:0026

------------------------ End of Report ------------------------
All counters zero.
148 bytes of results reported.
Intrspy returned successful status.
```

At (1), INTRSPY loads using the default allocations for interrupt handling code and results space. At (2), UNDOC.SCR is compiled. The version of UNDOC.SCR shown in Listing 5-7 includes some functions, such as INT 21h AH=34h and AH=50h, which were documented for DOS 5.0.

Listing 5-7: UNDOC.SCR (Includes Some Documented Calls)

```
;; UNDOC.SCR
intercept 21h
    function 1fh on_exit output "211F: Get Default DPB: " DS ":" BX
    function 32h on_entry output "2132: Get DPB: " DL
    function 34h on_exit output "2134: InDOS flag: " ES ":" BX
    function 50h on_entry output "2150: Set PSP: " BX
    function 51h on_exit output "2151: Get PSP: " BX
    function 52h on_exit output "2152: Get List of Lists: " ES ":" BX
    function 53h on_exit output "2153: Translate BPB"
    function 5dh subfunction 06h
        on_exit output "215D06: Get DOSSWAP: " DS ":" SI
    function 60h
        on_entry output "2160: Canon File: " (DS:SI->byte,asciiz,64)
        on_exit sameline " ==> " (ES:DI->byte,asciiz,64)
    function 25h
        on_entry
            if (al == 28h) output "SetVect INT 28h: KBD busy loop"
;;
;; Use the next functions and ints 20h and 27h to show which
;; program made the undoc DOS call, and to show termination
;;
    function 4bh
        subfunction 00h
            on_entry
                output (DS:DX->byte,asciiz,64)
        subfunction 01h
            on_entry
                output "214B01: EXEC debug: " (DS:DX->byte,asciiz,64)
    function 4ch on_entry output "--------------------------"
    function 31h on_entry output "--------- TSR -----------"
intercept 20h on_entry output "--------------------------"
intercept 27h on_entry output "--------- TSR -----------"
intercept 2eh on_entry output "2E: Execute command"
```

At (3), MSCDEX runs. At (4), a screen report of the results to this point is generated. So that it is possible to distinguish which calls were generated by which program in the event that we want to accumulate results for a while, or in the event that one program spawns others, the script monitors the DOS EXEC and termination functions and interrupts. The line of hyphens at (5) is the end of the run of CMDSPY from (2) that loaded the script. The line following it shows that MSCDEX has started. At (6), MSCDEX has terminated but stayed resident. In the next line, we see the invocation of CMDSPY corresponding to (4). At (7), the result space is cleared; this action isn't really necessary, but it ensures that the next report is limited to what happened in NET5, without reiterating the MSCDEX results. At (8), NET5 is run, and at (9), the results of its loading are reported.

In this experiment, we see that, MSCDEX calls INT 21h Function 52h at load time, and that NET5, in addition to Function 52h, also calls Functions 34h and 50h. The reasons these programs make these particular DOS calls should be clear to you from other chapters. The DOS List of Lists, retrieved with Function 52h, contains a pointer to the DOS Current Directory Structure; MSCDEX alters the CDS. Functions 34h and 50h are both important for TSRs like NET5.

LSTOFLST

In Chapter 2, we went through a fairly laborious process using C to display SysVars, the DOS List of Lists. It is simpler to do this with INTRSPY, as seen in Listing 5-8 (LSTOFLST.SCR).

Listing 5-8: LSTOFLST.SCR Displays SysVars

```
; LSTOFLST.SCR
; INTRSPY script to examine DOS List Of Lists (INT 21h Function 52h)
structure list_20 fields          ; DOS 2.x
    share_retry_count (word, dec)
    retry_delay (word, dec)
    curr_disk_buff (dword, ptr)
    unread_con (word, dec)
    mcb (word)
    dpb (dword, ptr)
    file_tbl (dword, ptr)
    clock (dword, ptr)
    con (dword, ptr)
    num_drives (byte, dec)
    max_bytes (word, dec)
    first_disk_buff (dword, ptr)
    nul (byte,dump,18)
structure list_30 fields          ; DOS 3.0
    share_retry_count (word, dec)
    retry_delay (word, dec)
    curr_disk_buff (dword, ptr)
    unread_con (word, dec)
    mcb (word)
    dpb (dword, ptr)
    file_tbl (dword, ptr)
    clock (dword, ptr)
    con (dword, ptr)
    num_blk_dev (byte, dec)
    max_bytes (word, dec)
    first_disk_buff (dword, ptr)
    curr_dir (dword, ptr)
    lastdrive (byte, dec)
    string_area (dword, ptr)
    size_string_area (word, dec)
    fcb_tbl (dword, ptr)
    fcb_y (word, dec)
    nul (byte,dump,18)
structure list_31 fields          ; DOS 3.1+
    share_retry_count (word, dec)
    retry_delay (word, dec)
    curr_disk_buff (dword, ptr)
    unread_con (word, dec)
    mcb (word)
    dpb (dword, ptr)
    file_tbl (dword, ptr)
    clock (dword, ptr)
    con (dword, ptr)
    max_bytes (word, dec)
    disk_buff (dword, ptr)
    curr_dir (dword, ptr)
    fcb (dword, ptr)
    num_prot_fcb (word, dec)
    num_blk_dev (byte, dec)
```

```
    lastdrive (byte, dec)
    nul (byte,dump,18)
    num_join (word, dec)
intercept 21h
    on_exit
        function 52h
            output "DOS Version is " (OS_MAJOR, dec) "." OS_MINOR
            if (OS_MAJOR == 2)
                output (es:bx[-12]->list_20)
            if (OS_MAJOR == 3) and (OS_MINOR == 0)
                output (es:bx[-12]->list_30)
            if (OS_MAJOR == 3) and (OS_MINOR != 0)
                output (es:bx[-12]->list_31)
                output ""
                output "CON device header"
                    (es:bx[-12]->list_31.con->byte,dump,18)
                output ""
                output "CLOCK device header"
                    (es:bx[-12]->list_31.clock->byte,dump,18)
            if (OS_MAJOR > 3)
                output (es:bx[-12]->list_31)
                output ""
                output "CON device header"
                    (es:bx[-12]->list_31.con->byte,dump,18)
                output ""
                output "CLOCK device header"
                    (es:bx[-12]->list_31.clock->byte,dump,18)
        function 52h
            output ""
;; Issue an Int 21h/AH=52h
generate 21h
    on_entry
        ah = 52h
report
```

Note that you can display an entire structure with one OUTPUT statement. CMDSPY takes care of formatting output according to the format options specified in the structure itself. When you are displaying an entire structure with a single OUTPUT statement, CMDSPY also takes care of displaying the field names. For example, sample output from LSTOFLST.SCR is shown in Figure 5-9. This output was produced under DOS 5.0; the structure is called LIST_31 because the fields we are examining here haven't changed since DOS 3.1.

Figure 5-9: INTRSPY Displays SysVars (the List of Lists)

```
DOS Version is 5.00

LIST_31.SHARE_RETRY_COUNT    : 3
LIST_31.RETRY_DELAY          : 1
LIST_31.CURR_DISK_BUFF       : FFFF:A078
LIST_31.UNREAD_CON           : 0
LIST_31.MCB                  : 0253
LIST_31.DPB                  : 0116:1362
LIST_31.FILE_TBL             : 0116:00CC
LIST_31.CLOCK                : 0070:0059
LIST_31.CON                  : 0070:0023
LIST_31.MAX_BYTES            : 512
LIST_31.DISK_BUFF            : 0116:006D
LIST_31.CURR_DIR             : 0381:0000
LIST_31.FCB                  : 034F:0000
LIST_31.NUM_PROT_FCB         : 0
LIST_31.NUM_BLK_DEV          : 3
LIST_31.LASTDRIVE            : 12
```

```
            on_exit if (cflag == 0) sameline " ==> " al
     function 60h
         on_entry output "2160: Canon " (ds:si->byte,asciiz,32) " ==> "
         on_exit sameline (es:di->byte,asciiz,32)
intercept 25h
    on_entry
        output "25: Abs Disk Read drv " al ", at sectr "
        if (cx == 0FFFFh)
            sameline (ds:bx->big.sector) ", "
                     (ds:bx->big.num) " sctrs"
        if (cx != 0FFFFh)
            sameline dx ", " cx " sctrs"
    on_exit if (cflag==1) sameline " [fail]"
intercept 26h
    on_entry
        output "26: Abs Disk Write drv " al ", at sectr "
        if (cx == 0FFFFh)
            sameline (ds:bx->big.sector) ", "
                     (ds:bx->big.num) " sctrs"
        if (cx != 0FFFFh)
            sameline dx ", " cx " sctrs"
    on_exit if (cflag==1) sameline " [fail]"
intercept 13h
    function 0 on_entry output "1300: Recalibrate drive " dl
    function 1 on_exit output "1301: Disk system status " al
    function 2
        on_entry
            output "1302: Read " al " sctrs: drv " dl ", head " dh
                   ", sctr " cl ", trk " ch
        on_exit if (cflag==1)
            sameline " - FAILED (" ah ")"
    function 3
        on_entry
            output "1303: Write " al " sctrs: drv " dl ", head " dh
                   ", sctr " cl ", trk " ch
        on_exit if (cflag==1)
            sameline " - FAILED (" ah ")"
    function 4
        on_entry
            output "1304: Verify " al " sctrs: drv " dl ", head " dh
                   ", sctr " cl ", trk " ch
        on_exit if (cflag==1)
            sameline " - FAILED (" ah ")"
    function 5
        on_entry
            output "1305: Format " al " sctrs: drv " dl ", head " dh
                   ", sctr " cl ", trk " ch
        on_exit if (cflag==1)
            sameline " - FAILED (" ah ")"
    function 8
        on_entry
            output "1308: Get drive params for " dl
        on_exit
            if (cflag==1) sameline " - FAILED (" ah ")"
            if (cflag==0)
                output "Type " bl ", " dl " drvs, max head " dh
                       ", max sctr " cl ", max cyls " ch
    function 0ch
        on_entry output "130C: Seek to cyl " ch ", drv " dl ", head " dh
        on_exit if (cflag==1) sameline " - FAILED (" ah ")"
    function 0dh
        on_entry output "130D: Alternate reset drive " dl
        on_exit if (cflag==1) sameline " - FAILED (" ah ")"
```

```
function 10h
    on_entry output "1310: Test drive " dl
    on_exit sameline " - status " ah
function 15h
    on_entry output "1315: Get type drv " dl
    on_exit
        sameline ": "
        if (ah==0) sameline "No disk present : sctrs " cx dx
        if (ah==1) sameline "Floppy - Not changed : sctrs " cx dx
        if (ah==2) sameline "Floppy - changed : sctrs " cx dx
        if (ah==3) sameline "Fixed disk : sctrs " cx dx
function 16h
    on_entry output "1316: Get media change drv " dl ": "
    on_exit
        if (ah==0) sameline "Unchanged"
        if (ah==6) sameline "Changed"
function 17h
    on_entry
        output "1317: Set type drv " dl ": "
        if (al==0) sameline "no disk"
        if (al==1) sameline "reg disk in reg drv"
        if (al==2) sameline "reg disk in high dens. drv"
        if (al==3) sameline "high dens. disk in high dens. drv"
        if (al==4) sameline "720k disk in 720k drv"
        if (al==5) sameline "720k disk in 1.44M drv"
        if (al==6) sameline "1.44M disk in 1.44M drv"
function 18h
    on_entry
        output "1318: Set media type drv " dl ": sctrs/trk " cl
            ", trks " ch ": "
    on_exit
        if (ah==0) sameline "OK"
        if (ah==1) sameline "Not available"
        if (ah==0ch) sameline "Not supported"
        if (ah==80h) sameline "No disk in drive"

run "%1 %2 %3 %4"
report
```

Note that the script dumps the results to the screen. It is sometimes useful to see the output immediately and then to be able to review it in an editor. To capture the results to a file, simply run CMDSPY REPORT > FORMAT.OUT after the run has completed.

Figure 5-10 shows a small portion of the output from DISK.SCR that results from formatting a double density 5.25" diskette. You can see that there is also a small amount of output not generated by FORMAT itself. The first four lines of the CMDSPY REPORT also show DOS loading FORMAT.COM from the hard disk (drive 80h).

Figure 5-10: INTRSPY DISK.SCR Watches FORMAT B:

```
1302: Read 01 sctrs: drv 80, head 03, sctr 06, trk 71
1302: Read 01 sctrs: drv 80, head 01, sctr 1D, trk 00
1302: Read 40 sctrs: drv 80, head 03, sctr 06, trk 71
1302: Read 01 sctrs: drv 80, head 04, sctr 07, trk 71
21440D: IOCTL drive 02 [60: Get Device Parameters]
214409: IOCTL drive 02 Remote?
214409: IOCTL drive 02 Remote?
2160: Canon B:CON ==> B:/CON
21440D: IOCTL drive 02 [60: Get Device Parameters]
21440F: IOCTL Set Logical Drive 02 ==> 00
Insert new diskette for drive
B
:
and press ENTER when ready...
```

```
21440D: IOCTL drive 02
21440D: IOCTL drive 02
Checking existing disk format.

25: Abs Disk Read drv 01, at sectr 0000, FFFF sctrs
1302: Read 02 sctrs: drv 01, head 00, sctr 01, trk 00
Saving UNFORMAT information.

2132: Get DPB drive 02

... details omitted ...

1316: Get media change drv 01: Unchanged
25: Abs Disk Read drv 01, at sectr
1302: Read 01 sctrs: drv 01, head 01, sctr 01, trk 00
25: Abs Disk Read drv 01, at sectr
1302: Read 02 sctrs: drv 01, head 00, sctr 08, trk 00
25: Abs Disk Read drv 01, at sectr

... details omitted ...

21440D: IOCTL drive 02 [40: Set Device Parameters]
21440D: IOCTL drive 02 [42: Format and Verify Track]
1318: Set media type drv 01: sctrs/trk OF, trks 4F: OK
21440D: IOCTL drive 02
1304: Verify OF sctrs: drv 01, head 00, sctr 01, trk 00
  0
percent completed.
21440D: IOCTL drive 02
1304: Verify OF sctrs: drv 01, head 01, sctr 01, trk 00
  1
percent completed.
21440D: IOCTL drive 02
1304: Verify OF sctrs: drv 01, head 00, sctr 01, trk 01

... details omitted ...

100
percent completed.
Format complete.

26: Abs Disk Write drv 01, at sectr 0000, FFFF sctrs
1303: Write 01 sctrs: drv 01, head 00, sctr 01, trk 00

... details omitted ...

21440D: IOCTL drive 02 [40: Set Device Parameters]
2132: Get DPB drive 02
1302: Read 01 sctrs: drv 01, head 00, sctr 01, trk 00
1302: Read 01 sctrs: drv 01, head 00, sctr 02, trk 00
1302: Read 01 sctrs: drv 01, head 00, sctr 01, trk 00

... details omitted ...
```

Whereas DISK.SCR groups functions together by interrupt and function number, the output resulting from running the script together with the DOS FORMAT command is quite different. Here you see the nesting of BIOS calls from DOS calls. In Figure 5-10, you can clearly see how FORMAT displays the "Head: XX Cylinder: XX" odometer (which we're able to show here by monitoring INT 21h Function 40h). It then calls DOS INT 21h Function 44h Subfunction 0Dh to format and verify a track, which, in turn, indirectly calls BIOS INT 13h Functions 18h, 05h, and 04h to format and verify the sectors that make up the track. After the format itself is complete, as the above INTRSPY output shows, to create the FAT and root directory on the newly formatted disk, FORMAT calls the DOS Absolute Disk Write interrupt (INT 26h). This interrupt, in turn, indirectly calls the BIOS Write Sector Function (INT 13h Function 03h). (Indirectly: DOS calls a device driver, which in this case calls the BIOS; see Chapter 8.)

DISK.SCR handles INT 25h and INT 26h calls on systems with partitions larger than 32 megabytes. This function is important even when you are formatting a floppy disk because even then

FORMAT uses the alternate form of INT 26h, where CX holds the value FFFFh, and DS:BX points to a structure that in DISK.SCR is called BIG. You can also see from this display that FORMAT uses two undocumented DOS calls: Resolve Path String to Canonical Path String (INT 21h Function 60h) and Get DPB (INT 21h Function 32h). Again, having INTRSPY means that you can do this kind of exploring without disassembling the code.

MEM

One last INTRSPY script worth examining is MEM.SCR (Listing 5-11), which, in 24 lines of INTRSPY code, can monitor all DOS memory allocation by intercepting INT 21h Functions 48h (Allocate), 49h (Release), and 4Ah (Resize). Again, Function 4Bh (EXEC) is monitored as well, so that you know which program performed the memory operation. Chapter 7 presents another, more comprehensive version of MEM.

Listing 5-11: MEM.SCR Watches DOS Memory Management Calls

```
; MEM.SCR
intercept 21h
    function 48h
        on_entry
            output "ALLOC " (bx, dec) " paras"
        on_exit
            if (cflag==1)
                sameline " FAIL (" (ax, dec) "), only " (bx, dec) " available"
            if (cflag==0)
                sameline " - seg " ax "h"
    function 49h
        on_entry output "FREE seg " es "h"
        on_exit if (cflag==1) sameline " denied (" (ax, dec) "h)"
    function 4ah
        on_entry
            output "REALLOC seg " es "h to " (bx, dec) " paras"
        on_exit
            if (cflag==1)
                sameline " FAIL (" (ax, dec) "), only " (bx, dec) " available"
    function 4bh
        on_entry output (ds:dx->byte,asciiz,64)
```

MEM can be used to track down memory allocation bugs, but it is also useful in a hands-on examination of the DOS memory allocation issues discussed in Chapter 3 of this book. For example, you can see immediately that DOS programs typically are allocated all available memory:

```
C:\UNDOC\MAXEY\HELLO.EXE
ALLOC 65535 paras FAIL (8), only 37705 available
ALLOC 37705 paras - seg 161Bh
FREE seg 161Bh
```

Space does not allow me to show all the uses that even my limited imagination has found for INTRSPY.

Writing a Generic Interrupt Handler

Let's step back now and discuss some of the design issues behind INTRSPY. Some of this sounds like a functional specification for INTRSPY because, in fact, it does come from the functional specification initially drawn up for INTRSPY.

Traditionally, DOS programmers would write a host of small, tailor-made programs to perform the kind of exploration we have been doing. In the past, I have written separate programs to monitor NetBIOS (INT 5Ch) calls, DOS (INT 21h) calls, and EMS (INT 67h) calls. The cycle has been to write a simple TSR, debug it, and eventually have something that could printf or writeln register values into or out of intercepted functions. In principle, that initial version cost a few hours of thought, programming, and debugging effort. Subsequent versions that refined the list of functions being monitored or that added a new or increased capability came easier and more quickly, but they still required recompilation and debugging.

All monitoring programs are essentially the same, however, whether they monitor DOS, NetBIOS, EMS, or anything else. This suggests that it should be possible to write a generic monitoring program. By extension, this means writing a generic interrupt handler. The actual interrupts, functions, or subfunctions you wish to monitor would be parameters to the generic interrupt handler. To ensure that building the tools doesn't detract or distract from your investigations, the rapid modification of parameters, without the necessity of debugging, is a high priority. The sheer number of parameters that need to be within reach, however, and the need for a broad range of capabilities suggest that a command-line, switch-based TSR is unlikely to be adequate. A script-interpreting, precompiled interrupt handling tool would be better.

Because DOS uses a number of different interrupt numbers and provides its services through functions and subfunctions within these interrupts (generally specified via AH and AL), and because you would want to be able to monitor these interrupts and their function calls selectively, INTRSPY must be capable of monitoring any subfunction of any function of any interrupt. It should, therefore, allow you to build some useful logging and exploration applications, not just in the field of undocumented DOS calls but in a whole range of DOS-related and non-DOS-related interrupt-based services. Logging DOS memory usage would be a snap, for example. Relating DOS disk access to the underlying device-driver calls and BIOS interrupts, watching EMS calls, recording a NetBIOS session: All these functions should be within reach simply by using different, easily modifiable parameters. INTRSPY should be a platform for snap-on debug tools for PC software developers.

The preliminary specification is beginning to form. The program should be script-driven. This allows for transportable, repeatable, and canned experiments and debugging tools. The program should intrude as little as possible. That is, it should make no DOS calls, should hook few interrupts, and should consume little memory. Any interrupts that are generated, any memory that is consumed, any interrupts that are intercepted, other than those that are supposed to be intercepted—all these factors constitute noise and can affect, potentially in many ways, the systems being studied. If CMDSPY made undocumented DOS calls, for example, these would show up in the report from UNDOC.SCR. Thus, it is perhaps ironic that in a book devoted to the advertisement of undocumented DOS calls as crucial tools in the development of TSRs and system level software, strenuous pains have gone into developing CMDSPY and INTRSPY with as few undocumented DOS calls as possible. Once it is resident, INTRSPY generates no interrupts and uses no DOS services whatsoever.

The program should provide dumps of register contents, flags, and DOS and other structures in memory. The STRUCTURE capability was specified initially because of the DOS List of Lists structure and the associated DOS Function 52h (see LSTOFLST.SCR previously). As was hinted at, however, once an initial capability of this type has been provided, building in a little flexibility can make it useful in many originally unimagined ways. As was already said, the central requirement is to be able to focus, from session to session, on different subfunctions of different functions of different interrupts; reconfiguration should be easy and painless so that it does not impede learning, experimentation, or the debugging progress.

Access should be available both before and after an interrupt is serviced. The program needs to be able to see and act on the parameters that the caller supplies, as well as the structures, registers, and flags that the interrupt function returns.

A non-resident transient portion should compile the scripts, hand them off to the resident portion, and decode the output. When we were first discussing the specification for INTRSPY, we had been using some of the other available interrupt monitoring software packages. It was not clear that any of them offered the flexibility we needed.

The options here were either a shell implementation or a TSR/transient controller combination. In a shell implementation, programs under scrutiny would be run from within the system. Much like those of a debugger, a shell implementation's facilities would be available until the user quit the user interface. The problems with this approach include potentially much reduced memory availability for the program being studied and less flexibility to run commands and batch files as well as programs. Benefits include control over the environment and the ability to limit monitoring to a specific run of a particular program. Thus, INTRSPY includes this as an option with the RUN statement. We decided to go with the TSR/transient controller combination. A relatively small TSR would perform the monitoring function, and a separate, less memory-constrained program would perform script compilation, result formatting, and printing; it would handle all communications with the TSR. We saw this approach as preferable because the transient portion itself can be made to act as a shell.

This approach does have its disadvantages, however. Complexity is introduced through the decoupling of the compilation from the execution of the script. This is awkward only because, unlike normal compilation and execution cycles, script source is needed to be able to decode the results of the execution.

The resident portion stores results, rather than write them to disk or pop-up screens. This removes the need to plan for file I/O within the generic interrupt service routine (ISR) code. File I/O by necessity generates interrupts, changes the state of the operating system by a little or a lot, and leads to coding complexity when implemented properly in TSRs (as is shown in Chapter 9).

The Problem with Intel's INT

Now that we have explained how to use INTRSPY and discussed some of the thinking behind it, we need to discuss briefly some problems with the Intel INT instruction. These problems stand in the way of anyone seeking to write a generic interrupt handler. The INT instruction is the source of a great deal of the flexibility in the PC architecture because the ability to get and set interrupt vectors means that system services, including DOS itself, are infinitely extensible, replaceable, and monitorable. Yet, given its importance, the INT instruction is also remarkably inflexible in two key ways:

- An interrupt handler does not know which interrupt number invoked it.
- The INT instruction itself expects an immediate operand: you cannot write MOV AX, 21h and then INT AX; you must write INT 21h.

The first problem raises the question, How will the program trap a variable number of user-specificable interrupts? There are at least three possibilities here.

The first possibility is to use a generic interrupt service routine for all interrupts the user specifies. When invoked, the ISR can use the return address on the stack to find out what INT instruction issued the interrupt.

This would indeed be an elegant, economical solution. Unfortunately, it is an unreliable strategy because many high-level-language compilers (and the important Simulate_Int and Exec_Int functions in Windows Enhanced mode) compile interrupts into PUSHF and far CALL instruction sequences, rather than do an actual INT. Others push the address of the handler on the stack and RETF to it. In order to cover the different ways to simulate an INT instruction, a generic ISR would need a small disassembler.

One reason for all these different ways of performing what should simply be an INT is in fact the second problem—that the INT instruction itself can't be parameterized. Thus, different compiler vendors implement functions such as int86x() differently.

The other crippling failure of this first possible implementation is that it relies on the caller's stack being large enough for our interrupt processing. Bear in mind that the program is going to have to be able to handle DOS internal function calls, for which DOS will have switched to its own small stack of less than 400 bytes (for exact sizes, see the appendix entry for INT 21h Function 5D06h).

A second possibility involves coding 256 small stubs. Only those interrupts the user specifies would be redirected to the appropriate stubs. When invoked, a stub would record its interrupt number, save away the caller's stack, switch to the program's internal stack, then call the generic ISR. This is a better solution but will waste several kilobytes of memory.

There are variations on these, but none were appealing, and I decided to go with what I thought was at least a more interesting solution—that is, to allocate a custom ISR object on the heap for each interrupt to be monitored. I called it an object because it was a structure containing machine code to perform stack switching, registers for saving state, and the specific compiled code associated with the interrupt processing. INTRSPY contained a skeleton ISR that was copied onto the heap and fixed up with some run time-dependent addresses. The interrupt processing was then actually performed by procedures called from the ISR machine code on the heap.

Will the program have to fix up the relative data structure offsets at run time because it is allocating on the heap and therefore cannot expect every ISR structure to be paragraph aligned? No. Each ISR starts on a paragraph boundary, wasting up to 15 bytes to ensure it. This amount is insignificant and allows the entry point, as well as all the data fields in the ISR structure, to be at a constant offset. INTRSPY can thus be viewed as a program loader for which the programs are just small pieces of ISR code, and the handler space substitutes for DOS memory.

How should the interrupt processing instructions be stored? My first reaction was to think in terms of compilation into machine language. Instead, for the first version, I implemented a linked tree of small structures that describes the entities in the processing. The resident ISR processor in version 1.0 walked the linked list of function records stored for the interrupt that has been intercepted, processing the subfunction branches of each. Each subfunction branch was a linked list of subfunction records, each of which pointed to a "before" and "after" branch. These branches were, in turn, linked lists of records that specified the conditionals and resulting data storage to be performed before and after the interrupt is serviced.

Changed Implementation in INTRSPY 2.0

Version 2.0 was born out of experience with version 1.0, which is as it should be. A number of those early decisions have been overturned, and some additional thoughts have lead to other design changes.

For example, I now realize that I should probably have bitten the bullet of machine code generation right from the start. Many of the powerful newer script language features have required less incremental effort to implement than they would have from the database approach of INTRSPY 1.0. Indeed, many would simply not have been feasible with that approach.

It also became clear that INTRSPY needed to be little more than a home in memory for handlers generated and managed by CMDSPY. Much of the conversation between CMDSPY and INTRSPY was unnecessary; INTRSPY did not need a hand in it. Instead, CMDSPY should treat INTRSPY as a block of memory that it could act on directly. This approach produced a dramatic drop in the size of the base (that is, ignoring handler/result space allocation) INTRSPY memory footprint from 20K in 1.0 to less than 7K in 2.0.

Note that for 1.0, many readers wanted to know the undocumented interface between INTRSPY and CMDSPY, in order to write their own CMDSPY replacements. This was documented in Ralf Brown and Jim Kyle's *PC Interrupts* (odd that we had undocumented stuff in *Undocumented DOS!*), but now most of this goes away. The interface in 2.0 is simple.

Implementation

Let us take a look at the structure of INTRSPY and its transient controller CMDSPY. The system functions as follows:

- INTRSPY is loaded and reserves some memory for holding intercept code and results data.

■   CMDSPY compiles the specified script file on the basis of STRUCTURE and INTERCEPT constructs; it then implements the language as specified in the earlier *INTRSPY System User Guide*. CMDSPY installs the compiled INTERCEPT code in the memory held by INTRSPY.

When the script has been compiled, CMDSPY stores the name of the input file that has just been processed, the drive and directory that were current when it was processed, and any command line arguments that were passed to the script within INTRSPY's data segment for later retrieval. Finally, CMDSPY enables the intercept handlers that have been installed; that is, CMDSPY ensures that all handlers are plugged into the addresses that they are to intercept, such as those in the interrupt vector table.

Programs are run, commands are issued, and INTRSPY builds up the results in memory. When results are to be output, CMDSPY disables the installed handlers by disengaging them from the addresses that they are intercepting.

CMDSPY then locates the buffer of results in INTRSPY's memory. Although the script language supports structure definitions and literal strings for output, these compile into offsets, lengths, and reference numbers. In order to decode the results that are stored in INTRSPY, CMDSPY must recompile the script. In order to do that relatively safely, CMDSPY must make current the drive and directory that were current at the time the script was first compiled, load the file as it was specified on the command line the first time, and pass to it the same command line arguments it was passed the first time. This is why CMDSPY stored those pieces of information after initial script compilation.

Having reloaded the original script file, CMDSPY walks the results buffer, formatting and printing the data using the literal and structure information from the script.

Pitfalls I Fell In

To wrap up this brief explanation of the INTRSPY implementation, let's look at some of the sticks that DOS jams in the spokes of a project like this. The first concerns a class of DOS functions that behave in a manner that is obviously logical, but not necessarily obvious. These are the process termination functions, and their unusual behavior is that they do not return.

I only realized this fairly obvious fact (failure to return is generally what one wants in a termination routine!) during a debugging session that had dragged on into the night while developing the first version of INTRSPY. After some time with a script running, INTRSPY would just lock up my machine. I traced the problem fairly rapidly to a corrupted register save field in the ISR record in the handler space. Because DOS, while not reentrant, nests function calls—as when a program invoked by a function 4Bh performs file I/O before the function 4Bh completes—I had allowed a function/subfunction stack of 16 entries; it became clear that this stack was being overfilled and its contents were spilling out into the rest of the record. As soon as any of the saved SP, SS, CS, or IP values were corrupted, INTRSPY returned to forever-neverland! I knew that DOS did not nest that deep, and it finally hit me . . . (sound of hand slapping forehead). Specifically, then, when a termination function is called, a DOS intercepter must tidy up any function or return address stack while still in pre-processing mode because, unlike normal interception, the DOS intercepter will not have an opportunity to do so during post-processing.

The situation is complicated still further by Ctrl-Break and Critical Errors. When a DOS function that checks for these conditions gives control to the DOS break processor, in all cases it aborts the currently executing function and backs up its internal state to the way it was on entry to the DOS function dispatcher. It then either restarts the original function or, in the case of an Abort, replaces the original function request in AH with a termination request. In that case, the INTRSPY intercepter does not receive control back from the function it is currently intercepting, and the function stack is now misaligned. The solution is for INTRSPY to intercept INT 23h (Ctrl-C) and 24h (Critical Error) and recalibrate the stack on entry to the next function intercepted if the application handler requests termination. This involves decrementing the function stack pointer until the previous EXEC or start-of-stack, whichever comes first.

Int 25h and 26h, the Absolute Sector Read/Write interrupts must also be special cased. Even though they are accessed through the interrupt mechanism, they are implemented as far call routines. This means that on return, the flags that were pushed onto the stack by the int 25h instruction are still on the stack, and that SP is not as it was before the instruction was issued. Therfore the stack must be adjusted by the caller.

Another DOS-specific complication that we saw when reviewing CMDSPY messages involves the attempt to unload an Int 21h handler. As we saw, CMDSPY itself is running as part of a DOS EXEC (Function 4Bh), in which case the ISR handling it is in mid-interrupt. Restoring the vector and potentially replacing that ISR with another one would be disastrous since the DOS EXEC function would return to an address that had been superseded.

The key thing to remember here is that all this complication is encapsulated within the generic interrupt handler in INTRSPY. You can write INTRSPY scripts happily without agonizing over the usual complications of interrupt handling because INTRSPY's job is to handle these details. This is a key benefit to using such an interrupt handling language.

Because INTRSPY is becoming a commercial product, source code is not provided. If you are interested in getting a general idea of how an interrupt monitoring program works, you might want to look at Bob Flanders' and Michael Holmes' "Collecting Program Statistics with INFORMER," in *PC Magazine C Lab Notes* (Ziff-Davis Press, 1993).

The Future of INTRSPY

INTRSPY is now at version 2.0 and is a robust and widely used debugging tool. Pressure for additional features and support has been growing, and although 2.0 is a considerable advance over 1.0, a still more significant upgrade is already planned for the first commercial release of INTRSPY version 3.0. A partial list of the intended new features for inclusion in that release includes:

- A fully-fledged language along the lines of C, incorporating support for named variables, math, and a powerful set of built-in functions.
- An improved user interface, with automatic script generation tools.
- Secondary monitor capabilities for real-time monitoring of events.
- Additional result storage options, including XMS, file, and transmission via serial or network connection to a second PC.
- Enhanced report and screen formatting capabilities.
- Full documentation.

For more information, please contact me through my CompuServe address (70401,3057).

## CHAPTER 6

Disassembling DOS

by Andrew Schulman

The previous chapter showed that it possible to discover a lot about a program without resorting to what is often called reverse engineering. Simply by examining a program's outward behavior, a utility such as INTRSPY shows, for example, that Windows uses the undocumented DOS Get SysVars function, and that Microsoft's QuickC makes the weird SetPSP(0) and SetPSP(-1) calls that are discussed in Chapter 4.

But such external examination of a program's behavior can take us only so far. INTRSPY can't tell us *why* Windows calls Get SysVars—that is, which fields it uses in the SysVars data structure)— nor can INTRSPY tell us why QuickC passes the illegal values 0 and -1 to the DOS Set PSP function. To figure out why a program behaves in a certain way, you need to actually get inside the program. This requires disassembly.

Disassembly is particularly important to understanding what goes on inside MS-DOS itself. What does DOS actually do when a program calls the Get SysVars function, for example? How does DOS carry out an INT 21h AH=4Bh EXEC request? How do DOS 5.0 and 6.0 interact with Windows? To answer questions like these, there's no substitute for looking at the DOS code. Though Microsoft does produce a DOS OEM Adaptation Kit (OAK) that we discuss later in this chapter, source code to MS-DOS is not widely available. For those of us without the DOS source code, understanding DOS requires disassembling it.

The goal of this chapter is to acquire an understanding of DOS internals, that is, to get an intuitive feel for what goes on when a program makes an INT 21h DOS call. Chapter 2 briefly presented a disassembly of two DOS functions, INT 21h AH=0Eh (Set Default Drive; see Listings 2-7 and 2-8) and INT 21h AH=19h (Get Default Drive). But how did we find the code for these functions in the first place? A key purpose of this chapter is to present a close look at the key part of MS-DOS, the INT 21h handler, with its function dispatch table, which contains pointers to the code that handles each individual INT 21h function. Armed with this table, you can readily consult the code for any particular DOS function whose implementation interests you. You can apply the same technique to other pieces of code, such as DR DOS or the INT 21h hook in Novell NetWare's NETX.COM (see Chapter 4).

The resident DOS code is found in two files, IO.SYS and MSDOS.SYS—sometimes named IBMBIO.COM and IBMDOS.COM. DOS 6.0 and higher also has DBLSPACE.BIN, which Microsoft usually considers a third member of the DOS kernel. While there are various ways to examine the code in these files on disk, this chapter instead examines the INT 21h handler in memory, using Microsoft's own DEBUG, a primitive though handy tool that comes with MS-DOS.

Part of the reason for using DEBUG, rather than a more sophisticated debugger or disassembly tool, is to underline the point that Microsoft itself provides the means for reverse engineering DOS.

Since programmers frequently have questions about the legalities of disassembly, this chapter also briefly discusses the law surrounding reverse engineering and trade secrets.

Of course, there is more to DOS than just IO.SYS and MSDOS.SYS. There are also external programs such as COMMAND.COM, MSCDEX.EXE, and PRINT.COM, which is probably the most heavily disassembled DOS utility and the one on which many TSR writers first figured out their craft.

Whether or not you disassemble DOS depends of course on what interests you. The examination of the INT 21h dispatch code in this chapter may provide all you ever wanted to know about how DOS functions internally. On the other hand, if you absolutely, positively must know exactly what is going on inside MS-DOS and you have the money to pay for this information, you may want to license Microsoft's DOS OEM Adaptation Kit, which includes assembly language and C source code for many parts of DOS, as well as .OBJ files with full symbolic information for those parts where direct source code is not provided. We take a quick look at the OAK contents later on.

What is MS-DOS?

MS-DOS is a bit like pornography. Everyone knows what it is when they see it, but almost no one can define it.

First of all, MS-DOS is *not* the C> prompt. While that infamous user interface seems practically synonymous with MS-DOS, it is not actually a necessary part of DOS. The C> prompt is provided by COMMAND.COM, which (as Chapter 10 explains in more detail) anyone can easily replace. As indicated by the shell= statement in CONFIG.SYS, COMMAND.COM is just a shell around the DOS kernel. Other shells, such as 4DOS or the MKS Korn shell, are widely available. Get rid of COMMAND.COM, and you still have MS-DOS.

From a programmer's perspective, MS-DOS seems like a collection of INT 21h functions. But this isn't quite accurate either. While the INT 21h functions are the most important service provided by DOS, DOS and INT 21h are not synonymous. Several application wrappers in Chapter 2 (Listings 2-20 and 2-21) already showed how easy it is for a normal program to fiddle with INT 21h calls before or after DOS itself gets them. That a piece of code handles INT 21h doesn't necessarily make it part of DOS.

So if DOS ain't necessarily the C> prompt or the INT 21h interface, what then is it? And where is it?

The "what" part is difficult to answer, except to note that DOS is in many ways what textbooks on operating systems call a microkernel. DOS provides a small bare minimum of services, on top of which other, more sophisticated, services can be built. Think of DOS as a software motherboard, into which the user is free to plug various extensions. These extensions come not only from Microsoft but also from key third-party vendors such as Novell, Quarterdeck, Qualitas, Symantec, Central Point, and Phar Lap. DOS is the arena in which all these companies' products must both compete and work together.

Well, that was vague enough!

Mercifully, the "where" part at least is easy to answer. MS-DOS consists of two files, IO.SYS and MSDOS.SYS. In both IBM PC-DOS and Novell's DR DOS, these files are called IBMBIO.COM and IBMDOS.COM. Despite the .SYS file names, these are not device drivers, but binary images. In MS-DOS 6.0, there is a third file, DBLSPACE.BIN, which Microsoft generally considers a full-fledged third member of the DOS kernel—the SYS and FORMAT /S commands in DOS 6.0 copy DBLSPACE.BIN over to a floppy, along with IO.SYS and MSDOS.SYS. Take these two or three files, and you've got DOS. Of course, you'll also need a shell such as COMMAND.COM in order to get much work done.

Among other things, MSDOS.SYS contains the DOS dispatch function, which is DOS's handler for INT 21h calls. There are other DOS functions, such as INT 25h, 26h, and 2Fh, that MSDOS.SYS and IO.SYS handle as well.

IO.SYS consists of two parts, a loader (MSLOAD.COM) and BIOS support code (MSBIO.BIN); Microsoft creates IO.SYS by concatenating these two files:

```
copy /b msload.com+msbio.bin io.sys
```

IO.SYS is *not* "the BIOS," as books on DOS programming frequently claim, but merely the DOS *interface* to the BIOS. IO.SYS contains the standard device drivers such as CON, AUX, LPT1, and COM1 (see Chapter 7). These device drivers are implemented using BIOS calls. For example, the CON driver built into IO.SYS (more precisely, MSBIO.BIN) makes INT 10h and INT 16h calls to the ROM BIOS video and keyboard routines.

The MSLOAD.COM portion of IO.SYS contains a famous set of routines called SYSINIT, which is responsible for the bootstrap loading of DOS.

We won't discuss SYSINIT here, as it has already been covered elsewhere (see "How MS-DOS Is Loaded" in Chapter 2 of Ray Duncan's *Advanced MS-DOS Programming*, and "The Components of MS-DOS" in Duncan's *MS-DOS Encyclopedia*). And practically every other book on DOS programming seems to repeat this same basic material on SYSINIT. Presumably this is not just because the bootstrap loading of DOS is an interesting subject, but also because Microsoft already documents SYSINIT in the DOS OAK. Geoff Chappell provides a far more original and useful description of DOS startup in his *DOS Internals*, Chapters 1 ("The System Configuration"), 2 ("The System Footprint"), and 3 ("The Startup Sequence"). For example, Chappell is the first author to make the connection between SYSINIT and the List of Lists structure (whose actual name in the DOS source code is SysInitVars).

So the DOS boot sequence is fairly well known. What hasn't been provided before, amazingly, is any description of what DOS looks like once it is up and running. This primarily requires a description of DOS's INT 21h handler and the INT 21h dispatch table. In other words, what code runs when you make an INT 21h call to DOS? Scores of DOS programming books of course describe what this or that DOS function call does, but few describe how any of these function calls work, and none to our knowledge—aside from a brief discussion of DOS stack switching in Microsoft's *MS-DOS Encyclopedia* (pp. 353-355)—describes the DOS function call mechanism itself. This seems far more important than providing yet another standard description of how DOS boots up or how SYSINIT moves segments around in memory.

One of our tech reviewers writes that "parts of the boot sequence are NOT well known! In DOS 6.0 and up, there's the mechanism that IO.SYS uses to preload DBLSPACE.BIN. And in DOS 7.0 (Chicago), if CONFIG.SYS contains the setting DOS=ENHANCED, there is code in IO.SYS that loads DOS386.EXE, which is a big executable similar to WIN386.EXE."

Disassembling IO.SYS and MSDOS.SYS

The choice between describing SYSINIT or describing the INT 21h handler is an important one, because the portion of DOS which one is interested in looking at largely determines how one goes about disassembling DOS.

To look at DOS initialization, you either have to acquire the DOS OAK (which provides assembly language source code to IO.SYS, including the SYSINIT modules), or you have to disassemble the actual IO.SYS and MSDOS.SYS files on disk. These files are hidden system files, which, however, can be easily unhidden:

```
C:\UNDOC\CHAP6>attrib -h -s \*.sys
```

IO.SYS is about 32K, and MSDOS.SYS is about 37K. Once unhidden, these two files can be disassembled, even with the u (unassemble) command in the primitive DEBUG utility that comes with DOS. After running ATTRIB to unhide MSDOS.SYS or IO.SYS, type DIR to find the file's size. DEBUG loads the file at address 100h, so add 100h to the file size (converted to hexadecimal) to yield the disassembly end-range. For example, if MSDOS.SYS is 37,506 (9282h) bytes:

```
C:\UNDOC2\CHAP6>type msdos.scr
u 0100 9382
q

C:\UNDOC2\CHAP6>debug \msdos.sys < msdos.scr > msdos.lst
```

The resulting MSDOS.LST is about one megabyte in size; if you use a disassembler such as Sourcer, the file is about 800K. In some ways, the output from such a straightforward disassembly of MSDOS.SYS looks quite useful. For example, you can quite plainly see DOS's INT 21h handler inspecting the caller's function number in AH. This is the DOS code called whenever a program generates an INT 21h:

```
6A76:040B FA            CLI
6A76:040C 80FC6C        CMP AH,6C        ; is function > 6Ch?
6A76:040F 77D2          JA  03E3         ; yes: error
6A76:0411 80FC33        CMP AH,33
6A76:0414 7218          JB  042E
6A76:0416 74A2          JZ  03BA
6A76:0418 80FC64        CMP AH,64
; ... etc. ...
```

Likewise the MSDOS.SYS INT 2Fh handler is also visible. IO.SYS has its own INT 2Fh handler, and in the last line of the code fragment below, you can see the INT 2Fh handler in MSDOS.SYS jump to the one in IO.SYS, using a hard-wired address:

```
1C53:07B9 FB            STI
1C53:07BA 80FC11        CMP AH,11
1C53:07BD 750A          JNZ 07C9
;;; Go to 07BFh if an INT 2Fh call belonging to an external
;;; program such as a redirector, SHARE, or NLSFUNC, ends up
;;; in MSDOS.SYS. This means the external program isn't loaded.
1C53:07BF 0AC0          OR  AL,AL        ; is AL=0?
; ... error handling ...
1C53:07C9 80FC10        CMP AH,10        ; INT 2Fh AH=10h? (SHARE)
1C53:07CC 74F1          JZ  07BF ; got here, so SHARE not loaded
1C53:07CE 80FC14        CMP AH,14        ; INT 2Fh AH=14h? (NLSFUNC)
1C53:07D1 74EC          JZ  07BF ; got here, so NLSFUNC not loaded
1C53:07D3 80FC12        CMP AH,12        ; INT 2Fh AH=12h?
1C53:07D6 7503          JNZ 07DB
1C53:07D8 E99701        JMP 0972         ; handle DOS internal functions
1C53:07DB 80FC16        CMP AH,16        ; INT 2Fh AH=16h? (Windows)
1C53:07DE 740D          JZ  07ED         ; might be Windows broadcast
1C53:07E0 80FC46        CMP AH,46        ; INT 2Fh AH=46h?
1C53:07E3 7503          JNZ 07E8
1C53:07E5 E93E01        JMP 0926
1C53:07E8 EA05007000    JMP 0070:0005    ; see if IO.SYS wants it
```

But while at first this looks useful, after a few minutes it becomes clear that the quality of the unassembly is unfortunately quite poor. (Much better versions of these INT 21h and INT 2Fh handlers are shown later in Figures 6-7 and 6-13.) For example, the most important part of the INT 21h handler uses the function number in AH as an index into a dispatch table:

```
;;; previously moved AH func number into BX
6A76:04FE 8B9FA73E      MOV BX,[BX+3EA7]
6A76:0502 36871EEA05    XCHG BX,SS:[05EA]
6A76:0507 368E1EEC05    MOV DS,SS:[05EC]
6A76:050C 36FF16EA05    CALL SS:[05EA]
```

Unfortunately, if you now go and look at 3EA7h, presumably the address of the all-important INT 21h function dispatch table, there turns out instead to be perfectly valid-looking code at that address, and not a table at all. Likewise, 05ECh and 05EAh are, in this context, totally bogus. This isn't a problem with DEBUG, however. A straight disassembly on disk of MSDOS.SYS or IO.SYS, even with a more sophisticated disassembler such as Sourcer, doesn't produce much better results.

The problem is that the SYSINIT process (as described in the *MS-DOS Encyclopedia*) moves segments around in memory and relies heavily on segment arithmetic. Address cross-references often won't match up properly in a static disassembly of DOS on disk. To get a good disassembly of the core DOS interrupt handlers, it is much easier to disassemble DOS *in memory*, after the DOS initialization segment movement (which might include the DOS=HIGH movement of the DOS kernel to the high memory area, or HMA) is complete.

The only problem with disassembling DOS out of memory, rather than in the system files on disk, is that this misses the SYSINIT code, which is discarded from memory when the initialization is complete. However, as noted earlier, SYSINIT and the DOS bootstrap process have already been adequately covered elsewhere.

Again, a tech reviewer writes, "NO! You're forgetting all the 'preload' stuff that IO.SYS does starting in DOS 6.0. Also, taking apart IO.SYS really isn't that difficult. To link up data with the code that uses it, you just need to subtract some fixed amount, which is easy to figure out once you have one code/data pair. Just look at the code in IO.SYS that preloads DBLSPACE.BIN." Hmm, it seems we ought to take a look at this. . . .

Examining How IO.SYS Preloads DBLSPACE.BIN

It turns out that static disassembly of IO.SYS is actually pretty easy, even though at first glance the results produced by a disassembler such as Sourcer look inadequate. It's true that references to data don't match up with the actual locations of the data in the file, but once you match up just one piece of data in the file with code that references it, you can figure out everything else.

For example, a Sourcer disassembly of IO.SYS from MS-DOS 6.0 contains the following data item:

```
54BF:8138  5C 44 42 4C 53 50 41 43   db      '\DBLSPACE.BIN'
54BF:813E  45 2E 42 49 4E 00
```

This is followed shortly by code that, based on the surrounding context (the code calls the INT 21h AX=4B03h Load Overlay function), is probably loading DBLSPACE.BIN. However, the code does not reference offset 8138h. Instead, it references CS:3B62h:

```
54BF:8153  0E           push cs
54BF:8154  1F           pop ds
54BF:8155  BE 3B62      mov si,3B62h
```

If you subtract 3B62h from 8138h, you get 45D6h. If the code at 54BF:8155 really is referencing the '\DBLSPACE.BIN' string at offset 8138h, then 45D6h is the amount which you must add to other data references in this version of IO.SYS in order to locate the data itself. To see if this amount is accurate, just look for another data reference, and see if adding the amount onto it yields a likely-looking address. For example, a little further on in the file, IO.SYS produces an error message:

```
54BF:81E9  0E           push cs
54BF:81EA  1F           pop ds
54BF:81EB  BA 5823      mov dx,5823h
54BF:81EE  B4 09        mov ah,9
54BF:81F0  CD 21        int 21h      ; DOS Services  ah=function 09h
                                     ;   display char string at ds:dx
```

From the helpful comment supplied by Sourcer on how INT 21h AH=9 works, it is clear that 5823h must be the offset within CS of a string. Adding 45D6h to 5823h yields 9DF9h and there, indeed, is an error message:

```
54BF:9DF9  57 72 6F 6E 67 20    db  'Wrong DBLSPACE.BIN version', 0Dh
```

Thus, we really can pick apart IO.SYS on disk. This lets us examine the DOS boot process, in particular the recent additions such as the preloading of DBLSPACE.BIN in DOS 6 and the apparent ability to preload DOS386.EXE in DOS 7. "Preloading" means that IO.SYS looks for and loads these external programs before processing any DEVICE= statements in CONFIG.SYS. Chapter 1 discussed how Stacker 3.1 uses this interface to get itself preloaded under DOS 6. By examining IO.SYS, you can see how the interface works.

For example, after calling INT 21h AX=4B03h to load DBLSPACE.BIN, IO.SYS looks for a function pointer at offset 14h in DBLSPACE.BIN:

```
54BF:819F  E8 FBD6              call    LOAD_OVERLAY   ; subr. does 21/4B03
; ...
54BF:81C6  2E: C7 06 0387 0014  mov word ptr cs:[387h],14h ; get func ptr from
54BF:81CD  2E: 8C 06 0389       mov word ptr cs:[389h],es  ;   offset 14h
; ...                                                      ;   in DBLSPACE.BIN
```

IO.SYS saves away the function pointer provided by DBLSPACE.BIN, and then calls it:

```
54BF:81DA  0E                   push cs            ; IO.SYS passes DBLSPACE.BIN
54BF:81DB  07                   pop es            ;   a pointer to a buffer:
54BF:81DC  BB 036A              mov bx,36Ah       ; 36Ah+45D6h=4940h (see below)
54BF:81DF  B8 0006              mov ax,6          ; DOS version
54BF:81E2  2E: FF 1E 0387       call dword ptr cs:[387h] ; call DBLSPACE.BIN
; ...                                             ;         function ptr

54BF:8228  BB 0004              mov bx,4                  ; subfunction 4
54BF:822B  2E: FF 1E 0387       call dword ptr cs:[387h]
; ...

54BF:4940  18 00                db  18h, 00h  ; a communications buffer
```

IO.SYS also checks for a 2E2Ch signature at offset 12 in DBLSPACE.BIN. A hex dump of DBLSPACE.BIN reveals the presence of this signature:

```
C:\UNDOC2\CHAP6dump \dos\dblspace.bin -bytes 32
0000 | FF FF FF FF 42 48 41 08 8B 08 01 44 42 4C 53 50 | ....BHA....DBLSP
0010 | 41 43 2C 2E E9 B2 59 00 00 EA 41 08 00 00 EA 8B | AC,...Y...A.....
```

Further discussion of this interface, and its possible role in the ongoing battle between Microsoft and Stac Electronics, appears in Chapter 1. Here, the point is simply that all existing descriptions of the DOS boot process will need to be rewritten to take into account new additions to DOS such as DBLSPACE.BIN (and, in DOS 7, DOS386.EXE).

In any case, one topic that hasn't been covered at all is the INT 21h dispatch code, which is executed every time a program makes a DOS call (except if another program that hooks INT 21h has completely intercepted the call, without chaining). As we'll see, there are many important aspects to the INT 21h dispatch code, including stack switching, use of the current PSP, incrementing and decrementing the InDOS flag, handling of critical sections, Ctrl-Break, and critical errors, checking the machine's A20 line when DOS=HIGH, and special casing for Windows Enhanced mode.

Interrupt Vectors and Chaining

Studying DOS internals requires finding the code in DOS that handles software interrupts such as INT 21h and INT 2Fh. As we just saw, trying to do this with IO.SYS and MSDOS.SYS on disk can produce inadequate results. In memory, however, it seems like it should be trivial to find DOS's INT 21h and INT 2Fh handlers. As every PC programmer knows, there is a documented DOS function, INT 21h AH=35h, which returns (in ES:BX) a far pointer to the code that handles the interrupt given in AL.

Finding the current handlers for INT 21h and INT 2Fh is thus a simple matter of calling INT 21h AX=3521h and AX=352Fh and looking at the returned far pointer, or vector, as it is called. This can be wrapped up in a simple program to print out interrupt vectors. Add a little extra smarts, such as trying to figure out the *owner* of each interrupt vector and disassembling some frequently encountered instructions at the beginning of the interrupt handler, and the result is INTVECT.C, shown in Listing 6-1; Listing 6-2 shows MAP.C, which attempts to figure out owners.

Listing 6-1: INTVECT.C

```
/*
INTVECT.C
bcc intvect.c map.c
*/

#include <stdlib.h>
#include <stdio.h>
#include <dos.h>

typedef unsigned char BYTE;
typedef unsigned short WORD;
typedef unsigned long DWORD;

#define MK_LIN(fp)  ((((DWORD) FP_SEG(fp)) << 4) + FP_OFF(fp))

extern char *find_owner(DWORD lin_addr);     // in map.c

#define ARPL       0x63
#define IRET       0xCF
#define JMPF       0xEA
#define JMP8       0xEB
#define JMP16      0xE9

BYTE far *get_vect(int intno)    // call INT 21h AH=35h
{
    _asm push es
    _asm mov al, byte ptr intno
    _asm mov ah, 35h
    _asm int 21h
    _asm mov dx, es
    _asm mov ax, bx
    _asm pop es
    // return value in DX:AX
}

void print_vect(int intno)
{
    char *s;
    BYTE far *fp = get_vect(intno);
    printf("INT %02Xh   %Fp   ", intno, fp);
    if (fp == 0)
    {
        printf("unused\n");
        return;
```

```
    }
    s = find_owner(MK_LIN(fp));
    printf("%-08s   ", s? s: " ");

    switch (*fp)      // see if first instruction of interrupt handler
    {                 // is anything really obvious
        case ARPL:  printf("arpl -- Windows V86 breakpoint"); break;
        case IRET:  printf("iret -- NOP function"); break;
        case JMP8:  printf("jmp %Fp",
            ((BYTE far *) fp) + fp[1] + 2); break;
        case JMP16: printf("jmp %Fp",
            ((BYTE far *) fp) + *((WORD far *) &fp[1]) + 3); break;
        case JMPF:  printf("jmp %Fp",
            *((void far * far *) &fp[1])); break;
    }
    printf("\n");
}

main(int argc, char *argv[])
{
    char *end;
    int intno, i;
    if (argc < 2)
        for (intno=0; intno<256; intno++)
            print_vect(intno);
    else for (i=1; i<argc; i++)
        print_vect(strtoul(argv[i], &end, 16));
    return 0;
}
```

For example:

```
C:\UNDOC2\CHAP6>intvect 21 28 2f 2f
INT 21h    C0B6:0942
INT 28h    18D4:0615    PRINT
INT 29h    0070:0762    IO
INT 2Fh    1A82:000D    NLSFUNC
```

INTVECT and Windows

If you run INTVECT without command line parameters, it dumps out the vectors for all 256 interrupts. This is useful, for example, in determining which interrupts Windows Enhanced mode takes over; you can run INTVECT > TMP.TMP, start Windows, run INTVECT > TMP.2 from inside a DOS box, and then use diff or a similar utility to compare the files TMP.TMP and TMP.2. The difference between these two files reveals the interrupts that Windows Enhanced mode hooks using the low memory interrupt vector table (it also hooks some interrupts using the protected mode interrupt descriptor table). Where < points to the pre-Windows DOS output from INTVECT, and > points to the output under Windows, part of the output from diff might look like this (the complete output also shows changes to INT 0, 3, 8, 10h, 15h, 1Ch, 22h, 23h, 24h, 67h, and 68h):

```
< INT 28h    07F9:15AE    SMARTDRV
> INT 28h    FEF8:0B62    DBLSSYS$    arpl -- Windows V86 breakpoint

< INT 2Fh    1305:0285    DOSKEY
> INT 2Fh    1627:02A7    win

< INT 4Bh    F000:EA97    DBLSSYS$
> INT 4Bh    FEE1:0CD2    DBLSSYS$    arpl -- Windows V86 breakpoint
```

INT 28h is the DOS idle interrupt, and the Virtual DMA Services (VDS) use INT 4Bh. As you can see, INTVECT examines the first byte of an interrupt handler looking for code such as the ARPL instruction, which Windows Enhanced mode uses as a V86 breakpoint, to force a transition from user (Ring 3) code to VMM (Ring 0) code. The seeming location of the Windows V86 breakpoints inside DBLSSYS$ (DoubleSpace) is misleading; this has to do with the way Windows implements V86 breakpoints (see Chappell, *DOS Internals*, Chapter 2).

To build INTVECT, INTVECT.C should be linked with MAP.C (Listing 6-2). MAP.C attempts to provide the owner's name for each interrupt vector, using code that is explained in detail in Chapter 7. We will reuse MAP.C with another program later in this chapter, INTCHAIN.C (Listing 6-5). MAP can also be compiled with -DTESTING to produce a stand-alone program. For example, running MAP on one machine happened to produce the following output, which shows that this machine is running DoubleSpace, MSCDEX, SMARTDRV (loaded high), DOSKEY (also loaded high), and XMS and EMM servers:

```
C:\UNDOC2\CHAP6>map
00000700    000009A0    IO
000009A0    00001E80    DOS
00001E80    00002010    D:
00002010    00005780    MS$MOUSE
00005780    00007EA0    MSCD001
00007EA0    00012FA0    DBLSSYS$
00012FA0    000131F0    SETVERXX
000131F0    00013670    XMSXXXX0
00013670    00014950    EMMXXXX0
00014950    000188A0    MSCDEX
000189A0    0002A7E0    MAP
000CAA30    000CBBA0    COMMAND
000CBBD0    000D2C60    SMARTDRV
000CDDA2    000CDDB4    M:
000CDDB4    000DE470    J:
000DE470    000DF4A0    DOSKEY
00100000    0010FFEE    HMA
```

Listing 6-2: MAP.C

```c
/*
MAP.C
bcc intvect.c map.c
bcc intchain.c map.c
bcc -DTESTING map.c
*/

#include <stdlib.h>
#include <stdio.h>
#include <string.h>
#include <dos.h>

typedef unsigned char BYTE;
typedef unsigned short WORD;
typedef unsigned long DWORD;
typedef void far *FP;

#ifndef MK_FP
#define MK_FP(s,o)    ((((DWORD) s) << 16) + (o))
#endif

#pragma pack(1)
```

```c
typedef struct {
    DWORD start, end;
    char name[9];
    } BLOCK;

static BLOCK *map;
static int num_block = 0;

int cmp_func(const void *b1, const void *b2)
{
    if (((BLOCK *) b1)->start < ((BLOCK *) b2)->start)      return -1;
    else if (((BLOCK *) b1)->start > ((BLOCK *) b2)->start)  return 1;
    else                                                     return 0;
}

typedef struct {
    BYTE type;              /* 'M'=in chain; 'Z'=at end */
    WORD owner;             /* PSP of the owner */
    WORD size;              /* in 16-byte paragraphs */
    BYTE unused[3];
    BYTE name[8];           /* in DOS 4+ */
    } MCB;

#define IS_PSP(mcb)     (FP_SEG(mcb) + 1 == (mcb)->owner)

WORD get_first_mcb(void)
{
    _asm mov ah, 52h
    _asm int 21h
    _asm mov ax, es:[bx-2]
    // retval in AX
}

typedef struct DEV {
    struct DEV far *next;
    WORD attr, strategy, intr;
    union {
        BYTE name[8], blk_cnt;
        } u;
    } DEV;

#define IS_CHAR_DEV(dev)    ((dev)->attr & (1 << 15))

DEV far *get_nul_dev(void)
{
    _asm mov ah, 52h
    _asm int 21h
    _asm mov dx, es
    _asm lea ax, [bx+22h]
    // retval in DX:AX
}

int get_num_block_dev(DEV far *dev)
{
    // can't rely on # block devices at SysVars[20h]?
    // walk once through dev chain just to count # blk devs
    int num_blk = 0;
    do {
        if (! IS_CHAR_DEV(dev))
            num_blk += dev-u.blk_cnt;
        dev = dev-next;
    } while(FP_OFF(dev-next) != (WORD) -1);
    return num_blk;
}
```

```c
WORD get_umb_link(void)
{
    _asm mov ax, 5802h
    _asm int 21h
    _asm xor ah, ah
    // return value in AX
}

WORD set_umb_link(WORD flag)
{
    _asm mov ax, 5803h
    _asm mov bx, flag
    _asm int 21h
    _asm jc error
    _asm xor ax, ax
error:;
    // return 0 or error code in AX
}

WORD get_dos_ds(void)
{
    _asm push ds
    _asm mov ax, 1203h
    _asm int 2fh
    _asm mov ax, ds
    _asm pop ds
    // retval in AX
}

/* find IO.SYS segment with built-in drivers */
WORD get_io_seg(DEV far *dev)
{
    WORD io_seg = 0;
    do {
        if (IS_CHAR_DEV(dev))
            if (_fstrncmp(dev->u.name, "CON      ", 8) == 0)
                io_seg = FP_SEG(dev);   // we'll take the last one
        dev = dev->next;
    } while(FP_OFF(dev->next) != (WORD) -1);
    return io_seg;
}

static int did_init = 0;

void do_init(void)
{
    MCB far *mcb;
    DEV far *dev = get_nul_dev();
    WORD dos_ds, io_seg, mcb_seg, next_seg, save_link;
    BLOCK *block;
    int blk, i;

    map = (BLOCK *) calloc(100, sizeof(BLOCK));
    block = map;

    io_seg = get_io_seg(dev);
    block->start = io_seg << 4; block->end = (DWORD) -1;
    strcpy(block->name, "IO"); block++;

    dos_ds = get_dos_ds();
    block->start = dos_ds << 4; block->end = (DWORD) -1;
    strcpy(block->name, "DOS"); block++;

    // should really check if there IS an HMA!
    block->start = 0x100000L;   block->end =  0x10FFEEL;
```

```
strcpy(block->name, "HMA"); block++;
num_block = 3;

/* walk MCB chain, looking for PSPs, interrupt owners */
if (_osmajor >= 4)
{
    mcb_seg = get_first_mcb();
    mcb = (MCB far *) MK_FP(mcb_seg, 0);
    if (_osmajor >= 5)  // be lazy; see ch. 7 for DOS < 5
    {
        save_link = get_umb_link();
        set_umb_link(1);    // access UMBs too
    }

    for (;;)
    {
        next_seg = mcb_seg + mcb->size + 1;
        if (IS_PSP(mcb))
        {
            block->start = ((DWORD) mcb_seg) << 4;
            block->end = ((DWORD) next_seg) << 4;
            _fstrncpy(block->name, mcb->name, 8);
            block->name[8] = '\0';
            block++; num_block++;
        }
        mcb_seg = next_seg;
        if (mcb->type == 'M')
            mcb = (MCB far *) MK_FP(next_seg, 0);
        else
            break;
    }
}

/* walk device chain looking for non-builtin drivers */
blk = get_num_block_dev(dev);
do {
    MCB far *dev_mcb;
    if ((FP_SEG(dev) != dos_ds) && (FP_SEG(dev) != io_seg))
    {
        block->start = (((DWORD) FP_SEG(dev)) << 4) + FP_OFF(dev);
        dev_mcb = (MCB far *) MK_FP(FP_SEG(dev)-1,0);
        if (dev_mcb->owner == 8)
        {
            dev = dev->next;
            continue;
        }
        if (dev_mcb->type == 'M')
            block->end = block->start + ((DWORD) dev_mcb->size << 4);
        else
            block->end = (DWORD) -1;
        if (IS_CHAR_DEV(dev))
        {
            _fstrncpy(block->name, dev->u.name, 8);
            block->name[8] = '\0';
        }
        else
        {
            blk -= dev->u.blk_cnt; // block drivers in reverse order
            block->name[0] = blk + 'A';
            block->name[1] = ':';
            block->name[2] = '\0';
        }
        block++; num_block++;
    }
    dev = dev->next;
```

```
    } while(FP_OFF(dev->next) != (WORD) -1);

    if (_osmajor >= 5)
        set_umb_link(save_link);

    qsort(map, num_block, sizeof(BLOCK), cmp_func);

    for (i=0, block=map; i<num_block-1; i++, block++)
        if (block->end == (DWORD) -1)
            block->end = map[i+1].start;
    if (block->end == (DWORD) -1)   // last one
        block->end = 0xFFFFFL;

    did_init = 1;
}

char *find_owner(DWORD lin_addr)
{
    BLOCK *block;
    int i;

    if (! did_init) do_init();

    for (i=0, block=map; i<num_block; i++, block++)
        if ((lin_addr >= block->start) &&
            (lin_addr <= block->end))
            return block->name;

    /* still here */
    return (char *) 0;
}

#ifdef TESTING
main()
{
    BLOCK *block;
    int i;
    do_init();
    for (i=0, block=map; i<num_block; i++, block++)
        printf("%08lX   %08lX   %s\n",
            block->start, block->end, block->name);
}
#endif
```

With the exception of unused interrupt vectors and those (such as INT 1Eh) that point to data rather than code, you can take addresses displayed by INTVECT and unassemble them to see how a given interrupt is handled. As an example, Figure 6-1 shows INT 29h, which is the undocumented Fast Console Output function, located by default in the CON driver provided by IO.SYS.

Figure 6-1: Default Implementation of INT 29h

```
C:\UNDOC2\CHAP6>intvect 29
INT 29h   0070:0762   IO

C:\UNDOC2\CHAP6>debug
-u 70:762
0070:0762 50          PUSH   AX
0070:0763 56          PUSH   SI
0070:0764 57          PUSH   DI
0070:0765 55          PUSH   BP
0070:0766 53          PUSH   BX
0070:0767 B40E        MOV    AH,0E
0070:0769 BB0700      MOV    BX,0007
0070:076C CD10        INT    10
```

```
0070:076E 5B          POP    BX
0070:076F 5D          POP    BP
0070:0770 5F          POP    DI
0070:0771 5E          POP    SI
0070:0772 58          POP    AX
0070:0773 CF          IRET
```

That is very straightforward. INT 29h here is just a wrapper around INT 10h AH=0Eh, which is the ROM BIOS function to write a character in teletype mode.

Of course, things are never quite that simple. For example, if you install ANSI.SYS, which is a replacement CON driver, INT 29h points somewhere else:

```
C:\UNDOC2\CHAP6>intvect 29
INT 29h    0070:0762

C:\UNDOC2\CHAP6>\undoc2\chap7\devlod \dos\ansi.sys

C:\UNDOC2\CHAP6>intvect 29
INT 29h    6EB3:0510    DEVLOD
```

Because we loaded ANSI.SYS using DEVLOD, the INTVECT program shows DEVLOD as the owner of the interrupt vector; the owner, of course, is actually the new CON driver in ANSI.SYS. Now the code at 6EB3:0510 is no longer just a wrapper around an INT 10h call. Instead, it directly manipulates video memory at segment B800h and contains special handling for ANSI escape control codes. Showing the code here would take us too far afield, even for a chapter such as this that rambles more-or-less aimlessly through the DOS code. The point anyway is merely that the INTVECT program, simple as it is, can help us point DEBUG at useful segment:offset addresses to unassemble.

But there's a major problem here. Recall that we are interested in looking at the DOS INT 21h and INT 2Fh handlers. INTVECT can, of course, print out the addresses of the INT 21h and INT 2Fh handlers:

```
C:\UNDOC2\CHAP6>intvect 21 2f
INT 21h    0F93:32B6    MSCDEX
INT 2Fh    1305:0285    DOSKEY
```

However, as INTVECT indicates, these interrupt vectors point not to DOS but to DOS add-ins such as MSCDEX and DOSKEY. In fact, it is practically *guaranteed* that, except on the lamest, freshly booted, stripped-down system with no AUTOEXEC.BAT or CONFIG.SYS file, INT 21h, INT 2Fh, and many other DOS interrupt vectors *won't* point into DOS. The INT 21h and INT 2Fh vectors are pointing at one of the plug-in subsystems rather than at the DOS motherboard.

Of course, if you're interested in examining MSCDEX's INT 21h handler or DOSKEY's INT 2Fh handler, the INTVECT results are very useful. They provide all the information needed by a debugger such as DEBUG or SYMDEB (a handy debugger that Microsoft once included with the Windows SDK). For example, by using DEBUG or SYMDEB to unassemble the 1305:0285 address displayed by INTVECT for INT 2Fh, we can see that DOSKEY watches for the Windows and task-switcher initialization broadcasts (INT 2Fh AX=1605h and AX=4B05h). DOSKEY clearly uses the same piece of code (here, at offset 0299h) to handle both calls. We can also see confirmation that, as documented in Microsoft's *MS-DOS Programmer's Reference*, DOSKEY responds to INT 2Fh AH=48h calls:

```
C:\UNDOC2\CHAP6>intvect 2f
INT 2Fh    1305:0285    DOSKEY
C:\UNDOC2\CHAP6>debug
-u 1305:0285
1305:0285 3D0516       CMP    AX,1605
1305:0288 740F         JZ     0299
1305:028A 3D054B       CMP    AX,4B05
1305:028D 740A         JZ     0299
1305:028F 80FC48       CMP    AH,48
```

```
1305:0292 741B              JZ     02AF
1305:0294 2EFF2E5F02        JMP    FAR CS:[025F]
; ...
```

But if, for example, we want to see MSCDEX's INT 2Fh handler rather than DOSKEY's, and if DOSKEY is loaded after MSCDEX, INTVECT is of no use. (Note, however, that unlike MSDOS.SYS and IO.SYS, programs such as MSCDEX.EXE and DOSKEY.EXE are easy to disassemble on disk with a program such as Sourcer from V Communications.)

More importantly, INTVECT doesn't help us get the address of what we might call The One True INT 21h Handler inside MSDOS.SYS. Nor does it help with finding the original INT 2Fh handlers inside MSDOS.SYS and IO.SYS.

Why? Because interrupts are handled in a kind of last-in, first-out (LIFO) stack. The point was made at the beginning of this chapter that the DOS philosophy is to provide the bare minimum operating system services, along with facilities for *extending* DOS. As discussed in greater detail in Chapter 9 on TSRs, one of the keys to extending DOS is INT 21h AH=25h, the DOS Set Interrupt Vector function. Along with the Get Interrupt Vector function (AH=35h), the Set Vector function allows the creation of what are called interrupt chains, which are essentially linked lists (or LIFO stacks) of code. An interrupt chain consists of two or more pieces of code that handle the same interrupt. The following code fragment, adapted from the FUNC0E32 and DOSVER programs in Listings 2-20 and 2-21, illustrates this:

```
void (interrupt far *prev)();          // ptr to previous handler in chain
prev = _dos_getvect(0x21);             // call 21/35 -- get previous
_dos_setvect(0x21, my_int21_handler);  // call 21/25 -- set new
// ...
void interrupt far my_int21_handler(REG_PARAMS r)
{
    // look at AH to see if we're interested
    // ...
    _chain_intr(prev);  // pass interrupt down to previous owner in chain
}
```

The _chain_intr() does a far JMP to the previous interrupt handler in the chain, without returning. It is important to note that sometimes interrupt handlers CALL, rather than JMP to, the previous handler. This allows a handler to post-process the interrupt *after* the previous handler has done its work, rather than pre-processing the interrupt beforehand, which is what happens in the more typical JMP style of interrupt chaining. Sometimes the JMP-style code is called a front-end handler, and the CALL-style code is called a back-end handler.

It is especially important that INT 21h AH=25h and 35h allow *even INT 21h itself* to be hooked. This is a source of tremendous flexibility in DOS, but it also makes it difficult for us to find The One True INT 21h Handler. Calling INT 21h AX=3521h returns the head of the INT 21h linked list, that is, the address of the most recently installed INT 21h handler. This might conceivably be the genuine DOS INT 21h handler, but more likely it belongs to MSCDEX, NETX, or perhaps even something as dumb as the FUNC0E32 or DOSVER programs from Chapter 2. INT 21h AX=35h simply returns the *head* of an interrupt chain. Finding the original INT 21h or INT 2Fh handler belonging to DOS usually requires finding the chain's *tail*. (Usually rather than always, because there might be back-end handlers.)

How can we find the actual INT 21h and INT 2Fh handlers provided by DOS itself, when all we have is the address of the head of the INT 21h or INT 2Fh interrupt chain? There is unfortunately no function that returns the tail of an interrupt chain. And while there is an undocumented DOS function (INT 2Fh AX=1203h) to return the DOS data segment, there is no equivalent function that returns the DOS code segment (which, remember, may well be in the HMA).

One solution would, of course, be to boot on an absolutely bare-bones system and hope that INT 21h and INT 2Fh point to the original MS-DOS handlers, thereby bypassing the whole problem of how to follow interrupt chains. Or you could write a device driver to keep track of interrupts and install it very early in DOS initialization. But this is ridiculous! Clearly there must be some way to *follow* the interrupt chain, as the processor does this many times a second.

Unfortunately, there is no standard mechanism for interrupt chaining. IBM and Microsoft at one point put forward a specification for this purpose (David Thielen described it in detail in *Microsoft Systems Journal*, July 1991, pp. 24-25), but unfortunately no one seems to use it. Ralf Brown has proposed an INT 2Dh protocol (described in the Interrupt List on disk) to combat the extremely long interrupt chains that currently plague INT 2Fh, but again you can't rely on programs to do the right thing and use this protocol.

Tracing a DOS INT 21h Call

It turns out that Microsoft provides, with every copy of DOS, an almost perfect solution to the problem of finding the actual DOS INT 21h and INT 2Fh handlers. The solution is none other than DEBUG.

Like most debuggers, DEBUG has an *a* command to assemble instructions on the fly, and a *t* command for tracing into (as opposed to stepping over) instructions. Even better, unlike some otherwise more sophisticated debuggers, the *t* command in DEBUG can trace *into* an INT instruction. For the purposes of trace, in other words, DEBUG does not treat INT as an atomic operation:

```
C:\UNDOC2\CHAP6>intvect 21
INT 21h   0F93:32B6   MSCDEX

C:\UNDOC2\CHAP6>debug
-a
19B5:0100 mov ah, 62
19B5:0102 int 21
19B5:0104 ret
19B5:0105
-t

AX=6200  BX=0000  CX=0000  DX=0000  SP=FFEE  BP=0000  SI=0000  DI=0000
DS=19B5  ES=19B5  SS=19B5  CS=19B5  IP=0102    NV UP EI PL NZ NA PO NC
19B5:0102 CD21            INT 21
-t

AX=6200  BX=0000  CX=0000  DX=0000  SP=FFE8  BP=0000  SI=0000  DI=0000
DS=19B5  ES=19B5  SS=19B5  CS=0F93  IP=32B6    NV UP DI PL NZ NA PO NC
0F93:32B6 80FC60          CMP AH,60
```

Notice that pressing *t* at the INT 21h instruction took us into the first line of the handler at 0F93:32B6, rather than over it to the RET instruction at 19B5:0104. This is exactly what one might expect from pressing *t* rather than *p* (proceed); yet because of the way the single step interrupt works on Intel processors (see INTCHAIN.C at Listing 6-5 later in this chapter), most debuggers don't behave this way; it's useful that every copy of DOS comes with one that does.

We can use this facility in order to follow the INT 21h or INT 2Fh chain down into the bowels of DOS itself. (Yuck!) All we must do is keep tracing (either by continuously pressing *t* or by telling DEBUG with a command such as *t 16* to trace a certain number of instructions) until the segment:offset returns to DEBUG and our RET instruction (which, in the example above, is located at 19C7:0104). This will surely locate the actual DOS INT 21h or INT 2Fh handler.

However, the astute reader may wish to interject right now, before we go any further, that using DEBUG to trace into INT 21h "won't work" because DEBUG itself uses DOS, and DOS, as we all know, is not reentrant. This is absolutely true; a debugger that does not use DOS, such as Nu-Mega's Soft-ICE, is better suited than DEBUG to tracing through DOS.

However, there are a handful of DOS functions that *are* reentrant, at least for the purposes of tracing with DEBUG. By examining the DOS code for INT 21h, we will soon see precisely what this reentrancy or lack thereof means. In the meantime, simply take it on faith that the DOS INT 21h functions shown in Table 6-1 are (with an important caveat that we'll get to) reentrant and thus traceable using DEBUG, SYMDEB, or any other debugger that uses DOS. With the exception of the undocumented INT 21h AH=64h, note that these are among the INT 21h functions that Microsoft (*MS-DOS Programmer's Reference*, Chapter 7) lists as callable from a critical error handler.

Table 6-1: Reentrant MS-DOS Functions

INT 21h AH=33h	(Get/Set Ctrl-Break, Get Boot Drive, Get DOS Version)
INT 21h AH=51h and AH=62h	(Get PSP)
INT 21h AH=50h	(Set PSP)
INT 21h AH=64h	(Set Driver Lookahead Flag)

Note: These are reentrant unless DOS=HIGH and the A20 line is disabled.

It is desirable for MS-DOS to single out the Get and Set PSP functions for special treatment, because this means that interrupt handlers can freely call these process-manipulation functions (see Chapter 9 on TSRs). But it is not at all obvious why functions 33h and 64h merit this special attention. It would seem that other functions, such as AH=25h and AH=35h to get and set interrupt vectors, might be more useful. On the other hand, including function 33h here means that interrupt handlers can freely get and set the DOS BREAK= flag.

Let us now use DEBUG to trace into a call to one of these functions, INT 21h AH=62h (Get PSP), and see exactly what occurs when this function is called under DOS 6.0, in a configuration with a few standard DOS TSRs such as MSCDEX and DOSKEY. The documentation states that function 62h takes no parameters other than the number 62h in AH, and that the function returns the current PSP in BX. You can probably guess that the DOS implementation for this function is rather simple, doing little more than loading BX from the CURR_PSP location in the DOS data segment. This location corresponds to offset 10h in the Swappable Data Area (SDA; see INT 21h AX=5D06h in the appendix). However, as you'll see, the processor executes a lot of code before DOS eventually gets to the point of carrying out the otherwise simple Get PSP operation.

As noted earlier, the key facility DEBUG provides here is that (unlike SYMDEB, for example) it traces *into* the INT instruction. In Figure 6-2, comments have been added to the following DEBUG output, using ;;; to make them stand out.

Figure 6-2: Starting to Trace a Call to INT 21h AH=62h

```
C:\UNDOC2\CHAP6>debug
-a
19B5:0100 mov ah, 62
19B5:0102 int 21
19B5:0104 ret
19B5:0105
-t

AX=6200  BX=0000  CX=0000  DX=0000  SP=FFEE  BP=0000  SI=0000  DI=0000
DS=19B5  ES=19B5  SS=19B5  CS=19B5  IP=0102   NV UP EI PL NZ NA PO NC
19B5:0102 CD21           INT 21
-t

;;; We have to keep tracing until the segment:offset comes back to
;;; our own code, the RET instruction at 19B5:0104.

AX=6200  BX=0000  CX=0000  DX=0000  SP=FFE8  BP=0000  SI=0000  DI=0000
DS=19B5  ES=19B5  SS=19B5  CS=0F93  IP=32B6   NV UP DI PL NZ NA PO NC
0F93:32B6 80FC60         CMP AH,60
```

```
-t

;;; Running MEM /D showed that above is MSCDEX. This is consistent
;;; with output from INTVECT program. Apparently MSCDEX is interested
;;; in the undocumented DOS INT 21h AH=60h (Truename) function. Note that
;;; we were running MSCDEX /S (for network sharing); usually MSCDEX doesn't
;;; care about the INT 21h AH=60h call.

AX=6200  BX=0000  CX=0000  DX=0000  SP=FFE8  BP=0000  SI=0000  DI=0000
DS=19B5  ES=19B5  SS=19B5  CS=0F93  IP=32B9   NV UP DI PL NZ NA PO NC
0F93:32B9 7405          JZ    32C0
-t

AX=6200  BX=0000  CX=0000  DX=0000  SP=FFE8  BP=0000  SI=0000  DI=0000
DS=19B5  ES=19B5  SS=19B5  CS=0F93  IP=32BB   NV UP DI PL NZ NA PO NC
0F93:32BB 2E            CS:
0F93:32BC FF2EB232      JMP FAR [32B2]                        CS:32B2=15FA
-t

;;; MSCDEX decided it's not interested in our call to 21/62, so it chains
;;; to the previous handler, whose address it earlier retrieved (by
;;; calling 21/35) and saved away (apparently in CS:32B2) before installing
;;; (with 21/25) its own INT 21h handler.

AX=6200  BX=0000  CX=0000  DX=0000  SP=FFE8  BP=0000  SI=0000  DI=0000
DS=19B5  ES=19B5  SS=19B5  CS=07F9  IP=15FA   NV UP DI PL NZ NA PO NC
07F9:15FA 80FC3F        CMP AH,3F

;;; We're now in the previous INT 21h handler. MEM /D shows that
;;; 07F9:15FA is SMARTDRV. Here it's (reasonably enough) interested in
;;; whether we've called INT 21h AH=3Fh to read from a file. (SMARTDRV
;;; wants to see if the data we want from the file is actually already
;;; in its cache.) But we called 21/62 not 21/3F so...
```

Well, you get the idea. Running DEBUG this way is a bit tedious, and saving its output to a file is difficult. As an improvement, you can drive DEBUG with input scripts, such as 2162.SCR in Listing 6-3, and redirect its output to a file. (For a lengthy discussion of DEBUG scripts, see *PC Magazine DOS Power Tools*, 2nd edition, Chapter 9.) Furthermore, rather than repeatedly hitting *t* to trace (single step) the next instruction, you can give the trace command a numeric parameter (for example, *t 16* or *t 32*) to trace a series of instructions.

Listing 6-3: 2162.SCR

```
C:\UNDOC2\CHAP6>type 2162.scr
a
mov ah, 62
int 21
ret
; blank line below is crucial to leave assembly mode!

t 100
q
```

The only problem is in guessing how many instructions to trace; if you ask DEBUG to trace too far, it starts executing garbage. You only want to trace until you return to the RET instruction you assembled, or at least not much past it. The best bet is first try *t 16*, examine DEBUG's output to see if the traced instructions come back, then try t 32, examine the output again, and so on. In any case, *t 100* happened to work here; a larger number would be needed on machines with more TSRs that hook INT 21h installed.

Figure 6-3 shows a complete trace into an INT 21h AH=62h call, from the time we issued the INT 21h until DOS returns to us with the current PSP in BX. Normally all that you see (or want to see!) of an INT 21h call is your input and its output. But Figure 6-3 views the DOS call "through the looking glass," as it were. Instead of looking down at DOS, you'll be inside DOS looking up at the INT 21h call. This can be slightly disorienting at first, but if you carefully study Figure 6-3 in the end you'll have a much better understanding of what DOS is all about.

Figure 6-3: Tracing a Call to INT 21h AH=62h

```
C:\UNDOC2\CHAP6>debug<2162.scr>2162.out

C:\UNDOC2\CHAP6>type 2162.out
-a
19B5:0100 mov ah, 62
19B5:0102 int 21
19B5:0104 ret
19B5:0105
-t 106

AX=6200  BX=0000  CX=0000  DX=0000  SP=FFEE  BP=0000  SI=0000  DI=0000
DS=19B5  ES=19B5  SS=19B5  CS=19B5  IP=0102   NV UP EI PL NZ NA PO NC
19B5:0102 CD21            INT 21

AX=6200  BX=0000  CX=0000  DX=0000  SP=FFE8  BP=0000  SI=0000  DI=0000
DS=19B5  ES=19B5  SS=19B5  CS=0F93  IP=32B6   NV UP DI PL NZ NA PO NC
0F93:32B6 80FC60          CMP AH,60

;;; As before (Figure 6-2), we're in MSCDEX /S now.

AX=6200  BX=0000  CX=0000  DX=0000  SP=FFE8  BP=0000  SI=0000  DI=0000
DS=19B5  ES=19B5  SS=19B5  CS=0F93  IP=32B9   NV UP DI PL NZ NA PO NC
0F93:32B9 7405            JZ   32C0

;;; The AX=xxxx BX=xxxx etc. dump that DEBUG shows each time usually
;;; isn't important here, so from now on we'll omit it (and blank lines)
;;; except when the register dump is useful.

0F93:32BB 2E             CS:
0F93:32BC FF2EB232       JMP FAR [32B2]                          CS:32B2=15FA
07F9:15FA 80FC3F         CMP AH,3F

;;; As before, we're in SMARTDRV now.

07F9:15FD 7414           JZ   1613
07F9:15FF 80FC0D         CMP AH,0D
07F9:1602 7426           JZ   162A
07F9:1604 3D1325         CMP AX,2513
07F9:1607 7451           JZ   165A
07F9:1609 80FC68         CMP AH,68
07F9:160C 7442           JZ   1650

;;; Above provides a catalog of the DOS INT 21h function calls that
;;; SMARTDRV cares about: 3Fh (read file), 0Dh (disk reset), 2513h
;;; (set INT 13h vector), 68h (commit file). All this makes sense.
;;; For example, SMARTDRV uses 21/0D as a signal to flush the cache.
;;; For some calls, such as 21/0D, SMARTDRV doesn't JMP to the previous
;;; handler; instead, it does a far CALL and examines the 21/0D on
;;; the way back.

07F9:160E 2E             CS:
07F9:160F FF2E1423       JMP FAR [2314]                          CS:2314=0800

;;; We called 21/62; SMARTDRV doesn't care, so SMARTDRV chains to
;;; previous handler, C801:0800, which SMARTDRV earlier got from
;;; calling 21/35 before installing its own 21 handler with 21/25, and
;;; which is stored in CS:2314.
```

```
C801:0800 9C              PUSHF
```

```
;;; Was running with DOS=UMB, so some INT 21h handlers are running
;;; in upper memory. Don't know who the owner of this is!
```

```
C801:0801 FB              STI
C801:0802 3D0258          CMP  AX,5802
C801:0805 7413            JZ   081A
C801:0807 3D0358          CMP  AX,5803
C801:080A 7431            JZ   083D
C801:080C 80FC31          CMP  AH,31
C801:080F 7503            JNZ  0814
C801:0814 9D              POPF
```

```
;;; We can see that this handler cares about calls to INT 21h functions
;;; 5802h (Get UBM Link), 5803h (Set UMB Link), 31h (TSR). Wonder why.
;;; Anyway, we called 21/62; the handler isn't interested in that, so it
;;; chains to the previous handler.
```

```
C801:0815 2E              CS:
C801:0816 FF2ECE01        JMP FAR [01CE]                        CS:01CE=0023
```

```
0255:0023 EA8E052ECC      JMP CC2E:058E
```

```
;;; DEV shows that seg 0255h is a a block-mode device driver for
;;; D: through I: -- it is a low-memory stub for DoubleSpace, located in
;;; high memory. Stacker uses the same area; both have signatures at
;;; 0255:0000. DEV also shows that CC2E:058E is DBLSSYS$ (DoubleSpace).
```

```
CC2E:058E 9C              PUSHF
CC2E:058F FB              STI
CC2E:0590 FC              CLD
CC2E:0591 1E              PUSH    DS
CC2E:0592 0E              PUSH    CS
CC2E:0593 1F              POP  DS
CC2E:0594 C606C20700      MOV BYTE PTR [07C2],00                DS:07C2=00
CC2E:0599 53              PUSH    BX
CC2E:059A 8ADC            MOV BL,AH
CC2E:059C 80FB6C          CMP BL,6C
CC2E:059F 7759            JA   05FA
CC2E:05A1 32FF            XOR BH,BH
CC2E:05A3 8A9F1305        MOV BL,[BX+0513]                      DS:0575=00
CC2E:05A7 FFA78005        JMP [BX+0580]                         DS:0580=05FA
```

```
;;; DoubleSpace is sufficiently tied into DOS that it uses a jump table to
;;; store a handler for every DOS function. The table at CC2E:0513 holds
;;; byte offsets into code at CC2E:0580. Most DOS functions (including
;;; our 21/62 call) are just passed on. Examining the table with the FTAB
;;; program from later in this chapter shows that DoubleSpace cares
;;; about the following INT 21h functions: 00, 0A, 0D, 10, 13, 17, 25, 31,
;;; 36, 39, 3A, 3E, 41, 43, 4B, 4C, 56, 57, 5D, 68. We know this from
;;; running "ftab cc2e:0513 6d DSI21 1 | grep -v 00". For example, it hooks
;;; 21/25 because (like SMARTDRV) it wants to know whenever someone sets the
;;; INT 13h (BIOS Disk) vector.
```

```
CC2E:05FA 5B              POP BX
CC2E:05FB 1F              POP DS
CC2E:05FC 9D              POPF
CC2E:05FD 2E              CS:
CC2E:05FE FF2E0005        JMP FAR [0500]                        CS:0500=109E
```

```
;;; Trivial handling for our 21/62 call. Pass it to previous handler . . .
```

```
0116:109E 90              NOP
```

```
;;; MEM /D shows that 0116h is MS-DOS. Finally!

0116:109F 90              NOP
0116:10A0 E8CC00          CALL     116F

;;; Hmm, DOS is calling some subroutine (which we've traced into):

0116:116F 9C              PUSHF
0116:1170 1E              PUSH     DS
0116:1171 06              PUSH     ES
0116:1172 51              PUSH     CX
0116:1173 56              PUSH     SI
0116:1174 57              PUSH     DI

;;; We need to see the registers for the next few instructions.
;;; Note what happens to DS and ES

AX=6200 BX=0000 CX=0000 DX=0000 SP=FFDA BP=0000 SI=0000 DI=0000
DS=19B5 ES=19B5 SS=19B5 CS=0116 IP=1175    NV UP DI NG NZ AC PE CY
0116:1175 2E              CS:
0116:1176 C5366711        LDS SI,[1167]                        CS:1167=0080

AX=6200 BX=0000 CX=0000 DX=0000 SP=FFDA BP=0000 SI=0080 DI=0000
DS=0000 ES=19B5 SS=19B5 CS=0116 IP=117A    NV UP DI NG NZ AC PE CY
0116:117A 2E              CS:
0116:117B C43E6B11        LES DI,[116B]                        CS:116B=0090

AX=6200 BX=0000 CX=0000 DX=0000 SP=FFDA BP=0000 SI=0080 DI=0090
DS=0000 ES=FFFF SS=19B5 CS=0116 IP=117F    NV UP DI NG NZ AC PE CY
0116:117F B90400          MOV CX,0004

0116:1182 FC              CLD
0116:1183 F3              REPZ
0116:1184 A7              CMPSW
0116:1185 7407            JZ  118E

;;; DOS has just compared 8 bytes (4 words) at DS:SI (0000:0080) and
;;; ES:DI (FFFF:0090). If they are identical, DOS jumps somewhere.
;;; What is this?! This particular run of DEBUG was conducted with
;;; DOS=HIGH. DOS is in the HMA, which is only reachable when the
;;; machine's A20 address line is enabled. DOS is comparing 0000:0080
;;; and FFFF:0090 because, if the 8 bytes at these two addresses are
;;; identical, it assumes that memory addresses are wrapping around, and
;;; therefore that A20 is off. DOS can't call routines in the HMA if A20
;;; is off. Thus, even when DOS=HIGH there must be a low-memory stub; the
;;; code at 0116:109E is that stub, which ensures that A20 is enabled before
;;; calling DOS in the HMA. Here, A20 was already on (0000:0080 and
;;; FFFF:0090 were different), but A20 has been off; we would
;;; have jumped to the subroutine at 0116:118E, whose job
;;; is to enable A20 (by calling XMS function 5, Local Enable A20).
;;; If that function call succeeds, DOS will jump back here, just as if
;;; A20 had been enabled all along. If that function call fails, we're
;;; in big trouble: DOS uses INT 10h AH=0Eh to display "A20 Hardware
;;; Error" and goes into a dynamic halt. We'll come back to this
;;; code later. Right now, A20 is enabled so...

0116:1187 5F              POP DI
0116:1188 5E              POP SI
0116:1189 59              POP CX
0116:118A 07              POP ES
0116:118B 1F              POP DS
0116:118C 9D              POPF
0116:118D C3              RET
0116:10A3 2E              CS:
```

```
0116:10A4 FF2E6A10    JMP FAR [106A]                    CS:106A=40F8
```

;;; The low-memory stub for DOS knows it can jump to DOS in the HMA, and
;;; here we go:

```
FDC8:40F8 FA          CLI
```

;;; We are now in The One True INT 21h Handler. That this is at
;;; FDC8:40F8 in this particular configuration is the one piece of
;;; information we're after here, because now we can go and disassemble
;;; (rather than trace) at that address. Static unassembly is
;;; generally easier than dynamic tracing. But let's see the thing
;;; through, to learn exactly how 21/62 is handled...

```
FDC8:40F9 80FC6C      CMP AH,6C
FDC8:40FC 77D2        JA  40D0
```

;;; Any INT 21h function > 6Ch is an error. ("In DOS 7.0,
;;; the upper limit is 72h," writes one tech reviewer.)

```
FDC8:40FE 80FC33      CMP AH,33
FDC8:4101 7218        JB  411B
```

;;; Any INT 21h function < 33h will be handled at FDC8:411B.

```
FDC8:4103 74A2        JZ  40A7
```

;;; 21/33 is special: it is handled at FDC8:40A7 (in this configuration).

```
FDC8:4105 80FC64      CMP AH,64
FDC8:4108 7711        JA  411B
```

;;; Any INT 21h function > 64h will also be handled at FDC8:411B;
;;; seems like 411B is the handler for "normal" DOS calls.

```
FDC8:410A 74B5        JZ  40C1
```

;;; 21/64 is another special function, handled here at FDC8:40C1

```
FDC8:410C 80FC51      CMP AH,51
FDC8:410F 74A4        JZ  40B5
FDC8:4111 80FC62      CMP AH,62
FDC8:4114 749F        JZ  40B5
```

;;; Finally! DOS sees our 21/62 call and will handle it by jumping to
;;; FDC8:40B5. Notice that the same code also handles calls to 21/51, which
;;; makes sense, since the two functions are documented as being identical.

```
FDC8:40B5 1E          PUSH    DS
FDC8:40B6 2E          CS:
FDC8:40B7 8E1EE73D    MOV DS,[3DE7]                     CS:3DE7=0116
```

;;; DOS DS (0116h) is stored in a variable kept at CS:3DE7. This is
;;; the segment where things like SysVars and SDA live. This value is
;;; also returned from 2F/1203 (see appendix).

```
FDC8:40BB 8B1E3003    MOV BX,[0330]                     DS:0330=1408
```

;;; Believe it or not, the previous line is actually the Get PSP function!
;;; We know that DOS keeps the current PSP at SDA+10h. In this
;;; configuration, 21/5D06 (Get SDA) returns 0116:0320. The Get PSP
;;; function just moves the WORD at 0116:0330 into BX. In other words,
;;; 21/62 (and 21/51) just return the WORD from SDA+10h. Duh.

```
FDC8:40BF 1F          POP DS
```

```
FDC8:40C0 CF            IRET
```

;;; DOS IRETs back to our code running in DEBUG.

```
19B5:0104 C3            RET
```

;;; This is the RET statement in our DEBUG script.

```
19B5:0000 CD20          INT 20
0116:1094 90            NOP
```

;;; Our script has already returned to DEBUG, which did an INT 20h return
;;; to DOS. At this point, we start tracing all sorts of things we don't
;;; care about. If we trace too far, we start to make DEBUG execute
;;; garbage, which can hang the machine.

-q

The most noticeable feature of the INT 21h trace in Figure 6-3 is the way that DOS extensions such as SMARTDRV and MSCDEX become indistinguishable from DOS itself. If any non-Microsoft DOS extensions such as Novell NetWare or Stacker had been running, they too would have appeared in the INT 21h chain, looking not a bit different from any of the Microsoft-provided software in the chain. The walk through the INT 21h chain in Figure 6-3 thus presents an excellent illustration of what DOS really is.

Unassembling the Get/Set PSP Functions

As you can see, under normal circumstances with a few TSRs loaded, you have to wade through a lot just to get to the single line of code that actually performs the DOS Get PSP function. It should now be clear why INT 21h is called an interrupt "chain." As you'll see later, the INT 2Fh chain is typically much longer than the INT 21h chain. Given the overhead of INT 21h on a typical machine, programmers might even consider writing their own Get PSP calls to bypass this long interrupt chain. Seeing how DOS implements Get PSP (when it eventually gets there!), you can also see how to implement your own:

```c
// uses get_sda() from GETSDA.C (Listing 3-4a)
WORD my_get_psp(void)
{
    static WORD far *psp_ptr = (WORD far *) 0;
    if (! psp_ptr)                  // one-time init
        psp_ptr = (WORD far *) (get_sda() + 0x10);
    return *psp_ptr;
}
```

Of course, this would cut out any TSRs or drivers that might actually need to see and respond to DOS Get PSP calls.

Having already seen the code that handles the Get PSP function (INT 21h AH=51h and 62h), we might as well also examine the code for Set PSP, shown in Figure 6-4, though we can guess what it's going to look like (we'll see later, in Figure 6-7, where the 40A9h address comes from).

Figure 6-4: Implementation of INT 21h AH=50h (Set PSP) in MS-DOS 6.0

```
-u fdc8:40a9
FDC8:40A9 1E            PUSH    DS          ; save caller's DS
FDC8:40AA 2E            CS:
FDC8:40AB 8E1EE73D      MOV DS,[3DE7]       ; switch to DOS DS
FDC8:40AF 891E3003      MOV [0330],BX       ; put caller's BX into CURR_PSP
FDC8:40B3 1F            POP DS              ; restore caller's DS
FDC8:40B4 CF            IRET                ; done!
```

In other words, the Get and Set PSP functions just manipulate this word at offset 330h in the DOS data segment (offset 10h in the SDA). This provides a small taste of how DOS internally uses such externally-visible structures as SysVars and the SDA. Thus:

```
void my_set_psp(WORD psp)
{
    static WORD far *psp_ptr = (WORD far *) 0;
    if (! psp_ptr)                    // one-time init
        psp_ptr = (WORD far *) (get_sda() + 0x10);
    *psp_ptr = psp;
}
```

This is intended merely as an example of what DOS itself does. Calling this function instead of INT 21h AH=50h is bad, because it bypasses NETX and other TSRs that need to see Set PSP calls.

Unassembling INT 21h AH=33h

A glance toward the end of the DEBUG output in Figure 6-3 shows that MS-DOS special-cases a handful of functions: 33h, 51h, 62h, 64h, and (not shown in Figure 6-3) 50h. These functions correspond to the reentrant DOS functions listed in Table 6-1. While we're still not quite in a position to understand what makes these functions different from all other DOS functions, we do at any rate now have a bunch of addresses that we can unassemble. Recall that this was our goal in tracing through DOS.

For example, INT 21h AH=33h is an omnibus function with a number of subfunctions relating to Ctrl-Break, the Boot Drive, and the DOS Version. For example, setting BREAK=ON ends up calling INT 21h AX=3300h with DL=1. In this configuration, code at FDC8:40A7 handles this function:

```
FDC8:40FE 80FC33        CMP AH,33
FDC8:4101 7218          JB  411B
FDC8:4103 74A2          JZ  40A7
```

We can now unassemble (rather than trace) at this address, using DEBUG or any other DOS debugger. Comments have been added to the output in Figure 6-5, which has also been cleaned up slightly.

Figure 6-5: Implementation of INT 21h AH=33h in MS-DOS 6.0

```
C:\UNDOC2\CHAP6>debug
-u fdc8:40a7
FDC8:40A7 EBA9          JMP 4052
-u fdc8:4052
FDC8:4052 3C06          CMP AL,06       ; functions 3300h through 3306h
FDC8:4054 7603          JBE 4059
FDC8:4056 B0FF          MOV AL,FF       ; error: subfunction number too high
FDC8:4058 CF            IRET
FDC8:4059 1E            PUSH    DS      ; save caller's DS
FDC8:405A 2E            CS:
FDC8:405B 8E1EE73D      MOV DS,[3DE7]   ; switch to DOS's DS; hmm, not truly
FDC8:405F 50            PUSH    AX      ;      reentrant after all!
FDC8:4060 56            PUSH    SI
FDC8:4061 BE3703        MOV SI,0337     ; offset of break flag:  SDA+17h
FDC8:4064 32E4          XOR AH,AH       ; see if subfunct 0
FDC8:4066 0BC0          OR  AX,AX
FDC8:4068 7504          JNZ 406E
FDC8:406A 8A14          MOV DL,[SI]     ; 21/3300 -- get break flag
FDC8:406C EB35          JMP 40A3
FDC8:406E 48            DEC AX          ; see if subfunct 1
FDC8:406F 7507          JNZ 4078
FDC8:4071 80E201        AND DL,01
FDC8:4074 8814          MOV [SI],DL     ; 21/3301 -- set break flag
FDC8:4076 EB2B          JMP 40A3
FDC8:4078 48            DEC AX          ; see if subfunct 2
FDC8:4079 7507          JNZ 4082
```

```
FDC8:407B 80E201        AND  DL,01
FDC8:407E 8614          XCHG DL,[SI]    ; 21/3302 (UNDOC) -- get/set brk flg
FDC8:4080 EB21          JMP  40A3       ;    as single atomic operation: XCHG
FDC8:4082 3D0300        CMP  AX,0003 ; see if subfnc 5 (already subtracted 2)
FDC8:4085 7506          JNZ  408D
FDC8:4087 8A166900      MOV  DL,[0069]   ; 21/3305 -- get startup drive
FDC8:408B EB16          JMP  40A3
FDC8:408D 3D0400        CMP  AX,0004 ; see if subfnc 6 (already subtracted 2)
FDC8:4090 7511          JNZ  40A3
FDC8:4092 BB0600        MOV  BX,0006       ; 21/3306 -- MS-DOS version 6.0
FDC8:4095 B200          MOV  DL,00
FDC8:4097 32F6          XOR  DH,DH
FDC8:4099 803E111200    CMP  BYTE PTR [1211],00 ; is DOS=HIGH?
FDC8:409E 7403          JZ   40A3
FDC8:40A0 80CE10        OR   DH,10         ; DOSINHMA flag
FDC8:40A3 5E            POP  SI            ; done: restore caller's regs
FDC8:40A4 58            POP  AX
FDC8:40A5 1F            POP  DS
FDC8:40A6 CF            IRET               ; return to caller
```

In addition to showing how DOS happens to handle function 33h, the code in Figure 6-5 also provides many snippets of information than can be used to understand the disassembly listing of other parts of MS-DOS. For example, Microsoft documents INT 21h AX=3306h as returning the DOSINHMA flag in DH. The end of Figure 6-5 shows DOS using the byte at DOS_DS:[1211h] to set DH. Therefore, DOS_DS:[1211h] must be the DOS=HIGH indicator. This is not important by itself, but you can use this fact to help you understand other parts of the code: Anywhere you see DOS:DS:[1211h], you now know that this is the DOSINHMA flag.

Similarly, functions 3300h and 3301h are known to get and set the Ctrl-C flag. Figure 6-5 shows these functions manipulating the byte at offset 0337h in the DOS data segment; this byte must then be the Ctrl-C (or break) flag. (Later on, in Figure 6-7, we'll see how DOS uses this flag.) Finally, Microsoft documents INT 21h AX=3305h as returning the startup drive in DL, and the code in Figure 6-5 clearly shows DOS setting DL from DOS_DS:[0069h]. Therefore, anywhere else in the code where you see DOS_DS:[0069h], you can translate this to STARTUP_DRIVE.

Examining the Low-Memory Stub for DOS=HIGH

Another interesting location to examine is the function that DOS's low memory stub calls when DOS=HIGH, but the A20 line is disabled. The processor's A20 address line accesses memory above one megabyte. PCs based on 286 and higher processors disable A20 in order to emulate address wraparound on 8088 PCs. If DOS=HIGH but A20 is off, DOS must first enable A20 before it can reach its code in HMA above one megabyte. But if DOS's code is located above one megabyte, how can it check A20 in the first place? With a function that it keeps in low memory when DOS=HIGH. Earlier (Figure 6-3) you saw this was located at 0116:118E; Figure 6-6 shows what this function actually does.

Figure 6-6: DOS Function Called When DOS=HIGH But A20 Is Off

```
-u 116:118e
0116:118E 53            PUSH    BX
0116:118F 50            PUSH    AX
0116:1190 8CD0          MOV     AX,SS
0116:1192 2E            CS:
0116:1193 A38610        MOV     [1086],AX
0116:1196 2E            CS:
0116:1197 89268810      MOV     [1088],SP   ; save caller's stack
0116:119B 8CC8          MOV     AX,CS       ; switch to a DOS stack; hmm, not
0116:119D 8ED0          MOV     SS,AX       ;    reentrant at all if A20 off!
0116:119F BCA007        MOV     SP,07A0     ; SDA+480h=end of Crit Err Stack
0116:11A2 B405          MOV     AH,05       ; XMS func 5 = Local Enable A20
```

```
0116:11A4 2E              CS:
0116:11A5 FF1E6311        CALL    FAR [1163]  ; XMS address from 2F/4310
0116:11A9 0BC0            OR      AX,AX
0116:11AB 740F            JZ      11BC        ; failed: can't turn A20 on!!
;;; okay:
0116:11AD 2E              CS:
0116:11AE A18610          MOV     AX,[1086]
0116:11B1 8ED0            MOV     SS,AX
0116:11B3 2E              CS:
0116:11B4 8B268810        MOV     SP,[1088]   ; switch back to caller's stack
0116:11B8 58              POP     AX
0116:11B9 5B              POP     BX
0116:11BA EBCB            JMP     1187    ; jump back into normal code (fig. 6-3)
                                         ; as if A20 had been enabled all along.
;;; fail:
0116:11BC B40F            MOV     AH,0F       ; come here if couldn't enable A20
0116:11BE CD10            INT     10          ; get video mode
0116:11C0 3C07            CMP     AL,07
0116:11C2 7406            JZ      11CA
0116:11C4 32E4            XOR     AH,AH
0116:11C6 B002            MOV     AL,02       ; set normal text mode
0116:11C8 CD10            INT     10
0116:11CA B405            MOV     AH,05
0116:11CC 32C0            XOR     AL,AL       ; set display page 0
0116:11CE CD10            INT     10
0116:11D0 BEB812          MOV     SI,12B8     ; 12B8 -> "\nA20 Hardware Error\n$"
0116:11D3 0E              PUSH    CS
0116:11D4 1F              POP     DS
0116:11D5 FC              CLD
0116:11D6 AC              LODSB
0116:11D7 3C24            CMP     AL,24       ; look for '$'
0116:11D9 7409            JZ      11E4
0116:11DB B40E            MOV     AH,0E       ; write in TTY mode (use BIOS
0116:11DD BB0700          MOV     BX,0007     ;   since can't make DOS calls
0116:11E0 CD10            INT     10          ;   here!)
0116:11E2 EBF2            JMP     11D6
0116:11E4 FB              STI
0116:11E5 EBFD            JMP     11E4        ; tight little loop (INTs on)

-d 116:12b8
0116:12B0                        -0D 0A 41 32 30 20 48 61         ..A20 Ha
0116:12C0  72 64 77 61 72 65 20 45-72 72 6F 72 0D 0A 24 36   rdware Error..$6
```

Notice, by the way, that DOS leaves the A20 line on. This reduces the overhead of keeping the DOS code in the HMA: DOS probably doesn't have to call the low-memory stub in Figure 6-6 very often.

That all *calls* to DOS in the HMA are guarded with this low- memory stub brings up an interesting question: What about *data* in the HMA? MS-DOS doesn't put internal data structures such as the Current Directory Structure (CDS) and System File Tables (SFT) up in the HMA, because this would break too many third-party applications that peek and poke these ostensibly-internal structures and that wouldn't know to first ensure that A20 is enabled. However, DOS does keep its BUFFERS in the HMA. If a program such as BUFFERS.C in Chapter 8 (see Listing 8-8) accesses the DOS sector buffers ("or if some future version of DOS has FILESHIGH or LASTDRIVEHIGH statements that use HMA," adds one tech reviewer), the program would need to check and possible reenable A20, just like DOS does in Figure 6-6. But since, from what we've just seen, any trivial DOS call will ensure that A20 is turned on, perhaps a program that accesses data in the HMA merely needs to preface that access with a trivial DOS call. DOS will take care of checking the A20 state and, if necessary, calling XMS function 5 to enable A20. But any TSR could turn it off! How frequently should programs that access the HMA check the A20 state? How much of a problem is this? Is the extra few kbytes gained by putting data in the HMA worth this kind of uncertainty? ("Ouch! This makes my head hurt," says one of the tech reviewers.)

Examining the INT 21h Dispatch Function

Of all the addresses we found through tracing the INT 21h call, the most important is that of DOS's INT 21h handler, seen in Figure 6-3 at FDC8:40F8. This is really the piece of information we wanted all along. To see exactly what happens during an INT 21h call, we can now disassemble at this address. By tracing an INT 21h AH=62h, we only saw those snippets that happen to get executed when calling the Get PSP function; we can now look at the entire function. Here it is (Figure 6-7), the DOS INT 21h handler (this time we've used SYMDEB and added some labels as well as comments). In Microsoft's source code, this all-important function, located in MSDISP.ASM, is called COMMAND.

Figure 6-7: MS-DOS 6.0 INT 21h Dispatch Function

```
-u fdc8:40f8
FDC8:40F8 FA              CLI                         ; disable interrupts
FDC8:40F9 80FC6C          CMP     AH,6C
FDC8:40FC 77D2            JA      40D0                ; invalid function number

; step 1
FDC8:40FE 80FC33          CMP     AH,33
FDC8:4101 7218            JB      411B                ; normal DOS function
FDC8:4103 74A2            JZ      40A7                ; do 21/33 (fig. 6-5)
FDC8:4105 80FC64          CMP     AH,64
FDC8:4108 7711            JA      411B                ; normal DOS function
FDC8:410A 74B5            JZ      40C1                ; do 21/64
FDC8:410C 80FC51          CMP     AH,51
FDC8:410F 74A4            JZ      40B5                ; do Get PSP
FDC8:4111 80FC62          CMP     AH,62
FDC8:4114 749F            JZ      40B5                ; do Get PSP (51==62)
FDC8:4116 80FC50          CMP     AH,50
FDC8:4119 748E            JZ      40A9                ; do Set PSP (fig. 6-4)

normal_DOS:
; step 2
; caller's flags, CS, and IP of course already pushed on the stack by INT
FDC8:411B 06              PUSH    ES   ; 10h   ; Save regs on caller's stack.
FDC8:411C 1E              PUSH    DS   ; 0Eh   ; The order is important, as
FDC8:411D 55              PUSH    BP   ; 0Ch   ; later on different INT 21h
FDC8:411E 57              PUSH    DI   ; 0Ah   ; functions will access the
FDC8:411F 56              PUSH    SI   ; 08h   ; caller's original registers
FDC8:4120 52              PUSH    DX   ; 06h   ; by treating this stack frame
FDC8:4121 51              PUSH    CX   ; 04h   ; as a structure. See 2f/1218.
FDC8:4122 53              PUSH    BX   ; 02h   ; For example, caller's BX
FDC8:4123 50              PUSH    AX   ; 00h   ; is at offset 2, ES at 10h.

; step 3
FDC8:4124 8CD8            MOV     AX,DS
FDC8:4126 2E8E1EE73D      MOV     DS,CS:[3DE7]        ; get DOS DS
FDC8:412B A3EC05          MOV     [05EC],AX           ; save caller's DS
FDC8:412E 891EEA05        MOV     [05EA],BX           ; save caller's BX
FDC8:4132 A18405          MOV     AX,[0584]   ; SDA+264h = ptr to stack frame
FDC8:4135 A3F205          MOV     [05F2],AX   ;     containing user registers
FDC8:4138 A18605          MOV     AX,[0586]   ;         on INT 21h
FDC8:413B A3F005          MOV     [05F0],AX

; step 4
FDC8:413E 33C0            XOR     AX,AX               ; set AX=0
FDC8:4140 A27205          MOV     [0572],AL
FDC8:4143 F606301001      TEST    Byte Ptr [1030],01  ; Is Win3 Enh running?
FDC8:4148 7503            JNZ     414D
```

```
; following line only if Windows 3 Enhanced mode not running!
FDC8:414A A33E03       MOV    [033E],AX        ; set machine ID to zero


; step 5
FDC8:414D FE062103     INC    Byte Ptr [0321]   ; increment InDOS flag


; step 6
FDC8:4151 89268405     MOV    [0584],SP        ; SDA+264h
FDC8:4155 8C168605     MOV    [0586],SS        ; save current stack ptr
FDC8:4159 A13003       MOV    AX,[0330]        ; get current PSP
FDC8:415C A33C03       MOV    [033C],AX        ; SDA+1Ch = SHARE, NET PSP
FDC8:415F 8ED8         MOV    DS,AX            ; point DS at caller's PSP
FDC8:4161 58           POP    AX
FDC8:4162 50           PUSH   AX               ; get back caller's AX
FDC8:4163 89262E00     MOV    [002E],SP        ; save current stack ptr
FDC8:4167 8C163000     MOV    [0030],SS        ;     in caller's PSP
FDC8:416B 2E8E16E73D   MOV    SS,CS:[3DE7]
; INT 21h AX=5D00h (Server Function Call) jumps to here
                                   ; switch stack to 07A0h-SDA =
FDC8:4170 BCA007       MOV    SP,07A0 ;   SDA+480h=end of Crit Err Stk


; step 7
FDC8:4173 FB           STI                      ; reenable interrupts
FDC8:4174 8CD3         MOV    BX,SS
FDC8:4176 8EDB         MOV    DS,BX            ; point DS at DOS_DS
FDC8:4178 93           XCHG   AX,BX            ; caller's AX into BX
FDC8:4179 33C0         XOR    AX,AX
FDC8:417B 36A2F605     MOV    SS:[05F6],AL     ; extended open off?
FDC8:417F 36812611060008 AND  Word Ptr SS:[0611],0800
FDC8:4186 36A25703     MOV    SS:[0357],AL     ; set different vars to 0
FDC8:418A 36A24C03     MOV    SS:[034C],AL
FDC8:418E 36A24A03     MOV    SS:[034A],AL
FDC8:4192 40           INC    AX
FDC8:4193 36A25803     MOV    SS:[0358],AL     ; okay to do INT 28h


; step 8
FDC8:4197 93           XCHG   AX,BX            ; get back caller's AX
FDC8:4198 8ADC         MOV    BL,AH            ; DOS func num into BL
FDC8:419A D1E3         SHL    BX,1    ; make DOS func number into word ofs


; step 9
FDC8:419C FC           CLD
FDC8:419D 0AE4         OR     AH,AH
FDC8:419F 7417         JZ     41B8             ; AH=0 (terminate process)
FDC8:41A1 80FC59       CMP    AH,59
; if 21/59 (get critical error), bypass code that turns off critical error!
FDC8:41A4 7444         JZ     41EA             ; AH=59h (get extended error)
FDC8:41A6 80FC0C       CMP    AH,0C
FDC8:41A9 770D         JA     41B8             ; AH > 0Ch


INT21_01_THRU_0C:
; step 10
FDC8:41AB 36803E200300 CMP    Byte Ptr SS:[0320],00  ; critical error set?
FDC8:41B1 7537         JNZ    41EA    ; if so, stay with crit error stack
FDC8:41B3 BCA00A       MOV    SP,0AA0 ; SDA+780h=end of Char I/O Stack
FDC8:41B6 EB32         JMP    41EA


INT21_00:
INT21_ABOVE_0C: ;;; except (normally) 33h, 50h, 51h, 59h, 62h, 64h
; step 11
FDC8:41B8 36A33A03     MOV    SS:[033A],AX
FDC8:41BC 36C606230301 MOV    Byte Ptr SS:[0323],01  ; crit err locus
FDC8:41C2 36C606200300 MOV    Byte Ptr SS:[0320],00  ; turn off crit error
FDC8:41C8 36C6062203FF MOV    Byte Ptr SS:[0322],FF  ; crit err drive#
```

```
; Windows Enhanced mode patches next four lines into a far call!
FDC8:41CE 50              PUSH    AX
FDC8:41CF B482            MOV     AH,82
FDC8:41D1 CD2A            INT     2A                       ; End crit section
FDC8:41D3 58              POP     AX

FDC8:41D4 36C606580300    MOV     Byte Ptr SS:[0358],00   ; no INT 28h
FDC8:41DA BC2009          MOV     SP,0920          ; SDA+600h = end of Disk Stack
FDC8:41DD 36F6063703FF    TEST    Byte Ptr SS:[0337],FF ; SDA+17h=break flag
FDC8:41E3 7405            JZ      41EA
FDC8:41E5 50              PUSH    AX                       ; BREAK=ON, so
FDC8:41E6 E8964E          CALL    907F                     ; check ctrl-break
FDC8:41E9 58              POP     AX

; step 12
;;; Next four lines are the key; call through dispatch table.
;;; BX holds caller's INT 21h function number SHL 1 (word offset)
FDC8:41EA 2E8B9F9E3E      MOV     BX,CS:[BX+3E9E] ; get func handler addr
FDC8:41EF 36871EEA05      XCHG    BX,SS:[05EA]     ; move func ptr into var
FDC8:41F4 368E1EEC05      MOV     DS,SS:[05EC]   ; switch to caller's saved DS
FDC8:41F9 36FF16EA05      CALL    SS:[05EA]            ; call func handler addr!
;;; We've just called the DOS function for the specific DOS function in AH.

; step 13
;;; Now into cleanup preparatory to returning to caller.
FDC8:41FE 3680268600FB    AND     Byte Ptr SS:[0086],FB
FDC8:4204 FA              CLI
FDC8:4205 2E8E1EE73D      MOV     DS,CS:[3DE7]     ; switch back to DOS DS
FDC8:420A 803E850000      CMP     Byte Ptr [0085],00
FDC8:420F 7527            JNZ     4238
FDC8:4211 FE0E2103        DEC     Byte Ptr [0321]          ; decrement InDOS
FDC8:4215 8E168605        MOV     SS,[0586]        ; switch back to caller's
FDC8:4219 8B268405        MOV     SP,[0584]        ;     stack
FDC8:421D 8BEC            MOV     BP,SP
FDC8:421F 884600          MOV     [BP+00],AL
FDC8:4222 A1F205          MOV     AX,[05F2]
FDC8:4225 A38405          MOV     [0584],AX        ; caller's SP
FDC8:4228 A1F005          MOV     AX,[05F0]
FDC8:422B A38605          MOV     [0586],AX        ; caller's SS
FDC8:422E 58              POP     AX               ; put back caller's
FDC8:422F 5B              POP     BX               ; registers, including
FDC8:4230 59              POP     CX               ; any changes the DOS
FDC8:4231 5A              POP     DX               ; function made to them
FDC8:4232 5E              POP     SI
FDC8:4233 5F              POP     DI
FDC8:4234 5D              POP     BP
FDC8:4235 1F              POP     DS
FDC8:4236 07              POP     ES
FDC8:4237 CF              IRET
```

The dispatch function in Figure 6-7 is the heart of DOS. It is executed every time a program issues an INT 21h call. The dispatch function is the DOS equivalent of the function syscall() in UNIX, which has been examined in books such as Bach's *Design of the UNIX Operating System* (pp. 165-168) and Andleigh's *UNIX System Architecture* (pp. 21-23). The discussions of syscall() in these and other UNIX books provides a useful background for understanding the INT 21h dispatch code. However, in UNIX there is a clear separation between applications and the operating system. The discussions of syscall() emphasize the transition from user mode to kernel mode. As you can see, there is nothing like this in DOS, though DOS extenders such as Windows do maintain a separation between the application running in protected mode and DOS running in real mode. Actually, there is one important separation. DOS usually switches from the application's stack to one of its own. This important aspect of DOS will be discussed in detail below.

Near the top of the function (commented "step 1"), you see how DOS picks off a handful of special functions (33h, 64h, 51, 62h, and 50h). These, of course, are none other than what we've been calling the reentrant DOS functions. Here, reentrancy simply means that, while the above code is executing—after it has passed the initial CLI, and before it has executed the closing IRET—it could be interrupted by an interrupt handler, and the interrupt handler could call one of these five functions. These five functions are reentrant simply in the sense that DOS handles them without switching stacks and incrementing the InDOS flag. Thus an interrupt handler can call these functions, even if the InDOS or critical error flag is set.

In a larger sense, of course, these functions aren't really reentrant, given the way that, for example, the Set PSP function writes to a global variable (see Figure 6-4). MS-DOS's extensive reliance on global variables makes it completely non-reentrant. Furthermore, if DOS=HIGH and the A20 line is off, DOS, as Figure 6-6 showed, has to switch stacks. But in any case, it should now be clear why we picked INT 21h AH=62h to trace with DEBUG and not, say, INT 21h AH=52h; DOS handles the latter function only after switching stacks and incrementing InDOS.

Next (step 2), the INT 21h dispatch code pushes the caller's registers on to the caller's stack. The caller is, of course, simply whatever program issued the INT 21h call. This can be slightly disorienting because, of course, we're used to thinking about INT 21h from the caller's perspective and now we're looking at it from DOS's point of view. These pushed registers form a structure that many DOS functions use later on. Undocumented INT 2Fh AX=1218 (Get Caller's Registers; see appendix) returns a pointer to this structure.

At step 3 in Figure 6-7, DOS saves away the caller's DS and BX again and switches from the caller's DS to its own DS. DOS keeps DS in a variable accessible through DOS's CS. It is also available by calling INT 2Fh AX=1203h (see get_dos_ds() in Listing 6-2). Note that, even though DOS=HIGH and the DOS code is in the HMA, the data segment is still in low memory. This is necessary because many existing DOS programs rely on the ability to reach DOS internal data structures and wouldn't know to first check the status of the A20 line. Microsoft has to introduce improvements such as DOS=HIGH without breaking existing applications.

The next interesting thing the code does (step 4) is check a variable at 1030h to see whether Windows 3.x Enhanced mode (or Windows/386 2.x) is running. Since most of us think of Windows as something that runs "on top of" DOS, it is a bit disconcerting at first to learn that DOS 5.0 and higher know about Windows. As discussed in Chapter 1, however, this part of the intricate DOS/Windows connection is implemented using documented functionality. In its INT 2Fh handler, MSDOS.SYS monitors the AX=1605h Windows initialization and AX=1606h exit broadcasts; the code for AX=1605h sets the variable at 1030h (actually, just the byte at 1031h), and the code for AX=1606h clears it. This variable thus serves as a kind of InWindows flag. It's important to underline that this is for Enhanced mode only; DOS doesn't care one way or the other about Standard mode.

If Windows Enhanced mode is *not* running, then DOS zeroes out a variable at 033Eh (SDA+1Eh), used by DOS as the machine ID. If Windows Enhanced mode is running, the DOSMGR VxD (as explained in Chapter 1) has smacked a virtual machine ID in here. DOS uses this VM ID to manage SFTs.

Next (step 5), the code increments the InDOS flag, which is simply a variable at 0321h (SDA+1) in the DOS data segment. The until-recently-undocumented function INT 21h AH=34h (Get InDOS Flag Address) returns a pointer to this variable.

The InDOS flag has been set, so we're now "in DOS"! Of course, we were in DOS before, but the significance of this spot is that DOS is about to switch stacks. Switching stacks requires a guard or semaphore, namely the InDOS flag. Notice, however, that while DOS increments the InDOS flag, it does not check it before proceeding. Thus, InDOS is not a true semaphore. If the processor is interrupted in the middle of this code (or, rather, a little further on when DOS reenables interrupts with an STI instruction), the code can be reentered.

In other words, DOS does nothing to enforce its requirement that only one caller at a time execute inside the INT 21h code. Obeying the InDOS flag is merely a convention. But it is vital that programs do observe this convention, because making an INT 21h call when InDOS is set will almost always cause problems. For one thing, DOS relies on many global variables. If, for example, DOS were working with a particular hard-disk cluster to service an INT 21h file I/O call, and an interrupt handler that ignored the InDOS flag made a file I/O call to DOS before DOS had finished with the first one, DOS would mistakenly use the second caller's cluster to satisfy (not!) the first caller's request. Global variables do not work like a last-in/first-out stack. It is vital that interrupt handlers check InDOS before issuing INT 21h calls. (So why did it take Microsoft so long to document InDOS and the INT 21h AH=34h function that returns a pointer to it?)

Ignoring InDOS can cause another problem. Because the code at step 5 in Figure 6-7 increments InDOS, reentering DOS means that InDOS will take on a value of two or greater. This is bad, because the internal DOS function that checks for Ctrl-C only does so when CMP Byte Ptr IN_DOS, 01. Thus, if InDOS is 2 or greater, DOS won't check Ctrl-C, even if BREAK=ON.

There is a method by which DOS can be safely reentered: If the entire DOS state (including all three DOS stacks) is saved and restored by each caller, and if each such caller observes the DOS critical sections by hooking INT 2Ah. The SDA TSR technique put forward in Chapter 9 is an approximation of this method, though only an approximation because the SDA does not include the entire DOS state.

Returning to step 6 in Figure 6-7, you can see the beginnings of the stack switching code. How does DOS switch away from the user's stack to one of its own? First, it saves away the caller's current SS:SP. Next, DOS gets the current PSP (at 0330h, or SDA+10h) and uses it to save the caller's SS:SP at offset 2Eh in the caller's PSP. Finally, it sets SS:SP to a DOS stack. Depending on the DOS function number, it may switch again to a different DOS stack.

What is the purpose of stack switching? Why not just use the caller's stack? Wouldn't that make DOS much more reentrant? Yes, it would. As it is, making an INT 21h call already uses 18h bytes on the caller's stack (see Table 6-2). If the caller could be relied on to provide a large enough stack, DOS could even be multithreaded. Unfortunately, DOS has to accommodate programs with unknown stack sizes. This complicates DOS tremendously and helps make it non-reentrant.

At the very end of step 6, where DOS points SP at the Critical Error stack, is a location (called Redisp in the source code) to which undocumented INT 21h AX=5D00h (Server Function Call) jumps. This function is a backdoor into the INT 21h dispatcher. If a network-aware program hooks this call, it can be used by one machine to do remote INT 21h calls on another machine (or perhaps to another Windows virtual machine).

Skipping over a bunch of the code in step 7, which zeroes out several variables in the DOS data segment, we come to step 8, where the code takes the caller's AH (with the crucial DOS function number) and turns it into a word offset in BX. This will be important later on.

Next (step 9), DOS examines the function number in AH. If AH=59 (Get Extended Error) is being called, DOS proceeds directly to step 12, where the code for function 59h will be called. It stays on the Critical Error Stack, bypassing more stack-switching code in steps 10 and 11, and bypassing code that would obliterate information pertaining to any pending Critical Error.

If one of the CP/M-based character I/O functions (INT 21h AH=1 through AH=0Ch) is being called, DOS (step 10) points SP at 0AA0h, which is the top of the character I/0 stack, located in the Swappable Data Area (see appendix). However, if there is a pending critical error, DOS stays with the Critical Error stack that was set initially. This is not surprising, since Microsoft documents these functions (*MS-DOS Programmer's Reference*) as callable from a critical error handler. Notice that DOS does not turn off critical error information for functions 1 through 0Ch. As you can see, much of the core DOS code accommodates critical errors.

Finally, if the DOS function number is 0 (Terminate Program), or anything greater than 0Ch, but not 59h, and not one of the special functions that were picked off earlier in step 1 and which DOS already processed on the caller's stack, DOS (step 11) switches to the disk stack. Thus, there are three DOS stacks:

- Critical Error (or auxiliary), used for function 59h and for functions 1 through 0Ch when a critical error is pending, and used temporarily for any DOS function call if DOS=HIGH but A20 is off.
- Character I/O Stack, used for functions 1 through 0Ch in the absence of a critical error
- Disk Stack, used for everything else. Calling any of the special functions with the INT 21h AX=5D00h indirect function call also ends up using this stack (though in practice indirectly calling the special functions via 21/5D00 crashes the machine).

For the majority of functions running on the disk stack, the code (step 11) carries out a number of tasks, turning off critical error, calling undocumented INT 2Ah AH=82h to end any critical sections (see below), and checking the Ctrl-C Check flag at SDA+17h. In Figure 6-5, you saw the code for INT 21h AX=3301h that sets this flag when a user types BREAK=ON. Now you can see where DOS actually uses this flag. If BREAK=ON (that is, if the flag at SDA+17h is non-zero), DOS calls a sub-routine (here located at 907Fh) to check Ctrl-C for the functions that come through here. Otherwise, DOS (elsewhere) only checks Ctrl-C for functions 1 through 0Ch. As noted earlier, the DOS internal function to check Ctrl-C will only do so if IN_DOS == 1.

What is this call to INT 2Ah AH=82h? Normally, the INT 2Ah handler in DOS does an immediate IRET, performing no operation. However, other programs can take over INT 2Ah and/or patch DOS. Windows Enhanced mode, in particular, uses INT 2Ah critical sections because it runs preemptively multitasked DOS boxes on top of a single copy of MS-DOS. Because the InDOS flag is instanced per VM (that is, each DOS box gets its own copy), it cannot be used to control access to DOS by different VMs. Nor would you want the InDOS flag to do that, as different VMs could be in different *parts* of DOS at the same time. What different parts? Different critical sections can be set and cleared with INT 2Ah AH=80h and 81h (see appendix). DOS's call to INT 2Ah AH=82h is a signal that a multitasking extension to DOS, such as Windows or networking software, can restart any task (VM) that was suspended because it was waiting for a critical section. For additional information on critical sections, see Chapter 1 and Chapter 9 (see CRITSECT.C in Listing 9-19). Also see Microsoft's *MS-DOS 6 Technical Reference* (p. 41), which briefly discusses critical sections in the context of the MRCI specification.

As discussed later in this chapter, the DOSMGR VxD in Windows Enhanced mode patches this INT 2Ah AH=82h in the INT 21h dispatch, turning it into a far call into Windows. When Windows exits, of course it (hopefully) puts back the original code.

With all this talk of critical errors, Ctrl-Break, and critical sections—which do dominate the DOS dispatch code—it is important not to lose sight of the main goal, which is that a program wants to call a DOS function! As is typical of software, DOS accomplishes this main goal in only a few lines, while rarer situations such as critical errors and so on occupy the bulk of the code.

Having switched to an appropriate stack, saved the caller's registers, and so on, step 12 in Figure 6-7 is the simplest and the most important. Recall that step 8 moved the function number in AH into BX and multiplied by two. DOS will now use this value as an offset into an array of function pointers, one for each DOS function. Here, the table is at CS:3E9E, so that for example the address for DOS function 0 is at CS:3E9E, function 1's address is at CS:3EA0, function 2's address is at CS:3EA2, and so on. Since this array holds two-byte words, not far pointers, you can't use it to hook individual DOS functions. All handlers must be located in a single segment (here, FDC8h). We come back to this array of function pointers momentarily; it is very important to us. In any case, having retrieved the address of the handler for the DOS function being called, DOS calls the handler. Ta da! The function the user wanted has now been called.

In step 13, having invoked the appropriate handler for the DOS function, DOS decrements the InDOS flag, switches back to the caller's stack, and pops back the caller's registers from the register image created on the stack back in step 2. As you'll see in a moment, the handler for the specific DOS function probably modifies the register image. Finally, DOS returns to the caller with an IRET. Since IRET pops the flags off the stack, the specific DOS functions have to set or clear the carry flag by modifying its image that the processor pushed on the stack as part of the initial INT (see the comment to step 2).

Seeing the DOS dispatch code in Figure 6-7, it should now be clear why a DEBUG trace through an INT 21h AH=62h call works, but tracing, for example, through a call to INT 21h AH=52h wouldn't. A call to AH=52h would involve switching stacks, mucking with global variables in the DOS data segment, and so on. DEBUG itself uses DOS, so you would end up instead tracing through one of the DOS calls that DEBUG would be making to display our information. A complete mess! One alternative, of course, is to use a debugger that bypasses DOS, such as Soft-ICE (or Tim Patterson's SERMON from the first edition of *Undocumented DOS*, which, however, did not support tracing through INT instructions).

Examining the INT 21h Dispatch Table
We really don't need to trace through INT 21h any more. We now have the address of COMMAND (The One True INT 21h Handler) and the address of the function pointer array (called Dispatch in the DOS source code) and can thus unassemble at leisure, rather than trace under pressure, so to speak.

To find the code that handles each specific DOS function, you need do nothing more than dump out the Dispatch table, which you can see from step 12 in Figure 6-7 is located at FDC8:3E9E. This table of two-byte words is conveniently dumped with SYMDEB's dw command:

```
-dw fdc8:3e9e
FDC8:3E9E  A1F6 54E0 54E9 559F 55BC 55C2 541C 544B
FDC8:3EAE  51BA 5214 5220 55D6 55E0 4DA1 4C78 5CCC
FDC8:3EBE  5688 5DDF 5E73 5625 5DCB 5DD0 5DB1 56F9
FDC8:3ECE  440D 4C73 4C68 4D2D 4D2F 440D 440D 4D71
FDC8:3EDE  440D 5DD5 5DDA 5639 560D 4C9A 4EB6 5DC6
FDC8:3EEE  5DC1 4D22 4839 4856 4876 4887 4A46 4C54
FDC8:3EFE  4A1C A19A 4D73 4052 4D59 4C8A 4C2B 4CC9
FDC8:3F0E  4A4D 60E1 6029 6065 AFE6 AF0F A72A A839
; ... etc. ...
```

You can double-check that all is in order by looking for a known function. Let's see what the table shows for function 62h (although we know it usually gets picked off in step 1 of Figure 6-7, only coming through this table in the unlikely event of an INT 21h AX=5D00h indirect function call of AH=62h):

```
-dw fdc8:(3e9e+62*2)
FDC8:3F62  40B5 ......

-u fdc8:40b5
FDC8:40B5 1E              PUSH    DS
FDC8:40B6 2E8E1EE73D      MOV     DS,CS:[3DE7]
FDC8:40BB 8B1E3003        MOV     BX,[0330]
FDC8:40BF 1F              POP     DS
FDC8:40C0 CF              IRET
```

That's it! So you now have the DOS dispatch table and can examine at will the code for any DOS function you're interested in.

Examination of this table and others like it is made easier with a short C program, FTAB.C, shown in Listing 6-4. FTAB can display tables of bytes (1), words (2), or dwords (4).

Listing 6-4: FTAB.C

```c
/* FTAB.C */

#include <stdlib.h>
#include <stdio.h>
#include <dos.h>

typedef unsigned char BYTE;
typedef unsigned short WORD;
typedef unsigned long DWORD;

void fail(const char *s) { puts(s); exit(1); }

main(int argc, char *argv[])
{
    char *prefix;
    void far *tab;
    BYTE far *btab;
    WORD far *wtab;
    DWORD far *dtab;
    WORD seg, ofs;
    int num_func, size, i;

    if (argc < 4)
        fail("usage: ftab <seg:ofs> <num_func | ?> [prefix] [size]");

    sscanf(argv[1], "%04X:%04X", &seg, &ofs);
    tab = (void far *) MK_FP(seg, ofs);

    if (argv[2][0] == '?')
    {
        num_func = *((BYTE far *) tab);     /* first BYTE is #func */
        tab = ((BYTE far *) tab + 1);       /* then array of WORDs */
    }
    else
        sscanf(argv[2], "%04X", &num_func);

    prefix = (argc > 3) ? argv[3] : "func";
    size = (argc > 4) ? atoi(argv[4]) : 2;  /* default to WORD table */

    switch (size)
    {
        case 1:
            for (i=0, btab=(BYTE far *)tab; i<num_func; i++, btab++)
                printf("%02X\t%s_%02X\n",
                    *btab, prefix, i);
            break;
        case 2:
            for (i=0, wtab=(WORD far *)tab; i<num_func; i++, wtab++)
                printf("%04X:%04X\t%s_%02X\n",
                    seg, *wtab, prefix, i);
            break;
        case 4:
            for (i=0, dtab=(DWORD far *)tab; i<num_func; i++, dtab++)
                printf("%Fp\t%s_%02X\n",
                    *dtab, prefix, i);
            break;
        default:
            fail("size only 1 (byte), 2 (word), 4 (dword)");
    }

    return 0;
}
```

To generate a list of the 6Dh (0 through 6Ch) different DOS INT 21h function handlers ("72h, not 6Ch, is the highest function number in the DOS 7.0 component of Chicago," says one tech reviewer), run FTAB on the table at FDC8:3E9E. Figure 6-8 shows sample output from FTAB.

Figure 6-8: The INT 21h Dispatch Table Displayed by FTAB

```
C:\UNDOC2\CHAP6>ftab fdc8:3e9e 6D int21 2
FDC8:A1F6    int21_00
FDC8:54E0    int21_01
FDC8:54E9    int21_02
FDC8:559F    int21_03
; ...
FDC8:4C9A    int21_25
; ...
FDC8:4D59    int21_34
FDC8:4C8A    int21_35
; ...
FDC8:AF0F    INT21_3D
FDC8:A72A    INT21_3E
FDC8:A839    INT21_3F
FDC8:A89F    INT21_40
FDC8:B038    INT21_41
FDC8:A8A4    INT21_42
; ...
FDC8:40A9    int21_50
FDC8:40B5    int21_51
FDC8:4D65    int21_52
FDC8:4DD6    int21_53
FDC8:4A41    int21_54
FDC8:4EA5    int21_55
FDC8:B05E    int21_56
FDC8:A90C    int21_57
FDC8:A448    int21_58
FDC8:4CDD    int21_59
FDC8:B0E9    int21_5A
FDC8:B0D1    int21_5B
FDC8:B2D8    int21_5C
FDC8:A531    int21_5D
FDC8:AA49    int21_5E
FDC8:A9AA    int21_5F
FDC8:AEA8    int21_60
FDC8:440D    int21_61
FDC8:40B5    int21_62
; ... etc. ...
```

Confirming that this table is correct, you can see that int21_51 and int21_62 are located at the same address (FDC8:40B5), as they should be.

Get SysVars and the Caller's Registers

To check that the FTAB output in Figure 6-8 is correct, examine another function that should be simple, INT 21h AH=52h, which returns a far pointer to SysVars in ES:BX. According to the FTAB output, the code to handle function 52h should be at FDC8:4D65, so you can use SYMDEB or DEBUG to unassemble at that address. Figure 6-9 shows the results.

Figure 6-9: MS-DOS 6.0 Implementation of INT 21h AH=52h (Get SysVars)

```
-u fdc8:4d65
FDC8:4D65 E81AF5        CALL    4282
FDC8:4D68 C744022600    MOV     Word Ptr [SI+02],0026
FDC8:4D6D 8C5410        MOV     [SI+10],SS
FDC8:4D70 C3            RET
```

In fact, calling Get SysVars in this particular configuration does return 0116:0026, so the hard-wired 0026h does look correct. But what is going on here?! How come we don't see SS:0026 being moved into ES:BX? What are [SI+02] and [SI+10h]? To answer these questions, let's examine the subroutine being called at 4282h:

```
-u fdc8:4282
FDC8:4282 2E8E1EE73D    MOV    DS,CS:[3DE7]
FDC8:4287 C5368405      LDS    SI,[0584]
FDC8:428B C3            RET
```

CS:3D37h is just our old friend (see step 3 in Figure 6-7) , the DOS data segment, whose value DOS keeps in its code segment. (DOS stores the value of DS in its code segment because, when an INT occurs, DS isn't known, but CS is.) So this subroutine is first setting itself up to use DOS's DS, just as the code did back in Figures 6-3, 6-4, and 6-7 for Get PSP, Set PSP, and the INT 21h dispatch.

The subroutine then loads DS:SI with something at DOS:584h. In step 6 of the INT 21h dispatch code in Figure 6-7, you saw DOS set the dword at DOS:584h to the caller's SS:SP. In other words, DOS:584h contains a pointer to the caller's stack, with all the registers that were pushed on it during step 2 of Figure 6-7 (and earlier, as part of the actual INT instruction). Sure enough, the comments to step 3 point out that DOS:584h in this configuration happens to be SDA+264h, which the appendix identifies as "a pointer to the stack frame containing the user registers on entry to the INT 21h call."

So the subroutine at FDC8:4282 loads DS:SI with a pointer to the caller's pushed register structure. Given the order in which steps push registers, it won't surprise you to learn that the client register structure has the format shown in Table 6-2.

Table 6-2: MS-DOS Caller's Register Structure

00h	AX
02h	BX
04h	CX
06h	DX
08h	SI
0Ah	DI
0Ch	BP
0Eh	DS
10h	ES
12h	IP
14h	CS
16h	flags

In Figure 6-9, the code for function 52h at FDC8:4D65 moves 26h into [SI+2] and DOS's SS (DS) into [SI+10h]. DS:SI points at the caller's register structure, where offset 2 is BX and offset 10h is ES. Thus, the code is actually setting an image of the caller's ES:BX to DOS_DS:0026. The register image gets popped into the actual CPU registers in the series of POPs at the end (step 13) of the INT 21h dispatch in Figure 6-7. So this is how INT 21h function 52h returns SysVars in ES:BX. (If you want to see how DOS creates SysVars in the first place, you need to disassemble the DOS initialization code.) You may have noted from the appendix that there is an internal DOS function, INT 2Fh AX=1218h, to get the caller's register structure; it returns a pointer to the structure in DS:SI. This sounds a lot like the subfunction you viewed at FDC8:4282. In fact, they are one and the same function. DOS calls this subroutine through a near function pointer rather than through an INT 2Fh. You'll see in a moment that, in a table of INT 2Fh AH=12h subfunctions, 4282h duly appears as the handler for subfunction 18h.

A Very Brief Glance at File I/O

Next, let's look at a more interesting function. From Figure 6-8, the code for INT 21h AH=3Fh (Read File) is supposed to be located at FDC8:A839. The code for this function is too extensive to examine in depth here, so let's just look at the first two lines:

```
-u FDC8:A839
FDC8:A839 BEFD71          MOV     SI,71FD       ; offset of internal Read func
FDC8:A83C E82DFE          CALL    A66C          ; see below
; ...
```

You know that function 3Fh expects a file handle in BX; you know furthermore that file handles are associated with the current PSP. Examining the subroutine called at A66Ch shows how DOS uses the passed-in file handle:

```
-u FDC8:A66C
FDC8:A66C 2E8E06E73D      MOV     ES,CS:[3DE7]  ; get DOS DS
FDC8:A671 268E063003      MOV     ES,ES:[0330]  ; ES <- current PSP
FDC8:A676 263B1E3200      CMP     BX,ES:[0032]  ; PSP[32h] = # max open files
FDC8:A67B 7204            JB      A681
FDC8:A67D B006            MOV     AL,06         ; 6 = invalid handle error
FDC8:A67F F9              STC                   ; set carry flag
FDC8:A680 C3              RET
FDC8:A681 26C43E3400      LES     DI,ES:[0034]  ; PSP[34h] -> file handle tbl
FDC8:A686 03FB            ADD     DI,BX         ; use file handle as offset
FDC8:A688 C3              RET
```

In other words, this subroutine uses the current PSP to convert the passed-in file handle into a pointer to the caller's Job File Table (see Chapter 8). Dereferencing this pointer yields an index into the System File Table. From the SFT entry, the DOS Read function can determine what type of file the caller wants to read from. With a network file, for example, the Read function must pass the call down to a redirector (see Chapter 8), whereas with a normal file, a device driver must handle the call. Of course, a Read call may never get here in the first place, having already been picked off by a disk cache such as SMARTDRV. That, after all, is the whole point of a disk cache.

The subroutine at FDC8:A66C is none other than the handler for the internal DOS function INT 2Fh AX=1220h (Get Job File Table Entry; see appendix). You saw earlier that many DOS functions call use a near pointer to INT 2Fh AX=1218h to get a pointer to the client register structure. And the "MOV DS,CS:[3DE7]" code you've seen so many times sounds a lot like what INT 2Fh AX=1203h (Get DOS Data Segment) must do. We keep on running into these INT 2Fh AH=12h subfunctions; it's time to take a closer look.

Tracing a DOS INT 2Fh Call

To examine the code for INT 2Fh AH=12h, we're going to unassemble the DOS INT 2Fh handler, just as we did for INT 21h. Recall that we first used DEBUG to trace through a simple INT 21h call so we could find the DOS INT 21h handler. We could do the same thing again for a simple call such as INT 2Fh AX=1200h (DOS internal services installation check; see appendix). But is there any way to automate what DEBUG did? Can you perhaps trace through interrupts and locate an entire interrupt chain without DEBUG's help?

How Does DEBUG Trace Through an INT?

First you have to understand a little of how the DEBUG trace command works. The first edition of *Undocumented DOS* had an entire chapter by Tim Paterson on debugging, with extensive source code examples on the accompanying disk (\UNDOC\CHAP7*.ASM) This is an excellent place to turn for a general understanding of how DEBUG works.

The trace command in debuggers such as DEBUG and SYMDEB uses the single-step feature built into all Intel 80x86 microprocessors. When the processor's trace flag (TF) is enabled, the processor issues an INT 1 for every instruction it executes. A debugger can install an INT 1 (single-step) handler and get the effect of having a breakpoint on every instruction.

However, a single-step handler contains code too, and leaving TF enabled on entry to the single-step handler would produce an endless loop. For this reason, the processor temporarily disables the trace flag when it issues an interrupt and reenables tracing when the interrupt handler returns. In fact, the processor disables single step for *all* interrupts.

This is why most debuggers won't trace into an INT. To trace through an INT, a debugger must do something like set a breakpoint at the first instruction of the interrupt handler and then reenable single step after the breakpoint is hit (see Crawford and Gelsinger, *Programming the 80386*). This is what DEBUG does. Unfortunately, the MON family of debuggers included with the first edition of *Undocumented DOS* happened not to trace through INT instructions.

INTCHAIN

We can incorporate this knowledge into a program that single steps through an interrupt handler. INTCHAIN.C, shown in Listing 6-5, installs an INT 1 single-step handler, turns on the trace flag, calls an interrupt function specified on the program's command line, and turns off the trace flag. Because INTCHAIN.C uses a far CALL rather than an INT, the processor calls the single-step handler for each instruction in the other interrupt handler; the handler saves away CS:IP whenever CS changes, as a likely indication that the interrupt function is chaining to the previous handler. When the interrupt function returns and INTCHAIN has turned off the trace flag, INTCHAIN prints out the interrupt chain saved by the single-step handler.

For example, consider the point made in Figure 6-3 that SMARTDRV does back-end handling of the DOS Disk Reset function (INT 21h AH=0Dh). This is plainly visible in an INTCHAIN trace of a call to this function, shown in Figure 6-10a.

Figure 6-10a: INTCHAIN Display for INT 21h AH=0Dh (Disk Reset)

```
C:\UNDOC2\CHAP6>intchain 21/0d00
1387 instructions
Skipped over 4 INT

0B94:32B6    MSCDEX
07FA:15FA    SMARTDRV
C801:0829
0255:0023    J:
CC2C:058E    DBLSSYS$
0116:109E    DOS
FDC8:40F8    HMA
0070:06F5    IO
FDC8:8653    HMA
0070:0700    IO
FFFF:0043    HMA
CC2C:0623    DBLSSYS$
07FA:1631    SMARTDRV
```

Notice that, after being processed by MSDOS.SYS, IO.SYS, and DBLSSYS$, the call winds up back in SMARTDRV.

For a direct comparison with the DEBUG trace in Figure 6-3, Figure 6-10b presents sample INTCHAIN output when tracing an INT 21h AH=62h call.

Figure 6-10b: INTCHAIN Display for INT 21h AH=62h

```
C:\UNDOC2\CHAP6>intchain 21/6200
77 instructions
```

```
OF93:32B6    MSCDEX
07F9:15FA    SMARTDRV
C801:0800
0255:0023    D:
CC2E:058E    DBLSSYS$
0116:109E    DOS
FDC8:40F8    HMA
```

Sure enough, this matches the interrupt chain we so laboriously traced back in Figure 6-3. INTCHAIN uses MAP.C from Listing 6-2 to try to match up CS:IP addresses with the names of resident TSRs and drivers. The addresses displayed by INTCHAIN can be passed to SYMDEB or DEBUG for unassembly (this is the whole point of the program).

INTCHAIN can also trace through an XMS function or an arbitrary segment:offset pointer. Actually, the program has little to do with interrupt chains as such. Rather than generate an actual INT instruction and then have to mess with setting a breakpoint, the program just turns an INT XXh into a far call (and PUSHF) to the handler for INT XXh. Thus, INTCHAIN won't trace through any INT generated inside the handler (such as the INT 2Ah call made by the INT 21h dispatch in Figure 6-7); this is generally what you want anyway.

Listing 6-5: INTCHAIN.C

```
/*
INTCHAIN.C
Andrew Schulman, May 1993
Copyright (C) 1993 Andrew Schulman. All rights reserved.

bcc intchain.c map.c

Uses single-step to trace through interrupt chains
usage:    intchain intno/ax/bx/cx/dx
example: intchain 21/6200
*/

#include <stdlib.h>
#include <stdio.h>
#include <string.h>
#include <dos.h>

typedef unsigned char BYTE;
typedef unsigned short WORD;
typedef unsigned long DWORD;

#ifdef __cplusplus
typedef void interrupt (far *INTRFUNC)(...);
#else
typedef void (interrupt far *INTRFUNC)(void);
#endif

typedef void (far *FARFUNC)(void);

#ifndef MK_FP
#define MK_FP(s,o)  ((((DWORD) s) << 16) + (o))
#endif

#define MK_LIN(fp)  ((((DWORD) FP_SEG(fp)) << 4) + FP_OFF(fp))

#pragma pack(1)

typedef struct {
#ifdef __TURBOC__
    WORD bp,di,si,ds,es,dx,cx,bx,ax;
#else
```

```
        WORD es,ds,di,si,bp,sp,bx,dx,cx,ax;       /* same as PUSHA */
#endif
        WORD ip,cs,flags;
        } REG_PARAMS;

#define INT_INSTR        0xCD
#define TRACE_FLAG       0x100

extern char *find_owner(DWORD lin_addr);    // in map.c

void fail(const char *s) { puts(s); exit(1); }

#define MAX_ADDR         512

static WORD volatile instr = 0, int_instr = 0;
static WORD prev_seg = 0, my_seg = 0;
static void far * *addr;
static int num_addr = 0;

void interrupt far single_step(REG_PARAMS r)    // INT 1 handler
{
    WORD seg;
    BYTE far *fp;

    if ((seg = r.cs) == my_seg)               // ignore my own code
        return;

    fp = (BYTE far *) MK_FP(r.cs, r.ip);
    if (fp[0] == INT_INSTR)                   // count INTs
        int_instr++;
    instr++;

    if (seg != prev_seg)                      // if segment changed,
    {                                         // assume we've chained
        if (num_addr < MAX_ADDR)
            addr[num_addr++] = (void far *) fp;
        prev_seg = seg;
    }
}

#define GET_FLAGS(reg)  _asm { pushf } ; _asm { pop reg }
#define SET_FLAGS(reg)  _asm { push reg } ; _asm { popf }

void set_flag(unsigned mask)
{
    GET_FLAGS(ax);
    _asm or ax, word ptr mask
    SET_FLAGS(ax);
}

void clear_flag(unsigned mask)
{
    GET_FLAGS(ax);
    _asm mov bx, word ptr mask
    _asm not bx
    _asm and ax, bx
    SET_FLAGS(ax);
}

FARFUNC get_xms(void)
{
    _asm mov ax, 4300h
    _asm int 2fh
    _asm cmp al, 80h
    _asm je present
```

```
absent:
    fail("XMS not present!");
present:
    _asm mov ax, 4310h
    _asm int 2fh
    _asm mov ax, bx
    _asm mov dx, es
    // retval in DX:AX
}

main(int argc, char *argv[])
{
    static int intrfunc = 0;       /* make sure not in a register */
    INTRFUNC old_sstep;
    FARFUNC func = (FARFUNC) 0;
    FARFUNC xms_func = (FARFUNC) 0;
    void far *fp;
    char *s;
    WORD intno, _ax, _bx, _cx, _dx;
    int a20off = 0;
    int i;

    puts("INTCHAIN 1.0 -- Walks interrupt chains");
    puts("From \"Undocumented DOS\", 2nd edition (Addison-Wesley, 1993)");
    puts("Copyright (C) 1993 Andrew Schulman. All rights reserved.\n");

    if (argc < 2)
        fail("usage: intchain [-a20off] <intno|xms|seg:ofs>/ax/bx/cx/dx");

    if (strcmp(strupr(argv[1]), "-A20OFF") == 0)
    {
        xms_func = get_xms();
        a20off++;
        argv++;
    }

    // Figure out what code they want to generate:
    // an XMS call
    if (strncmp(strupr(argv[1]), "XMS", 3) == 0)
    {
        func = get_xms();
        sscanf(argv[1], "XMS/%04X/%04X/%04X/%04X",
            &_ax, &_bx, &_cx, &_dx);
        printf("Tracing XMS at %Fp\n", func);
    }
    // ... or a far (segment:offset) CALL
    else if (strchr(argv[1], ':'))
    {
        WORD seg, ofs;
        sscanf(argv[1], "%04X:%04X/%04X/%04X/%04X/%04X",
            &seg, &ofs, &_bx, &_cx, &_dx);
        func = (FARFUNC) MK_FP(seg, ofs);
        printf("Tracing function at %Fp\n", func);
    }
    // ... or an INT XXh
    else
    {
        sscanf(argv[1], "%02X/%04X/%04X/%04X/%04X",
            &intno, &_ax, &_bx, &_cx, &_dx);

        /* single-step doesn't go through INT, so turn the INT into
           a PUSHF and far CALL */
        if (! (func = (FARFUNC) _dos_getvect(intno)))
            fail("INT unused");
        intrfunc++;       // so do PUSHF when call func
```

```
        printf("Tracing INT %02X AX=%04X\n", intno, _ax);
    }
    if (! (addr = (void far **) calloc(MAX_ADDR, sizeof(void far *))))
        fail("insufficient memory");
    fp = (void far *) main;
    my_seg = FP_SEG(fp);

    old_sstep = _dos_getvect(1);
    _dos_setvect(1, (INTRFUNC) single_step);

    if (a20off)
    {
        _asm mov ah, 6
        (*xms_func)();   // local disable A20 line
    }

    set_flag(TRACE_FLAG);

    /* call the code */
    _asm mov ax, _ax
    _asm mov bx, _bx
    _asm mov cx, _cx
    _asm mov dx, _dx
    if (intrfunc)
        _asm pushf
    (*func)();

    clear_flag(TRACE_FLAG);
    _dos_setvect(1, old_sstep);

    printf("%u instructions\n", instr);
    if (int_instr)
        printf("Skipped over %u INT\n", int_instr);
    printf("\n");

    for (i=0; i<num_addr; i++)
    {
        s = find_owner(MK_LIN(addr[i]));
        printf("%Fp\t%s\n", addr[i], s? s: " ");
    }
    if (num_addr == MAX_ADDR)
        fail("Overflow: very long INT chain!");

    return 0;
}
```

Examining The INT 2Fh Chain

You can now use INTCHAIN to trace through a call to INT 2Fh AX=1200h, without using DEBUG.
Figure 6-11 shows sample results. Note that the configuration is somewhat different from the one
used to produce the INTCHAIN output for INT 21h AH=62h in Figure 6-10b.

Figure 6-11: INTCHAIN Display for INT 2Fh AX=1200h

```
C:\UNDOC2\CHAP6>intchain 2f/1200
174 instructions
Skipped over 1 INT

1248:0007    NLSFUNC
109A:0980    PRINT
0F16:0943    SHARE
DB18:0285    DOSKEY
0B94:308D    MSCDEX
07FA:1368    SMARTDRV
0726:019F    COMMAND
0725:0135    COMMAND
C801:0696
0725:01BD    COMMAND
FFFF:DFD8    HMA
```

```
C801:061E
0255:002D    J:
CC2C:25ED    DBLSSYS$
0255:0028    J:
CC2C:0116    DBLSSYS$
0116:10C6    DOS
FDC8:44BD    HMA
```

Toward the goal of disassembling DOS, the essential piece of information here is the very last line, as this gives the address (FDC8:44BD) of MSDOS.SYS's INT 2Fh handler. We will come back to this in a few moments.

The most noticeable feature of Figure 6-11 is the very long interrupt chain. NLSFUNC, PRINT, SHARE, DOSKEY, MSCDEX, SMARTDRV, COMMAND.COM, and DoubleSpace all take a crack at processing the call. Processing even what is (as you'll see) an absolutely trivial INT 2Fh AX=1200h call requires that every TSR and device driver camped out on INT 2Fh inspect the call to see if it interests them. INT 2Fh chains can be extremely long; they are particularly bad when any interrupt handlers written in C (such as the wrappers from Chapter 2) are involved. As noted earlier, Ralf Brown has suggested an alternate INT 2Dh protocol in an attempt to shorten the long chains of handlers waiting around for INT 2Fh calls to appear.

Naturally, you can pass any of the addresses displayed by INTCHAIN to a debugger such as DEBUG or SYMDEB. For example, take the 0B94:308D handler for INT 2Fh, which INTCHAIN shows belong to the Microsoft CD-ROM Extensions:

```
-u b94:308d
0B94:308D 9C            PUSHF
0B94:308E 80FC11        CMP      AH,11
0B94:3091 7503          JNZ      3096
0B94:3093 EB6B          JMP      3100
0B94:3095 90            NOP
0B94:3096 80FC15        CMP      AH,15
0B94:3099 7503          JNZ      309E
0B94:309B EB09          JMP      30A6
0B94:309D 90            NOP
0B94:309E 80FC05        CMP      AH,05
; ...
```

You can see MSCDEX first checking for calls to INT 2Fh AH=11h. This makes perfect sense, as INT 2Fh AH=11h is the network redirector protocol, and MSCDEX is a network redirector (see Chapter 8). MSCDEX next looks for calls to INT 2Fh AH=15h, which again makes sense since this is the documented MSCDEX API (see Ray Duncan, *MS-DOS Extensions*). What about INT 2Fh AH=05h? As explained in the appendix, this is an undocumented interface that allows resident programs (network redirectors in particular) to expand critical error numbers into strings. External DOS programs such as COMMAND.COM issue INT 2Fh AH=05h calls; network redirectors such as MSCDEX handle the calls and provide the caller with strings to display (such as "CDR101: Not ready reading drive D" when you try to DIR a recording of Handel's *Messiah*).

How about INT 2Fh under Windows? Figure 6-12 shows INTCHAIN output for the same configuration as Figure 6-11, except that INTCHAIN is running in a DOS box under Windows Enhanced mode:

Figure 6-12: INTCHAIN Display for INT 2Fh AX=1200h Under Windows Enhanced Mode

```
Tracing INT 2F AX=1200
175 instructions

14D4:02A7    win
12E4:0D68    WINICE
1248:0007    NLSFUNC
109A:0980    PRINT
```

```
0F16:0943    SHARE
DB18:0285    DOSKEY
0B94:308D    MSCDEX
07FA:1368    SMARTDRV
0726:019F    COMMAND
0725:0135    COMMAND
C801:0696
1580:0045    win386
0725:01BF    COMMAND
FFFF:DFD8    HMA
C801:061E
0255:002D    J:
CC2C:25ED    DBLSSYS$
0255:0028    J:
CC2C:0116    DBLSSYS$
0116:10C6    DOS
FDC8:44BD    HMA
```

Not only have WIN.COM and WINICE (the Soft-ICE/Windows debugger) added themselves to the front of the INT 2Fh chain, but notice that WIN386 has insinuated itself into the middle of the chain. This, however, isn't the half of it. To service interrupts from DOS boxes, Windows Enhanced mode executes large amounts of code that never show up in INTCHAIN, at least in its present form. Many instructions, such as STI and CLI, cause a jump into the Windows Virtual Machine Manager, running in 32-bit protected mode. This jump is invisible to a real mode DOS program like INTCHAIN. In particular, Windows Enhanced mode hooks INT 2Fh using the protected mode interrupt descriptor table (IDT). A more sophisticated version of INTCHAIN would need to be written to deal with Windows Enhanced mode. The same goes for INTVECT (Listing 6-1), which does at least recognize the ARPL instruction that Windows uses as a V86 breakpoint.

The MSDOS.SYS and IO.SYS INT 2Fh Handlers

You already have the information you want, which is the last line in Figures 6-11 and 6-12. (In the next-to-last line, you see the low-memory stub for INT 2Fh when DOS=HIGH.) In this configuration, the MSDOS.SYS INT 2Fh handler is located at FDC8:44BD; this code is shown with comments in Figure 6-13.

Figure 6-13: MSDOS.SYS INT 2Fh Handler from MS-DOS 6.0

```
-u fdc8:44bd
FDC8:44BD FB          STI
FDC8:44BE 80FC11      CMP    AH,11      ; 2F/11 network redirector call?
FDC8:44C1 750A        JNZ    44CD       ; no

;; Unsupported functions come here. Some external program like SHARE,
;; NLSFUNC, or a redirector is supposed to handle these. If we got here,
;; the external program must not be loaded, so it's an error -- except
;; if the caller is doing a 2F/??/00 install check, in which case DOS
;; will just return AX unchanged to indicate the software isn't installed.

FDC8:44C3 0AC0        OR     AL,AL      ; 2F/??/00 install check?
FDC8:44C5 7403        JZ     44CA       ; yes: unsupported func; AX unchanged
FDC8:44C7 E8DCFF      CALL   44A6       ; no -- set carry flag for error
FDC8:44CA CA0200      RETF   0002       ; sort-of IRET without changing flags

FDC8:44CD 80FC10      CMP    AH,10      ; 2F/10 SHARE call?
FDC8:44D0 74F1        JZ     44C3       ; yes: error
FDC8:44D2 80FC14      CMP    AH,14      ; 2F/14 NLSFUNC call?
FDC8:44D5 74EC        JZ     44C3       ; yes: error
FDC8:44D7 80FC12      CMP    AH,12      ; 2F/12 DOS internal function?
FDC8:44DA 7503        JNZ    44DF       ; no: keep checking
FDC8:44DC E91102      JMP    46F0       ; yes: goto fig. 6-15a
FDC8:44DF 80FC16      CMP    AH,16      ; 2F/16 Windows call or broadcast?
```

```
FDC8:44E2 740D          JZ      44F1     ; yes: DOS communicate with Windows
FDC8:44E4 80FC46        CMP     AH,46    ; 2F/46: misc. DOS/Windows func?
FDC8:44E7 7503          JNZ     44EC     ; no: jump to IO.SYS INT 2Fh handler
FDC8:44E9 E9B801        JMP     46A4     ; yes: goto 2F/46 handler
FDC8:44EC EA05007000    JMP     0070:0005 ; pass to IO.SYS (fig. 6-14)
```

At the very end of Figure 6-13, you can see a hardwired jump to 0070:0005. Here, MSDOS.SYS has decided that it doesn't handle a particular INT 2Fh call, so it passes it down to IO.SYS, which has its own INT 2Fh handler. Geoff Chappell discusses these two DOS INT 2Fh handlers at greater length in his *DOS Internals*, but since we're here, we might as well steal a brief glance at the IO.SYS INT 2Fh handler, which is shown in Figure 6-14. Note that when DOS=HIGH, IO.SYS can assume that A20 is already on because the only path into IO.SYS's INT 2Fh handler is through the one in MSDOS.SYS, which already took care of enabling A20 in its low memory stub (located at 0116:10C6 in Figures 6-11 and 6-12).

Figure 6-14: IO.SYS INT 2Fh Handler from MS-DOS 6.0

```
-u 70:5
0070:0005 EA93087000    JMP     0070:0893

-u 70:893
0070:0893 2EFF2EE606    JMP     FAR CS:[06E6]

-dd 70:6e6 6e6
0070:06E6  FFFF:1302

-u ffff:1302
FFFF:1302 80FC13        CMP     AH,13    ; 2F/13 (set INT 13h handler) call?
FFFF:1305 7413          JZ      131A     ; yes: do it
FFFF:1307 80FC08        CMP     AH,08    ; 2F/08 DRIVER.SYS call?
FFFF:130A 743B          JZ      1347     ; yes: do it
FFFF:130C 80FC16        CMP     AH,16    ; 2F/16 Windows call?
FFFF:130F 7479          JZ      138A     ; yes: IO.SYS also handles these!
FFFF:1311 80FC4A        CMP     AH,4A    ; 2F/4A (misc. undoc func) call?
FFFF:1314 7503          JNZ     1319     ; no: return unchanged
FFFF:1316 E9A700        JMP     13C0     ; yes: do it
FFFF:1319 CF            IRET
```

There are many interesting side roads we could explore here, including the Set INT 13h Handler (INT 2Fh AH=13h) function, and the several different AH=16h subfunctions that MSDOS.SYS and IO.SYS use to communicate with Windows. Sadly, however, we have to drive by if we are to have any chance of making it to our goal of disassembling DOS. As noted already, to do this, we must find where DOS handles the INT 2Fh AH=12h internal functions.

Examining the MSDOS.SYS Handler for INT 2Fh AH=12h

In Figure 6-13, it is clear that FDC8:46F0 is the handler for these functions. As usual, we can pass this address to DEBUG or SYMDEB for unassembly; Figure 6-15 shows the results.

Figure 6-15a: MSDOS.SYS Handler for INT 2Fh AH=12h

```
-u fdc8:46f0
FDC8:46F0 2EFF36783F    PUSH    CS:[3F78]  ; word at FDC8:3F78 = 44CAh
FDC8:46F5 2EFF367A3F    PUSH    CS:[3F7A]  ; word at FDC8:3F7A = 3F7Ch
FDC8:46FA 50            PUSH    AX         ; push function/subfunction
FDC8:46FB 55            PUSH    BP
FDC8:46FC 8BEC          MOV     BP,SP
FDC8:46FE 8B460E        MOV     AX,[BP+0E] ; put possible stack arg into AX
FDC8:4701 5D            POP     BP
FDC8:4702 E84509        CALL    504A       ; call subroutine (fig. 6-15b)
FDC8:4705 E9BFFD        JMP     44C7
```

Hmm, not very promising looking. What is this subroutine at 504A?

Figure 6-15b: More MSDOS.SYS Code for INT 2Fh AH=12h

```
-u fdc8:504a
FDC8:504A 55           PUSH    BP
FDC8:504B 8BEC         MOV     BP,SP
FDC8:504D 53           PUSH    BX
FDC8:504E 8B5E06       MOV     BX,[BP+06]    ; address of subfunc table
FDC8:5051 2E8A1F       MOV     BL,CS:[BX]    ; number of valid sbfuncts
FDC8:5054 385E04       CMP     [BP+04],BL    ; caller's subfunction number
FDC8:5057 7317         JNB     5070          ; if too high, error
FDC8:5059 8A5E04       MOV     BL,[BP+04]    ; get subfunction
FDC8:505C 32FF         XOR     BH,BH
FDC8:505E D1E3         SHL     BX,1          ; turn into word offset
FDC8:5060 43           INC     BX            ; skip past # subfunctions
FDC8:5061 035E06       ADD     BX,[BP+06]    ; add in address of table
FDC8:5064 2E8B1F       MOV     BX,CS:[BX]    ; pull out func ptr
FDC8:5067 895E06       MOV     [BP+06],BX    ; push on stack, RET to it
FDC8:506A 5B           POP     BX
FDC8:506B 5D           POP     BP
FDC8:506C 83C404       ADD     SP,+04
FDC8:506F C3           RET                   ; call subfunc via RET
FDC8:5070 5B           POP     BX            ; invalid sbfunc come here
FDC8:5071 5D           POP     BP
FDC8:5072 C20600       RET     0006
```

Despite the heading, the code in Figure 6-15b is not specifically related to INT 2Fh AH=12h; other functions that have subfunctions use this same subroutine. For example, the handler for INT 21h AH=5Dh calls this same subroutine. The top of Figure 6-15a shows that calling this subroutine involves pushing several values on the stack, including AX, which holds the function and subfunction that the caller wants (for example, 1200h) and the address of a table of function pointers. This table's first byte holds the number of valid subfunctions; the rest of the table is an array of near function pointers to the appropriate handlers for each subfunction.

The subroutine in Figure 6-15b takes the caller's subfunction number (for example, the 00h in 1200h) and compares it to the first byte of the table to see if it is within range. If it is, the code shifts the subfunction number into a word and adds it to the address of the table; the value is incremented by 1 to skip past the table's first byte. The subroutine then pulls the function pointer out of the table, pushes the function pointer on the stack, and "returns" to it.

Locating the INT 2Fh AH=12h Dispatch Table

This is somewhat difficult to follow, but for our purposes the key piece of information is simply the location of the table, as this holds pointers to every INT 2Fh AH=12h subfunction. At the top of Figure 6-15a there is a comment indicating that, in this configuration, the table is at FDC8:3F7C. The first byte of this table is the number of subfunctions. This is followed immediately by an array of 30h words, holding function pointers to the various INT 2Fh AH=12h subfunctions:

```
-db fdc8:3f7c 3f7c
FDC8:3F70                              30                    0
-dw fdc8:3f7d
FDC8:3F7D    470E 6E2E 4CBE 4708 9066 54EB 9342 98EA
FDC8:3F8D    6F2F 9A9F B38F 6B6A 6B53 48CE 5030 98E3
FDC8:3F9D    5030 4FF9 5011 9011 9927 9A76 A6A3 AB12
FDC8:3FAD    4282 AABB AECD 4978 4A12 496C 4FD7 A9FC
; ...
```

Let's see if this is really the INT 2Fh AH=12h dispatch table. Earlier, it was noted that the subroutine at 4282h that DOS is so fond of calling is actually the code for INT 2Fh AX=1218h (Get Caller's Registers). Using SYMDEB to dump the table entry #18h confirms that this is correct:

```
-dw fdc8:3f7d+(18*2)
FDC8:3FAD    4282 ....
```

The FTAB program from Listing 6-4 can produce a nicer display of this same table. In fact, FTAB has an option to display tables such as this that keep the number of subfunctions as their first byte. The two commands shown in Figure 6-16 are thus equivalent. So that you have a handy 2F/12 crib sheet to refer to, the entire table is shown, along with comments indicating the purpose of each subfunction.

Figure 6-16: INT 2Fh AH=12h Dispatch Table Displayed by FTAB

```
C:\UNDOC2\CHAP6>ftab fdc8:3f7e 30 int2f12

C:\UNDOC2\CHAP6>ftab fdc8:3f7d ? int2f12
FDC8:470E    int2f12_00      ; install check
FDC8:6E2E    int2f12_01      ; close current file
FDC8:4CBE    int2f12_02      ; get interrupt addr
FDC8:4708    int2f12_03      ; get dos data seg
FDC8:9066    int2f12_04      ; normalize path separator
FDC8:54EB    int2f12_05      ; output char
FDC8:9342    int2f12_06      ; invoke crit err
FDC8:98EA    int2f12_07      ; make disk buff most recently used
FDC8:6F2F    int2f12_08      ; decrement sft ref count
FDC8:9A9F    int2f12_09      ; flush and free disk buff
FDC8:B38F    int2f12_0A      ; perform crit err interrupt
FDC8:6B6A    int2f12_0B      ; signal share violation
FDC8:6B53    int2f12_0C      ; set fcb file's owner
FDC8:48CE    int2f12_0D      ; get date and time
FDC8:5030    int2f12_0E      ; mark all disk buffer unreferenced
FDC8:98E3    int2f12_0F      ; make buffer most recently used
FDC8:5030    int2f12_10      ; find unreferenced disk buffer
FDC8:4FF9    int2f12_11      ; normalize asciiz filename
FDC8:5011    int2f12_12      ; strlen
FDC8:9011    int2f12_13      ; toupper
FDC8:9927    int2f12_14      ; _fstrcmp
FDC8:9A76    int2f12_15      ; flush buffer
FDC8:A6A3    int2f12_16      ; get address of SFT entry
FDC8:AB12    int2f12_17      ; set working drive
FDC8:4282    int2f12_18      ; get caller's registers
FDC8:AABB    int2f12_19      ; set drive
FDC8:AECD    int2f12_1A      ; get file's drive
FDC8:4978    int2f12_1B      ; set year, length of February
FDC8:4A12    int2f12_1C      ; checksum memory
FDC8:496C    int2f12_1D      ; sum memory
FDC8:4FD7    int2f12_1E      ; compare filenames
FDC8:A9FC    int2f12_1F      ; build CDS
FDC8:A66C    int2f12_20      ; get JFT entry
FDC8:AEA8    int2f12_21      ; truename
FDC8:4434    int2f12_22      ; set extended err info
FDC8:8147    int2f12_23      ; check if char dev
FDC8:5030    int2f12_24      ; delay
FDC8:501F    int2f12_25      ; strlen
FDC8:50D4    int2f12_26      ; open file
FDC8:A72A    int2f12_27      ; close file
FDC8:50DA    int2f12_28      ; move file pointer (lseek)
FDC8:A839    int2f12_29      ; read file
FDC8:5094    int2f12_2A      ; set fastopen entry point
FDC8:5117    int2f12_2B      ; ioctl
FDC8:5106    int2f12_2C      ; get dev chain
FDC8:5134    int2f12_2D      ; get extended err code
FDC8:5139    int2f12_2E      ; get/set error table addresses
FDC8:440D    int2f12_2F      ; nop
```

The whole reason for looking at INT 2Fh AH=12h was that we expected that many of the near function calls that DOS makes internally would show up here. Indeed, you can now see clearly that the CALL 4282h that has continually popped up in these explorations is actually INT 2Fh AX=1218h. Similarly, as promised earlier, CALL 466C is actually INT 2Fh AX=1220h (Get JFT Entry). DOS internally makes extensive use of the functions in Figure 6-16, but, as already noted, it does so using a near CALL rather than an INT. DOS provides the INT form mostly for use by redirectors (see Chapter 8). Having this table of obscure INT 2Fh AH=12h functions definitely makes it much easier to understand the code for any INT 21h functions in which you are interested.

Recall that, in Figures 6-11 and 6-12, the process of locating this table started by having the INTCHAIN program call INT 2Fh AX=1200h. This function, the DOS internal services install check, does nothing more than return with AL=FFh to indicate that the services are present. The table indicates that FDC8:470E is the handler for this function. Let's unassemble at this address to check that the table makes sense:

```
-u fdc8:470e
FDC8:470E B0FF        MOV     AL,FF
FDC8:4710 C3          RET
```

How about INT 2Fh AX=1203h, which is supposed to return with the DOS data segment in DS?

```
-u fdc8:4708
FDC8:4708 2E8E1EE73D  MOV     DS,CS:[3DE7]
FDC8:470D C3          RET
```

The table seems to be accurate, so let's look at a more interesting function. According to the appendix, INT 2Fh AX=1217h sets DOS's working drive; the caller must push a zero-based drive number on the stack before calling the function. According to Figure 6-16, this function is located at FDC8:AB12. Figure 6-17 shows a commented SYMDEB unassembly of this code.

Figure 6-17: INT 2Fh AX=1217h (Set Working Drive) in MS-DOS 6.0

```
-u fdc8:ab12
;;; SS points at DOS DS.
;;; Here, SysVars is at DOS:0026. So DOS:0047 is SysVars+21h.
FDC8:AB12 363A064700  CMP     AL,SS:[0047]   ; SysVars+21h = LASTDRIVE
FDC8:AB17 7202        JB AB1B                ; is drive < LASTDRIVE?
FDC8:AB19 F9          STC                    ; no: set carry flag, fail
FDC8:AB1A C3          RET
FDC8:AB1B 53          PUSH    BX             ; yes
FDC8:AB1C 50          PUSH    AX
FDC8:AB1D 36C5363C00  LDS     SI,SS:[003C]   ; SysVars+16h = CDS ptr
FDC8:AB22 B358        MOV     BL,58          ; 58h = size of CDS entry
FDC8:AB24 F6E3        MUL     BL
FDC8:AB26 03F0        ADD     SI,AX          ; DS:SI = ptr to drive's CDS
;;; Here, SDA at DOS:0320, so DOS:05A2 is SDA+282h.
FDC8:AB28 368936A205  MOV     SS:[05A2],SI   ; move drive's CDS ptr into
FDC8:AB2D 368C1EA405  MOV     SS:[05A4],DS   ;    DOS SDA+282h
FDC8:AB32 58          POP     AX
FDC8:AB33 5B          POP     BX
FDC8:AB34 F8          CLC
FDC8:AB35 C3          RET
```

If this function is called with the drive number on the stack, you may wonder how the code starts off with the drive number in AL. Looking back at Figure 6-15a, note that the generic INT 2Fh AH=12h handler took a word off the stack (BP+0Eh, located after the caller's CS:IP and flags) and moved it into AX. In the case of those functions that don't expect a parameter on the stack, AX holds ignorable garbage. Thus, when we say that DOS makes an INT 2Fh AX=12xxh call, this is just a shorthand way of saying that DOS issues a near call to the code for INT 2Fh AX=12xxh, and that any parameter which, in the INT 2Fh version, would appear on the stack (see the appendix) actually appears in AX.

Everything else in this function involves fairly straightforward manipulation of DOS internal structures. The function checks the drive number against the internal value of LASTDRIVE in SysVars. If the drive number is valid, the function uses it as an index into the CDS array, a pointer to which is also contained in SysVars. The function then moves a pointer to the CDS entry into a DOS global variable. Changing this variable is basically what it means to set DOS's working drive.

It is useful to see how DOS internally uses the LASTDRIVE variable in SysVars, the CDS, and other undocumented DOS features. Discussions of undocumented DOS are often (as in the first edition of this book) disconnected from any consideration of DOS internals. But the CDS, SFT, List of Lists, and other structures are not provided for our entertainment, like the hidden "gang screens" that software hobbyists and enthusiasts seem to enjoy finding. In fact, the CDS and so on are not so much undocumented DOS features as *internal* DOS features that happen to be externally accessible through an undocumented interface. That undocumented DOS is often discussed without the surrounding context of DOS internals tends to obscure the real purpose of these structures.

For example, even though this chapter has often referred to the location of variables such as CURR_PSP as SDA+10h, or BREAK_FLAG as SDA+17h, within DOS there really is no such thing as the Swappable Data Area. The SDA is merely an externally-visible interface that Microsoft added rather late on top of the DOS data segment (see "Origins of the SDA" in Chapter 8). Likewise, the INT 2Fh AH=12h functions are just an undocumented external interface provided on top of some internal DOS functions, for the convenience mostly of network redirectors. The internal near-call form of these functions is the true one.

What have we accomplished here? Basically, by locating the INT 2Fh AH=12h dispatch table, we now acquired *names* for 30h different internal DOS functions. Our earlier uncovering of the INT 21h dispatch table gave us names for 6Dh different locations in DOS. Rather than keep picking at disassembly of individual functions here and there, we can now turn around and do a full-blown disassembly of this entire code segment.

Really Disassembling DOS

Everything we've looked at in DOS is in the same code segment, which in this particular configuration happens to be FDC8h. Of course there are other parts of DOS, but this segment seems like a good place to start. How can you disassemble the entire code segment at once, but still keep track of where the individual functions are located? For example, in a monster disassembly of segment FDC8h, you would like to know where the Set PSP function is handled, where Exec is handled, and so on.

You can use DEBUG or SYMDEB to produce a disassembly of this DOS code segment and use the FTAB program to produce labels indicating the location of key functions within the segment. To merge the FTAB output with the disassembly and, while we're about it, clean up and improve the disassembly in various ways, we will use a program named NICEDBG, written in AWK, a C-like pattern-matching language that is excellent for text-processing tasks like this.

To unassemble the main DOS code segment, you first need to know where to tell DEBUG to start and stop unassembly. You can make a preliminary stab at finding the proper unassembly range by taking the FTAB outputs for the INT 21h dispatch table (Figure 6-8) and the INT 2Fh AH=12h dispatch table (Figure 6-16), combining them, and sorting them by address:

```
C:\UNDOC2\CHAP6>type tmp.bat
@echo off
ftab fdc8:3e9e 6d INT21 > int212f.tmp
ftab fdc8:3f7d 30 INT2F_12 >> int212f.tmp
sort < int212f.tmp > int212f.log

C:\UNDOC2\CHAP6>tmp

C:\UNDOC2\CHAP6>type int212f.log
FDC8:4052    INT21_33
```

```
FDC8:40A9     INT21_50
FDC8:40B5     INT21_51
FDC8:40B5     INT21_62
FDC8:40C1     INT21_64
FDC8:4282     INT2F_12_18
FDC8:440D     INT21_18
; ... etc. ...
FDC8:B0E9     INT21_5A
FDC8:B183     INT21_6C
FDC8:B2D8     INT21_5C
FDC8:B38F     INT2F_12_0A
```

From the first and last lines of INT212F.LOG, it is clear that you want DEBUG or SYMDEB to unassemble starting at FDC8:4052 and ending somewhere a bit after FDC8:B38F. B500h is probably a good place to stop. You will probably need to adjust the unassembly range later and rerun DEBUG, but this is fine for now. You can put the unassembly command into a tiny script file, feed it to the debugger, and redirect the debugger's output to a file:

```
C:\UNDOC2\CHAP6>type int212f.scr
u fdc8:4052 b500
q

C:\UNDOC2\CHAP6>debug < int212f.scr > int212f.out
```

Using SYMDEB rather than DEBUG produces nicer results. SYMDEB puts segment overrides in their proper place, rather than on a separate line like DEBUG. But you must use the SYMDEB /X command line to suppress SYMDEB's [more] prompt, which you wouldn't see if you redirected output to a file:

```
C:\UNDOC2\CHAP6>symdeb /x < int212f.scr > int212f.out
```

This takes a minute or so to run. The INT212F.OUT file will be about 870k bytes—much smaller if you use SYMDEB—and won't yet look very interesting. For example, there aren't yet any labels indicating where each DOS function starts. One of the things NICEDBG can do is merge the INT212F.OUT file produced by DEBUG or SYMDEB with the INT212F.LOG file produced using FTAB.

Windows Patches MS-DOS

Actually, there's one interesting thing you can do with the raw unassembly output from DEBUG or SYMDEB. Run the DEBUG unassembly script once under MS-DOS; then start Windows Enhanced mode and rerun the DEBUG script again from inside a DOS box. Redirect DEBUG's output to a different file. This sequence gives you an easy way to examine the patches that Windows applies to MS-DOS. Just compare the two files, using diff or a similar utility. Any differences in this DOS code segment are the result of Windows patches.

```
C:\UNDOC2\CHAP6>debug < int212f.scr > int212f.out

C:\UNDOC2\CHAP6>win

;;; from inside DOS box:
C:\UNDOC2\CHAP6>debug < int212f.scr > int212f.win

C:\UNDOC2\CHAP6>diff int212f.out int212f.win > int212f.dif
```

The list of Windows patches in INT212F.DIF is incomplete, because it shows only one DOS code segment. Still, it does provide some idea of what is going on:

```
;; original MS-DOS code in INT 21h dispatch (see Figure 6-7 above)
< FDC8:41CE 50            PUSH   AX
< FDC8:41CF B482          MOV    AH,82
< FDC8:41D1 CD2A          INT    2A
< FDC8:41D3 58            POP    AX

;; patched by Windows; 15AD belongs to WIN386.EXE
> FDC8:41CE 9A0A00AD15    CALL   15AD:000A
> FDC8:41D3 90            NOP

;; original DOS code in a frequently called internal Begin Crit 01 function
< FDC8:514B B80180        MOV    AX,8001
< FDC8:514E CD2A          INT    2A

;; patched by Windows
> FDC8:514B 9A4300AD15    CALL   15AD:0043

;; original DOS code in a frequently called internal End Crit 01 function
< FDC8:516B B80181        MOV    AX,8101
< FDC8:516E CD2A          INT    2A

;; patched by Windows
> FDC8:516B 9A7900AD15    CALL   15AD:0079

; ... etc. ...
```

The DOSMGR VxD built into WIN386.EXE applies these patches. When Windows exits, DOSMGR, of course, backs its changes out, restoring the original DOS code. As you can see, these patches have to do with DOS critical sections; DOSMGR wants DOS to call into the Windows VMM Begin_Critical_Section and End_Critical_Section functions. It's important to note that DOSMGR scans for the INT 2Ah instructions to patch, rather than using hardwired addresses. Thus, these patches should at least theoretically work with a different vendor's DOS.

The same before-and-after technique can be used to find DOS patches applied by other programs, such as MSCDEX. Programs that patch DOS can only be safely unloaded by a MARK/RELEASE type of program that knows enough about these patches to back them out.

Using NICEDBG

To run NICEDBG (on the companion disk), feed it output from DEBUG or SYMDEB. Optionally, you can supply a symbol-table file of code name/address pairs such as FTAB produces. You can also supply NICEDBG with an optional file of data name/address pairs. For example:

```
debug < int212f.scr > int212f.out
ftab fdc8:3e9e 6d INT21 > int212f.log
ftab fdc8:3f7d 30 INT2F_12 >> int212f.log
nicedbg int212f.out int212f.log int212f.dat > int212f.lst
```

NICEDBG can make many improvements to the output from DEBUG or SYMDEB. The program makes several passes over the DEBUG file, replacing calls and jumps to meaningless-looking addresses such as 4282h with calls and jumps to meaningful labels supplied by the user, such as INT2F_12_18. The program also creates semi-useful labels for any other addresses that are the target of calls, loops, or jumps. If the target address itself contains a RET or JMP, NICEDBG changes the label to reflect this. The program also generates a list of cross-references to each location.

For example, a sample of output from DEBUG looks like this:

```
FDC8:5126 9C            PUSHF
FDC8:5127 36            SS:
```

```
FDC8:5128 803E0C0D00     CMP BYTE PTR [0D0C],00
FDC8:512D 740F           JZ   513E
FDC8:512F EB01           JMP 5132
FDC8:5131 CF             IRET
FDC8:5132 0E             PUSH    CS
FDC8:5133 E8FBFF         CALL    5131
FDC8:5136 50             PUSH    AX
FDC8:5137 B80180         MOV AX,8001
FDC8:513A CD2A           INT 2A
FDC8:513C 58             POP AX
FDC8:513D C3             RET
FDC8:513E EB01           JMP 5141
FDC8:5140 CF             IRET
FDC8:5141 0E             PUSH    CS
FDC8:5142 E8FBFF         CALL    5140
FDC8:5145 C3             RET
```

This is not very promising looking. But NICEDBG can transform this raw disassembly listing into something much more readable and useful:

```
; xref: FDC8:4304 FDC8:438B FDC8:4D7A
                        func_5126:
FDC8:5126    9C            PUSHF
FDC8:5127    36803E0C0D00  CMP BYTE PTR SS:[0D0C],00
FDC8:512D    740F          JZ jmp_513E  -> loc_5141
FDC8:512F    EB01          JMP loc_5132

; xref: FDC8:5133
                        ret_5131:
FDC8:5131    CF            IRET

; xref: FDC8:512F
                        loc_5132:
FDC8:5132    0E            PUSH CS
FDC8:5133    E8FBFF        CALL ret_5131
FDC8:5136    50            PUSH AX
FDC8:5137    B80180        MOV AX,8001
FDC8:513A    CD2A          INT 2A
FDC8:513C    58            POP AX
FDC8:513D    C3            RET

; xref: FDC8:512D
                        jmp_513E:
FDC8:513E    EB01          JMP loc_5141

; xref: FDC8:5142
                        ret_5140:
FDC8:5140    CF            IRET

; xref: jmp_513E
                        loc_5141:
FDC8:5141    0E            PUSH CS
FDC8:5142    E8FBFF        CALL ret_5140
FDC8:5145    C3            RET
```

Here are some of the changes that NICEDBG made at various offsets in the code:

- 5126: Generated a cross-reference listing (xref) and a func_5126 label, because this location is CALLed from three other places elsewhere in the code. To generate such labels and xrefs, NICEDBG of course must make multiple passes over the DEBUG listing.
- 5127: Combined the SS: override together with the rest of the instruction at 5128.
- 5128: Replaced "JZ 513E" with "JZ jmp_513E -> loc_5141". 513E is the target of the JZ at 5128. Because 513E itself does an unconditional JMP, NICEDBG gives it a jmp_513E label.

Furthermore, NICEDBG chases down JMPs to JMPs, and shows the final destination (here, loc_5141). The DOS code contains many JMPs to JMPs; knowing the ultimate destination of the JMP can make the code a little easier to understand (and also suggests a possible area for DOS optimization).

- 5131: Skipped a blank line because 5131 is the target of another instruction and thus starts a new block, and because 5131 can't be reached from the preceding line at 512F, which does an unconditional JMP. NICEDBG generated a xref, based on the CALL to this location from 5133. Finally, because the code at this location does an immediate IRET, NICEDBG gave it a ret_5131 label.

- 5132: Again, NICEDBG skipped a blank line because 5132 is target of another instruction, and because 5132 can't be reached from the preceding line, which does an IRET. NICEDBG generated a loc_5132 label.

NICEDBG uses loc_ to specify targets of jumps, func_ to specify targets of CALLs, loop_ to specify targets of LOOPs, ret_ to specify code that immediately returns via either RET or IRET, and jmp_ to specify code that does an unconditional JMP. If the user supplies a symbol-table file of name/address pairs such as generated by FTAB, NICEDBG will use this as a source of labels.

NICEDBG.AWK (Listing 6-6) is the source code for this postprocessor for output from DEBUG or SYMDEB.

What is AWK?

Since the reader is likely to be unfamiliar with AWK, a brief explanation of Listing 6-6 is probably called for. AWK reads in each line of text in one or more files and splits the line into fields. You can change the delimiters that AWK uses to decide where fields start and end, but it defaults to using white space, which is exactly what we need here. The fields are available to the program as $1, $2, and so on, up to $NF (NF is a built-in AWK variable that holds the number of fields); $0 is the original line. For example, the line "FDC8:440D INT21_1D" is $0, "FDC8:440D" is $1, and "INT21_ID" is $2 (and $NF).

Note too that AWK handles regular expressions (as also found in utilities such as grep); for example, the regular expression "/[CDES]S\:/" matches "CS:", "DS:", "ES:", or "SS:", and "/\[.*\]/" matches anything within square brackets. AWK also has associative arrays (just built-in hash tables, really) that can be indexed with strings (for example, array["string"]) as well as numbers. The presence of an item in an associative array can be tested with the *in* operator; for example, if ("string" in array).

The standard reference is *The AWK Programming Language* by Alfred Aho, Brian Kernighan, and Peter Weinberger (from the first letters of whose last names the language got its name). The high-level pattern-matching and array features of AWK make it possible to implement NICEDBG in about 200 lines of code.

NICEDBG.EXE on the accompanying disk was produced with the excellent AWK compiler from Thompson Automation. You can run the program without having AWK or understanding anything about it; but to modify the program, you would need Thompson AWK or another AWK interpreter or compiler. The popular MKS Toolkit comes with AWK, and many BBSs carry MAWK, a freely available, fast AWK interpreter by Mike Brennan.

NICEDBG processes each line in the DEBUG file. For example, consider the following line from a DEBUG listing:

```
FDC8:512D 740F          JZ    513E
```

AWK breaks this line into fields, delimited by spaces. The *nth* field is referred to as *$n*:

```
$1    FDC8:512D            Address of the instruction
$2    740F                 Instruction opcode bytes
$3    JZ                   Instruction operator
$4    513E                 Instruction operand
```

Of course, not every instruction looks quite like this. For example:

```
  $1      $2             $3  $4   $5     $6
FDC8:5126 9C             PUSHF
FDC8:5127 36             SS:
FDC8:5128 803E0C0D00     CMP BYTE PTR [0D0C],00
```

In any case, NICEDBG.AWK can rely on $1 as the address of the instruction and on $3 as either the instruction operator or (when using DEBUG rather than SYMDEB) something like a segment override.

Before processing the DEBUG file, NICEDBG reads in the optional symbol-table and data files. NICEDBG uses INT212F.LOG (or any similarly formatted file) to build a table of names (called ftab) corresponding to segment:offset locations; the program runs through each line in INT212F.OUT, or any unassembly listing produced by DEBUG or SYMDEB, to see if the line's segment:offset address is in the table.

NICEDBG makes three passes over the DEBUG file:

Pass 1: NICEDBG looks for any calls, jumps, or loops in the code and adds the target of the call, jump, or loop to ftab, which it will later use to generate labels. Simplifying considerably, the AWK code looks like this:

```
if ($3 ~ /CALL/) ftab[$4] = "func_" $4;
if ($3 ~ /LOOP/) ftab[$4] = "loop_" $4;
if ($3 ~ /J.*/)  ftab[$4] = "loc_" $4;
```

In pass 1, NICEDBG also constructs the jmptab, for resolving JMPs to JMPs:

```
if ($3 ~ /JMP/)  jmptab[$1] = $4;   # jmptab[SOURCE] = TARGET
```

Pass 2: The second time through the DEBUG file, NICEDBG builds its xref table, and also improves some of the labels generated in pass 1. A label such as jmp_XXXX or ret_XXXX, indicating that location XXXX does an unconditional JMP or (I)RET, is generally more useful than a label such as loc_XXXX, indicating that XXXX is the *target* of a jump. Thus, if pass 1 assigned a location a name, and if this location does a JMP or a (I)RET, NICEDBG changes ftab to reflect this:

```
if (($3 ~ /I*RET/) && ($1 in ftab)) ftab[$1] = "ret_" $1;
if (($3 ~ /JMP/) && ($1 in ftab))   ftab[$1] = "jmp_" $1;
```

Also in pass 2, NICEDBG looks for code that may be "not reached," that is, not accessible from any other location in the listing (of course, the code might be called from outside the disassembly range). If the previous line of code did an unconditional JMP or (I)RET, and if there are no labels at the current address (i.e., ftab[$1] is empty, indicating that $1 is not the target of a jump, call, or loop), NICEDBG adds $1 to a not_reached array:

```
if ((did_jmpret == 1) && (! ($1 in ftab))) not_reached[$1]++;
did_jmpret = 0;
if ($3 ~ /I*RET|JMP/) did_jmpret = 1;
```

Pass 3: In its final pass over the DEBUG listing, NICEDBG prints out the new, improved listing:

- If the current line was not reached (i.e., $1 in not_reached), NICEDBG indicates this with a comment; this might be a sign either of data, or of "dead code."

- If the current line has one or more labels (i.e., $1 in ftab), NICEDBG prints them out, one per line. Either the user will have supplied these labels in a symbol-table file, or NICEDBG will have generated them automatically in passes 1 and 2.

- If any other line of code jumped, called, or looped to this line of code, NICEDBG displays the cross-reference.

- If the code itself calls, jumps, or loops to some other line of code, NICEDBG replaces the numeric target with a name from ftab ($4 = ftab[$4]).

- If the target of the call, jump, or loop is a line of code that itself does an unconditional JMP, NICEDBG chases down any JMPs to JMPs (see the resolve_jmp_jmp() function in Listing 6-6).

- If the user supplied a file of data address/name pairs, NICEDBG uses it to replace expressions such as [0330] with names provided by the user, such as CURRENT_PSP. Recall that an earlier inspection of Get PSP and Set PSP (Figures 6-3 and 6-4) showed that these functions do nothing more than get and set a word at offset 0330h in DOS DS. Thus, all occurrences of [0330] in an unassembly of DOS can *probably* be replaced with a name such as CURR_PSP. Likewise, examination of INT 21h AH=33h (Figure 6-5) showed that DOS:0069h is STARTUP_DRV and that 0337h is BRK_FLAG. You can feed this sort of information to NICEDBG in a file of data address/name pairs, such as INT212F.DAT:

```
0069        STARTUP_DRV
0330        CURR_PSP
0337        BRK_FLAG
3DE7        DOS_DS
1030        IN_WIN3E
033E        MACHINE_ID
0321        IN_DOS
0584        USER_SP
0586        USER_SS
0320        CRIT_ERR
1211        DOS_HIGH
```

But note that NICEDBG's replacements of, for example, [0330] with CURRENT_PSP are very simple-minded: The program merely does a blind global search and replace. Thus you should be conservative about what you put in a NICEDBG .DAT file.

- If DEBUG rather than SYMDEB was used to produce NICEDBG's input, NICEDBG saves away any segment override on the current line ($3 ~ /[CDES]S\:/) and uses the AWK sub() substitution function to smack it into its proper place on the next line.

Listing 6-6: NICEDBG.AWK

```
# NICEDBG.AWK -- Produces nicer output from DEBUG input and symbol table
# usage: nicedbg symtab dbgfile  lstfile
# example: nicedbg int212f.log int212f.out  int212f.lst

# get offset from seg:ofs
function get_off(addr)        { split(addr, so, ":"); return so[2]; }

function mk_fp(ofs)           { return seg ":" ofs; }  # make seg:ofs farptr

function get_ftab_name(addr) {  # get name from table
    if (addr !~ SEG_OFS)
        addr = mk_fp(addr);      # table indexed by seg:ofs
    if (! (addr in ftab))
        return addr;             # not there -- return unchanged
    split(ftab[addr], label, ",");
    return label[1];             # just return first name if  1
    }
```

```
function resolve_jmp_jmp(src) { # JMP to JMP to ...
    if (! (src in jmptab))
        return;
    if (done[src])
        return done[src];
    # if get here, haven't seen this one yet
    target = target2 = jmptab[src];
    while (target in jmptab)    {
        target2 = jmptab[target];
        if (target2 == target)      # endless loop
            break;
        if (target2 == src)         # cycle
            break;
        if (target2 in done) {      # we've seen this part already
            target2 = done[target2];
            break;
            }
        target = target2;
        }
    done[src] = target2;
    return target2;
    }

function hex(x)     { return 0 + ("0x" x); }     # relies on Thompson AWK

BEGIN {
    print "NICEDBG -- Makes nicer output from DEBUG input and symbol table";
    print "From \"Undocumented DOS\", 2nd edition (Addison-Wesley, 1993)";
    print "Copyright (C) 1993 Andrew Schulman. All rights reserved.\n";
    if (ARGC < 2)    {
        print "usage: nicedbg dbgfile [symtab] [datfile]  lstfile" ;
        print "example: nicedbg int212f.out int212f.log  int212f.lst" ;
        did_anything = 0;
        exit;
        }
    else did_anything = 1;

    # commonly-used regular expressions
    SQ_BRACK = /\[.*\]/;                # anything within square brackets
    SEG_OFS = /\:/;                     # has a : in it
    SEG_OVERRIDE = /[CDES]S\:/;         # CS: or DS: or ES: or SS:
    CALL_OR_JUMP = /CALL|LOOP|J.*/;     # CALL, LOOP, JMP, J*

    # read in optional symbol-table file
    # lines in symtab file look like:  xxxx:yyyy     name
    if (ARGC < 2) {
        while (getline < ARGV[2])       # for each line in symbol table
            ftab[$1] = ftab[$1] $2 ","; # put name into table for seg:ofs
        close(ARGV[2]);
        }

    # read in optional data file
    # lines in data file look like:    xxxx     name
    # example:                         0321     IN_DOS
    if (ARGC < 3)    {
        while (getline < ARGV[3])
            data[$1] = $2;
        close(ARGV[3]);
        }

    ARGC = 2;                          # finished with sym, dat file
    dbgfile = ARGV[1];                 # switch over to DEBUG file

    # debug file looks like:  xxxx:yyyy    XXXXXX    op operands
    # example:                FDC8:4052    3C06      CMP AL,06     ; comments
```

```
        while (getline < dbgfile)   {        # make pass 1 through debug file
            if ($1 ~ SEG_OFS) {
                split($1, so, ":");
                if (! seg)  {
                    seg = so[1];             # get segment for later use
                    start = hex(so[2]);
                    }
                else
                    stop = so[2];            # take last one
                }
            if ($3 ~ CALL_OR_JUMP) {
                if ($4 ~ /\:|\[.*\]|FAR/)  # don't do [xxxx] or xxxx:yyyy etc.
                    continue;
                # should also ignore e.g. CALL DI
                if ($3 ~ /JMP/)
                    jmptab[get_off($1)] = $4;   # jmptab for resolving JMP JMP
                if (! (mk_fp($4) in ftab))      # put call/jmp target into table
                    ftab[mk_fp($4)] = (($3 ~ /CALL/) ? "func_" :
                                       ($3 ~ /LOOP/) ? "loop_" : "loc_") $4;
                }
            }
        close(dbgfile);
        stop = hex(stop);

        # pass 2: build cross-ref table, improve some label names, etc.
        while (getline < dbgfile)   {
            if ((did_jmpret == 1) && (! ($1 in ftab)))
                not_reached[$1]++; # prev line did JMP/RET, but no label, so
            did_jmpret = 0;        #     "not reached"; may be data or dead code

            if ($3 ~ /I*RET|JMP/)  {
                did_jmpret = 1;
                if ($1 in ftab)    # if target is a ret/jmp, change label name
                    ftab[$1] = (($3 ~ /JMP/) ? "jmp_" : "ret_") get_off($1);
                # oops, this will also replace labels supplied in sym file!
                }
            # below *not* "else if" -- JMP handled both places
            # build xref table and outside-range table
            if (($3 ~ CALL_OR_JUMP) && ($4 !~ SQ_BRACK) && ($5 !~ SQ_BRACK)) {
                if ($4 ~ /FAR/)
                    outside[$5]++;
                else if ($4 ~ SEG_OFS)
                    outside[$4]++;
                else {
                    off = hex($4);
                    if ((off  start) || (off  stop))
                        outside[off]++;
                    }
                if ($4 !~ /\:|FAR/)     # don't do [xxxx] or xxxx:yyyy
                    xref[mk_fp($4)] = xref[mk_fp($4)] get_ftab_name($1) " ";
                }
            }
        close(dbgfile);
        }

    {                                    # pass 3: for each line in dbg file
        while (! ($1 ~ SEG_OFS)) {       # ignore any lines without xxxx:yyyy
            print; getline;
            if (! $0) exit;
            }

        jmpline = "";

        # indicate if this is possible unreached (dead) code; show
        # cross-reference (xref) table; show all labels for this address
```

```awk
    if ($1 in not_reached)  {                  # possible dead code
        print ""
        print ";;; not reached?";
        }
    else if ($1 in ftab) {                      # if segment:offset in table
        print ""
        if (xref[$1])
            print "; xref: " xref[$1]          # show xref
        nf = split(ftab[$1], label, ",");
        for (i=1; i<=nf;i++)
            if (label[i])                       # show all labels for this addr
                printf("%24s%s:\n", " ", label[i]);
        ftab_found[$1] = 1;
        }

    # if a CALL, LOOP, or some kind of JMP, show eventual destination
    # of any JMP JMP, and possibly replace number address with string name
    if ($3 ~ CALL_OR_JUMP)  {
        if ($4 !~ /FAR/)    {
            if ($4 in jmptab)
                jmpline = " - " get_ftab_name(resolve_jmp_jmp($4));
            $4 = get_ftab_name($4);      # replace number with name
            }
        }

    # cheap replacement of [xxxx] with names from data file
    if (match($0, SQ_BRACK))                 # match sets RSTART, RLENGTH
        if ((addr = substr($0, RSTART+1, RLENGTH-2)) in data)
            sub(SQ_BRACK, data[addr], $0);  # sub() does substitution

    # get rid of DEBUG segment override ugliness
    if ($3 ~ SEG_OVERRIDE) {
        ovride_addr = $1;                    # save to use on next line
        byte = $2;
        override = $3;
        }
    else if (ovride_addr)   {
        $1 = ovride_addr; ovride_addr = "";
        $2 = byte $2;
        sub(/\[/, override "[", $0);     # plug in override:
        }

    # print out (possibly altered) line
    if (! ovride_addr)  {
        printf("%s\t%-15s\t", $1, $2);
        for (i=3; i<=NF;i++)
            printf("%s ", $i);
        if (jmpline)
            printf("%s", jmpline);
        printf("\n");
        }
}

# print list of CALL, JMP, etc. references outside disasm range
END {
    if (did_anything) {
        printf("\n;; outside range %s:%04X-%04X:\n", seg, start, stop);
        for (x in outside)
            printf(";; " ((x ~ SEG_OFS) ? "%s" : "%04X") "\n", x);
        # should suppress following if within a not-reached block?
        printf("\n;; possible unresolved labels:\n");
        for (x in ftab)
            if (! (x in ftab_found))
                printf(";; %s\n", ftab[x]);
        }
}
```

With output from DEBUG in INT212F.OUT, a symbol table produced by FTAB in INT212F.LOG, and the optional data file INT212F.DAT, you can produce a nice looking disassembly of the main MSDOS.SYS code segment, INT212F.LST, with:

```
nicedbg int212f.out int212f.log int212f.dat > int212f.lst
```

We will examine this INT212F.LST file in more detail momentarily, but the following excerpt provides some idea of what NICEDBG produces:

```
                         INT2F_12_18:
FDC8:4282 2E8E1EE73D      MOV DS,CS:DOS_DS
FDC8:4287 C5368405        LDS SI,USER_SP
FDC8:428B C3              RET
; ...
                         INT21_34:
FDC8:4D59 E826F5          CALL INT2F_12_18
FDC8:4D5C C744022103      MOV WORD PTR [SI+02],IN_DOS
FDC8:4D61 8C5410          MOV [SI+10],SS
FDC8:4D64 C3              RET
```

This is quite usable. You can see that INT 21h AH=34h (Get InDOS Flag Address) calls the code for INT 2Fh AX=1218h (Get Caller's Registers) and then moves DOS_DS:IN_DOS into the caller's ES:BX registers. This is just as you would expect.

You could make this even more readable by going into INT212F.LOG and taking the only partially useful names, such as INT21_34 and INT2F_12_18 produced by FTAB, and replacing them with more evocative names, such as GET_INDOS_34 and GET_STACKPTR_1218. But this is left as an exercise for the reader (who may in any case know all the DOS function numbers by heart and not require such a crutch). The point is simply that you can manually change or add to INT212F.LOG as you discover new functions. For example, you can add the following two functions that you already know about from running INTCHAIN:

```
FDC8:40F8    INT21_DISPATCH
FDC8:44BD    INT2F_DISPATCH
```

Please note that INT212F.LST is *not* included on the accompanying disk, as redistributing a large piece of MS-DOS would obviously violate Microsoft's copyright! However, it should be easy for readers to produce their own personal copies, given the instructions in this chapter. To quickly summarize the steps involved in producing INT212F.LST:

1. INTCHAIN 21/6200 and use last line to locate DOS INT 21h handler.
2. DEBUG or SYMDEB to unassemble INT 21h handler; locate dispatch table.
3. Run FTAB on INT 21h dispatch table > tmpfile.
4. INTCHAIN 2F/1200 and use last line to locate DOS INT 2Fh handler.
5. DEBUG or SYMDEB to unassemble INT 2Fh handler; locate dispatch table.
6. Run FTAB on INT 2Fh dispatch table >> tmpfile.
7. SORT < tmpfile > symfile.
8. Inspect top and bottom of symfile to create script for DEBUG or SYMDEB.
9. DEBUG < script > outfile.
10. Optionally create datafile.
11. Optionally change and add to symfile.
12. NICEDBG outfile symfile [datafile] > lstfile
13. Check "outside range" comment at end of lstfile. Possibly alter script, and goto step 9.

The last point needs an explanation. Because code and data are intermixed within DOS, DEBUG and SYMDEB are likely to encounter data that they will misinterpret as code. This invalid code can throw off the unassembly of valid code further on in memory. The result is that INT212F.LST may contain, for example, several CALLs to func_9024 but, instead of showing code at offset 9024h, there is instead some bogus-looking instruction at offset 9023h. NICEDBG will list such possibly unresolved labels at the end of the listing; you can use this to split the DEBUG or SYM-DEB u command into two or more parts. For example, let's say that there are valid-looking calls to func_9024, but no func_9024 itself. If the original DEBUG script contained the following command:

```
u fdc8:4052 b500
```

you can split this in two, making DEBUG restart unassembly at offset 9024h:

```
u fdc8:4052 9024
u fdc8:9024 b500
```

At this point, of course, you may find idea of postprocessing DEBUG output a little ridiculous. You may want to switch to genuine disassembler such as V Communications' Sourcer.

Remember that we've disassembled just one MSDOS.SYS code segment. You can apply the same techniques to other parts of MS-DOS (the outside range list produced by NICEDBG is helpful here), to DR DOS, or to NetWare's NETX code.

Examining a Few DOS Functions

Let's look at a small portion of the MS-DOS 6.0 disassembly produced by DEBUG with a little help from FTAB, INTCHAIN, and NICEDBG. Figure 6-18 shows the code for a few simple DOS functions.

Figure 6-18: MS-DOS 6.0 Code for Functions 34h, 52h, 1Fh, 32h, and 0Dh

```
                              INT21_34:
FDC8:4D59    E826F5             CALL INT2F_12_18
FDC8:4D5C    C744022103         MOV Word Ptr [SI+02],0321
FDC8:4D61    8C5410             MOV [SI+10],SS
FDC8:4D64    C3                 RET

                              INT21_52:
FDC8:4D65    E81AF5             CALL INT2F_12_18
FDC8:4D68    C744022600         MOV Word Ptr [SI+02],0026
FDC8:4D6D    8C5410             MOV [SI+10],SS
FDC8:4D70    C3                 RET

                              INT21_1F:
FDC8:4D71    B200               MOV DL,00

                              INT21_32:
FDC8:4D73    16                 PUSH SS
FDC8:4D74    1F                 POP DS
FDC8:4D75    8AC2               MOV AL,DL
FDC8:4D77    E8415D             CALL INT2F_12_19
FDC8:4D7A    7222               JB loc_4D9E
FDC8:4D7C    C43EA205           LES DI,[05A2]
FDC8:4D80    26F6454480         TEST Byte Ptr ES:[DI+44],80
FDC8:4D85    7517               JNZ loc_4D9E
FDC8:4D87    E8B003             CALL func_513A
FDC8:4D8A    E83749             CALL func_96C4
FDC8:4D8D    E8CA03             CALL func_515A
FDC8:4D90    720C               JB loc_4D9E
FDC8:4D92    E8EDF4             CALL INT2F_12_18
FDC8:4D95    896C02             MOV [SI+02],BP
FDC8:4D98    8C440E             MOV [SI+0E],ES
FDC8:4D9B    32C0               XOR AL,AL
FDC8:4D9D    C3                 RET
```

```
; xref: FDC8:4D7A FDC8:4D85 FDC8:4D90
                              loc_4D9E:
FDC8:4D9E     B0FF            MOV AL,FF
FDC8:4DA0     C3              RET


                              INT21_0D:
FDC8:4DA1     B0FF            MOV AL,FF
FDC8:4DA3     16              PUSH SS
FDC8:4DA4     1F              POP DS
FDC8:4DA5     E89203          CALL func_513A
FDC8:4DA8     830E110604      OR Word Ptr [0611],+04
FDC8:4DAD     E8844C          CALL func_9A34
FDC8:4DB0     83261106FB      AND Word Ptr [0611],-05
FDC8:4DB5     C706B50D0000    MOV Word Ptr [0DB5],0000
FDC8:4DBB     BBFFFF          MOV BX,FFFF
FDC8:4DBE     891E2000        MOV [0020],BX
FDC8:4DC2     891E1E00        MOV [001E],BX
FDC8:4DC6     E89103          CALL func_515A
FDC8:4DC9     B8FFFF          MOV AX,FFFF
FDC8:4DCC     50              PUSH AX
FDC8:4DCD     B82011          MOV AX,1120
FDC8:4DD0     CD2F            INT 2F
FDC8:4DD2     58              POP AX
FDC8:4DD3     C3              RET
```

First off, notice our old friends INT 21h AH=34h and 52h. Except for the clarity of the code displayed in Figure 6-18, these hold no surprises for us. The functions are nearly identical. They both get the caller's register structure and return different values into the caller's BX. Perhaps NICEDBG could be improved to recognize the caller's register structure and, where appropriate (which would be the difficult part), replace expressions such as [SI+02] and [SI+10] with something like CALLER_BX and CALLER_ES. That's for version 2.0!

More interesting is the code that appears next in Figure 6-18 for INT 21h functions 1Fh and 32h. These Disk Parameter Block functions have been around for a while, but Microsoft only documented them starting in DOS 5.0. Note that the code for function 1Fh simply sets DL=0 and falls into the code for function 32h. This makes sense, since function 1Fh is Get Default DPB, and function 32h is Get DPB. Get DPB takes a drive number in DL and returns the DPB in DS:BX.

Where does the DPB come from? The Get DPB code calls several subfunctions not shown here, but armed with the NICEDBG output, you can examine the code for each of these subfunctions fairly easily. In essence, INT 21h AH=1Fh and AH=32h call the internal Set Drive function (INT 2Fh AX=1219h), which in turn calls the INT 2Fh AX=1217h function that we examined in Figure 6-17. As noted there, this function sets the working Current Directory Structure field at DOS:05A2h (SDA+282h). Note that this is not the same as changing drives; it merely sets up a working area in the DOS data segment. When INT 2Fh AX=1219h has returned, Get DPB pulls the CDS pointer out of the working CDS field where the INT 2Fh function just put it. It then calls a subroutine that gets the DPB pointer from offset 45h in the CDS. Having examined the different subroutines that Get DPB calls, we can decorate the code with comments, as shown in Figure 6-19.

Figure 6-19: MS-DOS 6.0 Code for DPB Functions 1Fh and 32h

```
                              INT21_1F:
FDC8:4D71     B200            MOV DL,00          ; 0 = default drive
                                                 ; fall through!
                              INT21_32:
FDC8:4D73     16              PUSH SS
FDC8:4D74     1F              POP DS             ; get DOS DS
FDC8:4D75     8AC2            MOV AL,DL
FDC8:4D77     E8415D          CALL INT2F_12_19   ; Set Drive, like 2f/1217
FDC8:4D7A     7222            JB loc_4D9E
FDC8:4D7C     C43EA205        LES DI,[05A2]      ; SDA+282h = curr CDS ptr
```

```
FDC8:4D80    26F6454480    TEST Byte Ptr ES:[DI+44],80 ; CDS[43-44h] = flags
FDC8:4D85    7517          JNZ loc_4D9E              ; if net/redir drive, fail
FDC8:4D87    E8B003        CALL func_513A           ; enter crit #1 (2A/8001)
FDC8:4D8A    E83749        CALL func_96C4           ; ES:BP get DPB from CDS[45h]
FDC8:4D8D    E8CA03        CALL func_515A           ; exit crit #1 (2A/8101)
FDC8:4D90    720C          JB loc_4D9E              ; fail?
FDC8:4D92    E8EDF4        CALL INT2F_12_18         ; get caller's regs
FDC8:4D95    896C02        MOV [SI+02],BP           ; caller's BX
FDC8:4D98    8C440E        MOV [SI+0E],ES           ; caller's DS
FDC8:4D9B    32C0          XOR AL,AL                ; al = 0 for success
FDC8:4D9D    C3            RET
```

The final function to examine back in Figure 6-18 is INT 21h AH=0Dh (Disk Reset). The function does its real work inside the call to func_9A34 (not shown), which loops over all buffers, calling the internal Flush Buffer function (INT 2Fh AX=1215h). But note in Figure 6-18 that Disk Reset also calls INT 2Fh AX=1120h, which is the network redirector Flush All Disk Buffers function. This provides a good illustration of how the network redirector works as a series of *hooks* in DOS. At various key moments, DOS issues an INT 2Fh AH=11h call; any installed redirector can pick up the call and do what it needs (see Chapter 8).

One of the things that probably isn't clear from the DOS code shown in this chapter, but which becomes clear from examining the INT212F.LST file, is that hooks play an important role in DOS. In addition to the INT 2Fh AH=11h redirector interface, DOS also checks the SHARE hooks. These, however, are implemented in a totally different manner from the redirector (see SHARHOOK.C at Listing 8-22 in Chapter 8). Of course, many DOS functions get passed down to installable device drivers; the DOS code calls these drivers using the Strategy and Interrupt pointers in the device driver header (see Chapter 7).

Remember also that external programs probably hook many of these DOS calls. You saw earlier, for example, that SMARTDRV and DBLSPACE hook the Disk Reset call. Thus it is a little misleading to view the INT 21h AH=0Dh handler in MSDOS.SYS in isolation. When examining the code for a DOS function, it is important to remember that DOS isn't just the code in MSDOS.SYS and IO.SYS, but it is the sum total of the interactions of this code with all the DOS extensions you are likely to find on a user's machine. This not only means understanding the role of programs such as Windows, SMARTDRV, MSCDEX, DOSKEY, and DBLSPACE, but also understanding where non-Microsoft programs such as Stacker, NetWare, and 386MAX fit in. A good example of this, as we saw in Chapter 4, is the way that the trivially-simple Set PSP function suddenly takes on new meaning and complexity when Novell NetWare is running.

Examining the DOS Lseek Function

As a more extensive, but still relatively self-contained, example, let's examine the DOS Move File Pointer function (INT 21h AH=42h), frequently known as lseek after its C/Unix equivalent. We had occasion to examine the DOS code for this function while working on Chapter 8 of this book. An early draft of the network-redirector specification in Chapter 8, in discussing the redirector INT 2Fh AX=1121h Seek From End function, asserted that "DOS never calls this function." Since this was based merely on empirical evidence (we never saw 2F/1121 called), it made sense to examine the DOS code to verify that DOS did not contain a call to INT 2Fh AX=1121h.

To our surprise, the DOS code for lseek *did* contain a call to this INT 2Fh function. It turns out that DOS only calls the redirector's Seek From End function under a special set of circumstances having to do with network FCBs and various SHARE modes. Frankly, we still don't quite understand this. In any case, the rest of the code for INT 21h AH=42h is fairly straightforward, yet long enough to be a little more interesting than the feeble little examples we've seen so far. In addition, there is some interesting Windows-related code in DOS that we'll encounter along the way.

Before we examine the disassembly listing for INT 21h AH=42h, recall that the function has the following specification:

```
Move File Pointer
Input:
    AH = 42h
    AL = method (0 = from beginning; 1 = from current pos; 2 = from end)
    BX = file handle
    CX:DX = hi:lo offset from beginning, current, or end
    INT 21h
Output success:
    Carry clear
    DX:AX = new hi:lo position
Output failure:
    Carry set
    AX = error value (1 = invalid function; 6 = invalid handle)
```

Microsoft's DOS programmer's reference further notes that

A program should never attempt to move the file pointer to a position before the start of the file. Although this action does not generate an error during the move, it does generate an error on a subsequent read or write operation. A program can move the file position beyond the end of the file. On a subsequent write operation, MS-DOS writes data to the given position in the file, filling the gap between the previous end of the file and the given position with undefined data. This is a common way to reserve file space without writing to the file.

This suggests that almost any CX:DX parameters to lseek are valid. Indeed, as we're about to see, the code does little more than move the CX:DX parameter into the file's SFT entry. The hard part is getting the SFT entry. To make sense of the code listing, you'll need to know the following offsets in the SFT (for further information, see the appendix under INT 21h AH=52h):

```
02h     WORD        open mode
05h     WORD        device info word
11h     DWORD       file size
15h     DWORD       current file position
2Fh     WORD        machine number (Windows VM ID)
```

Figure 6-20 shows the DOS code for INT 21h AH=42h (Move File Pointer). Many explanatory comments were added by hand to the code generated by NICEDBG.

Figure 6-20: MS-DOS 6.0 Code for INT 21h AH=42h (lseek)

```
; xref: FDC8:50D5 FDC8:9D52 FDC8:9DC1 FDC8:9E9C
                        INT21_42:
FDC8:A845   E8E100          CALL func_A929 ; TURNS BX HANDLE INTO
                                           ; ES:DI SFT (see fig. 6-21)
; xref: FDC8:A8B4
                        loc_A848:
FDC8:A848   7302            JNB loc_A84C
FDC8:A84A   EB9E            JMP jmp_A7EA  -> loc_43ED  ; couldn't: fail!

; xref: loc_A848
                        loc_A84C:              ; ES:DI=valid SFT entry
FDC8:A84C   3C02            CMP AL,02          ; which move method?
FDC8:A84E   760A            JBE loc_A85A
FDC8:A850   36C606230301    MOV Byte Ptr SS:[0323],01 ; SDA+3=error locus
FDC8:A856   B001            MOV AL,01          ; 1=invalid function

    ; note many jmp jmp in DOS code:
    ;   A858 -> A7EA -> A7D8 -> A7D4 -> A716 -> A6FB -> 43ED
    ; usually to use short jmp, but is it still worth it?
```

```
              ; but can it ever be changed??

; xref: jmp_A8AB
                              jmp_A858:
FDC8:A858     EB90            JMP jmp_A7EA  -> loc_43ED  ; fail!

; xref: FDC8:A84E
                              loc_A85A:
FDC8:A85A     3C01            CMP AL,01
FDC8:A85C     720A            JB loc_A868               ; below = 0
FDC8:A85E     771B            JA loc_A87B               ; above = 2

                              ; handling seek method #1: from current pos
FDC8:A860     26035515        ADD DX,ES:[DI+15]         ; SFT->file_pos
FDC8:A864     26134D17        ADC CX,ES:[DI+17]
                              ; fall through to method #0

; xref: FDC8:A85C FDC8:A88A
                              loc_A868:         ; #0: from beginning
FDC8:A868     8BC1            MOV AX,CX
FDC8:A86A     92              XCHG AX,DX               ; DX:AX <- CX:DX

; xref: FDC8:A8A9
                              loc_A86B:
FDC8:A86B     26894515        MOV ES:[DI+15],AX    ; update SFT->file_pos
FDC8:A86F     26895517        MOV ES:[DI+17],DX
FDC8:A873     E8FF99          CALL INT2F_12_18     ; get caller's regs
FDC8:A876     895406          MOV [SI+06],DX       ; move into caller's DX
                              ;;; later on, loc_43FD does MOV [SI], AX
                              ;;; see table 6-2 for caller reg struct

; xref: jmp_A8EF
                              jmp_A879:
FDC8:A879     EBA7            JMP jmp_A822  -> loc_43E4  ; success!

; xref: FDC8:A85E
                              loc_A87B:                      ; #2: from end
FDC8:A87B     26F6450680      TEST Byte Ptr ES:[DI+06],80 ; dev info: NETWORK
FDC8:A880     750A            JNZ loc_A88C

; xref: FDC8:A891 FDC8:A8A2
                              loc_A882:
FDC8:A882     26035511        ADD DX,ES:[DI+11]          ; SFT->file_size
FDC8:A886     26134D13        ADC CX,ES:[DI+13]          ; CX:DX += file_size
FDC8:A88A     EBDC            JMP loc_A868               ; go to method #0

; xref: FDC8:A880
                              loc_A88C:              ; this is a network drive!

              ;;; This is seek method #2 (from end of file), and network bit is set
              ;;; in SFT. DOS may call a network redirector's 2F/1121 Seek From End
              ;;; handler, but only if some strange conditions are met: It can't
              ;;; be an FCB open, and certain SHARE bits must be set.

FDC8:A88C     26F6450380      TEST Byte Ptr ES:[DI+03],80 ; open mode: FCB!
FDC8:A891     75EF            JNZ loc_A882               ; an FCB open
                                    ;;; this is not an FCB open ;;;
FDC8:A893     268B4502        MOV AX,ES:[DI+02]          ; open mode
FDC8:A897     25F000          AND AX,00F0
FDC8:A89A     3D4000          CMP AX,0040    ; OPEN_SHARE_DENYNONE
FDC8:A89D     7405            JZ DO_2F_1121  ; redir seek from end
FDC8:A89F     3D3000          CMP AX,0030    ; OPEN_SHARE_DENYREAD
FDC8:A8A2     75DE            JNZ loc_A882   ; no: update caller's regs

; xref: FDC8:A89D
```

```
                             DO_2F_1121:
FDC8:A8A4    B82111          MOV AX,1121    ; Call network redirector's
FDC8:A8A7    CD2F            INT 2F         ; Seek from End function
FDC8:A8A9    73C0            JNB loc_A86B   ; update caller's DX:AX from SFT

; xref: jmp_A8F9
                             jmp_A8AB:
FDC8:A8AB    EBAB            JMP jmp_A858  -> loc_43ED        ; fail!
```

As you can see, the code can fail if the caller passes an invalid file handle in BX or an invalid seek method in AL. But other than this, the function essentially does little more than update the current position in the file's SFT entry. Even for files on network drives, DOS almost always can service an lseek call without calling on a network redirector for assistance. We can summarize the function's operation in this way:

```
sft = get_sft(handle)  // see below
if (seek from begin) then set sft->file_pos = new_pos
if (seek from end) then (signed) new_pos += file_size; goto seek from begin
if (seek from current) then new_pos += sft->file_pos; goto seek from begin
set caller's new_pos (DX:AX) = sft->file_pos
```

We haven't explained the very first line of the INT 21h AH=42h handler, however, where DOS calls a subroutine, here called func_A929, to turn the caller's BX file handle into an SFT entry in ES:DI. This is shown in Figure 6-21. The code for func_A929 turns out to be very interesting, because it shows some of MS-DOS's interaction with Windows. As indicated in the xref generated by NICEDBG, this same subroutine is also called by other parts of DOS, including the code for functions 3Eh and 68h.

Figure 6-21: MS-DOS 6.0 Code To Verify SFT Virtual Machine ID

```
; xref: INT21_3E INT21_68 FDC8:A7E5 INT21_42 FDC8:A8B1 FDC8:A907
                             func_A929:
                                            ; func_A62A turns BX handle
FDC8:A929    E8FEFC          CALL func_A62A ; into ES:DI SFT (fig. 6-22)
FDC8:A92C    721C            JB ret_A94A    ; percolate error up
          ; valid handle, but it could be for another DOS box!
FDC8:A92E    50              PUSH AX
FDC8:A92F    36F606630100    TEST Byte Ptr SS:IN_WIN3E,01
FDC8:A935    7404            JZ loc_A93B
FDC8:A937    33C0            XOR AX,AX
FDC8:A939    EB08            JMP loc_A943

; xref: FDC8:A935
                             loc_A93B:                      ; Windows running
FDC8:A93B    36A13E03        MOV AX,SS:MACHINE_ID
FDC8:A93F    263B452F        CMP AX,ES:[DI+2F]              ; SFT->share_machine

; xref: FDC8:A939
                             loc_A943:                      ; okay
FDC8:A943    58              POP AX
FDC8:A944    7501            JNZ loc_A947
FDC8:A946    C3              RET

; xref: FDC8:A944
                             loc_A947:                      ; failure
FDC8:A947    B006            MOV AL,06                      ; "invalid handle"
FDC8:A949    F9              STC

; xref: FDC8:A92C
                             ret_A94A:
FDC8:A94A    C3              RET
```

This code deals with the fact that, under Windows Enhanced mode, it is possible to have multiple processes in different DOS boxes that happen to have the same PSP ID (though note that SYSTEM.INI has a UniqueDOSPSP= setting). Normally, the current PSP and a file handle are sufficient to specify an open file. Under Windows Enhanced mode, the current virtual machine (VM) ID is also needed to specify an open file.

In this subroutine, DOS (a) checks whether Windows Enhanced mode is running (see Chapter 1 to see how DOS initially sets the IN_WIN3E flag); (b) gets the current VM ID (see Chapter 1 to see how the DOSMGR VxD patches DOS's MACHINE_ID word with the current VM ID); and (c) compares the current VM ID against the machine ID field at offset 2Fh in the SFT. If the SFT's machine ID doesn't match the current VM, lseeks fails with error code 6, as if the handle in BX were invalid. It wasn't invalid per se, but it belonged to another process that happened to have the same PSP in another DOS box.

We still haven't seen, though, how DOS turns a file handle in BX into an SFT entry in ES:DI. This is accomplished by func_A62A in Figure 6-22, which turns turns the BX handle (which is really an index into the current PSP's Job File Table) into a JFT pointer (equivalent to INT 2Fh AX=1220h), then turns the JFT pointer into an SFT index, and then turns the SFT index into an SFT entry (equivalent to INT 2Fh AX=1216h). The disassembly starts off with DOS's INT 2Fh AX=1220h handler; func_A62A appears in the middle of the listing.

Figure 6-22: MS-DOS 6.0 Code To Turn File Handle into SFT Pointer

```
; xref: FDC8:4F01 func_A62A loc_A671 loc_A6EA loc_A7DD FDC8:A90F FDC8:A924
                        INT2F_12_20:
FDC8:A60D   2E8E06D73D    MOV ES,CS:DOS_DS          ; get DOS_DS
FDC8:A612   268E063003    MOV ES,ES:CURR_PSP        ; use current PSP
FDC8:A617   263B1E3200    CMP BX,ES:[0032]          ; # files in JFT
FDC8:A61C   7204          JB loc_A622
FDC8:A61E   B006          MOV AL,06                 ; invalid handle

; xref: FDC8:A637
                        loc_A620:                   ; fail
FDC8:A620   F9            STC
FDC8:A621   C3            RET

; xref: FDC8:A61C
                        loc_A622:                   ; file handle < # files
FDC8:A622   26C43E3400    LES DI,ES:[0034]          ; JFT ptr in PSP
FDC8:A627   03FB          ADD DI,BX                 ; add on BX handle

; xref: FDC8:A62D
                        ret_A629:
FDC8:A629   C3            RET                        ; return ptr -> SFT ndx

;;; code to turn handle in BX into SFT entry in ES:DI ;;;
; xref: FDC8:4EDC INT21_4400_01 INT21_4402_03 FDC8:61DD INT21_440A \
; FDC8:757B func_A929 FDC8:B27B
                        func_A62A:
FDC8:A62A   E8E0FF        CALL INT2F_12_20   ; turn BX handle->ES:DI JFT
FDC8:A62D   72FA          JB ret_A629
FDC8:A62F   26803DFF      CMP Byte Ptr ES:[DI],FF ; unused!
FDC8:A633   7504          JNZ loc_A639
FDC8:A635   B006          MOV AL,06                 ; invalid handle
FDC8:A637   EBE7          JMP loc_A620              ; fail

; xref: FDC8:A633
                        loc_A639:
FDC8:A639   53            PUSH BX
FDC8:A63A   268A1D        MOV BL,ES:[DI]            ; JFT entry -> SFT index
FDC8:A63D   32FF          XOR BH,BH
```

```
FDC8:A63F   E80200            CALL INT2F_12_16         ; SFT index -> SFT ES:DI
FDC8:A642   5B                POP BX
FDC8:A643   C3                RET

; xref: FDC8:6DF1 FDC8:A516 FDC8:A63F FDC8:A686
                              INT2F_12_16:             ; SFT ndx -> ES:DI SFT
FDC8:A644   2E8E06D73D        MOV ES,CS:DOS_DS         ; get DOS DS
FDC8:A649   26C43E2A00        LES DI,ES:[002A]         ; SysVars+4 -> first SFT

; xref: FDC8:A65E
                              loc_A64E:                ; walk SFT chain
FDC8:A64E   263B5D04          CMP BX,ES:[DI+04]        ; SFT # files
FDC8:A652   720E              JB loc_A662              ; in this table!
FDC8:A654   262B5D04          SUB BX,ES:[DI+04]        ; subtract #files this SFT
FDC8:A658   26C43D            LES DI,ES:[DI]           ; follow linked list
FDC8:A65B   83FFFF            CMP DI,-01               ; end of SFTs?
FDC8:A65E   75EE              JNZ loc_A64E             ; loop to next SFT
FDC8:A660   F9                STC                      ; invalid SFT index
FDC8:A661   C3                RET                      ; fail!

; xref: FDC8:A652
                              loc_A662:                ; in this SFT
FDC8:A662   50                PUSH AX
FDC8:A663   B83B00            MOV AX,003B              ; SFT each size entry
FDC8:A666   F6E3              MUL BL
FDC8:A668   03F8              ADD DI,AX                ; offset of this entry
FDC8:A66A   58                POP AX
FDC8:A66B   83C706            ADD DI,+06               ; skip past SFT header
FDC8:A66E   C3                RET
```

The basic sequence here is: BX handle -> JFT entry (2F/1220) -> SFT ndx -> SFT entry (2F/1216).

Recall that the file handle in BX is really an index into the current PSP's JFT. Thus, the code for INT 2Fh AX=1220h gets the current PSP from the familiar CURR_PSP global DOS variable and checks PSP:0032 (which holds the maximum number of file handles available to this PSP). If the handle in BX is < the file-handle maximum (i.e., the JFT size), then this code gets a far pointer to the JFT from PSP:0034 and adds BX onto the JFT pointer, yielding a far pointer in ES:DI to the file's JFT entry.

Each JFT entry is a single byte that holds an index into the SFT, or FFh to indicate an unused entry. The code in Figure 6-22 ensures that the caller hasn't passed in a file handle whose corresponding JFT entry is unused.

If DOS has a valid SFT index, it passes it to a function (equivalent to INT 2Fh AX=1216h), which returns a pointer to the corresponding SFT entry. From the listing above, we can see how this code works: DOS gets a pointer to the first SFT from SysVars+4, and walks the SFT chain, comparing the SFT index against the number of files in each SFT until it finds the right one. DOS then multiples the remaining SFT index by 3Bh (the size of an SFT entry in this version of DOS) and adds it onto the start of this SFT, to form an SFT entry.

That's it. We've now examined the DOS code for lseek in its entirety. We've seen how the specification for INT 21h AH=42h is actually implemented in working code, how DOS gets from a file handle in BX to an SFT entry in ES:DI, and how it can use this SFT to get and set the current file position and size, and also to check the Windows VM ID. But remember that this is DOS, so it is possible and even likely that some important third-party extensions such as NetWare hook the lseek function. Our disassembly of the DOS kernel neglects to deal with whatever changes these might make to the behavior of lseek.

We have only presented a fairly random selection of extremely simple DOS functions, viewed in isolation from key third-party DOS extensions. To properly discuss this simple DEBUG disassembly of 30 kbytes of DOS code would require an entire book. In fact, properly explaining each function, examining its interactions with resident software such as SmartDrv, Windows, and NetWare could easily be the subject of several books. For further in-depth discussions of this code, see Chappell's *DOS Internals* and Mike Podanoffsky's *Dissecting DOS: A Code Level Look at the DOS Operating System* (this forthcoming book is described in more detail later in this chapter).

Other Parts of DOS

As noted earlier, NICEDBG places an "outside range" list at the end of a disassembly listing. This list indicates locations that are called or jumped to in the listing, but which don't themselves appear in the listing. This list provides additional addresses for unassembly by DEBUG or SYMDEB.

For example, the disassembly of the MSDOS.SYS code segment includes the function INT2F_DISPATCH. As you know from the earlier investigation in Figure 6-13, the INT 2Fh handler in MSDOS.SYS jumps to the handler in IO.SYS. Here is how this shows up in the INT212F.LST file produced by NICEDBG:

```
; xref: FDC8:44DA FDC8:462F FDC8:4687 FDC8:46E0
                        jmp_44DF:
FDC8:44DF   EA05007000        JMP 0070:0005

; ...

;; outside-range FDC8:4045-B800:
;; 0070:0005
; ...
```

You can use this one address, 0070:0005, as the starting point for a disassembly of the IO.SYS code:

```
C:\UNDOC2\CHAP6>symdeb
-u 0070:0005 0005
0070:0005 EA93087000      JMP     0070:0893
-u 0070:0893 0893
0070:0893 2EFF2EE606      JMP     FAR CS:[06E6]
-dd 0070:06e6 06e6
0070:06E6   FFFF:1302
-u ffff:1302
FFFF:1302 80FC13          CMP     AH,13
FFFF:1305 7413            JZ 131A
FFFF:1307 80FC08          CMP     AH,08
FFFF:130A 743B            JZ 1347
FFFF:130C 80FC16          CMP     AH,16
FFFF:130F 7479            JZ 138A
FFFF:1311 80FC4A          CMP     AH,4A           ;'J'
FFFF:1314 7503            JNZ     1319
FFFF:1316 E9A700          JMP     13C0
FFFF:1319 CF              IRET
-q

C:\UNDOC2\CHAP6>type io.scr
u ffff:1302 1319
q

C:\UNDOC2\CHAP6>symdeb /x < io.scr > io.out

C:\UNDOC2\CHAP6>nicedbg io.out > io.lst

C:\UNDOC2\CHAP6>type io.lst
; ....
;; outside range FFFF:1302-1319:
;; 131A
;; 1347
;; 138A
;; 13C0
```

Now, of course, we expand the unassembly range for SYMDEB based on the addresses in the outside range list. Also, we can start to create a file with symbolic names:

```
C:\UNDOC2\CHAP6>type io.scr
u ffff:1302 13c0
q

C:\UNDOC2\CHAP6>type io.sym
FFFF:1302    IO_INT2F
FFFF:131A    IO_INT2F_13
FFFF:1347    IO_INT2F_08
FFFF:138A    IO_INT2F_16
FFFF:13C0    IO_INT2F_4A

C:\UNDOC2\CHAP6>symdeb /x < io.scr > io.out

C:\UNDOC2\CHAP6>nicedbg io.out io.sym > io.lst

C:\UNDOC2\CHAP6>type io.lst
; ...
;; outside range FFFF:1302-13C0:
;; 0070:0898
;; 174E
```

We continue in this way until no unresolved references remain. As noted earlier, sometimes DEBUG and SYMDEB get thrown off track because of data residing in the middle of a code segment. Based on the NICEDBG "unresolved label" list, you may need to split a single u command in a DEBUG script into two or more separate u commands.

Of course, the techniques shown here for disassembly in memory of MSDOS.SYS and IO.SYS also work for any other resident software. In Figure 6-11, for example, we saw SMARTDRV, MSCDEX, DOSKEY, SHARE, PRINT, COMMAND.COM, and so on, all camped out on the INT 2Fh chain. You can submit any of the addresses displayed by INTCHAIN to DEBUG or SYMDEB for disassembly and process the resulting output with NICEDBG.

However, it is much easier to disassemble separate programs such as SMARTDRV, MSCDEX, COMMAND, and PRINT on disk rather than in memory, because these programs don't involve the segment-moving contortions of the DOS kernel. PRINT in particular is probably the most disassembled piece of DOS, as this was how many TSR writers learned their craft. You can use a disassembler such as Sourcer to examine these programs.

Given the ability to reverse engineer DOS, an almost infinite amount of information on DOS programming is readily available. To answer some question about DOS, look at the code running on your machine. But one obvious problem with this approach is that what is true in one configuration may not be true in another. Applications patch DOS; DOS changes (though not much, in truth) from one version to version. Describing software based on its source code (whether supplied or disassembled) can either be the only accurate way to find out what the software really does, or it can be dangerous, relying on features that may change. There are no certainties here. Your best bet is to examine the source code but to realize how it may change, either because of future versions, or because of unforseen interactions with other software.

Am I Going to Jail for This?

Many programmers have doubts about the legality of what we've been doing in this chapter. Programmers frequently think that disassembling Microsoft's code is illegal, and even that it is somehow a full-blown criminal (rather than civil) offense, punishable by a stiff prison sentence! We had better look into this now.

The following discussion of the legalities of disassembly was not written by an attorney, and should not in any way be viewed as legal advice. However, I have benefited enormously from discussions with Gene K. Landy, a partner at the law firm of Shapiro, Israel & Weiner, P.C. in Boston. Any errors and misconceptions of course remain mine.

Landy is the author of a superb book/disk package, *The Software Developer's and Marketer's Legal Companion*, published by Addison-Wesley (1993), which includes several extremely useful discussions of reverse engineering. Chapter 1 discusses reverse engineering in the context of copyright, including the important Sega *v.* Accolade case. Chapter 2 discusses software trade secrets and confidentiality agreements. Chapter 11 covers shrink-wrap licenses and warranties and the standard shrink-wrap license limitation on reverse engineering, noting the important case of *Vault v. Quaid*. This is a fine book that every software developer will want to have in these troubled, legally complex, times.

Why do some programmers believe that you can wind up behind bars just for having seen the CLI instruction at the beginning of the INT 21h dispatch code? Quite simply because the standard license agreement that comes with all Microsoft products states, as plain as day

> 3. OTHER RESTRICTIONS. . . . You may not reverse engineer, decompile, or disassemble the software.

The very top of the license agreement states that "this is a legal agreement between you (either an individual or an entity) and Microsoft Corporation. By opening the sealed software packet(s) you are agreeing to be bound by the terms of this Agreement."

Well, that settles it, doesn't it? If you use any Microsoft software, you have entered into a binding legal agreement not to disassemble it, even if disassembly were otherwise a legitimate activity, right?

No. Attorneys have long questioned whether shrink-wrap licenses are binding, because of the mechanism they use. The few court cases that have decided issues of shrink-wrap licenses have spread further doubt about their effectiveness. As Landy explains in his chapter on shrink-wrap licenses,

> The central concept of a shrink wrap license is its system of acceptance or rejection: If you accept the contract, you tear open the envelope; if you reject it, you return the package for a refund. But does this "tear open" concept work? Does the law really allow the licensor to force the user to this choice? . . .
>
> A fundamental idea in contract law, from its eighteenth-century roots to the present, is the *bargain*—what lawyers sometimes call a "meeting of the minds." In a classic contract, the terms are bargained out, then the sale takes place as agreed. While the sale of goods in all states (except Louisiana) is now governed by a state statute, the Uniform Commercial Code, the same concept has carried over. A contract and its terms are agreed before or at the time of the sale. The problem with the Shrink Wrap License is that the retail software sale is over and done with before the customer is presented with the one-sided terms of the Shrink Wrap license. After the sale is already made, it is too late to try to impose adverse terms.

Similarly, Raymond T. Nimmer's excellent textbook, *The Law of Computer Technology* notes that "The attempt to alter the expectations of the common purchaser by virtue of a printed form included within the product package is unlikely to be successful."

How about the specific shrink-wrap license limitation against disassembly and reverse engineering? Two important cases have held that shrink-wrap or tear-me-open license agreements cannot be used to outlaw reverse engineering. Both Landy's book and Nimmer's discusses the important case of *Vault v. Quaid* (1987-1988). The state of Louisiana had enacted special legislation to validate various aspects of shrink-wrap licenses, including the restriction on reverse engineering. Vault (a California corporation) took Quaid (a Canadian corporation) to court in Louisiana to try to take advantage of this exceptional law. Unfortunately for Vault, but fortunately for those who think that disassembly is an important consumer right, the court ruled that the Louisiana statute was preempted by federal law. A similar Illinois statute has been repealed

So Microsoft's shrink-wrap license limitation against disassembly probably isn't worth the paper it's printed on.

How about the law of "trade secrets"? To begin with, reverse engineering is actually one of the few *legitimate* ways to discover a trade secret. The Uniform Trade Secrets Act (UTSA), adopted in the mid-1980s by almost all states, says explicitly that discovery through reverse engineering is a proper means of gaining access to non-patented trade secrets. Choosing one of the many books on intellectual property more or less at random, we find (Roger E. Schechter, *Unfair Trade Practices and Intellectual Property*, pp. 135-136, italics added):

> REVERSE ENGINEERING IS NOT IMPROPER MEANS
>
> Many products are manufactured pursuant to plans or with technologies that are trade secrets and then sold to the public at large. In some cases the method of manufacture of these items may be discovered by careful study of the object. Typical methods of discovery include taking the product apart or performing experiments on it. This process of analysis is usually called "reverse engineering." *Numerous cases hold that reverse engineering is not an improper means of learning a trade secret.* Risk of discovery by reverse engineering is a risk that a firm takes when it chooses to rely on trade secret protection for a valuable commercial asset. Note that if a firm secures patent protection for a new device or manufacturing process it is protected against "reverse engineering." This is one of the most important differences between patent and trade secret protection.

Given that MS-DOS is not patented (the two patent numbers, 4,955,066 and 5,109,433, in the front of all Microsoft's manuals are for a form of data compression, as used, for example, in Microsoft's help compilers), it then all seems to be quite straightforward: As far trade secret law is concerned, reverse engineering is okay. The rationale here is that trade secret law is basically about the loyalty of employees or others who receive important business information in confidence. You violate trade secret law by committing, inducing, or exploiting violations of trust. One does not violate anyone's trust by disassembling a product purchased on the open market.

So far, the shrink-wrap license statement against disassembling seems ineffective, and trade secrets law says disassembly is okay. What about the fact that MS-DOS is copyrighted? Does copyright law permit us to study how DOS works internally and then build products based on this new-found knowledge? For example, does it violate Microsoft's copyright to figure out how IO.SYS preloads DBLSPACE.BIN in MS-DOS 6.0 and then write a replacement for DBLSPACE.BIN that supports the same interface?

Disassembly is sometimes regarded as a form of copying (translation from one medium to another, or one language to another), and therefore as possible copyright infringement. However, disassembly for the purposes of achieving compatibility is generally regarded as "fair use." An important decision by the Court of Appeals for the Ninth Circuit in *Sega v. Accolade* (August 1992), overturning a lower court's ruling, held that Accolade's use of knowledge reverse-engineered from the Sega Genesis system did not violate Sega's copyright and constituted fair use. According to the court (as quoted in *UNIX Review*, May 1993),

> We conclude that where disassembly is the only way to gain access to the ideas and functional elements embodied in a copyrighted computer program and where there is a

legitimate reason for seeking such access, disassembly is a fair use of the copyrighted work, as a matter of law.

The importance of Sega *v.* Accolade was underlined in a comment in *Microprocessor Report* (December 9, 1992): "For the industry, many can breathe a deep sigh of relief. No longer are we unwitting copyright violators because we need to understand the parameters to an undocumented 'Int 21' call."

Naturally, not all members of the industry breathed a sigh of relief on hearing the appeals court's ruling. In particular, a group calling itself the Business Equipment Manufacturers, which includes IBM, Intel, and Microsoft, is seeking stronger protection against reverse engineering. Arguing for greater protection for reverse engineering is the so-called American Committee for Interoperable Systems, which includes Sun Microsystems, Amdahl, and Chips & Technologies (see "Reverse Engineering Reversals," *Upside*, May 1993).

If disassembly for the purposes of achieving compatibility is okay (and this, by the way, is also true in Europe under article 6 of the EC's directive on software protection), then how about this book's quotations from disassembly listings? Have we violated Microsoft's copyright by reprinting several chunks of code from MS-DOS and Windows in this book?

Again, no. For purposes of copyright, computer programs are considered to be "literary works." While it is a bogus notion that a compiled program without its source code merits being called a literary work, if the phrase "literary work" means anything at all in the context of computer software, it must include the possibility for *literary criticism*. Our inclusion of brief excerpts from disassembly listings is essentially a form of scholarly quotation, which is one of the oldest forms of fair use (see William S. Strong, *The Copyright Book*, 4th edition, Chapter 8).

Remember too that throughout this chapter we have relied on DEBUG, a tool which Microsoft provides with every copy of MS-DOS. Microsoft has made no effort to secure MS-DOS against disassembly, especially given DEBUG's ability to trace into an INT 21h or INT 2Fh call.

Use the Source, Luke!

Is there any alternative to disassembly? One alternative is, of course, to rely entirely on the vendor's documentation and not to consider whether this documentation is an accurate reflection of the actual software. But as the reader has probably figured out by now, relying on vendor documentation has as many risks as does relying on undocumented behavior that has been discerned through disassembly.

Depending on what you are interested in, there may be another, better alternative to disassembly: source code.

For example, programmers' questions sometimes aren't really about how the operating system behaves in a certain circumstance, but about what their compiler's run-time library (RTL) does. There is persistent confusion among many programmers about the difference between a FILE* in C and a DOS file handle. Programmers often call the DOS Set Handle Count function (INT 21h AH=67h) and then wonder why the C fopen() function still fails. Confusion such as this can be cleared up by a careful study of the RTL source code. Both Microsoft C and Borland C++ come with RTL source code.

Sometimes, rather than having specific questions about MS-DOS, programmers are just curious about how operating systems work in general. In this case, the best approach is probably to study one of the several excellent books available on the design and implementation of UNIX. Some of these, such as Bach's *Design of the UNIX Operating System* and Andleigh's *UNIX System Architecture*, present detailed pseudocode for UNIX. Others, such as Tanenbaum's wonderful *Operating Systems: Design and Implementation* (MINIX) and Comer's *Operating System Design: The XINU Approach*, come with complete source code for UNIX workalikes. Despite the numerous differences between DOS and UNIX, these books should be required reading for anyone planning to delve into DOS internals.

DOS's handling of memory, processes, files, devices, and so on, can often best be understood by contrasting it with the design and implementation of a well-understood system such as UNIX.

For a more specifically DOS-like approach to operating system design and implementation, another alternative to disassembly of MS-DOS is to examine the source code that is available for several DOS workalikes. Embedded DOS from General Software (Redmond WA) has Steve Jones's superb documentation on DOS internals (for an excellent discussion of making a fully-reentrant DOS, see Steve's article "DOS Meets Real-Time" in the February 1992 *Embedded Systems Programming*). General Software's Utility SDK and Device Driver SDK come with complete source code in C for versions of utilities such as CHKDSK, FORMAT, FDISK, DISKCOPY. ROM DOS 5 from Datalight (Arlington WA) is also available with source code.

Last, but not least, Mike Podanoffsky (mikep@world.std.com) has written RxDOS, an inexpensive DOS available with fully commented, assembly language source code. Podanoffsky is currently writing a full-length book on RxDOS, *Dissecting DOS: A Code Level Look at the DOS Operating System*, which will be available in 1994. While obviously not identical to the MS-DOS source, this source code may be more than adequate for your needs. For example, Figure 6-23 shows the implementation of INT 21h functions 50h, 51h, and 52h from RXDOS.ASM.

Figure 6-23: RxDOS Implementation of INT 21h AH=50h, 51h, and 52h

```
        ;''''''''''''''''''''''''''''''''''''''''''''''''''''''';
        ;   50h Set PSP Address                                  ;
        ;- - - - - - - - - - - - - - - - - - - - - - - - - - - -;
        ;   bx       contains PSP address to use                 ;
        ;......................................................;
_SetPSPAddress:
        mov word ptr [ _RxDOS_CurrentPSP ], bx    ; Seg Pointer to current PSP
        ret

        ;''''''''''''''''''''''''''''''''''''''''''''''''''''''';
        ;   51h Get PSP Address                                  ;
        ;- - - - - - - - - - - - - - - - - - - - - - - - - - - -;
        ;   bx       contains PSP address to use                 ;
        ;......................................................;
_GetPSPAddress:
        mov bx, word ptr [ _RxDOS_CurrentPSP ] ; Seg Pointer of current PSP
        RetCallersStackFrame es, si
        mov word ptr es:[ _BX ][ si ], bx
        ret

        ;''''''''''''''''''''''''''''''''''''''''''''''''''''''';
        ;   52h Get Dos Data Table Pointer                       ;
        ;- - - - - - - - - - - - - - - - - - - - - - - - - - - -;
        ;   es:bx returns pointer to dos device parameter block  ;
        ; --- DOS Undocumented Feature ------------------------- ;
        ;......................................................;
_GetDosDataTablePtr:
        RetCallersStackFrame es, si
        mov word ptr es:[ _ExtraSegment ][ si ], ds
        mov word ptr es:[ _BX ][ si ], offset _RxDOS_pDPB
        clc
        ret
```

There are no big surprises here (really, how else could Get and Set PSP be implemented, anyway?), but we can see that this accurately reflects MS-DOS, and that having this code earlier in the chapter might have saved us a lot of trouble.

More interesting, Figure 6-24 shows the RxDOS implementation of lseek, the MS-DOS implementation of which we saw, in Figure 6-20. The RxDOS code provides a useful guide to MS-DOS disassembly.

Figure 6-24: RxDOS Implementation of INT 21h AH=42h (lseek)

```
            ;;;;;;;;;;;;;;;;;;;;;;;;;;;;;;;;;;;;;;;;;;;;;;;;;;;;;;;;;;;;;;;;;
            ;  42h Lseek (Move) File Pointer                                 ;
            ;- - - - - - - - - - - - - - - - - - - - - - - - - - - - - - - -;
            ;  al        move method                                        ;
            ;  bx        handle                                             ;
            ;  cx:dx     distance to move pointer                           ;
            ;..............................................................;
_MoveFilePointer:
            Entry
            def _method, ax
            def _handle, bx
            ddef _moveDistance, cx, dx
            ddef _newPosition

            mov ax, bx                            ; handle
            call MapAppToSysHandles               ; map to internal handle info
            call FindSFTbyHandle                  ; get corresponding SFT (es: di )
            jc _moveFilePointer_36                ; if could not find -->

            getdarg cx, dx, _moveDistance
            mov ax, word ptr [ _method ][ bp ]
            Goto SEEK_BEG,    _moveFilePointer_beg
            Goto SEEK_CUR,    _moveFilePointer_cur
            Goto SEEK_END,    _moveFilePointer_end
            SetError -1,      _moveFilePointer_36
;- - - - - - - - - - - - - - - - - - - - - - - - - - - - - - - - - - - - -
;  seek from end
;- - - - - - - - - - - - - - - - - - - - - - - - - - - - - - - - - - - - -
_moveFilePointer_end:
            add dx, word ptr es:[ sftFileSize. _low  ][ di ]
            adc cx, word ptr es:[ sftFileSize. _high ][ di ]
            jmp short _moveFilePointer_beg
;- - - - - - - - - - - - - - - - - - - - - - - - - - - - - - - - - - - - -
;  seek from current position
;- - - - - - - - - - - - - - - - - - - - - - - - - - - - - - - - - - - - -
_moveFilePointer_cur:
            add dx, word ptr es:[ sftFilePosition. _low  ][ di ]
            adc cx, word ptr es:[ sftFilePosition. _high ][ di ]
      ;     jmp short _moveFilePointer_beg

;- - - - - - - - - - - - - - - - - - - - - - - - - - - - - - - - - - - - -
;  seek from beginning
;- - - - - - - - - - - - - - - - - - - - - - - - - - - - - - - - - - - - -
_moveFilePointer_beg:
            mov word ptr es:[ sftFilePosition. _low  ][ di ], dx
            mov word ptr es:[ sftFilePosition. _high ][ di ], cx
;- - - - - - - - - - - - - - - - - - - - - - - - - - - - - - - - - - - - -
;  Return
;- - - - - - - - - - - - - - - - - - - - - - - - - - - - - - - - - - - - -
_moveFilePointer_36:
            RetCallersStackFrame ds, bx
            mov word ptr [ _AX ][ bx ], dx
            mov word ptr [ _DX ][ bx ], cx
            Return
```

If you want a disassembly of genuine MS-DOS, but don't want to DIY (do it yourself), and for some reason would be happy with a disassembly of DOS 1.1 or 2.1, Information Modes (Denton TX) sells inexpensive disassembly listings of these early versions of DOS. Imodes used the information gleaned from its long-ago disassembly project as part of its well-known product, The $25 Network ("Skeptical? We make believers! Over 15,000 sold"). For example, Figure 6-25 shows Imodes' rendition of the Get and Set PSP functions from D1.ASM, a disassembly dated April 1987. (It is an interesting reflection on the state of knowledge about DOS internals at the time that function 52h is labelled "get device driver list".)

Figure 6-25: Imodes Disassembly of DOS 2.1 Set and Get PSP

```
;........................ Set current PSP ........................ Fn 50
L10D6:
    MOV CS:L0191,BX             ;current PSP seg
    RET_NEAR

;........................ Get current PSP ........................ Fn 51
L10DC:
    CALL LOC1A                 ;ds:si--> user's stack
    PUSH CS:L0191              ;
    POP [SI+2]                 ;return in bx
    RET_NEAR
```

Figure 6-26 shows the Imodes interpretation of the lseek function from DOS 2.1, which you can compare against the MS-DOS 6.0 disassembly in Figure 6-20 and the RxDOS implementation in Figure 6-24.

Figure 6-26: Imodes Disassembly of DOS 2.1 INT 21h AH=42h (lseek)

```
;........................ Lseek (handle) ........................ Fn 42
                           ;bx = handle
                           ;cx_dx = hi_low dword offset
                           ;al = seek mode,  0 - from file start
                           ;                 1 - from current position
                           ;                 2 - from file end
                           ;return: cy=0, dx_ax = new position (from start)
                           ;    - or -
                           ;return: cy=1, ax = 1 - invalid function (mode)
                           ;                   6 - invalid handle
L3BD5:
    CMP AL,3                   ;is method in range 0..2 ?
    JC L3BDD                   ;no:      yes-->
    MOV AL,1                   ;err = invalid function

L3BDB:
    JMP SHORT L3BD3            ;dos error return

L3BDD:
    PUSH SS
    POP DS
    CALL L38FB                 ;with bx=handle, get handle defn.
    PUSH ES
    POP DS
    JC L3BD1                   ;if handle bad--> ret, invalid handle
    TEST BYTE PTR [DI+1Bh],80h ;is char device?
    JZ L3BF2                   ;yes:  no-->
    XOR AX,AX                  ;record = 0 always
    XOR DX,DX
    JMP SHORT L3C08            ;--> set random record fields

L3BF2:
    DEC AL                     ;is method 0, from file start ?
    JL L3C05                   ;no:  yes-->
    DEC AL                     ;is method 1, from current position ?
    JL L3C18                   ;no:  yes-->

;. . . . . . . . . . . method 2, from end of file
    XCHG DX,AX                 ;ax = LSWord
    XCHG DX,CX                 ;dx = MSWord
    ADD AX,[DI+13h]            ;add fcb's file size
    ADC DX,[DI+15h]            ;
    JMP SHORT L3C08            ;--> set fields
```

```
;. . . . . . . . . . . . . method 0, from start of file
L3C05:
  XCHG DX,AX                    ;ax = LSWord
  XCHG DX,CX                    ;dx = MSWord
```

As with the PSP functions, this disassembly of lseek in DOS 2.1 bears many similarities to the disassembly of lseek in DOS 6.0. On the other hand, the DOS 2.1 version does not do Windows and doesn't contain any network-redirector code.

Microsoft's DOS OEM Adaptation Kit (OAK)

But perhaps you care deeply and desperately about getting the genuine article: commented source code from Microsoft for MS-DOS 5.0 and higher. Microsoft does not publicize the product a great deal, but Microsoft will sell you an OEM Adaptation Kit on signing a license agreement. Microsoft's OAK comes on an oddly-formatted tape cartridge, but a version on normal PC diskettes is available from Annabooks (San Diego CA).

The contents of the OAK are Microsoft confidential, so unfortunately we cannot reproduce any of it here, but we can give you some idea of its contents:

```
\DOS500AK
    \BIOS
        msbio1.asm
        msbio2.asm
        sysinit1.asm
        sysinit2.asm
        ...
    \BOOT
        msboot.asm
        ...
    \CMD
        \COMMAND
        \FORMAT
        \MODE
        ...
    \DEV
        \ANSI
        \HIMEM
        ...
    \DOS
        fat.obj
        getset.obj
        handle.obj
        msdisp.obj
        ...
    \H
        cds.h
        dpb.h
        sysvar.h
        ...
    \INC
        arena.inc
        bpb.inc
        mult.inc
        pdb.inc
        sysvar.inc
        win386.inc
        wpatch.inc
        ...
```

As you can see from this very partial directory tree, Microsoft supplies some components of the OAK in .ASM source code form, and others are supplied as .OBJ files. The idea, of course, is that the OEM will change parts of IO.SYS but not MSDOS.SYS, so IO.SYS comes with source, but MSDOS.SYS comes only with .OBJ files. Having .OBJ files is almost as good as having source code, though, since .OBJ files contain names for functions and variables. An .OBJ disassembler such as WDISASM (included with Watcom C) can basically regenerate the source code, missing only comments (which are probably out-of-date and misleading anyway).

Examination of the OAK contents mostly confirms what has been known for many years as a result of reverse engineering. However, it is sometimes interesting to know the actual names for undocumented functions as they appear in Microsoft's source code. For example, the undocumented structure generally called the List of Lists is called SysInitVars in the DOS source because the structure is actually intended for use by SYSINIT. INT 21h AH=52h, which returns a pointer to this structure, and which is generally called Get List of Lists or Get SysVars, is called GET_IN_VARS in the DOS source. It turns out that there is little correspondence between the documented names for INT 21h functions and their actual names in the DOS source. For example, AH=1Bh is Get Default Drive Data and AH=1Ch is Get Drive Data in the *MS-DOS Programmer's Reference*, but in the code they are called SLEAZEFUNC and SLEAZEFUNCDL.

Looking over the OAK contents, it seems a shame that source code for MS-DOS and Windows isn't more widely available. In the same way that the old IBM PC and IBM AT technical references (for example, IBM, *Technical Reference—Personal Computer AT*, 1985) greatly promoted the development of innovative new software and hardware by publishing complete assembly-language listings of the system ROM BIOS, likewise Microsoft could promote greater understanding of DOS and Windows by making the source code for these fundamental technologies available. This isn't as ridiculous as it may sound. Consider that just a few years ago compiler run-time library source code was kept proprietary too. Now almost all compilers come with RTL source.

Microsoft did at one point make some attempt at opening up DOS to closer inspection. The original *MS-DOS (Versions 1.0-3.2) Technical Reference Encyclopedia* (1986), one of the few books ever to be subject to a *recall* from the publisher, made an attempt to provide descriptions, not only of each DOS function's inputs and outputs, but also of its internal operation. Each function was accompanied by a flowchart titled, "How It Works." While an excellent idea, the execution was flawed. Some functions (such as INT 21h AH=48h Allocate Memory) were described in great detail, with the flowchart running for many pages, while others were described in only the vaguest terms such as "call internal function". The Microsoft encyclopedia carried the following warning:

> *Note:* These flowcharts were written for MS-DOS Version 3.2. This in no way means that all future or past versions of MS-DOS will behave in the same manner. You should take care not to write programs that make use of the specific structure of the function routine, because this could result in lack of compatibility with other versions of DOS. Microsoft guarantees only that if you input the values in the registers in the specified way, you will get back the specified values. How the function actually accomplishes a task is subject to change.

In addition to the generally vague and misleading flowcharts for each DOS function, the Microsoft encyclopedia also carried an extremely detailed flowchart for COMMAND.COM.

Is there any value to knowledge of DOS internals? With more and more software developers programming for Windows, using high-level tools such as Visual C++, and with more and more software developers viewing even the Windows API as hopelessly low level, does an understanding of an even lower level, the DOS kernel, matter anymore? Hopefully this chapter has given you some idea of why the answer to that question is a resounding "yes." True, you don't want to have to think about how the JFT is connected to the SFT every time you use a high-level C or C++ or Win32 API call to read or write a file. But without understanding how the system really works, you can have only a vague notion of how your own code works.

## CHAPTER 7

MS-DOS Resource Management: Memory, Processes, Devices

by Jim Kyle

Resource management is the primary task of any operating system. This chapter concentrates on such facets of MS-DOS resource management as device drivers, memory allocation, and process management. Throughout the discussion, sample code fragments and programs are used; the conclusion brings everything together in a utility that lets you install a device driver from the DOS command line without requiring that you edit your CONFIG.SYS file or reboot the system.

The earliest operating systems, in the dim prehistory of mainframe days, managed resources by default—only one process could be loaded into the machine at a time, and that process had full access to all resources.

Operating systems evolved, and it became possible to load several processes at the same time. Any true operating system must, in fact, contain at least two processes, the supervisor or system program (often called the kernel) and the user program. As soon as there is more than one process, it becomes necessary to manage memory and devices so that no process intrudes on another.

Entire textbooks have been written on the design of operating systems, and if you're interested in the general requirements, these books can be fascinating reading. Here, though, we concentrate specifically on MS-DOS, and even more specifically on version 5.0, which has gained such wide acceptance, and the newer version 6.0.

Memory Management

MS-DOS allows programs to allocate, free, and resize memory through three documented functions (INT 21h, Functions 48h, 49h, and 4Ah), but the actions of the DOS memory manager itself were not officially documented until Microsoft published its *Programmer's Reference for Version 5.0*. This section describes how memory is organized to make these functions possible.

The memory management scheme used by MS-DOS divides the first megabyte of the system's memory into contiguous blocks, each of which has a Memory Control Block (MCB) as its first paragraph. Each MCB provides enough information to get to the next MCB. It is important to note that this chain is not a linked list, but a contiguous block of memory. The size of one block is added onto its starting address to get to the next block. Figure 7-1 shows how an example of how this memory structure is laid out.

Figure 7-1. Organization of the DOS Memory Arena

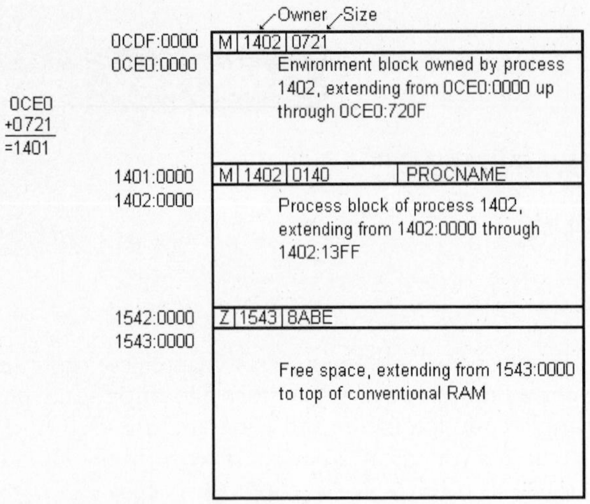

The total memory structure is referred to in official documentation (and in Ray Duncan's better-than-official *Advanced MS-DOS Programming*) as the memory arena, and the MCB that begins each block is called an arena header. Throughout this volume, though, we refer to the arena header by the term MCB.

The initial MCB structure is built at system boot time, just after the parsing of CONFIG.SYS directives. This structure omits memory below the DOS data segment because all RAM in that area was assigned earlier in the boot-up procedure and is not subject to reallocation.

Memory Control Blocks

Each block of memory begins with an MCB, which is a single paragraph. That is, the MCB is 16 bytes long and begins at an address that is an exact multiple of 16. Memory blocks themselves are also always an exact number of paragraphs in length. This paragraph alignment makes it possible to refer to a memory block using a 16-bit segment address rather than a full 20-bit address.

The excerpt from the UNDOCDOS.H header file (which we provide to supply full documentation, in one place, of the various undocumented structures our sample code deals with; it's on the companion diskette) in Figure 7-2 shows how each MCB is organized.

Figure 7-2. DOS Memory Control Block Structure

```
typedef struct {        /* Memory Control Block entry */
  BYTE type;            /* 'M'=in chain; 'Z'=at end   */
  WORD owner;           /* PSP of the owner           */
  WORD size;            /* in 16-byte paragraphs      */
  BYTE unused[3];
  BYTE owner_name[8];   /* filename of owner, if DOS4  */
} MCB, far * LPMCB;
```

When a program requests a block of memory with INT 21h Function 48h, DOS must find the number of requested paragraphs, plus one more for the MCB. Assuming that a block of memory is available, DOS sets up its first paragraph as an MCB and hands the segment address of the second paragraph back to the program. Let's say you've made this call:

```
mov ah, 48h              ; Allocate Memory Block
mov bx, 1                ; one paragraph
int 21h
jc fail
; AX now holds initial segment of allocated block
```

Let's say AX now holds the value 1234h. This means that an MCB is located at 1233h. What does this MCB look like?

The first byte of every MCB (MCB.type) except the last one in the chain, is 4Ch (the ASCII code for 'M'); the last MCB's first byte is instead 5Ah ('Z'). It may only be coincidental that these two letters are the initials of the principal architect of the DOS memory manager, Mark Zbikowski. In our example, this field could either be 'M' or 'Z', though 'M' is far more likely.

Following this tag byte is a 16-bit value in Intel low-high format (MCB.owner) that identifies the owner of the MCB. This field will be 0000 if the memory block is available for use. Otherwise, it will contain the ID number of the process to which the block has been allocated (the owner process). This information is used to locate free blocks, those where MCB.owner is 0, and to release allocated blocks when a process terminates. This ID number is the Program Segment Prefix (see below) of the owner. In our example, this field would hold the PSP of whatever program was the current process when INT 21h Function 48h was called.

Following the owner word is another word (MCB.size) giving the size in paragraphs of the memory block controlled by this MCB. In our example, this field will be set to 1, indicating that the MCB at 1233h controls only the next paragraph at 1234h. In other words, this size value does not include the paragraph taken by the MCB itself; consequently, it's possible to have a valid MCB that shows a free block with size equal to 0. This happens when all but one paragraph of a previously free block is allocated, and it is, in fact, not unusual. Because the MCB stores the number of paragraphs, not the number of bytes, it can manage blocks up to 1,048,575 bytes in size (the entire memory space available in real mode). This is the basis for huge pointers under DOS.

The three bytes following the size word are unused in all versions of MS-DOS to date. In versions 2.0 and 3.0, all remaining bytes of the MCB were unused; but in DOS 4.0 and later versions the final eight bytes of the MCB (MCB.owner_name) may contain the filename of the owning program. The name is included only in the MCB that controls the memory used by the program's PSP; otherwise, the final eight bytes are ignored.

To find the next MCB in memory (remember, it's not a linked list), you start with the MCB's own segment address, add 1 to it to get the segment address of the RAM it controls, then add to that the size from the word at byte 3 of the MCB. The result is the segment address of the next MCB. In our example, the next MCB is at 1235h. If the byte at 1235:0000 is anything other than 'M' or 'Z', the MCB chain has been corrupted and continued operation is not possible.

The first MCB is always the one that controls DOS's own data segment; this MCB contains the memory allocated based on commands given in CONFIG.SYS. Its owner word, in every version of DOS that I have examined, is 0008h, for no reason that I have ever been able to discover.

The final MCB, identified by the 'Z' in its first byte, will, in a normal 640K system, generate a next-MCB address of 0A000h, although that address should not be used because the 'Z' code indicates no next-MCB exists. Under DOS 5.0 (or with earlier versions, when using a third-party memory manager such as QEMM or 386MAX), it's possible to enable Upper Memory Blocks. When this is done, the MCB chain may extend past segment 0A000h, up to the point that ROM BIOS is found. We look at this later in a separate section.

In DOS 4.x and higher, the DOS data segment memory block (that is, the RAM that DOS retains for its own use, which can be located using the List of Lists as described later in this chapter) is subdivided into subsegments; each subsegment has its own variant of the standard MCB. However, the 'M'- coded MCB for the data segment includes the entire area, so you don't need to trace the subsegments when going through the MCB chain.

The subsegments follow a format similar to, but not identical with, the MCB layout. The first byte is a letter indicating usage, but the word at byte 1 is not the owner. Instead, it is the actual segment address of the item controlled by the block. The word at byte 3 is the size in paragraphs of the controlled item. Bytes 8 through 15 contain the filename, padded with blanks, of the file from which a driver was loaded.

Table 7-1 shows the codes used in these subsegment control blocks.

Table 7-1: Codes Used in Subsegment Control Blocks

Code	Directive Meaning Device Driver, If Present
E	device driver appendage, if present
I	IFS (Installable File System) driver, if present
F	FILES= control block storage area (for FILES>5)
X	FCBS= control block storage area, if present
C	BUFFERS EMS workspace area (if BUFFERS /X option used)
B	BUFFERS= storage area
L	LASTDRIVE= drive info table storage area
S	STACKS= code and data area
T	Transient area (DOS 5 and later only)

Because these subsegment control blocks appear only in the DOS data segment and are meaningless elsewhere, they appear to be of limited use. Their purpose appears to be simplification of the MEM command introduced in DOS 4.0, although most of the information contained in them is duplicated elsewhere in each of the applicable DOS structures.

Similar abbreviations are found in the buffer used internally by DOS for parsing CONFIG.SYS. 'X' represents FCBS=, for example, and 'D' represents DEVICE=. The abbreviations are not identical, however. For example, the CONFIG.SYS buffer uses 'K' to represent STACKS=, since 'S' apparently is needed for the SHELL= statement. (For more information on the CONFIG.SYS buffer, see Michael J. Mefford, "Choose CONFIG.SYS Options at Boot," *PC Magazine*, 29 November, 1988, pp. 323-344, a fascinating article explaining a brilliant DOS utility.)

The HMA and UMBs

Before we get into the details of tracing the MCB chains, let's step aside briefly and look at two powerful ideas that burst into the mainstream of memory management with DOS 5.0. These are the High Memory Area and Upper Memory Blocks.

What most of us call conventional RAM stops short at address A000:0000. This address is the start of the 384K that IBM's original system architects reserved for use both as video RAM and to hold memory-mapped adapter cards and the ROM BIOS. The memory space addressable by even the original 8088, though, goes all the way up to address FFFF:000F.

Not long after the 80286 processors appeared, with their ability to address more than a megabyte of memory, programmers worked out ways to make use of parts of that 384K that were *not* taken up with hardware and system services. Long before DOS itself had any ability to deal with these areas, third-party memory managers such as QEMM and 386MAX provided capabilities to "load programs high" in those parts of the 384K that were not otherwise used.

Then Microsoft developed its XMS specification that dealt with using the High Memory Area, a region just above the 1-megabyte mark. Subsequently Microsoft included provision for allocating memory in the Upper Memory region, the official name for the 384K adapter-infested area. With the release of DOS 5.0, allocation of UMBs became officially recognized and documented. Figure 7-3 is a memory map summarizing where these areas fit with respect to conventional RAM.

Figure 7-3. Memory Map Showing UMB Region and HMA

```
|                                         |
|              Extended Memory            |
|                                         |
|10FFF:0000     Next higher address       |
+-----------------------------------------+
|  FFFF:FFFF     (10000:FFEF) Top of HMA   |
|                                         |
|              HIGH MEMORY AREA           |
|                                         |
|  FFFF:0010    (10000:0000) Start of HMA  |
+-----------------------------------------+
|  FFFF:000F    Top of first megabyte      |
|                                         |
|              ROM BIOS                   |
|              UMB's                      |
|           Adapter Cards                 |
|           Video RAM                     |
|                                         |
|  A000:0000    Start of Upper Memory      |
+-----------------------------------------+
|  9FFF:000F    Top of conventional RAM    |
|                                         |
|              Programs                   |
|           DOS Data Structures           |
|                                         |
|  0000:0000    Lowest RAM address         |
+-----------------------------------------+
```

Making Use of UMBs

To make use of Upper Memory Blocks, it's necessary to include a special command, DOS=UMB, in CONFIG.SYS to enable them. You must also include EMM386.EXE with its option switch RAM or NOEMS, or some other memory manager that is a UMB provider to take its place. (Some third-party memory managers do not require the DOS=UMB line; check your manual for details.)

With these preliminaries out of the way, all you do is use the internal command LOADHIGH (or its alias LH) preceding your normal program command line. This command, used primarily when loading TSRs, causes the command interpreter to link the UMB memory chain onto the normal conventional RAM MCB chain. The command interpreter also sets the allocation strategy so that DOS searches the UMBs first when looking for space to load your program into. If DOS cannot find enough space in Upper Memory, conventional RAM will be used (with no error or warning message). When your program returns to DOS, the allocation strategy is returned to its original state, and the UMB chain is unhooked from the conventional MCB linkage.

The DOS actions involved were all documented in the *Programmer's Reference for MS-DOS 5.0*; the method by which LOADHIGH is implemented, however, has not been. The simple INTRSPY script in Figure 7-4 quickly reveals the sequence of events.

Figure 7-4. Organization of the DOS Memory Arena

```
; LOADHIGH.SCR
intercept 21h
    on_entry
        output "I21 at " cs ":" ip ", AX=" AX ": "
    function 0Ah
        on_entry
            sameline "Buffered Input to " ds ":" dx
    function 25h
        on_entry
            sameline "Set INT" al " ==> " ds ":" dx
    function 26h
```

```
    on_entry
        sameline "Create new PSP at " dx
function 30h
    on_entry
        sameline "Get version, flag = " al "  "
    on_exit
        sameline "Ver " al "." ah ", BH=" bh
function 35h
    on_exit
        sameline "INT" al " adr is " es ":" bx
function 37h
    on_exit
        sameline "Switchar is " dl
function 48h
    on_entry
        sameline "ALLOC " bx "h paras"
    on_exit
        if (cflag==1)
            sameline " FAIL (" ax "), only " bx "h available"
        if (cflag==0)
            sameline " returned seg " ax "h"
function 49h
    on_entry sameline "FREE seg " es "h"
    on_exit if (cflag==1) sameline " denied (" ax "h)"
function 4ah
    on_entry
        sameline "REALLOC seg " es "h to " bx "h paras"
    on_exit
        if (cflag==1)
            sameline " FAIL (" ax "h), only " bx "h available"
function 4bh
    on_entry sameline "Loading " (ds:dx->byte,asciiz,64)
    on_exit  output "---ret from child process---"
function 50h on_entry sameline "Set PSP: " BX
function 51h on_exit sameline "Get PSP: " BX
function 58h
  subfunction 00h
    on_entry
        sameline "Get Allocation Strategy"
    on_exit
        sameline " returned " ax
  subfunction 01h
    on_entry
        sameline "Set Allocation Strategy to " bx
    on_exit
        if (cflag==1)
            sameline " FAILED (" ax "h)"
  subfunction 02h
    on_entry
        sameline "Get UMB Link"
    on_exit
        sameline " returned " al
  subfunction 03h
    on_entry sameline "Link/Unlink UMB to MCBs: " bx
    on_exit
        if (cflag==1)
            sameline " FAILED (" ax "h)"
```

When this script compiles and runs under EMM386 and COMMAND.COM, here's the essential part of the resulting report. The command traced was "LOADHIGH DIDIT" (DIDIT.COM is a tiny COM file that simply outputs one line and terminates):

```
I21 at 9672:59E4, AX=5800: Get Allocation Strategy returned 0000
I21 at 9672:59EB, AX=5802: Get UMB Link returned 00
```

```
I21 at 9672:596F, AX=5800: Get Allocation Strategy returned 0000
I21 at 9672:597A, AX=5801: Set Allocation Strategy to 0080
I21 at 9672:5983, AX=5803: Link/Unlink UMB to MCBs: 0001
I21 at 9672:29FF, AX=4903: FREE seg 1A0Dh
I21 at 0B4D:01DC, AX=4B00: Loading  D:\UDOS2\ISPY\DIDIT.COM
I21 at CDE8:0107, AX=0900:
---ret from child process---
I21 at FFFF:BB0D, AX=5800: Get Allocation Strategy returned 0080
I21 at FFFF:BB1E, AX=5801: Set Allocation Strategy to 0000
I21 at FFFF:BB29, AX=5803: Link/Unlink UMB to MCBs: 0000
```

You can see that the five calls to Function 58h came from the transient portion of COM-MAND.COM in segment 9672. With the UMB region linked, and the strategy set to allocate space in the UM region first, on a first-fit basis, the resident portion of COMMAND.COM then invokes the DOS loader down at segment 0B4D then invoked the DOS loader .

The unidentified call to Function 09h from segment CDE8 is the single-line report sent by DIDIT.COM; the trace confirms that the program actually did load into a UMB (CS:IP was CDE8:0107, in the Upper Memory above A000h). DIDIT then terminated, returning control to the HMA at segment FFFF. There, COMMAND.COM reset the strategy to normal first-fit, and DOS removed the UM region link, completing the LOADHIGH sequence of events.

The High Memory Area

Unlike UMBs, the High Memory Area can be used only with an 80286 or later processor. Its operation depends on the CPU having more than 20 address bits. The original 8088-based systems had only 20 address lines available. If you tried to address a byte at FFFF:0010, for example, the CPU would perform its addition and generate an absolute address on the system bus of 100000h. That, however, required 21 bits rather than 20. The system simply ignored the excess bit, so that an address of this sort wrapped around to 0000:0000.

When the 80286 appeared with its 24 address bits, this wraparound stopped being automatic. So many programs depended on it for proper operation, though, that system designers added hardware for the express purpose of making it continue to happen. Of course, this added circuitry had to be capable of being switched out in order to let the 286 operate in its full 24-bit mode.

When the added circuits were switched out, it then became possible to address 65,520 (64K-16) bytes of extended RAM, above the 1-megabyte mark, without having to switch the processor out of real mode. By using a segment address of FFFFh and depending on the wraparound not taking place, programs could treat the first 64K-16 bytes of extended RAM the same as conventional RAM.

That special area has been termed the High Memory Area (HMA), and one of HIMEM.SYS's purposes is to control access to the HMA. Both the XMS specification and the DOS 5.0 *Programmer's Reference* document use of the HMA, but both tend to conceal certain critical points about the way it really works.

For instance, both documents tell us that the A20 line, which controls access to the HMA, is turned off each time a program is loaded; but if DOS is loaded high with the DOS=HIGH command, the A20 line will (as we see in Chapter 6) be enabled for each invocation of a DOS service. In fact, once turned back on by this means, it remains on. Since the loader itself calls DOS repeatedly in the course of bringing a new process into RAM, the A20 line might as well never be turned off when CONFIG.SYS contains the DOS=HIGH command. You can verify this using DEBUG. Just issue the command "d FFFF:0000" and watch the HMA display on the screen. You can scroll through the whole thing by using repeated "d" commands.

Leaving the A20 line enabled causes problems with programs that expect wraparound to occur, of course. One such program was the unpacking routine Microsoft's own linker originally included with any file that had been EXEPACKed to reduce its size! According to Phillip Gardner, author of the shareware DOSMAX UMB maintenance utility and a veteran in the DOS disassembly area, the notorious "Packed File corrupt" error message that began appearing everywhere shortly after the introduction of DOS 5.0 is directly due to the fact that the A20 line is enabled, and the original unpacking routines depended on the segment wraparound effect to properly expand the compressed files.

Specifically, the packing technique used by EXEPACK is a form of run-length encoding; the expansion method involves moving the packed copy of the program up in memory so that its end is at the final correct location, then working backward toward the front of the program. Each time the unpacking code finds a run-length count code, it calculates a target address for the program's first byte based on that count. All bytes from the start of the program up to the count code are then moved back so they start at that lower target address and the repeated run is inserted at the appropriate location, overwriting the count code. The original version of the unpacker calculated the offset of the new target address by negating the count in 32-bit form, then adding that to the current address in 20-bit form. When segment wraparound is in effect, the final calculation produces a 20-bit result of 00000h, which verifies that the expansion was successful. Otherwise, when the program happens to be located in the first 64K of the total address space, the final result wraps into the High Memory area, which causes the "corrupt" message to be displayed. Once the problem was identified, of course, Microsoft changed the decompression routine, and versions of the linkers produced since mid-1988 or so don't create the error. Many popular packages, though, were built with the older linkers; so the error may be with us for some time still. In fact, it popped back to the surface during final testing of DOS 6.0, because somehow a few system programs were linked with an old copy of the linker!

There is a small DOS API for suballocating the HMA; see Chapter 1, and the appendix entries for INT 2FH AX=4A01h and 4A02h.

How To Find the Start of the MCB Chain

The key to locating any MCB is in the still-undocumented DOS List of Lists, whose address is retrieved with INT 21h Function 52h. Although the List of Lists returned by this function differs from one version of DOS to the next, the MCB pointer's location is one of the very few items that is the same in all DOS versions to date. It's always located two bytes in front of the pointer returned in ES:BX, that is, at ES:[BX-2].

The value located there is actually not a pointer to the first MCB but its segment number (that of the DOS data segment memory block mentioned earlier); to use it as a pointer, you must provide an offset of 0000.

The following assembly language code fragment shows how to force the MCB pointer into ES:SI so that it may then be used to retrieve the key byte, the owner word, and the size word; this code only sets up ES:SI and does not retrieve the data:

```
mov     ah, 52h          ; Get List of Lists
int     21h
mov     ax, es:[bx-2]    ; First MCB Segment Address
mov     es, ax
xor     si, si           ; force offset to be zero
```

or, to be safe:

```
xor     bx, bx
mov     es, bx           ; set ES:BX to 0:0
mov     ah, 52h
int     21h
mov     cx, es
or      cx, bx           ; is ES:BX still 0:0?
jz      fail             ; then Function 52h not supported
mov     ax, es:[bx-2]    ; First MCB Segment Address
mov     es, ax
xor     si, si           ; force offset to be zero
fail:
```

The next code sequence then retrieves the key byte, the owner word, and the size word, respectively; the code assumes that ES:SI is unchanged from the preceding example:

```
mov     al, es:[si]      ; gets key byte, 'M' or 'Z'
mov     bx, es:[si+1]    ; gets owner word or 0000
mov     cx, es:[si+3]    ; gets size in paragraphs
```

For most applications, the code fragment in Figure 7-5 may be more useful; it can be used in Microsoft C 5.0 and higher, QuickC 2.0 and higher, Borland Turbo C 2.0 and higher, and Borland C++ 2.0 and higher:

Figure 7-5. Get_First_MCB() Routine

```
#include <dos.h>               /* use standard header file    */
#include "undocdos.h"          /* use our standard header file */
                              /* to define MCB structure and  */
                              /* MK_FP macro (make far ptr).  */

LPMCB Get_First_MCB( void )    /* locate first MCB, return ptr */
{ union REGS reg;              /* REGS, SREGS are defined by   */
  struct SREGS seg;            /* the DOS.H header file        */
  WORD *tmpp;

  segread( &seg );             /* set up seg regs              */
  reg.h.ah = 0x52;             /* get List of Lists in ES:BX   */
  intdosx( &reg, &reg, &seg );
  tmpp = (WORD far *) MK_FP( seg.es, reg.x.bx - 2 );
  return (LPMCB) MK_FP( *tmpp, 0 );
}
```

Get_First_MCB() is functionally identical to the first assembly language fragment. This function uses the MK_FP() macro (which became _MK_FP() in Visual C++) to create the returned pointer value, rather than stuffing the appropriate quantities into ES and SI. As explained in Chapter 2, you can also use in-line assembler or register pseudo-variables, if your compiler supports these options.

How To Trace the MCB Chain

Let's look at how to build a program that walks through the MS-DOS MCBs and tells you how RAM is being used. You probably already have such a program on your machine. Versions of this popular utility include MEM (a standard part of DOS 4.0 and later), PMAP (Chris Dunford), MAPMEM (TurboPower Software), and TDMEM (Borland Turbo Debugger 2.0). However, our version, UDMEM, can help you understand how such utilities are written.

Because some MCBs control PSPs, this program can be used to trace through all PSPs, showing which programs are resident in memory. When we refer to MCBs controlling PSPs, we only mean that the block of memory controlled by an MCB happens to be a program. To be precise, it is not a program, but a process: a program that has been loaded into memory. All DOS processes begin with a 256-byte (16-paragraph) PSP. The MCB controls the PSP only in the sense that the MCB is the arena header for the memory used by the PSP and by the process itself. For example, a PSP at 0AE9 is controlled by an MCB at 0AE8. In turn, the owner field of the MCB at 0AE8 would be 0AE9.

Our UDMEM program displays the segment number of each MCB, the Program Segment Prefix of its owner, and the size of the MCB in hex paragraphs and decimal bytes. For MCBs that hold actual PSPs, UDMEM also displays the segment for the corresponding environment, the ASCII filename of the owner (which in DOS 3.0 and higher is kept in a program's environment), and any interrupt vectors that point into the block of memory. The program also shows subsegments within the DOS data segment memory block and knows about UMBs.

One limitation of many MCB walkers is that they assume the presence of only one MCB chain. In fact, programs such as 386MAX and QEMM allow memory-resident programs to be loaded high by creating a secondary MCB chain in high DOS memory. With the advent of UMBs in DOS 5.0, this is the rule rather than the exception. Our UDMEM program shows secondary MCB chains. Figure 7-6 shows what UDMEM's output looks like.

Figure 7-6. Sample of UDMEM Output

```
D:\UDOS2\CHAP7> udmem
Seg     Owner   Size
0253    0008    092A ( 37536)    DOS Data Segment
                Seg  Size Type
                ----  ---- ----------------
                0254 0041 Device Driver (386MAX)
                0296 0015 Device Driver (386LOAD)
                02AC 0741 Device Driver (SSTORDRV) [26 F5 FA FE ]
                09EE 0015 Device Driver (386LOAD)
                0A04 005D System File Tables
                0A62 0005 FCBs
                0A68 0020 Buffers
                0A89 0037 CDS Table
                0AC1 00BC Stacks [02 0A 0B 0C 0D 0E 70 72 73 74 76 ]
0B7E    0008    0004 (    64)    DOS Code area
0B83    0B84    0010 (   256)    Env at D314     chap7.new /pd:\udos2\chap7\udkeys /q
0B94    0B84    0005 (    80)
0B9A    0B9B    0147 (  5232)    Env at 0B95     /f:2048 /l:20
0CE2    0CF1    000D (   208)
0CF0    0CF1    4CDB (314800)    Env at 0CE3     D:\UTILS\PE2.EXE  chap7.new  /pd:\udos2\chap7\udkeys
                                                /q [30 E5 E6 F7 FF ]
59CC    59DB    000D (   208)
59DA    59DB    0010 (   256)    Env at DA36
59EB    59F8    000B (   176)
59F7    59F8    1268 ( 75392)    Env at 59EC     D:\UDOS2\CHAP7\UDMEM.EXE  [00 E9 F9 ]
6C60    0000    339E (211424)    free [EC EF F4 ]
9FFF                             End of conventional RAM
                UMB Chain
C800    FFFF    058E ( 22752)    386LOADed Driver [13 15 28 ]
CD8F    FFFA    0004 (    64)    386MAX UMB control block
CD94    FFFE    0205 (  8272)    386MAX UMB
CF9A    FFFA    0004 (    64)    386MAX UMB control block
CF9F    FFFE    0022 (   544)    386MAX UMB
CFC2    FFFA    0004 (    64)    386MAX UMB control block
CFC7    FFFE    0022 (   544)    386MAX UMB
CFEA    FFFA    0004 (    64)    386MAX UMB control block
CFEF    FFFE    0042 (  1056)    386MAX UMB
D032    FFFA    0004 (    64)    386MAX UMB control block
D037    FFFE    0210 (  8448)    386MAX UMB
D248    FFFA    0004 (    64)    386MAX UMB control block
D24D    FFFE    00C0 (  3072)    C:\4D4\4DOS.COM [2E ]
D30E    FFFA    0004 (    64)    386MAX UMB control block
D313    FFFE    0020 (   512)    386MAX UMB
D334    D33C    0006 (    96)
D33B    D33C    04CD ( 19664)    Env at D80A     C:\UV\UV.COM [10 ]
D809    D33C    0002 (    32)
D80C    D814    0006 (    96)    [20 21 27 29 ]
D813    D814    01AD (  6864)    Env at D9C2     D:\UTILS\CTRLALT.COM  [08 09 ]
D9C1    D814    0002 (    32)
D9C4    FFFA    0004 (    64)    386MAX UMB control block
D9C9    FFFE    0066 (  1632)    386MAX UMB [22 23 24 2F ]
DA30    FFFA    0004 (    64)    386MAX UMB control block
DA35    FFFE    0020 (   512)    386MAX UMB
DA56    0000    05A8 ( 23168)    free
DFFF    FFFD    1200 ( 73728)    386MAX locked-out area [EB ]
F200    FFFF    0059 (  1424)    386LOADed Driver [1B ]
F25A    0000    05A4 ( 23104)    free
F7FF    FFFD    0400 ( 16384)    386MAX locked-out area
```

```
FC00    FFFF    00AD (    2768)   386LOADed Driver [40 67 ]
FCAE    FCB6    0006 (      96)
FCB5    FCB6    0042 (    1056)   Env at FCF9     C:\4D4\KSTACK.COM  [16 ]
FCF8    FCB6    0002 (      32)
FCFB    0000    0004 (      64)   free
FD00                             End of UMB Chain
```

To create this sample of output, I shelled out to DOS from within my text editor program (D:\UTILS\PE2.EXE at address 0CF1). The output shows both the normal RAM area below 0A000:0000 and the Upper Memory Blocks above that point. It also shows how various interrupts are routed to different drivers and programs, both above and below the UMB line. Those references to such interrupts as EC, EF, and F4 result from the fact that during the boot-up process, initialization code uses the top of the interrupt-vector area as its stack and never cleans the memory out afterward. These references are not valid.

It is useful to write UDMEM in two stages. First, just print out raw information about DOS memory control blocks. Then, after that simple program is working, write an improved version that displays the ASCII filenames of the owners of the MCBs (which gives us a display of all programs resident in memory including, of course, the UDMEM program itself). Figure 7-7 shows our first version of the UDMEM utility:

Figure 7-7. First Version of UDMEM

```c
/*
UDMEM1.C -- walks DOS MCB chain(s): simple version
Andrew Schulman and Jim Kyle, July 1990
        revised by Jim Kyle, August 1992, March 1993
*/
#include <stdlib.h>                 /* needed by MSC only    */
#include <stdio.h>
#include <dos.h>
#include "undocdos.h"
void fail(char *s) { puts(s); exit(1); }

LPMCB get_mcb(void)
{
    ASM mov ah, 52h
    ASM int 21h
    ASM mov dx, es:[bx-2]
    ASM xor ax, ax
    /* in both Microsoft C and Turbo C, far* returned in DX:AX */
}

void display(LPMCB mcb)
{
    char buf[80];
    sprintf(buf, "%04X    %04X    %04X (%6lu)",
        FP_SEG(mcb), mcb->owner, mcb->size, (long) mcb->size << 4);
    if (! mcb->owner)
        strcat(buf, "    free");
    puts(buf);
}

void walk(LPMCB mcb)
{
    printf("Seg     Owner    Size\n");
    for (;;)
        switch (mcb->type)
        {
            case 'M' :              /* Mark : belongs to MCB chain  */
                display(mcb);
                mcb = (LPMCB)MK_FP(FP_SEG(mcb) + mcb->size + 1, 0);
                break;
```

```
            case 'Z' :            /* Zbikowski : end of MCB chain */
                display(mcb);
                printf("%04X\n", FP_SEG(mcb) + mcb->size + 1);
                return;
            default :
                fail("error in MCB chain");
        }
}
main(int argc, char *argv[])
{
    walk(get_mcb());
    //could walk UMB chain here too
}
```

UDMEM1.C simply displays the raw MCB chain and makes no attempt to connect to any upper memory blocks that may be present. The function get_mcb(), written with in-line assembler, returns a far pointer to the first MCB. Even though we're calling undocumented DOS Function 52h here, we don't bother to check DOS version numbers because the segment of the first MCB is always located at offset -2 in the List of Lists. It's even supported in the DOS compatibility boxes of OS/2 and Windows NT (see Chapter 4). The start of the MCB chain is passed to the function walk(), which goes into an infinite loop, displaying an MCB and moving to the next MCB, until the end of the chain (or an error) is found. The MCB is displayed using the function display(). The output of this program looks like this:

```
Seg     Owner   Size
09F3    0008    03E1 ( 15888)
0DD5    0DD6    00D3 (  3376)
0EA9    0000    0003 (    48)      free
0EAD    0DD6    0040 (  1024)
0EEE    C0D6    0004 (    64)
0EF3    0F02    000D (   208)
0F01    0F02    1204 ( 73792)
2106    0000    7EF9 (520080)      free
A000
```

MCB Consistency Checks

Actually, this code is useful by itself. After chopping out main(), it can be linked into other programs and used to track their DOS memory allocation. This is particularly useful when you are trying to debug a program that trashes the MCB chain. By modifying the walk() function into mcb_chk() as shown in Figure 7-8, you can check the MCB chain for consistency before DOS does. The chain is inconsistent if mcb->type is equal to anything other than 'M' or 'Z'.

Figure 7-8. Routine to Check MCB Chain

```
BOOL mcb_chk(LPMCB mcb) /* see UNDOCDOS.H for typedefs  */
{ for (;;)
    if (mcb->type == 'M')
        mcb = (LPMCB)MK_FP(FP_SEG(mcb) + mcb->size + 1, 0);
    else
        return (mcb->type == 'Z');
}
```

With mcb_chk(), a program can periodically check the MCB chain with a call such as the following:

```
if (! mcb_chk(get_mcb()))
{
    /* maybe do stack backtrace here, or dump registers */
    puts("Error in MCB chain - prepare for halt...");
    getchar();
}
```

Of course, if mcb_chk() does return FALSE, then the next time any memory allocation is performed, the system will halt with a message such as:

```
Memory allocation error
Cannot load COMMAND, system halted
```

DOS merely performs the same consistency check as mcb_chk(), except that, if it does find anything other than 'M' or 'Z,' DOS has no choice but to halt the system. There seems to be no way that the MCB chain could be reliably repaired. In multitasking 80386 control programs such as DESQview or Windows 3.x, though, trashing the MCB chain in a DOS box (virtual machine) is far less catastrophic. You just throw the virtual machine away and get a new one.

Our minimal MCB walker has one other use. We can use it to reveal a bug in DOS itself. In the entry for INT 21h Function 4Ah (Resize Memory Block), the appendix notes that "if there is insufficient memory to expand the block as much as requested, the block will be made as large as possible." Don't believe it? Just substitute the version of main() shown in Figure 7-9 for the one provided in Figure 7-7.

Figure 7-9. How To Demonstrate a DOS Bug

```
main(void)
{
  unsigned segm;
  ASM mov ah, 48h                      /* Allocate Memory Block */
  ASM mov bx, 64h                      /* get 100 paragraphs    */
  ASM int 21h
  ASM jc done
  /* ax now holds initial segment of allocated block */
  ASM mov segm, ax
  printf("before: "); display(MK_FP(segm - 1, 0));

  ASM mov ax, segm
  ASM mov es, ax                       /* now resize the block */
  ASM mov ah, 4Ah                      /* Resize Memory Block  */
  ASM mov bx, 0FFFFh        /* impossible in real mode       */
  ASM int 21h
  ASM jnc done        /* something badly wrong if _didn't_ fail! */
  printf("after:  "); display(MK_FP(segm - 1, 0));
done:
  return 0;
}
```

The resulting display shows that all remaining memory has in fact been given to the block, even though the call failed:

```
before: 1D4C    0BEA    0064 (  1600)
after:  1D4C    0BEA    9AB3 (633648)
```

The enormous number of bytes allocated to MCB 1D4C in the second line shows that, even though Function 4Ah returned with the carry flag set, indicating an error, the block was still made as large as possible. (It's particularly large here because this test was run on a system with Quarterdeck QEMM.) This is definitely a bug in DOS, not an undocumented feature on which you should depend! As it stands, reallocations that fail but that nonetheless snarf memory can cause mysterious program behavior.

The bug, of course, is that DOS assigns all free space to the program before discovering that there's not enough, but then fails to restore the original program allocation and put the free space back once the error has been detected.

This example also shows that the display() function can be useful all by itself. Just pass the function an MCB and it displays some information. Given the segment address of a block of memory, though, remember that the MCB is located at the preceding paragraph. If a PSP is, for instance, 1234h, its MCB is 1233h. This is why segm-1, rather than segm, is used above in the call to display().

A More Detailed UDMEM Program

To produce a more complete display, we need to change the display() function, hook into any UMB chain that may be present, and add supporting functions.

Some of the relationships between MCB, PSP, and environment can get a little confusing, so we use a few simple macros that are defined in UNDOCDOS.H:

```
#define MCB_FM_SEG(seg)      ((seg) - 1)
#define IS_PSP(mcb)          ((FP_SEG(mcb) + 1 == (mcb)->owner) && \
             (*(WORD far *) MK_FP(FP_SEG(mcb) + 1, 0) == 0x20CD))
#define ENV_FM_PSP(psp_seg) (*((WORD far *) MK_FP(psp_seg, 0x2c)))
```

The first of these, MCB_FM_SEG(), simply converts the PSP segment value to the corresponding MCB segment value. The last, ENV_FM_PSP(), grabs the segment address of the environment block from offset 2Ch in the PSP. The IS_PSP() macro performs two tests on a segment value to determine whether it is a valid PSP segment. The first test simply verifies that this block owns itself. However, with the advent of protected mode programs such as Windows 3.x and some recent DOS programs that use protected mode PSPs, such a test isn't adequate. Thus, if a segment passes the first test, we go on to verify that the first two bytes of the segment are "CD 20" (the machine code for INT 20h). All valid PSPs begin with these two bytes; all imposters that we have run into so far fail the test.

Figure 7-10. New Display Routine

```
void display( LPMCB mcb )
{ static FP vect_2e = ( FP ) 0;
  WORD env_seg;
  printf( "%04X    %04X    %04X (%6lu)    ",
          FP_SEG( mcb ), mcb->owner,
          mcb->size, ( long ) mcb->size << 4 );

  if( IS_PSP( mcb ))
    { FP e = env( mcb );                     /* MSC wants lvalue    */
      if( ( env_seg = FP_SEG( e )) != 0 )
        printf( "Env at %04X    ", env_seg );
      else
        printf( "No Env Segment " );
    }

  if( ! vect_2e )
    vect_2e = GETVECT( 0x2e );               /* do just once        */

/* INT 2Eh belongs to master COMMAND.COM (or other shell) */
  if( belongs( vect_2e, FP_SEG( mcb ), mcb->size ))
    printf( "%s ", getenv( "COMSPEC" ));
  else
    switch( mcb->owner )                     /* decode special stuff */
      {
      case 0 :
        printf( "free " );
        break;
      case 6 :
        printf( "DR-DOS XMS UMB " );
        break;
      case 7 :
        printf( "DR-DOS hole " );
        break;
      case 8 :
        printf( "DOS " );
        display_subsegs( mcb, mcb->size );
```

```
      return;                         /* display_subsegs cleans up */
    case 0xFFFA :
      printf( "386MAX UMB control block " );
      break;
    case 0xFFFD :
      printf( "386MAX locked-out area " );
      break;
    case 0xFFFE :
      printf( "386MAX UMB " );
      break;
    case 0xFFFF :
      printf( "386LOADed Driver " );
      break;
    }
  display_progname( mcb );              // moved from original location
  if( IS_PSP( mcb ))
    display_cmdline( mcb );
  display_vectors( mcb );
  printf( "\n" );
}
```

The new display() (Figure 7-10) calls env() (Figure 7-11) to find out if the MCB contains the PSP of its owner and therefore has an associated environment block.

Figure 7-11. Environment-Locating Routine

```
char far * env( LPMCB mcb )
{ char far * e;
  WORD env_mcb;
  WORD env_owner;

  /*  if the MCB owner is one more than the MCB segment then
   *       psp := MCB owner
   *       env_seg := make_far_pointer(psp, 2Ch)
   *       e := make_far_pointer(env_seg, 0)
   *  else
   *       return NULL
   */
  if( IS_PSP( mcb ))
    e = MK_FP( ENV_FM_PSP( mcb->owner ), 0 );
  else
    return ( char far *) 0;

  /* Does this environment really belong to this PSP? An
   * environment is just another memory block, so its MCB is
   * located in the preceding paragraph. Make sure the env
   * MCB's owner is equal to the PSP whose environment this
   * supposedly is! Thanks to Rob Adams of Phar Lap Software
   * for pointing out the need for this check; this is a
   * good example of the sort of consistency check one must
   * do when working with undocumented DOS.
   *
   * Note that with DOS5, this test had to be changed to just
   * reject free MCBs, because 386MAX added special codes in
   * the owner field that caused our original test to fail!
   */
  env_mcb = MCB_FM_SEG( FP_SEG( e ));
  env_owner = (( MCB far *) MK_FP( env_mcb, 0 ))->owner;
/*return ( env_owner == mcb->owner ) ? e :( char far *) 0; changed! */
  return ( env_owner ) ? e :( char far *) 0;
}
```

The env() function uses the IS_PSP() macro to verify that this MCB is a PSP and that the environment pointer is not NULL. In its original version, env() further made sure we didn't pick up a stray environment for a program that has freed its environment. Usually such programs don't bother to zero out the environment segment number located at offset 2Ch in the PSP. The next-to-last line of the program, now commented out, was the original test. After Qualitas' 386MAX memory manager began using the owner field of the MCB for other purposes, it was necessary to change this function.

The display() function interprets the owner field of the MCB to decode all the special values that might appear there. If this shows the block to be the DOS data segment, display() calls display_subsegs() (Figure 7-12) to list the subsegments.

Figure 7-12. Decoding DOS Subsegments

```c
static BOOL ssdone = FALSE;

void display_subsegs( LPMCB mcb, WORD subsegsz )
{ char tmp[ 10 ];
  char far * src;
  int i;
  if( ssdone )                    /* if not first DOS area     */
    { printf( "Code area\n" );
      return;
    }
  printf( "Data Segment\n" );
  if( _osmajor < 4 )              /* subsegments only in V4+   */
    return;

  printf( "\t  Seg  Size Type \n\t  ---- ---- ----------------\n" );
  mcb = MK_FP( FP_SEG( mcb ) + 1, 0 );
  while( ( int ) subsegsz > 0 ) /* process each subsegment     */
    { printf( "\t  %04X %04X ", FP_SEG( mcb ), mcb->size );
      src = &( mcb->owner_name[ 0 ]); /* copy filename for D, I */
      for( i = 0; i < 8 && * src > ' '; i++ )
        tmp[ i ] = *src++;
      tmp[ i ] = 0;
      switch( mcb->type )         /* translate type codes      */
        {
        case 'D' :
          printf( "Device Driver (%s) ", tmp );
          break;
        case 'E' :
          printf( "Device Driver appendage " );
          break;
        case 'I' :
          printf( "IFS Driver (%s) ", tmp );
          break;
        case 'F' :
          printf( "System File Tables " );
          break;
        case 'X' :
          printf( "FCBs " );
          break;
        case 'C' :
          printf( "Buffer Workspace " );
          break;
        case 'B' :
          printf( "Buffers " );
          break;
        case 'L' :
          printf( "CDS Table " );
          break;
        case 'S' :
          printf( "Stacks " );
          break;
        case 'T' :
          printf( "Transient Code " );
```

```
            break;
          default :
            printf( "Unknown subsegment " );
          }
       display_vectors( mcb );    /* show vecs for this area      */
       printf( "\n" );
       subsegsz -= ( mcb->size + 1 );
       mcb = MK_FP( FP_SEG( mcb ) + mcb->size + 1, 0 );
     }
   ssdone = TRUE;
}
```

Next, display() calls display_progname(), which in turn calls progname_fm_psp() (Figure 7-13). This useful utility function, given a PSP, tries to return a far pointer to the name of the corresponding program.

Figure 7-13. Obtaining the Program's Name

```
char far * progname_fm_psp( WORD psp )
{ char far * e;
  WORD len;

/* is there an environment? */
  if( ! ( e = env( MK_FP( MCB_FM_SEG( psp ), 0 ))))
    return ( char far *) 0;

/* program name only available in DOS 3+ */
  if( _osmajor >= 3 )
    { do                     /* skip past environment variables      */
         e += ( len = fstrlen( e )) + 1;
      while( len );
      if( !*e ) /* test for empty env in UMB, created by 386MAX */
        e++;

      /*  e now points to WORD containing number of strings following
       *  environment; check for reasonable value: signed because
       *  could be FFFFh; will normally be 1
       */
      if(( *(( signed far *) e ) >= 1 ) && ( *(( signed far *) e ) < 10 ))
        { e += sizeof( signed );
          if( isalpha( *e ))
            return e;
        }
    }
  return ( char far *) 0;
}

void display_progname( LPMCB mcb )
{ char far * s;
  if( IS_PSP( mcb ))
    if(( s = progname_fm_psp(( FP_SEG( mcb ) + 1 ))) != 0 )
      printf( "%Fs ", s );
}
```

If an MCB corresponds to a PSP (IS_PSP() is TRUE), display_progname() calls progname_fm_psp(), which first verifies that there is an environment. Possibly there is a little too much verification and double-checking in this program, but any program that traffics in undocumented DOS should definitely be more paranoid than programs that rely only on documented interfaces. In DOS 3+, progname_fm_psp() walks past all variables in the environment to find the ASCIIZ pathname of the program owning the environment (see the description of the DOS environment block in the appendix entry for INT 21h Function 26h).

The new version of display() next calls display_cmdline() (Figure 7-14).

Figure 7-14. Showing Command Arguments

```
void display_cmdline( LPMCB mcb )
{ /*    psp := MCB owner
  *     cmdline_len := psp[80h]
  *     cmdline := psp[81h]
  *     print cmdline(display width := cmdline_len)
  */
  int len = *(( BYTE far *) MK_FP( mcb->owner, 0x80 ));
  char far * cmdline = MK_FP( mcb->owner, 0x81 );
  printf( "%.*Fs ", len, cmdline );
}
```

Note that display_cmdline() uses the C printf() mask "%.*Fs" to display a far string, using the maximum length given by the variable, len, whose value may be zero. Sometimes garbage is printed by MEM, or by any similar program, because the disk transfer area, located inside the PSP, overlays the beginning of the command line.

The simple function belongs() (Figure 7-15) determines if an interrupt vector points into the block controlled by a given MCB. The BOOL, FP, and WORD types are defined in UNDOCDOS.H.

Figure 7-15. Testing Interrupt Vectors

```
BOOL belongs( FP vec, WORD start, WORD size )
{ WORD seg = FP_SEG( vec ) + ( FP_OFF( vec ) >> 4 );/* normalize */
  return ( seg >= start ) && ( seg <= ( start + size ));
}
```

Finally, display() calls display_vectors() (Figure 7-16) to show any interrupts hooked by the program whose PSP is contained in this MCB. The function finds these hooked interrupts simply by seeing if CS:IP for the interrupt handler falls within this MCB.

Figure 7-16. Showing Interrupt Vectors

```
#ifdef __TURBOC__
#define GETVECT(x)      getvect(x)
#else
#define GETVECT(x)      _dos_getvect(x)
#endif

void display_vectors( LPMCB mcb )
{ static FP * vec = ( FP *) 0;
  WORD vec_seg;
  int i;
  int did_one = 0;

  if( ! vec )              /* one-time initialization      */
    { if( !( vec = calloc( 256, sizeof( void far *))))
        fail( "insufficient memory" );
      for( i = 0; i < 256; i ++ )
        vec[ i ] = GETVECT( i );
    }

  for( i = 0; i < 256; i ++ )
    if( vec[ i ] && belongs( vec[ i ], FP_SEG( mcb ), mcb->size ))
      { if( ! did_one )
          { did_one ++ ;
            printf( "[" );
          }
        printf( "%02X ", i );
        vec[ i ] = 0;
      }
  if( did_one )
    printf( "]" );
}
```

In DOS 4.0 and higher, some memory resident software can be loaded using the INSTALL= statement in CONFIG.SYS. Such programs can show up in the UDMEM display as MCBs that aren't associated with any program, but which may have hooked interrupt vectors. Note that UDMEM calls display_vectors() for all MCBs, even when there seems to be no associated program. For example, in DOS 4.0 and higher, if CONFIG.SYS contains the statement INSTALL=C:\CED\CED.COM to load Chris Dunford's CED command line editor, then UDMEM displays something like the following:

```
0E81    0E82    065F ( 26096)    [1B 21 61 ]
```

Another benefit of calling display_vectors() for all MCBs is that occasionally we find orphaned interrupt vectors that point into free memory:

```
2A2A    0000    7 (482640)              free    [30 F4 F5 F8 ]
```

INT 30h is a far-jump instruction, not an interrupt vector; but INTs F4h, F5h, and F8h are real interrupt vectors. Let's hope no program invokes them while they're pointing into free memory! Since these vectors are used as the stack during boot-up, it's essential that any program that tries to invoke them be certain they have first been set to valid interrupt service routines.

The boring little function shown in Figure 7-17 lets us easily get the length of far strings, even from a small-model program.

Figure 7-17. Determining String Length

```
WORD fstrlen( char far * s )
{
#if defined(_MSC_VER) && (_MSC_VER >= 600)
  return _fstrlen( s );
#else
  WORD len = 0;
  while( * s++ )
    len++;
  return len;
#endif
}
```

In addition to the changes made to the display() function, it's also necessary to modify walk(), as shown in Figure 7-18, so that it automatically includes any Upper Memory Blocks that may be in use.

Figure 7-18. Revised Walk Routine

```
void walk( LPMCB mcb )              /* walks chain displaying data  */
{ printf( "Seg     Owner    Size\n" );
  for( ; ; )
    switch( mcb->type )
      {
      case 'M' :                    /* Mark : belongs to MCBchain   */
              display( mcb );
              mcb = MK_FP( FP_SEG( mcb ) + mcb->size + 1, 0 );
              break;

      case 'Z' :                    /* Zbikowski : end of MCB chain */
              display( mcb );
              printf( "%04X                         ",
              FP_SEG( mcb ) + mcb->size + 1 );
              if( FP_SEG( mcb ) < 0xA000 )
                { printf( "End of conventional RAM\n" );
                  mcb = firsthi();     /* try to link to UMB area */
                  if( mcb == ( FP ) 0L )   /* No UMB MCB's found  */
                    return;
```

```
                printf( "        UMB Chain\n" );
                }
            else
                { printf( "End of UMB Chain\n" );
                  return;
                }
            break;

    default :
            fail( "error in MCB chain" );
    }
}
```

If UMBs are in use, but UDMEM is running from conventional RAM, there are actually two separate MCB chains; the first stops at the end of conventional RAM, while the other is entirely in the upper memory area. If LOADHIGH or LH is used to run UDMEM, the two chains merge into one.

To automatically deal with the case of two chains, the actions performed when the program detects the 'Z' type code and changed. If the current MCB is below the top of conventional RAM (0A000h), the program calls the firsthi() function to bridge to the UMB region. Otherwise, the second chain must be in use, and the end really has been encountered.

The firsthi() function, which creates the link to any UMBs that might be present, is a separate module shown in Figure 7-19, compiled by itself and subsequently linked into the UDMEM program. This function returns NULL if no UMB chain can be located or a far pointer to the first MCB in the chain. The function is based on code written by Kim Kokkonen, president of TurboPower Software, and is used in a number of his TSRCOM utilities. (The TSRCOM utilities include MARK and RELEASE, which permit TSRs to easily be unloaded; they are available on CompuServe and on many BBS systems.)

Figure 7-19. Finding the UMB Chain

```
/*
 * FIRSTHI - utility to locate first UMB address
 *
 *      adapted from:
 *         XMS.PAS - unit of XMS functions
 *         Copyright (c) 1991 Kim Kokkonen, TurboPower Software.
 *         MEMU.PAS - utility unit for TSR Utilities.
 *         Copyright (c) 1991 Kim Kokkonen, TurboPower Software.
 *      by Jim Kyle, with permission of Kim Kokkonen.  Thanks, Kim!
 *
 *      These are part of Kim's TSRCOM utility that includes
 *      MARK and RELEASE among others.
 */

#include <dos.h>
#include "undocdos.h"

static BYTE XmsInstalled( void )            /* true if XMS mgr here */
{ ASM mov ah,0x30;
  ASM int 0x21;
  ASM cmp al,3;
  ASM jae Check2F;
  ASM mov al,0;
  ASM jmp Done;
Check2F:
  ASM mov ax,0x4300;
  ASM int 0x2F;
Done:
  ASM mov ah,0;
}
```

```
static FP XmsControlAddr( void )          /* gets far ptr to code */
{ ASM mov ax,0x4310;
  ASM int 0x2F;
  ASM mov ax,bx;
  ASM mov dx,es;
}

static FP XmsControl;

static BYTE AnyUMB( void )        /* verify that a UMB exists      */
{ ASM mov ah,0x10;
  ASM mov dx,0xFFFF;                /* force an error return in BL  */
  ASM call dword ptr [XmsControl];
  ASM xor ah,ah;
  ASM mov al,bl;                    /* return error result          */
}

LPMCB firsthi( void )
{ WORD   Segment;
  WORD   Size;
  WORD   Mseg;
  BOOL   Done;
  BOOL   Invalid;
  LPMCB  M;
  LPMCB  N;
  LPMCB  Retval = (LPMCB)0L;

  if( !XmsInstalled() )          /* UMBs are not possible         */
    return Retval;
  XmsControl = XmsControlAddr(); /* get adr to test UMBs          */
  if( (1 | AnyUMB()) != 0xB1 )   /* UMBs are not possible         */
    return Retval;

  ASM int 0x12;                   /* find top of conventional RAM */
  ASM mov cx,6;
  ASM shl ax,cl;
  ASM mov Mseg,ax;                /* start the search there        */
  Done = FALSE;

  do
    { M = (LPMCB)MK_FP( Mseg, 0);
      if( M->type == 'M' )  /* may be an MCB; if any, must be 2 */
        { N = M;
          Invalid = FALSE;
          do                      /* determine whether valid MCBs */
            switch(N->type)
              {
              case 'M' :          /* try for next MCB via linkage */
                if( (WORD)(FP_SEG(N)+(N->size)+1) <= (WORD)0xFFFE )
                  N = (LPMCB)MK_FP( FP_SEG(N)+(N->size)+1, 0);
                else              /* can't be valid, keep looking */
                  Invalid = TRUE;
                break;
              case 'Z' :          /* found end of chain starting at M */
                Retval = M;
                Done = TRUE;
                break;
              default:            /* chain failed test, keep looking */
                Invalid = TRUE;
              } while( !Done && !Invalid );
        }
      if( !Done )
        { if( Mseg < 0xFFFF )
            Mseg++;
```

```
        else
            Done = TRUE;
        }
    } while( !Done );
  return Retval;                  /* either NULL or first MCB pointer */
}
```

The firsthi() function works on a brute force basis. It first verifies that UMBs might be present by testing for a UMB provider; then the function sets an internal pointer (Mseg) to the final paragraph of conventional RAM. From there, it tests each subsequent paragraph-aligned byte for the 'M' type signature. Each time firsthi() finds such a byte, it goes into an inner loop that attempts to verify that this is the start of an MCB chain. If the chain reaches a 'Z' type byte without failure, the original M-byte's address is returned as that of the first high MCB. If the inner loop fails, the outer loop resumes. If the outer loop reaches segment FFFFh without finding an MCB chain, the function returns NULL as its value to indicate that no UMBs are present.

It would be possible to avoid the brute force approach and simply use the same chain-linking technique that LOADHIGH itself does; but then UDMEM would not work with versions of DOS prior to 5.0, even if UMBs were in use, because the linking function did not exist before DOS 5.0. The search technique allows UDMEM to work with older versions and also helps make the following interesting point.

Not all UMB-providing XMS managers follow the same rules. Both QEMM and EMM386 use a two-level chain structure that collects free UMB space into regions and collects the regions into a separate chain of MCBs. This causes UDMEM to behave differently if loaded high than it does when run from low RAM with these managers. The firsthi() function locates the region chain and, as a result, never finds the lower level chains that control the individual UMBs.

When LOADHIGH is used, MS-DOS bypasses the chain of regions and links the individual UMB chain directly to the normal chain of MCBs. UDMEM then shows the individual UMBs and does not display the region-controlling blocks.

Under DOS 5.0, this was merely an interesting oddity; with DOS 6.0, it's more significant since the LOADHIGH command of DOS 6.0 allows you to specify which region to use for the program being loaded.

We now have a fairly complete implementation of the UDMEM program. Try it both with and without LOADHIGH, if you have DOS 5.0 or 6.0, to see the differences that LOADHIGH makes in its operation.

Allocation Precautions

Each time DOS INT 21h Function 4Bh loads a program for execution, it allocates memory for it as well. For a COM format file, the loader requests all available RAM. For an EXE format file, the file's relocation header specifies the amount of RAM needed. If this amount is not explicitly defined at link time, however, the EXE takes all available space.

Because most programs therefore hog all RAM each time they are loaded, whether they need it or not, it's up to you as a programmer to be sure that your programs trim themselves back to no more than they need, if they are going to be spawning other processes. Failure to do so will result in "out of memory" errors no matter how much RAM your system contains.

Each time a program terminates normally and returns control to its parent process, all RAM allocated to that program once again becomes available for allocation. If the program terminates through one of the TSR functions, only part (or possibly none) of its memory is released to be used again.

The upshot is that programs get all available space while they are executing and can turn it back when they finish. Memory allocation for your programs can thus be handled automatically and invisibly by DOS itself. Unfortunately, getting one large block of memory at start-up and having it deallocated for you at termination is often inconvenient because it means your program can't spawn other processes. Modern C compilers usually include in their start-up code the necessary calls to cut their RAM usage back to just what they require, or to 64K, whichever is larger; but at least one popular high-level language, Turbo Pascal, does not do this automatically. Instead, TP gives you a compiler option, "$M", that lets you specify how much memory to use.

Unfortunately, this option, like the DOS loader, defaults to "all available space." So an error condition results from attempts to EXEC or SPAWN a child process from TP without using the $M option to make RAM available for the child process. Because of this, the Turbo Pascal Exec() procedure gained a reputation for being broken; actually, it was just not adequately documented.

In most high-level language programming, you won't use the three DOS RAM allocation functions directly but if you use the C library function malloc() or any of its relatives, such as calloc() or realloc() you are using them indirectly.

The strategy behind malloc() is to obtain large blocks of RAM by using the DOS functions, then dole it out to the program in much smaller portions, as requested. Once RAM is allocated, the program never turns it loose; it remains allocated, even after calls to free(), until the program returns to DOS. This strategy is the heritage of UNIX, where the allocation of system RAM was a time-consuming process. Under MS-DOS, the reverse is true. A number of "improved performance" packages, which replace the standard library versions of malloc() with more-direct calls to the DOS functions, have appeared recently.

On the other hand, each block of memory allocated from DOS requires the additional 16-byte MCB, so all DOS allocations are consequently paragraph based. So if you want to allocate 4 bytes from DOS, for instance, you have to ask INT 21h Function 48h for one paragraph (16 bytes). In order to satisfy this request, DOS then actually needs two paragraphs: the one you asked for plus one for the MCB that controls the paragraph. The point is that the smallest possible direct DOS memory allocation actually uses 32 bytes.

Please don't get the idea from this discussion that malloc() is normally a direct equivalent to the DOS functions. In fact, some popular compilers, including Borland's, erroneously report that the system is out of memory if you attempt to use the direct DOS functions, then subsequently attempt to use malloc() or any of its relatives. This failure happens because the compiler's library routines depend on unrestricted access to contiguous RAM. If you grab a block using DOS, the library routines cannot get more and so they report an error.

RAM Allocation Strategies

When a program requests some paragraphs of memory and the memory manager has more than one block free, it's possible to satisfy that request in several different ways. These different ways of allocating memory are known as allocation strategies. DOS provides a function (INT 21h Function 58h) to select different strategies.

This function hasn't always been documented. For example, it is described in Microsoft's MS-DOS Encyclopedia, but not in IBM's technical reference manual for DOS 3.3. Only with publication of Microsoft's *MS-DOS Programmer's Reference* for DOS 5.0 did the subject come out of the closet.

Since INT 21h Function 58h is fully documented now, we won't spend nearly as much space on it as we did in the first edition of this book, when the allocation strategy capabilities could only be described as semi-documented. At that time, the function permitted you to select only from "first fit," "best fit," or "last fit" strategies. With DOS 5.0, six more strategies were added. The original three operate only in conventional RAM; three of the new ones duplicate the original three, but search the UMB area before looking into conventional RAM; and the final three search only the UMB area.

Since the sole difference between the three original strategies and the six new ones involves the question of which MCB chain to traverse, I describe only the original three here.

First-fit Strategy   The first-fit strategy is the default action unless you explicitly change things. In the first edition of this book, I wrote that "Even if you do change strategies, DOS will change back to first-fit whenever it loads a program, although it follows your selected strategy for all other loading actions." This statement was simply not true for all versions of DOS. In most versions, as a matter of fact, the strategy that you select rules all memory allocations until you change it.

Another major error in my earlier description of the process was the statement that the search for a block would stop as soon as one that was large enough was located. DOS actually maintains (see the Appendix) three segment pointers in the SDA, one for the first block that can satisfy a request, one for the best-fit choice, and one for the last block. DOS searches the entire MCB chain (or chains, if using the added strategies for UMB access) until reaching the end. Only then does it select which of the three pointers to return as the allocated block.

There's a reason for this seeming waste of effort. While it would be possible to stop short after finding the first fit, if that strategy were in effect, doing so would prevent DOS from merging adjacent free blocks back into single larger blocks. Since each such a merge makes an additional 16 bytes of RAM (the MCB for the extra block) available for use, the cumulative effect can be significant. By going through the entire chain for each allocation, DOS makes sure that all free memory blocks are as large as possible.

The first-fit strategy causes the memory manager to make the allocation from the first block that is large enough to satisfy the request. If the block is larger than requested, only enough is taken off the front to fill the request, and a new, still free, block is created for the remainder.

In normal everyday DOS operation, there's usually only one such block in the system when a program is loaded. Because the loader often asks for all available RAM, no new block is created. Under these conditions, there's no difference between first-fit and best-fit strategies. If, however, the available RAM has become highly fragmented, and at the same time the block being allocated is small enough to fit in the first free block encountered, the first-fit strategy uses that first block.

Best-fit Strategy   The best-fit strategy requires that the smallest block that will do the job be allocated, regardless of whether it is the first one encountered. As with the first-fit strategy, the block is allocated from the front, and any leftover space is put into a new, still free, block.

This approach guarantees that multiple allocations of small blocks don't fragment RAM unnecessarily. As long as blocks are released at approximately the same rate as they are allocated, the best-fit strategy continues using the same small blocks over and over, leaving the larger blocks free to accommodate requests that require them.

As pointed out in the previous section, in normal operation with only one or two blocks of RAM free, there's little difference in action between first-fit and best-fit. If, however, you are programming an application that does its own RAM management and that makes short-term use of large numbers of small blocks of RAM, you'll want to keep this strategy in mind. It could keep you from running out of RAM unexpectedly just because none of the remaining free blocks is large enough to fill your latest request!

Having said this, it is important not to oversell best-fit. In fact, as any textbook on operating systems will tell you, first-fit is almost always the correct strategy to use.

Last-fit Strategy   Unlike either of the other strategies, the last-fit technique is designed specifically for allocations that you expect to hang around for a long time, such as TSRs or device drivers.

When a block of RAM is allocated using the last-fit strategy, the highest possible block of memory that can satisfy the request is assigned. Normally this is the highest part of the final block of free RAM. The idea is that memory allocated at the end of the MCB chain won't ever need to be searched if you switch back to the default first-fit strategy for subsequent normal allocations.

In the first edition, I claimed that "the last-fit strategy is of limited usefulness," which moved reader Art Rothstein to respond with details of a significant use he had found for this strategy:

We use last fit. We load a TSR that provides common services to various applications. Our applications spawn each other, perhaps three levels deep. To save RAM, we link our applications with no slack in the Microsoft C (MSC) near heap. When there is insufficient room in the near heap, MSC attempts to expand the appropriate segment via INT 21h AH=4Ah. Most of the code in the TSR is provided by another vendor as OBJ and LIB files that are intended to be linked with our applications. We added just enough code to make the TSR and to provide a calling interface from our applications. One of the functions provided by the TSR allocates memory via INT 21h AH=48h. Suppose application X calls this function, then spawns application Y. MSC's spawn uses the near heap to build a copy of the DOS environment to pass to DOS 4BH. If the TSR used first-fit for its DOS 48H call, this allocation would usually be right below application A's data segment, preventing A's near heap from expanding to satisfy the spawn call. To avoid this problem, we change the allocation strategy to last-fit while the TSR has control.

Obviously, Microsoft knew what it was doing when it chose to make all three strategies available. Since the details are now documented, I'll end the discussion of memory management here and move on to process management.

Process Management

The idea of a process as a separate executable program that has been loaded into memory, but that may or may not be executing currently, is central to the operation of MS-DOS. The whole basis of TSR programming is that a process may be retained in residence after terminating; but TSRs are not the only processes that DOS manages. Every program loaded for execution, including the command interpreter itself, is a process.

Program Files and Processes
Before we get into the details of how processes are managed, let's first look at how program files are laid out and see how they relate to the eventual executing process.

The COM File Format
The original format for executable files, inherited from the CP/M operating system, was the COM file. This kind of executable file starts with all four segment registers containing the same value, and execution always starts at offset 0100, just past the PSP, with the stack pointer set to 00FE.

Because the file's total size is limited and advanced relocation techniques cannot be applied, Microsoft has attempted for years to push this format into obsolescence. However, it refuses to die. For small, simple utilities it remains an excellent choice. It's also useful for other special purposes, as we shall see toward the end of this chapter.

The EXE File Format
The EXE file format, unlike that of the COM file, allows multiple segments for both code and data. The format also supports relocation and simplifies the linking of overlays into a single process. A measure of its capability is that the original EXE format, which is still the standard version used in DOS, provides a foundation for the segmented executable format that is used by Windows and OS/2 programs to support dynamic linking.

While both the old and new formats have been officially documented in a number of places, we've found it useful to add typedefs for both sets of file headers to our UNDOCDOS.H file. Here is the appropriate excerpt:

```
typedef struct {          /* EXE Program Header       */
  WORD sig;               /* always 0x5A4D, 'MZ'      */
  WORD LeftOver;          /* No. of bytes on last page */
  WORD Pages;             /* No. of 512 byte pages    */
```

```
WORD Items;              /* No. of RelocationTableItems */
WORD HdrSiz;             /* in paragraphs               */
WORD ReqSiz;             /* in paragraphs               */
WORD DesSiz;             /* in paragraphs               */
WORD InitSS;             /* in relative paragraphs      */
WORD InitSP;             /* at entry                    */
WORD ChkSum;
WORD InitIP;             /* at entry                    */
WORD InitCS;             /* in paragraphs               */
WORD FirstReloItem;      /* Offset from beginning       */
WORD OlayNbr;
WORD Reserved[ 16 ];
ULONG NewExe;            /* offset from front of file   */
} EXE, far * LPEXE;
```

EXE files generated by Microsoft's linkers always use a 512-byte page, so that for them EXE.HdrSiz is always equal to a multiple of 512. Those generated by other linking programs may establish different sizes, so EXE.HdrSiz may vary.

When DOS loads an EXE file into memory, it reads the header information into RAM at a temporary location above that used by the program. The loader then adjusts all addresses in the program as directed by the relocation table, which follows the header, sets the stack segment and pointer from the data in EXE.InitSS and EXE.InitSP, pushes the values of EXE.InitCS and EXE.InitIP onto the stack in preparation for a return into the program, releases its temporary memory if it was separately allocated to the loader, sets DS and ES to the process segment address, and enters the program by executing a far return to the EXE.InitCS and EXE.InitIP pushed onto the stack.

If a file is in the new Windows format, it contains the full header of the original format at its front; but EXE.NewExe contains the offset to the additional header within the file. If the file is not in the new format, EXE.NewExe is 0.

The PSP: How It Identifies a Process

Even when discussing DOS memory management, there was no way to avoid mentioning the Program Segment Prefix. Now we can examine this crucial DOS data structure in more detail. The PSP, a 256-byte block located immediately preceding the actual process memory, is the key to process management in MS-DOS.

Figure 7-20. The PSP and Its Relation to the Process

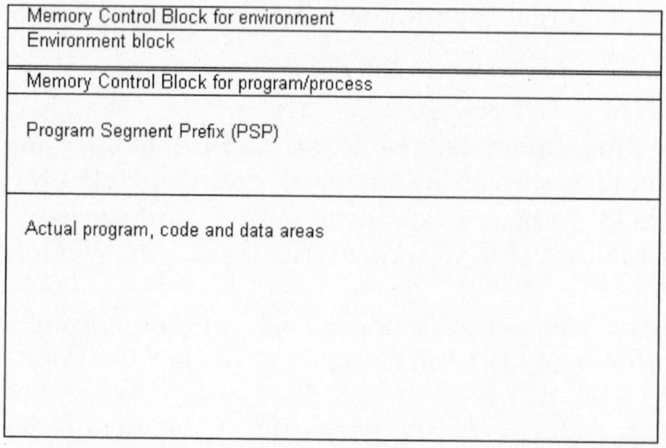

The PSP contains the DOS state (file handles, etc.) for its process; the segment address of the PSP itself provides a unique (within the single-tasking environment for which DOS was designed; see Chapter 6 for a discussion of non-unique PSPs under Windows Enhanced mode) identifier by which the process can be located and managed. Thus the PSP segment address is also known as the Process Identifier or PID value.

History, Purpose, and Use

The Program Segment Prefix came to MS-DOS by way of Seattle Computer Products' 86-DOS, which, for compatibility, took the idea from Digital Research's 8080 CP/M operating system. As MS-DOS developed through the years, however, the PSP evolved into far more than its CP/M equivalent. The PSP now embodies many of the ideas provided in other operating systems, such as UNIX and Multics, by the stack frame or the process directory. By proper use of information kept in the PSP, a process can pass data to other processes that it spawns, or it can return information back to its parent process. At the same time, many fields of the PSP are vestigial, holdovers from the days of CP/M.

The primary purpose of the PSP is to contain the system information necessary to start, run, and finish a specific process. This information includes, but is not limited to, the address of the routine to which control should transfer when the process terminates, the list of handles by which the process identifies its files and devices, the address of the environment space belonging to the process, the identity of the process' parent process, and last but far from least, any arguments passed directly to the process when it was invoked.

A secondary purpose is to provide methods of accessing DOS functions without INT 21h; this was much more important in earlier times than it is today. With CP/M, the interface to BDOS (Basic Disk Operating System, the ancestor of the INT 21h functions) was by way of a subroutine call to location 0005h. Consequently, to provide the same functionality, offset 0005h in the PSP of every process contains a rather cryptically coded far jump to the dispatcher area of MS-DOS itself (which has, interestingly enough, had a fatal error since Version 2.0 that is still uncorrected in Version 6.0: It goes to a location two bytes away from the right place).

Many UNIX systems provided similar capabilities through a far call in the user's stack frame area, so with the introduction of UNIX-like capabilities in MS-DOS 2.0, a special far call to INT 21h was added to the PSP at offset 0050h. At least, this was indicated in Tandy's MS-DOS 2.11 *Technical Reference* as "for UNIX compatibility."

Neither of these capabilities is widely used. Most programs today simply use INT 21h or, if the program is coded in a high level language, its equivalent.

(Usually) Unique Process Identifier

MS-DOS can have only one current process, because it uses the associated PSP as a scratch-pad area for much of its file management activity. Yet MS-DOS can be used for multitasking between multiple processes. A key to multitasking in an operating system with only one current process is simply to change this current process.

Throughout much of the MS-DOS documentation, you'll find references to an entity called the process identifier, often abbreviated to process ID or even PID. PID is a 16-bit value that uniquely identifies each process currently resident in the system, regardless of whether it is active. However, the documentation never explains precisely what the PID is.

This process identifier is nothing more than the segment address of the PSP associated with that process. Within the single task restriction upon which the design of MS-DOS was based, the value of the PSP segment address is unique. Only one PSP can be located at any specific segment address, so the PID identifies the process with no possible ambiguity.

Unfortunately, when the system evolved its multitasking capability, under Windows Enhanced mode, the uniqueness of the PID vanished. To deal with the situation, the Windows SYSTEM.INI file has two settings in the [386enh] section, UniqueDOSPSP= and PSPIncrement=. As noted in

Chapter 6, DOS also uses the virtual machine ID to differentiate processes. Thus, the combination of VM ID and PSP *is* a unique identifier.

Prior to version 5, DOS provided two undocumented functions and one documented one to store or retrieve the PID of the current process, thus activating one or another set of data stored in different PSPs. The two that had been undocumented became official with version 5. The current process is set using INT 21h Function 50h. The current process can be queried either with INT 21h Function 51h or, in DOS 3.x and higher, with the equivalent Function 62h.

It is important to understand that none of the PSP functions actually deals with the PSP of the program that calls them. As we saw in Chapter 6, all that they really do is move a 16-bit value either to or from the current PSP word in the Swappable Data Area maintained by DOS. If the value in that word is not correct, the Get PSP functions return the incorrect value with no indication of error.

There appears to be a great deal of confusion on this point. For example, even Duncan's *Advanced MS-DOS Programming* states that Function 62h "allows a program to conveniently recover the PSP address at any point during its execution, without having to save it at program entry."

In fact, the two Get PSP functions always return the value that was last established in the SDA with Set PSP. This corresponds to the current process in DOS, not necessarily to the PSP of the calling program. If Get PSP is called from a TSR that has been activated by an interrupt, Get PSP returns the PSP of the foreground process, *not* the TSR's PSP. That is what makes the Get/Set PSP functions important. They provide the basis for switching between multiple tasks in MS-DOS. It is often said that DOS is single-tasking, but this phrase merely means that only one process owns DOS at any given time.

Whenever the current process is switched, whether by your own multitasking code or by a TSR popping up for action, it's essential that the current PID also be switched if any I/O activity is to occur. Otherwise, the files or devices owned by the old foreground process, rather than your own files, will be affected.

The three get/set PSP functions are described in further detail in Chapter 9 on TSRs and DOS multitasking.

Undocumented Areas of the PSP

Less than one-third of the 256-byte area in the PSP has been documented officially; this section supplies information about the remaining parts. Not all of them, however, have ever been put to use.

The description in Figure 7-21 is taken from our UNDOCDOS.H header file, which provides typedefs for all the DOS structures described in this chapter. For information on PSP fields owned by Windows and by Novell NetWare, see Chapters 3 and 4.

Figure 7-21. PSP Details

```
#define ENV_FM_PSP(psp_seg) (*((WORD far *) MK_FP(psp_seg, 0x2c)))
#define PARENT(psp_seg)     (*((WORD far *) MK_FP(psp_seg, 0x16)))
typedef struct {            /* Program Segment Prefix       */
  WORD sig;                 /* 0000 always CD 20 (INT 20)   */
  WORD Nxtgraf;             /* 0002 first unused segment     */
  BYTE Skip1;               /* 0004 filler to align next     */
  BYTE CPMCall[5];          /* 0005 CP/M-like service call   */
  FP   ISV22;               /* 000A documented ISR vectors   */
  FP   ISV23;               /* 000E " (saved at start)       */
  FP   ISV24;               /* 0012 "                        */
  WORD Parent_ID;           /* 0016 PSP of parent process    */
  BYTE HTable[20];          /* 0018 indices into SFT         */
  WORD EnvSeg;              /* 002C environment segment      */
  FP   SavStk;              /* 002E saved SS:SP at INT21      */
  WORD Nhdls;               /* 0032 nbr of handles avail     */
  FP   HTblPtr;             /* 0034 ptr to handle table      */
  FP   ShareChn;            /* 0038 SHARE's closing chain    */
  BYTE Skip2;               /* 003C unknown                  */
```

```
BYTE TruNamFlg;         /* 003D APPEND's TrueName flag  */
BYTE Skip3a[2];         /* 003E Used by Windows?        */
WORD Version;           /* 0040 Major, minor vers level */
BYTE Skip3b[6];         /* 0042 Used by Windows?        */
BYTE WOldApp;           /* 0048 Windows OldApp Flag     */
BYTE Skip4[7];          /* 0049 unknown                 */
BYTE Disp[3];           /* 0050 Unix-like dispatcher    */
BYTE Skip5[2];          /* 0053 unknown                 */
BYTE ExtFCB[7];         /* 0055 extended FCB1 area      */
BYTE FCB1[16];          /* 005C documented FCB areas    */
BYTE FCB2[20];          /* 006C      "                  */
BYTE Tailc;             /* 0080 "command tail" count    */
BYTE Tail[127];         /* 0081 start actual data here  */
} PSP, far * LPPSP;
```

The ENV_FM_PSP(psp_seg) and PARENT(psp_seg) macros make it simple to obtain segment addresses for the associated environment block and for the process' parent process. When using either a Borland or Microsoft C compiler, you can get the segment address of your program's PSP from the global variable _psp.

If you create a far pointer to your PSP by using MK_FP(_psp, 0) you can then access any of the PSP elements as structure members. For instance, if you define the pointer as PSPptr, the environment's segment address could be obtained as PSPptr->EnvSeg, and the parent process segment would be PSPptr->Parent_ID.

DOS Termination Address

Although the three interrupt service vectors saved in the PSP are documented, their usage is not, and one of them provides a way to hook into a process at termination time, no matter what causes the process to terminate, thus providing DOS Exit List capability. The magic vector is ISV22, the INT 22h vector, documented as the termination address. What is not documented is the fact that the address in the PSP, rather than the one in the interrupt service region, is the one used when the process terminates.

To hook this vector and cause your own code to be executed when the process terminates and before control returns to the calling program, just use the routines shown in Figure 7-22, with your own code inserted as noted. Execute SetHook with ES pointing to the PSP; DoHook will be called automatically at termination time.

Figure 7-22. Process Termination Hook

```
SetHook  PROC
         MOV     AX,[ES:000Ah]           ; save old offset
         MOV     word ptr CS:OldVec,AX
         MOV     AX,[ES:000Ch]           ; save old segment
         MOV     word ptr CS:OldVec+2,AX
         MOV     AX,offset DoHook
         MOV     [ES:000Ah],AX           ; set in new vector
         MOV     AX,CS
         MOV     [ES:000Ch],AX
SetHook  ENDP
OldVec   DD      0                       ; place for old vector

DoHook   PROC    FAR
; whatever you need to do is coded here...
         JMP     [CS:OldVec]             ; then chain to original
DoHook   ENDP
```

The termination address stored at ISV22 in the PSP is just the return address to the Exec function call (INT 21h Function 4B00h) that the parent used to invoke this process. Obviously, then, when DOS transfers control to this address, it is ready to return to the parent. DoHook is grabbing control instead, so when DoHook is executed, all memory allocated to the terminating process has already been released—including the memory containing the DoHook code. All files have been closed and the current PSP has been set to that of the parent. In DOS 3.0 and later, the registers have been restored to the values they had when the parent performed the Exec.

Basically, all that DoHook should do is de-install any special handlers that the program had installed, so that they will not be left pointing to addresses that are no longer valid. No other actions should be attempted; and by all means no file access or other I/O should be tried since the context could easily vary depending on the parent programs. For more complex on-exit processing, you are better off using routines such as atexit() in C. Note, though, that the C routines are called only for normal process termination and will not be executed in case of fatal errors or other abnormal conditions.

For another approach to exit handling, see the discussion of INT 2Fh AX=1122h (Process Termination Hook) in Chapter 8.

Other PSP Fields

The first fully undocumented area of the PSP is the word at offset 0016h, which contains the PID of this process' parent process. If this process is the current command interpreter, its own PID appears here, even if it is really a spawned shell that can be terminated by the EXIT command. Were it not for this, you could trace back through these pointers from one PSP to the parent PSP and thus locate the master command interpreter. However, all you can do by tracing this is to locate the current shell, which may not be the master. (As noted earlier, INT 2Eh can be used to find the master copy of COMMAND.COM; more details appear in Chapter 10 on command interpreters.)

Immediately following the PARENT pointer, at offset 0018h, is the 20-byte handle table (JFT). Each byte in this list represents an index into the System File Tables maintained by DOS. The first five of these are automatically set up by the loader routines to predefine handles for stdin, stdout, stderr, stdaux, and stdprn. Note that the first three handles reference the same System File Table (see Chapter 8 on the DOS file system) entry for device CON. All unused handles have the value 0xFF.

The next undocumented area is the doubleword at offset 002Eh, which the DOS dispatch code uses to save SS and SP each time this process enters INT 21h (see step 6 in Figure 6-7). Saving the stack location in the PSP, rather than in DOS' own data area, makes multitasking possible by permitting DOS to switch current processes, resuming each process where it was last halted (that is, treating the processes as coroutines). However, MS-DOS itself has not yet taken advantage of this capability.

Right behind ENVPTR comes a six-byte group added at version 3.1, which permits you to relocate the handle table and thus make more than 20 file handles available to your process. A documented DOS function (INT 21h Function 67h) exists to manipulate this area. An alternative to Function 67h appears in FHANDLE.C, in Chapter 8.

The first two bytes of this region are the word NHDLS at offset 0032h, which defines the number of handles available to this process; attempting to open another file or device when this many handles are already in use triggers a DOS error. The following four bytes, HTBLPTR at offset 0034h, are a far pointers to the first byte of the handle table. By default, NHDLS is set to 20, and HTBLPTR to PSP:0018h, thus describing the handle table in the PSP.

The doubleword at offset 0038h is always set to 0FFFF:FFFFh in DOS versions prior to 3.3. Later DOS versions set this to point to a previous PSP when SHARE is in use, creating a chain of PSPs used by SHARE's cleanup function (close all files opened by a given machine).

APPEND uses the byte at offset 3Dh of the PSP to maintain its truename flag for INT 2Fh Function B711h (DOS version 4+). At Version 5.0, DOS began storing the major and minor version values at offset 40h (SETVER uses this to "lie" to applications about the DOS version number). WINOLDAP in Windows uses the byte at offset 48h, setting the bottom bit when running old (that is, DOS) applications. Finally, offset 55h is the start of an extended FCB field.

Spawning Child Processes

As is discussed further in Chapter 10, every program run under MS-DOS can be thought of as a child process. Even the very first one loaded as part of the boot action (that is, the loader that is read in from the boot sector of the disk) is a child of the ROM Bootstrap routine!

A child process is simply a process spawned by some other process, which is called the parent. Again, except for the bootstrap loader code that initially brings your system into action, every process in the system is a child of some other process.

The bootstrap loader spawns only one child, the command interpreter specified by the SHELL= line in CONFIG.SYS—or COMMAND.COM, by default, if no SHELL is specified. This process is what most users perceive to be DOS itself. Each time a program's name is typed on the command line, that program is spawned as a child of the command interpreter, for execution.

If the spawned program is, itself, a menu or other type of shell routine, it may in turn spawn children of its own, which then execute and return control to their parent. Should control ever return to the bootstrap loader, the result is the error message, "Bad or missing command interpreter," and a locked system requiring rebooting. However, DOS 6.0 does prompt for the full pathname to the command interpreter if it is unable to locate the specified one while performing the initial program load or bootstrap process.

Locating Parent Processes

From time to time, a process needs to be able to trace its ancestry. This isn't always possible. For example, a shell program such as COMMAND.COM is always its own parent, for excellent reasons (see Chapter 10), and so the chain stops right there. However, if the process is running as the child of anything other than a command interpreter such as COMMAND.COM, the job of locating its ancestors is straightforward, though undocumented.

Locating Ancestors   One undocumented field in the PSP, the PARENT word described previously, makes it possible for a program to trace its ancestry to the point of the closest command interpreter shell (any shell program modifies this field to show that it is its own parent).

Thus a program that needs to trace its ancestry need only locate its own PSP, extract the parent process ID, then use that to access the parent's PSP. The process continues until the point at which PARENT self-referentially points to the PSP that contains it; this PSP is the first command interpreter program encountered in the trace.

Use of this Capability   A sample program in C that uses this capability to trace its ancestry appears in Figure 7-23.

Figure 7-23. Tracing Process Ancestry

```
/*
 * ROOTS.C (with apologies to Alex Haley)
 * Trace Your Ancestry!
 * Jim Kyle, 1990
 * revised August, 1992, jk to include UNDOCDOS.H
 */
#include <stdio.h>
#include <stdlib.h>              /* required to get _psp for MS   */
#include "undocdos.h"

WORD parent, self;

main ( void )
{ self = _psp;                   /* start with own PSP value      */
  parent = PARENT( self );
  do
    { printf("PID = %04X, PARENT = %04X\n", self, parent );
```

```
      self = parent;
   }
  while (( parent = PARENT( self ) ) != self );
  return 0;
}
```

The program simply copies its own PID into the variable "self" and then uses it and the defined macro, PARENT, to retrieve the parent's PID in "parent."

From there, the program loops, reporting the values of the variables "self" and "parent" at each level and then redefining them both, until the program reaches the level at which the two values match. This is the command interpreter. At this point, the program returns. It's most instructive, by the way, to run this program from some environment, rather than from the command line, because that guarantees at least one level of ancestry before the command interpreter is reached. For example, we can run ROOTS inside of DEBUG, inside another copy of DEBUG:

```
D:\UDOS2\CHAP7>debug \dos\debug.exe roots.exe
-g
-g
PID = 6CFE, PARENT = 672E
PID = 672E, PARENT = 615D
PID = 615D, PARENT = 6139
```

Here, 6CFE is ROOTS, 672E and 615D are DEBUG, and 6139 is the current command interpreter shell, which was actually a secondary shell invoked from my text editor. Naturally, we could use the code developed earlier in UDMEM, especially the function progname_fm_psp( ), to find the ASCIIZ names of these ancestors.

Device Management

In addition to memory, the operating system must manage all devices connected to the CPU, such as the disk drives, the keyboard, and any displays. DOS manages, and issues requests to, device drivers, which in turn talk to lower-level interfaces such as the ROM BIOS (Basic Input Output System), or a device controller.

Why Device Drivers Exist

Older operating systems, and even MS-DOS 1.x, included all hardware-dependent code necessary to deal with input and output as an integral part of the system itself. This made it necessary to bring out version 1.1 of MS-DOS when IBM made available the 360K double-sided floppy disk drive, and made it impossible to use any kind of hard disk conveniently on a DOS 1.x system. Improvements were obviously in order.

A major part of the upgrade provided by MS-DOS 2.0 was the installable device driver capability. This idea, which apparently originated at MIT with the MULTICS mainframe system, found its way into DOS by way of Bell Labs' UNIX, but the idea was significantly improved on its way into DOS. The original idea concentrated all hardware dependencies into small modules that were separate from the main mass of operating system code, but that still required the user to rebuild and re-link the operating system in order to change any drivers. This was true for both MULTICS and UNIX. In DOS, on the other hand, all you do to change a driver is modify CONFIG.SYS and reboot. As we show before the end of this chapter, even that process can be made simpler, and a new driver can be installed from the command line with absolutely no change to the main operating system code itself.

An installable device driver is a code package that forms a self-contained unit capable of initializing itself and through which all communication to and from a specific hardware device can be channeled. The format of the driver and its command interface is specified by the MS-DOS documentation.

Devices (so far as DOS is concerned) come in two flavors, known as character and block. Character devices are those that can deal with a single character at a time, such as the CRT, the keyboard, the printer, or the serial port. Block devices are those that, like disk drives, must accumulate a block of data and transfer it all at once. Drivers for the two types are distinguished by a single bit in the device header's attribute word and by the fact that some of the command functions make sense for only one of them but are otherwise identical structures and require identical interfacing techniques.

By separating hardware dependencies into these modules, only new drivers, rather than a complete operating system upgrade, need to be developed when a new hardware device becomes available; the new device then immediately becomes usable with any older system that can accept the driver.

Hardware-Dependent Details

In general, three types of action tend to be highly device-specific and vary from one device to the next. These are the actions required to initialize the device and prepare it for use, those required to send data to it, and those required to receive data from it.

You might think that some devices need only two of these groups, because you don't usually send data to a keyboard or receive data from a printer. However, the keyboard does have to receive certain commands from the operating system to acknowledge that its output has been accepted, and similarly the system needs to read status conditions from the printer. These peripherals really are I/O devices, not just I or O devices.

Other details that are associated with specific hardware items, rather than with generic logical functions, include port addresses through which communication is achieved, the handshake protocol used to transfer data to and from the device, and the actual bit patterns transferred as commands and status.

All of these hardware-dependent details are concentrated within the single driver that serves each device. In order for DOS to use them, they are grouped into a small collection of logical functions as specified in the DOS documentation.

Logically Required Functions   The DOS documentation specifies 17 logical functions, all of which must be recognized and responded to by every device driver, regardless of whether that function makes sense for the driver (as in the amusing case of "media check" for a CRT). These functions provide adequate flexibility to deal with virtually any I/O requirement you can imagine.

Normally, function dispatching is implemented with a jump table. The driver uses the function's number as the index into a table of offset addresses, thus transferring control to the indexed address. If the specific function does not apply to this driver, the routine reached just returns an appropriate status code with no other action performed.

Congruence of Files and Devices   One of the most useful results of the device driver idea is that MS-DOS can treat files and devices in exactly the same way. However, it's not exactly obvious why you might consider this to be good. At first glance, files and devices don't seem to have a lot to do with each other.

That first glance, though, is deceiving. For both files and devices, what really counts is the stream of data. If your programs need not even know whether such a stream comes from a file, from the keyboard, or from a communications port, then they'll be that much simpler to deal with when some new type of input device arrives on the scene.

This idea makes the driver's device independence into a major advantage when compared to older techniques that, for example, require totally different programming to retrieve data from the keyboard than was required to retrieve otherwise identical data from a file.

Unfortunately, not all of the keyboard's capability as an input device can be used through the drivers, nor can maximum display speed be obtained from the CRT. If you are programming a real-time video image display system with hotkey control, you'll be forced to go directly to the video display controller with your output and to use BIOS routines to read the keyboard without waiting until the operator presses ENTER.

Thus not all programs that run under MS-DOS are able to take full advantage of the power offered by the driver idea. This is not a limitation inherent in the idea itself, but rather an artificial one imposed by the design of MS-DOS and its failure to anticipate all future needs. Or maybe it's limitation inherent in the idea of device independence. Windows device drivers deal with this problem by returning to the use of separate specifications for display drivers, keyboard drivers, and so on.

One interesting by-product of the files-devices congruence is that all your named devices can be accessed as files in any disk directory! This comes about because the DOS routines that open both devices and files always search for devices first. If a device name is the same as the name of the file you are trying to open, the device will be opened instead. Because most of the procedures that determine whether a given file exists depend on trying to open the file and then detecting the error if it cannot be opened, these routines show that any device exists as a file in any directory you happen to test. Nevertheless, the device does not show in the directory listing.

This can be used to test for the existence of a directory itself, because if you try to open a device by referring to it as a file in a nonexistent directory, the directory error occurs before the device access attempt. That error, in turn, indicates that the directory itself cannot be accessed; if the directory can be accessed, the device can also always be accessed. The following batch file uses this aspect of DOS devices:

```
@echo off
rem isdir.bat
if exist %1\nul goto exists
echo No such directory
goto done
:exists
echo Directory exists
:done

C:\UNDOC\KYLE>isdir \foobar
No such directory
C:\UNDOC\KYLE>isdir \undoc\kyle
Directory exists
```

Tracing the Driver Chain

In order to operate at all, MS-DOS must provide at least a minimal set of built-in device drivers. Yet to achieve the full advantages of expansion, it's necessary to be able to insert new drivers at will and to have the power of replacing an existing driver with a new version.

In order to make these things possible, DOS organizes the drivers as a singly linked chain, with a defined starting point that is always at the same place within any specific DOS version; the location differs from one version to the next, however. Each driver in the chain includes as part of its structure a pointer to the next one, and the end of the chain is signified by the value FFFFh in the offset position of the final driver's link. Unlike the MCB chain, this is a true linked list. Figure 7-24 shows how the chain of device drivers is organized in DOS.

The original device chain is prebuilt in the hidden system file IO.SYS (in PC-DOS, IBMBIO.COM). If you add drivers to your system using the DEVICE= command in the CONFIG.SYS file, they are patched into the chain by the initialization portion of IO.SYS each time you boot your system.

Subsequent sections of this chapter describe the detailed organization of the device driver chain, tell how drivers are initialized during system boot-up, and then show you how to locate the start of the chain for any version of DOS and how to trace the driver chain and find out what is in your system.

Figure 7-24. The Device Driver Chain in DOS

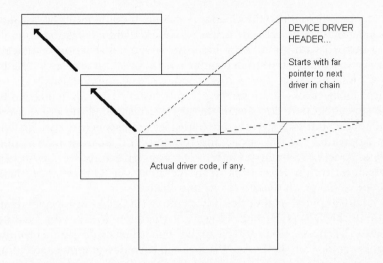

DEVICE DRIVER HEADER...

Starts with far pointer to next driver in chain

Actual driver code, if any.

Organization of the Device Driver Chain   The device driver chain is a singly linked list structure with a defined starting point. The link itself is a far pointer (32-bit segment:offset format) that forms the first four bytes of each device driver; the starting point is the driver for the NUL device.

The NUL device, a character type, is the bit bucket for both input and output; any output sent to NUL simply vanishes without trace, and any attempt to read input from this device encounters a permanent EOF condition. In itself, a device with these characteristics is handy. NUL also serves as the anchor location for the driver chain.

As delivered, NUL's link pointer holds the address of the supplied CON driver—the default console or keyboard/CRT routines. This driver is located near the front of the IO.SYS data area, which normally is at absolute address 00700h. The NUL driver, however, is located near the front of the DOS data segment itself, within the SysVars structure, which is at a much higher address.

Because the DOS handle-processing routines know where the NUL driver is located, they can trace through the chain to locate any required driver.

As already mentioned, the DOS routines always go through the device chain looking for a match between the name of each character device and the requested filename, whenever any attempt is made to open a handle for input or output. Only when no match is found in the driver chain does DOS search the directory for a named file. This makes it impossible to either create or access a file that has the same name as any device. It might be possible to develop a form of security system based on this fact by first creating a file then installing a device with the same name and providing a secure method for changing the device's name during operation.

Note that only character devices have names that are used in the search; block devices are referred to by drive letter instead of by name. During a name search, block drivers are simply skipped. Because the first match to a name ends the search, an existing driver is replaced simply by inserting the replacement driver into the chain where it will be encountered first and being sure that it has the same name.

How Drivers Are Initialized   When you add new drivers using CONFIG.SYS, each driver is added to the front of the chain as it is encountered. DOS copies the link values from NUL into the new driver's link and then puts the new driver's address into the NUL link instead.

Both block and character device drivers are added into the chain in the same way. The search always begins at the NUL driver, guaranteeing that any new drivers added will be found before the built-in ones.

The pointer-patching that inserts each driver into the chain is not done, though, until the last step of driver installation. First, the installation routine calls the driver's own internal initialization code. If an error occurs, the installation is skipped with an advisory message. If the initialization completes without error, DOS checks the driver's attribute word to determine whether the driver is for a character device or for a block device. If it's for a character device, it is added to the chain immediately.

However, if it's a block device, DOS checks the number of units installed by the initialization code; if this number is zero, that signals DOS not to install the driver even though no errors were detected. Otherwise, DOS uses the unit count to assign the next drive letter in sequence, then creates a Disk Parameter Block (see the Appendix) for the device and fills the DPB in from information returned by the initialization process. Next, DOS builds a Current Directory Structure (see the Appendix) entry for that drive letter, which relates the letter back to the device driver. Only after all these actions are successfully completed does DOS patch the driver into the chain.

The device driver specifications let you put several device drivers into a single file and specify them all by means of the single filename in the DEVICE= line. However, when you do this you must be aware of several "gotchas" that exist. The most serious gotcha applies only to block devices: The code that processes CONFIG.SYS assigns memory for the Disk DPB for each such device immediately following the driver's break address, which is the address returned to DOS by the driver when it initializes and the address that tells DOS where the driver's required space ends. Thus, if you have more than one block device driver in the same file, each should return different break addresses, and these addresses should not be followed by any code that will be needed after DOS calls the driver's initialization function.

If you mix character and block device drivers in the same file—which is not prohibited by the specs, but which is definitely a risky thing to do—you must be sure that all the character drivers appear in the file before any of the block drivers, for the same reason.

The best practice, of course, is to follow a rule of one driver, one file, thus avoiding these possible problems. Sometimes, however, it may be necessary to do otherwise. When that's the case, be very careful, and if you run into strange system crashes, look closely to be sure that an errant break address pointer is not wiping out driver code.

Locating the Start of the Chain   The start of the device driver chain, like that of the MCB chain discussed earlier in this chapter, can be determined using the undocumented INT 21h Function 52h (Get List of Lists). The NUL device driver header (the actual header, *not* a pointer) that forms the anchor point for the chain is always located in the List of Lists.

For DOS 2.x, the NUL header begins 17h bytes past the address returned in ES:BX by INT 21h Function 52h. With DOS 3.0, the offset is 28h; but with 3.1 that came down to 22h, and there it has remained.

The following code fragment shows how to load ES:BX with the address of the NUL driver for DOS 3.1 and up; for earlier versions, change the constant 22h to the appropriate value:

```
mov     ah, 52h   ; get List of Lists
int     21h
add     bx, 22h   ; NUL driver offset, DOS 3.1+
```

Tracing It Through   Once you have located the start of the device driver chain, actual tracing through all devices (to duplicate the action of DOS during an OPEN function) is simple. The only complicating factor is the need to distinguish between character and block devices and to report block devices differently because they have no names.

The sample program shown in Figure 7-25, written for MASM version 5.1 but usable with other assemblers that support the simplified segmentation directives, shows how simple it is.

Figure 7-25. Tracing the Device Chain

```
; DEV.ASM--for DOS 3.1+
.model small
.stack

.data
blkdev    db        'Block: '                 ; block driver message
blkcnt    db        '0 unit(s)$'

.code
dev       proc

          mov       ah,52h                    ; get List of Lists
          int       21h
          mov       ax,es                     ; segment to AX
          add       bx,22h                    ; driver offset, 3.1 and up
          mov       di,seg blkdev
          mov       dx,offset blkdev

dev1:     mov       ds,ax
          lea       si, [bx+10]               ; step to name/units field
          test      byte ptr [bx+5], 80h      ; check driver type
          jz        dev3                      ; is BLOCK driver

          mov       cx,8                      ; is CHAR driver
dev2:     lodsb                               ; so output its name
IFDEF INT29
          int       29h                       ; gratuitous use of undoc DOS
ELSE
          push      dx
          mov       dl, al
          mov       ah, 2                     ; Character Output
          int       21h
          pop       dx
ENDIF
          loop      dev2
          jmp       short   dev4              ; then go look for next one

dev3:     lodsb                               ; get number of units
          add       al,'0'                    ; assumes less than 10 units!
          push      ds
          mov       ds,di
          mov       blkcnt,al                 ; set into message
          mov       ah,9
          int       21h
          pop       ds

IFDEF INT29
dev4:     mov       al,13                     ; send CR and LF to CRT
          int       29h                       ; gratuitous use of undoc DOS
          mov       al,10
          int       29h
ELSE
dev4:     push      dx
          mov       ah,2                      ; Character Output
          mov       dl,13                     ; send CR and LF to CRT
          int       21h
          mov       dl,10
          int       21h
          pop       dx
```

```
ENDIF
        mov     si,bx                   ; back up to front of driver
        lodsw                           ; get offset of next one
        xchg    ax,bx
        lodsw                           ; and then its segment
        cmp     bx,0FFFFh               ; was this end of chain?
        jne     dev1                    ; no, loop back
        mov     ax,4C00H                ; yes, return to DOS
        int     21h
dev     endp
        end     dev
```

When DEV.EXE is run on a MS-DOS 6.0 system, it produces the following list of drivers. The bottom 13 are those contained in the hidden file IO.SYS, the 3-unit block driver controls drives A:, B:, and C:, and the other 10 are the standard DOS devices. The less than (<) reports result from the fact that some of the new Microsoft drivers allow 12 units, while DEV assumes that no more than nine are present. The duplication of block drivers is an artifact of having SMARTDRV.EXE installed; the system had only four disk drives.

```
NUL
Block: < unit(s)
Block: 3 unit(s)
DBLSSYS$
CON
$MMXXXX0
XMSXXXX0
Block: < unit(s)
CON
AUX
PRN
CLOCK$
Block: 3 unit(s)
COM1
LPT1
LPT2
LPT3
COM2
COM3
COM4
EMMXXXX0
```

The duplicate CON is UV-ANSI.SYS; because it appears in the chain ahead of the standard CON driver, it is always used.

It is worth noting that, if assembled with a /DINT29 flag, DEV.ASM makes gratuitous use of undocumented DOS. INT 29h is the *fast putchar* interrupt called from DOS when sending characters to a device whose attribute word has bit four set. It is tempting to use INT 29h here because it does simplify the code just below label dev2. However, Chapter 1 notes that there really are places you should use documented DOS instead of undocumented DOS, even when it seems like more trouble. Performing output in this program is one of those places. Although this program absolutely demands use of undocumented INT 21h Function 52h, there are several reasons why it should not use undocumented INT 29h:

- Essentially the same functionality is available with INT 21h Function 2, although it may be a trifle slower.
- INT 29h output is not redirectable. Because this program displays block devices using INT 21h Function 9, which is redirectable, using INT 29h elsewhere means that running DEV > TMP.TMP ends up displaying character devices on the screen and block devices in the file. Pretty silly!

Thus, DEV provides a nice demonstration of when undocumented DOS is needed and when it definitely isn't. Exercise some discretion here. Don't use undocumented DOS if you don't need to. End of lecture.

Loading Device Drivers from the DOS Command Line

To complete what you've learned about DOS resource management, let's create a program you can use to load device drivers from the DOS command line, without having to edit CONFIG.SYS and reboot.

Ever have an MS-DOS program that required the presence of a device driver, and you wished you had a way to install the driver from the command line prompt, rather than having to edit your CONFIG.SYS file and then reboot the system? Of course you can be thankful that it's so much easier to reboot MS-DOS than it is to rebuild the kernel, which is what must be done to add a device driver to UNIX. While DOS 2.x borrowed the idea of installable device drivers from UNIX, it's often forgotten that DOS in fact improved on the installation of device drivers by replacing the building of a new kernel with the simple editing of CONFIG.SYS.

Still, most of us occasionally wish we could just type a command line to load a device driver and be done with it, for truly installable device drivers. Also, developers of device drivers often wish they had a way to debug the initialization phase of a device driver. This type of debugging usually requires a debug device driver that loads before your device driver, or it requires hardware in-circuit emulation. But only you could load device drivers after the normal CONFIG.SYS stage.

Well, wish no more. Command-line loading of MS-DOS device drivers is not only possible, it's relatively simple to accomplish once you know a little about undocumented DOS. We present such a program, DEVLOD, written in a combination of C and assembly language. The program that follows is not the same one that appeared in the first edition of this book, nor the slightly modified version that later showed up in the November 1991 issue of *Dr. Dobb's Journal*. This is a much more extensively debugged version, which corrects several problems that made the original unusable for loading block devices under DOS 4.0 or 5.0; this version more reliably determines the correct drive letter to use when adding new block devices.

Many readers have provided feedback that helped improve DEVLOD for this edition. Some of the most vital feed back was from Dan B. Wright, who called a number of problems to our attention and suggested cures for most of them, which I gratefully acknowledge here. Another who spotted many of the same bugs, plus some that evaded everyone else, was Geoff Chappell. Thanks to Geoff, the new version tests for initialization errors in the same way that DOS itself does, rather than by using the documented-but-never-checked status return value! Others whose comments helped greatly include Nathaniel Polish, Dan Winter, William T. Wonneberger, and Jay Lowe, whose testing helped assure us that we had indeed solved most, if not all, of the reported problems. In addition to significant logic changes, we also modified DEVLOD to use the UNDOCDOS.H header file so that you would not be so likely to become confused by the arcane offset values sprinkled throughout the original.

To use the program, all you have to do is type DEVLOD, followed by the name of the driver to be loaded and any parameters needed, just as you would supply them in CONFIG.SYS. For example, instead of placing the following in CONFIG.SYS:

```
device=c:\dos\ansi.sys
```

you would simply type the following on the DOS command line:

```
C:\>devlod c:\dos\ansi.sys
```

There are several ways to verify that this worked. First, you can write ANSI strings to CON and see if they are properly interpreted as ANSI commands. For example, after a DEVLOD ANSI.SYS, the following DOS command should produce a DOS prompt in reverse video:

```
C:\>prompt $e[7m$p$g$e[0m
```

For maximum accuracy, you can tell that the new driver has been installed by running DEV and inspecting its display of the device chain; you can see your new driver at the top of the list, right after NUL and ahead of any identically-named drivers loaded earlier:

```
C:\UNDOC\KYLE>dev
NUL
QEMM386$
...
C:\UNDOC\KYLE>devlod \dos\clock.sys
C:\UNDOC\KYLE>dev
NUL
CLOCK$
QEMM386$
...
```

DEVLOD loads both character device drivers (such as ANSI.SYS) and block device drivers (drivers that support one or more drive units, such as VDISK.SYS), whether located in .SYS or .EXE files.

How DEVLOD Works

Here is the basic structure of the DEVLOD program:

```
startup code (C0.ASM)
main (DEVLOD.C)
    Move_Loader
        movup (MOVUP.ASM)
    Load_Drvr
        INT 21h Function 4B03h (Load Overlay)
    Get_List
        INT 21h Function 52h (Get List of Lists)
        based on DOS version number:
            get number of block devices
            get value of LASTDRIVE
            get Current Directory Structure (CDS) base
            get pointer to NUL device
    Init_Drvr
        call DD init routine
            build command packet
            call Strategy
            call Interrupt
    Get_Out
        if block device:
            Put_Blk_Dev
                for each unit:
                    Next_Drive
                        get next available drive letter
                    find last existing DPB
                    INT 21h Function 53h (Translate BPB -> DPB)
                    poke CDS
                    link into DPB chain
        Fix_DOS_Chain
            link into dev chain
        release environment space
        INT 21h Function 31h (TSR)
```

DEVLOD's first job is to move itself out of the way to the top of memory. This lets it load the device driver as low as possible, reducing memory fragmentation. Figures 7-26 and 7-27 diagram the significant steps that DEVLOD takes while running.

Figure 7-26. First Three Steps of DEVLOD Action

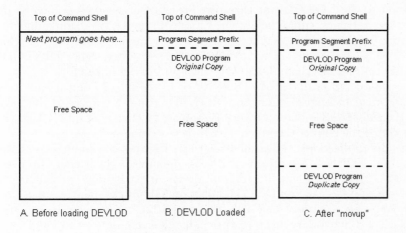

A. Before loading DEVLOD   B. DEVLOD Loaded   C. After "movup"

Memory maps not to scale

Figure 7-27. Final Stages of DEVLOD Operation

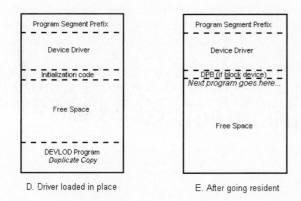

D. Driver loaded in place   E. After going resident

Memory maps not to scale

DEVLOD loads device drivers into memory using the documented DOS function for loading overlays, INT 21h Function 4B03h. An earlier version of DEVLOD read the driver into memory using DOS file calls to open, read, and close the driver, but this made handling .EXE driver types difficult. By using the EXEC function instead, DOS handles both .SYS and .EXE files properly. It might appear that the SetExecState function, 4B05h, should be called first to perform SETVER processing, but any device driver that is version specific should never be loaded with another version of

DOS. In general, drivers that do not depend on undocumented features of specific versions do not perform version tests, so using SETVER amounts, in essence, to tying down the boiler's safety valve.

DEVLOD then calls our good friend, undocumented INT 21h Function 52h, to retrieve the value of LASTDRIVE, a pointer to the DOS Current Directory Structure array and a pointer to the NUL device. The location of these variables within the SysVars varies with the DOS version number.

DEVLOD requires a pointer to the NUL device because, as we saw earlier in this chapter when discussing the DEV program, NUL acts as the anchor to the DOS device chain. Since DEVLOD's whole purpose is to add new devices into this chain, DEVLOD must update this linked list.

If the DOS version indicates operation under MS-DOS 1.x or in the OS/2 compatibility box, DEVLOD quits with an appropriate message. Otherwise, DEVLOD creates a pointer to the name field of the NUL driver, and the eight bytes at that location are compared to the constant NUL to verify that the driver is present and that the pointer is correct.

In glancing over the Appendix to this book, the astute reader may have noticed an undocumented DOS function, INT 2Fh Function 122Ch, which returns in BX:AX a pointer to the header of the second device driver (NUL is first). Since DOS links together all device driver headers, this effectively gets a pointer to the DOS driver chain. So why call INT 21h Function 52h instead? The reason is that, like all the internal INT 2Fh AH=12h functions, INT 21h Function 122Ch was meant to be called only from a DOS extension such as a network redirector, with all segment registers set to DOS's kernel segment. You still need those other variables from SysVars, in case you are loading a block device—which you won't know until later, after you've called the driver's INIT routine.

Once DEVLOD has retrieved this information, it sends the device driver an initialization packet. This is straightforward. The function Init_Drvr() forms a packet with the INIT command, calls the driver's Strategy routine, and then calls the driver's Interrupt routine. The offsets to these routines are part of the standard device driver header; DEVLOD creates a function pointer, using the offset to call each routine in turn. As elsewhere, DEVLOD merely mimics what DOS does when it loads a device driver.

If the device driver INIT fails, there is naturally nothing you can do but bail out. It is important to note that you have not yet linked the driver into the DOS driver chain, so it is easy to exit if the driver INIT fails. If the driver INIT succeeds, DEVLOD can then proceed with its true mission, which takes place, oddly enough, in the function Get_Out().

It is only at this point that DEVLOD knows whether it has a block or character device driver, so it is here that DEVLOD takes special measures for block device drivers, by calling Put_Blk_Dev(). For each unit provided by the driver, that function uses the undocumented DOS DPB structure to find the last used DPB; then the function calls INT 21h Function 53h (Translate BPB to DPB), alters the CDS entry for the new drive, and links the new DPB into the DPB chain. These new DPBs are added after the device driver's break address. (The BPB, DPB, and CDS are explained in detail in Chapter 8 on the DOS file system.) The key point is that in Put_Blk_Dev(), DEVLOD takes information returned by a block driver's INIT routine and produces a new DOS drive. This area of the program underwent significant change in this version because DOS 4.0 added one byte to the DPB, making it too large to fit in the space allowed by the original DEVLOD code! The result was total system lockup sometime subsequent to using DEVLOD to install a block device. This bug has been squashed.

When loading a block device driver, DEVLOD needs a drive letter to assign to the new driver. As Chapter 8 explains in great detail, the CDS is an undocumented array of structures, sometimes also called the Drive Info Table, which maintains the current state of each drive in the system. The array is n elements long, where n equals LASTDRIVE. DEVLOD pokes the CDS in order to install a block device driver.

The function Next_Drive() is where DEVLOD determines the drive letter to assign to a block device if there is an available drive letter. One technique for determining the next letter, #ifdefed out within DEVLOD.C, is simply to read the Number of Block Devices field (nblkdrs) out of the List of

Lists. However, this fails to take account of SUBSTed or network- redirected drives. Therefore, we instead walk the CDS, looking for the first free drive. In any case, DEVLOD updates the nblkdrs field, if it successfully loads a block device.

If the driver being loaded is for a character device, DEVLOD checks two of the bits in its attribute word to determine whether to update the CON and CLOCK$ pointers in the List of Lists. If the character device being installed has its STDIN bit set, the CON pointer is updated to point to the new driver. This pointer is used by DOS to check for CTRL-C and CTRL-BREAK keystrokes. Similarly, if the CLOCK bit is set, the CLOCK$ pointer is changed to reflect the address of the new driver. DOS uses this pointer for all references to the clock device, rather than going through the overhead of searching for it by name. The original version of DEVLOD failed to maintain these two pointers and, as a consequence, DEVLOD ANSI.SYS would disable Control-C checking! Thanks to Geoff Chappell for letting us know.

Also, when loading a character device driver, DEVLOD searches all SFT entries for any references to a driver of the same name. If DEVLOD finds any, it replaces the SFT's pointers to the driver with pointers to the new driver being installed. This is essential to maintaining proper operation of the critical error handlers, as pointed out by Dan Winter in the July, 1992, issue of *Dr. Dobb's Journal*, in a letter commenting on the original DEVLOD.COM. Since Dan's code was not completely compatible with DEVLOD, I rewrote it, but the idea remains the same as the one he suggested.

Whether loading a block or character driver, DEVLOD uses the break address—the first byte of the driver's address space that can safely be turned back to DOS for reuse—returned by the driver. For block devices, the break address has been increased to include the newly created DPBs. Get_Out() converts the break address into a count of paragraphs to be retained.

DEVLOD mimics the DOS SYSINIT routine's actions to determine whether driver initialization was successful. For character devices, the break address is compared to offset zero in the driver segment; if they are equal, initialization failed. For block devices, the number of units returned in the command packet is checked. If initialization failed, this number is set to zero. In neither situation is any check made of the status value returned by the driver!

DEVLOD then links the device header into DOS's linked list of driver headers. The function copyptr() is called three times in succession, first to save the content of the NUL driver's link field, then to copy it into the link field of the new driver, and finally to store the far address of the new driver in the NUL driver's link field. Note again that the DOS linked list is not altered until after you know that the driver's INIT succeeded.

Finally, DEVLOD saves some memory by releasing its environment. The resulting hole in RAM causes no harm, contrary to popular belief. In fact, any program subsequently loaded uses it as its environment space, if the size of the environment is not increased. DEVLOD's last action is to call the documented DOS TSR function, INT 21h Function 31h, to exit without releasing the memory now occupied by the driver.

DEVLOD.C

Before you look at how this dynamic loader accomplishes all this in less than 2,900 bytes of executable code, some constraints should be mentioned.

Many confusing details were eliminated by implementing DEVLOD as a .COM program, using the tiny memory model. The way the program moves itself up in memory became much clearer when the .COM format removed the need to individually manage each segment register.

In order to move the program while it is executing, it's necessary to know every address that the program can reach during its execution. This precludes using any part of the libraries supplied with the compiler. Fortunately, in this case that's not a serious restriction; nearly everything can be handled without them. Two assembly language listings take care of the few things that cannot easily be done in C itself.

Borland makes it easy to completely sever the link to the runtime libraries. They provide sample code showing how to do so. Microsoft also provides such a capability, but its documentation is quite cryptic. Any of the Borland compilers for DOS can be used. The first version of DEVLOD was created in Turbo C, while the current version was done with Borland C++ 3.0, used in its C mode.

Thus the program, as presented, requires either Borland or Turbo C with its register pseudo-variables, geninterrupt(), and _ _emit_ _() features. As explained in Chapter 2, register pseudo-variables such as _AX provide a way to directly read or load the CPU registers from C. Both geninterrupt() and _ _emit_ _() simply emit bytes into the code stream; neither are actually functions.

Figure 7-28 shows the main program, DEVLOD.C.

Figure 7-28. The DEVLOD.C Program

```
/*******************************************************************
 *      DEVLOD.C - Jim Kyle - 08/20/90                            *
 *        Copyright 1990,1992 by Jim Kyle - All Rights Reserved   *
 *      (minor revisions by Andrew Schulman - 9/12/90)            *
 *      (major rewrite by Jim Kyle - July-Aug 1992)               *
 *      (minor change by Jim Kyle - August 1993)                  *
 *      Dynamic loader for device drivers                         *
 *            Requires Turbo C or BC++; see DEVLOD.MAK also.       *
 *******************************************************************/
#include <stdio.h>
#include <stdlib.h>
#include <dos.h>

#include "undocdos.h"    /* defines DOS internal structures       */

#define GETFLAGS __emit__(0x9F)
#define FIXDS    __emit__(0x16,0x1F)    /* PUSH SS, POP DS         */
#define PUSH_BP  __emit__(0x55)
#define POP_BP   __emit__(0x5D)
#define GO_DOS   geninterrupt( 0x21 )

unsigned _stklen = 0x200;
unsigned _heaplen = 0;

LPPSP PSPptr;               /* used to access fields of the PSP    */
char  FileName[65];         /* filename global buffer              */
char  * dvrarg;             /* points to char after name in cmdline */
WORD  movsize;              /* number of bytes to be moved up      */
void  (far * driver)();     /* used as pointer to call driver code */
LPDDVR drvptr;              /* holds pointer to device driver      */
LPDDVR NULptr;              /* pointer to NUL device (chain start) */
FP    nuldrvr;              /* additional driver pointers          */
FP    nxtdrvr;
BYTE  far * nblkdrs;        /* points to block device count in List */
WORD  lastdrive;            /* value of LASTDRIVE in List of Lists */
BYTE  far * CDSbase;        /* base of Current Dir Structure       */
int   CDSsize;              /* size of CDS element                 */
WORD  nulseg;               /* hold parts of ListOfLists pointer   */
WORD  nulofs;
WORD  LoLofs;
LPLOL LOLptr;
DDCMDPKT CmdPkt;
int   SFT_size;             /* used by nex FixSFT, set by GetList  */

extern unsigned _psp;           /* established by startup code     */
extern unsigned _heaptop;       /* established by startup code     */
extern BYTE _osmajor;           /* established by startup code     */
extern BYTE _osminor;           /* established by startup code     */
void _exit( int );              /* established by startup code     */
void abort( void );             /* established by startup code     */
```

```
void movup( LPPSP, FP, int );    /* in MOVUP.ASM            */

int  TestName( LPDDVR, LPSFT ); /* in TESTNAME.ASM for FixSFT  */
void ChgSFT( LPSFT, LPDDVR );    /* in TESTNAME.ASM for FixSFT  */

void copyptr( FPP src, FPP dst )         /* copy far pointer   */
{ *dst = *src; }

void exit(int c)         /* called by startup code's sequence   */
{ _exit(c);}

void Put_Msg ( char *msg )  /* replaces printf(), uses DOS only */
{ _AH = 2;                  /* doesn't need to be inside loop    */
  while (*msg)
  { _DL = *msg++;
    GO_DOS;
  }
}


BOOL Get_Driver_Name ( void )
{ char *nameptr;
  int i, j, cmdlinesz;

  nameptr = (char *)&(PSPptr->Tailc);   /* set up to parse      */
  cmdlinesz = *nameptr++;
  if (cmdlinesz < 1)          /* if nothing there, return FALSE  */
    return FALSE;
  for (i=0; i<cmdlinesz && nameptr[i]<'!'; i++) /* skip blanks   */
    ;
  dvrarg = (char *)&nameptr[i]; /* save to put in SI            */
  for ( j=0; i<cmdlinesz && nameptr[i]>' '; i++)  /* copy name  */
    FileName[j++] = nameptr[i];
  FileName[j] = '\0';    /* name copied, but good time to        */
  for (; i<cmdlinesz && nameptr[i]>=' '; i++)   /*  make all UC */
    if( nameptr[i] >= 'a' && nameptr[i] <= 'z' )
      nameptr[i] &= 0x5F;                 /* take out case bit   */
  return TRUE;          /* and return TRUE to keep going         */
}


void Err_Halt ( char *msg )      /* print message and abort    */
{ Put_Msg ( msg );
  Put_Msg ( "\r\n" );            /* send CR,LF                 */
  abort();
}


void Move_Loader ( void )        /* vacate lower part of RAM    */
{ WORD movsize, destseg;
  movsize = _heaptop - _psp;     /* size of loader in paragraphs */
  destseg = PSPptr->Nxtgraf;     /* end of memory              */
  movup ( PSPptr, MK_FP( destseg - movsize, 0 ),
          movsize << 4);         /* move and fix segregs        */
}


void Load_Drvr ( void )          /* load driver file into RAM   */
{ WORD handle;
  struct {
    WORD LoadSeg;
    WORD RelocSeg;
  } ExecBlock;

  ExecBlock.LoadSeg = _psp + 0x10;
  ExecBlock.RelocSeg = _psp + 0x10;
  _DX = (WORD)&FileName[0];      /* ds:dx point to filename     */
  _BX = (WORD)&ExecBlock;        /* es:bx point to ExecBlock    */
```

```
    _ES = _SS;                      /* which, being local, is SS   */
    _AX = 0x4B03;                   /* load overlay (COM, SYS, EXE) */
    GO_DOS;                         /* DS is okay on this call      */
    GETFLAGS;                       /* check what happened          */
    if ( _AH & 1 )                  /* if carry flag set...         */
      Err_Halt ( "Unable to load driver file." );
}

void Get_List ( void )         /* set up pointers via List     */
{ _AH = 0x52;                  /* find DOS List of Lists       */
  GO_DOS;
  nulseg = _ES;                     /* DOS data segment             */
  LoLofs = _BX;                     /* current drive table offset   */
  LOLptr = (LPLOL)MK_FP( nulseg, LoLofs );

  switch( _osmajor )           /* NUL adr varies with version  */
    {
    case  0:
      Err_Halt ( "Drivers not used in DOS V1." );
    case  2:
      nblkdrs = (FP)0L;
      lastdrive = (LOLptr->ver.v2.lastdrv);
      NULptr = (LPDDVR)&(LOLptr->ver.v2.nul);
      nulofs = (WORD)NULptr;     /* just the offset part         */
      SFT_size = 0x28;
      break;
    case  3:
      if (_osminor == 0)
      {
          nblkdrs = (BYTE far *)&(LOLptr->ver.v30.blk_dev);
          lastdrive = (LOLptr->ver.v30.lastdrv);
          NULptr = (LPDDVR)&(LOLptr->ver.v30.nul);
          nulofs = (WORD)NULptr;          /* just the offset part */
          SFT_size = 0x38;
      }
      else
      {
          nblkdrs = (BYTE far *)&(LOLptr->ver.v31up.blk_dev);
          lastdrive = (LOLptr->ver.v31up.lastdrv);
          NULptr = (LPDDVR)&(LOLptr->ver.v31up.nul);
          nulofs = (WORD)NULptr;          /* just the offset part */
          SFT_size = 0x35;
      }
      CDSbase = (BYTE far *)(LOLptr->ver.v31up.cds);
      CDSsize = sizeof( CDS );  /* defined for DOS3.1 struct    */
      break;
    case  4:
    case  5:
    case  6:
      nblkdrs = (BYTE far *)&(LOLptr->ver.v31up.blk_dev);
      lastdrive = (LOLptr->ver.v31up.lastdrv);
      NULptr = (LPDDVR)&(LOLptr->ver.v31up.nul);
      nulofs = (WORD)NULptr;            /* just the offset part */
      CDSbase = (BYTE far *)(LOLptr->ver.v31up.cds);
      CDSsize = sizeof( CDS ) + 7;      /* V4,5 7 bytes bigger  */
      SFT_size = 0x3B;
      break;
    case 10:
    case 20:
      Err_Halt ( "OS2 DOS Box not supported." );
    default:
      Err_Halt ( "Unknown version of DOS!");
    }
}
```

```
void Fix_DOS_Chain ( void )        /* patches driver into DOS chn  */
{ WORD i;

   nuldrvr = MK_FP( nulseg, nulofs+0x0A );        /* verify drvr   */
   drvptr = "NUL      ";
   for ( i=0; i<8; ++i )
     if ( *((BYTE far *)nuldrvr+i) != *((BYTE far *)drvptr+i) )
       Err_Halt ( "Failed to find NUL driver." );

   nuldrvr = MK_FP( nulseg, nulofs );      /* point to NUL driver  */
   drvptr  = MK_FP( _psp+0x10, 0 );        /* new driver's address */

   copyptr( (FP)nuldrvr, (FP)&nxtdrvr ); /* hold old head now     */
   copyptr( (FP)&drvptr, (FP)nuldrvr ); /* put new after NUL     */
   copyptr( (FP)&nxtdrvr, (FP)drvptr ); /* and old after new     */
}

// returns number of next free drive, -1 if none available
int Next_Drive ( void )
{
#ifdef USE_BLKDEV
   return (nblkdrs && (*nblkdrs < lastdrive)) ? *nblkdrs : -1;
#else
   /* This approach takes account of SUBSTed and network-redirector
    * drives by finding the first unused entry in the CDS structure.
    */
   LPCDS cds;
   int i=0;
   for ( cds=(LPCDS)CDSbase;      /* start at front of struct    */
         i<lastdrive;             /* go all way through it       */
         i++, ((BYTE far *)cds)+=CDSsize)        /* count up      */
     if (! cds->flags)             /* found a free drive          */
        break;
   return (i == lastdrive) ? -1 : i;      /* return number, or -1 */
#endif
}

/*  This routine initializes the device driver and returns TRUE
 *  if all went well.  If initialization fails for any reason,
 *  this function returns FALSE and the driver will not be linked
 *  into the chain maintained by DOS.
 */
BOOL Init_Drvr ( void )
{ WORD tmp;
   drvptr  = MK_FP( _psp+0x10, 0 );       /* new driver's address */
   CmdPkt.command = DD_INIT;      /* defined in UNDOCDOS.H file   */
   CmdPkt.hdrlen = sizeof( DDCMDPKT );
   CmdPkt.unit = 0;
   CmdPkt.status = 0;             /* clear status just in case    */
   CmdPkt.inpofs = (WORD)dvrarg; /* points into command line     */
   CmdPkt.inpseg = _psp;
   CmdPkt.NextDrv = (BYTE)Next_Drive();  /* for block dev init    */
   if( CmdPkt.NextDrv == 0xFF &&
       ((drvptr->attr & CHAR_DEV) == 0))
     { Put_Msg( "Current Directory Structure is full, cannot install." );
       return FALSE;
     }

   if (_osmajor >= 5)
     { /* In DOS 5+, DOS passes the device driver irEndAddress
          (see DOS Programmer's Reference, p. 400) */
       CmdPkt.brkofs = 0;
       CmdPkt.brkseg =0xA000;                   /* allow all RAM */
     }
```

```
    tmp = drvptr->stratofs;          /* STRATEGY pointer in driver   */
    driver = MK_FP( FP_SEG( drvptr ), tmp );
    _ES = FP_SEG( (void far *)&CmdPkt );
    _BX = FP_OFF( (void far *)&CmdPkt );
    (*driver)();                      /* set up the packet address    */

    tmp = drvptr->introfs;           /* INTERRUPT pointer in driver   */
    driver = MK_FP( FP_SEG( drvptr ), tmp );
    (*driver)();                      /* do the initialization        */


    /* In the first edition version of DEVLOD, this function checked
     * the status code in the command packet to determine whether the
     * installation had failed. Actually, the status code is NOT
     * checked by DOS itself! Thanks to Geoff Chappell for pointing
     * out that SYSINIT does not check the status returned by drivers
     * after initialization -- a block device driver is not retained if
     * its unit count is found to be zero, while a character device
     * should set its break address to offset 0 in its load segment.
     */
    return( drvptr->attr & CHAR_DEV ?
            MK_FP(CmdPkt.brkseg,CmdPkt.brkofs) != MK_FP(FP_SEG(drvptr), 0) :
            CmdPkt.nunits != 0 );
}


/*  This routine looks far more complicated than it actually is.
 *  It's used only when block-device drivers are being installed,
 *  and does the housekeeping of DPBs and CDS entries that such
 *  devices require.  Major changes were made here in the second
 *  edition of the program, to accomodate changes in DPB size that
 *  happened at Version 4.0 but went unnoticed until DOS5 appeared.
 *  Special thanks are due Dan B. Wright, Nathaniel Polish, and
 *  Geoff Chappell for spotting problem areas here.
 *
 *  This routine returns FALSE if all goes well, or TRUE if any
 *  error condition is detected.
 */
BOOL Put_Blk_Dev ( void )
{ int newdrv;
  int i;
  int retval = TRUE;          /* pre-set for failure               */
  int BufferSize;
  int unit = 0;
  LPDPB oldDPB, newDPB, endmark = (LPDPB)0xFFFFFFFFL;
  LPCDS cds;
  LPDDVR newdriver = (LPDDVR)MK_FP( _psp+0x10, 0 );

  if ((Next_Drive() == -1) || CmdPkt.nunits == 0)
    return retval;              /* cannot install block driver      */
  if (CmdPkt.brkofs != 0)       /* align to next paragraph          */
  {
    CmdPkt.brkseg += (CmdPkt.brkofs >> 4) + 1;
    CmdPkt.brkofs = 0;
  }
  while( CmdPkt.nunits-- )  /* repeat this loop for each unit       */
  {
    if ((newdrv = Next_Drive()) == -1)
      return TRUE;        /* no room for another drive, quit        */
    if( nblkdrs )                 /* if not a null pointer,         */
      (*nblkdrs)++;               /* ...tally into drive counter    */

#ifdef ORIGINAL
    /* Tell DOS to get the DPB of the last drive in CDS.  This
     * technique, used in the first version of DEVLOD, creates a
     * problem if the final drive is a JOINed or SUBSTed entry in
     * the list.  The alternate method of finding the last DPB is
```

```
    *  not subject to this problem, but may be a bit slower.  The
    *  address of the last-drive DPB is saved in "oldDPB".
    */
   _AH = 0x32;            /* get DPB of last drive in CDS        */
   _DL = newdrv;
   GO_DOS;
   _AX = _DS;             /* save segment to make the pointer    */
   FIXDS;
   oldDPB = MK_FP(_AX, _BX);   /* this is base address of DPB  */
#else
   /*  Trace out entire chain each time around the loop.  While
    *  this is possibly slower than the original method, it will
    *  not be deceived by CDS entries.  The address of the last
    *  DPB is saved in "oldDPB".  Note that only the offset words
    *  of the link pointers are compared; DOS itself does not put
    *  "endmark" in the segment word, although this routine does.
    */
   oldDPB = LOLptr->dpb;         /* always start at first DPB     */
   if (_osmajor < 4)             /* trace through to the end      */
     while( (WORD)oldDPB->ver.v3.next != (WORD)endmark )
       oldDPB = oldDPB->ver.v3.next;
   else
     while( (WORD)oldDPB->ver.v45.next != (WORD)endmark )
       oldDPB = oldDPB->ver.v45.next;
#endif

   /*  Tell DOS to create the DPB, passing it BPB info from a
    *  list of near pointers passed back by the driver.  Note
    *  that DS must be set after all memory references are done,
    *  because it's used to access the globals.  Similarly, AX
    *  must be set after all segment registers, because it is
    *  used to load the segreg.
    */
   newDPB = (LPDPB)MK_FP( CmdPkt.brkseg, 0 );
   _SI = *(WORD far *)MK_FP(CmdPkt.inpseg, CmdPkt.inpofs);
   _ES = CmdPkt.brkseg;       /* ES:BP is DPB address to use */
   _DS = CmdPkt.inpseg;       /* DS:SI is adr of BPB to read */
   PUSH_BP;                   /* save stack-frame pointer    */
   _BP = 0;                   /* DPB offset value            */
   _AH = 0x53;                /* build the DPB for this unit */
   GO_DOS;
   POP_BP;                    /* restore stack-frame pointer */
   FIXDS;

   /*  Check to be sure that block sector size is acceptable.
    *  If bigger than BUFFERS were built for, refuse to install
    *  the driver...  No such check was made in the original
    *  version of this program. Geoff Chappell spotted the omission.
    */
   switch( _osmajor )         /* get BUFFERS size from LOL    */
   {                          /* location in LOL will vary... */
   case  2:
     BufferSize = LOLptr->ver.v2.secsiz;
     break;
   case  3:
     if (_osminor == 0)
       BufferSize = LOLptr->ver.v30.secsiz;
     else
       BufferSize = LOLptr->ver.v31up.secsiz;
     break;
   case  4:
   case  5:
     BufferSize = LOLptr->ver.v31up.secsiz;
     break;
   default:
```

```
        Err_Halt ( "Unknown version of DOS!");
     }
     if( newDPB->bytes_per_sect > BufferSize )
        return TRUE;                          /* get out if too big   */

     /*  Now set the DPB address into the old last-DPB's link
      *  address field ("next" pointer).
      */
     if (_osmajor < 4)             /* link new DPB to chain       */
        oldDPB->ver.v3.next = newDPB;
     else
        oldDPB->ver.v45.next = newDPB;

     /*  Set up the Current Directory Structure for this drive and
      *  tag it as a physical drive.  Clear IFS area if DOS V4 or
      *  higher.
      */
     if (_osmajor > 2)             /* Version 2 did not use CDS   */
       { cds = (LPCDS)(CDSbase + (newdrv * CDSsize));
         cds->flags = CDS_PHYS;  /* defined in UNDOCDOS.H file   */
         cds->dpb = newDPB;        /* set DPB adr into CDS        */
         cds->in.loc.start_cluster = 0xFFFF; /* not accessed yet */
         cds->in.loc.ffff = -1L;
         cds->slash_offset = 2;  /* start in root directory       */
         if (_osmajor > 3)        /* zero out IFS stuff           */
           { *((WORD far *)(&(cds->slash_offset))+1) = 0;
             *((WORD far *)(&(cds->slash_offset))+2) = 0;
             *((WORD far *)(&(cds->slash_offset))+3) = 0;
             *((BYTE far *)(&(cds->slash_offset))+8) = 0;
           }
       }

     /*  Finally, set up pointers for the DPB and the driver so
      *  that they can find each other, and adjust space
      *  reservations so that the DPB won't be wiped out upon
      *  return to DOS.  Step the BPB list pointer in case the
      *  driver has multiple units.
      */
     newDPB->drive = newdrv;      /* set in drive number         */
     newDPB->unit = unit++;       /* and also the unit number    */
     if (_osmajor < 4)            /* Versions 2 and 3 are alike   */
       { newDPB->ver.v3.driver = newdriver;
             newDPB->ver.v3.next = endmark;
         CmdPkt.brkseg += 2;      /* was 32 bytes, exact fit      */
       }
     else                         /* Versions 4 and 5 are alike   */
       { newDPB->ver.v45.driver = newdriver;
         newDPB->ver.v45.next = endmark;
         CmdPkt.brkseg += 3;      /* 33 bytes each now            */
       }
     CmdPkt.inpofs += 2;          /* point to next BPB pointer    */
    }                             /* end of nunits loop           */
  return FALSE;                   /* all went okay                */
}


/*  This function is called for a character driver only. It searches
 *  every entry in the SFT, looking for any reference to the named
 *  driver, and if such a reference is found, modifies 6 bytes in the
 *  SFT entry to point to the just-added new driver. This is necessary
 *  for proper operation of the critical error handler. It is based on
 *  code by Dan Winter, published in the July, 1992 issue of Dr. Dobb's
 *  Journal, but Dan's original code was not compatible with DEVLOD.
 *
 *  SFT_size is established by the GetList() function earlier.
 */
```

```
void FixSFT ( void )
{ LPSFTB blk, next_blk;          /* use typedefs for simplicity  */
  LPSFT sft;
  WORD num_items;

  for( next_blk = LOLptr->sft;              /* first SFT block      */
       (WORD)next_blk != 0xFFFF; )          /* check all blocks     */
     { blk = next_blk;                      /* start this block     */
       next_blk = blk->next;               /* link for next one    */
       num_items = blk->here;              /* get size of block    */
       sft = &(blk->first);               /* first SFT in it now  */
       while( num_items-- > 0 )            /* test all items here  */
         { if( sft->ver.v2.nusers )        /* is this SFT in use?  */
             if( TestName( drvptr, sft ))        /* yes, match?     */
               ChgSFT( sft, drvptr );      /* yes, fix the pointer */
           (char far *)sft += SFT_size;    /* to next item in list */
         }
     }
}


/*  This function is called only when the driver has been fully
 *  installed with no detected errors.  If the driver is a block
 *  device, Put_Blk_Dev() is called to create its drive letter
 *  and CDS and DPB structures; otherwise the CON and CLOCK$
 *  pointers in the List of Lists are updated as applicable.  If
 *  the block device installation fails, DEVLOD quits without
 *  linking the driver into the DOS chain.  Otherwise this driver
 *  is put at the head of the chain right after NUL, and the program
 *  returns to DOS, leaving the driver resident.  In either case,
 *  this function will never return to the main() procedure.
 */
void Get_Out ( void )
{ WORD temp;

  temp = drvptr->attr;            /* attribute word              */
  if( (temp & CHAR_DEV) == 0 )    /* if block device, set up tbls */
    { if( Put_Blk_Dev() )         /* fails if cannot do so       */
           Err_Halt( "Could not install block device" );
    }
  else                            /* not block, check for updates */
    { if( (temp & IS_STDIN) )
        LOLptr->con = drvptr;     /* this is for CTRL-C checking  */
        else if( (temp & IS_CLOCK) )
        LOLptr->clock = drvptr;   /* this is for fast time access */
        FixSFT();                 /* Dan Winter's fix for SFT     */
    }

  Fix_DOS_Chain();                /* all okay so patch into DOS   */

  _ES = PSPptr->EnvSeg;           /* release environment space    */
  _AH = 0x49;
  GO_DOS;
  PSPptr->EnvSeg = 0;             /* zero out the address in PSP   */

  /* then set up regs for KEEP function, and go resident         */
  temp = (CmdPkt.brkofs + 15);    /* normalize the offset          */
  temp >>= 4;
  temp += CmdPkt.brkseg;          /* add the segment address      */
  temp -= _psp;                   /* convert to paragraph count    */
  _DX = (WORD)temp;               /* paragraphs to retain          */
  _AX = 0x3100;                   /* KEEP function of DOS          */
  GO_DOS;                         /* won't come back from here!    */
}

void main( void )                 /* usual argc, argv not used!    */
```

```
{ PSPptr = (LPPSP)MK_FP( _psp, 0 );     /* create global ptr    */
  if( !Get_Driver_Name() )
    Err_Halt( "Device driver name required.");
  Move_Loader();                  /* move code high and jump    */
  Load_Drvr();                    /* bring driver into freed RAM */
  Get_List();                     /* get DOS internal variables */
  if(Init_Drvr())                 /* let driver do its thing    */
      Get_Out();                  /* check init status, go TSR  */
  else
      Err_Halt( "Driver initialization failed." );
}
```

MOVUP.ASM

The small assembly language module MOVUP (Figure 7-29) contains only one function, movup().
Recall that, in order not to fragment memory, DEVLOD moves itself up above the area into which it
loads the driver. The program accomplishes this feat with movup().

Figure 7-29. MOVUP.ASM

```
        NAME    movup
;[]-------------------------------------------------------------[]
;|      MOVUP.ASM -- helper code for DEVLOD.C                    |
;|      Copyright 1990 by Jim Kyle - All Rights Reserved        |
;[]-------------------------------------------------------------[]

_TEXT   SEGMENT BYTE PUBLIC 'CODE'
_TEXT   ENDS

_DATA   SEGMENT WORD PUBLIC 'DATA'
_DATA   ENDS

_BSS    SEGMENT WORD PUBLIC 'BSS'
_BSS    ENDS

DGROUP  GROUP   _TEXT, _DATA, _BSS

ASSUME  CS:_TEXT, DS:DGROUP

_TEXT   SEGMENT BYTE PUBLIC 'CODE'

;-------------------------------------------------------------------
;       movup( src, dst, nbytes )
;       src and dst are far pointers. area overlap is NOT okay
;-------------------------------------------------------------------
        PUBLIC  _movup

_movup  PROC    NEAR
        push    bp
        mov     bp, sp
        push    si
        push    di
        lds     si,[bp+4]               ; source
        les     di,[bp+8]               ; destination
        mov     bx,es                   ; save dest segment
        mov     cx,[bp+12]              ; byte count
        cld
        rep     movsb                   ; move everything to high ram
        mov     ss,bx                   ; fix stack segment ASAP
        mov     ds,bx                   ; adjust DS too
        pop     di
        pop     si
        mov     sp, bp
        pop     bp
        pop     dx                      ; Get return address
```

```
        push    bx                              ; Put segment up first
        push    dx                              ; Now a far address on stack
        retf
_movup  ENDP

_TEXT   ENDS

        end
```

TESTNAME.ASM

New in this modified version is the assembly file TESTNAME.ASM (Figure 7-30), which provides
two small routines that greatly simplify the FixSFT patching procedure, described by Dan Winter in
his July, 1992 letter to *Dr. Dobb's Journal*. TestName( ) takes far pointers to the new driver and to
the current SFT item; it then compares the 8-byte name fields, returning one if all eight bytes match
and zero otherwise. ChgSFT( ) takes the same two far pointers and corrects the affected fields of the
SFT entry to reflect the new driver's address.

Figure 7-30. TESTNAME.ASM

```
;-------------------------------------------------------------------
;        int TestName( LPDDVR, LPSFT )
;        src and dst are far pointers, TRUE if 8-byte match found
;-------------------------------------------------------------------
        PUBLIC  _TestName

_TestName       PROC      NEAR
        push    bp                      ; save regs
        mov     bp,sp
        push    si
        push    di
        push    ds
        lds     si,[bp+4]               ; get pointer to driver header
        add     si,10                   ; offset to name field
        les     di,[bp+8]               ; pointer to SFT start
        add     di,32                   ; offset to name field
        mov     cx,8                    ; name length
        cld
        repz    cmpsb                   ; go while equal
        mov     al,[si-01]              ; last chars tested
        sub     al,[es:di-01]
        add     al,0FFh                 ; CY if nonzero
        sbb     al,al                   ; 0 or FF
        inc     al                      ; 1 if match, else 0
        pop     ds
        pop     di
        pop     si
        pop     bp
        ret
_TestName       ENDP


;-------------------------------------------------------------------
;        void ChgSFT( LPSFT, LPDDVR )
;        modifies SFT to point to new driver
;-------------------------------------------------------------------
        PUBLIC  _ChgSFT

_ChgSFT PROC      NEAR
        push    bp                      ; save regs
        mov     bp,sp
        push    di
        les     di,[bp+4]               ; get SFT address into ES:DI
        add     di,7                    ; offset to v.type.devdrvr field
        mov     ax,[bp+8]               ; offset of LPDDVR
```

```
        mov     dx,[bp+10]          ; segment of LPDDVR
        cld
        stosw                       ; store offset
        xchg    ax,dx
        stosw                       ; store segment
        xchg    ax,dx
        stosw                       ; store offset
        pop     di
        pop     bp
        ret
_ChgSFT ENDP
```

While both of these functions normally would be more easily done using C library functions such as strncmp(), DEVLOD's need to use far pointers within near procedures made it much easier to perform the tasks in assembly language. By building the field offsets into this code, I was also able to eliminate a number of lines filled with confusing casts, although at least one remains in the FixSFT() function of DEVLOD.C because the size of the SFT depends upon the DOS version, making it necessary to defeat C's pointer arithmetic by casting the SFT pointer to (char far *) before adding the table size.

C0.ASM

Finally, start-up code is in C0.ASM, which has been extensively modified from start-up code provided by Borland with Turbo C. This, or similar, code forms part of every C program and provides the linkage between the DOS command line and the C program itself. Normal start-up code, however, does much more than this stripped-down version. This code parses the argument list, sets up pointers to the environment, and arranges things so that library functions can operate. It also arranges for automatic linking of the runtime library routines, which DEVLOD cannot tolerate.

Since our program has no need for any of these actions, our C0.ASM module omits them. What's left just determines the DOS version in use and trims the RAM used by the program down to the minimum. Then the module calls main(), PUSHes the returned value onto the stack, and calls exit(). Actually, if the program succeeds in loading a device driver, it never returns from main().

One additional function is performed. This module establishes global variables, _osmajor, _osminor, and _psp, on which DEVLOD depends for operation. Values for these variables are obtained from DOS itself, using documented capabilities, and stored in the variables before control transfers to main().

Because our C0.ASM module is more concerned with establishing an environment within which DEVLOD can run than it is with the actual objectives of DEVLOD itself, we've omitted its listing from the text. Both the source and the OBJ file are included on the companion diskette, however.

Make File

Since this sample program includes two assembly language modules, in addition to the C source, a MAKEFILE greatly simplifies its creation. Figure 7-31 shows one for use with Borland's MAKE utility.

Figure 7-31. The DEVLOD Makefile

```
# makefile for DEVLOD.COM - created 05/23/90 - jk
#                     last revised 08/20/92 - jk
# can substitute other assemblers for TASM, TCC for BCC

AS = D:\BC\BIN\TASM
CC = D:\BC\BIN\BCC
CL = D:\BC\BIN\TLINK

devlod.com:     devlod.obj c0.obj movup.obj testname.obj
        $(CL) c0 movup testname devlod /c/m/t,devlod.com

c0.obj  :       c0.asm
```

```
              $(AS) c0 /t/mx/la;

movup.obj:         movup.asm
              $(AS) movup /t/mx/la;

testname.obj:    testname.asm
              $(AS) testname /t/mx/la;

devlod.obj:        devlod.c
              $(CC) -c -ms -P- devlod.c
```

You do, of course, need to change the three macro definitions to reflect the drive and path for your own compiler installation. Then you can simply type "MAKE /FDEVLOD.MAK". The /t option switch included in the TLINK command line ensures that the linker generates a COM file, rather than the more usual EXE format.

How Well Does DEVLOD Work?

A fitting conclusion to this chapter is to use some of the utilities developed earlier, UDMEM and DEV, to see what my system looks like after I've loaded up a couple of device drivers with DEVLOD. The report is shown in Figure 7-32.

Figure 7-32. Testing DEVLOD

```
D:\UDOS2\CHAP7> devlod c:\ramdrive.sys 512 /e

Microsoft RAMDrive version 3.06 virtual disk E:
    Disk size: 512k
    Sector size: 512 bytes
    Allocation unit: 1 sectors
    Directory entries: 64

D:\UDOS2\CHAP7> devlod c:\ansi-uv.sys

D:\UDOS2\CHAP7> udmem
Seg    Owner   Size
0253   0008    092A ( 37536)    DOS Data Segment
               Seg  Size Type
               ----  ----  -----------------
               0254 0041 Device Driver (386MAX)
               0296 0015 Device Driver (386LOAD)
               02AC 0741 Device Driver (SSTORDRV) [26 FA FE ]
               09EE 0015 Device Driver (386LOAD)
               0A04 005D System File Tables
               0A62 0005 FCBs
               0A68 0020 Buffers
               0A89 0037 CDS Table
               0AC1 00BC Stacks [02 0A 0B 0C 0D 0E 70 72 73 74 76]
0B7E   0008    0004 (    64)    DOS Code area
0B83   0B84    0010 (   256)    Env at D314
0B94   0000    0005 (    80)    free
0B9A   0B9B    0147 (  5232)    No Env Segment   /f:2048 /l:20
0CE2   0CEF    000B (   176)
0CEE   0CEF    0010 (   256)    Env at DA36
0CFF   0DDF    000B (   176)
0D0B   0000    0001 (    16)    free
0D0D   0D0E    005A (  1440)    No Env Segment  c:\ramdrive.sys 512 /E
0D68   0D69    0075 (  1872)    No Env Segment  c:\ansi-uv.sys [1B 29 2F ]
0DDE   0DDF    1268 ( 75392)    Env at 0D00    D:\UDOS2\CHAP7\UDMEM.EXE  [00 E5 F7 FF ]
2047   0000    7FB7 (523120)    free [30 E6 E9 EC EF F4 F5 F9]
9FFF                            End of conventional RAM
       UMB Chain
C800   FFFF    058E ( 22752)    386LOADed Driver [13 15 28 ]
CD8F   FFFA    0004 (    64)    386MAX UMB control block
```

```
CD94     FFFE     0205 (   8272)    386MAX UMB
CF9A     FFFA     0004 (     64)    386MAX UMB control block
CF9F     FFFE     0022 (    544)    386MAX UMB
CFC2     FFFA     0004 (     64)    386MAX UMB control block
CFC7     FFFE     0022 (    544)    386MAX UMB
CFEA     FFFA     0004 (     64)    386MAX UMB control block
CFEF     FFFE     0042 (   1056)    386MAX UMB
D032     FFFA     0004 (     64)    386MAX UMB control block
D037     FFFE     0210 (   8448)    386MAX UMB
D248     FFFA     0004 (     64)    386MAX UMB control block
D24D     FFFE     00C0 (   3072)    C:\4D4\4DOS.COM [2E ]
D30E     FFFA     0004 (     64)    386MAX UMB control block
D313     FFFE     0020 (    512)    386MAX UMB
D334     D33C     0006 (     96)
D33B     D33C     04CD (  19664)    Env at D80A     C:\UV\UV.COM [10 ]
D809     D33C     0002 (     32)
D80C     D814     0006 (     96)    [20 21 27 ]
D813     D814     01AD (   6864)    Env at D9C2       D:\UTILS\CTRLALT.COM   [08 09 ]
D9C1     D814     0002 (     32)
D9C4     FFFA     0004 (     64)    386MAX UMB control block
D9C9     FFFE     0066 (   1632)    386MAX UMB [22 23 24 ]
DA30     FFFA     0004 (     64)    386MAX UMB control block
DA35     FFFE     0020 (    512)    386MAX UMB
DA56     0000     05A8 (  23168)    free
DFFF     FFFD     1200 (  73728)    386MAX locked-out area
F200     FFFF     0059 (   1424)    386LOADed Driver
F25A     0000     05A4 (  23104)    free
F7FF     FFFD     0400 (  16384)    386MAX locked-out area
FC00     FFFF     00AD (   2768)    386LOADed Driver [40 67 ]
FCAE     FCB6     0006 (     96)
FCB5     FCB6     0042 (   1056)    Env at FCF9       C:\4D4\KSTACK.COM       [16 ]
FCF8     FCB6     0002 (     32)
FCFB     0000     0004 (     64)    free
FD00                                End of UMB Chain

D:\UDOS2\CHAP7> dev
NUL
CON
Block: 1 unit(s)
CON
Block: 1 unit(s)
CACHE$$$
386MAX$$
EMMXXXX0
CON
AUX
PRN
CLOCK$
Block: 3 unit(s)
COM1
LPT1
LPT2
LPT3
COM2
COM3
COM4
```

In Figure 7-32, the output from UDMEM shows quite clearly that my device drivers really are resident in memory. Meanwhile, the output from DEV confirms that they are linked into the DOS device chain. For example, the first "CON" is ANSI-UV.SYS, and the first block device is RAM-DRIVE.SYS. Of course, the real test is that, after loading RAMDRIVE.SYS and ANSI-UV.SYS, I had an additional drive, created by RAMDRIVE.SYS; programs that assumed the presence of ANSI.SYS suddenly started producing reasonable output. And, of course, I had somewhat less memory.

It should be noted that some device drivers appear not to be properly loaded by DEVLOD. These include some memory managers and drivers that use extended memory. For example, Microsoft's XMS driver HIMEM.SYS often crashes the system if you attempt to load it with DEVLOD. This isn't amazing, considering that HIMEM.SYS, if installed, is documented to require loading before any other memory manager.

Furthermore, while DEVLOD VDISK.SYS definitely works in that a valid RAM disk is created, other programs that check for the presence of VDISK, such as protected mode DOS extenders, often fail mysteriously when VDISK has been loaded in this unusual fashion. Again, VDISK is such an ill-behaved program that Microsoft lists it as being incompatible with Windows 3.1 under any circumstances, so discrepancies are to be expected.

Jay Lowe has reported that a Trantor SCSI driver appears to load through DEVLOD without any detected errors, but that attempts to access the associated drive fail as if the driver were not there. Obviously some mysteries remain to be solved here. However, in the vast majority of cases DEVLOD should give you no problems. The few cases we've run across that give trouble represent a limited condition and are not representative of most device drivers.

For another perspective on loading drivers, see the article by Giles Todd, "Installing MS-DOS Device Drivers from the Command Line," published in the British magazine *.EXE* (August, 1989). For background on DOS device drivers in general, two excellent books are the classic *Writing MS-DOS Device Drivers*, Second Edition, by Robert S. Lai (Reading, MA: Addison-Wesley, 1992) and *Writing DOS Device Drivers in C*, by Phillip M. Adams and Clovis L. Tondo (Englewood Cliffs, NJ: Prentice Hall, 1990).

Many of the complexities of loading block devices—in particular, the importance of updating the CDS—become clear in the next chapter, where we discuss the DOS file system.

## CHAPTER 8

The DOS File System
and Network Redirector

by Jim Kyle, David Maxey, and Andrew Schulman

The file system is an almost irreplaceable part of MS-DOS. While most successful PC software bypasses many of DOS's services and goes directly to the hardware to produce screen output or read the keyboard, few programs spurn the DOS file system when it comes to reading and writing files. Even software like Microsoft's VFAT.386 from Windows for Workgroups (WfW) 3.11 and "Chicago" (DOS 7, Windows 4), which bypasses the file system code in MS-DOS, still closely emulate the behavior of DOS.

Actually, there are two DOS file systems. One, known as the FAT (File Allocation Table) file system from the name of its key data structure, is the logical structure that DOS uses for media such as floppy disks and hard drives. The FAT is probably the world's best-known DOS internal data structure, having entered popular culture through Peter Norton's book, *Inside the IBM PC*. Even some books for non-programmers discuss the internal FAT structures, as these are needed for disk recovery.

The other file system, introduced in DOS 3.1, is known as the MS-DOS network redirector. Whereas most DOS programming interfaces consist of INT 21h or INT 2Fh functions that a program calls, the network redirector is, instead, a set of functions that MS-DOS itself calls. For example, when performing a file open operation, DOS issues an INT 2Fh with AX=1116h. Any program can intercept INT 2Fh AH=11h and thereby make itself into a network redirector. When DOS tries to open a file, it ends up calling into the program. The program can handle the file open call itself, for example by sending (redirecting) the request over a network to a file server. Another way to do this, which NetWare versions prior to 4.0 use, is to hook INT 21h directly and watch for any file-related calls. However, as you'll see, there are some advantages to using the network redirector.

Thus, the network redirector is a set of *hooks* in MS-DOS that DOS uses for mapping a DOS directory hierarchy onto alien (non-FAT) systems such as network file servers and CD-ROM devices. Drives created with the network redirector do not require FATs or Disk Parameter Blocks. While networks are a tremendously important part of the DOS file system—and one that discussions of DOS internals frequently ignore—the network redirector is somewhat misnamed. It isn't just for networks anymore. The network redirector is a mechanism, albeit a somewhat primitive one, for creating installable file systems.

All drives, whether FAT-based or non-FAT, have entries in a key DOS data structure called the Current Directory Structure (CDS). An important exception to this statement is Novell NetWare, which prior to version 4.0 bypassed the CDS. Many programs in this chapter manipulate the CDS in some way.

The CDS, together with many other DOS structures we discuss in this chapter, is shared by all programs. Since DOS is normally thought of as a single-tasking operating system, having one global structure doesn't seem like a problem. However, as DOS is increasingly called upon to run multi-tasking software such as Windows, the assumption that only one program is using the CDS at a time becomes more and more inaccurate. Almost all DOS internal structures are global and non-reentrant, thereby seriously restricting DOS's ability to perform true multitasking. That's one reason why multitasking versions of DOS, such as General Software's Embedded DOS, avoid using such structures (see Steve Jones, "DOS Meets Real-Time," *Embedded Systems Programming*, February 1992). This is also why Windows employs "instance data." Recall from Chapter 1 that Windows Enhanced mode uses instance data to create the illusion of multiple CDSs (see Figure 1-9). Clearly, it would have been better if DOS supplied multiple CDSs, but an instanced CDS is the next best thing.

In this chapter, you will read about DOS drives, directories, and files, and, as in most such discussions, we begin with physical magnetic media and work our way to the directory structure seen by a typical DOS user. However, this chapter takes a somewhat different slant from most discussions of the DOS file system, because, having shown how DOS applies a logical ordering to physical media, it then proceeds to show how to apply this same logical ordering to things other than hard drives and floppy disks. Any file system is a fiction. This chapter emphasizes how generic the DOS notion of a drive is. It isn't just for physical media or even RAM disks anymore.

There are several additional layers of complexity to the DOS file system. First, as with any moderately sophisticated file system, there are *buffers*. Disk caches such as SmartDrive introduce another level of performance enhancing indirection. And of course the entire FAT file system doesn't rest directly on top of the physical media, but instead goes through block device drivers (see Chapter 7). So long as it provides the expected interface (such as the ability to read a given sector number), the block device driver can implement a file system as it sees fit. And don't forget disk compression software such as Stacker and Microsoft's DoubleSpace (DOS 6.0). We discuss Stacker and DoubleSpace later in this chapter.

This chapter contains an enormous number of sample programs, giving it more of a cookbook approach than other parts of the book. The chapter's pièce de résistance is PHANTOM.C, a complete example of using the DOS network redirector interface to create a new drive. Readers of the first edition of *Undocumented DOS* should note that we have completely rewritten the Phantom in C instead of Turbo Pascal. And it is now a full-blown XMS RAM disk, rather than a "proof of concept" toy. Other code in this chapter includes routines to

- Detect DoubleSpace, Stacker drives, and RAM disks
- Get the compression ratio for a DoubleSpace drive
- Free up orphaned file handles
- Turn a cluster number into a file name or vice versa
- Derive a filename from a file handle
- Increase the number of process file handles
- Determine the FILES= and BUFFERS= values
- Set or turn off drive letters
- Walk the 12-bit and 16-bit File Allocation Table
- Walk the Current Directory Structure
- Walk the System File Table
- Get the true (canonical) name of a file
- List all the open files for any given process

What ties all this together is an emphasis on the logical rather than the physical aspects of the DOS file system. But first let's take a quick overview of the file system, followed by a look at its physical aspects.

A Quick Overview of the System

To put all the bits and pieces of the DOS File System in perspective, we need to trace the significant actions that take place when DOS services a request to read from or write to a file. One good way to exercise these services is to use the COPY command, which reads the content in one file and writes it to another.

One of our major tools for delving into the internal workings of DOS is INTRSPY, and this program is what we use to see what happens inside the COPY command. Listing 8-1 shows the INTRSPY script we prepared, based on disassembles of earlier versions of COMMAND.COM and the DOS kernel itself. This script includes such intermediary interfaces as INT 25h/26h, INT 2Fh AH=12h, and the ROM BIOS INT 13h. With INTRSPY 2.0, we can even trace right into the device driver Interrupt and Strategy routines, so DISK.SCR includes DD.SCR from Chapter 5 (Listing 5-3).

Incidentally, while we say that INT 13h is the ROM BIOS disk interrupt, it's important to note that MS-DOS hooks INT 13h ahead of the BIOS; you can see this by running INTCHAIN 13/0/0/0/0 (see Chapter 6).

For a more complicated example, see Chapter 5, which uses INTRSPY to examine in detail the process of formatting a floppy disk.

Listing 8-1: DISK.SCR

```
; DISK.SCR
; usage: cmdspy compile disk [drive] [command]
; example: cmdspy compile disk c: command /c copy foo.bar bar.foo > disk.log

; DOS 4+/Compaq DOS 3.31+ >32M partition
structure big fields
    sector (dword,hex)
    num (word,hex)
    addr (dword,ptr)

intercept 21h
    function 32h
        on_entry output "2132: Get DPB drive " dl
        on_exit  output "2132: done"
    function 3Ch
        on_entry output "213C: Create File: " (ds:dx->byte,asciiz,64)
        on_exit  output "213C: done, file is " ax
    function 6Ch
        on_entry output "216C: Ext Open/Create: " (ds:si->byte,asciiz,64)
            output "AX=" ax " BX=" bx " CX=" cx " DX=" dx
        on_exit  output "216C: done, "
            if (cflag==1) sameline "Error " cx
            if (cflag==0) sameline "file is " ax
            if (cx==1) sameline ", opened"
            if (cx==2) sameline ", created"
            if (cx==3) sameline ", replaced"
    function 3Dh
        on_entry output "213D: Open File: " (ds:dx->byte,asciiz,64)
        on_exit  output "213D: done, file is " ax
    function 3Eh
        on_entry output "213E: Close File " bx
        on_exit  output "213E: done: File " bx
    function 3Fh
        on_entry output "213F: Read File " BX
        on_exit  output "213F: done: File " bx
    function 40h
        on_entry output "2140: Write File " bx (ds:dx->byte,asciiz,cx)
        on_exit  output "2140: done: File " bx
    function 44h
        subfunction 00h
            on_entry output "214400: IOCTL drive " bl " Attribs "
            on_exit  sameline dx
        subfunction 09h
            on_entry output "214409: IOCTL drive " bl " Remote? "
        subfunction 0dh
            on_entry output "21440D: IOCTL drive " bl
                if (cl == 40h) sameline " [40: Set Device Parameters]"
                if (cl == 41h) sameline " [41: Write Track]"
```

```
            if (cl == 42h) sameline " [42: Format and Verify Track]"
            if (cl == 60h) sameline " [60: Get Device Parameters]"
            if (cl == 61h) sameline " [61: Read Track]"
        subfunction 0fh
            on_entry output "21440F: IOCTL Set Logical Drive " bl
            on_exit if (cflag == 0) sameline " ==> " al

intercept 25h
    on_entry
        output "25: Abs Disk Read drv " al ", at sectr "
        if (cx == 0FFFFh)
            sameline (ds:bx->big.sector) ", " (ds:bx->big.num) " sctrs"
        if (cx != 0FFFFh) sameline dx ", " cx " sctrs"
    on_exit if (cflag==1) sameline " [fail]"

intercept 26h
    on_entry
        output "26: Abs Disk Write drv " al ", at sectr "
        if (cx == 0FFFFh)
            sameline (ds:bx->big.sector) ", " (ds:bx->big.num) " sctrs"
        if (cx != 0FFFFh) sameline dx ", " cx " sctrs"
    on_exit if (cflag==1) sameline " [fail]"

intercept 13h
    function 0 on_entry output "1300: Recalibrate drive " dl
    function 1 on_exit output "1301: Disk system status " al
    function 2
        on_entry
            output "1302: Read " al " sctrs: drv " dl ", head " dh
                ", sctr " cl ", trk " ch " to " es ":" bx
        on_exit if (cflag==1) sameline " - FAILED (" ah ")"
    function 3
        on_entry
            output "1303: Write " al " sctrs: drv " dl ", head " dh
                ", sctr " cl ", trk " ch " from " es ":" bx
        on_exit if (cflag==1) sameline " - FAILED (" ah ")"
    function 4
        on_entry
            output "1304: Verify " al " sctrs: drv " dl ", head " dh
                ", sctr " cl ", trk " ch
        on_exit if (cflag==1) sameline " - FAILED (" ah ")"
    function 5
        on_entry
            output "1305: Format " al " sctrs: drv " dl ", head " dh
                ", sctr " cl ", trk " ch
        on_exit if (cflag==1) sameline " - FAILED (" ah ")"
    function 8 on_entry output "1308: Get drive params for " dl
    function 0ch on_entry output "130C: Seek cyl " ch " drv " dl " head " dh
    function 0dh on_entry output "130D: Alternate reset drive " dl
    function 10h on_entry output "1310: Test drive " dl
    function 15h on_entry output "1315: Get type drv " dl
    function 16h on_entry output "1316: Get media change drv " dl
    function 17h on_entry output "1317: Set type drv " dl ": " al
    function 18h on_entry output "1318: Set media type drv " dl

include "dd.scr %1 %2 %3 %4 %5 %6 %7 %8 %9"   ; DD.SCR does RUN, REPORT
```

This INTRSPY script requires a command line with a drive letter and a DOS command. For example:

```
C:\UNDOC2\CHAP8>intrspy -R20480
C:\UNDOC2\CHAP8>cmdspy compile disk c: command /c copy foo.bar bar.foo
```

In this example, FOO.BAR is a tiny file containing only the line "this is foo.bar". Figure 8-1 shows part of the INTRSPY output when copying FOO.BAR to BAR.FOO.

Figure 8-1: INTRSPY Results for a DOS COPY

```
216C: Ext Open/Create: FOO.BAR
AX=6C00 BX=0040 CX=0000 DX=0101
01 - media check
04 - input
1302: Read 09 sctrs: drv 80, head 08, sctr 0B, trk 03 to 17D5:0000
04 - input
1302: Read 03 sctrs: drv 80, head 0A, sctr 4D, trk 36 to 1003:0000
1302: Read 01 sctrs: drv 80, head 08, sctr 4B, trk 37 to 1063:0000
04 - input
04 - input
04 - input
216C: done, file is 0005, opened
214400: IOCTL drive 05 Attribs 0042
213E: Close File 0005
213E: done: File 0005
01 - media check
01 - media check
216C: Ext Open/Create: FOO.BAR
AX=6C00 BX=0040 CX=0000 DX=0101
01 - media check
216C: done, file is 0005, opened
214400: IOCTL drive 05 Attribs 0042
213F: Read File 0005
04 - input
1302: Read 09 sctrs: drv 80, head 01, sctr 07, trk 04 to 16B5:0000
1302: Read 01 sctrs: drv 80, head 02, sctr 42, trk 28 to 1003:0000
213F: done: File 0005
213E: Close File 0005
213E: done: File 0005
216C: Ext Open/Create: BAR.FOO
AX=6C00 BX=0040 CX=0000 DX=0101
01 - media check
216C: done, file is 0005, opened
214400: IOCTL drive 05 Attribs 0042
213E: Close File 0005
213E: done: File 0005
01 - media check
216C: Ext Open/Create: BAR.FOO
AX=6C00 BX=0021 CX=0000 DX=0112
01 - media check
04 - input
1302: Read 09 sctrs: drv 80, head 02, sctr 08, trk 04 to 17D5:0000
08 - output
1303: Write 01 sctrs: drv 80, head 06, sctr 0A, trk 03 from 1223:0000
1303: Write 01 sctrs: drv 80, head 02, sctr 09, trk 04 from 1D1D:361C
08 - output
1303: Write 01 sctrs: drv 80, head 08, sctr 09, trk 05 from 1D1D:361C
08 - output
216C: done, file is 0005, replaced
214400: IOCTL drive 05 Attribs 0042
01 - media check
2140: Write File 0005this is foo.bar

2140: done: File 0005
214400: IOCTL drive 05 Attribs 0002
213E: Close File 0005
01 - media check
08 - output
08 - output
```

```
08 - output
08 - output
03 - ioctl input
1303: Write 01 sctrs: drv 80, head 0B, sctr 06, trk 46 from 100C:0000
1303: Write 03 sctrs: drv 80, head 0A, sctr 4D, trk 36 from 100B:0008
1303: Write 01 sctrs: drv 80, head 08, sctr 4B, trk 37 from 106B:0008
1303: Write 05 sctrs: drv 80, head 02, sctr 09, trk 04 from 17F5:0000
1303: Write 05 sctrs: drv 80, head 08, sctr 09, trk 05 from 17F5:0000
213E: done: File 0005
2140: Write File 0001           1
04 - input
1302: Read 01 sctrs: drv 80, head 0B, sctr 05, trk 46 to 1003:0000
2140: done: File 0001
2140: Write File 0001 file(s) copied

2140: done: File 0001
```

COPY uses the relatively new function 6Ch for opening and creating files, instead of the older functions 3Ch and 3Dh. When called to open FOO.BAR, this function calls block device driver function 4 (Read), which in turn uses the BIOS INT 13h to read the root directory from the C: drive. COPY then calls IOCTL function 44h to get the file's attributes and closes the file.

Next, Figure 8-1 shows COPY open the same file again. This time, COPY reads the file's entire contents into a buffer before closing the file. Again, the command interpreter (COMMAND.COM) checks attributes immediately after performing the open. The program then calls function 3Fh to do the read; this function in turn calls BIOS to perform the actual work, though not directly, of course. Function 3Fh actually calls the block device driver's Interrupt and Strategy routines, using device driver function 4 (Read); the device driver in turn calls the BIOS. For more information on how block device drivers fit into the DOS file system, see Robert S. Lai, *Writing MS-DOS Device Drivers* (second edition), Chapters 7 and 8.

With the data read into memory, the next step is to invoke function 6Ch, by attempting to open the file for reading, to determine if the destination file BAR.FOO exists. This call succeeds, indicating that the file exists. You don't see any action to read in directory information because that information is already in the DOS buffers, so no physical disk read is required. The values function 6Ch returns indicate that BAR.FOO is open, meaning that the file already exists from a previous test.

After the usual IOCTL attribute check, COPY closes the file then immediately reopens it for writing, with bits in DX set to create or truncate the file. This time, you see several BIOS disk writes, as the Open function first releases the space the previous copy of BAR.FOO uses, updates both FATs, then modifies the directory entry to reflect a file length of zero bytes together with a new date/time stamp.

Next, COPY writes the data that was earlier read in from FOO.BAR; but as clearly seen in Figure 8-1, no actual disk action occurs during Write function 40h: "2140: done" appears immediately after entry to the function, with no intermediary calls to a device driver or the BIOS. Another IOCTL attribute check, though, indicates that writing has taken place (the attribute has changed from 0042h to 0002h). Actually, the Write function has moved the data from COMMAND.COM's buffer area to the DOS buffers, but the data has not yet made it out to the disk. Clearly, buffers play a crucial role in DOS file I/O; see BUFFERS.C in Listing 8-8.

When function 3Eh closes the file this time, DOS does all of the deferred writing. It allocates disk space, updates both FATs, writes the actual data with device-driver function 8 (Write), and finally updates the directory entry for BAR.FOO.

The final action shown in our trace are calls to the Write function to Handle 1 (stdout) to create the "1 file(s) copied" display.

All that just to copy a tiny file! And, as noted earlier, even this inside view of the COPY command was quite superficial. We didn't get into what happens with disk compression, such as Stacker or DoubleSpace, or what happens if you're using a disk cache such as SmartDrive. Still, the INTRSPY results provide a useful overview of the typical sequence of events involved in actual file I/O. Now let's look at the physical aspects of disk storage.

The DOS File System

The starting point for the FAT file system is generally the physical disk and the drive mechanism itself. These marvels of mechanical precision convert a stream of information, represented as a sequence of bits, into a corresponding sequence of magnetic flux reversals that are placed on the surface of the disk.

Someone could write entire volumes on the methods by which this is done, but probably only disk-drive designers would read them. As programmers, we are more interested in how program-oriented descriptions of data are translated into the form the actual disk hardware requires.

These translations occur in several layers. Programs organize data into a stream of bytes and store these streams into files which are later read back as streams. DOS translates our references to files into references to logical drive locations such as *drive* and *cluster*. The cluster isn't part of the physical disk structure but instead is merely a fiction maintained by the FAT code in DOS. DOS converts the cluster number into a logical sector number (LSN) for transmission to a block device driver. If the device driver supports a physical disk, it translates the LSN into the more hardware-oriented values of *track*, *head*, and *sector* for transmission to the specified drive. The BIOS and the drive controller then translate those values into sequences of pulses that select the addressed drive, position the actuator to the desired cylinder of tracks, select the specified head, and begin reading from it when the correct sector is identified. (For a detailed examination of the BIOS and drive controller, see Frank van Gilluwe's *The Undocumented PC.*)

Surfaces, Tracks, and Sectors

One starting point for gaining an understanding of the DOS file system is the surface of the magnetic medium itself, as exemplified by the familiar floppy diskette (the hard disk operates in much the same way, but with much greater precision).

In the earliest days of MS-DOS, the original IBM PC came equipped with a single-head, single-sided disk drive that had a storage capacity of 160K per disk. The head made contact with the underside of the diskette when it was placed into the drive in its normal operating position. Balancing the pressure of the head against the lower side of the diskette was a felt pressure pad that rubbed against the upper surface.

On the single active surface, the head wrote to and later read back information from one of 40 concentric tracks. The head actuator mechanism was moved in or out to position the head accurately over the desired track. The track nearest the outer edge of the disk was designated as track 00, that nearest the hub hole, as track 39.

A small index hole near the large hub hole served as a reference point to determine disk rotation. A sensor in the disk drive generated an index pulse each time this hole passed over it, and since the disk rotated at a constant speed of 300 RPM (200 milliseconds per revolution), the associated controller card could measure off sectors around the track in which to store data. These first drives contained eight sectors per track, each sector with room for 512 bytes of storage. Between sectors, an address mark and some special identification codes helped the controller verify that all was well with the drive. Thus, each track contained 8*512 bytes of data, or 4,096 bytes, and the 40 tracks held a total of 163,840 bytes, or 160K.

Before long, the single-sided drive was supplanted by a two-headed model that could read and write on both surfaces, immediately doubling the storage capacity to 320K per disk. MS-DOS 2.0 added an extra sector to the format, bringing the storage capacity up to 360K. Later, high-density 1.2MB drives, rotating at 360 RPM and holding 80 rather than 40 tracks, came along, but the basic principles hold true for them too, as well as for 3.5-inch units and today's huge hard drives.

In all cases, the drive itself identifies storage locations in terms of which head is used, which track (or cylinder, an alternative term) is positioned over the head, and which sector of that track is read or written.

Humans, however, have difficulty remembering a large collection of numeric values. Instead, we like to name things. It seems much simpler to remember that this text is stored in a file named CHAP8.DOC than that it is located starting at sector 14, cylinder 93, head 5, of drive 3. That's part of what the DOS file system is all about. It permits us to deal with our programs and data as named files; it turns over to the computer the job of translating these names into the sequence of numeric data that the hardware requires. Since computers excel at dealing with numeric information, it is just another example of letting the computer do what it does best, so that humans can do what they do best.

Another aspect of the DOS file system extends this type of mapping to non-storage devices. RAM disks, for example, map a directory or file structure onto fast, volatile memory. DOS's simple I/O redirection facility allows you to treat the screen and keyboard ports (CON), serial ports (COMx), and parallel ports (LPTx) as files. Drives created with the DOS network redirector can map a file system structure onto packets sent over the network to another machine, possibly running a completely different file system. The file system, in other words, not only simplifies access to hardware, but also provides unified access to otherwise disparate devices.

To let us deal with stored programs and data as named files, rather than forcing us to use physical head/track/sector addresses for every read or write action, the DOS file system maps these physical addresses into logical sector numbers and groups blocks of adjacent sectors into clusters for allocation to named files.

We examine these processes in detail shortly, but first let's look at some special records that are not part of the file system, but without which the file system would not exist. These are the partition record, which can treat a single physical drive as multiple logical drives, and the boot record (often called the boot sector since under DOS this record occupies a single sector), which controls the boot process each time you power up your system.

Partition and Boot Records

The partition record came into use soon after hard disks became popular. The original purpose seems to have been to allow multiple operating systems such as MS-DOS and UNIX to exist on the same system without interfering with each other. However, the capability quickly provided a way to deal with the 32-megabyte volume limit for disk drives that existed prior to MS-DOS 3.31, by allowing multiple 32-MB logical drives on a single large physical device. The presence of hard disk partitions shows that even a hard disk is just a logical construct rather than a physical reality. Hard disk C: may be just one subsection of the physical hard disk.

The boot record has been with us since the first disk operating systems. Its purpose is to control system operation for that brief period of time when the full operating system has not yet been read into memory. The boot record sees to it that the operating system can be read from the disk.

Most hard drives contain a partition record in the first sector of the first track under the first head (Drive=80h, H=0, T=00, S=1). The FDISK utility modifies this record, sometimes also called the Master Boot Record (MBR). It establishes the physical limits on the logical drives and thus permits multiple logical drives to exist on a single physical drive. When you power up the system, the ROM BIOS reads the MBR into memory and transfers control to it. The code in this record, in turn, reads in the boot record for the currently specified bootable partition, then jumps to the code in that boot record.

Since the partition record is not inside any logical drive, and since DOS deals only with logical drives (the usual case is that each physical drive has only one logical drive, which occupies all available space), normally you cannot access this record. You can, however, read it with the BIOS disk-read function, INT 13h AH=02, as the following DEBUG script shows:

```
a
MOV AX,0201          ; AH=ReadSec, AL=number to read (1)
MOV BX,1000          ; buffer at ES:1000h, ES set by loader
MOV CX,0001          ; CH=cyl (0), CL=sector (1)
MOV DX,0080          ; DH=head (0), DL=drive (C:)
INT 13               ; call BIOS disk function
JMP 0100             ; provides place to set breakpoint

g 10e
d 1000 l200
q
```

The blank line after JMP 0100 is essential; it signals DEBUG that the A (assembly) command is complete. To use this script for DEBUG, type it into a file, RPART.SCR, then type

```
DEBUG < RPART.SCR > PART.CAP
```

This creates a file named PART.CAP containing a hex dump of your C: drive's partition table. To read from your D: drive, you can change the value set into DX from 0080 to 0081. Figure 8-2 shows an edited version of sample results from this script (we added spaces to create four-byte columns).

Figure 8-2: A Partition Record

```
000: FA 2B C0 8E  D0 8E C0 8E  D8 B8 00 7C  8B E0 FB 8B   .+.........|....
010: F0 BF 00 7E  FC B9 00 01  F3 A5 E9 00  02 B9 10 00   ...~............
020: 8B 36 85 7E  F6 04 80 75  08 83 EE 10  E2 F6 EB 37   .6.~...u.......7
030: 90 BF BE 07  57 B9 08 00  F3 A5 5E BB  00 7C 8B 14   ....W.....^..|..
040: 8B 4C 02 BD  05 00 B8 01  02 CD 13 73  09 2B C0 CD   .L.........s.+..
050: 13 4D 74 19  EB F0 BE FE  7D AD 3D 55  AA 75 14 BE   .Mt.....}.=U.u..
060: BE 07 EA 00  7C 00 00 8B  36 87 7E EB  0A 8B 36 89   ....|...6.~...6.
070: 7E EB 04 8B  36 8B 7E AC  0A C0 74 FE  BB 07 00 B4   ~...6.~...t.....
080: 0E CD 10 EB  F2 EE 7F 8D  7E A7 7E C8  7E 0D 0A 49   .........~.~.~..I
090: 6E 76 61 6C  69 64 20 50  61 72 74 69  74 69 6F 6E   nvalid Partition
0A0: 20 54 61 62  6C 65 00 0D  0A 45 72 72  6F 72 20 4C    Table...Error L
0B0: 6F 61 64 69  6E 67 20 4F  70 65 72 61  74 69 6E 67   oading Operating
0C0: 20 53 79 73  74 65 6D 00  0D 0A 4D 69  73 73 69 6E    System...Missin
0D0: 67 20 4F 70  65 72 61 74  69 6E 67 20  53 79 73 74   g Operating Syst
0E0: 65 6D 00 00  00 00 00 00  00 00 00 00  00 00 00 00   em..............
0F0: 00 00 00 00  00 00 00 00  00 00 00 00  AA 55 00 00   .............U..
100: 00 00 00 00  00 00 00 00  00 00 00 00  00 00 00 00   ................
; ... lines omitted: all zeroes ...
1B0: 00 00 00 00  00 00 00 00  00 00 00 00  00 00 80 01   ................
1C0: 01 00 06 08  D1 FE 11 00  00 00 56 63  02 00 00 00   ..........Vc....
1D0: 00 00 00 00  00 00 00 00  00 00 00 00  00 00 00 00   ................
1E0: 00 00 00 00  00 00 00 00  00 00 00 00  00 00 00 00   ................
1F0: 00 00 00 00  00 00 00 00  00 00 00 00  00 00 55 AA   ..............U.
```

The first 254 bytes, up to and including the signature AA 55 at offset 0FCh in the record, is the code used on a cold boot to determine which of the logical partitions to use for the startup process. The remaining bytes, except for the final signature 55 AA at offset 1FEh, form a table of sixteen 16-byte entries, each of which defines the limits of a logical partition. In Figure 8-2, one such entry starts with the byte 80h at offset 1BEh.

Microsoft has finally documented the layout of each entry (see the PARTENTRY structure in the *MS-DOS Programmer's Reference*). This is the arrangement for each of the 16 entries:

```
struct PartEntry {
  char BootableFlag;       /* 80h if bootable partition, else 00h */
  char StartHead;          /* starting head number */
  char StartSector;        /* Bits 0-5 are start sector, 6-7 cyl */
  char StartCyl;           /* Low 8 bits of start cyl, 8-9 to prev */
  char SystemID;           /* Encodes file system type; see below */
  char EndHead;            /* ending head number */
```

```
char EndSector;          /* ending sector and hi bits of cyl */
char EndCyl;             /* low bits of ending cyl number */
unsigned long AbsBegin;  /* nbr, relative to disk, of first sec */
unsigned long SectCount; /* total number of sectors in partition */
};
```

The SystemID byte can hold any value, since non-MS-DOS operating systems also use this partition table. As of version 5.0, MS-DOS recognizes the following values:

00h = Unknown type or unused entry
01h = MS-DOS, 12-bit FAT
04h = MS-DOS, 16-bit FAT, partition < 32 MB
05h = MS-DOS, extended partition
06h = MS-DOS, 16-bit FAT, partition >= 32 MB

(Geoff Chappell provides values for other operating systems in Chapter 16 of his *DOS Internals*.)

If an entry is all zeroes, there is no corresponding partition. In Figure 8-2, only one of the sixteen possible entries is non-zero because this drive was partitioned as a single 76-megabyte logical volume. The data at offset 1BEh indicates that this volume is bootable; the byte at 1BFh says that the partition begins with head 1; that at 1C0h specifies sector 1; and that at 1C1h, together with the high two bits from 1C0h, indicates cylinder (track) 00. The 06h at offset 1C2h shows that this is a DOS volume using 16-bit FAT and it is larger than 32 megabytes. The next three bytes specify the ending head, sector, and cylinder positions. The value 00000011h starting at offset 1C6h means that the partition begins on the 17th sector from the start of the physical disk; and the final value, 00026356h at offset 1CAh, is the total sector count for the volume.

Partitions are created with the FDISK utility. Commented C source code for an FDISK utility, along with code for FORMAT, CHKDSK, SYS, DISKCOPY, and other programs, is included with the excellent Utility SDK available from General Software (Redmond, WA).

The Boot Record and BIOS Parameter Block (BPB)

The boot record, which Microsoft calls *the startup record* in the MS-DOS 5.0 documentation, occupies the first sector of the DOS bootable partition (FDISK won't let you specify more than one DOS bootable partition for a single physical drive). The code in the partition record reads the boot record into memory. You can examine the boot record of any DOS disk volume with the DEBUG L command, to load the very first sector into memory. For instance, L 100 2 0 1 at the DEBUG prompt reads one sector (1) starting with the first sector (0) of drive C: (2) to offset 100h (100). DEBUG, unlike the rest of DOS, starts numbering sectors with zero; elsewhere, the first sector is sector 1. Figure 8-3 shows how to view DOS boot records with DEBUG.

Figure 8-3: Using DEBUG to View DOS Boot Records

```
C:\UNDOC2\CHAP8>debug
-L 100 2 0 1
-d 100 200
81E2:0100  EB 00 90 53 54 41 43 4B-45 52 20 00 02 10 01 00    ...STACKER .....
81E2:0110  02 00 02 00 00 F8 66 00-3F 00 0F 00 00 00 00 00    ......f.?.......
81E2:0120  4D 25 03 00 00 14 00 00-00 01 09 00 20 47 32 00    M%.......... G2.
81E2:0130  00 0C 00 ED 00 CD 00 00-00 00 00 00 00 00 00 00    ................
81E2:0140  00 53 54 41 43 56 4F 4C-20 30 30 30 43 7D 00 A8    .STACVOL 000C}..
;; ... etc.
;; that's a Stacker drive; let's look at its host, a normal DOS drive:
-L 100 3 0 1
-d 100 200
81E2:0100  EB 3C 90 4D 53 44 4F 53-35 2E 30 00 02 04 01 00    .<.MSDOS5.0.....
81E2:0110  02 00 02 00 00 F8 7A 00-11 00 0C 00 11 00 00 00    ......z.........
81E2:0120  9F E7 01 00 80 00 29 E7-11 51 1B 4E 4F 20 4E 41    ......)..Q.NO NA
```

```
81E2:0130   4D 45 20 20 20 20 46 41-54 31 36 20 20 20 FA 33     ME     FAT16   .3
81E2:0140   C0 8E D0 BC 00 7C 16 07-BB 78 00 36 C5 37 1E 56     .....|...x.6.7.V
; ...
-u 0100 102
81E2:0100 EB3C            JMP 013E    ; bsJump
81E2:0102 90              NOP
; ...
0103h         db    'MSDOS5.0'        ; bsOemName
;;; beginning of BPB
010Bh         dw    0200h             ; bsBytesPerSec
010Dh         db    04h               ; bsSecPerClust
010Eh         dw    0001h             ; bsResSectors
0110h         db    02h               ; bsFATs
0111h         dw    0200h             ; bsRootDirEnts
0113h         dw    0000h             ; bsSectors (0; see bsHugeSectors)
0115h         db    F8h               ; bsMedia (F8h = hard disk)
0116h         dw    007Ah             ; bsFATsecs
0118h         dw    0011h             ; bsSecPerTrack
011Ah         dw    000Ch             ; bsHeads
011Ch         dd    00000011h         ; bsHiddenSecs
0120h         dd    0001E79Fh         ; bsHugeSectors
;;; end of BPB
0124h         db    80h               ; bsDriveNumber (80h = first hard disk)
0125h         db    00h               ; bsReserved1 (used during boot)
0126h         db    29h               ; bsBootSignature  (29h = extended BPB)
;;; start of extended BPB (see Media ID)
0127h         dd    1B5111E7h         ; bsVolumeID (midSerialNum)
012Bh         db    'NO NAME    '     ; bsVolumeLabel (midVolLabel)
0136h         db    'FAT16   '        ; bsFileSysType (midFileSysType)
;;; end of extended BPB
```

The first three bytes of Figure 8-3 JMP to code (which code you can unassemble, of course) that first verifies that the disk is, indeed, a system disk; if it is, the code reads in the IO.SYS file, which then takes over the startup process.

Immediately after the JMP instruction is a set of data items that Microsoft has mostly documented in the DOS programmer's reference (see BOOTSECTOR). This set includes a structure called the BIOS Parameter Block (BPB), documented in the device driver chapter of the DOS programmer's reference.

As Figure 8-3 shows, the BPB contains information about the storage medium, such as the bytes per sector, sectors per cluster, number of FATs and root-directory entries, and so on. As noted later, however, DOS may overwrite some of the values in a BPB, so the BPB that IO.SYS maintains in memory doesn't necessary match the BPB on disk. For example, the number of FATs for floppy and hard disks is 2, no matter what the disk's own BPB claims! (For further discussion, see Chappell's *DOS Internals*, Chapter 16.)

Note the presence of what is called an extended BPB. You can retrieve this data with the generic IOCTL Get Media ID call (INT 21h AX=440Dh CX=0866h), which is equivalent (and obviously preferable) to undocumented INT 21h AH=69h. The inclusion of a volume label in the extended BPB means that a volume label no longer need be a file with a special attribute in the root directory. In MS-DOS 4.0 and higher, you can set and query volume labels with the Get/Set Media ID calls. Note, however, that this call only works for media that in fact does have an extended BPB. For disks formatted under MS-DOS 3.0, for example, Get Media ID returns error code 5 (access denied); you then must retrieve and set the volume label using an old method that requires an FCB.

DoubleSpace has further extended the BPB to a structure called the MDBPB (the 'MD' stands for MagicDisk; see the DoubleSpace discussion later in this chapter).

Logical Sector Numbers and the Cluster Concept

The first step toward simplifying the head/track/sector number sequence was to recognize that there was an alternate way of uniquely specifying every sector on a disk unit with a single number, rather than with three.

DOS assigns unique numbers to the sectors in logical sequence. That is, the first sector (S) of the first logical track (T) under the first logical head (H) (which in the fully hardware-oriented scheme, taking into account any partition offset to head 1, would be H=1 T=00 S=1) becomes Logical Sector Number (LSN) 001. Block devices on the PC start numbering physical sectors from 1, not 0. The calculations used for determining the LSN work with values that are relative to the start of the logical drive, not absolute with respect to the physical drive. The rest of the way around that first track, on the same surface, the numbers follow in sequence.

Then, however, the LSN jumps to the other surface of the disk. For a 360K diskette, with no partition record and nine sectors per track on both sides, LSN 10 would be H=1 T=00 S=1. After all sectors on track 0 of the second side are accounted for, the numbering returns H=0 T=01 S=1, for track 1 of the first side, which becomes LSN 19.

For other disk capacities, the exact transition points differ, but the essential point is that you can always translate a head/track/sector reference into a unique LSN if you know how many sectors are in each track, how many heads the disk includes, and where the logical volume begins with respect to the physical drive. You can also perform the reverse translation.

With extended DOS partitions, both translations can be difficult because no clean way exists with all versions of DOS to determine the start location of the partition, other than by reading the partition record using BIOS and interpreting the data found in the appropriate entry there. The problem with this technique is in determining which entry applies to the extended partition with which you are dealing. For more information on extended DOS partitions, see Chapter 16 of Geoff Chappell's *DOS Internals*.

For high capacity storage units, which may contain hundreds of thousands of 512-byte sectors, the LSN has finer granularity than DOS typically needs to allocate disk space and to access files. Thus emerged the idea of clusters. DOS inherited this idea from the older CP/M operating system, although CP/M used the term *extent*. A cluster is simply a group of adjacent sectors that are always assigned as a unit. If a file needs only one byte, it gets a whole cluster anyway. This solves several problems and creates one new one.

Allocating multiple sector clusters greatly reduces DOS overhead in allocating and freeing disk space, since DOS performs these actions a fraction less frequently than it would if it allocated space directly in sectors. Multiple-sector clusters also serve to speed up disk access by reducing (though by no means eliminating) the extent to which a file can become scattered all over the drive. Even if no two clusters in the file are adjacent to each other, at least within each cluster all the sectors are together. Since seek time is a major part of disk I/O delay, this improves overall system performance.

One obvious disadvantage of clusters is that when there is more than one sector per cluster they increase the amount of disk space occupied by tiny files. The disk space files use is always a multiple of the cluster size. For example, if there are 512 bytes per sector and 8 sectors per cluster, then the minimum space allocated to a file is 4K, even for a file whose size in a directory listing is one byte. Not exactly a peanut cluster! This wasted space is known as cluster overhang.

So how big is a cluster? It all depends. Some RAM disks such as Microsoft's RAMDRIVE.SYS use one-sector clusters. Lower density diskette formats use a cluster of only two sectors; 1.2 MB and higher density diskettes use one-sector clusters. Hard disks for the most part use either 4-sector or 8-sector clusters. Some optical drives use larger clusters as an alternative to larger sector sizes, to deal with gigabytes of space under older versions of DOS. DOS has a built-in limit of 128 sectors per cluster; in MS-DOS 5.0, some FCB handling breaks down under this condition, so in practice 64 sectors per cluster is tops.

One way that DoubleSpace compresses disks is by allocating a *variable* number of sectors per cluster. Rather than converting from clusters to sectors via a fixed formula, DoubleSpace uses a lookup table called the MDFAT. We discuss DoubleSpace in greater detail later in this chapter.

To tell which clusters are in use and which are available for assignment, DOS uses the famous File Allocation Table (FAT), with one entry per cluster. The cluster structure is the backbone of the FAT file system. If it is damaged, all data on the affected disk unit may be lost.

The File Allocation Table (FAT)

The FAT is always located near the front of each disk volume, generally immediately after the boot record. The FAT may begin at what would normally be a cluster boundary or at the first sector after the boot record. DOS normally maintains two copies of the FAT in case of hard disk errors (not logical errors). DOS must successfully write both copies each time space is allocated or released, but only needs to read one of them; DOS ignores an error reading the first copy if it can successfully read the second copy. Microsoft used three FATs in its Stand-Alone Disk BASIC (1979); this is where the multiple FAT idea (and in fact FAT itself) comes from. For some of the goals of FAT, see Tim Paterson, "An Inside Look at MS-DOS" (*Byte*, June 1983).

The FAT is an array of cluster numbers. That is, you use a cluster number as an index into the FAT. The value at FAT[cluster_number] is, in turn, another cluster number or an end-of-file indicator. These cluster numbers indicate the location on disk of files, directories, and free space.

Sometimes each element in the FAT array is a 16-bit cluster number, but unfortunately for smaller media the FAT is an array of inconveniently-sized 12-bit numbers.

For DOS 3.x and higher, the top 4 bits in the highest cluster word of the Drive Parameter Block tell which FAT size is in use for any specific volume. DOS 4.0 added a field to the extended BPB, containing an 8-character file system type identifier, which can be "FAT12" or "FAT16", with the unused three bytes padded with space characters (see bsFileSysType in Figure 8-3). You can access this field with INT 21h AX=440Dh CX=0866h (Get Media ID).

Because of the FAT16 identifier in the extended BPB, it's theoretically possible to have a 16-bit FAT even for media with 0FFFh or few clusters. However, the DOS kernel itself assumes 12-bit FAT entries when these are sufficient to hold the media's highest cluster number. Although the SystemID field in the partition record identifies whether each partition uses a 12-bit or 16-bit FAT, DOS doesn't use this information. The reason for this seeming oversight might be that floppies and other removable media need not have partition records, but still require FAT to be usable under DOS. So in practice it is adequate to just check the top four bits of the highest cluster (dpb->highest_cluster >> 12) to determine the FAT size.

Even with the huge volume sizes that DOS 4.x and up permit, the FAT element size in DOS itself never exceeds 16 bits, despite occasional claims to the contrary. What does increase as the volume size grows is the cluster size (with the inefficiencies noted earlier) and the maximum LSN. Hooks are available to permit creation of custom file systems using other FAT sizes (a third-party vendor perhaps could write a FAT24 or FAT32), but DOS itself recognizes only the 12-bit and 16-bit sizes.

Each element in the FAT, whether 12 or 16 bits long, corresponds to a single cluster of the drive's storage space. The first two elements, which would refer to cluster 0 and cluster 1, instead hold media information. The first byte of the FAT indicates the Media Code; if the drive serves removable media, there's no direct correlation with the drive's own type. The remaining 16 or 24 bits of the first two elements are normally set to all ones and remain unused. It appears that DOS may use cluster 1 as a temporary nonzero marker while building an allocation chain for a file, and it uses cluster 0 as a shorthand reference to the root directory for any drive when defining the ".." directory entry for a subdirectory from the root.

Cluster 2 is the first one usable for data. Since both copies of the FAT and the volume's root directory area precede this space, DOS must calculate the LSN for cluster 2 from the values provided in the DPB. Note, though, that DOS is not consistent in performing this calculation; as a result, if a root directory does not contain some exact multiple of 16 entries, things become confused. IO.SYS rounds down when doing the calculation, while MSDOS.SYS rounds up!

Once the LSN for cluster 2 is known, the LSN at which any cluster starts is determined by multiplying the cluster number (minus 2) by the sectors per cluster, then adding the known LSN for cluster 2. That's how DOS translates cluster numbers taken from directory entries into the LSNs that block device drivers require. As noted earlier, the LSN for cluster 2 is calculated from values in the DPB. But we're getting ahead of ourselves: DPBs are explained shortly.

The value contained in each FAT element tells whether the corresponding cluster is in use or not, and if it is, the element gives essential information about the file that is using it. A zero indicates that the cluster is free and can be allocated. A value of 1 should never occur, although you can trap such a value on disk if you reboot at the right moment (or are single-stepping through an INT 21h function) and have a low enough setting for BUFFERS.

The last eight possible values (FF8h-FFFh for 12-bit FATs, or FFF8h-FFFFh for 16-bit FATs) indicate that this cluster is the last one in the file. (F)FF7h marks a bad cluster; (F)FF0h through (F)FF6h are reserved, meaning that they are not used and quite possibly never will be. Any other value indicates that the file using this cluster is continued in the cluster having that value: next_cluster = FAT[cluster].

Incidentally, because FFF0h is highest cluster number, because 2 is the first valid cluster number, and because each file, no matter how small, occupies at least one cluster, there can be at most FFF0h - 2 = FFEEh (65,518) files and directories per DOS volume. 65,518 is not a large number.

Listing 8-2 shows a short program, FAT.C, which prints out the FAT chain for any drive and cluster number specified on the command line. For example, the following shows that the file starting at cluster 7470 on drive C: occupies 88 clusters, distributed in nine different places on the disk:

```
C:\UNDOC2\CHAP8>fat c: 7470
7470-7486 (17)
7491-7492 (2)
7494-7502 (9)
7512-7514 (3)
7544-7545 (2)
7554-7556 (3)
7683-7715 (33)
7729-7746 (18)
7752

88 clusters in 9 groups
(10% fragmentation)
```

But what filename corresponds to cluster 7470 on drive C:? You'll see how filenames are mapped to clusters in a few moments (see NAMCLUST.C in Listing 8-5).

Listing 8-2: FAT.C

```
/*
FAT.C -- Given drive and cluster number, print FAT chain
Andrew Schulman, July 1993
*/

#include <stdlib.h>
#include <stdio.h>
#include <ctype.h>
#include <dos.h>
#include "diskstuf.h"

void fail(const char *s) { puts(s); exit(1); }
```

```
main(int argc, char *argv[])
{
    DPB far *dpb;
    WORD prev_cluster, cluster, num_clusters = 0, num_groups = 0;
    WORD start_cluster;
    int drive;

    if (argc < 3)
        fail("usage: fat [drive] [cluster]");
    drive = toupper(argv[1][0]) - 'A';
    cluster = atoi(argv[2]);                // decimal, not hex

    if (! (dpb = get_dpb(drive + 1)))  // see DISKSTUF.C (listing 8-4)
        fail("can't get DPB");

    start_cluster = cluster;
    // the following works because get_fat_entry() returns
    // 12-bit EOF in 16-bit form!
    #define EOF(cluster) ((cluster) >= 0xFFF0)  // end of file
    while (! EOF(cluster))
    {
        num_clusters++;
        prev_cluster = cluster;
        cluster = get_fat_entry(drive, dpb, cluster);
        #define CONTIGUOUS(x,y) ((x) == ((y) + 1))
        if (! CONTIGUOUS(cluster, prev_cluster))
        {
            int num_clust = prev_cluster + 1 - start_cluster;
            num_groups++;
            if (num_clust > 1)
                printf("%u-%u (%u)\n",
                        start_cluster, prev_cluster, num_clust);
            else    // only one cluster
                printf("%u\n", start_cluster);
            start_cluster = cluster;
        }
    }
    printf("\n%u clusters in %u groups\n", num_clusters, num_groups);
    if (num_clusters > 2 && num_groups > 1)
        printf("(%u%% fragmentation)\n", (num_groups * 100) / num_clusters);
    return 0;
}
```

FAT.C includes the header file DISKSTUF.H (Listing 8-3) and uses the get_dpb() and get_fat_entry() functions from DISKSTUF.C (Listing 8-4). We use DISKSTUF again later in this chapter. All the hard work in FAT.C is done inside get_fat_entry(), although "hard work" is an overstatement when working with 16-bit FATs; all the difficulty is in handling 12-bit FATs. FAT.C depends on get_fat_entry() to return 12-bit EOF markers in 16-bit form. Because get_fat_entry() masks the difference between 12-bit and 16-bit FATs, FAT.C doesn't know or care which type of FAT it's dealing with.

Listing 8-3: DISKSTUF.H

```
/*
DISKSTUF.H -- Some functions and structures for low-level disk access
Andrew Schulman, July 1993
*/

#ifndef DISKSTUF_H
#define DISKSTUF_H

typedef unsigned char BYTE;
typedef unsigned short WORD;
typedef unsigned long DWORD;
```

```c
typedef char *STRING;

extern void fail(const char *s);      // application must define
#pragma pack(1)
typedef struct {
    BYTE name[8], ext[3], attrib;
#ifdef OS2
    BYTE reserved[8];
    WORD ea_handle;        // OS/2 handle to extended attributes (EAs)
#else
    BYTE reserved[10];
#endif
    WORD time, date, cluster;
    DWORD size;
    } DIR_ENTRY;

#define VOLUME_ATTR       0x08
#define DIRECTORY_ATTR    0x10

#ifndef MK_FP
#define MK_FP(seg,ofs) \
    ((void far *)(((DWORD)(seg) << 16) | (ofs)))
#endif

typedef struct dpb {                   // Disk Parameter Block
    BYTE drive, unit;
    WORD bytes_per_sect;
    BYTE sectors_per_cluster;      // plus 1
    BYTE shift;                    // for sectors per cluster
    WORD boot_sectors;
    BYTE copies_fat;
    WORD max_root_dir, first_data_sector, highest_cluster;
    union {
        struct {
            BYTE sectors_per_fat;
            WORD first_dir_sector;  // root dir
            void far *device_driver;
            BYTE media_descriptor, access_flag;
            struct dpb far *next;
            DWORD reserved;
            } dos3;
        struct {
            WORD sectors_per_fat;          // WORD, not BYTE!
            WORD first_dir_sector;
            void far *device_driver;
            BYTE media_descriptor, access_flag;
            struct dpb far *next;
            DWORD reserved;
            } dos4;
        } vers;
    } DPB;
#pragma pack()

DPB far *get_dpb(int drive);
int _dos_driveremoveable(int drive);
int _dos_getdrivemap(int drive);
char far *truename(char far *s, char far *d);
WORD get_fat_entry(int drive, DPB far *dpb, WORD cluster);
int read_sectors(int drive, BYTE far *buf, int sectors, DWORD first_sector);
#endif /* DISKSTUF_H */
```

In DISKSTUF.C (Listing 8-4), get_dpb( ) checks for removable media and installs an INT 24h critical error handler. This is because the DOS Get DPB function (INT 21h AH=32h) hits the disk. In the absence of an INT 24h critical error handler like the one provided in Listing 8-4, calling Get DPB for drive A:, for example, can produce an annoying "Not ready reading drive A: / Abort, Retry, Fail?"

message. Furthermore, calling Get DPB for drive B:, if the drive is currently assigned to drive A:, produces the equally annoying "Insert diskette for drive B: and press any key when ready" message. This issue is discussed at length in (as usual) Chapter 16 of Geoff Chappell's *DOS Internals*.

Listing 8-4: DISKSTUF.C

```c
/*
DISKSTUF.C -- Some functions and structures for low-level disk access
Andrew Schulman, July 1993
*/

#include <stdlib.h>
#include <stdio.h>
#include <ctype.h>
#include <dos.h>
#include "diskstuf.h"

int _dos_driveremoveable(int drive)
{
    int retval;
    _asm mov ax, 4408h
    _asm mov bl, byte ptr drive
    _asm int 21h
    _asm jnc ok
    return 0;                // treat error as non-removeable
ok:
    _asm mov retval, ax
    return (! retval);   // turn around so non-removeable = 0
}

int _dos_getdrivemap(int drive)
{
    _asm mov ax, 440Eh
    _asm mov bl, byte ptr drive
    _asm int 21h
    _asm jc error
    _asm cmp ax, 0                  // only one drive number
    _asm je error
    _asm xor ah, ah
    _asm mov word ptr drive, ax     // active drive number
error:
    return drive;
}

typedef struct {
#ifdef __TURBOC__
    unsigned short bp,di,si,ds,es,dx,cx,bx,ax;
#else
    unsigned short es,ds,di,si,bp,sp,bx,dx,cx,ax;   /* PUSHA order */
#endif
    unsigned short ip,cs,flags;
    } REG_PARAMS;

/*************************************************************/
typedef void interrupt (far *INTVECT)();
static volatile int failed = 0;
static INTVECT old_int24 = (INTVECT) 0;

void interrupt far crit_err(REG_PARAMS regs) // INT 24h handler
{
    REG_PARAMS *pregs = &regs;
    pregs->ax = 3;
    failed++;
}

void watch_crit_err(void)
{
    failed = 0;
```

```c
    old_int24 = (INTVECT) _dos_getvect(0x24);
    _dos_setvect(0x24, (INTVECT) crit_err);
}

void unwatch_crit_err(void) { _dos_setvect(0x24, old_int24); }
int get_failed(void)        { return failed; }
void reset_failed(void)     { failed = 0; }
/*****************************************************************/
DPB far *get_dpb(int drive)
{
    DPB far *dpb = (DPB far *) 0;
    // if drive removeable and not mapped, fail
    if (_dos_driveremoveable(drive))
        if (_dos_getdrivemap(drive) != drive)
            return (DPB far *) 0;
    // install temp crit-error handler for duration of 21/32 call
    watch_crit_err();
    // call newly-documented DOS Get DPB function
    _asm push ds
    _asm mov ah, 32h
    _asm mov dl, byte ptr drive
    _asm int 21h
    _asm mov dx, ds
    _asm pop ds
    _asm cmp al, 0FFh
    _asm je fini
    _asm mov word ptr dpb+2, dx
    _asm mov word ptr dpb, bx
fini:
    // remove temporary crit-err handler
    unwatch_crit_err();
    // "failed" is set inside Get DPB by crit-err handler
    return failed? ((DPB far *) 0) : dpb;
}

char far *truename(char far *s, char far *d)    // get canonical pathname
{
    /* INT 21h AH=60h doesn't like leading or trailing blanks */
    char far *s2;
    while (isspace(*s)) s++;            // ltrim
    s2 = s; while (*s2) s2++; s2--;     // go to end
    while (isspace(*s2)) *s2-- = 0;     // rtrim

    /* Apparently some versions of DR DOS insist on ES:DI != DS:SI */

    _asm push di
    _asm push si
    _asm push ds
    _asm push es
    _asm les di, d
    _asm lds si, s
    _asm mov ah, 60h
    _asm int 21h
    _asm pop es
    _asm pop ds
    _asm pop si
    _asm pop di
    _asm jc error
    return d;
error:
    return (char far *) 0;
}

typedef struct {
    DWORD diStartSector;
    WORD diSectors;
    BYTE far *diBuffer;
```

```
    } DISKIO;
int read_sectors(int drive, BYTE far *buf, int sectors, DWORD first_sector)
{
    DISKIO diskio, far *pdiskio = &diskio;
    diskio.diStartSector = first_sector;
    diskio.diSectors = sectors;
    diskio.diBuffer = buf;

    // INT 25h/26h are obsolete; should instead use generic
    // IOCTL functions 21/440D/0861 and 21/440D/0841.
    _asm push ds
    _asm mov al, byte ptr drive
    _asm lds bx, pdiskio
    _asm mov cx, 0FFFFh
    _asm mov dx, 0
    _asm int 25h
    _asm jc do_fail
    _asm popf                // INT 25h, 26h leave flags on stack
    _asm pop ds
    return 1;
do_fail:
    _asm popf
    _asm pop ds
    return 0;
}
// get_fat_entry() hides differences between 12-bit and 16-bit FATs
// returns 12-bit FAT EOF indicators (e.g., 0xFF0) in 16-bit form (0xFFF0)
WORD get_fat_entry(int drive, DPB far *dpb, WORD cluster)
{
    static WORD *fat_sect = (WORD *) -1;
    static WORD prev_drive = (WORD) -1;
    static DPB far *prev_dpb = (DPB far *) -1L;
    static WORD prev_sect = (WORD) -1;
    WORD first_fat_sect, entry_per_sect, sect, fat_size;

    // One-time initialization of buffer; allocate 2 sectors because
    // this may be needed for 12-bit FAT if a FAT entry slops over
    // two sectrors. (Yuch!)
    if (fat_sect == (WORD *) -1)
        if (! (fat_sect = (WORD *) malloc(dpb->bytes_per_sect * 2)))
            fail("insufficient memory");

    if (_osmajor >= 4)
        first_fat_sect = dpb->vers.dos4.first_dir_sector -
            (dpb->copies_fat * dpb->vers.dos4.sectors_per_fat);
    else
        first_fat_sect = dpb->vers.dos3.first_dir_sector -
            (dpb->copies_fat * dpb->vers.dos3.sectors_per_fat);

    fat_size = (dpb->highest_cluster >> 12 == 0) ? 12 : 16;
    if (fat_size == 12)
        sect = first_fat_sect + (((cluster * 3) / 2) / dpb->bytes_per_sect);
    else
    {
        entry_per_sect = dpb->bytes_per_sect / 2;
        sect = first_fat_sect + (cluster / entry_per_sect);
    }

    // Don't reread if same sector as last time (assumes of course
    // that some TSR hasn't modified the sector in the meantime!)
    if (! (drive == prev_drive && dpb == prev_dpb && sect == prev_sect))
    {
        int num_sect = (fat_size == 12) ? 2 : 1;    // for possible slop
        if (! read_sectors(drive, (BYTE far *) fat_sect, num_sect, sect))
            fail("can't read FAT");    // could try FAT #2
    }
    prev_sect = sect; prev_drive = drive; prev_dpb = dpb;
```

```
    if (fat_size == 12)
    {
        BYTE *fat = (BYTE *) fat_sect;
        WORD ofs = ((cluster * 3) / 2) % dpb->bytes_per_sect;
        WORD retval = *((WORD *) &fat[ofs]);
        if (cluster & 1)            // odd cluster #
            retval >>= 4;           //    take top 12 bits
        else                        // even cluster #
            retval &= 0x0FFF;       //    take bottom 12 bits
        // return 12-bit FF0-FFF as 16-bit FFF0-FFFF
        return (retval >= 0x0FF0) ? (retval | 0xF000) : retval;
    }
    else    // gosh, 16-bit FATs are easy
        return fat_sect[cluster % entry_per_sect];
}
```

In addition to get_dpb() and get_fat_entry(), DISKSTUF.C also contains the function read_sectors(), which uses INT 25h (the newer style first introduced in Compaq DOS 3.31). INT 25h and 26h are the DOS Absolute Disk Read and Write functions. According to the MS-DOS programmer's reference, the generic IOCTL functions, INT 21h AX=440Dh CX=0861h (Read Track on Logical Drive) and CX=0841h (Write Track on Logical Drive) are now the preferred functions for accessing disks below the file system level. For example, FORMAT relies heavily on generic IOCTL. The disk related generic IOCTL calls also largely replace any need for directly messing with BIOS INT 13h calls. Both INT 25h/26h and the generic IOCTL disk functions just call down to the block device driver, which in turn does what is needed to read the disk. As shown by running the FAT program under INTRSPY DISK.SCR in this particular configuration, this means calling BIOS INT 13h:

```
C:\UNDOC2\CHAP8>cmdspy compile disk c: fat c: 7470
; ...
25: Abs Disk Read drv 02, at sectr 0000001E, 0001 sctrs
04 - input
1302: Read 09 sctrs: drv 80, head 00, sctr 0F, trk 04 to 16B5:0000
25: Abs Disk Read drv 02, at sectr 0000001F, 0001 sctrs
04 - input
1302: Read 09 sctrs: drv 80, head 01, sctr 07, trk 04 to 17D5:0000
; ...
```

The INTRSPY output plainly shows that INT 25h calls device-driver function 4 (Read), which in turn calls INT 13h AH=2.

However, in the case of a RAM disk, for example, the device driver would certainly *not* call INT 13h! Instead, it would read and write sectors by accessing memory. The construction of RAM disks is an interesting topic that we won't take up further here. For an introduction, see the chapter on RAM disks in Robert Lai's *Writing MS-DOS Device Drivers*, and supplement this with an exploration of the newer RAM disk memory management issues, such as the issue of extended memory. For example, on 80286 machines, Microsoft's RAMDRIVE.SYS uses the undocumented LOADALL instruction. IBM for some time distributed an assembly language listing of VDISK. Later on (see maybe_ram_disk() in Listing 8-11), we look briefly at how to detect whether a given drive is a RAM disk.

The get_fat_entry() function uses the cluster number and DPB information to figure out which FAT sector is needed. If this sector differs from the one get_fat_entry() last used, the function calls read_sectors() to read it in. Finally, it indexes into the FAT sector; this is trivial for 16-bit FATs and annoying for 12-bit FATs. For 12-bit FATs, the code also has to worry about a FAT entry spanning two sectors; this is why it allocates space for two sectors and for 12-bit FATs reads in two sectors.

In summary, the FAT is a linked list of clusters that threads the pieces of each file together and indicates where space is available. Determine where the very first cluster for any specified file is located, and you can access everything in it. How then is the starting cluster found? That's done by the directory structure, to which we now turn.

DOS Directory Structure

Every disk volume (that is, each diskette in drives with removable media, or each partition in non-removeable media) has a root directory which is the starting point for translating human-oriented file names into system-oriented cluster numbers.

The root directory immediately follows the FAT and precedes the data storage area. Its size is established when the disk is formatted. Unlike non-root directories which are just files, the root directory can never change. A typical root directory size for a 360K floppy is 112 entries; for a hard disk, it's usually larger, typically 512 entries. For a floppy disk, IO.SYS won't accept a BPB calling for more than 240 root directory entries. (Neither will it accept values other than 2 for the number of FATs, 1 for the count of reserved sectors, or a sector size other than 512 bytes.)

Besides having a fixed size, the root directory has another important difference from non-root directories. The root directory is not accessible from the FAT. To get from one sector in the root directory to the next, you cannot walk the FAT as with non-root directories. Instead, all root-directory sectors are contiguous. You can use values from the DPB to compute the number of root directory sectors, as shown in the sample program NAMCLUST.C (Listing 8-5; see the code in do_cluster() to handle the case of cluster == 0).

As seen from the DIR_ENTRY structure in DISKSTUF.H (Listing 8-3), each entry in a directory, whether in the root or in a subdirectory, consists of a 32-byte structure. This structure is plainly visible in a hex dump of a directory structure. In Figure 8-4, the DEBUG L command loads sector 5B4Dh from drive 2 (C:); this sector is then dumped with the D command. The fact that sector 5B4Dh contained a directory for C:\UNDOC2\CHAP8 was ascertained using the NAMCLUST program, whose source code we present in a few moments. In Figure 8-4, the filenames FILES.C and FILES.EXE are visible within this directory, as are the standard "." and ".." files for the current and parent subdirectories.

Figure 8-4 was generated on a system running Stacker. The directory structure shown is just data inside a STACVOL.000 file on drive D: and is not physically on disk in the location it appears to be on drive C:. To make the point once more, file-system data need not reside on disk in any fixed way, because the block device driver can conjure up the necessary DOS file system data structures on demand.

Figure 8-4: A DOS Directory Structure

```
C:\UNDOC2\CHAP8>namclust .
C:\UNDOC2\CHAP8 ==> 1448 (sect 23373, 0x00005b4d)

C:\UNDOC2\CHAP8>debug
-L 1000 2 5b4d 1
-d 1000
7CCD:1000  2E 20 20 20 20 20 20 20-20 20 20 10 00 00 00 00   .          .....
7CCD:1010  00 00 00 00 00 00 2D B5-73 1A A8 05 00 00 00 00   ......-.s......
7CCD:1020  2E 2E 20 20 20 20 20 20-20 20 20 10 00 00 00 00   ..         .....
7CCD:1030  00 00 00 00 00 00 2D B5-73 1A 12 00 00 00 00 00   ......-.s......
7CCD:1040  46 49 4C 45 53 20 20 20-43 20 20 20 00 00 00 00   FILES   C   ....
7CCD:1050  00 00 00 00 00 00 5B 70-E7 1A AA 22 3C 19 00 00   ......[p..."<...
7CCD:1060  46 49 4C 45 53 20 20 20-45 58 45 20 00 00 00 00   FILES   EXE ....
7CCD:1070  00 00 00 00 00 00 17 B9-72 1A 53 05 52 1D 00 00   ........r.S.R...
; ...

C:\UNDOC2\CHAP8>dir
; ...
.              <DIR>      03-19-93   10:41p
..             <DIR>      03-19-93   10:41p
FILES    C         6460  07-07-93    2:02p
FILES    EXE       7506  03-18-93   11:08p
; ...
```

```
00h      BYTE name[8]            "FILES   "
08h      BYTE ext[3]             "C  "
0Bh      BYTE attrib             20
0Ch      BYTES reserved[10]      00 .. 00 (used for OS/2 EAs)
16h      WORD time               5B 70
18h      WORD date               E7 1A
1Ah      WORD cluster            AA 22 (22AAh = 8874 dec)
1Ch      DWORD size              3C 19 00 00 (193Ch = 6,460 bytes)
```

In this structure, the first byte of the filename field has special significance, as does the attribute byte. If the first byte of the filename is E5h, this indicates the that entry refers to a file which has been deleted and which can be reused for a new file or directory entry, or possibly undeleted if you get to it in time. (DOS 5 and higher save a pointer to the last directory entry written and use this rather than the beginning of the directory as the starting point for walking directory entries. This increases the chances of successfully undeleting an entry before DOS recycles it.) If the first byte is 05h, this indicates the first byte is actually E5h, which is a valid filename character in DOS 3.0 and higher. Finally, if the first byte is 00, this indicates that neither this entry, nor any subsequent one in the directory, has ever been used. This permits searches to stop as soon as a 00 byte is found. It also means that a stray 00 byte can make it appear as if not just one bad entry, but all the entries following it, have disappeared from your disk.

In case you're curious as to why E5h was chosen to indicate a deleted directory entry, according to Tim Paterson (who wrote the code in the first place and ought to know), the original 8-inch floppy diskettes for CP/M were shipped pre-formatted with that byte. With E5h indicating that a directory entry was available to use, a brand new diskette right out of the box would be ready to accept files. When MS-DOS was created, it inherited this convention along with many other CP/M artifacts. The FAT still needed clearing, using the built-in CLEAR command in pre-IBM DOS. The zero byte to indicate never-used directory space did not appear until later in the history of DOS.

The attribute byte indicates whether the entry refers to a file or to a subdirectory (10h), or if it is a volume label (08h); if it's a file, the attribute byte provides other information as well. The meaning of the date, time, and size fields is self-evident. OS/2 uses two of the ten reserved bytes as a handle to extended attributes (EAs), which OS/2 keeps in a separate EA database file. As Chapter 4 notes, DOS programs running under OS/2 can access these EAs with INT 21h AH=57h. One of the extended attributes might be a long filename.

Long Filenames in "Chicago"

For the first time, Microsoft's important new "Chicago" operating system (DOS 7.0, Windows 4) supports long filenames. For example, "This is a valid filename under Chicago" is, indeed, a valid filename under Chicago.

Of course, Microsoft had to implement these long filenames in a way that didn't break existing applications. Furthermore, media written under Chicago must still be usable under old versions of DOS and Windows.

Every long filename in Chicago has a unique short alias, such as "THISIS~1". In fact, it appears that Chicago will be case-preserving (though case-insensitive), so essentially *all* files and directories created under Chicago will have two forms. For example, "copy foo.bar foobarsk.doc" would create both a standard "FOOBARSKDOC" directory entry and, even though FOOBARSK.DOC fits within the standard 8.3 filename confines, a second, case-preserving "foobarsk.doc" entry.

Judging from a prerelease version, Chicago implements long filenames in a substantially different way from OS/2 EAs. Whereas OS/2 uses two reserved bytes in the directory entry to store an EA handle (one of the EAs can be a long filename), Chicago instead uses a series of directory entries to store the long case-preserving filename, following these with the unique short filename alias. For example:

```
I:\>md foo
I:\>cd foo
;; Note below that the directory name in the prompt is lower case.
I:\foo>copy con this.is.a.test.of.foo.barsky.tester
;; Note below that DIR shows both the long/lower name and short/upper alias
I:\foo>dir this*.*
THISIS~1 TES         7  09-13-93  14:55 this.is.a.test.of.foo.barsky.tester
;; Now use NAMCLUST (Listing 8-5) to see how this appears in the directory
I:\foo>namclust .
I:\FOO ==> 2 (sect 439, 0x000001b7)
;; SECTDUMP is a sector-dump program on the UndocDOS disk
I:\foo>sectdump i: 439 1
Sector 00000439 (000001B7h):
0000 | 2E 20 20 20 20 20 20 20 20 20 20 10 00 00 00 00 | .           .....
0010 | 00 00 00 00 00 00 F1 76 2D 1B 02 00 00 00 00 00 | .......v-.......
0020 | 2E 2E 20 20 20 20 20 20 20 20 20 10 00 00 00 00 | ..          .....
0030 | 00 00 00 00 00 00 F1 76 2D 1B 00 00 00 00 00 00 | .......v-.......
0040 | 12 6B 79 2E 74 65 73 74 65 72 00 0F 00 B9 FF FF | .ky.tester......
0050 | FF FF FF FF FF FF FF FF FF FF 00 00 FF FF FF FF | ...............
0060 | 01 74 68 69 73 2E 69 73 2E 61 2E 0F 00 B9 74 65 | .this.is.a....te
0070 | 73 74 2E 6F 66 2E 66 6F 6F 2E 00 00 62 61 72 73 | st.of.foo...bars
0080 | 54 48 49 53 49 53 7E 31 54 45 53 20 00 00 00 00 | THISIS~1TES ....
0090 | 00 00 2D 1B 00 00 F8 76 2D 1B 03 00 07 00 00 00 | ..-....v-.......
; ...
```

The long filename appears, in place, directly adjacent to the short form. SECTDUMP shows that the long filename is spread across two directory entries, which immediately precede the short form. Larry Seltzer discusses the pros and cons of this approach in an excellent article in *PC Week* (September 20, 1993). Each long filename entry consists almost entirely of part of the long filename itself, ignoring the normal directory entry fields, except for the attribute byte, which is 0Fh. Programs that directly manipulate directory entries, such as CLUSTNAM and NAMCLUST, can use (p->attrib == 0x0F) to skip over these strange long filename entries. Otherwise these programs will misinterpret part of the ASCII name as, for example, the file size or date! Of course, this implementation may change in the final release, and you should not rely on this scheme.

Few programs poke their noses into directory entries, though, so discussing the implementation of long filenames before discussing the standard INT 21h interface is putting the cart before the horse. Most DOS programs open and find files, get the current directory, and so on, using normal INT 21h calls. Fortunately, programs like CLUSTNAM and NAMCLUST are the exception rather than the rule.

Let's say a DOS program calls INT 21h AH=47h to get the current directory. According to Microsoft's DOS 6.0 programmer's reference, a program needs a buffer of at least 64 bytes, which is large enough to contain the largest possible path. The program now finds itself running under Chicago, where a single directory, not to mention the entire path, is easily larger than 64 bytes (the limit is 254 characters for the filename, and 259 characters for the pathname). What happens?

The program gets the short form, of course. Otherwise, Chicago would break every DOS program that had obeyed the rules and allocated as little as 64 bytes in which to receive the current directory string. So developers don't have to worry about Microsoft breaking old programs with long filenames. Furthermore, Microsoft is taking care so that, as much as possible, an end-user sees long filenames even when a program sees the short alias. For example, it intends for the Windows common file dialogs (COMMDLG.DLL) to work this way.

However, programs will eventually want to know full filenames. Getting the long filename instead of the short alias requires a new set of functions. Windows programs will use Win32 API functions such as GetCurrentDirectory and CreateFile. A DOS program will be able to use a new set of INT 21h AX=71XXh functions, where the subfunction in AL is the same as the old DOS AH function number. For example, because the old DOS Get Current Directory function is INT 21h AH=47h, the new one that knows about long pathnames is INT 21h AX=7147h; while the other registers are identical to the old call, the buffers pointed to by DS:SI must be large enough to receive the maximum-allowed path. Programs can call the new INT 21h AX=4302h Get Volume Information function (see below) to get the length of the maximum-allowed path.

(It isn't clear if there is a new 21/7160 equivalent to the old 21/60 undocumented Truename function. Also, it isn't clear if Chicago will provide functions to convert between long and short filenames.)

In addition to these new INT 21h AH=71h calls, Chicago also requires some new actions for INT 21h AH=57h (4 = get last access date, 5 = set last access date). Incidentally, Chicago neatly skips over the two OS/2 EA actions for INT 21h AH=57h (see Chapter 4), which the preliminary Chicago documentation marks as "reserved." This is important, because some initial reports on Chicago (*PC Week*, August 23, 1993) claimed that Chicago long filenames might involve some deliberate incompatibility with OS/2. The evidence here points in the exact opposite direction (it appears to be deliberately *compatible*!), a welcome change from the actual incompatibility (seemingly deliberate) discussed in Chapter 1.

Another new DOS call is INT 21h AH=72h (FindClose). Whereas previous versions of DOS support only FindFirst and FindNext, Chicago requires FindClose because the Win32 programming interface (API) supports multiple, simultaneous file finds. FindFirst (INT 21h AX=714Eh) returns a "search handle," which you must pass to FindNext (INT 21h AX=714Fh), and which you must close with FindClose.

Long filenames are not supported in the initial DOS boot code portion of Chicago, which runs before DOS386.EXE. This means that real-mode programs such as TSRs and device drivers can't call the new long filename APIs if they run at system startup. Similarly, the few programs run in so-called "Single Application Mode" also won't be able to call the long filename APIs. To determine if the new APIs are available, a program can check the return values from the new 21/71 functions, or it can call the INT 21h AX=4302h Get Volume Information function. This new function returns information on the maximum pathname component length, whether the file system is case-preserving, and whether the long filename APIs are available. The function also returns the file-system name, which in the preliminary release was "LFAT".

The undocumented (prior to DOS 5.0) item in the directory entry, and the one we're most interested in at the moment, is the cluster word at offset 1Ah. This is the number for the file's first cluster. Recall from FAT.C that once you have the first cluster, the FAT chain gives you access to the rest of the file. The cluster word in the directory entry is what DOS uses to translate a file name to a location on disk.

NAMCLUST.C (Listing 8-5) shows use to use the cluster number in directory entries to translate names to locations. NAMCLUST takes a pathname (file or directory) on its command line and displays the file or directory's first cluster number. For convenience when using DEBUG to load sectors from disk, NAMCLUST also translates the cluster number to a hex sector number. For example:

```
C:\UNDOC2\CHAP8>namclust ..
C:\UNDOC2 ==> 18 (sect 493, 0x000001ed)

C:\UNDOC2\CHAP8>debug
-L 1000 2 01ED 1
```

NAMCLUST.C doesn't illustrate the easiest way to turn a pathname into a cluster number. You'll see later on that the SFT entry for an open file contains the file's starting cluster number. Thus, opening a file, and then looking for the cluster number in the open file's corresponding SFT, is simpler. You can do the same thing with FCBs: Robert Hummel's *Assembly Language Lab Notes* (Chapter 3) shows how to use FCBs to find starting clusters, again without walking the FAT. However, the code in NAMCLUST.C uses the actual directory structures on disk, and so better illustrates the workings of the DOS file system.

If run with just a drive on its command line (for example, NAMCLUST C:), the program walks the entire directory structure, printing out a hierarchical list of every file and its starting cluster. For example, the following shows C:\BORLANDC\INCLUDE\SYS\LOCKING.H and other files:

```
C:\UNDOC2\CHAP8>namclust c:
; ...
BORLANDC ==> 172 (sect 2957, 0x00000b8d)
    INCLUDE ==> 175 (sect 3005, 0x00000bbd)
        SYS ==> 176 (sect 3021, 0x00000bcd)
            LOCKING.H ==> 10797 (sect 172957, 0x0002a39d)
            STAT.H ==> 10798 (sect 172973, 0x0002a3ad)
            TIMEB.H ==> 10799 (sect 172989, 0x0002a3bd)
            TYPES.H ==> 10800 (sect 173005, 0x0002a3cd)
        ALLOC.H ==> 10711 (sect 171581, 0x00029e3d)
        ASSERT.H ==> 10712 (sect 171597, 0x00029e4d)
        BCD.H ==> 10713 (sect 171613, 0x00029e5d)
        BIOS.H ==> 10715 (sect 171645, 0x00029e7d)
        ; ... etc. ...
```

In NAMCLUST.C the variable do_all controls this listing of the entire disk.

Listing 8-5: NAMCLUST.C

```
/*
NAMCLUST.C -- Convert file name to starting cluster
Andrew Schulman, July 1993

Overall structure:
main
    truename -- to get canonical filename
    get_dpb
    do_cluster -- process a directory cluster; start with root dir <-+
        read_sectors (if it's a root directory)                     |
        read_cluster                                                |
            read_sectors (INT 25h)                                  |
        do_dir                                                      |
            printf -- success!  print results                      |
            do_cluster -- partial match; recurse to next level ------+
            get_fat_entry -- get next cluster of directory
        fail -- no such file!
*/

#include <stdlib.h>
```

```c
#include <stdio.h>
#include <string.h>
#include <ctype.h>
#include <dos.h>
#include "diskstuf.h"

// see Hummel, Assembly Language Lab Notes, p. 88
#define CLUSTER_TO_LSN(clust)   \
    ((((DWORD) (clust) - 2) * sect_per_clust) + first_sect)

void do_cluster(WORD cluster);
void do_dir(WORD cluster, DIR_ENTRY *buffer);
void read_cluster(int drive, BYTE far *buffer, WORD cluster);

static STRING glob_name[64] = {0};
static DPB far *glob_dpb;
static WORD want_cluster = 0xFFFF;
static WORD bytes_per_clust = 0, sect_per_clust = 0, first_sect = 0;
static int level = 0, glob_num_dir = 0, glob_drive;
static int num_levels = 0;
static char canon[128];
static int do_all = 0;

void fail(const char *s) { puts(s); exit(1); }

main(int argc, char *argv[])
{
    char partname[64];
    char *s, *s2;
    int i, part;

    if (argc < 2)
        fail("usage: namclust [pathname or drive:]");

    for (i=0; i<64; i++)
        glob_name[i] = (STRING) malloc(16);

    // program uses DOS 3.31 style of INT 25h
    if ((_osmajor < 3) || (_osmajor == 3 && _osminor < 31))
        fail("This program requires DOS 3.31 or higher");

    if (strlen(argv[1]) == 2 && argv[1][1] == ':')
    {
        do_all++;
        num_levels = 0xFFFF;
        strcpy (canon, strupr(argv[1]));
    }
    else
    {
        if (! truename(argv[1], canon))
            fail("can't get truename"); // might be JOINed drive
        if (canon[1] != ':')
            fail("Sorry, this doesn't work on network-redirector drives");

        for (part=0, s=canon, s2=partname; ; s++)
            if ((*s == '\0') || (*s == '\\'))
            {
                *s2 = '\0';
                strcpy(glob_name[part], partname);
                part++;
                if (*s == '\0')
                    break;
                s2 = partname;
            }
            else
                *s2++ = *s;
        num_levels = part - 1;
        level = 1;
    }
```

```
    glob_drive = canon[0] - 'A';
    if (! (glob_dpb = get_dpb(glob_drive+1)))
        fail("can't get DPB");

    sect_per_clust = glob_dpb->sectors_per_cluster + 1;
    bytes_per_clust = glob_dpb->bytes_per_sect * sect_per_clust;
    first_sect = glob_dpb->first_data_sector;
    glob_num_dir = bytes_per_clust / sizeof(DIR_ENTRY);
    do_cluster(0);              // kick-start search
}
void do_cluster(WORD cluster)
{
    BYTE *buffer;
    if (cluster == 0)    // phony cluster # for root directory
    {
        int num_sect;
        buffer = (BYTE *) calloc(glob_dpb->max_root_dir, sizeof(DIR_ENTRY));
        if (! buffer)
            fail("insufficient memory");
        num_sect = (glob_dpb->max_root_dir * sizeof(DIR_ENTRY)) /
                glob_dpb->bytes_per_sect;
        read_sectors(glob_drive, buffer, num_sect,
            (_osmajor >= 4) ? glob_dpb->vers.dos4.first_dir_sector :
                            glob_dpb->vers.dos3.first_dir_sector);
    }
    else
    {
        if (! (buffer = (BYTE *) calloc(bytes_per_clust, 1)))
            fail("insufficient memory");
        read_cluster(glob_drive, buffer, cluster);
    }
    do_dir(cluster, (DIR_ENTRY *) buffer);
    // shouldn't get here: can't free!
    if (do_all)
        free(buffer);
    else
        fail("can't find file");     // error if get here
}
void do_dir(WORD cluster, DIR_ENTRY *buffer)
{
    DIR_ENTRY *dir, *p;
    char name[16], *s;
    WORD next, num_dir;
    int entry, i;

    dir = (DIR_ENTRY *) buffer;
    num_dir = (cluster == 0) ? glob_dpb->max_root_dir : glob_num_dir;

    for (entry=0, p=dir; entry<num_dir; p++, entry++)
    {
        if (p->name[0] == '\0') return;      // end of dir
        if (p->name[0] == 0xE5) continue;    // deleted entry
        if (p->name[0] == '.')  continue;    // don't bother with . and ..

        // looks like Chicago uses these for long-filename entries
        if (p->attrib == 0x0F) continue;

        memcpy(name, p->name, 8); name[8] = 0;
        s = name; while (*s && *s != ' ') s++; *s = '\0';
        if (name[0] == 0x05) name[0] = 0xE5;    // 0xE5 is valid first char
        if (p->ext[0] != ' ')
        {
            strcat(name, ".");
            strncat(name, p->ext, 3);
            s = name; while (*s && *s != ' ') s++; *s = '\0';
        }
```

```
        if (do_all || strcmp(name, glob_name[level]) == 0)  // got match!
        {
            if (do_all || level == num_levels)              // done
            {
                DWORD sector = CLUSTER_TO_LSN(p->cluster);
                char *s;
                if (do_all)
                {
                    int i;
                    for (i=0; i<level; i++)
                        printf("   ");
                    s = name;
                }
                else
                    s = canon;
                printf("%s ==> %u (sect %lu, 0x%08lx)\n",
                    s, p->cluster, sector, sector);
                if (! do_all)
                    exit(0);
            }
            if (p->attrib & DIRECTORY_ATTR) // already know not . or ..
            {
                level++;
                do_cluster(p->cluster);     // if directory, recurse
                level--;                    // for do_all
            }
        }
    }

    // locate next directory cluster
    if ((next = get_fat_entry(glob_drive, glob_dpb, cluster)) < 0xFFF0)
        do_cluster(next);
}
void read_cluster(int drive, BYTE far *buffer, WORD cluster)
{
    DWORD sector;
    if (cluster != 0)        sector = CLUSTER_TO_LSN(cluster);
    else if (_osmajor >= 4) sector = glob_dpb->vers.dos4.first_dir_sector;
    else                    sector = glob_dpb->vers.dos3.first_dir_sector;
    if (! read_sectors(drive, buffer, sect_per_clust, sector))
        fail("can't read cluster");
}
```

NAMCLUST walks through a disk's directory hierarchy, trying to match the name of the specified file or directory.

The program calls the truename() function (INT 21h AH=60h) in DISKSTUF.C (Listing 8-4) to canonicalize the name specified on its command line (see "Finding a True Name").

Finding a True Name

In the MS-DOS file system, things may not be what they seem. A file called D:\FLOPPY\FOO.BAR may actually be located on a joined floppy disk in drive A:, and a subdirectory called F:\SOURCES may actually be located on a network file server (probably not even running MS-DOS), in a directory called \\BIN\EXPORT\DOS. A canonical (true) path string resolves all these logical (that is, non-physical) drive and path references to an absolute pathname, taking account of any renaming due to JOIN, SUBST, or network redirections.

Fortunately, there is a DOS function that provides a true canonical pathname: undocumented INT 21h function 60h (Resolve Path String to Canonical Path String). This corresponds to the undocumented TRUENAME command in COMMAND.COM in DOS 4.01 and higher (see Chapter 10). For example:

```
C:\UNDOC2>truename foo.bar
C:\UNDOC2\FOO.BAR

C:\UNDOC2>subst g: c:\undoc2

C:\UNDOC2>truename g:\foo.bar
C:\UNDOC2\FOO.BAR

C:\UNDOC2>c:\dos\join a: c:\floppy

C:\UNDOC2>truename c:\floppy\foo.bar
A:\FOO.BAR

C:\UNDOC2>rem E: and F: are network drives

C:\UNDOC2>truename f:\foo.bar
\\HOME\U\ANDREW\FOO.BAR

C:\UNDOC2>truename e:\*.exe
\\BIN\EXPORT\DOS\????????.EXE
```

Because G: is a SUBSTed alias for C:\UNDOC2, the true name for G:\FOO.BAR is C:\UNDOC2\FOO.BAR. Likewise, because C:\FLOPPY is a JOINed alias for the A: drive, A:\FOO.BAR is the true name for C:\FLOPPY\FOO.BAR. F: is located on a Sun SPARCstation (made available to DOS using PC/TCP, from FTP Software), and the \\ that starts off the truename of F:\FOO.BAR is the universal naming convention (UNC) indicating that this is a network drive.

It is important to realize, however, that the file FOO.BAR need not necessarily exist. This is a source of tremendous confusion about what function 60h and the TRUENAME command do. The truename function and TRUENAME command deal with *path names*, not with actual files. This is important for disk utilities such as NAMCLUST because it provides an easy way of determining that the user has specified a device with which the program can work. Simply examining the specified drive letter such as C: or A: tells you nothing about the actual drive involved. It is also useful sometimes to have some assistance from the operating system in interpreting complex pathnames with many .. and . subdirectories:

```
C:\UNDOC2>truename foo\bar\..\..\.\.\.
C:\UNDOC2
```

The undocumented TRUENAME command in COMMAND.COM in DOS 4.0 and higher is simply a wrapper around undocumented function 60h, which became available in DOS 3.0. You can call function 60h using the truename() function from DISKSTUF.C (Listing 8-4). Like most of the code in this chapter, the truename() function in DISKSTUF.C is only callable from a real-mode DOS program. To call INT 21h AH=60h from a protected mode Windows program, you need to use the techniques from Chapter 3 of this book. In particular, Listing 3-20 shows a protected mode version of truename() that uses DPMI. This is important because the normally well-informed *Microsoft Systems Journal* claimed (July-August 1992) that "unfortunately, TrueName cannot be called from Windows." Can too!

One problem with function 60h is its slightly odd interaction with JOIN. If you JOIN A: C:\FLOPPY, then while TRUENAME C:\FLOPPY\FOO.BAR works, TRUENAME A:\FOO.BAR gets an "Invalid drive specification" message! Meanwhile, function 60h does seem to work properly with the odd ASSIGN command. For example, if you ASSIGN a=c, then TRUENAME A:\FOO.BAR properly returns C:\FOO.BAR.

Another potential problem is that function 60h hits the disk. In some situations, accessing the Current Directory Structure might be preferable to function 60h. With the exception of its coexistence with ASSIGN, function 60h relates fairly directly to the CDS. For any drive n:, the output of function 60h for the string "n:." (that is, for the . subdirectory) matches cds[drive n:]->current_path. This point will make more sense when we discuss the CDS in detail, later in this chapter.

TRUNAM.C is a small sample program on the accompanying disk that runs truename() in a loop over the current directory for each drive on your system. The result is similar to that of the ENUMDRV program, shown later in Listing 8-11. Apparently there may be problems calling INT 21h AH=60h repeatedly under NetWare.

After calling truename(), NAMCLUST next calls get_dpb() to retrieve the DPB for the specified drive. NAMCLUST uses the DPB to determine values such as the number of directory entries in a directory cluster and to locate the sector for the root directory. NAMCLUST then calls do_cluster(0) to kick-start the name search in the root directory. For root directories, do_cluster() reads in the entire root directory. Root directories have a fixed number of entries which is given in the DPB; you don't locate them through the FAT. For non-root directories, do_cluster() reads a single directory cluster into memory and then calls do_dir() to process the directory cluster.

The do_dir() function checks each directory entry to see if the name matches the current portion of the pathname the user specified. If NAMCLUST finds a match at the end of the specified pathname, it has matched the entire pathname; NAMCLUST prints out the cluster number from the directory entry and exits successfully. If more of the specified pathname remains to be matched, do_dir() recurses into subdirectories by calling do_cluster(). Finally, if do_dir() hits the end of a directory cluster without a match, it calls get_fat_entry() to determine if there are additional clusters for the directory; if there are, do_dir() calls do_cluster() to read them in. If NAMCLUST arrives at the bottom of do_cluster() without a match, the program has failed to match the specified pathname. Therefore, no such pathname exists.

Thus, the code in NAMCLUST shows how to turn pathnames into starting cluster numbers. For example, you could bolt this code onto the front of FAT.C in Listing 8-2 to produce a more useful program that, given a pathname rather than a cluster number, displayed the file or directory's (possibly fragmented) FAT chain.

It is also possible to work in the opposite direction. Given a starting cluster number, this program could produce the corresponding full pathname. This will be useful later when this chapter examines the DOS System File Table (SFT). The SFT contains only the name and extension of a file, without any path information. However, the SFT does contain the starting cluster number for any open file, and you can use this to figure out the full pathname. Unfortunately, this CLUSTNAM operation can take a long time. For example, the Norton Utilities NU program has an "Information on item" option; choosing this for a cluster number causes NU to put up a "Working; one moment please . . . " notice and grind away for a while on the disk. Potentially every subdirectory on the disk must be examined to match a cluster number.

In any case, CLUSTNAM.C in Listing 8-6 (the opposite of NAMCLUST.C in Listing 8-5) takes a drive and cluster number on its command line and walks the directory structure, trying to produce the corresponding pathname:

```
C:\UNDOC2\CHAP8>clustnam d: 28005
C:\UNDOC2\CHAP8\CHAP8.TXT
```

Running NAMCLUST confirms this:

```
C:\UNDOC2\CHAP8>namclust chap8.txt
C:\UNDOC2\CHAP8.TXT ==> 28005 (sect 112289, 0x0001b6a1)
```

The do_cluster() and do_dir() functions in CLUSTNAM.C differ those from in NAMCLUST.C.
Rather than creating two slightly different versions of the same basic code, we should have written a
more generic subroutine library for manipulating DOS directory entries.

Listing 8-6: CLUSTNAM.C

```
/*
CLUSTNAM.C -- Convert cluster # to full pathname
See also NAMCLUST.C (Convert pathname to cluster #)
Andrew Schulman, July 1993

Program needs large model: bcc -ml clustnam.c diskstuf.c

Overall structure:
main
    get_dpb
    search_for_cluster
        do_cluster <-------------+
            read_sectors         |
            read_cluster         |
                read_sectors     |
            do_dir               |
                do_cluster ------+
                get_fat_entry
*/

#include <stdlib.h>
#include <stdio.h>
#include <string.h>
#include <ctype.h>
#include <dos.h>
#include "diskstuf.h"

void search_for_cluster();
void do_cluster(WORD cluster);
void do_dir(WORD cluster, DIR_ENTRY *buffer);
void read_cluster(int drive, BYTE far *buffer, WORD cluster);

void fail(const char *s) { puts(s); exit(1); }

static STRING glob_name[64] = {0};
static DPB far *glob_dpb;
static WORD want_cluster = 0xFFFF;
static WORD bytes_per_clust = 0, sect_per_clust = 0, first_sect = 0;
static int level = 0, glob_num_dir = 0, glob_drive;

main(int argc, char *argv[])
{
    int i;

    if (argc < 3)
        fail("usage: clusters [drive] [cluster]");

    // program uses DOS 3.31 style of INT 25h
    if ((_osmajor < 3) || (_osmajor == 3 && _osminor < 31))
        fail("This program requires DOS 3.31 or higher");

    for (i=0; i<64; i++)
        glob_name[i] = (STRING) malloc(16);

    glob_drive = toupper(argv[1][0]) - 'A';
    want_cluster = atoi(argv[2]);
    if (glob_dpb = get_dpb(glob_drive+1))
    {
        if (want_cluster <= glob_dpb->highest_cluster)
        {
            search_for_cluster();
```

```
                fail("couldn't find cluster");  // error if get here
        }
        else
            fail("cluster number too high");
    }
    else
        fail("can't get DPB");
    return 0;
}

void search_for_cluster(void)
{
    glob_drive = glob_dpb->drive;
    sect_per_clust = glob_dpb->sectors_per_cluster + 1;
    bytes_per_clust = glob_dpb->bytes_per_sect * sect_per_clust;
    first_sect = glob_dpb->first_data_sector;
    glob_num_dir = bytes_per_clust / sizeof(DIR_ENTRY);
    do_cluster(0);  // phony cluster 0 to kick-start
}

void do_cluster(WORD cluster)
{
    BYTE *buffer;
    if (cluster == 0)   // phony cluster # for root directory
    {
        int num_sect;
        buffer = (BYTE *) calloc(glob_dpb->max_root_dir, sizeof(DIR_ENTRY));
        if (! buffer)
            fail("insufficient memory");
        num_sect = (glob_dpb->max_root_dir * sizeof(DIR_ENTRY)) /
            glob_dpb->bytes_per_sect;
        read_sectors(glob_drive, buffer, num_sect,
            (_osmajor >= 4) ? glob_dpb->vers.dos4.first_dir_sector :
                        glob_dpb->vers.dos3.first_dir_sector);
    }
    else
    {
        if (! (buffer = (BYTE *) calloc(bytes_per_clust, 1)))
        {
            if (sizeof(void far *) != 4)
                puts("Hey, you should have compiled with large model!");
            fail("insufficient memory");
        }
        read_cluster(glob_drive, buffer, cluster);
    }
    do_dir(cluster, (DIR_ENTRY *) buffer);
    free(buffer);
}

void do_dir(WORD cluster, DIR_ENTRY *buffer)
{
    DIR_ENTRY *dir, *p;
    char name[9], ext[4];
    WORD next, num_dir;
    int entry, i;

    dir = (DIR_ENTRY *) buffer;
    num_dir = (cluster == 0) ? glob_dpb->max_root_dir : glob_num_dir;
    for (entry=0, p=dir; entry<num_dir; p++, entry++)
    {
        if (p->name[0] == '\0') return;      // end of dir
        if (p->name[0] == 0xE5) continue;    // deleted entry
        if (p->name[0] == '.')  continue;    // don't bother with . and ..

        // looks like Chicago uses these for long-filename entries
        if (p->attrib == 0x0F) continue;
```

```c
        memcpy(name, p->name, 8); name[8] = 0;
        if (name[0] == 0x05) name[0] = 0xE5;       // 0xE5 is valid first char
        memcpy(ext, p->ext, 3);    ext[3] = 0;

        strcpy(glob_name[level], name);
        if (ext[0] != ' ' != 0)
        {
            strcat(glob_name[level], ".");
            strcat(glob_name[level], ext);
        }

        if (p->cluster == want_cluster) // found it!
        {
            char *s;
            int i;
            putchar(glob_drive + 'A'); putchar(':'); putchar('\\');
            for (i=0; i<level; i++)
            {
                s = glob_name[i];        // trim spaces out of name
                while (*s) { if (*s != ' ') putchar(*s); s++; }
                putchar('\\');
            }
            s = glob_name[level];        // trim spaces out of name
            while (*s) { if (*s != ' ') putchar(*s); s++; }
            putchar('\n');
            exit(0);                     // done: success!
        }

        if (p->attrib & DIRECTORY_ATTR) // already know not . or ..
        {
            level++;
            do_cluster(p->cluster);      // if directory, recurse
            level--;
        }
    }

    // locate next directory cluster
    next = get_fat_entry(glob_drive, glob_dpb, cluster);
    if (next < 0xFFF0)                   // end of dir
        do_cluster(next);
}
// see Hummel, Assembly Language Lab Notes, p. 88
#define CLUSTER_TO_LSN(clust)   \
    ((((DWORD) (clust) - 2) * sect_per_clust) + first_sect)

void read_cluster(int drive, BYTE far *buffer, WORD cluster)
{
    DWORD sector;
    if (cluster != 0)        sector = CLUSTER_TO_LSN(cluster);
    else if (_osmajor >= 4)  sector = glob_dpb->vers.dos4.first_dir_sector;
    else                     sector = glob_dpb->vers.dos3.first_dir_sector;
    if (! read_sectors(drive, buffer, sect_per_clust, sector))
        fail("can't read cluster");
}
```

Like NAMCLUST.C, CLUSTNAM.C uses the DISKSTUF module from Listings 8-3 and 8-4. The program's overall structure is very similar to that of NAMCLUST, except that where NAMCLUST can bail out of the directory search as soon as it finds a mismatch, CLUSTNAM must keep walking the entire disk directory hierarchy until it finds a match.

The Drive Parameter Block (DPB)

The programs presented so far in this chapter all relied heavily on the DPB structure and get_dpb() function in DISKSTUF (Listings 8-3 and 8-4) to determine characteristics of a drive, such as its bytes per sector, sectors per cluster, sectors per FAT, location of the first FAT, directory, data sectors, and so on. But we haven't said much yet about the DPB.

For every block device in the system, there is a Drive Parameter Block. These 32-byte blocks contain the information that DOS uses to convert cluster numbers into logical sector numbers for passing to the block device driver Read and Write functions and to associate the device driver for that device with its assigned drive letter.

DOS creates the DPB for each drive immediately after calling the driver's Initialize routine during the boot process. (Recall from Chapter 7 how the DEVLOD program, which mimics DOS operation, loads block device drivers.) DPBs for the drivers built into IO.SYS or IBMBIO.COM (normally floppies A: and B: together with hard disk C:) are created when IO.SYS initializes itself before processing CONFIG.SYS; those for all other block devices are created as one of the final steps of installing the device driver, while processing CONFIG.SYS.

To create the DPB, the code that installs drivers uses the still-undocumented INT 21h function 53h, passing it a far pointer to the drive's BPB (see the Put_Blk_Dev() function in DEVLOD.C in Chapter 7; Figure 7-28). You should recognize many of the fields in the DPB from our earlier discussion of the BPB. However, DOS doesn't take the BPB's description at face value. A copy of the BPB normally is built into the device driver itself, and the pointer is part of the information returned by the driver's Initialize routine (device driver function 0). As you saw earlier, for the built-in disk drives, the BPBs are contained in the boot sector of each volume, and each time a volume is changed, DOS uses this BPB to rebuild the DPB in case the new volume's characteristics differ from the original values.

No DPB exists for drive letters which have no drive associated with them; the exception to this is drive B: in a single-floppy system; it's always assumed to exist, even when it doesn't. On the other hand, non-physical devices that masquerade as drives (such as RAM disks) generally *do* have DPBs.

Each DPB is linked to the next one by a far pointer in the DPB structure; FFFFh in the pointer's offset position indicates the end of this linked list. But while DPBs are chained together in a linked list, whose root is available as the first DWORD in SysVars, a better way to get the DPB for a given drive is to use the DOS Get DPB function (INT 21h function 32h), which we saw in Chapter 7 as part of DEVLOD's facility for loading block device drivers and which is often used in disk programs such as Norton Utilities or PC Tools. Microsoft has finally documented this function in its *MS-DOS Programmer's Reference*. However, according to Microsoft this function is only for MS-DOS 5.0 and higher. Thus, if you believe the Microsoft documentation, you can't write disk utilities that work under any previous version of DOS.

The sample program in Listing 8-7 (DPBTEST.C) uses INT 21h function 32h to display capacity information for each drive on the system with a DPB. For example, on a system with a 1.2 megabyte floppy drive that had a 360K floppy in it at the time, a 70 megabyte hard disk, and a 64K RAMdrive (installed with DEVLOD, by the way), here is the program's output:

```
Drive A: 512 bytes/sector * 2 sectors/cluster =
         1024 bytes/cluster * 354 clusters = 362496 bytes
Drive C: 512 bytes/sector * 8 sectors/cluster =
         4096 bytes/cluster * 17648 clusters = 72286208 bytes
Drive E: 512 bytes/sector * 1 sectors/cluster =
         512 bytes/cluster * 122 clusters = 62464 bytes
```

The program displays this information twice, once by walking the DPB linked list (whose head is at offset 0 in SysVars), and once by calling INT 21h function 32h (via get_dpb() from DISKSTUF.C in Listing 8-4) for each drive < lastdrive.

A third possibility, which would work better than walking the DPB chain for SUBST drives, for example, is to retrieve the DPB from the drive's Current Directory Structure. For an illustration, see the function maybe_ram_disk() in ENUMDRV.C (Listing 8-11), which can retrieve a DPB with the expression currdir(drive)->dpb.

Listing 8-7: DPBTEST.C

```c
/*
DPBTEST.C -- uses undocumented INT 21h function 32h (Get DPB)
    to display bytes per drive; but first walks the DPB chain,
    showing the difference between the two access methods.
    A third access method gets the DPB from the CDS (see
    maybe_ram_disk() in ENUMDRV.C).
Andrew Schulman, updated July 1993
*/

#include <stdlib.h>
#include <stdio.h>
#include <dos.h>
#ifdef __TURBOC__
#include <dir.h>
#endif
#include "diskstuf.h"               // DPB structure, get_dpb()

void fail(const char *s) { puts(s); exit(1); }

void display(DPB far *dpb)
{
    DWORD bytes_per_clust =
        dpb->bytes_per_sect * (dpb->sectors_per_cluster + 1);

    printf("Drive %c: ", 'A' + dpb->drive);
    printf("%u bytes/sector * ", dpb->bytes_per_sect);
    printf("%u sectors/cluster = \n",
        dpb->sectors_per_cluster + 1);
    printf("        %lu bytes/cluster * ", bytes_per_clust);
    printf("%u clusters = ", dpb->highest_cluster - 1);
    printf("%lu bytes\n\n",
        bytes_per_clust * (dpb->highest_cluster - 1));
}

main()
{
    BYTE far *sysvars;
    DPB far *dpb;
    unsigned lastdrive;
    int i;

    if ((_osmajor < 3) || (_osmajor == 3 && _osminor < 2))
        fail("This program requires DOS 3.2 or higher");

    puts("Using DPB linked list");
    _asm mov ah, 52h                /* get SysVars */
    _asm int 21h
    _asm mov word ptr sysvars+2, es
    _asm mov word ptr sysvars, bx
    /* pointer to first DPB at offset 0h in SysVars */
    if (! (dpb = *((DPB far * far *) sysvars)))
        return 1;
    do {
        // don't show both A: and B: etc.
        if ((! _dos_driveremoveable(dpb->drive + 1)) ||
            (_dos_getdrivemap(dpb->drive + 1) == dpb->drive + 1))
            display(dpb);
        dpb = (_osmajor<4) ? dpb->vers.dos3.next : dpb = dpb->vers.dos4.next;
    } while (FP_OFF(dpb) != 0xFFFF);

    // Another (better) method gets DPB pointer out of drive's CDS:
    // #define GET_DPB(drive) (currdir(drive)->dpb)
    // see maybe_ram_disk() #ifdef USE_CDS_DPB in listing 8-11

    puts("Using INT 21h function 32h");
    _dos_setdrive(0xFF, &lastdrive);    // get lastdrive
    for (i=1; i<=lastdrive; i++)
```

```
        if (dpb = get_dpb(i))     // checks for removeable, critical error
            display(dpb);
    return 0;
}
```

This program brings up an important reason to use INT 21h function 32h instead of walking the DPB linked list. For removable media, function 32h goes to the disk and, therefore, picks up the most current information. Walking the linked list merely gets whatever (possibly stale) DPB happens to be in memory. If you access a 360K floppy disk in drive A:, remove it, put in a 1.2 megabyte floppy without accessing it, and then walk the DPB linked list, you get the DPB for the 360K floppy. Function 32h would not make this mistake.

On the other hand, function 32h hits the disk (see the disassembly of functions 32h and 1Fh in Chapter 6), which makes it inconvenient to get the DPB of drives with removable media. Further, you want to avoid reading both drives A: and B: in a system where these logical drives are mapped to the same physical floppy drive.

The version of DPBTEST in Listing 8-7 differs substantially from that in the first edition of *Undocumented DOS*, which feebly tried to deal with the above problem by checking for drives A: and B: neglecting the fact that other drive letters (such as those created with DRIVER.SYS) may involve removable media. This utter bogosity was further compounded by checking the floppy disk logical drive indicator at address 504h. Totally hopeless!

Instead, programs should use generic IOCTL calls to determine whether a device uses removable media (INT 21h AX=4408h) and to get the logical drive map (INT 21h AX=440Eh). These calls, along with an INT 24h critical error handler invoked when there is no media in the drive at all, are incorporated into the get_dpb() function that DPBTEST.C uses from DISKSTUF.C (Listing 8-4).

One last note about DPBs. Many crucial DOS disk utilities were thrown into temporary confusion by the introduction of DOS 4.0 because of a one-byte change to the DPB structure. The sectors-per-FAT field at offset 0Fh (see the appendix) grew from a *byte* to a *word*, so all subsequent fields were bumped one byte as well. As noted at the time (Ted Mirecki, "Function 32h in DOS," *PC Tech Journal,* February 1989), this one-byte modification produced a major ripple effect in the Norton Utilities and other programs that relied on this undocumented DOS data structure. Rather than bemoaning incompatibilities, cynics may view this sort of change as a good excuse to hit up customers with an upgrade release.

Buffers and Disk Caches

Like any proper operating system, MS-DOS has *buffered* I/O. Rather than directly reading sectors off the disk, DOS first checks to see whether the sector is already present in an in-memory buffer. DOS uses buffers for FAT, directory, and data sectors. DOS buffers sectors, not higher-level clusters or lower-level tracks. The BUFFERS= statement in CONFIG.SYS controls the number of sector buffers, which are chained together in a least-recently-used (LRU) circular linked list; SysVars holds a pointer to the head of this list.

Each sector-sized buffer follows a small header which identifies the drive currently using that buffer, the sector of the data it contains, a status byte indicating what type of sector (FAT, directory, or data) it contains, and a pointer to the next buffer header in the chain.

The buffer chain made its debut in DOS 2.0. In DOS 1.x, there was a single sector buffer; Tim Paterson admitted this was "a design inadequacy that is difficult to defend." On the other hand, while DOS 1.x kept the FAT memory-resident at all times, in marked contrast to CP/M which could require multiple disk reads just to find the location of a user's data, DOS 2.0 and higher rely entirely on the buffers for keeping often-used FAT sectors in memory. Paterson notes ("An Inside Look at MS-DOS," *Byte*, June 1983):

> The new MS-DOS does not keep the file allocation tables in memory at all times. Instead the tables share the use of the sector buffers. . . . This means that at any one time, all, part, or none of a FAT may be in memory. The buffer-handling algorithms will presumably keep often-used sectors in memory, and this applies to individual sectors of the FAT as well. This change in the DOS goes completely against my original design principles. . . . Now we're back to doing disk reads just to find out where the data is.

With today's large media, a memory-resident FAT could occupy up to 128K (64K clusters * 16 bits) of memory.

DOS uses the buffers in sequence, changing the linkages as necessary to maintain the most recently used buffers near the front of the chain. Any DOS sector access first walks through the chain of headers, looking for the requested drive and sector; if found, it can use the buffer contents without having to hit the disk. Moving each used buffer up to the front of the chain guarantees that any time a search reaches the end of the chain without finding its sector, the buffer at the end would be the least recently used and, thus, the proper one (in this scheme) to replace with the new data read from the disk.

Unfortunately, this simple approach did not take into account the pattern by which DOS performs disk reads. In practice, the buffer chain filled rapidly with FAT and directory data, leaving only a few buffers for all file data transfers. The system was modified several times under DOS 2.0 and 3.0, but performance problems remained significant. The DOS buffers underwent a major implementation change in DOS 4.0, when IBM introduced a complicated hashing scheme and a mechanism for keeping buffers in expanded memory. This was thrown out in DOS 5.0, which returned to the simpler LRU buffers scheme.

If DOS=HIGH, DOS 5.0 and higher keep the buffers in the HMA. Also for the first time in DOS 5.0, sectors accessed with the INT 25h and INT 26h absolute disk read and write functions first check the sector buffers.

In addition to a pointer to the head of the buffers chain, SysVars in DOS 4.0 and higher also contains the *number* of buffers, that is, the value from the BUFFERS= statement in CONFIG.SYS. (For more information, see "SysVars, or The List of Lists" later in this chapter.) Determining BUFFERS= is probably the only practical way a program could use buffers information. It is difficult when running a program to determine which CONFIG.SYS file was used to boot the system. In fact, prior to the availability of INT 21h function 3305h in DOS 4.0, one couldn't even tell what drive the system was booted from! So install, setup, and configuration programs might want to determine the value of BUFFERS= (and FILES=, which we'll look at later).

To find the value of BUFFERS= in earlier versions of DOS, a program must walk the buffers chain, as shown in BUFFERS.C (Listing 8-8). In DOS 4.0 and higher, this program also prints out a description of each buffer's contents. For example:

```
C:\UNDOC2\CHAP8>buffers
FFFF:A8C8 -- C: #208 -- DIR
FFFF:B968 -- C: #3133 -- DATA
FFFF:A4A0 -- C: #1 -- FAT
FFFF:9A3C -- C: #3226 -- DATA
FFFF:B540 -- D: #109 -- FAT
FFFF:BD90 -- D: #110 -- FAT
; ... etc. ...
FFFF:B118 -- A: #19 -- DIR
FFFF:9400 -- A: #20 -- DIR
BUFFERS=30
```

As you can see, the buffers include floppy diskettes as well as hard disks; however, network redirected drives are not included. It is instructive to run BUFFERS, then perform a disk operation, such as DIR, or run some other program, and then run BUFFERS again. You can see the contents of the buffers change. Of course, running BUFFERS.EXE itself changes the contents of the buffers!

When DOS=HIGH, DOS usually allocates the buffers in the high memory area (HMA) just above one megabyte. This area can be accessed only if the processor's A20 address line is enabled. If the buffers are in the HMA but A20 is off, BUFFERS.C in Listing 8-8 calls XMS to enable A20. This code is very similar to that MS-DOS itself uses when DOS=HIGH but A20 is off (see Chapter 6). Other programs in this chapter that access structures such as the CDS and SFT don't contain code to enable A20, because DOS (to date) doesn't allocate these structures in the HMA. Some third-party utilities can move the CDS and SFT to upper memory (UMBs), but A20 is irrelevant to UMB access.

Few programs directly access the DOS buffers, and so moving them to the HMA "broke" few, if any, programs. In contrast, moving the CDS or SFT to the HMA might have disastrous results for programs that didn't know to check A20 first. This might become important, because Chicago is reported to have CONFIG.SYS settings such as LASTDRIVEHIGH= and FILESHIGH= (though these probably use UMBs rather than the HMA). On the other hand, any problems will be quite rare, because (as we saw in Chapter 6) MS-DOS leaves A20 on, and because any trivial DOS call will put A20 back on if some program turns it off.

Listing 8-8: BUFFERS.C

```
/*
BUFFERS.C -- Display buffer chain, and count BUFFERS=
See also COUNTF.C to determine value of FILES=
Andrew Schulman, revised July 1993
Added code to check and enable A20 if BUFFERS are in HMA
*/

#include <stdlib.h>
#include <stdio.h>
#include <string.h>
#include <dos.h>

typedef unsigned char BYTE;
typedef unsigned short WORD;
typedef unsigned long DWORD;

#ifndef MK_FP
#define MK_FP(seg, ofs) \
    ((void far *) (((DWORD) (seg) << 16) | (ofs)))
#endif

#pragma pack(1)
    typedef struct dskbuf3 {
        struct dskbuf3 far *next;
        BYTE drive, flags;
        } DSKBUF3;

    typedef struct {
        WORD next, prev;
        BYTE drive, flags;
        DWORD sector;
        } DSKBUF4;
#pragma pack()

void fail(const char *s) { puts(s); exit(1); }

char *buff_status(BYTE flags)
{
    static char buf[128];
    buf[0] = '\0';
    if (flags & 2) strcpy(buf, "FAT ");
    if (flags & 4) strcat(buf, "DIR ");
    if (flags & 8) strcat(buf, "DATA ");
    if (flags & 16) strcat(buf, "REF ");      // referenced
    if (flags & 32) strcat(buf, "DIRTY ");    // modified, not yet written
    if (flags & 64) strcat(buf, "REMOTE ");
    return buf;
}
```

```c
/* XMS stuff in case BUFFERS in HMA ******************************/
/* if XMS present, store entry point in xms_entrypoint */
static void (far *xms_entrypoint)(void) = (void (far*)()) 0;

int xms_is_present(void)
    {
    int available = 0;
    if (xms_entrypoint) return 1;

    _asm {
        mov     ax, 4300h
        int     2fh
        cmp     al, 80h
        je      present
        jmp     SHORT done
        }

present:
    available = 1;
    _asm {
        mov     ax, 4310h;
        int     2fh;
        push    ds;
        mov     ax, seg xms_entrypoint;
        mov     ds, ax;
        mov     word ptr xms_entrypoint, bx;
        mov     word ptr xms_entrypoint+2, es;
        pop     ds;
        }
done:
    return available;
    }


int xms_local_a20(int func)
{
    if (! xms_entrypoint)
        if (! xms_is_present())
            return 0;    // no XMS
    _asm mov ah, byte ptr func
    (*xms_entrypoint)();
    // return value in AX; success=1
}
int xms_local_enable_a20(void)  { return xms_local_a20(5); }
int xms_local_disable_a20(void) { return xms_local_a20(6); }

static int testing = 0;
/****************************************************************/

unsigned buffers(void)
{
    BYTE far *doslist;
    WORD buffers;

    _asm mov ah, 52h
    _asm int 21h
    _asm mov word ptr doslist+2, es
    _asm mov word ptr doslist, bx

    /* pointer to first disk buffer in List of Lists */
    if (_osmajor < 3)
        fail("This program requires DOS 3.0 or higher");
    else if (_osmajor == 3)
    {
        DSKBUF3 far *dskbuf3;
        if (_osminor == 0)
            dskbuf3 = *((DSKBUF3 far * far *) (doslist + 0x13));
        else
```

```
                dskbuf3 = *((DSKBUF3 far * far *) (doslist + 0x12));
            for (buffers=1; ; buffers++)
            {
                printf("buffer @ %Fp\n", dskbuf3);
                if ((dskbuf3 = dskbuf3->next) == (DSKBUF3 far *) -1L)
                    break;
            }
        }
        else     // DOS 4, 5, 6
        {
            DSKBUF4 far *dskbuf4 = *((DSKBUF4 far * far *) (doslist + 0x12));
            WORD seg, first, in_use;

            if (_osmajor >= 5)  // DOS 5+ disk buffer info struct
                dskbuf4 = *((DSKBUF4 far * far *) dskbuf4);

            seg = FP_SEG(dskbuf4);
            first = FP_OFF(dskbuf4);
            in_use = 0;
// code added in case BUFFERS in HMA; have to check A20!
{
    DWORD lin = (DWORD) seg << 4L;
    lin += first;
    if (lin > 0x100000L)
    {
        DWORD far *low = (DWORD far *) 0x00000080L;
        DWORD far *high = (DWORD far *) 0xFFFF0090L;
        puts("BUFFERS are HIGH");

        if (testing)
            xms_local_disable_a20();     // force A20 to test code below

        if ((low[0] == high[0]) && (low[1] == high[1]))
        {
            puts("A20 is off; turning A20 on");
#if 1
            if (! xms_local_enable_a20())
                fail("Can't enable A20");
#else
            // as we know from chapter 6, this will work too!!
            // in fact, we could just do this, and let DOS do all checking
            _asm mov ax, 3000h
            _asm int 21h
#endif
            if ((low[0] == high[0]) && (low[1] == high[1])) // still!
                fail("A20 still disabled!");
        }
    }
}


        for (buffers=1; ; buffers++)
        {
            if (dskbuf4->drive == 0xFF)
                printf("%Fp -- unused\n", dskbuf4);
            else
            {
                in_use++;
                printf("%Fp -- %c: #%lu -- %s\n",
                    dskbuf4,                        // pointer
                    'A' + dskbuf4->drive,           // drive
                    dskbuf4->sector,                // sector number
                    buff_status(dskbuf4->flags));   // status
            }
            if (dskbuf4->next == first) // LRU list wraps around
```

```
                break;
            else
                dskbuf4 = (DSKBUF4 far *) MK_FP(seg, dskbuf4->next);
        }
        if (buffers != doslist[0x3F])    // number of buffers
            fail("Something wrong!");
        printf("%u buffers in use\n", in_use);
        return buffers;
    }
}
main(int argc, char *argv[])
{
    WORD num_buf;
    if (argc > 1) testing++;     // any command line arg
    // To make program useful, stick various experiments in here
    // (e.g., call 21/0D to flush disk; read/write a file, etc.).
    num_buf = buffers();
    printf("BUFFERS=%d\n", num_buf);
    return num_buf;        // can check with ERRORLEVEL
}
```

For machines with sufficient memory, SmartDrive or another disk cache provides better performance than relying entirely on DOS buffers. When using SmartDrive, Microsoft rightly suggests using a small BUFFERS= value. Whereas the DOS buffers cache DOS logical sectors from floppy diskettes as well as hard disks, SmartDrive works at the INT 13h level, and only cares about hard disks. SmartDrive and other BIOS-level caches do not cache data from any devices that don't call down to INT 13h. This includes CD-ROM drives, for example; hence the growing popularity of CD-ROM "speedup" products. As this book went to press, Microsoft announced that SmartDrive 4.2, which can cache CD-ROM drives, will be included with MS-DOS 6.2; SmartDrive 4.2 is also available separately from Microsoft's CompuServe forum.

After DOS 6.0 was introduced, many supposed DoubleSpace problems reported by *InfoWorld* actually turned out to be "cockpit errors" (end-user problems) with using the newer SmartDrive, which introduced a "write-behind cache" that defers disk writes, possibly for several seconds. The typical problem scenario is that a COPY command appears to complete, the machine is sitting at the DOS C:\ prompt and, taking that as a visual cue, the user turns the machine off. If COPY's deferred writes haven't yet completed (very possible given SmartDrive's aggressive caching), the end result is typically reported by CHKDSK as a cross-linked file. Part of the problem was that users weren't educated to check their hard-drive light before turning off the machine. As part of combatting these problems, SmartDrive 4.2 doesn't give back the DOS prompt until disk writes have completed.

For an excellent, though now slightly dated, discussion, see Geoff Chappell's "Untangling SmartDrive" (*Dr. Dobb's Journal*, January 1992); also see the brief discussion of "Undocumented SmartDrive" in Chapter 1. Some non-Microsoft disk caches also support the undocumented SmartDrive interface.

SysVars, or The List of Lists

Since the introduction of CONFIG.SYS with MS-DOS version 2.0, the DOS kernel has maintained a collection of pointers and variables near the start of its data segment. Since this collection of pointers is not officially documented, it's known by several names. The name in the DOS source code is SysInitVars; the structure is built by the DOS initialization code, called SysInit (see Chapter 6). This is often shortened to SysVars, which is the name used throughout this book. In the first edition, we referred to SysVars using the biblical-sounding name, List of Lists.

SysVars, together with INT 21h AH=52h, which returns in ES:BX a pointer to this structure, is the central clearinghouse for virtually all of the undocumented data concerning the DOS file system. In addition, as already discussed in Chapter 7, SysVars provides the start of the Memory Control Block chain and the device driver chain. More than any other single structure, SysVars is the key to reaching the undocumented areas of DOS. The following is a schematic listing of just some of the structures that you can access directly or indirectly via SysVars. You can see why this is sometimes called the List of Lists!

```
Memory Control Block (MCB)
      Program Segment Prefix (PSP)
            Environment segment
            Job File Table (JFT)
Drive Parameter Block (DPB)
      File Allocation Table (FAT)
      Directory entries
System File Table (SFT)
Device driver chain
Disk buffers
Current Directory Structure (CDS)
FCB table
SHARE.EXE hooks
```

These structures are interconnected. For example, the SFT entry for block devices contains a pointer to the corresponding DPB; so does the CDS. One of the items contained in the DPB is a pointer to its corresponding device driver. Meanwhile, the heads of both the DPB and device chains are found directly in SysVars.

IO.SYS builds SysVars on the fly each time you boot your system. The starting point is the processing of CONFIG.SYS, which makes any installable device drivers part of the DOS kernel and possibly modifies certain values (for example, LASTDRIVE and the CDS pointer) stored in SysVars.

But what happens if no CONFIG.SYS file exists? Obviously no drivers are installed, but the default values that control the building of the SysVars are assembled into IO.SYS. Thus DOS sets FILES=8, LASTDRIVE=5, FCBS=4, calculates an appropriate BUFFERS= value from memory size and drive data, and sets the primary shell to C:\COMMAND.COM /P (assuming C: is the boot drive).

If CONFIG.SYS is processed, these commands will overwrite the default values. (Incidentally, Chicago appears to have new commands such as FILESHIGH= and LASTDRIVEHIGH=.) When DOS has parsed the entire file, with all commands executed or passed over with error messages, DOS builds SysVars from the values which then exist in the CONFIG control variables (see Chapter 7). It then discards the control variables, along with the rest of the now-surplus initialization code.

Incidentally, addition of the capability to load DOS high (into the High Memory Area) and to force device drivers and TSRs into Upper Memory Blocks has had some strange side effects on what happens during IO.SYS initialization. Before DOS 5.0 it was possible to predict just where in RAM each item processed from CONFIG.SYS would wind up. If high or upper memory is involved, however, you can't predict the memory map layout at all, because it depends on the availability of UMBs and the HMA which, in turn, depend on the specific device drivers installed, such as HIMEM.SYS, EMM386.EXE, or 386MAX.SYS. That is, the addition of a single driver can now totally rearrange the locations in RAM at which all other drivers are loaded, moving some from high to low and others from low to high. For example, if CONFIG.SYS requested DOS=HIGH but an XMS server such as HIMEM.SYS was unavailable, you could end up with a rather strange memory map.

The Current Directory Structure (CDS)

SysVars contains a far pointer to an array of Current Directory Structures. Each drive in the system has its own CDS, which contains the current working directory and points to the DPB for that drive. This structure also contains attribute bits that specify whether the drive exists or not, whether it is modified by the JOIN or SUBST commands, or whether it is a network drive. Microsoft adopted the CDS as part of the networking additions begun in DOS 3.0; it plays a central role in manipulating foreign (not just network) file systems.

The CDS array contains one CDS for each possible block device or drive letter on the system. If you specify LASTDRIVE=Z, your system will have a 26-element CDS array; using the default value for LASTDRIVE, your CDS array will contain only five elements. In other words, the LASTDRIVE value is nothing more than the size of the CDS array. Each element in the array is 81 (51h) bytes long under DOS version 3.0, and 88 (58h) bytes for versions 4.0 and up. CURRDIR.H (Listing 8-9) includes a CDS structure that several different programs later in this chapter will use. As you can see, the CDS for each drive starts off with a 67-byte ASCIIZ string for the current path on the drive; it is from this that the CDS takes its name.

Listing 8-9: CURRDIR.H

```
/*
CURRDIR.H
Current Directory Structure (CDS); also Stacker and DoubleSpace stuff
Andrew Schulman, revised July 1993
*/

typedef unsigned char BYTE;
typedef unsigned short WORD;
typedef unsigned long DWORD;
typedef int BOOL;

#include "diskstuf.h"    // for get_dpb(), DPB structure

#pragma pack(1)
typedef struct {
    BYTE current_path[67]; // current path                               00h
    WORD flags;            // NETWORK, PHYSICAL, JOIN, SUBST, CDROM       43h
    DPB far *dpb;          // pointer to Drive Parameter Block            45h
    union {
        struct {
            WORD start_cluster; // root: 0000; never accessed: FFFFh      49h
            DWORD unknown;
            } LOCAL;       // if (! (cds[drive].flags & NETWORK))
        struct {
            DWORD redirifs_record_ptr;
            WORD parameter;
            } NET;         // if (cds[drive].flags & NETWORK)
        } u;
    WORD backslash_offset; // offset in current_path of '\'               4Fh
    // DOS4 fields for IFS
    // 7 extra bytes...
    } CDS;

// flags (CDS offset 43h)
#define NETWORK       (1 << 15)
#define PHYSICAL      (1 << 14)
#define JOIN          (1 << 13)
#define SUBST         (1 << 12)
#define REDIR_NOT_NET (1 << 7)      // CDROM

CDS far *currdir(unsigned drive);

extern void fail(const char *s);    // app must define

/* Stacker -- see IS_STACK.C */
typedef struct {
```

```
      WORD signature, version, ofs_tab;
      BYTE unknown[56], vol_num, unknown2[19];
      BYTE swap_str[4], drive_map[26];
      } STACKER_DRIVER;
#pragma pack()

STACKER_DRIVER far *stacker_detect(void);
int stacker_swapped(int drive);
DWORD stacker_drive(int drive, BOOL *pswap, BYTE *phost);

/* DoubleSpace -- see IS_DSPAC.C */
BOOL double_space_drive(BYTE drive, BOOL *pswap, BYTE *phost, int *pseq);
```

CURRDIR.H also contains function declarations and structures for testing Stacker and DoubleSpace drives; we examine these later on.

After reading through CONFIG.SYS and determining the value of LASTDRIVE=, DOS creates an array like the following (though in DOS 4.0 and higher, each CDS element is 7 bytes larger):

```
CDS cds[LASTDRIVE];
```

Because LASTDRIVE fixes the size of this array, you normally can't expand the CDS without changing CONFIG.SYS and rebooting. The DOS kernel usually occupies the space immediately above the array and contains areas referenced by absolute pointers from many other parts of DOS. However, the program LASTDRIV.COM shipped with QEMM can increase LASTDRIVE on the fly and expands the CDS array. The XLASTDRV program in Chapter 2 (Listing 2-18) shows how this is done.

Most programs of course do not create a CDS. Instead, you use the CDS already built by DOS. Rather than declare an array, you declare a far pointer to a CDS and set it using the CDS pointer at the appropriate offset in SysVars:

```
SysVars far *list;
CDS far *cds;
// ...
if (_osmajor == 2)                      fail("no CDS");        // DOS 2.0
if (_osmajor == 3 && _osminor == 0) cds = list->dos30.cds;   // DOS 3.0
else                                cds = list->dos31.cds;   // DOS 3.1+
```

To access the CDS for a given drive, you index into the array. However, because the size of a CDS entry is not known until run time (unless you restrict the program to running only under DOS 4.0 or higher), you must treat the CDS array, not as an array of CDS entries, but as an array of BYTEs:

```
BYTE far *cds;                      // rather than CDS far *
int drive;
int currdir_size = (_osmajor >= 4) ? 88 : 81;
// ...
if (drive >> lastdrive())           // see chapter 2 for lastdrive()
    fail("no such drive");          // but watch out for Novell NetWare
else
    printf("%Fs\n", &cds[drive * currdir_size]);
```

We can package all this knowledge into a currdir() function that several programs will use later in this chapter. The function is called with a drive number (where drive A: is 0) and returns a far pointer to the CDS for that drive. Its implementation appears in CURRDIR.C (Listing 8-10).

Listing 8-10: CURRDIR.C

```
/*
CURRDIR.C
Current Directory Structure (CDS)
Andrew Schulman, revised July 1993
*/

#include <stdlib.h>
#include <dos.h>
```

```c
#include "currdir.h"

typedef enum { UNKNOWN=-1, FALSE=0, TRUE=1 } OK;

/* return pointer to CDS for a given drive */
CDS far *currdir(unsigned drive)
{
    /* statics to preserve state: do one-time init */
    static BYTE far *dir = (BYTE far *) 0;
    static OK ok = UNKNOWN;
    static unsigned currdir_size;
    static BYTE lastdrv;

    if (ok == UNKNOWN)  /* do one-time init */
    {
        unsigned drv_ofs, lastdrv_ofs;

        /* curr dir struct not available in DOS 1.x or 2.x */
        if (! (ok = (_osmajor >= 3)))
            return (CDS far *) 0;

        /* compute offset of curr dir struct and LASTDRIVE in DOS
           list of lists, depending on DOS version */
        #define DOS(maj, min)   ((_osmajor == (maj)) && (_osminor == (min)))
        if (DOS(3,0))           { drv_ofs = 0x17; lastdrv_ofs = 0x1B; }
        else                    { drv_ofs = 0x16; lastdrv_ofs = 0x21; }

        _asm    push si     /* must preserve */

        /* get DOS list of lists into ES:BX */
        _asm    mov ah, 52h
        _asm    int 21h

        /* get LASTDRIVE byte */
        _asm    mov si, lastdrv_ofs
        _asm    mov ah, byte ptr es:[bx+si]
        _asm    mov lastdrv, ah

        /* get current directory structure */
        _asm    mov si, drv_ofs
        _asm    les bx, es:[bx+si]
        _asm    mov word ptr dir+2, es
        _asm    mov word ptr dir, bx

        _asm    pop si

        /* OS/2 DOS box sets dir to FFFF:FFFF */
        if (dir == (BYTE far *) -1L) ok = FALSE;

        /* compute curr directory structure size */
        currdir_size = (_osmajor >= 4) ? 0x58 : 0x51;
    }

    if ((ok == FALSE) || (drive >= lastdrv))
        return (CDS far *) 0;
    else    /* return array entry corresponding to drive */
        return (CDS far *) &dir[drive * currdir_size];
}
```

Like most of the LASTDRV programs in Chapter 2, currdir() uses offsets computed at run time, rather than C data structures set at compile time, because this seems better suited to the volatility of undocumented DOS. The code assumes that DOS 5.0 and higher are fairly compatible with DOS 4.0. There are problems with this assumption, though, since while the DOS box in OS/2 1.10 presents itself to a program as DOS 10.10, in fact it more closely resembles DOS 3.x than DOS 4.x. The test for (_osmajor >= 4) incorrectly groups the OS/2 DOS box together with DOS 4.x instead of DOS 3.x. However, the DOS boxes in OS/2 1.x and 2.x don't provide a CDS anyway, and currdir() anticipates this possibility by checking for the invalid -1L pointer (FFFF:FFFF).

Contents of the CDS

So what is in the CDS that you would want to access it in the first place?

Offset 43h from the start of each CDS entry holds a collection of bit flags indicating the type of drive (cds[drive].flags). As shown in CURRDIR.H (Listing 8-9), these flags are NETWORK, PHYSICAL, JOIN, SUBST, and REDIR_NOT_NET (such as, CD-ROM). For example, running SUBST G: C:\UNDOC2 means that (cds['G' - 'A'].flags & SUBST). Likewise, running JOIN A: C:\FLOPPY means that (cds[0].flags & JOIN). If (cds[drive].flags == 0), the drive is invalid.

How ASSIGN Works (It Does?)

The ASSIGN command (assertions in the first edition of this book notwithstanding) has *nothing* to do with the CDS. We probably just thought ASSIGN belonged in the same general family as SUBST and JOIN. It doesn't. Instead, ASSIGN.COM installs a small TSR that hooks all entry points to the DOS file system and contains a 26-byte lookup table. When the TSR is installed, all DOS file system functions use the ASSIGN table to change their drive codes from ones that the calling program specified to the ones contained in the table, as indexed by the caller's drive. For example, if ASSIGN A=C, then it would set the first slot in the table (A:) to 3 (C:). ASSIGN has an undocumented API call (INT 2Fh AX=0601h) that lets you access this table.

The DOS user's manual recommends using the SUBST command rather than ASSIGN. The command SUBST A: C:\ achieves exactly the same results as does ASSIGN A=C, but it goes through the CDS and has no side effects such as losing RAM to an unremovable TSR. The user manual also notes that Microsoft will continue to support SUBST, but makes no such promise with regard to ASSIGN.

Another weird program like this is APPEND, which lets you specify directories in which you can open files as if they were in the current directory. APPEND is intended to act somewhat like PATH, but for data files rather than executables. Like ASSIGN, APPEND has a little API (INT 2Fh AH=B7h). Also like ASSIGN, APPEND has nothing at all to do with the CDS, and it's not even clear why we're mentioning it here, except that like ASSIGN (and also like FASTOPEN) it's a somewhat strange program, a supplied piece of MS-DOS that seems to do an end-run around MS-DOS.

The NETWORK flag refers to any drive created with the network redirector; the flag is not restricted to network drives per se. For example, CD-ROM drives attached to DOS by the Microsoft CD-ROM extensions have the NETWORK flag set. However, as Geoff Chappell notes in *DOS Internals*, the CDS attributes also have a REDIR_NOT_NET bit that MSCDEX uses to keep CD-ROM drives from the INT 21h AH=5Fh assign-list make/break network connection calls.

While not all NETWORK drives are located on a network, conversely not all network drives show up in the CDS. In particular, drives created with Novell NetWare prior to version 4.0, don't appear in the CDS. As Chapters 2 and 4 discuss, drives in NetWare version 2 and 3 start *after* LASTDRIVE, and NETX.COM maintains them without involving DOS. Because LASTDRIVE is merely the size of the CDS array, these drives are not found in the CDS and are the one important exception to our statement that the CDS ties together all DOS drives. Novell didn't use the CDS because (until NetWare 4) it provided network services by hooking INT 21h, rather than with the redirector. Novell has provided DOS networking since 2.x, before there was a redirector or a CDS. Starting with version 4.0, NetWare uses the network redirector interface (described in detail later in this chapter), and therefore NetWare 4 drives do show up in the CDS.

Offset 45h from the start of the CDS entry holds a far pointer to the drive's DPB (cds[drive].dpb). Since the DPB in turn contains a far pointer to the actual device driver, this links the logical unit to the physical drive. Earlier in this chapter, we noted that get_dpb(drive) hits the disk, whereas cds[drive].dpb does not. On the other hand, for removable media (which is where hitting the disk is a major problem in the first place) cds[drive].dpb may hold stale data.

For local drives, that is, where (cds[drive].flags & NETWORK) == 0, offset 49h in the CDS contains the starting cluster for the current directory (cds[drive].u.LOCAL.start_cluster). DOS of course has its own uses for this, but other programs could use this for a different purpose: to implement the earlier NAMCLUST program (see Listing 8-5) for directories, without having to traverse the directory structure and FAT. Such a program could CD to a directory and pull the cluster out of CDS, letting DOS do all the hard work. You will see later that the SFT similarly contains the starting cluster for open files.

The first element (offset 0) in each drive's CDS is the current path (cds[drive].current_path); but it is not always what you might expect. The current path in the CDS tells you where the data really is, rather than where you address it. You can see this in the output from a utility named ENUMDRV, the source code for which you will see shortly:

```
C:\UNDOC2>\dos\join a: c:\floppy
C:\UNDOC2>subst g: c:\undoc2
C:\UNDOC2>rem e: and f: are network drives
C:\UNDOC2>phantom -S512 h:
C:\UNDOC2>enumdrv
A    C:\FLOPPY                        JOIN [ROOT]
B    B:\                              [NOT_ACC]
C    C:\UNDOC2                        [#18] STACKER (swapped D:)
D    D:\UNDOC2                        [#26348]
E    \\BIN\EXPORT\DOS                 NETWORK
F    \\HOME\U\ANDREW                  NETWORK
G    C:\UNDOC2                        SUBST [NOT_ACC] STACKER
H    Phantom H:\                      NETWORK
```

The COMMAND.COM prompt shows we were logged into drive C: at the \UNDOC2 subdirectory; this shows up clearly in the CDS for drive C:. The SUBST command permits you to address data on one drive as if it were on another—you can see this from the CDS for drive G:. The situation is reversed when you use JOIN to refer to an entire drive as though it were a subdirectory on another drive (see the CDS for drive A: above). The first byte in the current path string contains the drive letter of the SUBST or JOIN target.

As shown in drives E: and F: in the ENUMDRV map above, network drives are treated differently from local drives. Attaching a drive to a network file server means that all references to the drive actually refer to the server, which is generally, though not always, addressed with an opening "\\" string (that's "\\\\" in a C program). The \\ prefix is part of the so-called Universal Naming Convention (UNC) that Microsoft uses in its different networking projects such as PC-LAN, Lan Manager, and Windows for Workgroups. Here, using PC/TCP from FTP Software, drives E: and F: were mapped to different directories on a Sun SPARCstation running SunOS. This is a good illustration of how the DOS file system allows installable file systems. You can use the disk of a UNIX RISC machine as though it were part of DOS.

The word at offset 4Fh in the CDS (cds[drive].backslash_offset) contains the number of characters in the pathspec area that precede the root directory indicator. This is often initially set to a value of 2, to skip the drive letter and colon; when a SUBST command is processed, the value changes to skip not only the drive letter, but all directory names concealed by SUBST. That is, SUBST G: C:\UDOS copies the string C:\UDOS\ into cds['G' - 'A'].current_path; it copies the status word and DPB pointers from drive C: and sets the SUBST bit in the drive G: status word; it sets the directory cluster number to that for the first sector of the UDOS directory on drive C: and sets the word at 4Fh to a value of 7, the number of characters preceding the final \ of the pathspec string.

The CDS may store the non-DOS name of an alien file system, such as \\BIN\EXPORT\DOS or \\HOME\U\ANDREW in the ENUMDRV output above, so cds[drive].backslash_offset can also block off such names. The Phantom sample program later in this chapter uses this (see the ENUMDRV output). But this is possibly not normal behavior for a network redirector. An engineer at Novell, whose DR DOS does not quite support this behavior, has told us that no other network redirector uses the CDS in quite this way. Perhaps Phantom should instead use \\ UNC naming.

As you navigate the directory tree, the path string stored in the CDS tracks your position so that DOS can always convert your relative path references (those which do not begin with a backslash) into fully qualified path names. When you change directories by calling INT 21h function 3Bh or its user-level equivalent, the CD command, DOS updates cds[drive].current_path.

Conversely, changing cds[drive].current_path instantly changes the current directory. Going into your favorite debugger, locating the CDS for the current drive, and manually editing the path string in the CDS is sufficient to change directories. The change is immediately reflected in the PROMPT pg display, for example. It's now quite clear why this is called the Current Directory Structure.

However, there is one problem with the CDS array: There is only one. All DOS tasks share the single global CDS. The reader who thinks of DOS as a single-tasking operating system might well ask, "*What* DOS tasks? In DOS there is only one task, so of course there is only one CDS." But as shown in Chapter 7's discussion of PSPs and in Chapter 9's discussion of TSRs and DOS multitasking, this just isn't so. Consider especially the example of Windows Enhanced mode, where multiple DOS boxes may be preemptively multitasked, each manipulating the DOS current directory at the same time. Windows uses instance data to maintain a separate CDS for each DOS box (see Chapter 1). Furthermore, each Windows program has its own current drive and directory, maintained in its Task Database (see *Undocumented Windows*, Chapter 5).

Walking the CDS Array

The currdir() function in Listing 8-10 goes to some trouble to ensure that it can be called frequently without a lot of duplicated effort. This way, currdir() can be called in a loop for each drive in the system, producing the ENUMDRV output shown earlier. Listing 8-11 shows ENUMDRV.C, which contains the currdir() loop, along with some other code we'll get to in a moment.

Listing 8-11: ENUMDRV.C

```
/*
ENUMDRV.C -- uses currdir() in CURRDIR.C
Added CD-ROM bit, DoubleSpace test, Stacker test, primitive RAM disk test
Andrew Schulman, revised July 1993

bcc enumdrv.c currdir.c is_stack.c is_dspac.c diskstuf.c
*/

#include <stdlib.h>
#include <stdio.h>
#include <string.h>
#include <dos.h>

#include "currdir.h"     // includes DoubleSpace, Stacker too
#include "diskstuf.h"    // get_dpb

void fail(const char *s) { puts(s); exit(1); }

int maybe_ram_disk(int drive);

main()
{
    CDS far *dir;
    BYTE host;
    BOOL swapped;
```

```c
    unsigned lastdrv;
    int i, seq;

    _dos_setdrive(0xFF, &lastdrv);
    for (i=0; i<lastdrv; i++)
    {
        if (! (dir = currdir(i)))
            fail("can't get current directory structure");
        else if (dir->flags)    /* is this a valid drive? */
        {
            printf("%c   %-40Fs   ", 'A' + i, dir->current_path);

            if (dir->flags & JOIN) printf("JOIN ");
            if (dir->flags & SUBST) printf("SUBST ");
            if (dir->flags & REDIR_NOT_NET) printf("REDIR_NOT_NET ");

            if (dir->flags & NETWORK) printf("NETWORK ");
            else switch (dir->u.LOCAL.start_cluster)
            {
                case 0:      printf("[ROOT] "); break;       // root dir
                case 0xFFFF: printf("[NOT_ACC] "); break;    // not accessed
                default:     printf("[#%u] ", dir->u.LOCAL.start_cluster);
            }   // check cluster numbers by running CLUSTNAM
            if (double_space_drive(i, &swapped, &host, &seq))
                printf("DBLSPACE %c:\\dblspace.%03u", 'A' + host, seq);

            if (stacker_drive(i, &swapped, &host))
            {
                printf("STACKER");
                if (swapped) printf(" (swapped %c:)", 'A' + host);
            }

            if (maybe_ram_disk(i)) printf("RAM disk?");

            putchar('\n');
        }
    }
    return 0;
}

int maybe_ram_disk(int drive)
{
#ifdef USE_CDS_DPB
    return (currdir(drive)->dpb->copies_fat == 1);
#else
    DPB far *dpb = get_dpb(drive+1);
    return (dpb) ? (dpb->copies_fat == 1) : 0;
#endif
}
```

For each drive < LASTDRIVE, ENUMDRV calls the currdir() function and prints out values from the CDS, that is, the current path string, the drive type and, for local drives, the starting cluster of the current directory. ENUMDRV then calls some additional functions to check for DoubleSpace and Stacker compressed drives and for RAM disks. We'll get to the DoubleSpace and Stacker code in a moment.

Detecting RAM Disks

The tiny maybe_ram_disk() function is interesting. Since RAM disks are intended to look as much like physical disks as possible, there is no sure test for a RAM disk. However, RAM disks generally provide only one FAT, and the presence of a single FAT is a common test for a likely RAM disk. As noted earlier, for floppy and hard disks DOS forces the DPB to indicate two FATs no matter what the BPB says.

The number of FATs is retrieved from the DPB (note that network drives don't have DPBs). The maybe_ram_disk() function can get the DPB either from the CDS (currdir(drive)->dpb) or by calling the get_dpb() function from DISKSTUF.C (Listing 8-4). This involves the usual trade-off between hitting the disk with get_dpb() and possibly getting a stale DPB with currdir(drive)->dpb. Hitting the disk with get_dpb() isn't so bad because this function checks for removable media and contains a critical error handler.

For an alternative approach to drive enumeration, see the DRVINFO program in Chappell's *DOS Internals.*

DoubleSpace Drives

DoubleSpace is an on-the-fly disk compression subsystem that Microsoft licensed from Vertisoft, makers of the earlier DoubleDisk product, and incorporated in MS-DOS 6.0. ENUMDRV checks for DoubleSpace drives by calling the double_space_drive() function from IS_DSPAC.C, shown in Listing 8-12.

Listing 8-12: IS_DSPAC.C

```
/*
IS_DSPAC.C -- Is this a DoubleSpace drive?
Based on DRVINFO.C from Microsoft's DSDUMP sample code (March 1993)
Andrew Schulman, July 1993
NOTE:  *None* of this is undocumented!
*/

#include <stdlib.h>
#include <stdio.h>
#include <dos.h>
#include "currdir.h"
BOOL DSGetDriveMapping(int drive, BOOL *pcomp, int *phost, WORD *pseq)
{
    BYTE ldata, hdata;
    _asm mov ax, 4A11h      /* DBLSPACE INT 2Fh function */
    _asm mov bx, 1          /* DSGetDriveMapping */
    _asm mov dl, byte ptr drive
    _asm int 2fh
    _asm or ax, ax
    _asm jnz no_dblspace
    _asm mov byte ptr ldata, bl
    _asm mov byte ptr hdata, bh
    *pcomp = ldata & 0x80;  /* compressed drive flag */
    *phost = ldata & 0x7F;  /* host drive (if drive compressed) */
    *pseq = hdata;          /* compressed drv sequence # (0..254) */
    return 1;
no_dblspace:
    return 0;
}

// Can generate CVF filename with host:\DBLSPACE.seq
BOOL double_space_drive(BYTE drive, BOOL *pswap, BYTE *phost, int *pseq)
{
    WORD seq, seq2;
    int drHost, drHost2;
    BOOL fCompressed, fSwapped;

    if (! DSGetDriveMapping(drive, &fCompressed, &drHost, &seq))
        return 0;
    if (! fCompressed)
        return 0;   /* could be host drive, but don't care */

    fSwapped = 0;
    if (DSGetDriveMapping(drHost, &fCompressed, &drHost2, &seq2))
        if (drHost2 == drive) // host of host is drive itself: means swapped
            fSwapped = 1;
```

```
        *phost = drHost;
        *pswap = fSwapped;
        *pseq = seq;
        return 1;
}
```

If double_space_drive() returns TRUE, indicating the specified drive is compressed with DoubleSpace, this function also passes back the host drive, sequence number, and a BOOL indicating whether the DoubleSpace drive was swapped with its host. Taking ENUMDRV snapshots before and after mounting a DoubleSpace drive makes clearer what all this means:

```
C:\DOS6>\undoc2\chap8\enumdrv
A    A:\                                   [ROOT]
B    B:\                                   [NOT_ACC]
C    C:\DOS6                               [#27112]

C:\DOS6>dblspace a: /mount
DoubleSpace is mounting drive A.
DoubleSpace has mounted drive A.

C:\DOS6>\undoc2\chap8\enumdrv
A    A:\                                   [ROOT] DBLSPACE I S I:\dblspace.000
B    B:\                                   [NOT_ACC]
C    C:\DOS6                               [#27112]
I    I:\                                   [ROOT]
```

You can see that DBLSPACE /MOUNT created a new drive, I: and changed the nature of drive A:. Drive I: is the old drive A:, and drive A: is just a DoubleSpace file, I:\DBLSPACE.000, that DoubleSpace arranges to look like a (larger) drive A:. Drives A: and I: have been swapped. In other words, before using DBLSPACE /MOUNT, drive A: contained the hidden system file, A:\DBLSPACE.000, which now appears on drive I:.

The file DBLSPACE.000, from which DBLSPACE.BIN creates a DoubleSpace drive, is called a Compressed Volume File (CVF). The CVF contains all the compressed data that the user thinks of as belonging on the drive. It also contains internal DoubleSpace data structures such as the MDBPB, the BitFAT, and MDFAT (MD stands for Magic Disk, which was the original internal name for DoubleSpace).

Microsoft documents the CVF file format and these structures in a "DoubleSpace Compressed Volume File Overview," in the MS-DOS 6.0 *Programmer's Reference,* and in sample code, including a CVF.H header file, distributed through the Microsoft forum on CompuServe and on the Microsoft Developer Network (MSDN) CD-ROM. There is also a useful introduction to DoubleSpace internals in the article, "Inside MS-DOS 6.0," by Ben Slivka, Eric Straub, and Richard Freedman (*Byte,* July 1993). Unfortunately, this article fails to point out the work done on DoubleSpace by its creators at Vertisoft.

IS_DSPAC.C uses INT 2Fh AX=4A11h BX=1 (DSGetDriveMapping). INT 2Fh AX=4A11h is the DoubleSpace programming interface, documented in Microsoft's "DoubleSpace System API Specification." Version 1.00.01 of this specification (dated March 12, 1993) includes subfunctions 3 and 4 (DSGetEntryPoints and DSSetEntryPoints) that were previously reserved for use by SmartDrive. This leaves two undocumented calls (BX=FFFEh and BX=FFFFh) that DBLSPACE.SYS /MOVE uses to relocate DBLSPACE.BIN to its final location in memory, plus the DOS 6.0 Preload API that DoubleSpace uses (see Chapter 1).

While it is fortunate that DoubleSpace is fairly well-documented, it is also fortunate that most applications won't need this documentation in the first place. After all, the point of on-the-fly disk compression is to operate on the fly, that is, transparently. DoubleSpace makes all normal DOS file system structures appear as if they existed on the DoubleSpace drive, even though they are either just data in a DBLSPACE.xxx file or simulated outright by DBLSPACE.BIN.

However, some utilities need to know about the actual DoubleSpace structures such as the MDFAT and MDBPB. For example, Norton Utilities 7.0 includes versions of the Norton Disk Doctor (NDD) and Speedisk that can repair and defragment DoubleSpace and Stacker drives, presumably in a better way than Microsoft's DBLSPACE /CHKDSK or Stac Electronics' SCHECK utilities can.

As an application for DoubleSpace information, consider writing a program to compute the compression ratio for a file, as DIR /C does in DOS 6.0:

```
Volume in drive A is DOS6
Volume Serial Number is 16D3-265C
Directory of A:\

COMMAND  COM     52925 03-10-93    6:00a   1.4 to 1.0
READTHIS TXT       350 07-12-93    3:11p  16.0 to 1.0
CHAP8    ZIP    103029 07-16-93    6:13p   1.0 to 1.0
CHAP8C   ZIP     58469 07-16-93    2:12p   1.1 to 1.0
DM       ZIP     24075 07-10-93   10:27a   1.0 to 1.0
; ...
FAT      EXE      8270 07-10-93    9:26p   2.5 to 1.0
DPBTEST  EXE      8354 07-15-93   12:18p   2.5 to 1.0
                  1.7 to 1.0 average compression ratio
        49 file(s)      550393 bytes
                       1384448 bytes free
```

How does DIR /C know that CHAP8.ZIP has 1:1 compression (none), whereas DPBTEST.EXE has 2.5:1 compression? Certainly the information doesn't come from any of the standard DOS file system structures. Instead, it comes from the MDFAT. Whereas non-compressed DOS disks have a fixed formula for turning cluster numbers into sector numbers (see CLUSTER_TO_LSN() in Listing 8-5), DoubleSpace allocates a variable number of sectors per cluster, depending on the possible compression. Since there isn't a fixed cluster-to-sectors formula, DoubleSpace uses the MDFAT, which is a lookup table, indexed by cluster number. (MDFAT is a very poor name for the structure, given that it plays a totally different role from the FAT; it ought to have been called CLUSTMAP or SECTMAP.) For each cluster, the MDFAT contains a four-byte entry, shown in the following C structure with bit fields, adapted from Microsoft's CVF.H header file. (Note that Borland C++ does not accept the unsigned long bit field, so in practice you should access the MDFAT fields with shifts and masks, as in Listing 8-13.)

```
typedef struct {
    unsigned long secStart : 21;     // starting sector for cluster
    unsigned reserved : 1;
    unsigned cCmp : 4;               // # of compressed sectors
    unsigned cUnc : 4;               // # of uncompressed (original) sectors
    unsigned Flags : 2;              // Is entry in use? data compressed?
    } MDFAT_ENTRY;
MDFAT_ENTRY MDFAT[num_clusters];
```

Because 4 bits each are devoted to the count of original sectors (cUnc) and the count of possibly compressed sectors found in the CVF (cCmp), there are a maximum of 16 sectors per cluster. Given a cluster whose original uncompressed size is 16 sectors (cUnc == 16), the compressed cluster occupies less than 16 sectors (duh!). With 2:1 compression, cCmp == 8. With no compression (for example, a portion of CHAP8.ZIP), cCmp == 16.

There is still a limit on 64K clusters, of course. With a *maximum* of 16 sectors per cluster and 512 bytes per sector, a DoubleSpace volume can hold a maximum of 512 megabytes of *uncompressed* data.

The cUnc field in the MDFAT entry is important. DoubleSpace does not assume a fixed 16 uncompressed sectors per cluster. This is merely the maximum. Files whose true size is not a multiple of 16 sectors will have a final MDFAT entry whose cUnc field is less than 16. In this way, DoubleSpace changes the space-wasting cluster overhang of hard disks under DOS to a much less wasteful sector overhang.

You can see this clearly in the following session using two of our earlier programs, NAMCLUST (see Listing 8-5) and FAT (see Listing 8-2), as well as a Microsoft DoubleSpace dumper called, appropriate enough, DSDUMP. Microsoft provides the C source code for DSDUMP along with the DoubleSpace documentation on its CompuServe forum.

```
C:\UNDOC2>namclust a:\command.com
A:\COMMAND.COM ==> 12 (sect 236, 0x000000ec)

C:\UNDOC2>fat a: 12
12-18 (7)

7 clusters in 1 groups

C:\UNDOC2>dsdump a: /M14-20
DoubleSpace File Dumper - Version 0.58

Drive: A (mounted from I:\DBLSPACE.000)

MDFAT entries 14 to 20
Flags: A=Allocated, F=Free, C=Compressed, U=Uncompressed
--------------------------------------------------------
FAT#  MDFAT# Flags cUnc cCmp secStart
----- ------ ----- ---- ---- --------
  12     14   A,C   16   13     261
  13     15   A,C   16   14     274
  14     16   A,C   16   15     288
  15     17   A,C   16   14     303
  16     18   A,C   16   12     317
  17     19   A,C   16   10     329
  18     20   A,C    8    1     339
```

This shows where DIR /C gets those compression ratios. For COMMAND.COM, recall that DIR /C showed compression of 1.4 to 1.0. Adding up the cUnc column, we get 16*6+8 = 104 sectors for the original COMMAND.COM. Adding up the cCmp column, we get 13+14+15+14+12+10+1 = 79 sectors used in I:\DBLSPACE.000. Dividing 104 by 79, we get 1.31.

But if the actual compression ratio is 1.31, why does DIR /C get 1.4? Because, rather than add up the actual cUnc sector counts for the file, taking into the account the final count that is generally less than 16 (for FAT #18, it was 8), DIR /C instead simply multiples the number of clusters by 16:

```
compression ratio = (num_clusters * 16) / total cCmp
```

This formula explains why DIR /C shows 16.0 to 1.0 compression ratios for all files whose size is less than 512 bytes. Stacker's SDIR shows similarly wildly inflated compression ratios for small files. With DIR /C, even a one-byte file shows a compression ratio of 16.0 to 1.0 (it's been squeezed down to half a bit?). This sounds completely bogus at first, but in fact it is only mostly bogus. As we pointed out earlier, a file whose size is less than 512 bytes still occupies the full cluster size on an uncompressed disk. By multiplying the number of clusters by the sectors per cluster, DIR /C reflects the fact that DoubleSpace eliminates cluster overhang. A supposedly one-byte file would in fact occupy a total cluster; DoubleSpace could store this one-byte file in a single *sector*.

The only problem is that DIR /C assumes 16 sectors per cluster, which is appropriate for the DoubleSpace drive, but probably not appropriate for the original uncompressed media. As pointed out earlier, high-density floppies generally use 1 sector per cluster, and hard disks generally use 4 or 8 sectors per cluster. Thus, a one-byte file's true compression ratio is 1:1 for a floppy diskette, and 4:1 or 8:1 for a hard disk; it would only be 16:1 for host media with 16 sectors per cluster. More accurate compression ratios require handling a file's last cluster, using the sectors per cluster (from the DPB) of the original pre-DoubleSpaced host:

```
(((num_clust - 1) * 16) + original sect_per_clust) / total cCmp
```

DIR /CH uses a similar formula, producing more accurate compression ratios:

```
                        bytes         /C ratio        /CH ratio
COMMAND   COM           52925           1.4              1.3
ENUMDRV   EXE            9252           2.1              1.3
READTHIS  TXT             350          16.0              1.0
DM        ZIP           24075           1.0              1.0
DSDUMP    ZIP           13956           1.0              1.0
CHAP8     ZIP          103029           1.0              1.0
CHAP8C    ZIP           58469           1.1              1.0
FILES     C              7949           1.8              1.8
DPBTEST   C              1957           5.3              1.3
FAT       EXE            8270           2.5              1.5
DPBTEST   EXE            8354           2.5              1.5
.....
Average compression ratio             1.4              1.1
```

In this example, COMMAND.COM was located on a high density floppy, with one sector per cluster, so our original 1.31 compression ratio was accurate. The true compression ratio—that is, the effect of using DoubleSpace vs. not using it—for a tiny file like READTHIS.TXT is not 16:1 but instead depends on the original pre-DoubleSpaced media. For hard disks, it is 8:1 or 4:1; for high-density floppies, it is only 1:1.

However, there is still a problem because, at least in the original release of DoubleSpace, the number of compressed sectors can in some cases *exceed* the original number of uncompressed sectors on the host media (that is, cUnc > cCmp). For example:

```
C:\UNDOC2>namclust i:dsdump.zip
A:\DSDUMP.ZIP ==> 5 (sect 36, 0x00000024)

C:\UNDOC2>fat i: 5
5-32 (28)

28 clusters in 1 groups

C:\UNDOC2>namclust a:dsdump.zip
A:\DSDUMP.ZIP ==> 32 (sect 556, 0x0000022c)

C:\UNDOC2>fat a: 32
32-33 (2)

2 clusters in 1 groups

C:\UNDOC2>dsdump a: /M34-35
DoubleSpace File Dumper - Version 0.58

Drive: A (mounted from I:\DBLSPACE.000)

MDFAT entries 34 to 35
Flags: A=Allocated, F=Free, C=Compressed, U=Uncompressed
--------------------------------------------------------

FAT#  MDFAT#  Flags cUnc cCmp secStart
-----  ------  ----- ---- ---- --------
  32      34   A,U   16   16      454
  33      35   A,U   12   16      470
```

In other words, the original occupied 28 one-sector clusters and the "compressed" version occupies two 16-sector clusters, so the compression ratio is 28 to 32, or 0.875 to 1.0. Both DIR /C and DIR /CH report a 1:1 compression, however. The problem here isn't a faulty compression algorithm. As the *U* flag above shows, DoubleSpace has decided it can't compress this data, so it is stored uncompressed. It is not clear why DoubleSpace should bother stowing 16 sectors when the original has only 12. (One developer told us that this is just a bug that is being fixed, and that we're making too big a deal of it here.)

In any case, Microsoft's DSDUMP shows that you can derive compression ratios (whether true compression ratios or the inflated ones DIR /C produces) by examining the MDFAT entries in the CVF.

How then does a program find the MDFAT for a DoubleSpace drive? First, call the DoubleSpace DSGetDriveMapping() API function (INT 2Fh AX=4A11h) to find the host \DBLSPACE.seq CVF file name, as shown by the double_space_drive() function in IS_DSPAC.C (Listing 8-12). Next, open the CVF file and read in the MDBPB to find the MDFAT; the MDBPB is an extended BPB at the start of the CVF file and includes a secMDFATStart field.

The sample program in Listing 8-13, when run with a -VERBOSE command line switch, dumps the in-use MDFAT entries from a CVF file. By itself, this program is not terribly useful, but you could lash it together with NAMCLUST, FAT, and IS_DSPAC to produce a program to show accurate compression ratios for any DoubleSpaced file. Use the code from NAMCLUST to turn a filename into a starting cluster, use the FAT code to find the file's entire set of clusters, use IS_DSPAC to locate the CVF file on the host drive, and then use the code in Listing 8-13 to examine the MDFAT entries for the file's clusters.

Listing 8-13: MDFAT.C

```
/*
MDFAT.C -- Dump a DoubleSpace MDFAT
Based on Microsoft's DSDUMP sample code
Andrew Schulman, July 1993
NOTE:  *NONE* of this is undocumented!
cl mdfat.c is_dspac.c
*/

#include <stdlib.h>
#include <stdio.h>
#include <string.h>
#include <ctype.h>
#include <dos.h>

typedef unsigned char BYTE;
typedef unsigned short WORD;
typedef unsigned long DWORD;
typedef int BOOL;

#pragma pack(1)
typedef struct {
    BYTE    jmpBOOT[3];      // Jump to bootstrap routine
    char    achOEMName[8];   // OEM Name ("MSDSP6.0")
    // MS-DOS BPB
    WORD    cbPerSec;
    BYTE    csecPerClu;
    WORD    csecReserved;
    BYTE    cFATs;
    WORD    cRootDirEntries, csecTotalWORD;
    BYTE    bMedia;
    WORD    csecFAT, csecPerTrack, cHeads;
    DWORD   csecHidden, csecTotalDWORD;
    // DoubleSpace extensions
    WORD    secMDFATStart;
    BYTE    nLog2cbPerSec;
    WORD    csecMDReserved, secRootDirStart, secHeapStart, cluFirstData;
    BYTE    cpageBitFAT;
    WORD    RESERVED1;
    BYTE    nLog2csecPerClu;
    WORD    RESERVED2;
    DWORD   RESERVED3, RESERVED4;
    BYTE    f12BitFAT;
    WORD    cmbCVFMax;
    } MDBPB;
#pragma pack()

void fail(const char *s) { puts(s); exit(1); }

// my buffer size
```

```c
#define MDFAT_PER_BLOCK      (2048)
#define MDFAT_BLOCK_SIZE     (MDFAT_PER_BLOCK * sizeof(DWORD))
// handy macros from Microsoft's DSDUMP.C
#define GET_SECSTART(dw)     ((dw) & 0x3FFFFFL)
#define GET_CSEC_CODED(dw)   (1 + (int) (15 & ((dw) >> 22)))
#define GET_CSEC_PLAIN(dw)   (1 + (int) (15 & ((dw) >> 26)))
#define GET_FLAGS(dw)        (3 & ((dw) >> 30))
#define USED(dw)             (GET_FLAGS(dw) & 2)
#define UNCOMPRESSED(dw)     (GET_FLAGS(dw) & 1)

static DWORD sectors_coded = 0, sectors_plain = 0;
static WORD clusters_in_use = 0;
static WORD first_data_clust = 0;
static int verbose = 0, did_banner = 0;

void do_mdfat_entry(WORD cluster, DWORD mdfat_entry)
{
    int coded, plain;

    if (USED(mdfat_entry)) clusters_in_use++;
    else                   return;

    sectors_coded += (coded = GET_CSEC_CODED(mdfat_entry));
    sectors_plain += (plain = GET_CSEC_PLAIN(mdfat_entry));

    if (verbose || ( coded > plain))
    {
        if (! did_banner)
        {
            if (coded > plain)
                printf("Expanded clusters (cCmp > cUnc):\n");
            printf("Cluster     Sector cCmp cUnc C/U\n");
            printf("------      ------ ---- ---- ---\n");
            did_banner++;
        }
        printf("%5u   %8lu   %2u   %2u   %c\n",
            cluster - first_data_clust,
            GET_SECSTART(mdfat_entry),
            coded, plain,
            UNCOMPRESSED(mdfat_entry) ? 'U' : 'C');
    }
}

main(int argc, char *argv[])
{
    char *cvf_name;
    FILE *cvf;
    MDBPB *mdbpb;
    DWORD *mdfat_block, num_sect, mdfat_bytes;
    WORD num_clust, mdfat_blocks, ratio, i, j;

    if (argc < 2 || argv[1][1] == '?')
        fail("usage: mdfat [DoubleSpace drive or CVF file]");
    if (strcmp(strupr(argv[1]), "-VERBOSE") == 0)
        { verbose++; argv++; argc--; }
    cvf_name = argv[1];

    if ((cvf = fopen(cvf_name, "rb")) == NULL)
    {
        // If we can't open the specified filename, maybe it's not
        // a filename at all.  See if maybe it's a DoubleSpace drive
        // letter.  If so, use function from IS_DSPAC.C to get CVF name
        extern BOOL double_space_drive(BYTE drive, BOOL *pswap,
            BYTE *phost, int *pseq);
        BYTE drive = (BYTE) (toupper(cvf_name[0]) - 'A');
        BYTE swap, host;
        int seq;
```

```
    if (double_space_drive(drive, &swap, &host, &seq))
    {
        static char filename[16];
        sprintf(filename, "%c:\\dblspace.%03u", 'A' + host, seq);
        printf("CVF file: %s\n", filename);
        cvf_name = filename;
        if ((cvf = fopen(cvf_name, "rb")) == NULL)
            fail("can't open CVF file");
    }
    else
        fail("can't open CVF file");
}
if (! (mdbpb = malloc(sizeof(MDBPB))))        fail("insufficient memory");
if (! fread(mdbpb, sizeof(MDBPB), 1, cvf))  fail("can't read MDBPB");
if (! ((mdbpb->jmpBOOT[0] == 0xE9) || (mdbpb->jmpBOOT[0] == 0xEB)))
    fail("not a valid CVF file");    // has to start with JMP

first_data_clust = mdbpb->cluFirstData; // used by do_mdfat_entry()
num_sect = (mdbpb->csecTotalWORD) ?
    mdbpb->csecTotalWORD : mdbpb->csecTotalDWORD;
num_clust = 1 + (num_sect / mdbpb->csecPerClu);
mdfat_bytes = (DWORD) num_clust * sizeof(DWORD);
mdfat_blocks = 1 + (mdfat_bytes / MDFAT_BLOCK_SIZE);

if (! (mdfat_block = (DWORD *) malloc(MDFAT_BLOCK_SIZE)))
    fail("insufficient memory");

fseek(cvf, (1 + mdbpb->secMDFATStart) * mdbpb->cbPerSec, SEEK_SET);
for (i=0; i<mdfat_blocks-1; i++)
    if (fread(mdfat_block, MDFAT_PER_BLOCK, sizeof(DWORD), cvf))
        for (j=0; j<MDFAT_PER_BLOCK; j++)
            do_mdfat_entry((i*MDFAT_PER_BLOCK)+j, mdfat_block[j]);
    else
        fail("can't read MDFAT");

if (fread(mdfat_block, MDFAT_PER_BLOCK, sizeof(DWORD), cvf)) // last one
    for (j=0; j<(num_clust % MDFAT_PER_BLOCK); j++)
        do_mdfat_entry((mdfat_blocks-1) + j, mdfat_block[j]);
else
    fail("can't read MDFAT");    // okay to read less

fclose(cvf);
printf("\nTotal clusters:            %u\n", num_clust);

// print global counters incremented by do_mdfat_entry()
printf("In use:                    %u (%lu%% used)\n",
    clusters_in_use, (100L * clusters_in_use) / num_clust);
printf("Plain sectors (cUnc):      %lu\n", sectors_plain);
printf("Compressed sectors (cCmp): %lu (%lu%% compressed)\n",
    sectors_coded, (100L * sectors_coded) / sectors_plain);
ratio = (10L * sectors_plain) / sectors_coded;
printf("Sector compression ratio:  %u.%u to 1\n",
    ratio / 10, ratio % 10);
if (sectors_coded != 0)
{
    ratio = (160L * clusters_in_use) / sectors_coded;
    printf("DIR /C compression ratio:  %u.%u to 1\n",
        ratio / 10, ratio % 10);
}
// Exercise for the reader (I suddenly got very lazy here):
// To produce DIR /CH use get_dpb(host)->sectors_per_cluster

return 0;
}
```

MDFAT shows compression ratios for a CVF file and also lists any clusters where cCmp is greater than cUnc:

```
C:\UNDOC2\CHAP8>mdfat a:\dblspace.000
Expanded clusters (cCmp > cUnc):
Cluster   Sector cCmp cUnc C/U
-------   ------ ---- ---- ---
    33      470   16   12   U
    46      678   16   10   U
   103     2107   16   10   U
   112     2123   16    8   U

Total clusters:               297
In use:                       179 (60% used)
Plain sectors (cUnc):        2288
Compressed sectors (cCmp):   2000 (87% compressed)
Sector compression ratio:    1.1 to 1
DIR /C compression ratio:    1.4 to 1
```

The sector compression ratio here is only equal to DIR /CH when the original media had 1 sector per cluster. To produce a DIR /CH ratio, the MDFAT program would need to keep count of partial clusters (cUnc < 16); the program would also need to use get_dpb(host)->sectors_per_cluster.

As a final note on DoubleSpace, it's important to realize that the actual compression and decompression of data isn't part of DoubleSpace; it is done by something called a Microsoft Real-Time Compression Interface (MRCI) server that happens to be built inside DBLSPACE.BIN. There can be other MRCI (pronounced "merci") clients besides DoubleSpace and other MRCI servers. MRCI includes services for compressing and decompressing arbitrary blocks of data in memory; it includes support for incremental decompression. This interface uses INT 2Fh AX=4A12h (and the BIOS service INT 1Ah AX=B001h for possible hardware-based MRCI servers), and is documented in Microsoft's *MS-DOS 6.0 Programmer's Reference*. Developers can license MRCI libraries for DOS and Windows free of charge from Microsoft (though Microsoft's cover letter to the MRCI license agreement warns that MRCI might be subject to a patent-infringement suit from Stac Electronics).

Vertisoft, trying to leverage their status as "the company that licensed [read: gave away] the data compression technology to Microsoft for inclusion in MS-DOS 6 DoubleSpace," sells a nice add-in product to DoubleSpace, called SpaceManager. According to the packaging, "We didn't share all our space secrets with Microsoft. We held back on 6 of our crown jewels that'll make your life a lot easier." These include SuperCompress, SelectCompress, FortuneTeller, and other nifty additions to DoubleSpace.

Stacker Drives
Back in Listing 8-11, ENUMDRV also checks for Stacker drives, using the function stacker_drive() from IS_STACK.C, shown in Listing 8-14.

Listing 8-14: IS_STACK.C
```
/*
IS_STACK.C -- Detect Stacker driver, and Stacker drives
Andrew Schulman, July 1993

These calls were documented in the back of the Stacker 2.0 User's
Guide, and are also described in the Interrupt List
*/

#include <stdlib.h>
#include <stdio.h>
#include <dos.h>
#include "currdir.h"

STACKER_DRIVER far *stacker_detect(void)
{
```

```c
    static STACKER_DRIVER far *drv = (STACKER_DRIVER far *) 0;
    char far *pbuf;
    char *buf;
    if (drv) return drv;
    if (! (buf = (char *) malloc(1024)))
        fail("insufficient memory");
    pbuf = (char far *) buf;

    // Get address of Stacker driver by making an otherwise-illegal
    // INT 25h call
    #define STACKER_MAGIC 0x0CDCD
    _asm push ds
    _asm mov ax, STACKER_MAGIC
    _asm lds bx, pbuf
    _asm mov cx, 1
    _asm xor dx, dx
    _asm int 25h
    _asm popf
    _asm pop ds
    _asm cmp ax, STACKER_MAGIC
    _asm jne no_stacker
stacker:
    drv = *((STACKER_DRIVER far * *) &buf[4]);
    free(buf);
    return (drv->signature == 0xA55A) ? drv : (STACKER_DRIVER far *) 0;
no_stacker:
    free(buf);
    return (STACKER_DRIVER far *) 0;
}

int stacker_swapped(int drive)
{
    static STACKER_DRIVER far *driver = (STACKER_DRIVER far *) 0;
    if (! driver) driver = stacker_detect();
    return (driver) ? driver->drive_map[drive] : 0;
}

DWORD stacker_drive(int drive, BOOL *pswap, BYTE *phost)
{
    volatile DWORD drv = 0; // volatile so compiler doesn't just return 0!
    static STACKER_DRIVER far *driver = (STACKER_DRIVER far *) 0;
    int host;
    if (! driver) driver = stacker_detect();     // one-time init
    if (! driver) return 0L;
    drive++;
    _asm mov ax, 4404h
    _asm mov cx, 4
    _asm mov bl, byte ptr drive
    _asm lea dx, drv
    _asm int 21h
    if (! drv) return 0L;
    drive--;
    host = stacker_swapped(drive);
    *phost = host;
    *pswap = (host != drive);
    return drv;
}

#ifdef TESTING
void fail(const char *s) { puts(s); exit(1); }

main()
{
    int i, lastdrive, swap, host;
    if (! stacker_detect())
        fail("Stacker not installed");
    _dos_setdrive(0xFF, &lastdrive);
```

```
    for (i=0; i<lastdrive; i++)
        if (stacker_drive(i, &swap, &host))
        {
            printf("%c:\tSTACKER", i + 'A');
            if (swap) printf(" (swapped %c:)", host + 'A');
            printf("\n");
        }
    return 0;
}
#endif
```

This code checks for the presence of Stacker using an otherwise invalid INT 25h call; it also checks for Stacker drives by making IOCTL calls to the Stacker driver. These portions of the Stacker API are described in the INTRLIST database that accompanies this book. Some partial documentation on the Stacker API is available from the Stac Electronics forum on CompuServe.

Earlier, we saw that DIR /C in DOS 6.0 produces very odd compression ratios for small files. The same thing has been true for years of Stacker's SDIR utility:

```
C:\STACKER>sdir foo*.*
SDIR - 3.00, (c) Copyright 1990-92 Stac Electronics, Carlsbad, CA
Volume in drive C is STACKER
Directory of  C:\STACKER

FOO     BAR       1 07-20-93  10:09p   8.0:1
FOOBAR  BAR       5 07-20-93  10:19p  16.0:1
        2 file(s)    3137536 bytes free

Overall compression ratio of files listed = 10.7:1
```

Showing 8:1 compression for a one-byte file and 16:1 compression for a five-byte file is certainly wrong. The host drive had four sectors per cluster and, thus, uses 2,048 bytes each to store these small files. Assuming Stacker uses a single 512-byte sector each to store these small files, the actual compression ratios are 4:1. SDIR is presumably using the maximum 16 sectors per cluster of the Stacker drive, rather than the 4 sectors per cluster of the original host drive. But then why the reported 8:1 compression for the one-byte file? Truly, there is something very strange (and slightly dishonest) about these compression ratios.

The Stacker SDIR utility has an undocumented /=D switch that dumps out diagnostics for some of the internal Stacker structures. The Cmap is presumably the cluster map, similar to DoubleSpace's poorly named MDFAT:

```
C:\STACKER>sdir /=d sdir.exe
SDIR - 3.00, (c) Copyright 1990-92 Stac Electronics, Carlsbad, CA
Volume in drive C is STACKER
Directory of  C:\STACKER

SDIR    EXE    35689 06-03-93   3:05a
    First cluster: 19B6
    Fat: 19B9  Cmap: 0084C1D7  Extent: 008B02ED
    Fat: 19BA  Cmap: 0086C1FA  Extent: 008904ED
    Fat: 19BB  Cmap: 0085C2A1  Extent: 008A02ED
    Fat: 19BC  Cmap: 0083C2D8  Extent: 008C04ED
    Fat: FFFF  Cmap: 0081C364  Extent: 000402ED

Sector Ratio = 1:0.933
Host Cluster Ratio = 0.960:1
Compressed Disk Cluster Ratio = 1.067:1
Adjusted Cluster Ratio = 1.067:1
Percent of original file size: 104.17%

        1 file(s)    3137536 bytes free

Overall compression ratio of files listed = 1.1:1
```

SDIR.EXE itself achieved such low compression here because Stac Electronics has already pre-compressed the executable, using the excellent LZEXE program by Fabrice Bellard (whose signature '*FAB*' appears at the end of such compressed executables). Mitugu Kurizono's UNLZEXE can decompress these executables.

Novell NetWare Drives

Because ENUMDRV simply walks the CDS, whose size is set by LASTDRIVE, the program does not show Novell NetWare drives that are assigned to drive numbers that exceed the value of LASTDRIVE. As noted in Chapter 4, the NetWare API includes INT 21h AH=EFh and AH=E2h functions that can help to display NetWare drives. However, as also explained in Chapter 4, the NetWare workstation shell also provides its own versions of many standard INT 21h calls. A documented MS-DOS function call, Get Assign-List Entry (INT 21h AX=5F02h), can enumerate NetWare drives. Of course, it also enumerates any non-NetWare network drives that DOS supports.

Thus, a commercial version of the ENUMDRV program would also have to incorporate code such as that found in Listing 8-15 (NETDRV.C), which runs the Get Assign-List Entry function in a loop and prints out the local and network names for each network connected device, including printers as well as drives.

Listing 8-15: NETDRV.C

```
/*
NETDRV.C -- Display network connections, using 21/5F02
Andrew Schulman, July 1993
NOTE: 21/5F02 is *not* undocumented! Is NetWare support for it documented?
*/

#include <stdlib.h>
#include <stdio.h>
#include <dos.h>

typedef unsigned char BYTE;
typedef unsigned short WORD;

int _dos_getassignlist(WORD index, char far *local, char far *net,
    BYTE *pavail, BYTE *pdevtype, WORD *puserval)
{
    BYTE avail, devtype;
    WORD userval;
    _asm push ds
    _asm push di
    _asm push si
    _asm mov bx, index
    _asm lds si, local
    _asm les di, net
    _asm mov ax, 5f02h
    _asm int 21h
    _asm pop si
    _asm pop di
    _asm pop ds
    _asm jc error
    _asm mov byte ptr avail, bh
    _asm mov byte ptr devtype, bl
    _asm mov word ptr userval, cx
    *pavail = avail; *pdevtype = devtype; *puserval = userval;
    return 0;    // success
error:;
    // return value in AX
}
main()
{
    char local[128], net[128];
```

```
    BYTE avail, devtype;
    WORD userval, i;

    for (i=0; i<0xFFFF; i++)
        if (_dos_getassignlist(i, local, net, &avail, &devtype, &userval))
            break;
        else
            printf("%u\t%s\t%s\n", i, local, net);
    return 0;
}
```

Running under NetWare 3.11, with LASTDRIVE=F, NETDRV produced the following sample results:

```
0       G:      \\MRY-APPL-TS\VOL1
1       H:      \\MRY-APPL-TS\VOL1
2       I:      \\MRY-APPL-TS\SYS
3       J:      \\MRY-APPL-TS\VOL2\TOOLS\SRC
; ...
12      Y:      \\MRY-APPL-TS\VOL1
13      Z:      \\MRY-APPL-TS\SYS
14      LPT1    \\MRY-MAIL-CORP\GCC1-TS-HPLJ2
15      LPT2    \\MRY-MAIL-CORP\GCC1-TS-QMSPS
16      LPT3    \\MRY-MAIL-CORP\GCC1-HPLJ2-TS
```

You may recall that we were talking about the CDS and then went off to discuss a whole range of drives, whose type (RAM disk, DoubleSpace, Stacker, NetWare) in one way or another is not reflected in the CDS. Let's now return to the CDS itself.

Manufacturing and Removing Drive Letters

All the utilities and functions presented so far in this chapter report back on the state of the DOS file system, but they don't *do* anything. Our next utility changes the CDS. But it's perverse to classify utilities by the internal data structures they alter. A user would say that this program creates and destroys drive mappings. For example:

```
C:\UNDOC2>dir d:\

 Volume in drive D is RAMANUJAN
 Directory of  D:\
CHAP1   DOC     4439    6-12-90    9:05a
        1 File(s)    1261568 bytes free

C:\UNDOC2>drvoff d:

C:\UNDOC2>dir d:\
Invalid drive specification
```

Sometimes it is useful to convince MS-DOS that a logical drive is no longer present. If you have ever worked with the Microsoft CD-ROM Extensions, for example, you might have noted that the only way to deinstall this utility is by rebooting the machine. Even TSR management programs like the superb MARK/RELEASE from TurboPower Software are insufficient to remove MSCDEX because, in addition to grabbing memory, MSCDEX also creates a logical drive and that, too, must be undone.

DRVOFF merely calls the currdir() function from CURRDIR.C (Listing 8-10) and uses the returned CDS pointer to zero the flags word, instantly making the drive invalid. In essence, DRVOFF is nothing more than:

```
currdir(toupper(argv[1][0]) - 'A')->flags = 0;
```

This is the utility that interested one of the authors enough in undocumented DOS to work on this book. However, DRVOFF may not actually work so well in its intended purpose of unloading MSCDEX from memory (see the notes at the top of DRVSET.C in Listing 8-16).

Access to the CDS isn't just for invalidating drive letters. With a utility called DRVSET, you can activate an invalid drive in an odd way, simply by turning on some bits in the flags word. DOS immediately recognizes the resulting *air drive* as valid, in that you can change to it and send it requests (all of which fail, of course):

```
C:\UNDOC>e:
Invalid drive specification

C:\UNDOC>dir e:
Invalid drive specification

C:\UNDOC>drvset e: net phys
NET PHYSICAL

C:\UNDOC>dir e:

 Volume in drive E has no label
 Directory of  E:\

File not found

C:\UNDOC>e:

E:\>chkdsk
Cannot CHKDSK a Network drive
```

Simply by twiddling bits in the CDS, we convince DOS that E: is in some way a valid drive. Since DIR doesn't show any files up there, it's not clear what value this has. However, this is the foundation for creating drives with the network redirector. Simply by making drive E: a network drive (again, the term "network" just means a non-FAT installable file system), we can route all DOS file requests for the drive to an INT 2Fh function 11h handler. Later on in this chapter, we write such a handler. In the meantime, DRVSET is useful for experimenting with air drives, which are the foundation for installable file systems under DOS.

Since DRVOFF and DRVSET are so similar, it makes sense to package them in the same source module, DRVSET.C (Listing 8-16). The resulting program behaves differently if its pathname (argv[0] in C) contains the string, "DRVOFF".

Because DRVOFF/DRVSET calls the currdir() function to get a far pointer to the CDS entry for the specified drive, link it with the CURRDIR module (see Listing 8-10).

Listing 8-16: DRVSET.C

```
/*
DRVSET.C -- Set attributes of drive (CDS entry) given on command line
Andrew Schulman, revised July 1993

NOTE: This (in its DRVOFF form) was the stupid program that got me
interested in undocumented API calls, back in 1989 when I was working
on CD/Networker for David Maxey at Lotus. It was part of something
that our customers (especially Shearson) wanted to unload MSCDEX,
called NOMSCDEX. (When Shearson talks, Lotus listens.) Basically,
NOMSCDEX was a batch file that ran MARK/RELEASE and then DRVOFF.

Based on a casual disassembly of MSCDEX (which I did on the urging of
Brian Livingston, who correctly suggested there was something fishy
going on here), it is now clear to me that DRVOFF doesn't truly work
for unloading MSCDEX, because MSCDEX *patches* DOS. A true NOMSCDEX
would back out these patches too. Or do the patches occur
only when running MSCDEX /S on a server, so that using DRVOFF for
NOMSCDEX *would* work except when running MSCDEX /S?  Anyhow,
programs like MSCDEX do enough gross low-level things to DOS that
trying to back out their changes and unload them is a risky
proposition at best.
```

```c
*/
#include <stdlib.h>
#include <stdio.h>
#include <string.h>
#include <ctype.h>
#include "currdir.h"

void fail(char *s) { puts(s); exit(1); }

main(int argc, char *argv[])
{
    char *cmd;
    CDS far *drv;
    int drive, drvoff, i;

    /* to just turn off drives, rename program DRVOFF */
    drvoff = (strstr(strupr(argv[0]), "DRVOFF") != 0);

    /* what drive do they want? (accepts letters and numbers) */
    if (argc < 2) fail(drvoff?
        "usage: drvoff [drive]" :
        "usage: drvset [drive] NET PHYS REDIR SUBST JOIN OFF COPY [drv2] "
                            "BACKOFF [ofs]");

    drive = toupper(argv[1][0]) - 'A';
    if (! (drv = currdir(drive)))
        fail("can't get current directory structure");

    if (drvoff) { drv->flags = 0; return 0; }   /* just turn off drive */

    for (i=2; i<argc; i++)
    {
        cmd = strupr(argv[i]);
        if (strstr(cmd, "COPY"))       /* COPY one CDS entry to another */
        {
            CDS far *drv2 = currdir(toupper(argv[i+1][0]) - 'A');
            if (! drv2) fail("can't copy from invalid drive");
            _fmemcpy(drv, drv2, (_osmajor >= 4) ? 0x58 : 0x51);
            i++;
            continue;
        }
        else if (strstr(cmd, "BACKOFF")) /* set backwack offset */
        {
            drv->backslash_offset = atoi(argv[i+1]); i++;
            continue;
        }
        /* COPY and BACKOFF let you simulate SUBST. (Big deal!) */

        /* change drive attributes */
        if (strstr(cmd, "OFF"))    drv->flags = 0;
        if (strstr(cmd, "CDROM"))  drv->flags |= REDIR_NOT_NET;
        if (strstr(cmd, "REDIR"))  drv->flags |= REDIR_NOT_NET;
        if (strstr(cmd, "NET"))    drv->flags |= NETWORK;
        if (strstr(cmd, "SUBST"))  drv->flags |= SUBST;
        if (strstr(cmd, "JOIN"))   drv->flags |= JOIN;
        if (strstr(cmd, "PHYS"))   drv->flags |= PHYSICAL;
    }

    /* print current drive state */
    if (! drv->flags)              fputs("INVALID ", stdout);
    if (drv->flags & REDIR_NOT_NET) fputs("REDIR ", stdout); // CDROM
    if (drv->flags & NETWORK)   fputs("NET ", stdout);
    if (drv->flags & SUBST)     fputs("SUBST ", stdout);
    if (drv->flags & JOIN)      fputs("JOIN ", stdout);
    if (drv->flags & PHYSICAL)  fputs("PHYSICAL ", stdout);
    putchar('\n');
    return 0;
}
```

DRVSET also has an option to copy from one CDS entry to another and an option to set the CDS backslash offset. In an unnecessary and somewhat bogus but perhaps enlightening way, this simulates the effect of the SUBST command:

```
D:\UNDOC2>dir e:
Invalid drive specification

D:\UNDOC2>drvset e: copy d: subst backoff 9
SUBST PHYSICAL

D:\UNDOC2>dir e:
 Volume in drive E has no label
 Volume Serial Number is 1B51-11E7
 Directory of E:\

.                <DIR>      02-16-93  11:52a
..               <DIR>      02-16-93  11:52a
NAMCLUST EXE      9812 07-14-93   7:31p
CLUSTNAM EXE      8102 07-10-93  10:42p
CHAP8    TXT    321850 07-20-93   8:49a
; ... etc. ...
```

This is close enough to the actual effect of SUBST that an examination of the code in DRVSET.C should give you some idea of how the real SUBST command must work:

```
CDS far *dest = currdir('E' - 'A');
CDS far *src = currdir('D' - 'A');
_fmemcpy(dest, src, (_osmajor >= 4) ? 0x58 : 0x51);
dest->flags |= SUBST;
dest->backslash_offset = _fstrlen(src->currdir);
```

As another example of modifying the CDS, see the XLASTDRV program in Chapter 2, which changes the location and size of the CDS (that is, the LASTDRIVE= value) on the fly.

For now we're finished talking about drives and directories. So get yourself another cup of coffee and another slice of pizza and proceed to the next installment in our saga of the DOS file system. It's now time to look at the data structures that DOS uses when you open a file.

System File Tables (SFTs) and Job File Table (JFT)

The System File Tables are the backbone of the DOS file system and have been present in DOS since version 2.0 when Microsoft added handle-based file operations. Before that, DOS used File Control Blocks (FCBs), which are discussed briefly later in this chapter. An SFT maintains the state of an *open* file. This includes associating a filename with a directory entry and with a cluster on disk, keeping track of the current position within the file (the file pointer), determining current file size, and maintaining the time and date stamps when a file is modified. All information contained in the directory entry for a file gets there from the SFT when the file is closed; it is brought back into the SFT when the file is opened.

When a program opens a file using DOS function 3Dh (Open File) or 6Ch (Extended Open/Create), it gets back a file handle that later refers to the file when reading with function 3Fh, writing with function 40h, and so on. The file handle is what Microsoft calls a "magic cookie," meaning that you can use the handle to access the object (in this case, a file), without assigning any particular meaning to the handle. For example:

```
#include <io.h>
// ...
char buf[12];
int f = open("foo.bar", O_RDONLY);
if (f == -1) fail("couldn't open file!");
read(f, buf, 12);
close(f);
```

After checking that (f !== -1), that is, that the file was successfully opened, most applications treat file handles as magic cookies. A function such as open() returns the handle to you, and you faithfully pass it along to functions such as read(), write(), and close(). With the exception of the predefined handles 0 (stdin), 1 (stdout), 2 (stderr), and sometimes 3 (stdaux) and 4 (stdprn), applications generally attach no particular meaning to the numeric value of a file handle. DOS, however, certainly does attach meaning the value of the file handle, and it is sometimes useful for an application to do so too.

A DOS file handle, such as that returned from INT 21h functions 3Dh and 6Ch, is simply an index into another data structure, the Job File Table. The JFT is an array of BYTEs, indexed by file handles, and holding SFT indices. In other words,

```
int f = open(...);
sft_index = jft[f];
sft_entry = sft[sft_index];
```

or:

```
sft_entry = sft[jft[f]];
```

An important exception is Novell NetWare versions 2 and 3 which, as discussed in Chapter 4, assign *negative* handles to files located on network servers. NETX uses this as a reverse index into its own internal file handle table, thereby bypassing the SFT.

All DOS processes share a single chain of SFTs. A far pointer to the first SFT in the chain can be found at offset 4 in SysVars. Each DOS process has its own JFT; a far pointer to a process's JFT can be found at offset 34h in its PSP (see Chapter 7).

FILE* vs. File Handles

Before we go any further, we need to to distinguish DOS file handles from the file identifiers used in compiler run-time libraries. Many DOS applications use a compiler run-time library rather than calling directly down to DOS. In some cases, like the C open() function declared in IO.H, the DOS version of the C run-time library usually does happen to return a DOS file handle. However, in other cases, such as the C fopen() function declared in STDIO.H, something completely different is returned: fopen() returns a pointer to a FILE structure (FILE *).

FILE is a structure declared in STDIO.H. It is an indication of the success of the C run-time library that most programmers think purely of FILE* without having to give any consideration to, and perhaps without ever having looked at, FILE itself. The C run-time library includes a fileno() function which, given a FILE*, can return the corresponding file handle that the application would have, had it called open() rather than fopen(). In most C compilers for the PC, the FILE structure contains a field for the DOS file handle, and fileno() simply returns the value of this field:

```
#include <stdio.h>
// ...
FILE *f = fopen(...);
sft_entry = sft[jft[fileno(f)]];
```

The superficial similarity between FILE* and file handles is a surprisingly large source of confusion. The technical support department for one vendor of programmer's products reports the confusion between FILE* and a DOS file handle as one of the most frequently occurring problems among its (supposedly quite sophisticated) clientele. This confusion is particularly rampant among those trying to increase the number of available file handles: They call INT 21h AH=67h to get more DOS file handles and then wonder why fopen() still fails after twenty open files. We'll get to this topic later in this horrendously long chapter.

All DOS systems have at least five SFT entries; many have 20 or more. Just as the LASTDRIVE= value in CONFIG.SYS sets the size of the CDS, FILES= establishes the number of SFT entries. (Incidentally, for an excellent answer to an end-user's question, "What exactly does the FILES directive in CONFIG.SYS do?," see Jeff Prosise, "What FILES= Does," *PC Magazine*, November 12, 1991.) FILES= defaults to eight if no such command is present in CONFIG.SYS. Every file handle that a program obtains from DOS leads (through the JFT) to one of the SFTs.

When you ask DOS to open a file by calling functions 3Dh or 6Ch or by calling a higher level function like fopen(), which in turn calls one of the DOS functions for you, the following takes place.

First, DOS uses the current PSP (see Chapter 6) to locate your JFT—actually, the JFT of whatever PSP happens to be current, but we assume for this discussion that the current PSP belongs to your program. (It might not: see Chapter 9 on TSRs.) DOS searches through the current PSP's JFT to find a slot that is not currently in use and remembers the index into the table for the first such free slot that it finds. This index into the JFT eventually becomes the handle associated with the open file, assuming all goes well. DOS searches for a free JFT slot first because, if your JFT is full, DOS can't open the file and doesn't need to do anything more. DOS would return to you with error code 4 (too many open files). An application can increase the size of its JFT using function 67h (Set Maximum Handle Count), discussed later in this chapter.

In the likely event of finding a free JFT entry, DOS next searches the chain of SFTs, looking for the first SFT entry that is available for use. If no such entry is found, again DOS fails the file open, and returns error code 4. In this SFT-full situation (which is normally indistinguishable from JFT-full), calling function 67h to increase the JFT size does not help. The best bet is to raise FILES= in CONFIG.SYS and reboot, though you will see later that there is another way to get more SFT entries.

If both a free handle (JFT entry) and a free SFT entry exist, DOS calls the SHARE file-open hook function (see the discussion of SHARE later in this chapter). Assuming SHARE allows the file open to succeed, DOS determines the drive for the filename you asked to open and uses this to index into the CDS, locating the proper CDS entry for the drive where the requested file resides. If you passed in a relative pathname such as "FOO.BAR", DOS uses the current directory in the CDS. If installed, the triple kludges ASSIGN, APPEND, and FASTOPEN do their thing.

From the CDS, DOS also determines if the file you want to open is on a network drive. If so, DOS issues the appropriate INT 2Fh AH=11h calls to have any installed network redirectors open the file. As noted later in the lengthy discussion of the network redirector interface, when DOS calls one of the Open or Create redirector functions (INT 2Fh AX=1116h, AX=1117h, or AX=112Eh), it passes the redirector a free uninitialized SFT entry, which it expects the redirector to fill in.

If you're dealing with a physical drive, DOS also uses the CDS to extract a pointer to the drive's DPB. DOS uses the DPB to locate the drive's root directory to perform the necessary calculations to convert cluster references into LSNs and to find the block device driver that handles the driver. From the device driver header, DOS locates function pointers to the driver's Interrupt and Strategy routines, which it calls to do the actual I/O to and from the drive.

Armed with all this information from the DPB, the DOS kernel calls the device driver to read the drive's root directory into one of the DOS buffers—unless, of course, the root directory is already located in one of the buffers; recall from the BUFFERS program (Listing 8-8) that the buffers often include directory and FAT sectors.

If the supplied path contains any subdirectories, the DOS kernel searches the root directory of the drive, trying to match the first component of the supplied path (e.g., the "UNDOC2" in "C:\UNDOC2\CHAP8\FOO.BAR"). If it isn't found, the function fails with "Path not found" (error code 3).

If DOS finds this top-level directory, however, it then converts the starting cluster value in its directory entry to an LSN. It then passes the LSN to the device driver, which reads that subdirectory into another buffer or uses it to locate the subdirectory if it's already in the buffers. This process continues until DOS has traversed all directories in the supplied path string, and only the filename remains to be located.

All this is quite similar to the code shown earlier in NAMCLUST.C (Listing 8-5), which turns a file or directory name into a starting cluster number. For example:

```
C:\UNDOC2\CHAP8>namclust foo.bar
```

NAMCLUST first calls truename() to convert "foo.bar" into "C:\UNDOC2\CHAP8\FOO.BAR", and then calls get_dpb() so drive C: gets the information necessary to read in its root directory. After reading in the root directory, it searches for "UNDOC2", just as MS-DOS itself would if we issued an INT 21h AH=3Dh to open that file:

```
C:\>namclust undoc2
C:\UNDOC2 ==> 48 (sect 973, 0x000003cd)
```

Armed with UNDOC2's starting cluster number, as found in its entry in the root directory, DOS would read in this subdirectory cluster (of course, DOS first checks the buffers). DOS would next search the UNDOC2 subdirectory for CHAP8. If CHAP8 is not found in the first cluster of this subdirectory, DOS locates a possible next cluster for the subdirectory and searches there too. Again, this is similar to the operation of NAMCLUST:

```
C:\UNDOC2>namclust chap8
C:\UNDOC2\CHAP8 ==> 51 (sect 1021, 0x000003fd)
```

Assuming CHAP8 is found, DOS again gets its starting cluster number and reads in that cluster. It is now at the final level in the file name, "FOO.BAR".

At this point, and no earlier, DOS determines whether you are dealing with a real file or with a named (character) device such as CON or LPT1. It does so by searching the list of installed device drivers (see the device-driver chain walking program in Chapter 7). If DOS finds an exact match for the filename portion of the pathspec you gave it (it ignores any extension in this test), it opens the device rather than the file. This means that all the named devices seem to exist in all directories of the file system. They also exist in a seeming subdirectory named \DEV, even though DIR \DEV fails; it also means that you cannot open any file, regardless of extension, with the same name as one of the installed devices. This means that, for example, "READ" would be a very bad name for a device; installing this device would prevent you from accessing a READ.ME file. This is one reason device names using common words tend to include dollar signs (for example, "CLOCK$").

If no matching device name is found, DOS searches the last directory for the filename and the extension. Again, this can be simulated with NAMCLUST:

```
C:\UNDOC2\CHAP8>namclust foo.bar
C:\UNDOC2\CHAP8\FOO.BAR ==> 5576 (sect 89421, 0x00015d4d)
```

Assuming the file or device is found, DOS sets the reference count in the first free SFT (located earlier) to 1, and the index of this SFT entry is stored somewhere in the program's JFT. DOS will later return the "somewhere" part to the calling program as the file handle. If DOS can't match the name, it instead returns error code 1 ("File not found").

What happens next this depends on whether you're opening a file or a device. For a file, DOS copies all pertinent information from the file's directory entry into the corresponding fields of the SFT entry. The information includes the starting cluster for the file. DOS also copies in a pointer to the DPB for the drive on which the file resides; the DPB in turn points to the device driver header for this drive. DOS also sets the file pointer field in the SFT to zero, indicating the beginning of the file. For a device, the SFT entry includes a pointer to the device driver header.

For both files and devices, DOS then returns to you with the AX register set to the handle value that it reserved at the start of the process. You now refer to the file using that handle (the magic cookie). As you saw earlier, this file handle is merely an index into the current PSP's JFT, and the byte at that index (JFT[handle]) is itself an index into the SFT.

If you're creating a new file, rather than opening an existing one, this same basic sequence of events is followed, though one significant difference occurs when the SFT entry has been filled out, before the DOS function comes back to you with a handle. The new directory entry for the just-created file is put back into the DOS buffer for that LSN, and the dirty bit for that buffer (see BUFFERS.C, Listing 8-8) is set. This tells DOS to write the buffer out to disk as soon as possible, certainly before reassigning it. A directory entry is created immediately for your new file, though with a length of zero.

Each time you read from or write to the file, referencing it by means of the handle, DOS uses the supplied handle to index into the JFT associated with the current PSP; and it uses the value it finds there to index into the SFTs. The handle is then used to perform the requested operation on the file or device referenced by its corresponding SFT entry. The file pointer and date-timestamps in the SFT are updated accordingly. Data transfers also normally involve the DOS buffer chain. To summarize:

```
current PSP -> JFT -> SFT -> buffers, DPB, device driver
```

When you close a file, DOS accesses its SFT just as for reading or writing. If the file has been written to, as indicated by a status bit in the SFT attribute word, DOS updates its directory entry with information from the SFT, which reflects the latest size, time, and date. Also, any dirty buffer is flushed to disk. If the file hasn't been written to, DOS skips these steps.

DOS decrements the handle-count field of the SFT entry (for quickest access, the first field) to reflect the fact that this handle is being disconnected from the SFT. The SFT index in the JFT handle table is replaced by the value FFh, which indicates an unused, available slot. Because FFh (255) indicates free JFT entries, it cannot be a valid SFT index; FILES=254 is therefore the maximum useful value you can set. However, remember that Novell NetWare uses negative file handles; as discussed in Chapter 4, setting a very high FILES= value can *reduce* the number of files you can open on NetWare servers.

If the newly-freed file handle was the only one using the SFT entry, decrementing the handle count brings it back to 0 and makes the entry available for reuse the next time someone calls DOS Open or Create. Some programs keep multiple files open simultaneously, but despite many programs' insistence on having 30 to 50 files available, it is rare for the number of SFTs in use to grow much larger than 15 or 20. As you'll see with the FILES program a little later on, when you look at the SFT there usually isn't much to see.

How Many FILES?

Earlier, we walked through the DOS disk buffers to determine the value of BUFFERS=; we can likewise walk through the SFTs to determine the value of FILES=. Just as with BUFFERS=, this value is normally set in CONFIG.SYS, although you can alter it on the fly with a utility like Quarterdeck's FILES.COM.

SFTWALK.C (Listing 8-17) determines the value of FILES= and prints out the address and size of each SFT. We already saw similar code in Chapter 3 (see Listing 3-5), which showed how to port this real-mode code to protected-mode Windows. The result was a second version of SFTWALK.C (Listing 3-18), which used DPMI and/or Windows API calls. Here, we focus entirely on SFT issues.

SFTWALK determines the FILES= value by threading through the SFT headers and keeping count of the entries in each table. The first SFT always holds five possible open file entries (it's assembled right into MSDOS.SYS). If FILES=40 appears in CONFIG.SYS, for example, then DOS allocates a second SFT, large enough for 35 more files, and chains it to the first SFT. Since each header consists of a count of the number in its associated table, together with a pointer to the next header, it's easy to count the possible files.

If DO_FCBS is enabled, SFTWALK can also determine the value of FCBS= by walking the chain of System FCBs. These have the same format as the SFTs; we briefly discuss System FCBs later in this chapter.

Listing 8-17: SFTWALK.C

```
/*
SFTWALK.C -- Count FILES= by Walking SFTs
For protected mode Windows version, see \UNDOC2\CHAP3\SFTWALK.C
Andrew Schulman, March 1993
From "Undocumented DOS", 2nd edition (Addison-Wesley, 1993)
*/

#include <stdlib.h>
#include <stdio.h>
#include <string.h>
#include <dos.h>

typedef unsigned char BYTE;
typedef unsigned short WORD;

typedef struct _sft {
    struct _sft far *next;
    WORD num;
    // the actual SFT entires start here
    } SFT;

int sftwalk(int offset, char *name)
{
    static BYTE far *sysvars = (BYTE far *) 0;
    SFT far *sft;
    int files = 0;
    if (! sysvars)
    {
        _asm mov ah, 52h
        _asm int 21h
        _asm mov word ptr sysvars+2, es
        _asm mov word ptr sysvars, bx
        if (! sysvars) return 0;
    }
    sft = *((SFT far * far *) &sysvars[offset]);
    while (FP_OFF(sft) != 0xFFFF)
    {
        files += sft->num;
        printf("%s @ %Fp -- %u files\n", name, sft, sft->num);
        sft = sft->next;
    }
    return files;
}

main()
{
    int files, fcbs;
    files = sftwalk(4, "SFT");
    printf("FILES=%d\n\n", files);
#ifdef DO_FCBS
    fcbs = sftwalk(0x1A, "System FCB table");
    printf("FCBS=%d\n", fcbs);
#endif
    return files;
}
```

Even if Windows or a program such as QEMM's FILES.COM has added an SFT (and possibly loaded it into upper memory), SFTWALK finds it. For example:

```
C:\UNDOC2\CHAP8>sftwalk
SFT @ 0116:00CC -- 5 files
SFT @ 1014:0000 -- 35 files
FILES=40

C:\UNDOC2\CHAP8>\qemm\files +10
FILES=40 before
10 files added
FILES=50 now

C:\UNDOC2\CHAP8>sftwalk
SFT @ 0116:00CC -- 5 files
SFT @ 1014:0000 -- 35 files
SFT @ 1838:0000 -- 10 files
FILES=50
```

From the SFTWALK output, you can see that the earlier mention of sft[jft[f]] was an oversimplification. Because there is a chain of several SFTs, rather than a single array, indexing into the SFT requires walking the linked list to first find the correct table. For example, if (jft[f] == 10), then in the above configuration, sft[10] would be somewhere in the second SFT table that starts at 1014:0000.

But where? This depends on the size of each SFT entry. We've talked a lot about how DOS uses SFTs and about how to walk the SFT list, but we haven't yet seen what an SFT entry looks like. Usually the SFT is mostly empty, so there's not much to look at, but we can create a fuller SFT by running Windows, which keeps many files open. After running SFTWALK within a Windows DOS box to get the address of each SFT in the SFT chain, we can then use DEBUG to look at one of the SFTs:

```
C:\UNDOC2\CHAP8>debug sftwalk.exe
-g
SFT @ 0116:00CC -- 5 files
SFT @ 1014:0000 -- 35 files
SFT @ 1838:0000 -- 10 files
FILES=50

Program terminated normally
-d 1014:0000
1014:0000  00 00 19 1B 23 00 01 00-00 00 20 42 10 A4 13 16   ....#..... B....
1014:0010  01 F9 08 40 19 6A 18 C0-14 00 00 00 02 00 00 00   ...@.j..........
1014:0020  00 F1 01 00 00 03 45 47-41 38 30 57 4F 41 46 4F   ......EGA80WOAFO
1014:0030  4E 00 00 00 00 01 00 0D-1F 00 00 F9 08 00 00 00   N...............
1014:0040  00 01 00 00 00 20 42 10-A4 13 16 01 F7 08 40 19   ..... B.......@.
1014:0050  6A 18 B0 20 00 00 A0 1E-00 00 00 00 F1 01 00 00   j.. ............
1014:0060  02 45 47 41 34 30 57 4F-41 46 4F 4E 00 00 00 00   .EGA40WOAFON....
1014:0070  01 00 0D 1F 00 00 F7 08-00 00 00 00 01 00 00 00   ................
```

What have we got here? Each SFT starts off with a header shown in SFTWALK.C: a DWORD pointer to the next SFT (an offset of FFFFh indicates the end of the chain), followed by a WORD with the number of files in this SFT, followed by SFT entries themselves. In the SFT at 1014:0000, the first four bytes (0 0 19h 1Bh) indicate that the next SFT is at 1B19:0000; the next two bytes (23h 0) indicate that there are 23h (35) files, just as SFTWALK claimed.

SFTWALK doesn't look at the SFT entries themselves, but from the DEBUG hex dump one can plainly see the file names EGA80WOA.FON and EGA40WOA.FON. Notice that the SFT includes only the filename and extension, not the full pathname. However, the SFT also includes the starting cluster for each file, and, as we know from the CLUSTNAM program, if necessary you can turn this starting cluster into the full pathname.

One could derive the size of an SFT entry simply by subtracting the start of one filename in the hex dump above from the start of the next: for example, offset("EGA40WOAFON") - offset("EGA80WOAFON") = 61h - 26h = 3Bh bytes. As crazy as it sounds, there is code in Windows that does just this (see "CON CON CON CON CON" in Chapter 1). Programs that want to deal with SFTs in the widest range of DOS versions have to somehow deal with the fact that the SFT size and layout differs in DOS 2.0, DOS 3.0, and DOS 3.1, and of course may change again in future DOS versions, though so far it has remained stable from DOS 3.1 through DOS 6.0.

In DOS 3.1 and higher, each SFT entry is 3Bh bytes, and the filename is located at offset 20h in each entry. We use this information in our next program, which also takes us back to look more closely at the JFT and its relation to the PSP.

Filename From Handle

Sometimes you need to know the name of a file and have only its handle available. One important example of this is when you use the DOS redirection facility to redirect stdout to a file rather than to CON, its normal destination. While the stdout handle is always 1, there is no documented way of telling from inside a running program the *name* of the file to which this (or any other) handle corresponds.

This next program, H2NAME.C (Listing 8-18) converts file handles to names by combining several undocumented DOS features. It consists primarily of the function h2name(), which, when passed a PSP and a handle, returns the filename to which that PSP/handle combination corresponds.

While you can clip out the function h2name() and use it in other programs, H2NAME.C also includes a test driver. If you run H2NAME with a PSP number on the command line (you can get the PSP numbers of different processes from the UDMEM program in Chapter 7), H2NAME enumerates all open files belonging to that process. Otherwise, it enumerates all open files belonging to H2NAME itself (using the _psp global found in most C compilers for the PC). To see anything interesting in this case, you should redirect H2NAME's output to a file so that this redirected output file shows up in the open-file enumeration. H2NAME sends its output to stderr, so the output is still visible. You can also redirect the program's (unused) input:

```
C:\UNDOC2\CHAP8>h2name > foo.bar < h2name.c
Files for 7976
  0 ==>  3 ==> H2NAME   C
  1 ==>  4 ==> FOO      BAR
  2 ==>  1 ==> CON
  3 ==>  0 ==> AUX
  4 ==>  2 ==> PRN
; ...
```

Standard input (stdin) is always file handle 0. Here, we can see that stdin has been redirected from H2NAME.C, located at SFT entry 3. Standard output (stdout) is always file handle 1, and again, you can see that H2NAME knows its standard output has been redirected to the file FOO.BAR, with SFT entry 4. We made no effort to redirect stderr, so this (file handle 2) shows up in the H2NAME output as CON.

Only the name and extension are reported. Getting a complete pathname would require using the CLUSTNAM code (Listing 8-6) to process the starting cluster number stored in the SFT.

Listing 8-18: H2NAME.C

```
/*
H2NAME.C -- Convert file handle into file name.
Jim Kyle, 1991; Revised Andrew Schulman, July 1993

The file handle is a JFT index. JFT[handle] is an SFT index. The
SFT contains information on the file, including the name. However,
H2NAME only gets the name and extension. To get the full pathname,
convert cluster number in SFT entry to a pathname (see code in
CLUSTNAM.C to see how to turn clusters numbers into full pathnames).
*/

#include <stdlib.h>
```

```c
#include <stdio.h>
#include <string.h>
#include <dos.h>
#ifdef __TURBOC__
#include <mem.h>
#else
#include <memory.h>
#endif

#ifndef MK_FP
#define MK_FP(s,o) ((void far *)\
    (((unsigned long)(s) << 16) | (unsigned)(o)))
#endif
char * h2name( unsigned psp, int h, int *sft_handle )
{ static char name[15];  /* will hold file's name */
  static unsigned far *sft_ptr = (unsigned far *) 0;
  static unsigned nmofs;
  static int sftsize;
  unsigned far *ptr;
  signed char far *sptr, far *htbl;
  int sftn;

  memset( name, 0, 15 ); /* blank out the static name */

  /* create pointer to handle table (JFT) */
  htbl = *((char far * far *) MK_FP(psp, 0x34));

  if (! sft_ptr)    /* one-time initialization to get SFT info */
  {
      _asm mov ah, 52h
      _asm int 21h
      _asm les bx, dword ptr es:[bx+4]  /* SFT chain = SysVars[4] */
      _asm mov word ptr sft_ptr+2, es
      _asm mov word ptr sft_ptr, bx

      switch( _osmajor )
      {
        case 2: sftsize = 0x28; nmofs = 4; break;
        case 3: sftsize = 0x35; nmofs = (_osminor == 0) ? 0x21 : 0x20; break;
        default: sftsize = 0x3B; nmofs = 0x20; break;   // DOS 4.0, 5.0, 6.0
      }
  }
  ptr = sft_ptr;
  *sft_handle = htbl[h];
  if (htbl[h] >= 0)             /* now if handle is valid... */
    { sftn = htbl[h];           /* get index into SFT list */
      while ( FP_OFF(ptr) != 0xFFFF )
        { if (ptr[2] > sftn)  /* then target is here */
            { sptr = (unsigned char far *)&ptr[3];
              while (sftn--)  /* so skip down to it */
                sptr += sftsize;
              _fmemcpy( name, &sptr[nmofs], 11 );
              return name;     /* found and copied; done */
            }
          sftn -= ptr[2];      /* not here; reduce index  */
          ptr = (unsigned int far *) MK_FP( ptr[1], ptr[0] );
        }
    }
  strcpy( name, "UNKNOWN" );
  return name;                 /* reached only by error       */
}
void fail(const char *s) { puts(s); exit(1); }

main( int argc, char *argv[] )
{
    char *s;
```

```
    unsigned psp;
    signed int max_files, sft_handle, jft_handle;

    if (argc < 2)
        psp = _psp;                    /* display files for this program */
    else
        sscanf(argv[1], "%X", &psp); /* take PSP from command line */

    max_files = (_osmajor >= 3) ? *((int far *) MK_FP(psp, 0x32)) : 20;

    if (*((unsigned far *) MK_FP(psp, 0)) != 0x20CD) /* check for INT 20h */
        fail("that's not a PSP!");

    fprintf(stderr, "Files for %04X\n", psp);

    for (jft_handle=0; jft_handle<max_files; jft_handle++)
    {
        s = h2name(psp, jft_handle, &sft_handle);
        if (sft_handle < 0)
            fprintf(stderr, "%2d ==> %2d\n",
                jft_handle, sft_handle);    // unused, or Novell
        else
            fprintf(stderr, "%2d ==> %2d ==> %s\n",
                jft_handle, sft_handle, s);
    }

    return 0;
}
```

Here's how h2name() works: The PSP contains a pointer to the JFT (and usually the JFT itself). From this, the function first creates a far pointer to the handle table (JFT) for the specified PSP. It then calls INT 21h AH=52h (Get SysVars) to set up the SFT pointer, and two variables sftsize and nmofs establish the SFT size and the offset within the SFT of the file or device name, based on the DOS version in use.

With these preliminaries out of the way, h2name() uses the supplied handle value as an index into the JFT. If the value found there is non-negative, indicating a valid handle, it is an SFT index. (Recall that negative file handles have special meaning in Novell NetWare.)

The function then walks through the linked list of SFTs until it finds the SFT containing the desired index (ptr[2] > sftn; ptr[2] is just this program's admittedly odd way of saying sft->num_files). Each time h2name() skips over an SFT, the number of entries in the skipped block is subtracted from the desired index (sftn -= ptr[2]), so the index is always relative to the current block rather than to the absolute beginning of the SFT linked list.

When the correct block is found, a pointer is set to the first byte of its first SFT entry (sptr = &ptr[3]), and then SFT entries are skipped (sptr += sftsize), decrementing the index each time, until the index reaches zero. When this happens the SFT entry under the pointer is the one you're looking for. The name-field offset value is then added to sptr; the eleven bytes at the resulting location are copied into the static buffer (name); and the program returns a pointer to the first byte of the buffer.

Clearly, one could apply this same technique to other information found in the SFT; h2attr(), for example, would return the file attributes rather than the filename, and h2cluster()—well, you get the idea.

H2NAME calls h2name() for each JFT entry. H2NAME's ability to look at the JFT for any PSP specified on its command line will come in handy later when we need to test the FHANDLE and FILES programs. If H2NAME were built as a Windows program, using the techniques shown in FILES.C (Listing 8-19) and explained further in Chapter 3, it could reveal the JFT for KRNL386 or any other program running in the System VM. As Chapter 3 noted, Windows programs have PSPs, just as DOS programs do.

What Files Are Now Open?

Our next utility, FILES, displays information about all open files and devices on your system. Normally there aren't many open files in the SFTs; to see anything other than AUX, CON, and PRN, redirect FILES's output to a file (for example, files > files.log) or (unnecessarily) redirect input from a file (files < foo.bar):

```
D:\UNDOC2>files > files.log < foo.bar
D:\UNDOC2>type files.log
#   Filename            Size    Attr    cRef    Owner   Cluster, DD, DPB
--  --------            ----    ----    ----    -----   ----------------
[SFT @ 0116:00CC -- 5 files]
0   AUX     .              0    0000       7    9077    DEV 0070:0035  0
1   CON     .              0    0000      19    9077    DEV 0070:0023  0
2   PRN     .              0    0000       7    9077    DEV 0070:0047  0
3   FOO     .BAR        7391    0020       2    6AC2    D: 29444   DPB 0FF1:0000  0
4   FILES   .LOG           0    0020       2    6AC2    D:     0   DPB 0FF1:0000  0
[SFT @ 1014:0000 -- 35 files]
[SFT @ 1838:0000 -- 10 files]
```

When its input or output is redirected, FILES inherits an open file from COMMAND.COM. Note how FOO.BAR and FILES.LOG each have a reference count of 2.

You can run CLUSTNAM to confirm the cluster numbers FILES displays. Only one file in the SFT, FOO.BAR, has a cluster number. (FILES.LOG, to which output from the FILES program was redirected, was at the time of course just a directory entry with no associated data clusters):

```
D:\UNDOC2>clustnam d: 29444
D:\UNDOC2\FOO.BAR
```

Besides a nice doublecheck that the output from FILES is accurate, this also shows that the CLUSTNAM code (Listing 8-5) could be moved into FILES to output the full pathname for each SFT entry with an associated data cluster. (The same point was made earlier regarding the H2NAME program.) Unfortunately, the CLUSTNAM code may take a long time to run.

As you will see in FILES.C (Listing 8-19), the owner FILES display comes right out of the SFT. Often this is a PSP, and you could extend FILES with the UDMEM code from Chapter 7 to turn the owner's PSP address into a readable name.

However, these owners aren't always legitimate PSP addresses. The AUX, CON, and PRN entries show an owner of 9077h. Running UDMEM indicates that this is not a valid PSP. Instead, the value is apparently the effective PSP at the time that the SYSINIT initialization code in IO.SYS or IBMBIO.COM opened them. (SYSINIT relocates itself to the top of memory, accounting for the high address.)

As a more interesting example, consider the output from FILES when running in a DOS box under Windows 3.1 Enhanced mode:

```
D:\UNDOC2>files
#   Filename            Size    Attr    cRef    Owner   Cluster, DD, DPB
--  --------            ----    ----    ----    -----   ----------------
[SFT @ 0116:00CC -- 5 files]
0   AUX     .              0    0000      17    9077    DEV 0070:0035  0
1   CON     .              0    0000      51    9077    DEV 0070:0023  0
2   PRN     .              0    0000      17    9077    DEV 0070:0047  0
3   WIN386  .SWP     1769472    0020       1    1AAE    C: 6506    DPB 0116:13A4  0
4   COURE   .FON       23408    0020       1    1F0D    C: 2513    DPB 0116:13A4  1
[SFT @ 1014:0000 -- 35 files]
6   SH      .EXE       33792    0020       1    1F0D    C: 1218    DPB 0116:13A4  1
7   VGAFIX  .FON        5360    0020       1    1F0D    C: 2310    DPB 0116:13A4  1
8   GDI     .EXE      275261    0020       1    1F0D    C: 3037    DPB 0116:13A4  1
```

```
9    SSERIFE .FON      64544    0020     1  1FOD    C:   2547   DPB 0116:13A4  1
10   USER    .EXE     338406    0020     1  1FOD    C:   3072   DPB 0116:13A4  1
11   WINFILE .EXE     146864    0020     1  1FOD    C:   1794   DPB 0116:13A4  1
12   KEYBOARD.DRV       7568    0020     1  1FOD    C:   2301   DPB 0116:13A4  1
13   VGA     .DRV      73200    0020     1  1FOD    C:   2204   DPB 0116:13A4  1
14   COMM    .DRV       9280    0020     1  1FOD    C:   2253   DPB 0116:13A4  1
15   FILES   .EXE      14698    0020     1  1FOD    C:  12643   DPB 0116:13A4  2
16   ANTQUA  .TTF      59776    0020     1  1FOD    C:   2947   DPB 0116:13A4  1
[SFT @ 1B19:0000 -- 30 files]
```

Note WIN386.SWP, the SFT entry #3 in the output above. As its name suggests, this is the Windows 386 Enhanced mode swap file, which Windows uses for do paging when you don't have a permanent swap file. The SFT entry FILES displayed indicates WIN386.SWP's owner is 1AAEh. We can run H2NAME (Listing 8-18) to make sure this all makes sense:

```
D:\UNDOC2>h2name 1aae
Files for 1AAE
  0 ==>   1 ==> CON
  1 ==>   1 ==> CON
  2 ==>   1 ==> CON
  3 ==>   0 ==> AUX
  4 ==>   2 ==> PRN
  5 ==>   3 ==> WIN386   SWP
  6 ==>  -1
; ...
```

Sure enough, the JFT for PSP 1AAEh has a file handle that points back to this SFT entry. Running UDMEM from Chapter 7 (or MEM /P) shows that PSP 1AAEh corresponds to WIN386.EXE:

```
D:\UNDOC2>udmem
; ...
1AAD    1AAE    0452 ( 17696)    Env at 1AA2    C:\WIN31\system\win386.exe
; ...
```

But note the owner 1F0Dh for SFT entries 4-16 in the FILES output. Specifying the number 1F0Dh on H2NAME's command line produces the message "that's not a PSP!" (H2NAME.C merely checks the first two bytes of the specified segment to ensure they are the 0x20CD signature, which are the opcode bytes for the INT 20h instruction that begins every PSP.)

The problem is that we are running H2NAME from within a DOS box. The last column in the FILES output is the virtual machine (VM) ID of the file's owner: 0 indicates files or devices opened before Windows started; 1 indicates the System VM, where Windows applications run; 2 indicates the first DOS box. In this test, FILES was run within the first DOS box, VM 2. As indicated by the last column of FILES output, the number 1F0Dh is only a valid PSP within another virtual machine, VM 1. In fact, this other virtual machine is the System VM in which Windows applications are run, and this PSP is only visible within the System VM's address space. Even if the DOS box happened to have a PSP 1F0Dh, it wouldn't be the right one (see lseek in Chapter 6). As discussed in Chapter 3, viewing a PSP in the System VM requires (1) a DOS program run from within WINSTART.BAT; (2) a protected mode DOS program that maps in memory from other VMs; or simply (3) a Windows application. When you run the WINPSP program from Chapter 3, PSP 1F0Dh (or the equivalent on your machine) shows up plain as day:

```
1F0D    7FF3    KRNL386    3196:0000 (32 files, 18 open)
```

But if the SFT entries for COURE.FON, SH.EXE, VGAFIX.FON, and so on all belong to a PSP that is only visible within the System VM, why then are these open files located in the global SFT, visible to all processes in all VMs? In other words, why doesn't Windows declare the SFT as instance data? Because, while Windows instances other DOS data structures such as the CDS on a per-VM basis,

Windows can't instance the SFT. How else would SHARE work? (See the SHARE discussion later in this chapter.)

On the other hand, *parts* of SFTs can be allocated on a per-VM basis. The Windows SYSTEM.INI file has a PerVMFiles= setting that controls how many SFT entries each VM can add to its view of the SFT chain. To support this, the sft->next pointer in the last SFT table allocated before Windows started up *is* declared as instance data.

The effect of a PerVMFiles=30 statement is readily seen in the following output from SFT-WALK. Here, CONFIG.SYS said FILES=40, but running the SFTWALK program within a Windows DOS box showed FILES=70:

```
D:\UNDOC2>sftwalk
SFT @ 0116:00CC -- 5 files
SFT @ 1014:0000 -- 35 files
SFT @ 1B19:0000 -- 30 files
FILES=70
```

Thus, Windows implements PerVMFiles by linking an additional SFT table to the end of the chain, just as you saw FILES.COM from QEMM do earlier. Effectively, the DOS FILES= value has been temporarily increased without having to change CONFIG.SYS and reboot.

Windows extension of the SFT gets even more complicated because, as noted in Chapter 1 and in the description of GrowSFTToMax() in Matt Pietrek's *Windows Internals*, KRNL386 does its own expansion of the SFT, independent of PerVMFiles. When SFTWALK is run as a Windows program (see Chapter 3), the output once again changes:

```
SFT @ 0116:00CC -- 5 files
SFT @ 1014:0000 -- 35 files
SFT @ 319A:0000 -- 87 files
FILES=127
```

In this session, we happened not to have run the QEMM FILES.COM program. If we had, its added SFT would also show up in the SFT chain. As you can see, the SFT was almost made to be expanded.

The source code for FILES appears in Listing 8-19. Just as SFTWALK did, FILES walks the SFTs. However, FILES descends into each SFT to get information on each open file. FILES starts with the first SFT pointed to by SysVars, displays any files in that table, and then goes into a loop following the sft->next field, until it finds a next field whose segment is zero or whose offset is -1 (FFFFh). Only in-use SFT entries (NUM_HANDLES(ff) != 0) are shown.

Listing 8-19: FILES.C

```
/*
FILES.C -- List all files in DOS System File Table (SFT)
Andrew Schulman, Revised July 1993

real mode DOS: bcc files.c
protected mode Windows: bcc -WS -2 -DWINDOWS files.c \undoc2\chap3\prot.c

This version is substantially different from that published in
the first edition of UNDOCUMENTED DOS:
-- Includes DOS 3.0 file structure, which is not same as 3.1
   (USHORT dir_entry, not BYTE). Thanks to Neil Rubenking!
-- DOS 2.x, 3.0, 3.1+ structs combined into union, with access
   macros. This points up the relative inflexibility of structures:
   struct->field just turns into an offset, but at compile-time,
   with no control over changing field offsets at run-time.
-- Replaced previous check for possible orphaned files, which was
   just too flaky. Now just use simple garbage-collection test:
   for each SFT entry, see if its owner's JFT actually contains a
   reference to this SFT. You can examine FILES output and decide
   for yourself if these files are really orphaned. If they are,
```

```
        you can run SFT_FREE with their SFT index # on the command line.
    -- Ported code to protected mode Windows (see #ifdef WINDOWS).
    -- On suggestion of Geoff Chappell, got rid of AUX-CON "sanity check,"
       which was insane.
    -- Can be run with -FCB switch to view System FCBs instead of SFTs.
    */
    #include <stdlib.h>
    #include <stdio.h>
    #include <string.h>
    #include <dos.h>
    #ifdef WINDOWS
    #include "windows.h"
    #include "prot.h"              // see \undoc2\chap3\prot.h
    #endif

    typedef unsigned char BYTE;
    typedef unsigned short WORD;
    typedef unsigned long DWORD;
    typedef BYTE far *FP;

    #pragma pack(1)

    typedef struct file2 {
        BYTE num_handles, open_mode;
        BYTE fattr;       // might be wrong?
        BYTE drive;
        BYTE filename[8], ext[3];
        WORD unknown1, unknown2;
        DWORD fsize;
        WORD date, time;
        BYTE dev_attr;
        union {
            FP dev_drv;            // for CHAR dev
            WORD cluster[2];       // for disk file (BLOCK dev)
            } u;
        // ...
        // NOTE! no owner_psp!
        } file2; // for DOS 2.x

    typedef struct file30 {
        WORD num_handles, open_mode;
        BYTE fattr;
        WORD dev_info;    // includes drive number
        FP ptr;                   // device driver (CHAR) or DPB (BLOCK)
        WORD start_cluster, time, date;
        DWORD fsize, offset;
        WORD rel_cluster, abs_cluster, dir_sector;
        WORD dir_entry;    // only difference from file31: WORD, not BYTE
        BYTE filename[8], ext[3];
        DWORD share_prev_sft;
        WORD share_net_machine, owner_psp;
        // ...
        } file30; // for DOS 3.0 only

    typedef struct file31 {
        WORD num_handles, open_mode;
        BYTE fattr;
        WORD dev_info;    // includes drive number
        FP ptr;                  // device driver (CHAR) or DPB (BLOCK)
        WORD start_cluster, time, date;
        DWORD fsize, offset;
        WORD rel_cluster, abs_cluster, dir_sector;
        BYTE dir_entry, filename[8], ext[3];
        DWORD share_prev_sft;
        WORD share_net_machine, owner_psp;
        // ...
```

```c
    } file31; // for DOS 3.1+

typedef union file {
    file2 f2;
    file30 f30;
    file31 f31;
    } file;

// access macros
#define DOS(maj)            (_osmajor == (maj))
#define DOSVER(maj, min)    (_osmajor == (maj) && _osminor == (min))
#define DOS3_FIELD(pf,x)    (DOSVER(3,0) ? (pf)->f30.x : (pf)->f31.x)
#define DOSVER_FIELD(pf,x)  (DOS(2) ? (pf)->f2.x : DOS3_FIELD(pf,x))
#define FILENAME(pf)        DOSVER_FIELD(pf,filename)
#define EXT(pf)             DOSVER_FIELD(pf,ext)
#define FSIZE(pf)           DOSVER_FIELD(pf,fsize)
#define FATTR(pf)           DOSVER_FIELD(pf,fattr)
#define NUM_HANDLES(pf)     DOSVER_FIELD(pf,num_handles)
#define DEV_WORD(pf)        DOS3_FIELD(pf,dev_info)
#define DEV_ATTR(pf)        (DEV_WORD(pf) & 0x80)
#define CHAR_DEV(pf)        (DEV_ATTR(pf) == 0x80)
#define DISK_FILE(pf)       (DEV_ATTR(pf) == 0)
#define DRIVE(pf)           (DOS(2) ? (pf)->f2.drive : DEV_WORD(pf) & 0x003F)
#define OWNER_PSP(pf)       (DOS(2) ? -1 : DOS3_FIELD(pf,owner_psp))
#define START_CLUSTER(pf)   (DOS(2) ? (pf)->f2.u.cluster[0] : \
                            DOS3_FIELD(pf,start_cluster))
#define PTR(pf)             DOS3_FIELD(pf,ptr)
#define VM_ID(pf)           DOS3_FIELD(pf,share_net_machine) // Windows VM
#define DEV_DRIVER(pf)      (DOS(2) ? (pf)->f2.u.dev_drv : PTR(pf))
#define DPB(pf)             PTR(pf)

typedef struct sysftab {
    struct sysftab far *next;
    WORD num_files;
    file f[1];
    } SYS_FTAB;

void fail(char *s) { puts(s); exit(1); }

#ifndef MK_FP
#define MK_FP(seg,ofs)  ((FP)(((DWORD)(seg) << 16) | (ofs)))
#endif

#ifdef WINDOWS
#define MAP(ptr, bytes)     map_real((ptr), (bytes))
#define FREE_MAP(ptr)       free_mapped_linear(ptr)
#define GET_REAL(ptr)       get_real_addr(ptr)
#else
#define MAP(ptr, bytes)     (ptr)
#define FREE_MAP(ptr)       /**/
#define GET_REAL(ptr)       (ptr)
#endif

main(int argc, char *argv[])
{
    SYS_FTAB far *sys_filetab, far *next;
    file far *ff;
    char buf[9];
    int size, i, num=0, do_fcbs = 0, orph = 0;

    // either examine SFT table or System FCB table (same format)
    int sft_ptr_ofs = 4;
    if (argc > 1 && strcmp(strupr(argv[1]), "-FCB") == 0)
        { do_fcbs++; sft_ptr_ofs = 0x1A; }
#ifdef WINDOWS
    WORD mapped;
```

```
    RMODE_CALL r;
    memset(&r, 0, sizeof(r));
    r.eax = 0x5200;
    if (dpmi_rmode_intr(0x21, 0, 0, &r))
    {
        SYS_FTAB far * far *tmp = (SYS_FTAB far * far *)
            MAP(MK_FP(r.es, (WORD) r.ebx + sft_ptr_ofs), 4);
        SYS_FTAB far *psysftab = *tmp;
        FREE_MAP(tmp);
        sys_filetab = (SYS_FTAB far *) MAP(psysftab, 0xFFFF);
    }
    else
        fail("Could not generate real mode 21/52!");
#else
    _asm mov ah, 52h
    _asm int 21h
    _asm add bx, word ptr sft_ptr_ofs    /* either SFT or System FCB chain */
    _asm les bx, dword ptr es:[bx]
    _asm mov word ptr sys_filetab, bx
    _asm mov word ptr sys_filetab+2, es
#endif
    /* DOS box of OS/2 1.x doesn't provide system file tbl */
    if (sys_filetab == (SYS_FTAB far *) -1L)
        fail("system file table not supported");

    /* could try to confirm this size by subtracting one filename
       from another, as Windows does in "CON CON CON CON CON" code. */
    size = DOS(2) ? 0x28 : DOS(3) ? 0x35 : 0x3B;    // SFT entry size

puts("#  Filename          Size  Attr  cRef  Owner   Cluster, DD, DPB");
puts("-  --------          ----  ----  ----  -----   ----------------");

    do { /* FOR EACH SFT */
        printf("\n[SFT @ %Fp -- %d files]\n",
            GET_REAL(sys_filetab), sys_filetab->num_files);

        /* FOR EACH ENTRY IN THIS SFT */
        ff = (file far *) sys_filetab->f;  // DON'T MAP; already mapped!
        for (i=0; i<sys_filetab->num_files; i++, num++, ((FP) ff) += size)
        if (NUM_HANDLES(ff) != 0)    // don't show unused entries
        {
            printf("%-3d ", num);    // SFT index
#ifdef __BORLANDC__
            // bcc pmode printf GP faults on non-null-terminated strings
            _fmemcpy(buf, FILENAME(ff), 8); buf[8] = 0; printf("%.8s.", buf);
            _fmemcpy(buf, EXT(ff), 3); buf[3] = 0; printf("%.3s  ", buf);
#else
            printf("%.8Fs.",         FILENAME(ff));
            printf("%.3Fs  ",        EXT(ff));
#endif
            printf("%10lu\t",        FSIZE(ff));
            printf("%04X\t",         FATTR(ff));
            printf("%2d  ",          NUM_HANDLES(ff));
            printf("%04X",           OWNER_PSP(ff));

            /* A new check for orphaned files:  for each SFT entry,
               see if the entry is referenced in the supposed owner's
               JFT. If it isn't, it's a possible orphan. If the
               reference count (NUM_HANDLES(ff)) is 1, then it's a
               definite orphan? */
            orph = 0;
            if ((_osmajor >= 3) && (NUM_HANDLES(ff) == 1) && (! do_fcbs))
            {
                WORD psp = OWNER_PSP(ff);
                if (*((WORD far *) MK_FP(psp, 0)) == 0x20CD) // real PSP
                {
                    WORD jft_size = *((WORD far *) MK_FP(psp, 0x32));
```

```
                    BYTE far *jft = *((BYTE far * far *) MK_FP(psp, 0x34));
                    int i, ok;
                    for (i=0, ok=0; i<jft_size; i++)
                        if (jft[i] == num)  // found SFT entry in PSP's JFT
                            { ok++; break; }
                    if (! ok) orph++;
                }
            }
            printf( orph? " OR " : "     ");

            if (DISK_FILE(ff))
            {
                printf("%c: ",     'A' + DRIVE(ff));
                printf("%5u  ",    START_CLUSTER(ff));
                printf("DPB %Fp",  DPB(ff));
            }
            else
                printf("DEV %Fp",   DEV_DRIVER(ff));
            printf("  %d\n", VM_ID(ff)); // Windows VM # (see 2F/1683)
        }

        /* FOLLOW LINKED LIST... */
        next = sys_filetab->next;        // get next...
        FREE_MAP(sys_filetab);           // then free old
        if (next && (FP_OFF(next) != 0xFFFF))
            sys_filetab = (SYS_FTAB far *) MAP(next, 0xFFFF);
        else
            break;
    } while (FP_SEG(sys_filetab) &&
             (FP_OFF(sys_filetab) != 0xFFFF)); /* ...UNTIL END */

#ifdef WINDOWS
    if ((mapped = get_mapped()) != 0)
        printf("ERROR!  %u mapped selectors remaining!\n", mapped);
#endif
    return 0;
}
```

FILES.C would be a much shorter program if there were only one SFT entry structure. Most of the complexity in the program comes from the differences between SFT entries in DOS 2.0, DOS 3.0, DOS 3.1, and higher. Most of these differences are disguised by a set of access macros so that the program can, for example, get the name out of an SFT entry with the simple-looking expression FILENAME(ff), which behind the scenes expands into:

```
(_osmajor == 2) ? ff->f2.filename : (osmajor == 3 && osminor == 0) ?\
   ff->f30.filename : ff->f31.filename
```

FILES.C also uses access macros to make it appear as if the SFT entry has a field containing the drive number for the open file. In fact, the SFT only contains a drive number in DOS 2.x; in DOS 3.0 and higher, the SFT contains a device information word, from which the DRIVE() macro extracts the drive number.

The other reason for FILES.C's length is that you can compile it for protected mode Windows, as well as for real mode DOS. Using PROT.C and PROT.H from Chapter 3 and a library such as Microsoft's QuickWin or Borland's EasyWin, FILES can run as a Windows program in the System VM, as shown in Figure 8-4. In FILES.C, the map_real(), get_real_addr(), and free_mapped_linear() functions from PROT.C have been hidden behind yet another set of macros, MAP(), GET_REAL(), and FREE_MAP(). These macros have no effect when WINDOWS is not defined—that is, when compiling for real mode DOS. This reduces the #ifdef WINDOWS preprocessor statements that would otherwise clutter up FILES.C even worse than it is now.

Figure 8-4: WINPSP and the Windows version of FILES

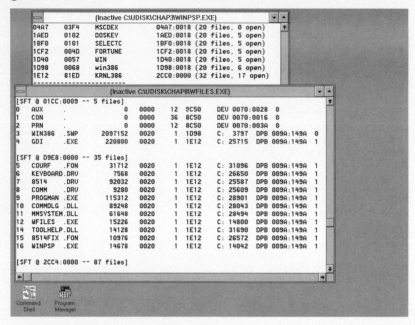

Since the SFT is not instanced, FILES running as a Windows program in the System VM shows essentially the same output as FILES running in a DOS box. The only difference is in the final (usually empty) SFT table, added in a DOS box by PerVMFiles and in the System VM by the GrowSFTToMax() code in KRNL386.

Releasing Orphaned File Handles

One other thing you can do with FILES is use it to locate possible orphaned files. DOS closes all open files that belong to a process that terminates with INT 21h function 4Ch. However, the common practice of redirecting output from a TSR's installation code to the NUL device normally leaves behind one orphaned file in the SFT. FILES attempts to identify these and displays an "OR" (orphan) after the owner:

```
C:\UNDOC2\CHAP8>..\chap9\tsrmem > nul

C:\UNDOC2\CHAP8>files
; ...
0   AUX     .           0   0000      8   9077      DEV 0070:0035
1   CON     .           0   0000     23   9077      DEV 0070:0023
2   PRN     .           0   0000      8   9077      DEV 0070:0047
3   NUL     .           0   0000      1   1289   OR DEV 0116:0048

C:\UNDOC2\CHAP8>udmem | \dos\find "1289"
1288   1289   0094 (  2368)   Env at 1323   C:\COMMAND.COM   [22 23 24 2E ]
1322   1289   0010 (   256)
```

Following the TSR>NUL, there is an SFT entry (#3) for NUL, with one owner, PSP 1289h. FILES has marked this with an OR, indicating a possible orphan. Running UDMEM from Chapter 7 indicates that PSP 1289h is COMMAND.COM. There is nothing intrinsically wrong with this. A command shell can legitimately own open files (a point that was missed in the first edition of *Undocumented DOS*); a good example is 4DOS.COM, which in disk-swapping mode keeps open a swap file.

However, in this case NUL is definitely an orphaned file. COMMAND.COM opened NUL to support the redirection of the TSR's output. Redirected files have two owners (see Chapter 10 for a description of how command shells provide I/O redirection). That NUL here has only one owner, COMMAND.COM, is a sure tip-off that the other party in the redirection hasn't exited. (It's worth noticing here that it is COMMAND.COM, not the TSR, that is the file's single owner, as the first edition of *Undocumented DOS* hopelessly confused this point.)

While the SFT contains an entry for NUL pointing back at PSP 1289h, running the H2NAME program on PSP 1289h shows that this PSP's JFT has no entry pointing to this SFT entry:

```
D:\UNDOC2>h2name 1289
Files for 1289
 0 ==>  1 ==> CON
 1 ==>  1 ==> CON
 2 ==>  1 ==> CON
 3 ==>  0 ==> AUX
 4 ==>  2 ==> PRN
 5 ==> -1
; ...
```

Sure enough, nothing in the presumed owner's JFT points to this SFT. This is how FILES.C attempts to locate orphaned files. As you saw earlier, not every SFT entry has an owner which appears to FILES as a legitimate PSP, but for those that do, FILES.C checks whether the owner's JFT contains an entry pointing back at this SFT entry. If the SFT entry cannot be reached from the presumed owner's JFT, and if the SFT entry's reference count (NUM_HANDLES(ff)) is 1, it indicates that the entry is garbage.

You can collect this garbage by specifying the (hopefully) orphaned SFT entry number on the command line of our next program, SFT_FREE:

```
C:\UNDOC2\CHAP8>files | \dos\find " OR "
3  NUL      .            0  0000    1  1289 OR DEV 0116:0048

C:\UNDOC2\CHAP8>sft_free 3

C:\UNDOC2\CHAP8>files
; ...
0  AUX      .            0  0000    8  9077      DEV 0070:0035
1  CON      .            0  0000   23  9077      DEV 0070:0023
2  PRN      .            0  0000    8  9077      DEV 0070:0047
```

All gone! Use this program with extreme care!

The code for SFT_FREE.C (Listing 8-20) is amazingly simple. Once the program gets a pointer to the SFT entry it wants to free, it simply smacks a 0 into its first WORD. As seen in the structures in FILES.C (Listing 8-19), the first WORD of an SFT entry is num_handles; setting this reference count to 0, even without changing anything else, effectively frees up the entry for reuse by DOS.

Listing 8-20

```c
/*
SFT_FREE.C -- Free SFT entries specified on command line -- DANGER!!
To find SFT numbers, run FILES and look for "OR" after the owner PSP
Andrew Schulman, July 1993
*/

#include <stdlib.h>
#include <stdio.h>
#include <string.h>
#include <dos.h>

typedef unsigned char BYTE;
typedef unsigned short WORD;

typedef struct _sft {
    struct _sft far *next;
```

```
    WORD num;
    WORD file;  // SFT entries start here; num_handles is first entry
    // other stuff not used here
    } SFT;
void fail(const char *s) { puts(s); exit(1); }
main(int argc, char *argv[])
{
    BYTE far *sysvars;
    SFT far *sft;
    int curr_handle, handle_to_free, size, i, files, testing;

    if (argc < 2)
        fail("usage: sft_free [-testing] [list of SFT handles to free!!]");
    _asm mov ah, 52h
    _asm int 21h
    _asm mov word ptr sysvars+2, es
    _asm mov word ptr sysvars, bx
    if (! sysvars)
        fail("can't get SysVars");

    #define DOS(maj) (_osmajor == (maj))
    size = DOS(2) ? 0x28 : DOS(3) ? 0x35 : 0x3B;      // SFT entry size

    sft = *((SFT far * far *) &sysvars[4]);
    if ((! sft) || (sft == (SFT far *) -1L))
        fail("can't get SFT");

    // walk through SFT chain once to find FILES= value
    files = 0;
    while (FP_OFF(sft) != 0xFFFF)
    {
        files += sft->num;
        sft = sft->next;
    }
    if ((! files) || (files > 255))
        fail("Something wrong!");

    testing = 0;
    if (strcmp(strupr(argv[1]), "-TESTING") == 0)
        { testing++; argv++; argc--; }

    for (i=1; i<argc; i++)
    {
        if ((handle_to_free = atoi(argv[i])) > files)
            fail("invalid SFT entry specified!");
        curr_handle = 0;
        sft = *((SFT far * far *) &sysvars[4]);
        while (FP_OFF(sft) != 0xFFFF)
        {
            if (handle_to_free < (curr_handle + sft->num))
            {   // one we want to free is in this SFT
                BYTE far *sft_entry = (BYTE far *) &sft->file;
                WORD far *num_handles;
                sft_entry += ((handle_to_free - curr_handle) * size);
                num_handles = (WORD far *) sft_entry;   // first item
                if (testing)
                {
                    if (*num_handles != 0) fail("already in use!");
                    *num_handles = 1;        // create phony used entry
                    // should create full-blown orphaned entry!
                }
                else
                {
                    if (*num_handles == 0) fail("already free!");
                    *num_handles = 0;            // free it!
```

```
                  // should check owner JFT to make sure really orphan!
            }
            break;
        }
        curr_handle += sft->num;
        sft = sft->next;
    }
}

    return 0;
}
```

SFT_FREE shouldn't be necessary with the TSRs produced using the TSR skeleton in Chapter 9. As noted there, the acid test for correct TSR deinstallation is the freeing up of any otherwise orphaned file handles. The generic TSR in Chapter 9 deinstalls with a normal DOS terminate (INT 21h function 4Ch), thereby eventually closing and freeing any open file handles.

More File Handles

You've seen that the handle-based file I/O routines introduced in DOS 2.0 rely on two data structures, the system-wide linked list of System File Tables and the pre-process Job File Table. In contrast to the older File Control Blocks (FCBs), which applications allocated on an as-needed basis, the SFTs and each JFT are normally allocated by DOS itself and therefore are limited in size. You've seen that the FILES= statement in CONFIG.SYS controls the number of files held in the SFTs. Normally, there are 20 possible open file handles in a process's JFT. This is dictated by the fact that a 20-byte JFT resides directly inside the PSP. This is the downside to the switch from FCBs to handles/SFTs.

DOS 3.3 introduced a function, Set Handle Count (INT 21h AH=67h), which can increase the size of the calling process's JFT, thereby increasing the files and devices that may simultaneously be opened using handle-based file I/O. Sometimes programmers claim the function "doesn't work" merely because they forgot to increase the FILES= setting before attempting to keep 50 files open at once, or because they think that calling this function automatically allows them to open more files with a run-time library function such as fopen() (see "FILE* vs. File Handles," earlier in this chapter). In other words, these supposed bugs are nothing more than cockpit errors.

However, as indicated in the appendix entry for INT 21h AH=67h, there have been bugs in this function that often preclude its use. An old *PC Tech Journal* article (April 1988) noted that the function can incorrectly allocate 64K too much memory because its code uses an ROR instruction instead of the correct RCR.

Fortunately, it is just as easy to perform the same function yourself. Since a JFT is embedded directly at offset 18h in the PSP, it seems like it should be difficult to increase its size. However, since DOS 3.0, the PSP has also contained a far pointer to the JFT and to a word holding its size. The relevant fields in the PSP, which we already used in the orphan-seeking code in FILES.C, are:

```
18h   20 BYTEs   DOS 2+ JFT
32h   WORD       DOS 3+ max open files
34h   WORD       DOS 3+ JFT address
```

You can't do anything to increase the size of the array at offset 18h in the PSP, but you can allocate a new, larger block of memory for the JFT, bump up the count at offset 32h in PSP, copy the old table into the new one, and then set the pointer at offset 34h to the new table. The same type of manipulation is possible with other seemingly static DOS arrays, such as the SFTs and CDS, whose far pointers are located in SysVars.

The program in Listing 8-21, FHANDLE.C, carries out this series of operations. FHANDLE takes a number on its command line and attempts to resize its own JFT:

```
D:\UNDOC2>fhandle 40
Currently 20 max JFT file handles
And SFT FILES=40
Max file handles increased to 40
Opened 34 files
```

To test that more files can be opened, FHANDLE continually opens its own executable file (argv[0]) in a loop until the Microsoft C _dos_open() function fails.

Listing 8-21: FHANDLE.C

```
/*
FHANDLE.C
Alternative to using INT 21h function 67h (added in DOS 3.3)
Andrew Schulman, revised July 1993

bcc fhandle.c
fhandle 40
fhandle 40 -testing
NOTES:
-- Generally need FILES= greater than 20 in CONFIG.SYS to have any
   effect. Actually, this isn't strictly necessary. Certainly you
   could have a larger JFT than your SFT and have multiple JFT
   entries pointing to the same SFT entry. This occurs already,
   where normally file handles 0, 1, and 2 all correspond to
   SFT entry 0 (CON). But this generally isn't why programmers want
   to increase their JFT size! So, if your intended JFT size is
   larger than the current SFT size, you can:
-- Change FILES= in CONFIG.SYS and reboot.
-- Or use Quarterdeck FILES.COM program to increase SFT size.
-- Or see XLASTDRV program in Chapter 2, which expands CDS, and adopt
   it to expand the SFT chain.
-- If you want to open >20 files simultaneously with high-level function
   like fopen(), you probably must increase run-time library tables. For
   example, in Microsoft C the size of table for FILE* is hard-wired
   to 20 in /msc/source/startup/_file.c (#define _NFILE_ 20). So
   increase the size of this table as well (and recompile
   startup code) if you want to use >20 fopen() at once, even after
   using the following code.
*/

#include <stdlib.h>
#include <stdio.h>
#include <string.h>
#include <dos.h>

typedef unsigned char BYTE;
typedef unsigned WORD;
typedef unsigned long DWORD;
typedef BYTE far *FP;

#ifndef MK_FP
#define MK_FP(seg,ofs)  ((FP)(((DWORD)(seg) << 16) | (ofs)))
#endif

extern unsigned files(void);    // in COUNTF.C

void fail(char *s) { puts(s); exit(1);

typedef struct _sft {
    struct _sft far *next;
    WORD num;
    // other stuff not used here
    } SFT;

WORD files(void)
{
    SFT far * far *sysvars; // treat SysVars as array of far ptrs
```

```
    SFT far *sft;
    WORD files = 0;

    _asm mov ah, 52h
    _asm int 21h
    _asm mov word ptr sysvars+2, es
    _asm mov word ptr sysvars, bx

    if (! sysvars) return 0;
    for (sft = sysvars[1]; FP_OFF(sft) != 0xFFFF; sft = sft->next)
        files += sft->num;
    return files;
}
main(int argc, char *argv[])
{
    WORD far *pmax = (WORD far *) MK_FP(_psp, 0x32);
    BYTE far * far *pjft = (BYTE far * far *) MK_FP(_psp, 0x34);
    BYTE *new_jft;
    WORD max = *pmax;
    WORD new_max;
    int f, i;

    if (argc < 2)
        fail("usage: fhandle [-testing] [#handles]");
    new_max = atoi(argv[1]);
    printf("Currently %u max JFT file handles\n", max);
    printf("And SFT FILES=%u\n", files());

    if (new_max <= max)
        fail("nothing to do");
    else if (new_max > files())
        fail("FILES= too low: edit CONFIG.SYS and reboot\n"
             "or run a program like QEMM FILES.COM to grow the SFT");

    if (! (new_jft = (BYTE *) malloc(new_max)))
        fail("insufficient memory");
    _fmemcpy(new_jft, *pjft, max);               // copy over old entries
    _fmemset(new_jft+max, 0xFF, new_max - max); // fill in new entries
    *pmax = new_max;                             // set new max file handles
    *pjft = (BYTE far *) new_jft;                // set new JFT!

    printf("Max file handles increased to %u\n", new_max);

    // now test how many files we can open by opening ourselves (argv[0])
    for (i=0; ; i++)
        if (_dos_open(argv[0], 0, &f) != 0)
            break;
    printf("Opened %d files\n", --i);

    if (argc > 2 && strcmp(strupr(argv[2]), "-TESTING") == 0)
    {
        BYTE cmd[16];
        // printf("Closing %d ==> %d\n", f, new_jft[f]);
        _dos_close(f);  // close last one so we can spawn shell!
        sprintf(cmd, "H2NAME %04X", _psp);
        printf("\n> %s\n", cmd);       // show command line
        system(cmd);                    // run H2NAME on my PSP
        printf("\n> FILES\n");
        system("FILES");                // run FILES
    }

    return 0;
}
```

If FHANDLE is also run with the -TESTING command line option, it runs the previous H2NAME (Listing 8-18) and FILES (Listing 8-19) programs. First it closes the most recently opened file so that there is a free JFT entry from which to spawn the programs! (Even so, FHANDLE still sometimes has problems spawning H2NAME and FILES.) This not only helps verify that you can really open more files, but also helps to show how these three different programs tie together:

```
D:\UNDOC2>fhandle 40 -testing
Currently 20 max JFT file handles
And SFT FILES=40
Max file handles increased to 40
Opened 34 files

> H2NAME 6C7B
Files for 6C7B
 0 ==>  1 ==> CON
 1 ==>  1 ==> CON
 2 ==>  1 ==> CON
 3 ==>  0 ==> AUX
 4 ==>  2 ==> PRN
 5 ==>  3 ==> FHANDLE EXE
 6 ==>  4 ==> FHANDLE EXE
; ... etc. ...
37 ==> 35 ==> FHANDLE EXE
38 ==> 36 ==> FHANDLE EXE
39 ==> -1

> FILES
#   Filename           Size    Attr    cRef   Owner    Cluster, DD, DPB
-   --------           ----    ----    ----   -----    -----------------
[SFT @ 0116:00CC -- 5 files]
0   AUX     .             0    0000      10   9077     DEV 0070:0035
1   CON     .             0    0000      29   9077     DEV 0070:0023
2   PRN     .             0    0000      10   9077     DEV 0070:0047
3   FHANDLE .EXE       9126    0020       1   6C7B     D: 30714   DPB OFF1:0000
4   FHANDLE .EXE       9126    0020       1   6C7B     D: 30714   DPB OFF1:0000
[SFT @ 1014:0000 -- 35 files]
5   FHANDLE .EXE       9126    0020       1   6C7B     D: 30714   DPB OFF1:0000
6   FHANDLE .EXE       9126    0020       1   6C7B     D: 30714   DPB OFF1:0000
; ... etc. ...
36  FHANDLE .EXE       9126    0020       1   6C7B     D: 30714   DPB OFF1:0000
```

You might wonder why there are all these SFT entries for the same file. From the FILES output, they all look identical. However, one of the fields in the SFT not shown by FILES is the current file position. This cannot be shared among multiple opens of the same file, since the following code (for example) is valid:

```
int f1 = open("foo.bar", O_RDONLY);
int f2 = open("foo.bar", O_RDONLY);
lseek(f1, 10, SEEK_CUR);
lseek(f2, 20, SEEK_CUR);
```

The f1 and f2 handles must lead to separate SFT entries. Even loading SHARE can't change this, assuming the second open() is allowed is succeed.

Once again, increasing the DOS file handles does not automatically allow you to open more files with the fopen() function in C. If you need to increase the number of fopen-able files, consult your compiler's startup code. For example, in Microsoft C, you can increase the FILE* maximum by changing the value of _NFILE in the startup code (see STARTUP\CRT0DAT.ASM).

Note that an enlarged JFT is not inheritable, so FHANDLE can't pass its increased wealth along to any children it might have. For an in-depth look at this topic, see the article, "DOS File Handle Limits" by David Burki (*TECH Specialist*, February 1993; this magazine is now the *Windows/DOS Developer's Journal*).

System FCBs

And now for a trip down memory lane.

So far we have seen how handle-based DOS file operations manipulate SFTs. But remember DOS File Control Blocks, inherited from CP/M when it was the standard of the 8-bit microcomputer world? How does DOS handle (as it were) FCBs? Recall (keeping some nausea medicine nearby) how FCBs work. Instead of getting back a handle when it calls the operating system to open a file, an application creates an FCB *in its own data area* and tells the operating system where this FCB is. DOS fills in the FCB in the application's data area.

Thus, the application allocates FCBs on behalf of the operating system, rather than the other way around. Sick! The problems with keeping crucial operating system data in the application's data area should be rather obvious. For example, whereas today's DOS can close any open files when an application exits, in the days of FCBs the operation system couldn't do anything about programs that left behind open files when exiting.

Furthermore, putting the FCB under the application's control meant that every application using FCBs was dependent on its precise structure. Contrast the way that, for example, the vast majority of DOS applications are not dependent on the structure of an SFT. The dependence of applications on the FCB structure has obviously made it impossible to change this structure, even when necessary, for instance, to support media larger than 32 megabytes. FCBs in fact are a perfect example of why it is bad to expose operating system internals to applications!

What is less obvious is that there was one benefit to FCBs over the new, improved handle-based file functions. Since the application allocates FCBs, there are practically unlimited open files. An FCB system doesn't need a FILES= setting in CONFIG.SYS. When the application needs to open a file, it creates another FCB.

SFTs and file handles were introduced in DOS 2.0, and with them the need for a FILES= setting so that users could exercise some control over the trade-off between having lots of potential open files on the one hand and taking too much precious memory on the other.

However, Microsoft couldn't get rid of FCBs entirely. While over time Microsoft has reduced its support for FCBs (for example, in the Windows DOS extenders), the MS-DOS programmer's reference continues to document the FCB calls, while classifying them as superseded. According to Microsoft, programmers "should not use a superseded function except to maintain compatibility with versions of MS-DOS earlier than version 2.0."

Naturally, Microsoft itself continues to use FCBs, even in parts of DOS 5.0 and 6.0 that, presumably, do not require compatibility with DOS 1.0. Microsoft seldom follows its own advice; this advice is intended, apparently, for everyone else. For example, a simple INTRSPY script reveals that COMMAND.COM extensively uses FCB functions. It uses function 29h (FCB Parse Filename) as part of its normal operation, functions 11h (FCB Find First) and 12h (FCB File Next) for the DIR command (perhaps as a cheap way to get starting cluster values?), function 13h (FCB Delete) for DEL, and function 17h (FCB Rename) for REN with wildcards. In addition, extended FCBs are necessary to change volume labels on pre-DOS 4.0 disks (disks formatted under DOS 4.0 or higher can have their volume labels changed or queried with the Media ID generic IOCTL calls mentioned earlier).

So how does DOS continue to support FCBs without totally compromising the system? By providing so-called System FCBs. When a program uses FCBs, DOS copies all pertinent information from the program's own FCB into an available System FCB, does the actual work using the System FCB, and finally copies the information back into the user's original FCB before returning control. Programs using FCBs thus have no knowledge of System FCBs.

Since FCBs belong to the application, System FCB sounds like an oxymoron. However, System FCBs are just SFT entries in disguise. The layout for System FCBs and SFTs is identical. Thus, all the internal DOS routines that work with SFT entries work exactly the same way with System FCBs. The only differences are that System FCBs are kept on a separate list from the SFTs, that the far pointer to the System FCB chain is at a different location in SysVars from the SFT pointer, and that DOS must keep a System FCB synchronized with the old FCB that its owner believes is controlling file I/O. Just as FILES= determines the number of SFT entries, so FCBS= determines the number of System FCBs.

That System FCBs are SFTs in disguise makes it easy to use our SFT walking programs to view System FCBs. If the symbol DO_FCBS is enabled, SFTWALK (Listing 8-17) can determine the value of FCBS= by walking the chain of System FCBs, just as it determines the value of FILES= by walking the SFT chain:

```
D:\UNDOC2>sftwalk
SFT @ 0116:00CC -- 5 files
SFT @ 1014:0000 -- 35 files
FILES=40
System FCB table @ 1979:0000 -- 8 files
FCBS=8
```

The only difference from the SFT walking code is that SysVars[1Ah] rather than SysVars[4] is consulted:

```
printf("FILES=%d\n", sftwalk(4,    "SFT"));
printf("FCBS=%d\n",  sftwalk(0x1A, "System-FCB table"));
```

Similarly, FILES.C (Listing 8-19) takes an optional -FCB switch on its command line.

The problem with System FCBs, however, is that because the FCBS= statement in CONFIG.SYS fixes the number of System FCBs, programs can no longer open unlimited FCBs. Once the System FCBs are used up, DOS has to *recycle* least-recently-used System FCBs. There was a complicated mechanism for this in IBM's DOS 4.0 that involved protected FCBs (the y in a FCBS=x,y statement) that was dropped in DOS 5.0.

While this may sound like a lot of extra work just to support an archaic manner of opening files, it does permit programs that use the older calls to coexist with the newer techniques. Hard to believe though it may be, many programs still use FCBs for one reason or another. System FCBs give DOS the control to deal with file sharing, networking, and multiple users, while still allowing ancient programs to run without change.

One final reason to care about System FCBs is that a heavily encrypted piece of code in Windows 3.1 (known as the AARD code) uses the offset of the first System-FCB header as part of its test for genuine MS-DOS. Any version of DOS in which this offset is non-zero (that is, FP_OFF(Sys-Vars[0x1A]) != 0) Microsoft considered a competitor's DOS, and certain versions of Windows issue a non-fatal error message. Chapter 1 discusses this in great detail (see MSDETECT.C in Chapter 1).

The SHARE Hooks

In our lengthy discussion of the DOS file system, you may have been wondering where SHARE fits in. How does the SHARE.EXE TSR insinuate itself into the DOS file system?

It's pretty messy. If you glance through the appendix to this book, you will see many, many references to SHARE—far more than you would expect from what seems like a fairly simple file-sharing and record-locking subsystem. While the network redirector interface that we describe next is no model of software engineering, compared to SHARE it seems downright elegant.

While SHARE provides a small set of API functions (some documented) using INT 21h AH=5Dh and INT 2Fh AH=10h, this is not its primary mode of operation. Instead, SHARE patches itself into the DOS kernel.

The DOS kernel makes calls using far pointers at various significant times during execution. These pointers, known as the SHARE hooks, are located at negative offsets from the first SFT. By default, the SHARE hooks point at one of two dummy routines, which merely set or clear the carry flag, depending on whether the routine should succeed or fail when SHARE is not loaded. SHARE changes these pointers to transfer control to its own routines. As a result of SHARE's modifications to the DOS kernel, most TSR removal programs can't remove SHARE: DOS will hang the next time it tries to call one of the SHARE functions through the no-longer-valid pointers.

   SHARHOOK.C (Listing 9-22) is a simple program to dump out the SHARE hooks. Usually mere inspection of the SHARHOOK output tells you whether SHARE is installed because prior to loading SHARE all the hooks point to the same two routines; after loading SHARE each hook points to a unique location, which can of course be disassembled:

```
C:\UNDOC2\CHAP8>sharhook
-3c      0116:0090    FDC8:44AA     unknown
-38      0116:0094    FDC8:44AE     OpenFile
-34      0116:0098    FDC8:44AE     CloseFile
; ...
-c       0116:00C0    FDC8:44AE     CloseFileIfDup
-8       0116:00C4    FDC8:44AA     Close?
-4       0116:00C8    FDC8:44AA     UpdateDirInSFT
C:\UNDOC2\CHAP8>share
SHARE installed
C:\UNDOC2\CHAP8>sharhook
-3c      0116:0090    0000:0000     unknown
-38      0116:0094    1842:0954     OpenFile
-34      0116:0098    1842:0958     CloseFile
; ...
-c       0116:00C0    1842:0980     CloseFileIfDup
-8       0116:00C4    1842:0984     Close?
-4       0116:00C8    1842:0988     UpdateDirInSFT
```

Listing 8-22: SHARHOOK.C

```c
/*
SHARHOOK.C -- Dump DOS SHARE hooks
Andrew Schulman, June 1993
*/

#include <stdlib.h>
#include <stdio.h>
#include <dos.h>

typedef void (far *FUNCPTR)(void);

char *share_func_name[] = { "unknown", "OpenFile", "CloseFile",
    "CloseAllMachine", "CloseAllProcess", "CloseByName", "LockRegion",
    "UnlockRegion", "CheckRgnLocked", "GetOpenFileListEntry",
    "update FCB from SFT?", "get first cluster of FCB?", "CloseFileIfDup",
    "Close?", "UpdateDirInSFT" } ;

main()
{
    unsigned char far *sftptr;
    FUNCPTR far *sharehooks, far *hook;
    int ofs, i;

    _asm mov ah, 52h
    _asm int 21h
    _asm les bx, dword ptr es:[bx+4]
    _asm mov word ptr sftptr+2, es
    _asm mov word ptr sftptr, bx

    sharehooks = (FUNCPTR far *) (sftptr - 0x3c);
    for (i=0, hook=sharehooks, ofs=0x3c; i<15; i++, hook++, ofs-=4)
        printf("-%-4x    %Fp    %Fp    %s\n",
            ofs, hook, *hook, share_func_name[i]);
    return 0;
}
```

The three most important SHARE hooks are those called when a file is opened, closed, and modified. Additional hooks are used to pass through several undocumented DOS calls for closing files by process number or by name, lock and unlock regions of a file for checking whether a region is locked, as well as a few hooks whose use is not entirely known. All of the SHARE hooks are listed in the appendix under INT 21h function 52h.

As noted earlier, to open a file, DOS first canonicalizes the filename. After determining that there are file handles available in the caller's JFT and allocating an SFT entry, DOS then calls the SHARE file-open hook. That is, DOS calls through whatever function pointer is plugged in at offset -38h from the start of the first SFT. If this function returns with carry set, the file is not available due to sharing restrictions, so DOS delays and tries calling the hook until the sharing retry count is exhausted or the file becomes available. SHARE proceeds by beginning a DOS critical section, checking whether the file may be opened, filling in the SHARE fields of the SFT entry if so, and finally ending the critical section. To determine whether the file may be opened, SHARE searches its list of open files for a match with the name of the file. If a match is found, the file open modes of the initial open of the file and the current attempted open are compared according to the standard SHARE rules (for example, an open Deny Write beats a subsequent open Read/Write). If no match is found, a new sharing record is created for the new file and the open is always allowed to succeed. When filling in its SFT fields, SHARE stores, among other things, the file's owner and links the SFT to any SFTs already referencing the same file.

When a file is closed, DOS again calls on SHARE. After beginning a DOS critical section, SHARE removes any locks placed on the file by the calling process and unlinks the SFT entry from the chain of SFT entries for the file, if the close removes the final reference to the SFT entry. Finally, SHARE ends the DOS critical section. If the SFT removal destroys the last reference to the file, SHARE also erases the sharing record for that file.

DOS calls the final of the three most important SHARE hooks whenever the file size or time-stamp changes. DOS calls on SHARE to propagate these changes, as well as any change in the starting cluster number, to all of the other SFTs referencing the same file. This ensures that all processes have a consistent view of the file, especially the starting cluster and file size. You can see an interesting result of this updating when downloading a file under a multitasker. From another windows of the multitasker, you can access the portion of the file already downloaded, even though its directory entry still shows a zero length, provided that the second program reads until DOS returns an end-of-file indication or seeks to the end of the file, rather than using the size in the directory entry.

It is important to use SHARE when running a preemptive multitasking system such as Windows Enhanced mode. For SHARE to arbitrate file requests from multiple Windows VMs, you must run it *before* Windows. Running SHARE from within a Windows DOS box is a bad idea, so Microsoft prevents you from doing this.

Unfortunately, Microsoft prevents users from running SHARE in a Windows DOS box by *pretending* that SHARE is already installed! Whether or not SHARE is loaded before Windows, the SHARE detect call (INT 2Fh AX=1000h) always succeeds under Windows. This unfortunately has led to the widespread belief that Windows automatically loads SHARE or that Windows contains built-in emulation for SHARE. (Actually, in Windows for Workgroups 3.11 and in Chicago, Windows *does* contain built-in emulation for SHARE, in form of the VSHARE.386 VxD.) In fact, Windows just wants to prevent you from running SHARE in a DOS box. By hooking the INT 2Fh SHARE detection call, Windows (more precisely, the DOSMGR VxD built into WIN386.EXE) fakes SHARE.EXE into not installing. SHARE.EXE makes this INT 2Fh call, sees that SHARE is supposedly already installed, and exits. DOSMGR uses the same INT 2Fh code (installed with the VMM function Hook_V86_Int_Chain) to similarly fake out FASTOPEN and NLSFUNC.

You can run SHARHOOK run under Windows to confirm whether SHARE is really installed or not:

```
C:\UNDOC2\CHAP8>share
SHARE already installed
C:\UNDOC2\CHAP8>sharhook
-3c      0116:0090    FDC8:44AA    unknown
-38      0116:0094    FDC8:44AE    OpenFile
-34      0116:0098    FDC8:44AE    CloseFile
-30      0116:009C    FDC8:44AA    CloseAllMachine
-2c      0116:00A0    FDC8:44AA    CloseAllProcess
-28      0116:00A4    FDC8:44AA    CloseByName
; ...
```

That only two different hook functions are installed is a sure tip-off that SHARE is *not* already installed. (Again, none of this applies under VSHARE.386.)

Microsoft's DOS programmer's reference explicitly mentions the fake SHARE problem. "Some operating environments, such as Windows, intercept this multiplex interrupt and always return a nonzero value whether the Share program is loaded or not." It is sick when, due to the manufacturer's own actions, you can't use a function labeled Get SHARE.EXE Installed State to get the SHARE installed state.

However, Microsoft does recommend a true SHARE detection method. "To determine whether file sharing is available, a program should check for error values upon returning from carrying out a file-sharing function, such as Lock/Unlock File (Interrupt 21h Function 5Ch)." It would be nice if PC diagnostic programs would heed this advice, rather than blindly reporting "SHARE installed" under Windows. The code in Listing 8-23 (IS_SHARE.C) presents both the now-bogus SHARE detection call and one that actually works, based on function 5Ch.

Listing 8-23: IS_SHARE.C

```c
/*
IS_SHARE.C -- Determine if SHARE really loaded
Andrew Schulman, April 1993
*/

#include <stdlib.h>
#include <stdio.h>
#include <dos.h>

int bogus_share(void)
{
    unsigned char bogu;
    _asm mov ax, 1000h
    _asm int 2fh
    _asm mov bogu, al
    return (bogu == 0xFF);
}

int is_share(void)
{
    _asm push si
    _asm push di
    _asm xor bx, bx
    _asm mov cx, bx
    _asm mov dx, bx
    _asm mov si, bx
    _asm mov di, bx
    _asm mov ax, 5C00h        /* try to lock */
    _asm int 21h
    _asm jc lock_error
have_share:
    _asm mov ax, 5C01h        /* SHARE there: unlock! */
    _asm int 21h
    _asm pop di
    _asm pop si
    return 1;
```

```
lock_error:
    _asm pop di
    _asm pop si
    _asm cmp ax, 1          /* invalid function: no SHARE */
    _asm jne have_share_2:
no_share:
    return 0;
have_share_2:
    return 1;
}
main(int argc, char *argv[])
{
    int share = is_share();
    if (bogus_share())
        puts( share ? "SHARE loaded" :
            "SHARE supposedly loaded, but it really isn't" );
    else
        puts( share ? "SHARE supposedly not loaded, but Func 5Ch present" :
            "SHARE not loaded" );
    return 0;
}
```

In a Windows DOS box, unless SHARE was run before starting Windows, IS_SHARE displays the message "SHARE supposedly loaded, but it really isn't."

Microsoft's VSHARE.386 makes this problem a thing of the past. As part of its major Chicago project (DOS 7.0 and Windows 4.0), Microsoft is moving many (possibly all?) pieces of MS-DOS, including SHARE, into Windows 386 Enhanced mode virtual device drivers (see Chapters 1 and 3). Microsoft is providing some of these VxDs, including VSHARE.386, as part of Windows for Workgroups 3.11, prior to the release of Chicago. VSHARE.386 provides file sharing and locking, without having to load SHARE before Windows. Because it is a VxD, VSHARE also does not waste conventional memory; VxDs are 32-bit protected mode code allocated out of extended memory. With a DEVICE=VSHARE.386 statement in SYSTEM.INI, when Windows reports that SHARE services are available, they actually will be. What a concept.

The MS-DOS Network Redirector

As we've seen, MS-DOS contains a set of function-pointer hooks that are set by SHARE.EXE and that MS-DOS calls at various points during file I/O. Another set of hooks in MS-DOS is the network redirector interface. Whereas DOS calls SHARE through function pointers with a far CALL, DOS calls network redirectors with INT 2Fh calls. Thus, whereas SHARE requires setting the value of function pointers in the DOS kernel, writing a redirector requires hooking INT 2Fh.

Not to be confused with I/O redirection (see Chapter 10), the MS-DOS network redirector is a mechanism for inserting a monitor into the stream of file system and printer requests so that some requests can be pulled out and serviced in a special way. Generally, a redirector services such requests by turning them into network packets sent to a file server; but there is nothing in the redirector mechanism that restricts it to networking. In this section, we are concerned with the file system, rather than printer, aspects of redirection.

Microsoft has used the redirector interface since DOS 3.1 to allow DOS programs to transparently access alien file systems. That this coincided with the version of DOS to first support networking is no coincidence, since the redirector interface is the vehicle DOS provided for the implementation of network services such as IBM PC LAN.

Microsoft uses the redirector interface to provide CD-ROM access under DOS through the Microsoft CD-ROM Extensions (MSCDEX). Other users of the interface include network operating systems from Banyan and 3Com. Novell's NetWare Lite uses the redirector and, starting with version 4.0, so does Novell NetWare.

It is worth stressing the usefulness and power of the redirector interface. Although arcane, inconsistent, and just plain awkward in places, as you will see, the possibilities for its application are enormous. However, Microsoft has not documented it and will not support it. In response to one customer's request that redirector information be posted on its Online technical support service, Microsoft responded

> The INT 2fh interface to the network is an undocumented interface. Only INT 2fh, function 1100h (get installed state) of the network services is documented.
> Some third parties have reverse engineered and documented the interface (i.e., "Undocumented DOS" by Shulman [sic], Addison-Wesley), but Microsoft provides absolutely no support for programming on that API, and we do not guarantee that the API will exist in future versions of MS-DOS.

The party line thus appears to be, "Here's where you get the info, but you better not use it."

Rumor has it that the redirector is not even documented within Microsoft, except through oral history. On the other hand, Microsoft has made redirector source code and expertise available to selected vendors, thus making the network redirector yet another example of how supposedly undocumented functionality is in reality *selectively* documented functionality. Such discriminatory documentation seems far worse than any outright complete absence of documentation.

Novell's Undocumented Redirector Interfaces

So that we're not dumping unfairly on Microsoft, it's worth pointing out that its major competition, Novell, has its own undocumented redirector interface: two of them in fact. NetWare 3.x and 4.x has an undocumented server interface for Name Spaces (Macintosh, HPFS, etc.). The name spaces are supposed to be dynamically allocated, but Novell hard codes the hook-in slots. Name Space NLMs (NetWare loadable modules, sort of a cross between DLLs and VxDs) then plug in to these pre-allocated slots.

Novell's NLM SDK describes a second redirector-like interface: "A new feature in NetWare v4.0 is the volume switch, which makes it possible for NetWare to access non-NetWare file systems, such as the NFS file system." While Novell mentioned this Volume Switch at one of its "Brainshare" conferences, it declined to release developer's documentation. According to one engineer, "they [Novell] like to handle this kind of thing 'strategically,' which means they bring in the developer who is whining about it and give them documentation under strict NDA."

In any case, the information and techniques presented in this chapter were empirically derived. We have gained considerable experience with the redirector since the first edition of *Undocumented DOS*.

Because of the possibilities for confusion in terminology, we need to define some terms. The term *redirector interface* means the functionality and hooks DOS provides for foreign file systems, and *a redirector* or *the redirector* is any program that uses the interface. More concretely, DOS at certain times calls INT 2Fh function 11h; this is called the redirector interface. Programs can receive these calls from DOS by taking over INT 2Fh function 11h; such programs are called redirectors.

After the following brief words on the subject, we won't use the term Installable File System (IFS) again, to keep the terminology manageable levels. IBM introduced IFS as part of OS/2 1.2. IFS allowed specialized file systems to be developed and to link seamlessly into the operating system. The first file system to use OS/2 IFS was the High Performance File System (HPFS), designed as a replacement for the old FAT file system; another OS/2 IFS user was the Novell NetWare Requestor.

In essence, IFS was to be a legitimized version, under OS/2, of the hidden, undocumented redirector interface under DOS. The fact that the initials IFS appeared frequently in DOS 4.0 documentation indicates that IBM's intention was to provide a stepping stone to help developers migrate toward OS/2 (particularly LAN Manager).

The IFS interface appears to have been implemented under DOS 4.0 using the IFSFUNC program, which loaded itself as a redirector. In other words, IFS was an extra layer on top of the redirector. Some additional subfunctions have appeared under the redirector interface to support what may be enhanced functionality over and above the existing redirector interface.

However, the reality is that IFS in the DOS world received no publicity at all, and DOS 4.0 was retired due to lack of enthusiasm. There is not much benefit to a further discussion of IFSFUNC, REDIRIFS, or any other DOS 4.0-specific spin put on the network redirector. We consider IFS here only in so far as it is still visible and overlaps the redirector interface. In other words, we will refer to subfunctions of Int 2Fh function 11h as redirector interface subfunctions, even if they were first introduced in DOS 4.0 as IFS subfunctions.

In Chicago, Microsoft will introduce an IFS Manager (IFSMGR.386 and IFSHELP.SYS). This, rather than the network redirector, will be the approved way for writing installable file systems. According to Microsoft, the benefits of IFSMGR over the redirector are (1) it will be documented (probably in the Chicago DDK); (2) it cleanly handles the case of multiple redirectors; and (3) its services are genuine (no mucking around with DOS global variables in the SDA and so on).

In the remainder of this chapter, we delve further into what happens inside DOS file I/O calls, using INTRSPY to see the circumstances under which DOS calls a redirector. A detailed specification for the INT 2Fh AH=11h interface is presented, along with an extensive sample program, the Phantom. Readers of the first edition of *Undocumented DOS* should note that the rewritten PHANTOM.C incorporates far more extensive knowledge of the redirector interface than did the original PHANTOM.PAS. PHANTOM.C is too large to reprint here in its entirety, but we present a detailed discussion of how the Phantom handles selected file I/O calls such as Open, Read, Chdir, and Mkdir. Complete source code is presented on the accompanying disk in \UNDOC2\CHAP8\PHANTOM.C.

Several readers of *Undocumented DOS* provided important additional information and clarifications to the redirector interface. Thanks are due to Carsten Bukholdt Andersen, Dave Andrews, Dwayne Bailey, Erick Engelke, Tim Farley, Mike Karas, David Markun, Kirit Patel, Mitchell Schoenbrun, Mike Shiels, and Martin Westermeier.

For an additional perspective on the redirector interface, readers may wish to read the article, "A DOS Redirector for SCSI CD-ROM" by Jim Harper (*Dr. Dobb's Journal*, March 1993). Another interesting source of information is the redirector module from the DOS emulation code (MDOS) in Carnegie-Mellon University's Mach operating system; the relevant file is DOS_FS.C, available by ftp from cs.cmu.edu.

Using the Network Redirector Interface

In essence, we want to use the redirector interface to manufacture DOS drives. A DOS drive is any entity that has a drive letter and a CDS entry and that behaves like a hard drive or floppy, in that you can access it with normal DOS disk, directory, and file commands and INT 21h function calls. Whether there is magnetic media at the other end is irrelevant, since a file system is a purely logical construct.

One can view almost any area in computing as a set of file operations. To take one example, say that every evening you log onto an information service, such as CompuServe, with a hierarchical structure of forums, message and library areas within forums, topics within message areas, and so on. Normally to access such services, you would dial up through the modem and send the service various command strings or menu selections. However, it might be more convenient to pretend that the information service is just another drive on your machine. Changing to drive I: and typing CD

\IBM.DOS\SECRETS, for example, might be equivalent to joining the ibm.dos/secrets conference on BIX. Conceptually, this is quite simple. All you need is to designate a drive letter for the information service, install a piece of software that catches all disk, directory, and file requests sent to that drive, and have the software service these requests by issuing the proper CompuServe or BIX incantations. With a sufficiently fast modem, this would feel just like using a disk.

Front-End Hooks and Device Drivers vs. Back-End Redirectors

There are several ways to catch INT 21h file I/O requests. One method does quite literally "catch" disk, directory, and file requests by hooking INT 21h and watching every function call that comes in. Novell NetWare earlier than 4.0 works this way (see NETX in Chapter 4). Because this method sees INT 21h calls before DOS itself (in fact DOS may not see some of them at all), it is sometimes called a *front-end hook*. Novell uses the term *shell*, because NETX puts a shell around the DOS APIs.

A front-end hook is conceptually simple (see FUNC0E32.C and DOSVER.C in Chapter 2), but there are problems with hooking INT 21h and looking for all file- and directory-related calls for your special drive. For one thing, you must deal separately with FCB- and handle-based calls. DOS file functions available to applications provide two very different interfaces. As you saw earlier in this chapter, the older FCB calls have the following implications:

- (practically) limitless concurrent open files because the state for the open file is kept in a user-supplied structure
- wildcard filename specification in Delete and Rename
- FCB functions cannot use pathnames

The file handle calls imply that

- the concurrent open file count is limited to the FILES= line in CONFIG.SYS (that is, to the size of the SFT), and, for any given application, to the size of its JFT
- filenames can contain pathnames
- simplicity of use ("magic cookie" handles): applications don't have to know the underlying JFT and SFT structure.

The redirector interface unifies the two access methods so that, with one exception discussed later, a redirector need not know by what method a file is being accessed. This shows the interface is functioning at a level *below* INT 21h, that is, as a back-end to DOS. This access method independence is a great labor saver and confirms the desirability of the redirector interface over INT 21h replacement as the means of implementing alternative file systems. Rather than having to duplicate the entire range of function calls in the DOS programmer's interface, including both FCB- and handle-based file access methods, a redirector instead plugs in at a level where much of the higher level administrative functionality has already been accomplished and deals with a homogenized, much narrower interface. For example, all filename strings used to open and otherwise manipulate files arrive at the redirector as fully-qualified paths; the DOS kernel has already done the work of resolving the drive and directory.

One major annoyance with hooking INT 21h is that you must implement your own version of function 4Bh (EXEC). While Microsoft does provide a Set Execution State function (INT 21h AX=4B05h) for those who implement their own EXEC, there is little additional support. Each new version of DOS may require changes to one's EXEC code. In fact, it is reported that one reason for Novell's shift from hooking INT 21h to redirection via INT 2Fh is that the company felt burned by the DOS 5 changes to EXEC.

Another problem is that a front-end hook requires a fairly large amount of state, just to correctly handle complex path names.

Finally, when you use the redirector, support for undocumented calls such as Truename (INT 21h AH=60h) happens automatically. A front-end hook must explicitly code in support for all undocumented calls. With the redirector interface, DOS takes care of cooking all file system requests for you.

On the other hand, the redirector in its entirety is undocumented, so it may not seem to hold any genuine advantage over hooking INT 21h. And of course getting total support for DOS calls, both documented and undocumented, requires implementing the entire redirector interface. For example, support for INT 21h AX=5F02h (Get Assign-List Entry; see NETDRV.C in Listing 8-15) requires that the redirector support INT 2Fh AX=111Eh (Do Redirection). In any case, the point remains that the redirector provides a more homogenized, narrower interface than does implementing an INT 21h front-end hook. We'll look at some problems with the INT 2Fh redirector interface a little later on.

Another way to attach foreign file systems to DOS is of course to use an installable block device driver. But the device driver interface imposes certain restrictions on the file system. It must have a BPB, DPB, and FAT, which are not appropriate to all file systems. There is the added fact that device drivers are just plain inconvenient (though DEVLOD from Chapter 7 helps a lot!).

The alternative to hooking INT 21h or writing a block device driver is to use the INT 2Fh function 11h redirector interface. It is often stated that "the network redirector grabs file system calls for the remote drive before INT 21h sees them," or words to that effect. While that is a good description of how the workstation shell (NETX) works in NetWare 2 and 3, it is not a good description of the redirector, which operates at a level *below* or inside INT 21h. As we'll see, MS-DOS's code for INT 21h takes care of calling INT 2Fh Function 11h when appropriate.

What DOS Provides   On one side of the redirector interface are the redirector services. These consist of DOS data structures and a set of INT 2Fh calls issued at strategic times by the DOS kernel. While the usual model of an operating system is that of a lower-level program that responds to requests for services initiated by an application, the redirector interface specifies function calls that the operating system generates and that a redirector may intercept and service. In normal DOS programming, you call INT 21h, and DOS (or whichever program has hooked INT 21h) services the call. In the redirector interface, DOS calls INT 2Fh AH=11h and *you* (the redirector) service the call. Function 11h of the multiplex interrupt is set aside for redirector services, and each redirector function call is a subfunction of function 11h. Because DOS calls you essentially from inside INT 21h, such a program is called a "back-end redirector," in contrast to the NETX-style front-end hook.

The data structures involved in the redirector interface include SysVars, the Current Directory Structure (CDS), the System File Table (SFT), and the Swappable Data Area (SDA).

The SysVars structure, obtained through undocumented INT 21h function 52h, provides the address of the CDS table and the LASTDRIVE value. A redirector is responsible for initializing, maintaining, and, if it is deinstallable, restoring the CDS for its chosen drive letter(s). For the most part, only a drive with an entry in the CDS can be redirected with INT 2Fh AH=11h. (In contrast, front-end hooks can grab requests before they reach the CDS, so that Novell NetWare 2 and 3, for example, can have drive letters start *after* LASTDRIVE.) DOS primarily cares about three fields in the CDS: the current directory string, the offset of the root directory in that string, and the flags word.

As you saw much earlier in this chapter, an SFT entry holds the state that DOS maintains for each open file in the system. DOS appears to be interested only in a subset of the SFT: the open-mode flags (which describe the access level to, and shareability of, the file), the device information flags word (which indicates whether the device is a block or character level device, whether it has been written to, and so forth), the date, time, and file size, and the current position fields. While the SFT is a DOS structure, it contains fields that are wholly for the use by the drive's owner. And while the SFT was designed for DOS to manage files in its FAT-based file system, and so contains fields that deal with units of sector and cluster, a redirector based on some other file system may use those fields in whatever way it needs.

The most important structure for the redirector interface is the Swappable Data Area. DOS is usually non-reentrant, but it can be re-entered using the SDA. This is explained in more detail in Chapter 9, which includes a section on building TSRs with the SDA. The SDA is that area of the DOS data segment which must be saved and restored to provide for DOS reentrancy. More than that, however, the SDA is also that part of the DOS data segment that contains the global data required for implementation of a redirector. This data includes key DOS variables such as the current critical error state, a pointer to the current Disk Transfer Area, the current open mode for a file, search attributes for Find First/Find Next, and so on.

Origins of the SDA

Tim Farley

[Some programmers wonder why a single-tasking operating system like MS-DOS has a Swappable Data Area in the first place. The following brief historical note was written by Tim Farley, author of the forthcoming book *Undocumented NetWare*, to be published by Addison-Wesley in early 1994.]

I always find it helpful to understand the historical background behind APIs. The fact that the "server" portion of NetWare Lite uses the DOS SDA got me to thinking about why DOS includes an SDA in the first place.

That NetWare Lite is a redirector provides a clue: Perhaps the SDA was part of the other Microsoft Networks code introduced with DOS 3, and was originally designed to allow the implementation of a background network server program, which would obviously get into some situations where it would need to re-enter DOS to serve multiple tasks. MS-NET, and its derivatives like the IBM PC LAN Program were peer-to-peer networks very similar in concept to NetWare Lite.

To test this theory—that Microsoft introduced the SDA into DOS to support redirectors, and especially peer-to-peer "servers"—I went to Atlanta's Computer remnants and job-lot outlet (a place called, oddly enough, "Quality Computer Components") and, lo and behold, there was a copy of the IBM PC LAN Program 1.00, which I promptly bought for a grand total of $2.50. I believe this was one of the first, if not the first, implementation of Microsoft Networks (MS-NET) and therefore might even be the first redirector.

I couldn't get the product (dated March 1985) to run on my hardware, but I was able to shoot it through the Sourcer disassembler from V Communications, and, sure enough, the server portion of IBM PC LAN 1.00 uses the DOS SDA function call (INT 21h AX=5D06h). This is RECEIVER.COM, similar to SERVER.EXE in NetWare Lite. After calling INT 21h AH=5D06h to get a pointer to the SDA, the code does a REP MOVSB, so you can see why the function uses the CX register to return the size of the swap-InDOS area.

As one would expect, the client portion (REDIR.EXE, the equivalent of CLIENT.EXE in NetWare Lite) implements a redirector, and makes very extensive calls to twenty-seven different DOS internal (INT 2Fh AH=12h) functions. Clearly, the INT 2Fh AH=12h calls, like the SDA, were intended for redirectors.

REDIR.EXE, RECEIVER.COM, and NET.COM also all extensively use INT 2Ah, including critical sections 5 and 0Fh.

IBM PC LAN Program 1.00 dates from March 1985, so that's the "date to beat" to find an earlier user of the DOS SDA.

Whereas multitaskers generally just copy entire blocks of the SDA without caring as to their contents (see Chapter 9), network redirectors must use specific fields in the SDA. Unfortunately, the SDA structure changed from DOS 3.0 to DOS 4.0, so programs that want to work in DOS 3.0 as well as in DOS 4.0, 5.0, and 6.0 must cope with two different SDA structures. The Appendix shows the DOS 3.0 style SDA under INT 21h AX=5D06h and the DOS 4.0 style SDA (which also applies to DOS 5.0 and 6.0) under INT 21h AX=5D0Bh. Note, however, that the AX=5D0Bh call is for DOS 4.0 *only*. Thus, in DOS 5.0 and 6.0 you use the same INT 21h AX=5D06h call as in DOS 3.0, but the SDA has the same format as in DOS 4.0. Totally confused yet? Fortunately, in DOS 4.0, you can also use INT 21h AX=5D06h, so it is best for those writing redirectors to just forget about the AX=5D0Bh call. Besides checking the DOS version to determine whether a DOS 3.0 or a DOS 4.0 style SDA is in use, a program can also consult a WORD flag that DOS keeps at offset 4 in its data segment. For example, this is how MSCDEX determines which style DOS segment is in use:

```
CURR_DTA_PTR    dw  2DAh        ; offset in DOS 3 DS of CURR_DTA
CURR_DRV_PTR    dw  2E4h        ; offset in DOS 3 DS of CURR_DRV
; ... etc.: other DOS variables
mov ah, 52h
int 21h
mov word ptr DOS_DS, es         ; get SysVars ptr, ignore BX; ES = DOS DS
mov ax, word ptr es:[4]         ; DOS_DS[4] = style; 0 = DOS 3.0; 1 = DOS 4+
mov DOS_DS_VERS, ax
; ...
cmp DOS_DS_VERS, 1              ; is this DOS 4+ style DOS DS?
jz DOS_4_DS
jmp short done                  ; What about values other than 0 or 1?
; ...
DOS_4_DS:
mov CURR_DTA_PTR, 32Ch          ; offset in DOS 4+ DS of CURR_DTA
mov CURR_DRV_PTR, 336h          ; offset in DOS 4+ DS of CURR_DRV
done:
```

Observe that MSCDEX is *not* using the SDA, but instead contains two sets of offsets into the DOS data segment. MSCDEX uses DOS_DS[4] to determine which set of offsets to use. Probably only Microsoft can afford for its redirectors to use hard-wired offsets into the DOS data segment. In general, third-party redirectors should use offsets from the start of the SDA address that INT 21h AH=5D06h returns.

Of the many fields in the SDA, a redirector needs access to only a (large) handful:

ERR_LOCUS, ERR_CODE	Locus and extended error code of last error
ERR_ACTION, ERR_CLASS	Suggested action and class of last error
CURR_DTA	Current Disk Transfer Area (DTA)
FN1, FN2	Filename work areas
SRCH_BLK	Find First/Find Next search data block (SDB)
FOUND_FILE	Directory entry for found file
FN1_11CHAR	FCB-style filename for device-name comparison
FN2_11CHAR	FCB-style filename for Rename wildcard destination
SRCH_ATTR	Directory search attributes
OPEN_ATTR	File open mode
DRIVE_CDSPTR	Pointer to CDS for drive accessed
SPOP_ACT	Extended open (21/6C) action code
SPOP_ATTR	Extended open attributes
SPOP_MODE	Extended open mode
REN_SRCFILE	Rename source search data block (SDB)
REN_FILE	Rename source directory entry

The DOS kernel fills in many of these fields as it services INT 21h calls. In fact, these are not fields in a genuine structure, but variables in DOS's own data segment, to which redirectors are given (or at least take) privileged access via the SDA.

Listing 8-24 (DOSSTRUC.SCR) is an INTRSPY script that describes only the fields in the DOS structures that are important to a redirector. Other script files used to investigate the interface will include this script. The script uses a feature of INTRSPY that we failed to mention in Chapter 5 (Undocumented INTRSPY?): The ability to specify fields in a structure that INTRSPY skips over when asked to dump the entire structure.

Listing 8-24: DOSSTRUC.SCR

```
; DOSSTRUC.SCR
; Undocumented DOS structures relevant to the redirector interface
; This uses the undocumented INTRSPY "skip" feature.

;; Current Directory Structure entry - All DOS versions
structure CDS fields
    CURR_PATH (byte,asciiz,67)
    CDS_FLAGS (word,hex)
    f1 (byte,skip,10)
    ROOT_OFS (word,dec)
    ; In DOS 4.0 and above there are a further 7 bytes of IFS/SHARE fields

;; Directory entry for 'found' file - All DOS versions
structure DIRENTRY fields
    FNAME_11CHAR (byte,char,11)
    ATTR_BYTE (byte,hex)
    f0 (byte,skip,10)
    F_TIME (word,hex)
    F_DATE (word,hex)
    START_CLSTR (word,hex) ; A redirector can reuse this field
    F_SIZE (dword,dec)

;; Search Data Block - All DOS versions
structure SDB fields
    DRIVE_NUM (byte,dec)
    SRCH_MASK (byte,char,11)
    DIR_ENTRY (word,dec) ; A redirector can reuse this field
    DIR_SECTOR (word,dec) ; A redirector can reuse this field
    f0 (byte,skip,4)

;; Lock/Unlock region of file structure
structure LOCKREC fields
    REGION_START (dword,dec)
    REGION_LEN (dword,dec)
    f0 (byte,skip,13)
    FILENAME (byte,asciiz,80)

;; Swappable DOS Area - DOS 3.1 to 3.3
;; Used in the form SDA_SEG:SDA_OFS->SDA3
structure SDA3 fields
    f0 (byte,skip,3)
    ERR_LOCUS (byte,hex)
    ERR_CODE (word,hex)
    ERR_ACTION (byte,hex)
    ERR_CLASS (byte,hex)
    DEVDRVR_PTR (dword,ptr)
    CURR_DTA (dword,ptr)
    f1 (byte,skip,30)
    DD (byte,dec)
    MM (byte,dec)
    YY_1980 (word,dec)
    f2 (byte,skip,96)
    FN1 (byte,asciiz,128)
    FN2 (byte,asciiz,128)
```

```
    SRCH_BLK (SDB)
    FOUND_FILE (DIRENTRY)
    f3 (byte,skip,81)
    FN1_11CHAR (byte,char,11)
    f4 (byte,skip)
    FN2_11CHAR (byte,char,11)
    f5 (byte,skip,11)
    SRCH_ATTR (byte,hex)
    OPEN_MODE (byte,hex)
    f6 (byte,skip,48)
    DRIVE_CDSPTR (dword,ptr)
    f7 (byte,skip,72)
    REN_SRCFILE (SDB)
    REN_FILE (DIRENTRY)

;; Swappable DOS Area - DOS 4.0, 5.0, 6.0
;; Used in the form SDA_SEG:SDA_OFS->SDA4
structure SDA4 fields
    f0 (byte,skip,3)
    ERR_LOCUS (byte,hex)
    ERR_CODE (word,hex)
    ERR_ACTION (byte,hex)
    ERR_CLASS (byte,hex)
    DEVDRVR_PTR (dword,ptr)
    CURR_DTA (dword,ptr)
    f1 (byte,skip,32)
    DD (byte,dec)
    MM (byte,dec)
    YY_1980 (word,dec)
    f2 (byte,skip,106)
    FN1 (byte,asciiz,128)
    FN2 (byte,asciiz,128)
    SRCH_BLK (SDB)
    FOUND_FILE (DIRENTRY)
    f3 (byte,skip,88)
    FN1_11CHAR (byte,char,11)
    f4 (byte,skip)
    FN2_11CHAR (byte,char,11)
    f5 (byte,skip,11)
    SRCH_ATTR (byte,hex)
    OPEN_ATTR (byte,hex)
    f6 (byte,skip,51)
    DRIVE_CDSPTR (dword,ptr)
    f7 (byte,skip,87)
    SPOP_ACT (word,hex)
    SPOP_ATTR (word,hex)
    SPOP_MODE (word,hex)
    f8 (byte,skip,29)
    REN_SRCFILE (SDB)
    REN_FILE (DIRENTRY)

;; System File Table entry - All DOS versions
structure SFT fields
    C_HANDLES (word,dec)
    OPEN_MODE (word,hex)
    ATTR_BYTE (byte,hex)
    DEV_INFO (word,hex)
    DEVDRV_PTR (dword,ptr)
    ST_CLSTR (word,dec) ; A redirector can reuse this field
    F_TIME (word,hex)
    F_DATE (word,hex)
    F_SIZE (dword,dec)
    F_POS (dword,dec)
    LAST_RELCLSTR (word,dec) ; A redirector can reuse this field
    LAST_ABSCLSTR (word,dec) ; A redirector can reuse this field
    DIR_SCTR_NO (word,dec) ; A redirector can reuse this field
```

```
DIR_ENTRY_NO (byte,dec) ; A redirector can reuse this field
FNAME_11CHAR (byte,char,11)
; other fields
```

Note the "A redirector can reuse this field" comment at some places in DOSSTRUC.SCR. When we discuss the Phantom source code, you will see that Phantom uses a slightly different version of the SFT than that shown earlier in this chapter. The meaning of the fields that DOS maintains must, of course, be left unchanged. Similarly, DOS expects that the redirector will fill in certain fields. This expectation is a crucial part of the redirector interface.

What a Redirector Must Supply   On the other side of the interface is the redirector itself, be it MSCDEX, the PC LAN program, the hypothetical CompuServe file system, or this chapter's demonstration redirector, the Phantom. A redirector normally loads itself as a TSR program and, to install into the chain of INT 2Fh handlers, gets the vector to the current INT 2Fh handler, stores it as the next handler in the chain, and then sets the INT 2Fh vector to point to itself. When INT 2Fh is invoked, the redirector's INT 2Fh handler receives control. If the INT 2Fh call is not for the redirector (AH != 11h), it will pass control to the next handler in the chain. In this way, the redirector monitors all INT 2Fh calls and filters out all but redirector interface function calls.

One major problem with this interface is its use of INT 2Fh. As you saw with the INTCHAIN program in Chapter 6, every TSR and its brother may be camped out on this multiplex interrupt. It is not uncommon to have ten or more handlers in the INT 2Fh chain (see Figure 6-11). The performance problems with INT 2Fh may be one possible reason for Microsoft's apparent move away from the redirector interface, in the direction of a Novell NETX-style front-end hook, even while Novell itself is moving toward the redirector.

Another problem with the redirector interface is that it provides no assistance when multiple redirectors are present. Each redirector must decide on a subfunction-by-subfunction basis which INT 2Fh AH=11h calls it will chain to another, previously-loaded, redirector. With both MSCDEX and NetWare 4.x using the redirector interface, the "chaining redirectors" problem is a real one.

Because INT 2Fh redirectors are called by DOS, they have less flexibility and leeway than INT 21h redirectors, which grab I/O requests before DOS even sees them. For example, INT 2Fh redirectors have little choice over the DOS file naming scheme (note subfunction 23h, however), whereas an INT 21h hook at least theoretically can devise any file-naming conventions it wants.

Tracing an Open, Revisited

Much earlier in this chapter, we used INTRSPY to trace through the COPY command working on a local drive. COMMAND.COM called INT 21h AH=6Ch, which in turn called a block device driver, which in this case (see Figure 8-1) called INT 13h. We now need to repeat this exercise for a redirector drive. This can be a network drive, a CD-ROM drive provided by MSCDEX, or even an XMS RAM disk provided by the Phantom sample program described later in this chapter.

We can't use the exact same DISK.SCR (Listing 8-1) used to produce Figure 8-1 because DISK.SCR includes DD.SCR, and network redirector drives don't have associated block device drivers. However, removing DD.SCR results in an INTRSPY script that we can use to see what happens to a COPY command on a redirector drive:

```
C:\UNDOC2>phantom -S256 h:
256Kb XMS allocated.
Phantom installed as H:

C:\UNDOC2>copy con h:foo.bar
this is foo.bar
^Z
        1 file(s) copied

C:\UNDOC2>intrspy

C:\UNDOC2>cmdspy compile disk command /c copy h:foo.bar h:bar.foo
```

However, the resulting INTRSPY report doesn't show anything occurring "inside" the INT 21h function 6Ch call:

```
216C: Extended Open/Create: H:FOO.BAR
AX=6C00 BX=0040 CX=0000 DX=0101
216C: done, file is 0005
```

Well, of course it doesn't show anything inside the INT 21h AH=6Ch call! Why should it? There is no block device driver installed for the drive, and it seems unlikely that an XMS RAM disk would call INT 13h, which is the BIOS disk function.

So what *does* happen inside an INT 21h on a network redirector drive? DOS issues INT 2Fh AH=11h calls to the network redirector. To see this, we can create a very simple INTRSPY script which tracks entry and exit into a few INT 21h calls and tracks any calls to INT 2Fh AH=11h. 2F11.SCR is shown in Listing 8-25.

Listing 8-25: 2F11.SCR

```
; 2F11.SCR
intercept 21h
    function 3Ch
        on_entry output "21/3C: Create " (ds:dx->byte,asciiz,64)
        on_exit  output "21/3C: Create done: " ax
    function 3Dh
        on_entry output "21/3D: Open " (ds:dx->byte,asciiz,64)
        on_exit  output "21/3D: Open done: " ax
    function 3Eh
        on_entry output "21/3E: Close " bx
        on_exit  output "21/3E: Close done " bx
    function 3Fh
        on_entry output "21/3F: Read " bx
        on_exit  output "21/3F: Read done " bx
    function 40h
        on_entry output "21/40: Write File " bx
        on_exit  output "21/40: Write done " bx
    function 6Ch
        on_entry output "21/6C: Ext Open/Create " (ds:si->byte,asciiz,64)
        on_exit  output "21/6C: Ext Open/Cr done: " ax
intercept 2fh
    function 11h
        on_entry output "   2F/" ax
run "command /c %1 %2 %3 %4 %5 %6 %7 %8 %9"
report
```

The results from this script are far more interesting:

```
C:\UNDOC2>cmdspy compile 2f11 copy h:foo.bar h:bar.foo

21/6C: Ext Open/Create H:FOO.BAR
   2F/1123
   2F/112E
21/6C: Ext Open/Cr done: 0005
21/3F: Read 0005
   2F/1108
21/3F: Read done 0005
21/3E: Close 0005
   2F/1106
21/3E: Close done 0005
; ...
21/6C: Ext Open/Create H:BAR.FOO
   2F/1123
   2F/112E
21/6C: Ext Open/Cr done: 0005
```

```
   2F/1123
21/40: Write File 0005
   2F/1109
21/40: Write done 0005
21/3E: Close 0005
   2F/1106
21/3E: Close done 0005
```

The indenting of INT 2Fh calls within INT 21h calls provides a clear picture of how the network redirector interface works. For example, calling INT 21h AH=3Fh (Read File) on a network redirector drive results in DOS sending an INT 2Fh AX=1108h to the redirector:

```
21/6C Open/Create -> 2F/1123 and 2F/112E
21/3F Read -> 2F/1108
21/40 Write -> 2F/1109
21/3E Close -> 2F/1106
```

In DOS 5.0 and higher, the COPY command happens to use INT 21h AH=6Ch. If a file had instead been opened with the older INT 21h AH=3Dh call, DOS would have issued an INT 2Fh AX=1116h, rather than the AX=112Eh seen above. It's important to understand that DOS usually only makes these 2F/11 calls when the network bit is set in the current CDS's flags or in an SFT entry's device-info word. For example, here is how MS-DOS decides whether to issue the INT 2Fh AX=1108h Read call:

```
; ES:DI points to an SFT entry
test    byte ptr es:[di+6], 80h ; test network bit in SFT dev info
jz      not_redir
mov     ax, 1108h
int     2fh
; ...
not_redir:
```

Likewise, here is how DOS decides whether to make the INT 2Fh AX=1103h Mkdir call:

```
; ES:DI points to the current CDS
test    byte ptr es:[di+44h], 80h   ; test network bit in CDS flags
jz      not_redir
mov     ax, 1103h
int     2fh
not_redir:
```

Even if no drive in the CDS has the network bit set, there are still a few redirector calls that DOS issues. Experimentation with INTRSPY and inspection of a DOS disassembly show that several redirector calls, including subfunctions 1Dh, 20h, 22h, 23h, and 25h, are essentially broadcasts that DOS issues, regardless of whether a redirector is installed or not.

Furthermore, there are a few relatively obscure redirector calls (subfunctions 18h and 19h) that don't require a CDS at all. These are used, for example, by LAN Manager named pipes. But for the most part, installing a redirector means setting the network bit in a CDS entry. Likewise, a redirector must set the network bit in the SFT device-info word for any files opened on its drives.

So far, it sounds like there are just a few redirector calls and that these correspond closely to the documented INT 21h calls. However, we haven't done much to the redirector drive yet—just copy a single small file. We need to try DEL, DIR, MD, CD, RD, and so on. To get a general idea of which redirector calls DOS makes, we can simplify the INTRSPY script even further to print out nothing but the INT 2Fh AX function number:

```
intercept 2fh function 11h
    on_entry output ax
```

If we then do a few minutes' work on the drive and sort the results, we can get some idea of the range of redirector calls that DOS issues:

```
C:\UNDOC2>cmdspy report | sort | uniq
1101                ; remove dir
1103                ; make dir
1105                ; change dir
1106                ; close file
1108                ; read file
1109                ; write file
110C                ; get disk space
1113                ; delete file
1116                ; open file
1117                ; create/truncate file
111B                ; find first
111C                ; find next
111D                ; close all for PSP
1120                ; flush all buffers
1122                ; proc term hook
1123                ; qualify pathname
1125                ; redirected printer mode
112E                ; extended open file
```

All this in just a minute or two of random activity on the drive. Even more, there are other, less common but still important, redirector calls that DOS issues. For example, calling INT 21h AX=5F02h (see the NETDRV.C program in Listing 8-15) results in a call to INT 2Fh AX=111Eh. Basically, it looks like producing a reliable redirector requires implementing the whole bloody interface. You cannot get away, for example, with just implementing the calls listed above.

Trapping calls with INTRSPY is a fairly random way to determine what parts of the redirector interface are used. To see which redirector calls DOS makes, it is better to examine the actual DOS versions you wish to support. Using the INT212F.LST file generated with NICEDBG in Chapter 6, you can see exactly which INT 2Fh AH=11h calls DOS makes and when. For example:

```
                 INT21_OD:            ; Reset Drive
; ...
; do INT 2Ah AX=8001h, call func to flush all buffers (calls code for
; INT 2Fh AX=1215h in loop), do INT 2Ah AX=8101h
; ...
FDC8:4DBC     B8FFFF        MOV AX,FFFF
FDC8:4DBF     50            PUSH AX
FDC8:4DC0     B82011        MOV AX,1120      ; Flush all disk buffers
FDC8:4DC3     CD2F          INT 2F           ; 2f/1120
FDC8:4DC5     58            POP AX
FDC8:4DC6     C3            RET
```

Inspection of the DOS 5.0 kernel indicates that it calls redirector subfunctions 0, 1, 3, 5-0Ah, 0Ch, 0Eh, 0Fh, 11h, 13h, 16h-19h, 1Bh-26h, and 2Eh. Therefore, a commercial redirector should implement at least these calls, which are described in a moment.

So far you have seen which redirector calls DOS makes but haven't seen any details of how they work. To see the interface in more detail, we can follow a File Open call a little more closely using another INTRSPY script, REDIR.SCR (Listing 8-26).

Listing 8-26: REDIR.SCR

```
;; REDIR.SCR -- for DOS >= 4.00
include "dosstruc"      ; see listing 8-24
intercept 21h
    function 6Ch
        on_entry
            output "== DOS OPEN (6Ch) ======================="
            output "File name: " (ds:si->byte,asciiz,40)
            output "Open mode: " (bl,hex) "h"
```

```
        on_exit
            output ""
            output "== 6Ch OPEN Completed "
            if (cflag == 1) sameline "(FAILED " (ax,dec) ") ==========="
            if (cflag == 0) sameline "(Handle " (ax,dec) ") ==========="
intercept 2fh
    function 11h
        subfunction 2Eh
            on_entry
                output ""
                output "-- 2F Open (2Eh) -------------------"
                output "File name: " (sda_seg:sda_ofs->SDA4.FN1)
                output "Open mode: " (sda_seg:sda_ofs->SDA4.SPOP_MODE)
                output "Uninitialized SFT:"
                output (es:di->SFT)
            on_exit
                output ""
                output "-- 2F Open (2Eh) completed "
                if (cflag == 0)
                    sameline "-------------------"
                    output "Completed SFT:"
                    output (es:di->SFT)
                if (cflag == 1) sameline "(FAILED " (ax,dec) ") ---------"
run "command /c type %1"
report
```

This script takes as a parameter the name of a file that exists on the redirected drive. For variety, we'll look at a file on an MSCDEX CD-ROM drive L: rather than on Phantom drive H:

```
C:\UNDOC2>cmdspy compile redir l:read.me > redir.log
```

This types out the file entered as the parameter. If the file is on a redirected drive, as in the MSCDEX-based example L:\READ.ME, the file REDIR.LOG contains something like this

```
== DOS OPEN (6Ch) =====================
File name: l:read.me
Open mode: 00h

-- 2F Open (2Eh) -------------------
File name: \\L.A.\READ.ME
Open mode: 0000
Uninitialized SFT:

SFT.C_HANDLES             : 65535
SFT.OPEN_MODE             : 0000
SFT.ATTR_BYTE             : 20
SFT.DEV_INFO              : 0042
SFT.DEVDRV_PTR            : 0116:13A4
SFT.ST_CLSTR              : 7002
SFT.F_TIME                : 2800
SFT.F_DATE                : 1689
SFT.F_SIZE                : 47845
SFT.F_POS                 : 47845
SFT.LAST_RELCLSTR         : 5
SFT.LAST_ABSCLSTR         : 867
SFT.DIR_SCTR_NO           : 0
SFT.DIR_ENTRY_NO          : 11
SFT.FNAME_11CHAR          : COMMAND COM

-- 2F Open (2Eh) completed -----------------
Completed SFT:

SFT.C_HANDLES             : 65535
SFT.OPEN_MODE             : 0002
SFT.ATTR_BYTE             : 01
SFT.DEV_INFO              : 8048
```

```
SFT.DEVDRV_PTR              : 0D57:00F3
SFT.ST_CLSTR                : 9933
SFT.F_TIME                  : 2395
SFT.F_DATE                  : 1ADC
SFT.F_SIZE                  : 21900
SFT.F_POS                   : 0
SFT.LAST_RELCLSTR           : 21560
SFT.LAST_ABSCLSTR           : 0
SFT.DIR_SCTR_NO             : 56026
SFT.DIR_ENTRY_NO            : 2
SFT.FNAME_11CHAR            : READ    ME
== 6Ch OPEN Completed (Handle 5) ==========
```

This shows the DOS Open function called with the raw filename string in DS:SI as specified
(l:read.me), and the resultant redirector Open call subfunction 16h called with the SDA.FN1 field
reflecting a fully qualified filename (\\L.A\READ.ME). Note that the truename for files on network-
redirected drives usually begins with a \\ (double backslash). It also shows an uninitialized SFT passed
to the redirector Open function, with data left over from previous use (COMMAND.COM in this
case), and the SFT initialized by MSCDEX. This gives you an idea of the sort of detail DOS takes care
of before calling a redirector, as well as the tasks for which the redirector is responsible.

The Phantom

To study the interface in detail, it is best to use a real example. Here, then, is The Phantom. The
Phantom implements a phantom drive, that is, the drive is not based on a physical disk drive, but
rather uses XMS as its media. Radically changed from its guise in the first edition of *Undocumented
DOS* as the world's least effective storage device, Phantom is now a fully functioning and useful
extended memory RAMDisk TSR:

- It supports all DOS file system commands that you can run on a network drive, with the exception of CHKDSK, FORMAT, SYS, and DBLSPACE. These all operate on native DOS devices
  using calls such as INT 25h/26h and generic IOCTL, which do not get redirected through the
  redirector interface.
- It behaves like a very fast hard disk and is transparent to all DOS and Windows applications.
  (Note, however, that loading SHARE has no effect; Phantom does not signal sharing violations.)
- It works under DOS 3.10 to 6.0, inclusive. It has also been tested under a prerelease version of
  DOS 7.0 (Chicago).
- It supports FCB, as well as handle-based file operations.
- Unlike the first version of Phantom, the number of directories and files on the drive is limited
  only by the amount of XMS memory allocated for the drive on the command line. (As this
  book was going to press, we found that Phantom currently supports only two subdirectory levels.)
- As an unloadable TSR redirector, it has some advantages over conventional device driver RAM
  disks like RAMDRIVE.SYS in that you can load it when you need it, unload it when you don't
  need it, and pick a disk size (XMS allocation) on the fly to suit the application.
- It illustrates not only updated and enhanced knowledge of the redirector interface, but principles of a FAT-based file system as well.

Its usage is:

```
PHANTOM [-Snnnn] d: [-U]
-Snnnn   specifies size of RAM disk in KB of XMS
d:       specifies drive letter to use
-U       unloads latest copy of Phantom loaded
```

The -S switch is particularly important because by default the Phantom takes all XMS memory; this is not necessarily what you want.

You can run multiple copies of Phantom, specifying a different drive letter each time. Note that -U unloads the most-recent invocation.

Here is a brief sample session with the Phantom drive, where the entire contents of the Interrupt List from C:\UNDOC2\INTRLIST is XCOPYed to a new \INTRLIST subdirectory on Phantom drive H:

```
C:\UNDOC2\CHAP8>phantom h:
3968Kb XMS allocated
Phantom installed as H:

C:\UNDOC2\CHAP8>md h:\intrlist

C:\UNDOC2\CHAP8>xcopy C:\UNDOC2\INTRLIST\*.* h:\intrlist
Reading source file(s)...
C:\UNDOC2\INTRLIST\COMBINE.BAT
C:\UNDOC2\INTRLIST\FILE_ID.DIZ
C:\UNDOC2\INTRLIST\GLOSSARY.LST
C:\UNDOC2\INTRLIST\INTERRUP.1ST
C:\UNDOC2\INTRLIST\INTERRUP.A
Reading source file(s)...
C:\UNDOC2\INTRLIST\INTERRUP.B
; ... okay, we get the idea ...
C:\UNDOC2\INTRLIST\_ADVERT.TXT
      30 File(s) copied

C:\UNDOC2\CHAP8>dir h:\intrlist

 Volume in drive H is PHANTOM
 Directory of H:\INTRLIST

COMBINE  BAT      150 05-06-93  11:06a
FILE_ID  DIZ      200 05-24-93  12:34a
GLOSSARY LST    23998 03-21-93   4:42p
INTERRUP 1ST    60877 05-24-93  12:34a
INTERRUP A     290154 05-24-93  12:34a
INTERRUP B     242488 05-24-93  12:34a
; ... lots of big files ...
_ADVERT  TXT     1845 01-28-92  10:19p
      30 file(s)    3096942 bytes
                     941056 bytes free
```

Naturally, processing the three-megabyte Interrupt List on this Phantom drive, whether with a tool such as grep or with Hackensack Software's INTERVUE, is very fast.

All the elements of a full-blown file system are here. We have created an entity which looks like a drive, behaves like a drive, and yet which has no reality outside our INT 2Fh function 11h handler and XMS. (As this book was going to press, a beta site discovered that Phantom crashes if you have HIMEM.SYS, but don't have DOS=HIGH. Thus, right now Phantom inadvertently requires DOS=HIGH.)

Phantom Implementation

With the C source code for Phantom, we can resume our trace into the DOS Open call and see how a redirector like Phantom handles this and other INT 2Fh calls that DOS sends it. The source code for Phantom is too large (2400 lines of code) to print here in its entirety, but it is on the accompanying disk as \UNDOC2\CHAP8\PHANTOM.C. Here, we look at selected portions of PHANTOM.C to see how a redirector handles DOS Open, Read, Find First, Change Directory, and Make Directory.

Initializing the CDS First, however, we must see how the Phantom sets itself up to be called in the first place. As we saw earlier, DOS issues most of the INT 2Fh AH=11h redirector calls only if the network bit is set in the current CDS or in the device-info word of the current SFT. Before you can see how the Phantom handles INT 2Fh calls, then, you must see how it sets up the CDS. This, appropriately enough, is done in PHANTOM.C's set_up_cds() function, shown in Listing 8-27.

Listing 8-27: PHANTOM.C set_up_cds()

```
// V3_CDS_PTR and V4_CDS_PTR are CDS structures for DOS 3, DOS 4+
// LOLREC_PTR is pointer to LOLREC (LOL = List of Lists = SysVars)

// global variables
LOLREC_PTR   lolptr;               /* pointer to List Of Lists */
uchar        our_drive_no;         /* A: is 0, **not** 1 !! */
uint         cds_root_size;        /* Size of our CDS root string */
char far *   cds_path_root = "Phantom  :\\"; /* Root string for CDS */

extern void failprog(char * msg);   /* print message, exit to DOS */

void set_up_cds(void)
    {
    V3_CDS_PTR our_cds_ptr = lolptr->cds_ptr;

    if (our_drive_no >= lolptr->last_drive)
        failprog("Drive letter higher than last drive.");

    if (_osmajor == 3)
        our_cds_ptr += our_drive_no;
    else
        {
        V4_CDS_PTR t = (V4_CDS_PTR) our_cds_ptr;
        t += our_drive_no;
        our_cds_ptr = (V3_CDS_PTR) t;
        }
    // Check that this drive letter is currently invalid (not in use)
    // Test both Physical (0x4000) and Network (0x8000) at same time.
    if ((our_cds_ptr->flags & 0xc000) != 0)
        failprog("Drive already assigned...");

    // Establish our 'root'
    cds_root_size = _fstrlen(cds_path_root);
    _fstrcpy(our_cds_ptr->current_path, cds_path_root);
    our_cds_ptr->current_path[_fstrlen(our_cds_ptr->current_path) - 3] =
        (char) ('A' + our_drive_no);
    _fstrcpy(cds_path_root, our_cds_ptr->current_path);
    our_cds_ptr->root_ofs = _fstrlen(our_cds_ptr->current_path) - 1;
    current_path = our_cds_ptr->current_path + our_cds_ptr->root_ofs;

    // Set both Physical (0x4000) and Network (0x8000) at same time.
    // David Markun says that a non-network redir such as Phantom
    // should set 0xC080, not 0xC000. 0x80 is the REDIR_NOT_NET bit
    // used by MSCDEX. If 0x80 is not set, Phantom shows up in
    // NET USE in DEC Pathworks and IBM LAN Server. This point
    // comes from an Interrupt List entry supplied by Geoff Chappell.
    our_cds_ptr->flags |= 0xc000;
    }
```

On entry to set_up_cds(), the global variable our_drive_no holds the zero-based (A=0, not 1) drive the user specified for the new Phantom drive, and set_up_cds() uses this to get a far pointer to the CDS entry for that drive. The function ensures that the drive doesn't exceed LASTDRIVE (in other words, that the CDS is large enough) and ensures that the drive is not already in use by testing both the Physical and Network bits in our_cds_ptr->flags.

Assuming that the specified drive letter can be Phantomized, the function sets the current_path in the CDS entry to a default string such as "Phantom H:\" and sets the root_ofs field to the backslash, so that the root directory is "\". For this drive, the TRUENAME command would print the string "Phantom H:\" directly from the CDS.

Most important, set_up_cds() turns on the CDS entry's Network and Physical bits (our_cds_ptr->flags |= 0xC000), thereby declaring that disk, directory, and file requests for this drive will henceforth be handled by a redirector. If you remove a Phantom drive with PHANTOM-U, the program switches off these bits (our_cds_ptr->flags &= ~0xC000). (See the comment in set_up_cds(), which notes that this should really be 0xC080, not 0xC000. As you can tell, this was a last-minute change.)

The Redirector INT 2Fh Handler   Once the appropriate bits have been set, there must of course be an INT 2Fh handler to act as the redirector. The Phantom installs its INT 2Fh handler, called redirector(), in the normal way:

```
prev_int2f_vector = _dos_getvect(0x2f);       // 21/35
_dos_setvect(0x2f, redirector);               // 21/25
_dos_keep(0, tsr_paras);                       // 21/31: TSR
```

The Phantom's INT 2Fh handler is shown in Listing 8-28.

Listing 8-28: PHANTOM.C redirector()

```
// ALL_REGS are compiler-specific register params to interrupt functions
#define     MAX_FXN_NO        0x2E
#define     STACK_SIZE        1024
#define     FCARRY            0x0001
// global variables
int         curr_fxn;               /* Record of function in progress */
ALL_REGS    r;                      /* Global save area for all caller's regs */
uint        dos_ss;                 /* DOS's saved SS at entry */
uint        dos_sp;                 /* DOS's saved SP at entry */
char        our_stack[STACK_SIZE];  /* our internal stack */
uint far*   stack_param_ptr;        /* ptr to word at top of stack on entry */
int         filename_is_char_device; /* generate_fcbname found CHAR dev! */
void succeed(void)  { r.flags &= ~FCARRY; r.ax = 0; }

// dispatch_table, fxnmap, and is_call_for_us() are discussed below
void interrupt far redirector(ALL_REGS entry_regs)
    {
    static uint save_bp;

    _asm STI;

    // Make sure that AH=11h and that AL <= MAX_FXN_NO
    // i.e., only support INT 2Fh AX=1100h through AX=1123h
    if (((entry_regs.ax >> 8) != (uchar) 0x11) ||
        ((uchar) entry_regs.ax > MAX_FXN_NO))
            goto chain_on;

    curr_fxn = fxnmap[(uchar) entry_regs.ax];    // AL=subfunction

    if ((curr_fxn == _unsupported) ||
        (! is_call_for_us(entry_regs.es, entry_regs.di))) // listing 8-29
        goto chain_on;

    // Set up our copy of the registers
    r = entry_regs;

    // Save ss:sp and switch to our internal stack. We also save bp
    // so that we can get at any parameter at the top of the stack
    // (such as the file attribute passed to subfxn 17h).
    _asm mov dos_ss, ss;
    _asm mov save_bp, bp;
    stack_param_ptr = (uint far*) MK_FP(dos_ss, save_bp + sizeof(ALL_REGS));

    _asm {
        mov dos_sp, sp;
        mov ax, ds
```

```
        cli
        mov ss, ax          // New stack segment is in Data segment.
        mov sp, offset our_stack + STACK_SIZE -2
        sti
        }
    succeed(); // Expect success!
    // DO IT! Call the appropriate handling function
    // unless we already know we need to fail (NUL, CON, AUX, etc.)
    // filename_is_char_device is set inside is_call_for_us()
    if (filename_is_char_device)    fail(5);
    else                            dispatch_table[curr_fxn]();

    // Switch the stack back
    _asm {
        cli;
        mov ss, dos_ss;
        mov sp, dos_sp;
        sti;
        }
    // put the possibly changed registers back on the stack, and return
    entry_regs = r;
    return;
    // If the call wasn't for us, we chain on.
chain_on:
    _chain_intr(prev_int2f_vector);
    }
```

The redirector() function sees all INT 2Fh calls, whether they are redirector-related or not, and whether they are intended for one of the Phantom's drives or not. For every call,

- if it is a redirector call, that is, AH=11h, and
- if it is a call for one of its drive letters (see below), and
- if it is a supported call,

then redirector() dispatches the appropriate procedure to carry out the requested subfunction. If any of these parameters is false, the redirector passes control to the previous handler in the (possibly very long) INT 2Fh chain.

Phantom also ensures that you don't try to create files on the Phantom drive with names such as "NUL" or "CON" that belong to installed character device drivers. The is_call_for_us() function calls generate_fcbname(), which in turn calls is_a_charcter_device(), which is a C wrapper around INT 2Fh AX=1223h; generate_fcbname() then sets the global variable filename_is_char_device. (Incidentally, generate_fcbname(), like almost all other references to FCBs in the Phantom code, has nothing to do with FCBs. This very confusing name merely refers to 11-character file names, such as one finds in FCBs but also in many other parts of DOS.)

Having established that it has a supported redirector call for one of its drives, redirector() prepares a copy of the registers as they were on entry and then switches SS:SP to an internal stack, which is simply a static array of bytes in the TSR's DS. Upon entry to redirector(), SS is the DOS stack segment, but DS becomes our DS, courtesy of the C _interrupt keyword. Switching to our own stack satisfies the compiler's SS==DS assumption. Furthermore, the DOS stacks are not very large (about 300 bytes; see Chapter 6), and having our own stack ensures that we do not run out of stack space.

Non-reentrancy is the only concern that use of this internal stack might raise. By using an internal stack and always positioning to the top of it on entry, our redirector is not reentrant—the contents of the stack are always destroyed by each invocation. However, our redirector is called only by DOS, and (as we saw in Chapter 6) DOS does exactly the same thing upon entry to Int 21h for all the functions which generate calls to us. To all intents and purposes, DOS itself is not reentrant, so our lack of reentrancy is not an issue. (However, the reader may wish to ponder how this interacts with software that uses the Swappable Data Area to reenter DOS.)

Having switched stacks, redirector() dispatches the appropriate handler function for the requested subfunction. When the subfunction returns, redirector() switches SS:SP to their original values upon entry, reinstates the registers, and returns.

How Do We Know the Call Is for Us?
DOS allows the installation of multiple redirectors. If redirector() receives a INT 2Fh AH=11h call, but one which is not intended for one of its drives, the function passes the call on in the normal way with the _chain_intr() function (provided with both Microsoft C and recent versions of Borland C++).

How does Phantom decide that it should handle a call rather than pass it on to MSCDEX, NetWare Lite, or some other redirector? Since there may be a chain of redirectors, each wanting to service only those calls that relate to the drive(s) that it is redirecting, there must be a way of determining whether a particular redirector call that's making the rounds is for you.

The redirector() function passes the ES and DI registers to is_call_for_us() to figure out, well, whether the call is for us. This function is shown in Listing 8-29.

Listing 8-29: PHANTOM.C is_call_for_us()

```
// _clsfil, _unlockfil, _inquiry, etc. are 2F/11 AL subfunction numbers
// SFTREC_PTR: far ptr to an System File Table (SFT) entry
// SRCHREC_PTR: far ptr to a FindFirst Search Data Block (SDB)
// V3_SDA_PTR, V4_SDA_PTR: far ptrs to the Swappable Data Area (SDA)
int is_call_for_us(uint es,uint di)
    {
    filename_is_char_device = 0;

    // The first 'if' checks for the bottom 6 bits of the
    // device information word in the SFT. Values > LASTDRIVE
    // relate to files not associated with drives, such as LAN Manager
    // named pipes (thanks to David Markun).
    if ((curr_fxn >= _clsfil && curr_fxn <= _unlockfil)
        || (curr_fxn == _skfmend)
        || (curr_fxn == _unknown_fxn_2D) )      // file related
        {
        SFTREC_PTR sft_ptr = (SFTREC_PTR) MK_FP(es,di); // check SFT
        // Markun says 0x3F mask is WRONG! See subfunction 1Ch below.
        return (sft_ptr->dev_info_world & 0x3F) == our_drive_no;
        }
    else if (curr_fxn == _inquiry)       // 2F/11/00: succeed automatically
        return TRUE;
    else if (curr_fxn == _fnext)         // Find Next
        {
        SRCHREC_PTR psrchrec;            // check search record in SDA
        if (_osmajor==3)
            psrchrec=&(((V3_SDA_PTR) sda_ptr)->srchrec);
        else
            psrchrec=&(((V4_SDA_PTR) sda_ptr)->srchrec);
        // Markun says 0x3F mask is WRONG! See subfunction 1Ch below.
        return ((uchar) (psrchrec->drive_no & 0x3F) == our_drive_no);
        }
    else                                          // everything else
        {
        uchar far * p;
        if (_osmajor==3)
            p=((V3_SDA_PTR) sda_ptr)->cdsptr;    // check CDS
        else
            p=((V4_SDA_PTR) sda_ptr)->cdsptr;
        if (_fmemcmp(cds_path_root, p, cds_root_size) == 0)
            {
```

```
        // If a path is present, does it refer to a character device?
        if (curr_fxn != _dskspc)
            generate_fcbname(ds);    // eventually call 2F/1223
        return TRUE;
        }
    else
        return FALSE;
    }
}
```

The method is_call_for_us() uses depends on the type of operation to be performed. If the 2F/11 call is one that deals with an open file, such as Read, Write, Commit, or Close, DOS sets up ES:DI to point to the SFT entry for the file before issuing the INT 2Fh call (see the redirector specification later in this chapter). The device information word in the SFT entry contains the file's drive number in the bottom six bits, so it is a simple masking and comparison operation for is_call_for_us() to ascertain that the call is one of ours:

```
(((SFTREC_PTR) MK_FP(es,di))->dev_info_word & 0x3F) == our_drive_no
```

If the call is for subfunction 1Ch (Find Next), the SRCH_BLK structure in the SDA contains a drive number byte at the beginning of the structure and, again, we need only mask and compare the bottom 6 bits of that drive to see if the findnext is for us:

```
(uchar) (psrchrec->drive_no & 0x3F) == our_drive_no
```

Actually, this 0x3F mask should probably be changed to 0x1F. In addition, bit 6 (0x40) should be checked. See subfunction 1Ch later in this chapter for the gory details. (Another last-minute correction by David Markun!)

For the remaining calls, DOS will have already pointed the DRIVE_CDSPTR field of the SDA at the CDS entry for whatever drive is being accessed during the redirector call. The most reliable way to compare the CDS entries is to match the hidden characters in their CURR_PATH fields up to the root offset. In a Phantom drive, this involves the string such as "Phantom H:", which appears when you run TRUENAME on a Phantom drive. In MSCDEX, the equivalent is a string such as "\\H.A."

The is_call_for_us() function always returns TRUE for subfunction 0, the redirector install check.

Another Detection Method: The Network UserVal

Tim Farley

The methods used in is_call_for_us() may not be practical for all redirectors, such as those that own a whole list of drives in the CDS.

Also, comparing the string in the CDS is not practical on some network redirectors, because it might contain one of several server or volume names, and even if you recognized them, that might not conclusively identify the drive as yours. (For instance, suppose you had two different LANs loaded, and you had servers on both LANs that had the same name.)

A different method requires callers to set the UserVal parameter in CX when calling the INT 21h AH=5F03h Make Network Connection function (this shows up at the redirector as an INT 2Fh AX=111Eh, with 5F03h on the stack). This UserVal is stored at offset 4Dh in the CDS and is a magic value that identifies your drives. For example:

```
if (cds[drive].flags & NETWORK)
    if (cds[drive].u.NET.parameter == my_magic_number)
        return CALL_IS_FOR_ME;
```

NetWare 4.0 appears to use this, as it requires callers to put 'NW' (574Eh) in CX when calling INT 21h AX=5F03h. Of course, your redirector could store the magic value at offset 4Dh itself, if appropriate, and not rely on the caller. Comparing this one word is far easier than comparing an entire string.

Handling a Read   The redirector() function has finally decided that a call is intended for one of its drives. Let's say the call is a Read—in other words, that a program has called INT 21h AH=3Fh (File Read) or INT 21h AH=21h (FCB Random Read), and that DOS has boiled this down to an INT 2Fh AX=1108h call, which has wound up on redirector()'s doorstep. How does Phantom handle the subfunction 8 Read call?

Looking back at redirector() in Listing 8-28, you can see that, given a supported redirector subfunction number in AL, the subfunction is called through a dispatch table:

```
if (fxnmap[AL] != _unsupported)
    dispatch_table[AL]();
```

As you would expect, dispatch_table is nothing more than an array of function pointers:

```
PROC dispatch_table[]= {
    inquiry,        /* 0x00h */
    rd,             /* 0x01h */
    unsupported,    /* 0x02h */
    md,             /* 0x03h */
    unsupported,    /* 0x04h */
    cd,             /* 0x05h */
    clsfil,         /* 0x06h */
    cmmtfil,        /* 0x07h */
    readfil,        /* 0x08h */
    writfil,        /* 0x09h */
    // ...
    } ;
```

Having made a short story long, the punch line is that when DOS calls INT 2Fh AX=1108h, the Phantom redirector() ends up calling the readfil() function, shown in Listing 8-30. Thus, we can start to fill in further detail for the INTRSPY trace we produced earlier:

```
21/3F: Read 0005
    2F/1108
        redirector() (listing 8-28)
            is_call_for_us() (listing 8-29)
            readfil() (listing 8-30; see alternate in listing 8-38)
21/3F: Read done 0005
```

Listing 8-30: PHANTOM.C readfil() (INT 2Fh AX=1108h)

```
/* DOS System File Table entry - all DOS versions. NOTE!!! This is
   slightly different from the standard DOS SFT structure. Some
   of the fields are for the redirector's use to treat as
   it sees fit. Others, of course, are maintained and used by
   DOS, so their meaning must never be changed. */
typedef struct {
    uint          handle_count, open_mode;
    uchar         file_attr;
    uint          dev_info_word;
    uchar far *   dev_drvr_ptr;
    uint          start_sector, file_time, file_date;
    long          file_size, file_pos;
    uint          rel_sector, abs_sector, dir_sector, dir_entry_no;
    char          file_name[11];
    ulong         share_prev_sft;
    uint          share_net_machine_num, owner_psp;
```

```
    // other fields
    } SFTREC, far* SFTREC_PTR;
void fail(uint err) { r.flags |= FCARRY; r.ax = err; }
void read_data(long far *file_pos_ptr, uint *len_ptr, uchar far *buf,
    uint start_sector, uint far* last_rel_ptr, uint far* last_abs_ptr);
// Read from File - subfunction 08h
void readfil(void)
    {
    SFTREC_PTR p = (SFTREC_PTR) MK_FP(r.es, r.di);

    if (p->open_mode & 1) { fail(5); return; }  // access denied

    if ((p->file_pos + r.cx) > p->file_size)
        r.cx = (uint) (p->file_size - p->file_pos);

    if (! r.cx) return;      // nothing to do
    // Fill caller's buffer and update the SFT for the file
    read_data(&p->file_pos, &r.cx, ((V3_SDA_PTR) sda_ptr)->current_dta,
        p->start_sector, &p->rel_sector, &p->abs_sector);
    }
```

Gosh, that was easy. That's all reading files involves? When presented this way, it looks like you could write a DOS clone (the world's most valuable piece of code) one weekend while your spouse is out of town.

Not surprisingly, writing a DOS file system is a bit harder than this. For example, later on (Listing 8-38), you'll see another version of readfil() with critical error handling. As a RAM disk that handles XMS rather than an error-prone disk, Phantom can be a bit cavalier about errors.

You can see that readfil() takes the caller's ES:DI and treats it as an SFTREC_PTR. This matches what is said about the Read subfunction in the redirector specification later in this chapter:

```
Subfunction 08h
Read from File
Inputs:        ES:DI -> SFT for file to read from
               CX = count of bytes to read
               SDA.CURR_DTA -> user buffer to read data into
Outputs:       Carry set + error code in AX if error encountered
               if no error, CX = bytes actually read
               SFT updated
```

In fact, the Phantom readfil() function is little more than a C version of this specification, taking parameters in the SFT and updating the SFT. The Read function reads at the current file position stored in the SFT, so the only other parameters needed are the number of bytes to read (CX) and the address of the caller's buffer (DTA). All the updating of the SFT is done in the lower-level read_data() function which, however, knows nothing about SFTs. The function readfil() passes read_data() the addresses of all the SFT fields that need updating.

Back in FILES.C (Listing 8-19), we dumped out some SFT fields. However, a key value not shown in FILES is the current file position. This is maintained not only in the SFT file_pos field, but also in rel_sector and abs_sector. Phantom treats part of the SFT in its own way; as noted earlier, a redirector can reinterpret the meaning of some fields in the SFT. These fields are used and updated by readfil() and of course also by writfil() (not shown).

These fields are also updated when a program calls INT 21h AH=42h (Move File Pointer, a/k/a lseek). Interestingly, however, in DOS 4.0 and higher these lseek calls usually don't appear at the redirector's doorstep. Instead, DOS fiddles with the SFT directly without bothering the redirector. There is one circumstance, having to do with seeking from the end of a file, in which DOS will call the redirector. (See the disassembly of lseek in Chapter 6, Listing 6-20.)

The Phantom XMS File System   At this point, we have satisfied the redirector specification. The internals of the read_data() function don't matter for the purposes of understanding the redirector. For all it matter, read_data() could produce random data such as stock-market prices on demand.

However, let's keep going and see how Phantom organizes the file system. Because Phantom implements a FAT-based file system, it is worth examining, if only to reinforce the points made much earlier in this chapter about the FAT and DOS directory structures. The read_data() function is shown in Listing 8-31.

The file system implemented in Phantom uses XMS extended memory. The way that it organizes the storage of directory and file information and data is similar, but not identical to, the DOS FAT-based file system. Of course, there is no requirement that a redirector use a FAT file system; that in fact is a prime reason to use the redirector in the first place. Since it treats XMS memory as though it were simply a hard disk formatted into sectors, it would be relatively easy to modify Phantom to work on any random access medium. (There are separate interesting issues involved with sequential access media, such as tape.)

The Phantom file system is sectored, but into 1024-byte chunks of XMS instead of 512-byte chunks of disk. Phantom divides its disk space XMS allocation into two areas:

- The FAT (only one copy). Since a FAT entry that's a WORD in size allows for approximately 64K clusters, a 1024-byte cluster allows the FAT to manage a full 64MB of XMS memory. Therefore, Phantom removes the distinction between sectors and clusters and deals exclusively in sectors.
- The data storage area, which accommodates not only the file and subdirectory data, but the root directory as well, which Phantom treats as simply another subdirectory (recall that DOS provides special treatment for the root directory, assigning it a fixed contiguous size not accessible through the FAT).

Apart from this, Phantom emulates the DOS file system fairly closely. It uses the same directory entry structure and the same FAT management techniques as DOS. It is worth stressing again that none of this similarity is required of a redirector.

Listing 8-31: PHANTOM.C read_data()

```
#define    SECTOR_SIZE    1024    /* 1024b/sector allows for 64M of XMS */

uchar      sector_buffer[SECTOR_SIZE]; /* general purpose sector buffer */
uint       last_sector = 0xffff; /* last sector read into sector buffer */

/* Uses FAT to find next sector in chain for current file/directory */
extern uint next_FAT_sector(uint abs_sector);

void read_data(long far *file_pos_ptr, uint *len_ptr, uchar far * buf,
       uint start_sector, uint far* last_rel_ptr, uint far* last_abs_ptr)
    {
    uint start, rel_sector, abs_sector;
    uint i, count, len = *len_ptr;

    start = (uint) (*file_pos_ptr / SECTOR_SIZE);
    if (start < *last_rel_ptr)
        {
        rel_sector = 0;
        if ((abs_sector = start_sector) == 0xFFFF)  // end of FAT chain
            {
            *len_ptr = 0;
            return;
            }
        }
    else
        {
```

```
        rel_sector = *last_rel_ptr;
        abs_sector = *last_abs_ptr;
        }
    while (len)
        {
        start = (uint) (*file_pos_ptr / SECTOR_SIZE);
        if (start > rel_sector)
            {
            if ((abs_sector = next_FAT_sector(abs_sector)) == 0xFFFF)
                {
                *len_ptr -= len; goto update_sectors;
                }
            rel_sector++;
            continue;
            }
        i = (int) (*file_pos_ptr % SECTOR_SIZE);
        count = min((uint) SECTOR_SIZE - i, len);
        if (count < SECTOR_SIZE)
            {
            if (! get_sector(abs_sector, &sector_buffer))
                {
                *len_ptr -= len; goto update_sectors;
                }
            last_sector = abs_sector;
            _fmemcpy(buf, (uchar far *) &sector_buffer[i], count);
            }
        else if (! get_sector(abs_sector, buf))
            {
            *len_ptr -= len; goto update_sectors;
            }
        len -= count;
        *file_pos_ptr += count;
        buf += count;
        }
update_sectors:
    *last_rel_ptr = rel_sector;
    *last_abs_ptr = abs_sector;
    }
```

The read_data() function contains a standard loop over the number of bytes of data the caller requested. In this FAT-like system, there is effectively one sector per cluster, each 1024 bytes. If the number of bytes requested exceeds one sector-cluster, read_data() has to use the FAT to find the location of the next sector-cluster. The function calls next_FAT_sector() (see PHANTOM.C on disk), which uses abs_sector as an index into the FAT. Of course, next_FAT_sector() may have to read in a FAT sector from the XMS disk. This in turn involves first writing the current FAT sector back out to disk.

As happens with any disk, Phantom reads entire sectors at a time. If the remaining bytes the caller requested are fewer than a full sector, read_data() can't read directly into the user's buffer, so it uses sector_buffer, which is then copied (_fmemcpy) into the user's buffer.

Since Phantom operates on memory, it does not implement a buffer pool, but most redirectors should. While data from redirector drives is not by default integrated into the DOS buffers pool, a redirector could call internal DOS functions such as INT 2Fh AX=1210h (Find Unreferenced Disk Buffer) and INT 2Fh AX=120Fh (Make Buffer Most Recently Used). Note also that data from redirector drives is not cached by programs such as SmartDrive, which work off INT 13h. This is especially important for slow media such as CD-ROM. MSCDEX incorporates its own sector buffers (the location and number of which you can set with MSCDEX /m /e), but there is now a market for third-party CD-ROM "accelerators" (i.e., caches). As noted earlier, SmartDrive 4.2 and higher, included with MS-DOS 6.2, can cache data from CD-ROM drives.

In Listing 8-31, you can see that read_data() gets the actual data by calling get_sector(). This is a macro in PHANTOM.C:

```
#define get_sector(sec, buf) \
    xms_copy_to_real(xms_handle, (ulong) SECTOR_SIZE * (sec), \
        SECTOR_SIZE, (uchar far *) (buf))
```

The xms_copy_to_real() function is in turn just a C wrapper around XMS function 0Bh (Move Extended Memory Block). Thus, our trace of a DOS read for a Phantom drive now looks like this:

```
21/3F: Read 0005
   2F/1108
      redirector() (listing 8-28)
         is_call_for_us() (listing 8-29)
         readfil() (listing 8-30; see alternate in listing 8-38)
            read_data() (listing 8-31)
               XMS function 0Bh
21/3F: Read done 0005
```

In other words, eventually a DOS read turns into a call to XMS function 0Bh—exactly as one would hope from an XMS RAM disk!

Handling an Open   Having seen how Phantom handles a DOS read, we'll now step back to consider how files get opened in the first place. Rather than the Extended Open/Create call, we'll look at the simpler Open File call (INT 21h AH=3Dh), which DOS turns into a redirector Open (INT 2Fh AX=1116h). Phantom's handler for this subfunction, opnfil(), is dispatched (see Listing 8-28) in the same way as readfil(). The opnfil() function is shown in Listing 8-32.

In Listing 8-32, fcbname_ptr and srch_attr_ptr are among several Phantom global far-pointer variables that point to fields in SysVars, the SDA, and other parts of DOS. This sounds disgusting, but the entire redirector interface depends on the redirector having direct access to DOS's own global data. And again, note that names such as fcbname_ptr have nothing to do with FCBs, and merely refer to 11-character filenames.

Listing 8-32: PHANTOM.C opnfil() (INT 2Fh AX=1116h)

```
/* these are version-independent pointers to various frequently used
   locations within the various DOS structures */
// note: fcbname_ptr has nothing to do with FCBs! just 11-char filename
char far *  fcbname_ptr;        /* ptr to 1st FCB-style name in SDA */
uchar far * srch_attr_ptr;      /* ptr to search attribute in SDA */

extern int contains_wildcards(char far* path);
// ffirst(), fill_sft(), init_sft(): see below

void opnfil(void)
    {
    // DOS calls the redirector with ES:DI pointing
    // to an uninitialized SFT entry.
    SFTREC_PTR p = (SFTREC_PTR) MK_FP(r.es, r.di);

    if (contains_wildcards(fcbname_ptr)) { fail(3); return; }

    // opening a file requires first finding the file...
    *srch_attr_ptr = 0x27; // Archive+System+Hidden+Readonly+Normal
    ffirst();
    if (! r.ax)
        {
        // ...and then using the ffirst search record to fill in the SFT
        fill_sft(p, TRUE, FALSE);
        init_sft(p);
        }
    }
```

Like readfil(), opnfil() is trivial. It does little more than call ffirst() (Find First) and then fill_sft() and init_sft(). In essence, Open = get uninitialized SFT from DOS + Find First + set SFT.

The ffirst() function is shown in Listing 8-33; this is the same function that would be called if a program did an INT 21h AH=4Eh (Find First) on a redirector drive. Before calling ffirst(), opnfil() sets the search attribute in the SDA (srch_attr_ptr) to 0x27, indicating (for those readers who do not carry the entire DOS programmer's reference around in their heads) that system, hidden, and read-only files will be found in addition to normal files. This matches DOS behavior on local drives, where you can TYPE (open) a hidden file, although you can't DIR (find first) one.

Listing 8-33: PHANTOM.C ffirst() (INT 2Fh AX=111Bh) and fnext() (AX=111Ch)

```
char far *  filename_ptr;        /* ptr to 1st filename area in SDA */
SRCHREC_PTR srchrec_ptr;         /* ptr to 1st Search Data Block in SDA */
/* Finds the sector number of the start of the directory entries for
   the supplied path */
extern int get_dir_start_sector(char far* path, uint far* abs_sector_ptr);
void ffirst(void)                     /* FindFirst - subfunction 1Bh */
    {
    char far* path;
    int success;

    /* Special case for volume-label-only search: must be in root */
    if (path = (*srch_attr_ptr == 0x08) ?
            filename_ptr : _fstrrchr(filename_ptr, '\\'))
        *path = 0;

    if (path) *path = '\\';
    success = get_dir_start_sector(filename_ptr, &srchrec_ptr->dir_sector);
    if (! success) { fail(3); return; }

    _fmemcpy(&srchrec_ptr->srch_mask, fcbname_ptr, 11);

    srchrec_ptr->dir_entry_no = -1;
    srchrec_ptr->attr_mask = *srch_attr_ptr;
    srchrec_ptr->drive_no = (uchar) (our_drive_no | 0x80);

    /* ffirst()'s embedded call to fnext() admittedly looks a little
       odd. This arises from the view that findfirst is simply a
       findnext with some initialization overhead: findfirst has to
       locate the directory in which findnext is to iterate, and
       initialize the SDB state to 'point to' the first entry. It
       then gets that first entry, using findnext. ffirst() does
       initialization, and fnext() is the "workhorse." */
    fnext();

    /* To mimic DOS behavior, a findfirst that finds no matching entry
       returns an error 2 (file not found), whereas a subsequent findnext
       that finds no matching entry should return error 18 (no more
       files). Having just done the embedded fnext(), we need to turn any
       error return value into what is appropriate for ffirst() */
    if (r.ax == 18) r.ax = 2;
    }

DIRREC_PTR  dirrec_ptr;          /* ptr to 1st found dir entry area in SDA */

/* Get next directory entry that matches specified mask, continuing
   from the supplied starting position (from the previous find) */
extern int find_next_entry(char far* mask, uchar attr_mask,
    char far* filename, uchar far * attr_ptr, ulong far* file_time_ptr,
    uint far* start_sec_ptr, long far* file_size_ptr,
    uint far* dir_sector_ptr, int far* dir_entryno_ptr);
void fnext(void)                     /* FindNext  - subfunction 1Ch */
    {
    if (! find_next_entry(srchrec_ptr->srch_mask,
            srchrec_ptr->attr_mask, dirrec_ptr->file_name,
```

```
        &dirrec_ptr->file_attr, &dirrec_ptr->file_time,
        &dirrec_ptr->start_sector, &dirrec_ptr->file_size,
        &srchrec_ptr->dir_sector, &srchrec_ptr->dir_entry_no))
    fail(18);
}
```

Aside from some special handling for volume labels, Find First calls get_dir_start_sector() (not shown; see PHANTOM.C on disk) to locate the requested file. If the file is located, ffirst() fills in the first Search Data Block in the SDA.

We're looking at ffirst() because, as you saw in Listing 8-32, the opnfil() function in Phantom internally calls ffirst() to locate files. Having called ffirst() to locate the requested file to open, opnfil() proceeds to do the actual "open," which involves nothing more than setting the correct fields in the uninitialized SFT entry that DOS passes in ES:DI. Phantom's opnfil() calls fill_sft() and init_sft() to initialize the SFT, using the SDB (srchrec_ptr) filled in by ffirst(), and the directory entry (dirrec_ptr) filled in by fnext() (see the comments to Listing 8-33 to see why ffirst() calls fnext()). The fill_sft() and init_sft() functions are shown in Listing 8-34.

Listing 8-34: PHANTOM.C fill_sft() and init_sft()

```
#define     FREE_SECTOR_CHAIN(sec)  \
    while ((sec) != 0xFFFF) (sec) = set_next_sector((sec), 0)
extern ulong dos_ftime(void);    // call 2F/120D
void fill_sft(SFTREC_PTR p, int use_found_1, int truncate)
    {
    _fmemcpy(p->file_name, fcbname_ptr, 11);
    if (use_found_1)
        {
        p->file_attr = dirrec_ptr->file_attr;
        if (truncate)
            {
            FREE_SECTOR_CHAIN(dirrec_ptr->start_sector);
            p->start_sector = 0xFFFF;
            p->file_time = dos_ftime(); // includes date; calls 2F/120D
            p->file_size = 0L;
            }
        else
            {
            p->start_sector = dirrec_ptr->start_sector;
            p->file_time = dirrec_ptr->file_time;
            p->file_size = dirrec_ptr->file_size;
            }
        p->dir_sector = srchrec_ptr->dir_sector;
        p->dir_entry_no = (uchar) srchrec_ptr->dir_entry_no;
        }
    else
        {
        p->file_attr = (uchar) *stack_param_ptr;   /* Attr is top of stack */
        p->file_time = dos_ftime();
        p->start_sector = 0xffff;
        p->file_size = 0;
        p->dir_sector = srchrec_ptr->dir_sector;
        p->dir_entry_no = 0xff;
        }
    }
extern void set_sft_owner(SFTREC_PTR sft);   // call 2F/120C
void init_sft(SFTREC_PTR p)
    {
    /* Initialize the supplied SFT entry. Note the modifications to the open
       mode word in the SFT. If bit 15 is set when we receive it, it is an
       FCB open, and requires the Set SFT Owner internal DOS function to be
```

```
                      called. We don't understand this, but this is what MSCDEX does. */
             if (p->open_mode & 0x8000)
                      p->open_mode |= 0x00F0;       // File is being opened via FCB
             else
                      p->open_mode &= 0x000F;

             // Mark file as being on network drive, unwritten to
             p->dev_info_word = (uint) (0x8040 | (uint) our_drive_no);
             p->file_pos = 0;
             p->rel_sector = 0xffff;
             p->abs_sector = 0xffff;
             p->dev_drvr_ptr = NULL;

             if(p->open_mode & 0x8000)    // File is being opened via FCB
                      set_sft_owner(p);    // Call 2F/120C
             }
```

The fill_sft() and init_sft() functions set fields in the SFT from a variety of sources:

- As noted, some SFT fields are set from the first found directory entry in the SDA (dirrec_ptr) and the first Search Data Block in the SDA (srchrec_ptr), which are themselves set by ffirst() and fnext().
- The SFT file time and date (combined into file_time) is set using DOS internal function INT 2Fh AX=120Dh (dos_ftime()).
- The SFT dev_info_word is set based on our_drive_no and the magic number 0x8040, which indicates a remote file (bit 15) that has not been written to (bit 6).
- The SFT open_mode is fiddled with in an odd, only semi-understood way for FCBs (bit 15 in the open mode indicates an FCB Open).
- For an FCB Open, init_sft() calls set_sft_owner(), which is a C wrapper around INT 2Fh AX=120Ch. Among other things, this DOS internal function uses the current PSP to set the SFT owner field.

For a redirector, there are three SFT field types: those fields (such as the above) that the redirector sets that that DOS uses, those fields that DOS leaves alone for the redirector's own internal use (see DOSSTRUC.SCR, Listing 8-24), and those fields that DOS sets.

When Phantom's opnfil() returns, the result is a filled-in SFT entry. As you saw in Listing 8-30, many of the fields set up in opnfil(), such as p->file_pos and p->start_sector, are subsequently used in readfil(). Of course, these SFT fields are also changed by other DOS functions, such as Write and Lseek.

Handling Chdir   Having looked at how the Phantom handles file I/O, let us briefly examine directory management. How is the CD (change directory) command implemented?

When a program issues an INT 21h AH=3Bh (Change Directory) on a redirector drive (a drive whose CDS has the network bit set), DOS generates an INT 2Fh AX=1105h. In the Phantom, this is handled by the cd() function, shown in all its glory in Listing 8-35.

Listing 8-35: PHANTOM.C cd() (INT 2Fh AX=1105h)

```
char far *  filename_ptr;        /* ptr to 1st filename area in SDA */
char far *  current_path;        /* ptr to current path in CDS */
void cd(void)                    /* Change Directory - subfunction 05h */
    {
    /* Special case for root */
    if ((*filename_ptr != '\\') || (*(filename_ptr + 1)))
        {
        /* can't make directory with * or ? in name */
        if (contains_wildcards(fcbname_ptr)) { fail(3); return; }

        *srch_attr_ptr = 0x10;  // look for directory
        ffirst();   // calls fnext(), which sets dirrec_ptr
```

```
    if (r.ax || (! (dirrec_ptr->file_attr & 0x10))) { fail(3); return; }
    }
  _fstrcpy(current_path, filename_ptr);
}
```

Well, gosh, CD hardly does anything but call ffirst() to verify that the specified directory string is valid and then blast the string into the current CDS. This makes sense. If you were to use a debugger to manually edit the CDS in memory, it would change your current directory, so conversely the DOS Change Directory function does little more than edit the CDS.

Handling Mkdir   But how do directories come into existence in the first place, so that the call to ffirst() in Listing 8-35 can find them? DOS directories are, of course, created with the MD command (Make Directory). This command calls INT 21h AH=39h (Mkdir), which in turn, for a redirector drive, calls INT 2Fh AX=1103h (you saw this in an earlier code fragment from a disassembly of DOS). In the Phantom, this is handled by the md() function, shown in Listing 8-36.

Listing 8-36: PHANTOM.C md() (INT 2Fh AX=1103h)

```
#define put_sector(sec, buf)          \
    xms_copy_fm_real(xms_handle, (ulong) SECTOR_SIZE * (sec), \
        SECTOR_SIZE, (uchar far *) (buf))

void md(void)                          /* Make Directory - subfunction 03h */
{
    /* special case for root */
    if ((*filename_ptr=='\\') && (! *(filename_ptr+1))) { fail(5); return; }

    if (contains_wildcards(fcbname_ptr)) { fail(3); return; }

    *srch_attr_ptr = 0x3f;             // 0x3F = everything
    ffirst();                          // if ffirst() succeeds,
    if (r.ax == 0) { fail(5); return; }   //    directory already exists!
    if (r.ax != 2) return;             // we WANT error 2 ("not found")
    // if any component part of path is wrong, we'll return error 3

    /* Although we initialize a directory sector, we actually don't need to,
        since we do not create . or .. entries. This is because
        a redirector never receives requests for . or .. in Chdir - DOS
        resolves the absolute path before we get it. If you want to
        see dots in DIR listings, create directory entries for them after
        put_sectors. But then you must take account of them in Rmdir. */
    last_sector = 0xffff;
    memset(sector_buffer, 0, SECTOR_SIZE);
    if (!(dirrec_ptr->start_sector=next_free_sector())) { fail(5); return; }
    set_next_sector(dirrec_ptr->start_sector, 0xFFFF);
    last_sector = dirrec_ptr->start_sector;
    if (! put_sector(dirrec_ptr->start_sector, &sector_buffer))
        { fail(5); return; }    // access denied

    /* Finally, create entry for this directory: srchrec_ptr and
        dirrec_ptr were set in fnext, called from ffirst */
    if (! create_dir_entry(&srchrec_ptr->dir_sector, NULL, fcbname_ptr, 0x10,
        dirrec_ptr->start_sector, 0, dos_ftime())))  // listing 8-37
        { fail(5); return; }    // access denied
    succeed();
}
```

When you MD on one of its drives, Phantom first has to run your new directory string through a series of tests:

- Have you tried to create a root directory? (error 5 = access denied)
- Does the string contain wildcards? (3 = path not found)
- Does the path already exist? (access denied)

At first, it may look strange that md() calls ffirst() and, if ffirst() succeeds (ax == 0), md() *fails*. But if you're creating a new directory, it cannot already exist, so for md() to succeed, the ffirst() call must fail. Normally one looks for something in hopes of finding it. Here, md() look for the directory in the hopes of *not* finding it. The md() function can only proceed if and only if ffirst() returns error 2 (file not found).

On the other hand, if there are multiple path components, all the higher level component parts must exist. For example, for an MD \FOO\BAR\BAZ to succeed, both FOO and FOO\BAR must already exist. If they don't, md() fails with error code 3 returned from ffirst(). The md() function can only proceed if ffirst() returns error 2 (file not found).

At this point, md() can go ahead and make the directory, which basically involves some sector manipulation. (If this were DOS rather than the Phantom, it would of course manipulate clusters rather than sectors.) As seen in md(), the steps involve getting a free sector, setting its FAT entry (next-sector pointer) to 0FFFFh, writing the sector to disk, and finally creating the entry for the new directory in its parent directory.

It isn't immediately obvious from md() how the new entry is plugged into the parent directory, that is, how MD \FOO\BAR would end up smacking an entry for BAR into FOO's directory. The very end of the function calls create_dir_entry() to create this directory entry, but it isn't clear how md() locates the parent directory into which to plug it. As usual in the Phantom, the answer lies in the ffirst/fnext engine. Yes, md() calls ffirst() to ensure that the target directory doesn't already exist, but this isn't the only reason; ffirst/fnext also implicitly locate the new directory's parent.

Given the location of the new directory's parent directory, md() creates the new directory entry by calling create_dir_entry(). As shown in Listing 8-37, this function walks through a directory, looking for an unused or deleted entry. If a free entry can't be found in the current directory sector, create_dir_entry() uses the FAT to find the next directory sector. If there isn't a next directory sector, create_dir_entry() calls next_free_sector() to create one. This new directory sector (assuming it can be allocated) needs to be linked in the FAT to the current one; this FAT link is made by set_next_sector(), also shown in Listing 8-37.

Listing 8-37: PHANTOM.C create_dir_entry() and set_next_sector()

```
int create_dir_entry(uint far *dir_sector_ptr,
    uchar far * dir_entryno_ptr, char far* filename, uchar file_attr,
    uint start_sector, long file_size, ulong file_time)
    {
    uint next_sector, dir_sector = *dir_sector_ptr;
    DIRREC* dr = (DIRREC*) &sector_buffer;
    int i;

    for (;;)
        {
        if (dir_sector != last_sector)
            {
            if (! get_sector(dir_sector, sector_buffer))
                return FALSE;
            else
                last_sector = dir_sector;
            }
        for (i = 0; i < DIRREC_PER_SECTOR; i++)
            {
            if (dr[i].file_name[0] && (dr[i].file_name[0] != (char) 0xE5))
                continue;   // looking for unused or deleted entry
            _fmemcpy(dr[i].file_name, filename, 11);
            dr[i].file_attr = file_attr;
            dr[i].file_time = file_time;    // includes date
            dr[i].file_size = file_size;
            dr[i].start_sector = start_sector;
            *dir_sector_ptr = dir_sector;
```

```
            if (dir_entryno_ptr) *dir_entryno_ptr = (uchar) i;
            return put_sector(dir_sector, &sector_buffer);
            }
        // no free dir entry: get next, or allocate new
        if ((next_sector = next_FAT_sector(dir_sector)) == 0xFFFF)
            {
            if (! (next_sector = next_free_sector()))
                return FALSE;
            set_next_sector(dir_sector, next_sector);
            set_next_sector(next_sector, 0xFFFF);
            }
        dir_sector = next_sector;
        }
    }

uint    FAT_page[FATPAGE_SIZE]; /* buffer for FAT entries */
int     cur_FAT_page = -1;      /* index of FAT page in buffer */
int     FAT_page_dirty = FALSE; /* Has current FAT page been updated */
uint    free_sectors;          /* unallocated sectors on XMS disk */

/* Checks that the page of FAT entries for the supplied sector is in
    the buffer. If it isn't, go get it, but write back the currently
    buffered page first if it has been updated. */
extern int check_FAT_page(uint abs_sector);

/* Update the FAT entry for this sector to reflect the next sector
    in the chain for the current file/directory */
uint set_next_sector(uint abs_sector, uint next_sector)
    {
    uint save_sector;

    if (! check_FAT_page(abs_sector)) return 0;

    save_sector = FAT_page[abs_sector - (cur_FAT_page * FATPAGE_SIZE)];
    FAT_page[abs_sector - (cur_FAT_page * FATPAGE_SIZE)] = next_sector;
    if (save_sector != next_sector)
        {
        FAT_page_dirty = TRUE;
        if (! save_sector)        free_sectors--;
        else if (! next_sector) free_sectors++;
        }
    return save_sector;
    }
```

Assuming create_dir_entry() has found or created a free directory entry, it initializes the directory using the function's parameters (filename, file_attr, start_sector, and so on). Finally, the directory sector is written back to disk using put_sector(), a macro that calls xms_copy_fm_real(). As with xms_copy_to_real(), this is a C wrapper around XMS function 0Bh (Move Extended Memory Block). In the Phantom XMS RAM disk, "writing" a sector involves a copy from conventional (real mode) memory to XMS, whereas "reading" a sector involves a copy from XMS to conventional memory.

While the creation of a directory entry in Listing 8-37 is unexceptional, it still helps to examine the code. Earlier in this chapter, we used directory entries without giving much thought to how fields such as a file's starting sector come to be there in the first place. In create_dir_entry() and many other parts of Phantom, you can view the same structures from the operating system's viewpoint (yes, redirectors are basically part of the operating system).

This completes our trace through the Phantom code. Again, complete source code is available on disk as \UNDOC2\CHAP8\PHANTOM.C.

Differences Between DOS Versions

Phantom works with DOS versions from 3.10, when Microsoft introduced the redirector interface, through to DOS 6.0. The interface has changed little in that time, except in one or two important areas. Perhaps the most predictable change is that some subfunctions have been added to cater to new functions added to the INT 21h interface.

In DOS 4.0, for example, the Extended Open (6Ch) function was introduced to make all types of file opens available through one call. At that time, a corresponding new redirector interface subfunction number (2Eh) was added to handle Extended Open. The SDA also changed with DOS 4.0, and, as seen in Listing 8-24, SPOP_ACTION, SPOP_MODE, and SPOP_ATTR fields were added to support the special open functionality.

Another subfunction number introduced with DOS 4.0 was 2Dh. Some of the DOS internal commands use the (also undocumented) DOS function 57h, which appears to trigger 2Dh at the redirector interface. However, both DOS function 57h and the redirector subfunction 2Dh are among those DOS 4.0 calls that disappear in later DOS versions, so we won't worry about them further. The following redirector specification quite deliberately writes off anything specific to DOS 4.0 as a dead-end.

The Network Redirector Specification

The following table presents the known redirector subfunctions, with usage, parameters, and notes. Remember that DOS merely defines this specification and that any given redirector must supply the actual functions that meet this specification.

```
Subfunction 00h
Installation Check
Inputs:      None
Outputs:     AL = 00h not installed, OK to install
             AL = 01h not installed, not OK to install
             AL = FFh installed, OK to install
```

1. A redirector should call this subfunction at initialization and should not load if the subfunction returns 01h in AL. If it returns 00h, or FFh, it is OK to load. These two values allow a redirector to opt not to load if another redirector is already present. Once installed, the redirector should respond to other redirectors that call this subfunction, normally with FFh in AL unless there is a reason to disallow subsequent redirectors to load, in which case the redirector should set AL to 01h.

2. A redirector should always handle this call. This convention means that it is up to the most recently-loaded redirector to decide whether any further redirectors may be loaded. (You can see this by taking the INTCHAIN program from Chapter 6: run INTCHAIN 2F/1100, and notice that the most recently-loaded redirector takes the call.) Again, the whole issue of chaining redirectors is complicated.

3. MSCDEX checks for a previous instance of itself by pushing 0DADAh on the stack before calling INT 2Fh AX=1100h. After return from the INT 2Fh, it tests if the top of the stack is still 0DADAh. If not (i.e., the INT 2Fh handler has changed 0DADAh to something else), it concludes that MSCDEX is already loaded and exits instead of going TSR. Meanwhile, the MSCDEX handler for subfunction 0 sets the word at the top of the stack to 0ADADh. Note what David Markun calls the "slack" in this interface: the resident code sets to ADAD but the prospectively-resident code tests only for non-DADA. At least one program that impersonates MSCDEX (Lotus CD/Networker 4.x and 5.x) looks for DADA on the stack and changes it, if and only if there was a genuine MSCDEX that loaded before CD/Networker. Networker does not change DADA to ADAD, but instead merely increments it, allowing a caller to detect that something special is going on.

```
Subfunction 01h
Remove Directory
Inputs:      SDA.FN1 = fully qualified directory name
Outputs:     Carry set, error code in AX if error encountered
```

1. The redirector should either compare the supplied CDS_PTR pointer in the SDA with the address of the CDS for one of its drives or, preferably, the referenced CDS contents with the contents of its own CDS to determine if the call is intended for its drive.
2. The redirector should ensure that it doesn't remove the *current* directory by comparing SDA.FN1 with the current path in the CDS; attempts to remove the current directory should be failed with error code 16.

```
Subfunction 03h
Make Directory
Inputs:          SDA.FN1 = fully qualified directory name
Outputs:         Carry set, error code in AX if error encountered
```

See note 1 for subfunction 01h.

```
Subfunction 05h
Change Current Directory
Inputs:          SDA.FN1 = fully qualified directory name
Outputs:         Carry set, error code in AX if error encountered
```

1. See note 1 for subfunction 01h.
2. The redirector must update the CURR_PATH field of the CDS for the drive.

```
Subfunction 06h
Close File
Inputs:          ES:DI -> SFT for file to close
Outputs:         Carry set, error code in AX if error encountered
                 SFT completed if no error
```

1. The redirector should use the bottom 6 bits of the DEV_INFO field of the SFT pointed to by ES:DI to determine whether the call refers to a file on one of its drive numbers (0 = A:, 1 = B:, and so forth). (There may be an issue involving the DPB field within the SFT.)
2. It should also decrement C_HANDLES (first field) in the SFT and create or update directory information for the file if it was opened for writing (bit 0 or 1 set). Failing to decrement the SFT handle count creates orphaned files. The redirector can decrement the handle count directly (sft->handle_count--) or by calling INT 2Fh AX=1208h.

```
Subfunction 07h
Commit File
Inputs:          ES:DI -> SFT for file to commit (flush buffers)
Outputs:         Carry set, error code in AX if error encountered
```

See note 1 for subfunction 6.

```
Subfunction 08h
Read from File
Inputs:          ES:DI -> SFT for file to read from
                 CX = count of bytes to read
                 SDA.CURR_DTA -> user buffer to read data into
Outputs:         Carry set, error code in AX if error encountered
                 if no error, CX = bytes actually read
                 CX = 0 to indicate end of file
                 SFT updated
```

1. See note 1 for subfunction 6.
2. The redirector should also update the F_POS field in the SFT.
3. Don't forget to set CX = 0 to indicate EOF.

```
Subfunction 09h
Write to File
```

```
Inputs:          ES:DI -> SFT for file to write to
                 CX = count of bytes to write
                 SDA.CURR_DTA -> user buffer from which to write data
Outputs:         Carry set, error code in AX if error encountered
                 if no error, CX = bytes actually written
                 SFT updated
```

1. See note 1 for subfunction 6.
2. The redirector should also update the F_POS and F_SIZE fields in the SFT.
3. The call should fail with access denied (5) if the file was opened for reading only (bits 0 and 1 both zero).
4. If CX is 0, truncate the file to the current file position.

```
Subfunction 0Ah
Lock/Unlock Region of File
Inputs:          ES:DI -> SFT for file
                 CX:DX = region offset (DOS 3.0.X)
                 SI = high word of region size (DOS 3.X)
                 Word at top of stack = low word of region size (DOS 3.X)
                 BL = 0 (Lock) or 1 (Unlock) (DOS 4+)
                 DS:DX -> LOCKREC for region to lock (DOS 4.0+)
Outputs:         Carry set, error code in AX if error encountered
```

1. See note 1 for subfunction 6.
2. The redirector is expected to resolve lock conflicts. Loading SHARE has no effect on a redirector. The redirector must do all arbitration itself (this is obvious in the case of a true network redirector, which must keep all state at the server).
3. This function only provides locking in DOS 3.1-3.3, with parameters in registers and on the stack. Both locking and unlocking are achieved through this subfunction in DOS 4.0 and above, with parameters in the LOCKREC structure.

```
Subfunction 0Bh
Unlock Region of File
Inputs:          ES:DI -> SFT for file
                 CX:DX = region offset
                 SI = high word of region size
                 Word at top of stack = low word of region size
Outputs:         Carry set, error code in AX if error encountered
```

1. See note 1 for subfunction 6.
2. The redirector is expected to resolve lock conflicts.
3. This subfunction is only called in DOS 3.1-3.3 and is superceded by subfunction 0Ah BL=1 in DOS 4.0 and higher.

```
Subfunction 0Ch
Get Disk Space
Inputs:          ES:DI -> CDS for drive
Outputs:         AL = Sectors per cluster
                 BX = Total clusters
                 CX = Bytes per sector
                 DX = Number of available clusters
```

1. The redirector should either compare the supplied CDS pointer in ES:DI (*not* in the SDA as with subfunction 01h) with the address of the CDS for its drive or, preferably, the CDS contents with the contents of its own CDS, to determine if the call is intended for its drive(s).
2. The units of sector and cluster are DOS arbitrary and may not be appropriate to the redirector's underlying storage. It is sufficient to return values such that (AL*CX*BX)

reflects the size in bytes of the drive as the redirector wants it reported, and that (AL*CX*DX) reflects the amount of free space in bytes that the redirector wants reported as available. The register usage here limits the size of redirector drives to 1,024 gigabytes.

```
Subfunction 0Eh
Set File Attributes
Inputs:          SDA.FN1 = Fully qualified filename
                 SDA.CURR_CDS -> CDS for drive with file
                 Word at top of stack = New file attributes
Outputs:         Carry set, error code in AX if error encountered
```

See note for subfunction 01h.

```
Subfunction 0Fh
Get File Attributes
Inputs:          SDA.FN1 = Fully qualified filename
                 SDA.CURR_CDS -> CDS for drive with file
Outputs:         Carry set, error code in AX if error encountered
                 If no error, AX = file attributes
                 BX:DI = file size
```

1. See note for subfunction 01h.
2. INT 21h AH=23h (Get File Size) depends on the BX:DI file size return value.

```
Subfunction 11h
Rename File
Inputs:          SDA.FN1 = Current fully qualified filespec
                 SDA.FN2 = New fully qualified filename
                 SDA.CURR_CDS -> CDS for drive with file
Outputs:         Carry set, error code in AX if error encountered
```

1. See note for subfunction 01h.
2. The redirector can use the SRCH_BLK, FOUND_FILE, REN_SRCFILE, and REN_FILE fields of the SDA as a workspace for iterating over source and target filespecs.

```
Subfunction 13h
Delete File
Inputs:          SDA.FN1 = Fully qualified filespec
                 SDA.CURR_CDS -> CDS for drive with file
Outputs:         Carry set, error code in AX if error encountered
```

1. See note for subfunction 01h.
2. The redirector can use the SRCH_BLK and FOUND_FILE fields of the SDA as workspace for iterating over source and target filespecs.

```
Subfunction 16h
Open Existing File
Inputs:          SDA.FN1 = Fully qualified filename
                 SDA.OPEN_MODE = Open mode for file
                 SDA.CURR_CDS -> CDS for drive with file
                 ES:DI -> Uninitialized SFT for the file
Outputs:         Carry set, error code in AX if error encountered
                 SFT completed if no error
```

1. See note for subfunction 01h.
2. The redirector should not set the C_HANDLES field in the SFT. DOS maintains this field itself.
3. Bit 15 of the open mode will be set for an FCB open.

```
Subfunction 17h
Create/Truncate File
Inputs:         SDA.FN1 = Fully qualified filename
                ES:DI -> Uninitialized SFT for the file
                SDA.CURR_CDS -> CDS for drive with file
                Word at top of stack = File attribute for file
Outputs:        Carry set, error code in AX if error encountered
                SFT completed if no error
```

1. See note for subfunction 01h.
2. INT 21h AH=5Bh (Create New File) calls this subfunction. For 5Bh to fail if the file already exists, subfunction 17h must be able to communicate the pre-existence of a file. It appears this is done by *changing* the value at the top of the stack.
3. The redirector should not set the C_HANDLES field in the SFT. DOS maintains this field itself.

```
Subfunction 18h
Create File without CDS
Input and Output: Identical to subfunction 17h (see above)?
```

Calling INT 21h AH=5Bh (Create New File) with a UNC filename such as "\\FOO\BAR" triggers a DOS call to subfunction 18h. It is similar to subfunction 17h, but is only called when the current CDS pointer in the SDA has an offset of 0FFFFh (see also subfunction 19h). This call may have been provided to support LAN Manager named pipes.

```
Subfunction 19h
Find First without CDS
Input and Output: Identical to subfunction 1Bh (see below).
```

Like subfunction 18h, this allows redirectors to manage virtual files on drives without a CDS. DOS calls this function in its Find First code when the current CDS has an offset of 0FFFFh:

```
FDC8:6C22    C43EA205         LES DI,[05A2]    ; current CDS
FDC8:6C26    83FFFF           CMP DI,-01       ; offset = 0FFFFh
FDC8:6C29    7506             JNZ DO_2F_111B   ; do regular redir call
FDC8:6C2B    B81911           MOV AX,1119      ; do no-CDS redir call
FDC8:6C2E    CD2F             INT 2F
FDC8:6C30    C3               RET
                         DO_2F_111B:
FDC8:6C31    26F745430080     TEST Word Ptr ES:[DI+43],8000 ; CDS network bit
FDC8:6C37    7406             JZ no_redir
FDC8:6C39    B81B11           MOV AX,111B
FDC8:6C3C    CD2F             INT 2F
FDC8:6C3E    C3               RET
                         no_redir:
                             ; ...
```

This call (and thus the CDS offset == 0FFFFh condition) can be triggered with a command such as "DIR \\FOO\BAR".

UNC Filespecs

Tim Farley

When a redirector is installed that supports the non-CDS calls, you can use UNC-style filespecs directly in DOS calls. For instance, you could DIR \\SERVER1\VOL1*.* to search the root drive of the volume VOL1 on server SERVER1. Even though it is a front-end hook and not a redirector, the Novell NetWare shell (NETX) supports this behavior. You can also do this under many of the networks which are redirectors, including Artisoft's LANtastic. NetWare Lite 1.0, on the other hand, doesn't support a DIR of a UNC filespec.

The non-CDS calls can help if you know the exact network name of a file you need to access but don't want to set up a CDS entry for a fake DOS drive on which to access that file. Some of Novell's own utilities such as LOGIN.EXE use this trick.

Understanding UNC filespecs is crucial to writing a proper network redirector, especially when it comes to implementing the INT 21h AH=5Eh and AH=5Fh calls. Microsoft's *LAN Manager's Programmer's Reference* briefly discusses UNC.

```
Subfunction 1Bh
Find First Matching File
Inputs:        SDA.FN1 = Fully qualified filespec for search
               SDA.SDB = Unitialized Search Data Block
               SDA.FOUND_FILE -> Directory info buffer for found file
               SDA.SRCH_ATTR = Search attribute mask for file
Outputs:       Carry set, error code in AX if error encountered
               If no error, SDB initialized
```

See note 1 for subfunction 01h.

```
Subfunction 1Ch
Find Next Matching File
Inputs:        SDA.SDB = Search Data Block from last Find operation
               SDA.FOUND_FILE -> Directory info buffer for found file
Outputs:       Carry set, AX = 12h if no more files
```

The redirector should use the bottom 6 bits (mask 0x3F) of the DRIVE_NUM field of the SRCH_BLK field of the SDA to determine whether the call continues a previous search on its drive number (0 = A:, 1 = B:, and so forth).

But the above is probably wrong. According to David Markun,

> The above logic (and the corresponding mask-with-3Fh code) will lead to flaky results under IBM Lan Server— you may into get a situation where the Phantom will claim a findnext whose findfirst was handled by Lan Server. MSCDEX does not have this problem because it explicitly tests bit 6 (0040h) to be sure it is on before claiming the call. Masking with 3Fh will ignore that bit and thus mistakenly claim some calls. For findnext, cooperating redirectors store a 1-based drive in the low 5 bits of the SDB driveletter field. (Lan Server is an uncooperating redirector that uses the low 5 bits in some other fashion, thus requiring cooperating redirectors to distinguish themselves with bit 6 set). Cooperating redirectors identify themselves by setting bit 6 in the drive letter; this is the same bit that turns a 1-based drive into a drive letter A-Z.

```
Subfunction 1Dh
Close all Files for Process
```

To implement this function, the redirector must maintain a record of all files opened and by which processes on which machines. This is a DOS broadcast, called even if no drive in the CDS has the network bit set. DOS calls this function immediately after using INT 21h AH=3Eh to close all of a terminating process's open files. The current PSP still points to the terminating process.

```
Subfunction 1Eh
Do Redirection
Inputs:        Word at top of stack = Command to execute (e.g., 5F02h)
               Other inputs depend on command to execute
Outputs:       Carry set, error code in AX if error encountered
               Other outputs depend on command to execute
```

This is a back end to INT 21h AH=5Fh. For example, if you want your redirector's drives to show up in an INT 21h AX=5F02h assign list (see NETDRV.C, Listing 8-15), then you need to implement this call. To determine is_call_for_us() for the AX=5F03h Make Network Connection call, use the UserVal in CX (see "Another Detection Method). LAN Manager also uses INT 21h AH=5Fh (see *Dr. Dobb's Journal*, April 1993).

```
Subfunction 1Fh
Printer Setup
Inputs:         Word at top of stack = Command to execute (e.g., 5E02h)
                Other inputs depend on command to execute
Outputs:        Carry set, error code in AX if error encountered
                Other outputs depend on command to execute
```

DOS calls this subfunction for INT 21h AH=5Eh, similar to the way that 2F/111E is the back-end to 21/5F.

```
Subfunction 20h
Flush All Disk Buffers
Inputs & Outputs:          Unknown.
```

This is a DOS broadcast: when the Reset Drive function (INT 21h AH=0Dh) is called, DOS calls INT 2Fh AX=1120h, even if no CDS has the network bit set.

```
Subfunction 21h
Seek From End of File
Inputs:         ES:DI -> SFT for file
                CX:DX = Offset relative to end of file to position to
Outputs:        Carry set, error code in AX if error encountered
                DX:AX = new file position
```

This function is almost never called in DOS 4.0 and higher, so don't depend on it to keep you informed of file-position changes. The redirector should always use the F_POS field in the SFT to determine the current file position at which to read or write. As seen in Chapter 6, given an INT 21h AH=42 lseek, DOS almost always fiddles directly with the SFT without calling the redirector. Subfunction 21h only gets called when a program uses method #2, move from end, and even then only for non-FCB opens when certain SHARE open-access flags permit write access. The conditions under which this subfunction are called are so specialized that it appears to have been a special-purpose hack.

```
Subfunction 22h
Process Termination Hook
Input:          DS = PSP of process about to terminate
```

Whenever a program exits, DOS issues this subfunction 22h broadcast. The following small INTRSPY script hooks this call to output a list of programs that have terminated:

```
intercept 2fh function 11h subfunction 22h
    on_entry output (ds-1:8->byte,asciiz,8) " (PSP " ds ") exiting"
```

This might help TSRs that must know when programs exit. Trapping subfunction 22h is far easier than hooking INT 21h, INT 20h and INT 27h, which is how a front-end hook would watch for process terminations.

```
Subfunction 23h
Qualify Path and Filename
Inputs:         DS:SI -> Unqualified filename
                ES:DI -> Buffer for fully qualified filename
Outputs:        Carry set, error code in AX if error encountered
```

DOS appears to supply a default name qualification function that does a very adequate job without support from a redirector. DOS appears to need the assistance of this redirector function only for some some special directory or filename translations. The output of this function, or of the DOS default routine, directly supplies the input for the directory and file subfunctions. This call is a DOS broadcast, made even if no redirector is running.

```
Subfunction 24h
Turn Off Remote Printer
```

Called by DOS 3.1+ kernel if subfunction 26h (below) returns carry set.

```
Subfunction 25h
Redirected Printer Mode
Inputs:       Word at top of stack = Command to execute (e.g., 5D07h)
              Other inputs depend on command to execute
Outputs:      Carry set, error code in AX if error encountered
              Other outputs depend on command to execute
```

DOS turns a call to INT 21h AX=5D07h (Get Redirected Printer Mode), AX=5D08h (Set Redirected Printer Mode), or AX=5D09h (Flush Redirected Printer Output) into a broadcast of subfunction 25h. Unless an INT 2Fh handler supports this subfunction, these INT 21h calls perform no action.

```
Subfunction 26h
Remote Printer Echo On/Off
Inputs:       ES:DI -> SFT for file handle 4 (stdprn)?
              ???
Outputs:      CF set on error
```

DOS calls this subfunction when print echoing (^P, ^PrtSc) changes state, and stdprn has bit 11 ("network spooler") of the device information word set in the SFT.

```
Subfunction 27h
Remote Copy
Inputs:       SI = Source file handle
              DI = Destination file handle
              DX:CX = Bytes to copy (from/to current seek positions)
              BX = 'NW' (574Eh) signature for NetWare
Outputs:      CF clear if successful, set if failed
              AX = Return code, if error
                  05h Access denied: No read rights or no write rights.
                  06h Invalid handle: One of the file handles is invalid.
                  0Bh Invalid format: Improper signature in BX.
                  11h Device not the same: Both files are not handled by
                      the redirector.
                  3Bh Unexpected network error.
              If successful, current file positions updated for both files
```

When implemented (it seems to be Novell specific), this function copies one file to another file, where both files are on the redirected drive. This can greatly reduce network traffic. This function does *not* rely on being called from within DOS and can therefore be called directly from an application. Unlike all other file access subfunctions, this function is passed file handles, not SFT pointers.

The Remote Copy subfunction appears to be supported in Netware 4.0, the beta documentation for which provided the basis for the above description. Microsoft LAN Manager has a similar NetRemoteCopy() function (INT 21h AX=5FA4h).

```
Subfunction 2Eh
Extended Open File (DOS 4+)
Inputs:       SDA.FN1 = Fully qualified filename
              ES:DI -> Uninitialized SFT for the file
              Word at top of stack = File attr for created/truncated file
              SDA.SPECOPEN_ACT = Action codes
              SDA.SPECOPEN_MODE = Open mode for file
Outputs:      Carry set, error code in AX if error encountered
              SFT completed if no error
              CX = result code
```

```
01h file opened
02h file created
03h file replaced (truncated)
```

1. See note for subfunction 01h.
2. DOS 4.0 introduced this function, to provide a unified interface to the functionality supplied by subfunctions 16h and 17h and to support DOS Function 6Ch.
3. The redirector should not set the C_HANDLES field in the SFT. DOS maintains this field itself.

There are other INT 2Fh AH=11h functions that are not part of the network redirector interface. For example, the LAN Manager API for DOS provides asynchronous named pipes using INT 2Fh AH=11h calls. For more information, see Michael Shiels, "The Undocumented LAN Manager and Named Pipe APIs for DOS and Windows," *Dr. Dobb's Journal*, April 1993 (this appeared in the *DDJ* "Undocumented Corner").

Using DOS Internal Functions

Because redirectors effectively become part of DOS, they have at their disposal many of the same functions that DOS itself uses internally. As we saw in Chapter 6, DOS uses INT 2Fh AH=12h to export many DOS internal functions. This interrupt-based interface was probably initially designed (or at least thrown together) for use by redirectors and presents a wealth of quite useful functions that are only accessible to redirectors and other in-DOS subsystems.

Phantom uses only three DOS internal DOS functions; and the only mandatory one is Set SFT Owner (INT 2Fh AX=120Ch). As stated above, one of the benefits of the redirector interface is that it hides, with one exception, the existence of the two file-access methods (FCB- vs. handle-based) available to DOS programs. The one exception is that, at file-open time, the redirector must call Set SFT Owner for FCB opens. Bit 15 set in the open-mode word in the SFT passed to the redirector open call (INT 2Fh AX=1116h; see above) indicates an FCB open. Failure to call this function in this situation leads to "FCB unavailable" errors.

Phantom also calls Get Date and Time (INT 2Fh AX=120Dh) to obtain the system date and time in directory format. It could equally well convert the BIOS timer tick-count value for the time, and the DD, MM, and YY-1980 fields of the SDA for the date to generate the necessary values for new directory and file time-stamping, but the DOS internal function is slightly simpler.

Finally, Phantom calls Check If Char Device (INT 2Fh AX=1223h) to detect file access to NUL, CON, and so on, which DOS does not filter adequately before passing control to a redirector. Without this check, Phantom would mistakenly let users create files with names such as NUL and CON.

The following is a list of the INT 2Fh AH=12h subfunctions that a foreign file system redirector might use. The entries do not describe usage in detail (see the Appendix or the Interrupt List on disk) but instead discuss why a redirector might want or not want to use the function.

- 06h - Invoke critical error

This is potentially a very important function for a redirector that relies on a physical, network, or other possibly error-prone medium. It triggers the mechanism that leads to invocation of the documented Int 24h critical error handler. There are two requirements for its proper use:

- Set the appropriate error class, locus, and suggested action. These are, happily, accessible in the ERR_LOCUS, ERR_CODE, ERR_ACTION and ERR_CLASS fields in the SDA.
- Create a dummy device driver header for the drive, and record its address in the DEVDRVR_PTR field of the SDA. This is required because DOS uses the device attributes word of the device driver associated with the error to decode the type of error message to display.

Errors generated during open, read, write, close and findfirst/findnext processing are candidates for critical error invocation. Because Phantom does not use an unreliable medium (in general a rash assumption about XMS, especially given well-known bugs in the XMS resize function), it has no need for critical error capabilities.

However, the code fragment in Listing 8-38 shows modifications that might be made to readfil() in PHANTOM.C if a failure at read time were possible. This code fragment assumes that read_data() now returns an int indicating success (non-zero) or failure (zero). This code is an alternate to the version of readfil() shown earlier, in Listing 8-30.

Listing 8-38: Alternate Version of readfil() to Handle Critical Errors

```c
// Possible returns from critical_error()
#define CRITERR_IGNORE      0
#define CRITERR_RETRY       1
#define CRITERR_ABORT       2    //ABORT returns control to DOS, not us
#define CRITERR_FAIL        3

uint sp_before_switch;          // save area for our sp

// This is the dummy device driver header to keep DOS happy at
// critical error invocation. In this case, the critical error message
// will be 'Error reading drive D:'. Change the dev_attr field value
// from 0 to 0x8000 to generate 'Error reading from PHANTOM'
structure {
    long    next_hdr;
    uint    dev_attr;
    uint    strat_entry, intr_entry;
    char    dev_name[8];
    } dummy_devhdr = {-1,0,0,0,{'P','H','A','N','T','O','M',' '};
//Set DOS extended error info.
void set_dos_extended_err(uint ax_val, uchar bl_val, uchar bh_val,
    uchar ch_val)
    {
    //  ax_val -- DOS extended error code.
    //  bh_val -- error class
    //  bl_val -- suggested action
    //  ch_val -- locus of error
    ((V3_SDA_PTR) sda_ptr)->err_code = ax_val;
    ((V3_SDA_PTR) sda_ptr)->err_action = bl_val;
    ((V3_SDA_PTR) sda_ptr)->err_class = bh_val;
    ((V3_SDA_PTR) sda_ptr)->err_locus = ch_val;
    ((V3_SDA_PTR) sda_ptr)->devdrvr_ptr = (void far *) &dummy_devhdr;
    }

//Invoke DOS critical error handler and get user
//  return code (Ignore, Retry, Abort, Fail).
int critical_error(uchar ah_val)
    {
    int ret;

    //Invoke critical error.
    _asm {
        mov ah, ah_val
        push bp
        push si
        push di
        mov di, 000Bh               // Read error
        mov bp, ds                  // BP:SI must point to our fake
        mov si, OFFSET dummy_devhdr //  device header.
        mov sp_before_switch, sp    //Save current stack pointer.
        cli
        mov ss, dos_ss              //Establish DOS's stack, which was
        mov sp, dos_sp              //  current when we got called.
        sti
```

```
            mov al, our_drive_no        //Driveletter
            push ax                     //Int 24h AX value goes on the stack
            mov ax, 1206h               //Invoke critical error.
            int 2Fh
            mov bx, ds                  //Restore our stack segment (same as DS)
            cli
            mov ss, bx
            mov sp, sp_before_switch    //  and stack pointer (which we saved).
            sti
            pop di
            pop si
            pop bp
            xor ah, ah
            mov ret, ax
            }
        return ret;
        }
    void readfil(void)                  // Read from File - subfunction 08h
        {
        SFTREC_PTR p = (SFTREC_PTR) MK_FP(r.es, r.di);

        if (p->open_mode & 1) { fail(5); return; }

        if ((p->file_pos + r.cx) > p->file_size)
            r.cx = (uint) (p->file_size - p->file_pos);

        if (! r.cx) return;

        /* Fill caller's buffer and update the SFT for the file */
        while (read_data(&p->file_pos, &r.cx,
                ((V3_SDA_PTR) sda_ptr)->current_dta,
                p->start_sector, &p->rel_sector, &p->abs_sector) == 0)
            {
            set_dos_extended_err(   0x001E,  // Error - Read fault
                                    0x04,    // Action - Orderly abort
                                    0x0B,    // Class - Media error
                                    0x05);   // Locus - Memory

            // call the user's critical error handler. This is interesting
            // because we are used to seeing critical error from the app's
            // point of view; here we see if from DOS's point of view.
            switch (critical_error(111110b)) //  0 -- 0 indicates read
                                             //  1,2 -- 11 indicates file error
                                             //  3 -- 1 indicates allow Fail
                                             //  4 -- 1 indicates allow Retry
                                             //  5 -- 1 indicates allow Ignore
                {
                case CRITERR_IGNORE: break;
                case CRITERR_FAIL: fail(2); return; // not reached
                case CRITERR_RETRY: break;
                default: break; // Impossible...
                }
            }
        }
```

If readfil() encounters an error, it first calls set_extended_err() to set the appropriate codes into the SDA; it then calls the critical_error() function with flags to indicate where the error occurred and what responses are to be allowed. These bits, together with the extended error, class, action, and locus values, are documented in the DOS programmer's reference for INT 21h AH=59h (Get Extended Error). The return from that function is the user's or application's response to the error.

Although CRITERR_ABORT is defined, we never receive control back if that is the selected response. DOS fails the application or command immediately after the Int 24h handler returns.

As a final note on critical errors, redirectors should use the INT 2Fh AH=05h interface to expand critical error messages. For example, MSCDEX uses this interface. There is a detailed discussion of this interface and other error-handling issues in Chapter 17 of Geoff Chappell's *DOS Internals*.

- 08h - Decrement SFT Reference Count

Redirector subfunction 6 (Close File) must decrement the SFT handle count to avoid creating orphaned files. INT 2Fh AX=1208h does just this. However, it is much more efficient to decrement the SFT reference count directly, rather than to call this function. For example, the following is lifted from the Phantom's clsfil() function:

```
SFTREC_PTR p = (SFTREC_PTR) MK_FP(r.es, r.di);
if (p->handle_count)          /* If handle count not 0, decrement it */
    --p->handle_count;
```

- 0Ah - Perform Critical Error Interrupt

This function is similar to the preferable function 06h. The function 0Ah version appears to need a DPB for the redirected drive (in general, redirector drives don't require DPBs).

- 0Bh - Signal Sharing Violation To User

Peer-to-peer DOS networks and SHARE.EXE use this function to signal that a command or application has attempted to open a file previously opened by FCB or with a sharing "deny." Its principal return is the value of the carry flag, indicating whether to retry the operation.

- 0Ch - Set SFT Owner (Set FCB Owner)

As discussed earlier, this is the one essential DOS internal call for a redirector. While DOS internally uses this call all the time, a redirector only needs it for FCB opens, so it is sometimes called Set FCB Owner. Clearly the function sets the specified SFT owner to the value of the current PSP, but it appears to do a good deal more than that. Based on the behavior of MSCDEX, a redirector may have to modify the open_mode before calling Set SFT Owner (see init_sft() in Listing 8-34 and set_sft_owner() in PHANTOM.C on disk).

- 0Dh - Get Date And Time

This useful function returns in AX:DX the current date:time in packed, DOS directory format. It can generate the timestamp for a new directory entry generated when, for example, a subdirectory is created, or when a newly created file is flushed or closed. Phantom uses this in fill_sft() (see Listing 8-34).

- 11h - Normalize ASCIZ Filename

This function translates a filename from an input buffer into an output buffer, turning forward slashes in the input buffer into backslashes in the output buffer and transferring all other characters unchanged.

- 16h - Get Address Of System File Table (SFT) Entry

This function takes an SFT entry *number* and converts it into an SFT *address*. The SFT entry number is contained in the JFT for a process at the index for the appropriate handle. Since almost all redirector functions get an SFT entry rather than a file handle, this function, together with function 20h, is only obviously useful to a redirector which supports Int 2Fh function 11h subfunction 27h (Remote Copy), which is passed file handles rather than SFT addresses.

- 18h - Get Caller's Registers

This is a potentially useful function to a redirector that wants to know more about the originating DOS call. It returns a pointer to the saved register contents upon entry to the DOS function dispatcher. See the lengthy discussion of this function in Chapter 6.

- 1Ah - Get File's Drive

Given a fully qualified filespec, this function separates the path from the drive letter and returns the drive number to which it refers. It could help a redirector that uses a standard DOS drive identification string, made up of the drive letter immediately followed by a colon. The is_call_for_us() function could use it. Phantom uses a distinctive drive identifier that disallows use of this unsophisticated function. To determine whether the path is relative to a specific drive and not to the default drive, subfunction 1Ah looks for a colon in the second character position. DOS uses it to parse paths at the INT 21h level.

- 1Eh - Compare Filenames

This function compares filenames, ignoring case and treating forward and back slashes as equivalent. It could help if the redirector's underlying file system has a UNIX flavor. (Most of the rest of DOS also treats / and \ as equivalent. You can even pass forward slashes to INT 21h, as do some programs such as PKZIP.)

- 1Fh - Make Current Directory Structure Invalid

This function invalidates the CDS referenced by the DRIVE_CDSPTR field of the SDA. To achieve this, it simply moves 0 to the FLAGS field of the CDS entry. If a redirector encounters a fatal error, this function provides a simple way of invalidating its drive, since DRIVE_CDSPTR is already appropriately set.

- 20h - Get Job File Table Entry

This function, which, together with subfunction 16h, provides a mechanism to convert from a file handle belonging to the current process to an SFT entry address, only helps a redirector that supports Int 2Fh function 11h subfunction 27h (Remote Copy).

- 22h - Set Extended Error Info

This subfunction provides a means for modifying the DOS internal associations between an extended error code and its associated class action and locus fields. Phantom sets this information directly into the SDA, which appears to be more reliable than subfunction 22h when more than one redirector is present on the machine. With subfunction 22h, one redirector might override modifications made by another. MSCDEX, however, uses this subfunction.

- 23h - Check If Character Device

This subfunction walks the device driver header chain searching for a character device with the name specified in the FCB_FN1 field of the SDA. Phantom uses this function to weed out and fail any calls that attempt to create a file or subdirectory with the same name as a character device such as CON or AUX. DOS filters out references to these only if no explicit path is included.

- 26h - Open File

This function, together with functions 27h, 28h, and 29h, has the useful capability of performing read-only file access from within a redirector. It is interesting and perhaps disappointing that there is no Write To File function in the group. (MSCDEX, which of course is read-only, uses these functions.) This provides the means to read configuration files on the fly. This function consumes an SFT entry and a JFT entry in the current PSP.

- 27h - Close File

Closes a file belonging to the current PSP. This might be a file opened using function 26h.

- 28h - Move File Pointer

Performs a seek within the specified file, which belongs to the current process, and which may have been opened using function 26h.

- 29h - Read From File

Performs a read from the specified file, which belongs to the current process, and which may have been opened with subfunction 26h. This call modifies the CURR_DTA field of the SDA. If the call is made from within a redirector read or write call, the redirector should save the current contents of the CURR_DTA field before this call and restore it afterwards.

The Future of the DOS File System

As we said at the beginning of this section, Microsoft introduced the redirector interface in DOS 3.10. In DOS 6.0, it is still in place, little changed, and Phantom works in prerelease versions of DOS 7.0 from Chicago too.

However, the redirector's future looks a little confused. Microsoft, with the introduction of Windows for Workgroups, has moved from the REDIR.EXE TSR over to a Windows virtual device driver, VREDIR.386, to implement their redirector. This redirector traditionally translates between the redirector interface and the Server Message Block (SMB) protocol, on which many PC peer-to-peer networks are based. On the other hand, in other network-related areas of Microsoft development, there is apparently a move away from the redirector interface, presumably because of the relatively poor level of internal expertise in that area (or perhaps because of the increasing length of the INT 2Fh chain), toward an INT 21h call intercept/replacement strategy that we advised against at the beginning of the section!

The giant of the network operating system marketplace, Novell, has been taking the opposite approach. In NetWare 4.0, the workstation component (NETx.COM/EXE in previous versions) consists of several modules, loaded by VLM.EXE, which is the Virtual Loadable Module manager. One of the modules that it manages is REDIR.VLM, a full redirector. For backward compatibility, Novell provides NETx.VLM, which provides the traditional INT 21h replacement/enhancement functionality (see Chapter 4).

The difference between these two approaches suggests several possible alternative views. The most pessimistic is that Microsoft is in the process of phasing out the redirector interface, that VREDIR.386 simply represents a platform for increasing the support for Windows and networking, and that it will soon host an entirely different file system interface. This would imply that Novell (and the authors!) simply does not realize this and has potentially wasted a lot of time and development cost on a lame duck.

It is possible that Microsoft is indeed wary of encouraging use of the redirector interface because of its rather murky past and backwater support status, but that it will continue to tolerate it. That view would endorse Novell's strategy of making workstation file system interface modular, but it still leaves uncertainty.

One might, from a more optimistic perspective, conclude that the redirector interface is not only to remain a fixture, but that, through guesswork or information, Novell expects the level of support for it to increase.

All of this is part of larger changes in the implementation of the DOS file system. Just as WfW includes VREDIR.386, Microsoft also has VFAT.386, a 32-bit protected mode Windows virtual device driver supporting the FAT file system. VFAT.386 is part of Microsoft's Chicago project (DOS 7.0, Windows 4), but it is appearing early in WfW 3.11, along with VREDIR, VSHARE, and other file system VxDs. As noted earlier, Chicago will also introduce an IFSMGR as the documented, improved, and approved way of writing installable file systems.

In addition to talking a lot about the FAT, directory, CDS, SFT, JFT, DPB, System FCBs, and so on, one central point emerges from this ridiculously lengthy chapter: The DOS file system isn't just for plain old disks anymore. Any file system is primarily a logical rather than a physical construct. Interfaces such as the redirector have steadily moved the DOS file system away from the mundane world of cylinders/tracks/sectors and toward a more abstract notion of file store. A disk, directory, or file is anything that behaves like one.

## CHAPTER 9

Memory Resident Software: Pop-ups and Multitasking

by Raymond J. Michels

With the release of MS-DOS 5.0, Microsoft documented many previously undocumented DOS functions—mainly TSR-related functions. Not only are these functions documented for DOS 5.0, they are also documented back to the version of DOS where they first appeared. Some programmers used to argue that, because these functions were undocumented, it was unsafe to use them. In retrospect, using these then-undocumented functions must not have been unsafe. By using these undocumented functions so widely, developers pushed Microsoft into documenting and supporting them. So much for the idea that calling an undocumented function is automatically unsafe!

If there is any area of previously-undocumented DOS with which PC programmers are generally familiar, it is writing memory resident programs. Because such programs call the DOS Terminate and Stay Resident (TSR) function (INT 21h Function 31h) or the older TSR interrupt (INT 27h), they are often called TSRs. However, these facilities are insufficient for writing TSRs that, once resident, make INT 21h DOS calls. It is well known within the PC programming community that you must use additional DOS functions to properly write the vast majority of TSRs.

Given the continuing importance of memory resident software in the PC marketplace, it is not surprising that much has been written about using DOS to write TSRs. Microsoft itself published a definitive piece on the subject, Richard Wilton's "Terminate-and-Stay-Resident Utilities," in the massive *MS-DOS Encyclopedia*. Wilton's article discusses the following once-undocumented DOS functions and interrupts:

- INT 21h Function 34h (Return InDOS Pointer)
- INT 21h Function 50h (Set PSP Segment)
- INT 21h Function 51h (Get PSP Segment)
- INT 21h Function 5D0Ah (Set Extended Error Information)
- INT 28h (Keyboard Busy Loop)

These functions are now officially documented in Microsoft's *MS-DOS Programmers' Reference*. In addition, several books on C programming for the PC (see the bibliography) include generic TSRs that use this same core set of DOS functions. The popular utilities published in each issue of *PC Magazine* are often TSRs whose assembly listings and prose descriptions show the intricacies of using these DOS functions.

Numerous commercial packages that provide generic TSR libraries are also available. These libraries use undocumented DOS and so, by extension, do any applications built using them. Anyone who is writing TSRs should consider using a commercial TSR library. Tried and tested libraries provide a very cost-effective short cut through the TSR debugging labyrinth, which could otherwise turn into a lengthy exercise in trial and error. Some of the commercial TSR libraries available are as follows:

- TesSeRact Ram Resident Development System (TesSeRact)
- CodeRunneR (for C or assembler; Microsystems Software, Framingham, MA)
- /*resident_C*/, Hold Everything, and TSRific (South Mountain Software, South Orange, NJ)
- C Tools Plus 6.0 (Blaise Computing, Berkeley, CA)
- TSRs and More (C/C++; TurboPower Software)
- Object Professional 1.0 (Turbo Pascal 5.5; Turbo Power Software)
- Magic TSR Toolkit (for ASM; Quantasm Corporation, Cupertino, CA)
- Stay-Res Plus (for BASIC; Micro Help)
- BATCOM (batch file compiler with TSR option; Wenham Software, Wenham, MA)

In addition, and especially if Pascal is your favored language, check out the source code for Tim Kokkonen's excellent MARK and RELEASE programs available on CompuServe (GO BPROGA).

Is there anything new to say on this subject? Surprisingly, yes. Several areas of TSR programming with undocumented DOS have not been adequately covered elsewhere. These include:

- INT 21h Functions 5D06h, 5D0Bh (Get DOS Swappable Data Area)
- Effective TSR termination
- Using C (both Microsoft and Borland) interrupt functions
- Writing non-pop-up TSRs

In addition, the Task Switching APIs provided by Windows and DOSSHELL, though documented, are new enough to require some mention here. We'll touch upon their use in TSRs for solving the "instance data" problem, and for dealing with task switches.

Many tasks for which a TSR was once suitable should today perhaps be instead carried out by a Windows virtual device driver (VxD; see the end of Chapter 3). In addition, there are now several competing standards for building protected-mode TSRs; these are discussed briefly in Chapter 4 (see the section on "Protected Mode DOS").

This chapter presents a generic TSR skeleton that you can use to "TSRify" your own programs, using either Borland C++ (version 3.xx) or Microsoft C (version 6.0 and higher). You can use this generic TSR to turn utilities from other parts of this book into pop-ups that are activated by the press of a user-defined hotkey (we discuss these terms in more detail in a moment). The last section of this chapter presents a memory resident program that is not activated by a hotkey; instead, it is periodically activated by the PC's timer tick, thereby multitasking in the background with whatever programs you run from the DOS command line in the foreground. The program is an add-on to the PRINT multitasking TSR that comes with DOS.

TSR: It Sounds Like a Bug, But It's a Feature

Only three functions are absolutely necessary to write memory resident software for MS-DOS; these three functions have been fully documented since their inception. They are

- Terminate and Stay Resident (INT 21h Function 31h)
- Set Interrupt Vector (INT 21h Function 25h)
- Get Interrupt Vector (INT 21h Function 35h)

A TSR is any DOS program that calls INT 21h Function 31h (or the obsolete but equivalent interrupt, INT 27h). The description of this function's purpose in the IBM DOS 3.3 Technical Reference is "Terminates the current process and attempts to set the initial allocation block to the memory size in paragraphs." Doesn't sound too exciting. The TSR function is very much like the normal DOS termination function (INT 21h Function 4Ch), which kills off whatever program calls it. The difference is that, after calling the TSR function, all memory belonging to the program is *not* released.

Instead, part or all of the program's initial allocation block is preserved so that it will not be overlaid by the next program to be loaded.

Thus, a TSR is any DOS program that leaves bits of itself behind after terminating. This sounds like a classic bug (sometimes referred to as the "leaky bucket"), wherein memory is allocated and then never deallocated. It doesn't sound like a feature you would want in your operating system, nor one around which an entire software subindustry could be built.

What is the advantage of terminating without freeing all your memory? If you've terminated and some other program is now running, there's not much your memory is going to do other than take up space, right? Chewing up memory can occasionally serve a purpose. In fact, TSRs have been written with names like MEMHOG and EATMEM to allow a developer with, say, a 640K machine to test software under conditions similar to those on, say, a 512K machine. But aside from this limited use, what good is it to hog memory after you're gone? You can't take it with you!

This is where the second necessary function, Set Interrupt Vector, comes in. All machines based on the Intel 80x86 architecture allow any program to install code that gets invoked whenever a hardware or software interrupt is generated. For example, the only reason INT 21h is a gateway to MS-DOS services is that interrupt vector 21h points to code inside DOS that provides these services. The ability to hang a piece of code off of an interrupt vector is what makes the TSR function something other than an elaborate way to consume memory. You can use the Set Interrupt Vector function to point interrupt vectors at your code and then call the TSR function to keep this code and its associated data and stack space resident in memory after you terminate. Whenever one of your interrupts is generated, it activates the code you left behind. Thus, there really is life after termination; you *can* take it with you.

What sort of interrupts would a TSR be interested in trapping? The most obvious one is the hardware interrupt, INT 9, generated every time a user presses a key. By trapping INT 9, a TSR can watch every key that a user types. Let's say your TSR is a memory resident Gilbert and Sullivan sampler that plays a selection from *The Mikado* whenever the user presses Alt-M, or *The Pirates of Penzance* whenever the user presses Alt-P. These are the only two keys the TSR is interested in, and they are referred to as the program's hotkeys. Each time the user hits a key, the INT 9 handler wakes up, looks at the key, and, if it is not one of its hotkeys, goes back to sleep. But if it is one of its hotkeys, then your application should do its thing. In this example, that means playing light opera (Tarantara!), but in TSRs in general this sudden seeming springing to life is called the pop-up.

Now, one item has been glossed over. When the user types a key that is *not* one of the TSR's hotkeys, how does the key go to its true destination? The TSR can't just discard it, but must somehow let other programs get a crack at it. The TSR does this by jumping to whichever function previously owned the INT 9 vector before our TSR installed its INT 9 handler. In other words, before setting an interrupt vector, almost all TSRs have to get the interrupt vector's previous value by calling the DOS Get Interrupt Vector function. Thus, the TSR looks something like this:

```
INTERRUPT PTR old_int9_handler;
INTERRUPT my_int9_handler()
    IF (key == alt_m)
        mikado();
    ELSE IF (key == alt_p)
        penzance();
    ELSE
        JMP PTR old_int9_handler();
BEGIN
    old_int9_handler = _dos_getvect(9);  // INT 21h Function 35h
    _dos_setvect(9, my_int9_handler);    // INT 21h Function 25h
    go_tsr();                            // INT 21h Function 31h
```

If every program that has hooked INT 9 takes care to call the interrupt's previous owner, then every program that needs to will get a peek at the stream of user keystrokes. Jumping to the previous owner is known as chaining the interrupt, and the end result is an interrupt chain (see the INTCHAIN program in chapter 6). Every time you press a key, a whole host of programs might see it. This mechanism for multiple program access to the keyboard input stream was formalized in the OS/2 concept of the "monitor."

There is a distinction between CALLing the previous interrupt handler, and JMPing to it. Handlers that want to process an interrupt *after* the previous handler (i.e., postprocessing) pass control to the previous handler with a far CALL. Otherwise, the handler preprocesses the interrupt, and passes control with a far JMP. Unlike a CALL, a JMP of course does not return.

While the best-known TSRs, such as Borland's now-ancient SideKick, are pop-ups that are activated by hotkeys, pressing a hotkey is just one way of generating an interrupt. Anything that generates an interrupt can reactivate a TSR. For example, when our own program calls INT 21h, it's generating a software interrupt, so a TSR could easily attach itself to INT 21h, providing a mechanism for extending the operating system or for debugging, as in the INTRSPY TSR in Chapter 8. For example:

```
INTERRUPT PTR old_int21_handler;

INTERRUPT my_int21_handler()
    IF (ah == some function I'm interested in)
        // do pre-processing
        // maybe CALL PTR old_int21_handler()
        // do post-processing
    ELSE
        JMP PTR old_int_21_handler();

BEGIN
    old_int21_handler = _dos_getvect(0x21);
    _dos_setvect(0x21, my_int21_handler);
    go_tsr();
```

In this example, as soon as we attach my_handler to INT 21h by calling _dos_setvect, the processor passes all INT 21h calls to the code in my_handler. This means that our own call to INT 21h Function 31h in go_tsr is actually first processed in my_handler. It is entirely up to the code in my_handler to determine what happens with each INT 21h request. Presumably, the call to Function 31h would pass through unchanged to old_int21_handler, which might be MS-DOS or some other TSR that previously hooked INT 21h, such as one of the simple "application wrappers" from the end of chapter 2.

With all this power, it is essential that programs reserve the TSR facility for genuinely useful code that is worth having resident in memory. Software that helps the user prepare his last will and testament, for example, is not a good candidate for memory residency. Neither, for that matter, is our Gilbert and Sullivan sampler, since readily available, dedicated hardware already exists for this purpose.

Where Does Undocumented DOS Come In?

Since many functions you need to produce the TSR are all fully documented, where does undocumented DOS come in? Do you really need undocumented DOS to write a program that plays "I Am the Very Model of a Modern Major General" whenever the user presses the Alt-P hotkey? Unfortunately, you almost definitely do. Unless you have achieved remarkable data compression, you don't want the notes for the music occupying memory. Instead, when the user presses Alt-P, you want to allocate some memory, read the music in from a file, close the file, play the notes, free the memory, then go back to sleep.

It would be nice if things worked this way, but they don't. The problem is that in this example you have no control over when my_int9_handler() will be invoked. Recall that my_int9_handler() is not called from within the program, the way functions like _dos_setvect() or go_tsr() are. Instead, my_int9_handler() is called whenever the user pounds on the keyboard. A keypress is an asynchronous event that bears no relation either to the internal state of whatever program happens to be running or to the internal state of DOS. You can't control when the user will press a key.

For instance, the foreground program might be copying a large file to the printer when the user decides that it's time for a musical interlude. If, while the foreground program is executing an INT 21h function such as Read File or Write File, the penzance() function suddenly takes over and starts issuing its own INT 21h requests, the resulting scenario is one which DOS was not designed to handle. MS-DOS is a single tasking operating system, which means that it does not allow for the possibility that it might be interrupted in the middle of one request, be asked to carry out some other request, and then resume the first request at the point where it was interrupted.

This property of MS-DOS is often referred to as "non-reentrancy," meaning that, if INT 21h is already executing, another INT 21h request can't be issued. A function or program which is "reentrant" is designed so that it can be interrupted at any time, allowing another process to enter without losing the state of the function just before the interruption. Primary among many techniques to achieve reentrancy, a function will normally keep its state (the contents of variables that relate to a particular instance of its invocation) on the caller's stack. With a very few exceptions, MS-DOS uses neither this nor any other reentrancy tricks. As we saw in chapter 6, DOS relies almost entirely on global data, and mostly uses its own stacks, rather than the caller's.

Any textbook on operating systems or on concurrent programming contains a discussion of the difference between reentrant code, which may be shared by several processes simultaneously, and what by contrast is called serially-reusable code, which may be used by only one process at a time. MS-DOS is serially reusable code.

When MS-DOS is called using INT 21h, DOS switches to one of three internal stacks: the I/O stack, the Disk stack, or the Auxiliary stack. Functions 00 through 0Ch use the I/O stack. The remainder of the functions use the Disk stack. If MS-DOS is called during a critical error—such as DIR A: when the drive door is open—the Auxiliary stack is used. In chapter 6, we saw exactly how DOS switches stacks. Because of this stack switching, if a TSR calls MS-DOS when the foreground is already executing inside INT 21h, MS-DOS loads the TSR's data onto its stack, overwriting the foreground process's data.

If DOS happens to be servicing a Function 0Ch request or lower and the TSR issues a Function 0Dh request or higher, then there won't be a problem because two different stacks are involved. Furthermore (as we again know from chapter 6), a few INT 21h functions (33h, 50h, 51h, 62h, and 64h) are so simple that they use the caller's stack and are therefore fully reentrant. But for the most part, DOS is non-reentrant.

To further complicate the issue, it's not just DOS you have to worry about. What if the heads on the hard disk are in the middle of writing data as part of the response to an application's INT 13h call? If the TSR starts issuing INT 13h requests that move the head somewhere else, then you're going to have a big reentrancy problem that has nothing to do with stacks or reusable code, but that could well result in a scrambled hard disk.

Does this mean the TSR can't perform DOS memory and file operations whenever the user presses the hotkey? Does all this have to be done once during initialization, before hooking any interrupt vectors, so that the memory resident portion of the TSR avoids all use of DOS calls? For example, one book on C programming for the PC makes the blanket statement that a TSR interrupt service routine (ISR) "cannot use any DOS functions." If this were true, it would certainly restrict what you can do with TSRs.

This isn't quite as terrible a restriction as it sounds. Many commercial programs for the PC that aren't even TSRs bypass DOS for many operations such as screen display and keyboard input. Avoiding DOS is not only possible, but, for certain key operations on the PC, it is practically a necessity. It is easy to write screen display functions, for example, that not only bypass DOS, but which are many times faster than DOS output routines and which provide far greater control over the screen. Not being able to reenter DOS sounds almost like a blessing in disguise.

However, as we noted in Chapter 8, the one area of DOS functionality that nearly is irreplaceable is file I/O. In addition, while programs can allocate expanded or extended memory rather than use the DOS memory allocation routines, expanded or extended memory is not always available; so many TSRs need to allocate memory through DOS. In summary, most TSRs need to make some INT 21h calls while popped up.

Fortunately, it is simply not true that TSR interrupt service routines "can't make INT 21h calls." But it is true that TSRs must do something special to make such calls. There are two options:

- Defer issuing INT 21h calls while INT 21h is in the middle of processing a request, or
- Somehow save and restore all of DOS's context (including the three DOS stacks) so that you can freely interrupt it.

The second option will be discussed later in this chapter, in the section on the DOS Swappable Data Area (SDA). Until then, we will concentrate on how not to enter DOS in the middle of some other program's INT 21h call, but instead to wait until that call has completed—how to use DOS as a serially reusable resource. Until we discuss the SDA, you will be reading about the state that a TSR must save and restore as part of its pop-up regime.

The chief requirement here is to have some way of determining when INT 21h is busy or, more accurately, of determining when one of its three stacks is in use. A short while ago, you saw a small block of pseudocode for trapping INT 21h calls, and it may have occurred to you that this might help determine whether DOS is in use. For example, you might put both the INT 21h handler and INT 9 handler into the same program and use the former to tell the latter whether it's safe to pop up:

```
INTERRUPT PTR old_int9_handler;      // keyboard
INTERRUPT PTR old_int21_handler;     // DOS
WORD using_io_stack = 0;
WORD using_disk_stack = 0;

INTERRUPT my_int21_handler()
    IF (ah <= 0x0c)
        INCR using_io_stack;
        CALL PTR old_int_21_handler;
        DECR using_io_stack;
    ELSE
        INCR using_disk_stack;
        CALL PTR old_int21_handler;
        DECR using_disk_stack;

INTERRUPT my_int9_handler()
    IF key == alt_m AND NOT using_disk_stack
        mikado();
    ELSE IF key == alt_p AND NOT using_disk_stack
        penzance();
    ELSE
        JMP PTR old_int9_handler();

BEGIN
    old_int9_handler = _dos_getvect(9);
    old_int21_handler = _dos_getvect(0x21);
    _dos_setvect(0x21, my_int21_handler);
    _dos_setvect(9, my_int9_handler);
    go_tsr();
```

This code hooks INT 21h to find out whether someone is "in DOS." The INT 21h handler increments a flag on entry to an INT 21h call, and decrements it on the way back out. The INT 9 handler checks the using_disk_stack flag and won't pop up if the flag is non-zero. The flag therefore acts as a semaphore, serializing access to DOS.

This is the basic idea behind making DOS calls from a TSR, but there are many problems with the preceding pseudocode. For example, DOS termination functions (Functions 00h, 31h, and 4Ch) do not return and, therefore, would need to get special treatment. Likewise, this code does not take into account DOS critical errors. Nor does it account for the fact that a PC sitting at the COMMAND.COM prompt is actually parked inside INT 21h Function 0Ah (Buffered Keyboard Input), making it seem as if one can't pop up while at the DOS prompt, which we all know is not the case. Fortunately, this code doesn't need to work properly because MS-DOS already provides both an InDOS semaphore and a critical error semaphore that the TSR can check. Instead of hooking INT 21h in an attempt to maintain the InDOS flag, you can use the one that DOS already provides. (On the other hand, this technique of hooking an interrupt to maintain an in-use flag is essential later on to serialize access to INT 13h, the ROM BIOS disk interrupt.)

This is where newly-documented DOS enters the picture, because the DOS function that returns the address of the InDOS semaphore was once undocumented, and the documentation still doesn't really tell you how to use this function to also find the critical-error semaphore. Furthermore, DOS generates idle interrupts (INT 28h) while inside INT 21h Function 0Ah. As we discuss later, Microsoft originally created these workarounds for its own TSRs, such as PRINT.COM.

That Microsoft's own TSRs use these functions should tell you that developers who want to create robust TSRs probably need to use them as well. It goes against common sense to assert that using undocumented features makes a program more rather than less stable, but who said that TSR programming was supposed to make sense? The techniques for writing correct TSRs may not be a model of software engineering at its finest, and some of the undocumented functions for TSR support have the feel of glorified afterthoughts, rather than parts of a well-thought-out interface, but you need them if you want your program to survive in the PC marketplace.

If you're writing a TSR, you have probably already bought into a host of compatibility problems, and frankly, using undocumented DOS is the least of them. The reason industry pundits have spoken of a "TSR crisis" is not because of undocumented DOS, but because of keyboard conflicts, problems associated with popping up over screens in graphics mode, memory usage conflicts, and the like. Undocumented DOS is one of the saner areas in TSR programming. This is perhaps confirmed by the fact that Microsoft finally documented a number of the TSR-necessary functions that were previously undocumented.

MS-DOS TSRs

How did PC programmers find out about the undocumented TSR functions? From examining Microsoft's own TSRs, of course.

TSRs have been a part of MS-DOS since its initial release in 1981. M. Steven Baker notes in his fine article, "Safe Memory-Resident Programming" (*The Waite Group's MS-DOS Papers*, 1988), that TSRs were even available within the 64K confines of the earlier CP/M operating system, in programs like Smartkey, Uniform, and Unspol. The only TSR program to ship with DOS 1.x was MODE.COM; PRINT, GRAPHICS, and ASSIGN were added in DOS 2.x.

PRINT is the only DOS utility program that preemptively multitasks. You can run an application at the same time that PRINT is printing a file. Only one of the two programs is running at any given instant, but the illusion of simultaneous operation is maintained by switching between them on each timer tick.

When the PRINT program is installed, it chains into the BIOS timer tick interrupt (INT 1Ch), the DOS Keyboard Busy Loop interrupt (INT 28h), and numerous other interrupts. Hooking a large number of interrupts is fairly normal for a TSR. INT 1Ch and INT 28h allow the PRINT program to gain control at regular intervals, independent of the user, and to perform its processing (open file, read, print, and close). These intervals are sufficiently close together that your foreground program appears to be operating at the same time as the PRINT program.

Every time PRINT wakes up, it saves the current DTA, PSP, and the vectors for INT 1Bh (Ctrl-Break), 23h (Ctrl-C), and 24h (Critical Error); PRINT sets up its own values for these items. On exiting from its current processing, PRINT restores these values to their original state. The TSRs presented in this chapter follow a similar structure. The multitasking TSR at the end of this chapter is an enhancement to the PRINT utility. It periodically looks for files that appear in a certain subdirectory and automatically submits them to PRINT.

One of the significant improvements in MS-DOS 2.0 was the availability of a hard disk. However, this new disk (usually drive C:) did cause some problems with software that was hard coded to use drive A: or B:. The ASSIGN utility allowed drive letters to be mapped to other drive letters. When programs referenced drive A:, they could be transparently made to access drive C: instead. ASSIGN sits on three MS-DOS interrupts: INT 21h (DOS Function Call), INT 25h (Absolute Sector Read), and INT 26h (Absolute Sector Write). When INT 25h or 26h is called and the AL register references the ASSIGNed drive, the value in AL is replaced by the new drive number. Simple, huh?

MODE is a good example of a TSR that can modify output to a device. Many programs do not support a serial printer (COM1); they just reference LPT1. Among other capabilities, MODE can grab data sent through INT 17h (BIOS Parallel Printer Service) and send the data to the serial port. The same principle can be used to write translation programs for various output devices. A TSR program that one of the authors once wrote was for a printer that did not support the form-feed command. The TSR sat on the parallel printer output interrupt and checked for a form feed character. When one came by, the TSR would output the appropriate number of line feeds to get to the next page. It was a simple program, but it saved someone from having to buy a new printer.

The Generic TSR

Now it's time for some code! Our goal is to build a generic TSR with Microsoft or Borland C/C++. This chapter provides everything so that when a user-defined hotkey is pressed, a function named application() is called. You simply provide application(), link with the generic TSR object modules, and you've got a TSR. We have deliberately stayed away from issues involving screen modes or even screen saves and restores, since these have nothing to do with undocumented DOS. The generic TSR code deals with all the issues connected with undocumented or once-undocumented DOS. The resulting TSRs have been tested extensively and seem quite robust (there are no 100% guarantees in the world of TSRs, however).

We use our generic TSR to build three sample pop-ups, a simple file browser (TSRFILE), a memory resident version of the MCB walker from Chapter 7 (TSRMEM), and a memory resident version of the INT 2Eh command interpreter that we will meet in Chapter 10 (TSR2E). We also build MULTI, the nonpop-up multitasking program mentioned earlier. The TSRs can be built either using the traditional DOS functions for TSRs or by using the DOSSWAP technique described later on. Finally, you can indicate whether a given TSR uses the disk or not. To show how all these pieces fit together, we take the somewhat unusual approach of first showing the MAKEFILE for this project. Shown in Listing 9-1, the file works with NMAKE from Microsoft C 6.0. Make files for Borland C++ are also supplied on the diskette.

Listing 9-1: MAKEFILE for the generic TSR

```
# NMAKE makefile for generic TSR
# example: C:\UNDOC2\CHAP9>nmake tsrfile.exe

# can be overridden from environment with NMAKE /E
# example:
#   C:\UNDOC2\CHAP9>set swap=1
#   C:\UNDOC2\CHAP9>nmake /e tsrfile.exe
#
```

```
#   C:\UNDOC2\CHAP9>set no_disk=1
#   C:\UNDOC2\CHAP9>nmake /e tsrmem.exe
SWAP = 0
NO_DISK = 0

!IF $(SWAP)
DOSSWAP = -DDOS_SWAP
!ELSE
DOSSWAP =
!ENDIF

!IF $(NO_DISK)
USES_DISK =
!ELSE
USES_DISK = -DUSES_DISK
!ENDIF

# defines the key components of the generic TSR:
#   TSREXAMP.C - main
#   INDOS.C - InDOS, critical error flag
#   PSP.C - Set PSP, Get PSP
#   EXTERR.C - Extended error save and restore
#   TSRUTIL.ASM - Miscellaneous routines
#   STACK.ASM - Stack save and restore
#   DOSSWAP.C - Optional use of DOS Swappable Data
#   SWITCHER.C - Task switcher, instance data
#   NOTIFY.ASM - Task switcher notification handlers
#   BREAK.C - Ctrl-C handling

UNDOC_OBJS = indos.obj psp.obj exterr.obj break.obj switcher.obj

MULTI_OBJS = indos.obj psp.obj exterr.obj break.obj

TSR_OBJS = tsrexamp.obj $(UNDOC_OBJS) \
    tsrutil.obj stack.obj notify.obj

STSR_OBJS = tsrexamp.obj $(UNDOC_OBJS) dosswap.obj \
    tsrutil.obj stack.obj notify.obj

# command to turn a .C file into an .OBJ file
.c.obj:
    cl -AS -Ox -Zp -c -W3 -Zi -DTSR $(USES_DISK) $(DOSSWAP) $*.c

# command to turn an .ASM file into an .OBJ file
.asm.obj:
    masm -ml $*.asm;

# special handling for MULTUTIL.ASM
multutil.obj:  tsrutil.asm
    masm -ml -DMULTI tsrutil,multutil;

multstk.obj:  stack.asm
    masm -ml -DMULTI stack,multstk;

# make the file-browser sample TSR
tsrfile.exe: $(TSR_OBJS) file.obj
    link /far/noi/map @tsrfile.rsp

# make the MCB-walker sample TSR
tsrmem.exe:  $(TSR_OBJS) mem.obj put.obj
    link /far/noi @tsrmem.rsp

# make the INT 2Eh command-interpreter sample TSR

INT2E_OBJS = test2e.obj send2e.obj have2e.obj do2e.obj

INT2E = test2e send2e have2e do2e

tsr2e.exe: $(TSR_OBJS) $(INT2E_OBJS) put.obj
    link /far/noi @tsr2e.rsp

# link the dos swapple examples only if the env var set
!IF $(SWAP)

# make the file-browser sample TSR
stsrfile.exe:  $(STSR_OBJS) file.obj
```

```
    link /far/noi @stsrfile.rsp
# make the MCB-walker sample TSR
stsrmem.exe:  $(STSR_OBJS) mem2.obj put.obj
    link /far/noi @stsrmem.rsp

# make the INT 2Eh command-interpreter sample TSR
stsr2e.exe: $(STSR_OBJS) $(INT2E_OBJS) put.obj
    link /far/noi @stsr2e.rsp

!ENDIF
# make the non-pop-up PRINT add-on
multi.exe: multi.obj $(MULTI_OBJS) multutil.obj multstk.obj put.obj
    link /far/noi/map/li multi $(MULTI_OBJS) multutil multstk,multi;
```

TSR Programming in Microsoft and Borland C/C++

Before beginning our examination of the various components of the generic TSR, we need to discuss writing TSRs in Microsoft and Borland C++, rather than in assembly language. This discussion strays fairly far from the topic of undocumented DOS, unfortunately, but that's unavoidable. As a consolation, we will cover all sorts of interesting aspects of low-level PC programming in C.

Managing TSRs in assembly language seems relatively easy at first because you have total control of the CPU. The process becomes a bit more difficult when the actual TSR application goes beyond the scope of simple assembly language code. C is generally easier to code than assembly language, and a wealth of libraries is available. By using C to write a TSR, you give up a little efficiency but gain ease of use and manageability.

For a TSR to do anything, it must be accessed through some type of interrupt. Therefore, anyone interested in TSR programming in a high-level language like C must become familiar with the facilities for interrupt manipulation.

Most C compilers for the PC offer an interrupt or _interrupt keyword that helps create interrupt handlers, and thus, TSRs. The interrupt keyword causes the compiler to create special entry and exit code for any procedure whose definition has the interrupt modifier. On entry the function saves all of the registers and sets DS to that of the C program. Because these registers are defined as parameters and are pushed on the stack, you can get and set them just like any other variable. When the procedure exits, it pops the registers values from the stack. Listing 9-2 shows example code for a simple interrupt handler.

Listing 9-2: An interrupt handler in C

```
typedef struct {
#ifdef TURBOC
    unsigned bp, di, si, ds, es, dx, cx, bx, ax;
#else
    unsigned es, ds;
    unsigned di, si, bp, sp, bx, dx, cx, ax;      /* PUSHA */
#endif
    unsigned ip, cs, flags;
    } INTERRUPT_REGS;
void interrupt far my_handler(INTERRUPT_REGS r)
{
    unsigned i = r.ax;
    r.bx = i >> 8;
}
```

Sample code for the interrupt keyword often shows an enormous parameter list for each interrupt handler, with each register named separately. Using the INTERRUPT_REGS structure (not a pointer to one!) makes the parameter list more manageable.

What sort of code does this produce? By compiling with the Microsoft C -Fa or -Fc command-line switches, you can examine the resulting assembly language code. Listing 9-3 shows the code generated by the compilation of this interrupt procedure in Microsoft C. The order in which registers are pushed is dictated in part by the Intel PUSHA and POPA instructions. Borland C++ also offers an interrupt keyword, but the order in which it pushes and pops registers is different from and incompatible with the PUSHA/POPA instructions.

Listing 9-3: Assembly Language Generated from Listing 9-2 by Microsoft C

```
_my_handler PROC FAR
        push    ax              ; bp+18
        push    cx              ; bp+16
        push    dx              ; bp+14
        push    bx              ; bp+12
        push    sp              ; bp+10
        push    bp              ; bp+8
        push    si              ; bp+6
        push    di              ; bp+4
        push    ds              ; bp+2
        push    es              ; bp+0
        mov bp,sp
        sub sp,2
        mov ax,DGROUP
        mov ds,ax
        ASSUME DS:DGROUP
        cld
        mov ax,WORD PTR [bp+18] ; i = r.ax
        mov al,ah
        sub ah,ah
        mov WORD PTR [bp+12],ax ; r.bx = i >> 8
        mov sp,bp
        pop es
        pop ds
        pop di
        pop si
        pop bp
        pop bx
        pop bx
        pop dx
        pop cx
        pop ax
        iret
_my_handler PROC FAR
```

Pushing the registers on the stack allows the C function to access the register values through variables. Because these values are popped from the stack on exit, the C function can change the return values of registers on interrupt exit. Notice that on exit BX is popped twice. On entry, SP was pushed at this point. If the C function was allowed to change SP (the stack pointer), the IRET instruction would put us in some unknown spot (recall that IRET uses the stack to return to the caller). Note that the processor itself pushes CS:IP and the flags on the stack.

If you compile for 80286 and higher machines with the -G2 switch, the resulting code would look like Listing 9-4.

Listing 9-4: Assembly Language Generated From Listing 9-2 with -G2 switch

```
        .286
_my_handler PROC FAR
        pusha                   ; push ax,cx,dx,bx,old_sp,bp,si,di
        push ds
        push es
        mov bp,sp
        sub sp,2
        mov ax,DGROUP
        mov ds,ax
```

```
        ASSUME DS:DGROUP
        cld
        mov ax,WORD PTR [bp+18]
        mov al,ah
        sub ah,ah
        mov WORD PTR [bp+12],ax
        mov sp,bp
        pop es
        pop ds
        popa                    ; pop di,si,bp; skip sp; pop bx,dx,cx,ax
        iret
_my_handler ENDP
```

The enormous amount of code generated (even for the best case, with PUSHA/POPA) and the large amount of stack space used for our three-line interrupt handler should not go unnoticed. If you were writing my_handler in assembly language, it might look like Listing 9-5.

Listing 9-5: Interrupt Handler in Hand-Crafted Assembly Language

```
_my_handler PROC FAR
        mov bx, ax
        shr bx, 8
        iret
_my_handler ENDP
```

Every feature has a price; and here too you pay for the convenience of writing the application in C, rather than in assembly language. Remember that, for each interrupt your TSR hooks, every application which generates that interrupt will wind up in your TSR's interrupt handler, even if the application isn't interested in the TSR's services, and even if the TSR is just going to chain to the previous handler. As we saw in chapter 6, this is an especially bad problem with the long INT 2Fh chain. Adding C-generated interrupt handlers to this chain just makes things worse.

In addition to the interrupt or _interrupt keyword, C compilers for the PC generally offer a set of functions for manipulating interrupts. In Microsoft and Borland C/C++, the DOS.H header file provides a large set of DOS-specific functions, including those excerpted in Listing 9-6.

Listing 9-6: Excerpts from Microsoft C DOS.H

```
void (_cdecl _interrupt _far *
    _cdecl _dos_getvect(unsigned intno))();

void _cdecl _dos_setvect(unsigned intno,
    void (_cdecl _interrupt _far *new_handler)());

void _cdecl _chain_intr(void (_cdecl _interrupt _far *target)());

void _cdecl _dos_keep(unsigned retcode, unsigned memsize);
```

The functions _dos_getvect() and _dos_setvect() directly translate into calls to INT 21h Functions 25h and 35h, and are vastly preferable to using the more general intdosx() or int86x() functions. For example:

```
#include <dos.h>
// ...
extern void interrupt far my_int21_handler(); // declare new function
void (_interrupt _far *old_int21)();          // pointer to old function
main()
{
    old_int21 = _dos_getvect(0x21);         // save old
    _dos_setvect(0x21, my_int21_handler); // install new
    // ...
    _dos_setvect(0x21, old_int21);        // restore old
}
```

You can do more with the old_int21 function pointer than just restore it when you're finished. In fact, almost all interrupt handlers and TSRs need to do something else with the pointer to the previous handler. They need to chain to it! Microsoft and Borland provide the extremely useful _chain_intr() function, which is necessary when your new interrupt handler needs to do preprocessing before chaining to the old handler. For instance:

```
void (_interrupt _far *old_int21)();
void interrupt far my_int21_handler(INTERRUPT_REGS r)
{
    // do some work
    _chain_intr(old_int21);
    // never reached!
}
main()
{
    old_int21 = _dos_getvect(0x21);          // save old
    _dos_setvect(0x21, my_int21_handler);    // install new
    // ...
}
```

It's called interrupt chaining because each interrupt handler is akin to a link in a chain; each one is a unit, but the units are linked together. The _chain_intr() function is basically a JMP instruction. Control is passed from the current interrupt handler to the one passed as a parameter to _chain_intr(). When the final interrupt handler is reached (there could be many handlers linked together), the handler performs an interrupt return, passing control back to the foreground application that was active when the interrupt occurred.

If you need to do more work after chaining to the old handler (called post-processing), then you can't use _chain_intr(). Instead, you must directly call through the saved function pointer:

```
// maybe do some preprocessing
(*old_int21)();
// we're back: do postprocessing
```

The C compiler turns the call through the interrupt function pointer into the following:

```
pushf
call dword ptr old_int21
```

The problem with this, however, is that the compiler uses the CPU registers in ways that may not be obvious from an examination of your C code. The registers on entry to the old interrupt handler may therefore not be correct. This is not a problem with _chain_intr() because that function (which can only be correctly called from within an interrupt function) loads up the CPU registers with the image of the registers that were stored on the stack. Wherever possible, use _chain_intr(old) rather than (*old)().

There are various tradeoffs involved in writing interrupt handlers in C rather than in assembly language. All in all, it seems like a win, but the overhead of pushing all registers on the stack on entry to an interrupt handler, and the inconvenience of not knowing the exact state of the registers before chaining to the previous handler, are sometimes too much. Fortunately, any time C is less convenient, you can always switch into assembly language. The generic TSR uses two assembly language modules, TSRUTIL.ASM and STACK.ASM, because that made more sense than any arbitrary C-only principles.

Keeping a C Program Resident

The hardest thing to do from a TSR in C is estimate the amount of memory you want to keep resident. Both Microsoft and Borland provide a handy _dos_keep() function, declared in DOS.H (see the excerpts in Listing 9-6), which calls the DOS TSR function. But this leaves unanswered the question of what number to pass in as memsize to _dos_keep(). When coding in assembly language, you can come up with this number fairly easily because you can find the size of your code. You have total control over its arrangement, allowing you to perform such efficiencies as placing startup code at the end, and jettisoning it when going resident. You can define addresses at the end of each segment and use the address to calculate the size of the segment; you can then total the size used in each segment to obtain the size required.

In C, however, you do not control the memory structure of the program beyond your source code. The memory map for a small-model Microsoft C program with hypothetical segment addresses is shown in Figure 9-7.

Figure 9-7: Memory Map of a Small Model Microsoft C Program

```
         ----------------
1E20h    FAR HEAP
         ----------------
         NEAR HEAP
         STACK
0E19h    DS
         ----------------
0BFAh    CODE
         ----------------
0BEAh    PSP
         ----------------
```

For Borland C++, the STACK and NEAR HEAP are reversed. Several readers did not agree with this memory map, but it can be validated by running a C program in a debugger. If a break point is set at the main() function, you can look at the value of the SP register. For Microsoft C, SP is a low address. For Borland C++, SP is near the top of the stack segment.

Of course, you could just pass a very high number to _dos_keep(), but with TSRs, one of the primary goals is to keep memory consumption to the absolute minimum. The code fragment in Listing 9-8 details one way to keep a memory segment resident in C for small memory models.

Listing 9-8: Sample Code for Keeping Memory Segment Resident

```
#define PSP_ENV_ADDR    0x2c  /* environment address from PSP */
#define STACK_SIZE      8192  /* must be 16 byte boundary */

#define PARAGRAPHS(x)   ((FP_OFF(x) + 15) >> 4)

char far *stack_ptr;           /* pointer to TSR stack */
unsigned memtop;               /* number of paragraphs to keep */
// ...
/* MALLOC a stack for our TSR section */
stack_ptr = malloc(STACK_SIZE);
stack_ptr += STACK_SIZE;

// ...
/* release environment back to MS-DOS */
FP_SEG(fp) = _psp;
FP_OFF(fp) = PSP_ENV_ADDR;
_dos_freemem(*fp);

/* release unused heap to MS-DOS */
/* All mallocs for TSR section must be done in TSR init */
segread(&sregs);
memtop = sregs.ds + PARAGRAPHS(stack_ptr) - _psp;
_dos_setblock(memtop, _psp, &dummy);
_dos_keep(0, memtop);
```

First, create a block of memory in the near heap using malloc(). This becomes the TSR's stack during activation. The alternative to using this local stack is to use whatever stack happens to be in effect during TSR activation. This is fine for small programs, but if you are doing wild and wonderful things with your code, it is best to create your own stack to avoid overflowing the foreground's stack. The stack size is added to the stack pointer variable to get it to the bottom of the stack. This stack bottom becomes the top of the TSR in memory.

Use the value of the new stack pointer to calculate the number of 16-byte paragraphs that must be kept resident (memtop). The expression PARAGRAPHS(stack_ptr) gives you the number of paragraphs in the local heap. This number must be retained because it includes the mallocs you've already done. This is added to DS to establish the top of the memory you need, and the PSP is subtracted to find the actual number of paragraphs needed by the entire program. Call MS-DOS to shrink the current block down to the size specified. In simple programs created with the generic TSR, memtop was generally less than 600h paragraphs, giving the resulting TSR an in-memory footprint of about 24K. This eliminates any far heap, the original C stack, and the unused near heap.

Using this method, you must perform any near mallocs before creating the stack. Once the TSR is resident, it cannot call the malloc family or use library routines that use malloc functions, because the near heap is gone. Use of malloc calls by library functions varies with compiler implementation, so be sure to select your functions carefully. (The *Run-Time Library Reference* for Microsoft C 6.0 includes, in the entry for malloc, a list of all functions that call malloc; it's rather large.) The final step is to call _dos_keep, which does an INT 21h Function 31h to terminate and stay resident, retaining in memory the number of paragraphs specified. If all goes well, you should be able to find your TSR in the display from Chapter 7's UDMEM program. For example:

```
C:\UNDOC2\CHAP9>tsrfile -k 59 4
Activation: CTRL SCAN=59
C:\UNDOC2\CHAP9>udmem
Seg     Owner   Size
...
0BDA    1E76    000D (   208)
0BE8    0000    0000 (     0)     free
0BE9    0BEA    0597 ( 22896)              -k 59 4  [08 09 13 28 2F ]
...
```

The MEM display shows that the TSR begins at 0BEAh (its MCB, of course, is at 0BE9h), that it retains 0597h paragraphs (22K), and that we freed the environment. You can still get the command line (which, by the way, designates a hotkey of Ctrl-F1), but the program name is no longer available. As for the various interrupts UDMEM says you've hooked, these will be discussed in a short while.

One final note about staying resident in a C program: to reduce their memory footprint even further, many TSRs jettison their startup code. For example, you don't need main() once you've gone resident. Any subsequent calls to TSRFILE (to deinstall, for instance) are going to go to the main() of a completely different instance of the program, not to the main() of the resident copy. (There is one program, but possibly more than one process.) Anyhow, it would be nice to throw away the code for main(). This is a technique that is relatively easy using assembly language. Figuring out how to do this in C, given the memory map shown earlier, is left as an exercise for the reader. Don't stay up too late!

Not Going Resident

If you are writing your own TSR from scratch, rather than using one of the commercial TSR libraries, or a generic TSR such as the one we present here, it is a good idea to put off going resident for as long as possible. Don't try debugging your application as a TSR. Instead, have it spawn a command shell from which you can exit, or have it run a single program whose name and arguments appear on the DOS command line, as shown in Listing 9-9.

Listing 9-9: Sample Code for Shell vs. TSR Implementation

```
main(int argc, char *argv[])
{
    // TSR init goes here
    old_int09 = _dos_getvect(0x09);
    _dos_setvect(0x09, my_int09_handler);
#ifdef TESTING
    // to launch a command shell:
    system(getenv("COMSPEC"));

    // or, to run just one program:
    // spawnvp(P_WAIT, argv[1], &argv[1]);

    // we're back: deinstall
    _dos_setvect(0x09, old_int09);
#else
    // ...
    _dos_keep(0, memtop);
#endif
}
```

In fact, this is so handy you might consider making some of your applications into shells rather than TSRs. A program that needs to set up a context of some sort for another program is often best treated as a shell, not a TSR. See the two application-wrapper examples at the end of chapter 2 (DOSVER and FUNC0E32).

Jiggling the Stack

Remember the stack we created with malloc just before remaining resident? For that stack to be used, the TSR interrupt routine that performs activation must call two routines; one sets up the local stack on entry and one restores the original stack on exit. The actual code to switch stacks must be programmed in assembly language because you don't have full access to the registers in C (though you could use in-line assembler, as demonstrated in the redirector() function of PHANTOM.C in Chapter 8).

Listing 9-10 is a short assembly language module that manages the stack context switch. The _set_stack procedure saves the current foreground stack in the data area and sets the stack pointer to the stack created with malloc (stack_ptr). Notice the stack manipulation at entry and exit of this procedure. A return address was placed on the stack when set_stack was called. Because this code switches stacks, this address is popped from the stack on entry and pushed on the stack before exit. The _restore_stack procedure restores the stack segment and pointer to what was saved in _set_stack.

Listing 9-10: Stack Switch Module STACK.ASM

```
;STACK.ASM
;Define segment names used by C
;
_TEXT    segment byte public 'CODE'
_TEXT    ends
CONST    segment word public 'CONST'
CONST    ends
_BSS     segment word public 'BSS'
_BSS     ends
_DATA    segment word public 'DATA'
_DATA    ends
DGROUP   GROUP   CONST, _BSS, _DATA
    assume  CS:_TEXT, DS:DGROUP
    public  _set_stack, _restore_stack
```

```
        extrn   _stack_ptr:near     ;our TSR stack
        extrn   _ss_save:near       ;save foreground SS
        extrn   _sp_save:near       ;save foreground SP
_TEXT   segment
;*****
;void far set_stack(void) -
;    save current stack and setup our local stack
;*****
_set_stack proc     far

;save foreground stack

;we need to get the return values from the stack
;since the current stack will change
        pop ax  ;get return offset
        pop bx  ;get return segment

;save away foreground process' stack
        mov word ptr _ss_save,ss
        mov word ptr _sp_save,sp

;setup our local stack
        mov ss,word ptr _stack_ptr+2
        mov sp,word ptr _stack_ptr

IFDEF MULTI
        mov bp,sp   ;make bp relative to our stack frame
ENDIF
;setup for ret
        push    bx
        push    ax

        ret
_set_stack  endp
;*****
;void far restore_stack(void) -
;    restore foreground stack, throw ours away
;*****
_restore_stack  proc    far

;we need to get the return values from the stack
;since the current stack will change
        pop cx  ;get return offset
        pop bx  ;get return segment

;save background stack
        mov word ptr _stack_ptr+2,ss
        mov word ptr _stack_ptr,sp

;restore foreground stack here
        mov ss,word ptr _ss_save
        mov sp,word ptr _sp_save

IFDEF MULTI
        mov bp,sp   ;make bp relative to our stack frame
ENDIF

;setup for ret
        push bx
        push cx

        ret
_restore_stack  endp
_TEXT   ends

_DATA   segment

_DATA   ends

        end
```

One final caveat on the stack is that it's crucial to compile Microsoft C with -Gs (or with a switch like -Ox that includes -Gs) to turn off stack checking. Otherwise, the C compiler's _chkstk routine would get hopelessly confused by the new stack.

DOS Functions for TSRs

Finally, we are ready to discuss TSR programming with DOS functions. Recall that the whole issue is how one makes DOS INT 21h calls from the resident portion of a TSR. First we present the traditional use of previously-undocumented DOS, then we show the undocumented DOSSWAP technique.

MS-DOS Flags

DOS keeps a byte in memory called the InDOS flag, also known as the "DOS safe" flag. This flag indicates when it is safe to access MS-DOS functions; it is a semaphore that turns DOS into a serially reusable resource. The disassembly in chapter 6 shows where DOS increments and decrements the InDOS flag. The idea is that no one should enter DOS (that is, make INT 21h calls) if the semaphore indicates that DOS is busy. As you'll see, there are numerous exceptions to this rule, but the basic idea is sound.

Generally, the activation section of a TSR that uses MS-DOS checks this flag. If the flag indicates that MS-DOS is busy, the TSR program must defer the activation, or at least that portion of the activation which makes INT 21h calls. DOS INT 21h Function 34h returns the address of the InDOS flag. Because this address (returned in ES:BX) is constant for a particular operating environment, the initialization section of a TSR calls this function once. You can then store the address in a local variable for later access during the pop-up phase.

The C module INDOS.C in Listing 9-11 contains a function, DosBusy, that returns a zero if it is safe to make INT 21h calls. If DOS cannot be interrupted, it returns non-zero. Your application must call InitInDos to set the addresses of the InDos flags during initialization. If you neglect to do so, DosBusy always returns non-zero. (Of course, DosBusy could instead just call InitInDos for you at this point.)

The Int28DosBusy function in Listing 9-11 returns non-zero if the InDos flag is greater than one or the critical error flag is non-zero, and is intended to be used only inside an INT 28h loop. Inside INT 28h, InDOS == 1 is normal and indicates DOS is *not* busy; InDOS > 1 inside INT 28h means it is busy.

Listing 9-11: DOS Flag Management Module INDOS.C

```c
/* INDOS.C - Functions to manage DOS flags */

#include <stdlib.h>
#include <dos.h>

#define GET_INDOS       0x34
#define GET_CRIT_ERR    0x5D06

char far *indos_ptr=0;
char far *crit_err_ptr=0;
int   DosBusy(void);
void  InitInDos(void);

/*****
Function: Init InDos Pointers
Initialize pointers to InDos Flags
*****/
void InitInDos(void)
{
    union  REGS regs;
    struct SREGS segregs;
```

```
    regs.h.ah = GET_INDOS;
    intdosx(&regs,&regs,&segregs);
    /* pointer to flag is returned in ES:BX */
    FP_SEG(indos_ptr) = segregs.es;
    FP_OFF(indos_ptr) = regs.x.bx;

    if (_osmajor < 3)  /* flag is one byte after InDos */
        crit_err_ptr = indos_ptr + 1;
    else if (_osmajor==3 && _osminor == 0) /* flag is 1 byte before*/
        crit_err_ptr = indos_ptr - 1;
    else
    {
        regs.x.ax = GET_CRIT_ERR;
        intdosx(&regs,&regs,&segregs);
        /* pointer to flag is returned in DS:SI */
        FP_SEG(crit_err_ptr) = segregs.ds;
        FP_OFF(crit_err_ptr) = regs.x.si;
    }
}

/*****
Function: DosBusy
This function will non-zero if DOS is busy
*****/
int DosBusy(void)
{
    if (indos_ptr && crit_err_ptr)
        return (*crit_err_ptr || *indos_ptr);
    else
        return 0xFFFF;  /* return dos busy if pointers are not set */
}
/*****
Function: Int28DosBusy
*****/
int Int28DosBusy(void)
{
    if (indos_ptr && crit_err_ptr)
      return (*crit_err_ptr || (*indos_ptr > 1));
    else
        return 0xFFFF;  /* return dos busy if flags are not set */
}
```

Listing 9-11 puts the cart before the horse by referencing another byte in addition to the InDOS flag. This is the Critical Error flag. The Dos Critical Error flag is set when DOS is processing a critical error (of course!). It is yet another flag that must be checked before deciding if it is safe to access MS-DOS. In MS-DOS version 2.x, this flag is one byte after the InDOS flag. In MS-DOS version 3.x and higher, this flag is one byte before the InDOS flag. When retrieving these flags, you must check the DOS version. In MS-DOS versions 3.10 and above, you can also retrieve the address of the Critical Error flag by calling INT 21h Function 5D06h. All the DOS versionitis problems are taken care of during initialization, in InitInDos, so that DosBusy, which is called quite frequently, has an easy job.

In addition to checking if DOS is in the middle of a critical error, another use for the critical error flag is to force MS-DOS to use its critical error stack. A bug in MS-DOS 2.x requires that the critical-error flag be set (and therefore DOS's critical-error stack be used) so that the Get PSP and Set PSP functions (discussed momentarily) work properly. You can avoid having to think about the problem by requiring DOS 3 or higher.

As yet another forward reference, note that INDOS.C also provides a function called Int28DosBusy(), to be used in an INT 28h handler. Inside INT 28h, InDOS is always at least one. In this context, (InDOS == 1) means DOS isn't busy (this is one of the many InDOS exceptions we were talking about), but if (InDOS > 1), then DOS is really busy; come back some other time!

Get/Set PSP

As discussed in Chapter 7 (particularly in the section "Unique Process Identifier"), each process in MS-DOS has a Program Segment Prefix. You learned that Memory Control Blocks are stamped with the PSP of their owner. In Chapter 7, you saw that this 256-byte area contains, among other things, the default file handle table (Job File Table) for the process. Because it is a unique value (though, as chapters 3 and 6 note, this can get complicated in 386 multitasking environments), the segment address of the PSP also acts as a unique process identifier.

At any given moment in an MS-DOS system, there is a current PSP. In the appendix entry for INT 21h Functions 5D06h and 5D0Bh, you can see that the current PSP is kept at offset 10h in both versions of the DOS Swappable Data Area. When DOS receives an INT 21h Function 3Dh request to open a file, for example, the handle returned in AX is an index into the JFT of the current PSP.

Well, that's obviously the PSP that belongs to whatever process called INT 21h Function 3Dh, right? No! Remember that we are talking about TSRs here. The current PSP, unless you somehow change it, belongs to whatever process happens to be running when we pop up. Thus, if the TSR decides to start opening files, it would be using the foreground process's PSP. This could be totally disastrous.

Consider the following example of a TSR that ignores the current PSP when it pops up. If the TSR opens a file handle or allocates memory using MS-DOS, these items become associated with the foreground process. The foreground process is not aware of these items, but entries in its JFT are consumed. When the foreground terminates, all open files are closed and allocated memory segments are freed. This includes those which the TSR thought of as its own, yet allowed to be associated with the foreground process. Furthermore, if the TSR opens a file while popped up over one PSP, and tries to read from the file while popped up over a different PSP, the file handle will reference the wrong file!

What the TSR must do when it pops up is somehow change DOS's current PSP so that it corresponds to the TSR's, carry out whatever task the TSR is supposed to perform when it pops up, and then, before lapsing back into its dormant state, restore the current PSP to whatever value it had when the TSR popped up.

Fortunately, DOS provides just the functions you need. DOS INT 21h Functions 50h and 51h are the Get PSP and Set PSP functions in MS-DOS 2.x and above. In DOS 3.x and above, documented Function 62h is also available to Get PSP. As noted in Chapter 7, it is often thought that Get PSP returns the PSP of whatever program called it. As chapter 6 showed, however, it gets DOS's current PSP out of the SDA. Likewise, Set PSP sets this value in the SDA.

In DOS 3.0 and higher, Functions 50h, 51h, and 62h do not use any of the DOS stacks and are fully reentrant. They are among the few INT 21h functions you can call without paying attention to the InDOS flag, and thereby, they constitute another exception to the InDOS rule. But, as noted earlier, to call Functions 50h or 51h in DOS 2.x, you must first force use of the critical error stack. The following pseudocode describes the steps to use Get/Set PSP from a TSR.

```
TSR_INITIALIZATION:
    .
    .
    .
    psp_addr :=
    Get current PSP with Function 51h or 62h
    (this PSP will be that of the TSR)
    .
    Terminate and stay resident
TSR_ACTIVATION:
    fgrnd_psp_addr :=
    Get current PSP with Function 51h or 62h
    (since the TSR interrupted the foreground, this address
        will be that of the foreground process)

    Set current PSP with Function 50h, using psp_addr
    Do TSR work
```

```
      Set current PSP with Function 50h, using fgrnd_psp_addr
      Go back to sleep
```

Listing 9-12 (PSP.C) contains functions that Get and Set the current PSP, taking into account the various oddities which we have discussed. These are not just simple-minded sugar coating for the equivalent DOS functions. We test for DOS 2.x and set the critical error flag accordingly. Again, you must call InitInDos before using these functions.

Listing 9-12: PSP Management Module PSP.C

```c
/* PSP.C */

#include <stdlib.h>
#include <dos.h>
#include "tsr.h"

#define GET_PSP_DOS2    0x51
#define GET_PSP_DOS3    0x62
#define SET_PSP         0x50

extern union  REGS regs;

/*****
Function: GetPSP - returns current PSP
*****/
unsigned GetPSP(void)
{
    if (_osmajor == 2)
    {
        if (! crit_err_ptr) /* forgot to call InitInDos */
            return 0;  /* gosh, I should just call InitInDos for them */

        *crit_err_ptr = 0xFF;    /* force use of proper stack */
        regs.h.ah = GET_PSP_DOS2;
        intdos(&regs,&regs);
        *crit_err_ptr = 0;
    }
    else
    {
        regs.h.ah = GET_PSP_DOS3;
        intdos(&regs,&regs);
    }

    return regs.x.bx;
}

/*****
Function: SetPSP - sets current PSP
*****/
void SetPSP(unsigned segPSP)
{
    if (!crit_err_ptr)           /* forgot to call InitInDos */
        return;          /* should call InitInDOS for them! */

    if (_osmajor == 2)
        *crit_err_ptr = 0xFF;   /* force use of correct stack if DOS 2.x */

    regs.h.ah = SET_PSP;
    regs.x.bx = segPSP;          /* pass segment value to set */

    intdos(&regs,&regs);

    if (_osmajor == 2)
        *crit_err_ptr = 0;       /* restore crit error flag */
}
```

Extended Error Information

Consider the following scenario. The foreground program has performed a DOS function that failed. Because of this, DOS has stored extended error information. Normally, the foreground program can access the extended information at this point. The TSR becoming active, however, delays the access of the extended error information. Now the TSR has control and could possibly perform DOS functions that fail, overwriting the existing extended error information, making it invalid for the interrupted (foreground) program.

Don't despair, though. DOS has this problem well in hand. In DOS 3.0 and higher, documented Function 59h is available to query the extended error information. A TSR must save this information prior to activation and reset it at exit. DOS Function 5D0Ah allows the extended error information to be set. On entry to Function 5D0Ah, point DS:DX (not DS:SI as claimed in the *MS-DOS Programmer's Reference* for DOS 5) to a table containing the contents of the registers when an error occurred. The register values for this table can be retrieved using Function 59h.

The C functions in Listing 9-13 can get the extended error information on TSR activation and reset the extended error information on exit.

Listing 9-13: Extended Error Management Module EXTERR.C

```c
/* EXTERR.C - extended error saving and restoring */

#include <stdlib.h>
#include <dos.h>

#define GET_EXTERR      0x59
#define SET_EXTERR      0x5d0a

#pragma pack(1)

struct   ExtErr
{
    unsigned int errax, errbx, errcx, errdx, errsi, errdi;
    unsigned int errds, erres;
    unsigned int reserved, userID, programID;
};

void  GetExtErr(struct ExtErr * ErrInfo);
void  SetExtErr(struct ExtErr near * ErrInfo);

extern union  REGS regs;
extern struct SREGS sregs;


/*****
Function: GetExtErr
get extended error information
*****/
void GetExtErr(struct ExtErr * ErrInfo)
{
    if (_osmajor >= 3)   /* only for DOS 3 and above */
    {
        regs.h.ah = GET_EXTERR;
        regs.x.bx = 0;  /* must be zero */
        intdosx(&regs,&regs,&sregs);
        ErrInfo->errax = regs.x.ax;
        ErrInfo->errbx = regs.x.bx;
        ErrInfo->errcx = regs.x.cx;
        ErrInfo->errds = regs.x.dx;
        ErrInfo->errsi = regs.x.si;
        ErrInfo->errdi = regs.x.di;
        ErrInfo->errds = sregs.ds;
        ErrInfo->erres = sregs.es;
        ErrInfo->userID = 0;      /* zero per DOS 5 Tech Ref */
        ErrInfo->programID = 0;
    }
}
/*****
Function: SetExtErr
```

```
set extended error information
*****/
void SetExtErr(struct ExtErr near * ErrInfo)
{
    if (_osmajor >= 3)    /* only for DOS  3 and above */
    {
        regs.x.ax = SET_EXTERR;
        regs.x.bx = 0;          /* must be zero */
        segread(&sregs);     /* put address of err info in DS:DX */
        regs.x.dx = (int) ErrInfo;
        intdosx(&regs,&regs,&regs);
    }
}
```

Extended Break Information

At times, it is necessary to tell the operating system, "Hey, stop what you're doing and go back to the command prompt!" This is better known as Ctrl-C or Ctrl-Break.

MS-DOS, by default, checks the incoming keys for these break characters only when you use its CP/M emulation I/O functions (INT 21h AH=01h through 0Ch). If BREAK=ON, however, DOS checks for the break key when processing almost all INT 21h functions (see the INT 21h dispatch disassembly in chapter 6). While at the COMMAND prompt, entering BREAK=ON allows extended break checking and BREAK=OFF turns off the extra check.

Now, what does this have to do with a TSR?

If extended break checking is on *and* you press a break key just before the TSR becomes active, an MS-DOS function call in the TSR fails! This is a small window of disaster, but it would probably happen just as you're ready to save that large program you were editing.

To avoid this possibility, you must query and save the current break status. Then, the first DOS function call within the TSR activation section must be to turn extended break checking off. On TSR exit, restore the original break status.

The one problem to this solution concerns DOS 2.x, where getting or setting the extended break status causes a failure if a break key is pending and extended break checking in ON. This is corrected in DOS 3.0 and later. Unfortunately, there is no clean solution for DOS 2.x. To avoid problems with the TSR examples in this chapter, extended break checking must be OFF for DOS 2.x.

Listing 9-14 shows BREAK.C, containing C functions to get and set the Extended Break status.

Listing 9-14: Extended Break Management Module BREAK.C

```
/* BREAK.C */
#include <stdlib.h>
#include <dos.h>
#include "tsr.h"

#define GET_SET_BREAK  0x33
#define GET_BREAK 0
#define SET_BREAK 1

extern union  REGS regs;


/*****
Function: GetBreak - returns current Break Status 0 = OFF, 1 = ON
*****/
int GetBreak(void)
{
    if (_osmajor != 2)
    {
        regs.h.ah = GET_SET_BREAK;
        regs.h.al = GET_BREAK;
```

```
        intdos(&regs,&regs);
        return regs.h.dl;
    }
    else
        return (0);
}
/*****
Function: SetBreak - sets current Break Status 0 = OFF, 1 = ON
*****/
void SetBreak(int breakStatus)
{
    if (_osmajor != 2)
    {
        regs.h.ah = GET_SET_BREAK;
        regs.h.al = SET_BREAK;
        regs.h.dl = breakStatus;
        intdos(&regs,&regs);
    }
}
```

Interrupt 28h

The TSR can now pop up whenever DOS is not in use. So you're sitting at the COMMAND.COM prompt, not doing anything, you hit the TSR's hotkey, and the TSR doesn't pop up!

This wasn't the answer you expected, was it? If you're not doing anything, the TSR should pop up as soon as you press its hotkey. Sitting at the COMMAND.COM seems like the epitome of idleness. Why doesn't the TSR pop up?

The answer is quite simple. COMMAND is waiting for input in DOS. As will be explained in Chapter 10, whenever COMMAND has finished carrying out some task and is awaiting your next instruction, it calls the documented DOS Buffered Keyboard Input function (INT 21h Function 0Ah). This function provides the standard DOS editing keys such as F3. While idling at the prompt waiting for you to type something, COMMAND is parked inside INT 21h Function 0Ah. In other words, the InDOS flag is set.

Now what do you do? One alternative, naturally, is to throw in the towel and declare that the TSR won't pop up at the COMMAND prompt. You're probably not going to sell a lot of copies of the program that way, though.

This curious paradox—that InDOS flag is set and yet DOS is really idle—must have confronted Microsoft when it was putting together the PRINT program. True, PRINT is not a pop-up, but the same principles apply. When COMMAND is doing nothing, it would seem to be a good time for the TSR to print some files. And, if you've ever used PRINT, you know that in fact it does print in the background while COMMAND is idling. So how did Microsoft resolve this dilemma?

They put in a hack so that whenever DOS is waiting for a user keypress in places like Function 0Ah, it periodically generates an interrupt, INT 28h. PRINT hooks this interrupt, thereby receiving wake-up calls while the state of the InDOS flag otherwise indicates that it shouldn't. INT 28h is referred to as the MS-DOS Idle interrupt or Keyboard Busy Loop interrupt. Whenever this Idle interrupt is generated, it is safe to use INT 21h Functions 0Dh and above, as long as InDOS is not greater than one. INT 28h is undocumented, but it is such a foundation of TSR programming that it is supported even in the DOS compatibility box of OS/2.

The above discussion is slightly misleading because, as chapter 10 also explains, in DOS 5 and higher COMMAND.COM first calls the DOSKEY Read Command Line function (INT 2Fh AX=4810h), and only calls INT 21h AH=0Ah if the DOSKEY function fails (probably because DOSKEY isn't installed). However, DOSKEY also issues the period INT 28h TSR "heartbeat," just as DOS does while processing INT 21h AH=0Ah, so INT 28h is issued whether or not DOSKEY is running. DOSKEY also issues the INT 2Fh AX=1680h call that Windows uses for idle detection.

Thus, our TSR has acquired another wrinkle. In addition to checking the InDOS and critical error flags, saving and restoring DOS's current PSP, and saving and restoring the extended error information, you must now must hook INT 28h too. Well, no one ever said the DOS TSR interface was a model of clarity. It is unlikely that anyone at Microsoft sat down and tried to design a nice interface for TSR programming. Instead, they put in what they needed to write their own TSRs. The end result is an interface that looks like something someone would design only for their own use. On the other hand, the DOS TSR interface, if we can call it that, benefits from the fact that its designers used it themselves. They ran into the same problems you run into with your TSRs, so they put in solutions.

Interrupt handlers for INT 28h should pass control to the previous INT 28h owner when complete. Generally they should not hog the INT 28h interrupt by executing large amounts of code. TSRs that solicit user input should not only hook INT 28h, but also periodically invoke INT 28h in their input loop. This gives other TSRs a chance to use the idle time. In our generic TSR, we use INT 28h to detect whether the user had earlier pressed the hotkey at a time when we couldn't pop up. In the MULTI TSR program at the end of this chapter, INT 28h is hooked so that we can use the time slices we get while the system is sitting at the COMMAND prompt.

The INDOS.C module shown earlier contains the function called Int28DosBusy(), which returns zero if it is safe to access DOS during an INT 28h. The InDOS flag is never zero during an INT 28h, so you might think that you don't need to even check InDOS during an INT 28h. However, InDOS could be greater than one, in which case you still can't pop up.

The INT 28h handler appears in the main TSR module, TSREXAMP.C, to which we now turn.

Inside the Generic TSR

The main module for our generic TSR, TSREXAMP.C, initializes the program; then the pop-up routine calls your application and several interrupt handlers. The remainder of the interrupt handlers are written in assembly language for reasons noted earlier and are found in TSRUTIL.ASM. Naturally, TSREXAMP.C relies heavily on the modules we have already examined, INDOS.C, PSP.C, EXTERR.C, and STACK.ASM.

Rather than plunge directly into the 550 lines of code belonging to TSREXAMP.C or the 250 lines that comprise TSRUTIL.ASM, we'll start off with a pseudocode explanation. The following pseudocode makes heavy use of the keyword ON (borrowed from BASIC, which in turn borrowed it from PL/1). A phrase such as ON TIMER indicates code that is called, not from within the program itself, but from outside the program. It is merely an interrupt handler, written in C, using the interrupt keyword discussed earlier, and installed using (in this example) _dos_setvect(8, new_int8). The ON keyword, as used in the following pseudocode, is particularly expressive of what happens in our TSR.

The following discussion assumes that the TSR is going to access the disk during its pop-up phase, and that the TSR does not use the DOSSWAP interface, which we've mentioned, but not yet discussed in detail.

The initialization of the generic TSR looks something like this:

```
INIT ; main() in TSREXAMP.C
    IF they want to deinstall
        CALL deinstall()
    ELSE IF TSR not already installed
        MALLOC stack
        GETVECT TIMER(8), KEY(9), DISK(13h), IDLE(28h), MULTIPLEX(2Fh)
        ; 2Fh is for communication with already-resident copy of TSR

        ; (install check, deinstall)
        SETVECT TIMER, KEY, DISK, IDLE, MULTIPLEX
```

```
RELEASE environment
RELEASE unused heap
TSR
```

There are no surprises here, except perhaps the fact that we are somehow using INT 2Fh to communicate between an already resident copy of the TSR program and a second copy that, rather than go TSR, deinstalls the resident copy. If TSRFILE has already been made resident, it can be deinstalled by typing TSRFILE -d at the COMMAND prompt. If you are installing rather than deinstalling, then the TSR first checks to see if the TSR is already installed (also using INT 2Fh, incidentally). If it isn't installed, when the INIT routine completes, the program has become memory resident, and five interrupt handlers have been installed.

Before examining the interrupt handlers, let us create a few semaphores that the interrupt handlers will use to communicate among themselves:

```
FLAG wanted_pop up      ; wanted to pop up earlier, but DOS was busy
FLAG disk_unsafe        ; INT 13h in use?
FLAG idle_int           ; is INT 28h in progress?
```

InDOS is not included here because this flag is maintained by DOS itself and is not located inside the program. We use our DosBusy() routine to check InDOS.

The first interrupt handler to examine is the one that handles keyboard events. Because we installed an INT 9 handler, each time the user presses any key, a piece of code something like the following gets executed:

```
ON KEY ; new_int9() in TSREXAMP.C
    IF we are not already running AND
        IF it's our hotkey AND
            IF NOT disk_unsafe THEN
                CALL POP UP
            ELSE
                ; we can't pop up now, so just set flag indicating that
                ; we WANT to pop up at the next available moment
                wanted_pop up = TRUE
                JMP previous KEY handler
        ELSE
            ; not our hotkey - chain to next handler
            JMP previous KEY handler
    ELSE
        ; we're already running - let key beprocessed normally
        JMP previous KEY handler
```

In the simplest scenario, the user presses the hotkey at a time when INT 13h isn't in use. Our keyboard handler then calls the POP UP routine:

```
POP UP ; tsr_function() in TSREXAMP.C
    CALL set_stack() ; switch to our own stack
    IF DosBusy() AND NOT idle_int
        wanted_pop up = TRUE
    ELSE
        ; we really can POP UP now!
        GETVECT CTRL-BREAK(1Bh), CTRL-C(1Ch), CRITERR(24h)
        SETVECT CTRL-BREAK, CTRL-C, CRITERR
        current_PSP = GetPSP()
        CALL SetPSP(TSR_PSP) ; TSR_PSP and TSR_DTA were set in init
        current_DTA = GetDTA()
        CALL SetDTA(TSR_DTA)
        save_err = GetExtErr()
        eat keys
        CALL application()
        CALL SetExtErr(save_err)
        CALL SetDTA(current_DTA)
        CALL SetPSP(current_PSP)
```

```
    SETVECT CTRL-BREAK, CTRL-C, CRITERR ; REVERT
ON CTRL-BREAK DO NOTHING
ON CTRL-C DO NOTHING
ON CRITERR ; new_int24() in TSREXAMP.C
    RETURN FAILURE
```

Continuing with the simplest scenario, let's say that DosBusy() returns FALSE. The program then proceeds to install three short-term interrupt handlers. The Ctrl-Break and Ctrl-C handlers merely discard these events. A more sophisticated TSR might do something fancy with them. The Critical Error handler merely returns failure. The key point is that the pop-up portion of the TSR must run its own handlers for these events, not whatever handler the foreground process happens to have installed at the time. Next, the TSR swaps its own Disk Transfer Area and PSP with that of the foreground process, and saves the extended error information discussed earlier. It eats whatever keys are lurking in the keyboard buffer and—finally!—calls the application, which, as you know, does something useful like providing a notepad, dialing a modem, or playing a tune from *Pinafore*. When the application finishes, the TSR puts everything back the way it found it.

That was the simplest scenario. Say the user has pressed the hotkey, but the TSR can't pop up. Either INT 13h is in use or DOS is really busy—that is, InDOS is set and DOS is not inside an INT 28h idle interrupt. In this case, either the keyboard handler or the pop-up routine sets the wanted_popup flag, and more or less immediately returns (in the case of the keyboard handler, with an IRET).

So all the TSR has done is set the wanted_popup flag. How is this going to help the TSR pop up?

Remember the INT 8 timer tick handler the TSR installed? At each timer tick (about 18.2 times a second, unless someone has reprogrammed the chip that generates these interrupts), our TIMER routine gets woken up. Its job is to check the wanted_popup flag:

```
ON TIMER ; new_int8() in TSREXAMP.C
    CALL previous TIMER handler
    IF NOT tsr_active
        IF wanted_popup
            IF NOT DosBusy()
                IF NOT disk_unsafe
                    wanted_popup = FALSE
                    CALL POP UP
```

Once the wanted_popup flag has been set, the TIMER routine checks 18.2 times a second to see if it's now safe to pop up. It does this until it is safe to pop up, at which time the flag is turned off.

One thing not shown in pseudocode, but appearing in the genuine code in TSREXAMP.C and TSRUTIL.ASM, is that, for all hardware interrupts like INT 8 or INT 9, the TSR chains to the previous handler. In addition to giving the previous interrupt handler an opportunity to do its thing, it also relies on the previous handler to send the end-of-interrupt (EOI) command to the Intel 8259A interrupt controller. This is why you won't find the otherwise obligatory call to out(0x20,0x20) sprinkled throughout the code.

In addition to timer ticks, you can also use the Idle interrupt as a trigger for servicing a wanted_popup request. Note also that the IDLE handler increments and decrements the idle_int flag, which is checked on entry to the POP UP routine:

```
ON IDLE ; new_int28() in TSREXAMP.C
    INCR idle_int
    IF wanted_popup
        IF NOT Int28DosBusy()
            IF NOT tsr_active
                IF NOT disk_unsafe
                    POP UP!
```

```
    DECR idle_int
    CALL previous IDLE handler
```

Finally, how does the important disk_unsafe flag stay updated? There is unfortunately no flag in the BIOS that we can get a far pointer to as we did with InDOS, so we hook INT 13h to create our own disk_unsafe semaphore:

```
ON DISK ; new_int13() in TSRUTIL.ASM
    INCR disk_unsafe
    CALL previous DISK handler
    DECR disk_unsafe
```

That's about all there is to the generic TSR. Note how decentralized the code for a TSR is. Rather than have one top-level routine that calls various subroutines, there is instead a collection of independent handlers that get called due to some event taking place outside the program. The system has no "top" and instead consists of these asynchronously invoked agents. Much is made of event-driven programming in environments like Windows; but in reality, it's not much different from what we're doing here.

Having taken this walk through the pseudocode, you should now be able to fully understand the actual live C source code in TSREXAMP.C (Listing 9-15). However, many of the variable and function names are different from our pseudocode, and we haven't yet explained the sections which are conditionally compiled with #ifdef DOSSWAP.

TSREXAMP.C includes the rather uninteresting, but necessary, TSR.H, which contains typedefs and function prototypes for all the modules that make up the generic TSR. Listing 9-16 shows TSR.H.

Listing 9-15: TSREXAMP.C

```c
/*
TSREXAMP.C
by Raymond J. Michels
with revisions by Andrew Schulman

Second Edition - includes MS-DOS Task Manager/Windows Support
*/

#include <stddef.h>
#include <stdlib.h>
#include <stdio.h>
#include <conio.h>
#include <dos.h>
#include <bios.h>
#include <memory.h>
#include "tsr.h"

#define STACK_SIZE      8192    /* must be 16 byte boundary */
#define SET_DTA         0x1a    /* SET Disk Transfer Address */
#define GET_DTA         0x2f    /* GET Disk Transfer Address */

#define DOS_EXIT        0x4C    /* DOS terminate (exit) */

#define KEYBOARD_PORT   0x60    /* KEYBOARD Data Port */

#define PSP_TERMINATE   0x0A    /* Termination addr. in our PSP */
#define PSP_PARENT_PSP  0x16    /* Parent's PSP from  our PSP */
#define PSP_ENV_ADDR    0x2c    /* environment address from PSP */

#define HOT_KEY         32      /* Hot key along with ALT (D)*/

#define RIGHT_SHIFT     1
#define LEFT_SHIFT      2
#define CTRL_KEY        4
#define ALT_KEY         8

#define MULTIPLEX_ID    0xC0
#define INSTALL_CHECK   0x00
```

```
#define INSTALLED        0xFF
#define DEINSTALL        0x01
#define SESSION_ACTIVE   0x03

#define PARAGRAPHS(x)    ((FP_OFF(x) + 15) >> 4)

unsigned char multiplex_id = MULTIPLEX_ID;
char far *stack_ptr;              /* pointer to TSR stack */
unsigned ss_save;                 /* slot for stack segment register */
unsigned sp_save;                 /* slot for stack pointer register */
volatile int int_28_in_progress = 0;    /* true if INT 28h in progress */
volatile int unsafe_flag = 0;            /* true if INT 13h in progress */
unsigned keycode;
char buf[20];                     /* work buffer */
unsigned long TerminateAddr;      /* used during de-install */
union REGS regs;                  /* register work structures */
struct SREGS sregs;
int hot_key;                      /* keycode for activation */
int shift_key;                    /* shift status bits (alt, ctrl..) */
int user_key_set = 0;

/* Save areas for old interrupt pointers */
INTVECT old_int8, old_int9, old_int10, old_int13;
INTVECT old_int28, old_int2f;

#ifdef DOS_SWAP
extern int dos_critical;    /* used by DOSSWAP.C */
INTVECT old_int2a;
void interrupt far new_int2a(INTERRUPT_REGS);
#endif

extern int enhanced_windows;
extern int switcher_critical;

/* Global Data block that will be maintained in Instance Memory.
   That way each session in a Task Manager will have unique Global
   Data. */

struct
{
    volatile int tsr_already_active;     /* true if TSR active */
    volatile int popup_while_dos_busy;   /* true if hotkey hit while dos busy */
    int breakState;                      /* status of MS-DOS break checking */
        INTVECT old_int1b, old_int23, old_int24;
    unsigned foreground_psp;             /* PSP of process we've interrupted */
    unsigned foreground_dta_seg;         /* DTA of process we've interrupted */
    unsigned foreground_dta_off;
    struct ExtErr ErrInfo;               /* save area for extended error info */
} TsrGlb;

int global_tsr_active = 0;               /* flag to indicate a session is in TSR */

/* PROTOTYPES FOR THIS MODULE */
void interrupt far new_int8(INTERRUPT_REGS);
void interrupt far new_int9(INTERRUPT_REGS);
extern void interrupt far new_int13(void);   /* in TSRUTIL.ASM */
void interrupt far new_int1b(INTERRUPT_REGS);
void interrupt far new_int23(INTERRUPT_REGS);
void interrupt far new_int24(INTERRUPT_REGS);
void interrupt far new_int28(INTERRUPT_REGS);
void interrupt far new_int2f(INTERRUPT_REGS);
void tsr_function(void);
void tsr_exit(void);
void usage(char *);
int UnlinkVect(int Vect, INTVECT NewInt, INTVECT OldInt);
void parse_cmd_line(int argc, char *argv[]);
void main(int argc,char *argv[]);

/*********
* TIMER INTERRUPT HANDLER
```

```
*********/
void interrupt far new_int8(INTERRUPT_REGS r)
{
    (*old_int8)();      /* process timer tic */
#ifdef DOS_SWAP
    if (!TsrGlb.tsr_already_active && TsrGlb.popup_while_dos_busy &&
        !dos_critical && !unsafe_flag)
#else
    if (!TsrGlb.tsr_already_active && TsrGlb.popup_while_dos_busy &&
        !DosBusy() && !unsafe_flag)
#endif
    {
        /* If we're not running enhanced mode windows, set flag so that
           task swap will not occur. If we're not running Windows,
           enhanced defaults to true, so there is no effect. */

        if (!enhanced_windows)
            switcher_critical++;  /* don't allow task switch */

        TsrGlb.popup_while_dos_busy = 0;
        TsrGlb.tsr_already_active = 1;
        global_tsr_active = 1;

        _enable(); /* turn interrupts back on */
        tsr_function();
        TsrGlb.tsr_already_active = 0;
            global_tsr_active = 0;

        if (!enhanced_windows)
            switcher_critical--; /* task switch ok */
    }
}

/**********
* KEYBOARD INTERRUPT HANDLER
**********/
void interrupt far new_int9(INTERRUPT_REGS r)
{
    if (!TsrGlb.tsr_already_active)
    {
        if ((keycode = inp(KEYBOARD_PORT)) != hot_key)
            _chain_intr(old_int9);
        if ((_bios_keybrd(_KEYBRD_SHIFTSTATUS) & shift_key) == shift_key)
            {
#ifdef USES_DISK
            if (!unsafe_flag)
                {
#endif
                TsrGlb.popup_while_dos_busy = 0;
                TsrGlb.tsr_already_active = 1;
                global_tsr_active = 1;

                (*old_int9)();      /* send key to old int routine */
                tsr_function();
                TsrGlb.tsr_already_active = 0;
                global_tsr_active = 0;
#ifdef USES_DISK
                }
            else
                {
                TsrGlb.popup_while_dos_busy = 1;
                _chain_intr(old_int9);
                }
#endif
            }
        else
            _chain_intr(old_int9);
```

```
        }
        else
            _chain_intr(old_int9);
}

/*********
 * CTRL-BREAK INTERRUPT HANDLER
 *********/
void interrupt far new_int1b(INTERRUPT_REGS r) { /* do nothing */ }

/**********
 * CTRL-C INTERRUPT HANDLER
 **********/
void interrupt far new_int23(INTERRUPT_REGS r) { /* do nothing */ }

/**********
 * CRTITICAL ERROR INTERRUPT HANDLER
 **********/
void interrupt far new_int24(INTERRUPT_REGS r)
{
    if (_osmajor >= 3)
        r.ax = 3;   /* fail dos function */
    else
        r.ax = 0;
}

/**********
 * DOS IDLE INTERRUPT HANDLER
 **********/
void interrupt far new_int28(INTERRUPT_REGS r)
{
    int_28_in_progress++;
#ifdef DOS_SWAP
    if (TsrGlb.popup_while_dos_busy && !dos_critical
        && !TsrGlb.tsr_already_active && !unsafe_flag)
#else
    if (TsrGlb.popup_while_dos_busy && (!Int28DosBusy())
        && !TsrGlb.tsr_already_active && !unsafe_flag)
#endif
    {
        TsrGlb.tsr_already_active = 1;
        global_tsr_active = 1;

        tsr_function();
        TsrGlb.tsr_already_active = 0;
        global_tsr_active = 0;

    }

    int_28_in_progress--;
    _chain_intr(old_int28);
}

#ifdef DOS_SWAP
/*********
 * DOS INTERNAL INTERRUPT HANDLER
 *********/
void interrupt far new_int2a(INTERRUPT_REGS r)
{
    switch (r.ax & 0xff00)
    {
        case 0x8000:    /* start critical section */
            dos_critical++;
            break;
        case 0x8100:    /* end critical section */
        case 0x8200:    /* end critical section */
            if (dos_critical)    /* don't go negative */
                dos_critical--;
            break;
```

```
        default:
            break;
    }
    _chain_intr(old_int2a);
}
#endif
/*********
* DOS MULTIPLEX INTERRUPT HANDLER
*********/
void interrupt far new_int2f(INTERRUPT_REGS r)
{
    if (process_switcher_int2f(&r)) /* check if task switcher function */
    {
        unsigned ah = r.ax >> 8;
        unsigned al = r.ax & 0xFF;
        if (ah == multiplex_id)
        {
            if (al == INSTALL_CHECK)
                r.ax |= INSTALLED;
            else if (al == DEINSTALL)
            {
                if (global_tsr_active)
                /* a session is active, don't allow de-install */
                {
                    r.ax &= 0xff00;
                    //let caller know  we're still there
                    r.ax |= SESSION_ACTIVE;
                }
                else
                {
                    // because of stack swap, pass arg in static variable.
                    TerminateAddr = ((long)r.bx << 16) + r.dx;
                    if (! TsrGlb.tsr_already_active)
                    /* don't exit if we're active */
                    {
                        _enable(); /* STI */
                        tsr_exit();
                        // If we got here, we weren't able to unlink
                        // let caller know we're still there
                        r.ax = 0xFFFF;
                        // MSC 6.0 /Ox optimizes out the above
                        // get it back by using the value in ax
                        TsrGlb.tsr_already_active = -r.ax;
                        //set to 1 to prevent any more action
                    }
                }
            }
        }
        else
            _chain_intr(old_int2f);
    }
}

/*********
* TSR ACTIVE SECTION
*********/
void tsr_function()
{
    switcher_critical++;
    windows_begin_critical();

    set_stack();

    windows_end_critical();
    switcher_critical--;
```

```
#ifdef DOS_SWAP
    if (SaveDosSwap() && !int_28_in_progress)
#else
    if (DosBusy() && !int_28_in_progress)
#endif
        /* set flag: next INT 8,28 activates us */
        TsrGlb.popup_while_dos_busy = 1;
    else
    {
        TsrGlb.popup_while_dos_busy = 0;

        /* save current extended break status */
        TsrGlb.breakState = GetBreak();

        /* set extended break status to be off */
        SetBreak(0);

#ifndef DOS_SWAP
        /* Get Extended Error Information */
        GetExtErr(&TsrGlb.ErrInfo);
#endif

        /* save old interrupt-CTRL-BREAK, CTRL-C and CRIT ERROR */
        TsrGlb.old_int1b = _dos_getvect(0x1b);
        TsrGlb.old_int23 = _dos_getvect(0x23);
        TsrGlb.old_int24 = _dos_getvect(0x24);

        /* set our interrupts functions */
        _dos_setvect(0x1b, new_int1b);
        _dos_setvect(0x23, new_int23);
        _dos_setvect(0x24, new_int24);


        /* not needed for DOSSWAP, but can be used by application */
        TsrGlb.foreground_psp = GetPSP();


        SetPSP(_psp);    // _psp in STDLIB.H

#ifndef DOS_SWAP
        /* get foreground DTA */
        regs.h.ah = GET_DTA;
        intdosx(&regs, &regs, &sregs);
        TsrGlb.foreground_dta_seg = sregs.es;
        TsrGlb.foreground_dta_off = regs.x.bx;
#endif

        /* set up our DTA */
        regs.h.ah = SET_DTA;
        regs.x.dx = 0x80;    /* use default in PSP area */
        sregs.ds = _psp;
        intdosx(&regs, &regs, &sregs);


        /* suck up key(s) in buffer */
        while (_bios_keybrd(_KEYBRD_READY))
            _bios_keybrd(_KEYBRD_READ);

        /* your code goes here */
        application();
#ifdef DOS_SWAP
        /* put back original INTS */
        _dos_setvect(0x1b, TsrGlb.old_int1b);
        _dos_setvect(0x23, TsrGlb.old_int23);
        _dos_setvect(0x24, TsrGlb.old_int24);

        /* put back extended error information */
        SetExtErr(&TsrGlb.ErrInfo);
```

```
        RestoreDosSwap();
#else

        /* put back original DTA */
        regs.h.ah = SET_DTA;
        regs.x.dx = TsrGlb.foreground_dta_off;
        sregs.ds  = TsrGlb.foreground_dta_seg;
        intdosx(&regs, &regs, &sregs);

        /* put back original PSP */
        SetPSP(TsrGlb.foreground_psp);

        /* put back original INTS */
        _dos_setvect(0x1b, TsrGlb.old_int1b);
        _dos_setvect(0x23, TsrGlb.old_int23);
        _dos_setvect(0x24, TsrGlb.old_int24);

        /* put back extended error information */
        SetExtErr(&TsrGlb.ErrInfo);
#endif

        /* put back extended break checking the way it was */
        SetBreak(TsrGlb.breakState);


    }

    switcher_critical++;
    windows_begin_critical();

    restore_stack();

    windows_end_critical();
    switcher_critical--;
}
// only restores OldInt if someone hasn't grabbed away Vect
int UnlinkVect(int Vect, INTVECT NewInt, INTVECT OldInt)
{
    if (NewInt == _dos_getvect(Vect))
        { _dos_setvect(Vect, OldInt); return 0; }
    return 1;
}

void tsr_exit(void)
{
    set_stack();
    /* put interrupts back the way they were, if possible */

    if (!(UnlinkVect(8, new_int8, old_int8)       |
          UnlinkVect(9, new_int9, old_int9)       | // Do not use ||, we
          UnlinkVect(0x28, new_int28, old_int28)  | // DON'T want early out
          UnlinkVect(0x13, new_int13, old_int13)  |
#ifdef DOS_SWAP
          UnlinkVect(0x2a, new_int2a, old_int2a)  |
#endif
          UnlinkVect(0x2f, new_int2f, old_int2f) ))
    {
        // Set parent PSP, stored in our own PSP, to the current PSP
        *(int far *)(((long)_psp << 16) + PSP_PARENT_PSP) = GetPSP();

        // Set terminate address in our PSP
        *(long far *)(((long)_psp << 16) + PSP_TERMINATE) = TerminateAddr;

        SetPSP(_psp); /* set psp to be ours */

        bdos(DOS_EXIT, 0, 0); /* exit program */
    }
    restore_stack();
}
```

```c
void usage(char *progname)
{
    fputs("Usage: ", stdout);
    puts(progname);
    puts(" [-d deinstall] [-k key shift-keys] [-f multiplex id]");
    puts(" Valid multiplex id");
    puts("     00 through 15 specifies a unique INT 2Fh ID");
    puts(" Valid shift-keys is any combination of:");
    puts("     1 = Right Shift");
    puts("     2 = Left Shift");
    puts("     4 = CTRL");
    puts("     8 = ALT");
    exit(1);
}

void do_deinstall(char *progname)
{
    fputs(progname, stdout);
    switch (deinstall())
    {
        case 1:
            puts(" was not installed"); break;
        case 2:
            puts(" deinstalled"); break;
        case SESSION_ACTIVE:
            puts(" TSR active in another session. "
                "TSR was not deinstalled"); break;
        default:
            puts(" deactivated but not removed"); break;
    }
    exit(0);
}

int set_shift_key(unsigned sh)
{
    /* figure out, report on shift statuses */
    /* make sure shift key < 0x10 and non-zero */
    if (((shift_key = sh) < 0x10) && shift_key)
    {
        printf("Activation: %s%s%s%sSCAN=%d\n",
            shift_key & RIGHT_SHIFT ? "RIGHT " : "",
            shift_key & LEFT_SHIFT ? "LEFT " : "",
            shift_key & CTRL_KEY ? "CTRL " : "",
            shift_key & ALT_KEY ? "ALT " : "",
            hot_key);
        return 1;
    }
    else /* error, bad param */
    {
        puts("Invalid Shift-Status");
        return 0;
    }
}

void parse_cmd_line(int argc, char *argv[])
{
    int i;
    int tmp;

    for (i = 1; i < argc; i++)   /* for each cmdline arg */
        if ((argv[i][0] == '-') || (argv[i][0] == '/'))
            switch(toupper(argv[i][1]))
            {
                case 'D':
                    do_deinstall(argv[0]);
                    break;
                case 'K':    /* set pop up key sequence */
```

```
                        user_key_set = 1;
                        i++;      /* bump to next    argument */
                        if ((hot_key = atoi(argv[i])) != 0)
                        {
                            i++;   /* bump to next argument */
                            if (!set_shift_key(atoi(argv[i])))
                                usage(argv[0]);
                        }
                        else
                            usage(argv[0]);
                        break;
                  case 'F':   /* set multiplex ID */
                        i++;      /* bump to next argument */
                        if ((tmp = atoi(argv[i])) < 0x10)
                            multiplex_id += tmp; /* range of C0-CF */
                        else
                            usage(argv[0]);
                        break;
                  default:    /* invalid argument */
                        usage(argv[0]);
            }   /* end switch */
        else
            usage(argv[0]);
}
void FAIL(char *s) { puts(s); exit(1); }
void main(int argc,char *argv[])
{
    union REGS  regs;
    struct SREGS sregs;
    unsigned far *fp;
    unsigned memtop, dummy;
    int ret_value;

    /* initialize flags */
    TsrGlb.popup_while_dos_busy = 0;
    TsrGlb.tsr_already_active = 0;

    InitInDos();


    /* the foollowing must be called before adding instance data */
    init_switcher_structures();

    parse_cmd_line(argc,argv);

    /* check if TSR already installed! */
    regs.h.ah = multiplex_id;
    regs.h.al = INSTALL_CHECK;
    int86(0x2f, &regs, &regs);
    if (regs.h.al == INSTALLED)
    {
        puts("TSR already installed");
        fputs(argv[0], stdout); puts(" -D de-installs");
        exit(1);
    }

    if (! user_key_set)
    {
        puts("Press ALT-D to activate TSR ");
        printf("Multiplex ID = %0x \n",multiplex_id);
        hot_key = HOT_KEY;
        shift_key = ALT_KEY;
    }
#ifdef DOS_SWAP

    if ((ret_value = InitDosSwap()) != 0)
    {
```

```
        puts("Error initializing DOS Swappable Data Area");
        switch (ret_value)
        {
            case 1:
                puts("No Available Memory"); break;
            case 2:
                puts("Too Many Swap Blocks"); break;
            case 3:
                puts("Unsupported DOS"); break;
            case 4:
                puts("Unable to add swap blocks to instance memory");
                break;
            default:
                puts("Failure Return from GetDosSwap Call"); break;
        }
        exit(1);
    }
#endif
    /* MALLOC a stack for our TSR section */
    if ((stack_ptr = malloc(STACK_SIZE)) == NULL)
        FAIL("Unable to allocate stack");

    if (add_instance_block(stack_ptr, STACK_SIZE))
        FAIL("Unable to add stack to instance data");

    stack_ptr += STACK_SIZE;

    if (add_instance_block(&TsrGlb, sizeof(TsrGlb)))
        FAIL("Unable to add TSR global data to instance data");
    if (add_instance_block(&ss_save, sizeof(ss_save)))
        FAIL("Unable to add ss_save global data to instance data");
    if (add_instance_block(&sp_save, sizeof(sp_save)))
        FAIL("Unable to add sp_save global data to instance data");
    if (add_instance_block(&stack_ptr, sizeof(stack_ptr)))
        FAIL("Unable to add stack_ptr global data to instance data");
    if (add_instance_block(&regs, sizeof(regs)))
        FAIL("Unable to add regs global data to instance data");
    if (add_instance_block(&sregs, sizeof(sregs)))
        FAIL("Unable to add sregs global data to instance data");

     /* check if windows running */
    check_windows_running();

     /* check if task switcher running */
    check_switcher_running();

    /* get interrupt vector */
    old_int8  = _dos_getvect(8);        /* timer interrupt */
    old_int9  = _dos_getvect(9);        /* keyboard interrupt */
    old_int13 = _dos_getvect(0x13);     /* disk intr, in TSRUTIL.ASM */
    old_int28 = _dos_getvect(0x28);     /* dos idle */
    old_int2f = _dos_getvect(0x2f);     /* multiplex int */
#ifdef DOS_SWAP
    old_int2a = _dos_getvect(0x2a);     /* dos internal int */
#endif

    init_intr();  /* initialize int routines in TSRUTIL.ASM */

    /* set interrupts to our routines */
    _dos_setvect(8, new_int8);
    _dos_setvect(9, new_int9);
    _dos_setvect(0x13, new_int13);            /* in TSRUTIL.ASM */
    _dos_setvect(0x28, new_int28);
    _dos_setvect(0x2f, new_int2f);
#ifdef DOS_SWAP
    _dos_setvect(0x2a, new_int2a);
#endif
```

```
    /* release environment back to MS-DOS */
    FP_SEG(fp) = _psp;
    FP_OFF(fp) = PSP_ENV_ADDR;
    _dos_freemem(*fp);

    /* release unused heap to MS-DOS */
    /* All MALLOCS for TSR section must be done in  TSR_INIT() */
    /* calculate top of memory, and go TSR */
    segread(&sregs);

    memtop = sregs.ds + PARAGRAPHS(stack_ptr) - _psp;

    _dos_keep(0, memtop);
}
```

Listing 9-16: TSR.H

```
/* TSR Prototype file and common variables */

#ifdef _cplusplus
extern "C" {
#endif

#define INTERRUPT void interrupt far

typedef struct {
#ifdef TURBOC
    unsigned bp, di, si, ds, es, dx, cx, bx, ax;
#else
    unsigned es, ds;
    unsigned di, si, bp, sp, bx, dx, cx, ax;      /*  PUSHA */
#endif
    } INTERRUPT_REGS;

typedef void (interrupt far *INTVECT)();

/* Prototypes for functions in INDOS.C */
int   DosBusy(void);
int   Int28DosBusy(void);
void  InitInDos(void);

/* Prototypes for functions in PSP.C */
unsigned GetPSP(void);
void  SetPSP(unsigned segPSP);

/* Prototypes for functions in TSRUTIL.ASM */
int   far   deinstall(void);
void  far   init_intr(void);
void  far   idle_int_chain(void);

void  interrupt far   new_int10(void);
void  interrupt far   new_int13(void);
void  interrupt far   new_int25(void);
void  interrupt far   new_int26(void);

void  far   timer_int_chain(void);

/* Prototypes for functions in STACK.ASM */
void  far   set_stack(void);
void  far   restore_stack(void);

/* Prototypes for functions in EXTERR.C */
void  GetExtErr(struct ExtErr * ErrInfo);
void  SetExtErr(struct ExtErr * ErrInfo);

struct    ExtErr
{
    unsigned int errax, errbx, errcx, errdx, errsi, errdi;
    unsigned int errds, erres;
    unsigned int reserved, userID, programID;
};

/* Prototypes for functions in DOSSWAP.C */
```

```
int   InitDosSwap(void);
int   SaveDosSwap(void);
void  RestoreDosSwap(void);

/* Pointer defined in INDOS.C */
extern char far *   indos_ptr;
extern char far *   crit_err_ptr;

/* Prototypes for functions in BREAK.C */
int GetBreak(void);
void SetBreak(int breakStatus);

/* Prototypes and global vars defined in SWITCHER.C */
extern int   enhanced_windows;
extern int   switcher_critical;

int    process_switcher_int2f(INTERRUPT_REGS far *r);
void   init_switcher_structures(void);
int add_instance_block(void far *ptr, unsigned int size);
void windows_begin_critical();
void windows_end_critical();
void check_windows_running(void);
void check_switcher_running(void);

#ifdef _cplusplus
}
#endif
```

Many readers of the first edition of this book noticed an error in the tsr_function() of TSREXAMP.C. We were incorrectly calling RestoreDosSwap() before having restored original interrupt handlers. Since _dos_setvect generates an INT 21h function 25h DOS call, which in turn switches stacks, it potentially damages the state of DOS after we have called RestoreDosSwap. We should call RestoreDosSwap only after all we have made all DOS calls. This has been corrected in Listing 9-15.

Finally, there's TSRUTIL.ASM (Listing 9-17), which contains miscellaneous routines which we either didn't want to write in C, or couldn't.

Listing 9-17: TSRUTIL.ASM

```
;TSRUTIL.ASM

;Define segment names used by C
;
_TEXT     segment byte public 'CODE'
_TEXT     ends

CONST     segment word public 'CONST'
CONST     ends

_BSS      segment word public 'BSS'
_BSS      ends

_DATA     segment word public 'DATA'
_DATA     ends

DGROUP    GROUP    CONST, _BSS, _DATA

     assume   CS:_TEXT, DS:DGROUP

     public   _new_int13, _init_intr
IFDEF MULTI
     public   _timer_int_chain
     public   _new_int10, _new_int21, _new_int25, _new_int26
ELSE
     public   _deinstall
ENDIF

     extrn    _ss_save:near        ;save foreground SS
     extrn    _sp_save:near        ;save foreground SP
     extrn    _unsafe_flag:near    ;if true, don't interrupt
     extrn    _old_int13:near
```

```
IFDEF MULTI
    extrn    _old_int8:near
    extrn    _old_int10:near
    extrn    _old_int21:near
    extrn    _old_int25:near        ; note difference between
    extrn    _old_int26:near        ; old_int25 and _old_int25!
    extrn    _dos_count:near
    extrn    _in_progress:near
ELSE
    extrn    _multiplex_id:near    ;our INT 2Fh id byte
ENDIF

_TEXT    segment

IFNDEF MULTI
;*****
;void far deinstall(void)
;function to use INT 2Fh to ask TSR to deinstall itself
;the registers are probably all changed when our tsr exits
;so we save then and perform the INT 2f. The TSR exit will
;eventually bring us back here. Then the registers are restored
;This function is called from the foreground, not the TSR

DEINSTALL    equ    1

_deinstall       proc    far
    push    si
    push    di
    push    bp
    mov     word ptr _ss_save,ss      ; save our stack frame
    mov     word ptr _sp_save,sp

    mov     cs:_ds_save,ds            ; save DS for later restore

    mov     bx,cs
    mov     dx, offset TerminateAddr; bx:dx points to terminate address
    mov     ah, byte ptr _multiplex_id
    mov     al, DEINSTALL
    int     2fh                       ; call our TSR
;
;if TSR terminates ok, we'll skip this code and return to Terminate Addr
;
    jmp     short NoTerminate
TerminateAddr:
;Restore DS and stack
    mov     ax,cs:_ds_save            ; bring back our data segment
    mov     ds,ax                     ; destroyed by int 2f

    mov     al,2                      ; Set value for success

    mov     ss, word ptr _ss_save     ; restore our stack
    mov     sp, word ptr _sp_save     ; destroyed by int 2f
NoTerminate:
    cbw                               ;Extend return value to word
    pop     bp
    pop     di
    pop     si
    ret
_deinstall endp
ENDIF
;*****
;void inc_unsafe_flag(void) - increment unsafe flag
;*****
inc_unsafe_flag proc    far
    push    ax
    push    ds
    mov     ax,DGROUP                 ;make DS = to our TSR C data segment
    mov     ds,ax
```

```
        inc     word ptr _unsafe_flag

        pop     ds                      ;put DS back to whatever it was
        pop     ax
        ret
inc_unsafe_flag endp
;*****
;void dec_unsafe_flag(void) - decrement unsafe flag
;*****
dec_unsafe_flag proc    far
        push    ax
        push    ds
        mov     ax,DGROUP               ;make DS = to our TSR C data segment
        mov     ds,ax

        dec     word ptr _unsafe_flag

        pop     ds                      ;put DS back to whatever it was
        pop     ax
        ret
dec_unsafe_flag endp
;we can't trap the following interrupts in C for a number of
;reasons
;    INT 13 returns info in the FLAGS, but a normal IRET
;    restores the flags
;
;    INT 25 & 26 leave the flags on the stack. The user
;    must pop the off after performing an INT 25 or 26
;
;    These interrupts pass information via registers such
;    as DS. We don't want to change DS.
;
;    Since DS is unknown, we must call the old interrupts
;    via variables in the code segment. The _init_intr routine
;    sets up these CS variables from ones with nearly-identical
;    names in the C data segment in TSREXAMP.C.
;*****
;void far init_intr(void)
;move interrupt pointer saved in the C program to our CS data area
;*****
; note confusing distinction between e.g. _old_int13 and old_int13
SET_OLD MACRO _old_int, old_int
        les  bx, dword ptr _old_int
        mov  word ptr cs:old_int, bx
        mov  word ptr cs:old_int+2, es
        ENDM

_init_intr proc far
        push    es
        push    bx
IFDEF MULTI
        SET_OLD _old_int10, old_int10
        SET_OLD _old_int21, old_int21
        SET_OLD _old_int25, old_int25
        SET_OLD _old_int26, old_int26
ENDIF
        SET_OLD _old_int13, old_int13

        pop     bx
        pop     es
        ret
_init_intr endp
;*****
;void far new_int13(void) - disk interrupt
;*****
```

```
_new_int13 proc far
    call    inc_unsafe_flag
    pushf                               ;simulate interrupt call
    call    cs:old_int13
    call    dec_unsafe_flag
    ret     2                           ; leave flags intact
_new_int13 endp
IFDEF MULTI
;*****
;void far new_int21(void) - dos interrupt
;*****
_new_int21 proc far

    sti
;see if function 0. if so jump to int 21h vector

    cmp     ah,0
    jne     int21_0

    jmp     cs:old_int21

int21_0:

    push    ds
    push    ax

    mov     ax, DGROUP
    mov     ds,ax
    cmp     word ptr [_in_progress], 0
    je      int21_1                     ;not in background, so skip next

    inc     word ptr _dos_count         ;flag that the background has called dos

int21_1:
    pop     ax
    pop     ds
    pushf                               ;simulate interrupt call
    call    cs:old_int21

    pushf
    push    ds
    push    ax

    mov     ax, DGROUP
    mov     ds,ax
    cmp     word ptr [_in_progress], 0
    je      int21_2                     ;not in background, so skip next

    dec     word ptr _dos_count

int21_2:
    pop     ax
    pop     ds
    popf
    ret     2
_new_int21 endp
;*****
;void far new_int10(void) - video interrupt
;*****
_new_int10 proc far
    call    inc_unsafe_flag
    pushf                               ;simulate interrupt call
    call    cs:old_int10
    call    dec_unsafe_flag
    iret
_new_int10 endp
;*****
;void far new_int25(void) - MS-DOS absolute sector read
;*****
```

```
_new_int25  proc far
    call        inc_unsafe_flag
    call        cs:old_int25
    call        dec_unsafe_flag
    ret                             ; user must pop flags — MS-DOS convention
                                    ; so leave them on the stack
_new_int25 endp
;*****
;void far new_int26(void) - MS-DOS absolute sector write
;*****
_new_int26 proc far
    call        inc_unsafe_flag
    call        cs:old_int26
    call        dec_unsafe_flag
    ret                             ; user must pop flags — MS-DOS convention
                                    ; so leave them on the stack
_new_int26 endp
;*****
;void far timer_int_chain(void) - jump to next timer ISR
;we need to clean up the stack because of this call
;*****
_timer_int_chain proc far
    mov         _ax_save,ax
    pop         ax
    pop         ax
    mov         ax, _ax_save
    jmp         dword ptr _old_int8
_timer_int_chain    endp
ENDIF
;
;save areas for original interrupt vectors
;
IFDEF MULTI
old_int10   dd  0       ;video
old_int21   dd  0       ;dos int
old_int25   dd  0       ;sector read
old_int26   dd  0       ;sector write
ENDIF
old_int13   dd  0       ;disk

_ds_save    dw  0
_TEXT   ends

_DATA   segment
IFDEF MULTI
_ax_save    dw  0
ENDIF
_DATA   ends
    end
```

TSR Command Line Arguments

Any program built with the generic TSR can take optional command line arguments that set its hotkey and its multiplex interrupt ID number. A command line option is also available to deinstall the TSR, the implementation of which will be discussed in detail later on.

The command line syntax is [tsrname] [-k scan shift] [-f multiplex_id] [-d deinstalls]. A valid shift status is any combination of

1 =	Right Shift
2 =	Left Shift
4 =	CTRL
8 =	ALT

A valid multiplex id is 00 through 15, and specifies a unique INT 2Fh ID, starting at AH=C0h.

The default hotkey is Alt-D, and the default multiplex ID is zero which turns into INT 2Fh Function C0h. Specifying alternate hotkeys and multiplex IDs makes it possible to simultaneously run multiple programs built with the generic TSR. Finally, to deinstall a TSR whose multiplex ID is not the default, you must specify the use of both the -F and -D switches. For example:

```
C:\UNDOC2\CHAP9>tsrfile -k 59 8
    TSRFILE hotkey is Alt-F1 (F1 decimal scancode is 59)
    TSRFILE multiplex ID is default C0h

C:\UNDOC2\CHAP9>tsrmem -k 60 4 -f 1
    TSRMEM hotkey is Ctrl-F2 (F2 decimal scancode is 60)
    TSRMEM multiplex ID is C1h

C:\UNDOC2\CHAP9>tsrmem -f 1 -d
    TSRMEM deinstalled
```

Writing TSRs with the DOS Swappable Data Area

Undocumented INT 21h Function 5D06h for DOS 3.1 through 3.3, as well as for DOS 5.0 and higher, and Function 5D0Bh for DOS 4.x, gives you access to the DOS SDA. This block of data contains most (though definitely not all) of the current context of MS-DOS. The SDA includes the current PSP segment and the three MS-DOS stacks, as discussed earlier and as shown in gory detail in the appendix. If the List of Lists (LoL) is the key to DOS's data, then the SDA is DOS's data. For example, when either INT 21h Function 51h INT 21h Function 62h returns the current PSP, where do you think it gets it from? From the SDA. Ever wonder exactly how large each of DOS's three stacks is? Just look at SDA. They're in there! In the previous chapter, we made extensive use of the SDA in order to implement our network redirector. The SDA is a large chunk of the DOS data segment. In DOS 4.0 only, there can be multiple SDAs.

Although the call used to obtain the SDA is different for DOS 4.x only, the actual structure of the SDA introduced at version 4.x continued unchanged into DOS 5.00 and 6.00.

What does the SDA have to do with TSRs? Rather than wait for some time when there's no danger of reentering DOS, as our TSR has been doing up to now, a TSR can use Functions 5D06h and 5D0Bh to safely reenter MS-DOS by saving and restoring the SDA. This allows you to call MS-DOS at almost any time without having to wait until the DOS flags indicate it is safe. We should note that the word "safely" used two sentences ago is a relative term! Saving and restoring the SDA can never be 100% reliable, since the SDA does *not* (notwithstanding implications to the contrary in the first edition of this book) encompass all of DOS' state.

These functions are used in conjunction with INT 2Ah. When undocumented INT 2Ah Function 80h is invoked, it indicates that DOS is in a critical section. When DOS is in a critical section, you cannot change the SDA. The end of a critical section is indicated by a call to INT 2Ah Functions 81h or 82h. Note that INT 2Ah is invoked by MS-DOS and not by your application.

While an important piece of the puzzle, INT 2Ah suffers from one major drawback. It can be most obviously demonstrated by using a script such as that shown in Listing 9-18 in conjunction with the INTRSPY program presented in Chapter 5.

Listing 9-18: CRITSECT.SCR Watches INT 2Ah Critical Section Calls

```
;; CRITSECT.SCR -- Trap INT 2Ah critical section entry/exit calls
intercept 2Ah
    function 80h on_entry output "ENTER CRIT " al
    function 81h on_entry output "EXIT CRIT " al
    function 82h on_entry output "EXIT ALL CRIT"
```

Running this script and leaving it loaded for as long as you like while running programs in native DOS will yield no results other than a lot of calls to INT 2Ah AH=82h, which exits all critical sections. This call comes from the INT 21h dispatch code we examined in chapter 6. But we never see any critical sections being entered! This is because, while DOS has code to generate these calls at the appropriate times, it is normally disabled, and requires patches to enable it. These patches are, perhaps unsurprisingly, version specific. Windows and network shells perform the necessary patches, and use the resultant calls in just the way we need to. In the case of Windows Enhanced mode, the calls can be made visible inside a DOS box by adding the line ReflectDosInt2A=1 to the SYSTEM.INI file. The CRITSECT script, when then run in a DOS box, will be much more then productive. The CRITSECT program in Listing 9-19 allows the necessary patches to be applied and removed by invoking the program with ON or OFF on the command line.

Listing 9-19: CRITSECT.C

```
/*
CRITSECT.C
Andrew Schulman, January 1993
from "Undocumented DOS", 2nd edition (Addison-Wesley, 1993)

Thanks to John Brennan (John.Brennan@vi.ri.cmu.edu)
and to Norman D. Culver (CIS 70672,1257)

Reports on DOS critical sections, turns off or on

Table of critical section patch offsets at:
DOS:02C3h in DOS 3.1-3.3
DOS:0315h in DOS 4, 5, 6

to turn ON critical section calls in DOS:
in DOS 3-4, poke in 50h (PUSH AX) to replace C3h (RET)
in DOS 5-6, poke in any non-zero value
*/

#include <stdlib.h>
#include <stdio.h>
#include <string.h>
#include <dos.h>

#ifndef MK_FP
#define MK_FP(seg, ofs) \
    ((void far *) (((unsigned long) (seg) < 16) | (ofs)))
#endif

// get DOS data segment
// call 21/52 (Get List of Lists), keep segment, discard offset
unsigned short get_dos_ds(void)
{
    _asm push es
    _asm xor ax, ax
    _asm mov es, ax
    _asm mov ax, 5200h
    _asm int 21h
    _asm mov ax, es
    _asm pop es
    // return value in AX
}

// get DOS version number
// if DOS 5+, use 21/3306 because of SETVER
void get_dos_vers(unsigned char *pmaj, unsigned char *pmin)
{
    unsigned char maj, min;
    // must call 21/3306 before 21/30, but don't know if 21/3306 supported!
    // best bet is to clear BX beforehand; unsupported should set AL=FFh
    _asm xor bx, bx
    _asm mov ax, 3306h
```

```
    _asm int 21h
    _asm mov maj, bl
    _asm mov min, bh
    if ((maj==0) && (min==0))
    {
        _asm mov ax, 3000h
        _asm int 21h
        _asm mov maj, al
        _asm mov min, ah
    }
    *pmaj = maj;
    *pmin = min;
}

void fail(char *s) { puts(s); exit(1); }

typedef enum { STATUS, ON, OFF } REQU;

main(int argc, char *argv[])
{
    unsigned short far *patch_tab;
    unsigned short far *p;
    unsigned char far *fpop;
    unsigned short dos_ds;
    unsigned short tab_ofs;
    unsigned char dos_maj, dos_min;
    char *s;
    unsigned char op;
    REQU requ;

    // command line:  ON, OFF, or (default) STATUS
    if (argc < 2)
        requ = STATUS;
    else
    {
        s = strupr(argv[1]);
        if (strcmp(s, "STATUS") == 0) requ = STATUS;
        else if (strcmp(s, "ON") == 0) requ = ON;
        else if (strcmp(s, "OFF") == 0) requ = OFF;
        else fail("usage: critsect [status | on | off]");
    }

    // get DOS data segment
    dos_ds = get_dos_ds();

    // get DOS version number -- program works with DOS 3.1-6.0
    // may have to check for DR-DOS, etc.!
    get_dos_vers(&dos_maj, &dos_min);
    if ((dos_maj < 3) || (dos_maj > 6) || ((dos_maj == 3) && (dos_min == 0)))
        fail("Unsupported DOS version");

    // get pointer to table
    tab_ofs = (dos_maj == 3) ? 0x02c3 : 0x0315;
    patch_tab = (unsigned short far *) MK_FP(dos_ds, tab_ofs);

    if (requ == STATUS)
        printf("Critical section patch table at %Fp\n", patch_tab);
#define RET         0xC3
#define PUSH_AX     0x50
    // walk table
    for (p=patch_tab; *p != 0; p++)
    {
        fpop = (unsigned char far *) MK_FP(dos_ds, *p);
        op = *fpop;
        if (dos_maj < 5)
        {
            if (op == RET) s = "OFF";
            else if (op == PUSH_AX) s = "ON";
```

```
            else fail("Critical section patch table invalid!");
            if (requ == ON)          *fpop = PUSH_AX;
            else if (requ == OFF)    *fpop = RET;
        }
        else
        {
            if (op == 0) s = "OFF";
            else s = "ON";
            // no way to check for valid/invalid,
            // though anything other than 0 or 1 is suspicious

            if (requ == ON)          *fpop = 1;
            else if (requ == OFF)    *fpop = 0;
        }
        if (requ == STATUS)
            printf("%Fp = %02X   %s\n", fpop, op, s);
    }
    if (requ == ON) puts("Turned critical sections ON");
    else if (requ == OFF) puts("Turned critical sections OFF");

    return 0;
}
```

Once DOS is generating INT 2Ah critical section calls, you will need to write an interrupt handler for INT 2Ah to keep track of critical sections. You can only swap the SDA when DOS isn't in a critical section.

Your INT 2Ah handler may be bypassed under Windows Enhanced mode, because Windows patches DOS, turning its INT 2Ah calls into far calls into the Virtual Machine Manager (VMM). Microsoft's *MS-DOS Programmer's Reference* for MS-DOS 6 obliquely refers to this when it says that MRCI programs must acquire the Windows disk critical section by calling INT 2Ah AX=8001h, and furthermore that calls to this function must be coded in a particular way, because "Windows expects this exact sequence" (p. 446). This point is that Windows will patch an INT 2Ah AX=8001h so that it becomes a far call into VMM, which implements its own Begin_Critical_Section and End_Critical_Section calls, documented in the Windows DDK.

Returning to the SDA, INT 21h Function 5D06h returns the following information:

```
DS:SI - points to DOS swappable data area
DX    - size of area to swap when InDOS > 0
CX    - size of area to always swap
```

INT 21h Function 5D0Bh (for DOS 4 and higher) returns in DS:SI a pointer to an SDA list, which contains:

Offset	Size	Description
00h	WORD	Count of SDAs
SDA_ENTRY:		
02h	DWORD	Address of this SDA
06h	WORD	Data area length and type: bit 15 – set if swap always clear if swap while InDOS > 0 bits 14-0 – length in bytes
08h		next SDA_ENTRY

To reiterate, these functions give you pointers to the data area(s) that contains much (but not all) of the information related to the current process, as well as information specific to a DOS call that may be in progress. Since MS-DOS switches stacks when invoked with INT 21h, it is seemingly not reentrant. But since the stacks are part of this data area, you can save their current information by moving the entire swappable data area and immediately call DOS without fear of trashing DOS's internal stacks. Unfortunately, there are also key DOS variables that reside outside the part of the DOS data segment that is made available as the SDA.

In previous sections, we checked the DOS flags to determine whether it was safe to activate, and, once activated, we saved the current PSP, DTA, and extended error information. Using the DOSSWAP method eliminates these steps. You can determine whether it is safe to pop up by tracking the INT 2Ah critical section calls. If you are not in critical section, it is safe to call DOS. If InDOS is zero, just save the data area that is always swapped (typically 18h bytes). If InDOS is non-zero, then all swappable data areas must be saved (typically 73Ch bytes, less than 2K).

The TSR saves the data to a memory block that was allocated during TSR initialization (see the InitDosSwap function in DOSSWAP.C). In our C TSR, this malloc must be performed before the TSR stack is allocated. Once the data area has been saved, we set the current PSP and DTA values to those for our TSR. When it is time for the TSR to exit, we just move back the SDAs that we've saved. Since this data block contains the current PSP, DTA, and extended error information, we don't need to deal directly with these values.

Note: At the time of this writing, it is not clear whether the DOS SDA list returned by function 5D0Bh is static when MS-DOS is booted or whether it is changed dynamically during the course of MS-DOS execution. It appears that Functions 5D06h and 5D0Bh return identical information for MS-DOS 4.1. Since function 5D0Bh went away in DOS 5, it thus is a DOS 4.0 only phenomenon, and you may want to totally ignore it. Frankly, function 5D0Bh looks like just another example of how IBM added over-complexity to DOS when they got their hands on it in version 4.0.

The C module in Listing 9-20 contains functions for saving and restoring the DOS SDA.

Listing 9-20: SDA Save and Restore Module DOSSWAP.C

```
/* DOSSWAP.C - Functions to manage DOS swap areas */

#include <stdlib.h>
#include <dos.h>
#include <memory.h>
#include "tsr.h"
#include "put.h"

#define GET_DOSSWAP3        0x5d06
#define GET_DOSSWAP4        0x5d0b

#define SWAP_LIST_LIMIT     20

struct  swap_list     /* format of DOS 4+ SDA list */
{
    void far* swap_ptr;
    int swap_size;
};
/* variables for 3.x swap work */
static      char    far * swap_ptr;  /* pointer to dos swap area */
static      char    far * swap_save; /* pointer to our local save area */
static      int     swap_size_indos;
static      int     swap_size_always;
static      int     size;

/* variables for 4.x swap work */
static int swap_count;         /* count of swappable areas */
static struct swap_list swp_list[SWAP_LIST_LIMIT];
/*list of swap areas*/
static char far *swp_save[SWAP_LIST_LIMIT];   /* out save area */
static int swp_flag[SWAP_LIST_LIMIT];   /* flags if has been swapped */

static int dos_level;    /* for level dependent code */
int dos_critical;        /* in critical section, can't swap */
/*****
Function: InitDosSwap
```

```
Initialize pointers and sizes of DOS swap area.
Return zero if success
        1      - no memory
        2      - too many swap lists
        3      - unsupported dos
        4      - too many instance memory blocks
*****/
int InitDosSwap(void)
{
    union  REGS regs;
    struct SREGS segregs;
    int    ret;
     /* establish what dos level we're running
       make sure that DOSVER is not setup for this TSR
     */
    if ((_osmajor == 3) && (_osminor >= 10))
        dos_level = 3;
    else if (_osmajor == 4)
        dos_level = 4;
     else if (_osmajor == 5 || _osmajor == 6) /* 5 == 6 for now */
        dos_level = 5;
    else
        dos_level = 0;

    if (dos_level == 3 || dos_level == 5)    /* use 215D06 */
    {
        regs.x.ax = GET_DOSSWAP3;
        intdosx(&regs,&regs,&segregs);

        /* make sure no error occurred on interrupt function */
        if (regs.x.cflag)
            return(!0);

        /* pointer to swap area is returned in DS:SI */
        FP_SEG(swap_ptr) = segregs.ds;
        FP_OFF(swap_ptr) = regs.x.si;

        swap_size_indos = regs.x.cx;
        swap_size_always= regs.x.dx;

        size = 0;  /* initialize for later */
        swap_save = malloc(swap_size_indos);

        ret = ((swap_save == 0) ? 3 : 0);

        /* if we got mem, then see if we can add instance */
        if (!ret && add_instance_block(swap_save, swap_size_indos))
            ret = 4;

        return(ret);

    }
    else if (dos_level >= 4)  /* use 5d0b */
    {
        struct swap_list far *ptr;
        int far *iptr;
        int i;
        regs.x.ax = GET_DOSSWAP4;
        intdosx(&regs,&regs,&segregs);

        /* make sure no error occurred on interrupt function */
        if (regs.x.cflag)
            return(!0);


        /* pointer to swap list is returned in DS:SI */
        FP_SEG(iptr) = segregs.ds;
        FP_OFF(iptr) = regs.x.si;
        swap_count = *iptr;                    /* get size of list */
        iptr++;
```

```
        ptr = (struct swap_list far *) iptr;  /* create point to list */
        if (swap_count > SWAP_LIST_LIMIT)       /* too many data areas */
            return 2;
        /* get pointers and sizes of data areas */
        for (i = 0; i < swap_count; i++)
        {
            swp_list[i].swap_ptr = ptr->swap_ptr;
            swp_list[i].swap_size= ptr->swap_size;
            if (!(swp_save[i] = malloc(swp_list[i].swap_size & 0x7fff)))
                return 3;   /* out of memory */

            if (add_instance_block(swp_save[i],
                    swp_list[i].swap_size & 0x7fff))
                return 4;   /* not instance blocks available */

            swp_flag[i] = 0;
            ptr++;   /* point to next entry in the list */
        }
        return 0;
    }
    else
        return 1;   /* unsupported DOS */
}

/*****
Function: SaveDosSwap
This function will save the dos swap area to a local buffer
It returns zero on success, non-zero meaning can't swap
*****/
int SaveDosSwap(void)
{
    if (dos_level == 3 || dos_level == 5)
    {
        if (swap_ptr && !dos_critical)
        {
            /* if InDOS flag is zero, use smaller swap size */
            size = (*indos_ptr) ? swap_size_indos : swap_size_always;
            movedata(FP_SEG(swap_ptr),  FP_OFF(swap_ptr),
                    FP_SEG(swap_save), FP_OFF(swap_save),
                    size);
        }
        else       /* can't swap it */
            return 1;
    }
    else if (dos_level == 4)
    {
        /* loop through pointer list and swap appropriate items */
        int i;
        for (i = 0; i < swap_count; i++)
        {
            if (swp_list[i].swap_size & 0x8000)  /* swap always */
            {
                movedata(FP_SEG(swp_list[i].swap_ptr),
                        FP_OFF(swp_list[i].swap_ptr),
                        FP_SEG(swp_save[i]),
                        FP_OFF(swp_save[i]),
                        swp_list[i].swap_size & 0x7fff);
            }
            else if (*indos_ptr)       /* swap only if dos busy */
            {
                movedata(FP_SEG(swp_list[i].swap_ptr),
                        FP_OFF(swp_list[i].swap_ptr),
                        FP_SEG(swp_save[i]), FP_OFF(swp_save[i]),
```

```
                              swp_list[i].swap_size);
                }
            }
        }
    else
        return 1;

    return 0;
}
/*****
Function: RestoreDosSwap
This function will restore a previously swapped dos
data area
*****/
void RestoreDosSwap(void)
{
    if (dos_level == 3 || dos_level == 5)
    {
        /* make sure its already saved and we have a good ptr */
        if (size && swap_ptr)
        {
            movedata(FP_SEG(swap_save), FP_OFF(swap_save),
                    FP_SEG(swap_ptr), FP_OFF(swap_ptr), size);
            size = 0;
        }
    }
    else if (dos_level == 4)
    {
        int i;
        for (i = 0; i < swap_count; i++)
        {
            movedata(FP_SEG(swp_save[i]), FP_OFF(swp_save[i]),
                    FP_SEG(swp_list[i].swap_ptr),
                    FP_OFF(swp_list[i].swap_ptr),
                    swp_list[i].swap_size);
            swp_flag[i] = 0;    /* clear flag */
        }
    }
}
```

To try out the new DOSSWAP method for building TSRs, recompile TSREXAMP.C (Listing 9-15) with -DDOSSWAP and then link with the DOSSWAP module (Listing 9-20). See the makefile shown in Listing 9-1.

To use the DOSSWAP method in the multitasking non-pop-up example presented later, we would need to save not only the foreground data area (data belonging to the process we are interrupting), but the background data area (our TSR's data) as well. The SDA for the TSR could be saved during TSR initialization. Using this method, we would not need to deal with PSP, DTA, and Extended Error values at all since they would already exist in the SDA! Always saving and restoring the data area may make it easier to design some sort of round-robin task switcher. A hotkey could step through a number of independent applications. Interestingly, as we saw in chapter 1, the Microsoft Windows 3.x multitasker uses the undocumented SDA function. The "Origins of the SDA" discussion in chapter 8 points out that the SDA is not a genuine DOS internal data structure, but merely a portion of DOS's data segment that Microsoft exports for the benefit of networking software and other multitaskers.

If you have examined the actual contents of the DOS SDA in our appendix, you can see that this area is quite large. Because of this you may need to weigh the advantages and disadvantages of using the SDA. The primary advantage of using the SDA in TSRs is that you can activate almost anytime while DOS is busy, unless, of course, a critical section has been flagged using INT 2Ah. This would be most beneficial for multitasking or round-robin task switching, since the response to a task switch would be almost instantaneous. In our generic pop-up TSR, for example, using DOSSWAP, allows us to pop up instantly in the middle of a TYPE command.

There are two disadvantages. One is that this function requires memory to save the data area(s). This problem could be lessened by swapping the data to extended or expanded memory. Second, this technique is new and its effectiveness has yet to be determined. It's something that you must play with and prove to yourself that it works.

TSRs and Task Managers

A task manager is a resident program, which is part of both Windows and DOSSHELL and provides control over a number of applications or tasks. Both Windows and DOSSHELL allow multiple sessions to be available, giving the user control over which session is active. When writing and using TSRs with a task manager, special consideration may be required! Let's find out why.

First we'll go into a little more explanation of how a task manager works in general.

A task manager is an application program, generally designed in some type of menu format. One menu often displays what applications can be started, while another menu may display applications that have already been started. It is from this list that the user can select which application to make active, with the task manager taking care of activating and deactivating the chosen applications. When an application is deactivated, all information specific to that application is saved or swapped. A simple example would be that all of the application memory is copied and saved to a disk file or extended/expanded memory. When it is time to activate an application, the saved information is restored to memory. In reality, the memory swapping is more selective, just saving needed information, such as program data and the MS-DOS swappable data area. Most times, the swapping is transparent to the application being activated or deactivated.

Okay, enough about task manager operations. What does that have to do with TSRs?

Most task managers allow multiple DOS (COMMAND.COM) sessions. Of course, only one session is running at any given moment, but you can easily move from session to session.

TSRs are generally meant to pop up over a foreground application. However, the foreground application may now be one of many running in multiple independent DOS sessions. Because of this, there are two different arenas in which to run the TSR. The first is that you could run the TSR in each independent DOS session. Since each session preserves its own memory, each TSR instance would not interact with each other. That does not require any work for the TSR, since each TSR is attached to its own DOS session.

Now, what if you load the TSR into memory before loading the Task Manager Application? In that case, all DOS session have access to a single shared TSR. If the TSR is not reentrant, switching DOS sessions while the TSR is active may cause severe problems. Fortunately, the Windows and DOSSHELL Task Manager provides means to notify TSRs of impending task creation and switching and also provides what is called instance memory.

Instance memory is a block of memory that is unique for each session. By keeping global data and the stack in this block of memory, each DOS session can have truly independent access to the TSR. The TSR provides a list of memory block sizes and addresses, and the Task Manager takes care of keeping the data unique for each session.

Otherwise, all DOS sessions share a single copy of the TSR's data. This is great if you want the TSR to provide a communications buffer or pipe between the different DOS sessions, but in general this is not how you want your TSR to behave. Consider a command-line editor loaded before Windows. If (like the venerable CED), the command-line editor doesn't know about declaring instance data, then commands typed in one DOS session will show up when you hit the up-arrow key in another DOS session. Interesting behavior, certainly, but probably not what you want. The DOSKEY command-line editor, in contrast, knows about instance data (it hooks INT 2Fh AX=1605h and AX=4B05h). As a result, even if DOSKEY is loaded before Windows, commands typed in one DOS session do not leak across to the history buffer seen by other DOS sessions.

The multiplex interrupt (INT 2Fh) is used for communications to and from the active task manager. Additional communication structures are also set up through an INT 2Fh call. Since these functions are documented in MS-DOS technical documentation, I will not go into a long detailed discussion on these items. The January/February 1992 *Microsoft Systems Journal* has an excellent article by Douglas Boling on writing TSRs in an MS-DOS 5.0 environment, which includes details on the task manager API. The Microsoft Developer Network (MSDN) CD-ROM also has an excellent article by David Long on "TSR Support in Microsoft Windows Version 3.1." TSR developers, even if they "don't do Windows," must become familiar with these issues, because you have no control over whether an end-user is going to load Windows after loading your TSR.

The following INT 2Fh calls are utilized by our TSR code. These calls are supported by Windows and DOSSHELL:

```
1605h      Windows Start
4B01h      Build Notification Chain (attaches TSR to task manager)
4B05h      Get Instance Data
```

When the task manager (such as DOSSHELL, or Windows 3.1 Standard mode) starts, it calls INT 2Fh AX=4B01h to build a chain of structures that indicates what programs are interested in receiving session information during session creation and switching. The task manager also calls INT 2Fh AX=4B05h to get information about instance data required by any programs. The 4B05h call is very similar to the Windows INT 2Fh AX=1605h initialization broadcast. In fact, DOSKEY uses the same piece of code to handle both 4B05h and 1605h.

As our program processes the INT 2Fh AX=4B01h call, it provides the task managers with an address to a structure called SWCALLBACKINFO. This structure provides an address to code that processes notifications messages by the task manager. That is, the task manager calls this address when it has information to pass on to the program. This allows the program to be aware of task states and events such as impending session swaps. If the session is not in a state that can be interrupted, the notification message also returns a value that prevents a session swap.

The source code module SWITCHER.C, in Listing 9-21, manages part of the interface to the task manager. The structures were taken right from the MS-DOS programmer's reference. None of this is undocumented, but to discuss TSRs without mentioning Windows, task switching, and instance data, would be misleading.

Listing 9-21: DOS Task Manager Interface Module SWITCHER.C

```c
/* SWITCHER.C -- handles MS task switcher functions */

#include <stdlib.h>
#include <dos.h>
#include <memory.h>
#include "tsr.h"
/* The following structures are defined in the Microsoft "MS-DOS
   Programmer's Reference" for DOS 5 */

/* SWINSTANCEITEM contains information about a block of instance data.
   You pass a list of these structure through the SWSTARTUPINFO
   structure. The list of SWINSTANCEITEM structures is terminated
   by a 32 bit (double word) 0 value. */
typedef struct {
   void  far      *iisPtr;          /* points to instance data */
   unsigned int   iiSize;           /* instance data size */
} SWINSTANCEITEM;

/* SWSTARTUPINFO Contains information about a client program's instance
   data. Used during an INT 2Fh AX=4B05h call */
typedef struct {
   unsigned int   sisVersion;       /* ignored */
```

```
    void far        *sisNextDev;            /* prev. handler's SWSTARTUPINFO */
    void far        *sisVirtDevFile;        /* ignored */
    void far        *sisReferenceData;      /* ignored */
    SWINSTANCEITEM far *sisInstanceData;/* SWINSTACEITEM structures */
} SWSTARTUPINFO;

/* SWAPIINFO Contains information about the support level a client program
   provides. Since our TSR does not provide any support, this block will
   be set to zeros. Refer to Microsoft's technical reference for more
   details on the values allowed in this structure. */
typedef struct {
    unsigned int    sisLength;              /* size of this structure */
    unsigned int    sisAPI;                 /* API identifier */
    unsigned int    sisMajor;               /* major version number */
    unsigned int    sisMinor;               /* minor version number */
    unsigned int    sisSupport;             /* level of support */
} SWAPIINFO;

/* SWCALLBACKINFO Contains information about the client program */
typedef struct {
    void            far *scbiNext;          /* next SWCALLBACKINFO structure */
    void far        *scbiEntryPoint;        /* notification-function handler */
    void far        *Reserved;              /* reserved */
    SWAPIINFO far   *scbiAPI;               /* list of swapping structures */
} SWCALLBACKINFO;


#define MAX_INSTANCE    20                  /* limit to 20 instance blocks */


SWINSTANCEITEM SWInstanceItem[MAX_INSTANCE];  /* instance blocks */
int current_instance = 0;                   /* current number of blocks */

SWSTARTUPINFO   SWStartupInfo;
SWAPIINFO       SWSwapIInfo;
SWCALLBACKINFO SWCallBackInfo;


int     enhanced_windows = 1;               /* indicating if we're running enhanced mode */
int     switcher_critical = 0;              /* indicating if a switch can happen */

extern union REGS    regs;
extern struct SREGS sregs;


INTVECT switcher_service;

extern  notify_function();                              /* used to get linkage into the supporting ASM
                                                module. We just need the address */
/* the following is from NOTIFY.ASM */
extern void far process_existing_int2f(INTERRUPT_REGS far *r, void far *next);
extern void far check_switcher(void far *ptr);

/* Initialize Switcher Data structures.
   This is where we configure the notification address and any instance
   data that we might need. */
void    init_switcher_structures(void)
{
    /* zero out swap info structure since no API in this TSR support */
    memset(&SWSwapIInfo,0, sizeof(SWSwapIInfo));

    /* set address of swap info in the call back structure */
    SWCallBackInfo.scbiAPI = &SWSwapIInfo;

    /* set address of notification function handler (in NOTIFY.ASM) */
    SWCallBackInfo.scbiEntryPoint = &notify_function;

    /* zero out instance data structures for now, we'll add some later */
    memset(&SWInstanceItem,0, sizeof(SWINSTANCEITEM) * MAX_INSTANCE);

    /* Set Structure ID */
    SWStartupInfo.sisVersion = 3;
```

```
     /* set up pointers to our instance data */
     SWStartupInfo.sisInstanceData = SWInstanceItem;
}
/* add_instance_block() adds a block to the instance data array.
   This must be called before tsr goes resident.
   Returns 0 on success, or 1 if no more instance blocks available. */
int add_instance_block(void far *ptr, unsigned int size)
{
int ret = 0;

     if (current_instance > MAX_INSTANCE-1)
        ret = 1;
     else
     {
        SWInstanceItem[current_instance].iisPtr = ptr;
        SWInstanceItem[current_instance].iiSize = size;
        current_instance++;
     }

     return(ret);
}
/* process_switcher_int2f() checks to see if a switcher command has
   been passed. If yes, it will process it and return a 0 indicating
   to the caller not to continue with INT 2Fh processing. A return
   of 1 indicates the caller should process the 2F interrupt. */
int   process_switcher_int2f(INTERRUPT_REGS far *r)
{
     int ret_code;

     segread(&sregs);

     switch (r->ax)          /* see if we're interested */
     {
         case 0x1605:           /* windows initialization */
             enhanced_windows = !(r->dx & 1); /* zero in enhanced windows */

             /* call other 2F handlers */
             process_existing_int2f(r, &SWStartupInfo.sisNextDev);

             /* set up saved registers with required address */
             r->es = sregs.ds;
             r->bx = (unsigned int) &SWStartupInfo;

             ret_code = 0;     /* tell caller that all is processed */
             break;
         case 0x4b01:           /* build notification chain */
             /* call other 2F handlers */
             process_existing_int2f(r, &SWCallBackInfo.scbiNext);

             /* set up saved registers with required address */
             r->es = sregs.ds;
             r->bx = (unsigned int) &SWCallBackInfo;

             ret_code = 0;     /* tell caller that all is processed */
             break;
         case 0x4b05:           /* get instance data */
             /* call other 2F handlers */
             process_existing_int2f(r, &SWStartupInfo.sisNextDev);

             /* set up saved registers with required address */
             r->es = sregs.ds;
             r->bx = (unsigned int) &SWStartupInfo;

             ret_code = 0;     /* tell caller that all is processed */
             break;
         default:                      /* let every thing else fall through */
```

```
            ret_code = 1;
            break;
        }

    return(ret_code);
}

/* Signal Windows to not task swap */
void windows_begin_critical()
{
    if (enhanced_windows)
    {
        regs.x.ax = 0x1681;
        int86(0x2f, &regs, &regs);
    }
}

/* Signal Windows that task swap ok */
void windows_end_critical()
{
    if (enhanced_windows)
    {
        regs.x.ax = 0x1682;
        int86(0x2f, &regs, &regs);
    }
}

/* See if windows is running in enhanced mode.
   If not, decrement enhanced mode flag */
void check_windows_running(void)
{
    regs.x.ax = 0x1600; /* windows check */
    int86(0x2f, &regs, &regs);
    if (regs.h.al == 0)      /* windows not installed */
        enhanced_windows = 0;
}

/* See if task switcher running (done in assembly) */
void check_switcher_running(void)
{
    check_switcher(&SWCallBackInfo);
}
```

As stated previously, the task manager sends messages to our program through a notification call. Since parameters are passed through registers, and the notification is not through an interrupt, the TSR processes this call through an assembly language function. That is because you can't control the register usage in C, and registers containing parameters may be used by C before the program gets a chance to process the call. NOTIFY.ASM, in Listing 9-22, manages the rest of the interface to the task manager. There is also a helper routine called process_existing_int2f() in this file. Process_existing_int2f() passes the INT 2Fh message on to other programs that may be interested in it. The program doesn't use a direct call, since it must save register information after the call to the other INT 2Fh handlers return. Part of the documented API usage for the task manager is that the program calls other programs first and then acts on the task manager INT 2Fh function.

Listing 9-22: DOS Task Manager Interface Module NOTIFY.ASM

```
;NOTIFY.ASM

;
; Routines to handle notification messages from the task switcher
; these are not easily (if possible at all) written in C since the
; parameters are passed in registers, and NOT called through an
; interrupt (if they were interrupt functions a C interrupt function
; could handle them. Most of these functions are stubs, returning
; all is ok. The only thing we might want to prevent is switching
; during a TSR critical section, say if we were handling a time
```

```
;  sensitive piece of hardware.
;
;  None of the notify functions are called from the C program, and should
;  not be!
;
;Define segment names used by C
;
_TEXT    segment byte public 'CODE'
_TEXT    ends

CONST    segment word public 'CONST'
CONST    ends

_BSS     segment word public 'BSS'
_BSS     ends

_DATA    segment word public 'DATA'
_DATA    ends
DGROUP   GROUP    CONST, _BSS, _DATA
     assume   CS:_TEXT, DS:DGROUP

     public _notify_function
     public _process_existing_int2f
     public _check_switcher

     extrn  _switcher_service:near      ;switcher service function
     extrn  _switcher_critical:near     ;critical = 1, means no swap!
     extrn  _old_int2f:near             ;original INT 2Fh vector

_TEXT    segment
;*****
;function called by task switcher to notify us of switcher states
;*****
_notify_function proc far
     push     ds
     push     bx

     push     ax
     mov      ax, DGROUP     ;setup to our C data segment
     mov      ds,ax
     pop      ax


;
; save current switcher service function. Documentation says this
; may change, so save every time you get one
;
     mov                              word ptr [_switcher_service], di
     mov                              word ptr [_switcher_service+2], es

;
; setup to call notification function through a jump table defined
; below in data segment
;

     cm                               pax,7        ;make sure valid function value
     ja       notify_exit

     mov      bx,ax
     shl      bx,1

     call     [SwitcherTable+bx]
notify_exit:

     pop      bx
     pop      ds
     ret
```

```
_notify_function endp


;*****
; RET_ZERO used for:
; Function 00 - Initialize Switcher
; Function 03 - Activate Session
; Function 04 - Session Active
; Function 05 - Create Session
; Function 06 - Destroy Session
; Function 07 - Switcher Exiting
;*****
RET_ZERO proc near
     xor        ax,ax         ;signal ok to process
     ret
RET_ZERO endp

;*****
; Function 01 - Query if OK to suspend session
;*****
QuerySuspend proc near
     mov        ax, word ptr _switcher_critical
     ;;; Oops! According to MS-DOS Programmer's Reference for
     ;;; DOS 6 ("Task Switcher API Patch," pp. 495-496), under
     ;;; v. 5 of the DOS task switcher, the QuerySuspend handler
     ;;; must install a patch that preserves CX.
     ret
QuerySuspend endp

;*****
; Function 02 - Suspend Session
;*****
SuspendSession proc near
     mov      ax, word ptr _switcher_critical
     ret
SuspendSession endp

;Call Old INT 2Fh function used to process switcher INT 2Fh functions
;from our C code. Its main reason for being is to put
;the INT 2Fh registers back to the way when we received the interrupt.
;This is so that the function we call has them in the right place
;
; void process_existing_int2f(INTERRUPT_REGS far *r, void far *next)
;
;*****
_process_existing_int2f proc far

     push       bp
     mov        bp,sp

;
;     move the original INT 2Fh address into the code segment
;     we'll lose the data segment when we reset the registers
;
     mov        ax, word ptr _old_int2f
     mov        word ptr cs:[_save_int2f], ax

     mov        ax, word ptr _old_int2f+2
     mov        word ptr cs:[_save_int2f+2], ax
;
; save address of SWSTARTUPINFO.next
;
     lds        bx, [bp + 10]   ; get address we want to put ES (cx):BX into
     mov        cs:tmp_data1, bx ; save address of STRUCTURE
     mov        cs:tmp_data2, ds

;
; get stack back to just after all registers were pushed by the C
; interrupt routine
```

```
;
     lds      bx, [bp+6]     ;get pointer to regs structure
     mov      ax, ds
     cli
     mov      ss,ax
     mov      sp, bx
     sti
;
; Restore regs as they were in original INT 2Fh call
;
IFDEF TURBOC
     pop      bp
     pop      di
     pop      si
     pop      ds
     pop      es
     pop      dx
     pop      cx
     pop      bx
     pop      ax
ELSE
     pop      es
     pop      ds
     pop      di
     pop      si
     pop      bp
     pop      bx
     pop      bx
     pop      dx
     pop      cx
     pop      ax
ENDIF

;
; save INT 2Fh function for later compare
;
     mov      cs:tmp_data3, ax ;save request

;
; let others process request
;
     pushf
     call     dword ptr cs:_save_int2f

;
; now update the structure with the address returned in ES:BX
;
     push     ds
     push     ax
     push     bx

     mov      ax,DGROUP ;get data seg so we can store ES:BX
     mov      ds,ax

     pop      ax   ;save value of bx from INT 2Fh call

     mov      bx, cs:tmp_data1 ;get address of structure
     mov      [bx], ax     ;store ES:BX values
     mov      [bx + 2], es

;
; if function 4b01, then structure address is same as next address
;
     cmp      cs:[tmp_data3], 4b01h
     je       skip_dec
     dec      bx ;point to start of structure
```

```
        dec     bx
skip_dec:
        push    ds
        pop     es

        pop     ax
        pop     ds
        iret
_process_existing_int2f endp

; *****
; check if task switcher already running.
; If so, setup call back structure to hook notification chain.
; *****
_check_switcher proc far

        push    bp
        mov     bp,sp

        mov     bx,0        ;documentation says must be zeros
        mov     di,0
        mov     es,di

        mov     ax, 4b02h
        int     2fh

        or      al,al

        jnz     no_switcher ;none installed, so just exit

;
; save switcher service function
;
        mov     word ptr [_switcher_service], di
        mov     word ptr [_switcher_service+2], es

        les     di, [bp+4]  ;get address of callback structure

        call    dword ptr [_switcher_service]

no_switcher:
        pop     bp
        ret
_check_switcher endp


_save_int2f  dd  0

tmp_data1    dw  0
tmp_data2    dw  0
tmp_data3    dw  0

_TEXT   ends


_DATA   segment

;
; Jump table used to dispatch switcher notification messages
;
SwitcherTable dw offset RET_ZERO      ; InitSwitcher (00)
              dw offset QuerySuspend         ; (01)
              dw offset SuspendSession       ; (02)
              dw offset RET_ZERO     ; ActivateSession (03)
              dw offset RET_ZERO     ; SessionActive (04)
              dw offset RET_ZERO     ; CreateSession (05)
              dw offset RET_ZERO     ; DestroySession (06)
              dw offset RET_ZERO     ; SwitcherExit (07)

_DATA   ends

        end
```

Removing a TSR

Before we get started, we would like to extend special thanks to Tim Paterson for all the help he provided in this section for the first edition of *Undocumented DOS*.

There are times when you need to remove a TSR from memory. TSRs use memory and at times conflict with other software. Usually, the TSR can be removed so that there is no trace of it ever being installed; the removal process unlinks the TSR from the interrupt vector table and releases all TSR memory back to MS-DOS.

One situation that can arise when trying to remove a TSR is that other programs can chain into the same interrupt(s) that the TSR is processing. This prevents you from removing the TSR from the interrupt chain. Consider the following TSR example that chains into interrupt 8.

In this process the code saves the current interrupt address in the TRS's local data storage (to be called from inside the TSR). The interrupt vector table now points to the TSR. The following diagram describes the chaining process before and after a TSR adds itself into the chain:

```
Before our TSR loads:
INT 08  ----------------> Original Interrupt Service Routine (ISR)
After our TSR is resident:
INT 08 ------------> TSR ISR  --------> Original ISR
```

At this point, if you wanted to remove the TSR from the interrupt chain, you would just put the original ISR address, saved earlier, back into the interrupt vector table. The TSR is out of the link. But what if another program has placed itself into the interrupt chain, as in the following diagram?

```
INT 08 -----> NEW ISR  -----> TSR IRS -----> Original ISR
```

If you put the value stored for the original ISR back into the interrupt vector table, you would be cutting off the new program that has inserted itself into the chain! When it comes time to remove your TSR from the interrupt chain, therefore, check to make sure the interrupt table is pointing to the correct, that is, *your*, interrupt service routine. If it is, then you know that no other TSR has been loaded after your TSR. If it isn't, what then?

Currently, there are two new strategies that have been discussed for use at unload time of a TSR that has interrupt handlers in the middle of a chain. Neither of them lends itself easily to TSR programming in C.

1. If you can't remove a TSR because there is another application in the chain, then at least remove everything possible. Basically, create (allocate) a small ISR that just jumps to the original ISR. On TSR removal, de-allocate all memory except for the section the small ISR stub uses. This retains the interrupt chain integrity.

2. IBM has proposed a standardized format for interrupt handlers. All handlers will start with a jump instruction, followed by data that contains a signature and the original ISR address. The jump is to get over this small data block and continue with interrupt processing. This works well with assembly language, since you have control over how your ISR appears. This does not fit easily into C, though, since a programmer has no control over the structure of the C interrupt function. To achieve this standard in a high-level language, all interrupts would have to be vectored to code in an assembly module. The C program would have to store the original interrupt addresses into the CODE segment of the assembly module. The assembly module would JUMP to the associated C interrupt function. The proposed interrupt structure is shown in Figure 9-23.

Figure 9-23: Proposed Interrupt Chain Structure

```
new_interrupt:          jmp _interrupt_handler
previoushandler         dd 0
signature               dw 424Bh      ; 'KB'
hardwareflag            db 0
                        jmp hardwarereset
                        db 7 dup (0) ; Reserved
```

The signature field is an aid for other programs in identifying this interrupt structure. The hardwareflag field is important for interrupt handlers that will be issuing an EOI hardware operation. This field should be zero unless the ISR handles a hardware interrupt and is the FIRST installed ISR (which becomes the last in the chain if other handlers are installed). The jump instruction to a hardware reset is usually not needed for software interrupts.

The following code snippet demonstrates how this would be done. Don't forget that the TSR initialization section would need to save the old interrupt address in the _old_int8 variable contained in the assembly language routine:

```
public _new_int8, _old_int8
extern _process_int8

_new_int8 proc far
                jmp far  _process_int8 ;go to C handler
_old_int8       dd 0
signature       dw 424Bh
hardwareflag    db 0
                jmp _hardwarereset ;(if hardware funtion)
                db 7 dup (0)  ; Reserved
_hardwarereset:
                retf ;just return in case someone calls into this label
_old_int8
_new_int8 endp
```

The interrupt handler in C would look like it always does:

```
void interrupt far process_int8(INTERRUPT_REGS 2)
{
    // interrupt processing
    _chain_intr(_old_int8)
}
```

Since this is only a proposed standard, our sample TSR does not include such code, but it probably should.

The generic TSR developed in this chapter can be removed by a command line argument. If you have previously loaded TSRFILE.EXE, the command TSRFILE -D unloads the resident copy of TSRFILE.EXE. The -D tells the generic TSR shell to signal the resident TSR program to unload and not to load up another copy.

The generic TSR uses INT 2Fh to communicate between the newly executed copy and the resident copy. The actual function number (AH value) can be set with a command line parameter, but the subfunctions (AL) are hardcoded into the TSR program. A value of zero in the AL register is an install check, and a value of one is a deinstall command. The use of zero for the install check is dictated by the standard Multiplex Interrupt interface.

The following steps are required for deinstalling. These steps follow the INT 2Fh deinstallation call. Step one must be performed by the TSR, since only it knows what addresses to restore to the interrupt vector table. Steps two through five can be performed either by the TSR or the calling application.

1. See if all of the interrupt vectors the TSR has chained still point to the interrupt service routines. Restore all vectors that have not changed since the TSR chained into them. If any interrupt vectors have changed, disable the TSR operations and skip the following steps to leave the TSR in memory.
2. Set the parent PSP of the TSR to be that of the application that executed the INT 2Fh deinstallation call. The parent PSP value is contained at offset 16h of the TSR's PSP.
3. To return control to the calling application, set the termination address to be a location in the calling application.
4. Set the current PSP to the PSP of the TSR. Doing this allows DOS to free the TSR's memory and close any open files.
5. Execute the normal DOS Terminate function (INT 21h Function 4Ch). When the TSR has been terminated by DOS, control returns to the terminate address set in step three.
6. At this point, all registers have unknown values. The calling process must save them before issuing the INT 2Fh deinstallation command. They can now be restored.

If the TSR is not performing steps two through five, it must return its PSP value as part of the INT 2Fh interface.

The generic TSR performs steps one through five. TSRUTIL.ASM contains the deinstallation call through INT 2Fh, and TSREXAMP.C contains the rest of the code that handles deinstallation. The pseudocode in Figure 9-24 describes the generic TSR's operation.

Figure 9-24: Generic TSR Unload Pseudocode

```
Foreground Application          Resident Application (TSR)

Save SI, DI, BP, SS and SP registers
Set AX=C001h
Set BX:DS TO terminate address (TERM_ADDR,
   used in step 3 above)
Perform INT 2Fh
                                TSR receives INT 2Fh request
                                Set up local stack
                                Attempt to unlink interrupts
                                If unable to unlink all
                                   interrupt vectors, then:
                                       Set AL = 0xFF
                                       Return from INT 2Fh
If we get here, the deinstallation failed.
Check AL register and display proper message.
EXIT
                                Get PSP (foreground app.)
                                Set parent PSP field in our PSP
                                Set terminate address in our PSP
                                   to address passed via INT 2Fh
                                Set PSP to TSR's PSP
                                Call MS-DOS terminate
TERM_ADDR:
Restore SI, DI, BP, SS and SP registers
EXIT
```

Many times, a TSR is not able to deinstall due to interrupt vectors chained by another application. A return from the INT 2Fh call with AL = 0FFh indicates that the TSR could not unlink itself from one or more interrupts. Deinstallation also fails if the TSR is not installed to begin with. This is indicated by AL = 00h on return from the INT 2Fh call.

Sample TSR Programs

To exercise the generic TSR, we built three different simple TSRs, two of which are pop-up versions of programs from other parts of this book.

TSRFILE

The first sample program, TSRFILE (see Listing 9-25), demonstrates that you really can make DOS file I/O and memory allocation calls while you're popped up in the middle of some other program. When TSRFILE pops up, it prompts the user for a filename and then displays the file on the screen. No screen saving/restoring amenities are provided.

FILE.C uses the Microsoft C _dos functions for file I/O and memory allocation. These functions translate directly into the appropriate INT 21h calls and are thus preferable to using the intdos or int86 functions. Instructions for turning FILE.C into TSRFILE.EXE are found in the makefile shown in Listing 9-1; it can also be compiled as a stand-alone FILE.EXE.

Listing 9-25: Example Pop-up - FILE.C

```
/* FILE.C */

#include <dos.h>
#include <conio.h>
#include <fcntl.h>
#include <share.h>

char file_prompt[] = "File? ";
char cant_open[] = "Can't open file\r\n";
char error_reading[] = "Error reading file\r\n";
char insuff_mem[] = "Insufficient memory; Press any key...\r\n";
char crlf[] = "\r\n";

#define PUTSTR(s)     \
    _dos_write(STDERR, (char far *) s, sizeof(s)-1, &wcount)

#define MIN_PARAS    4
#define WANT_PARAS   64
#define BYTES        (paras << 4)

#define STDERR       2

#ifdef TSR
void application(void)
#else
main(void)
#endif
{
    char buf[81];
    char far *s;
    unsigned rcount, wcount, ret, paras, seg;
    int f;

    /* prompt for filename */
    if (PUTSTR(file_prompt) != 0)
        return;

    /* get filename */
    if ((_dos_read(STDERR, buf, 80, &rcount) != 0) || (rcount < 3))
        return;
    /* replace CRLF with NULL */
    buf[rcount-2] = '\0';

    /* try to allocate: first try a lot, then a little */
    if (_dos_allocmem(WANT_PARAS, &seg) == 0)
        paras = WANT_PARAS;
    else if (_dos_allocmem(MIN_PARAS, &seg) == 0)
        paras = MIN_PARAS;
    else
```

```
{
    PUTSTR(insuff_mem);
    return;
}
FP_SEG(s) = seg;
FP_OFF(s) = 0;
/* open file */
if (_dos_open(buf, O_RDWR | SH_DENYNO, &f) != 0)
    return PUTSTR(cant_open);
/* display file */
while (((ret = _dos_read(f, s, BYTES, &rcount)) == 0) && rcount)
    if (_dos_write(STDERR, s, rcount, &wcount) != 0)
        break;
/* write one more CRLF */
PUTSTR(crlf);
if (ret)
    PUTSTR(error_reading);
/* free memory */
_dos_freemem(seg);
/* close file */
_dos_close(f);
PUTSTR("Press any key...");
}
```

FILE.C makes two stabs at allocating memory, because if it pops up over COMMAND.COM, there is almost no free memory available. COMMAND uses the largest block in memory, and all that are left are little dribs and drabs, like the environment we freed during TSR initialization. You can see this situation when running our second example, the MEM program as a TSR.

TSRMEM

One problem with the MEM program presented in Chapter 7 was that, since it was a stand-alone program, you could only examine the memory map from within MEM itself. By putting the generic TSR and MEM together to form TSRMEM.EXE, you can examine the memory map within other programs. For example, you can clearly see how COMMAND grabs the largest chunk of memory, leaving almost nothing free:

```
C:\UNDOC2\CHAP9>tsrfile
C:\UNDOC2\CHAP9>tsrmem -k 59 8 -f 1
C:\UNDOC2\CHAP9>\sidekick\sk

[Hit TSRMEM hotkey, Alt-F1]
Seg     Owner   Size
09F3    0008    00F4 (   3904)    config [15 4B 67 ]
0AE8    0AE9    00D3 (   3376)    0BC1 c:\dos33\command.com  [22 2E ]
0BBC    0000    0003 (     48)    free
0BC0    0AE9    0019 (    400)
0BDA    171A    000D (    208)
0BE8    0000    0000 (      0)    free
0BE9    0BEA    0575 (  22352)          [F1 FA ]
115F    1160    05B9 (  23440)     -k 59 8 -f 1 [1B 23 24 2F F4 F5 ]
1719    171A    19B5 ( 105296)    0BDB C:\SIDEKICK\SK.COM  [08 09 10 13
                                         16 1C 21 25 26 28 ]
30CF    0AE9    8730 ( 553728)          [30 F8 ]
B800
```

The largest block in the MCB chain, totaling 8730h paragraphs, is not marked "free." Instead, it's owned by PSP 0AE9. Looking back along the MCB chain, which also functions as a PSP chain, you can see that 0AE9 is COMMAND.COM. In fact, there are only three paragraphs of free memory, located directly after COMMAND. Even the environment TSRMEM freed was picked up by Side-

Kick for use as its environment. If you hit TSRFILE's hotkey (Alt-D) at this point, it will ask for the filename and then report "Insufficient memory."

However, if you leave COMMAND by running an application and then hitting Alt-D, there is generally plenty of memory because COMMAND is no longer hogging the largest block. Again, this shows up clearly if you hit TSRMEM's hotkey within some other application. The MCB belonging to COMMAND.COM has now been replaced by the following:

```
30CF    30DE    000D (    208)
30DD    30DE    292D (168656)    30D0 c:\eps\EPSILON.EXE  [00 05 16 ]
5A0B    0000    5DF4 (384832)    free      [30 F8 ]
```

Since there are 5DF4h paragraphs of free memory, you now have no trouble allocating memory in TSRFILE.

Porting MEM.C to use the generic TSR was straightforward. We had to get rid of a call to calloc(), replace any calls to exit() with simple returns, expand any "\n" characters into "\r\n", and make a few other minor adjustments. The key change, however, was to link with a version of printf() that doesn't call malloc(), because, after initialization, the TSR would have no near heap from which to allocate memory.

This non-malloc version of printf() is provided in the module PUT.C, which can be used with any program that uses the generic TSR. The non-malloc version of printf() uses the stdarg facilities of ANSI C, in particular the function vsprintf(), which can help create functions that take variable argument lists. PUT.C also contains a number of other helpful functions. Prototypes for the functions appear (naturally) in PUT.H (see Listing 9-26).

Listing 9-26: No-malloc SRDERR Output - PUT.H

```
/* PUT.H -- STDERR output routines, no malloc */

// calls _dos_write, returns number of bytes actually writen
unsigned doswrite(int handle, char far *s, unsigned len);

// displays ASCIIZ string on STDERR
unsigned put_str(char far *s);

// displays character on STDERR
unsigned put_chr(int c);

// displays number (width, radix) on STDERR
unsigned put_num(unsigned long u, unsigned wid, unsigned radix);

// PUT includes alternate version of printf: goes to STDERR,
// doesn't use malloc. Same prototype as <stdio.h>

// get string from STDERR, returns actual length
unsigned get_str(char far *s, unsigned len);

#define putstr(s)       { put_str(s); put_str("\r\n"); }
#define put_hex(u)      put_num(u, 4, 16)
#define put_long(ul)    put_num(ul, 9, 10)
```

In MEM.C, the C preprocessor #ifdef statement was used to conditionally compile either a stand-alone or a TSR version. For example:

```
#ifdef TSR
void fail(char *s) { printf("%s\r\n", s); return; }
#else
void fail(char *s) { puts(s); exit(1); }
#endif
```

The changes needed to make MEM a pop-up were all of a similar nature and are so straightforward and uninteresting that we leave them as an exercise for the reader. In any case, the resulting TSRMEM.EXE can be found on the disk that accompanies this book.

TSR2E

Finally, we jump the gun a little bit by porting a program from the next chapter in this book. As Jim Kyle will explain, INT 2Eh is the backdoor to the DOS command interpreter. The TEST2E command interpreter from Chapter 10 can be easily turned into a TSR to provide an instant pop-up copy of COMMAND.COM!

This really does work. The only peculiarity is that on occasion when you pop up TSR2E and type in a command, the following message appears from the resident portion of COMMAND.COM:

```
Memory allocation error
Cannot start COMMAND, exiting
```

Note, however, that this is different from the horrifying message one sees when the MCB chain has been trashed:

```
Memory allocation error
Cannot load COMMAND, system halted
```

The message "exiting" rather than "system halted" is for real. If you try to execute the command again, it works. In any case, this should probably join the list of other INT 2Eh caveats found in the next chapter.

You can use TSR2E not only to issue internal commands such as DIR or COPY but also to issue external commands that launch other programs or even batch files.

As shown in the makefile presented earlier in the chapter, you build TSR2E by combining the generic TSR components with Jim Kyle's three files, SEND2E.C, HAVE2.ASM, and DO2E.ASM. These files are unchanged. All changes for going TSR are confined to the module TEST2E.C, where we change the name of the module entry point from main() to application(), add a test that lets TSR2E avoid popping up when COMMAND.COM is already running, and use the facilities in the PUT module rather than the C standard library's mallocy studio facilities. The altered version of TEST2E.C appears in Listing 9-27.

Listing 9-27: Example Pop-up - TEST2E.C

```c
#include <stdlib.h>
#include <string.h>
#include <dos.h>

#include "put.h"

#define MK_FP(seg,ofs) \
    ((void far *)(((unsigned long)(seg) < 16) | (ofs)))

extern unsigned foreground_psp;     // in TSREXAMP.C
extern int Send2E(char *command);   // in SEND2E.C

static char buf[80];
static int running = 0;

typedef enum { SAVE=0, RESTORE } SAVEREST;
typedef void (interrupt far *INTVECT)();

void interrupts(int restore)
{
    static INTVECT int_1b, int_23, int_24;
    if (restore)
    {
        _dos_setvect(0x1b, int_1b);
        _dos_setvect(0x23, int_23);
        _dos_setvect(0x24, int_24);
```

```
    }
    else
    {
        int_1b = _dos_getvect(0x1b);
        int_23 = _dos_getvect(0x23);
        int_24 = _dos_getvect(0x24);
    }
}

void application(void)
{
    // don't run if we are already running
    if (running)
        return;
    running++;
    // don't execute INT 2Eh if COMMAND.COM already running
    // see if COMMAND.COM running by checking if current PSP is the
    // same as its own parent (see chapter 10)
    if (foreground_psp ==
        *((unsigned far *) MK_FP(foreground_psp, 0x16)))
    {
        put_str("COMMAND.COM already running");
        running--;
        return;
    }
    put_str("TSR COMMAND SHELL: type DOS commands,    or BYE to quit\r\n");
    for (;;)
    {
        put_str("$ ");
        if (! get_str(buf, 80))
            break;
        if (strcmp(buf, "bye") == 0 || strcmp(buf,    "BYE") == 0)
            break;
        interrupts(SAVE);
        Send2E(buf);
        interrupts(RESTORE);
    }
    putstr("Bye");
    running--;
}
```

We save and restore the Ctrl-C, Ctrl-Break, and Critical Error interrupts around the call to Send2E(). With this precaution, even Ctrl-C, Ctrl-Break, and Critical Errors are handled properly within the INT 2Eh pop-up:

```
TSR COMMAND SHELL: type DOS commands, or BYE to quit
$ dir a:
Not ready error reading drive A
Abort, Retry, Fail? a
$ dir *.c /w
 Volume in drive C is RAMANUJAN
 Directory of  C:\UNDOC\RMICHELS
DOSSWAP  C       EXTERR  C       ^C
$ bye
Bye
```

One word about trying to install a TSR from within the pop-up command interpreter: DON'T! This will hang your system sometime after you exit the pop-up.

Multitasking TSR

Finally, let us discuss TSRs that don't pop up at a user hotkey, but which do their work in the background. We call such programs multitasking TSRs to distinguish them from pop-ups. MULTI.C is a multitasking TSR shell that can be modified to perform multiple background tasks, from disk file copying to background communications.

The example presented here is an enhancement to the DOS PRINT utility. It periodically (activated by INT 8 and INT 28h) searches a \SPOOL directory for files having the extension .SPL. When it finds a match, the TSR uses PRINT's INT 2Fh Function 01h interface, to ask PRINT to print the file. Once the file has been submitted for printing, the TSR periodically obtains a status report from PRINT. If the file is no longer in the print queue (its printing is complete), the file is deleted:

```
C:\UNDOC2\CHAP9> print
C:\UNDOC2\CHAP9> multi
C:\UNDOC2\CHAP9> copy \undoc\rmichels\*.asm \spool\*.spl
C:\UNDOC2\CHAP9> dir \spool

 Volume in drive C is RAMANUJAN
 Directory of  C:\SPOOL

.               <DIR>        3-23-89    9:54p
..              <DIR>        3-23-89    9:54p
TSRUTIL  SPL     5852        9-17-90   11:40p
STACK    SPL     1758        9-17-90   11:36p
        4 File(s)      94208 bytes free

C:\UNDOC2\CHAP9> print

    C:\SPOOL\TSRUTIL.SPL is currently being printed

C:\UNDOC2\CHAP9> dir \spool

 Volume in drive C is RAMANUJAN
 Directory of  C:\SPOOL

.               <DIR>        3-23-89    9:54p
..              <DIR>        3-23-89    9:54p
STACK    SPL     1758        9-17-90   11:36p
        3 File(s)     102400 bytes free
```

Basically, the program manages two independent processes, the foreground process and the background process. When it is time for one process to start, the current process is suspended and its registers are saved on the stack for later restart. Once the TSR has been loaded for later restart, the environment of the suspended process's environment is restored, and it continues where it left off.

This multitasking is achieved by maintaining a count based on the timer interrupt. Each process gets a specific amount of time; in the preceding example, the foreground process gets the most time so as not to degrade performance. It is possible to add more tasks, but you would need to maintain a list of SS:SP sets to service all running processes.

Most of the code is similar to TSREXAMP. The two main differences are that activation is through the timer interrupt, not a hot key, and that instead of completing its work during activation, the TSR is suspended for later restart. Because DOS is not reentrant, the TSR still must follow the rule of not interrupting DOS when it is active.

In most computer systems, multitasking is a method of quickly switching from one task to another, so that the computer appears to be running multiple tasks at the same time. Of course, it's not as simple as that. Multitasking systems are designed so that resources, such as disks, screens, and keyboards, can be shared by multiple applications. True multitasking systems such as OS/2 supply interface routines that are reentrant. The code segment of each routine has only one instance, and this code segment can be shared by multiple processes at the same time. Each user (each routine) will have its own instance of data. But, as we know, the INT 21h API is not like this, so this multitasking example is controlled to some extent by the DOS flags.

Task Switching

Every process has what can be called its context or frame. This consists of the following items:

- Register values (including code, data, and stack segment values)
- Program Segment Prefix (PSP) or process ID
- Disk Transfer Address
- Extended Error Information

During a task or context switch, these items must be saved and replaced by ones that pertain to the new task. The example simply flip-flops between two tasks. If more independent tasks were required, we would need to keep a list of information for each task. Each item in the list might contain the relevant DOS information (PSP, DTA, etc.) and a pointer to the process stack segment and offset. You might also want to keep, and switch to, a copy of the SDA for each task. The code to perform the list management is more complex and is not presented here.

The type of multitasking presented here is called time-slicing because each task gets a predetermined slice of time in which to run. If needed, more intelligence could be added that would control the percentage of time each process gets. This could be based on usage of the operating system (INT 21h) or the disk (INT 13h). You could chain these interrupts, and if a process is making extensive use of these resources, you could lower its time slice to give other processes more time.

This method is used during the background process. When the file being printed is still in the print queue, a timer limit variable is set so that background processing terminates immediately. There is no point in running in the background if the program is simply waiting for the print spooler to complete its job.

One word regarding the use of MULTI with other task switchers: DON'T! Things can get very confusing with multitaskers on top of multitaskers. MULTI is not compatible with Microsoft Windows. To avoid Windows, MULTI intercepts the Windows startup message (INT 2Fh AX=1605h) and returns a non-zero value in the CX register. This tells Windows to abort its startup.

MULTI Installation

MULTI installs using the techniques already described. Some interrupt handling routines must be in assembly language because they augment the normal interrupt process. On returning from most interrupts, the flags are restored to their condition just before the interrupt was invoked. But three of the interrupts we are interested in handling—INT 13h, 25h, and 26h—do not follow this convention. INT 13h, like INT 21h, returns error conditions with flags, so an INT 13h handler must end with a RET 2 rather than an IRET. Meanwhile, the DOS absolute disk routines, INT 25h and 26h, leave the flags on the stack, so they exit with a RET rather than an IRET. This code is marked as IFDEF MULTI in TSRUTIL.ASM, shown earlier in the chapter.

Another difference between TSREXAMP and MULTI is that, in MULTI, the address of the main_loop function is placed on the stack that is created in the main() procedure. This is typical of multitasking code; it causes execution to begin at this address when the background process is first activated.

Timer Interrupt

MULTI is activated, not by a user keypress of course, but by the INT 8 timer tick interrupt. MULTI's INT 8 handler increments a variable called tic_count, which keeps track of how many timer ticks have occurred. Each process that you manage is allowed a given number of ticks. Once the current tick count exceeds the process limit, and if InDOS is zero (except within INT 28h, in which it will be one, but must not be more than one) and the unsafe_flag is FALSE, that process suspends and the other process activates.

At this point, you can suspend the process. Depending on what process you are currently executing, you call either suspend_background or suspend_foreground. To suspend the foreground, set the stack to be the local TSR stack. In either case, carry out the save/restore regime used earlier in tsr_function in TSREXAMP: setting INT 1Bh, 23h, and 24h, and swapping PSP, DTA, and extended error information.

One returning to the new_int8 function, it restores the stack if you have just activated the foreground process and passes control along the INT 8 interrupt chain.

One special condition applies the first time you activate the background process. At this point, you have never interrupted this process, so its registers are not on the stack. Because of this, an assembly language function, timer_int_chain(), is called to jump to the next timer interrupt handler.

We earlier referred to a flag variable called unsafe_flag. Since there is no INBIOS flag to use, you have to create your own; unsafe_flag is set TRUE when critical BIOS services (INT 10h video and INT 13h disk) or the DOS absolute disk services (INT 25h and 26h) are in progress.

Idle Interrupt

The timer interrupt is not the only way you can run in the background. You also use the DOS idle interrupt (INT 28h), discussed earlier. This allows you to continue processing while the system is sitting at the COMMAND prompt. Otherwise, you would never run in the background while COMMAND was awaiting orders.

During an INT 28h, if the Int28DosBusy function returns FALSE and the background is not already active, you set the foreground limit to zero and the int_28_active variable to TRUE. Then wait for the int_28_active variable to go FALSE before continuing. This allows a nearly immediate task switch to the background process.

Keyboard Interrupt

Notice that we have installed a service routine for INT 9, the keyboard hardware interrupt. Whenever the user presses a key, the background task-time limit is set to zero, causing the task to go into a suspended state more quickly. This gives the user better, response time.

Printing

The main_loop() function in our example is the background process. This function performs the work of searching for files and submitting them to the spooler using INT 2Fh Function 01h. Notice that the example includes numerous loops that do nothing during the main_loop() function. This is to avoid constant disk access by the background task. The background time limit is also set to zero in a number of places to ensure that the background becomes suspended at that time.

MULTI.C

Listing 9-28 shows MULTI.C, the source code for the multitasking TSR. To build MULTI.EXE, use the instructions found in the makefile in Listing 9-1.

Listing 9-28: MULTI.C

```
/* MULTI.C */
#include <stddef.h>
#include <stdlib.h>
#include <stdio.h>
#include <string.h>
#include <dos.h>
#include <io.h>
#include "tsr.h"
#include "put.h"

#define SEARCH_DIR   "C:\\SPOOL\\"
#define STACK_SIZE   4096   /* must be 16 byte boundary */
#define SET_DTA      0x1a   /* SET Disk Transfer Address */
#define GET_DTA      0x2f   /* GET Disk Transfer Address */
```

```
#define BACKGROUND_TICKS 2
#define FOREGROUND_TICKS 16
#define BACKGROUND_YIELD 0
#define FOREGROUND_YIELD 0

struct  prReq
{
    char level;
    char far *fname;
};

char    far *stack_ptr;   /* stack for our background TSR */
char    far *ptr;
unsigned ss_save;              /* slot for stack segment register */
unsigned sp_save;              /* slot for stack pointer register */
unsigned unsafe_flag = 0; /* set true by various interrupts */
int first_time = 1;       /* flag for first time in running background */

int my_psp;                   /* our TSR's psp */
int foreground_psp;           /* PSP of interrupted foreground process */
int foreground_dta_seg;       /* DTA of interrupted foreground process */
int foreground_dta_off;
int ctr=0;
int tic_count = 0;        /* counts timer tices */
int in_progress = 0;      /* true if we're in background process */
int breakState;           /* Extended Break Status of ForeGround */
int dos_count = 0;        /* count of our calls into DOS */
int multi_critical = 0;   /* indicates we can't swap right now */
char search_work[65];
struct ExtErr my_ErrInfo;
struct ExtErr foreground_ErrInfo;

int foreground_limit = FOREGROUND_TICKS; /* foreground cycle limit */
int background_limit = BACKGROUND_TICKS; /* background cycle limit */

char search_dir[65] = {SEARCH_DIR}; /* dir to search for spool files */
volatile int    int_28_active = 0;   /* true if activated by INT 28h */
volatile int    interval_timer;      /* for sleeping a number of ticks */

/* old interrupt pointers are stored here */
INTVECT old_int8, old_int9, old_int10, old_int13;
INTVECT old_int1B, old_int21, old_int23, old_int24, old_int25;
INTVECT old_int26, old_int28, old_int2f;

/* prototypes for this module */
void main_loop();
void interrupt far new_int8(INTERRUPT_REGS);
void interrupt far new_int9(INTERRUPT_REGS);
void interrupt far new_int10(void);
void interrupt far new_int13(void);
void interrupt far new_int1B(INTERRUPT_REGS);
void interrupt far new_int21(INTERRUPT_REGS);
void interrupt far new_int23(INTERRUPT_REGS);
void interrupt far new_int24(INTERRUPT_REGS);
void interrupt far new_int25(void);
void interrupt far new_int26(void);
void interrupt far new_int28(INTERRUPT_REGS);
void interrupt far new_int2f(INTERRUPT_REGS);
int  spooler_active(void);
int  search_spl_que(char * fname);
void suspend_foreground(void);
void suspend_background(void);

/* returns nonzero if PRINT installed */
int spooler_active()
{
    union REGS  regs;

    regs.x.ax = 0x0100;          /* PRINT install check */
    int86(0x2f,&regs,&regs);     /* call multiplex interrupt */
```

```
            return(regs.h.al == 0xff);   /* FF if installed */
    }

    /* returns nonzero if file is in the spooler queue  */
    int search_spl_que(char * fname)
    {
        union REGS  regs;
        struct SREGS   sregs;
        char far *  que_ptr;
        char que_name[65];
        int i;
        int found = 0;

        if (spooler_active())
        {
            regs.x.ax = 0x0104;  /* get spooler status */
            int86x(0x2f,&regs,&regs,&sregs);
            /* on return from call DS:SI points to print  queue */
            FP_SEG(que_ptr) = sregs.ds;
            FP_OFF(que_ptr) = regs.x.si;
            /* release hold on spooler, side effect of status*/
            regs.x.ax = 0x0105;
            int86x(0x2f,&regs,&regs,&sregs);
            while (*que_ptr && !found)  /* while items in queue */
            {
                for (i = 0; i < 64; i++)
                    que_name[i] = *(que_ptr + i);
                if (found = !strcmpi(que_name,fname))
                    break;
                que_ptr += 64;
            }
        }
        return(found);
    }

    void main_loop()
    {
        struct find_t c_file;
        union REGS regs;
        struct SREGS sregs;
        struct prReq prRequest;
        struct prReq far * ptr;
        int sleep_cntr;

        while (1)
        {
            strcpy(search_work,search_dir);
            strcat(search_work,"*.SPL");   /* create dir  search string */

            interval_timer = 18 * 30;     /* search every 30 seconds */
            while (interval_timer)    /* wait between each dir search */
                background_limit = BACKGROUND_YIELD;  /* yield for fgrnd */

            if (!_dos_findfirst(search_work,_A_NORMAL,&c_file))
            {
                /* if spooler installed, dos 3.xx+ and file size > 0 */
                if (spooler_active() && _osmajor >= 3 && c_file.size)
                {
                    strcpy(search_work,search_dir);
                    strcat(search_work,c_file.name); /* full pathname */
                    prRequest.level = 0;
                    prRequest.fname = search_work;
                    regs.x.ax = 0x0101;
                    ptr = &prRequest;
                    sregs.ds = FP_SEG(ptr);
                    regs.x.dx= FP_OFF(ptr);
                    int86x(0x2f,&regs,&regs,&sregs);
```

```
                    while (search_spl_que(search_work))   /*  wait till done */
                    {
                        interval_timer = 18 * 30;  /* sleep  for 30 seconds */
                        while (interval_timer)
                            background_limit = BACKGROUND_YIELD;
                    }

                    unlink(search_work);      /* delete file */
                    background_limit = BACKGROUND_YIELD;
                }
            }
        }
}
union REGS regs;
struct SREGS sregs;

void suspend_foreground()
{
    /* save current extended break status */
    breakState = GetBreak();

    /* set extended break status to be off */
    SetBreak(0);

    /* SWAP TO BACKGROUND */
    tic_count = 0;
    /* save old handlers */
    old_int1B= _dos_getvect(0x1B);
    old_int23= _dos_getvect(0x23);
    old_int24= _dos_getvect(0x24);

    /* set our interrupt handlers */
    _dos_setvect(0x1b,new_int1B);
    _dos_setvect(0x23,new_int23);
    _dos_setvect(0x24,new_int24);

    /* save current PSP and set to ours */
    foreground_psp = GetPSP();
    SetPSP(my_psp);

    /* get foreground DTA */
    regs.h.ah = GET_DTA;
    intdosx(&regs, &regs, &sregs);
    foreground_dta_seg = sregs.es;
    foreground_dta_off = regs.x.bx;

    /* set up our DTA */
    regs.h.ah = SET_DTA;
    regs.x.dx = 0x80;    /* use default in PSP area  */
    sregs.ds = my_psp;
    intdosx(&regs, &regs, &sregs);

    /* save error info */
    GetExtErr(&foreground_ErrInfo);

    if (! first_time)
        SetExtErr(&my_ErrInfo);

    in_progress = 1;
    background_limit = BACKGROUND_TICKS; /* set default limit */
}

void suspend_background()
{
    /* SWAP TO FOREGROUND */

    /* put back original DTA */
    regs.h.ah = SET_DTA;
    regs.x.dx = foreground_dta_off;
    sregs.ds  = foreground_dta_seg;
    intdosx(&regs, &regs, &sregs);
```

```
      /* put back original PSP */
      SetPSP(foreground_psp);

      /* put back original INTS */
      _dos_setvect(0x1b,old_int1B);
      _dos_setvect(0x23,old_int23);
      _dos_setvect(0x24,old_int24);

      /* get error info */
      GetExtErr(&my_ErrInfo);
      SetExtErr(&foreground_ErrInfo);

      tic_count = 0;
      in_progress = 0;
      int_28_active = 0;

      foreground_limit = FOREGROUND_TICKS; /* set default limit */

      /* put back extended break checking the way it was */
      SetBreak(breakState);
}

/**********
* TIMER TICK INTERRUPT HANDLER
**********/
void interrupt far new_int8(INTERRUPT_REGS r)
{
      _enable();               /* enable interrupts */
      tic_count++;

      if (interval_timer)
          interval_timer--;

      if (in_progress &&
          !multi_critical &&
          dos_count == 0 &&
          ((tic_count >= background_limit &&
              !DosBusy() && !unsafe_flag) ||
          (int_28_active && !Int28DosBusy() &&
              tic_count >=background_limit)))
      {
          suspend_background();
          restore_stack();
      }
      else if (!in_progress &&
              ((tic_count >= foreground_limit &&
                  !DosBusy() && !unsafe_flag) ||
              (int_28_active && !Int28DosBusy() &&
                  tic_count >=foreground_limit)))
      {
          set_stack();
          suspend_foreground();
          if (first_time)
          {
              first_time = 0;
              timer_int_chain();
          }
      }
      old_int8();    /* call old handler */
}

/**********
* KEYBOARD INTERRUPT HANDLER
**********/
void interrupt far new_int9(INTERRUPT_REGS r)
{
   unsafe_flag++;
   old_int9();
```

```
    if (in_progress)
        background_limit = BACKGROUND_YIELD; /* set to swap to fgrnd */
    foreground_limit = 18;                   /* since user hit keyboard */
    unsafe_flag--;
}

/*********
* CTRL-BREAK INTERRUPT HANDLER
*********/
void interrupt far new_int1B(INTERRUPT_REGS r) { /* do nothing */ }


/**********
* CTRL-C INTERRUPT HANDLER
**********/
void interrupt far new_int23(INTERRUPT_REGS r) { /* do nothing */ }

/**********
* CRTITICAL ERROR INTERRUPT HANDLER
**********/
void interrupt far new_int24(INTERRUPT_REGS r)
{
    if (_osmajor >= 3)
        r.ax = 3;    /* fail dos function */
    else
        r.ax = 0;
}

/**********
* DOS IDLE INTERRUPT HANDLER
**********/
void interrupt far new_int28(INTERRUPT_REGS r)
{
    if (!in_progress && !Int28DosBusy() && !unsafe_flag &&
        tic_count > foreground_limit)
    {
        foreground_limit = FOREGROUND_YIELD;   /* stop foreground */
        int_28_active = 1;
        _enable();              /* STI */
        while (int_28_active)
            ;            /*spin waiting for task swap to  bckgrnd*/
    }
    (*old_int28)();    /* call old handler */
}

/**********
* DOS MULTIPLEX INTERRUPT HANDLER
**********/
void interrupt far new_int2f(INTERRUPT_REGS r)
{
    /* See if windows is starting up. If so, then set CX to be non-zero
       to keep windows from starting. This TSR and Windows are not
       compatible. */
    if (r.ax == 0x1605) /* windows init msg */
        r.cx = 1;
    else
        _chain_intr(old_int2f); /* pass int to other handlers */
}

main()
{
    unsigned         memtop, dummy;
    void far* far*   tmpptr;

    puts("Multi-Tasking PRINT spooler installing");

    if (_osmajor < 3)
    {
        puts("Error: MS-DOS version 3.00 or greater required");
```

```
        exit(1);
    }

    if (! spooler_active())
        puts("Warning: Print Spooler not active");

    InitInDos();
    my_psp = GetPSP();

    /* MALLOC a stack for our TSR section */
    stack_ptr = malloc(STACK_SIZE);
    stack_ptr += STACK_SIZE;
    ptr = stack_ptr;
    *(--stack_ptr) = 0xF2;   /* set up stack as if an an IRET was done*/
    *(--stack_ptr) = 0x02;
    stack_ptr -= 4;
    tmpptr = stack_ptr;
    *(tmpptr) = main_loop;

    /* get interrupt vectors */
    old_int8  = _dos_getvect(0x08); /* timer int */
    old_int9  = _dos_getvect(0x09); /* keyboard int */
    old_int10 = _dos_getvect(0x10); /* video int */
    old_int13 = _dos_getvect(0x13); /* disk int */
    old_int21 = _dos_getvect(0x21); /* dos int */
    old_int25 = _dos_getvect(0x25); /* sector read  int */
    old_int26 = _dos_getvect(0x26); /* sector write int */
    old_int28 = _dos_getvect(0x28); /* dos idle int */
    old_int2f = _dos_getvect(0x2f); /* dos multiplex int */

    init_intr();     /* init asm variables */

    _dos_setvect(0x08,new_int8);
    _dos_setvect(0x09,new_int9);
    _dos_setvect(0x10,new_int10);
    _dos_setvect(0x13,new_int13);
    _dos_setvect(0x21,new_int21);
    _dos_setvect(0x25,new_int25);
    _dos_setvect(0x26,new_int26);
    _dos_setvect(0x28,new_int28);
    _dos_setvect(0x2f,new_int2f);
#define PARAGRAPHS(x)   ((FP_OFF(x) + 15) >> 4)

    /* release unused heap to MS-DOS */
    /* All MALLOCS for TSR section must be done in  TSR_INIT() */
    /* calculate top of memory, shrink block, and go TSR */
    segread(&sregs);
    memtop = sregs.ds + PARAGRAPHS(ptr) - _psp;

    _dos_setblock(memtop, _psp, &dummy);
    _dos_keep(0, memtop);
}
```

When compiling the MULTI TSR example under Microsoft C 6.0, we ran across a code optimization "gotcha." Notice that the new_int28() function simply sets up the tick counting variables so that the background becomes active. The code then sets the int_28_active semaphore and waits for it to be cleared:

```
int_28_active = 1;
while (int_28_active)
    ;
```

The idea behind this code is to wait until a task swap occurs. During the task swap, int_28_active is set to zero.

But when compiling with full optimization, the compiler sees that int_28_active is initialized to 1 is not altered in the while loop. Therefore it figures this is an infinite loop and generates a JMP $.

What it does not know is that the timer-interrupt routine will clear this flag. To avoid this problem but still allow optimization, declare the int_28_active variable with a "volatile" attribute:

```
volatile int int_28_active;
```

This ANSI C keyword tells the compiler that the variable may change from an external source.

This multitasking TSR is a simple example to which a few enhancements could be added. Memory could be swapped to disk or EMS as needed. The TSR could provide a pop-up service where background operations can be controlled dynamically. If keyboard and CRT I/O is required by the background task, you must be careful to save and restore the appropriate settings. You also must not switch tasks while in the middle of a BIOS Video service. For a true multitasking system, MS-DOS alone is probably not the way to go. Commercial multitaskers such as Windows or DesqView give you much more functionality. But such systems use many of the same principles outlined here.

## CHAPTER 10

Command Interpreters

by Jim Kyle

Every operating system that permits more than a single program to run requires some sort of command interpreter. In the earliest days of computing, the human operator interpreted commands by picking out the correct plugboard or card deck and setting the system in action. Now a program (often called the shell because it surrounds the system kernel, but more formally termed the command interpreter) does the job. The command interpreter prompts the user for input and then reacts to that input.

For most users, a command interpreter is the closest contact they ever have with an actual operating system. The familiar C> prompt from COMMAND.COM, the character based, command line shell that comes with MS-DOS, is almost universally called the DOS prompt although the interpreter is not in fact part of MS-DOS itself. Alternate interpreters such as 4DOS.COM and the MKS Korn Shell are also available.

This chapter examines first the functional requirements that must be met by any command interpreter. The standard COMMAND.COM from DOS 5.0 provides specific examples of such requirements. While examining these requirements, the chapter explores several undocumented services that DOS provides to simplify the task of interfacing with the command interpreter. The first section concludes with a tiny shell program you can use to replace COMMAND.COM; this program illustrates exactly what the requirements are for creating a command interpreter.

With the functional requirements established, the chapter dissects COMMAND.COM to see how it meets those requirements. In this section, you learn about the environment, how it works, and how to locate COMMAND.COM once it is loaded into memory. This section includes a number of utility routines for locating and dealing with environment blocks, since the environment strings contain essential information used by the command interpreters, such as the prompt and the path to the interpreter itself.

Next, we examine some alternative command interpreters that are now available, together with some shells that are actually only extensions to COMMAND.COM.

The chapter concludes with a sample program that combines the use of documented and undocumented features to permit editing of either the master environment or the currently active copy of it. This program, ENVEDT, works with any command interpreter that supports the undocumented DOS hook INT 2Eh; actually, the command interpreter need not provide full support, so long as it includes a minimal interrupt handler for the service.

Several notorious undocumented aspects of the DOS programmer's interface are covered in this chapter, including the back door to the command interpreter (INT 2Eh) and the DOS master environment block. The less- well-known but quite important installable command interface (INT 2Fh Function AEh) is also discussed in detail.

Inside COMMAND.COM

The major requirements for any command interpreter are as follows:

- To provide a means of obtaining commands from the human operator
- To act on them by dispatching appropriate processes

An additional requirement is that these actions be enclosed in a loop so that more commands may be issued after all current commands have been processed.

Before we look at the details of these requirements, let's see just what happens inside COMMAND.COM itself, to help put these details into perspective. The summary that follows resulted from an INTRSPY script using DOS 5.0. The script reported all calls to INT 21h and INT 2Fh. I then edited the INTRSPY report to include only one cycle around COMMAND.COM's inner loop and to remove excessive detail that obscured the nature of the actions. I also added comments in the report to help clarify just what COMMAND.COM is doing at each point.

The cycle begins at the return to COMMAND.COM's loop, following execution of the previous command:

```
---ret from child process---
I21 at FFFF:B33F, AX=4D00: Get exit code: Exit Code 00h, Exit Type 00
I21 at FFFF:B4D3, AX=4800: ALLOC FFFFh paras FAIL (0008), only 89E0h available
I21 at FFFF:B4EC, AX=48AD: ALLOC 89E0h paras returned seg 161Fh

I21 at FFFF:B723, AX=2522: Set INT22 ==> 0B4D:017F
I21 at FFFF:B72A, AX=2523: Set INT23 ==> 0B4D:014B
I21 at FFFF:B731, AX=2524: Set INT24 ==> 0B4D:0156

I21 at FFFF:B60A, AX=3E24: Close 0005 through 0013
```

COMMAND.COM first retrieves the exit code returned by the previous process and stores it in an internal variable. COMMAND.COM then grabs back all available RAM that the previous process released on the way out during the DOS Terminate function. This is apparently done so that COMMAND.COM will own the transient memory area if it needs to reload that part of itself. Next, the three interrupt vectors saved in the PSP are restored to point to routines within COMMAND.COM itself, and all 15 file handles above the 5 predefined ones are closed.

Note that all of the preceding calls to INT 21h came from the HMA; this could indicate that they are all part of the DOS Terminate function's processing. However, a similar trace (not shown), run from 4DOS.COM instead of COMMAND.COM, reported a different sequence of calls to do the same jobs, proving that this sequence is not part of DOS itself. As you shall see later, COMMAND.COM automatically puts portions of its code in the HMA if you run DOS=HIGH, and that's where these calls originate.

With cleanup from the previous process nearly done, COMMAND.COM next resets its internal error tables with a sequence of calls to undocumented INT 2Fh AX=122EH. This is followed by calls that apparently support international character set capabilities and finally by output of a CR/LF pair to predefined STDOUT handle 1. The << and >> symbols in this part of the trace identify the line generated at entry to the interrupt, <<, and the one generated on exit, >>.

```
INT 2F << 9672:5119, AX=122E: DOS HOOK: GET/SET ERROR TABLE
=== 2F >> AX=122E, BX=0014, CX=0000, DX=5E00
INT 2F << 9672:5128, AX=122E: DOS HOOK: GET/SET ERROR TABLE
=== 2F >> AX=122E, BX=0014, CX=0000, DX=5E02
INT 2F << 9672:5137, AX=122E: DOS HOOK: GET/SET ERROR TABLE
=== 2F >> AX=122E, BX=0014, CX=0000, DX=5E04
INT 2F << 9672:5146, AX=122E: DOS HOOK: GET/SET ERROR TABLE
=== 2F >> AX=122E, BX=0014, CX=0000, DX=5E06
INT 2F << 9672:5173, AX=122E: DOS HOOK: GET/SET ERROR TABLE
=== 2F >> AX=122E, BX=0014, CX=007B, DX=5E08
```

```
I21 at 9672:51B3, AX=6300: Get Lead Byte Table: 9672:5E08
I21 at 9672:0199, AX=3800: Get/Set Country Code: 9672:985A
I21 at 9672:541B, AX=4000: Write to 0001: 0Dh 0Ah
```

The cleanup is now complete, so COMMAND.COM generates a prompt for display, building it from the current drive code and current working directory to satisfy my "pg" PROMPT= specification. This is written to STDOUT handle 1. COMMAND.COM then calls the redirector (see Chapter 8) using undocumented functions INT 21h AX=5D08h and 5D09h, just in case a redirected printer needs to be flushed and restarted. I removed exit lines from the following excerpt:

```
I21 at 9672:01EE, AX=1900: Current drive is: 03
I21 at 9672:1ED3, AX=475C: Get CWD for 00 returned UDOS2\ISPY
I21 at 9672:541B, AX=4000: Write to 0001: D:\UDOS2\ISPY
I21 at 9672:1EA8, AX=023E: Display Char '>'

I21 at 9672:02AB, AX=5D09: Flush redir printer output
INT 2F << FDC8:A5DC, AX=1125: REDIRECTOR: Get/Set stream state:

I21 at 9672:02B2, AX=5D08: Set redir printer: 01
INT 2F << FDC8:A5DC, AX=1125: REDIRECTOR: Get/Set stream state:
```

With the prompt displayed, COMMAND.COM then calls DOSKEY using INT 2Fh to load the keyboard buffer if DOSKEY is active. Since DOSKEY is not active, this call has no effect and the next call, to 21/0A, is necessary to get the typed input. Were DOSKEY active, the call to 21/0A would be skipped over. COMMAND.COM spends most of its execution time inside of either DOSKEY or 21/0A, waiting for keystrokes.

```
INT 2F << 9672:02BC, AX=4810: DOSKEY: Get input
=== 2F >> AX=4810, BX=858C, CX=00F9, DX=8B59

I21 at 9672:02C4, AX=0A10: Buffered Input to 9672:8B59
```

When I press ENTER to end the input, control returns to COMMAND.COM. The program echoes a CR/LF pair to acknowledge input, then parses the command line to determine what to do next:

```
I21 at 9672:541B, AX=4000: Write to 0001: 0Dh 0Ah

I21 at 9672:0313, AX=2901: Parse FCB (mode 01) from 9672:8BDE to 9672:8E05
I21 at 9672:0394, AX=2901: Parse FCB (mode 01) from 9672:0081 to 9672:005C
I21 at 9672:03B1, AX=2901: Parse FCB (mode 01) from 9672:0081 to 9672:006C
```

The first action below determines whether DIDIT (the string I typed in this example, representing the name of a simple program) is a user-installed command (see the discussion later in this chapter). COMMAND.COM makes two calls to 2F/AE00 to perform this test, but other command interpreters use only a single call:

```
INT 2F << 9672:2BEC, AX=AE00: INST CMD: Check of DIDIT
                        CH=FF
=== 2F >> AX=AE00, BX=8BDC, CX=FF00, DX=FFFF, returns 00
INT 2F << 9672:2BEC, AX=AE00: INST CMD: Check of DIDIT
                        CH=00
=== 2F >> AX=AE00, BX=8BDC, CX=0000, DX=FFFF, returns 00
```

The return value of 00 from both these calls tells the command interpreter that DIDIT is not an installed command. COMMAND.COM then examines its list of internal commands and does not find DIDIT there either. The next step is to try to locate a file of that name in the current working directory. The confusing call below to the Redirector routine is built into the FindFirst function, apparently just in case reference to a remote drive happens to be made:

```
I21 at 9672:32ED, AX=1A00: Set DTA to 9672:96D5
I21 at 9672:34E9, AX=4700: Get CWD for 00 returned  UDOS2\ISPY
I21 at 9672:34F4, AX=4E00: FindFirst: didit.???
```

```
INT 2F << FDC8:ABA5, AX=1123: REDIRECTOR: Qualify name:  didit.???
  name not resolved returned 0000
```

This time, the return value of 0000 indicates that such a file exists. Were the return value non-zero, COMMAND.COM would repeat the previous step in each directory named by the PATH environment variable. However, in this case DIDIT.??? exists in the current working directory (CWD), so COMMAND.COM searches for DIDIT.COM, DIDIT.EXE, or DIDIT.BAT. Comparison of the file type returned in the DTA by the FindFirst call indicates that the file found is DIDIT.COM, so no additional search is needed. COMMAND.COM releases the memory it grabbed earlier then calls 21/4B00 to load and run DIDIT.COM as a child process. Again, an embedded call to the redirector appears:

```
I21 at 9672:3362, AX=4700: Get CWD for 04 returned  UDOS2\ISPY
I21 at 9672:29FF, AX=4908: FREE seg 161Fh
I21 at 0B4D:01DC, AX=4B00: Loading  D:\UDOS2\ISPY\DIDIT.COM
INT 2F << FDC8:ABA5, AX=1123: REDIRECTOR: Qualify name: D:\UDOS2\ISPY\DIDIT.COM
  name not resolved
```

DIDIT.COM itself performs only one action, printing the words "Loaded and run"; then it terminates using INT 20h rather than by the normal DOS Termination function. Since our script does not capture this interrupt, the indication of termination comes from the two calls to the DOS redirector that ensure the cleanup and closing of all remote files. Then the program returns from the INT 21/4B00 call, completing one cycle around the inner loop and ending our example:

```
I21 at 1628:0107, AX=0900: Print String:  Loaded and run
INT 2F << FDC8:93E2, AX=1122: REDIRECTOR: Cleanup at termination
INT 2F << FDC8:6DC3, AX=111D: REDIRECTOR: Close all remote files
---ret from child process---
```

At this point the action returns to exactly where we started. The shell retrieves the exit code, grabs memory once more just in case it's needed, and restores the interrupt vectors, although the DIDIT.COM program never changed them. COMMAND.COM, as well as all other command interpreters, follows the principle of undoing the user-program's actions, even if it never did them in the first place.

Don't let the redirector calls confuse you; these all involve networking capabilities (see Chapter 8), not command line redirection of stdin and stdout. Later in this chapter we look at command line redirection.

To summarize, the command interpreter shows a prompt, gets operator input, determines how to respond to that input, and does so by either running an installed command, running an internal command built into the interpreter itself, or launching an external program. When one of those three actions is complete and control returns to the loop, the interpreter retrieves the exit code (for an external program), restores its internal conditions, and does it all over again. The key MS-DOS functions involved are 0Ah (buffered keyboard input) and 4Bh (load and execute process).

Requirements of a Command Interpreter

Obtaining Operator Input

The most essential requirement for any command interpreter is that it obtain commands to be interpreted; without that nothing else has any meaning.

You've seen that operator input can be obtained from keystrokes entered directly by the user in response to a prompt from the command interpreter. There are, however, several alternate methods, all of them frequently used.

The DOS Prompt   The command interpreter usually signals the user that it's waiting for input by issuing a prompt message, usually known simply as "the prompt." Some menu-style shell programs turn on the cursor or the mouse pointer to indicate that input is needed, but more often these programs display their menus only when seeking input, so that the mere presence of the menu on the screen serves as the prompt.

In event-driven, multitasking environments such as Windows, this prompt is always present because input can be accepted even when other programs are running. In this case the mouse pointer often changes to an hourglass shape when input cannot be accepted due to the temporary existence of a system-modal condition.

In the more conventional command line operation, the prompt consists of a relatively short sequence of characters. The default prompt message of COMMAND.COM is simply C>, where C indicates the drive letter of the current drive and > is simply a visual delimiter. Virtually all command interpreters, though, give the user a means to modify the prompt into whatever form might be desired.

Although a dedicated PROMPT command is used to define custom prompt messages, the actual message is stored as a string in the environment space and can be changed in the same manner as any other environment string. Many hard disk users use PROMPT pg rather than the default C> prompt, which is equivalent to PROMPT ng. Our example COMMAND.COM loop showed how this prompt is produced. In addition, ANSI.SYS can be used to put the current drive and directory at the top left corner of the screen, for example, while the usual prompt appears in its normal place.

Keystrokes   The normal source of input to the command interpreter is the system keyboard, but it's examined only as a last resort, if the interpreter is unable to get input from any of the alternates!

This apparently backward approach actually has a very logical basis; it lets you start a job using the alternate methods and then switch to the keyboard to finish the job. This method can, however, be highly confusing to the neophyte user. Let's defer examination of the possible confusion until you see what alternatives to the keyboard exist.

When the keyboard furnishes input, most command interpreters use the standard DOS Buffered Keyboard Input function (Int 21h, Function 0Ah) to obtain that input. This function provides, through several of the function keys, a rudimentary string edit capability, which we examine in more detail later in this chapter. Note that this editing capability, such as it is, is a feature of the input function, not of COMMAND.COM itself.

Command line editors, such as Chris Dunford's CED, hook INT 21h and supply their own Read String Function, thereby enhancing the editing of any program, not just COMMAND.COM, that calls Function 0Ah. These programs include DEBUG or SYMDEB. DOSKEY, the command line editor included with DOS 5.0, does not hook INT 21h; instead, it provides a separate interface (INT 2Fh AX=4810h), which a program such as COMMAND.COM must explicitly call, as shown in our earlier example.

Unlike older operating systems, keyboard input to the command interpreter in DOS is not forced to uppercase but passes to the interpreter exactly as you type it, except for characters erased with the backspace keys.

All command interpreters used with MS-DOS that I have examined have a size limit of 126 characters for their keyboard input. This limit is imposed by the layout of the PSP (refer to Chapter 7), which allows only 128 bytes for the command tail. Of these 128 bytes, one is taken by the character count and one by the CR character that terminates the input string.

Although it would be possible to extend this limit by a few bytes because the command itself is never copied into the PSP, no actual interpreter does so. For simplicity, most provide a maximum 128-byte input buffer, although at least one (4DOS) allows you to configure it for larger buffer sizes.

Batch Files   In many applications, a relatively complex series of commands must be entered to get the desired action started. Batch files provide the most generally used method for supplying those commands. You type the commands into the batch file once, and then the entire sequence is pumped into the command interpreter when you invoke the batch file. Command interpreters treat a batch file as a special type of external command. Although different interpreters process these files in different ways, the general idea is that the interpreter reads the file one line at a time, then executes the command contained on that line before coming back to read the next.

For safety, COMMAND.COM closes the batch file each time a line is read, and reopens it to read the next line. This makes it possible to use batch files with a single drive system by having a copy of the file on each diskette; so long as all copies are named the same and have the same content, the command interpreter would never be aware that the disks were swapped between lines. This action does, unfortunately, also make batch file operation quite slow.

Batch Enhancers and Compilers   Batch files are so widely used that several firms offer batch language enhancement programs, such as BE (Batch Enhancer) in the Norton Utilities, EBL (Extended Batch Language), and several PC Magazine utilities such as Michael Mefford's BATCH-MAN. Recently, batch file compilers have become popular as well. In addition to Wenham Software's BATCOM and Hyperkinetix's BUILDER, *PC Magazine* (August 1990) has published a batch file compiler, Doug Boling's BAT2EXEC. These compilers turn .BAT files into true .COM or .EXE files.

This raises an interesting issue. As is well known, the SET statement in a .BAT file alters the master environment (explained in the section, "How COMMAND.COM Uses the Environment"), but a seemingly equivalent attempt to change the environment by a .COM or .EXE program results only in an alteration to the program's local copy of the environment, which then gets thrown away when the program exits.

How then can the proper semantics of the SET statement be preserved when a .BAT file is compiled into a .COM file? Simple: The compiled SET statement uses undocumented DOS to alter the master environment. For example, any time a .BAT file with a SET statement is compiled with BAT2EXEC, the resulting .COM file calls undocumented INT 21h Function 52h.

Why Function 52h? To get a pointer to the DOS List Of Lists, which contains at offset -2 the segment of the first MCB (see Chapter 3). By walking the MCB chain, the program can find the master environment. This is explained in much greater detail later on, in the section "Other Ways of Locating the Environment." In any case, the popularity of batch file compilers will, for better or worse, poliferate more programs that rely on undocumented DOS functions and data structures.

"Losing" Stuffed Commands

Only the command interpreter can obtain input directly from the batch file; it's not possible to provide direct input to your programs by lines typed into any batch file. However, it's possible to use special utilities to stuff input into the keyboard buffer, where your programs can find it, and these utilities can be called from the batch file. This is useful with programs that do not take command line arguments.

One such keyboard stuffer is Charles Petzold's KEY-FAKE.COM, available in the book *PC Magazine DOS Power Tools*. KEY-FAKE is used here to illustrate a feature of batch files that, although seemingly obvious, appears to cause a lot of confusion. Any other keyboard stuffer serves equally well.

The following batch file creates a file called FOO.BAR, containing the single line "hello" (the 13 26 13 emits a newline, ^Z, newline sequence):

```
echo off
key-fake "hello" 13 26 13
copy con foo.bar
```

Note that input is stuffed into the keyboard buffer before the COPY CON command is invoked. If you want to stuff both the input and the command into the keyboard, however, the command must go first:

```
echo off
key-fake "copy con foo.bar" 13 "hello" 13 26 13
```

So far so good. Now let's add a line to the end of the batch file:

```
echo off
key-fake "copy con foo.bar" 13 "hello" 13 26 13
echo Done creating FOO.BAR
```

What happens when you run this? The second command happens before the first command:

```
C:\UNDOC\KYLE>tmp
Done creating FOO.BAR
C:\UNDOC\KYLE>copy con foo.bar
hello
^Z
    1 File(s) copied
```

The message that signals that the operation is complete is displayed before the operation begins! Just adding a line to the end of the batch file somehow caused the COPY CON command to be deferred.

It gets worse. Do the keyboard stuffing inside a loop, and the COPY CON command never gets executed, resulting in an infinite loop:

```
echo off
del foo.bar
:loop
key-fake "copy con foo.bar" 13 "hello" 13 26 13
if not exist foo.bar goto loop
```

Simply putting a command inside a loop causes the batch file to stop working! What is going on here?

If, as a final experiment, you return to the original idea of putting the COPY CON command itself in the batch file and stuffing only its input into the keyboard buffer, everything starts working properly again.

```
echo off
del foo.bar
:loop
key-fake "hello" 13 26 13
copy con foo.bar
echo Done creating FOO.BAR
if not exist foo.bar goto loop
```

What you have just seen merely illustrates that the command interpreter exhausts all batch file lines before looking in the buffer for keyboard input. Therefore, unless the keyboard stuffer happens to execute as the last command in the batch file, the stuffed command isn't executed at the correct time.

This detail of command interpreter operation seems rather obvious, yet it spawns at least one question per week on the major network forums that deal with hardware and software problems. The rule to follow in order to avoid the problem is simple: Invoke commands directly from the batch file, not by stuffing the keyboard buffer; provide only program input through the buffer.

Interpreting Operator Requests

Once the operator's input has been obtained, it must be put into a form acceptable to MS-DOS (that is, it must be parsed for file names and so forth), interpreted, and acted on. This section first describes the factors involved in parsing the input, then discusses how the input is interpreted, and finally deals with the execution of internal commands. Any input not recognized as an installed or internal command passes to the dispatching procedure as a possible external command that it must load from a file.

Parsing for Inclusion in the PSP

The standardized parsing done by DOS command interpreters traces directly back to CP/M; the major difference is that MS-DOS includes INT 21h Function 29h, fully documented, to perform the parse for you.

In this standardized parse, certain characters are treated as separators, and only a few of these are white space. These include the blank space, the tab character, the switch character (normally a forward slash, but in some versions of DOS this can be changed to a hyphen; see below), the comma, the colon, the semicolon, and the equal sign. Several of these have additional syntactic significance, but all are recognized as marking the end of the possible command name.

The parse begins by skipping over all blank or tab characters at the front of the input line. When a nonblank character is found, the parse routine converts it to uppercase if it's alphabetic and moves it to an internal parse buffer. From that point until one of the separator characters is encountered, all characters are moved to the parse buffer and case-converted if necessary. When the terminating separator character is found, the parse pointer is left pointing to it.

If the command in the parse buffer turns out to be either an installed command or an external program name, a new process will execute it; if it is an internal command, the command interpreter itself performs the execution. In either event, a PSP is available for the rest of the parsing procedure.

All remaining characters from the input buffer are moved to the command tail area of the PSP associated with the command's execution, starting at offset 81h, and the count of those characters (omitting the terminating CR) is stored at offset 80h. None of these characters is case-converted during the move.

Next, the first complete word (if any) in the command tail is examined to determine if it could be a filename. That is, it must contain no characters that would not be valid in a filename; its second character can be a colon and any subsequent character up to the ninth can be a period. This permits the CP/M and DOS 1.x (nondirectory) file specification, such as A:FILENAME.EXT, to be accepted.

If the word passes all these tests, it is converted to FCB format, which includes case conversion, and copied into the FCB1 region of the PSP at offset 5Ch (see Chapter 7). The drive code corresponding to the drive letter, if any, goes into the first byte, followed by the filename portion, padded to 8 bytes with spaces if necessary. The period, like the colon, is omitted, and the extension goes into the next 3 bytes, again padded with spaces. The process is repeated for the second complete word of the command tail to fill in the FCB2 area of the PSP at offset 6Ch.

This is a direct copy of the steps performed by CP/M programs, and the syntax of many of the older internal commands is based on these parsing rules. In DOS 1.x, many programs took advantage of these parsing rules to extract their first two command line arguments from the filename fields of FCB1 and FCB2. By doing so, they could avoid the need to furnish their own parsing routines; the command interpreter had already done the work for them. However, these routines are not capable of handling subdirectory references and full path names, so with DOS 2.x their usefulness began to fade, and today they are primarily a footnote to history. Unfortunately, some programs still depend on them, showing the persistence to this day of CP/M vestiges.

On completion of this standard parse, then, the command interpreter has in an internal parsing buffer the first word of input converted to uppercase, and it has, in the new current PSP, the two FCB areas and the command tail data. The next step is to determine whether the input was actually a valid command. But first, a little more on the subject of input.

SWITCHAR   If you've ever needed to switch between DOS and UNIX machines, you may have been annoyed that, whereas UNIX uses the forward slash (/) for paths and hyphens (-) for command line options, MS-DOS uses the backslash (\) for paths and the forward slash (/) for command line options. (Prior to DOS 5.0, the convention applied to COMMAND.COM more than to DOS itself; since DOS 5.0, though, it's built into DOS and cannot be modified.)

What a mess! An undocumented DOS function, INT 21h Function 3701h, can help clean up this situation if you use a version prior to DOS 5.0. This function, described in the Appendix, changes the switch character. This facility was documented for a brief time in the DOS user interface (the SWITCHAR= option in the DOS 2.0 CONFIG.SYS); but then it was made undocumented.

This function can be incorporated into a tiny utility (see Figure 10-1) that sets the DOS SWITCHAR. Packages of UNIX utilities for DOS, such as the MKS Toolkit, include a similar utility.

Figure 10-1. SWITCHAR.C

```
/*
SWITCHAR.C -- uses undocumented DOS Function 3701h
switchar    changes DOS switch char to - and path char to /
switchar \  restores DOS switch char to / and path char to \
*/

#include <stdlib.h>
#include <stdio.h>
#include <dos.h>
main(int argc, char *argv[])
{ int c = (argc > 1) ? argv[1][0] : '-';
#ifdef __TURBOC__
  _DL = c;
  _AX = 0x3701;
  geninterrupt(0x21);
  _AH = 0;   /* value returned in AX */
#else
  _asm {
    mov dl, c
    mov ax, 3701h
    int 21h
    xor ah, ah   ; value returned in AX
    }
#endif
}
```

Most of COMMAND.COM since DOS 4.0 (including the DIR command) completely ignores the SWITCHAR. Setting SWITCHAR with Function 3701h is useful only when other programs, in particular COMMAND.COM, bother to call Function 3700h (Get SWITCHAR). As of DOS 5.0, this SWITCHAR program won't even work; while Function 3700h still works, Function 3701h now has no effect at all, making the program an exercise in futility for DOS 5.0 and above.

Command Line Redirection and Pipes

One feature that has existed in COMMAND.COM since DOS 2.0, and which consequently is also in all the popular alternate command interpreters, is the ability to redirect input and output. This means that the command interpreter can "throw a switch" so that input for a process comes from a file rather than from the keyboard and can, independently, send output from a process to a file rather than to the CRT.

Together with this feature, which came from UNIX, "pipes" can be created to hook two processes together so that the output of the first becomes the input to the second.

The capabilities themselves are well documented; the method by which they are achieved is not. Let's look first at how COMMAND.COM performs this magic in DOS 5.0, then create a simple C program that performs its own redirection, using command line arguments to specify the input and output names.

Here's how command line redirection works when COMMAND.COM processes this line:

```
D:\UDOS2\ISPY> DEV >xyz
```

The redirection symbol (>) specifies that output is to go into the file XYZ, rather than to the screen. DEV is the driver-tracing program from Chapter 7, but any program could have been used. And though this example deals only with redirection of output, input redirection is done in exactly the same way.

COMMAND.COM processes "DEV>XYZ" in almost the same way that it processes a plain "DEV" command. Only after DEV has been determined to be an external command, the file located, and the current working directory's name retrieved, does the command line redirection cause a change in how COMMAND.COM processes "DEV>XYZ". COMMAND.COM creates a file named XYZ in the current working directory.

The System File Table entry for the handle returned by the Create File call (INT 21h AX=3C04h) is then plugged into STDOUT handle 1. All output sent to STDOUT from this point on goes into file XYZ, rather than to the CRT. COMMAND.COM then continues just as in the earlier example to load and run the program DEV.

After return from the child process, COMMAND.COM detects that STDOUT handle 1 points to a different System File Table entry from STDERR handle 2. This indicates that STDOUT has been redirected. Consequently, COMMAND.COM closes STDOUT and restores it to the same SFT entry as handle 2 before dropping into the loop that closes the 15 non-predefined handles (hmm, what about programs that know how to redirect STDERR?).

Because of the device independence achieved by the use of file handles and device drivers (discussed in Chapter 7), only these two additions to the normal inner loop of COMMAND.COM were required to put the output from DEV into file XYZ rather than onto the screen.

The only difference between redirection, as described here, and pipes that connect processes, is that the command interpreter automatically creates a temporary file to serve as a pipe and redirects output from the first process into the file. The interpreter then directs the file to the second process as its input. Those parts of the normal command interpreter loop that generate the prompt and wait for keyboard input are dropped for the second process, so that the single piped command actually does the same thing as two separate commands with a common redirection file connecting them. Finally, the command interpreter automatically destroys the temporary file when it's no longer needed.

You've seen how COMMAND.COM deals with command line redirection. Now let's see how to do the same thing in C code (Figure 10-2). The key is the dup2() function.

Figure 10-2. REDIR.C

```
/*
 *   REDIR.C - August 1992 - Jim Kyle
 *       Shows how to redirect STDIN and STDOUT
 *       Tested only with BCC++ in ANSI-C mode:
 *               bcc redir.c
 */
#include <stdio.h>
#include <string.h>
#include <io.h>
#include <process.h>

int main( int argc, char **argv )
{ char cmdbfr[126] = "";
  FILE *NewIn = NULL, *NewOut = NULL;
  int oldin, oldout;
  int retval = 255, i;

  if( argc < 4 )
    { puts( " Usage: REDIR In Out Command ... " );
```

```
      puts( "    where In = STDIN or name of input file" );
      puts( "         Out = STDOUT or name of output file" );
      puts( "   and Command = normal command line to be run." );
    }
  else
  { if( stricmp( argv[1], "STDIN" ) != 0 )    /* if file named... */
    { NewIn = fopen( argv[1], "r" );   /* open the file to read */
      if( !NewIn )                            /* quit if any error */
        { perror( argv[1] );
          return retval;
        }
      oldin = fileno( stdin );              /* save for restoring */
      dup2( fileno( NewIn ), fileno( stdin ));/* force to stdin */
    }

    if( stricmp( argv[2], "STDOUT" ) != 0 )  /* if file named...  */
    { NewOut = fopen( argv[2], "w" )   /* open the file, output */
      if( !NewOut )                          /* quit if any error */
        { perror( argv[2] );
          return retval;
        }
      oldout = fileno( stdout );             /* save for restoring */
      dup2( fileno( NewOut ), fileno( stdout ));/* force stdout */
    }

    for( i=3; i<argc; i++ )            /* rebuild the command line */
      { strcat( cmdbfr, argv[i] );
        strcat( cmdbfr, " " );
      }
    retval = system( cmdbfr );          /* then exec, save exit code */

    if( NewIn )                        /* restore STDIN if needed */
      { fclose( NewIn );
        dup2( oldin, fileno( stdin ));      /* use original value */
      }
    if( NewOut )                               /* and also STDOUT */
      { fclose( NewOut );            /* close to update directory */
        dup2( oldout, fileno( stdout ));   /* use original value */
      }
  }
  return retval;                          /* return exit code */
}
```

Rather than confuse the issue by attempting to parse its input command line to detect a redirection request, REDIR.C just requires that you specify both its input and output paths as the first two command-line arguments. If the first argument is "STDIN", no input redirection is performed. If it is anything else, the argument is passed as a file or device name to the fopen() function to be opened for reading.

Similarly, the second argument is compared to "STDOUT" to detect a request for output redirection.

After these two arguments are processed, the rest of the input command line is reassembled into a new command line and passed on to the normal command interpreter through the system() function. Any value returned by system() is saved in the local variable, retval, to be passed back as REDIR's own exit code. We look at this exit code business a little later.

Before returning to DOS, REDIR closes any redirection files or devices that have been opened and attempts to restore the corresponding stream to its original device. With these tasks taken care of, REDIR then returns the saved exit code as its own and goes back to DOS.

The dup2() function is a standard C library function whose MS-DOS implementations use documented INT 21h AH=46h (Force Duplicate File Handle).

Distinguishing Internal and External Commands   Every command interpreter implemented for any microcomputer has included at least some internal commands; most have also provided a means of executing external commands.

What distinguishes an internal from an external command is the location of the code that executes it. All internal commands are built into the command interpreter itself; external commands reside elsewhere. In some systems, including Tandy's TRSDOS among microprocessors and Honeywell's GCOS in the mainframe world, external commands have been stored in special library files. In MS-DOS, however, they are stored as individual program files.

CP/M, from which the MS-DOS architecture was derived, contained only five internal commands. All other commands were external, stored as COM (for COMmand) files in a memory image format. The internal commands were DIR, REN, TYPE, ERA, and SAVE. The first four of these were functionally the same as their MS-DOS descendants. The other one provided the means for creating the necessary COM files. It would SAVE the specified number of 256-byte "pages" to a named file. To load a newly created program into RAM so that SAVE could do its thing, you had to use DDT.COM (certainly the best named debugger ever).

The earliest versions of MS-DOS had only a bit more in the way of internal commands. COPY, which under CP/M had been a function of the external utility called PIP (Peripheral Interchange Program, an idea inherited from DEC systems), moved into the command interpreter as an internal, and DATE, TIME, VER, and CLS were added. With each new version, as features were added to the system, additional internal commands came with them. The use of batch files gave birth to several internal commands to help make such files more useful.

By the time MS-DOS made it up to version 3.3, the list of internal commands had grown to 36. One undocumented command was added with version 4.0, two documented commands at version 5.0, and none in version 6.0.

The undocumented TRUENAME command displays the full path name of a file, given the file's name as its argument. Any SUBST replacement is translated from logical back to physical form, and any implicit path is made explicit. For instance, if you issue the command SUBST F: C:\ZAP\ZIP and make F: your current drive, the command "TRUENAME LZSS.C" displays the string "C:\ZAP\ZIP\LZSS.C". This command corresponds exactly to INT 21h Function 60h, which is explained in greater detail in Chapter 8 on the DOS file system. Operation of the new LOADHIGH and LH commands was summarized in Chapter 7, in the discussion of the HMA and UMBs.

Let's get back to the way the command interpreter determines whether it's dealing with an internal command or an external one. It performs a simple search of its internal command list. If the input command exactly matches any item in this list, it's internal and the corresponding internal command routine is executed. If it's not found, the interpreter treats it as a possible external command.

DOS 3.3 introduced a capability for extending the internal command list by way of TSRs that communicate with COMMAND.COM through a set of undocumented hooks. However, because this feature was not publicized, few such extensions were produced, with the exception of APPEND in DOS 3.3, for which this functionality was probably created in the first place, and DOSSHELL, which appeared first in DOS 4.0. Both of these programs exhibited serious problems, and in DOS 5.0 the original DOSSHELL was replaced by a totally different package under the same name created by Central Point Software, the publishers of PC Tools. We provide source code for an installable command later in this chapter when we examine the hooks that MS-DOS provides for command interpreters.

Note that the entire command line that was input to the interpreter is parsed before any attempt is made to locate the command. During parsing, the command interpreter treats the percent (%) character as having special meaning because it identifies references to command line arguments when found in a batch file; it also identifies environment variables. If followed by a character that is neither an argument identifier nor an environment variable's name, the % character normally is thrown away rather than passed on to the command as part of the command line. This is true only when input is taken from a batch file.

Sometimes the % character needs to be kept, though. The classic case is the FOR command, with its internal variable reference, as in "FOR %f IN (*.c) DO type %f". That line works perfectly from keyboard input, but if it is included in a batch file, both % characters will be dropped, and the command then generates a syntax error. To solve this problem, whenever COMMAND.COM or its functional equivalent alternates sees a pair of % characters, it replaces them with a single %, which COMMAND.COM passes on to the program. Thus, a batch file requires "FOR %%f IN (*.c) DO type %%f. This action is analogous to the C language conventions regarding \, which require that you use \\ in any string where you want a single \ to appear.

Finding and Executing Internal Commands
Because the internal command list, including any installed commands, is searched first, it's a tricky matter to coax COMMAND.COM to run a program that has the same name as one of the internal commands. That is, if you name a program file TYPE.COM, you find that the internal command TYPE takes its place when you try to execute the program using the command interpreter, although it runs your own program perfectly when invoked through the DOS EXEC function or DEBUG.

When COMMAND.COM searches its command list for a possible internal command, it breaks off the command word at the first imbedded period after the command. Thus, to continue the example, if you entered TYPE.COM at the prompt, the .COM would be ignored, and the internal search would find a match to TYPE, which it would then execute.

With more recent versions of DOS that permit you to specify a full path name for a command, you can solve this problem by specifying the full path to TYPE.COM, such as .\TYPE, if the file is in the current directory.

At least some of the alternative command replacements attack this problem in two ways. First, they let you selectively disable any internal command using a configuration option; second, they vary the way the search is performed. The variation is simply that the input is not truncated at a period. If you enter TYPE.COM, that is what it searches for, and of course it will not find TYPE.COM because none of the internal commands have embedded periods.

Under any command interpreter, once an internal command is detected, it's normally executed immediately. The usual method of executing the command is to call the appropriate internal routine, followed by a loop back to the top level prompt code. Because all of this code is contained within the interpreter itself, no program swapping occurs, and no child process is spawned for the majority of internal commands.

Before the internal command CALL was introduced, the external command COMMAND with the /C option switch was used to run one batch file from inside another, then return to the original file. This technique still works, but it requires about 4K additional RAM for the child copy of COMMAND.COM that is loaded. This technique may be significantly slower due to the additional disk accesses required.

Dispatching Appropriate Processes
Any name that is not an internal command or matched in the installed command list is presumed to be an external command. The command interpreter searches for a file of that name, using the PATH to determine where to search. If such a file is located, it is loaded and run. If not, the error message "Bad command or file name" tells the operator that the input was faulty; the command interpreter then returns to its top-level "get input" procedures for a fresh command to interpret.

Locating and Loading External Commands
To locate and execute an external command, the command interpreter first searches the current working directory for a file having a name identical to the command word and the extension .COM. If this fails, the search is repeated using the

extension .EXE; if this also fails, a third search is made with the extension .BAT. Thus, if three files named DO-ME.COM, DO-ME.EXE, and DO-ME.BAT all exist in the current directory, only the .COM file will be executed as an external command.

This COM, EXE, BAT sequence is established by code in the command interpreter, not by MS-DOS itself. It can be exploited in several ways that we examine a little later, but if you want to change it for any reason, you can do so by locating in your command interpreter the nine bytes that contain the characters COMEXEBAT and changing them as you desire. This can be done on the disk copy of the interpreter or in memory using DEBUG.

If all three searches fail in the current working directory, the command interpreter looks for an environment variable named PATH, and, if one exists, it takes the first path listed in that string (that is, all characters up to but not including the leftmost semicolon) and repeats the triple search in the directory specified by that path. If unsuccessful, the interpreter moves on to the next pathspec in the PATH variable and repeats its actions. This continues until either it finds a file that satisfies the search, or the PATH variable is exhausted without finding such a file.

If no file is found, the command interpreter issues a "Bad filename or command" error message and returns to the prompt. Note that this happens only after the three searches (COM, EXE, BAT) have been made in each directory specified by PATH. If you have a large number of directories in your PATH, and if each has a large number of files, the search may take a significant amount of time.

Dealing with BAT Files

When a file is found that satisfies the search criteria, the command interpreter's next action depends on whether or not the file found was a batch file (.BAT extension). If so, the command interpreter sets appropriate flags to indicate to itself that it is processing a batch file rather than keyboard input; the interpreter also stores enough data about the file to be able to find it again. The flag locations and the amount of data saved vary significantly from one version of DOS to the next.

The interpreter opens the batch file, reads its first line into the command input buffer, and replaces any indicated arguments (%1, %2, %3, and so on) with corresponding words from the original input line, which is retained in a separate buffer. If any %0 argument is found, it's replaced with the name of the batch file itself, less the extension. The interpreter then closes the batch file and interprets and executes the modified batch file line, just as if it had been typed from the keyboard.

When that line is fully executed and control returns to the command interpreter, the flags tell the command interpreter to reopen the batch file, read the next line (actually, a minimum of 32 bytes) and execute it. This process continues until all lines of the batch file have been executed.

The commands contained in the batch file can be either internal or external and since DOS 3.3, these commands can invoke additional subsidiary batch files in subroutine fashion using the CALL internal command. For these reasons, it's quite possible to invoke a batch file that never finishes executing, with the result that control never gets back to the original command interpreter's keyboard input level

Dealing with COM and EXE Files

If the file found was not a batch file, the command interpreter uses the DOS EXEC function (INT 21h, Function 4B00h) to spawn the file's execution as a child process of the command interpreter; nothing more happens in the interpreter until the child process terminates.

Notice that, with COMMAND.COM, it makes no difference whether a COM or EXE file was found; the distinction between the two types of executable files is made by the EXEC function based only on the first two bytes of the file (which in .EXE files have the MZ signature), and the actual file extension is ignored except to locate the file. This means that you could force a file that is really an EXE type to be found during the first search by changing its extension to COM. It also means that you could take a text file, word-processor document, or spreadsheet, rename it with an extension of COM or EXE, and COMMAND.COM would try to execute it as a COM file.

An alternative to changing the file's extension is to create a stub loader, which is a small file of the same name except for the extension COM. The stub loader then uses the EXEC function to spawn the original EXE file as a child of its own. This approach makes it possible to set up all sorts of special conditions before the program file is executed, then subsequently undo them with minimal overhead.

One widespread use of this technique is in support of the third-party replacement video BIOS package, UltraVision, from Personics. UltraVision permits its users to set up a wide variety of screen options, ranging up to 132x60. These formats are compatible with any other program that is well behaved, in the sense that it looks in the BIOS work area to determine what number of columns and rows are currently set. Unfortunately, many popular programs don't bother to do so because the ability to set non-standard formats is relatively recent.

To run programs that do not check the current number of columns and rows, it's necessary to set the screen format to the standard 80x25 dimensions. Personics' UltraVision includes a utility which generates a stub loader for any desired EXE format program file. The loader first notes all pertinent information from the BIOS area and then resets to the 80x25 format. Next, it EXECs the specified program file, using its full name, including the EXE extension, and passes to it all the command line arguments that the loader itself received. Upon return, the loader temporarily saves the exit code from the real program, restores the video set up to the conditions the loader found at entry, and returns its child's exit code to DOS as though the code were its own. The command interpreter always finds the loader with the .COM extension first, so as a user you do nothing different.

As a result, by using the utility supplied with UltraVision to create a loader, you can make any program well-behaved in the video area at the cost of less than a thousand bytes of overhead code.

Another use of the stub loader idea is built into Microsoft's new segmented executable files, which are used in Windows, OS/2, and in the now-obsolete European OEM multitasking DOS4. These new .EXE files have a normal, old-style .EXE file at their head, followed by a new .EXE header with the NE signature. The old-style .EXE can be used to print a message, such as "This program requires Microsoft Windows," or it can be used as a loader that, for example, runs Windows.

The Exitcode Idea   When I said that the UltraVision loader saved the real program's exit code, you may have wondered why a loader should preserve the exit code of a spawned process, or possibly even what an exit code is all about. Although it's documented (at least with regard to the method by which a program can supply one to its parent), the details are so spread out that some explanation is in order.

The idea that a process should return a result code to its parent followed directly from the idea that every process in a system is equivalent to a subroutine that is called by some higher level process, all the way back to the primary bootstrap loader. This idea apparently originated at about the same time as the idea of the operating system itself, long before microcomputing came upon the scene.

Any DOS process returns an exit code to its parent; the code can be controlled by the program if the process terminates using INT 21h functions 4Ch (Terminate with Exit Code) or 31h (Terminate But Stay Resident). If any other method is used to return to DOS, such as INT 20h or INT 21h Function 0, a default exit code value of zero is generated by DOS itself.

The code can be retrieved, once *and only once*, after the spawned process returns to the parent and before any subsequent process is spawned. The reason for this restriction is that DOS itself provides only one 16-bit word to hold the exit code, so that every process overwrites the code left there by its predecessor, or child. The DOS function that retrieves the code (INT 21h Function 4Dh, Get Exit Code of Subprogram) zeroes out that storage location in the process of retrieving the code.

COMMAND.COM provides the internal command, ERRORLEVEL, which is actually a function that can be evaluated by the internal IF command. ERRORLEVEL retrieves the exit code of the most recent command and compares it to a specified value. All compatible command interpreters provide this command, which they implement in a functionally identical manner.

In the sample trace of one cycle of COMMAND.COM's processing loop that began this chapter, you saw that the first thing COMMAND.COM does upon return from a child process is to retrieve the exit code and save it in COMMAND.COM's own data area for possible use by ERRORLEVEL later. When ERRORLEVEL is called, it uses that saved value, rather than attempt to retrieve the exit code from DOS again.

The idea of exit code and ERRORLEVEL applies only to external commands; most internal commands have no effect at all on the ERRORLEVEL value. Because these commands do not spawn child processes, most commands do not affect the DOS exit code value. Some third-party command interpreters do extend the ERRORLEVEL idea to at least some internal commands; extending it to all commands, including those that test it, would negate the whole idea because it would make multiple way decisions impossible.

Installable Commands

Function AEh (Installable Command) of INT2Fh, available since DOS 3.3, connects what would otherwise be an external command into the internal command list of COMMAND.COM. Both the command code itself and the handler for this function must be installed as a single, non-pop-up TSR. The only well-known examples of its use are APPEND in DOS 3.3 and higher and in the DOS 4.0 DOSSHELL facility, which is now of only historical interest since the DOS 5.0 version of DOSSHELL is totally different.

You can use this undocumented interrupt to install your own commands with DOS 3.3 and above. The basic principle is "Don't call us, we'll call you." COMMAND.COM issues calls to this interrupt at four places while parsing the input line. To use the functionality, you provide your own interrupt handler, hooking INT 2Fh/AH=AEh.

Two of the calls COMMAND.COM issues to Subfunction AE00h are to determine if the command on the input line is a valid installed command. The other two are called only if the first calls return FFh in the AL register, indicating that the command is indeed valid. The second calls are both to Subfunction AE01h, which is expected to execute the command.

When Subfunction AE00h is called the first time, both the DS and ES registers point to COMMAND.COM's transient area. The DX register is set to 0FFFFh for unknown reasons; the BX register points to a buffer that contains two count bytes, followed by an exact copy of the input line; CH contains FFh; and the SI register points to a different buffer that contains only the command word from the line, converted to uppercase and preceded by its character count. Your code must verify that the content of this second buffer is an exact match for the name of your installed command. If it is if not a match, the code should chain the interrupt on up the line in case some other installed command is being called. If the second buffer does match your installed routine, your routine should change the AL register to FFh and return to the caller.

The second call to Subfunction AE00h is identical to the first except that CH contains 00h instead of FFh. I've been unable to determine why COMMAND.COM makes both calls. The alternative command interpreter 4DOS.COM does the same job satisfactorily, but calls this subfunction only once.

If Subfunction AE00h returns 00h in AL, indicating that the command is not an installed command, no call to AE01h will be made. Instead, the command interpreter is expected to deal with the command itself.

If Subfunction AE01h is called to execute the command, the ES, DS, BX, DX, and SI registers contain exactly the same data as for the previous subfunction, although only DX and SI are again explicitly loaded with the values prior to the call. The BX register has been preserved through a couple of subroutine calls, but in future DOS versions may not always retain the pointer to the full input line buffer.

Therefore, if your command accepts arguments on the input line, we recommend that those arguments be copied into a local buffer before the routine returns from the AE00h call. After executing the actual command within the AE01h call, your code should zero out the count byte in the command buffer at DS:SI. The zero count signals COMMAND.COM not to attempt to execute the command itself.

These calls to Function AEh are made before the internal command list is checked, which means that you can install a command that has the same name as one of the internal commands, and your command will replace the original one. Because your own command can be a do-nothing, this offers an elegant way to disable the DEL and ERASE commands on a system that must be accessible to the general public.

This also permits you to add a modified front end to any internal command. You can provide an installed command with an identical name that does your front end processing during the call to Subfunction AE00 but does not zero out the count byte of the command buffer, and returns zero from the AE00 call so that COMMAND.COM will process the internal command.

The C program shown in Figure 10-3, INSTCMD.C, illustrates all the points of dealing with the installable command interrupt service. Note that this program does not install as a TSR but instead operates as a wrapper (see "Application Wrappers", Jim Kyle, *PC Techniques*, June/July 1992) to avoid problems in deinstalling the added command. Note that, despite the repeated references to COMMAND.COM in the comments, this program actually works with any command interpreter that supports 2F/AE, since the program uses the COMSPEC environment variable to locate the command interpreter itself.

Figure 10-3. INSTCMD.C

```
/*
INSTCMD.C

The "Installable Command" function is not called by a program that
wants to extend COMMAND.COM's repertoire. Instead, you hook the
function and wait for COMMAND.COM to call you ("don't call us, we'll
call you"). Function AE00h lets you tell COMMAND.COM whether you
want to handle the command, and function AE01h is where you actually
handle it (similar to device driver division of labor between
Strategy and Interrupt).

Note that AE01h is called with only the name of the command: not with
any arguments. Therefore, arguments must be saved away in AE00h. Yuk!

Furthermore, while redirection is handled in the normal way in
AE01, in AE00 we get the entire command string, including any
redirection or piping. Therefore, these must be stripped off before
saving away the args during AE00 processing.

Problem with the following AE00 and AE01 handlers: they should
chain to previous handler. For example, INTRSPY program won't see
AE00 and AE01 once INSTCMD is installed.

The sample COMMAND.COM extension used here is FULLNAME, based on the
undocumented TRUENAME command in DOS 4+. We simply run undocumented
Function 60h in order to provide FULLNAME. Actually, not quite so
simple, since Function 60h doesn't like leading or trailing spaces.
These are handled inside function fullname().

The following INTRSPY script was helpful in debugging 2FAE:

; INSTCMD.SCR
structure cmdline fields
    max (byte)
```

```
        text (byte,string,64)

intercept 2fh
    function 0aeh
      subfunction 00h
        on_entry
          if (dx == 0FFFFh)
            output "AE00"
            output (DS:BX->cmdline)
            output CH          ; CH=FF (first), 0 (second)
            output " "
      subfunction 01h
        on_entry
          if (dx == 0FFFFh)
          output "AE01"
          output (DS:SI->byte,string,64)

tested only for Microsoft C 6.0+ or above
    cl -qc instcmd.c
*/

#include <stdlib.h>
#include <stdio.h>
#include <string.h>
#include <ctype.h>
#include <conio.h>
#include <dos.h>

#pragma pack(1)

typedef struct {
    unsigned es,ds,di,si,bp,sp,bx,dx,cx,ax;
    unsigned ip,cs,flags;
    } REG_PARAMS;

typedef unsigned char BYTE;

typedef struct {
    BYTE len;
    BYTE txt[1];
    } STRING;

typedef struct {
    BYTE max;
    STRING s;
    } CMDLINE;

void interrupt far handler_2f(REG_PARAMS r);

void (interrupt far *old)();

void fail(char *s) { puts(s); exit(1); }

main(void)
{ /* hook INT 2F */
  old = _dos_getvect(0x2f);
  _dos_setvect(0x2f, handler_2f);

  puts("This demo of installable commands isn't a TSR.");
  puts("Instead, it just creates a subshell from which you can EXIT");
  puts("when done. In the subshell, one new command has been added:");
  puts("FULLNAME [filename].");

  system (getenv("COMSPEC"));
```

```
    /* unhook INT 2F */
    _dos_setvect(0x2f, old);
}


char far *fullname(char far *s, char far *d)
{   char far *s2;

    /* INT 21h AH=60h doesn't like leading or trailing blanks */
    while (isspace(*s))
      s++;
    s2 = s;
    while (*s2) s2++;
    s2--;
    while (isspace(*s2))
      *s2-- = 0;

    _asm {
      push di
      push si
      les di, d
      lds si, s
      mov ah, 60h
      int 21h
      pop si
      pop di
      jc error
    }

    return d;
error:
    return (char far *) 0;
}


void fcputs(char far *s)
{   /* can't use stdio (e.g., putchar) inside 2FAE01 handler */
    while (*s)
      putch(*s++);
    putch(0x0d); putch(0x0a);
}


char buf[128];        /* not reentrant */
char args[128];

#define CMD_LEN      8

void interrupt far handler_2f(REG_PARAMS r)
{   if ((r.ax == 0xAE00) && (r.dx == 0xFFFF))
      {
      CMDLINE far *cmdline;
      int len;
      FP_SEG(cmdline) = r.ds;
      FP_OFF(cmdline) = r.bx;
      len = min(CMD_LEN, cmdline->s.len);
      if ((_fmemicmp(cmdline->s.txt, "fullname", len) == 0) ||
          (_fmemicmp(cmdline->s.txt, "FULLNAME", len) == 0))
        {
        char far *redir;
        int argslen = cmdline->s.len - CMD_LEN;
        _fmemcpy(args, cmdline->s.txt + CMD_LEN, argslen);
        args[argslen] = 0;
      /* yuk! we have to get rid of redirection ourselves! */
      /* it will still take effect in AE01 */
      /* the following is not really correct, but okay for now */
        if (redir = _fstrrchr(args, '>'))
          *redir = 0;
```

```
                if (redir = _fstrrchr(args, '<'))
                  *redir = 0;
                if (redir = _fstrrchr(args, '|'))
                  *redir = 0;
                r.ax = 0xAEFF;  /* we will handle this one */
                }
            }
        else if ((r.ax == 0xAE01) && (r.dx == 0xFFFF))
            {
            STRING far *s;
            int len;
            FP_SEG(s) = r.ds;
            FP_OFF(s) = r.si;
            len = min(CMD_LEN, s->len);
            if ((_fmemicmp(s->txt, "fullname", len) == 0) ||
                (_fmemicmp(s->txt, "FULLNAME", len) == 0))
                {
                char far *d;
                if (! *args)
                  d = "syntax: fullname [filename]";
                else if ((d = fullname(args, buf)) == 0)
                  d = "invalid filename";
                fcputs(d);
                s->len = 0; /* we handled it; COMMAND.COM shouldn't */
                }
            }
        else
            _chain_intr(old);
}
```

If you run INSTCMD, you first see the four-line explanation of what the program does, followed by the banner line, as the child copy of your command interpreter initializes itself. From that point until you type EXIT to return to your parent process, you have available the added command FULLNAME. This command is functionally identical to the undocumented TRUENAME command introduced with DOS 4.0 and described elsewhere in this chapter.

Notice that in INSTCMD.C, we copy the arguments supplied on the input line into a buffer when servicing subfunction AE00; then we use them when executing the command subsequently. Both arguments are in the function handler_2f().

For another view of installable commands, see Jeff Prosise's article, "Replacing Internal DOS Commands," *PC Magazine,* Dec. 31, 1991, and several other articles on 2F/AE cited in the bibliography

TSHELL, a Simple Command Interpreter

The basic ideas behind a command interpreter are extremely simple. What makes them seem complicated in practice is the need to handle all possible circumstances with a minimum disruption of system operation. To illustrate just how simple a command interpreter can be and still function, Figure 10-4 shows TSHELL.C, a tiny shell that you can install as the primary shell of your system.

Figure 10-4. TSHELL.C

```
/**********************************************************
 *   TSHELL.C - Demonstration tiny command interpreter    *
 *   Jim Kyle, July 10, 1990                              *
 *                                                        *
 *   Intended only to show basic principles; not for use  *
 *   with DOS versions prior to 3.1 (EXEC function of such *
 *   versions does not preserve stack registers).         *
 *                                                        *
 *   For Borland C compilers only due to pseudovariables  *
 *                                                        *
```

```
 *        tcc -mt -c tshell                        *
 *        tlink /t /c c0t+tshell,tshell,,cs.lib    *
 *                                                 *
 ****************************************************/
#include <stdio.h>
#include <string.h>
#include <dos.h>
#include <dir.h>

char cmdbuf[128];
char *cmdlst[] = {"DIR","RUN"};
int i;

void do_dir( void )                    /* reports files in cur dir */
{ struct ffblk wkarea;
  int endir;

  if (strlen(cmdbuf) < 5)              /* default to all files */
    strcpy( cmdbuf+4, "*.*" );
  puts("\n     Files and sizes\n");
  endir = findfirst( cmdbuf+4, &wkarea, 0 );
  while ( !endir )
    { printf("%-13s    %8ld\n",
            wkarea.ff_name, wkarea.ff_fsize );
      endir = findnext( &wkarea );
    }
  putchar( '\n' );
}


/* CHEAT! Implemented RUN by EXECing COMMAND.COM. */
void do_run( void )                  /* caution, safe only for DOS3+ */
{ struct {
    unsigned eseg, clo, cls;
    long     fcb1, fcb2;
  } parms;

  cmdbvf[0] = strlen (cmdbuf+1);       /* was wrong in first edition */
  cmdbuf[1] = '/';
  cmdbuf[2] = 'C';
  cmdbuf[3] = ' ';
  parms.eseg = 0;
  parms.clo = (unsigned) cmdbuf;       /* was wrong in first edition */
  parms.cls = _DS;
  parms.fcb1 = parms.fcb2 = 0L;
  _ES = _SS;
  _BX = (unsigned) &parms;
  _DX = (unsigned) "C:\\COMMAND.COM";   /* may need to change this */
  _AX = 0x4B00;
  geninterrupt( 0x21 );
}


void main( void )
{ puts( "  TINY SHELL DEMONSTRATOR\n" );
  puts( "Copyright 1990  by Jim Kyle\n" );
  puts( "  Commands: DIR, RUN only\n" );
  for( ; ; )
    { printf("tinyshell> ");
      gets(cmdbuf);
      for(i=0; i<2; i++)
        if(strnicmp(cmdlst[i],cmdbuf,strlen(cmdlst[i]))==0)
          break;
      switch(i)
      { case 0: do_dir();
                break;
        case 1: do_run();
```

```
            break;
       default: puts("Unknown command!!!\n");
      }
    }
}
```

Of course, this shows just the bare rudiments of a DOS command interpreter. A real one would have to handle INT 23h (Ctrl-C) and INT 24h (Critical Error) at the very minimum. It also would be important to take over undocumented INT 2Eh, discussed later in this chapter, even if only to point it at an IRET instruction. While it might be possible to stumble through these things at a bare-bones level also, the details of even those bare bones would totally obscure the point being made. COMMAND.COM for DOS 5.0, when disassembled, generates 358 pages of listing; at least half of that handles errors!

Unlike the other programs in this chapter, TSHELL.C is written to be compiled with only Borland C++ or Turbo C. The interface to the DOS EXEC function in this program cannot rely on any environment being established (remember, COMMAND.COM isn't running!), and the library functions of both the Microsoft and Borland products do use the environment.

The connection between the command interpreter and the environment variables can be mystifying; it's essentially a matter of conventions. The normal command interpreters allow you to modify the prompt and to specify the path through which any program can spawn a copy of the interpreter. Both functions are accomplished by storing ASCII text strings in environment variables named PROMPT and COMSPEC. Similarly, you can specify the paths to be searched for external commands, and they are stored in the PATH environment variable. COMMAND.COM and other command interpreters then obtain the information from these variables in the environment. But as shown by TSHELL, there's not really any necessary connection between the command interpreter and the environment; it's all a matter of convenience and convention.

Note that TSHELL is not intended in any way to be useful; its sole purpose is to present the skeleton of a command interpreter. It recognizes only two commands, DIR and RUN. The RUN command actually launches COMMAND.COM as a child process in order to make the conventional DOS command set available. Without this capability, it's much more difficult to get TSHELL out of your system once you've tried it out!

Once you have TSHELL.COM, add a line such as the following to your CONFIG.SYS file (temporarily REM out any existing SHELL= statement):

```
SHELL=C:\TSHELL.COM
```

Note that you must use the SHELL= command in CONFIG.SYS to install a different command interpreter. Many people are under the impression that a new shell can also be installed by changing the COMSPEC= variable in the environment, but the environment variable is used only after a command interpreter exists in memory. Until a command interpreter is loaded and initialized, neither the COMSPEC variable nor the master environment block itself exists!

Now reboot the system. You'll see that the prompt is now tinyshell> rather than anything you may be used to seeing. You'll note, also, that AUTOEXEC.BAT did not run and none of your TSR programs have been installed.

If you type DIR, you get a list of files in the current directory, but no subdirectories will be shown, nor will the amount of available space. Any other conventional command produces only an error message because TSHELL does not recognize it.

When you type RUN, you have all normal commands available to you, which lets you run an editor to change CONFIG.SYS back to get rid of the SHELL=TSHELL line.

TSHELL doesn't create a master environment. You can verify the absence of a master environment by executing the EPTST.EXE program, presented later in this chapter, from the child COMMAND.COM spawned by TSHELL's RUN; it shows no master environment, and SET shows that

PATH= is blank in the current copy. The lack of an environment is intentional, in order to demonstrate the independence of the interpreter from the environment in principle.

The key point about TSHELL, though, is the skeletal structure of a command interpreter provided in main( ). This structure includes an endless for (;;) loop, which prints a prompt—a more complete implementation that uses the environment could interpret and print getenv("PROMPT")—gets commands, interprets them, and executes them. That's all a command interpreter does.

How COMMAND.COM Works

This section is based on the disassembly of several versions of COMMAND.COM. The major emphasis is on those points not already adequately covered in official system documentation. This section also defines such terms as master environment and primary shell.

Although COMMAND.COM is not the only possible command interpreter (later in this chapter we look briefly at some alternatives), it is the one most used with MS-DOS because it comes as part of the system package. To many users, it *is* the operating system because the real system files are hidden from view. (Actually, in IBM's version of DOS 2.x, COMMAND.COM was an essential part of the operating system; the DOS EXEC Function 4Bh was contained in COMMAND.COM, rather than in the DOS kernel. By the time the Microsoft OEM versions were released, however, EXEC had been moved to its proper location, and the operating system itself became independent of COMMAND.COM.)

The process of creating the primary shell actually begins when hidden file IO.SYS in MS-DOS (or IBMBIO.COM in PC-DOS) loads and its initialization code takes over. After a bit of preliminary calculation, the IO.SYS code moves the part of itself that has not yet been executed up to the topmost memory area physically present in the 640K DOS memory. The process is similar to the way the DEVLOD program in Chapter 7 moved itself during execution.

From that vantage point, out of harm's way, the IO.SYS code then installs the rest of the DOS kernel, making it possible for the primary shell to use all the DOS services when it loads for the first time. In DOS 5.0+, IO.SYS even constructs a fake PSP for its upper memory copy, making possible the use of handle-based DOS functions within the installation code of device drivers, despite warnings in official documentation that only the low numbered DOS functions and a few others are available. (My thanks to Hans Salvisberg, creator of BOOT.SYS, for verifying this!) It's still a no-no, though, to attempt to allocate memory at this time because the MCB chain (Chapter 7) has not yet been built.

The CONFIG.SYS file defines the primary shell, defaulting to COMMAND.COM if no SHELL= line occurs in CONFIG.SYS. Loading the primary shell is essentially the final step of initialization by IO.SYS, after the IO.SYS initialization routine loads the MSDOS.SYS hidden file, calls its initialization subroutine, and regains control. After building all required data structures, the IO.SYS initialization procedures use INT 21h Function 4B00h to load and execute the primary shell program. This primary shell, like most other copies of the command interpreter—some don't follow the COMMAND.COM standard—points to itself as its own parent using the PSP. Very soon now we'll take you on a small side trip and discover why this is done.

One of the parameters passed to DOS with this request is the address of the associated environment block. For the primary shell, a master environment block just above the DOS kernel area is assigned by code in the COMMAND.COM initialization routines. The size of this block defaults to 160 bytes, but it can be expanded by adding the /E: option switch to a SHELL=COMMAND.COM /P line in CONFIG.SYS.

For primary shells other than COMMAND.COM, the exact method may differ, but all provide methods for tailoring the size of the master environment to whatever you need.

In versions of DOS prior to 6.0, if the primary shell ever returned control to the IO.SYS initialization code, it was assumed that a fatal error—such as the stack becoming corrupted or critical system code being modified by accident—had occurred and that continued operation would be impossible. Therefore, the call to INT 21h EXEC was followed by a dynamic halt (JMP $), which would lock the system solid. Only pressing the reset button (if present) or powering down and then back up again could return the system to operation.

The only time this dynamic halt code could gain control was when the primary shell was loading. Such things as a spelling error in the CONFIG.SYS file or a move of the program to some directory other than that specified in CONFIG.SYS could cause this failure. If this happened with DOS 5.0 or before, you needed to have a bootable floppy handy to bring the system back up so that you could correct the errors in CONFIG.SYS.

With version 6.0, however, this halt is replaced by a prompt that asks for the name of the command interpreter. The program then tries again to load, using the name you supply. If that attempt fails, the prompt appears again. This process continues until you give up and use a bootable floppy or until you succeed in establishing a primary shell.

As soon as the primary shell begins execution, the area at the top of DOS RAM from which IO.SYS called the shell becomes available for reuse. Subsequent operations while initializing the primary shell normally overwrite the EXEC call and the JMP $ which follows it.

Why Shells Are Their Own Parents

In the first edition of this book, I wrote that "COMMAND.COM is always its own parent." Fine, but I never did say why COMMAND.COM is always its own parent, for the very good reason that I didn't know. Not long after the first edition appeared, D. Rifkind posted an excellent explanation on the BIX network. What follows is based on his message.

One of the standard features of COMMAND.COM, and of any other command interpreter shell that even attempts to maintain compatibility with accepted standards, is that the program contains the default INT 24h handler. This routine prints "Abort, Retry, Ignore," and so on. One option this handler offers is the opportunity to abort, which means that if you are executing an external command, that process is unceremoniously terminated.

But what happens if a critical error occurs while executing an internal DOS command? The program can't just dump COMMAND.COM, or whatever shell is running, because the shell must continue its loop. Obviously, the INT 24h handler knows that COMMAND.COM is running and does something other than abort if you press *A*, right?

Wrong! In fact, the critical error handler does nothing different, regardless of the process that happens to be running. If you press *A*, the handler returns a code of 2, and DOS terminates the current process, whatever it may be. So why doesn't COMMAND.COM go away, hanging the system?

The reason is that when DOS terminates a process, it uses the parent PSP field in that process's PSP and the termination address (at offset 0Ah in the PSP) to determine which process is going to get control next. If the parent PSP is the same as the current PSP, however, DOS does not deallocate the program's memory blocks before exiting. COMMAND.COM (and all compatible shell programs) sets the parent PSP field equal to its own PSP and points the termination address back into itself. The result is that, when DOS terminates the process, the current program stays active and retains control.

And that is why COMMAND.COM's parent PSP field points to itself. My grateful thanks to D. Rifkind for clearing this up!

How and Why COMMAND.COM Reloads Itself

One of the least understood parts of COMMAND.COM's internal operations is the reloading of the transient portion of COMMAND.COM upon return from an external command. If something goes wrong in this process, the error messages can range from confusing ("Bad or missing command interpreter" when it was working fine just a second or two before) to downright misleading ("Unable to load COMMAND.COM" when the real problem was that the COMSPEC variable pointed to a different version of the program). And a point that's usually unclear is why the reloading happens sometimes, but not always.

Whenever an external command is loaded, the RAM occupied by the transient portion of COMMAND.COM is made available to that external command for its use, if needed; upon return from an external command, the resident portion of COMMAND.COM does a checksum of the transient area to detect any changes in it.

If any change has occurred, the resident routine reloads the entire transient area from disk, using the COMSPEC environment variable to locate COMMAND.COM. Only the upper part of the file is loaded. The exact offset into the file at which the reload begins is hardwired into the code that performs the reloading; this offset varies from one DOS version to the next.

This checksum for the transient portion is first calculated immediately after the move to high RAM. That result is stored in the resident portion. Each time the checksum is run after that, the new result is compared to the original value; any mismatch causes the transient area to be reloaded. Thus, it's essential that the copy of COMMAND.COM pointed to by the COMSPEC variable be identical, byte for byte, to the copy used at boot time.

After the transient area is reloaded from disk, the checksum is run again to verify that the reload was in fact successful. Any mismatch at this time triggers (before DOS 6) an error message, "Unable to load COMMAND.COM, system halted," and the computer goes into a dynamic halt (JMP $). This message usually indicates that the path set by COMSPEC is not valid, but the message can also be triggered by differences between the copy of COMMAND.COM reached through COMSPEC and the copy from which the checksum was calculated at boot time.

Such differences are most often caused by having mixed versions of COMMAND.COM on the system (that is, having version 5 on the hard drive, but version 3 on the floppy from which the system was booted). These problems may also be caused by patches applied to the disk copy. If a patch causes this problem, the reboot needed to use the system clears things up by causing a fresh copy of the checksum, which does include the patch effects, to be calculated.

Another possible cause of the reload error, not even hinted at by the message itself, occurs in network situations when the network software redefines COMSPEC to point to the file server copy of COMMAND.COM. This copy may differ from the copy at any given workstation. The cure for errors resulting from this problem is to remove the redefinition of COMSPEC from the network software, if possible. If redefinition is not possible, each workstation must run a batch file to perform the network login. That batch file must fix up COMSPEC to point back to the workstation's own copy.

The Division Points
When first loaded by the initialization code in IO.SYS, COMMAND.COM divides itself into three parts. One part stays where it initially loaded, in low memory, just below the area where most user programs run. Another part moves to the highest available area within the 640KB DOS RAM limit. The middle portion is discarded after it finishes setting things up. Official DOS manuals distributed with earlier OEM versions of the system told us that much, but very little else; here's more of the story.

Resident, Initial, and Transient Portions   The three parts into which COMMAND.COM divides itself are known as the resident, transient, and initialization portions.

The resident portion of COMMAND.COM contains the interrupt service routine for INT 2Eh, which is really the main parser of the interpreter, not a separate ISR. In some older versions of DOS it also contains some of the INT 21h service routines, including, as mentioned earlier, the EXEC function. In addition to these interrupt handlers, the resident portion contains the code to which a terminated process returns control using the INT 22 pointer in the PSP. This portion also contains some permanent data storage associated with the command interpreter, such as the pointers to the transient portion.

The transient portion is needed only for internal commands. For all others it is freed up for use by any external command that needs the space. This area contains the actual input buffer, the code that interprets commands, the internal command list, and all of the code for executing commands. In DOS 5.0 and higher, if DOS is loaded in the HMA, COMMAND.COM automatically puts much of the transient portion into the HMA, rather than at the top of conventional RAM.

Because the actual DOS input buffer is in the transient portion, the standard input-editing commands, such as F3, sometimes lose their data if the transient portion is overlaid during the processing of an external command. We'll take another small side trip to look inside DOS Function 0Ah and see why this happens before we move on to study the environment. Right now, though, let's continue with the three portions of COMMAND.COM.

Next is the initialization portion. Each time COMMAND.COM is loaded, at least some of this code is executed to verify that the version levels of COMMAND.COM and the resident DOS kernel match exactly, as well as to parse any arguments passed to the program. Other actions depend on whether the /P option switch was one of the arguments passed. If this switch is absent, the actions described in the next two paragraphs are skipped.

If, however, the switch is present—as it is when the primary shell is being installed by IO.SYS— initialization calculates and stores the starting address for the transient portion, moves the transient portion into place at the top of RAM, calculates and stores its checksum for future use in reloading, and sets up the interrupt vector for INT 2Eh to point to the ISR inside the resident portion. Note that this automatically makes this copy of COMMAND.COM the primary shell even if another copy already exists.

The initialization code then checks for the existence of a file named AUTOEXEC.BAT in the current working directory. If it exists, the initialization portion sets flags that direct the input routines to process this file before looking for keyboard input.

In either case, COMMAND.COM next shrinks its RAM allocation to be just adequate for covering the resident portion. If this copy of COMMAND.COM is not the primary shell, that is, the one to which the INT 2Eh vector points, "resident portion" refers to this copy and not to the primary copy itself. COMMAND.COM then transfers control to the command input prompting routine. This routine issues the prompt, waits for input, and dispatches it. But the initialization portion, as such, ceased to exist when the RAM allocation was reduced.

Where These Portions Are Loaded   The preceding descriptions show you how COMMAND.COM splits itself up for action. In the first edition of this book, I provided detailed instructions, showing you how to examine exactly the way the various parts wind up in your own system. This isn't practical under DOS 5.0 because there are just too many possible variations, depending on whether you have DOS loaded high or low, whether you have UMB's enabled, and what model of CPU you are using!

For instance, Geoff Chappell at the University of London (and author of a forthcoming book on DOS internals) found that in DOS 5.0, COMMAND.COM contains a portion of shareable code, retained only by the first-loaded, top-level command processor and which may have been transferred to the HMA. This code is accessed by means of a calling point table; you use INT 2Fh, Function 5500h, to get the table address:

```
INT 2Fh     AX = 5500h
returns     AX = 0000h
            DS:SI = address of calling point table
```

The procedures listed in this table include services provided for the transient portion, as well as interrupt handlers (int 23h, 24h, 2Eh, 2Fh). For the most part, the procedures manipulate data in the

COMMAND.COM resident portion. Because of this and the fact that the method by which the dispatcher communicates its data segment is susceptibile to change, these procedures must be of only limited use outside of COMMAND.COM itself.

In the first releases of DOS 5.0, they were called from a dispatcher in COMMAND.COM's resident portion. The dispatcher was intrinsically non-reentrant. Its structure is something like this:

```
int_23h:
              push     ax
              mov      ax,0
              jmp      get_address
int_24h:
              push     ax
              mov      ax,1
              jmp      get_address
              .
              .
get_address:
              sti
              mov      cs:[bx_save],bx          << DANGER!!!
              .
              .
```

BX was then used to index into the table of calling addresses. This opened a window for disaster each time COMMAND.COM fielded an interrupt because subsequent passage through the dispatcher could overwrite the saved value of BX, which the first interrupt still needed. This would be serious if an INT 24h were followed a few microseconds later by an INT 2Fh or when one INT 2Fh interrupted another.

Later copies of DOS 5.0, when disassembled, show that this technique was replaced by individual jumps for each ISR. The table still exists, but it contains far jumps that can take control directly into the HMA, with no window for disaster en route. Access is direct, rather than by means of an indexing technique.

Why Does F3 Sometimes Quit Working?
A few pages back, I promised another side trip to discover why the standard input-editing keys such as F3 occasionally and unpredictably quit working after a large external program is run. These editing functions are actually part of DOS itself, inside Function 0Ah (buffered input). But their occasional failure is intimately connected with the way that COMMAND.COM partitions and reloads itself, so it's not too much of a digression to examine them here.

As you have seen, COMMAND.COM spends much of its time parked inside INT 21/0Ah. In order for the function key editing operations to work, Function 0Ah must first get all keyboard input into a temporary buffer. The function can copy the input to the user's own buffer only after input is complete. This temporary buffer is located on the user's stack, so it vanishes when Function 0Ah returns. To be able to use F3 to reuse the input line just typed, there must be another copy of that line in another temporary buffer maintained by Function 0Ah.

It's tempting to jump to the conclusion that this previous copy is kept in the DOS data area, but that's not the case. Each application that supports the F3 editing capability must keep its own copy of "last input" data, so that input for various applications won't be mixed up. For instance, you can go into DEBUG by typing "debug" on the DOS command line. In DEBUG you can use F3 to recall each line you type there; but when you return to the command shell prompt and press F3, the last DOS command line, "debug" shows up. It has been saved by COMMAND.COM itself, all the time you were using DEBUG.

Incidentally, the official documentation for Function 0Ah is strangely silent on just how the DOS editing functions are brought into play. In fact, the *MS-DOS Programmer's Reference* for DOS

5.0 calls Function 0Ah "obsolete" and recommends using Function 3Fh instead, although the Read File function itself has no editing capabilities at all. (It appears, though I have been unable to confirm this with the equipment available to me, that the Read File function detects reading from STDIN as a special case and really uses the Function 0Ah code!)

The documented requirement for using Function 0Ah is that DS:DX point to a buffer large enough to accept the expected input, starting at its third byte. The first byte of the buffer specifies the total number of bytes it can hold, and the second byte the number of bytes now in the buffer. Normally most programs set the second byte to zero when setting up the buffer.

It turns out that this buffer itself serves dual duty as the "last copy" and as the destination for new input. Several requirements must be met in order to enable function key editing with Function 0Ah; the small assembly language program in Figure 10-5, F3TEST.ASM, shows them all.

Figure 10-5. F3TEST.ASM

```
        title   F3TEST
.model small                            ; use simplified seg style

.data
buf1    db      126,0                   ; buffer for input
        db      126 dup (0)
buf2    db      'This is Buf1 initial string'
buf2l   equ     $ - buf2                ; calculated data length
crlf    db      13,10,'$'
buf3    db      128 dup (0)             ; buffer for output

.stack

.code
start   proc
        mov     ax, DGROUP              ; set up segment regs
        mov     ds,ax
        mov     es,ax
        mov     di, offset DGROUP:buf1  ; prepare to preload buffer
        mov     si, offset DGROUP:buf2

        mov     cx,buf2l                ; get the move count
        mov     al,126                  ; establish max size
        mov     ah,cl                   ; and current size (essential)
        stosw
        inc     cx                      ; include the CR in data moved
        rep     movsb

L1:     mov     dl,':'                  ; prompt character
        mov     ah,2
        int     21h
        mov     dx, offset DGROUP:buf1  ; get buffered input line
        mov     ah,0Ah
        int     21h
        mov     al,buf1+1               ; check returned length
        cmp     al,1
        jb      L2                      ; quit if zero

        mov     si,offset DGROUP:buf1+2 ; copy to BUF3 for output
        mov     di,offset DGROUP:buf3   ; (essential that BUF1
        xor     cx,cx                   ;  not be changed in any
        mov     cl,al                   ;  way, to allow edits)
        rep     movsb
        mov     si, offset DGROUP:crlf  ; append CR/LF/$
        mov     cl,3
        rep     movsb
        mov     dx, offset DGROUP:crlf  ; print CR/LF first
        mov     ah,9
```

```
        int     21h
        mov     dx,offset DGROUP:buf3    ; then print BUF3
        mov     ah,9
        int     21h
        jmp     L1                       ; go back for another

L2:     mov     ax,4c00h                 ; terminate process
        int     21h

start   endp

        end     start
```

When you assemble and link this program, then run it, you can press F3 as the initial response to the prompt (:) and see the preloaded data string that was moved into the input buffer by the code immediately ahead of label L1.

The essential point here is that the length byte at BUF1+1 must point to an ASCII CR character in order to enable the function key editing feature. Also, the input buffer must either be preserved without change or be restored to the same condition in which Function 0Ah returned it, in order to permit subsequent edits. That's why F3TEST copies the input line over to buffer BUF3 before appending the CR and LF to it, inside the input loop. It's also why the two bytes at BUF1 and BUF1+1 are never modified inside the loop but are left just as they were returned by the previous call to Function 0Ah. Simple enough, but it took a while to discover that these were essential to enable the edit capability.

Here's a short sample to show how it works:

```
D:\UDOS2\CHAP10>f3test
:This is Buf1 initial string
This is Buf1 initial string
:NEW---s Buf1 initial string
NEW---s Buf1 initial string
:

D:\UDOS2\CHAP10>
```

On the second line, I simply pressed F3 to echo out the preloaded initial string, then pressed ENTER. F3TEST duly echoed the buffer content back and then prompted me again. This time I typed "NEW---" and then pressed F3 followed by ENTER.

The reason why the editing functions fail when the transient portion of COMMAND.COM is overlaid by a large program is simply that the last input buffer kept by COMMAND.COM (actually, the working buffer that it uses for parsing the command line) is located in that transient portion. The permanent copy of this buffer in the disk image of the transient portion is empty. Thus, when you press F3 or one of the other editing keys after the transient portion has been reloaded from disk, you get only the empty buffer, instead of the actual last input data.

DOSKEY

The DOSKEY TSR that comes with DOS provides a command history capability that allows you to recall and reuse previously entered command lines, edit them, and supply them to COMMAND.COM in place of input from the keyboard.

As you saw at the start of this chapter when tracing one cycle of COMMAND.COM's operating loop, the shell first checks DOSKEY by means of INT 2Fh to determine if it is installed and, at the same time, to obtain its input if DOSKEY is active. Only if DOSKEY is not active does COMMAND.COM call INT 21/0Ah.

DOSKEY maintains a ring-linked collection of input buffers. Each time that DOSKEY is called, it takes the next buffer in the ring, clears its character count to zero, and calls INT 21/08h to get input into that buffer.

The up or down arrow keys select either a previous or later buffer from the ring, without clearing its count. This allows you access to any buffer in the collection by repeated use of either arrow key; empty buffers are automatically skipped when stepping in either direction.

While looping to input characters, DOSKEY issues the same INT 28h as INT 21h AH=0Ah would.

Using the Environment

This section discusses the environment as implemented by MS-DOS and used by COMMAND.COM. Although the environment itself is firmly based at the operating system level (the PSP contains an environment segment field, for instance), the details of its usage are left to the command interpreter, with the result that this discussion may not apply fully if an alternate interpreter is in use.

How COMMAND.COM Uses the Environment

The idea of an environment for each process didn't exist in CP/M. The idea came to MS-DOS from UNIX but was greatly simplified in the transfer. As currently implemented in MS-DOS, the environment consists of a paragraph-aligned block of space that may be up to 32,767 bytes in length, although in practice it is always much smaller. This block contains a collection of environment variables, each of which consists of a variable name followed by the variable's data. Both the name and the data are stored as an ASCIIZ text string, with an equal sign (=) separating the name from the data. Note that this is just the convention used by COMMAND.COM and is not something built into DOS itself.

DOS provides the link between the process and its environment. DOS plugs the segment address of the environment into the word at offset 2Ch of the PSP when DOS dispatches the process through DOS EXEC, INT 21/4Bh.

The program that calls EXEC is responsible for allocating the environment space and defining all the variables contained in it, with one exception. If the segment address passed to the DOS EXEC function is 0h, then DOS itself allocates just enough space to contain a copy of each variable in the caller's environment and then does the copying automatically. The sole (and undocumented) exception to this rule is that the environment space used initially by the primary shell must be set up explicitly by the primary shell itself when it initializes. Otherwise, no master copy of the environment will exist.

COMMAND.COM uses several predefined environment variables to control its actions. COMSPEC provides the drive, path, and file specification that is used each time COMMAND.COM must reload its transient portion. PATH lists the drives and paths to be searched for possible external command filenames. PROMPT stores the string of characters that COMMAND.COM uses to prompt for user input.

Both PATH and PROMPT have separate internal commands that can be used to modify their contents. However, any environment variable can be modified by the internal command SET; if the variable does not exist, it is created in the environment, provided that enough space exists for it. From the primary command shell, the SET command operates on the master environment.

The predefined environment variables (PATH and COMSPEC only) are created in the master environment for the primary shell by the primary shell's own initialization code. The size of the master environment is also determined at this time. It is 160 bytes by default, but can be altered by the /e:nnn option in the SHELL=COMMAND.COM line in CONFIG.SYS. Alternate shells use different syntax but have the same capability.

Once the primary shell has been loaded, its environment space allocation cannot be increased. While it might appear simple to replace it with a new, larger copy and adjust the segment address at

PSP:002C accordingly, that original master environment address was also saved in undocumented internal locations for use by internal commands. Those addresses would be difficult to locate reliably in order to modify them.

When COMMAND.COM dispatches an external command, it simply passes the 0h code to DOS, thus generating an exact copy of the master environment for use by the spawned process. Because it is a copy and not the original, any changes made to it by the process will not be reflected in the master environment itself. Although this protects the master environment from being altered accidentally, it is difficult to alter it intentionally, except by using the SET command from the primary shell command line prompt, which is not always convenient.

Locating the Environment   Before you can make any use of the information stored in the environment area, you must first find it. DOS stores the segment address of the environment area for each process in the word at offset 2Ch in the PSP, but if you need access to the master environment, you must locate the PSP for the primary shell.

The assembly language package shown in Figure 10-6, ENVPKG.ASM, contains three routines designed to support small-model C programs. Curenvp() and mstenvp() locate the current and the master environment areas, respectively, and return far pointers to the first byte; envsiz() requires as input a pointer, such as the one returned by the first two, and returns the size of the area in paragraphs.

Figure 10-6. ENVPKG.ASM

```
;ENVPKG.ASM - Jim Kyle - July 1990, April 1993

.model small,c

.data
; assumes being used from C with _psp global variable
        extrn    _psp:word

.code

curenvp proc
        public   curenvp
; char far * curenvp( void );
        mov      ax,_psp          ; get PSP seg
        mov      es,ax
        mov      dx,es:[002Ch]    ; get env address
        xor      ax,ax            ; offset is zero
        ret
curenvp endp

mstenvp proc
        public   mstenvp
; char far * mstenvp( void );
; This is the only guaranteed method for COMMAND.COM if DOS=HIGH is
; in effect, but has problems under some circumstances.
; See notes in text.
        mov      ax,352Eh         ; get INT2E vector
        int      21h              ; vector in ES:BX
        mov      dx,es:[002Ch]    ; es:2C is seg of environment
        xor      ax,ax            ; make the offset zero
        ret
mstenvp endp

envsiz  proc     oenv:word, senv:word
        public   envsiz
; short envsiz( char far * vptr);
        mov      ax,senv          ; get segment of env
        dec      ax               ; back up to MCB
```

```
        mov     es,ax
        mov     ax,es:[0003h]    ; get size in paragraphs
        ret
envsiz  endp

        end
```

The comment lines following each of the *public* directives are sample prototype declarations to be copied into any C program that uses ENVPKG. To use these routines, first assemble the program into an OBJ file as follows:

```
MASM /mx ENVPKG;

TASM /mx /jMASM51 ENVPKG;
```

The /mx option switch for both assemblers forces procedure names to remain in lower case so that the OBJ file can be linked with your C programs. The operation of curenvp() and mstenvp() also relies on the fact that C compilers for the PC return four-byte far pointers in the DX:AX register pair.

The curenvp() routine assumes an external global variable called _psp. This variable is provided in all C compilers for the PC, though some compilers declare _psp in DOS.H and others in STDLIB.H. You could change this code to call INT 21/51h or INT 21/62h if you prefer to avoid compiler differences.

The envsiz() routine is based on the fact that every environment block starts at an offset of zero and immediately follows a Memory Control Block that contains the size of the block in paragraphs (see Chapter 7). Thus, when you pass a far pointer to the environment block to envsiz(), it decrements the segment by 1 to address its associated MCB and then retrieves the size from offset 3 in that segment. Note that the returned value is always in paragraphs. If a byte size is needed, the returned value must be multiplied by 16 (shifted left 4 places).

The short C program EPTST.C, shown in Figure 10-7, uses the ENVPKG routines. Compile this using the small memory model, and link with envpkg.obj.

Figure 10-7. EPTST.C

```c
/**********************************************************
 *   EPTST.C - Tests environment-access object modules   *
 *   Jim Kyle, July 1, 1990, April 1993                  *
 **********************************************************/
#include <stdio.h>

char far * curenvp( void );    /* prototype declarations   */
char far * mstenvp( void );
short envsiz( char far * vptr);

void main (void)
{ char far *mine;
  char far *master;

  puts("\nEnvironment locations:");
  mine = curenvp();
  master = mstenvp();
  printf("Current environment is at %Fp, size: %i bytes\n",
         mine, envsiz(mine)<<4 );
  printf(" Master environment is at %Fp, size: %i bytes\n",
         master, envsiz(master)<<4 );
}
```

Typical output from EPTST, when run at the primary shell's command prompt, follows:

```
Environment locations:
Current environment is at 1868:0000, size: 256 bytes
Master environment is at 11D7:0000, size: 512 bytes
```

This shows how the current working copy of the environment has been trimmed to a size just adequate to hold the defined variable strings and the program's pathspec.

Other Ways of Locating the Environment

The preceding discussion has a problem which does not often arise but is serious when it does. The interrupt vector for INT 2Eh doesn't always point to the primary copy of the command interpreter! For example, using David Maxey's INTRSPY program from Chapter 5, it is trivial to take over INT 2Eh for the purpose of seeing who calls it. If mstenvp() comes along while INTRSPY is in control of INT 2Eh, it will think that INTRSPY is the primary command interpreter, even though INTRSPY has simply hooked INT 2Eh for diagnostic purposes and is just chaining the interrupt to the previous owner, presumably, the primary command interpreter.

Of course, this is unlikely to happen out in the field. After all, nothing but a command interpreter really takes over INT 2Eh, right? Still, it's easy to fool mstenvp() in its current form once you know how to do so.

What other ways are there of locating the master environment?

One technique avoids the issue of locating the master environment entirely. It issues SET commands using INT 2Eh. The ability to call COMMAND.COM using INT 2Eh is discussed later in this chapter. Note that mstenvp() does not call INT 2Eh; it merely uses its interrupt vector in hopes of finding the primary command interpreter. This technique is repeated in mstenvp1(), in MSTENVP.C below.

An entirely different technique, used by the .BAT compilers discussed earlier in this chapter, walks the MCB chain looking for the environment segment belonging to the primary command interpreter. Chapter 7 documented how to walk the MCB chain. The key here is to take the first environment you find in the chain.

How do you find the first environment? Don't look for certain ASCII characters to see if an MCB corresponds to an environment; instead, look for PSPs (walk the PSP chain, as it were) and look at offset 2Ch. Take the first environment you find. How do you know you have a PSP? Don't look for the opcode bytes for INT 20h (CDh 20h) like some programs do; instead, look for an MCB whose owner is one greater than the MCB itself. See the routine mstenvp2() in Figure 10-8.

Another technique, designed especially to accommodate command interpreters loaded with the /p option, also walks the MCB chain. This time you look for the last environment that is at a higher address than its corresponding PSP. (That's a mouthful.) Why? You look for the last environment because of the /p option, and you look for an environment higher than its PSP because the command interpreter builds an environment for itself. Therefore, the environment is at a higher address than the program. (See mstenvp3() in Figure 10-8.) Note that this technique can easily fail if you load programs into UMBs, since some of the memory manager routines that do so place the environments *after* the program rather than before, when loading high. It also fails if you use 4DOS and have it swap itself into a UMB.

Finally, another technique involves walking back along the PSP chain until you find a PSP that is its own parent. However, this technique (which first appeared in Barry Simon, "Providing Program Access to the Real DOS Environment," PC Magazine, 28 November 1989, pp. 309-314) is designed to find what is called the active environment, not the master environment. This method finds only the currently active shell. If you are within a program spawned from the ! statement in a dBASE or FoxPro program, for example, you won't find the master environment using this technique.

On the other hand, this is the only reliable way to locate the effective (active) environment if you are running in a DOS box from Windows, since each DOS box gets its very own copy of the master environment. For example, ENVEDT, as presented in our first edition, didn't work in a DOS box under Windows. It affected the wrong environment, one too high up in the chain. We've revised ENVEDT to overcome this problem in the current version.

Three techniques for finding the master environment appear in the routine in Figure 10-8. The function walk() in MSTENVP.C is a variation on the UDMEM.C program from Chapter 7. Here, though, walk() expects a pointer to a function. For each MCB it finds, walk() calls this function, passing it an MCB pointer. The function should return TRUE, to indicate that walk() should keep going, or FALSE, to indicate that walk() should stop.

Thus, you can plug different functions into walk(), making MSTENVP.C (Figure 10-8) a test bed for trying out different methods for locating the master environment using the MCB chain.

Figure 10-8. MSTENVP.C

```
/*
 * MSTENVP.C
 * test bed for different methods to find master environment
 * Andrew Schulman, July 1990
 * modified July 1992 to use "undocdos.h" typedefs
 *          and also for UMB support - Jim Kyle
 */

#include <stdlib.h>
#include <dos.h>
#include "undocdos.h"                            /* see Chapter 7 */

extern LPMCB firsthi( void );

/**********************************************************************/
LPMCB get_mcb(void)            /* returns far pointer to first MCB */
{   ASM mov ah, 52h
    ASM int 21h
    ASM mov dx, es:[bx-2]
    ASM xor ax, ax
}         /* in both Microsoft C and Turbo C, far* returned in DX:AX */

char far *env(LPMCB mcb)          /* returns far ptr to env, or NULL */
{   char far *e;
    unsigned env_mcb;
    unsigned env_owner;

    if (! IS_PSP(mcb))
        return (char far *) 0;

    e = MK_FP(ENV_FM_PSP(mcb->owner), 0);
    env_mcb = MCB_FM_SEG(FP_SEG(e));
    env_owner = ((MCB far *) MK_FP(env_mcb, 0))->owner;
    return e;
}

typedef BOOL (*WALKFUNC)(LPMCB mcb);

/*  General-purpose MCB walker.
 *  The second parameter to walk() is a function that expects an
 *  MCB pointer, and that returns TRUE to indicate that walk()
 *  should keep going, and FALSE to indicate that walk() should
 *  stop.
 */
BOOL walk(LPMCB mcb, WALKFUNC walker)
{   for (;;)
        switch (mcb->type)
        {   case 'M':
                if (! walker(mcb))
                    return FALSE;
                mcb = (LPMCB)MK_FP(FP_SEG(mcb) + mcb->size + 1, 0);
                break;
            case 'Z':                            /* end of an MCB chain */
```

```
                    walker(mcb);
                    if( FP_SEG( mcb ) < 0xA000 )
                      { mcb = firsthi();            /* bridge to UMB chain */
                        if( mcb == ( FP ) 0L )
                          return FALSE;                     /* none found */
                      }
                    else
                      return FALSE;               /* UMBs all done too */
                    break;
               default:
                    return FALSE;                /* error in MCB chain! */
          }
}

/*******************************************************************/
/* using the GETVECT 2Eh technique (ENVPKG.ASM) */
void far *mstenvp1(void)
{   ASM mov ax, 352eh                        /* get INT 2Eh vector */
    ASM int 21h
    ASM mov dx, es:[002Ch]                    /* environment segment */
    ASM xor ax, ax                       /* return far ptr in DX:AX */
}

/*******************************************************************/
/* walk MCB chain, looking for very first environment */
void far *env2 = (void far *) 0;

BOOL walk2(LPMCB mcb)
{   env2 = env(mcb);
    return env2 ? FALSE : TRUE;
}

void far *mstenvp2(void)
{   walk(get_mcb(), walk2);
    return env2;
}

/*******************************************************************/
/* walk MCB chain, looking for very LAST env addr > PSP addr */
void far *env3 = (void far *) 0;

#define NORMALIZE(fp)    (FP_SEG(fp) + (FP_OFF(fp) >> 4))

BOOL walk3(LPMCB mcb)
{   void far *fp;
    /* if env seg at greater address than PSP, then
       candidate for master env -- we'll take last */
    fp = env(mcb);
    if (fp)
        if (NORMALIZE(fp) > (FP_SEG(mcb)+1))
            env3 = fp;
    return TRUE;                    /* always return TRUE to get last */
}

void far *mstenvp3(void)
{   walk(get_mcb(), walk3);
    return env3;
}

/*******************************************************************/
/* walk MCB chain, looking for very first environment belonging
   to PSP which is its own parent */
void far *env4 = (void far *) 0;

BOOL walk4(LPMCB mcb)
```

```
{   env4 = env(mcb);
    if (env4)
    {   unsigned psp = FP_SEG(mcb) + 1;
        return (PARENT(psp) == psp) ? FALSE /*found it!*/ : TRUE;
    }
    else
        return TRUE;     /* keep going */
}

void far *mstenvp4(void)
{   walk(get_mcb(), walk4);
    return env4;
}

/***************************************************************/
void main( void )
{   printf("GETVECT 2Eh method; mstenvp1    = %Fp\n", mstenvp1());
    printf("WALK MCB method; mstenvp2       = %Fp\n", mstenvp2());
    printf("WALK MCB/LAST method; mstenvp3  = %Fp\n", mstenvp3());
    printf("WALK MCB/OWN PARENT; mstenvp4   = %Fp\n", mstenvp4());
}
```

How does this program behave under various conditions? First let's try it from the normal COM-MAND.COM prompt:

```
D:\UDOS2\CHAP10>mstenvp
GETVECT 2Eh method; mstenvp1    = 1A7B:0000
WALK MCB method; mstenvp2       = 1A7B:0000
WALK MCB/LAST method; mstenvp3  = 1A7B:0000
WALK MCB/OWN PARENT; mstenvp4   = 1A7B:0000
```

So far so good. All four methods agree on where the master environment is. Let's see what happens if we load a child copy of the command interpreter:

```
D:\UDOS2\CHAP10>mstenvp
GETVECT 2Eh method; mstenvp1    = 1A7B:0000
WALK MCB method; mstenvp2       = 1A7B:0000
WALK MCB/LAST method; mstenvp3  = 1B29:0000
WALK MCB/OWN PARENT; mstenvp4   = 1A7B:0000
```

Oh, oh! The third method picked up the child copy's environment instead of the master's. But that might not always be bad, because sometimes you need to be able to locate the active, rather than the master, copy.

Now let's load a new permanent command interpreter with the /p flag and run MSTENVP again:

```
D:\UDOS2\CHAP10>mstenvp
GETVECT 2Eh method; mstenvp1    = 1B29:0000
WALK MCB method; mstenvp2       = 1A7B:0000
WALK MCB/LAST method; mstenvp3  = 1B29:0000
WALK MCB/OWN PARENT; mstenvp4   = 1A7B:0000
```

Here, mstenvp2() and mstenvp4() were in error. They both stuck with the old abandoned environment segment in 1A7B:0000, instead of upgrading as the other two subroutines did. The /p flag (in COMMAND.COM only but not in 4DOS.COM or NDOS.COM) creates a new primary command interpreter, not a secondary command interpreter. Strike one for mstenvp2() and mstenvp4().

What happens if you run a second child copy of the command interpreter under the new primary? By now, you should be expecting to find at least three different environments, and you do:

```
D:\UDOS2\CHAP10>mstenvp
GETVECT 2Eh method; mstenvp1    = 1B29:0000
WALK MCB method; mstenvp2       = 1A7B:0000
WALK MCB/LAST method; mstenvp3  = 1BD7:0000
WALK MCB/OWN PARENT; mstenvp4   = 1A7B:0000
```

Only mstenvp1() correctly located the real master environment in this case; mstenvp3() grabbed the child copy, just as it did earlier, while the other two techniques were still stuck on the original, no longer valid, version.

After loading a debugger (INTRSPY, with an appropriate script) that hooks INT 2Eh, we get this:

```
D:\UDOS2\CHAP10>mstenvp
GETVECT 2Eh method; mstenvp1    = FB00:0000
WALK MCB method; mstenvp2       = 1A7B:0000
WALK MCB/LAST method; mstenvp3  = 1B29:0000
WALK MCB/OWN PARENT; mstenvp4   = 1A7B:0000
```

Now, mstenvp1() is wrong, too. Segment FB00 points into the debugger, not the primary command interpreter! Only mstenvp2() and mstenvp4() properly identified the master environment, and they too would have been wrong had a second primary been present.

Finally, reboot the machine, load a TSR in CONFIG.SYS with the INSTALL= command, and try MSTENVP again:

```
D:\UDOS2\CHAP10>mstenvp
GETVECT 2Eh method; mstenvp1    = 1C35:0000
WALK MCB method; mstenvp2       = 1968:0000
WALK MCB/LAST method; mstenvp3  = 1C35:0000
WALK MCB/OWN PARENT; mstenvp4   = 1C35:0000
```

In this situation, mstenvp2() was wrong again. Segment 1968 points into the environment of the TSR loaded with the INSTALL= command! Thus, any program that uses the "walk MCB" method of finding the master environment fails whenever a user of DOS 4.0 or higher uses the handy INSTALL= command.

Could some enhancement be made to mstenvp2() to detect this situation? Yes. Take, not the first environment you find, but the first environment belonging to a PSP that is its own parent (another mouthful). That's the mstenvp4() option, shown on all the sample runs.

This works beautifully in the DOS 4.0 and higher INSTALL= situation, but as you saw in earlier test runs, it still leaves the problem with the /p option that caused mstenvp2() to fail. It also fails miserably under Qualitas' 386MAX memory manager, which sometimes alters the owner fields of MCBs in Upper Memory Blocks (the changes it makes are detailed in the UDMEM.C file, in Chapter 7); if your master environment happens to be loaded high under 386MAX, it won't ever be found by this technique!

All these methods fail if someone has used a device driver to change the memory allocation strategy to last-fit before the top level shell is loaded. In such a case, you may have to settle for finding the active environment, rather than the master copy, by walking back up the parent-process chain, as shown in the ROOTS.C program of Chapter 7 or in the section which follows.

Thus, although all these techniques work pretty well in many cases, none presents a 100-percent fool-proof method for finding the master environment. Of course, the problems discussed here are the result of some admittedly offbeat special cases, but trying to anticipate such cases is what distinguishes the professional programmer from the amateur. So, what's a programmer to do? One technique, of course, is to perform the mstenvp() function in two (or more) different ways, compare the results, and bail out if they don't match.

It's some small comfort that Microsoft itself messed up finding the master environment in its own APPEND utility. The APPEND /E switch, when executed from a secondary command interpreter, does not affect the master environment and can, in fact, cause mysterious crashes. Of course, these crashes may also be due to APPEND's interception of FCB open and get file size requests, which corrupt register DX if the file is not actually found (a bug which Geoff Chappell notes has been present since at least DOS 3.30).

All of our examples here, by the way, were run with COMMAND.COM. Alternative command interpreters may drastically alter the results from the four search methods. For instance, while the /p switch causes COMMAND.COM to create a new primary shell and effectively discard the original, the popular 4DOS alternative never changes the primary, nor does it modify where the INT 2Eh vector points, once the program has been loaded. In addition, its capability to put the environment in a UMB invalidates some of the search techniques. Thanks to Lewis Paper, who raised questions about these methods in the 4DOS support area of CompuServe. The questions prompted me to dig a bit deeper for good answers, which boil down to, *use the active, rather than the master, environment in most cases.*

Finding the "Active" Environment

When the four techniques for locating the master environment all fail to do what you need, it's time to walk back along the PSP chain until one finds a PSP which is its own parent. This technique was first described by Barry Simon, in the 28 November 1989 issue of *PC Magazine*.

The principle is the same that we used in our ROOTS.C program back in Chapter 7. Here's a code fragment based on our revised version of ENVEDT.C, which appears in full later in this chapter:

```
#include "undocdos.h"              // see Chapter 7
char far * FindActive( void )
{ WORD parent, self;
  self = _psp;                     // or use INT 21/62h
  parent = PARENT( self );
  do                               // trace back up the chain
    { self = parent;
    }
  while (( parent = PARENT( self ) ) != self );
  return (char far *)MK_FP( ENV_FM_PSP( parent ), 0 );
}
```

Walking back along the PSP chain always locates the currently active shell; that's what you need to do when running in a DOS box under Windows or OS/2. It's the wrong way to go, though, if you're working inside a menu program or similar dispatching tool (such as Norton's Commander). These programs spawn an individual shell for each command, which then vanishes without trace upon returning to the menu or dispatcher. The active environment you find will be destroyed before you execute the next command when this happens.

Searching the Environment

Just locating the environment block, of course, isn't enough to let you recover data from it. The next step is to know the format in which information is stored there and to make use of that knowledge to find and retrieve the item you want.

The internal storage format used is generally pure ASCII text. Each variable consists of a single ASCIIZ string. The first part of this string is the variable's name, and the rest is its data. The name and data are separated by an equal sign. The string is terminated, C style, with an all-zero byte (the meaning of ASCIIZ). Each variable immediately follows the previous one, and the end of the list of variables is indicated by two consecutive all-zero bytes.

Since version 3.1, the EXEC function has added another item of information to the environment, the full path specification for the process that owns this copy of the environment. This information immediately follows the double-zero byte pair and begins with a binary (not ASCII) 01h word. That word indicates the number of items that follow. The drive letter, in ASCII, appears as the next byte, and the pathspec in ASCII continues until a zero end-of-string byte is reached.

Once you have a far pointer to the first byte of the environment area and you know the internal storage format just described, it's simple to develop code to locate an environment variable by name.

In fact, current C compilers include library functions, getenv() and setenv(), to do just that; but they are limited to accessing only the current working copy of the environment. What's more, many, if not most, implementations make still another UNIX-style copy of the variables into their own data areas. This copy supports the optional envp argument to main().

For maximum flexibility, you need to be able to access any copy you desire because, if you happen to be shelled out of a program, changes made to the current copy vanish without a trace when you return to the parent program. Changes made to the master copy remain, but they will have no effect until you return to the primary shell.

Several methods could be used to provide totally flexible access to the environment; the one we'll explore is designed for easy expansion to other needs. Its foundation is the small assembly language function shown in NXTEVAR.ASM (Figure 10-9). This function accepts as input a pointer to one environment variable; it returns either a pointer to the first byte of the following variable, which may be an all-zero byte, or NULL, if the input pointer already points to an all-zero byte.

Figure 10-9. NXTEVAR.ASM

```
;        NXTEVAR.ASM - Jim Kyle - July 1990

.model small,c
.code

nxtevar proc    uses di, vptr:far ptr byte

        public nxtevar
; char far * nxtevar( char far * vptr );
        les     di, vptr
        mov     cx, 8000h
        xor     ax, ax      ; search for 0 and...
        mov     dx, ax      ; ...initialize return DX:AX to 0:0
        repne   scasb       ; search ES:DI for char 0 in AL
        inc     cx          ; CX = 8000h if only one 0 found
        js      nev
        mov     dx, es
        mov     ax, di
nev:    ret
nxtevar endp
        end
```

This function, when presented with a far pointer to any ASCIIZ string (not just one in the environment area), returns a far pointer to the byte that follows the end-of-string marker byte. In the environment's structure, that pointer is either to the first byte of the next string or to a byte that is all zeroes. In the latter event, the end of the environment's variable area has been reached, so another call to nxtevar(), using this pointer, would return NULL.

Before that happens, the previous call to nxtevar() will have returned the far pointer to the all-zero byte itself. If each pointer is retained in an array, the final one can be used to recover the process' full path name. This final pointer's value can be passed to a routine that first verifies that the next two bytes are 01h and 00h, then copies the path information from the remaining bytes. Because the path data, like each variable, is an ASCIIZ string, the normal C string functions deal with it properly.

This function is flexible because you can pass the function a pointer to any environment, including the current environment you obtain with the curenvp() function of ENVPKG, the master environment you obtain by using mstenvp(), or the active environment which this chapter shows how to obtain with the ENVEDT.C program.

To use NXTEVAR.ASM, you must assemble it into an OBJ file, following the procedures noted earlier in this chapter for ENVPKG.ASM. To illustrate how NXTEVAR.ASM is used, Figure 10-10 shows a little C program that reports the location and contents of each string in the current environment.

Figure 10-10. NEV.C

```
/**********************************************************
 *  NEV.C - Next Environment Variable                     *
 *  Jim Kyle, July 1, 1990                                *
 **********************************************************/
#include <stdio.h>
#include <stdlib.h>

char far * nxtevar( char far * vptr );
char far * curenvp( void );

void main (void)
{ char far * myenv;

  myenv = curenvp();
  while ( myenv )
    { printf("Env Var at %Fp: %Fs\n", myenv, myenv );
      myenv = nxtevar( myenv );
    }
  exit(0);
}
```

To create NEV.EXE from the C program, use either Microsoft or Borland C compilers; both the
ENVPKG.OBJ and NXTEVAR.OBJ modules must be used this time because NEV.C calls curenvp()
to locate the current environment. NEV.C tells you the address and contents of each variable string in
the current environment, in the sequence in which they occur in the environment block. More often,
you'll want to locate a specific environment variable by name, and you may want to locate it in the
master environment rather than in the current copy. You could use the library function getenv() to
return a pointer to the named variable in the current environment copy, but getenv() won't access the
master.

To both search by name and use the master environment, we modify NEV.C into a far more useful program, FMEV.C, as shown in Figure 10-11. This also requires ENVPKG and NXTEVAR.

Figure 10-11. FMEV.C

```
/**********************************************************
 *  FMEV.C - Find Master Environment Variable             *
 *  Jim Kyle, July 7, 1990                                *
 **********************************************************/
#include <stdio.h>
#include <stdlib.h>
#include <string.h>

char far * nxtevar( char far * vptr );
char far * mstenvp( void );

void main ( int argc, char * argv[] )
{ char far * menv;
  char vname[128], *vdata, tgt[64];
  int tlen;

  menv = mstenvp();
  if (argc < 2)
    { printf("Var to find: ");
      gets( tgt );
    }
  else
    strcpy( tgt, argv[1] );
  tlen = strlen( tgt );

  while ( menv )
```

```
      { sprintf(vname, "%Fs", menv );
        if ( vname[tlen] == '=' )
          { vdata = &vname[tlen+1];
            vname[tlen] = '\0';
            if ( stricmp( tgt, vname ) == 0 )
              break;
          }
        menv = nxtevar( menv );
      }

  if ( menv )
    { printf("Found %s at %Fp:\n%s\n", vname, menv, vdata );
      exit(0);
    }
  else
    { printf("%s not found.\n", tgt );
      exit(1);
    }
}
```

In FMEV, the declaration of main( ) has been changed to permit the desired variable's name to be entered as a command line argument. Using sprintf( ) with the %Fs format specifier forces the library routine to do all necessary conversion to copy each string, in turn, from the environment to the local work area, vname. Although newer compilers include the _fstrcpy( ) library function to do some mixed-pointer copying tasks, the sprintf( ) solution still seems much simpler to comprehend.

We'll return to the environment at the end of this chapter, with the ENVEDT utility.

INT 2Eh, the Back Door

Interrupt 2Eh provides a back door into COMMAND.COM, allowing access to both the main interpreter routine and the command dispatcher from outside the program. Contrary to popular belief, this interrupt is *not* used in the command interpreter itself for any purpose; it is never invoked.

The procedures to which INT 2Eh provides access, though, are not re-entrant. The execution of batch files and the FOR and CALL internal commands also use these procedures. Consequently, no external program that calls INT 2Eh can be called within such operations. It's important to note that this interrupt is serviced by code in the resident portion of COMMAND.COM itself, rather than by DOS. If an alternative command interpreter such as 4DOS is installed in place of COMMAND.COM, the description provided in this section will not be true.

Although INT 2Eh can be dangerous if you use it without knowing its limitations, it does permit access to the primary copy of the command interpreter shell, the one dispatched by CONFIG.SYS during system bootstrap.

The real meat on this weird aspect of undocumented DOS can be found in Daniel E. Greenberg's article, "Reentering the DOS Shell," which appeared in *Programmer's Journal*, May/June 1990, on pages 28-36. This article is the definitive piece on INT 2Eh. Unfortunately, *PJ* is no longer published, and copies of this issue may be nearly impossible to locate.

The Function   The purpose of INT 2Eh is to provide external programs with a method for accessing the command parsing and dispatching routines within COMMAND.COM. It also defines which copy of COMMAND.COM is the primary shell if multiple copies exist in the system. The copy to which the INT 2Eh vector points is defined as primary.

Existence of this capability permits programs to use COMMAND.COM's internal commands, like SET, to modify environment variables. Since it invokes both the interpreter and dispatcher routines of COMMAND.COM, INT 2Eh can even be used to launch a batch file. However, its use is highly restricted by the fact that COMMAND.COM is not re-entrant. Any program that uses it to launch a batch file will, like a batch file that directly launches another, never return to its next operation.

Because only COMMAND.COM supports this interrupt, it's only prudent to verify that the interrupt service routine exists before attempting to use it.

The assembly language program HAVE2E.ASM, shown in Figure 10-12, provides a C-callable routine that returns TRUE if the first byte of the service routine for INT 2Eh is not the IRET that DOS points the vector to by default; the routine returns FALSE if the byte is equal to the IRET opcode.

Figure 10-12. HAVE2E.ASM

```
.model small,c
.code
have2e  proc                        ; returns 1 if ISR exists, else 0
        public  have2e
; int have2e( void ); /* prototype */
        mov     ax,352Eh
        int     21h
        mov     ax,es               ; test for empty just to be safe
        or      ax,bx               ; although MS-DOS never leaves this
        jz      h1                  ; vector all zeroes
        mov     al,es:[bx]
        xor     al,0CFh             ; opcode for IRET
        jz      h1
        mov     ax,1
h1:     cbw
        ret
have2e  endp
        end
```

Its Use   To use INT 2Eh, take a command string such as DIR *.* or anything else a user might normally type at the prompt, put a CR at the end of it and a byte count at the front, just as INT 21h/0Ah does, point DS:SI to the count byte, then invoke INT 2Eh. The command is executed. But to use INT 2Eh successfully, you must follow several rather strict guidelines. This capability has never been officially sanctioned. Microsoft's DOS 5.0 *Programmer's Reference* describes INT 2Eh merely as "reload transient; for use by COMMAND.COM only," despite the fact that it's never called within COMMAND.COM. As a result, INT 2Eh omits most of the error-trapping abilities of more normal functions.

The most important restriction on the use of this interrupt is that no registers, not even the stack segment and stack pointer, are preserved. Immediately at entry to the service routine, the return address offset and segment are popped into dedicated storage areas in COMMAND.COM's own data segment. On completion of the task invoked by using INT 2Eh, control returns to the caller by means of a far jump through the saved segment and offset values.

This has two major implications. The most obvious is that when you call INT 2Eh, you must save all essential registers in locations that you can access upon return, when only CS and IP are valid. Not so obvious is the fact that INT 2Eh, by its very nature, is not reentrant. That is, if it is called a second time before return from a prior invocation, the second call destroys the return address for the first invocation, leading to system lockup.

It is possible to overcome the lack of reentrancy. The trick is to copy all critical data areas from the COMMAND.COM data segment to dedicated memory space, obtained specifically for the purpose, then invoke INT 2Eh and, upon return, restore the data areas from the saved copy. This is essentially how the internal command CALL works, so that it can operate successfully from within a batch file.

The program DO2E.ASM, shown in Figure 10-13, contains the function do2e(), which sets everything up properly for invoking the interrupt, executing a command string, and regaining control upon return.

Figure 10-13. DO2E.ASM

```
.model small,c
.code
do2e      proc    uses ds si di, cmdstr:ptr byte
          public  do2e
; void do2e( char * cmdstr ); /* prototype */

          push    ds              ; save data segment regardless of model
          mov     si,cmdstr       ; small model
;         lds     si,cmdstr       ; large model
          mov     cs:svss,ss      ; save stack pointer
          mov     cs:svsp,sp
          cld
          int     2Eh             ; issue command
          cli
          mov     ss,cs:svss      ; restore stack pointer
          mov     sp,cs:svsp
          pop     ds              ; restore data segment
          sti
          cld
          ret

          even                    ; for best 286+ usage
svss      dw      0
svsp      dw      0

do2e      endp
          end
```

This routine should not be used unless have2e() returns TRUE to indicate that the interrupt is in fact present in your system. The command string passed to the do2e() function must be in a special format, the same format in which COMMAND.COM's input buffer is left after keyboard input. The first byte of the string must contain a binary count of the string's length, excluding the count byte and the terminating carriage-return character; and the string must be terminated by an 0Dh CR character.

Although you can build your own routines using only the do2e() function in DO2E.OBJ, it's easier if you work through an intermediate level support module such as the C function shown in Figure 10-14.

Figure 10-14. SEND2E.C

```
/********************************************************
 *    Send2E.C - support for INT 2Eh                    *
 *    Jim Kyle, July 1990                                *
 ********************************************************/
#include <stdio.h>
#include <string.h>

int have2e( void );             /* prototype */
void do2e( char * cmdstr );     /* prototype */

int Send2E( char * command )
{ char temp[130];
  int retval;

  if( retval = have2e() )
    { sprintf( temp, "%c%s\r", strlen( command ), command );
      do2e( temp );
    }
  return retval;
}
```

This snippet of code takes just the command line itself, as you would type it at the prompt, and adds the character count and terminating CR. It then passes the edited string on to INT 2Eh using the assembly language module. These actions happen only if the interrupt is present; if not, they are skipped. Finally, Send2E() returns TRUE if the command was passed to INT2E and FALSE if it was not.

The program in Figure 10-15 runs Send2E() in a loop, making a little command interpreter.

Figure 10-15. TEST2E.C

```
/*
TEST2E.C
        Revised August 1992 - jk
Turbo C++ 2.0:
    tcc test2e.c send2e.c do2e.asm have2e.asm
Microsoft C 6+:
    cl -qc test2e.c send2e.c -MAmx do2e.asm have2e.asm
Borland C++ 3+:
    bcc test2e.c send2e.c do2e.asm have2e.asm
*/

#include <stdlib.h>
#include <stdio.h>
#include <string.h>
main()
{
  char buf[128];
  for (;;)
    { fputs("$ ", stdout);
      gets(buf);
      if ((strcmp(buf, "bye") == 0 || strcmp(buf, "BYE") == 0) ||
          (strcmp(buf, "exit") == 0 || strcmp(buf, "EXIT") == 0))
        break;
      Send2E(buf);
    }
    puts("Bye");
}
```

We already saw this program in Chapter 9 on TSRs, where it was used with Ray Michels' TSR skeleton to create a memory resident command interpreter, TSR2E.

It is worth noting that this program, and INT 2Eh in general, is compatible with the installable command interface discussed earlier in this chapter. For example, if you run our INSTCMD program, you can issue its new internal command FULLNAME using an INT 2Eh program such as TEST2E or TSR2E.

INT 2Eh is literally an alternative entry point, with corresponding exit, to the command loop of COMMAND.COM, to which control returns when COMMAND's child program terminates. So, this is only to be expected. The few differences are sorted out early on, so that (subject to the re-entrancy question) INT 2Eh supports everything one expects to obtain from the command processor.

An interesting thing happens if a program uses Send2E() to issue a SET command. The master environment, instead of the local copy of the environment belonging to the program, is updated. Using INT 2Eh is thus one technique for updating the master environment; other, safer, techniques were detailed earlier in this chapter, in the section "Using the Environment."

Notice that the issue of reentrancy is not addressed in Send2E(). That's because the issue is much more complex than just saving the data areas and restoring them. Although that's necessary, other considerations must also be addressed to make INT 2Eh calls robust enough for dependable use.

The first question that arises is how much data to save from the DOS area. Greenberg's article in *Programmer's Journal*, referenced at the start of this section, suggested that 120 bytes would include all necessary information for DOS versions 2.0 through 4.01. However, not all of that 120 bytes needed to be restored, and the locations that required restoration varied from one DOS version to the next. DOS 5.0 and 6.0 had not yet appeared when Greenberg's article was published, but the 120-byte figure can be used as a starting point for experimentation.

Another question, equally important, concerns the methods required to handle CTRL-BREAK interruptions or critical error conditions. In both cases, the normal COMMAND.COM response is inadequate to provide full safety.

Since the first edition of this book was published, the issue of running INT 2Eh clients like TEST2E.EXE from within a batch file has garnered some publicity. Even before that, Michael Mefford ("Running Programs Painlessly," *PC Magazine,* February 16, 1988) had written that programs using INT 2Eh "will not execute batch files nor work from within a batch file."

Jeff Prosise, in a good article on undocumented DOS ("Undocumented DOS Functions," *PC Magazine,* February 12, 1991) states, "Be careful about how you call interrupt 2Eh. If you aren't, you can crash your system in certain very common situations. The main one is if the program you're using is running under a batch file. Since INT 2Eh is nonreentrant, DOS uses it to run batch files. So if you run a batch file using INT 2Eh from your program, your system will crash."

We too have had problems running programs that use INT 2Eh from within a batch file, but nothing so dramatic as crashing the system. Instead, we have found simply that EXIT is not handled properly and that memory can be lost. And we found no indication at all, in actual disassembly of COMMAND.COM from DOS 5.0, that DOS uses it to run batch files. INT 2Eh is not invoked at all within COMMAND.COM. Its entry point, however, jumps to the self-same internal code used for batch file processing.

It would be nice if we could clear up this issue of INT 2Eh and batch files once and for all and say what does and does not work, and why. However, doing so would take far more effort than the result warrants, since it appears likely that still another version of DOS will be appearing annually. Any research spent on DOS 5.0 or 6.0 in this totally version-specific area would probably fail to apply to the next version.

Greenberg presented a major program written in assembly language to accompany his article, and a study of it is recommended if you want to use INT 2Eh as a tool for serious programming. However, because future revisions of DOS will undoubtedly cause changes to this capability at least as significant as those that have accompanied each revision in the past, your safest course is to avoid the use of INT 2Eh entirely, aside from its function in guiding you through some of the undocumented internal workings of COMMAND.COM. If you need to execute internal commands from within your program, use functions such as system() or the spawn() family in C.

Alternatives to COMMAND.COM

Several alternatives to COMMAND.COM now exist, and this section looks at a sampling of them. Some provide complete replacement of the command interpreter, while others retain the existing command interpreter but hide its command line interface from the user.

4DOS.COM

This command interpreter from J. P. Software totally replaces COMMAND.COM. Originally distributed only as shareware, it is now also available through retail outlets. As this was being written, 4DOS.COM was at version 4.02.

Another alternative is NDOS, distributed by Symantec with recent versions of the Norton Utilities. This is a very slightly modified version of 4DOS version 3.03, which has been customized for interaction with the NU batch enhancer capabilities, but which does not have all of the features added to 4DOS in its version 4. The NDOS supplied with NU 7.0 is a newer version, fully DOS 6.0 compatible. Most of the description of 4DOS that follows applies to NDOS also.

Other products that replace COMMAND.COM include Command-Plus, PolyShell, and FlexShell. I have chosen to describe 4DOS because it typifies the group and because I use it daily and am more familiar with it than with the others. But all of the programs offer improved capabilities when compared to COMMAND.COM.

A Total Replacement, Plus More   Like all of its competitors, 4DOS provides near-total compatibility with COMMAND.COM, even going so far as to duplicate strange actions that most users consider to be bugs, in order to maximize the number of applications that can run without change.

Where COMMAND.COM has only 39 internal commands at most, however, 4DOS now provides more than 80, thereby making many utilities used with COMMAND.COM obsolete. For example, this command interpreter includes a built-in environment editor (ESET), which allows you to edit either the master or the active environment.

For building batch file menuing systems, internal commands are able to draw boxes on the screen and obtain input from the keyboard that then modifies batch file execution decisions. It's even possible to perform arithmetic using the EVAL function and to plug the result into a command to be processed.

One of the most useful enhancements is the ability to do batch file processing entirely in RAM. COMMAND.COM must reload a batch file from disk for each line of input, making it necessary to keep the file available throughout its processing. Reading the file into RAM makes it possible to remove a floppy disk-based file from the system physically yet continue its execution.

The swapping techniques used are one area in which 4DOS has greatly improved on the standard command interpreter. Rather than reload from the same copy that was used to load the program initially, 4DOS actually swaps out the entire transient area of RAM, including any data storage that's not necessary for swapping it back in. This makes it possible for the program to shrink itself to only 256 bytes in normal DOS RAM when run on a 286 or higher system that has the ability to load the resident portion in upper memory.

Version 3.0 of 4DOS, and its relative NDOS, used command line switches supplied on the SHELL= line in CONFIG.SYS to control just how swapping was done. In version 4.0 of 4DOS, the command line switches are replaced by a 4DOS.INI file.

In all versions, though, you have the choice of swapping to Extended Memory (XMS), to Expanded Memory (EMS), to disk, or of not swapping at all. You can also specify the size of your environment area and of the buffer in which command line history will be saved. Many additional features are controlled by the INI file in version 4.0, such as automatically identifying DIR-entry filetypes by the color in which the entries are displayed.

Not the least of the enhancements, incidentally, is a full-featured, hypertext-like HELP system that gives you full details of how to use each of the internal commands from the command line. With all the added power, this feature is needed often.

No Undocumented Features   One of the most amazing things about 4DOS is that it is implemented almost entirely with documented features of DOS and works across all versions of DOS from 2.0 on. Prior to DOS 6.0, it made no use of the undocumented features and hooks on which COMMAND.COM depends for success, though it does implement several of them and documents them accordingly. Full compatibility with DOS 6.0 required that a few undocumented parts of DOS be used, but they remain at a minimum.

For instance, 4DOS originally made no use of INT 2Eh as a back door into the command interpreter. In version 3.01, INT 2Eh was vectored only to an IRET command. It is, however, part of the 4DOS code segment, so that the interrupt vector can be used to locate the primary shell, just as with the standard command interpreter.

Since Novell's menu program used with NETWARE required INT 2Eh to operate properly, compatibility suffered. By version 3.03, 4DOS included an extra TSR program, SHELL2E, which duplicated the functions and made the Novell menu usable. But in version 4.0, SHELL2E went away. It had been fully integrated into 4DOS itself. An INI file setting was added to control how the shell dealt with Novell's dependencies on undocumented aspects of COMMAND.COM. NDOS, being derived from version 3.03, still requires SHELL2E to function with the Novell menu, although this may have changed with the NU7 version.

Here's the official description of SHELL2E, taken from the on-disk documentation that accompanied the 4DOS version 3.03 release (thanks to Tom Rawson and Rex Conn, the creators of 4DOS, for letting me use this excerpt):

> SHELL2E accomplishes most of the purpose of INT 2E. It traps calls programs make to Interrupt 2E and loads a secondary shell to execute them. With one exception, this should make programs that use INT 2E work properly.
>
> The exception is programs that use INT 2E to issue SET commands intended to modify the master environment. Under COMMAND.COM the INT 2E is executed by the primary command processor, and therefore implicitly modifies the master environment when a SET command is executed. Since SHELL2E uses a secondary command processor to execute the commands, a SET command will modify the secondary command processor's environment, and not the master environment. As of this writing the only program we know of using INT 2E to execute SET commands is Personal Rexx from Mansfield Software.
>
> SHELL2E starts the command processor to run a secondary shell. The name of the command processor is obtained from the COMSPEC environment variable that was in effect at the time SHELL2E was loaded—NOT the COMSPEC environment variable setting in effect when SHELL2E is invoked by an INT 2E from another program. In general this subtlety won't matter, but remember that if you change COMSPEC during operation of your system those changes won't be noticed by SHELL2E when it loads the secondary shell. You can set parameters for a 4DOS shell created by SHELL2E using the 4DSHELL environment variable, just as you can for any secondary 4DOS shell.

Sample Program: An Environment Editor

It's time to put everything together into a single sample program that illustrates this chapter's topics and that is also potentially useful. The program, ENVEDT.C, lets you edit either the master environment, no matter how many levels down you happen to be shelled, or the current active environment. ENVEDT can be used with any command interpreter that vectors INT 2Eh to its own code space and that follows COM-file conventions (that is, CS and DS point to the same segment address). Even if INT 2Eh is not set up, ENVEDT's active environment capability remains available.

In our first edition, ENVEDT operated only on the master environment. This restriction made it unusable in such common situations as running a DOS session under Windows, so the current version adds a capability to edit the current active environment. You should note, however, that ENVEDT can't edit the environment within one DOS session under Windows and have your changes take effect in any other session, because each session has its own unique current active copy, and you would have to access the copy that Windows uses to create these individual ones.

ENVEDT first locates the desired environment block and then locates the specific variable to be edited. If you fail to give it a variable name, it displays a brief summary of how it is to be used, followed by a list of all variable names currently contained in the specified environment. You select which environment to edit by means of the option switches, "/M" for master or "/A" for active. In the absence of any option switch, the master environment is edited if running from DOS. If running under Windows, the active environment is automatically used.

Most of the specific techniques that ENVEDT uses have already been explained earlier in this chapter. The value of this program is that it shows you how to put the pieces together. In addition to ENVEDT.C itself, the program requires the support routines in ENVPKG.ASM and NXTEVAR.ASM, plus a new module, EEA.ASM (Environment Editor assembly code).

ENVEDT.C (Figure 10-16) has been tested only with Borland C++, but it should work equally well with Microsoft compilers. EEA.ASM has been tested with Turbo Assembler and with MASM V5.1. The finished program has been tested with both COMMAND.COM and 4DOS.COM as the primary shells, and with DOS versions ranging from 3.2 to 6.0.

Figure 10-16. ENVEDT.C

```
/***********************************************************
 *   ENVEDT.C - Editor for Master Environment Variables    *
 *   Jim Kyle, July 8, 1990                                 *
 *   major revision August 22, 1992 - jk                    *
 *                                                          *
 *   qcl envedt.c eea.obj envpkg.obj nxtevar.obj            *
 *    or  cl envedt.c -MAmx eea.asm envpkg.asm nxtevar.asm  *
 *    or  bcc envedt.c eea.asm envpkg.asm nxtevar.asm       *
 *                                                          *
 ***********************************************************/
#include <stdio.h>
#include <stdlib.h>
#include <conio.h>
#include <string.h>

#include "undocdos.h"                  /* defines structures */

#ifndef FP_SEG
#define FP_SEG(f) (*((unsigned *)&(f) + 1))
#endif

#ifndef FP_OFF
#define FP_OFF(f) (*((unsigned *)&(f)))
#endif

extern char far * nxtevar( char far * vptr );
extern char far * mstenvp( void );
extern void max_xy( int *x, int *y );
extern int IsWin3( void );
extern int col( void );
extern int row( void );
extern void setrc( int r, int c );
extern int envsiz( char far * envptr);

char far * menvp;                      /* perm ptr to environmnt */
char far * menv;                       /* pointer to current var */
char far * rest;                        /* pointer to next var */
char far * lstbyt;                     /* adr of last byte used */
char vname[512], *txtptr;              /* working buffer and ptr */
int nmlen,  insmode = 0,               /* name len, insert flag */
    max_x,  max_y,                         /* screen limits */
    i,      c,                             /* scratchpads */
    begrow, begcol,                    /* cursor, start of text */
    currow, curcol,                    /*       current loc */
    endrow,                            /*       end of text */
    editing,                           /* loop control flag */
    i_cur, i_max,                      /* cur, max i in txtptr */
    free_env;                          /* bytes free in env */

void findvar( char * varnam )          /* find var, set txtptr */
{ nmlen = strlen( varnam );
  txtptr = NULL;                       /* present not-found flag */
```

```
      while ( *menv )
        { rest = nxtevar( menv );              /* "rest" always next one */
          sprintf( vname, "%Fs", menv );
          if( vname[nmlen] == '=')             /* possible match found */
            { vname[nmlen] = '\0';
              if (stricmp( vname, varnam ) == 0)
                { txtptr = &vname[nmlen+1];
                  vname[nmlen] = '=';
                  return;                       /* found it, get out now */
                }
            }
          menv = rest;                          /* try again with next */
        }
}

void calccrsr( void )                           /* calc currow, curcol */
{ begrow = endrow - (i_max / max_x );
  if (( i_max % max_x ) == 0 )
    begrow++;
  begcol = 0;
  currow = begrow + (i_cur / max_x );
  curcol = begcol + (i_cur % max_x );
}

void show_var( void )                          /* display var content */
{ setrc( begrow, begcol );                             /* set to start */
  printf( txtptr );                                 /* show the string */
  endrow = row();                             /* update end row if scrl */
  if( ! col() &&                              /* adjust for line scroll */
      endrow == (max_y-1) )
    endrow--;
  calccrsr();                                /* establish cursor posn */
}

void do_del( void )
{ for (i=i_cur; txtptr[i]; i++ )              /* slide over one to left */
    txtptr[i] = txtptr[i+1];
  if ( i_max && i_cur >= --i_max )                    /* decr length */
    i_cur = (i_max - 1);                      /* and adjust if needed */
  free_env++;                                 /* account for freed byte */
  setrc( begrow, begcol );                    /* re-display the string */
  printf( txtptr );
  endrow = row();                             /* hold ending point */
  if( ! col() )                               /* adjust for line wrap */
    endrow--;                                 /*   if now in col 0 */
  putchar( ' ' );                             /* erase garbage char */
  calccrsr();                                 /* establish cursor posn */
}

void dochar( void )
{ if ( free_env < 3 )                          /* just beep if no space */
    { putchar( 7 );
      return;
    }
  if ( insmode )                               /* open up a hole for new */
    { if ( --free_env < 3 )                    /* decr freespace count */
        { putchar( 7 );                        /* and if too little is */
          return;                              /* left, beep and quit */
        }
      for (i = ++i_max; i > i_cur; i--)
        txtptr[i] = txtptr[i-1];
    }
  txtptr[i_cur++] = (char) c;                          /* put char down */
  if ( i_cur >= i_max )                        /* check for extending it */
    { txtptr[ ++i_max ] = '\0';                         /* set new EOS */
```

```
        if ( --free_env < 3 )             /* decr freespace count */
          { putchar( 7 );                     /* if too little is */
            return;                       /* left, beep and quit */
          }
      }
  show_var();                             /* re-display the string */
}

int edtxt( void )                         /* read kbd, do editing */
{ int retval;
  begrow = row();
  begcol = 0;
  i_max = strlen( txtptr );               /* set buffer index limit */
  i_cur = 0;                              /* and current index val */
  show_var();                             /* display the string */
  for ( editing=1; editing; )             /* main editing loop here */
    { setrc( 0, 70 );                         /* status message loc */
      printf("MODE: %s ", insmode ? "INS" : "REP" );
      setrc( currow, curcol );            /* keep cursor posn curr */
      switch( c = getch() )
        { case 0:                         /* function key or keypad */
            switch( getch() )
              { case 30:                          /* Alt-A, redisplay */
                  show_var();             /* re-display the string */
                  break;
                case 32:                  /* Alt-D, delete variable */
                  printf("\nDELETE this variable (Y/N)? ");
                  if(( getch() & 89 ) == 89 )       /* 89 = 'Y' */
                    { vname[0] = '\0';
                      retval = 1;
                      editing = 0;
                    }
                  break;
                case 71:                  /* home, goto first char */
                  i_cur = 0;
                  calccrsr();             /* establish cursor posn */
                  break;
                case 72:                          /* up arrow */
                  if ( (i_cur - max_x ) > 0 )
                    i_cur -= max_x;
                  calccrsr();             /* establish cursor posn */
                  break;
                case 75:                          /* left arrow */
                  if ( i_cur > 0 )
                    i_cur--;
                  calccrsr();             /* establish cursor posn */
                  break;
                case 77:                          /* right arrow */
                  if ( i_cur < i_max )
                    i_cur++;
                  calccrsr();             /* establish cursor posn */
                  break;
                case 79:                  /* end, goto last char */
                  i_cur = i_max;
                  calccrsr();             /* establish cursor posn */
                  break;
                case 80:                          /* down arrow */
                  if ( (i_cur + max_x ) < i_max )
                    i_cur += max_x;
                  calccrsr();             /* establish cursor posn */
                  break;
                case 82:                  /* insert, toggle flag */
                  insmode = !insmode;
                  break;
                case 83:                  /* delete, remove 1 char */
```

```
                do_del();
                break;
          }                              /* end of special codes */
        break;
      case 8:                          /* backspace del to left */
        if (i_cur)
          { i_cur--;                          /* back up one first */
            do_del();                   /* then do the delete */
          }
        break;
      case 13:                        /* Enter accepts changes */
        retval = 1;
        editing = 0;
        break;
      case 27:                         /* ESC quits without save */
        retval = 0;
        editing = 0;
        break;
      default:
        if (c >= ' ' && c < 127)
          dochar();                      /* handle INS or REP */
        else
          putchar( 7 );               /* beep on any other char */
    }
  }
  setrc( endrow, 0 );
  return (retval);
}
void putenvbak( void )                   /* copies back to env */
{ char * locptr;
  int save_size;

  save_size = FP_OFF( lstbyt ) - FP_OFF( rest ) + 1;
  locptr = (char *)malloc( save_size );

  for( i=0; i<save_size; i++ )            /* save trailing data */
    locptr[i] = rest[i];
  for( i=0; vname[i]; i++ )               /* copy edited string */
    *menv++ = vname[i];
  if( vname[0] )                         /* if not deleting... */
    *menv++ = '\0';                      /* ...add EOS byte to var */
  for( i=0; i<save_size; i++)            /* copy in trailing data */
    *menv++ = locptr[i];
  free( locptr );                        /* release save area */

  printf("\nENVIRONMENT UPDATED." );
}
void doedit( char * varnam )             /* find var, edit, save */
{ printf("Editing '%s':\n", varnam );
  menv = menvp;                          /* set starting point */
  free_env = envsiz(menv) << 4;       /* get the size in bytes */
  findvar( varnam );                    /* look for the variable */
  for( lstbyt=menv; *lstbyt; )          /* menv set by findvar() */
    lstbyt=nxtevar(lstbyt);             /* locate end of var area */
  if( lstbyt[1] == 1 && lstbyt[2] == 0 )
    { lstbyt += 3;                       /* skip loadfile name */
      while (*lstbyt)
        lstbyt++;
    }
  lstbyt++;
  free_env -= FP_OFF( lstbyt );           /* what's left is free */
  if ( txtptr == NULL )                  /* didn't find the name */
    { free_env -= (nmlen+1);              /* take out free space */
      if ( free_env < 5 )
        { puts("Not found, no room to add.");
          return;
```

```
    }
    printf( "Not found; add it (Y/N)? " );
    if(( getch() & 89 ) != 89 )                    /* 89 = 'Y' */
      return;
    for ( i=0; i<nmlen; i++ )          /* force to uppercase */
      vname[i] = (char) toupper( varnam[i] );
    vname[nmlen] = '=';                  /* add the equals sign */
    vname[nmlen+1] = '\0';             /* make content empty */
    txtptr = &vname[nmlen+1];        /* set text pointer to it */
    putchar( '\n' );                /* start on fresh line */
    insmode = 1;                    /* and in INS mode */
  }
  printf("Free environment space = %d bytes.\n", free_env );
  if ( edtxt() )                        /* do the editing now */
    putenvbak();                        /* copy to master env */
  else
    printf("\nENVIRONMENT NOT CHANGED." );
  putchar( '\n' );
}

void showvars( void )                    /* prints usage message */
{ puts(" USAGE: ENVEDT [env] varname [[name2] ... ]");
  puts("where varname is the name of an env variable");
  puts("  and name2, etc., are optional added names.");
  puts("optional switch [env] is /M to use Master copy");
  puts("  or /A to use Active copy of environment.");
  puts("\nCurrent variable names are:" );
  menv = menvp;
  for( i=0; i<8; i++ )
    vname[i] = ' ';
  while ( *menv )                        /* get and print names */
    { sprintf(vname+8, "%Fs", menv );
      for( i=8; vname[i] != '='; i++ )
      /* all done by for() */ ;
      vname[i] = '\0';
      puts( vname );
      menv = nxtevar( menv );
    }
  puts("Re-run with name(s) of variable(s) to be edited.");
}

char far * actenvp( void )                /* trace back to active */
{ WORD parent, self;
      self = _psp;                        /* start with current */
      parent = PARENT( self );              /* prog's parent, */
      do { self = parent;              /* and go until shell hit */
         } while (( parent = PARENT( self ) ) != self );
      return  (char far *)MK_FP( ENV_FM_PSP( parent ), 0 );
}

void main ( int argc, char **argv )
{ int i, j;

  menvp = IsWin3() ? actenvp() : mstenvp();      /* set default */
  for( i=1; i < argc; i++ )              /* first check for args */
    { switch( *argv[i] )
        {
        case '-':                      /* process option switches */
        case '/':
          switch( *(argv[i]+1) )
            {
            case 'M':                  /* use 2E to get master env */
            case 'm':
              menvp = mstenvp();
              break;

            case 'A':                  /* back up to active env */
            case 'a':
```

```
        menvp = actenvp();
        break;

      default:
        printf( "Unknown option \'%s\' ignored\n", argv[i] );
      }
      for( j=i; j < argc; j++ )    /* remove from arg list */
        argv[j] = argv[j+1];
      argc--;                      /* and reduce counts to fit */
      i--;
      break;
    }
  }
  if (argc < 2)
    showvars();                    /* list all vars to CRT */
  else
    { printf( "Changes will modify %s environment at %Fp\n",
         (menvp == mstenvp() ? "MASTER" : "ACTIVE" ), menvp );
    max_xy( &max_x, &max_y );      /* set up screen limits */
    while ( --argc )               /* process all vars named */
      doedit( *++argv );
    }
}
```

The program's first action is to establish a default environment based on the return from IsWin3(). It then processes any option switches found on the command line. When all arguments have been checked, main() determines what to do next.

If the only thing left on the command line is the program name itself (argc < 2), the showvars() procedure is called. If one or more additional arguments were present, the doedit() function would be called for each of them in turn until all have been processed. In either case, menvp points to the environment area that will be listed or edited.

The showvars() procedure locates the environment using menvp and cycles through it using nxtevar(), displaying the name of each variable. The SET internal command does almost the same thing, but if you are not working in the primary shell, SET always deals with the local copy of the environment rather than with the master. ENVEDT lets you choose between the two in this case.

The doedit() function searches the specified environment for a variable, again using menvp to start each search at the front of the environment area. Before searching, it sets the variable free_env to the total size in bytes of the environment block, using envsiz(), so that the amount of free space can be calculated later. The function then calls findvar() to do the actual search.

The findvar() procedure sets a pointer, txtptr, either to the address of the variable's contents in global work buffer vname (if it is found) or to NULL. This tells doedit() whether the search was successful. Before checking the result, however, doedit() moves another pointer, lstbyt, past any remaining variables and past the shell's loadfile pathspec, if one is present (normally, none is). When this is done, the offset portion of lstbyt is the count of the total number of environment block bytes in use; subtracting it from the total size of the block leaves in free_env, as the remainder, the number of bytes still free for use.

With free_env properly calculated, doedit() then checks the search result. If the name is not found, the procedure asks if you want to add it as a new variable, first verifying that there's room to do so and correcting the free_env value to account for the name itself. If you do want to add the new variable, the name is copied into the global work buffer vname, the equal sign (=) and a terminating \0 are added, txtptr is set to the address of the \0 character (the presently empty new contents), and the insmode flag is set to indicate INSERT mode operation. Otherwise, doedit() returns to main() to process the next variable in the input list.

If the variable was found, or if a new one is to be added, doedit() reports the number of bytes still free to use and calls edtxt() to do the actual editing. If edtxt() returns a nonzero value indicating normal completion of the editing operation, putenvbak() is called to copy the work buffer vname back into the environment block, sliding other data around as necessary to make things fit. If the value returned by edtxt() is zero, indicating an ESC-key bailout, the message "ENVIRONMENT NOT CHANGED" is displayed and doedit() returns.

Before we look at edtxt(), which contains the bulk of ENVEDT's complexity, let's see how findvar() searches for the name. The three pointers that address the block (menv, rest, and lstbyt) are all declared as far pointers. They are global in scope so that all procedures in ENVEDT can use them. The findvar() routine gets a near pointer (actually, one of those in the argv array) as its argument. Before the first call to findvar() is made and the menv pointer is initialized to the value of menvp, the permanent pointer to the block to be edited.

Each time that findvar() is entered, the pointer txtptr is set to NULL and the global variable nmlen is set to the length of findvar()'s argument. Then findvar() goes into a loop that continues until either the end of the variable list is reached (when the byte pointed to by menv is zero) or the argument is found as a variable name.

Within this loop, the pointer, rest, is first set to the address of the next variable, using nxtevar(). The current variable is then copied from the environment block to the global work buffer vname, by means of the sprintf() library function and its %Fs format modifier. Next, the character at position nmlen in the vname buffer is checked; if it is an equal sign (=), the variable's name is the right length to be a possible match; if not, no match is possible so no time is wasted trying to compare the strings.

If the length is right, the equal sign (=) is temporarily replaced by \0, and the library function stricmp() is used to compare the name and the argument without regard to case. If they match, the equal sign (=) is put back, txtptr is set to the first byte after it, and findvar() returns successfully. If the lengths differ or the strings fail to match, rest is copied to menv and the process repeats for the next variable in the master block.

Upon successful return from findvar(), menv still points to the first byte of the variable being edited, the vname buffer contains an exact copy of the entire variable, including its name and the trailing equal sign (=) separator; and txtptr points to the first byte of its value, in vname. These facts are critical to the operation of edtxt(), which does the actual editing.

On entry to edtxt(), variables are set up to save the cursor position and show_var() is called to display the variable on the screen. The main loop is then entered; control remains within this loop until you press Alt-D, Enter, or Esc. Any of these keys clears control variable editing; Enter and Alt-D set the return value to 1, and Esc sets the return value to 0. The cursor is then positioned just past the end of the variable on the screen, and control returns to doedit().

Each time that show_var() is called, it positions the cursor to the saved starting position, displays the entire contents of the variable using txtptr, saves the ending cursor position, and calls the function calccrsr() to calculate any necessary adjustments to the saved starting points and to establish the current cursor position within the variable.

The Alt-A keystroke simply refreshes the display should anything cause it to become confused. The Alt-D entry tells ENVEDT that you want to delete the variable entirely rather than just change it. When you have verified that you really mean it, the program zeroes the first byte in vname[] and forces the same actions as those that occur when you press Enter. This way, no bytes move back to the master block, but any following variables close up the gap.

The arrow keys move the cursor as would be expected, with the restriction that the cursor cannot move out of the variable. That is, up-arrow has no effect if the cursor is on the top line of the variable, left-arrow does nothing if the cursor is on the first character, and so forth. The Home and End keys move the cursor to the first and last characters, respectively, of the variable. The code for all six of these keystrokes simply changes the value of i_cur as appropriate, then calls calccrsr() to do the heavy work.

Once edtxt() has completed and returns a nonzero value, putenvbak() handles the job of moving the edited variable back into the master block. It does this by first calculating the number of bytes that must be saved, using the values of rest and lstbyt that were set up earlier, and then copying that material from the master block into a temporary block of memory obtained using malloc().

The full content of vname is then copied back to the specified environment block, starting at the address indicated by menv. Finally, the saved material is copied in following the vname data and the temporary block released by free(). The final action of putenvbak() is to display on screen the line "ENVIRONMENT UPDATED."

The module EEA.ASM contains IsWin3() and functions that are used when you are interactively editing the environment variables. It's not shown here, but you can find it on the companion diskette. To some degree, the functions in EEA.ASM duplicate others found in the Borland and Microsoft libraries, but the library functions differ greatly between the compilers. The addition of these video routines simplifies the rest of the program by providing identical operation regardless of the compiler you choose.

Here's what the operation of our revised ENVEDT looks like. First, we just tell it to edit variable OLDPATH:

```
D:\UDOS2\CHAP10> envedt oldpath
Changes will modify MASTER environment at D314:0000
Editing 'oldpath':
Free environment space = 270 bytes.
D:\WIN31;D:\VB;D:\UTILS;D:\DOS;D:\TAPE;C:\UV;C:\MAX6;C:\ADDSTOR
ENVIRONMENT NOT CHANGED.
```

The second line indicates that ENVEDT has defaulted to editing the master environment; the final line indicates that I pressed Esc rather than Enter to leave the program, and so the environment didn't change. Next, I repeated the command, but added the /a option switch to specify the active environment:

```
D:\UDOS2\CHAP10> envedt /a oldpath
Changes will modify ACTIVE environment at DAC8:0000
Editing 'oldpath':
Free environment space = 262 bytes.
D:\WIN31;D:\VB;D:\UTILS;D:\DOS;D:\TAPE;C:\UV;C:\MAX6;C:\ADDSTOR
```

With the content of OLDPATH displayed, I used the DEL key repeatedly to erase the reference to D:\WIN31; then I pressed Enter to change the variable in memory:

```
D:\VB;D:\UTILS;D:\DOS;D:\TAPE;C:\UV;C:\MAX6;C:\ADDSTOR
ENVIRONMENT UPDATED.
```

Repeating the original command sequence shows that no change occurred in the master environment; that's just what should have happened:

```
D:\UDOS2\CHAP10> envedt oldpath
Changes will modify MASTER environment at D314:0000
Editing 'oldpath':
Free environment space = 270 bytes.
D:\WIN31;D:\VB;D:\UTILS;D:\DOS;D:\TAPE;C:\UV;C:\MAX6;C:\ADDSTOR
ENVIRONMENT NOT CHANGED.
```

Finally, adding the /a switch at the end of the line, just to show that its position makes no difference, gets a report that verifies the earlier change was saved to the active environment:

```
D:\UDOS2\CHAP10> envedt oldpath /a
Changes will modify ACTIVE environment at DAC8:0000
Editing 'oldpath':
Free environment space = 271 bytes.
D:\VB;D:\UTILS;D:\DOS;D:\TAPE;C:\UV;C:\MAX6;C:\ADDSTOR
ENVIRONMENT NOT CHANGED.
```

If you are actually running in the primary shell so that the active environment and the master environment are the same block, you will find that ENVEDT reports it is working in the master even if you use the /a switch. This is not an error. The program determines whether it is using the master or the active block by comparing the value in menvp with the address of the master environment. If these are equal, as they will be if only one block serves both purposes, the program reports that the master will be modified.

One caveat: Some versions of COMMAND.COM copy the path in the COMSPEC variable into their own data area at system boot time, so it's possible that any changes you make to this variable with ENVEDT may have no effect on system operation. This is not true for all versions, though, and never applies to 4DOS.COM, which provides its own version of ENVEDT anyway.

Conclusion

In this chapter, we have looked at a wide variety of topics. They include the basic structure of the input-evaluate-do loop found in any command interpreter, the DOS hooks for installing new internal commands, the skeletal structure of a DOS command interpreter (TSHELL), the division of COMMAND.COM into initialization, resident, and transient portions, the DOS environment, the command interpreter backdoor (INT 2Eh), alternative interpreters like 4DOS, and methods for editing the environment.

That we have covered so many topics reflects the nature of command interpreters. They are, after all, interpreters of human input and produce (hopefully) human-readable output. While the basic operation is simply an input-evaluate-do for (;;) loop, there are enough different forms of input (keyboard, batch file, environment variable, or interpreter backdoor), and there are enough different locations for command code (internal, external, and installable), that we could have easily made this chapter even longer.

It is also important to remember that in MS-DOS as in UNIX, the command interpreter or shell is not part of the operating system itself. This is one reason why some of the techniques presented in this chapter do not work on every DOS machine. You can take a good many of the programs in this book, walk up to any of the 50 million or so DOS machines in existence, and run the program. Not necessarily so with the programs in this chapter, though. If a machine is running some interpreter other than COMMAND.COM (such as, heaven forbid, our own little TSHELL.COM), then techniques such as installing new internal commands, finding the master environment, or invoking INT 2Eh may or may not work.

This is because anyone is free to throw away COMMAND.COM and substitute something completely different. Now, it's true that users are also free to change parts of MS-DOS itself (by hooking INT 21h, for example), and it's also true that such changes are more widespread than the use of alternative command interpreters. But still, the command interpreter is not part of the operating system, and it's important to remember this. In other words, there are no 100% guarantees here. But then again, there can be none anywhere in an operating system as flexible as MS-DOS.

Undocumented DOS
Functions and Data Structures

Acknowledgment

The material in this appendix is an excerpt of a comprehensive list of IBM PC interrupt calls maintained by Ralf Brown; the full list of over 1000 pages is included on the disk accompanying this book. Updates are distributed electronically through CompuServe, the Internet, and bulletin boards worldwide several times per year. Over two hundred people have contributed to this massive listing; major contributors of information used in this appendix include Geoff Chappell (various undocumented behavior), Jan-Pieter Cornet (DR-DOS CDS), John Fa'atuai (DR-DOS and DR Multiuser DOS), Tim Farley (EMM386.EXE), Marcus Groeber (DR-DOS), David Maxey (various redirector calls), Duncan Murdoch (various undocumented fields and data structures), Richard A. Plinston (European MS-DOS 4.0), Jacob Rieper (some DR-DOS), Andrew Rossman (SMARTDRV 4.0), Michael Shiels (DR Multiuser DOS), Todor Todorov (some European MS-DOS 4.0), Robin Walker (DOS 3.0, 3.3, 4.0, and some 5.0), Manfred Young (miscellaneous), and Ralf Brown (DOS 2.x, 3.1, some DOS 3.3 and 4.0, and much of 5.0 and 6.0). Additional miscellaneous contributions were made by David Andrews, Tamura Jones, John Spinks, and Dan Lanciani.

Sample Entry

The following sample entry illustrates the various conventions used in this appendix by way of a mythical function call. A detailed explanation of various features follows the sample entry.

INT 2Bh Function 01h   DOS 2.7x only
GET DWIM INTERPRETER PARAMETERS

The DWIM (Do-What-I-Mean) interpreter is a loadable module called by COMMAND.COM when it encounters an unknown command or syntax error. The DWIM interpreter attempts to determine what the user meant, and returns that guess to COMMAND.COM for execution.

Call With:

AH	01h
DS:SI	pointer to buffer for parameter table (see below)
CX	size of buffer

Returns:

CF set on error
   AX   error code
          01h buffer too small (less than two bytes)
CF clear if successful

CX   size of returned data
DX   number of times DWIM interpreter invoked since parameters were last set

Notes: The DWIM interpreter was apparently never released due to its large memory requirements and slow operation.

If the given buffer size is at least two bytes but less than the size actually used by the parameter table, the first CX bytes will be copied into the buffer but no error will be returned.

Format of parameter table:

Offset	Size	Description
00h	WORD	size in bytes of following data
02h	WORD	maximum number of error corrections per line to attempt
04h	WORD	order in which to correct errors
		00h left-to-right
		01h right-to-left
		02h most serious first

—DOS 2.70—

06h	*BYTE*	*unknown*
07h	DWORD	pointer to DWIM statistics record (see INT 2B/AH=03h)

—DOS 2.71—

06h	*WORD*	*unknown*
08h	DWORD	pointer to DWIM statistics record (see INT 2B/AH=03h)

Note: The statistics record may be placed in a user buffer by changing the pointer with INT 2B/AH=02h.
See Also: *INT 21/AH=0Ah*, INT 2Bh/AH=02h, INT 2Fh/AX=AE01h

The right-hand side of the header indicates the versions of DOS for which the function is valid (in this case, versions 2.70 and 2.71 only). Two other variations are also used: DOS 2+ indicates that the entry is valid for all known versions of DOS from 2.00 to 6.00 inclusive, and DOS 3.1-3.3 indicates that the entry is valid for DOS versions 3.1 through 3.3, inclusive.

Various interrupt functions are called internally by DOS, and should be implemented by a user program rather than called. To further distinguish these functions, "Called with" is used instead of "Call with."

"Pointer to" means that the register or register pair contains the address of the indicated item, rather than the item itself.

Register descriptions which are indented mean that the register only applies for the value indicated by the preceding unindented register description. For this example, the value in AX is meaningful only if the carry flag is set on return, while CX and DX are only meaningful if the carry flag is clear.

Italicized text indicates that the information is not entirely certain, and that particular care (even more than usual for undocumented information) should be exercised when attempting to use it.

A Note: or Notes: section may apply either to the function in general or to the description of a data structure. Notes which come immediately after a Return section apply to the function in general, while those which follow a data structure description apply only to the data structure they follow.

Many data structures change their layouts between versions of DOS. To save space, the different versions are usually merged into a single description. The fields are assumed to be common to all versions unless a version indicator precedes them. In this example, the first three fields are common to both 2.70 and 2.71. In DOS 2.70, the fourth field is a byte, while in DOS 2.71 it is a word, shifting the remaining field.

One or more fields in a data structure may be pointers to additional data structures. Such data structures are often described in other entries of the appendix; in this case, under Interrupt 2Bh function 03h.

Throughout this appendix, you will see references such as 21/0A and 2F/AE01. The number before the slash is the INT (interrupt) number, such as INT 21h or INT 2Fh. A two-digit number after the slash is a hex function number to be placed in AH. Thus, 21/0A is INT 21h function 0Ah, or INT 21h AH=0Ah. A four-digit number after the slash is a hex function/subfunction number to be placed in AX. Thus, 2F/AE01 is INT 2Fh function AEh subfunction 01h, or INT 2Fh AX=AE01h. In some cases there may already be an 'h' hex indicator; this does not imply that those without an 'h' are decimal! All XX/YY and XX/YYYY numbers are in hex, whether or not there's an 'h'.

The final section of an entry is a list of related functions. For this example, the reader may wish to refer to Interrupt 2Bh function 02h (which would be the "Set DWIM Interpreter Parameters" call) and Interrupt 2Fh function AEh subfunction 01h (the COMMAND.COM installable command hook). In addition, Interrupt 21h function 0Ah is related, but not included in this appendix because it is a documented call. All cross references to functions not listed in this appendix are italicized. See the interrupt list on disk.

This can not be repeated often enough: because these calls are not officially documented, they may change from one version of DOS to the next, or quite simply be in error. Extra caution and testing are a must when using calls and data structures described in this appendix. Particular care is required where the information is known to be incomplete or uncertain (as indicated by italics).

INT 15h Function 2000h   DOS 3+
PRINT.COM - DISABLE CRITICAL REGION FLAG

Specify that PRINT should not set the user flag when it enters a DOS function call.
Call With:
    AX   2000h
See Also: INT 15/AX=2001h

INT 15h Function 2001h   DOS 3+
PRINT.COM - SET CRITICAL REGION FLAG

Specify a location which PRINT should use as a flag to indicate when it enters a DOS function call.
Call With:
    AX   2001h
    ES:BX   pointer to byte which is to be incremented while in a DOS call
See Also: INT 15/AX=2000h

INT 15h Function 4900h   Far East MS-DOS
GET DOS TYPE

Determine which Japanese variant of MS-DOS is running.

Call With:
    AX   4900h
Return:
    CF clear if successful
      AH   00h
      BL   type of DOS running
            00h DOS/V
            01h DOS/J or DOS/K (early IBM Japan versions of MS-DOS)
    CF set on error
      AH   86h (function not supported)

Note: In practice, DOS/J returns AH=86h; AX DOS does not support this call.
See Also: 21/30h

INT 21h Functions 1-0Ch   NetWare
CHARACTER I/O FUNCTIONS

The NetWare shell (NETX) has a special handler for redirection of the DOS character I/O calls (INT 21h functions 1, 2, 6, 7, 8, 9, 0Ah, 0Bh, 0Ch). For the DOS character I/O calls, NETX checks if there has been redirection to or from a network file (for example, "FOO > G:\BAR.BAR", where FOO is a program that calls INT 21h AH=9 (for example) to display a string, and where G: represents a NetWare file server). If there is redirection to or from a network file, NETX temporarily substitutes a token that routes the I/O to a @!NETW!@ device that handles the redirection. See chapter 4 for more information.

INT 21h Function 0Eh   NetWare
SELECT DISK

Whereas plain-vanilla DOS version of this function returns the LASTDRIVE value in AL, the NetWare shell (NETX) always returns 32, representing the size of NETX's internal drive tables: drives A: through Z:, plus the six temporary drives [, \,], ^, _, and '. Under NetWare, the actual number of local drives is available with INT 21h AH=DBh. See chapters 2 and 4.

INT 21h Function 13h   DOS 1+
DELETE FILE USING FCB

Although documented, the File Control Block contains undocumented fields, and this function has an undocumented quirk.

Call With:
> AH   13h
> DS:DX   pointer to unopened FCB (see below), filename filled with template for
>   deletion ('?' wildcards allowed)

Returns:
> AL   status
>   00h one or more files successfully deleted
>   FFh no matching files or all were read-only or locked

Notes: DOS 1.25+ deletes everything in the current directory (including subdirectories) and sets the first byte of the name to 00h (entry never used) instead of E5h if called on an extended FCB with filename '??????????' and bits 0-4 of the attribute set (bits 1 and 2 for DOS 1.x). This may have originally been an optimization to minimize directory searching after a mass deletion (DOS 1.25+ stop the directory search upon encountering a never-used entry), but can corrupt the file system under DOS 2+ because subdirectories are removed without deleting the files they contain.

Currently-open files should not be deleted, as file-system corruption may result when a subsequent attempt is made to write to the nonexistent file. MS-DOS allows a read-only file to be deleted with 21/13; NetWare NETX prevents this.

See Also: 21/41h, 2F/1113h. See 21/52 for system FCBs (chapter 8).

Format of File Control Block:

Offset	Size	Description
-7	BYTE	extended FCB if FFh
-6	5 BYTEs	reserved
-1	BYTE	file attribute if extended FCB
00h	BYTE	drive number (0=default, 1=A:, etc)
01h	8 BYTEs	blank-padded file name
09h	3 BYTEs	blank-padded file extension
0Ch	WORD	current block number
0Eh	WORD	logical record size

10h	DWORD	file size
14h	WORD	date of last write (see *21/5700h*)
16h	WORD	time of last write (see *21/5700h*) (DOS 1.1+)
18h	8 BYTEs	reserved (see below)
20h	BYTE	record within current block
21h	DWORD	random access record number (if record size is > 64 bytes, high byte is omitted)

Note: To use an extended FCB, you must specify the address of the FFh flag at offset -7, rather than the address of the drive number field.

Format of reserved field for DOS 1.0:

Offset	Size	Description
16h	WORD	location in directory (if high byte=FFh, low byte is device ID)
18h	WORD	number of first cluster in file
1Ah	WORD	last cluster number accessed (absolute)
1Ch	WORD	current relative cluster number within file (0 = first cluster of file)
1Eh	BYTE	dirty flag (00h=not dirty)
1Fh	BYTE	unused

Format of reserved field for DOS 1.10-1.25:

Offset	Size	Description
18h	BYTE	bit 7: set if logical device
		bit 6: not dirty
		bits 5-0: disk number or logical device ID
19h	WORD	starting cluster number on disk
1Bh	WORD	current absolute cluster number on disk
1Dh	WORD	current relative cluster number within file
1Fh	BYTE	unused

Format of reserved field for DOS 2.x:

Offset	Size	Description
18h	BYTE	bit 7: set if logical device
		bit 6: set if open
		bits 5-0: unknown
19h	WORD	starting cluster number on disk
1Bh	*WORD*	*unknown*
1Dh	*BYTE*	*unknown*
1Eh	*BYTE*	*unknown*
1Fh	*BYTE*	*unknown*

Format of reserved field for DOS 3.x:

Offset	Size	Description
18h	BYTE	number of system file table entry for file
19h	BYTE	attributes
		bits 7,6: 00 SHARE.EXE not loaded, disk file
		01 SHARE.EXE not loaded, character device
		10 SHARE.EXE loaded, remote file
		11 SHARE.EXE loaded, local file
		bits 5-0: low six bits of device attribute word

—SHARE.EXE loaded, local file (DOS 3.x and 5.0)—

1Ah	WORD	starting cluster of file on disk
1Ch	WORD	(DOS 3.x) offset within SHARE of sharing record (see 21/52h)

		(DOS 5.0) unique sequence number of sharing record
1Eh	BYTE	file attribute
1Fh	*BYTE*	*unknown*

—SHARE.EXE loaded, remote file—

1Ah	WORD	number of sector containing directory entry
1Ch	WORD	relative cluster within file of last cluster accessed
1Eh	BYTE	absolute cluster number of last cluster accessed
1Fh	*BYTE*	*unknown*

—SHARE.EXE not loaded—

1Ah	BYTE	(low byte of device attribute word AND 0Ch) OR open mode
1Bh	WORD	starting cluster of file
1Dh	WORD	number of sector containing directory entry
1Fh	BYTE	number of directory entry within sector

Note: If the FCB is opened on a character device, the DWORD at 1Ah is set to the address of the device driver header, and then the BYTE at 1Ah is overwritten.

INT 21h Functions 18h,1Dh,1Eh   DOS 1+
NULL FUNCTIONS FOR CP/M COMPATIBILITY

These functions correspond to CP/M BDOS functions which are meaningless under MS-DOS. An equivalent to function 1Eh was reintroduced with DOS 2.0.

Call With:
    AH   18h, 1Dh, or 1Eh
Returns:
    AL   00h

Note: Function 18h corresponds to the CP/M BDOS function "get bit map of logged drives" function 1Dh corresponds to "get bit map of read-only drives", and function 1Eh corresponds to "set file attributes."
See Also: 21/20h, 21/4459h

INT 21h Function 1Fh   DOS 1+
GET DRIVE PARAMETER BLOCK FOR DEFAULT DRIVE

Return the address of a disk description table for the current drive.

Call With:
    AH   1Fh
Returns:
    AL   status
            00h successful
                DS:BX pointer to Drive Parameter Block (DPB) (see below for DOS
                    1.x, 21/32h for DOS 2+)
            FFh invalid drive

Note: This call was undocumented prior to the release of DOS 5.0; however, only the DOS 4+ version of the DPB has been documented.
See Also: 21/32h

Format of DOS 1.1 and MS-DOS 1.25 drive parameter block:

Offset	Size	Description
00h	BYTE	sequential device ID
01h	BYTE	logical drive number (0=A:)
02h	WORD	bytes per sector

04h	BYTE	highest sector number within a cluster
05h	BYTE	shift count to convert clusters into sectors
06h	WORD	starting sector number of first FAT
08h	BYTE	number of copies of FAT
09h	WORD	number of directory entries
0Bh	WORD	number of first data sector
0Dh	WORD	highest cluster number (number of data clusters + 1)
0Fh	BYTE	sectors per FAT
10h	WORD	starting sector of directory
12h	WORD	address of allocation table

Note: The DOS 1.0 table is the same except that the first and last fields are missing; see 21/32 for the DOS 2+ version.

INT 21h Function 20h   DOS 1+
NULL FUNCTION FOR CP/M COMPATIBILITY

This function corresponds to the CP/M BDOS function "get/set default user (sublibrary) number", which is meaningless under MS-DOS.

Call With:
     AH   20h
Returns:
     AL   00h
See Also: 21/18h, 21/4459h

INT 21h Function 26h   DOS 1+
CREATE NEW PROGRAM SEGMENT PREFIX

Although documented, the PSP contains undocumented fields.

Call With:
     AH   26h
     DX   segment at which to create PSP (see below for format)
Notes: The new PSP is updated with memory size information; INTs 22h, 23h, and 24h are taken from the current interrupt vector table.
     DOS 2+ assumes that the caller's CS is the segment of the PSP to copy.
See Also: 21/4Bh, 21/50h, 21/51h, 21/55h, *21/62h*, 21/67h

Format of PSP:

Offset	Size	Description
00h	2 BYTEs	INT 20h instruction for CP/M CALL 0 program termination; the CDh 20h here is often used to test for a valid PSP
02h	WORD	segment of first byte beyond memory allocated to program
04h	BYTE	unused filler
05h	BYTE	CP/M CALL 5 service request (FAR JMP to 000C0h) **BUG:** (DOS 2+) PSPs created by 21/4Bh point at 000BEh
06h	WORD	CP/M compatibility—size of first segment for .COM files
08h	2 BYTEs	remainder of FAR JMP at 05h
0Ah	DWORD	stored INT 22h termination address
0Eh	DWORD	stored INT 23h control-Break handler address
12h	DWORD	DOS 1.1+ stored INT 24h critical error handler address
16h	WORD	segment of parent PSP
18h	20 BYTEs	DOS 2+ Job File Table, one byte per file handle, FFh if closed
2Ch	WORD	DOS 2+ segment of environment for process

2Eh	DWORD	DOS 2+ process's SS:SP on entry to last INT 21h call
32h	WORD	DOS 3+ number of entries in JFT (default 20)
34h	DWORD	DOS 3+ pointer to JFT (default PSP:0018h)
38h	DWORD	DOS 3+ pointer to previous PSP (default FFFFFFFFh in 3.x) used by SHARE in DOS 3.3
3Ch	2 BYTEs	unused by DOS versions <= 6.00
3Eh	2 BYTEs	(NetWare NETX) Used for Novell task id; see Chapter 4
40h	WORD	DOS 5.0 version to return on 21/30h
42h	WORD	(MSWindows3) selector of next PSP (PDB) in linked list; see Matt Pietrek's *Windows Internals*
44h	4 BYTEs	unused by DOS versions <= 6.00
48h	BYTE	(MSWindows3) bit 0 set if non-Windows application (WINOLDAP); see *Undocumented Windows* (IsWinOldApTask)
49h	7 BYTEs	unused by DOS versions <= 6.00
50h	3 BYTEs	DOS 2+ service request (INT 21/RETF instructions)
53h	9 BYTEs	unused in DOS versions <= 6.00
5Ch	16 BYTEs	first default FCB, filled in from first commandline argument overwrites second FCB if opened
6Ch	16 BYTEs	second default FCB, filled in from second commandline argument overwrites beginning of commandline if opened
7Ch	4 BYTEs	unused
80h	128 BYTEs	commandline / default DTA command tail is BYTE for length of tail, N BYTEs for the tail, followed by a BYTE containing 0Dh

Notes: In DOS versions 3.0 and up, the limit on simultaneously open files may be increased by allocating memory for a new open file table, filling it with FFh, copying the first 20 bytes from the default table, and adjusting the pointer and count at 34h and 32h. However, DOS will only copy the first 20 file handles into a child PSP (including the one created on EXEC).

Network redirectors based on the original MS-Net implementation use values of 80h-FEh in the open file table to indicate remote files; Novell NetWare is also reported to use values of 80h-FEh.

MS-DOS 5.00 incorrectly fills the FCB fields when loading a program high; the first FCB is empty and the second contains the first parameter.

Some DOS extenders place protected-mode values in various PSP fields such as the "parent" field, which can confuse PSP walkers. Always check either for the CDh 20h "signature" or that the suspected PSP is at the start of a memory block which owns itself (the preceding paragraph should be a valid MCB whose "owner" is the same as the possible PSP).

Format of environment block:

Offset	Size	Description
00h	N BYTEs	first environment variable, ASCIZ string of form "var=value"
	N BYTEs	second environment variable, ASCIZ string
	...	
	N BYTEs	last environment variable, ASCIZ string of form "var=value"
	BYTE	00h

—DOS 3+—

	WORD	number of strings following environment (normally 1)
	N BYTEs	ASCIZ full pathname of program owning this environment other strings may follow

INT 21h Function 30h   DOS 2+
GET DOS VERSION

Although documented, the OEM numbers this function returns are not documented.

Call With:

    AH   30h
—DOS 5.0—
    AL   what to return in BH
              00h OEM number (as for DOS 2.0-4.0x)
              01h version flag
Returns:
    AL   major version number (00h if DOS 1.x)
    AH   minor version number
    BL:CX   24-bit user serial number (most versions do not use this)
—if DOS <5 or AL=00h—
    BH   OEM number
              00h IBM
              05h Zenith
              16h DEC
              23h Olivetti
              29h Toshiba
              4Dh Hewlett-Packard
              99h STARLITE architecture (OEM DOS, NETWORK DOS, SMP DOS)
              FFh Microsoft, Phoenix
—if DOS 5.0 and AL=01h—
    BH   version flag
              bit 3: DOS is in ROM
              other: reserved (0)

Notes: The OS/2 1.x Compatibility Box returns major version 0Ah (10); the OS/2 2.x Compatibility Box returns major version 14h (20); early beta versions of the Windows NT DOS box returned major version 1Eh (30), but NT now masquerades as DOS 5 (INT 21h AX=3306h returns DOS 5.50). See Chapter 4.

   DOS 4.01 and 4.02 identify themselves as version 4.00.

   Generic MS-DOS 3.30, Compaq MS-DOS 3.31, and others identify themselves as PC-DOS by returning OEM number 00h.

   The version returned under DOS 4.0x may be modified by entries in the special program list (see 21/52h).

   The version returned under DOS 5+ may be modified by SETVER; use *21/3306h* to get the true version number.

See Also: *21/3306h*, 2F/122Fh

INT 21h Function 32h   DOS 2+
GET DOS DRIVE PARAMETER BLOCK FOR SPECIFIC DRIVE

Determine the address of a disk description table for the specified drive.

Call With:

    AH   32h
    DL   drive number (00h=default, 01h=A:, etc)
Returns:
    AL   status
              00h successful

DS:BX pointer to Drive Parameter Block (DPB) for specified drive
FFh invalid or network drive

Notes: The OS/2 compatibility box supports the DOS 3.3 version of this call with the exception of the DWORD at offset 12h. This call updates the DPB by reading the disk; the DPB may be accessed via the CDS or SysVars (see 21/52h) if disk access is not desirable. See Chapter 8.

This call was finally documented for DOS 5.0, but was undocumented in prior versions. Only the DOS 4+ version of the DPB was documented, however.

See Also: 21/1Fh, 21/52h, 21/53h

Format of DOS Drive Parameter Block:

Offset	Size	Description
00h	BYTE	drive number (00h=A:, 01h=B:, etc)
01h	BYTE	unit number within device driver
02h	WORD	bytes per sector
04h	BYTE	highest sector number within a cluster
05h	BYTE	shift count to convert clusters into sectors
06h	WORD	number of reserved sectors at beginning of drive
08h	BYTE	number of FATs
09h	WORD	number of root directory entries
0Bh	WORD	number of first sector containing user data
0Dh	WORD	highest cluster number (number of data clusters + 1)
		16-bit FAT if greater than 0FF6h, else 12-bit FAT
0Fh	BYTE	number of sectors per FAT
10h	WORD	sector number of first directory sector
12h	DWORD	address of device driver header
16h	BYTE	media ID byte
17h	BYTE	00h if disk accessed, FFh if not
18h	DWORD	pointer to next DPB
—DOS 2.x—		
1Ch	WORD	cluster containing start of current directory, 0000h if root, FFFFh if not known
1Eh	64 BYTEs	ASCIZ pathname of current directory for drive
—DOS 3.x—		
1Ch	WORD	cluster at which to start search for free space when writing
1Eh	WORD	number of free clusters on drive, FFFFh if not known
—DOS 4.0-6.0—		
0Fh	WORD	number of sectors per FAT
11h	WORD	sector number of first directory sector
13h	DWORD	address of device driver header
17h	BYTE	media ID byte
18h	BYTE	00h if disk accessed, FFh if not
19h	DWORD	pointer to next DPB
1Dh	WORD	cluster at which to start search for free space when writing, usually the last cluster allocated
1Fh	WORD	number of free clusters on drive, FFFFh if not known

---

INT 21h Function 3302h   DOS 3+
GET AND SET EXTENDED CONTROL-BREAK CHECKING STATE

Set a new state for the extended Control-Break checking flag and return its old value.

Call With:
    AX   3302h

DL   new state (00h for OFF or 01h for ON)

Returns:

DL   old state of extended BREAK checking

Note: This function does not use any of the DOS-internal stacks and may thus be called at any time, even during another INT 21h call. One possible use is modifying Control-Break check from within an interrupt handler or popup TSR. See Figure 6-5.

INT 21h Function 34h   DOS 2+
GET ADDRESS OF CRITICAL SECTION (InDOS) FLAG

Return the address of a flag which indicates when code within DOS is being executed, and it is thus unsafe to call DOS functions.

Call With:

AH   34h

Returns:

ES:BX   pointer to one-byte InDOS flag

Notes: The value of InDOS is incremented whenever an INT 21h function begins and decremented whenever one completes. However, InDOS alone is not sufficient for determining when it is safe to enter DOS, as the critical error handling decrements InDOS and increments the critical error flag for the duration of the critical error. Thus, it is possible for InDOS to be zero even if DOS is busy.

During an INT 28h call, it is safe to call some INT 21h functions (0Dh and above except as noted in the entry for INT 28h) even though InDOS may be 01h instead of zero.

The critical error flag is the byte immediately following InDOS in DOS 2.x, and the byte BEFORE the InDOS flag in DOS 3+ (except COMPAQ DOS 3.0, where the critical error flag is located 1AAh bytes BEFORE the critical section flag)

For DOS 3.1+, the undocumented Get SDA function (21/5D06) can be used to get the address of the critical error flag.

This function was documented prior to the release of DOS 5.0.

The implementation of this function is very simple; see Figure 6-18.

See Also: 21/5D06h, 21/5D0Bh, INT 28h

INT 21h Function 3700h   DOS 2+
"SWITCHAR" - GET SWITCH CHARACTER

Determine the character which is used to introduce command switches. This setting is ignored by DOS programs in version 4.0 and higher, but is honored by many third-party programs.

Call With:

AX   3700h

Returns:

AL   status

00h successful

DL   current switch character

FFh unsupported subfunction

Notes: This function is documented in some OEM versions of some releases of DOS, and is supported by the OS/2 compatibility box.

The returned value is always 2Fh for DOS 5+.

See Also: 21/3701h

INT 21h Function 3701h   DOS 2+
"SWITCHAR" - SET SWITCH CHARACTER

Set a new value for the character which is used to introduce command switches.

Call With:

AX   3701h

DL   new switch character

Returns:

AL   status

00h successful

FFh unsupported subfunction

Notes: This function is documented in some OEM versions of some releases of DOS, and is supported by the OS/2 compatibility box.

This call is ignored by DOS 5+.

See Also: 21/3700h

INT 21h Functions 3702h and 3703h   DOS 2.x and 3.3+ only
"AVAILDEV" - SPECIFY \DEV\ PREFIX USE

Get or set the state of the flag which makes a \DEV\ prefix to character device names mandatory.

Call With:

AH   37h

AL   subfunction

02h get availdev flag

Returns:

DL   00h if \DEV\ must precede character device names

nonzero if \DEV\ is optional

03h set availdev flag

DL   00h   \DEV\ is mandatory

nonzero   \DEV\ is optional

Returns:

AL   status

00h successful

FFh unsupported subfunction

Notes: All versions of DOS from 2.00 allow \DEV\ to be prepended to device names without generating an error even if the directory \DEV does not actually exist (other paths generate an error if they do not exist).

Although DOS 3.3+ accepts these calls, they have no effect, and subfunction 02h always returns DL=FFh.

INT 21h Function 3Fh   Workgroup Connection
WORKGRP.SYS - GET ENTRY POINT

WORKGRP.SYS is the driver for Microsoft's Workgroup Connection, which permits communication with PCs running Windows for Workgroups or LAN Manager networks. This call is one way to determine the address of the API handler.

Call With:

AH   3Fh

BX   file handle for device "NETHLP"

CX   0008h

DS:DX   pointer to buffer for entry point record (see AX=4402h"WORKGRP.SYS")

Returns:

CF clear if successful

AX   number of bytes actually read (0 if at EOF before call)

CF set on error

AX   error code (05h,06h) (see AH=59h)

INT 21h Function 3Fh   Driver Names
READ DEVICE

A number of device names are used by various drivers to provide interfaces to the drivers by performing reads or writes rather than IOCTL calls. See the list below for a sampling of special device names and the full interrupt list on disk for details on several of these devices.

See Also: 21/4402h, 2F/9400h

Special Device Names:

03COMPAQ	
386MAX$$	Qualitas' 386-to-the-MAX
CACHCMPQ	
EMMXXXX0	Expanded Memory Manager (not all memory managers provide data on access to this device name)
EMMQXXX0	QEMM-386 with disabled EMM
EMM\XXX0	disabled EMM
NETHLP	Workgroup Connection WORKGRP.SYS
QEMM386$	Quarterdeck's QEMM-386
SMARTAAR	SmartDrive 3.x
XMSXXXX0	HIMEM.SYS (not used for an API by HIMEM, but possibly by other extended memory managers)
$DebugDD	Windows low-level debugger
$MMXXXX0	disabled EMM
\MMXXXX0	disabled EMM

INT 21h Function 40h   DOS 2+
ADJUST FILE SIZE

Set the size of the specified file to the current file position as set by LSEEK (21/42h), truncating or expanding the file as necessary. This is a little-known (but documented) feature of the "write to file" call accessed by specifying a write of zero bytes. This feature has a bug, however.

Call With:
>   AH   40h
>   CX   0000h
>   BX   file handle

Returns:
>   CF clear if successful
>   AX   0000h
>   CF set on error
>   AX   error code (see *21/59h*)

BUG: A write of zero bytes to adjust the file size will appear to succeed when it actually failed if the write is extending the file and there is not enough disk space for the expanded file; one should therefore check whether the file was in fact extended by seeking to 0 bytes from the end of the file (21/4202h/CX=0/DX=0).

See Also: 2F/1109h

INT 21h Function 41h   DOS 2+
"UNLINK" - DELETE FILE

When invoked via 21/5D00h, this function has the undocumented behavior of allowing wildcards in the filename and enabling an attribute mask, deleting all files matching the wildcards and attribute mask.

Call With:

AH	41h
DS:DX	pointer to ASCIZ filename (no wildcards, but see below)
CL	attribute mask for deletion (server call only, see below)

Returns:

CF clear if successful

AX destroyed (DOS 3.3)

AL appears to be drive of deleted file

CF set on error

AX   error code (02h,03h,05h) (see *21/59h*)

Notes: For DOS 3.1+, wildcards are allowed if the function is invoked via 21/5D00h, in which case the filespec must be canonical (as returned by 21/60h), and only files matching the attribute mask in CL are deleted.

DOS does not erase the file's data; it merely becomes inaccessible because the FAT chain for the file is cleared.

Deleting a file which is currently open may lead to filesystem corruption. Unless SHARE is loaded, DOS does not close the handles referencing the deleted file, thus allowing writes to a nonexistant file.

See Also: 21/13h, 21/5D00h, 21/60h, 2F/1113h

INT 21h Function 4302h   Chicago
GET VOLUME INFORMATION

Under "Chicago" (DOS 7, Windows 4), 21/4302 will be the INT 21h equivalent of the Win32 GetVolumeInformation API call. The function will return information on the ability to store long filenames on the specified volume, whether the volume preserves lower-case filenames, the maximum length of a pathname (necessary for allocating buffers for 21/71), and so on. See 21/71, 21/72, and chapter 8.

INT 21h Function 4302h   DR-DOS 3.41+
GET ACCESS RIGHTS

Determine which operations the calling program may perform on a specified file without being required to provide a password.

Call With:

AX	4302h
DS:DX	pointer to ASCIZ pathname

Returns:

CF	clear if successful
CX	access rights

	bit 0	owner delete requires password
	bit 1	owner execution requires password (FlexOS)
	bit 2	owner write requires password
	bit 3	owner read requires password
	bit 4	group delete requires password
	bit 5	group execution requires password (FlexOS)
	bit 6	group write requires password
	bit 7	group read requires password
	bit 8	world delete requires password
	bit 9	world execution requires password (FlexOS)
	bit 10	world write requires password
	bit 11	world read requires password

AX   equals CX (DR-DOS 5.0)
CF   set on error
AX   error code

Notes: This protection scheme has been coordinated on all current Digital Research/Novell operating systems (DR-DOS 3.41+, DRMDOS 5.x, and FlexOS 2+).

Only FlexOS actually uses the "execution" bits; DR-DOS 3.41+ treats them as "read" bits.

This function is documented in DR-DOS 6.0 and corresponds to the "Get/Set File Attributes" function, subfunction 2, documented in Concurrent DOS.

DR-DOS 3.41-5.x only use bits 0-3. Only DR-DOS 6.0 using a DRMDOS 5.x security system allowing for users and groups uses bits 4-11.

See Also: 21/4303h

INT 21h Function 4303h   DR-DOS 3.41+
SET ACCESS RIGHTS AND PASSWORD

Specify which operations may be performed on a file without a password, and optionally set the file's password.

Call With:
    AX   4303h
    CX   access rights
          bits 0-11: see 21/4302h
          bit 15 new password is to be set
    DS:DX   pointer to ASCIZ pathname
    [DTA]   new password if CX bit 15 is set (blank-padded to 8 characters)

Returns:
    CF clear if successful
    CF set on error
       AX   error code

Notes: If the file is already protected, the old password must be added after the pathname, separated by a semicolon.

This function is documented in DR-DOS 6.0 and corresponds to the "Get/Set File Attributes" function, subfunction 3, documented in Concurrent DOS.

See Also: 21/4302h, 21/4454h

INT 21h Function 4304h   DR-DOS 5.0+
GET ENCRYPTED PASSWORD

Get the encrypted password for a file.

Call With:
    AX   4304h
    additional arguments (if any) unknown

Returns:
    CF clear if successful
       AX   unknown
       CX   unknown (same as AX)
    CF set on error
       AX   error code (see *21/59h*)

See Also: 21/4303h, 21/4305h

INT 21h Function 4305h   DR-DOS 5.0+
SET EXTENDED ATTRIBUTES

This function permits the extended attributes, and optionally the encrypted password, for a file to be set.

Call With:
        AX   4305h
        additional arguments (if any) unknown
Returns:
        CF clear if successful
        CF set on error
            AX   error code (see *21/59h*)
See Also: *21/4304h*

INT 21h Function 4400h   DOS 2+
IOCTL - GET DEVICE INFORMATION

Although documented, the returned device information word has a number of undocumented attribute bits.

Call With:
        AX   4400h
        BX   handle
Returns:
        CF clear if successful
            DX   device information word
                        character device
                            14: device driver can process IOCTL requests (see *21/4402h, 4403h*)
                            13: output until busy supported
                            11: driver supports OPEN/CLOSE calls (see *21/4408h*)
                             7: set (indicates device)
                             6: EOF on input
                             5: raw (binary) mode
                             4: device is special (uses INT 29h)
                             3: clock device
                             2: NUL device
                             1: standard output
                             0: standard input
                        disk file
                            15: file is remote (DOS 3+)
                            14: don't set file date/time on closing (DOS 3+)
                            11: media not removable
                             8: (DOS 4+) generate INT 24h if no disk space on write
                             7: clear (indicates file)
                             6: file has not been written
                            5-0: drive number (0=A:)
        AX destroyed
        CF set on error
            AX   error code (01h,05h,06h) (see *21/59h*)

Note: The value in DH corresponds to the high byte of device driver's attribute word if the handle refers to a character device.
See Also: *21/4401h*, 21/52h, 2F/122Bh

INT 21h Functions 4402h, 4403h   **Third-Party Drivers**
IOCTL INTERFACES

Many third-party device drivers, such as 386 memory managers, network drivers, caches, and so on, use 21/4402 and 21/4403 to provide an IOCTL interface. See 21/3F for a list of the device names of some important device drivers. The interrupt list on disk provides information on many IOCTL interfaces, including:

EMMXXXX0	386 memory managers - Global EMM Import Specification
QEMM386$	Quarterdeck QEMM-386
386MAX$$	Qualitas 386MAX
SMARTAAR	SMARTDRV.SYS 3.x (see 2F/4A10 for SMARTDRV 4.x)
PROTMAN$	Network Driver Interface Spec (NDIS) Protocol Manager
NETHLP	Windows for Workgroups - Workstation Connection (WORKGRP.SYS)
(varies)	CD-ROM device drivers

INT 21h Function 4404h   **DBLSPACE.BIN**
IOCTL - FLUSH OR INVALIDATE INTERNAL CACHES

DBLSPACE.BIN is the DoubleSpace disk compression manager introduced with MS-DOS 6.0.

Call With:

AX	4404h
BL	drive number (00h = default, 01h = A:, etc)
CX	000Ah (size of DSPACKET structure)
DS:DX	pointer to DSPACKET structure (see below)

Returns:

CF clear if IOCTL successful—check DSPACKET for actual status

AX   number of bytes actually transferred

CF set on error

AX   error code (01h,05h,06h,0Dh) (see AH=59h)

See Also: *2F/4A11h/BX=0000h*

Format of DSPACKET structure:

Offset	Size	Description
00h	WORD	signature 444Dh ("DM")
02h	BYTE	command code
		46h ('F') flush internal caches
		49h ('I') flush and invalidate internal caches
03h	WORD	result code
		(return) 4F4Bh ("OK") if successful, else unchanged
05h	5 BYTEs	padding

INT 21h Function 4409h   **DOS 3.1+**
IOCTL - CHECK IF BLOCK DEVICE REMOTE

Although documented, this call returns more information than is indicated in the official documentation.

Call With:

AX	4409h
BL	drive number (00h=default, 01h=A:, etc)

Returns:

CF clear if successful

DX   device attribute word

bit 15: drive is SUBSTituted

        bit 12: drive is remote
        bit 9: direct I/O not allowed
    CF set on error
        AX   error code (01h,0Fh) (see *21/59h*)

Note: On local drives, DX bits not listed above are the attribute word from the device driver header (see 21/52h); for remote drives, the other bits appear to be undefined.

See Also: 21/4400h, 2F/122Bh

INT 21h Function 440Dh   DOS 3.2+
IOCTL - GENERIC BLOCK DEVICE REQUEST

Although documented, this call provides undocumented subfunctions to manipulate a disk's serial number and specify whether access to a drive is allowed.

Call With:

AX	440Dh
BL	drive number (00h=default,01h=A:,etc)
CH	category code
	08h disk drive
CL	function
	46h (DOS 4+) set volume serial number (see also 21/69h)
	47h (DOS 4+) set access flag
	48h (Chicago) lock/unlock drive
	49h (Chicago) eject drive
	66h (DOS 4+) get volume serial number (see also 21/69h)
	67h (DOS 4+) get access flag
DS:DX	pointer to parameter block (see below)

Returns:

    CF set on error
        AX   error code (see *21/59h*)
    CF clear if successful
        DS:DX pointer to data block if CL=60h or CL=61h

Notes: DOS 4.01 seems to ignore the high byte of the number of directory entries in the BPB for diskettes.

    Functions 46h and 66h were undocumented in DOS 4.x, but have been documented for DOS 5.0 and higher.

See Also: 21/69h, 2F/0802h, 2F/122Bh

Format of parameter block for functions 46h, 66h:

Offset	Size	Description
00h	WORD	info level (00h); set before calling
02h	DWORD	disk serial number (binary)
06h	11 BYTEs	volume label or "NO NAME "
11h	8 BYTEs	filesystem type "FAT12 " or "FAT16 " (CL=66h only)

Format of parameter block for functions 47h, 67h:

Offset	Size	Description
00h	BYTE	special-function field (must be zero)
01h	BYTE	disk-access flag, nonzero if access allowed by driver

INT 21h Functions 4410h-4418h   DR DOS
OBSOLETE DR DOS FUNCTIONS

DR DOS (now Novell DOS) for the most part has the same INT 21h interface as MS-DOS. However, it also provides some DR DOS-specific functions via INT 21h functions 4450h through 4458h. 21/4410-4418 are identical to 21/4450-4458, but won't be supported in future versions of Novell DOS, because they are starting to collide with documented MS-DOS IOCTL functions. See 21/4450-4458, and chapter 4.

INT 21h Function 4451h   Concurrent DOS v3.2+
INSTALLATION CHECK

Determine whether Digital Research, Inc.'s Concurrent DOS version 3.2 or higher is running.

Call With:
    AX   4451h
Returns:
    CF set if not Concurrent DOS
        AX   error code (see *21/59h*)
    CF clear if successful
        AH   single-tasking/multitasking nature
            10h single-tasking
            14h multitasking
        AL   operating system version ID (see below for multitasking,
            21/4452h for single-tasking)

Notes: As of Concurrent DOS/XM 5.0 (possibly earlier), the version is also stored in the environment variable VER.

Use this function if you are looking for multitasking capabilities, 21/4452h for single-tasking; this call should never return the single-tasking values. It returns an error under DR-DOS.

See Also: 21/4452h,21/4459h

Values for version ID:
32h Concurrent PC DOS 3.2
41h Concurrent DOS 4.1
50h Concurrent DOS/XM 5.0 or Concurrent DOS/386 1.1
60h Concurrent DOS/XM 6.0 or Concurrent DOS/386 2.0
62h Concurrent DOS/XM 6.2 or Concurrent DOS/386 3.0
66h DR Multiuser DOS 5.1
67h Concurrent DOS 5.x
See Also: 21/4452h, 21/4459h

INT 21h Function 4452h   DR-DOS 3.41+
DETERMINE DOS TYPE/GET DR-DOS VERSION

Determine whether running under one of Digital Research, Inc.'s (now Novell's) single-tasking MS-DOS-compatible operating systems.

Call With:
    AX   4452h
    CF set
Returns:
    CF set if not DR DOS
        AX   error code (see *21/59h*)
    CF clear if DR DOS
        AH   single-tasking/multitasking

> 10h single-tasking
> 14h multitasking

    AL   operating system version ID (see below for single-tasking,
                21/4451h for multitasking)

    DX   same as AX

Notes: The DR-DOS version is also stored in the environment variable VER

    Use this function if looking for single-tasking capabilities, 21/4451h if looking for multitasking; this call should never return multitasking values. See IS_DRDOS.C in Chapter 4.

See Also: AX=4412h, AX=4451h, AX=4459h

Values for version ID:

60h	DOS Plus
63h	DR-DOS 3.41
64h	DR-DOS 3.42
65h	DR-DOS 5.00
67h	DR-DOS 6.00
70h	Palm DOS
71h	DR-DOS 6.0 March 1993 update for WfW
72h	Novell DOS 7.0

INT 21h Function 4454h   DR-DOS 3.41+
SET GLOBAL PASSWORD

Specify the master password for accessing files.

Call With:

    AX   4454h
    DS:DX   pointer to password string (blank-padded to 8 characters)

See Also: 21/4303h, 21/4414h

INT 21h Function 4456h   DR-DOS 5.0+
HISTORY BUFFER CONTROL

Call With:

    AX   4456h
    DL   flag
        bit 0: set for COMMAND.COM history buffers, clear for application

Returns:

    AL   *unknown*
        (20h if DL bit 0 set, A0h if clear (DR-DOS 6.0))

Note: This function is called by COMMAND.COM of DR-DOS 6.0.

INT 21h Function 4457h   DR-DOS 5.0+
SHARE/HILOAD CONTROL

Specify whether SHARE should be enabled or whether or not HILOAD should place the DR-DOS kernel into high memory.

Call With:

    AX   4457h
    DH   subfunction
           00h enable/disable SHARE
           DL   new state
                00h disable
                01h enable
                else Returns: AX unknown

01h get HILOAD status
Returns: AX   status
0000h off
0001h on
02h set HILOAD status
DL   new state (00h off, 01h on)
Returns: AX   unknown
other
Returns: AX   unknown

Note: This function is called by COMMAND.COM of DR-DOS 6.0; it will reportedly not be supported in future versions of DR-DOS (Novell DOS).
See Also: AX=4457h/DX=FFFFh

INT 21h Function 4457h Subfunc FFFFh   DR-DOS 6.0
GET SHARE STATUS
Call With:
     AX   4457h
     DX   FFFFh
Returns:
     AX   SHARE status
See Also: 2F/1000h

INT 21h Function 4458h   DR-DOS 5.0+
GET POINTER TO TABLE OF VARIOUS INTERNAL VALUES
Determine the address of an internal table of useful DR-DOS values and pointers.

Call With:
     AX   4458h
Returns:
     ES:BX   pointer to internal table (see below)
     AX   unknown (0B50h for DR-DOS 5.0, 0A56h for DR-DOS 6.0)
See Also: 21/4452h

Format of internal table:

Offset	Size	Description
00h	*DWORD*	*pointer to unknown item*
04h	*7 BYTEs*	*unknown*
0Bh	WORD	K of extended memory at startup
0Dh	BYTE	number of far jump entry points
0Eh	WORD	segment containing far jumps to DR-DOS entry points (see below)
—DR-DOS 6.0—		
10h	WORD	(only if kernel loaded in HMA) offset in HMA of first free HMA memory block (see below) or 0000h if none; segment is FFFFh
12h	WORD	pointer to segment of environment variables set in CONFIG, or 0000h if already used
14h	WORD	(only if kernel loaded in HMA) offset in HMA of first used HMA memory block (see below) or 0000h if none; segment is FFFFh

Note: The segment used for the DR-DOS 6.0 CONFIG environment variables (excluding COMSPEC, VER and OS) is only useful for programs/drivers called from CONFIG.SYS. The word is set to zero later and the area lost.

Format of jump table for DR-DOS 5.0-6.0:

Offset	Size	Description
00h	5 BYTEs	far jump to kernel entry point for CP/M CALL 5
05h	5 BYTEs	far jump to kernel entry point for INT 20
0Ah	5 BYTEs	far jump to kernel entry point for INT 21
0Fh	*5 BYTEs*	*far jump to kernel entry point for INT 22 (RETF)*
14h	*5 BYTEs*	*far jump to kernel entry point for INT 23 (RETF)*
19h	5 BYTEs	far jump to kernel entry point for INT 24
1Eh	5 BYTEs	far jump to kernel entry point for INT 25
23h	5 BYTEs	far jump to kernel entry point for INT 26
28h	5 BYTEs	far jump to kernel entry point for INT 27
2Dh	5 BYTEs	far jump to kernel entry point for INT 28
32h	5 BYTEs	far jump to kernel entry point for INT 2A (IRET)
37h	5 BYTEs	far jump to kernel entry point for INT 2B (IRET)
3Ch	5 BYTEs	far jump to kernel entry point for INT 2C (IRET)
41h	5 BYTEs	far jump to kernel entry point for INT 2D (IRET)
46h	5 BYTEs	far jump to kernel entry point for INT 2E (IRET)
4Bh	5 BYTEs	far jump to kernel entry point for INT 2F

Note: All of these entry points are indirected through this jump table to allow the kernel to be relocated into high memory while leaving the actual entry addresses in low memory for maximum compatibility.

Format of HMA Memory Block (DR-DOS 6.0 kernel loaded in HMA):

Offset	Size	Description
00h	WORD	offset of next HMA Memory Block (0000h if last block)
02h	WORD	size of this block in bytes (at least 10h)
04h	BYTE	type of HMA Memory Block (interpreted by MEM)
		00h system
		01h KEYB
		02h NLSFUNC
		03h SHARE
		04h TaskMAX
		05h COMMAND
05h	var	TSR (or system) code and data. DR-DOS TSR's, such as KEYB, hooks interrupts using segment FFFEh instead FFFFh.

INT 21h Function 4459h   DR MultiUser DOS 5.0
CP/M-compatible API

Invoke one of the functions in the superset of the CP/M API provided by Digital Research's Multi-User DOS.

Call With:

AX	4459h
CL	function (not listed here for lack of space; see interrupt list on disk)
DS,DX	parameters

Notes: DR-DOS 5.0 returns CF set and AX=0001h (invalid function).

This API is also available on INT E0h.

See Also: 21/4452h

INT 21h Function 4Ah   DOS 2+
RESIZE MEMORY BLOCK

Although documented, this function has undocumented behavior when there is not enough memory to satisfy the request.

Call With:
>   AH   4Ah
>   BX   new size in paragraphs
>   ES   segment of block to resize

Returns:
>   CF clear if successful
>   CF set on error
>   AX   error code (07h,08h,09h) (see *21/59h*)
>   BX   maximum paragraphs available for specified memory block

Notes: Under DOS 2.1 through 6.0, if there is insufficient memory to expand the block as much as requested, the block will still be made as large as possible, rather than remaining unchanged.

   DOS 2.1-6.0 coalesces any free blocks immediately following the block to be resized.

See Also: *21/48h*, *21/49h*

INT 21h Functions 4B01h and 4B04h   DOS 2+
"EXEC" - LOAD AND/OR EXECUTE PROGRAM

In addition to the documented subfunctions to execute a child process and load an overlay, the EXEC function also has a formerly undocumented subfunction to load and relocate a program without beginning execution. The European OEM version 4.00 also supports a second undocumented subfunction to run a child process in the background.

Call With:
>   AH   4Bh
>   AL   type of load
>   00h load and execute (documented)
>   01h load but do not execute
>   03h load overlay (documented)
>   04h load and execute in background (European MS-DOS 4.0 only)
>   05h set execution state (documented; see also Chappell, *DOS Internals*)
>   DS:DX   pointer to ASCIZ program name (must include extension)
>   ES:BX   pointer to parameter block (see below)

Returns:
>   CF clear if successful
>   BX,DX destroyed
>   if subfunction 01h, process ID set to new program's PSP; get with *21/62h*
>   CF set on error
>   AX   error code (01h,02h,05h,08h,0Ah,0Bh) (see *21/59h*)

Notes: DOS 2.x destroys all registers, including SS:SP.

   The calling process must ensure that there is enough unallocated memory available; if necessary, by releasing memory with 21/49h or 21/4Ah.

   For function 01h, the value to be passed to the child program is put on top of the child's stack.

   Function 01h has been documented (incorrectly; CS:IP and SS:SP were reversed in the LOAD structure) for DOS 5+, but was undocumented in prior versions.

   For a full explanation of function 01h, see Tim Patterson's chapter on the MS-DOS debugger interface in *Undocumented DOS*, 1st Edition.

Some versions (such as DR-DOS 6.0) check the parameters and parameter block and return an error if an invalid value (such as an offset of FFFFh) is found.

Background programs under European MS-DOS 4.0 must use the New Executable (NE) format.

New format (NE) executables begin running with the following register values, where the command tail corresponds to an old executable's PSP:0081h and following, except that the trailing carriage return is turned into a NUL (00h).

    AX = environment segment
    BX = offset of command tail in environment segment
    CX = size of automatic data segment (0000h = 64K)
    ES,BP = 0000h
    DS = automatic data segment
    SS:SP = initial stack

BUG: DOS 2.00 assumes that DS points at the current program's PSP.

Load Overlay (subfunction 03h) loads up to 512 bytes too many if the file contains additional data after the actual overlay. Pad all overlays up to the next 512-byte boundary.

See Also: *21/4Ch*, 21/64h, 21/80h, INT 2Eh

Format of EXEC parameter block (LOAD) for AL=01h,04h:

Offset	Size	Description
00h	WORD	segment of environment to copy for child process (copy caller's environment if 0000h)
02h	DWORD	pointer to command tail to be copied into child's PSP
06h	DWORD	pointer to first FCB to be copied into child's PSP
0Ah	DWORD	pointer to second FCB to be copied into child's PSP
0Eh	DWORD	(AL=01h) will hold subprogram's initial SS:SP on return
12h	DWORD	(AL=01h) will hold entry point (CS:IP) on return

Note: Microsoft calls this the LOAD Structure, but erroneously swaps the last two fields in the DOS 5.0 *MS-DOS Programmer's Reference*. This was corrected in the DOS 6.0 reference.

Format of .EXE file header:

Offset	Size	Description
00h	2 BYTEs	.EXE signature, either "MZ" or "ZM" (5A4Dh or 4D5Ah)
02h	WORD	number of bytes in last 512-byte page of executable
04h	WORD	total number of 512-byte pages in executable (includes any partial last page)
06h	WORD	number of relocation entries
08h	WORD	header size in paragraphs
0Ah	WORD	minimum paragraphs of memory to allocate in addition to executable's size
0Ch	WORD	maximum paragraphs to allocate in addition to executable's size
0Eh	WORD	initial SS relative to start of executable
10h	WORD	initial SP
12h	WORD	checksum (one's complement of sum of all words in executable)
14h	DWORD	initial CS:IP relative to start of executable
18h	WORD	offset within header of relocation table 40h or greater for new-format (NE,LE,LX,PE,W3,etc.) executable
1Ah	WORD	overlay number (normally 0000h=main program)
—new executable—		
1Ch	*4 BYTEs*	*unknown*
20h	WORD	behavior bits
22h	26 BYTEs	reserved for additional behavior info

| 3Ch | DWORD | offset of new executable or other non-MZ header within disk file, or 00000000h if old-style MZ executable |

—other—

| 1Ch | var | optional information added by linker, program compressor, etc. |

| N | N DWORDs | relocation items |

Notes: If the word at offset 02h is 4, it should be treated as 00h, since pre-1.10 versions of the MS linker set it that way.

If both the minimum and maximum allocation (offset 0Ah/0Ch) are zero, the program is loaded as high in memory as possible. The Windows KERNEL uses this; see Pietrek, *Windows Internals*.

The maximum allocation is set to FFFFh by default.

The new executable (NE) and linear executable (LE,LX) headers are described in detail in the on-disk interrupt listing. The NE and Win32 portable executable (PE) formats are both documented by Microsoft.

INT 21h Function 4Eh   DOS 2+
"FINDFIRST" - FIND FIRST MATCHING FILE

Although documented, this function has undocumented fields in its data structure, which are used to record the progress of the directory search, an undocumented quirk, and a subtle bug.

Call With:
    AH   4Eh
    AL   special flag for use by APPEND (see note below)
    CX   file attribute mask (bits 0 and 5 ignored)
    DS:DX   pointer to ASCIZ file specification (may include path and wildcards)
Returns:
    CF clear if successful
       [DTA]   FindFirst data block (see below)
    CF set on error
       AX   error code (02h,03h,12h) (see *21/59h*)

Notes: For search attributes other than 08h, all files with at MOST the specified combination of hidden, system, and directory attributes will be returned. Under DOS 2.x, searching for attribute 08h (volume label) will also return normal files, while under DOS 3+ only the volume label (if any) will be returned.

This call also returns successfully if given the name of a character device without wildcards. DOS 2.x returns attribute 00h, size 0, and the current date and time. DOS 3+ returns attribute 40h and the current date and time.

Immediately after an 2F/B711h (APPEND return found name), the name at DS:DX will be overwritten; if AL=00h on entry, the actual found pathname will be stored, otherwise, the actual found path will be prepended to the original filespec without a path.

Under LANtastic, this call may be used to obtain a list of a server's shared resources by searching for "\\SERVER*.*"; a list of printer resources may be obtained by searching for "\\SERVER\@*.*".

BUG: Under DOS 3.x and 4.x, the second and subsequent calls to this function with a character device name (no wildcards) and search attributes which include the volume-label bit (08h) will fail unless there is an intervening DOS call which implicitly or explicity performs a directory search without the volume-label bit. Such implicit searches are performed by CREATE (*21/3Ch*), OPEN (*21/3Dh*), UNLINK (21/41h), and RENAME (21/56h).

See Also: *21/11h*, *21/4Fh*, 2F/111Bh, 2F/B711h

Format of FindFirst data block (in DTA):

Offset	Size	Description
—PCDOS 3.10, PCDOS 4.01, MS-DOS 3.2/3.3/5.0—		
00h	BYTE	drive letter (bits 6-0), remote if bit 7 set
01h	11 BYTEs	search template
0Ch	BYTE	search attributes
—DOS 2.x (and some DOS 3.x)—		
00h	BYTE	search attributes
01h	BYTE	drive letter
02h	11 BYTEs	search template
—DOS 2.x and most 3.x—		
0Dh	WORD	entry count within directory
0Fh	*DWORD*	*pointer to DTA*
13h	WORD	cluster number of start of parent directory
—PCDOS 4.01, MS-DOS 3.2/3.3/5.0—		
0Dh	WORD	entry count within directory
0Fh	WORD	cluster number of start of parent directory
11h	4 BYTEs	reserved
—all versions, documented fields—		
15h	BYTE	attribute of file found
16h	WORD	file time
		bits 11-15: hour
		bits 5-10: minute
		bits 0-4: seconds/2
18h	WORD	file date
		bits 9-15: year-1980
		bits 5-8: month
		bits 0-4: day
1Ah	DWORD	file size
1Eh	13 BYTEs	ASCIZ filename+extension

INT 21h Function 50h   DOS 2+
SET CURRENT PROCESS ID (SET PSP ADDRESS)

Force a new value for DOS's record of the current process's PSP segment, thus effectively becoming another process.

Call With:

AH	50h
BX	segment of PSP for new process

Notes: DOS uses the current PSP address to determine which processes own files and memory; it corresponds to process identifiers used by other OSs.

Under DOS 2.x, this function cannot be invoked inside an INT 28h handler without setting the Critical Error flag.

Under DOS 3+, this function does not use any of the DOS-internal stacks and may thus be called at any time, even during another INT 21h call. (See Chapter 6, Figure 6-4.)

Some Microsoft applications use segments of 0000h and FFFFh; although one should only call this function with valid PSP addresses, any program hooking it should be prepared to handle invalid addresses. See PSPTEST.C in Chapter 4.

NetWare NETX hooks this call, using it to patch the Novell task ID into offsets 3Eh-3Fh of the PSP.

This function is supported by the OS/2 compatibility box.

This call was undocumented prior to the release of DOS 5.0.
See Also: 21/26h, 21/51h, *21/62h*

INT 21h Function 51h   DOS 2+
GET CURRENT PROCESS ID (GET PSP ADDRESS)

Return the segment address of the current process's PSP, which is used by DOS as a process identifier.

Call With:
AH   51h
Returns:
BX   segment of PSP for current process

Notes: DOS uses the current PSP address to determine which processes own files and memory; it corresponds to process identifiers used by other OSs.

Under DOS 2.x, this function cannot be invoked inside an INT 28h handler without setting the Critical Error flag.

Under DOS 3+, this function does not use any of the DOS-internal stacks and may thus be called at any time, even during another INT 21h call.

This function is identical to the documented function *21/62h*, and is supported by OS/2 compatibility box.

This call was not documented for DOS 2.x-4.x, but has been newly documented for DOS 5.0.
See Also: 21/26h, 21/50h, *21/62h*

INT 21h Function 52h   DOS 2+
"SYSVARS" - GET LIST OF LISTS

Determine the address of DOS's internal list of tables and lists. Most internal data structures are reachable through this list.

Call With:
AH   52h
Returns:
ES:BX   pointer to DOS list of lists

Note: This function is partially supported by the OS/2 1.1+ compatibility box (however, most pointers are FFFFh:FFFFh, LASTDRIVE is FFh, and the NUL header "next" pointer is FFFFh:FFFFh). The implementation of this function is very simple; see Figure 6-9.

Format of List of Lists (SysVars):

Offset	Size	Description
-12	WORD	(DOS 3.1-5.0) sharing retry count (see *21/440Bh*)
-10	WORD	(DOS 3.1-5.0) sharing retry delay (see *21/440Bh*)
-8	DWORD	(DOS 3.+) pointer to current disk buffer
-4	WORD	(DOS 3.+) pointer in DOS code segment of unread CON input When CON is read via a handle, DOS reads an entire line, and returns the requested portion, buffering the rest for the next read. 0000h indicates no unread input.
-2	WORD	segment of first memory control block
00h	DWORD	pointer to first Drive Parameter Block (see INT 21/AH32h)
04h	DWORD	pointer to first System File Table (see below)
08h	DWORD	pointer to active CLOCK$ device (most recently loaded drive with CLOCK bit (bit 3) set)
0Ch	DWORD	pointer to active CON device (most recently loaded driver with STDIN bit (bit 0) set, such as ANSI.SYS)

—DOS 2.x—

10h	BYTE	number of logical drives in system
11h	WORD	maximum bytes/block of any block device
13h	DWORD	pointer to first disk buffer (see below)
17h	18 BYTEs	actual NUL device driver header (not a pointer!) NUL is always the first device on DOS's linked list of device drivers. (see below for format)

—DOS 3.0—

10h	BYTE	number of block devices
11h	WORD	maximum bytes/block of any block device
13h	DWORD	pointer to first disk buffer (see below)
17h	DWORD	pointer to array of current directory structures (see below)
1Bh	BYTE	value of LASTDRIVE command in CONFIG.SYS (default 5)
1Ch	DWORD	pointer to STRING= workspace area
20h	WORD	size of STRING area (the x in STRING=x from CONFIG.SYS)
22h	DWORD	pointer to FCB table
26h	WORD	the y in FCBS=x,y from CONFIG.SYS
28h	18 BYTEs	actual NUL device driver header (not a pointer!) NUL is always the first device on DOS's linked list of device drivers. (see below for format)

—DOS 3.1-3.3—

10h	WORD	maximum bytes per sector of any block device
12h	DWORD	pointer to first disk buffer in buffer chain (see below)
16h	DWORD	pointer to array of current directory structures (see below)
1Ah	DWORD	pointer to system FCB tables (see below)
1Eh	WORD	number of protected FCBs (the y in the CONFIG.SYS FCBS=x,y)
20h	BYTE	number of block devices installed
21h	BYTE	number of available drive letters (largest of 5, installed block devices, and CONFIG.SYS LASTDRIVE=). Also size of current directory structure array.
22h	18 BYTEs	actual NUL device driver header (not a pointer!) NUL is always the first device on DOS's linked list of device drivers. (see below for format)
34h	BYTE	number of JOIN'ed drives

—DOS 4.x—

10h	WORD	maximum bytes per sector of any block device
12h	DWORD	pointer to disk buffer info record (see below)
16h	DWORD	pointer to array of current directory structures (see below)
1Ah	DWORD	pointer to system FCB tables (see below)
1Eh	WORD	number of protected FCBs (the y in the CONFIG.SYS FCBS=x,y) (always 00h for DOS 5.0)
20h	BYTE	number of block devices installed
21h	BYTE	number of available drive letters (largest of 5, installed block devices, and CONFIG.SYS LASTDRIVE=). Also size of current directory structure array.
22h	18 BYTEs	actual NUL device driver header (not a pointer!) NUL is always the first device on DOS's linked list of device drivers. (see below for format)
34h	BYTE	number of JOIN'ed drives

35h	WORD	pointer within MS-DOS.SYS data segment to list of special program names (see below) (always 0000h for DOS 5.0-6.0)
37h	DWORD	pointer to FAR routine for resident IFS utility function (see below) This routine may be called by any IFS driver which does not wish to service functions 20h or 24h-28h itself.
3Bh	DWORD	pointer to chain of IFS (installable file system) drivers
3Fh	WORD	the x in BUFFERS x,y (rounded up to multiple of 30 if in EMS)
41h	WORD	number of lookahead buffers (the y in BUFFERS x,y) and offsets 3Bh and 3Dh under "DOS 5.0-6.0" should read
41h	WORD	the y in BUFFERS x,y
43h	BYTE	boot drive (1=A:)
44h	*BYTE*	*01h if 80386+, 00h otherwise*
45h	WORD	extended memory size in K

—DOS 5.0-6.0—

10h	39 BYTEs	as for DOS 4.x (see above)
37h	DWORD	pointer to SETVER program list or 0000h:0000h
3Bh	WORD	(DOS=HIGH) offset in DOS CS of function to fix A20 control when executing special .COM format
3Dh	WORD	PSP of most-recently EXECed program if DOS in HMA, 0000h if DOS low
3Fh	8 BYTEs	as for DOS 4.x (see above)

Format of memory control block (see also below):

Offset	Size	Description
00h	BYTE	block type: 5Ah if last block in chain, otherwise 4Dh
01h	WORD	PSP segment of owner or 0000h if free 0006h if DR-DOS XMS UMB 0007h if DR-DOS excluded upper memory ("hole") 0008h if belongs to DOS FFFAh if 386MAX UMB control block FFFDh if 386MAX locked-out memory FFFEh if 386MAX UMB (immediately follows its control block)
03h	WORD	size of memory block in paragraphs
05h	3 BYTEs	unused

—DOS 2.x,3.x—

08h	8 BYTEs	unused

—DOS 4+—

08h	8 BYTEs	ASCII program name if PSP memory block or DR-DOS UMB, else garbage null-terminated if less than 8 characters

Notes: The next MCB is at segment (current + size + 1).

Under DOS 3.1+, the first memory block is the DOS data segment, containing installable drivers, buffers, etc. Under DOS 4+ it is divided into subsegments, each with its own memory control block (see below), the first of which is at offset 0000h.

For DOS 5.0, blocks owned by DOS may have either "SC" or "SD" in bytes 08h and 09h. "SC" is system code or locked-out inter-UMB memory, "SD" is system data, device drivers, etc.

Some versions of DR-DOS use only seven characters of the program name, placing a NUL in the eighth byte.

Format of MS-DOS 5.0 UMB control block:

Offset	Size	Description
00h	BYTE	type: 5Ah if last block in chain, 4Dh otherwise
01h	WORD	first available paragraph in UMB if control block at start of UMB, 000Ah if control block at end of UMB
03h	WORD	length in paragraphs of following UMB or locked-out region
05h	3 BYTEs	unused
08h	8 BYTEs	block type name: "UMB" if start block, "SM" if end block in UMB

Format of DOS 4+ data segment subsegment control blocks:

Offset	Size	Description
00h	BYTE	subsegment type (blocks typically appear in this order) "D" device driver "E" device driver appendage "I" IFS (Installable File System) driver "F" FILES= control block storage area (for FILES>5) "X" FCBS= control block storage area, if present "C" BUFFERS EMS workspace area (if BUFFERS /X option used) "B" BUFFERS= storage area "L" LASTDRIVE= current directory structure array storage area "S" STACKS= code and data area, if present (see below) "T" INSTALL= transient code
01h	WORD	paragraph of subsegment start (usually the next paragraph)
03h	WORD	size of subsegment in paragraphs
05h	3 BYTEs	unused
08h	8 BYTEs	for types "D" and "I", base name of file from which the driver was loaded (unused for other types)

Format of data at start of STACKS code segment (if present):

Offset	Size	Description
00h	*WORD*	*unknown*
02h	WORD	number of stacks (the x in STACKS=x,y)
04h	WORD	size of stack control block array (should be 8*x)
06h	WORD	size of each stack (the y in STACKS=x,y)
08h	DWORD	pointer to STACKS data segment
0Ch	WORD	offset in STACKS data segment of stack control block array
0Eh	WORD	offset in STACKS data segment of last element of that array
10h	WORD	offset in STACKS data segment of the entry in that array for the next stack to be allocated (initially same as value in 0Eh and works its way down in steps of 8 to the value in 0Ch as hardware interrupts preempt each other)

Note: The STACKS code segment data may, if present, be located as follows:

DOS 3.2:   The code segment data is at a paragraph boundary fairly early in the IBMBIO segment (seen at 0070:0190h).

DOS 3.3:   The code segment is at a paragraph boundary in the DOS data segment, which may be determined by inspecting the segment pointers of the vectors for those of interrupts 02h, 08h-0Eh, 70h, 72-77h which have not been redirected by device drivers or TSRs.

DOS 4.x: Identified by sub-segment control block type "S" within the DOS data segment.

Format of array elements in STACKS data segment:

Offset	Size	Description
00h	BYTE	status: 00h=free, 01h=in use, 03h=corrupted by overflow of a higher stack.
01h	BYTE	not used
02h	WORD	previous SP
04h	WORD	previous SS
06h	WORD	ptr to word at top of stack (new value for SP). The word at the top of the stack is preset to point back to this control block.

SHARE.EXE hooks (DOS 3.1-6.0):

(offsets from first System File Table pointed at by ListOfLists+04h; see SHARHOOK.C in Chapter 8)

Offset	Size	Description
-3Ch	*DWORD*	*pointer to FAR routine for unknown purpose* **Note:** not called by MS-DOS 3.3, set to 0000h:0000h by SHARE 3.3
-38h	DWORD	pointer to FAR routine called on opening file; on call, internal DOS location points at filenam (see 21/5D06h) **Returns:** CF clear if successful / CF set on error / AX DOS error code (24h) (see *21/59h*) **Note:** SHARE assumes DS=SS=DOS DS, and directly accesses DOS internals to get the name of the file just opened
-34h	DWORD	pointer to FAR routine called on closing file ES:DI pointer to system file table **Note:** SHARE does something to every lock record for file
-30h	DWORD	pointer to FAR routine to close all files for given computer (called by 21/5D03h)
-2Ch	DWORD	pointer to FAR routine to close all files for given process (called by 21/5D04h)
-28h	DWORD	pointer to FAR routine to close file by name (called by 21/5D02h) DS:SI pointer to DOS parameter list (see 21/5D00h) DPL's DS:DX pointer to name of file to close **Returns:** CF clear if successful / CF set on error / AX DOS error code (03h) (see 21/59)
-24h	DWORD call with BX CX:DX SI:AX	pointer to FAR routine to lock region of local file file handle starting offset size **Returns:** CF set on error / AL DOS error code (21h) (see *21/59h*) **Note:** not called if file is marked as remote
-20h	DWORD call with BX	pointer to FAR routine to unlock region of local file file handle

	CX:DX	starting offset
	SI:AX	size
		Returns:
		CF set on error
		AL DOS error code (21h) (see *21/59h*)
		Note: not called if file is marked as remote (see 2F/110B)
-1Ch	DWORD	pointer to FAR routine to check if file region is locked
	call with ES:DI	pointer to system file table entry for file
	CX	length of region from current position in file
		Returns:
		CF set if any portion of region locked
		AX 0021h
-18h	DWORD	pointer to FAR routine to get open file list entry
		(called by 21/5D05h)
		call with DS:SI pointer to DOS parameter list (see 21/5D00h)
		DPL's BX index of sharing record
		DPL's CX index of SFT in SFT chain of sharing rec
		Returns:
		CF set on error or not loaded
		AX DOS error code (12h) (see *21/59h*)
		CF clear if successful
		ES:DI pointer to filename
		CX number of locks owned by specified SFT
		BX network machine number
		DX destroyed
-14h	DWORD	pointer to FAR routine for updating FCB from SFT
		call with DS:SI pointer to unopened FCB
		ES:DI pointer to system file table entry
		Returns:
		BL C0h
		Note: copies following fields from SFT to FCB:
		starting cluster of file 0Bh 1Ah
		sharing record offset 33h 1Ch
		file attribute 04h 1Eh
-10h	*DWORD*	*pointer to FAR routine to get first cluster of FCB file*
		call with ES:DI pointer to system file table entry
		DS:SI pointer to FCB
		Returns:
		CF set if SFT closed or sharing record offsets mismatched
		CF clear if successful
		BX starting cluster number from FCB
-0Ch	DWORD	pointer to FAR routine to close file if duplicate for process
	DS:SI	pointer to system file table
		Returns:
		AX number of handle in JFT which already uses SFT
		Note: called during open/create of a file
		Note: if the SFT was opened with inheritance enabled
		and sharing mode 111, SHARE does something to all
		other SFTs owned by same process which have the same
		file open mode and sharing record
-08h	DWORD	pointer to unknown FAR routine

		Note: closes various handles referring to file most-recently opened
-04h	DWORD	pointer to FAR routine to update directory info in related SFT entries
		call with ES:DI pointer to system file table entry for file (see below)
		AX subfunction (apply to each related SFT)
		00h: update time stamp (offset 0Dh) and date stamp (offset 0Fh)
		01h: update file size (offset 11h) and starting cluster (offset 0Bh). Sets last-accessed cluster fields to start of file if file never accessed
		02h: as function 01h, but last-accessed fields always changed
		03h: do both functions 00h and 02h
		Note: follows pointer at offset 2Bh in system file table entries
		Note: NOP if opened with no-inherit or via FCB

Note: Most of the above hooks (except -04h, -14h, -18h, and -3Ch) assume either that SS=DOS DS or SS=DS=DOS DS, and directly access DOS-internal data.

Format of sharing record:

Offset	Size	Description
00h	BYTE	flag
		00h free block
		01h allocated block
		FFh end marker
01h	WORD	size of block
03h	BYTE	checksum of pathname (including NUL)
		if sum of ASCII values is N, checksum is (N/256 + N%256)
04h	WORD	offset in SHARE's DS of lock record (see below)
06h	DWORD	pointer to start of system file table chain for file
0Ah	WORD	unique sequence number
0Ch	var	ASCIZ full pathname

Format of SHARE.EXE lock record:

Offset	Size	Description
00h	WORD	offset in SHARE's DS of next lock table in list
02h	DWORD	offset in file of start of locked region
06h	DWORD	offset in file of end of locked region
0Ah	DWORD	pointer to System File Table entry for this file
0Eh	WORD	PSP segment of lock's owner

Format of DOS 2.x system file tables:

Offset	Size	Description
00h	WORD	pointer to next file table (offset = FFFFh if last)
04h	WORD	number of files in this table
06h	28h bytes per file	

Offset	Size	Description
00h	BYTE	number of file handles referring to this file
01h	BYTE	file open mode (see *21/3Dh*)
02h	BYTE	file attribute
03h	BYTE	drive (0 if character device, 1=A:, 2=B:, etc)
04h	11 BYTEs	filename in FCB format (no path,no period,blank-padded)
0Fh	*WORD*	*unknown*
11h	*WORD*	*unknown*
13h	*DWORD*	*file size*
17h	WORD	file date in packed format (see *21/5700h*)

19h	WORD	file time in packed format (see *21/5700h*)
1Bh	BYTE	device attribute (see 21/4400h)

—character device—

1Ch	DWORD	pointer to device driver

—block device—

1Ch	WORD	starting cluster of file
1Eh	WORD	relative cluster in file of last cluster accessed

20h	WORD	absolute cluster number of current cluster
22h	*WORD*	*unknown*
24h	*DWORD*	*current file position*

Format of DOS 3.0 system file tables and FCB tables:

Offset	Size	Description
00h	DWORD	pointer to next file table (offset = FFFFh if last)
04h	WORD	number of files in this table
06h	38h bytes per file	

Offset	Size	Description
00h-1Eh as for DOS 3.1+ (see below)		
1Fh	WORD	byte offset of directory entry within sector
21h	11 BYTEs	filename in FCB format (no path/period, blank-padded)
2Ch	DWORD	(SHARE.EXE) pointer to previous SFT sharing same file
30h	WORD	(SHARE.EXE) network machine number which opened file (Windows Enhanced mode DOSMGR uses the virtual machine ID as the machine number; see *2F/1683h*)
32h	WORD	PSP segment of file's owner
34h	WORD	(SHARE.EXE) offset in SHARE code seg of share record
36h	*WORD*	*apparently always 0000h*

Format of DOS 3.1-3.3x system file tables and FCB tables:

Offset	Size	Description
00h	DWORD	pointer to next file table (offset = FFFFh if last table)
04h	WORD	number of files in this table
06h	35h bytes per file	

Offset	Size	Description
00h	WORD	number of file handles referring to this file
02h	WORD	file open mode (see *21/3Dh*) bit 15 set if this file opened via FCB
04h	BYTE	file attribute
05h	WORD	device info word (see 21/4400h) bit 15 set if remote file bit 14 set means do not set file date/time on closing bit 12 set means don't inherit on EXEC bits 5-0 drive number for disk files
07h	DWORD	pointer to device driver header if character device else pointer to DOS Drive Parameter Block (see 21/32h)
0Bh	WORD	starting cluster of file
0Dh	WORD	file time in packed format (see *21/5700h*)
0Fh	WORD	file date in packed format (see *21/5700h*)
11h	DWORD	file size

 APPENDIX — Undocumented DOS Functions

—system file table—

| 15h | DWORD | current offset in file (may be larger than size of file; *21/42h* does not check new position) |

—FCB table—

15h	WORD	counter for last I/O to FCB
17h	WORD	counter for last open of FCB (these are separate to determine the times of the latest I/O and open)
19h	WORD	relative cluster within file of last cluster accessed
1Bh	WORD	absolute cluster number of last cluster accessed *0000h if file never read or written*
1Dh	WORD	number of sector containing directory entry
1Fh	BYTE	number of dir entry within sector (byte offset/32)
20h	11 BYTEs	filename in FCB format (no path/period, blank-padded)
2Bh	DWORD	(SHARE.EXE) pointer to previous SFT sharing same file
2Fh	WORD	(SHARE.EXE) network machine number which opened file (Windows Enhanced mode DOSMGR uses the virtual machine ID as the machine number; see 2F/1683h)
31h	WORD	PSP segment of file's owner (see 21/26h) (first three entries for AUX/CON/PRN contain segment of IO.SYS startup code); sometimes contains PSP's MCB rather than PSP itself
33h	WORD	offset within SHARE.EXE code segment of sharing record (see above), 000h if none

Format of DOS 4.0-6.0 system file tables and FCB tables:

Offset	Size	Description
00h	DWORD	pointer to next file table (offset = FFFFh if last)
04h	WORD	number of files in this table
06h		3Bh bytes per file

Offset	Size	Description
00h	WORD	number of file handles referring to this file
02h	WORD	file open mode (see *21/3Dh*) bit 15 set if this file opened via FCB
04h	BYTE	file attribute
05h	WORD	device info word (see 21/4400h) bit 15 set if remote file bit 14 set means do not set file date/time on closing bit 13 set if named pipe bit 12 set if no inherit bit 11 set if network spooler bits 5-0 drive number for disk files
07h	DWORD	pointer to device driver header if character device else pointer to DOS Drive Parameter Block (see 21/32h) or REDIR data
0Bh	WORD	starting cluster of file
0Dh	WORD	file time in packed format (see *21/5700h*)
0Fh	WORD	file date in packed format (see *21/5700h*)
11h	DWORD	file size
15h	DWORD	current offset in file

—local file—

19h	WORD	relative cluster within file of last cluster accessed
1Bh	DWORD	number of sector containing directory entry
1Fh	BYTE	number of dir entry within sector (byte offset/32)

—network redirector—

19h	DWORD	pointer to REDIRIFS record
1Dh	*3 BYTEs*	*unknown*

20h	11 BYTEs	filename in FCB format (no path/period, blank-padded)
2Bh	DWORD	(SHARE.EXE) pointer to previous SFT sharing sam file
2Fh	WORD	(SHARE.EXE) network machine number which opened file (Windows Enhanced mode DOSMGR uses the virtual machine ID as the machine number; see *2F/1683h*)
31h	WORD	PSP segment of file's owner (see 21/26h) (first three entries for AUX/CON/PRN contain segment of IO.SYS startup code)
33h	WORD	offset within SHARE.EXE code segment of sharing record (see above), 0000h if none
35h	WORD	(local) absolute cluster number of last clustr accessed *(redirector) unknown*
37h	DWORD	pointer to IFS driver for file, 0000000h if native DOS

Format of current directory structure (CDS) (array, LASTDRIVE entries):

Offset	Size	Description
00h	67 BYTEs	ASCIZ path in form X:\PATH (local) or \\MACH\PATH (network)
43h	WORD	drive attributes (see also note below and 21/5F07h)
		bit 15: uses network redirector } invalid if 00, installable
		14: physical drive } file system if 11
		13: JOIN'ed } path above is true path that would be
		12: SUBST'ed } needed if not under SUBST or JOIN
		7: redirector, but not network (e.g. CD-ROM)
45h	DWORD	pointer to Drive Parameter Block for drive (see 2/32h)

—local drives—

49h	WORD	starting cluster of current directory 0000h if root, FFFFh if never accessed
4Bh	*WORD*	*apparently always FFFFh*
4Dh	*WORD*	*apparently always FFFFh*

—network drives—

49h	DWORD	pointer to redirector or REDIRIFS record, or FFFFh:FFFFh
4Dh	*WORD*	*stored user data from 21/5F03h*

4Fh	WORD	offset in current directory path of backslash corresponding to root directory for drive. This value specifies how many characters to hide from the "CHDIR" and "GETDIR" calls; normally set to 2 to hide the drive letter and colon. SUBST, JOIN, and networks change it so that only the appropriate portion of the true path is visible to the user.

—DOS 4+—

51h	*BYTE*	*unknown, used by network*
52h	DWORD	pointer to IFS driver for this drive, 00000000h if native DOS
56h	*WORD*	*unknown*

Notes: The path for invalid drives is normally set to X:\, but may be empty after JOIN x: /D in DR-DOS 5.0 or NET USE x: /D in older LAN versions.

Normally, only one of bits 13&12 may be set together with bit 14, but DR-DOS 5.0 uses other combinations (see below)

Format of DR-DOS 5.0-6.0 current directory structure entry (array):

Offset	Size	Description
00h	67 BYTEs	ASCIZ pathname of actual root directory for this logical drive
43h	WORD	drive attributes
		1000h SUBSTed drive
		3000h JOINed drive
		4000h physical drive
		5000h ASSIGNed drive
		7000h JOINed drive
		8000h network drive
45h	BYTE	physical drive number (0=A:) if this logical drive is valid
46h	*BYTE*	*apparently flags for JOIN and ASSIGN*
47h	WORD	cluster number of start of parent directory (0000h if root)
49h	WORD	entry number of current directory in parent directory
4Bh	WORD	cluster number of start of current directory
4Dh	*WORD*	*used for media change detection*
4Fh	WORD	cluster number of SUBST/JOIN "root" directory
		0000h if physical root directory

Format of device driver header:

Offset	Size	Description
00h	WORD	pointer to next driver, offset=FFFFh if last driver
04h	WORD	device attributes

    Character device:
        bit 15 set
        bit 14 IOCTL supported (see 21/44h)
        bit 13 (DOS 3+) output until busy supported
        bit 12 reserved
        bit 11 (DOS 3+) OPEN/CLOSE/RemMedia calls supported
        bits 10-8 reserved
        bit 7 (DOS 5+) Generic IOCTL check call supported
                (command 19h)
        bit 6 (DOS 3.2+) Generic IOCTL call supported
                (command 13h)
        bit 5 reserved
        bit 4 device is special (use INT 29h "fast console output")
        bit 3 device is CLOCK$ (all reads/writes use transfer
        record described below)
        bit 2 device is NUL
        bit 1 device is standard output
        bit 0 device is standard input
    Block device:
        bit 15 clear
        bit 14 IOCTL supported
        bit 13 non-IBM format
        bit 12 reserved
        bit 11 (DOS 3+) OPEN/CLOSE/RemMedia calls supported

                    bit 10 reserved
bit 9   direct I/O not allowed
        (set by DOS 3.3 DRIVER.SYS for "new" drives)
bit 8   unknown, set by DOS 3.3 DRIVER.SYS for "new drives
      bit 7   (DOS 5+) Generic IOCTL check call supported
          (command 19h)
      bit 6   (DOS 3.2+) Generic IOCTL call supported
          (command 13h)
         implies support for commands 17h and 18h
      bits 5-2 reserved
      bit 1   (DOS 3.31+) driver supports 32-bit sector addressing
      bit 0   reserved

Offset	Size	Description
06h	WORD	device strategy entry point
		call with ES:BX pointer to request header (see 2F/0802h)
08h	WORD	device interrupt entry point

—character device—

Offset	Size	Description
0Ah	8 BYTEs	blank-padded character device name

—block device—

Offset	Size	Description
0Ah	BYTE	number of subunits (drives) supported by driver
0Bh	7 BYTEs	unused
—		
12h	WORD	(CD-ROM driver) reserved, must be 0000h
14h	BYTE	(CD-ROM driver) drive letter (must initially be 00h)
15h	BYTE	(CD-ROM driver) number of units
16h	6 BYTEs	(CD-ROM driver) signature 'MSCDnn' where 'nn' is version (currently '00')

Format of CLOCK$ transfer record:

Offset	Size	Description
00h	WORD	number of days since 1-Jan-1980
02h	BYTE	minutes
03h	BYTE	hours
04h	BYTE	hundredths of second
05h	BYTE	seconds

Format of DOS 2.x disk buffer:

Offset	Size	Description
00h	DWORD	pointer to next disk buffer, offset = FFFFh if last least-recently used buffer is first in chain
04h	BYTE	drive (0=A, 1=B, etc), FFh if not in use
05h	*3 BYTEs*	*apparently unused (seems always to be 00h 00h 01h)*
08h	WORD	logical sector number
0Ah	BYTE	number of copies to write (1 for non-FAT sectors)
0Bh	BYTE	sector offset between copies if multiple copies to be written
0Ch	DWORD	pointer to DOS Drive Parameter Block (see 21/32h)
10h		buffered data

Format of DOS 3.x disk buffer:

Offset	Size	Description
00h	DWORD	pointer to next disk buffer, offset = FFFFh if last least-recently used buffer is first in chain
04h	BYTE	drive (0=A,1=B, etc), FFh if not in use

05h	BYTE	flags
		bit 7: unknown
		bit 6: buffer dirty
		bit 5: buffer has been referenced
		bit 4: unknown
		bit 3: sector in data area
		bit 2: sector in a directory, either root or subdirectory
		bit 1: sector in FAT
		bit 0: boot sector
06h	WORD	logical sector number
08h	BYTE	number of copies to write (1 for non-FAT sectors)
09h	BYTE	sector offset between copies if multiple copies to be written
0Ah	DWORD	pointer to DOS Drive Parameter Block (see INT 21AH=32h)
0Eh	*WORD*	*apparently unused (almost always 0)*
10h	buffered data	

Format of DOS 4.00 (pre UR 25066) disk buffer info:

Offset	Size	Description
00h	DWORD	pointer to array of disk buffer hash chain heads (see below)
04h	WORD	number of disk buffer hash chains (referred to as NDBCH below)
06h	DWORD	pointer to look ahead buffer, zero if not present
0Ah	WORD	number of look ahead sectors, else zero (the y in BUFFERS=x,y)
0Ch	BYTE	00h if buffers in EMS (/X), FFh if not
0Dh	WORD	EMS handle for buffers, zero if not in EMS
0Fh	WORD	EMS physical page number used for buffers (usually 255)
11h	*WORD*	*apparently always 0001h*
13h	WORD	segment of EMS physical page frame
15h	*WORD*	*apparently always zero*
17h	*4 WORDs*	*EMS partial page mapping information*

Format of DOS 4.01
(from UR 25066 Corrective Services Disk on) disk buffer info:

Offset	Size	Description
00h	DWORD	pointer to array of disk buffer hash chain heads (see below)
04h	WORD	number of disk buffer hash chains (referred to as NDBCH below)
06h	DWORD	pointer to lookahead buffer, zero if not present
0Ah	WORD	number of lookahead sectors, else zero (the y in BUFFERS=x,y)
0Ch	BYTE	01h, possibly to distinguish from pre-UR 25066 format
0Dh	*WORD*	*EMS segment for BUFFERS (only with /XD)*
0Fh	*WORD*	*EMS physical page number of EMS seg above (only with /XD)*
11h	*WORD*	*EMS segment for unknown data (only with /XD)*
13h	*WORD*	*EMS physical page number of above (only with /XD)*
15h	*BYTE*	*number of EMS page frames present (only with /XD)*
16h	WORD	segment of one-sector workspace buffer allocated in main memory if BUFFERS/XS or /XD options in effect, possibly to avoid DMA into EMS
18h	WORD	EMS handle for buffers, zero if not in EMS
1Ah	WORD	EMS physical page number used for buffers (usually 255)
1Ch	*WORD*	*appears always to be 0001h*
1Eh	WORD	segment of EMS physical page frame
20h	*WORD*	*appears always to be zero*
22h	BYTE	00h if /XS, 01h if /XD, FFh if BUFFERS not in EMS

Format of DOS 4.x disk buffer hash chain head (array, one entry per chain):

Offset	Size	Description
00h	WORD	EMS logical page number in which chain is resident, -1 if not in EMS
02h	DWORD	pointer to least recently used buffer header. All buffers on this chain are in the same segment.
06h	BYTE	number of dirty buffers on this chain
07h	BYTE	reserved (00h)

Notes: Buffered disk sectors are assigned to chain N where N is the sector's address modulo number of disk buffer chain heads (NDBCH), 0 <= N <= NDBCH-1

Each buffer chain resides completely within one EMS page.

This structure is in main memory even if the buffers are in EMS.

Format of DOS 4.0-6.0 disk buffer:

Offset	Size	Description
00h	WORD	forward pointer, offset only, to next least recently used buffer
02h	WORD	backward pointer, offset only
04h	BYTE	drive (0=A,1=B, etc), FFh if not in use
05h	BYTE	flags
		bit 7: remote buffer
		bit 6: buffer dirty
		bit 5: buffer has been referenced
		bit 4: search data buffer (only valid if remote buffer)
		bit 3: sector in data area
		bit 2: sector in a directory, either root or subdirectory
		bit 1: sector in FAT
		bit 0: reserved
06h	DWORD	logical sector number
0Ah	BYTE	number of copies to write
		for FAT sectors, same as number of FATs
		for data and directory sectors, usually 1
0Bh	WORD	offset in sectors between copies to write for FAT sectors
0Dh	DWORD	pointer to DOS Drive Parameter Block (see 21/32h)
11h	WORD	buffer use count if remote buffer (see flags above)
13h	BYTE	reserved
14h		buffered data

Note: For DOS 4.x, all buffered sectors which have the same hash value (computed as the sum of high and low words of the logical sector number divided by NDBCH) are on the same doubly-linked circular chain; for DOS 5+, only a single circular chain exists.

The links between buffers consist of offset addresses only, the segment being the same for all buffers in the chain.

See BUFFERS.C in Chapter 8.

Format of DOS 5+ disk buffer info:

Offset	Size	Description
00h	DWORD	pointer to least-recently-used buffer header (may be in HMA) (see above)
04h	WORD	0000h (DOS 5 does not hash disk buffers, so offset 00h points directly at the only buffer chain)
06h	DWORD	pointer to lookahead buffer, zero if not present
0Ah	WORD	number of lookahead sectors, else zero (the y in BUFFERS=x,y)

0Ch	BYTE	buffer location 00h base memory, no workspace buffer 01h HMA, workspace buffer in base memory
0Dh	DWORD	pointer to one-segment workspace buffer in base memory
11h	3 BYTEs	apparently unused
14h	WORD	unknown
16h	*BYTE*	*unknown counter of flag*
17h	BYTE	temporary storage for user memory allocation strategy during EXEC
18h	BYTE	unknown counter
19h	BYTE	bit flags bit 0: unknown bit 1: SWITCHES=/W specified in CONFIG.SYS (don't auto load WINA20.386 when MS Windows 3.0 starts) bit 2: in EXEC state (21/4B05h)
1Ah	WORD	unknown offset (used only during 21/4B05h)
1Ch	BYTE	bit 0 set iff UMB MCB chain linked to normal MCB chain
1Dh	WORD	minimum paragraphs of memory required by program being EXECed
1Fh	WORD	segment of first MCB in upper memory blocks or FFFFh if DOS memory chain in base 640K only (the first UMB MCB is usually at 9FFFh, locking out video memory with a DOS-owned memory block).
21h	WORD	paragraph of start of most recent MCB chain search

Format of IFS driver list:

Offset	Size	Description
00h	DWORD	pointer to next driver header
04h	8 BYTEs	IFS driver name (blank padded), as used by FILESYS command
0Ch	*4 BYTEs*	*unknown*
10h	DWORD	pointer to IFS utility function entry point (see below) call with ES:BX pointer to IFS request (see below)
14h	WORD	offset in header's segment of driver entry point *possibly more*

Call IFS utility function entry point with:

AH   20h miscellaneous functions

   AL = 00h get date

      Returns:

CX	year
DH	month
DL	day

   AL = 01h get process ID and computer ID

      Returns:

BX	current PSP segment
DX	active network machine number

   AL = 05h get file system info

      ES:DI   pointer to 16-byte info buffer

      Returns:

      buffer filled

Offset	Size	Description
00h	2 BYTEs	unused

02h	WORD	number of SFTs (actually counts only the first two file table arrays)
04h	WORD	number of FCB table entries
06h	WORD	number of protected FCBs
08h	6 BYTEs	unused
0Eh	WORD	largest sector size supported

AL = 06h get machine name
    ES:DI   pointer to 18-byte buffer for name
Returns:
    buffer filled with name starting at offset 02h
AL = 08h get sharing retry count
Returns:
    BX   sharing retry count
AL = other
Returns:
    CF set

AH	20h	
	AL = 00h	
	...	
	...	
	AL = other	
	Returns:	
	CF set	
AH	21h get redirection state	
	BH	type ...
	Returns:	
	BH	state
AH	22h appears to be a time calculation	
	AL = 00h ...	
	nonzero ...	
AH	23h ...	
AH	24h ...	
	DS:SI	
	ES:DI	
	Returns:	
	ZF ...	
AH	25h ...	
	DS:SI	
	ES:DI	
	Returns:	
	filename...	
AH	26h	
	Returns:	
	...	
AH	27h	
AH	28h	

Note: IFS drivers which do not wish to implement functions 20h or 24h-28h may pass them on to the default handler pointed at by [LoL+37h].

Format of IFS request block:

Offset	Size	Description
00h	WORD	total size in bytes of request
02h	BYTE	class of request

		02h unknown
		03h redirection
		04h unknown
		05h file access
		06h convert error code to string
		07h unknown
03h	WORD	returned DOS error code
05h	BYTE	IFS driver exit status
		00h success
		01h unknown
		02h unknown
		03h unknown
		04h unknown
		FFh internal failure
06h	*16 BYTEs*	*unknown*

—request class 02h—

16h	BYTE	function code
		04h unknown
17h	*BYTE*	*apparently unused*
18h	*DWORD*	*pointer to unknown item*
1Ch	*DWORD*	*pointer to unknown item*
20h	*2 BYTEs*	*unknown*

—request class 03h—

16h	BYTE	function code
17h	*BYTE*	*unknown*
18h	*DWORD*	*pointer to unknown item*
1Ch	*DWORD*	*pointer to unknown item*
22h	*WORD*	*unknown returned value*
24h	*WORD*	*unknown returned value*
26h	*WORD*	*unknown returned value*
28h	*BYTE*	*unknown returned value*
29h	*BYTE*	*apparently unused*

—request class 04h—

16h	*DWORD*	*unknown pointer*
1Ah	*DWORD*	*unknown pointer*

—request class 05h—

16h	BYTE	function code
		01h flush disk buffers
		02h get disk space
		03h MKDIR
		04h RMDIR
		05h CHDIR
		06h delete file
		07h rename file
		08h search directory
		09h file open/create
		0Ah LSEEK
		0Bh read from file
		0Ch write to file
		0Dh lock region of file

0Eh commit/close file
0Fh get/set file attributes
10h printer control
11h unknown
12h process termination
13h unknown

—class 05h function 01h—

17h	*7 BYTEs*	*unknown*
1Eh	*DWORD*	*unknown pointer*
22h	*4 BYTEs*	*unknown*
26h	*BYTE*	*unknown*
27h	*BYTE*	*unknown*

—class 05h function 02h—

17h	*7 BYTEs*	*unknown*
1Eh	*DWORD*	*unknown pointer*
22h	*4 BYTEs*	*unknown*
26h	WORD	returned total clusters
28h	WORD	returned sectors per cluster
2Ah	WORD	returned bytes per sector
2Ch	WORD	returned available clusters
2Eh	*BYTE*	*unknown returned value*
2Fh	*BYTE*	*unknown*

—class 05h functions 03h,04h,05h—

17h	*7 BYTEs*	*unknown*
1Eh	*DWORD*	*unknown pointer*
22h	*4 BYTEs*	*unknown*
26h	DWORD	pointer to directory name

—class 05h function 06h—

17h	*7 BYTEs*	*unknown*
1Eh	*DWORD*	*unknown pointer*
22h	*4 BYTEs*	*unknown*
26h	WORD	attribute mask
28h	DWORD	pointer to filename

—class 05h function 07h—

17h	*7 BYTEs*	*unknown*
1Eh	*DWORD*	*unknown pointer*
22h	*4 BYTEs*	*unknown*
26h	WORD	attribute mask
28h	DWORD	pointer to source filespec
2Ch	DWORD	pointer to destination filespec

—class 05h function 08h—

17h	*7 BYTEs*	*unknown*
1Eh	*DWORD*	*unknown pointer*
22h	*4 BYTEs*	*unknown*
26h	BYTE	00h FINDFIRST
		01h FINDNEXT
28h	DWORD	pointer to FindFirst search data + 01h if FINDNEXT
2Ch	WORD	search attribute if FINDFIRST
2Eh	DWORD	pointer to filespec if FINDFIRST

—class 05h function 09h—

17h	*7 BYTEs*	*unknown*

1Eh	*DWORD*	*unknown pointer*
22h	DWORD	pointer to IFS open file structure (see below)
26h	*WORD*	*unknown* } *together, specify open vs. create, whether or*
28h	*WORD*	*unknown* } *not to truncate*
2Ah	*4 BYTEs*	*unknown*
2Eh	DWORD	pointer to filename
32h	*4 BYTEs*	*unknown*
36h	WORD	file attributes on call
		unknown returned value
38h	*WORD*	*unknown returned value*

—class 05h function 0Ah—

17h	*7 BYTEs*	*unknown*
1Eh	*DWORD*	*unknown pointer*
22h	*DWORD*	*pointer to IFS open file structure (see below)*
26h	BYTE	seek type (02h=from end)
28h	DWORD	offset on call
		returned new absolute position

—class 05h functions 0Bh,0Ch—

17h	*7 BYTEs*	*unknown*
1Eh	*DWORD*	*unknown pointer*
22h	DWORD	pointer to IFS open file structure (see below)
28h	WORD	number of bytes to transfer
		returned bytes actually transferred
2Ah	DWORD	transfer address

—class 05h function 0Dh—

17h	*7 BYTEs*	*unknown*
1Eh	*DWORD*	*unknown pointer*
22h	DWORD	pointer to IFS open file structure (see below)
26h	*BYTE*	*file handle*
27h	*BYTE*	*apparently unused*
28h	WORD	*unknown*
2Ah	*WORD*	*unknown*
2Ch	*WORD*	*unknown*
2Eh	*WORD*	*unknown*

—class 05h function 0Eh—

17h	*7 BYTEs*	*unknown*
1Eh	*DWORD*	*unknown pointer*
22h	DWORD	pointer to IFS open file structure (see below)
26h	BYTE	00h commit file
		01h close file
27h	*BYTE*	*apparently unused*

—class 05h function 0Fh—

17h	*7 BYTEs*	*unknown*
1Eh	*DWORD*	*unknown pointer*
22h	*4 BYTEs*	*unknown*
26h	BYTE	02h GET attributes
		03h PUT attributes
27h	*BYTE*	*apparently unused*
28h	*12 BYTEs*	*unknown*
34h	*WORD*	*search attributes*
36h	DWORD	pointer to filename

3Ah	*WORD*	*(GET) unknown returned value*
3Ch	*WORD*	*(GET) unknown returned value*
3Eh	*WORD*	*(GET) unknown returned value*
40h	*WORD*	*(GET) unknown returned value*
42h	*WORD*	*(PUT) new attributes*
		(GET) returned attributes

—class 05h function 10h—

17h	*7 BYTEs*	*unknown*
1Eh	*DWORD*	*unknown pointer*
22h	DWORD	pointer to IFS open file structure (see below)
26h	*WORD*	*unknown*
28h	*DWORD*	*unknown pointer*
2Ch	*WORD*	*unknown*
2Eh	*BYTE*	*unknown*
2Fh	BYTE	subfunction
		01h get printer setup
		03h unknown
		04h unknown
		05h unknown
		06h unknown
		07h unknown
		21h set printer setup

—class 05h function 11h—

17h	*7 BYTEs*	*unknown*
1Eh	*DWORD*	*unknown pointer*
22h	DWORD	pointer to IFS open file structure (see below)
26h	BYTE	subfunction
27h	*BYTE*	*apparently unused*
28h	*WORD*	*unknown*
2Ah	*WORD*	*unknown*
2Ch	*WORD*	*unknown*
2Eh	*BYTE*	*unknown*
2Fh	*BYTE*	*unknown*

—class 05h function 12h—

17h	*15 BYTEs*	*apparently unused*
26h	WORD	PSP segment
28h	BYTE	type of process termination
29h	*BYTE*	*apparently unused*

—class 05h function 13h—

17h	*15 BYTEs*	*apparently unused*
26h	WORD	PSP segment

—request class 06h—

16h	DWORD	returned pointer to string corresponding to error code at 03h
1Ah	*BYTE*	*unknown returned value*
1Bh	BYTE	unused

—request class 07h—

16h	DWORD	pointer to IFS open file structure (see below)
1Ah	*BYTE*	*unknown*
1Bh	*BYTE*	*apparently unused*

Format of IFS open file structure:

Offset	Size	Description
00h	WORD	unknown
02h	WORD	device info word
04h	WORD	file open mode

Offset	Size	Description
06h	*WORD*	*unknown*
08h	WORD	file attributes
0Ah	WORD	owner's network machine number
0Ch	WORD	owner's PSP segment
0Eh	DWORD	file size
12h	DWORD	current offset in file
16h	WORD	file time
18h	WORD	file date
1Ah	11 BYTEs	filename in FCB format
25h	*WORD*	*unknown*
27h	WORD	hash value of SFT address (low word of linear address + segment &F000h)
29h	3 WORDs	network info from SFT
2Fh	*WORD*	*unknown*

Format of one item in DOS 4+ list of special program names:

Offset	Size	Description
00h	BYTE	length of name (00h is end of list)
01h	N BYTEs	name in format name.ext
N	2 BYTEs	DOS version to return for program (major,minor) (see 21/30h, 2F/122Fh)

—DOS 4 only—

N+2	BYTE	number of times to return fake version number (FFh if always)

Note: If the name of the executable for the program making the DOS "get version" call matches one of the names in this list, DOS returns the specified version rather than the true version number.

INT 21h Function 53h   DOS 2+
Translate Bios Parameter Block To Drive Parameter Block

Compute the information in a Drive Parameter Block from the information in the given BIOS Parameter Block.

Call With:

AH	53h	
DS:SI	pointer to BIOS Parameter Block (see below)	
ES:BP	pointer to buffer for Drive Parameter Block (see 21/32h for format)	

Returns:

ES:BP buffer filled

Note: For DOS 3+, the cluster at which to start searching is set to 0000h and the number of free clusters is set to FFFFh (unknown).

Format of BIOS Parameter Block:

Offset	Size	Description
00h	WORD	number of bytes per sector
02h	BYTE	number of sectors per cluster
03h	WORD	number of reserved sectors at start of disk
05h	BYTE	number of FATs
06h	WORD	number of entries in root directory
08h	WORD	total number of sectors
		for DOS 4+, set to zero if partition >32M, then set DWORD at 15h to actual number of sectors
0Ah	BYTE	media ID byte
0Bh	WORD	number of sectors per FAT

—DOS 3+—

0Dh	WORD	number of sectors per track
0Fh	WORD	number of heads
11h	DWORD	number of hidden sectors
15h	11 BYTEs	reserved

—DOS 4+—

15h	DWORD	total number of sectors if word at 08h contains zero
19h	*6 BYTEs*	*unknown*
1Fh	WORD	number of cylinders
21h	BYTE	device type
22h	WORD	device attributes (removable or not, etc)

INT 21h Function 55h   DOS 2+
CREATE CHILD PSP

Create a child Program Segment Prefix with the specified amount of available memory, and place it at a given location.

Call With:

> AH   55h
>
> DX   segment at which to create new PSP
>
> SI   (DOS 3+) value to place in memory size field at DX:[0002h]

Returns:

> CF clear if successful

Notes: This function creates a "child" PSP rather than making an exact copy of the current PSP; the new PSP's parent pointer is set to the current PSP and the reference count for each inherited file is incremented.

> (DOS 2+) The current PSP is set to the segment in DX.
>
> (DOS 3+) "No inherit" file handles are marked as closed in the child PSP.

See Also: 21/26h, 21/50h

INT 21h Function 56h   DOS 2+
"RENAME" - RENAME FILE

Although documented, this call has the undocumented behavior of allowing wildcards in both source and destination when invoked via 21/5D00h.

Call With:

> AH   56h
>
> DS:DX pointer to ASCIZ filename of existing file (no wildcards, but see below)
>
> ES:DI   pointer to ASCIZ new filename (no wildcards)
>
> CL   attribute mask (server call only, see below)

Returns:

> CF clear if successful
>
> CF set on error
>
>   AX   error code (02h,03h,05h,11h) (see *21/59h*)

Notes: This function allows a file to be moved between directories on a single logical volume.

> Open files should not be renamed.
>
> DOS 3+ allows renaming of directories.
>
> For DOS 3.1+, wildcards are allowed if invoked via 21/5D00h, in which case error 12h (no more files) is returned on success, and both source and destination specs must be canonical (as returned by 21/60h). Wildcards in the destination are replaced by the corresponding char of each source file being renamed. Under DOS 3.x, the call will fail if the destination wildcard is *.* or equivalent. When invoked via 21/5D00h, only those files matching the attribute mask in CL are renamed.

See Also: *21/17h*, 21/5D00h, 21/60h

INT 21h Functions 5702h-5705h   DOS 4.x, OS/2, Chicago
EXTENDED FILE ATTRIBUTE FUNCTIONS

In the DOS box of OS/2 1.1 and higher, 21/5702 gets the Extended Attributes (EAs) for a file, corresponding to the OS/2 DosQueryPathInfo and DosQueryFileInfo API functions. Likewise, 21/5703 sets the EAs, corresponding to DosSetFileInfo and DosSetPathInfo. Programs that hook the normal MS-DOS 21/57 Get/Set File Date/Time functions should explicitly ignore these OS/2 EA functions. For more information, see chapter 4, and the interrupt list on disk.

In DOS 4.x only (i.e., *not* DOS 5 or 6), 21/5702 and 21/5703 also manipulate EAs. 21/5704 has been reported in DOS 4.x as both "Truncate Open File to Zero Length" and "Set Extended Attributes." In DOS 4.x, 21/5703 and 21/5704 issue a 2F/112D call to IFSFUNC.EXE. Under "Chicago" (DOS 7, Windows 4), 21/5704 and 21/5705 will be the INT 21h equivalents of the Win32 GetFileTime and SetFileTime API functions. Preliminary Chicago documentation marks 21/57 subfunctions 2 and 3 as "reserved," neatly skipping over the two OS/2 EA functions.

INT 21h Function 5D00h   DOS 3.1+
SERVER FUNCTION CALL

Execute a specified INT 21h call using the sharing rules for the specified network machine number and process ID.

Call With:
   AX   5D00h
   DS:DX   pointer to DOS parameter list (see below)
   DPL contains all register values for a call to INT 21h

Returns:
   as appropriate for function being called

Notes: This function does not check the specified value for AH; out of range values will crash the system.

The DOS call executes using specified computer ID and process ID; sharing delay loops are skipped, a special sharing mode is enabled, wildcards are enabled for DELETE (21/41h) and RENAME (21/56h), and an extra file attribute parameter is enabled for OPEN (*21/3Dh*), DELETE (21/41h), and RENAME (21/56h).

Functions which take filenames require canonical names (as returned by 21/60h) when invoked by this method; this is apparently to prevent multi-hop file forwarding.

See Also: *21/3Dh*, 21/41h, 21/56h, 21/60h

Format of DOS parameter list:

Offset	Size	Description
00h	WORD	AX
02h	WORD	BX
04h	WORD	CX
06h	WORD	DX
08h	WORD	SI
0Ah	WORD	DI
0Ch	WORD	DS
0Eh	WORD	ES
10h	WORD	reserved (0)
12h	WORD	computer ID (0000h for current system)
14h	WORD	process ID (PSP segment on specified computer)

Note: Under Windows Enhanced mode, the computer ID is the virtual machine ID (see *2F/1683h*).

INT 21h Function 5D01h   DOS 3.1+
COMMIT ALL FILES FOR SPECIFIED COMPUTER/PROCESS

Flush all disk buffers and update the directory entry for each file which has been written to since opening or the last commit.

Call With:

AX	5D01h
DS:DX	pointer to DOS parameter list (see 21/5D00h), only computer ID and process ID fields used

Returns:

CF set on error
   AX   error code (see *21/59h*)
CF clear if successful

Notes: This function flushes disk buffers and updates directory entries for each file which has been written to; if the file is remote, it calls 2F/1107h.

The computer ID and process ID are stored but ignored under DOS 3.3.

See Also: *21/0Dh*, *21/68h*, *2F/1107h*

INT 21h Function 5D02h   DOS 3.1+
SHARE.EXE - CLOSE FILE BY NAME

Close a file given its fully-qualified name.

Call With:

AX	5D02h
DS:DX	pointer to DOS parameter list (see 21/5D00h), only fields DX, DS, computer ID, and process ID used
DPL's DS:DX	pointer to ASCIZ name of file to close

Returns:

CF set on error
   AX   error code (see *21/59h*)
CF clear if successful

Notes: This function returns an error unless SHARE is loaded (it calls [SysFileTable-28h]) (see 21/52h).

The name must be a canonical fully-qualified name, such as is returned by 21/60h.

See Also: *21/3Eh*, *21/5D03h*, *21/5D04h*, *21/60h*

INT 21h Function 5D03h   DOS 3.1+
SHARE.EXE - CLOSE ALL FILES FOR GIVEN COMPUTER

Close all files which were opened using a particular network machine number.

Call With:

AX	5D03h
DS:DX	pointer to DOS parameter list (see 21/5D00h), only computer ID used

Returns:

CF set on error
   AX   error code (see *21/59h*)
CF clear if successful

Note: This function returns an error unless SHARE is loaded (it calls [SysFileTable-30h]) (see 21/52h).

See Also: 21/5D02h, 21/5D04h

INT 21h Function 5D04h
SHARE.EXE - CLOSE ALL FILES FOR GIVEN PROCESS

DOS 3.1+

Close all files which were opened by a particular process.

Call With:

AX	5D04h
DS:DX	pointer to DOS parameter list (see 21/5D00h), only computer ID and process ID fields used

Returns:

CF set on error

    AX   error code (see *21/59h*)

CF clear if successful

Note: This function returns an error unless SHARE is loaded (it calls [SysFileTable-2Ch]) (see 21/52h).

See Also: 21/5D02h, 21/5D03h

INT 21h Function 5D05h
SHARE.EXE - GET OPEN FILE LIST ENTRY

DOS 3.1+

Return the filename and some additional information about a specified entry in SHARE's internal data structures.

Call With:

AX	5D05h
DS:DX	pointer to DOS parameter list (see 21/5D00h)
DPL's BX	index of sharing record (see 21/52h)
DPL's CX	index of SFT in sharing record's SFT list

Returns:

CF clear if successful

    ES:DI   pointer to ASCIZ filename

    BX   network machine number of SFT's owner

    CX   number of locks held by SFT's owner

CF set if either index out of range

    AX   0012h (no more files)

Notes: This function returns an error unless SHARE is loaded (it calls [SysFileTable-18h]) (see 21/52h).

    The returned names are always canonical fully-qualified, such as returned by 21/60h.

See Also: *21/5Ch*, 21/60h

INT 21h Function 5D06h
GET ADDRESS OF DOS SWAPPABLE DATA AREA

DOS 3.0+

Return the address and size of the region which must be swapped out and restored to allow DOS to be reentered.

Call With:

    AX   5D06h

Returns:

CF set on error

    AX   error code (see *21/59h*)

CF clear if successful

    DS:SI   pointer to nonreentrant data area (includes all three DOS stacks)

    CX   size in bytes of area which must be swapped while in DOS

    DX   size in bytes of area which must always be swapped

Notes: The Critical Error flag is used in conjunction with the InDOS flag (see 21/34h) to determine when it is safe to enter DOS from a TSR.

Setting the CritErr flag allows the use of functions 50h/51h from INT 28h under DOS 2.x by forcing use of correct stack.

Swapping the data area allows reentering DOS unless DOS is in a critical section delimited by 2A/80h and 2A/81h,82h.

Under DOS 4.x, 21/5D0Bh should be used instead of this function; the DOS 5+ swappable data area is also described under that call.

SHARE and other DOS utilities determine the SDA format in use by examining the byte at offset 04h in the DOS data segment (see INT 2Fh/AX=1203h). A value of 00h indicates a DOS 3.x SDA, 01h indicates DOS 4.0-6.0, and other values are an error. See PSPTEST.C in Chapter 4.

See Also: 21/5D0Bh, 2A/80h, 2A/81h, 2A/82h

Format of DOS 3.10-3.30 Swappable Data Area:

Offset	Size	Description
-11	5 WORDs	zero-terminated list of offsets which need to be patched to enabled critical-section calls (see 2A/80h) (not actually part of the SDA)
00h	BYTE	critical error flag
01h	BYTE	InDOS flag (count of active INT 21h calls)
02h	BYTE	drive on which current critical error occurred, or FFh
03h	BYTE	locus of last error
04h	WORD	extended error code of last error
06h	BYTE	suggested action for last error
07h	BYTE	class of last error
08h	DWORD	ES:DI pointer for last error
0Ch	DWORD	current DTA
10h	WORD	current PSP
12h	WORD	stores SP across an INT 23h
14h	WORD	return code from last process termination (cleared after reading with 21/4Dh; e.g. by COMMAND.COM)
16h	BYTE	current drive
17h	BYTE	extended break flag

—remainder need only be swapped if in DOS—

Offset	Size	Description
18h	WORD	value of AX on call to INT 21h
1Ah	WORD	PSP segment for sharing/network
1Ch	WORD	network machine number for sharing/network (0000h=caller)
1Eh	WORD	first usable memory block found when allocating memory
20h	WORD	best usable memory block found when allocating memory
22h	WORD	last usable memory block found when allocating memory
24h	WORD	memory size in paragraphs (used only during initialization)
26h	*WORD*	*unknown*
28h	BYTE	INT 24h returned Fail
29h	BYTE	bit flags for allowable actions on INT 24h
2Ah	*BYTE*	*unknown flag*
2Bh	BYTE	FFh if Ctrl-Break termination, 00h otherwise
2Ch	*BYTE*	*unknown flag*
2Dh	*BYTE*	*apparently not referenced*
2Eh	BYTE	day of month
2Fh	BYTE	month
30h	WORD	year - 1980
32h	WORD	number of days since 1-1-1980

34h	BYTE	day of week (0 for Sunday)
35h	*BYTE*	*working SFT pointer at SDA+2AAh is valid*
36h	BYTE	safe to call INT 28h if nonzero
37h	BYTE	flag: if nonzero, INT 24h abort turned into INT 24h fail (set only during process termination)
38h	26 BYTEs	device driver request header (See 2F/0802)
52h	DWORD	pointer to device driver entry point (used in calling driver)
56h	22 BYTEs	device driver request header
6Ch	22 BYTEs	device driver request header
82h	BYTE	type of PSP copy (00h=simple for 21/26h, FFh=make child)
83h	*BYTE*	*apparently not referenced by kernel*
84h	3 BYTEs	24-bit user number (see 21/30h)
87h	BYTE	OEM number (see 21/30h)
88h	*2 BYTEs*	*unknown*
8Ah	6 BYTEs	CLOCK$ transfer record (see 21/52h)
90h	*BYTE*	*buffer for single-byte I/O functions*
91h	*BYTE*	*apparently not referenced by kernel*
92h	128 BYTEs	buffer for filename
112h	128 BYTEs	buffer for filename
192h	21 BYTEs	findfirst/findnext search data block (see 21/4Eh)
1A7h	32 BYTEs	directory entry for found file
1C7h	81 BYTEs	copy of current directory structure for drive being accessed
218h	11 BYTEs	FCB-format filename for device name comparison
223h	*BYTE*	*apparently unused*
224h	11 BYTEs	wildcard destination specification for rename (FCB format)
22Fh	*2 BYTEs*	*unknown*
231h	*WORD*	*unknown*
233h	*5 BYTEs*	*unknown*
238h	BYTE	extended FCB file attribute (find first search attribute)
239h	BYTE	type of FCB (00h regular, FFh extended)
23Ah	BYTE	directory search attributes
23Bh	*BYTE*	*file open mode*
23Ch	*BYTE*	*unknown flags, bits 0 and 4*
23Dh	*BYTE*	*unknown flag or counter*
23Eh	*BYTE*	*unknown flag*
23Fh	BYTE	flag indicating how DOS function was invoked (00h if direct INT 20h/INT 21h, FFh if server call INT21/AX=5D00h)
240h	*BYTE*	*unknown*
241h	*BYTE*	*unknown flag*
242h	BYTE	flag: 00h if read, 01h if write
243h	*BYTE*	*unknown drive number*
244h	*BYTE*	*unknown*
245h	*BYTE*	*unknown flag or counter*
246h	BYTE	line edit (21/0Ah) insert mode flag (nonzero when on)
247h	BYTE	canonicalized filename referred to existing file/dir if FFh
248h	*BYTE*	*unknown flag or counter*
249h	BYTE	type of process termination (00h-03h) (see *21/4Dh*)
24Ah	*BYTE*	*unknown flag*
24Bh	BYTE	value with which to replace first byte of deleted file's name (normally E5h, but 00h as described under 21/13h)
24Ch	DWORD	pointer to Drive Parameter Block for critical error invocation
250h	DWORD	pointer to stack frame containing user registers on INT 21h
254h	WORD	stores SP across INT 24h

256h	*DWORD*	*pointer to DOS Drive Parameter Block for unknown use*
25Ah	*WORD*	*unknown*
25Ch	*WORD*	*unknown temporary*
25Eh	*WORD*	*unknown flag (only low byte referenced)*
260h	*WORD*	*unknown temporary*
262h	BYTE	Media ID byte returned by *21/1Bh, 21/1Ch*
263h	BYTE	apparently not referenced by kernel
264h	DWORD	pointer to device header
268h	DWORD	pointer to current SFT
26Ch	DWORD	pointer to current directory structure for drive being accessed
270h	DWORD	pointer to caller's FCB
274h	WORD	number of SFT to which file being opened will refer
276h	WORD	temporary storage for file handle
278h	DWORD	pointer to a JFT entry in process handle table (see INT21/AH=26h)
27Ch	WORD	offset in DOS DS of first filename argument
27Eh	WORD	offset in DOS DS of second filename argument
280h	WORD	offset of last component in pathname or FFFFh
282h	*WORD*	*offset of transfer address*
284h	*WORD*	*relative cluster within file being accessed*
286h	*WORD*	*absolute cluster number being accessed*
288h	*WORD*	*current sector number*
28Ah	*WORD*	*current cluster number*
28Ch	*WORD*	*current offset in file DIV bytes per sector*
28Eh	*2 BYTEs*	*unknown*
290h	*WORD*	*current offset in file MOD bytes per sector*
292h	DWORD	current offset in file
296h	*WORD*	*unknown*
298h	*WORD*	*unknown*
29Ah	*WORD*	*unknown*
29Ch	*WORD*	*unknown*
29Eh	*WORD*	*unknown*
2A0h	*WORD*	*unknown*
2A2h	DWORD	number of bytes appended to file
2A6h	*DWORD*	*pointer to unknown disk buffer*
2AAh	DWORD	pointer to working SFT
2AEh	WORD	used by INT 21h dispatcher to store caller's BX
2B0h	WORD	used by INT 21h dispatcher to store caller's DS
2B2h	WORD	temporary storage while saving/restoring caller's registers
2B4h	DWORD	pointer to prev call frame (offset 250h) if INT 21h reentered also switched to for duration of INT 24h
2B8h	21 BYTEs	FindFirst search data for source file(s) of a rename operation (see 21/4Eh)
2CDh	32 BYTEs	directory entry for file being renamed
2EDh	331 BYTEs	critical error stack
403h	35 BYTEs	scratch SFT
438h	384 BYTEs	disk stack (functions greater than 0Ch, INT 25h,INT 26h)
5B8h	384 BYTEs	character I/O stack (functions 01h through 0Ch)
—DOS 3.2,3.3 only—		
738h	BYTE	device driver lookahead flag (see 21/64h)
739h	*BYTE*	*apparently a drive number*
73Ah	*BYTE*	*unknown flag*
73Ah	*BYTE*	*unknown*

Note: for the DOS 4 SDA, see 21/5D0B; for the DOS 5+ SDA, use 21/5D06 but see 21/5D0B for the structure.

INT 21h Function 5D07h   DOS 3.1+ network
GET REDIRECTED PRINTER MODE

Determine whether redirected printer output is treated as a single print job or as multiple print jobs.
Call With:
   AX   5D07h
Returns:
   DL   mode
               00h redirected output is combined
               01h redirected output in separate print jobs
Note: Functions 5D07h through 5D09h all use the same code, which invokes 2F/1125h with the supplied AX on top of the stack.
See Also: 21/5D08h, 21/5D09h, 2F/1125h

INT 21h Function 5D08h   DOS 3.1+ network
SET REDIRECTED PRINTER MODE

Specify whether redirected printer output should be treated as a single print job or as multiple print jobs.

Call With:
   AX   5D08h
   DL   mode
               00h redirected output is combined
               01h redirected output placed in separate jobs, start new print job now
Notes: Called by COMMAND.COM.
   Functions 5D07h through 5D09h all invoke INT 2F/AX = 1125h with AX on top of the stack.
See Also: 21/5D07h, 21/5D09h, 2F/1125h

INT 21h Function 5D09h   DOS 3.1+ network
FLUSH REDIRECTED PRINTER OUTPUT

Force all redirected printer output to be sent to the printer, and start a new print job.
Call With:
   AX   5D09h
Notes: (same as previous entry)
See Also: 21/5D07h, 21/5D08h, 2F/1125h

INT 21h Function 5D0Ah   DOS 3.1+
SET EXTENDED ERROR INFORMATION

Set the values to be returned by the next "Get Extended Error Code" call.

Call With:
   AX   5D0Ah
   DS:DX   pointer to 11-word DOS parameter list (see 21/5D00h)
Returns:
               Nothing; next call to 21/59h will return values from fields AX,BX,CX,
               DX,DI, and ES in corresponding registers
Note: This function was undocumented prior to the release of DOS 5.0. The *MS-DOS Programmer's Reference* states that this call was introduced in DOS 4.0, but it was present as early as version

3.1. The MS-DOS 5.0 programmer's reference also incorrectly states that the parameter list goes in DS:SI rather than in DS:DX.
See Also: *21/59h*

INT 21h Function 5D0Bh   DOS 4.x only
GET DOS SWAPPABLE DATA AREAS

Return the address of a list of regions which must be swapped out and restored to allow DOS to be reentered. Use function 5D06h for DOS 3.x and 5+ even though the 5+ data structure is listed here, because the layout is the same as in DOS 4.x.

Call With:
>   AX   5D0Bh

Returns:
>   CF set on error
>   AX   error code (see *21/59h*)
>   CF clear if successful
>   DS:SI pointer to swappable data area list (see below)

Note: Copying and restoring the swappable data areas allows DOS to be reentered unless it is in a critical section delimited by calls to 2A/80h and 2A/81h,82h.

SHARE and other DOS utilities determine the SDA format in use by examining the byte at offset 04h in the DOS data segment (see INT 2Fh/AX=1203h). A value of 00h indicates a DOS 3.x SDA, 01h indicates DOS 4.0-6.0, and other values are an error.

See Also: 21/5D06h, 2A/80h, 2A/81h, 2A/82h

Format of DOS 4.x swappable data area list:

Offset	Size	Description
00h	WORD	count of data areas
02h	N BYTEs	"count" copies of data area record

Offset	Size	Description
00h	DWORD	address
04h	WORD	length and type
		bit 15 set if swap always, clear if swap in DOS
		bits 14-0: length in bytes

Format of DOS 4.0-6.0 swappable data area:

Offset	Size	Description
-11	5 WORDs	zero-terminated list of offsets which need to be patched to enabled critical-section calls (see 2A/80h) (not actually part of the SDA; all offsets are 0D0Ch, but this list is still present for DOS 3.x compatibility)
00h	BYTE	critical error flag
01h	BYTE	InDOS flag (count of active INT 21h calls)
02h	BYTE	drive on which current critical error occurred or FFh
03h	BYTE	locus of last error
04h	WORD	extended error code of last error
06h	BYTE	suggested action for last error
07h	BYTE	class of last error
08h	DWORD	ES:DI pointer for last error
0Ch	DWORD	current DTA
10h	WORD	current PSP
12h	WORD	stores SP across an INT 23h

14h	WORD	return code from last process termination (cleared after reading with 21/4Dh; e.g. by COMMAND.COM)
16h	BYTE	current drive
17h	BYTE	extended break flag
18h	*2 BYTEs*	*unknown*

—remainder need only be swapped if in DOS—

1Ah	WORD	value of AX on call to INT 21h
1Ch	WORD	PSP segment for sharing/network
1Eh	WORD	network machine number for sharing/network (0000h=caller)
20h	WORD	first usable memory block found when allocating memory
22h	WORD	best usable memory block found when allocating memory
24h	WORD	last usable memory block found when allocating memory
26h	WORD	memory size in paragraphs (used only during initialization)
28h	*WORD*	*unknown*
2Ah	*BYTE*	*unknown*
2Bh	*BYTE*	*unknown*
2Ch	*BYTE*	*unknown*
2Dh	*BYTE*	*unknown*
2Eh	*BYTE*	*unknown*
2Fh	*BYTE*	*apparently not referenced by kernel*
30h	BYTE	day of month
31h	BYTE	month
32h	WORD	year - 1980
34h	WORD	number of days since 1-1-1980
36h	BYTE	day of week (0 for Sunday)
37h	*BYTE*	*unknown*
38h	*BYTE*	*unknown*
39h	*BYTE*	*unknown*
3Ah	30 BYTEs	device driver request header (see 2F/0802h)
58h	DWORD	pointer to device driver entry point (used in calling driver)
5Ch	22 BYTEs	device driver request header
72h	30 BYTEs	device driver request header
90h	*6 BYTEs*	*unknown*
96h	6 BYTEs	CLOCK$ transfer record (see 21/52h)
9Ch	*2 BYTEs*	*unknown*
9Eh	128 BYTEs	buffer for filename
11Eh	128 BYTEs	buffer for filename
19Eh	21 BYTEs	findfirst/findnext search data block (see 21/4Eh)
1B3h	32 BYTEs	directory entry for found file
1D3h	88 BYTEs	copy of current directory structure for drive being accessed
22Bh	11 BYTEs	FCB-format filename for device name comparison
236h	*BYTE*	*unknown*
237h	11 BYTEs	wildcard destination specification for rename (FCB format)
242h	*2 BYTEs*	*unknown*
244h	*WORD*	*unknown*
246h	*5 BYTEs*	*unknown*
24Bh	BYTE	extended FCB file attributes (find first search attributes)
24Ch	BYTE	type of FCB (00h regular, FFh extended)
24Dh	BYTE	directory search attributes
24Eh	BYTE	file open mode
24Fh	*BYTE*	*unknown flag bits*
250h	*BYTE*	*unknown flag or counter*
251h	*BYTE*	*unknown flag*

252h	BYTE	flag indicating how DOS function was invoked (00h if direct INT 20h/INT 21h, FFh if server call INT21/AX=5D00h)
253h	*BYTE*	*unknown*
254h	*BYTE*	*unknown*
255h	*BYTE*	*unknown*
256h	*BYTE*	*unknown*
257h	*BYTE*	*unknown*
258h	*BYTE*	*unknown*
259h	*BYTE*	*unknown*
25Ah	BYTE	canonicalized filename referred to existing file/dir if FFh
25Bh	*BYTE*	*unknown*
25Ch	BYTE	type of process termination (00h-03h; TSR=3)
25Dh	*BYTE*	*unknown*
25Eh	*BYTE*	*unknown*
25Fh	*BYTE*	*unknown*
260h	DWORD	pointer to Drive Parameter Block for critical error invocation
264h	DWORD	pointer to stack frame containing user registers on INT 21h
268h	*WORD*	*stores SP*
26Ah	*DWORD*	*pointer to DOS Drive Parameter Block for unknown use*
26Eh	WORD	segment of disk buffer
270h	*WORD*	*unknown*
272h	*WORD*	*unknown*
274h	*WORD*	*unknown*
276h	*WORD*	*unknown*
278h	BYTE	Media ID byte returned by *21/1Bh, 21/1Ch*
279h	*BYTE*	*apparently not referenced by kernel*
27Ah	*DWORD*	*unknown pointer*
27Eh	DWORD	pointer to current SFT
282h	DWORD	pointer to current directory structure for drive being accessed
286h	DWORD	pointer to caller's FCB
28Ah	WORD	SFT index to which file being opened will refer
28Ch	WORD	temporary storage for file handle
28Eh	DWORD	pointer to a JFT entry in process handle table (see INT21/AH=26h)
292h	WORD	offset in DOS DS of first filename argument
294h	WORD	offset in DOS DS of second filename argument
296h	*WORD*	*unknown*
298h	*WORD*	*unknown*
29Ah	*WORD*	*unknown*
29Ch	*WORD*	*unknown*
29Eh	*WORD*	*unknown*
2A0h	*WORD*	*unknown*
2A2h	*WORD*	*directory cluster number*
2A4h	*DWORD*	*unknown*
2A8h	*DWORD*	*unknown*
2ACh	*WORD*	*unknown*
2AEh	*DWORD*	*offset in file*
2B2h	*WORD*	*unknown*
2B4h	WORD	bytes in partial sector
2B6h	WORD	number of sectors
2B8h	*WORD*	*unknown*
2BAh	*WORD*	*unknown*
2BCh	*WORD*	*unknown*
2BEh	DWORD	number of bytes appended to file
2C2h	*DWORD*	*pointer to unknown disk buffer*
2C6h	*DWORD*	*pointer to unknown SFT*

2CAh	WORD	used by INT 21h dispatcher to store caller's BX
2CCh	WORD	used by INT 21h dispatcher to store caller's DS
2CEh	WORD	temporary storage while saving/restoring caller's registers
2D0h	DWORD	pointer to previous call frame (offset 264h) if INT 21h reentered; also switched to for duration of INT 24h
2D4h	WORD	open mode/action for 21/6C00h
2D6h	*BYTE*	*unknown (set to 00h by INT 21h dispatcher, 02h when a read is performed, and 01h or 03h by 21/6C00h)*
2D7h	*WORD*	*apparently unused*
2D9h	*DWORD*	*stored ES:DI for 21/6C00h*
2DDh	WORD	extended file open action code (see *21/6C00h*)
2DFh	WORD	extended file open attributes (see *21/6C00h*)
2E1h	WORD	extended file open file mode (see *21/6C00h*)
2E3h	DWORD	pointer to filename to open (see *21/6C00h*)
2E7h	*WORD*	*unknown*
2E9h	*WORD*	*unknown*
2EBh	*BYTE*	*unknown*
2ECh	WORD	stores DS during call to [List-of-Lists + 37h]
2EEh	*WORD*	*unknown*
2F0h	*BYTE*	*unknown*
2F1h	*WORD*	*unknown bit flags*
2F3h	DWORD	pointer to user-supplied filename
2F7h	*DWORD*	*unknown pointer*
2FBh	WORD	stores SS during call to [List-of-Lists + 37h]
2FDh	WORD	stores SP during call to [List-of-Lists + 37h]
2FFh	BYTE	flag, nonzero if stack switched in calling [List-of-Lists+37h]
300h	21 BYTEs	FindFirst search data for source file(s) of a rename operation (see 21/4Eh)
315h	32 BYTEs	directory entry for file being renamed
335h	331 BYTEs	critical error stack
480h	384 BYTEs	disk stack (functions greater than 0Ch, INT 25h, INT 26h)
600h	384 BYTEs	character I/O stack (functions 01h through 0Ch)
780h	BYTE	device driver lookahead flag (see 21/64h)
781h	*BYTE*	*apparently a drive number*
782h	*BYTE*	*unknown flag*
783h	*BYTE*	*unknown*
784h	*WORD*	*unknown*
786h	*WORD*	*unknown*
788h	*WORD*	*unknown*
78Ah	*WORD*	*unknown*

INT 21h Function 5E01h   DOS 3.1+ network
SET MACHINE NAME

Specify the system's network machine name and number.

Call With:

AX	5E01h
CH	00h undefine name (make it invalid)
	else define name
CL	name number
DS:DX	pointer to 15-character blank-padded ASCIZ name

See Also: *21/5E00h*

INT 21h Function 5E04h
SET PRINTER MODE
DOS 3.1+ network

Specify whether the printer should be operated in text or binary mode.

Call With:

AX	5E04h
BX	redirection list index (see *21/5F02h*)
DX	mode
	bit 0: set if binary, clear if text (tabs expanded to blanks)

Returns:

CF set on error
    AX   error code (see *21/59h*)
CF clear if successful

Note: This function calls 2F/111Fh with 5E04h on top of the stack. 21/5E02-5E05 is a single front-end to 2F/111F, with AX pushed on stack.

See Also: 21/5E05h, 2F/111Fh

INT 21h Function 5E05h
GET PRINTER MODE
DOS 3.1+ network

Determine whether the printer is being operated in text or binary mode.

Call With:

AX	5E05h
BX	redirection list index (see *21/5F02h*)

Returns:

CF set on error
    AX   error code (see *21/59h*)
CF clear if successful
    DX   printer mode (see 21/5E04h)

Note: This function calls 2F/111Fh with 5E05h on top of the stack.

See Also: 21/5E04h, 2F/111Fh

INT 21h Function 5F00h
GET REDIRECTION MODE
DOS 3.1+ network

Determine whether disk or printer redirection is current enabled.

Call With:

AX	5F00h
BL	redirection type (03h printer, 04h disk drive)

Returns:

CF set on error
    AX   error code (see *21/59h*)
CF clear if successful
    BH   redirection state (00h off, 01h on)

Note: This function merely calls 2F/111Eh with AX on top of the stack.

See Also: 21/5F01h, 2F/111Eh

INT 21h Function 5F01h
SET REDIRECTION MODE
DOS 3.1+ Network

Specify whether disk or printer redirection is to be enabled or disabled.

Call With:

AX	5F01h
BL	redirection type (03h printer, 04h disk drive)
BH	redirection state (00h off, 01h on)

Returns:

CF set on error

AX   error code (see *21/59h*)

CF clear if successful

Note: When redirection is off, the local device (if any) rather than the remote device is used. This function merely calls 2F/111Eh with AX on top of the stack.

See Also: 21/5F00h, 2F/111Eh

INT 21h Function 5F05h   DOS 4.x + Microsoft Networks
GET REDIRECTION LIST EXTENDED ENTRY

Return the source and target of a given redirection, as well as its status and type.

Call With:

AX	5F05h
BX	redirection list index
DS:SI	pointer to buffer for ASCIZ source device name
ES:DI	pointer to buffer for destination ASCIZ network path

Returns:

CF set on error

AX   error code (see *21/59h*)

CF clear if successful

BH	device status flag (bit 0 clear if valid)
BL	device type (03h if printer, 04h if drive)
CX	stored parameter value (user data)
BP	NETBIOS local session number

DS:SI buffer filled

ES:DI buffer filled

Notes: The local session number allows sharing the redirector's session number; however, if an error is caused on the NETBIOS LSN, the redirector may be unable to correctly recover from errors.

This function merely calls 2F/111Eh with AX on top of the stack.

See Also: 21/5F06h, 2F/111Eh

INT 21h Function 5F06h   Network
GET REDIRECTION LIST

This function appears to be similar to documented *21/5F02h* (get redirection list) and 21/5F05h (get redirection list extended entry).

Call With:

AX   5F06h

additional arguments (if any) unknown

Returns:

unknown

Note: This function merely calls 2F/111Eh with AX on top of the stack.

See Also: 21/5F05h, 2F/111Eh

INT 21h Function 5F07h   DOS 5 +
ENABLE DRIVE
Enable a drive which was previously temporarily disabled by setting the "valid" bit in the drive's Current Directory Structure.

Call With:
    AX   5F07h
    DL   drive number (0=A:)
Returns:
    CF clear if successful
    CF set on error
       AX   error code (0Fh) (see *21/59h*)
See Also: 21/52h, 21/5F08h

INT 21h Function 5F08h   DOS 5+
DISABLE DRIVE
Temporarily disable a drive by clearing the "valid" bit in the drive's Current Directory Structure. For an alternate approach, see DRVSET.C in Chapter 8.

Call With:
    AX   5F08h
    DL   drive number (0=A:)
Returns:
    CF clear if successful
    CF set on error
       AX   error code (0Fh) (see *21/59h*)
See Also: 21/52h, 21/5F07h

INT 21h Functions 5F32h-5F55h   LAN Manager
NAMED PIPES FUNCTIONS
Microsoft LAN Manager uses 21/5F to provide Named Pipes and other services. Some of these calls are also supported by the Novell DOS Named Pipe Extender, Banyan VINES, and the OS/2 DOS box:

5F32h	DosQNmPipeInfo
5F33h	DosQNmPHandState
5F34h	DosSetNmPHandState
5F35h	DosPeekNmPipe
5F36h	DosTransactNmPipe
5F37h	DosCallNmPipe
5F38h	DosWaitNmPipe
5F39h	DosRawReadNmPipe
5F3Ah	DosRawWriteNmPipe
5F4Ch	NetServerEnum

    These 21/5F calls are issued, for example, by NETAPI.DLL in Windows, and by Microsoft's SQL Server. In the OS/2 2.0 DOS box, DDEAGENT and CLIPBRD make constant calls to 21/5F34 (DosSetNmPHandState).
For more information, see the interrupt list on disk, and Mike Shiels, "The Undocumented LAN Manager and Named Pipe APIs for DOS and Windows," *Dr. Dobb's Journal*, April 1993.

INT 21h Function 60h   DOS 3.0+
CANONICALIZE FILENAME OR PATH (TRUENAME)

Given a file specification, return an absolute pathname which takes into account any renaming due to JOIN, SUBST, ASSIGN, or network redirections. This function corresponds to the undocumented TRUENAME command in COMMAND.COM.

Call With:

AH	60h
DS:SI	pointer to ASCIZ filename or path
ES:DI	pointer to 128-byte buffer for canonicalized name

Returns:

CF set on error

AX	error code
	02h invalid component in directory path or drive letter only
	03h malformed path or invalid drive letter
ES:DI	buffer unchanged

CF clear if successful

AH	00h
AL	destroyed (00h or 5Ch or last char of current dir on drive)
ES:DI	buffer filled with qualified name of form D:\PATH\FILE.EXT or \\MACHINE\PATH\FILE.EXT

Notes: The input path need not actually exist.

Letters are uppercased, forward slashes are converted to backslashes, asterisks are converted to the appropriate number of question marks, and file and directory names are truncated to 8.3 if necessary.

'.' and '..' in the path are resolved.

Filespecs on local drives always start with "d:", those on network drives always start with "\\".

If the path string is on a JOINed drive, the returned name is the one that would be needed if the drive were not JOINed; similarly for a SUBSTed, ASSIGNed, or network drive letter. Because of this, it is possible to get a qualified name that is not legal under the current combination of SUBSTs, ASSIGNs, JOINs, and network redirections.

Under DOS 3.3 through 6.00, a device name is translated differently if the device name does not have an explicit directory or the directory is \DEV\ (if in the root directory, DEV\ also works). In these cases, the returned string consists of the unchanged device name and extension appended to the string X:/ (forward slash instead of backward slash as in all other cases) where X is the default or explicit drive letter.

This function is supported by the OS/2 1.1+ compatibility box.

NetWare 2.1x does not support characters with the high bit set; early versions of NetWare 386 support such characters except in this call. In addition, NetWare returns error code 3 for the path "X:\"; one should use "X:\." instead.

For DOS 3.3-6.0, the input and output buffers may be the same, as the canonicalized name is built in an internal buffer and copied to the specified output buffer as the very last step.

See Also: 2F/1123h, 2F/1221h

INT 21h Function 61h   DOS 3+
UNUSED

This function performs no action and returns immediately.

INT 21h Function 6300h   DOS 2.25
GET DOUBLE-BYTE CHARACTER SET LEAD BYTE TABLE

Determine the address of a table which specifies the ranges of characters which are the first half of a double-byte character.

Call With:
　　AX　　　　6300h
Returns:
　　CF clear if successful
　　　　DS:SI　pointer to lead byte table (see below for format)
　　　　all other registers except CS:IP and SS:SP destroyed
　　CF set on error
　　　　AX　　　error code (01h) (see *21/59h*)
Notes: does not preserve any registers other than SS:SP; the US version of MS-DOS 3.30 treats this as an unused function, setting AL=00h and returning immediately. The Microsoft Far East Windows SDK refers to "DBCS MS-DOS 2.21."
See Also: *21/07h*, *21/08h*, *21/0Bh*, 21/6301h

Format of lead byte table entry:

Offset	Size	Description
00h	2 BYTEs	low/high ends of a range of leading byte of double-byte chars
02h	2 BYTEs	low/high ends of a range of leading byte of double-byte chars
N ...	2 BYTEs	00h,00h end flag

INT 21h Function 6300h   Far East DOS 3.2+
GET DOUBLE BYTE CHARACTER SET LEAD-BYTE TABLE

Determine the address of a table which specifies the ranges of characters which are the first half of a double-byte character.

Call With:
　　AX　　　　6300h
Returns:
　　AL　　　　status
　　　　00h successful
　　　　　　DS:SI　　pointer to DBCS table (see below)
　　　　　　all other registers except CS:IP and SS:SP destroyed
　　　　FFh not supported
Notes: the US version of MS-DOS 3.30 treats this as an unused function, setting AL=00h and returning immediately; the US version of DOS 4.0+ accepts this function, but returns an empty list
See Also: 21/6301h, 21/65

Format of DBCS table:

Offset	Size	Description
00h	2 BYTEs	low/high ends of a range of leading byte of double-byte chars
02h	2 BYTEs	low/high ends of a range of leading byte of double-byte chars
N ...	2 BYTEs	00h,00h end flag

INT 21h Function 6301h   DOS 2.25, Far East DOS 3.2+
SET KOREAN (HANGEUL) INPUT MODE

Specify whether DOS input functions may return partially-formed double-byte characters, this function sets the "interim console flag."

Call With:

AX	6301h
DL	new mode
	00h return only full characters on DOS keyboard input functions
	01h return partially-formed (interim) characters also

Returns:

AL	status
	00h successful
	FFh invalid mode

Note: see the Microsoft Windows Far East SDK.
See Also: *21/07h, 21/08h, 21/0Bh*, 21/6300h, 21/6302h

INT 21h Function 6302h   DOS 2.25, Far East DOS 3.2+
GET KOREAN (HANGEUL) INPUT MODE

Determine whether DOS input functions may return partially-formed double-byte characters.

Call With:

AX   6302h

Returns:

AL   status
    00h successful
       DL   current input mode
            00h return only full characters (clears interim flag)
            01h return partial characters (sets interim flag)
    FFh not supported

See Also: *21/07h, 21/08h, 21/0Bh*, 21/6300h, 21/6301h

INT 21h Function 64h   DOS 3.2+
SET DEVICE DRIVER LOOKAHEAD FLAG

Specify whether the DOS input loop should check for pending input before attempting to call the device driver for input.

Call With:

AH	64h	
AL	flag	
	00h	(default) call device driver function 5 (non-destructive read) before 21/01h,08h,0Ah
	nonzero	don't call driver function 5

Returns:

nothing

Notes: This function is called by DOS 3.3+ PRINT.COM.

This call does not use any of the DOS-internal stacks and may thus be called at any time, even during another INT 21h call.

See Also: *21/01h, 21/08h, 21/0Ah*, 21/5D06h

INT 21h Function 64h   OS/2 2.x Virtual DOS Machine
GET/SET TASK TITLE

Determine or specify the title to be given the window of an OS/2 2.x virtual DOS machine (VDM).

Call With:

AH	64h
BX	0000h
CX	636Ch
DX	function

        0000h enable automatic title switch on 21/4Bh

        0001h set session title

                ES:DI   pointer to new ASCIZ title or "" to restore original title

        0002h get session title

                ES:DI   pointer to buffer for current title

Returns:

    buffer filled (single 00h if title never changed)

See Also: 21/4Bh

Note: OS/2 2.x uses 21/64 to provide a wide variety of services to DOS programs running in a VDM. Most important are INT 21h versions of the OS/2 Dos32StartSession API call, and of OS/2 semaphore API calls such as Dos32OpenEventSem, Dos32WaitEventSem, and Dos32PostEventSem. For more information, see chapter 4, and the interrupt list on disk.

INT 21h Function 6505h   DOS 3.3+
GET FILENAME TERMINATOR TABLE

Return information about the characters which terminate a filename.

Call With:

AH	65h
AL	info ID

        05h get pointer to filename terminator table

BX	code page (-1=global code page)
DX	country ID (-1=current country)
ES:DI	pointer to country information buffer (see below)
CX	size of buffer (>= 5)

Returns:

    CF set on error

      AX   error code (see *21/59h*)

    CF clear if succesful

        CX   size of country information returned

        ES:DI   pointer to country information

Notes: This function appears to return the same info for all countries and codepages; it has been documented for DOS 5.0, but was undocumented in earlier versions.

    NLSFUNC must be installed to get information for countries other than the default country.

See Also: *21/38h*, 2F/1401h, 2F/1402h

Format of country information:

Offset	Size	Description
00h	BYTE	info ID
01h	DWORD	pointer to filename terminator table (see below)

Format of filename terminator table:

Offset	Size	Description
00h	WORD	table size (not counting this word)
02h	*BYTE*	*unknown (01h for MS-DOS 3.30-6.00)*
03h	BYTE	lowest permissible character value for filename
04h	BYTE	highest permissible character value for filename
05h	*BYTE*	*unknown (00h for MS-DOS 3.30-6.00)*
06h	BYTE	first excluded character in range } all characters in this
07h	BYTE	last excluded character in range } range are illegal
08h	*BYTE*	*unknown (02h for MS-DOS 3.30-6.00)*
09h	BYTE	number of illegal (terminator) characters
0Ah	N BYTES	characters which terminate a filename: ."/\[]:|<>+=;,

Note: Partially documented for DOS 5.0, but undocumented for earlier versions

---

INT 21h Functions 6520h to 6522h   DOS 4+
COUNTRY-DEPENDENT CHARACTER CAPITALIZATION

Capitalize a character or string using the capitalization rules for the current country.

Call With:
> AH   65h
> AL   function
>> 20h capitalize character
>>> DL   character to capitalize
>>> **Returns:**
>>>> DL   capitalized character
>> 21h capitalize string
>>> DS:DX   pointer to string to capitalize
>>> CX   length of string
>> 22h capitalize ASCIZ string
>>> DS:DX pointer to ASCIZ string to capitalize

Returns:
> CF set on error
>> AX   error code (see *21/59h*)
> CF clear if successful

Note: These calls have been documented for DOS 5+, but were undocumented in DOS 4.x.

INT 21h Function 6523h   DOS 4+
Determine If Character Represents Yes/no Response

Compare the specified character against the YES and NO responses for the current country.

Call With:
> AX   6523h
> DL   character
> DH   second character of double-byte character (if applicable)

Returns:
> CF set on error
> CF clear if successful
>> AX   type
>>> 00h no
>>> 01h yes
>>> 02h neither yes nor no

INT 21h Functions 65A0h to 65A2h   DOS 4+
Country-dependent Filename Capitalization

Capitalize a filename character or string using the filename capitalization rules for the current country.

Call With:

AH	65h
AL	function

    A0h capitalize filename character
        DL   character to capitalize
        Returns:
           DL   capitalized character
    A1h capitalize counted filename string
        DS:DX   pointer to filename string to capitalize
        CX   length of string
    A2h capitalize ASCIZ filename
        DS:DX pointer to ASCIZ filename to capitalize

Returns:
    CF set on error
      AX   error code (see *21/59h*)
    CF clear if successful

Note: These calls are nonfunctional in DOS 4.00 through 6.00 due to a bug (the code sets a pointer depending on the high bit of AL, but doesn't clear the bit before branching by function number).

INT 21h Function 67h   DOS 3.3+
SET HANDLE COUNT

Although documented, this function is included because of a bug in early releases. This function is used to increase the per-process limit on open files beyond the default of 20 files.

Call With:
    AH 67h
    BX   size of new file handle table for process

Returns:
    CF clear if successful
    CF set on error
      AX   error code (see *21/59h*)

Notes: If BX is 20 or less, no action is taken if the handle limit has not yet been increased, and the table is copied back into the PSP if the limit is currently greater than 20 handles.

For file handle tables of more than 20 handles, DOS 3.30 never reuses the same memory block, even if the limit is being reduced; this can lead to memory fragmentation as a new block is allocated and the existing one freed.

Only the first 20 handles are copied to child processes in DOS 3.3-6.0.

Increasing the file limit with this function will generally not increase the number of files which may be opened using the runtime library of a high-level language. See Chapter 8.

BUG: The original release of DOS 3.30 allocates a full 64K for the handle table on requests for an even number of handles.

See Also: 21/26h

INT 21h Function 69h   DOS 4.0+
GET/SET DISK SERIAL NUMBER

Determine or specify a disk's serial number and volume label.

Call With:

AH   69h
AL   subfunction
            00h get serial number
            01h set serial number
BL   drive (0=default, 1=A, 2=B, etc)
DS:DX   pointer to disk info (see below)

Returns:

CF set on error
   AX   error code (see *21/59h*)
CF clear if successful
   AX destroyed
   (AL=00h) buffer filled with appropriate values from extended BPB
   (AL=01h) extended BPB on disk set to values from buffer

Notes: This function does not generate a critical error; all errors are returned in AX

Error 0005h is returned if there is no extended BPB on the disk.

This call does not work on network drives (error 0001h).

After the first two bytes, the buffer is exact copy of bytes 27h thru 3Dh of the extended BPB on the disk.

This function is supported under Novell NetWare versions 2.0A through 3.11; the returned serial number is the one a DIR would display, the volume label is the NetWare volume label, and the file system is set to "FAT16".

The volume label which is read or set by this function is the one stored in the extended BPB on disks formatted with DOS 4.0+, rather than the special root directory entry used by the DIR command in COMMAND.COM (use 21/11h to find that volume label).

See Also: 21/440Dh (CX=0866h; Get Media ID)

Format of disk info:

Offset	Size	Description
00h	WORD	info level (zero)
02h	DWORD	disk serial number (binary)
06h	11 BYTEs	volume label or "NO NAME" if none present
11h	8 BYTEs	(AL=00h only) filesystem type—string "FAT12" or "FAT16"

INT 21h Function 6Ah
COMMIT FILE   DOS 4+

This call is identical to documented function 68h in DOS 5.0 and 6.0; it is not known whether the two functions are identical in DOS 4.x.

Call With:

AH   6Ah
BX   file handle

Returns:

CF clear if succcessful
   AH   68h
CF set on error
   AX   error code

See Also: *21/68h*

INT 21h Function 6Bh
UNKNOWN FUNCTION   DOS 4.x only

The purpose of this function is not known, but it appears to be related to installable file systems.

Call With:
> AH   6Bh
> AL   subfunction
>> *00h unknown*
>>> DS:SI *pointer to Current Directory Structure*
>>> CL   drive (1=A:)
>> *01h unknown*
>>> DS:SI *pointer to unknown item*
>>> CL   *file handle*
>> *02h unknown*
>>> DS:SI *pointer to Current Directory Structure*
>>> DI   *unknown*
>>> CX   drive (1=A:)

Returns:
> CF set on error
>> AX   error code (see *21/59h*)
> CF clear if successful

Note: This call is passed through to 2F/112Fh with AX on top of the stack.
See Also: 2F/112Fh

INT 21h Function 6Bh   DOS 5+
NULL FUNCTION

This function performs no action and returns immediately.

INT 21h Functions 6Dh-6Fh   MS-DOS 5+ in ROM, OS/2
DOS IN ROM FUNCTIONS

Microsoft's ROM versions of MS-DOS 5.0 and higher use 21/6D through 21/6F for a set of functions documented in the MS-DOS OEM Adaptation Kit (OAK):

6Dh	Find First ROM Program
6Eh	Find Next ROM Program
6F00h	Get ROM Scan Start Address
6F01h	Set ROM Scan Start Address
6F02h	Get Exclusion Region List
6F03h	Set Exclusion Region List

For more information, see the interrupt list on disk (and Chappell's *DOS Internals*). To detect DOS in ROM, use documented 21/3306.

21/6D-6F is also used by the OS/2 DOS box to give DOS programs access to the DosMkDir2, DosEnumAttrib, and DosQMaxEASize OS/2 API functions. For more information, see chapter 4 and the interrupt list on disk.

INT 21h Functions 71h-72h   Chicago
CHICAGO LONG FILENAME FUNCTIONS

Under "Chicago" (DOS 7, Windows 4), 21/71 and 21/72 will provide DOS programs with access to long filenames. A DOS program will be able to use a new set of 21/71XX functions, where the subfunction in AL is the same as the old DOS AH function number. For example, because the old DOS Get Current Directory function is 21/47, the new one that knows about long pathnames is 21/7147; while the other registers are identical to the old call, the buffers pointed to by DS:SI must be large enough to receive the maximum-allowed path. Programs can call the Chicago 21/4302 Get Volume Information function to get the length of the maximum-allowed path.

The following are to be the documented INT 21h long filename functions, with their Win32 API equivalents:

7139h	CreateDirectory
713Ah	RemoveDirectory
713Bh	SetCurrentDirectory
7141h	DeleteFile
7143h	(BL=0) GetFileAttributes
7143h	(BL=1) SetFileAttributes
7147h	GetCurrentDirectory
714Eh	FindFirstFile
714Fh	FindNextFile
7156h	MoveFile
716Ch	CreateFile and OpenFile

If the 21/71XX function fails (carry set), AX=7100h indicates the function is not supported (for example, because the volume does not support long filenames). In this case, continue by calling the old 21/XX function. For example, if 21/7147 fails with carry set and AX=7100h, call 21/47.

A 21/7160 long filename version of 21/60 (Truename) does *not* appear to be provided.

Another new DOS call is 21/72 (FindClose). Whereas previous versions of DOS support only FindFirst and FindNext, Chicago requires FindClose because the Win32 API supports multiple, simultaneous file finds. FindFirst (21/714E) returns a "search handle," which you must pass to FindNext (21/714F), and which you must therefore close with FindClose.

For more information, see chapter 8 and (eventually) Microsoft's documentation for Chicago.

INT 21h Function 80h   European MS-DOS 4.0

AEXEC – EXECUTE PROGRAM IN BACKGROUND

Asynchronously execute a program, creating a new process for it. Although this function and the known functions on the next several pages are in fact (obscurely) documented, they are included here because to our knowledge there are no current publications which document them. European MS-DOS 4.0 is an OEM version with multitasking capabilities which was released on a limited number of systems between the mainstream versions 3.2 and 3.3. Some features of Windows and OS/2, including the New Executable (NE) file format, first appeared in European MS-DOS 4.0. See 21/87 for the European MS-DOS install check.

Call With:
> AH   80h
> CX   mode
>   0000h place child in zombie mode on exit to preserve exit code
>   0001h discard child process and exit code on termination
> DS:DX   pointer to ASCIZ full program name
> ES:BX   pointer to parameter block (as for 21/4B04h)

Returns:
> CF clear if successful
>   AX   Command Subgroup ID (CSID)
> CF set on error
>   AX   error code (see *21/59h*)

Notes: This function is called by the DETACH command.

There is a system-wide limit of 32 processes.

The CSID is used to identify all processes that have been spawned by a given process, whether directly or indirectly.

Programs to be run in the background must use the new executable format (see 21/4B04h); "NE" format executables made their first appearance in European MS-DOS 4.0.

Background processes may only perform asynchronous (background) EXECs, either this function or 21/4B04h.

Background processes may execute INT 11h, INT 12h, INT 21h, INT 2Ah, and INT 2Fh at any time; they may execute INT 10h and INT 16h only while they have opened a popup screen via 2F/1401h; no other interrupts may be executed from the background.

Background processes may not use drive B: or overlay their code segments.

See 21/87h for a possible installation check.

See Also: 21/4B04h, 21/87h, 2F/1400h "POPUP"

INT 21h Function 81h   European MS-DOS 4.0
"FREEZE" - STOP A PROCESS

Temporarily suspend a process or a process and all of its children. See INT 21h Function 80h for general comments on European MS-DOS 4.0.

Call With:
>   AH   81h
>   BX   flag (00h freeze command subtree, 01h only specified process)
>   CX   Process ID of head of command subtree

Returns:
>   CF clear if successful
>   CF set on error
>   AX   error code (no such process)

Note: If BX=0001h, this call will not return until the process is actually frozen, which may not be until after it unblocks from an I/O operation.

See Also: AH=82h, AH=89h, AX=8E00h

INT 21h Function 82h   European MS-DOS 4.0
"RESUME" - RESTART A PROCESS

Restart a previously-suspended process or a process and all of its children. See INT 21h Function 80h for general comments on European MS-DOS 4.0.

Call With:
>   AH   82h
>   BX   flag (00h resume command subtree, 01h only specified process)
>   CX   Process ID of head of command subtree

Returns:
>   CF clear if successful
>   CF set on error
>   AX   error code (no such process)

See Also: 21/81h

INT 21h Function 83h   European MS-DOS 4.0
"PARTITION" - GET/SET FOREGROUND PARTITION SIZE

Specify or determine how much memory may be allocated by the foreground process. See INT 21h Function 80h for general comments on European MS-DOS 4.0.

Call With:
>   AH   83h

AL   function
      00h get size
      01h set new size
         BX   new size in paragraphs

Returns:
   CF clear if successful
      BX   current size (function 00h) or old size (function 01h)
   CF set on error
      AX   error code (01h,07h,0Dh)(see AH=59h)

Notes: If the partition size is set to 0000h, no partition management is done and all memory allocation is compatible with DOS 3.2.

The partition size can be changed regardless of what use is being made of the changed memory; subsequent allocations will follow the partition rules (foreground processes may allocate only foreground memory; background processes allocate background memory first, then foreground memory).

See Also: *INT 21 Function 81h*, 21/4Ah

INT 21h Function 8400h   European MS-DOS 4.0
"CREATMEM" - CREATE A SHARED MEMORY AREA

Create an area of memory which may be accessed by multiple processes. See INT 21h Function 80h for general comments on European MS-DOS 4.0.

Call With:
   AX   8400h
   BX   size in bytes (0000h = 65536)
   CX   flags
      bit 6: zero-initialize segment
   DS:DX   pointer to ASCIZ name (must begin with "\SHAREMEM\")

Returns:
   CF clear if successful
      AX   segment address of shared memory global object
   CF set on error
      AX   error code (06h,08h) (see *INT 21 Function 82h and INT 21h Function 83h*)

Notes: Shared memory objects are created as special files (thus the restriction on the name).

On successful creation, the reference count is set to 1.

See Also: 21/8401h, 21/8402h

INT 21h Function 8401h   European MS-DOS 4.0
"GETMEM" - OBTAIN ACCESS TO SHARED MEMORY AREA

Get address of a previously-created area of memory which may be accessed by multiple processes.

Call With:
   AX   8401h
   CX   flags
      bit 7: writable segment (ignored by MS-DOS 4.0)
   DS:DX   pointer to ASCIZ name (must begin with "\SHAREMEM\")

Returns:
   CF clear if successful
      AX   segment address of shared memory global object
      CX   size in bytes
   CF set on error
      AX   error code (invalid name)

Note: This call increments the reference count for the shared memory area.
See Also: AX=8400h, AX=8402h

INT 21h Function 8402h   European MS-DOS 4.0
"RELEASEMEM" - FREE SHARED MEMORY AREA

Indicate that the specified area of shared memory will no longer be used by the caller.

Call With:
  AX   8402h
  BX   handle (segment address of shared memory object)
Returns:
  CF clear if successful
  CF set on error
    AX   error code (no such name)
Note: The reference count is decremented and the shared memory area is deallocated if the new reference count is zero.
See Also: 21/8400h, 21/8401h

INT 21h Function 86h   European MS-DOS 4.0
"SETFILETABLE" - INSTALL NEW FILE HANDLE TABLE

Adjust the size of the per-process open file table, thus raising or lowering the limit on the number of files the caller can open simultaneously.

Call With:
  AH   86h
  BX   total number of file handles in new table
Returns:
  CF clear if successful
  CF set on error
    AX   error code (06h,08h) (see AH=59h)
Notes: Any currently-open files are copied to the new table.
    If the table is increased beyond the default 20 handles, only the first 20 will be inherited by child processes.
    Error 06h is returned if the requested number of handles exceeds system limits or would require closing currently-open files.
See Also: 21/26h, 21/67h

INT 21h Function 87h   European MS-DOS 4.0
"GETPID" - GET PROCESS IDENTIFIER

Determine an identifier by which to access the calling process. This call can also be used as an install check for European MS-DOS 4.0.

Call With:
  AH   87h
Returns:
  AX   Process ID (PID)
  BX   parent process's PID
  CX   Command Subgroup ID (CSID)
Notes: This function is called by the Microsoft C 5.1 getpid() function.
    This function apparently must return AX=0001h for 21/80h to succeed.
    One possible check for European MS-DOS 4.0 is to issue this call with AL=00h and check whether AL is nonzero on return.
See Also: 21/30h, *21/62h, 21/80h*

INT 21h Function 89h   European MS-DOS 4.0
SLEEP

Suspend the calling process for the specified duration.

Call With:
>   AH   89h
>   CX   time in milliseconds or 0000h to give up time slice

Returns:
>   CF clear if successful
>   CX   0000h
>   CF set on error
>   AX   error code (interrupted system call)
>   CX   sleep time remaining

Notes: The sleep interval is rounded up to the next higher increment of the scheduler clock, and may be extended further if other processes are running.

This call may be interrupted by signals (see 21/8Dh).

This function is reportedly called by the Microsoft C 4.0 startup code.

Background processes have higher priority than the foreground process, and should thus periodically yield the CPU.

See Also: 21/81h, *INT 15/AX=1000h, 2F/1680h*

INT 21h Function 8Ah   European MS-DOS 4.0
"CWAIT" - WAIT FOR CHILD TO TERMINATE

Get return code from an asynchronously-executed child program, optionally waiting if no return code is available. See INT 21h Function 80h for general comments on European MS-DOS 4.0.

Call With:
>   AH   8Ah
>   BL   range (00h command subtree, 01h any child)
>   BH   suspend flag
>   00h suspend if children exist but none are dead
>   01h return if no dead children
>   CX   Process ID of head of command subtree

Returns:
>   CF clear if successful
>   AH   termination type
>   00h normal termination
>   01h aborted by Control-C
>   02h aborted by I/O error
>   03h terminate and stay resident
>   04h aborted by signal
>   05h aborted by program error
>   AL   return code from child or aborting signal
>   BX   PID of child (0000h if no dead children)
>   CF set on error
>   AX   error code (no child,interrupted system call)

See Also: 21/4B04h, *21/4Dh*, 21/80h, 21/8Dh

INT 21h Function 8Ch   European MS-DOS 4.0
SET SIGNAL HANDLER

Set the routine which will be invoked on a number of exceptional conditions.

Call With:

>   AH   8Ch
>   AL   signal number (see below)
>   BL   action (see below)
>   DS:DX   pointer to signal handler (see below)

Returns:

>   CF clear if successful
>   AL   previous action
>   ES:BX   pointer to previous signal handler
>   CF set on error
>   AX   error code (01h,invalid SigNumber or Action) (see *AH=59h*)

Note: All signals will be sent to the most recently installed handler.

See Also: 21/8Dh

Values for signal number:

01h	SIGINTR	Control-C or user defined interrupt key
08h	SIGTERM	program termination
09h	SIGPIPE	broken pipe
0Dh	SIGUSER1	reserved for user definition
0Eh	SIGUSER2	reserved for user definition

Values for signal action:

00h	SIG_DFL	terminate process on receipt
01h	SIG_IGN	ignore signal
02h	SIG_GET	signal is accepted
03h	SIG_ERR	sender gets error
04h	SIG_ACK	acknowledge received signal and clear it, but don't change current setting

Signal handler is called with:

>   AL   signal number
>   AH   signal argument

Returns:

>   RETF, CF set: terminate process
>   RETF, CF clear, ZF set: abort any interrupted system call with an error
>   RETF, CF clear, ZF clear: restart any interrupted system call
>   IRET: restart any interrupted system call

Note: The signal handler may also perform a nonlocal GOTO by resetting the stack pointer and jumping; before doing so, it should dismiss the signal by calling this function with BL=04h.

INT 21h Function 8Dh   **European MS-DOS 4.0**
SEND SIGNAL

Invoke the exceptional-condition handler for the specified process.

Call With:

>   AH   8Dh
>   AL   signal number (see AH=8Ch)
>   BH   signal argument
>   BL   action
>   00h send to entire command subtree
>   01h send only to specified process
>   DX   Process ID

Returns:

>   CF clear if successful
>   CF set on error

AX   error code (01h,06h)(see AH=59h)

Note: Error 06h may be returned if one or more of the affected processes have an error handler for the signal.

See Also: 21/8Ch

INT 21h Function 8E00h   European MS-DOS 4.0
"SETPRI" - GET/SET PROCESS PRIORITY

Specify or determine the execution priority of the specified process or the process and all of its children.

Call With:
    AX   8E00h
    BH   00h
    BL   action
         00h set priority for command subtree
         01h set priority for specified process only
    CX   Process ID
    DH   00h
    DL   change in priority (00h to get priority)
Returns:
    CF clear if successful
        DL   process priority
        DH   destroyed
    CF set on error
        AX   error code (01h,no such process)(see *21/59h*)
See Also: 21/81h

INT 21h Function 93h   European MS-DOS 4.0
"PIPE" - CREATE A NEW PIPE

Create a communications channel which may be used for interprocess data and command exchanges.

Call With:
    AH   93h
    CX   size in bytes
Returns:
    CF clear if successful
        AX   read handle
        BX   write handle
    CF set on error
        AX   error code (08h) (see AH=59h)
See Also: *21/3Ch*, *21/3Fh*, 21/40h, 21/84h

INT 21h Function 95h   European MS-DOS 4.0
HARD ERROR PROCESSING

Specify whether hard (critical) errors should automatically fail the system call or invoke an INT 24h.

Call With:
    AH   95h
    AL   new state
         00h enabled
         01h disabled, automatically fail hard errors

Returns:
>   AX   previous setting

See Also: *INT 24h*

INT 21h Function 99h   European MS-DOS 4.0
"PBLOCK" - BLOCK A PROCESS

Suspend the calling process until another process sends a "restart" signal or a timeout occurs.

Call With:
>   AH   99h
>   DS:BX   pointer to memory location on which to block
>   CX   timeout in milliseconds
>   DH   nonzero if interruptible

Returns:
>   CF clear if awakened by event
>   AX   0000h
>   CF set if unusual wakeup
>   ZF   set if timeout, clear if interrupted by signal
>   AX   nonzero

See Also: 21/9Ah, 2F/0802h

INT 21h Function 9Ah   European MS-DOS 4.0
"PRUN" - UNBLOCK A PROCESS

Restart all processes waiting for the specified "restart" signal.

Call With:
>   AH   9Ah
>   DS:BX   pointer to memory location on which processes may have blocked

Returns:
>   AX   number of processes awakened
>   ZF   set if no processes awakened

See Also: 21/99h, 2F/0802h

INT 28h   DOS 2+
DOS IDLE INTERRUPT

This interrupt is invoked each time one of the DOS character input functions (21/01h,06h,07h,08h,0Ah) loops while waiting for input, indicating that it is safe to call DOS to access the disk. Since a DOS call is in progress even though DOS is actually idle during such input waits, hooking this function is necessary to allow a TSR to perform DOS calls while the foreground program is waiting for user input.

Called with:
>   SS:SP   top of MS-DOS stack for I/O functions

Returns:
>   all registers preserved

Notes: The INT 28h handler may invoke any INT 21h function except functions 00h through 0Ch. Under DOS 2.x, the critical error flag (the byte immediately after the In DOS flag) must be set in order to call DOS functions 50h/51h from the INT 28h handler without destroying the DOS stacks.

Calls to 21/3Fh and 21/40h from within an INT 28h handler may not use a handle which refers to the CON device.

At the time of the call, the InDOS flag (see 21/34h) is normally set to 01h; if larger, DOS is truly busy and should not be reentered.

The default handler is an IRET instruction.

This interrupt is supported in the OS/2 compatibility box.

The *MS-DOS Programmer's Reference* for DOS 5.0 incorrectly documents this interrupt as superseded by 2F/1680.

See Also: 21/34h, 2A/84h, 2F/1680h

INT 29h   DOS 2+
FAST CONSOLE OUTPUT

This interrupt is called from the DOS output routines when sending characters to a device whose attribute word has bit 4 set.

Call With:
    AL   character to display

Returns:
    nothing

Notes: COMMAND.COM 3.2 and 3.3 compare the INT 29h vector against the INT 20h vector and assume that ANSI.SYS is installed if the INT 29h segment is larger.

The default handler under DOS 2.x and 3.x simply calls INT 10/AH=0Eh, see Figure 6-1.

See Also: 21/52h, 2F/0802h

INT 2Ah Function 00h   Network
INSTALLATION CHECK

Determine whether a Microsoft Networks-compatible network is installed.

Call With:
    AH   00h

Returns:
    AH   nonzero if installed

See Also: *INT 5Ch*

INT 2Ah Function 01h   Network
EXECUTE NETBIOS REQUEST,NO ERROR RETRY

This call is equivalent to invoking *INT 5Ch*, the NETBIOS interrupt.

Call With:
    AH   01h
    ES:BX   pointer to Network Control Block (see *INT 5Ch*)

Returns:
    AL   NetBIOS error code
    AH   00h if no error
              01h on error

See Also: 2A/04h, 2A/0500h, *INT 5Ch*

INT 2Ah Function 02h   Network
SET NETWORK PRINTER MODE

Specify the operating mode of the network printer.

Call With:
    AH   02h
    additional arguments (if any) unknown

Returns:
   unknown

INT 2Ah Function 0300h   Network
CHECK DIRECT I/O
DOS calls this function to determine whether direct transfers to a disk are allowed before attempting I/O for INT 25h or INT 26h.

Call With:
   AX   0300h
   DS:SI   pointer to ASCIZ device name (may be full path or only drive specifier
            must include the colon)
Returns:
   CF clear if direct physical addressing (INT 13h, INT 25h) permissible
   CF set if access via files only
Notes: Do not use direct disk accesses if this function returns CF set or the device is redirected (see 21/5F02h).
   This call may take some time to execute. This function is called by 21/4409 (Is Drive Remote).
See Also: *INT 13h, INT 25h, INT 26h, 21/5F02h*

INT 2Ah Function 04h   Network
EXECUTE NETBIOS REQUEST
Invoke the NETBIOS handler, optionally retrying the operation on certain errors.

Call With:
   AH   04h
   AL   error retry
            00h automatically retry request on errors 09h, 12h, and 21h
            01h no retry
   ES:BX   pointer to Network Control Block
Returns:
   AX   0000h if successful
   AH   01h on error
            AL   error code
Note: This function invokes either INT 5Bh or INT 5Ch as appropriate
See Also: 2A/01h, 2A/0500h, *INT 5Bh, INT 5Ch*

INT 2Ah Function 0500h   Network
GET NETWORK RESOURCE AVAILABILITY
Determine the available amounts of several important network resources.

Call With:
   AX   0500h
Returns:
   AX   reserved
   BX   number of network names available
   CX   number of network control blocks available
   DX   number of network sessions available
See Also: 2A/01h, 2A/04h, *INT 5Ch*

INT 2Ah Function 06h   NETBIOS, LANtastic
NETWORK PRINT-STREAM CONTROL
Specify behavior of redirected network printer output.

Call With:

AH	06h
AL	01h set concatenation mode (all printer output put in one job)
	02h set truncation mode (default): printer open/close starts new print job
	03h flush printer output and start new print job

Returns:

CF set on error
   AX   error code
CF clear if successful

Notes: Subfunction 03h is equivalent to Carl/Alt/keypad-*.
    LANtastic v4.x no longer supports this call.
See Also: 21/5D08h, 21/5D09h, 2F/1125h

INT 2Ah Function 2001h   MS Networks or NETBIOS
UNKNOWN FUNCTION
The purpose of this function is not known.

Note: This function is intercepted by DESQview 2.x.

INT 2Ah Functions 2002h and 2003h   Network
UNKNOWN FUNCTIONS
The purpose of these functions is not known.

Note: These functions are called by MS-DOS 3.30-6.00 APPEND.

INT 2Ah Function 7802h   PC LAN PROG v1.31+
GET LOGGED ON USER NAME
Call With:

AX	7802h
ES:DI	pointer to 8-byte buffer to be filled

Returns:

AL	00h if no user logged on to Extended Services
AL	nonzero if user logged on to Extended Services
	buffer at ES:DI filled with name, padded to 8 chars with blanks

INT 2Ah Function 80h   Network
BEGIN DOS CRITICAL SECTION
The DOS kernel and some of the DOS programs call this function to indicate that an uninterruptible region of code is being entered. The primary use of this function is to serialize access to the SDA and device drivers, to avoid conflicting simultaneous modifications of the SDA or reentering a single-tasking device driver.

Called With:

AH	80h
AL	critical section number (00h-0Fh)
	01h DOS kernel, SHARE.EXE, DOSMGR
	apparently for maintaining the integrity of DOS/SHARE/NET data structures
	02h DOS kernel, DOSMGR

ensures that no multitasking occurs while DOS is calling an installable device driver
05h DOS 4.x only IFSFUNC, REDIR, PC LAN
06h DOS 4.x only IFSFUNC
08h ASSIGN.COM
09h ASSIGN
0Ah MSCDEX
0Fh PC LAN

Notes: This function is normally hooked to avoid interrupting a critical section, rather than called.

The handler should ensure that none of the critical sections are reentered, usually by suspending a task which attempts to reenter an active critical section.

The DOS kernel does not invoke critical sections 01h and 02h unless it is patched. DOS 3.1+ contains a zero-terminated list of words beginning at offset -11 from the Swappable Data Area (see 21/5D06h); each word contains the offset within the DOS data segment of a byte which must be changed from C3h (RET) to 50h (PUSH AX) under DOS 3.x or from 00h to a nonzero value under DOS 4+ to enable use of critical sections. For DOS 4+, all words in this list point at the byte at offset 0D0Ch.

The Windows DOSMGR VxD implements 2A/80 by calling the VMM _BeginCriticalService function.

See CRITPATCH.C in Chapter 9.

See Also: 2A/81h, 2A/82h, 2A/87h, 21/5D06h, 21/5D0Bh

INT 2Ah Function 81h   Network
END DOS CRITICAL SECTION

The DOS kernel and some of the DOS programs call this function to indicate that an uninterruptible region of code has been completed.

Called With:
AH   81h
AL   critical section number (00h-0Fh) (see 2A/80h)

Notes: This function is normally hooked rather than called.

The Windows DOSMGR VxD implements 2A/81 and 2A/82 by calling the VMM _EndCriticalSection function.

The handler should reawaken any tasks which were suspended due to an attempt to enter the specified critical section.

See Also: 2A/80h, 2A/82h, 2A/87h

INT 2Ah Function 82h   Network
END DOS CRITICAL SECTIONS 0 THROUGH 7

Clean up any DOS critical section flags which may have been left set by an aborted process or DOS function call.

Called With:
AH   82h

Notes: This function is called by the INT 21h function dispatcher for function 0 and functions greater than 0Ch except 59h, and on process termination.

The handler should reawaken any tasks which were suspended due to an attempt to reenter one of the critical sections 0 through 7.

See Also: 2A/81h

INT 2Ah Function 84h   Network
KEYBOARD BUSY LOOP

This is a hook to let other work proceed while waiting for keyboard input.

Called With:
AH   84h
Note: This function is similar to DOS's INT 28h, and is called from inside the DOS keyboard input loop (21/07h, 08h, AH=#Fh if reading from CON, etc.) to allow network to process requests. The Windows DOSMGR implements 2A/84 by calling the VMM Release_Time_Slice function.
See Also: INT 28h

INT 2Ah Function 8700h   PRINT v3+
BEGIN BACKGROUND PRINTING

This function is used to inform interested programs that PRINT is about to start its background processing, and allow those programs to postpone the processing if necessary.

Called with:
    AX   8700h
    CF   clear
Returns:
    CF clear if OK to print in background now
    CF set if background printing not allowed at this time
Notes: When PRINT gains control and want to begin printing, it calls this function. If CF is clear on return, PRINT begins its background processing, and calls AX=8701h when it is done. If CF is set on return, PRINT will relinquish control immediately, and will not call AX=8701h.
    PCVENUS (an early network shell by IBM and CMU) hooks this call to prevent background printing while its own code is active.
See Also: AH=80h, AH=81h, AX=8701h

INT 2Ah Function 8701h   PRINT v3+ END
BACKGROUND PRINTING

This function is used to inform interested programs that PRINT has completed its background processing.

Called with:
    AX   8701h
Returns:
    nothing
Note: This function is called by PRINT after it has performed some background printing; it is not called if AX=8700h returned with CF set.
See Also: AX=8700h

INT 2Ah Function 89h   Network
UNKNOWN FUNCTION

The purpose of this function has not been determined.

Call With:
    AH   89h
    AL   *unknown   (ASSIGN uses 08h)*
                  additional arguments (if any) unknown
Returns:
    unknown

INT 2Ah Function C2h   Network
UNKNOWN FUNCTION
The purpose of this function has not been determined.

Call With:

AH	C2h
AL	subfunction
	07h unknown
	08h unknown
BX	0001h
	additional arguments (if any) unknown

Returns:

unknown

Note: This function is called by DOS 3.30-6.00 APPEND.

INT 2Dh   DOS 2+
RESERVED
This vector is not used, and points at an IRET instruction, in DOS versions through 6.00.

An alternate multiplex interrupt specification has been proposed for this interrupt, to reduce conflicts and chaining overhead on INT 2Fh (adding many TSRs to INT 2Fh will reduce the performance of network redirectors and other programs which make frequent calls through INT 2Fh). Up to 256 TSRs following this specification may be installed at once without conflicts, and may be removed in any order. The full specification may be found in the Interrupt List under INT 2Dh or in a separate file on bulletin boards and CompuServe called ALTMPXnn (where nn is the version, 3.5 as of this writing).

INT 2Eh   DOS 2+
PASS COMMAND TO COMMAND INTERPRETER FOR EXECUTION
Force COMMAND.COM to execute a command as if it were typed from the keyboard.

Call With:

DS:SI	pointer to commandline to execute (see below)

Returns:

	all registers except CS:IP destroyed
AX	status (4DOS v4.0)
	0000h successful
	FFFFh error before processing command (not enough memory, etc)
	other error number returned by command

Notes: This call allows execution of arbitrary commands (including COMMAND.COM internal commands) without loading another copy of COMMAND.COM.

If COMMAND.COM is the user's command interpreter, the primary copy executes the command; this allows the master environment to be modified by issuing a "SET" command, but changes in the master environment will not become effective until all programs descended from the primary COMMAND.COM terminate.

Since COMMAND.COM processes the string as if typed from the keyboard, the transient portion needs to be present, and the calling program must ensure that sufficient memory to load the transient portion can be allocated by DOS if necessary.

The results of an INT 2Eh call are unpredictable if it is invoked by a program run from a batch file, because this call is not reentrant and COMMAND.COM uses the same internal variables when processing a batch file.

This interrupt is hooked but ignored by version 3.0 of 4DOS (a COMMAND.COM replacement) unless SHELL2E has been loaded.

This interrupt is called "Reload Transient" in the *MS-DOS 5 Programmer's Reference*.

See DO2E.ASM in Chapter 10.

Format of commandline:

Offset	Size	Description
00h	BYTE	length of command string, not counting trailing CR
01h	var	command string
N	BYTE	0Dh (CR)

INT 2Fh Function 00h   DOS 2.x only
PRINT.COM - UNKNOWN FUNCTION

The purpose of this function has not been determined.

Call With:
>   AH   00h
>   *additional arguments (if any) unknown*

Returns:
>   *unknown*

Notes: DOS 2.x PRINT.COM does not chain to the previous INT 2Fh handler.

Values in AH other than 00h or 01h cause PRINT to return the number of files in the queue in AH.

See Also: INT 2F/AH=01h

INT 2Fh Function 0080h   DOS 3.1+
PRINT.COM - GIVE PRINT A TIME SLICE

Allow PRINT to execute for a while.

Call With:
>   AX   0080h

Returns:
>   after PRINT executes

INT 2Fh Function 0106h   DOS 3.3+
PRINT.COM - GET PRINTER DEVICE

Determine which device PRINT is using for output, if there are any files in the print queue.

Call With:
>   AX   0106h

Returns:
>   CF set if files in print queue
>   AX   error code 0008h (queue full)
>   DS:SI pointer to device driver header
>   CF clear if print queue empty
>   AX   0000h

Note: documented for DOS 5+, but not documented for prior versions. (The first edition of Undocumented DOS incorrectly documented this as "Check if Error on Output Device.")

See Also: *2F/0104h*

INT 2Fh Function 0200h   PC LAN REDIR/REDIRIFS
INSTALLATION CHECK

Determine whether the PC LAN Program redirector is installed.

Call With:

AX   0200h

Returns:

AL   FFh if installed

INT 2Fh Functions 0201h to 0204h   PC LAN REDIR/REDIRIFS
UNKNOWN FUNCTIONS

The purpose of these functions has not been determined.

Call With:

AX   0201h to 0204h

additional arguments (if any) unknown

Returns:

nothing

Notes: These functions are called by DOS 3.3+ PRINT.COM.

Functions 0201h/0202h and 0203h/0204h appear to be paired opposite functions.

INT 2Fh Function 0500h   DOS 3+
CRITICAL ERROR HANDLER - INSTALLATION CHECK

Determine whether code to expand an error number into the corresponding error message has been loaded.

Called With:

AX   0500h

Returns:

AL   00h not installed, OK to install

01h not installed, can't install

FFh installed

Note: This set of functions allows a user program to partially or completely override the default critical error handler's message in COMMAND.COM.

See Also: *INT 24h*, INT 2F/AH=05h

INT 2Fh Function 05h   DOS 3+
CRITICAL ERROR HANDLER - EXPAND ERROR INTO STRING

Convert an error number into the corresponding error message.

Called With:

AH   05h

—DOS 3.x—

AL   extended error code (not zero)

—DOS 4+ —

AL   error type

01h DOS extended error code

02h parameter error

BX   error code

Returns:

CF clear if successful

ES:DI   pointer to ASCIZ error message (read-only)

AL   unknown

CF set if error code can't be converted to string

Notes: This function is called at the start of COMMAND.COM's default critical error handler if installed by a user program, allowing partial or complete overriding of the default error message. Network redirectors should use this functionality.

Subfunction 02h is called by many DOS 4+ external programs, such as SHARE and MSCDEX.
See Also: *INT 24h*, 2F/122Eh

INT 2Fh Function 0600h   DOS 3+
ASSIGN - INSTALLATION CHECK
Determine whether ASSIGN has been loaded.

Call With:
      AX   0600h
Returns:
      AL   status
                  00h not installed
                  01h not installed, but not OK to install
                  FFh installed
Note: ASSIGN is not a TSR in DR-DOS 5.0; it is internally replaced by SUBST. This function was undocumented prior to the release of DOS 5.0.
See Also: 21/52h, 2F/0601h

INT 2Fh Function 0601h   DOS 3+
ASSIGN - GET DRIVE ASSIGNMENT TABLE
Return a pointer to the drive translation table used by ASSIGN.
Call With:
      AX   0601h
Returns:
      ES   segment of ASSIGN work area and assignment table
Note: Under DOS 3+, the 26 bytes starting at ES:0103h specify which drive each of A: to Z: is mapped to. This table is initially set to 01h 02h 03h....
See Also: 2F/0600h

INT 2Fh Function 0800h   DOS 3.2+
DRIVER.SYS SUPPORT - AVAILABILITY CHECK
Determine whether the DRIVER.SYS support is present in IO.SYS/IBMBIO.COM.
Call With:
      AX   0800h
Returns:
      AL   00h not installed, OK to install
                  01h not installed, not OK to install
                  FFh installed
Note: This call is supported by DR-DOS 5.0.

INT 2Fh Function 0801h   DOS 3.2+
DRIVER.SYS SUPPORT - ADD NEW BLOCK DEVICE
Add a new logical drive alias for an existing physical drive.
Call With:
      AX   0801h
      DS:DI   pointer to drive data table (see 2F/0803h)
Notes: This function moves down the internal list of drive data tables, copying and modifying the drive description flags word for tables referencing same physical drive.

The new drive data table is appended to the existing chain of tables.

This call is supported by DR-DOS 5.0.

See Also: 2F/0803h

INT 2Fh Function 0802h   DOS 3.2+
DRIVER.SYS SUPPORT - EXECUTE DEVICE DRIVER REQUEST

Execute the specified device driver request for a drive alias established by 2F/0801h. In the following descriptions (which apply to all device drivers, not just drive aliases), most documented device driver requests have been omitted for brevity; the full description may be found on the accompanying disk.

Call With:

    AX   0802h
    ES:BX   pointer to device driver request header (see below)

Returns:

    request header updated as per requested operation

Notes: This function is supported by DR-DOS 5.0.

DOS 3.2 executes this function on any AL value from 02h through F7h.

European MS-DOS 4.0 is an OEM version with multitasking capabilities which was released on a limited number of systems between the mainstream versions 3.2 and 3.3.

For a detailed discussion of 2F/08 and DRIVER.SYS, see Geoff Chappell, *DOS Internals*.

See Also: AX=0800h, AX=0801h, AX=0803h, 21/52h, 21/99h, 21/9Ah

Values for command code:

    00h INIT
    11h (European MS-DOS 4.0) Stop Output (console screen drivers only)
    12h (European MS-DOS 4.0) Restart Output (console screen drivers only)
    13h (DOS 3.2+) generic IOCTL
    14h unused
    15h (European MS-DOS 4.0) Reset Uncertain Media Flag
    16h unused
    19h (DOS 5.0+) Check Generic IOCTL Support

Format of device driver request header:

Offset	Size	Description
00h	BYTE	length of request header
01h	BYTE	subunit within device driver
02h	BYTE	command code (see below)
03h	WORD	status (filled in by device driver)
		bit 15: error
		bits 14-11: reserved
		bit 10: unknown, set by DOS kernel on entry to some driver calls
		bit 9: busy
		bit 8: done (may be clear on return under European MS-DOS 4.0)
		bits 7-0: error code if bit 15 set (see below)

—DOS—

05h	4 BYTEs	reserved (unused in DOS 2.x and 3.x)
09h	DWORD	(European MS-DOS 4.0 only) pointer to next request header in device's request queue
		(other versions) reserved (unused in DOS 2.x and 3.x)

—STARLITE architecture—

05h	DWORD	pointer to next request header
09h	4 BYTEs	reserved

—command code 00h—

0Dh	BYTE	(return) number of units
0Eh	DWORD	(call) pointer to DOS device helper function (see below) (European MS-DOS 4.0 only)
		(call) pointer past end of memory available to driver (DOS 5.0)
		(return) address of first free byte following driver
12h	DWORD	(call) pointer to commandline arguments
		(return) pointer to BPB array (block drivers) or 0000h: 0000h (character devices)
16h	BYTE	(DOS 3+) drive number for first unit of block driver (0=A)

—European MS-DOS 4.0—

17h	DWORD	pointer to function to save registers on stack

—DOS 5+—

17h	WORD	(return) error-message flag, set to 0001h for MS-DOS to display error message on initialization failure

—command codes 11h,12h—

0Dh	BYTE	reserved

—command code 15h—

no further fields

—command codes 13h,19h—

0Dh	BYTE	category code
		00h unknown
		01h COMn:
		03h CON
		05h LPTn:
		07h mouse (European MS-DOS 4.0)
		08h disk
		9Eh (STARLITE) Media Access Control driver
0Eh	BYTE	function code
		00h (STARLITE) MAC Bind request
0Fh	WORD	copy of DS at time of IOCTL call (apparently unused in DOS 3.3)
		SI contents (European MS-DOS 4.0) reserved (DOS 5.0)
11h	WORD	offset of device driver header
		DI contents (European MS-DOS 4.0) reserved (DOS 5.0)
13h	DWORD	pointer to parameter block from 21/440Ch or AX=440Dh

Values for error code:

00h write-protect violation
01h unknown unit
02h drive not ready
03h unknown command
04h CRC error
05h bad drive request structure length
06h seek error
07h unknown media
08h sector not found
09h printer out of paper
0Ah write fault
0Bh read fault
0Ch general failure
0Dh reserved
0Eh (CD-ROM) media unavailable

0Fh invalid disk change
Call European MS-DOS 4.0 device helper function with:
DL = function
00h "SchedClock" called on each timer tick
AL = tick interval in milliseconds
01h "DevDone" device I/O complete
ES:BX = pointer to request header
Note: must update status word first; may be called from an interrupt handler
02h "PullRequest" pull next request from queue
DS:SI = pointer to DWORD pointer to start of device's request queue
Return: ZF clear if pending request
ES:BX = pointer to request header
ZF set if no more requests
03h "PullParticular" remove specific request from queue
DS:SI = pointer to DWORD pointer to start of device's request queue
ES:BX = pointer to request header
Return: ZF set if request header not found
04h "PushRequest" push the request onto the queue
DS:SI = pointer to DWORD pointer to start of device's request queue
ES:BX = pointer to request header
interrupts disabled
05h "ConsInputFilter" keyboard input check
AX = character (high byte 00h if PC ASCII character)
Return: ZF set if character should be discarded
ZF clear if character should be handled normally
Note: called by keyboard interrupt handler so DOS can scan for special input characters
06h "SortRequest" push request in sorted order by starting sector
DS:SI = pointer to DWORD pointer to start of device's request queue
ES:BX = pointer to request header
interrupts disabled
07h "SigEvent" send signal on keyboard event
AH = event identifier
Return: AL,FLAGS destroyed
09h "ProcBlock" block on event
AX:BX = event identifier (typically a pointer)
CX = timeout in ms or 0000h for never
DH = interruptible flag (nonzero if pause may be interrupted)
interrupts disabled
Return: after corresponding ProcRun call
CF clear if event wakeup, set if unusual wakeup
ZF set if timeout wakeup, clear if interrupted
AL = wakeup code, nonzero if unusual wakeup
interrupts enabled
BX,CX,DX destroyed
Note: blocks process and schedules another to run
0Ah "ProcRun" unblock process
AX:BX = event identifier (typically a pointer)
Return: AX = number of processes awakened
ZF set if no processes awakened
BX,CX,DX destroyed
0Bh "QueueInit" initialize/clear character queue

DS:BX = pointer to character queue structure (see below)
Note: the queue size field must be set before calling
0Dh "QueueWrite" put a character in the queue
DS:BX = pointer to character queue (see below)
AL = character to append to end of queue
Return: ZF set if queue is full
ZF clear if character stored
0Eh "QueueRead" get a character from the queue
DS:BX = pointer to character queue (see below)
Return: ZF set if queue is empty
ZF clear if characters in queue
AL = first character in queue
10h "GetDOSVar" return pointer to DOS variable
AL = index of variable
03h current process ID
BX = index into variable if AL specifies an array
CX = expected length of variable
Return: CF clear if successful
DX:AX = pointer to variable
CF set on error
AX,DX destroyed
BX,CX destroyed
Note: the variables may not be modified
14h "Yield" yield CPU if higher-priority task ready to run
Return: FLAGS destroyed
1Bh "CritEnter" begin system critical section
DS:BX = pointer to semaphore (6 BYTEs, initialized to zero)
Return: AX,BX,CX,DX destroyed
1Ch "CritLeave" end system critical section
DS:BX = pointer to semaphore (6 BYTEs, initialized to zero)
Return: AX,BX,CX,DX destroyed
Note: must be called in the context of the process which called CritEnter on the semaphore

Note: The DWORD pointing at the request queue must be allocated by the driver and initialized to 0000h:0000h. It always points at the next request to be executed.

Format of character queue:

Offset	Size	Description
00h	WORD	size of queue in bytes
02h	WORD	index of next character out
04h	WORD	count of characters in the queue
06h	N BYTEs	queue buffer

INT 2Fh Function 0803h   DOS 4+
DRIVER.SYS support - GET DRIVE DATA TABLE LIST

Return a pointer to the first in a list of drive data tables describing the layout of the logical drives supported by the combination of the default disk device driver and aliases established with DRIVER.SYS.

Call With:
AX   0803h

Returns:
   DS:DI   pointer to first drive data table in list
Note: This function is not available under DR-DOS 5.0.
See Also: 2F/0801h

Format of DOS 3.30 drive data table:

Offset	Size	Description
00h	DWORD	pointer to next table
04h	BYTE	physical unit number (for INT 13h)
05h	BYTE	logical drive number (0=A:)
06h	19 BYTEs	BIOS Parameter Block (see also 21/53h)

Offset	Size	Description
00h	WORD	bytes per sector
02h	BYTE	sectors per cluster, FFh if unknown
03h	WORD	number of reserved sectors
05h	BYTE	number of FATs
06h	WORD	number of root dir entries
08h	WORD	total sectors
0Ah	BYTE	media descriptor, 00h if unknown
0Bh	WORD	sectors per FAT
0Dh	WORD	sectors per track
0Fh	WORD	number of heads
11h	WORD	number of hidden sectors
19h	BYTE	flags
		bit 6: 16-bit FAT instead of 12-bit FAT

Offset	Size	Description
1Ah	WORD	number of DEVICE OPEN calls without corresponding DEVICE CLOSE
1Ch	11 BYTEs	volume label or "NO NAME " if none (always "NO NAME" for fixed media)
27h	*BYTE*	*terminating null for volume label*
28h	BYTE	device type (see 21/440Dh)
29h	WORD	bit flags describing drive
		bit 0: fixed media
		bit 1: door lock supported
		bit 2: unknown (used in determining BPB to set for 21/440Dh)
		bit 3: all sectors in a track are the same size
		bit 4: physical drive has multiple logical units
		bit 5: current logical drive for physical drive
		bit 6: unknown
		bit 7: unknown
		bit 8: related to disk change detection
2Bh	WORD	number of cylinders
2Dh	19 BYTEs	BIOS Parameter Block for highest capacity supported
40h	*3 BYTEs*	*unknown*
43h	*9 BYTEs*	*filesystem type, default is "NO NAME"*
		(apparently only MS-DOS 3.30 fixed media, nulls for removable media and PCDOS 3.30)
4Ch	BYTE	least-significant byte of last-accessed cylinder number
—removable media—		
4Dh	DWORD	time of last access in clock ticks (FFFFFFFFh if never)
—fixed media—		
4Dh	WORD	partition (FFFFh if primary, 0001h if extended)

4Fh	WORD	absolute cylinder number of partition's start on physical drive (always FFFFh if primary partition)

Format of COMPAQ DOS 3.31 drive data table:

Offset	Size	Description
00h	DWORD	pointer to next table
04h	BYTE	physical unit number (for INT 13h)
05h	BYTE	logical drive number (0=A:)
06h	25 BYTEs	BIOS Parameter Block (see DOS 4.01 drive data table below)
1Fh	*6 BYTEs*	*apparently always zeros*
25h	BYTE	flags
		bit 6: 16-bit FAT instead of 12-bit FAT
		5: *large volume*
26h	*WORD*	*device-open count*
28h	11 BYTEs	volume label or "NO NAME" if none (always "NO NAME" for fixed media)
33h	BYTE	terminating null for volume label
34h	BYTE	device type (see 21/440Dh)
35h	WORD	bit flags describing drive
37h	WORD	number of cylinders
39h	25 BYTEs	BIOS parameter block for highest capacity drive supports
52h	*6 BYTEs*	*apparently always zeros*
58h	BYTE	least-significant byte of last-accessed cylinder number

—removable media—

59h	DWORD	time of last access in clock ticks (FFFFFFFFh if never)

—fixed media—

59h	WORD	partition (FFFFh if primary, 0001h if extended)
5Bh	WORD	absolute cylinder number of partition's start on physical drive (always FFFFh if primary partition)

Format of DOS 4.0-6.0 drive data table:

Offset	Size	Description
00h	DWORD	pointer to next table
04h	BYTE	physical unit number (for INT 13h)
05h	BYTE	logical drive number (0=A:)
06h	25 BYTEs	BIOS Parameter Block (see also 21/53h)

Offset	Size	Description
00h	WORD	bytes per sector
02h	BYTE	sectors per cluster, FFh if unknown
03h	WORD	number of reserved sectors
05h	BYTE	number of FATs
06h	WORD	number of root dir entries
08h	WORD	total sectors (see offset 15h if zero)
0Ah	BYTE	media descriptor, 00h if unknown
0Bh	WORD	sectors per FAT
0Dh	WORD	sectors per track
0Fh	WORD	number of heads
11h	DWORD	number of hidden sectors
15h	DWORD	total sectors if WORD at 08h is zero

1Fh	BYTE	file system flags
		bit 6: 16-bit FAT instead of 12-bit
		bit 7: unsupportable disk (all accesses will return Not Ready)
20h	*2 BYTEs*	*device-open count*

22h	BYTE	device type (see 21/440Dh)
23h	WORD	bit flags describing drive
		bit 0: fixed media
		bit 1: door lock supported
		bit 2: current BPB locked
		bit 3: all sectors in a track are the same size
		bit 4: physical drive has multiple logical units
		bit 5: current logical drive for physical drive
		bit 6: disk change detected
		bit 7: set DASD before formatting
		bit 8: disk reformatted
		bit 9: read/write disabled
25h	WORD	number of cylinders
27h	25 BYTEs	BIOS Parameter Block for highest capacity supported
40h	*7 BYTEs*	*unknown*

—removable media—

| 47h | DWORD | time of last access in clock ticks (FFFFFFFFh if never) |

—fixed media—

47h	WORD	partition (FFFFh if primary, 0001h if extended) always 0001h for DOS 5+
49h	WORD	absolute cylinder number of partition's start on physical drive (FFFFh if primary partition in DOS 4.x)
4Bh	11 BYTEs	volume label or "NO NAME " if none (apparently taken from extended boot record rather than root directory)
56h	*BYTE*	*terminating null for volume label*
57h	DWORD	serial number
5Bh	8 BYTEs	filesystem type ("FAT12 " or "FAT16 ")
63h	*BYTE*	*terminating null for filesystem type*

INT 2Fh Function 1000h   DOS 3+
SHARE - INSTALLATION CHECK

Determine whether SHARE has been loaded.

Call With:

    AX   1000h

Returns:

    AL   00h not installed, OK to install
                01h not installed, not OK to install
                FFh installed

Notes: Values of AL other than 00h put DOS 3.x SHARE and PCDOS 4.00 into a dynamic halt.

This call is supported by the OS/2 1.3+ compatibility box, which always returns AL=FFh.

If DOS 4.01 SHARE was automatically loaded for >32M FCB support, file sharing is in an inactive state until this call is made.

DOS 5+ chains to the previous handler if AL <> 00h on entry.

This function was undocumented prior to the release of DOS 5.0.

Windows Enhanced mode hooks this function and reports that SHARE is installed even when it is not. See IS_SHARE.C in Chapter 8.

See Also: 21/52h, 2F/1080h

INT 2Fh Function 1080h   DOS 4.x only
SHARE - TURN ON FILE SHARING CHECKS

Enable checks of file sharing modes when files are opened in addition to FCB support for large partitions.

Call With:

AX	1080h

Returns:

AL	status
	F0h successful
	FFh checking was already on

See Also: 2F/1000h, 2F/1081h

INT 2Fh Function 1081h   DOS 4.x only
SHARE - TURN OFF FILE SHARING CHECKS

Disable checks of file sharing modes when files are opened, but continue providing FCB support for large partitions.

Call With:

AX	1081h

Returns:

AL	status
	F0h successful
	FFh checking was already off

See Also: 2F/1000h, 2F/1080h

INT 2Fh Function 1100h   DOS 3.1+
NETWORK REDIRECTOR - INSTALLATION CHECK

Determine whether a network redirector using the DOS kernel network hooks is installed.

Call With:

AX	1100h

Returns:

AL	00h not installed, OK to install
	01h not installed, not OK to install
	FFh installed

Notes: This function is called by the DOS 3.1+ kernel.

For all 2F/11 calls, see the redirector specification in Chapter 8.

In DOS 4.x only, the 11xx calls are all in IFSFUNC.EXE, not in the network redirector; DOS 5+ moves the calls back into the redirector. The extra layer imposed by IFSFUNC proved to be overly detrimental to performance. This function was undocumented prior to the release of DOS 5.0.

INT 2Fh Function 1100h   MSCDEX
INSTALLATION CHECK

Determine whether the Microsoft CD-ROM Extensions have been loaded.

Call With:

AX	1100h
STACK	WORD DADAh

Returns:

AL	00h not installed, OK to install

> STACK unchanged
> 01h not installed, not OK to install
> STACK unchanged
> FFh installed
> STACK   WORD ADADh

INT 2Fh Function 1101h   DOS 3.1+
NETWORK REDIRECTOR - REMOVE REMOTE DIRECTORY

Remove a directory on a network or installable file system drive.

Called With:

AX	1101h	
SS	DOS DS	
SDA first filename pointer		pointer to fully-qualified directory name
SDA CDS pointer		pointer to current directory structure for drive with dir

Returns:

CF set on error
    AX   DOS error code (see *21/59h*)
CF clear if successful

Note: This function is called by the DOS 3.1+ kernel. For Phantom implementation, see listing 8-36.
See Also: *21/3Ah*, 21/60h, 2F/1103h, 2F/1105h

INT 2Fh Function 1102h   DOS 4.x only
IFSFUNC.EXE - REMOVE REMOTE DIRECTORY

Remove a directory on a network or installable file system drive.

Called With:

AX	1102h	
SS	DOS DS	
SDA first filename pointer		pointer to fully-qualified directory name
SDA CDS pointer		pointer to current directory structure for drive with dir

Returns:

CF set on error
    AX   DOS error code (see *21/59h*)
CF clear if successful

Note: This function appears to be identical to 2F/1101h.
See Also: 2F/1101h

INT 2Fh Function 1103h   DOS 3.1+
NETWORK REDIRECTOR - MAKE REMOTE DIRECTORY

Create a new directory on a network or installable file system drive.

Called With:

AX	1103h	
SS	DOS DS	
SDA first filename pointer		pointer to fully-qualified directory name
SDA CDS pointer		pointer to current directory structure for drive with dir

Returns:

CF set on error
    AX   DOS error code (see *21/59h*)
CF clear if successful

Note: This function is called by the DOS 3.1+ kernel.
See Also: *21/39h*, 21/60h, 2F/1101h, 2F/1105h

INT 2Fh Function 1104h   DOS 4.x only
IFSFUNC.EXE - MAKE REMOTE DIRECTORY
Create a new directory on a network or installable file system drive.

Called With:

AX	1104h
SS	DOS DS (see 2F/1203h)
SDA first filename pointer	pointer to fully-qualified directory name
SDA CDS pointer	pointer to current directory structure for drive with dir

Returns:
>   CF set on error
>> AX   DOS error code (see *21/59h*)
>   CF clear if successful

Note: This function appears to be identical to 2F/1103h.
See Also: 2F/1103h

INT 2Fh Function 1105h   DOS 3.1+
NETWORK REDIRECTOR - CHDIR
Change the current directory on a network or installable file system drive.

Called With:

AX	1105h
SS	DOS DS (see 2F/1203h)
SDA first filename pointer	pointer to fully-qualified directory name
SDA CDS pointer	pointer to current directory structure for drive with dir

Returns:
>   CF set on error
>> AX   DOS error code (see *21/59h*)
>   CF clear if successful
>> CDS updated with new path

Notes: This function is called by the DOS 3.1+ kernel. For Phantom implementation, see listing 8-35.

The directory string in the CDS should not have a terminating backslash unless the current directory is the root directory.
See Also: *21/3Bh*, 21/60h, 2F/1101h, 2F/1103h

INT 2Fh Function 1106h   DOS 3.1+
NETWORK REDIRECTOR - CLOSE REMOTE FILE
Close a file which was previously opened on a network or installable file system drive.

Called With:

AX	1106h
ES:DI	pointer to SFT
SFT DPB field	pointer to DPB of drive containing file (DPB may be 0 for redirector drive)

Returns:
>   CF set on error
>> AX   DOS error code (see *21/59h*)
>   CF clear if successful
>> SFT updated (redirector must decrement open count, which may be done with 2F/1208h)

Note: This function is called by the DOS 3.1+ kernel.

A redirector must decrement the open count in the SFT (see PHANTOM.C and 2F/1208 in Chapter 8).
See Also: *21/3Eh*, 2F/1201h, 2F/1227h

INT 2Fh Function 1107h   DOS 3.1+
NETWORK REDIRECTOR - COMMIT REMOTE FILE

Update the directory entry and flush disk buffers for a file on a network or installable file system drive.
Called With:

    AX   1107h
    ES:DI   pointer to SFT
      SFT DPB field   pointer to DPB of drive containing file
Returns:
    CF set on error
      AX   DOS error code (see *21/59*h)
    CF clear if successful
      all buffers for file flushed
      directory entry updated
Note: This function is called by the DOS 3.1+ kernel.
See Also: 21/5D01h, *21/68h*

INT 2Fh Function 1108h   DOS 3.1+
NETWORK REDIRECTOR - READ FROM REMOTE FILE

Read data from a file opened on a network or installable file system drive.
Called With:

    AX   1108h
    CX   number of bytes
    SS   DOS DS (see 2F/1203h0
    SDA DTA field   pointer to user buffer
    ES:DI   pointer to SFT
      SFT DPB field   pointer to DPB of drive containing file
Returns:
    CF set on error
      AX   DOS error code (see *21/59h*)
    CF clear if successful
      CX   number of bytes read (0000h if at end of file)
      SFT updated
Note: This function is called by the DOS 3.1+ kernel. For Phantom implementation, see listings 8-30 and 8-38.
See Also: *21/3Fh*, 21/5D06h, 2F/1109h, 2F/1229h

INT 2Fh Function 1109h   DOS 3.1+
NETWORK REDIRECTOR - WRITE TO REMOTE FILE

Write data to a file opened on a network or installable file system drive.

Called With:

    AX   1109h
    CX   number of bytes
    SS   DOS DS
    SDA DTA field   pointer to user buffer
    ES:DI   pointer to SFT
      SFT DPB field   pointer to DPB of drive containing file

Returns:
>CF set on error
>>AX   DOS error code (see *21/59h*)
>CF clear if successful
>>CX   number of bytes written
>>SFT updated

Note: This function is called by the DOS 3.1+ kernel.
See Also: *21/40h*, 21/5D06h, 2F/1107h, 2F/1108h

INT 2Fh Function 110Ah   DOS 3.1-3.31 only
NETWORK REDIRECTOR - LOCK REGION OF FILE

Request that no other processes be allowed access to a portion of the specified file.

Called With:
>AX   110Ah
>BX   file handle
>CX:DX   starting offset
>SI   high word of size
>SS   DOS DS (see 2F/1203h)
>ES:DI   pointer to SFT
>> SFT DPB field   pointer to DPB of drive containing file
>STACK   WORD low word of size

Returns:
>CF set on error
>>AL   DOS error code (see *21/59h*)
>STACK unchanged

Notes: This function is called by the DOS 3.10-3.31 kernel. The redirector is expected to resolve lock conflicts.
See Also: *21/5Ch*, 2F/110Bh

INT 2Fh Function 110Ah   DOS 4+
NETWORK REDIRECTOR - LOCK/UNLOCK REGION OF FILE

Deny or allow access to a portion of a remote file by other processes.

Called With:
>AX   110Ah
>BL   function
>>   00h lock
>>   01h unlock
>DS:DX   pointer to parameter block (see below)
>SS   DOS DS
>ES:DI   pointer to SFT
>> SFT DPB field   pointer to DPB of drive containing file

Returns:
>CF set on error
>>AL   DOS error code (see *21/59h*)

Notes: This function is called by the DOS 4.0+ kernel.
>The redirector is expected to resolve lock conflicts.

See Also: *21/5Ch*, 2F/110Bh

Format of parameter block:

Offset	Size	Description
00h	DWORD	start offset
04h	DWORD	size of region

INT 2Fh Function 110Bh   DOS 3.1-3.31 only
NETWORK REDIRECTOR - UNLOCK REGION OF FILE
Allow other processes to access the specified portion of the file.

Called With:

AX	110Bh
BX	file handle
CX:DX	starting offset
SI	high word of size
STACK	WORD low word of size
ES:DI	pointer to SFT for file
SFT DPB field	pointer to DPB of drive containing file

Returns:
CF set on error
    AL   DOS error code (see *21/59h*)
STACK unchanged

Note: This function is called by the DOS 3.1-3.31 kernel; DOS 4.0+ calls 2F/110Ah instead.
See Also: *21/5Ch*, 2F/110Ah

INT 2Fh Function 110Ch   DOS 3.1+
NETWORK REDIRECTOR - GET DISK SPACE
Get information on allocation size and disk space (free and total) for a network or installable file system drive.

Called With:

AX	110Ch
ES:DI	pointer to current directory structure for desired drive

Returns:

AL	sectors per cluster
AH	media ID byte
BX	total clusters
CX	bytes per sector
DX	number of available clusters

Note: This function is called by the DOS 3.1+ kernel.
See Also: *21/36h*

INT 2Fh Function 110Eh   DOS 3.1+
NETWORK REDIRECTOR - SET REMOTE FILE'S ATTRIBUTES
Change the attributes of a file on a network or installable file system drive.

Called With:

AX	110Eh
SS	DOS DS (see 2F/1203h)
SDA first filename pointer	pointer to fully-qualified name of file
SDA CDS pointer	pointer to current directory structure for drive with file
STACK	WORD new file attributes

Returns:
>   CF set on error
>   AX   DOS error code (see *21/59h*)
>   CF clear if successful
>   STACK unchanged

Note: This function is called by the DOS 3.1+ kernel.
See Also: *21/4301h*, 21/60h, 2F/110Fh

INT 2Fh Function 110Fh   DOS 3.1+
Network Redirector - Get Remote File's Attributes And Size

Get the attributes of a file on a network or installable file system drive.

Called With:
>   AX   110Fh
>   SS   DOS DS
>   SDA first filename pointer   pointer to fully-qualified name of file
>   SDA CDS pointer   pointer to current directory structure for drive with file

Returns:
>   CF set on error
>   AX   DOS error code (see *21/59h*)
>   CF clear if successful
>   AX   file attributes
>   BX:DI   file size

Note: This function is called by the DOS 3.1+ kernel.
See Also: *21/4300h*, 21/60h, 2F/110Eh

INT 2Fh Function 1111h   DOS 3.1+
NETWORK REDIRECTOR - RENAME REMOTE FILE

Change the name of a file on a network or installable file system drive.

Called With:
>   AX   1111h
>   SS   DOS DS
>   DS   DOS DS
>   SDA first filename pointer   offset of fully-qualified old name
>   SDA second filename pointer   offset of fully-qualified new name
>   SDA CDS pointer   pointer to current directory structure for drive with file

Returns:
>   CF set on error
>   AX   DOS error code (see *21/59h*)
>   CF clear if successful

Note: This function is called by the DOS 3.1+ kernel.
See Also: 21/56h, 21/60h

INT 2Fh Function 1113h   DOS 3.1+
NETWORK REDIRECTOR - DELETE REMOTE FILE

Remove a file from a network or installable file system drive.

Called With:
>   AX   1113h
>   SS   DOS DS

DS   DOS DS
SDA first filename pointer   pointer to fully-qualified filename in DOS DS
SDA CDS pointer   pointer to current directory structure for drive with file

Returns:
CF set on error
    AX   DOS error code (see *21/59h*)
CF clear if successful

Notes: This function is called by the DOS 3.1+ kernel.
    The file specification may contain wildcards.

See Also: 21/41h, 21/60h

INT 2Fh Function 1116h   DOS 3.1+
NETWORK REDIRECTOR - OPEN EXISTING REMOTE FILE

Prepare for access to an existing file located on a network drive.

Called With:
AX   1116h
ES:DI   pointer to uninitialized SFT
SS   DOS DS
SDA first filename pointer pointer to fully-qualified name of file to open
STACK   WORD file open mode (see *21/3Dh*)

Returns:
CF set on error
    AX   DOS error code (see *21/59h*)
CF clear if successful
    SFT filled (except handle count, which DOS manages itself)
STACK unchanged

Note: This function is called by the DOS 3.1+ kernel.
See Also: *21/3Dh*, 21/60h, 2F/1106h, 2F/1117h, 2F/1118h, 2F/112Eh

---

INT 2Fh Function 1117h   DOS 3.1+
Network Redirector - Create/truncate Remote File With Cds

Create a file on a network drive, or truncate an existing file to zero length.

Called With:
AX   1117h
ES:DI   pointer to uninitialized SFT
SS   DOS DS
SDA first filename pointer pointer to fully-qualified name of file to open
SDA CDS pointer   pointer to current directory structure for drive with file
STACK   WORD file creation mode
                            low byte = file attributes
                            high byte = 00h normal create, 01h create new file

Returns:
CF set on error
    AX   DOS error code (see *21/59h*)
CF clear if successful
    SFT filled (except handle count, which DOS manages itself)
STACK unchanged

Note: This function is called by the DOS 3.1+ kernel.
See Also: *21/3Ch*, 21/60h, 2F/1106h, 2F/1116h, 2F/1118h, 2F/112Eh

INT 2Fh Function 1118h   DOS 3.1+
Network Redirector - Create/truncate File Without Cds

Create a file on a drive which does not have a current directory structure.

Called With:

AX	1118h
ES:DI	pointer to uninitialized SFT
SS	DOS DS
SDA first filename pointer	pointer to fully-qualified name of file
STACK	WORD file creation mode
	low byte = file attributes
	high byte = 00h normal create, 01h create new file

Returns:

unknown
STACK unchanged

Note: This function is called by the DOS 3.1+ kernel when creating a file on a drive for which the SDA CDS pointer has offset FFFFh. For example, DOS will call 2F/1118 if someone calls 21/5B (Create New File) for the name \\FOO\BAR.

See Also: 21/60h, 2F/1106h, 2F/1116h, 2F/1117h, 2F/112Eh

INT 2Fh Function 1119h   DOS 3.1+
NETWORK REDIRECTOR - FIND FIRST FILE WITHOUT CDS

Begin a directory search on a logical drive which does not have a Current Directory Structure.

Called With:

AX	1119h
SS	DOS DS
DS	DOS DS
[DTA]	uninitialized 21-byte findfirst search data (see 21/4Eh)
SDA first filename pointer	pointer to fully-qualified search template
SDA search attribute	attribute mask for search

Returns:

CF set on error	
AX	DOS error code (see *21/59h*)
CF clear if successful	
[DTA]	updated findfirst search data
	(bit 7 of first byte must be set)
[DTA+15h]	standard directory entry for file

Notes: This function is called by the DOS 3.1+ kernel; for example: DIR \\FOO\BAR.
DOS 4.x IFSFUNC returns CF set, AX=0003h.

INT 2Fh Function 111Bh   DOS 3.1+
NETWORK REDIRECTOR - FINDFIRST

Begin a directory search on a network or installable file system drive.

Called With:

AX	111Bh
SS	DOS DS
DS	DOS DS
[DTA]	uninitialized 21-byte findfirst search data (see 21/4Eh)
SDA first filename pointer	pointer to fully-qualified search template

SDA CDS pointer   pointer to current directory structure for drive with file
SDA search attribute   attribute mask for search

Returns:
CF set on error
  AX DOS error code (see *21/59h*)
CF clear if successful
  [DTA] updated findfirst search data
      (bit 7 of first byte must be set)
  [DTA+15h] standard directory entry for file

Note: This function is called by the DOS 3.1+ kernel. For Phantom implementation, see listing 8-33.
See Also: 21/4Eh, 21/60h, 2F/111Ch

INT 2Fh Function 111Ch   DOS 3.1+
NETWORK REDIRECTOR - FINDNEXT
Continue a directory search on a network or installable file system drive.

Called With:
  AX 111Ch
  SS DOS DS
  DS DOS DS
  [DTA] 21-byte findfirst search data (see 21/4Eh)
Returns:
CF set on error
  AX DOS error code (see *21/59h*)
CF clear if successful
  [DTA] updated findfirst search data
      (bit 7 of first byte must be set)
  [DTA+15h] standard directory entry for file

Note: This function is called by the DOS 3.1+ kernel. For Phantom implementation, see listing 8-33.
See Also: *21/4Fh*, 2F/111Bh

INT 2Fh Function 111Dh   DOS 3.1+
Network Redirector - Close All Remote Files For Process
Close each file a particular process has opened on a network or installable file system drive.
Called With:
  AX 111Dh
  DS *unknown*
  SS DOS DS (see 2F/1203h)
Returns:
  unknown
Notes: This function is called by the DOS 3.1+ kernel.
  The redirector also closes all FCBs opened by the process.
See Also: 21/5D04h

INT 2Fh Function 111Eh   DOS 3.1+
NETWORK REDIRECTOR - DO REDIRECTION
Various subfunctions allow control of network redirection.
Called With:
  AX 111Eh
  SS DOS DS
  STACK WORD function to execute

5F00h get redirection mode
    BL   type (03h printer, 04h disk)
    Returns:
        BH   state (00h off, 01h on)
5F01h set redirection mode
    BL   type (03h printer, 04h disk)
    BH   state (00h off, 01h on)
5F02h get redirection list entry
    BX   redirection list index
    DS:SI   pointer to 16-byte local device name buffer
    ES:DI   pointer to 128-byte network name buffer
    Returns:
        must set user's BX to device type and CX to stored
        parameter value, using 2F/1218h to get stack frame address
5F03h redirect device
    BL   device type (see *21/5F03h*)
    CX   stored parameter value
    DS:SI   pointer to ASCIZ source device name
    ES:DI   pointer to destination ASCIZ network path + ASCIZ passwd
5F04h cancel redirection
    DS:SI   pointer to ASCIZ device name or network path
5F05h get redirection list extended entry
    BX   redirection list index
    DS:SI   pointer to buffer for ASCIZ source device name
    ES:DI   pointer to buffer for destination ASCIZ network path
    Returns:
        BH   status flag
        BL   type (03h printer, 04h disk)
        CX   stored parameter value
        BP   NETBIOS local session number
   5F06h similar to 5F05h

Returns:
    CF set on error
      AX   error code (see *21/59h*)
    STACK unchanged
Note: This function is called by the DOS 3.1+ kernel on 21/5Fh (including LAN Manager calls).
See Also: 21/5F00h, 21/5F01h, *21/5F02h*, *21/5F03h*, *21/5F04h*, 21/5F05h, 21/5F06h

---

INT 2Fh Function 111Fh
NETWORK REDIRECTOR - PRINTER SETUP
DOS 3.1+

Subfunctions allow getting or setting the network printer setup string or mode.

Called With:
    AX   111Fh
    STACK WORD function
           5E02h set printer setup
           5E03h get printer setup
           5E04h set printer mode
           5E05h get printer mode
Returns:
    CF set on error

      AX   error code (see *21/59h*)
    STACK unchanged
Note: This function is called by the DOS 3.1+ kernel on 21/5E.
See Also: *21/5E02h*, *21/5E03h*, 21/5E04h, 21/5E05h

INT 2Fh Function 1120h   DOS 3.1+
NETWORK REDIRECTOR - FLUSH ALL DISK BUFFERS

Force an immediate update of the network or installable file system drives from disk buffers which have not yet been written out to disk.

Called With:
    AX   1120h
    DS   DOS DS
    additional arguments (if any) unknown
Returns:
    CF clear (successful)
Notes: This function is called by the DOS 3.1+ kernel.
    The current directory structure array pointer and LASTDRIVE= entries of the DOS list of lists are used by the DOS 4 IFSFUNC handler for this call.
See Also: *21/0Dh*, *21/5D01h*

INT 2Fh Function 1121h   DOS 3.1+
NETWORK REDIRECTOR - SEEK FROM END OF REMOTE FILE

Set the file pointer relative to the end of the specified file.

Called With:

AX	1121h
SS	DOS DS
CX:DX	offset (in bytes) from end
ES:DI	pointer to SFT
SFT DPB field	pointer to DPB of drive with file

Returns:
    CF set on error
         AL   DOS error code (see *21/59h*)
    CF clear if successful
         DX:AX   new file position
Note: This function is called by the DOS 3.1+ kernel in a rare situation (see Chapter 8) when setting the file position for a remote file relative to the end (mode 02h), because the file's size may have changed since the last access to the file. The other two modes (absolute position and relative to current position) are handled without network calls because the file's actual size does not affect those two modes.
See Also: *21/42h*, 2F/1228h

INT 2Fh Function 1122h   DOS 3.1+
NETWORK REDIRECTOR - PROCESS TERMINATION HOOK

Inform the network that a process has terminated.

Called With:
    AX   1122h
    SS   DOS DS
    DS   PSP of process about to terminate
    additional arguments (if any) unknown

Returns:
  unknown
Note: This function is called by the DOS 3.1+ kernel.

INT 2Fh Function 1123h   DOS 3.1+
NETWORK REDIRECTOR - QUALIFY REMOTE FILENAME

Convert a name into a absolute pathname with any network redirections resolved.
Called With:
  AX   1123h
  DS:SI   pointer to ASCIZ filename to canonicalize
  ES:DI   pointer to 128-byte buffer for qualified name
Returns:
  CF set if not resolved
Notes: This function is called by the MS-DOS 3.1+ kernel, but not called by DRDOS 5.0 unless the filename matches the name of a character device.

  DOS calls this function first when it attempts to resolve a filename (unless inside an 21/5D00h server call); if this fails, DOS resolves the name locally.
See Also: 21/60h, 2F/1221h

INT 2Fh Function 1124h   DOS 3.1+
NETWORK REDIRECTOR - PRINTER OFF

Appears to force printer echo of standard output into the OFF state.
Called With:
  AX   1124h
  ES:DI   pointer to SFT
  SS   DOS DS
  additional arguments (if any) unknown
Returns:
  CX   unknown

Note: This function is called by the DOS 3.1+ kernel if 2F/1126h returns CF set.
See Also: 2F/1126h

INT 2Fh Function 1125h   DOS 3.1+
NETWORK REDIRECTOR - REDIRECTED PRINTER MODE

Set or determine the state of print streams for the network printer.

Called With:
  AX   1125h
  STACK   WORD subfunction
            5D07h get print stream state
                  Returns:
                  DL   current state
            5D08h set print stream state
                  DL   new state
            5D09h finish print job
Returns:
  CF set on error
    AX   error code (see *21/59h*)
  STACK unchanged
Note: This function is called by the DOS 3.1+ kernel.
See Also: 21/5D07h, 21/5D08h, 21/5D09h

INT 2Fh Function 1126h   DOS 3.1+
NETWORK REDIRECTOR - PRINTER ON/OFF
Toggle printer echo of standard output.

Called With:
>   AX   1126h
>   *ES:DI   pointer to SFT for file handle 4*
>   SS   DOS DS (see 2F/1203h)
>   *additional arguments (if any) unknown*

Returns:
>   CF set on error

Note: This function is called by the DOS 3.1+ kernel when print echoing (^P, ^PrtSc) changes state and STDPRN has bit 11 of the device information word in the SFT set.

See Also: 2F/1124h

INT 21h Function 1127h   Novell
NETWORK REDIRECTOR - REMOTE COPY
Network redirector subfunction 27h has been reported to be a Remote Copy function, for reducing network traffic when the source and destination for the copy are both on the same file server. For more information, see chapter 8.

INT 2Fh Function 112Bh   DOS 4.x only
IFSFUNC.EXE - GENERIC IOCTL
Implements the "Generic IOCTL" call on network devices.

Called With:
>   AX   112Bh
>   SS   DOS DS
>   CX   function/category
>   DS:DX   pointer to parameter block
>   STACK   WORD value of AX on entry to INT 21h (440Ch or 440Dh)
>   *additional arguments (if any) unknown*

Returns:
>   CF set on error
>   AX   DOS error code (see *21/59h*)
>   CF clear if successful

Note: This function is called by the DOS 4.0 kernel.

INT 2Fh Function 112Ch   DOS 4+
IFSFUNC.EXE - UNKNOWN FUNCTION
The purpose of this function has not been determined.

Called With:
>   AX   112Ch
>   SS   DOS DS
>   SDA current SFT ptr   pointer to SFT for file
>   *additional arguments (if any) unknown*

Returns:
>   CF set on error
>   AX   DOS error code (see *21/59h*)
>   CF clear if successful

Note: Called by SHARE in DOS 5.0

INT 2Fh Function 112Dh
IFSFUNC.EXE - UNKNOWN FUNCTION

DOS 4.x only

The purpose of this function has not been determined.

Called With:

AX	112Dh
BL	subfunction (value of AL on INT 21h)

            04h truncate open file to zero length

                  ES:DI pointer to SFT for file

                        Returns:

                            CF clear

        else unknown

                        Returns:

                            CX   *unknown (00h or 02h for DOS 4.01)*

ES:DI	pointer to SFT
SS	DOS DS

Returns:

DS	DOS DS

Note: This function is called by the DOS 4.0 kernel on 21/5702h, 21/5703h, and 21/5704h. Perhaps 2F/112D supports OS/2 extended attributes (EAs) and/or the DosGet/SetPath/FileInfo functions.

INT 2Fh Function 112Eh
NETWORK REDIRECTOR - EXTENDED OPEN/CREATE FILE

DOS 4+

Implements the extended file open call (21/6Ch) for network and installable file system drives.

Called With:

AX	112Eh
SS	DOS DS
DS	DOS DS
ES:DI	pointer to uninitialized SFT for file
SDA first filename pointer	pointer to fully-qualified filename
SDA extended file open action	action code (see *21/6C00h*)
SDA extended file open mode	open mode for file (see *21/6C00h*)
STACK	WORD file attribute for created/truncated file
	low byte = file attributes
	high byte = 00h normal create/open, 01h create new file

Returns:

CF set on error

    AX   error code

CF clear if successful

    CX   result code

        01h file opened

        02h file created

        03h file replaced (truncated)

    SFT initialized (except handle count, which DOS manages itself)

Note: This function is called by the DOS 4+ kernel, and by DOS 5+ SHARE.

See Also: *21/6C00h*, 2F/1115h, 2F/1116h, 2F/1117h

INT 2Fh Function 1130h
IFSFUNC.EXE - GET IFSFUNC SEGMENT

DOS 4.x only

Return the segment of the resident IFSFUNC code.

Called With:
AX   1130h
Returns:
ES   CS of resident IFSFUNC

INT 2Fh Function 1200h
INTERNAL FUNCTIONS AVAILABILITY CHECK

DOS 3+

Determine whether the DOS internal services are present.

Call With:
AX   1200h
Returns:
AL   FFh (for compatibility with other INT 2Fh functions which return AL=FFh if installed)
Note: See Chapters 6 and 8 for discussions of the DOS internal functions.

INT 2Fh Function 1201h
CLOSE CURRENT FILE

DOS 3+

Close the file currently being operated on.

Call With:
AX   1201h
SS   DOS DS
SDA current SFT pointer   pointer to SFT of file to close
Returns:
CF set on error
CF clear if successful
    BX   *unknown*
    CX   new reference count of SFT
    ES:DI   pointer to SFT for file
See Also: *21/3Eh*, 2F/1106h, 2F/1227h

INT 2Fh Function 1202h
GET INTERRUPT ADDRESS

DOS 3+

Return a pointer to the interrupt vector corresponding to the given interrupt number.

Call With:
AX   1202h
STACK   WORD vector number
Returns:
ES:BX   pointer to interrupt vector
STACK unchanged

INT 2Fh Function 1203h
GET DOS DATA SEGMENT

DOS 3+

Return the segment of the IBMDOS.COM/MS-DOS.SYS data area.

Call With:
AX   1203h

Returns:

DS   segment of IBMDOS.COM/MS-DOS.SYS data segment

Note: For DOS 3.X and 4.X (but *not* for DOS 5+), the kernel code segment is the same as the data segment.

Many Microsoft programs get the DOS data segment by calling 21/52, and using ES (ignoring BX). The "style" (DOS 3 or DOS 4+) of the DOS data segment is indicated by the byte at offset 4 in DOS DS (see 21/5D06).

INT 2Fh Function 1204h   DOS 3+
NORMALIZE PATH SEPARATOR

Convert forward slashes into backslashes.

Call With:

AX   1204h

STACK   WORD character to normalize

Returns:

AL   normalized character (forward slash turned to backslash, all others unchanged)

ZF   set if path separator

STACK   unchanged

INT 2Fh Function 1205h   DOS 3+
OUTPUT CHARACTER TO STANDARD OUTPUT

Send a single character to the standard output of the current process.

Call With:

AX   1205h

STACK   WORD character to output

Returns:

STACK unchanged

Note: This function can only be called from within a DOS function call.

INT 2Fh Function 1206h   DOS 3+
INVOKE CRITICAL ERROR

Cause an INT 24h, performing all necessary housekeeping and return code translations.

Call With:

AX   1206h

DI   error code

BP:SI   pointer to device driver header

SS   DOS DS

STACK   WORD value to be passed to INT 24h in AX

Returns:

AL   0-3 for Abort, Retry, Ignore, Fail

STACK unchanged

See Also: INT 24h

INT 2Fh Function 1207h   DOS 3+
MAKE DISK BUFFER MOST-RECENTLY USED

Move the specified disk buffer to the end of the disk buffer list (which is kept in reverse order of recency of use).

Call With:

AX	1207h
DS:DI	pointer to disk buffer

Returns:

nothing

Note: This function can only be called from within a DOS function call.

This function is nearly identical to INT 2Fh Function 120Fh.

See Also: 2F/120Fh

INT 2Fh Function 1208h
DECREMENT SFT REFERENCE COUNT

DOS 3+

Reduce the number of references to the given System File Table by one.

Call With:

AX	1208h
ES:DI	pointer to SFT

Returns:

AX	value of reference count before decrement.

Notes: The reference count is set to FFFFh to indicate no references, since 0 indicates that the SFT is not in use. In this case, the caller should set the count to zero after cleaning up.

This call is used by redirectors such as MSCDEX on 2F/1106h (Close Remote File). See Chapter 8. The SFT reference count can also be decremented by hand.

INT 2Fh Function 1209h
FLUSH AND FREE DISK BUFFER

DOS 3+

Force the given disk buffer's contents to disk if it is dirty, and then mark the buffer unused.

Call With:

AX	1209h
DS:DI	pointer to disk buffer

Note: This function can only be called from within a DOS function call.

See Also: 2F/120Eh, 2F/1215h

INT 2Fh Function 120Ah
PERFORM CRITICAL ERROR INTERRUPT

DOS 3+

Invoke an INT 24h, passing the appropriate values for the current drive and operation (stored in the SDA).

Call With:

AX	120Ah
DS	DOS DS
SS	DOS DS
STACK	WORD extended error code

Returns:

AL	user response (0=ignore, 1=retry, 2=abort, 3=fail)

CF clear if retry, set otherwise

STACK unchanged

Notes: This function can only be called during a DOS function call, as it uses various fields in the SDA to set up the registers for the INT 24h.

The code for this call reportedly sets the current DPB's first root directory sector to 1.

Used by network redirectors such as MSCDEX.
See Also: INT 24h

INT 2Fh Function 120Bh   DOS 3+
SIGNAL SHARING VIOLATION TO USER

Produce a critical error interrupt if an attempt was made to open a file previously opened in compatibility mode with inheritance allowed.

Call With:

AX	120Bh
ES:DI	pointer to system file table entry for previous open of file
STACK	WORD extended error code (should be 20h—sharing violation)

Returns:

CF clear if operation should be retried
CF set if operation should not be retried
   AX   error code (20h) (see *21/59h*)
STACK unchanged

Note: This function can only be called during a DOS function call. It should only be called if an attempt was made to open an already-open file contrary to the sharing rules.

INT 2Fh Function 120Ch   DOS 3+
OPEN DEVICE AND SET SFT OWNER

Invokes the "device open" call on the device driver for the given SFT and then sets the owner of the last-accessed FCB file to the calling process's ID.

Call With:

AX	120Ch
SDA current SFT pointer	pointer to SFT for file
DS	DOS DS
SS	DOS DS

Returns:

ES, DI, AX destroyed (ES:DI may point to the SFT)

Note: Network redirectors must call this function for FCB opens (see Chapter 8).

INT 2Fh Function 120Dh   DOS 3+
GET DATE AND TIME

Return the current date and time in directory format.

Call With:

AX	120Dh
SS	DOS DS

Returns:

AX	current date in packed format (see *21/5700h*)
DX	current time in packed format (see *21/5700h*)

See Also: *21/2Ah, 21/2Ch*

INT 2Fh Function 120Eh   DOS 3+
MARK ALL DISK BUFFERS UNREFERENCED

Clear the "referenced" flag on all disk buffers. This flag is automatically set when a buffer is read or written, and is used in the buffer replacement algorithm. Unreferenced buffers are generally replaced before referenced buffers.

Call With:

    AX   120Eh
    SS   DOS DS

Returns:

    DS:DI   pointer to first disk buffer

Note: In DOS 5+, this function has become essentially a NOP, invoking the same code used by AX=1224h (SHARING DELAY).

See Also: *21/0Dh*, 2F/1209h, 2F/1210h

INT 2Fh Function 120Fh   DOS 3+
MAKE BUFFER MOST RECENTLY USED

Move the specified disk buffer to the end of the buffer chain without flushing it to disk if it is dirty.

Call With:

    AX   120Fh
    DS:DI   pointer to disk buffer
    SS   DOS DS

Returns:

    DS:DI   pointer to next buffer in buffer list

Notes: This function is the same as 2F/1207h except that it returns a pointer to the buffer following the specified buffer in the buffer chain. Under DOS 3.3, the specified buffer is moved to the start of the buffer chain if it is marked unused.

See Also: 2F/1207h

INT 2Fh Function 1210h   DOS 3+
FIND UNREFERENCED DISK BUFFER

Return a pointer to the least-recently used disk buffer (if any) which has not been referenced since its first use or the last "Mark all Disk Buffers Unreferenced" call.

Call With:

    AX   1210h
    DS:DI   pointer to first disk buffer to check

Returns:

    ZF clear if found
        DS:DI pointer to first unreferenced disk buffer
    ZF set if not found

Note: In DOS 5+, this function has become essentially a NOP, invoking the same code used by AX=1224h (SHARING DELAY).

See Also: 2F/120Eh

INT 2Fh Function 1211h   DOS 3+
NORMALIZE ASCIZ FILENAME

Copy the given filename, converting it to uppercase and changing forward slashes into backslashes.

Call With:

    AX   1211h
    DS:SI   pointer to ASCIZ filename to normalize
    ES:DI   pointer to buffer for normalized filename

Returns:

    destination buffer filled

See Also: 2F/121Eh, 2F/1221h

INT 2Fh Function 1212h
DOS 3+
GET LENGTH OF ASCIZ STRING

Return the length of a null-terminated character string.

Call With:
AX	1212h
ES:DI	pointer to ASCIZ string

Returns:
CX	length of string

See Also: 2F/1225h

INT 2Fh Function 1213h
DOS 3+
UPPERCASE CHARACTER

Return the uppercase equivalent, using the current country's capitalization rules, of the given character.

Call With:
AX	1213h
STACK	WORD character to convert to uppercase

Returns:
AL	uppercase character
STACK unchanged	

INT 2Fh Function 1214h
DOS 3+
COMPARE FAR POINTERS

Determine whether two FAR pointers are bit-wise identical.

Call With:
AX	1214h
DS:SI	first pointer
ES:DI	second pointer

Returns:

ZF set if pointers are equal, ZF clear if not equal

INT 2Fh Function 1215h
DOS 3+
FLUSH BUFFER

Force the contents of the specified disk buffer to be written to disk if it is dirty.

Call With:
AX	1215h
DS:DI	pointer to disk buffer
SS	DOS DS
STACK	WORD drives for which to skip buffer
	ignore buffer if drive same as high byte, or bytes differ and the buffer is for a drive OTHER than that given in low byte

Returns:

STACK unchanged

Note: This function can only be called from within a DOS function call.

See Also: 2F/1209h

INT 2Fh Function 1216h   DOS 3+
GET ADDRESS OF SYSTEM FILE TABLE ENTRY

Return the address of a system file table entry given its number (such as returned by function 1220h).

Call With:

> AX   1216h
> BX   system file table entry number (such as returned from 2F/1220)

Returns:

> CF clear if successful
>> ES:DI pointer to system file table entry
> CF set if BX greater than FILES=

Note: for the implementaion of this function, see Figure 6-22.

See Also: 2F/1220h

INT 2Fh Function 1217h   DOS 3+
GET CURRENT DIRECTORY STRUCTURE FOR DRIVE

Call With:

> AX   1217h
> SS   DOS DS
> STACK   WORD drive (0=A:, 1=B:, etc)

Returns:

> CF set on error
>> (drive > LASTDRIVE)
> CF clear if successful
>> DS:SI pointer to current directory structure for specified drive
> STACK unchanged

Note: for implementation, see Figure 6-17.

See Also: 2F/1219h

INT 2Fh Function 1218h   DOS 3+
GET CALLER'S REGISTERS

Return a pointer to the stack frame containing the INT 21h caller's registers.

Call With:

> AX   1218h

Returns:

> DS:SI   pointer to saved caller's AX,BX,CX,DX,SI,DI,BP,DS,ES (on stack)

Note: The result of this function is only valid while within a DOS function call. See Figure 6-7.

INT 2Fh Function 1219h   DOS 3+
SET DRIVE

Call With:

> AX   1219h
> SS   DOS DS
> STACK   WORD drive (0=default, 1=A:, etc)

Returns:

> *unknown*
> STACK unchanged

Notes: This call eventually performs the equivalent of 2F/1217h; in addition, it builds a current directory structure if inside a server call (21/5D00h).

See Also: 2F/1217h, 2F/121Fh

INT 2Fh Function 121Ah   DOS 3+
GET FILE'S DRIVE
Determine which drive a filename specifies.

Call With:
AX	121Ah
DS:SI	pointer to filename

Returns:
AL	drive (0=default, 1=A:, etc, FFh if invalid)
DS:SI	pointer to filename without leading X: (if present)

Note: Increments SI by 2 if name starts with drive letter followed by colon.
See Also: 21/60h

INT 2Fh Function 121Bh   DOS 3+
SET YEAR/LENGTH OF FEBRUARY
Specify the current year, and return the length of February in days after storing that length internally.

Call With:
AX	121Bh
CL	year - 1980
DS	DOS data segment

Returns:
AL	number of days in February

See Also: *21/2Bh*

INT 2Fh Function 121Ch   DOS 3+
CHECKSUM MEMORY
Compute a checksum of the given range of memory. This function is also used by DOS in determining the day count since 1/1/1980 given a date.

Call With:
AX	121Ch
DS:SI	pointer to start of memory to checksum
CX	number of bytes
DX	initial checksum
SS	DOS DS

Returns:
AX, CX destroyed	
DX	checksum
DS:SI	pointer to first byte after checksummed range

See Also: 2F/121Dh

INT 2Fh Function 121Dh   DOS 3+
SUM MEMORY
Add up the values of a range of bytes until the specified limit is exceeded, and return the value which caused the limit to be exceeded. This function is also used by DOS to determine the year and month given a day count since 1/1/1980.

Call With:
AX	121Dh
DS:SI	pointer to memory to add up
CX	0000h

DX	limit

Returns:

AL	byte which exceeded limit
CX	number of bytes before limit exceeded
DX	remainder after adding first CX bytes
DS:SI	pointer to byte beyond the one which exceeded the limit

See Also: 2F/121Ch

INT 2Fh Function 121Eh   DOS 3+
COMPARE FILENAMES

Determine whether two filenames are identical except for case and forward/backslash differences.

Call With:

AX	121Eh
DS:SI	pointer to first ASCIZ filename
ES:DI	pointer to second ASCIZ filename

Returns:

ZF set if filenames equivalent, ZF clear if not

See Also: 2F/1211h, 2F/1221h

INT 2Fh Function 121Fh   DOS 3+
BUILD CURRENT DIRECTORY STRUCTURE

Create a new Current Directory Structure for the specified drive, and return the address of the temporary storage in which it was built.

Call With:

AX	121Fh
SS	DOS DS
STACK	WORD drive letter

Returns:

ES:DI	pointer to current directory structure (will be overwritten by next call)
STACK	unchanged

INT 2Fh Function 1220h   DOS 3+
GET JOB FILE TABLE ENTRY

Given a file handle, return the address of the entry in the Job File Table for that handle in the current process.

Call With:

AX	1220h
BX	file handle

Returns:

CF set on error

   AL   06h (invalid file handle)

CF clear if successful

   ES:DI pointer to JFT entry for file handle in current process

Note: The byte pointed at by ES:DI contains the number of the SFT entry for the file handle, or FFh if the handle is not open.

For the implementation of this function, see Figure 6-22.

See Also: 2F/1216h, 2F/1229h

INT 2Fh Function 1221h
CANONICALIZE FILE NAME

DOS 3+

Given a file specification, return an absolute pathname which takes into account any renaming due to JOIN, SUBST, ASSIGN, or network redirections.

Call With:

AX	1221h
DS:SI	pointer to file name to be fully qualified
ES:DI	pointer to 128-byte buffer for resulting canonical file name
SS	DOS DS

Returns:

(see 21/60h)

Note: This function can only be called from within a DOS function call, and is otherwise identical to 21/60h.

See Also: 21/60h, 2F/1123h

INT 2Fh Function 1222h
SET EXTENDED ERROR INFO

DOS 3+

Given a set of translation records, set the error class, locus, and suggested action corresponding to the current extended error code.

Call With:

AX	1222h	
SS	DOS data segment	
SS:SI	pointer to 4-byte records	
	BYTE	error code, FFh = last record
	BYTE	error class, FFh = don't change
	BYTE	suggested action, FFh = don't change
	BYTE	error locus, FFh = don't change
SDA error code set		

Returns:

SI destroyed

SDA error class, error locus, and suggested action fields set

Note: This function can only be called from within a DOS function call.

See Also: *21/59h*, 2F/122Dh

INT 2Fh Function 1223h
CHECK IF CHARACTER DEVICE

DOS 3+

Determine whether the given name is the name of a character device.

Call With:

AX	1223h
DS	DOS data segment
SS	DOS data segment
SDA+218h (DOS 3.10-3.30)	eight-character blank-padded name
SDA+22Bh (DOS 4.0-5.0)	eight-character blank-padded name

Returns:

CF set if no character device by that name found

CF clear if found

BH   low byte of device attribute word

Note: This function can only be called from within a DOS function call.

See Also: 21/5D06h, 21/5D0Bh

INT 2Fh Function 1224h
SHARING DELAY

Perform a sharing retry delay loop.

Call With:

AX	1224h
SS	DOS DS

Returns:

after delay set by 21/440Bh, unless in server call (21/5D00h)

Note: The delay depends on the processor speed, and is skipped entirely inside a server call.

See Also: *21/440Bh*, 21/52h

INT 2Fh Function 1225h
GET LENGTH OF ASCIZ STRING

Return the length of a null-terminated character string.

Call With:

AX	1225h
DS:SI	pointer to ASCIZ string

Returns:

CX	length of string

See Also: 2F/1212h

INT 2Fh Function 1226h
OPEN FILE

Open an existing file with the specified access mode and return a file handle if successful.

Call With:

AX	1226h
CL	access mode (AL from 21/3D)
DS:DX	pointer to ASCIZ filename
SS	DOS data segment

Returns:

CF set on error

AL   error code (see *21/59h*)

CF clear if successful

AX   file handle

Notes: This function can only be called from within a DOS function call; it is otherwise equivalent to 21/3Dh.

This function is used by NLSFUNC to access COUNTRY.SYS when invoked inside an INT 21h call by the DOS kernel.

See Also: *21/3Dh*, 2F/1227h

INT 2Fh Function 1227h
CLOSE FILE

Close a previously-opened file given its handle.

Call With:

AX	1227h
BX	file handle
SS	DOS data segment

Returns:
> CF set on error
>> AL   06h invalid file handle
>
> CF clear if successful

Notes: This function can only be called from within a DOS function call; it is otherwise equivalent to 21/3Eh.

This function is used by NLSFUNC to access COUNTRY.SYS when invoked by the DOS kernel.
See Also: *21/3Eh*, 2F/1106h, 2F/1201h, 2F/1226h

INT 2Fh Function 1228h   DOS 3.3+
MOVE FILE POINTER

Set the current position in the given file.

Call With:
> AX   1228h
> BP   4200h, 4201h, 4202h (see *21/42h*)
> BX   file handle
> CX:DX   offset in bytes
> SS   DOS DS

Returns:
> as for 21/42h

Notes: This function is equivalent to 21/42h, but may only be called from inside a DOS function call.

The user stack frame pointer is set to dummy buffer, BP is moved into AX, the LSEEK is performed, and finally the frame pointer is restored.

This function is used by NLSFUNC to access COUNTRY.SYS when invoked by the DOS kernel.
See Also: 21/42h

INT 2Fh Function 1229h   DOS 3.3+
READ FROM FILE

Read data from a previously-opened file.

Call With:
> AX   1229h
> BX   file handle
> CX   number of bytes to read
> DS:DX   pointer to buffer
> SS   DOS DS

Returns:
> as for 21/3Fh

Note: This function is equivalent to 21/3Fh, but may only be called when already inside a DOS function call.

This function is used by NLSFUNC to access COUNTRY.SYS when invoked by the DOS kernel.
See Also: *21/3Fh*, 2F/1226h

INT 2Fh Function 122Ah   DOS 3.3+
SET FASTOPEN ENTRY POINT

Specify the address(es) of the handlers for the FASTOPEN filename cache.

Call With:

AX	122Ah
BX	entry point to set (0001h or 0002h)
DS:SI	pointer to FASTOPEN entry point (entry point not set if SI=FFFFh for DOS 4+)

Returns:

CF set if specified entry point already set

Notes: The entry point number in BX is ignored under DOS 3.30.

Both entry points are set to same handler by the DOS 4.01 FASTOPEN.

DOS 3.30+ FASTOPEN is called with:

AL	01h	*unknown*
	CX	*appears to be offset*
	DI	*appears to be offset*
	SI	offset in DOS DS of filename
AL	02h	*unknown*
AL	03h	*open file*
	SI	offset in DOS DS of filename
AL	04h	*unknown*
	AH	subfunction (00h,01h,02h)
	ES:DI	*pointer to unknown item*
	CX	*unknown (subfunctions 01h and 02h only)*

Returns:

CF set on error or not installed

Note: function 03h calls function 01h first. MS-DOS 5-6 FASTOPEN called with additional unknown arguments.

INT 2Fh Function 122Bh   DOS 3.3+
IOCTL

Execute an I/O Control function from within the network redirector.

Call With:

AX	122Bh
BP	44xxh (AL from 21/44)
SS	DOS DS
additional registers as appropriate for 21/44xxh	

Returns:

as for 21/44h

Notes: This function is equivalent to 21/44h, but may only be called when already inside a DOS function call.

The user stack frame pointer is set to dummy buffer, BP is moved into AX, the IOCTL call is performed, and finally the frame pointer is restored.

This function is used by NLSFUNC to accessing COUNTRY.SYS when invoked by the DOS kernel.

INT 2Fh Function 122Ch   DOS 3.3+
GET DEVICE CHAIN

Return a pointer to the device driver chain (omitting the NUL device).

Call With:

AX	122Ch

Returns:

BX:AX	pointer to header of second device driver (NUL is first) in driver chain

See Also: 21/52h

INT 2Fh Function 122Dh   DOS 3.3+
GET EXTENDED ERROR CODE
Return the current extended error code.

Call With:
    AX   122Dh
Returns:
    AX   current extended error code
See Also: *21/59h*, 2F/1222h

INT 2Fh Function 122Eh   DOS 4+
GET OR SET ERROR TABLE ADDRESSES
Specify or determine the locations of various tables used to convert error numbers into error messages.

Call With:
    AX   122Eh
    DL   subfunction
           00h get standard DOS error table (errors 00h-12h,50h-5Bh)
              Returns:
                  ES:DI   pointer to error table
           01h set standard DOS error table
              ES:DI pointer to error table
           02h get parameter error table (errors 00h-0Ah)
              Returns:
                  ES:DI   pointer to error table
           03h set parameter error table
              ES:DI pointer to error table
           04h get critical/SHARE error table (errors 13h-2Bh)
              Returns:
                  ES:DI   pointer to error table
           05h set critical/SHARE error table
              ES:DI pointer to error table
           06h get unknown error table
              Returns:
                  ES:DI   pointer to error table or 0000h:0000h
           07h set unknown error table
              ES:DI pointer to error table
           08h get error message retriever (see below)
              Returns:
                  ES:DI   pointer to FAR procedure to fetch error message
           09h set unknown error table
              ES:DI pointer to error table

Notes: If the returned segment on a "get" is 0001h, then the offset specifies the offset of the error message table within COMMAND.COM, and the procedure returned by DL=08h should be called.

    DOS 5.0 COMMAND.COM does not allow setting any of the addresses; they are always returned with segment 0001h.

See Also: *21/59h*, 2F/0500h

Format of DOS 4.x error table:

Offset	Size	Description
00h	BYTE	FFh
01h	*2 BYTEs*	*04h,00h (DOS version)*
03h	BYTE	number of error headers following
04h	2N WORDs	table of all error headers for table

Offset	Size	Description
00h	WORD	error message number
02h	WORD	offset of error message from start of header
		error messages are count byte followed by msg

Note: The DOS 5 error tables consist of one word per error number; each word contains either the offset of a counted string or 0000h (invalid error number).

Call error retrieval function with:

AX	error number
DI	offset of error table

Returns:

ES:DI	pointer to error message (counted string)

Notes: This function needs to access COMMAND.COM if the messages were not loaded into memory permanently with /MSG; the caller should assume that the returned message will be overwritten by the next call of the function.

This function is supported by DR-DOS 5.0.

INT 2Fh Function 122Fh
SET DOS VERSION NUMBER TO RETURN
DOS 4.x only

Specify the DOS version number to be returned by subsequent calls to the "Get DOS Version" call (21/30h).

Call With:

AX	122Fh
DX	DOS version number (0000h to return true DOS version)

Note: Under later versions of DOS, you must directly manipulate the SETVER table (see SysVars offset 37h).

See Also: 21/30h

INT 2Fh Function 13h
SET DISK INTERRUPT HANDLER
DOS 3.2+

Specify the address of the handler for most DOS disk access, and return the old handler's address.

Call With:

AH	13h
DS:DX	pointer to interrupt handler disk driver calls on read/write
ES:BX	address to restore INT 13h to on system halt (exit from root shell) or warm boot (INT 19h)

Returns:

DS:DX	from previous invocation of this function
ES:BX	from previous invocation of this function

Notes: IO.SYS hooks INT 13h and inserts one or more filters ahead of the original INT 13h handler. The first is for disk change detection on floppy drives, the second is for tracking formatting calls and correcting DMA boundary errors, the third is for working around problems in a particular version of IBM's ROM BIOS.

Before the first call, ES:BX points at the original BIOS INT 13h; DS:DX also points there unless IO.SYS has installed a special filter for hard disk reads (on systems with model byte FCh and BIOS date "01/10/84" only), in which case it points at the special filter.

Most DOS 3.3+ disk access is via the vector in DS:DX, although a few functions are still invoked via an INT 13h instruction.

This function presents a dangerous security loophole for any virus-monitoring software which does not trap this call (many Bulgarian viruses are known to use it to get the original ROM entry point).

For a detailed discussion of 2F/13, see Geoff Chappell, *DOS Internals*.

See Also: *INT 13/AH=01h, INT 19h*

INT 2Fh Function 1400h   DOS 3.3+
NLSFUNC.COM - INSTALLATION CHECK
Determine whether NLSFUNC has been loaded.

Called With:
     AX   1400h
Returns:
     AL   00h not installed, OK to install
                 01h not installed, not OK
                 FFh installed
Notes: This function is called by the DOS 3.3+ kernel; it is supported by the OS/2 1.3+ compatibility box, which always returns AL=FFh, and by DR-DOS 5.0. Windows 3.x DOSMGR hooks this function, pretending that NLSFUNC is already installed.

This function has been documented for MS-DOS 5.0, but was undocumented in prior versions.

INT 2Fh Function 1400h   European MS-DOS 4.0
POPUP - "CheckPu" - INSTALLATION CHECK
Determine whether the POPUP module has been loaded. The POPUP interface in European MS-DOS 4.0 conflicts with the NLSFUNC interface for MS-DOS 3.3 and higher (DOS 3.3 was released after European MS-DOS 4.0).

Call With:
     AX   1400h
Returns:
     AX   FFFFh if installed
       BX   maximum memory required to save screen and keyboard info
     CF clear if successful
     CF set on error
       AX   error code
          0002h invalid function
          0004h unknown error
Note: The POPUP interface is used by background programs (see 21/80h) to communicate with the user.

See Also: 2F/1401h, 2F/1402h, 2F/1403h

INT 2Fh Function 1401h   DOS 3.3+
NLSFUNC.COM - CHANGE CODE PAGE
Select a new code page as the default.

Called With:
     AX   1401h

DS:SI	pointer to internal code page structure (see below)	
BX	new code page	
DX	*country code*	

Returns:

AL	status
	00h successful
	else DOS error code

Note: This function is called by the DOS 3.3+ kernel on 21/38.

See Also: *21/66h*

Format of DOS 3.30 internal code page structure:

Offset	Size	Description
00h	*8 BYTEs*	*unknown*
08h	64 BYTEs	name of country information file
48h	WORD	system code page
4Ah	WORD	number of supported subfunctions
4Ch	5 BYTEs	data to return for 21/6502h
51h	5 BYTEs	data to return for 21/6504h
56h	5 BYTEs	data to return for 21/6505h
5Bh	5 BYTEs	data to return for 21/6506h
60h	41 BYTEs	data to return for 21/6501h

INT 2Fh Function 1401h   European MS-DOS 4.0
POPUP - "PostPu" - OPEN/CLOSE POPUP SCREEN

Request access to the display from a background program.

Call With:

AX	1401h
DL	function (00h open, 01h close)
DH	wait flag
	00h block until screen opens
	01h return error if screen is not available
	02h urgent—always open screen immediately

Returns:

CF clear if successful	
BX	amount of memory needed to save screen and keyboard info,
	0000h if default save location can be used (only if DH was 02h)
CF set on error	

Note: The application using the screen is frozen until the popup screen is closed.

SeeAlso: 2F/1400h,2F/1402h,2F/1403h

INT 2Fh Function 1402h   DOS 3.3+
NLSFUNC.COM - GET COUNTRY INFO

Get country-specific information for a country or code page other than the default.

Called With:

AX	1402h
BP	subfunction (same as AL for 21/65h)
BX	code page
DX	country code
DS:SI	pointer to internal code page structure (see 2F/1401h)
ES:DI	pointer to user buffer
CX	size of user buffer

Returns:

AL   status

          00h successful

          else DOS error code

Notes: This function is called by the DOS 3.3+ kernel on 21/65h.

The code page structure is apparently only needed for the COUNTRY.SYS pathname.

See Also: 21/65h, 2F/1403h, 2F/1404h

INT 2Fh Function 1402h   European MS-DOS 4.0
POPUP - "SavePu" - SAVE POPUP SCREEN

Make a copy of the foreground program's screen so that it may be restored after the background program writes on the screen.

Call With:

AX   1402h

ES:DI   pointer to save buffer (0000h:0000h for default buffer in POPUP)

Returns:

CF clear if successful

CF set on error

    AX   error code

        0001h process does not own screen

        0004h unknown error

        0005h invalid pointer

See Also: 2F/1400h,2F/1401h,2F/1403h

INT 2Fh Function 1403h   DOS 3.3+
NLSFUNC.COM - SET COUNTRY INFO

Select a new country code as the default.

Called With:

AX   1403h

DS:SI   pointer to internal code page structure (see 2F/1401h)

BX   code page

DX   country code

Returns:

AL   status

Note: This function is called by the DOS 3.3+ kernel on 21/38h.

See Also: *21/38h*, 2F/1402h, 2F/1404h

INT 2Fh Function 1403h   European MS-DOS 4.0
POPUP - "RestorePu" - RESTORE SCREEN

Restore the screen to the state it was in before the background program wrote on the screen. The POPUP interface in European MS-DOS 4.0 conflicts with the NLSFUNC interface for MS-DOS 3.3 and higher (DOS 3.3 was released after European MS-DOS 4.0).

Call With:

AX   1403h

ES:DI   pointer to buffer containing saved screen

          (0000h:0000h for default buffer in POPUP)

Returns:

CF clear if successful

CF set on error
AX   error code (see AX=1402h"POPUP")
See Also: 2F/1400h,2F/1401h,2F/1402h

INT 2Fh Function 1404h   DOS 3.3+
NLSFUNC.COM - GET COUNTRY INFO

Return country-specific information for a country other than the current default.

Called With:

AX	1404h
BX	code page
DX	country code
DS:SI	pointer to internal code page structure (see 2F/1401h)
ES:DI	pointer to user buffer

Returns:

AL	status

Notes: This function is called by the DOS 3.3+ kernel on 21/38h.

The code page structure is apparently only needed for the COUNTRY.SYS pathname.

See Also: *21/38h*, 2F/1402h, 2F/1403h

INT 2Fh Function 14FEh   DR-DOS 5.0
NLSFUNC - GET EXTENDED COUNTRY INFORMATION

This function is called by the DR-DOS kernel when an application requests country-dependent information for a country other than the current country.

Call With:

AX	14FEh
BX	code page (FFFFh=global code page) (see 21/6602h)
DX	country ID (FFFFh=current country) (see 21/38h)
ES:DI	pointer to country information buffer
CL	info ID
	01h get general internationalization info
	02h get pointer to uppercase table
	04h get pointer to filename uppercase table
	05h get pointer to filename terminator table
	06h get pointer to collating sequence table
	07h get pointer to Double-Byte Character Set table
CF	set (used to return error if not installed)

Returns:

CF clear if successful
   DS:SI   pointer to requested information
CF set on error

Notes: DR-DOS 5.0 NLSFUNC returns CF set and AX=0001h if AL was not 00h, FEh, or FFh on entry.

The value in CL is not range-checked by the DR-DOS 5.0 NLSFUNC.

See Also: AX=14FFh, 21/65h

Format of DR-DOS COUNTRY.SYS file:

Offset	Size	Description
00h	110 BYTEs	copyright notice (terminated with Ctrl-Z, padded with NULs)
7Eh	WORD	signature EDC1h
80h	var	country pointer records

Offset	Size	Description
00h	WORD	country code (0000h if end of array)
02h	WORD	code page
04h	*WORD*	*unknown (0000h)*
06h	7 WORDs	offsets in file for data tables for subfunctions 01h-07h
var	var	country information

INT 2Fh Function 14FFh   DR-DOS 5.0
NLSFUNC - PREPARE CODE PAGE

This function is called by the DR-DOS kernel when setting the current code page; it passes a codepage preparation request to each character device supporting the generic IOCTL call.

Call With:
>   AX   14FFh
>   BX   code page
Returns:
>   *AX   unknown*
>   ZF set if AX=0000h
Note: DR-DOS 5.0 NLSFUNC returns CF set and AX=0001h if AL was not 00h, FEh, or FFh on entry.
See Also: AX=14FEh, 21/440Ch, 21/6602h

INT 2Fh Function 1500h   DOS 4.00 only
GRAPHICS.COM - INSTALLATION CHECK

Determine whether GRAPHICS has been loaded.

Call With:
>   AX   1500h
Returns:
>   AX   FFFFh
>   *ES:DI   unknown pointer (pointer to graphics data?)*
Note: This installation check was moved to 2F/AC00h in DOS 4.01 and later due to the conflict with the CD-ROM Extensions install check (also 2F/1500).
See Also: 2F/AC00h

INT 2Fh Function 1603h   MS Windows/386
GET INSTANCE DATA

Determine which areas of memory must be maintained as separate copies for each task.

Call With:
>   AX = 1603h
Returns:
>   AX = 5248h ('RH') if supported
>   DS:SI -> Windows/386 instance data (see below)
Notes: DOSMGR calls this function when AX=1607h/BX=0015h is not supported, as is the case in DOS versions prior to 5.0.

See Geoff Chappell's book *DOS Internals* for additional discussions of this function, DOSMGR's behavior, and instancing in general.
See Also: AX=1607h/BX=0015h

Format of Windows/386 instance data:

Offset	Size	Description
00h	WORD	segment of IO.SYS (0000h = default 0070h)
02h	WORD	offset in IO.SYS of STACKS data structure (DOS 3.2x); 0000h if not applicable
04h	WORD	number of instance data entries (max 32)
06h	Array of instance data entries	

Offset	Size	Description
00h	WORD	segment (0002h = DOS kernel)
02h	WORD	offset
04h	WORD	size

INT 2Fh Function 1607h   Windows 3.0+
WINDOWS ENHANCED MODE VXD CALLOUT

Microsoft documents this function, like most 2F/16 functions, in the Windows Device Driver Kit (DDK) *Device Driver Adaptation Guide*. 2F/1607 is a callout made by Enhanced mode virtual device drivers (VxDs). Real-mode TSRs and device drivers loaded before Windows can intercept this call to communicate with the VxD. As indicated in the next entry, MS-DOS (5.0 and higher) itself uses this mechanism, to communicate with the Windows DOSMGR VxD.

But while Microsoft documents the 2F/1607 mechanism, it does not document the callout API provided by any specific VxDs. A VxD puts its VxD identification number in BX before issuing the 2F/1607. By intercepting 2F/1607 before Windows starts and watching the VxD IDs in BX, it is known that the following VxDs are among those that issue callouts in Windows 3.1:

0006h	V86MMGR
000Ch	VMD (Virtual Mouse Device)
0010h	BlockDev
0014h	VNETBIOS
0015h	DOSMGR (see below)
0018h	VMPoll
0021h	PageFile (source code provided with DDK)

DDK more information on the V86MMGR, VMD, VNETBIOS, and DOSMGR callout interfaces, see the interrupt list on disk. The BlockDev 1607h callout is documented in the Windows DDK.

INT 2Fh Function 1607h   DOS 5+
MS WINDOWS "DOSMGR" VIRTUAL DEVICE API

Helper functions for MS Windows Enhanced mode which facilitate multitasking over MS-DOS.
Call With:
     AX   1607h
     BX   0015h (VxD identifier of "DOSMGR")
     CX   function
         0000h query instance processing
            Return: CX   state
                      0000h not instanced
                      other instanced (DOS 5.0 kernel returns 0001h)
                          DX   segment of DOS drivers (unchanged if call handled by DOS 5.0)
                          ES:BX pointer to patch table (see below)
         0001h set patches in DOS
            DX   bit mask of patch requests
               bit 0: enable critical sections
               bit 1: NOP setting/checking user ID

bit 2: turn 21/3Fh on STDIN into polling loop
bit 3: trap stack fault in "SYSINIT" to WIN386
bit 4: BIOS patch to trap "Insert disk X:" to WIN386

Returns:
AX   B97Ch
BX   bit mask of patches applied
DX   A2ABh

0002h remove patches in DOS (ignored by DOS 5.0 kernel)
DX   bit mask of patch requests (see function 0001h)

0003h get size of DOS data structures
DX   bit mask of request (only one bit can be set)
bit 0: Current Directory Structure size

Returns:
if supported request:
AX   B97Ch
CX   size in bytes of requested structure
DX   A2ABh
else:
all registers preserved

0004h determine instanced data structures

Returns:
AX   B97Ch if supported
DX   A2ABh if supported (DOS 5.0 kernel returns 0000h)
BX   bit mask of instanced items
bit 0: CDS
bit 1: SFT
bit 2: device list
bit 3: DOS swappable data area

0005h get device driver size
ES segment of device driver

Returns:
DX:AX   0000h:0000h on error (not dev. driver segment)
DX:AX   A2ABh:B97Ch if successful
BX:CX size of device driver in bytes

Notes: DOSMGR (DOS Manager) will check whether the OEM DOS/BIOS data has been instanced via this API and will not perform its own default instancing of the normal DOS/BIOS data if so; if this API is not supported, DOSMGR will also try to access instancing data through 2F/1603h. These functions are supported by the DOS 5+ kernel; DOSMGR contains tables of instancing information for earlier versions of DOS.

See Geoff Chappell's book *DOS Internals* for additional discussions of DOSMGR's behavior and instancing in general. Also see Chapter 1, NODOSMGR.C.

See Also: 2F/1603h

Format of patch table:

Offset	Size	Description
00h	2 BYTEs	DOS version (major, minor)
02h	WORD	offset in DOS data segment of "SAVEDS"
04h	WORD	offset in DOS data segment of "SAVEBX"
06h	WORD	offset in DOS data segment of InDOS flag
08h	WORD	offset in DOS data segment of User ID word
0Ah	WORD	offset in DOS data segment of "CritPatch" table

| 0Ch | WORD | (DOS 5+ only) offset in DOS data segment of "UMB_HEAD", containing segment of last MCB in conventional memory |

INT 2Fh Function 160Bh
WINDOWS TSR IDENTIFY
Windows 3.1

While the Windows DDK fails to document 2F/160B, Microsoft does document the function in an article "TSR Support in Microsoft Windows Version 3.1" by David Long, on the Microsoft Developer Network (MSDN) CD-ROM. This article also describes 2F/168B (Set Focus). 2F/160B and 2F/168B are also described in the interrupt list on disk.

INT 2Fh Function 1684h
GET VXD API ENTRY POINT
Windows 3.0+

Microsoft documents this function, like most 2F/16 functions, in the Windows Device Driver Kit (DDK) *Device Driver Adaptation Guide*. Any program running under Windows (whether a DOS, protected-mode DOS, or Windows program) can call 2F/1684 to get a function pointer to an API provided by an Enhanced mode virtual device drivers (VxDs).

But while Microsoft documents the 2F/1684 mechanism, it only documents the APIs provided by a few specific VxDs, such as VPICD. A DOS or Windows program puts the desired VxD identification number in BX before issuing the 2F/1684. Calling 2F/1684 from a real-mode DOS program gets the Virtual-8086 (V86) mode entry point, if available; calling 2F/1684 from a protected-mode DOS or Windows program gets the protected mode (PM) entry point, if available. Otherwise, 0 is returned. By looping over all possible VxD IDs, it is possible to determine which VxDs provide APIs, in which mode. The following VxDs are among those known to provide APIs:

0003h	VPICD	Virtual PIC Device	V86, PM
0005h	VTD	Virtual Timer Device	V86, PM
0009h	Reboot	Ctrl-Alt-Del virtualization	PM
000Ah	VDD	Virtual Display Device	PM
000Ch	VMD	Virtual Mouse Device	V86, PM
000Dh	VKD	Virtual Keyboard Device	PM
000Eh	VCD	Virtual COMM Device	PM
0015h	DOSMGR	DOS virtualization, DOS extender	V86
0017h	SHELL	KERNEL/VxD interface	PM
001Ch	LoadHi	memory manager	V86
001Dh	WINDEBUG	low-level debugging	PM
0021h	PageFile	demand paged swap device	PM
0442h	VTDAPI	Multimedia timer	PM

Microsoft's DDK documents the VPICD API. For more information on VxD APIs, see Andrew Schulman, "Go Anywhere and Do Anything with 32-bit Virtual Device Drivers for Windows," *Microsoft Systems Journal*, October 1992. The VTD API is described in the interrupt list on disk (see 2F/1684), which also provides a handy list of VxD IDs.

INT 2Fh Function 168Ah
DPMI - GET VENDOR-SPECIFIC API ENTRY POINT
DPMI

This function allows Microsoft and other vendors to extend DPMI, the DOS Protected Mode Interface. While this function is documented, the specific extensions are not. The most important extension is Microsoft's (vendor name "MS-DOS"), which allows the Windows KERNEL to bypass DPMI services and directly manipulate the protected-mode Local Descriptor Table (LDT). For more information, see Matt Pietrek, *Windows Internals*, chapter 1.

INT 2Fh Function 17h   Windows 2.0+
WINDOWS CLIPBOARD API FOR DOS PROGRAMS

Documented in Windows 2.x, and then de-documented in Windows 3.0 and 3.1, the Windows clipboard API for DOS programs has finally been documented again by Microsoft, in a Microsoft KnowledgeBase article. The services are:

1700h	Identify WinOldAp Version
1701h	Open Clipboard
1702h	Empty Clipboard
1703h	Set Clipboard Data
1704h	Get Clipboard Data Size
1705h	Get Clipboard Data
1708h	Close Clipboard
1709h	Compact Clipboard
170Ah	Get Device Capabilities

For more information, see the interrupt list on disk.

INT 2Fh Function 1900h   DOS 4.x only
SHELLB.COM - INSTALLATION CHECK

Determine whether SHELLB has been loaded.

Call With:
>   AX   1900h

Returns:
>   AL   00h not installed
>   FFh installed

INT 2Fh Function 1901h   DOS 4.x only
SHELLB.COM - SHELLC.EXE INTERFACE

Inform SHELLB of SHELLC's address, and return the location of a workspace for SHELLC.

Call With:
>   AX   1901h
>   BL   00h if SHELLC transient
>   01h if SHELLC resident
>   DS:DX   pointer to far call entry point for resident SHELLC.EXE

Returns:
>   ES:DI   pointer to SHELLC.EXE workspace within SHELLB.COM

Note: SHELLB.COM and SHELLC.EXE are parts of the DOS 4.x shell.

INT 2Fh Function 1902h   DOS 4.x only
SHELLB.COM - COMMAND.COM INTERFACE

Get the next line which COMMAND.COM should execute in preference to reading a command from the current batch file.

Call With:
>   AX   1902h
>   ES:DI   pointer to ASCIZ full filename of current batch file, with at least the final
>   filename element uppercased
>   DS:DX   pointer to buffer for results

Returns:
>   AL   00h failed, either

(a) final filename element quoted at ES:DI does not match identity of shell batch file quoted as parameter of most recent call of SHELLB command, or

(b) no more Program Start Commands available.

AL   FFh success, then:

memory at DS:[DX+1] onwards filled as:

DX+1:   BYTE   count of bytes of PSC

DX+2: N BYTEs   Program Start Command text

BYTE   0Dh terminator

Notes: COMMAND.COM executes the result of this call in preference to reading a command from a batch file. Thus the batch file does not advance in execution for so long as SHELLB provides Program Start Commands from its workspace.

The PSCs are planted in SHELLB workspace by SHELLC, the user menu interface.

The final PSC of a sequence is finished with a GOTO COMMON, which causes a loop back in the batch file which called SHELLC so as to execute SHELLC again.

The check on batch file name permits PSCs to CALL nested batch files while PSCs are still stacked up for subsequent execution.

INT 2Fh Function 1903h   DOS 4.x only
SHELLB.COM - COMMAND.COM INTERFACE

Determine whether a Program Start Command is attempting to re-execute the current batch file.

Call With:

AX   1903h

ES:DI   pointer to ASCIZ batch file name as for 2F/1902h

Returns:

AL   FFh if quoted batch file name matches last SHELLB parameter

AL   00h if it does not

INT 2Fh Function 1904h   DOS 4.x only
SHELLB.COM - SHELLB TRANSIENT TO TSR interface

Determine the name of the batch file from which the DOS Shell is executing.

Call With:

AX   1904h

Returns:

ES:DI   pointer to name of current shell batch file:

WORD   number of bytes of name following

BYTEs   (8 max) uppercase name of shell batch file

INT 2Fh Function 1A00h   DOS 4+
ANSI.SYS - INSTALLATION CHECK

Determine whether ANSI.SYS is present.

Call With:

AX   1A00h

Returns:

AL   FFh if installed

Note: This function has been documented for DOS 5+, but was undocumented for DOS 4.x.

INT 2Fh Function 1A01h   DOS 4+
ANSI.SYS - GET/SET DISPLAY INFORMATION

This appears to be the DOS IOCTL interface to ANSI.SYS.

Call With:

AX	1A01h
CL	function
	5Fh for SET
	7Fh for GET
DS:DX	pointer to parameter block as for 21/440Ch with CX=037Fh-/035Fh respectively

Returns:

CF set on error

   AX   error code (many non-standard)

CF clear if successful

   AX destroyed

See Also: *21/440Ch*, 2F/1A02h

INT 2Fh Function 1A02h   DOS 4+
ANSI.SYS - MISCELLANEOUS REQUESTS

Get or set miscellaneous ANSI.SYS flags.

Call With:

AX	1A02h
DS:DX	pointer to parameter block (see below)

Note: DOS 5+ chains to the previous handler if AL > 02h on call.

See Also: 2F/1A01h

Format of parameter block:

Offset	Size	Description
00h	BYTE	subfunction
		00h set/reset interlock
		01h get /L flag
01h	BYTE	interlock state
		00h=reset, 01h=set
		This interlock prevents some of the ANSI.SYS post-processing
		in its hook onto INT 10/AH=00h mode set
02h	BYTE	(returned)
		00h if /L not in effect
		01h if /L in effect

INT 2Fh Function 1B00h   DOS 4+
XMA2EMS.SYS - INSTALLATION CHECK

Determine whether XMA2EMS.SYS has been loaded.

Call With:

AX	1B00h

Returns:

AL	FFh if installed

Note: The XMA2EMS.SYS extension is only installed if DOS has page frames to hide. This extension hooks onto INT 67/AH=58h and returns from that call data which excludes the physical pages being used by DOS.

See Also: INT 2F/AH=1Bh

INT 2Fh Function 1Bh   DOS 4+
XMA2EMS.SYS - GET HIDDEN FRAME INFORMATION

Determine information which XMA2EMS hides from regular EMS function calls.

Call With:

AH	1Bh
AL	nonzero
DI	hidden physical page number

Returns:

AX	FFFFh if failed (no such hidden page)
AX	0000h if OK, then
	ES segment of page frame
	DI physical page number

Notes: The returned data corresponds to the data edited out of the INT 67/AH=58h call by XMA2EMS.

FASTOPEN makes this call with AL=FFh.

See Also: 2F/1B00h

INT 2Fh Function 2300h   DR-DOS 5.0
GRAFTABL - INSTALLATION CHECK
Determine whether the DR-DOS GRAFTABL has been loaded.

Call With:

AX	2300h

Returns:

AH	FFh

Note: This installation check does not follow the usual format of returning AL=FFh if installed.

See Also: INT 2F/AH=23h

INT 2Fh Function 23h   DR-DOS 5.0
GRAFTABL - GET GRAPHICS DATA
Determine the location of the graphics data used by GRAFTABL.

Call With:

AH	23h
AL	nonzero

Returns:

AH	FFh
ES:BX	pointer to graphics data

See Also: 2F/2300h

INT 2Fh Function 43h   XMS
XMS 3.0 SERVICES
Information on version 3.0 of the eXtended Memory Services (XMS) has long been difficult to find, but it is not undocumented. Microsoft has discretely placed an XMS30.TXT file on its CompuServe forum. The new XMS 3.0 functions are:

88h	Query any Free Extended Memory
89h	Allocate any Extended Memory Block
8Eh	Get Extended EMB Handle
8Fh	Realloc any Extended Memory

These are identical to XMS 2.0 functions 8, 9, 0Eh, and 0Fh, except that they work with 32-bit quantities, thus allowing access to up to four gigabytes of memory. The older XMS specification, since it used 16-bit values, was limited to a 64 MB maximum block size. Believe it or not, this was a problem. The new functions work with memory above 64 MB (so-called "Super Extended Memory"). For more information, see Microsoft's XMS30.TXT, or the interrupt list on disk.

INT 2Fh Function 4601h   DOS 5+
KERNEL - UNKNOWN FUNCTION

The purpose of this function has not been determined.

Call With:

    AX   4601h

Returns:

    unknown

Note: This function copies the MCB following the caller's PSP memory block into the DOS data segment.

See Also: 2F/4602h

INT 2Fh Function 4602h   DOS 5+
KERNEL - UNKNOWN FUNCTION

The purpose of this function has not been determined.

Call With:

    AX   4602h

Returns:

    unknown

Note: This function copies a previously copied MCB from the DOS data segment into the MCB following caller's PSP memory block.

See Also: 2F/4601h

INT 2Fh Function 4A00h   DOS 5+
SINGLE-FLOPPY LOGICAL DRIVE CHANGE NOTIFICATION

Inform any interested programs that the logical drive letter assigned to the only floppy drive in a single-floppy system is about to change from A: to B: or vice versa.

Called With:

    AX   4A00h
    CX   0000h
    DH   new drive number
    DL   current drive number

Returns:

    CX   FFFFh to skip "Insert diskette for drive X:" message

Note: This function is broadcast by MS-DOS 5+ IO.SYS just before displaying the message "Insert diskette for drive X:" on single-floppy systems.

INT 2Fh Function 4A01h   DOS 5+
QUERY FREE HMA SPACE

Determine how much space remains unallocated in the High Memory Area (1M to 1M+64K).

Call With:

    AX   4A01h

Returns:

    BX   number of bytes available in HMA (0000h if DOS not using HMA)
    ES:DI   pointer to start of available HMA area (FFFFh:FFFFh if not using HMA)

Note: This function is called by Windows 3.1 DOSX.EXE.

A discussion of this function and Function 4A02h may be found in the "DOS Q&A" column of the March 1993 *Microsoft Systems Journal*.

See Also: 2F/4A02h

INT 2Fh Function 4A02h   DOS 5.0
ALLOCATE HMA SPACE

Request a portion of the High Memory Area for storing a portion of the TSR's code or data.
Call With:
>   AX   4A02h
>   BX   number of bytes

Returns:
>   ES:DI   pointer to start of allocated HMA block or FFFFh:FFFFh

Change
>   BX   destroyed

to
>   BX   number of bytes actually allocated (rounded up to next paragraph under DOS 5 and 6)

Notes: This call is not valid unless DOS is loaded in the HMA (DOS=HIGH in CONFIG.SYS).

   This function is called by Windows 3.1 DOSX.EXE.

   There is unfortunately no call to deallocate HMA space.

See Also: 2F/4A01h

INT 2Fh Function 4A05h   DOS 5+
DOSSHELL - TASK SWITCHING API

The subfunctions of this function appear to support the DOSSHELL task-switching mechanism.

Call With:
>   AX   4A05h
>   SI   function
>   *0000h reset*
>   *0001h-000ch unknown*

Notes: DOSSHELL chains to the previous handler if SI is not one of the values listed above

   The DOSSWAP.EXE module calls functions 03h,04h,05h,07h,08h,09h,0Ch.

   The Windows 3.1 DSWAP.EXE and WSWAP.EXE task switchers use these calls.

See Also: *AX=4B01h*

INT 2Fh Function 4A06h   DOS 5+
ADJUST MEMORY SIZE

Specify the amount of memory available to DOS. Used by the DOS supervisor "reboot panel."
Called With:
>   AX   4A06h
>   DX   segment following last byte of conventional memory

Returns:
>   DX   segment following last byte of memory available for use by DOS

Note: This function is called by the MS-DOS 5.00 and 6.00 IO.SYS startup code if the signature "RPL" is present three bytes beyond the INT 2Fh handler; this call overrides the value returned by INT 12h. See Chappell, *DOS Internals*, Chapter 3.

See Also: *INT 12h*

INT 2Fh Function 4A10h Subfn 0000h   SMARTDRV v4+
Smartdrv Installation Check And Hit Ratios

Determine whether version 4.0 or higher of the SMARTDRV disk cache is installed, and how effective its caching has been. SMARTDRV 3.x uses a completely different API which is detailed in the complete listing on disk under 21/4402h.

Call With:
  - AX   4A10h
  - BX   0000h
  - CX   EBABh (v4.1+; see Note)

Returns:
  - AX   BABEh if installed
  - DX:BX   cache hits
  - DI:SI   cache misses
  - BP   version (4.00 = 0400h)
  - *CX   unknown*

Notes: Most of the SMARTDRV API, including this call, is supported by PC-Cache v8.0.

 If DBLSPACE.BIN is installed but SMARTDRV has not yet been installed, unless CX=EBABh on entry, DBLSPACE.BIN displays the error message "Cannot run SMARTDrive 4.0 with DoubleSpace" and aborts the caller with 21/4C00h.

See   Also: AX=4A10h/BX=0001h,   AX=4A10h/BX=0003h,   AX=4A10h/BX=0004h, AX=4A10h/BX=0005h,   AX=4A10h/BX=0007h,   AX=4A10h/BX=1234h,   21/4402h "SMARTDRV", 21/4403h "SMARTDRV"

INT 2Fh Function 4A10h Subfn 0001h   SMARTDRV v4+
RESET CACHE

Call With:
  - AX   4A10h
  - BX   0001h

Returns:
  registers unchanged

Note: This function is also supported by PC-Cache v8.0.
See Also: AX=4A10h/BX=0000h, AX=4A10h/BX=0002h

INT 2Fh Function 4A10h Subfn 0002h   SMARTDRV v4+
FLUSH BUFFERS

Force all modified data to be written to disk immediately.
Call With:
  - AX   4A10h
  - BX   0002h

Returns:
  registers unchanged
Note: This function is also supported by PC-Cache v8.0.
See Also: AX=4A10h/BX=0000h, AX=4A10h/BX=0001h

INT 2Fh Function 4A10h Subfn 0003h   SMARTDRV v4+
STATUS

Determine the caching status of a specified drive.

Call With:
  - AX   4A10h
  - BX   0003h
  - BP   drive # (0=A, 1=B, etc.)
  - DL   subfunction
    00h only get information
    01h turn on read cache

02h turn off read cache
03h turn on write cache
04h turn off write cache

Returns:
AX   BABEh if OK
DL   FFh if drive does not exist
DL   status
      bit 7 not cached
      bit 6 write-through
      bit 5 unknown
      bits 0-4 drive # (0=A, 1=B...)

Notes: If the read cache is off, reads will not be cached, but writes will continue to be cached if the write-cache is enabled.

This function is also supported by PC-Cache v8.0.

See Also: AX=4A10h/BX=0000h

INT 2Fh Function 4A10h Subfn 0004h   SMARTDRV v4+
GET CACHE SIZE

Determine how large the disk cache is, and the preset sizes for Windows and DOS operation.

Call With:
AX   4A10h
BX   0004h

Returns:
AX   current size in elements
BX   largest number of elements
CX   size of elements in bytes
DX   number of elements under Windows

Note: This function is also supported by PC-Cache v8.0.

See Also: AX=4A10h/BX=0000h,AX=4A10h/BX=0005h

INT 2Fh Function 4A10h Subfn 0005h   SMARTDRV v4+
GET DOUBLE-BUFFER STATUS

Determine whether the double-buffering code was installed for a particular drive.

Call With:
AX   4A10h
BX   0005h
BP   drive # (0=A, 1=B...)

Returns:
AX   BABEh if double-buffered
      ES:DI -> unknown item

See Also: AX=4A10h/BX=0000h, AX=4A10h/BX=0003h, AX=4A10h/BX=0006h

---

INT 2Fh Function 4A10h Subfn 0006h   SMARTDRV v4+
CHECK IF DRIVE CACHEABLE

SMARTDRV calls this function at startup to determine whether it should cache a particular drive.

Called with:
AX   4A10h
BX   0006h
CL   drive number (01h = A:)

Returns:

    AX   0006h if drive should not be cached by SMARTDRV

See Also: AX=4A10h/BX=0000h

INT 2Fh Function 4A10h Subfn 0007h   SMARTDRV v4+
GET DEVICE DRIVER FOR DRIVE

Determine which device driver handles the specified drive.

Call With:

    AX   4A10h
    BX   0007h
    BP   drive number

Returns:

    DL   *unknown*
    ES:DI   pointer to device driver header for drive

Note: This function is also supported by PC-Cache v8.0.

See Also: AX=4A10h/BX=0000h

INT 2Fh Function 4A10h Subfn 000Ah   SMARTDRV v4+
GET UNKNOWN TABLE POINTER

The purpose of this function has not yet been determined.

Call With:

    AX   4A10h
    BX   000Ah

Returns:

    ES:BX   pointer to table of about 10 bytes or 5 words. Seems to be words pointing
                     to memory addresses containing info (see below)

Note: This function is also supported by PC-Cache v8.0.

See Also: AX=4A10h/BX=0000h

Format of data table:

Offset	Size	Description
00h	*8 BYTEs*	*unknown*
08h	WORD	offset of WORD containing number of elements in cache

INT 2Fh Function 4A10h Subfn 1234h   SMARTDRV v4+
SIGNAL SERIOUS ERROR

This function pops up a message box saying that a serious error occurred and to hit R to retry.

Call With:

    AX   4A10h
    BX   1234h

Note: This function is also supported by PC-Cache v8.0.

See Also: AX=4A10h/BX=0000h

INT 2Fh Function 4A11h Subfunc FFFEh   DBLSPACE.BIN
RELOCATE

Move the DBLSPACE.BIN driver to its final location in memory.

Call With:

    AX = 4A11h
    BX = FFFEh
    ES = segment to which to relocate DBLSPACE.BIN

Returns:
> *unknown*

Note: This function is called by DBLSPACE.SYS; it also unhooks and discards the code providing this function and Subfunction FFFFh.

Other DoubleSpace API calls (including subfunctions 3 and 4, which at one point were "reserved for SMARTDRV") are documented in Microsoft's MS-DOS 6.0 *Programmer's Reference*.

See Also: AX=4A11h/BX=FFFFh

INT 2Fh Function 4A11h Subfunc FFFFh   DBLSPACE.BIN
GET RELOCATION SIZE

Determine how much memory the main portion of the DBLSPACE.BIN driver requires.

Call With:
> AX = 4A11h
> BX = FFFFh

Returns:
> AX = number of paragraphs needed by DBLSPACE.BIN

Note: This function is used by DBLSPACE.SYS when relocating the DBLSPACE driver to its final position in memory.

See Also: AX=4A11h/BX=0000h, AX=4A11h/BX=FFFEh

INT 2Fh Function 4A13h   DBLSPACE.BIN
GET UNKNOWN ENTRY POINTS

The purpose of this call has not been determined.

Call With:
> AX   4A13h

Returns:
> AX   134Ah if supported
> ES:BX   pointer to entry point record (see below)

See Also: *AX=4A11h/BX=0000h*

Format of entry point record:

Offset	Size	Description
00h	DWORD	pointer to unknown FAR function
04h	5 BYTEs	FAR JUMP instruction to unknown function

INT 2Fh Function 5500h   DOS 5+
COMMAND.COM INTERFACE

Communicate with the shareable portion of COMMAND.COM, which may have been moved into the HMA; only the primary COMMAND.COM retains this portion.

Call With:
> AX   5500h

Returns:
> AX   0000h
> DS:SI   pointer to entry point table

Note: The procedures in the entry point table are called from a dispatcher in COMMAND's resident portion; most assume that the segment address of the resident portion is on the stack and are thus not of general use.

INT 2Fh Function 5600h   DOS 6+
INTERLNK Install Check

INTERLNK is Microsoft's device driver for allowing one computer (generally a laptop) to transparently access files on another computer. For more information on 2F/56, see the interrupt list on disk.

INT 2Fh Function 9400h   Workgroup Connection
MICRO.EXE - INSTALLATION CHECK

Determine whether the MICRO electronic-mail module of Workgroup Connection has been installed.

Call With:
    AX   9400h
Returns:
    AL   07h or 08h if installed
Note: 2F/9401-9404 are also used, but their meaning is unknown.
See Also: AX=9401h, AX=9402h, AX=9403h, AX=9404h, 21/3Fh"WORKGRP.SYS"

INT 2Fh Function AC00h   DOS 4.01+
GRAPHICS.COM - INSTALLATION CHECK

Determine whether GRAPHICS has been loaded.

Call With:
    AX   AC00h
Returns:
    AX   FFFFh
    ES:DI   unknown pointer (pointer to graphics data?) (not documented)

Note: This installation check was moved here to avoid the conflict with the CD-ROM extensions that occurred in DOS 4.00.
See Also: 2F/1500h

INT 2Fh Function AD00h   DOS 3.3+
DISPLAY.SYS - INSTALLATION CHECK

Determine whether DISPLAY.SYS is present.

Call With:
    AX   AD00h
Returns:
    AL   FFh if installed
        BX unknown (0100h in MS-DOS 3.30, PCDOS 4.01)
Note: DOS 5+ DISPLAY.SYS chains to the previous handler if AL is not one of the subfunctions listed here.

INT 2Fh Function AD01h   DOS 3.3+
DISPLAY.SYS INTERNAL - SET ACTIVE CODE PAGE

Specify which code page DISPLAY.SYS should use.

Call With:
    AX   AD01h
    BX   new code page
Returns:
    CF clear if successful

     AX   0001h
   CF set on error (unsupported code page)
     AX   0000h
See Also: 2F/AD02h

INT 2Fh Function AD02h   DOS 3.3+
DISPLAY.SYS INTERNAL - GET ACTIVE CODE PAGE

Determine which code page DISPLAY.SYS is currently using.

Call With:
     AX   AD02h
Returns:
     CF set if code page never set
       AX   0001h
       BX   FFFFh (assume first hardware code page)
     CF clear if successful
       BX   current code page
See Also: 2F/AD01h,2F/AD03h

INT 2Fh Function AD03h   DOS 3.3+
DISPLAY.SYS INTERNAL - GET CODE PAGE INFORMATION

Retrieve information the number of code pages supported and the currently-available code pages.

Call With:
     AX   AD03h
     ES:DI   pointer to buffer for code page information (see below)
     CX   size of buffer in bytes
Returns:
     CF set if buffer too small
     CF clear if successful
       ES:DI buffer filled
See Also: 2F/AD01h,2F/AD02h

Format of DOS 5.0 code page information:

Offset	Size	Description
00h	WORD	number of software code pages
02h	*WORD*	*unknown (0003h)*
04h	WORD	number of hardware code pages
06h	N WORDs	hardware code page numbers
	N WORDs	software (prepared) code pages (FFFFh if not yet prepared)

INT 2Fh Function AD10h   DOS 4.x only
DISPLAY.SYS INTERNAL - INSTALLATION CHECK

This function appears to be an alternate installation check. If this function is analogous to the 10h subfunction for APPEND, then it also returns the DISPLAY.SYS version number.

Call With:
     AX   AD10h
     additional arguments (if any) unknown
Returns:
     AX   FFFFh
     BX   unknown (0100h in PCDOS 4.01)

INT 2Fh Function AD10h   DOS 5.0
DISPLAY.SYS INTERNAL - UNKNOWN FUNCTION

The purpose of this function has not been determined.

Call With:
     AX   AD10h
     additional arguments (if any) unknown
Returns:
     CF clear if successful
     CF set on error
Note: This function is a NOP if the active code page has never been set (2F/AD02h returns BX=FFFFh); its purpose otherwise is not known.

INT 2Fh Function AD40h   DOS 4+
UNKNOWN FUNCTION

The purpose of this function has not been determined.

Call With:
     AX   AD40h
     DX   *unknown*
     additional arguments (if any) unknown
Returns:
     unknown
Note: Called by PCDOS 4.01 PRINT.COM and DOS 5+ PRINT.EXE.

INT 2Fh Function AD80h   DOS 3.3+
KEYB.COM - INSTALLATION CHECK

Determine whether KEYB.COM has been loaded.

Call With:
     AX   AD80h
Returns:
     AL   FFh if installed
               BX   version number (major in BH, minor in BL)
               ES:DI   pointer to internal data (see below)
Notes: MS-DOS 3.30, PCDOS 4.01, and MS-DOS 5.00-6.00 all report version 1.00.

     This function was undocumented prior to the release of DOS 5.0: the internal data format is still undocumented.

Format of KEYB internal data:

Offset	Size	Description
00h	DWORD	original INT 09h
04h	DWORD	original INT 2Fh
08h	*6 BYTEs*	*unknown*
0Eh	WORD	flags
10h	*BYTE*	*unknown*
11h	*BYTE*	*unknown*
12h	*4 BYTEs*	*unknown*
16h	2 BYTEs	country ID letters
18h	WORD	current code page
—DOS 3.3—		
1Ah	*WORD*	*pointer to first item in list of code page tables*
1Ch	*WORD*	*pointer to unknown item in list of code page tables*

1Eh	2 BYTEs	*unknown*
20h	WORD	pointer to key translation data
22h	WORD	pointer to last item in code page table list (see below)
24h	9 BYTEs	*unknown*

—DOS 4.01+—

1Ah	2 BYTEs	*unknown*
1Ch	WORD	*pointer to first item in list of code page tables*
1Eh	WORD	*pointer to unknown item in list of code page tables*
20h	2 BYTEs	*unknown*
22h	WORD	pointer to key translation data
24h	WORD	pointer to last item in code page table list (see below)
26h	9 BYTEs	*unknown*

Format of code page table list entries:

Offset	Size	Description
00h	WORD	pointer to next item, FFFFh if last
02h	WORD	code page
04h	2 BYTEs	*unknown*

Format of translation data:

Offset	Size	Description
00h	WORD	size of data in bytes, including this word
02h	N-2 BYTEs	*unknown*

INT 2Fh Function AD81h
KEYB.COM - SET KEYBOARD CODE PAGE
DOS 3.3+

Select a new code page for use by the keyboard driver.

Call With:

    AX   AD81h
    BX   code page (see *21/6601*h)

Returns:

    CF set on error
       AX   0001h (code page not available)
    CF clear if successful

Note: This function is called by DISPLAY.SYS. It has been documented for DOS 5+, but was undocumented for earlier versions.

See Also: 2F/AD82h

INT 2Fh Function AD82h
KEYB.COM - SET KEYBOARD MAPPING
DOS 3.3+

Specify whether the keyboard driver should use the standard or the foreign key mappings.

Call With:

    AX   AD82h
    BL   new state
               00h US keyboard (Control-Alt-F1)
               FFh foreign keyboard (Control-Alt-F2)

Returns:

    CF set on error (BL not 00h or FFh)
    CF clear if successful

Note: This function has been documented for DOS 5+, but was undocumented for earlier versions.

See Also: 2F/AD81h, 2F/AD83h

INT 2Fh Function AD83h   DOS 5+
KEYB.COM - GET KEYBOARD MAPPING

Determine whether the keyboard driver is using the standard or the foreign key mappings.

Call With:
    AX   AD83h
Returns:
    BL   current state
                 00h US keyboard
                 FFh foreign keyboard
See Also: 2F/AD82h

INT 2Fh Function AE00h   DOS 3.3+
INSTALLABLE COMMAND - INSTALLATION CHECK

Determine whether a command is a TSR extension to COMMAND.COM's internal command set.

Called With:
AX	AE00h
DX	FFFFh
CH	FFh (first call); 0 (second call)
CL	length of command line tail (4DOS 4.0)
DS:BX	pointer to command line buffer (see below)
DS:SI	pointer to command name buffer (see below)
DI	0000h (4DOS 4.0)

Returns:
AL	FFh if this command is a TSR extension to COMMAND.COM
AL	00h if the command should be executed as usual

Notes: This call provides a mechanism for TSRs to install permanent extensions to the command repertoire of COMMAND.COM. COMMAND.COM makes this call before executing the current command line, and does not execute it itself if the return is FFh. See Chapter 10.

    APPEND hooks this call, to allow subsequent APPEND commands to execute without re-running APPEND.

See Also: INT 2Eh.

Format of command line buffer:

Offset	Size	Description
00h	BYTE	max length of command line, as in 21/0Ah
01h	BYTE	count of bytes to follow, excluding terminating 0Dh
	N BYTEs	command line text, terminated by 0Dh

Format of command name buffer:

Offset	Size	Description
00h	BYTE	length of command name
01h	N BYTEs	uppercased command name (blank-padded to 11 chars by 4DOS 4.0)

INT 2Fh Function AE01h   DOS 3.3+
INSTALLABLE COMMAND - EXECUTE

Execute a TSR extension to COMMAND.COM's set of internal commands. The extension may resolve to an existing internal command.

Called With:
AX	AE01h
DX	FFFFh

CH	00h
CL	length of command name (4DOS 4.0)
DS:SI	pointer to command name buffer (see 2F/AE00h)
DS:BX	pointer to command line buffer (see 2F/AE00h)

Returns:
>   DS:SI buffer updated
>   if length byte is nonzero, the following bytes contain the uppercase internal command
>   to execute and the command line buffer contains the command's parameters (the first
>   DS:[SI] bytes are ignored)

Notes: This call requests execution of the command which a previous call to 2F/AE00h indicated was resident.

>   APPEND hooks this call.

INT 2Fh Function B000h   DOS 3.3+
GRAFTABL.COM - INSTALLATION CHECK

Determine whether GRAFTABL has been loaded.

Call With:
>   AX   B000h

Returns:
>   AL   00h not installed, OK to install
>   01h not installed, not OK to install
>   FFh installed

Note: This function is called by DISPLAY.SYS. It has been documented for DOS 5.0, but was undocumented in prior versions.
See Also: 2F/B001h

INT 2Fh Function B001h   DOS 3.3+
GRAFTABL.COM - GET GRAPHICS FONT TABLE

Call With:
>   AX   B001h
>   DS:BX   pointer to DWORD buffer for address of 8x8 font table

Returns:
>   buffer filled
>   AL   FFh

Note: PCDOS 3.30/4.01 set the font table offset to 0130h, MS-DOS 3.30 to 0030h
See Also: 2F/B000h

INT 2Fh Function B700h   DOS 3.3+
APPEND - INSTALLATION CHECK

Determine whether APPEND has been loaded.

Call With:
>   AX   B700h

Returns:
>   AL   status
>   00h not installed
>   FFh installed

Note: MS-DOS 3.30 APPEND refuses to install itself when run inside TopView or a TopView-compatible environment.

>   This function is documented for DOS 5.0.

INT 2Fh Function B701h   APPEND
GET APPEND PATH

Alternative to function B704h to retrieve the current list of directories in which APPEND will search for a file.

Call With:
>   AX   B701h

Returns:
>   ES:DI   pointer to active APPEND path

Notes: Not all versions of APPEND support this call; use AX=B704h first, and only call this function if that one is not supported.

>   MS-DOS 3.30 APPEND displays "Incorrect APPEND Version" and aborts the caller.

See Also: AX=B704h

INT 2Fh Function B702h   DOS 3.3+
APPEND - VERSION CHECK

Determine which version of APPEND has been loaded.

Call With:
>   AX   B702h

Returns:
>   AX   FFFFh if not DOS 4.0 APPEND (also if DOS 5.0 APPEND)
>   AL   major version number
>   AH   minor version number, otherwise

Note: This function is documented for DOS 5.0.

See Also: 2F/B710h

INT 2Fh Function B703h   DOS 3.3, 5.0
APPEND - HOOK INT 21h

Specify the handler APPEND should call when it has finished pre-processing an INT 21h call.

Call With:
>   AX   B703h
>   ES:DI   pointer to INT 21h handler APPEND should chain to

Returns:
>   ES:DI   pointer to APPEND's INT 21h handler

Note: Each invocation of this function toggles a flag which APPEND uses to determine whether to chain to the user handler or the original INT 21h.

INT 2Fh Function B704h   DOS 3.3+
APPEND - GET APPEND PATH

Return the current APPEND path.

Call With:
>   AX   B704h

Returns:
>   ES:DI   pointer to active APPEND path (128 bytes max)

Note: This function is documented for DOS 5.0. Some versions of append do not support this call, and return ES unchanged; in this case, you should call AX=B701h to get the APPEND path.

See Also: AX=B701h

INT 2Fh Function B706h   DOS 4+
APPEND - GET APPEND FUNCTION STATE
Determine which actions APPEND is performing.
Call With:
> AX   B706h

Returns:
> BX   APPEND state
>   bit 0: set if APPEND enabled
>   bits 1-11 reserved
>   bit 12: (DOS 5.0) set if APPEND applies directory search even if a
>   drive has been specified
>   bit 13: set if /PATH flag active
>   bit 14: set if /E flag active (environment var APPEND exists)
>   bit 15: set if /X flag active

INT 2Fh Function B707h   DOS 4+
APPEND - SET APPEND FUNCTION STATE
Specify which actions APPEND is to perform.
Call With:
> AX   B707h
> BX   APPEND state bits (see 2F/B706h)

INT 2Fh Function B710h   DOS 3.3+
APPEND - GET VERSION INFO
Determine which version of APPEND has been loaded.
Call With:
> AX   B710h

Returns:
> AX   current APPEND state (see 2F/B706h)
> BX   *unknown (0000h in MS-DOS 3.30 and 5.00)*
> CX   *unknown (0000h in MS-DOS 3.30 and 5.00)*
> DL   major version
> DH   minor version

See Also: 2F/B702h

INT 2Fh Function B711h   DOS 4+
APPEND - SET RETURN FOUND NAME STATE
Specify that the fully qualified filename be written over the filename passed to the next INT 21h call.
Call With:
> AX   B711h

Note: If the next INT 21h call (and ONLY the next) is function 3Dh, 43h, or 6Ch (also 4B03h and 4Eh if /X active), the fully qualified filename is written over top of the filename passed to the INT 21h call. The application must provide a sufficiently large buffer. This state is reset after the next INT 21h call processed by APPEND.

BUG: DOS 4.0 APPEND reportedly overwrites DS:DX instead of DS:SI for 21/6Ch.
See Also: 21/4Eh

INT 2Fh Function B800h   Network
INSTALLATION CHECK
Determine whether a network is installed.

Call With:

AX   B800h

Returns:

AL   status

   00h   not installed

   nonzero installed

        BX   installed component flags (test in this order!)

        bit 6   server

        bit 2   messenger

        bit 7   receiver

        bit 3   redirector

INT 2Fh Function B803h   Network
GET NETWORK EVENT POST HANDLER

This function is used in conjunction with 2F/B804h to hook into the network event post routine.

Call With:

AX   B803h

Returns:

ES:BX   pointer to event post handler (see 2F/B804h)

See Also: 2F/B804h, 2F/B903h

INT 2Fh Function B804h   Network
SET NETWORK EVENT POST HANDLER

This function is used in conjunction with 2F/B803h to hook into the network event post routine.

Call With:

AX   B804h

ES:BX   pointer to new event post handler

Note: The specified handler is called on any network event. Two events are defined: message received and critical network error.

See Also: 2F/B803h, 2F/B904h

Values post routine is called with:

AX   *0000h single block message*

       DS:SI pointer to ASCIZ originator name

       DS:DI   pointer to ASCIZ destination name

       ES:BX   pointer to text header (see below)

AX   0001h start multiple message block

       CX   block group ID

       DS:SI   pointer to ASCIZ originator name

       DS:DI   pointer to ASCIZ destination name

AX   0002h multiple block text

       CX   block group ID

       ES:BX   pointer to text header (see below)

AX   0003h end multiple block message

       CX   block group ID

AX   0004h message aborted due to error

       CX   block group ID

AX   0101h server received badly formatted network request

       Returns:

           AX   FFFFh (PC LAN will process error)

AX   0102h unexpected network error

ES:BX   pointer to NCB (see *INT 5Ch*)

AX   0103h server received INT 24h error

other registers as for INT 24h, except AH is in BH

Returns:

as below, but only 0000h and FFFFh allowed

Returns:

AX   response code

0000h user post routine processed message

0001h PC LAN will process message, but message window not displayed

FFFFh PC LAN will process message

Format of text header:

Offset	Size	Description
00h	WORD	length of text (maximum 512 bytes)
02h	N BYTEs	text of message

Note: All CRLF sequences in the message text are replaced by Control-T's.

INT 2Fh Function B807h   Network
GET NetBIOS NAME NUMBER OF MACHINE NAME

Return the network machine number.

Call With:

AX   B807h

Returns:

CH   NetBIOS name number of the machine name

See Also: *21/5E00h*

INT 2Fh Function B808h   Network
RELINK KEYBOARD HANDLER

Specify the routine to which the network passes an INT 09h after completing its own interrupt handling.

Call With:

AX   B908h

ES:BX   pointer to INT 09h handler RECEIVER should call after it finishes INT 09h

Note: This call replaces the address to which the network software chains on an INT 09 without preserving the original value. This allows a prior handler to unlink, but does not allow a new handler to be added such that the network gets the INT 09h first unless the new handler completely takes over INT 09h and never chains. This function is called by the DOS 3.2 KEYBxx.COM.

See Also: 2F/B808h

INT 2Fh Function B809h   Network
LANtastic, NetWare Lite - VERSION CHECK

Determine which version of the network software has been installed.

Call With:

AX   B809h

Returns:

AH   major version

AL   minor version (decimal)

Note: See 21/5F in the interrupt list on disk for LANtastic API calls. See Tim Farley, *Undocumented NetWare* (1994) for more on the NetWare Lite API.

INT 2Fh Function B809h   Network PC
LAN Program, LAN Manager, DOS LAN Requester - Version Check

Determine which version of the network software has been installed. Note that these networks return the version reversed from the way LANtastic and NetWare Lite return the version.

Call With:

AX   B809h

Returns:

AH   minor version (decimal)
AL   major version

See Also: AX=4E53h, AX=B800h

INT 2Fh Function B900h   PC Network
RECEIVER.COM - INSTALLATION CHECK

Determine whether the PC Network receiver module has been loaded.

Call With:

AX   B900h

Returns:

AL   00h if not installed
           FFh if installed

INT 2Fh Function B901h   PC Network
RECEIVER.COM - GET RECEIVER.COM INT 2Fh HANDLER ADDRESS

Determine the entry point for the RECEIVER.COM INT 2Fh handler, allowing more efficient execution by bypassing any other handlers which have hooked INT 2Fh since RECEIVER.COM was installed.

Call With:

AX   B901h

Returns:

AL   *unknown*
ES:BX   pointer to RECEIVER.COM INT 2Fh handler

INT 2Fh Function B903h   PC Network
RECEIVER.COM - GET RECEIVER.COM POST ADDRESS

This function is used in conjunction with 2F/B904h to hook into the network event post routine.

Call With:

AX   B903h

Returns:

ES:BX   pointer to POST handler

See Also: 2F/B803h, 2F/B904h

INT 2Fh Function B904h   PC Network
RECEIVER.COM - SET RECEIVER.COM POST ADDRESS

This function is used in conjunction with 2F/B903h to hook into the network event post routine.

Call With:

AX   B904h
ES:BX   pointer to new POST handler

See Also: 2F/B804h, 2F/B903h

INT 2Fh Function B905h   PC Network
RECEIVER.COM - GET FILENAME
Return two filenames used internally by RECEIVER.COM.
Call With:
  AX   B905h
  DS:BX   pointer to 128-byte buffer for filename 1
  DS:DX   pointer to 128-byte buffer for filename 2
Returns:
  buffers filled from RECEIVER.COM internal buffers
Note: The use of the filenames is unknown, but one appears to be for storing messages.
See Also: 2F/B906h

INT 2Fh Function B906h   PC Network
RECEIVER.COM - SET FILENAME
Specify the filenames which RECEIVER.COM uses internally.
Call With:
  AX   B906h
  DS:BX   pointer to 128-byte buffer for filename 1
  DS:DX   pointer to 128-byte buffer for filename 2
Returns:
  RECEIVER.COM internal buffers filled from user buffers

Note: The use of the filenames is unknown, but one appears to be for storing messages.
See Also: 2F/B905h

INT 2Fh Function B908h   PC Network
RECEIVER.COM - UNLINK KEYBOARD HANDLER
Remove the INT 09h handler immediately following RECEIVER.COM in the INT 09h chain.

Call With:
  AX   B908h
  ES:BX   pointer to INT 09h handler RECEIVER should call after it finishes INT 09h
Note: This call replaces the address to which RECEIVER.COM chains on an INT 09h without pre-
serving the original value. This allows a prior handler to unlink, but does not allow a new handler to
be added such that RECEIVER gets the INT 09h first.
See Also: 2F/B808h

INT 2Fh Function BC00h   Windows 3.0, DOS 5+
EGA.SYS - INSTALLATION CHECK
Determine whether or not EGA.SYS has been loaded.

Call With:
  AX   BC00h
Returns:
  AL   00h not installed, OK to install
            01h not installed, not OK to install
            FFh installed
                BX   5456h ("TV")
Note: AH=BCh is the default value, which may be changed by a command line parameter to any value
between 80h and FFh.
See Also: *INT 10/AH=FAh*, 2F/BC06h

INT 2Fh Function BC06h   Windows 3.0, DOS 5+
EGA.SYS - GET VERSION INFO
Determine which version of EGA.SYS has been loaded.
Call With:
      AX   BC06h
Returns:
      BX   5456h ("TV")
      CH   major version
      CL   minor version
      DL   revision
See Also: *INT 10/AH=FAh*, 2F/BC00h

INT 2Fh Function BF00h   PC LAN
REDIRIFS.EXE - INSTALLATION CHECK
Determine whether the PC LAN Program Installable File System module has been loaded.
Call With:
      AX   BF00h
Returns:
      AL   FFh if installed

INT 2Fh Function BF01h   PC LAN
REDIRIFS.EXE - UNKNOWN FUNCTION
The purpose of this function has not been determined.

Call With:
      AX   BF01h
      additional arguments (if any) unknown
Returns:
      unknown

INT 2Fh Function BF80h   PC LAN
REDIR.SYS - SET REDIRIFS ENTRY POINT
Specify the address of an Installable File System handler for the PC LAN Program redirector.
Call With:
      AX   BF80h
      ES:DI   pointer to FAR entry point to IFS handler in REDIRIFS
Returns:
      AL   FFh if installed
            ES:DI pointer to internal workspace
Note: After executing this function, all future IFS calls to REDIR.SYS are passed to the specified entry point.

INT 30h   DOS 1+
FAR JMP instruction for CP/M-style calls
This is not a vector, but contains an actual JMP instruction. For CP/M compatibility, a program may invoke DOS function calls by loading CL with the function number (00h to 24h) and performing a near CALL to offset 5 in the program's PSP. That location contains a far jump instruction which points at absolute address 000C0h, which is this vector. This vector in turn contains a far jump instruction to the CP/M-compatibility entry point in the DOS kernel. The CP/M-compatibility entry point manipulates the stack, moves CL to AH, and falls through into the normal INT 21h entry point.

Note: Under DOS 2+, the instruction at PSP:0005h points two bytes too low in memory if the PSP was created by the EXEC call (21/4Bh).
See Also: 21/26h

INT 31h   DOS 1+
OVERWRITTEN BY CP/M JUMP INSTRUCTION IN INT 30h

The first byte of this vector contains the end of the FAR JMP instruction stored in INT 30h.

In protected mode, INT 31h provides access to DOS Protected Mode Interface (DPMI) services (detailed in the full list on the accompanying disk).
Note: DPMI is well documented in a specification from Intel, but Windows 3.x uses four obsolete DPMI functions which are undocumented:

0004h	Lock selector
0005h	Unlock selector
0700h	Mark paging candidates
0701h	Discard pages

For more information, see the interrupt list on disk, and *Undocumented Windows*, chapter 4.

INT 67h Function FFA5h   Microsoft EMM386.EXE v4.20+
EMM386 INSTALLATION CHECK
Call With:
>   AX   FFA5h

Returns:
>   AX   845Ah if loaded
>   BX:CX pointer to API entry point

Notes: This call is available even if EMM386 is not providing EMS support.

If no other program has hooked INT 67h, an alternate installation check is to search for the string "MICROSOFT EXPANDED MEMORY MANAGER 386" early in the INT 67h handler's segment, usually at offset 14h.

Call API entry point with:
>   AH   00h get memory manager's status
>   **Returns:**
>   AH   status
>   bit 0: not active (OFF)
>   bit 1: in "Auto" mode
>   AH   01h set memory manager's state
>   AL   new state (00h ON, 01h OFF, 02h AUTO)
>   AH   02h Weitek coprocessor support
>   AL   subfunction
>   00h get Weitek support state
>   **Returns:**
>   AL   status
>   bit 0: Weitek coprocessor is present
>   bit 1: Weitek support is enabled
>   01h turn on Weitek support
>   02h turn off Weitek support

> — v4.20-4.41 only —
>   *AH*   *03h Windows support*
>   *AL   subfunction (00h, 01h)*
>   AH   04h print copyright notice to standard output (using 21/09h)
>   AH   05h print report (the one shown when running EMM386 from the DOS prompt)

Glossary

The following list is a partial (and semi-random) list of some terms and abbreviations used throughout this book. An *italicized term* means to "see also" the italicized term. XX/YY and XX/YYYY means to see the entry for INT XXh AH=YYh or AX=YYYYh in the appendix on Undocumented DOS Functions and Data Structures.

A20 On 80286 and higher processors, the A20 address line controls access to the first megabyte of extended memory (address 1 << 20 = 100000h). For compatibility with "address wraparound" on the older 8088 processor, 286+ processors leave A20 disabled. However, to access the *HMA* (needed for DOS=HIGH), A20 must be enabled. See chapter 6.

ASCIZ A zero-terminated ASCII string, such as 'A','B','C',00h.

BPB The BIOS Parameter Block stores the low-level layout of a drive. See 21/53, and chapter 8.

CDS The Current Directory Structure for a drive stores the current directory, type, and other information about a logical drive. See 21/52, and chapter 8.

Chicago Microsoft's forthcoming desktop operating system, incorporating DOS 7 and Windows 4, includes long filenames, threads, pre-emptive multitasking, and other features. See 21/4302, 21/71, 21/72, and chapter 8.

Conventional memory Memory below one megabyte (100000h), immediately accessible by a *real mode* program. Contrast *extended memory*.

DOS extender Software that provides INT 21h and other DOS services in protected mode, creating the illusion that MS-DOS is a protected-mode operating system. Windows contains a DOS extender. See chapter 3.

DOSMGR The component of Windows Enhanced mode responsible for interfacing with MS-DOS. DOSMGR also provides the Enhanced mode *DOS extender*. See 2F/1607, chapter 1, and chapter 3.

DPB The DOS Drive Parameter Block stores the description of the media layout for a logical drive, as well as some housekeeping information. See 21/1F, 21/32, and chapter 8.

DblSpace DoubleSpace provides "on the fly" disk compression in MS-DOS 6.0 and higher. See 2F/4A11, and chapter 8.

DPL The DOS Parameter List is used to pass arguments to SHARE and network functions. See 21/5D00.

DPMI DOS programs can use the DOS Protected-Mode Interface to switch themselves into protected mode. Once in protected mode, they can use DPMI INT 31h services to communicate back to real mode. In Windows Enhanced mode, DPMI services are provided by the *VMM*. See chapter 3.

DR DOS DR DOS 5 and 6 were DOS workalikes produced by Digital Research, later bought by Novell. DR DOS has been renamed Novell DOS 7. See 21/4452, and chapter 4.

DTA The Disk Transfer Address indicates where functions which do not take an explicit data address will read or store data. Although the name implies that only disk accesses use this address, other functions use it as well. See 21/4E for the FindFirst/FindNext DTA format.

Extended memory Memory above one megabyte (100000h), usually accessible only from a *protected mode* program. XMS provides services that allow a real-mode program to access extended memory.

FAT The File Allocation Table of a disk, which records the clusters that are in use. See chapter 8.

FCB A File Control Block, which is used by DOS 1.x functions to record the state of an open file. See 21/13. Since an FCB resides in an application's own address space, DOS maintains internal System FCBs (also called SFT-FCBs). See 21/52, and chapter 8.

File handle An index into a *JFT*.

HMA The High Memory Area is a sliver of extended memory, just under 64k bytes, between addresses 10000h and (FFFF0h + FFFFh = 10FFEFh), that is accessible from real mode on 80286 and higher processors. Real-mode programs access the HMA with an address segment of FFFFh. The HMA is only accessible if the *A20* address line is enabled. See 2F/4A01 and 2F/4A02.

IFS An Installable File System which allows non-DOS format media to be used by DOS. In most ways, an IFS is very similar to a networked drive, although an IFS would typically be local rather than remote. The 2F/11 IFS interface was for DOS 4.x only; DOS 3, DOS 5, and DOS 6 use 2F/11 for the network redirector interface. *Chicago* will have a documented IFSMGR interface.

JFT The Job File Table (also called Open File Table), usually stored in a program's *PSP*, which translates file handles into *SFT* indices. See 21/26, and chapter 8.

LoL List of Lists—see SysVars.

MCB A Memory Control Block (or ARENA) contains the size and owner of a conventional-memory allocation. See 21/52, and chapter 7.

MZ Initials of Mark Zbikowski (5A4Dh), used as a signature for executable files. DOS also uses the letters M and Z as signatures for *MCBs*.

NCB A Network Control Block used to pass requests to NETBIOS and receive status information from the NETBIOS handler. (See INT 5Ch in the interrupt list on disk.)

NETX Generic name for NetWare workstation shell (NETX.EXE, NET4.EXE, NET5.EXE, etc.), which takes over the INT 21h interface. See chapter 4.

Protected mode The native mode of the Intel 80286 and higher microprocessors, protected mode provides transparent (i.e., immediately-addressable) access to memory above one megabyte. However, most 286+ machines still spend much of their time in *real mode*. See chapter 3.

PSP The Program Segment Prefix is a 256-byte data area prepended to a program when it is loaded. It contains the command line with which the program was invoked, a pointer to the *JFT* (and generally the JFT itself), the segment address of the program's environment, and a variety of housekeeping information for DOS. See also 21/26, and chapters 7 and 10.

Real mode   The native mode of the Intel 8086 and 8066 microprocessors, limited to one megabyte of immediately-addressable memory. 80286 and higher machines can emulate real mode, and in fact spend much of their time doing so. MS-DOS is a real-mode operating system. See chapter 3.

SDA   The DOS Swappable Data Area, containing many (though not all) of the variables used internally by DOS to record the state of a function call in progress. See 21/5D06, 21/5D0B, and chapters 8 and 9.

SFT   A System File Table maintains the state of an open file for the DOS 2+ handle functions, just as an *FCB* maintains the state for DOS 1.x functions. See 21/52, and chapter 8. SFT-like entries are also used for System FCBs.

SysVars   Also known as the "List of Lists" (LoL), SysVars is a DOS internal data structure containing far pointers to many other DOS internal structures, including the CDS, SFT, and so on. See 21/52.

TSR   A program that calls INT 27h (Terminate and Stay Resident) or 21/31 (Keep Program). See chapter 9.

UMB   An Upper Memory Block is an MCB that resides in a PC's "upper memory," the area between address A0000h and FFFFFh normally reserved for adapters. Expanded memory managers, including EMM386 in DOS 5 and higher, can allocate UMBs for use by DOS software. Unlike the HMA, UMBs are always accessible in real mode.

V86, VM, VMM   Virtual-8086 mode is provided by Intel 80386 and higher processors to emulate one or more 8088-like sessions. Each such session is called a Virtual Machine (VM). A VM can also include a protected-mode component. 386 memory managers such as EMM386, QEMM, and 386MAX, and multitaskers such as Windows Enhanced mode, run MS-DOS in V86 mode. All interrupts from real-mode software running in V86 mode are handled by a 32-bit protected-mode program called a Virtual Machine Monitor (VMM). The VMM can emulate the interrupt function and/or "reflect" the interrupt back to V86 mode. In Windows Enhanced mode, the VMM is contained inside WIN386.EXE, and works in conjunction with VxDs. In Chicago, the VMM is contained inside DOS386.EXE. See chapters 1, 3, and 4.

VxD   Virtual Device Drivers are used in Windows Enhanced mode to emulate the behavior of, and/or provide a multitasking interface to, real-mode software such as MS-DOS and the BIOS, and devices such as the keyboard, display, disk, mouse, printer, and so on. See 2F/1607, 2F/1684, and chapters 1 and 3. (In OS/2 2.x and Windows NT, Virtual Device Drivers are called VDDs; see chapter 4.)

ANNOTATED BIBLIOGRAPHY

Phillip M. Adams and Clovis L. Tondo, *Writing DOS Device Drivers in C*, Englewood Cliffs NJ: Prentice Hall, 1990, 385 pp.

Walter Adams and James Brock, *Antitrust Economics on Trial: A Dialogue on the New Laissez-Faire*, Princeton NJ: Princeton University Press, 1991, 132 pp. A brief, entertaining polemic (in the form of an play!) against the Chicago School of Economics' defense of tying arrangements and other predatory practices discussed in chapter 1 of *Undocumented DOS*. Pages 30-37 on "the predation problem" are particularly useful.

Alfred Aho, Brian Kernighan, and Peter Weinberger, *The AWK Programming Language*, Reading MA: Addison-Wesley, 1988, 210 pp. AWK is an excellent language with which to build disassembly and reverse-engineering utilities.

Prabhat K. Andleigh, *UNIX System Architecture*, Englewood Cliffs NJ: Prentice-Hall, 1990, 274 pp. Every programmer interested in operating systems should know something about UNIX internals. This is a short introduction, with very readable pseudocode. It's a good introduction before trying to tackle Bach's book (see below).

Rick Ayre, "DOS 6 Utilities vs. the Competition: What's the Price of a Free Lunch?," *PC Magazine*, September 14, 1993. On Microsoft's "bid to dominate the utilities turf."

Maurice J. Bach, *The Design of the UNIX Operating System*, Englewood Cliffs NJ: Prentice-Hall, 1986, 471 pp.

Richard Belgard, "Appeals Court Reverses Disassembly Decision," *Microprocessor Report*, December 9, 1992. A report on Sega v. Accolade.

Sudeep Bharati, "Virtual Device Driver Support on Windows NT," Microsoft NT Device Driver Developer's Conference, October 1992.

Douglas Boling, "Background Copying Without OS/2," *PC Magazine*, 17 January 1989. A DOS multitasking TSR which copies files in the background; discusses INT 28h and Get/Set PSP.

Douglas Boling and Jeff Prosise, "Give Yourself a Smart DOS Command Line with ALIAS," *PC Magazine*, 26 December 1989. Discusses 21/51 (Get PSP) in DOS 2.x, finding COMMAND.COM's PSP, and changes caused by the INSTALL= statement in DOS 4+.

Douglas Boling, "Strategies and Techniques for Writing State-of-the-Art TSRs that Exploit MS-DOS 5," *Microsoft Systems Journal*, January-February 1992. What TSR writers need to know about instance data, task switchers, and other new developments.

Douglas Boling, "Quick-Boot Your PC and Protect Your Data with BOOT2C and BOOTTPW," *PC Magazine*, March 30, 1993. These utilities use the DOS boot record.

Paul Bonneau, "Windows Questions and Answers," *Windows/DOS Developer's Journal*. This excellent monthly column (whose author is now a Microsoft employee) often covers topics of importance to DOS programmers. For example, the December 1992 column showed how to derive a Windows DOS box's virtual machine (VM) handle from its window handle (HWND).

James W. Brock, "Structural Monopoly, Technological Performance, and Predatory Innovation: Relevant Standards under Section 2 of the Sherman Act," *American Business Law Journal, Fall 1983*. This look at Kodak's relations with its competitors has some interesting parallels to Microsoft's role in the software industry.

Fred Brooks, *The Mythical Man-Month: Essays on Software Engineering* Reading MA: Addison-Wesley, 1975, 195 pp. Many developers refer to this book, but few seem to have actually read it or paid much attention to what Brooks is saying. Note Brooks's warnings regarding David Parnas's then-new theory of "information hiding": it presupposed complete documentation. Chapter 15 discusses documentation (note the picture of Stonehenge, "the world's largest undocumented computer").

Stan Brown, dos.faq (Frequently Asked Questions list for newsgroup comp.os.msdos.programmer). Available via anonymous FTP from pit-manager.mit.edu. The DOS FAQ contains handy answers to such popular questions as "What the heck is 'DGROUP 64K'?," "Will Borland C code and Microsoft C code link together?," "How can I tell if input or output has been redirected?," "How do I switch to 43- or 50-line mode?," "How can I read or write my PC's CMOS memory?," and even "Why won't my code work?"

Ralf Brown and Jim Kyle, *PC Interrupts: A Programmer's Reference to BIOS, DOS, and Third-Party Calls*, Reading MA: Addison-Wesley, 1991. This massive book lists almost any imaginable programming interface for the PC, so long as in one way or another it works off an INT call. Even though the Interrupt List is widely available online (and is included on the disk accompanying *Undocumented DOS*), *PC Interrupts* is still incredibly handy. In 1994, Addison-Wesley will publish the second edition, and a new book, *Network Interrupts*.

David Burki, "DOS File Handle Limits," *TECH Specialist*, February 1993. This magazine is now *Windows/DOS Developer's Journal*.

Carnegie-Mellon University, MDOS (Mach operating system DOS emulation code). Available by ftp from cs.cmu.edu. DOS_FS.C is the network redirector module.

Craig Chaiken, *Blueprint of a LAN*, Redwood City CA: M&T Books, 1989, 337 pp. Assembly-language source code for a network based on DOS device drivers.

Geoff Chappell, "Spreading Secrets," *.EXE* (UK), April 1991. A critique of some subtle and not-so-subtle errors in the first edition of *Undocumented DOS*.

Geoff Chappell, *DOS Internals*, Reading MA: Addison-Wesley, 1993. Chappell's book is the natural follow-on to *Undocumented DOS*, covering many topics in more detail (and more accurately!) than we could here. Includes system configuration and startup, the system "footprint," extensive coverage of INT 19h, the IO.SYS loader, the 2F/13 interface, DOS in ROM, Windows/DOS interaction, the 21/4B05 set execution state function, writing TSRs and device drivers in C, XMS, an entire chapter on the A20 line, LOADALL, a close look at HIMEM.SYS, SmartDrive, low-level disk access, boot sectors, generic IOCTL, and an entire chapter on error codes. An amazing book!

Geoff Chappell, "Untangling SMARTDrive," *Dr. Dobb's Journal*, January 1992. This article revealed the SmartDrv 3.x IOCTL interface; for the SmartDrv 4.x "BABE" interface, see the interrupt list on disk.

Laura Chappell, *Novell's Guide to NetWare LAN Analysis*, Sybex/Novell Press, 1993. Includes a good look at the "proprietary" NetWare Core Protocol (NCP).

Ken W. Christopher, Jr., Barry A. Feigenbaum, Shon O. Saliga, *Developing Applications Using DOS*, New York NY: Wiley, 1990, 573 pp. This book, by three IBM employees who were "the lead engineers directing the entire development of the DOS 4.0 system," describes many undocumented DOS features, including for example INT 21h Function 5Dh.

Paul Chui, "Undocumented DOS from Protected-Mode Windows 3," *Dr. Dobb's Journal*, February 1992. Enhancing standard file dialogs with a GetDriveTypeX() function.

Robert Collins, "The LOADALL Instruction," *TECH Specialist*, October 1991. This magazine is now the *Windows/DOS Developer's Journal*. Collins uses an in-circuit emulator (ICE) to take apart the undocumented LOADALL instruction; an amazingly good article.

David Cortesti, "CP/M-86 vs. MSDOS: A Technical Comparison," *Dr. Dobb's Journal*, July 1982. An early look at the similarities and differences between CP/M and MS-DOS 1.0.

Helen Custer, *Inside Windows NT*, Redmond WA: Microsoft Press, 1993, 385 pp. As the author puts it, this book explains "exactly" how NT "sort-of" works. Regardless of whether NT is appropriate for more than a small handful of users, the book nevertheless is essential reading for anyone interested in operating systems and how they work. The chapter on "protected subsystems" discusses virtual DOS machines.

Ralph Davis, *Windows Network Programming: How to Survive in a World of Windows, DOS, and Networks*, Reading MA: Addison-Wesley, 1993, 562 pp. An in-depth look at Windows for Workgroups, NetWare, LAN Manager, and other topics. Chapter 7 covers API translation and DPMI.

Harvey Deitel and Michael Kogan, *The Design of OS/2*, Reading MA: Addison-Wesley, 1992, 389 pp. Chapter 10, on compatibility, covers the OS/2 1.x and 2.x DOS box.

DOS Protected Mode Interface (DPMI) Specification, Version 1.0 (March 12, 1991). Available from Intel, order no. 240977-001. The 1.0 specification is more readable than the 0.9 version (order no. 240763-001), but be aware that 0.9 is what Windows implements.

Ray Duncan, *Advanced MS-DOS Programming*, second edition, Redmond WA: Microsoft Press, 1988, 669 pp. This is the bible of DOS programming, with examples in assembler and C. Includes a discussion of how MS-DOS is loaded.

Ray Duncan (ed.), *The MS-DOS Encyclopedia*, Redmond WA: Microsoft Press, 1988, 1570 pp. Part C of this mammoth book ("Customizing MS-DOS") is particularly good, containing chapters on TSRs, exception handlers, hardware interrupt handlers, DOS filters, and installable device drivers. Includes Richard Wilton's definitive piece on TSR programming. The article on "The Components of MS-DOS" describes the DOS boot sequence.

Ray Duncan et al., *Extending DOS*, second edition, Reading MA: Addison-Wesley, 1992, 538 pp. Discusses DPMI, VCPI, XMS, 16-bit and 32-bit protected-mode programming for DOS, DesqView, and other topics.

Ray Duncan, "Microsoft Windows/386: Creating a Virtual Machine Environment," *Microsoft Systems Journal*, September 1987. This remains an excellent description of how Windows Enhanced mode pre-emptively multitasks multiple DOS boxes, on top of a single copy of DOS. Discusses instancing of DOS data structures.

Ray Duncan, "Programming Considerations for MS-DOS 5.0," *PC Magazine*, October 29, 1991 (Part 1) and November 12, 1991 (Part 2). How to check the DOS version number; UMBs and the HMA; newly-documented INT 2Fh calls; the task switcher API.

Martin R.M. Dunsmuir, "OS/2 to UNIX LAN," in Stephen G. Kochan and Patrick H. Wood (eds.), *UNIX Networking*, Indianapolis IN: Hayden Books, 1989, pp. 237-284. You wouldn't know it from the title, but this discusses the Server Message Block (SMB) protocol, including Extended SMB.

Jeff Duntemann and Keith Weiskamp, *PC Techniques C/C++ Power Tools: HAX, Techniques, and Hidden Knowledge*, New York NY: Bantam, 1992, 626 pp. Includes useful snippets of code for TSR programming, calling DOS from Windows, moving DOS programs to Windows, working with disks, code optimization, date/time manipulation, and background printing.

Grant Echols, "DOS/NetWare Workstation Shell INT 21h Functions," 1990, unpublished.

Tim Farley, *Undocumented NetWare: A Programmer's Guide to Reserved Networking APIs and Protocols*, Reading MA: Addison-Wesley, 1994. This book will cover the NetWare Core Protocol (NCP), the NetWare Lite API, NETX modification of INT 21h, the F2 interface, server APIs, and so on.

Franklin Fisher et al., *Folded, Spindled, and Mutilated: Economic Analysis and U.S. vs. IBM*, MIT Press, 1983. IBM's view of the US v. IBM case; makes sobering reading for anyone who thinks there is an open and shut case against Microsoft.

Bob Flanders and Michael Holmes, *PC Magazine C Lab Notes*, Emeryville CA: Ziff-Davis Press, 1993. Chapter on "Collecting Program Statistics with INFORMER" presents C source for something sort of like INTRSPY, NETRUN demonstrates NetWare programming, and CHKSTRUC provides C source for a CHKDSK-like utility.

Bob Flanders and Michael Holmes, "Optimize Your Disk Drive Efficiency with DEFRAGR," *PC Magazine*, February 23, 1993. Describes the C source code for a defrag utility.

Bill Gates, "Free Market Economics—Not Intervention—Drives Innovation," *InfoWorld*, August 16, 1993. "The positive impact of Microsoft Windows on the fortunes of the entire industry has been profound.... Windows is nothing less than a job-creating engine."

General Software, *Device Driver SDK Reference Manual*, Redmond WA, 1992, 60 pp. The manuals for the Embedded DOS products, written by Steve Jones, provide a wealth of information about DOS.

General Software, *Embedded DOS System Architecture Specification and Technical Reference Manual*, Redmond WA, 1992, 155 pp.

General Software, *Utility SDK Reference Manual*, Redmond WA, 1992, 72 pp. Includes source code for an FDISK, FORMAT, CHKDSK, etc.

Steve Gibson, "Microsoft Should Let Users Decide Which Calls Are Important," *InfoWorld*, September 28, 1992.

Drew Gislason, "Flash File Systems," *Dr. Dobb's Journal*, May 1993. Discusses various approaches to building a FAT file system on top of flash memory.

Earl F. Glynn, "Getting a Good Look at How DOS Allocates Your Memory Blocks," *PC Magazine*, 12 June 1990. Building a MCB walker with Turbo Pascal.

Daniel E. Greenberg, "Reentering the DOS Shell," *Programmer's Journal*, May-June 1990. The definitive examination of the COMMAND.COM backdoor, INT 2Eh, from a now-defunct magazine.

Douglas F. Greer, *Industrial Organization and Public Policy*, third edition, New York: Macmillan, 1992, 736 pp. A standard textbook on competition, monopoly, oligopoly, firm/market tradeoffs, transaction costs, industry structure, barriers to market entry, predatory practices, vertical-market integration, technology policy, and many other subjects relevant to anyone interested in Microsoft's position within the software industry.

Jim Harper, "A DOS Redirector for SCSI CD-ROM," *Dr. Dobb's Journal*, March 1993.

Karen Hazzah, "Fast Interrupt Handling without VxDs," *Windows/DOS Developer's Journal*, June 1993. Using an interface provided by the VPICD VxD in Windows.

Frederick Hewett, "DPMI Meets C++," *Dr. Dobb's Journal*, October 1992. An object-oriented abstraction of DPMI.

Allen Holub, *On Command: Writing a Unix-Like Shell for MS-DOS*, Redwood City CA: M&T Books, 1986, 319 pp. An excellent explanation (much of it transferable to COMMAND.COM) of how command interpreters work.

Robert L. Hummel, *Assembly Language Lab Notes*, Emeryville CA: Ziff-Davis Press, 1992, 344 pp. Source code for utilities that walk the MCB chain, the DOS environment, and the FAT, that format diskettes, manage TSRs, and so on.

Robert L. Hummel, "How the DOS CLS Command Handles Various Displays," *PC Magazine*, 11 October 1988. "Every time you use the CLS command, DOS sifts through a bewildering array of information. Here's a peek behind the scenes of how COMMAND.COM clears the screen"; discusses INT 29h.

IBM, *Technical Reference—Personal Computer AT*, 1985 (IBM order number 6280070 and supplement 6280099). This is the IBM manual with the full BIOS source-code listings. Apparently it's still available, for about $200, from 1-800-426-7282.

IBM's *OS/2 2.0 Control Program Programming Guide*, Que, 1992. The official IBM documentation; includes information on long filenames, extended attributes (EAs), the STARTDATA structure, etc.

IBM, *OS/2 2.0 Virtual Device Driver Reference*, IBM publication #s10g-6310. Part of the OS/2 2.0 Device Driver Kit (DDK); there is also an OS/2 2.1 DDK.

Intel, *Pentium Processor User's Manual*, 1993. Appendix H ("Advanced Features") refers to the *Supplement to the Pentium Processor User's Manual*, "available with the appropriate non-disclosure agreements in place."

Dave Jewell, "Altered States of DOS," *Program NOW* (UK), April 1993. A utility in C for editing the master environment.

Steve Jones, "DOS Meets Real-Time," *Embedded Systems Programming*, February 1992. How to build a real-time DOS; see also Steve's manuals for General Software's Embedded DOS products.

Richard Kitson, "Command-Line Tricks of MS-DOS," *Program NOW* (UK), June 1991. Using the 2F/AE interface to add new "internal" commands to COMMAND.COM.

Rick Knoblaugh, "Locate Available IRQs with FINDIRQ," *PC Magazine*, September 28, 1993. Describes PIC programming, and a practical use for walking the DOS device chain.

Donald Knuth, *Literate Programming*, Stanford CA: Center for the Study of Language and Information, 1992, 368 pp. Knuth treats programs as a new form of literature. Therefore, programs also require a form of literary criticism. In an odd way, by taking apart MS-DOS and Windows, we are subjecting the world's most prevalent operating systems to a form of "literary criticism."

Kim Kokkonen, TSR Utilities, 1989. Kokkonen provides full Turbo Pascal source code for the following excellent TSR utilities: MARK, RELEASE, FMARK, MARKNET, RELNET, WATCH, DISABLE, RAMFREE, MAPMEM, DEVICE, EATMEM. Available from CompuServe, on the BPROGA forum.

Thomas Krattenmaker and Steve Salop, "Anticompetitive Exclusion: Raising Rivals' Costs to Achieve Power over Price," *Yale Law Journal*, December 1986. Read this article as one interpretation of what Microsoft is trying to achieve with its relentless delivery of increasingly complex APIs. Or perhaps read Joseph Schumpeter's writings on "creative destruction" instead.

Jim Kyle, "Application Wrappers," *PC Techniques*, June-July 1992. Writing applications that spawn other applications as an alternate to writing TSRs.

Robert S. Lai and The Waite Group, *Writing MS-DOS Device Drivers*, second edition, Reading MA: Addison-Wesley, 1992, 560 pp. The second edition is substantially the same as the first (1987), except for the addition of a chapter on CD-ROM device drivers and writing DOS device drivers in C. This is still the standard introduction to writing DOS device drivers.

Gene K. Landy, *The Software Developer's and Marketer's Legal Companion*, Reading MA: Addison-Wesley, 1993, 548 pp. This book/disk package (the disk contains sample forms, letters, and agreements) has superb discussions of trade-secret law, reverse engineering, fair use, shrink-wrap licenses, warranties, and everything else a software developer would want to know about the law.

Murray L. Lesser, "Extending COMMAND.COM," *Windows/DOS Developer's Journal*, February 1993. The 2F/AE installable command interface.

Gordon Letwin, *Inside OS/2*, Redmond, WA: Microsoft Press, 1988. Discusses backwards compatibility, de facto standards, etc.

David Long, "TSR Support in Microsoft Windows Version 3.1," Microsoft Developer Network (MSDN) CD-ROM (see below).

Steven Manes and Paul Andrews, *Gates: How Microsoft's Mogul Reinvented an Industry—and Made Himself the Richest Man in America*, New York: Doubleday, 1993, 534 pp. This is not really the story of Gates's life (who cares?), but of Microsoft's (now, *that's* interesting!). Meticulously-researched, with every fact or quotation backed up by at least one footnote, this book covers everything from Microsoft's purchase of QDOS, to its OEM pricing of DOS, to how Murray Sargent and Dave Weise moved Windows to protected mode.

Steven J. Mastrianni, *Writing OS/2 2.0 Device Drivers in C*, New York: Van Nostrand Reinhold, 1992, 407 pp. Chapter 9 discusses OS/2 virtual device drivers (VDDs) and the Virtual DOS Machine (VDM). A second edition, for OS/2 2.1, should be available.

Michael P. Maurice, "The PIF File Format, or, Topview (sort of) Lives!," *Dr. Dobb's Journal*, July 1993. Program Information Files (PIFs) are what Windows uses to run "old" (DOS) programs.

Michael Mefford, "Choose CONFIG.SYS Options at Boot," *PC Magazine*, November 29, 1988. Discusses the undocumented DOS CONFIG.SYS buffer.

Michael Mefford, "Running Programs Painlessly," *PC Magazine*, February 16, 1988. Discusses the problems with using INT 2Eh.

Philippe Mercier, *La maîtrise des programmes résidents sous MS-DOS*, Marabout, 1990, 410 pp. A handy book on TSRs from Belgium. Did you know that the French for "hotkey" is "touche magique"?

Microprocessor Report, *Understanding x86 Microprocessors*, Emeryville CA: Ziff-Davis Press, 1993. A collection of articles on the 286, 386, 486, and Pentium, from Michael Slater's brilliant newsletter, *Microprocessor Report* ("The Insider's Guide to Microprocessor Hardware"). Includes discussions of undocumented processor instructions, and an entire section on legal issues (Intel v. Cyrix, etc.). Don't miss the brilliant articles by John Wharton, such as "Gonzo Marketing." Why can't all technical writing be like this?

Microsoft, "API to Identify MS-DOS Instance Data," undated internal document. Describes the DOSMGR callout API.

Microsoft, *Device Driver Adaptation Guide* (DDAG), version 3.1, Redmond WA, 1992. Included with the Windows 3.1 Device Driver Kit (DDK), this includes an essential appendix on "Windows Interrupt 2Fh Services and Notifications." Why they've put this important stuff in an obscure manual like this is beyond me. There's also a useful chapter on Windows network drivers.

Microsoft Developer Network (MSDN) CD-ROM. A must-have for any serious DOS or Windows developer, the MSDN CD-ROM includes huge amounts of information that programmers often mistakenly think is undocumented. For more information, call (800) 759-5474 or (206) 936-8661. Here's a very small sampling of the articles related to DOS: "Determining Windows Version, Mode from MS-DOS App," "Demand Paging MS-DOS Applications," "Global TSR Pop-ups Incompatible with Windows," "Full-Screen DOS Apps Slow Timer Messages in Enhanced Mode," "Do Not Use the MS-DOS APPEND Utility in Windows," "Calling a DLL Written for Windows from a TSR for MS-DOS," "Binding a TSR to a VxD," "Using the Interrupt 2Fh Critical Section Services," "How a TSR Can Serialize Access to Its Data," "IOCtl Calls in Protected-Mode Microsoft Windows," "Access to the Windows Clipboard by DOS Applications," "Windows 3.1 Standard Mode and the VCPI," "How Microsoft Windows Uses an MS-DOS Mouse Driver," "How to Start a Windows Application Directly from DOS," "Passing File Handles from a TSR to a Windows Application." This partial list of titles should make clear that (1) Microsoft documentation isn't so bad after all; and (2) even die-hard DOS programmers can't ignore Windows.

"Microsoft Statement on the Subject of Undocumented APIs," August 31, 1992. Microsoft's news release on undocumented Windows: "There are undocumented APIs in every major operating system, and applications developers routinely make use of them." At the same time, Microsoft issued

"Questions and Answers About Documented and Undocumented APIs," and a really awful white paper entitled "Undocumented Functions."

Microsoft, "MS-DOS API Extensions for DPMI Hosts," version pre-release 0.02, October 31, 1990. A Microsoft confidential document.

Microsoft, *MS-DOS Programmer's Reference*, Redmond WA: Microsoft Press, 1991, 464 pp. The official programming reference for DOS 5. Microsoft advertised this book (which came out shortly after the first edition of *Undocumented DOS*) as "DOS Documented." For the first time, Microsoft officially documented some well-known undocumented functions, while still leaving many holes. While an essential reference, the book has some curious errors, which we examine in chapter 1.

Microsoft, *MS-DOS Programmer's Reference*, Redmond WA: Microsoft Press, second edition, 1993, 512 pp. This is the MS-DOS 6.0 version of the programmer's reference. It corrects some of the errors from the DOS 5.0 version, and adds chapters on DoubleSpace and MRCI.

Microsoft, OEM Adaptation Kit (OAK), Portable Computing Update for MS-DOS 5, November 1991. If you can afford it, the OAK provides a wealth of information on DOS internals, including discussions of DOS 5 initialization, DBCS support, OEM customization of DOS, the MIRROR file formats, DOS in ROM (21/6D-6F), APM, and new IOCTL calls for PCMCIA. The source code on disk includes SYSVAR.ASM (SysInitVars structure), WPATCH.INC (DOS patches), DOSTAB.ASM (more DOS patches), PDB.ASM (the PSP structure), CONST2.ASM (DOS data), MULT.ASM (INT 2Fh calls, including the network redirector), and OEMNUM.INC (OEM number assignments).

Microsoft, *Virtual Device Adaptation Guide* (VDAG), version 3.1, Redmond WA, 1992. Included with the Windows 3.1 Device Driver Kit (DDK), this is the definitive guide to VxDs and VMM. The DDK also includes source code for some of the VxDs built into Windows.

Microsoft, *Win32 Subsystem Driver Reference* and *Win32 Subsystem Driver Design Guide*, Redmond WA, 1993. Included with the Windows NT DDK. Includes "Virtual Device Drivers for MS-DOS Applications that Use Special Hardware."

Microsoft Windows for Workgroups Resource Kit, Redmond WA, 1992. Who says Microsoft doesn't know how to produce good documentation? Its "resource kits" are excellent, and often contain detailed information that isn't in the programmer's documentation.

Microsoft Windows Resource Kit, Redmond WA, 1992, 538 pp.

Microsoft Windows Software Development Kit (SDK), Redmond WA, 1992. The Windows 3.1 version of the SDK is generally quite good, and describes many formerly-undocumented interfaces. The *Programmer's Reference, Volume 1: Overview* contains several chapters that are relevant to DOS programmers, including a chapter on network applications, and an extremely inaccurate and skimpy ("the food is no good, and the portions are too small") chapter on "Windows Applications with MS-DOS Functions." *Volume 4: Resources* documents the New Executable (NE) file format.

Microsoft, "Windows/386 Paging Import Specification" (formerly Global EMM Import spec), document revision 3.10.003, interface version 1.11, August 3, 1991. A Microsoft confidential document.

Ted Mirecki, "DOS Memory Control," *PC Tech Journal*, October 1987, p. 45. A brief discussion of the layout of MCBs, from the popular "Tech Notebook" in a now-defunct magazine.

Ted Mirecki, "Function 32H in DOS," *PC Tech Journal*, February 1989, pp. 129-133. Describes the structure of the DPB.

Ted Mirecki, "More Handles for New Applications" and "More Handles for Old Applications," PC Tech Journal, April 1988, pp. 161-165. Describes the file handle table within a process's PSP.

Charles Mirho, "Interfacing a Windows Program to a Real-Mode Device Driver," *Windows/DOS Developer's Journal*, August 1993.

Barry Nance, *Network Programming in C*, Que, 1990. Includes a chapter on "Novell's Extended DOS Services."

Tomas Nelson, "Self-Loading Device Drivers for DOS," *Windows/DOS Developer's Journal*, May 1993, pp. 27-43. Another approach to loading device drivers from the command line.

Raymond T. Nimmer, *The Law of Computer Technology*, Boston MA: Warren, Gorham & Lamont, 1985. See also 1991 Cumulative Supplement No. 1. Covers reverse engineering, antitrust, "integrated systems innovation," tying arrangements, documentation obligations, mass-market contracts, warranties, and more.

Daniel Norton, *Writing Windows Device Drivers*, Reading MA: Addison-Wesley, 1992, 434 pp. If you just want a general idea of the services that the Windows Virtual Machine Manager (VMM) provides to virtual device drivers (VxDs), and don't want to buy the Device Driver Kit (DDK), this is AIA (an inexpensive alternative).

Novell, *A Brief Description of the NetWare DOS Requester*, February 1993. Explains the limitations of the NETX INT 21h hook, and describes the new DOS redirector-style "requester" in NetWare 4.x.

Novell, *DR DOS 6.0 Optimization and Configuration Tips*, September 1991 (earlier published by Digital Research). Discusses "DR DOS 6.0 Version Numbers."

Novell, DR DOS *System and Programmer's Guide* (DR product #1182-2013-001).

Novell, *NetWare System Interface Technical Overview*.

Thomas Olsen, "Making Windows and DOS Programs Talk," *Windows/DOS Developer's Journal*, May 1992. Presents several approaches to DOS/Windows communication, including the 2F/17 clipboard API and a pipe interface VxD.

Walter Oney, "Communicating Between Virtual Machines," Win-Dev East 1993 (April 26-30, 1993; Boston MA), Boston University Corporate Education Center. Another great presentation by Walt Oney, formerly of Rational Systems.

Walter Oney, "Instancing a TSR," *Windows Magazine*, November 1991. How to use 2F/1605 to force an old TSR to properly instance its data under Windows.

Walter Oney, "Programming for DPMI Compatibility," Software Development '91.

Walter Oney, "Using DPMI to Hook Inturrepts in Windows 3," *Dr. Dobb's Journal*, February 1992.

Ordover, Sykes, and Willig, "Predatory Systems Rivalry: A Reply," *Columbia Law Review*, June 1983

Tim Paterson, "An Inside Look at MS-DOS," *Byte*, June 1983

Tim Paterson, "The MS-DOS Debugger Interface," in Schulman et al., *Undocumented DOS*, first edition, Reading MA: Addison-Wesley, 1990. Tim's chapter was dropped from the second edition, because Microsoft has documented 21/4B01 (Load But Don't Execute). But the official documentation is so skimpy (and, until the DOS 6 programmer's reference, so wrong) that you'll still need Tim's chapter from the first edition if you want to do anything with 21/4B01, which is essential to DOS debuggers. In DOS 5 and higher, a debugger would also need to be aware of 21/4B05 (Set Execution State); see Chappell's *DOS Internals*.

Charles Petzold, "Widening the Path," *PC Magazine*, 28 April 1987. Discusses "the undocumented (and strange)" INT 2Eh.

Phar Lap Software, *286|DOS-Extender Developer's Guide*. The writing in this manual is curiously similar to parts of *Undocumented DOS* and *Undocumented Windows*, and contains protected-mode versions of several programs that use undocumented DOS.

Matt Pietrek, *Windows Internals: Implementation of the Windows Operating Environment*, Reading MA: Addison-Wesley, 1993. In chapter 1, Matt shows how Windows boots on top of DOS, with a particularly detailed look at WIN.COM and the Windows KERNEL.

Scott Pink, "Reverse Engineering Reversals," *Upside*, May 1993. A report on the Sega v. Accolade and Nintendo v. Atari cases.

Mike Podanoffsky, *Dissecting DOS: A Code-Level Look at the DOS Operating System*, Reading MA: Addison-Wesley, 1994. Mike is the author of a DOS workalike called RxDOS. This book presents the assembly-language source code for RxDOS, providing a unique inside look at how a DOS really works.

Jeff Prosise, *DOS 6 Techniques and Utilities*, Emeryville CA: Ziff-Davis Press, 1993, 1035 pp. This massive book for both users and programmers includes chapters on writing TSRs and device drivers.

Jeff Prosise, "Hidden Gold in DOS 5.0," *PC Magazine*, April 27, 1993. Brief explanation of 2F/4A HMA functions, of EMM386.EXE VCPI support, and of the FDISK /MBR switch.

Jeff Prosise, "How Device Drivers Work," *PC Magazine*, November 28, 1989. Finding the device chain via 21/52.

Jeff Prosise, "The Inner Life of a TSR," *PC Magazine*, August 1990. Discusses the InDOS flag, INT 28h, critical error flag, and Get/Set PSP.

Jeff Prosise, "Instant Access to Directories," *PC Magazine*, 14 April 1987. Excellent discussion of TSR programming; discusses the InDOS flag, INT 28h (including the need, not only to hook INT 28h, but also to periodically invoke INT 28h as well), the DOS stacks, DTA, critical errors, and hooking the BIOS disk interrupt.

Jeff Prosise, MS-DOS Q&A column in *Microsoft Systems Journal*. Sample columns: May-June 1992 on MCB chain, find first UMB, 'SC' signature; Sept 1992 on SMARTDrive 4 interface; Dec 1992 on making a program load itself high, and on detecting RAM drives; March 1993 on 2F/4A HMA functions; May 1993 on 21/4B03 load overlay, critical errors, and DoubleSpace; June 1993 on 8514/A detection, WinExec, and the critical-error flag.

Jeff Prosise, *PC Magazine DOS 6 Memory Management with Utilities*, Emeryville CA: Ziff-Davis Press, 1993, 405 pp. Includes assembly-language source for UMBFILES, FILEMON, HMAGAUGE, INSTALL/REMOVE, and other utilities.

Jeff Prosise, "Replacing Internal DOS Commands," *PC Magazine*, December 31, 1991. Using the 2F/AE interface.

Jeff Prosise, "Teaching a TSR New Tricks," *PC Magazine*, 12 June 1990. A brief discussion of the active PSP.

Jeff Prosise, "What FILES= Does," *PC Magazine*, November 12, 1991.

Jeff Prosise, "Unlocking the Mysteries of CHKDSK," *PC Magazine*, May 11, 1993.

Quantasm Corporation, *Magic TSR Toolkit*, Cupertino CA. A TSR toolkit for assembly-language and C programmers.

Robin Raskin, Charles Petzold, and Stephen Randy Davis, "Taking Up Residence," *PC Magazine*, November 25, 1986. Singing the "TSR blues."

Eric Raymond (ed.), *New Hacker's Dictionary*, Cambridge MA: MIT Press, 1991. Some will find this book annoying, but it does have good descriptions of several important pieces of programmer lore, such as "You are not expected to understand this" and "Lyons books."

Tony Rizzo, "MS-DOS CD-ROM Extensions: A Standard PC Access Method," *Microsoft Systems Journal*, September 1987, pp. 54-60. Describes the Microsoft CD-ROM Extensions (MSCDEX), including its implementation using the DOS network redirector.

Jeff Roberts, "10 Steps to Windows Coexistence," *PC Techniques*, February-March 1991. "Take your DOS text-mode applications halfway to Windows."

Wendy Goldman Rohm, "Will the FTC Come to its Sense About Microsoft's Mischief?," *Upside*, August 1993, pp. 11-27. A lengthy piece on Microsoft and the FTC, by the author of a forthcoming book on the subject. One *Undocumented DOS* coauthor appears in this article under the name "Michael Hatch." Includes a telephone interview with Brad Silvberg, Microsoft VP of Systems Software, regarding the AARD code (see chapter 1). Also see the letters to the editor in *Upside*, October 1993, which were overwhelmingly pro-Microsoft ("In a free market, Microsoft can design its products to do anything it pleases," "What right does the FTC have to regulate Microsoft?," etc.).

Charles Rose, *Programmer's Guide to NetWare*, McGraw-Hill, 1990.

Stephen F. Ross, *Principles of Antitrust Law*, Westbury NY: Foundation Press, 1993, 606 pp. An excellent "neo-populist" (and post-Reagan) survey of the field, including coverage of "Market Structure and Monopoly Power" (Berkey v. Kodak), "preadatory innovation" (Transamerica v. IBM), vertical integration, exclusionary conduct, vertical restraints, tying arrangements, and so on.

Arthur Rothstein, "Walking the OS/2 Device Chain," *Dr. Dobb's Journal*, October 1990. An interesting contrast to walking the device chain under MS-DOS.

Neil Rubenking, *PC Magazine Turbo Pascal 6.0 Techniques and Utilities*, Emeryville CA: Ziff-Davis, 1991. Objects for accessing undocumented DOS.

Neil Rubenking, *PC Magazine Turbo Pascal for Windows Techniques and Utilities*, Emeryville CA: Ziff-Davis, 1992, 1100 pp. Calling undocumented DOS from protected-mode TPW programs; includes a chapter on "Access to Real Mode."

Richard Sadowsky, "Attaining DOS Enlightenment," *Windows Tech Journal*, April 1992. Accessing undocumented DOS from a protected-mode Windows program.

Richard Sadowsky, "It's a Real Jungle Out There," *Windows Tech Journal*, January 1992. From the cutesy titles, you can never tell what these *Windows Tech Journal* articles are about. This one's about using DPMI for real-mode (get it?) TSR communications with Windows.

Richard Sadowsky, "A Primer on Protected Mode," *Windows Tech Journal*, January 1993. Includes a correction to Sadowsky's January 1992 article.

Brett Salter, "An Exception Handler for Windows 3," *Dr. Dobb's Journal*, September 1992. Assembly-language source code for a VxD, WINX.386.

Murray Sargent and Richard Shoemaker, *The PC From the Inside Out*, Reading MA: Addison-Wesley, 1994. This is the third edition of Sargent and Shoemaker's famous *The IBM PC From the Inside Out*. The new edition will cover protected mode, the post-IBM PC architecture, 386/486/Pentium machines, Windows VxDs, and a host of other topics.

Arne Schäpers, *DOS 5 für Programmierer: Die endgltige Referenz*, Bonn: Addison-Wesley (Germany), 1991, 1123 pp. This massive book includes a lot of material on DR DOS.

Roger E. Schechter, *Unfair Trade Practices and Intellectual Property*, St Paul MN: West Publishing Co., 1986, 272 pp. A quick outline that covers competition, trade secrets, the FTC, warranties, and other topics.

Herbert Schildt, "Supercharging TSRs," *Born to Code in C*, Berkeley CA: Osborne McGraw-Hill, 1989. Chapter 3 presents a useful TSR skeleton in Turbo C.

Andrew Schulman, "Accessing the Windows API from the DOS Box," *PC Magazine*, August 1992 (Part 1), September 15, 1992 (Part 2), and September 29, 1992 (Part 3). Using the Windows 2F/17 clipboard API from a DOS program.

Andrew Schulman, "The Programming Challenge of Windows Protected Mode," *PC Magazine*, June 25, 1991. Accessing undocumented DOS from a protected-mode Windows program, using DPMI and some then-undocumented Windows API calls.

Andrew Schulman, "Go Anywhere and Do Anything with 32-bit Virtual Device Drivers for Windows," *Microsoft Systems Journal*, October 1992. Describes VxD APIs accessible via 2F/1684.

Andrew Schulman, "Exploring Demand-Paged Virtual Memory in Windows Enhanced Mode," *Microsoft Systems Journal*, December 1992. Discusses DPMI and VxDs.

Andrew Schulman, "Call VxD Functions and VMM Services Easily Using Our Generic VxD," *Microsoft Systems Journal*, February 1993. This article describes in more detail the generic VxD used in *Undocumented DOS*, chapter 3.

Andrew Schulman, "Walking the VxD Chain in Windows (and Chicago)," *Dr. Dobb's Journal*, December 1993.

Andrew Schulman, David Maxey, and Matt Pietrek, *Undocumented Windows*, Reading MA: Addison-Wesley, 1992, 715 pp. By showing that Windows is just a fancy-looking DOS extender, in many ways really just a new version of DOS, *Undocumented Windows* should give even the most die-hard DOS fanatic ("I don't do Windows") a reason to look at Windows.

Larry Seltzer, "Long File Names are Not 'FAT-uous' Hope for Future DOS," *PC Week*, September 20, 1993. An advance peek at the implementation of long filenames in Chicago.

Mike Shiels, "The Undocumented LAN Manager and Named Pipe APIs for DOS and Windows," *Dr. Dobb's Journal*, April 1993. A survey of the 21/5F calls supported by LAN Manager; the named pipe calls are supported by other networks, including NetWare.

Barry Simon, "Providing Program Access to the Real DOS Environment," PC Magazine, 28 November 1989, pp. 309-314. Discusses the three (count 'em) DOS environments—the real or active environment, the program environment, and the root environment.

Ben Slivka, Eric Straub, and Richard Freedman, "Inside MS-DOS 6," *Byte*, July 1993. Three Microsoft developers provide a good overview of DoubleSpace internal data structures, though they fail to mention Vertisoft, who developed DoubleSpace in the first place.

South Mountain Software, */* resident C */ User's Manual* , Orange NJ, 1991, 111 pp. A succinct manual for South Mountain's TSR library, with a good explanation of TSR "theory." Also see South Mountain's TSRific and Hold Everything libraries.

Stac Electronics, *Stacker 2.0 User's Guide*, Appendix B: "Programming with Stacker." This information isn't included in later versions of the Stacker user's guide; a description of a Stacker API is available on CompuServe (GO STAC).

Al Stevens, *Turbo C: Memory-Resident Utilities, Screen I/O and Programming Techniques*, Portland OR: MIS Press, 1987, 315 pp. Chapter 11 ("Memory-Resident Programs") and Chapter 12 ("Building Turbo C Memory-Resident Programs") present a TSR skeleton. The author's later *Extending Turbo C Professional* (Portland OR: MIS Press, 1989, 418 pp.) contains an improved TSR skeleton, plus a fascinating TSR overlay manager.

John Switzer, "Closing DOS's Backdoor," *Dr. Dobb's Journal*, October 1990. Explains a bizarre quirk of the DOS Delete FCB function (21/13), with details on the INT 30h and INT 31h alternate function dispatchers.

Pawel Szczerbina, "The NetWare Core Protocol (NCP)," *Dr. Dobb's Journal*, November 1993.

Andrew Tanenbaum, *Modern Operating Systems*, Englewood Cliffs NJ: Prentice-Hall, 1993. Another great book by Tanenbaum.

Andrew Tanenbaum, *Operating Systems: Design and Implementation*, Englewood Cliffs NJ: Prentice-Hall, 1987, 719 pp. A superb operating-systems textbook, with special focus on the important topics like the file system, and less on scheduling algorithms. Includes C source code for MINIX.

David Thielen, "Less Filling, Tastes Great: A Programmer's Survery of MS-DOS Version 5," *Microsoft Systems Journal*, July 1991. (See correction in *MSJ*, November-December 1991, p. 116.) Includes a discussion of IBM's proposed protocol for interrupt chaining.

David Thielen, "Safer Functions for Working with MS-DOS FIles," *Microsoft Systems Journal*, July-August 1992.

David Thielen and Bryan Woodruff, *Writing Windows Virtual Device Drivers*, Reading MA: Addison-Wesley, 1993. The accompanying disk includes Microsoft's VxD Lite. See also Thielen's series on VxDs in *Windows Tech Journal*, March 1992-August 1992.

Jean Tirole, *The Theory of Industrial Organization*, Cambridge MA: MIT Press, 1992, 479 pp. Whoever ponders Microsoft's role in the software industry is actually asking a question about "industrial organization." The math in this book is very difficult, but the material on tying arrangements, "network externalities, lock-in," product differentiation, incompatibilities, standards, and bottlenecks is extremely useful.

Paula Tomlinson, "The VDD Backdoor," *Windows/DOS Developer's Journal*, May 1993. As part of an article on NT device drivers, Tomlinson describes ring transitions via illegal instructions

(BOPs). See the letters to the editor in the July 1993 issue, pointing up the similarities to IBM's DIAGNOSE instruction thirty years earlier in System/360, and later in VM/360.

Matt Trask, "Creating Virtual PCs on the 386," *Byte*, IBM special edition, Fall 1990. A detailed explanation of V86 mode, virtual machines, and device virtualization.

Giles Todd, "Installing MS-DOS Device Drivers from the Command Line," .EXE, August 1989, pp. 16-20.

TurboPower Software, *TSRs and More*, Colorado Springs CO, 1992, 353 pp. A detailed manual on how to write TSRs in C++ using TurboPower's library, which comes with complete source code. (TSRs Made Easy and Object Professional for Pascal provide similar libraries for Turbo Pascal programmers.) Some of the examples are very involved. If you're writing TSRs, you really ought to be using this or one of the other commercial libraries from South Mountain or Quantasm.

John G. Tyler, "Multiple Virtual DOS Machines: A Better DOS," in Dick Conklin (ed.), *OS/2 Notebook*, Redmond WA: Microsoft Press, 1990. Contrasts the OS/2 1.x and 2.x DOS boxes.

V Communications, *Windows Source Disassembly Pre-Processor*, San Jose CA, 1993. Manual (by Andrew Schulman and Frank van Gilluwe) includes in-depth discussions of "Understanding VxDs," "Understanding OS/2 Device Drivers," discussions of Windows executable file formats, and so on.

Frank van Gilluwe, *The Undocumented PC*, Reading MA: Addison-Wesley, 1993. This book is based on Frank's many years experience of disassembling BIOSes (he's the author of the Sourcer disassembler, which has an add-in product for disassembling BIOSes). Covers BIOS functions, absolute memory locations, I/O ports, and the CPU. Includes chapters on CPU detection methods, adapter card development, the BIOS data area, the hard disk, the keyboard, CMOS, system function, DMA and DRAM refresh, the interrupt controller and NMI, and system timers.

The Waite Group's MS-DOS Developer's Guide, second edition, Indianapolis IN: Howard W. Sams & Co., 1989, 783 pp. Chapter 3 ("Program and Memory Management"), chapter 4 ("Terminate and Stay Resident Programming"), chapter 6 ("Installable Device Drivers"), and chapter 11 ("Disk Layout and File Recovery") all discuss undocumented DOS.

The Waite Group's MS-DOS Papers, Indianapolis IN: Howard W. Sams & Co., 1988, 578 pp. Somewhat uneven, but several chapters have excellent discussions of undocumented DOS: chapter 6 (Raymond J. Michels, "Undocumented MS-DOS Functions"), chapter 7 (M. Steven Baker, "Safe Memory-Resident Programming (TSR)"), and chapter 10 (Walter Dixon, "Developing MS-DOS Device Drivers").

Robert Ward (ed.), *MS-DOS Systems Programming*, 2nd Edition, Lawrence KS: R&D Publications, 1990, 239pp.

Al Williams, *DOS and Windows Protected Mode*, Reading MA: Addison-Wesley, 1993, 503 pp. An overview of protected-mode DOS extenders (for the purposes of his book, Windows is just another protected-mode DOS extender). Includes DPMI programming, interfacing TSRs to Windows, 32-bit programming.

Al Williams, *DOS 5: A Developer's Guide*, Redwood City CA: M&T Books, 1991, 914 pp. Includes sample code for TSR programming, "Big Real Mode," and a protected-mode DOS extender.

Richard Wilton, "Terminate-and-Stay-Resident Utilities," in Ray Duncan (ed.), *MS-DOS Encyclopedia*, pp. 347-385. This article carries the note that "Microsoft cannot guarantee that the information in this article will be valid for future versions of MS-DOS." Nonetheless, it is probably the definitive article on TSR programming. Interestingly, Microsoft eventally documented all the then-undocumented functions discussed in this article.

Kelly Zytaruk, "The Windows Virtual Machine Control Block," *Dr. Dobb's Journal*, forthcoming in January 1994 (Part 1) and February 1994 (Part 2).

INDEX